MANAGING FINANCIAL INSTITUTIONS

An Asset/Liability Approach

MANAGING
FINANCIAL
INSTITUTIONS

An
Asset/Liability
Approach

Mona J. Gardner   Dixie L. Mills
Illinois State University

THE DRYDEN PRESS
Chicago   New York   San Francisco   Philadelphia
Montreal   Toronto   London   Sydney   Tokyo

Acquisitions Editor: Ann Heath
Project Editor: Karen Vertovec
Design Director: Alan Wendt
Production Manager: Barb Bahnsen
Permissions Editor: Cindy Lombardo
Director of Editing, Design, and Production:
  Jane Perkins

Text and Cover Designer: C. J. Petlick, Hunter Graphics
Copy Editor: Karen Schenkenfelder
Compositor: Weimer Typesetting Co., Inc.
Text Type: 10/11 Bembo

Library of Congress Cataloging-in-Publication Data

Gardner, Mona J.
  Managing financial institutions.

  Includes bibliographies and index.

  1. Asset-liability management (Banking)   2. Risk
management.   3. Financial institutions—Management.
I. Mills, Dixie L.   II. Title.
HG1615.25.G37   1988   332.1'068'1   86-32805
ISBN 0-03-005479-6

Printed in the United States of America
789-039-98765432

Address orders:
111 Fifth Avenue
New York, NY 10003

Address editorial correspondence:
One Salt Creek Lane
Hinsdale, IL 60521

The Dryden Press
Holt, Rinehart and Winston
Saunders College Publishing

To our families

THE DRYDEN PRESS SERIES IN FINANCE

PREFACE

Perhaps the only task more challenging than managing financial institutions today is writing for students who will manage them tomorrow. When we began teaching upper-level undergraduate and MBA courses in financial institutions in 1980, it was already apparent that no book could capture developments in the field as rapidly as they emerge; only constant reference to current periodicals and newspapers could do that. Even so, there is one thing a book on financial institutions *can* accomplish that has been lacking in available texts: It can address the growing similarities among institutions with a consistent and integrated focus on financial management.

The asset/liability management theme for this book is an attempt to address the need for a focused text covering more than commercial banking. The early parts of the book provide a theoretical framework that transcends the changes in the institutional environment we have come to expect. At the same time, we want to give students a sense of the dynamic nature of financial markets and institutions and of the challenges faced by those who choose a career in institutions management. We began integrating many of these ideas in our classes as early as 1980. When this project arose, we were grateful for the opportunity to develop and implement our ideas more fully.

The book is written for upper-level undergraduate and master's students. Students will benefit from an introductory course in corporate finance. In many cases, introductory material in typical courses on money and banking or money and capital markets is also useful, although not essential. The manuscript for this text was used in our undergraduate Management of Financial Institutions course at Illinois State University over four semesters. Portions of the manuscript have also been used at Duke University in financial markets classes at the MBA level. Students' suggestions were incorporated into successive drafts, and the result is a much stronger first edition.

ORGANIZATION AND USE OF THE BOOK

The book is divided into five parts. The first (Chapters 1-4) explores the regulatory and market environment in which asset/liability management is conducted. The second (Chapters 5-10) develops theories of interest rate determination, interest rate risk, and interest rate risk management. The third part (Chapters 11-16) investigates separate issues in the management of assets and liabilities at depository institutions. Part IV (Chapters 17-21) looks at integrated asset/liability management strategies in depositories. Finally, Part V (Chapters 22-25) covers asset/liability management in nondepositories. A more detailed discussion of each part of the book is included at the end of Chapter 1.

Possible Course Outlines

The classroom testing of the book suggests several course outlines. Our students have completed an introductory course in financial management and an introductory course in money and banking or financial markets. Without the money and banking or markets prerequisite, instructors may need to place more emphasis on Chapters 1-6 and to supplement the discussion of the Federal Reserve System in Chapter 2 with material on monetary policy. We also supplement the text material with simulations, cases, and exercises using Lotus 1-2-3.

Ways to use the text for both quarter and semester systems include the following outlines:

1. **Two-quarter sequence for undergraduates:**
    First quarter—Introduction to Financial Markets and Institutions
Chapters 1-10	Financial markets, interest rates, interest rate risk
Chapters 11, 22-25	Introductory material on financial institutions

    Second quarter—Management of Financial Institutions
Chapters 12-21	Financial institution management techniques

    Selected reference to other chapters
    Lotus 1-2-3 exercises or cases

2. **One-quarter course for undergraduates:**
    Introductory Course in Institutions
Chapters 1-7	Financial markets, interest rates
Chapters 11-16	Depository institutions: techniques for asset and liability management
Chapters 22-25	Management of nondepositories

    Some complex analytical material is omitted.

3. **One-semester courses for undergraduates:**
    A. Management of Financial Institutions
Chapters 1-6	Financial markets and interest rates—review (2-3 weeks)
Chapters 7-10	Interest rate risk management—duration, futures, and options (2-3 weeks)
Chapters 11-21	Depository institutions management (7-8 weeks)
Chapters 22-25	Selected topics in management of non-depositories and diversified financial services firms (2-3 weeks)

    Cases and Lotus 1-2-3 exercises
    B. Management of Depository Institutions
Chapters 1-6	Financial markets and interest rates—review (2-3 weeks)
Chapters 7-9	Interest rate risk management: duration and futures (2-3 weeks)
Chapters 11-21	Depository institution management (10 weeks)

    Simulations, cases, and/or Lotus 1-2-3 exercises

4. **MBA or MS elective course:**
    Chapters 1-25 (entire book)
    Simulations and/or cases, research assignments
    Journal articles (suggested in footnotes and end-of-chapter reference lists)

SPECIAL FEATURES

The book has several features that distinguish it from other texts that are currently available. First, the consistent framework of asset/liability management encourages students to integrate material throughout the course, rather than to view topics as fragmented pieces of information. Second, combining the treatment of all depositories in Parts III and IV assists students in understanding the massive changes that have occurred in the financial system in recent years, while at the same time grasping the differences that remain among the most numerous institutions.

The thorough coverage of interest rates and tools for managing interest rate risk in the early part of the book provides a good foundation for appreciating the specific management problems discussed later. For example, we have found it most helpful to be able to cover GAP management supplemented by futures hedging in Chapter 18 without interrupting the discussion with introductory material on the futures markets. This text's coverage of GAP management, duration, and other strategies for integrated financial management is more comprehensive and clear than in competing texts.

Given the dynamic nature of the material, we have put special effort into identifying issues for which significant change is possible in the next several years, such as risk-adjusted premiums for deposit insurance. Our approach is to outline clearly as many facets of these issues as possible, so that students understand the nature of current controversies. Should change occur, instructors should need to do little more than explain which course of action was taken by regulators or by Congress.

Our students tell us the book is interesting and well-organized. The opening quotations and vignettes often inject a humorous note to catch students' attention. In addition, we have tried throughout to provide useful and interesting examples of the application of most management tools. Our students have also enjoyed using Lotus 1-2-3 to solve designated end-of-chapter problems.

ANCILLARY MATERIALS

The text is accompanied by an *Instructor's Manual (IM)* with complete answers to end-of-chapter questions and problems. The *IM* also contains additional references, teaching sugges-

tions, and some tables and figures suitable for transparencies. In many chapters, problems requiring complex or repetitive calculations are designated in the margin as "diskette" problems by this symbol: ▮. Two solution diskettes using Lotus 1-2-3 are available to adopters of this text, one with complete answers and one with partial solutions suitable for distribution to students. Most of these problems have been classroom-tested. The text also contains four cases for which solutions are provided in the *IM*.

ACKNOWLEDGMENTS

Of course, this project could not have been completed without the assistance of many colleagues. For their thoughtful and helpful comments on the entire manuscript, we are indebted to Sheldon Balbirer (Duke University), Elizabeth Cooperman (Bowling Green State University), John H. Hand (Auburn University), James Nielsen (Oregon State University), and Walter Woerheide (University of Michigan–Flint). Selected portions of the book benefited from the reviews of Deborah Ford (University of Baltimore) and of Han Bin Kang, Theresa Morgan, Alan Reichert, and William Scott, our colleagues at Illinois State University. We are especially grateful to Robert L. Mills, Jr., vice president of the First National Bank of Cincinnati, for commenting on selected chapters and for writing one of the case studies at the end of the book.

Special intellectual and professional debts are owed to two people. Philip W. Glasgo, of Xavier University, in conversations going back ten years, has consistently provided thought-provoking analyses of the regulatory and economic environment in which financial institutions management is practiced. His thorough and careful review of the entire manuscript merely added to the many contributions he has made to both authors' professional lives. Also deserving of special gratitude is Geoffrey A. Hirt, of DePaul University, whose encouragement early in our careers is deeply appreciated. His unflagging enthusiasm for teaching and writing in finance has served as a source of inspiration, as has his advice on many professional matters over the years.

Of course, we are also indebted to our students. Although many gave us their reactions to the manuscript and end-of-chapter materials, we are particularly grateful to Bala Balakumar, Carl Davison, Diane M. Hustad (now of Del E. Webb Corporation), Rhonda Jenkins (now of Household International), Sergio Murer (now of Shearson/Lehman/American Express), Kaushik Patel, Thomas Smith (now of Continental Illinois National Bank), Kevin Stoelting (now of the National Association of Professional Baseball Leagues), Michelle Woodham, and Michael J. Wright (now of Arthur Andersen and Company) for their research assistance.

Finally, the exceptional people at The Dryden Press made the writing and production process a wonderful learning experience. Particular thanks are due to Liz Widdicombe, our editor in the early stages of project development; to Ann Heath, our current editor, who guided the manuscript from beginning to end; to Betsy Webster, Ann's assistant, who answered inquiries cheerfully and communicated with us in a timely fashion; to Karen Schenkenfelder, the copy editor who painstakingly reviewed every detail of the manuscript; to Karen Vertovec, who coordinated the production of the book; and to Alan Wendt, who provided artistic direction. All errors, of course, remain our own.

Mona J. Gardner
Dixie L. Mills
Bloomington, Illinois
August 1987

CONTENTS

Part I

The Environment of Asset/Liability Management

Chapter 1

ASSET/LIABILITY MANAGEMENT: WHAT AND WHY?

I don't mean to suggest that a free market approach won't result in some casualties. In the short term, an inefficient or poorly managed institution will fail—and it should. . . . At the moment, though, the banking system is in an awkward period of transition. The game has already started and the referees still haven't decided on the rules.

Edward R. Telling
Chairman, Sears, Roebuck and Company (1985)

THE Fleet/Norstar Financial Group of Providence, Rhode Island, makes real estate and consumer loans, lends to established firms, provides venture capital to start new companies, manages investments, offers data-processing services, and plans to enter the securities and insurance businesses. It is a prime example of a contemporary American financial institution with a thoroughly modern-sounding name.

Actually, Fleet was founded in 1791, the year the Bill of Rights was ratified and five years before George Washington gave his farewell address as President of the United States. It was called Providence Bank, and as times and the country changed, it became the Industrial National Bank. In 1982, Industrial paid a consultant $1 million to recommend a name to match its new image and broadened focus. By the end of 1985, half its earnings came from financial activities outside traditional banking. In March 1987, Fleet agreed to merge with Norstar Bancorp of Albany, New York, expecting to become a strong competitor on a national level.[1]

Although not all financial institutions have adopted such aggressive strategies, all have faced similar challenges and opportunities in recent years. Some, like Fleet, have been profitable; others have faltered or failed. Their success or failure is often traced to how well their managers understand the new financial environment and whether they respond by adapting financial management techniques. This book addresses financial management in financial institutions in the late 1980s and beyond.

CHANGING TIMES FOR FINANCIAL INSTITUTIONS

Many people think of financial institutions as "money specialists," as opposed to specialists in consumer or industrial products like soap or machinery. Until recently, people paid little attention to the fact that financial institutions have their own financial management problems. Instead, the common belief was that financial institutions exist to solve the financial management problems of others—not a surprising thought because most individuals have relationships with several financial institutions, beginning at an early age. A typical consumer might have a checking account at a local bank; a credit card issued by a bank headquartered in another state; a home mortgage from an area savings and loan association; an automobile loan from the credit union at work; a life insurance policy from an insurer with offices in 50 states, and automobile and homeowner's insurance from a different firm; savings for retirement entrusted to a mutual fund; and an account with the regional office of a national brokerage firm.

A View from the 1930s

So many financial institutions operate in the United States, and people are so accustomed to them, that their existence, functions, and con-

tinued operations are often taken for granted. This was not always the case. In the early 1930s, such widespread concern emerged about the safety and soundness of financial institutions that state and federal legislatures enacted laws to assure the public that the businesses to which its funds were entrusted were, in fact, viable.

By law, the activities of most financial institutions were limited so that, for several decades, their financial management was not a terribly complex process. Managers engaged in specific activities that were legally permissible, charging prices whose maximums were legally mandated, and incurring costs that were legally determined. Regulators set prices and costs such that financial institutions were usually profitable and relatively few failed.

A Different View from the 1970s and 1980s

As time passed and memories of the 1930s faded, the perceived need for regulation of financial institutions also diminished. In addition, as interest rates rose in the 1970s, depositors became dissatisfied with the low rates paid by financial institutions and withdrew their funds in search of higher returns elsewhere. Many financial institutions were unable to respond because the rates they could offer were limited by laws of the 1930s.

Congress and government regulators responded to these developments, and since 1978 many restrictions on financial institutions have been loosened or removed. Recent deregulation has coincided with, and has been encouraged by, rapid developments in technology and in-

---

[1] Jan Wong, "Diversifying Widely, a Rhode Island Bank Finds Room to Grow," *The Wall Street Journal,* December 27, 1985, pp. 1, 6; Linda Watkins, "Fleet, Norstar Agree to Merger for $1.3 Billion," *The Wall Street Journal,* March 19, 1987, p. 2.

novation in the products financial institutions offer. Although virtually all financial institutions are still regulated, regulations are less restrictive than in previous decades.

During deregulation, the United States economy has undergone significant changes, such as population migration to the South and West and a decline in the fortunes of basic manufacturing industries. These fundamental changes have resulted in the movement of money from one region to another and from some industries to others. Because financial institutions are "money specialists," they have definitely been affected. As a result of these combined forces, the complexity of managing a financial institution has increased dramatically.

Change Isn't Easy

On the one hand, then, there is a growing tendency to take the health and success of financial institutions for granted. On the other hand, events have made financial success more difficult to achieve than at any time in recent history. Evidence suggests that the public may not be altogether comfortable with or accustomed to the new financial environment.[2] Few industries in financial difficulty reap the media attention accorded financial institutions, and, indeed, few businesses seem as fragile.

The reaction of the public, the press, and government regulators to the 1985 failure of Home State Savings in Ohio provides a striking example of this fragility. *Business Week* reported on Home State's closing with comments such as "The S&L Collapse Heard Round the World" and "Tremors from Ohio's Bank Run."[3] Home State was insured by the Ohio Deposit Guaranty Fund, a private (rather than a state or federal) insurance fund. Home State's collapse depleted the fund, which in turn started a "run" on other privately insured savings associations in Ohio. The governor ordered immediate closing of privately insured institutions to prevent widespread failures and to give regulators time to propose solutions that would restore public confidence. Only months later, similar problems occurred with a private deposit insurance fund in Maryland.[4]

The effects of these crises were felt in other financial institutions throughout the United States, and even extended to the foreign exchange markets. The series of events in Ohio and Maryland further emphasize the importance of financial management in financial institutions as a topic of study. It is appropriate to begin that study with some basic definitions.

FINANCIAL VERSUS REAL ASSETS

Assets include a broad range of both tangible and intangible things that provide their owners with expected future benefits. An individual's education, good health, and favorable reputation provide future benefits, as do a home, an automobile, and a savings account. A business expects future benefits in the form of cash from the sale of its products and services, as well as from owning a recognizable trademark or slogan (Join the Pepsi Generation!) or having a patent on a production process.

Because so many things are assets, it is convenient to divide them into two major subsets: *real assets* and *financial assets.* Real assets are those expected to provide benefits based on their fundamental qualities. A person's home provides benefits commensurate with the quality of its construction, its location, and its size. A corporation's main computer provides benefits based on its speed, the size of its memory, the ease of its use, and the frequency with which it needs repair.

In contrast, financial assets are those expected to provide benefits based solely on an-

[2]William E. Blundell, "As Basic Institutions Like Phones and Banks Change, Public Chafes," *The Wall Street Journal,* February 5, 1985.

[3]G. David Wallace et al., "Tremors from Ohio's Bank Run," *Business Week,* April 1, 1985, pp. 28–30.

[4]Steve Schwartz, "Maryland Puts Limit on Thrift Withdrawals," *The Wall Street Journal,* May 5, 1985, p. 3; "Maryland Halts Withdrawals at S&L," *Chicago Tribune,* August 20, 1985, Section 4, pp. 1, 9.

other party's performance—that is, they are claims against others for future benefits. A bank savings account will provide future benefits only if the bank continues to operate and to pay interest on the account; the account holder depends upon the bank's performance for any benefits from the financial asset. It follows from this concept of financial assets that one party's financial asset is another party's *financial liability*—that is, the latter has an obligation (often a legal one) to provide future benefits to the owner of the financial asset.

FINANCIAL INSTITUTIONS VERSUS NONFINANCIAL FIRMS

Most business firms—steel makers, automobile manufacturers, restaurants, and department stores—exist to acquire and use real assets in a way that makes the value of future benefits received greater than the cost of obtaining them. Cash to acquire assets may come from lenders or creditors, who have a legal expectation of repayment from the firm's use of real assets. Cash may also come from those who take an ownership (or equity) interest in the firm, hoping for (but with no legal promise of) a share in the excess of asset benefits over costs. Regardless of the sources of its funds, however, the firm has issued obligations that become the financial assets of others. Funds generated by issuing financial obligations are then used to acquire real assets.

Like other businesses, financial institutions exist to acquire and use assets so that the value of their benefits exceeds their costs. The key difference between financial institutions and other firms is that the vast majority of the assets financial institutions hold are financial assets. Financial institutions use funds from their own creditors and owners to acquire financial claims against others. They may loan funds to individuals, businesses, and governments, or they may purchase ownership shares in other businesses. The future benefits financial institutions expect to receive thus depend upon the performance of the parties whose financial liabilities they pur-

chase. The major distinction between financial institutions and other firms is not so much in how they raise funds, because all businesses issue financial liabilities to do so, but in what they do with them.

FINANCIAL INSTITUTIONS: WHAT ARE THEY?

Although all financial institutions share operating characteristics and economic functions, they vary in the products they offer and the financial assets in which they specialize. The chapters to follow explore those similarities and differences in detail. First, however, it is useful to consider Table 1.1, which introduces the specific institutions that are the focus of this book.

Depository Institutions

Depository institutions control by far the largest proportion of assets. This category includes commercial banks, savings banks, savings and loan associations, and credit unions; they are grouped together because of their traditional emphasis on deposits, their primary financial liabilities.

At year-end 1985, *commercial banks* held assets in excess of $2,460 billion (over $2 trillion). They have long served the corporate community as a major source of short- and intermediate-term loans, and for years, by regulatory restriction, were the only depositories allowed to offer checking accounts payable on demand. The Fleet/Norstar Financial Group's activities indicate that such a description is hardly adequate in the current era of deregulation. Banks are expanding their services and markets rapidly, and many offer a diversified set of products. They have also recently encountered considerable competition in their traditional areas of specialization, as is apparent from the decline in banks' share of total institutional assets.

Other depositories are broadly classified as *thrift institutions* because of their traditional reliance on savings deposits as sources of funds, although they are now able to offer checkable

Table 1.1
Percentage Distribution of Assets of Financial Institutions

Institution	1950	1955	1960	1965	Year 1970	1975	1980	1985
Commercial banks	56.88%	49.80%	41.88%	40.11%	42.56%	44.74%	42.05%	37.14%
Savings and loan associations	5.69	8.91	11.62	13.78	13.02	15.68	15.57	16.15
Savings banks	7.54	7.40	6.60	6.19	5.84	5.62	4.24	3.27
Credit unions	0.34	0.64	1.02	1.17	1.33	1.71	1.77	2.05
Finance companies	3.13	4.33	4.49	4.75	4.73	4.58	4.90	5.40
Life insurers	21.55	21.37	19.44	16.89	15.31	13.42	11.83	11.67
Property and casualty insurers	NA	NA	4.89	4.44	4.33	4.36	5.25	4.70
Private pension funds	2.39	4.33	6.19	7.82	8.17	6.90	10.18	11.15
Investment companies	1.11	1.84	2.76	3.74	3.52	2.13	3.32	7.48
Securities firms	1.36	1.39	1.09	1.10	1.20	0.85	0.89	0.99
Total percent	100.00%	100.00%	100.00%	100.00%	100.00%	100.00%	100.00%	100.00%
Total assets (billions)	$296.94	$423.10	$615.10	$940.64	$1,353.73	$2,156.53	$4,051.60	$6,624.10

NA = Not Available

Sources: U.S. League of Savings and Loans, *Savings and Loan Fact Book,* 1979, 1980.

National Council of Savings Institutions, *1986 National Fact Book of Savings Institutions*.

Insurance Information Institute, *Property and Casualty Fact Book, 1986-87*.

Board of Governors of the Federal Reserve System, *Flow of Funds, 1949-1985*.

Investment Company Institute, *Mutual Fund Fact Book,* 1986.

deposits. Table 1.1 indicates that thrifts have commanded a larger share of total financial institution assets in the 1970s and 1980s than in the past. The largest of the thrifts by total asset size, the *savings and loan associations (S&Ls),* are expanding beyond their traditional role as suppliers of mortgage loans since economic changes and Congressional action have given them the power to do so. *Savings banks* resemble S&Ls, but they have a more diversified asset base than S&Ls.

Credit unions are distinguished by the fact that their services are available only to members, who must share some "common bond" representing the basis for forming the union. Another important difference between credit unions and other financial institutions is that they are nonprofit organizations. Thus, their managerial objectives and resulting strategies may have a focus somewhat different from other depositories.

Finance Companies

Similar to depositories in the financial assets they hold are *finance companies,* which specialize in loans to businesses and consumers. Their financial liabilities, however, are quite different from those of depositories, because they acquire most of their funds by selling commercial paper and bonds.

Contractual Intermediaries

A third category of institutions consists of *insurance companies* (both life insurers and property and casualty insurers) and *pension funds,* considered *contractual savings institutions* because of the formal agreements with policy-holders or pensioners who entrust their funds to these firms. The insurance industry has sold risk protection to the public for hundreds of years. Life insurers, because their commitments to customers are long-term, have traditionally held an asset portfolio structure quite different from the property and casualty insurers, who offer shorter-term policies such as automobile and home coverage.

Pension funds generally are designed to collect funds from employers and sometimes employees, and to repay those funds, along with investment returns, after employees have retired or become disabled. The most widely known retirement fund is the Social Security program, but there are numerous other public and private funds. Table 1.1 includes only the assets of private pension funds.

Investment Companies

Investment companies provide a means through which small savers can pool funds to invest in a variety of financial instruments. The resulting economies of scale offer investors the benefits of professional portfolio management, reduced transactions costs, and the lower risk exposure of a large diversified portfolio. The best known and largest type of investment company is the *mutual fund. Money market mutual funds,* in particular, now dominate the industry. The easy access to funds, along with the market rate of return they offer to investors, has allowed them to achieve an enviable rate of growth. In fact, the existence of money market funds almost entirely accounts for the increased share of financial institution assets that investment companies have claimed in the 1980s.

Securities Firms

Securities firms assist customers with purchasing and selling stocks, bonds, and other financial assets. The industry is often subdivided according to two major activities, investment banking and brokerage. *Investment bankers* assist in the issuance of new securities, and *brokers* assist in the transfer of ownership of previously issued securities. Both *full-service brokers* and *discount brokers* exist. Full-service brokers advise clients in addition to arranging securities purchases and sales; discount brokers execute trades but give no advice. Many securities firms engage in both investment banking and brokerage.

Balance Sheets Reveal Industry Differences

Differences in financial industries are reflected in their asset and liability structures. Although comparisons are made in greater detail in later chapters, Figure 1.1 identifies major distinctions among three types of firms—commercial banks, life insurance companies, and mutual funds.

The assets of the three industries as of year-end 1985 are shown in the upper panel. Over half the assets of commercial banks are loans to individuals and businesses. Of the three institutions, banks alone hold a significant quantity of cash. Insurance companies also make loans, but almost half their assets are invested in corporate bonds and stocks, which banks are not permitted to hold to as large an extent. The mutual fund industry had over half its assets invested in short-term securities, with the remainder in bonds and stocks.

Differences are also evident in the liability structures of the three institutions, shown in the lower panel of Figure 1.1. A large majority of the funds of commercial banks is deposits. In contrast, obligations to policyholders are the major liabilities of life insurers. Mutual funds are quite different, because they have virtually no debt obligations and derive all their funds from shareholders' investment. The shareholders of banks and insurers, however, provide only a small proportion of funds.

FINANCIAL INSTITUTIONS AND THE TRANSFER OF FUNDS

The phrase *primary securities* refers to direct financial claims against individuals, governments, and nonfinancial firms. *Secondary se-*

Figure 1.1
Assets and Liabilities of Selected Financial Institutions

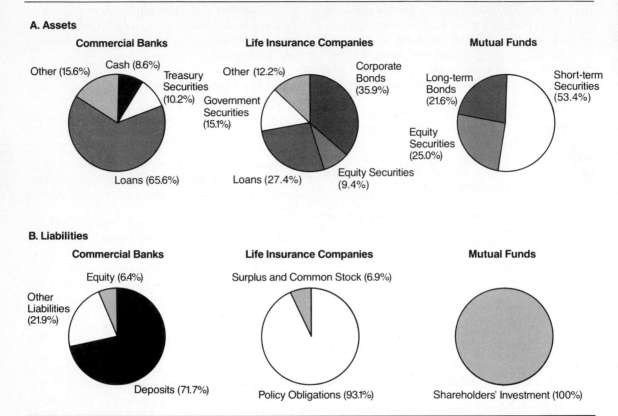

A. Assets

Commercial Banks — Other (15.6%), Cash (8.6%), Treasury Securities (10.2%), Loans (65.6%)

Life Insurance Companies — Other (12.2%), Government Securities (15.1%), Loans (27.4%), Equity Securities (9.4%), Corporate Bonds (35.9%)

Mutual Funds — Long-term Bonds (21.6%), Short-term Securities (53.4%), Equity Securities (25.0%)

B. Liabilities

Commercial Banks — Equity (6.4%), Other Liabilities (21.9%), Deposits (71.7%)

Life Insurance Companies — Surplus and Common Stock (6.9%), Policy Obligations (93.1%)

Mutual Funds — Shareholders' Investment (100%)

Source: Prepared by the authors with data from *Federal Reserve Bulletin,* December 1986; American Council of Life Insurance, *1986 Life Insurance Fact Book;* Investment Company Institute, *1986 Mutual Fund Fact Book.*

curities are the financial liabilities of financial institutions—that is, the claims against them. For example, in Figure 1.1, the asset holdings of banks, insurers, and mutual funds are primary securities: direct claims by these institutions against other parties. The institutions' liabilities—deposits, policyholder obligations, and mutual fund shares—are secondary securities, or claims against financial institutions.

Figure 1.2 illustrates the general difference between financial and nonfinancial firms and the origin of primary and secondary securities. Investors purchase financial assets, either primary or secondary securities, because they have

cash not needed for the immediate purchase of consumption goods or real assets. Rather than storing excess cash in a piggy bank, most investors wish to earn interest by purchasing a financial asset.[5] For every financial asset, there is an offsetting financial liability issued by a party who needs more cash and who is willing to pay interest to obtain it. Financial assets and liabili-

[5]In practice, returns on financial assets take other forms besides interest payments, such as dividend payments and the appreciation or decline in the price of the asset. In this context, "interest" is used generically to refer to rewards investors expect for deferring consumption.

Figure 1.2
Intermediation and Direct Investment

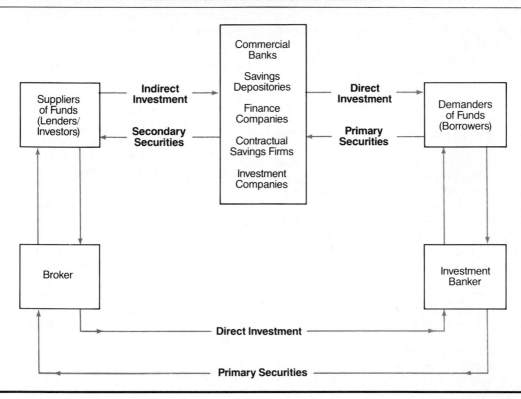

ties are the means through which excess funds are transferred in the economic system at rates of return (or costs) anticipated in advance by the lender (or borrower).

As time passes, the actual rate of return a lender earns may differ from initial expectations. In other words, owning financial assets involves *risk,* where risk is defined as potential variation in expected returns to the investor. If investors anticipate that the returns on an investment will vary, they will not lend unless the *expected* return is high enough to compensate for the risk.

Direct versus Indirect Investment

Funds transfers can occur directly between parties, as when an individual lends to a friend or purchases stock in a large industrial corpora-

tion. In these cases, the lender/investor has a claim on the friend or on the corporation—that is, the investor is engaged in *direct investment.* Direct investment results in the creation of a primary security.

The transfer of funds from one party to another can also occur with the assistance of a financial institution, taking one of two forms. One form occurs when an investor with excess funds purchases a secondary security, such as a life insurance policy or a savings account, allowing the financial institution to determine the ultimate recipient of the funds. For instance, a life insurer may invest the premium payments of its policyholders in corporate bonds, or a credit union may invest the savings of some of its members in home-improvement loans to other members. The policyholder or the saver is engaged in *indirect investment;* his or her claim is on the financial institution, while the institution holds a direct claim on the corporation or the homeowner. The institution has thus transformed a secondary security into a primary security. This transformation is called *intermediation.*

Not all funds transfers involving financial institutions occur through intermediation. Sometimes an institution arranges or assists in the transfer of funds between parties, without issuing its own financial liabilities in the process. When a financial institution acts in this more limited capacity, it is acting as a broker. This role is illustrated in the lower portion of Figure 1.2. As noted earlier, securities brokers and investment bankers seldom issue secondary securities themselves, but rather assist in the transfer of funds from suppliers to demanders. Many financial institutions act as both intermediaries and brokers from time to time.

BENEFITS OF INTERMEDIATION AND BROKERAGE

In creating indirect investment possibilities through intermediation, or in acting as brokers, financial institutions provide important benefits that are unavailable with direct investment. Most of these benefits can be categorized as reductions in transactions costs.[6] Because the return expected from a financial asset is reduced by the costs of acquiring the asset, a demand for an institution's services will exist if they are less costly than those incurred through direct investment. Conversely, those issuing financial liabilities want to minimize their noninterest transactions costs.

A Closer Look at Transactions Costs

Most transactions costs reduced by intermediation or brokerage fall into five categories.

---

[6]Parts of the following discussion are based on the analysis of George J. Benston and Clifford W. Smith, Jr., "A Transactions Cost Approach to the Theory of Financial Intermediation," *Journal of Finance* 31 (May 1976): 215-231.

Search or Information Costs. Financial institutions provide ways to identify those with excess funds and those needing funds, making it unnecessary for individual lenders and borrowers to find one another.

Portfolio Selection Costs. Lenders may wish to invest in financial assets in different dollar amounts, with different maturities, or with a different risk level from the financial liabilities borrowers wish to issue. Financial institutions issue secondary securities in forms attractive to lenders, then repackage the funds they obtain in forms attractive to borrowers.

Risk Management Costs. Many investors want a variety of financial assets in order to reduce the risk of holding a single claim against a party who may fail to meet its obligations. The investor avoids that risk by holding secondary securities because the financial institution holds a diversified portfolio. In addition, many secondary securities offer low risk exposure because they are insured against failure of the institution.

Monitoring Costs. Because financial assets are claims against others, their owners must monitor the performance of the parties against whom they have a claim. Financial institutions provide economies of scale in this task, employing appraisers, financial analysts, and other specialized personnel to monitor a large number of claims on a full-time basis. Lenders must then monitor only the financial institution.

Liquidity Costs. If lenders holding primary securities unexpectedly need cash, they may find it difficult or impossible to obtain without incurring substantial expense. The borrower may have used the funds for a purpose that cannot easily be liquidated on short notice. By investing in secondary securities, investors obtain financial assets, such as demand deposits, that they can convert to cash almost instantaneously at little more than the cost of writing a check.

ASSET/LIABILITY MANAGEMENT: WHAT IS IT?

Organizing and running a business whose primary function is reducing the transactions costs of others is itself a costly endeavor. By far the largest expenses to institutions are the interest costs resulting from their liabilities. There are also noninterest costs of intermediation and brokerage, such as the need to pay managers and other personnel and to maintain places of business. Like other firms, institutions can operate only if they can perform their functions as profitably as or more profitably than their competitors. Given the variety of financial institutions shown in Table 1.1, the competition faced by a single institution is often substantial. Success therefore requires careful attention to the financial implications of intermediation and brokerage.

Managing the Spread

Because financial institutions interact in the financial markets by issuing financial liabilities and purchasing financial assets, one critical element of the financial management of financial institutions is managing the *spread,* the dollar difference between the interest earned on assets and the interest cost of liabilities. This spread, expressed as a percentage of total assets, is called the *net interest margin (NIM):*

(1.1)

$$NIM = \frac{\text{Interest on Assets} - \text{Interest Cost of Liabilities}}{\text{Total Assets}}$$

If the net interest margin is high enough, the institution may use it to offset the noninterest costs of the intermediation and brokerage services it provides. Most institutions charge fees for these services, but unless the fees are competitive, investors may find it more eco-

nomical to switch to another institution or to engage in direct investment. When the spread is negative for an extended period of time, and interest costs actually exceed interest earned on assets, few institutions can make up the difference with other sources of income, and many have failed as a result.

Asset/Liability Management Defined

Added to the importance of managing the size of the NIM is the problem of managing its riskiness. Both aspects of the NIM must be considered to achieve successful financial performance. *Asset/liability management* is the management of the net interest margin to ensure that its level and riskiness are compatible with the risk/return objectives of the institution.[7]

Asset/liability management is more than just managing individual asset and liability categories well. It is an integrated approach to financial management, requiring simultaneous decisions about the types and amounts of financial assets and liabilities the institution holds, or the asset/liability mix and volume. In addition, asset/liability management requires an understanding of a broad range of financial markets in which institutions operate. Among the most significant financial market issues are how interest rates are determined, why they change over time, and what impact those changes have on the NIM and the value of an institution's assets and liabilities.

---

[7]Some authors have defined asset/liability management as the attempt to *stabilize* net interest margin with no expected variation—that is, as the attempt to minimize risk. See, for example, J. A. O'Brian, Harold M. Sollenberger, and Ronald Olson, *Asset/Liability Management: A Model for Credit Unions* (Richmond: Robert F. Dame, 1982), p. 1.

As Deshmukh, Greenbaum, and Kanatas have noted, however, such an objective is appropriate only for institutions choosing to perform brokerage, rather than intermediation, functions. The intermediation function, by definition, implies that the institution assumes some risk. See "Interest Rate Uncertainty and the Financial Intermediary's Choice of Exposure," *Journal of Finance* 38 (March 1983): 141-147.

ASSET/LIABILITY MANAGEMENT: WHO SETS OBJECTIVES?

Because asset/liability management involves managing the net interest margin in accordance with the institution's objectives, managers cannot carry it out unless they clearly understand what those objectives are and who sets them. For financial institutions, identification of objectives is somewhat more complex than for other businesses. To understand this complexity, it is helpful to have a brief outline of theories on the setting of managerial objectives. These theories have arisen from the study of financial management of nonfinancial firms.

A Normative Approach

In nonfinancial firms operating in competitive product markets, it is often argued that the firm's owners should set managerial objectives. Owners, unlike creditors, provide the initial funds to operate the business and therefore are entitled to any benefits resulting from superior operations.

Under this **classical theory,** managers are directed to ignore their personal risk/return preferences in making the firm's investment decisions. Instead, they should concentrate on maximizing expected benefits to owners, consistent with the risk owners are willing to bear. Managers who allow nonowner-determined objectives to influence their decisions will presumably be removed by unhappy owners. In addition, financing decisions, such as whether to borrow or not, are regarded as much less important than decisions involving investment in real assets.

The classical theory of the firm focuses on how managers *should* act, and thus is considered a **normative theory** of decision making.[8] Under this approach, the criterion for managerial decision making is clear: If a decision provides net benefits to owners, it should be made; otherwise, it should not. The classical theory leaves no doubt that the institution's owners are the ones to set objectives for asset/liability management.

A Positive Approach

Positive theories of managerial behavior focus on explaining how decisions *are* made by business managers, rather than on prescribing how they *should* be made. When owners and managers are the same people, the way managers should behave with respect to owners will be the same as the way they do behave. But if owners and managers are different, it is possible that managers' risk/return preferences will differ from those of owners. Under these circumstances, what do managers do? Positive theories of managerial objectives attempt to explain the behavior of managers arising from the separation of ownership and control.

Agency theory, a positive view of managerial decision making, suggests that managers are no different from other individuals and, if left unmonitored, will pursue their personal risk/return preferences. Thus, owners may incur costs in making sure that *their* preferences are recognized. The phrase "agency theory" refers to the view that nonowner-managers act as "agents" for owners, who are the "principals" of the business. Any reductions in benefits to owners as a result of the separation of ownership and control are known as **agency costs.**

Agency costs can take many different forms, such as the legal expenses of drawing up contracts to limit managers' salaries and expense accounts or the resources managers spend on annual reports convincing owners that owners' wishes are being considered. Agency costs may also be more subtle, such as potential benefits lost by owners when unmonitored managers follow their own risk/return preferences rather than those of owners. All types of agency

---

[8]The classical theory of managerial objectives is developed by Irving Fisher, *The Theory of Interest* (New York: Macmillan, 1930). Extensions of Fisher's work are provided in Jack Hirschleifer, "On the Theory of Optimal Investment Decision," *Journal of Political Economy* 67 (August 1958): 329-352 and in Hirschleifer, "Investment Decision Under Uncertainty: Choice-Theoretic Approaches," *Quarterly Journal of Economics* 79 (November 1965): 509-536.

costs reduce owners' welfare and would not be incurred if owners and managers were the same people.

Some experts argue that the agency "problem" is so prevalent today that a discussion of managerial objectives is realistic only if it includes the agent/principal relationship. Attention must be focused on ways to minimize agency costs.[9] Under this positive theory, the criterion managers use in decision making is whether or not they receive net benefits from an action. If they do, they will undertake the action; otherwise, they will not. Owners must therefore structure monitoring schemes with costs that are lower than the costs of letting managers operate unchecked. Agency theory implies that managers set asset/liability objectives and that owners protect their interests by setting appropriate constraints.

Managerial Objectives in Financial Institutions

Although the classical theory has been applied to managerial decision making in financial institutions, one can argue that it is inadequate on both theoretical and empirical grounds.[10]

------

[9]Formal development of agency theory is attributed to Michael C. Jensen and William H. Meckling, "Theory of the Firm: Managerial Behavior, Agency Costs, and Ownership Structure," *Journal of Financial Economics* 3 (1976): 305-360. Jensen and Meckling, however, were not the first to recognize that the classical theory of firm behavior may not be adequate when owners and managers are different.

One of the best known early analyses of the economic impact of managerially determined objectives on decisions is Oliver Williamson, "Managerial Discretion and Business Behavior," *American Economic Review* 53 (December 1963): 1032-1067. Williamson suggested that managers, if permitted, will engage in "expense preference" behavior, enlarging not only their own direct pecuniary benefits such as salaries and expense accounts, but also other perquisites such as the ability to hire large staffs and lavishly furnish their offices. Jensen and Meckling view expense preference behavior as one type of agency cost.

[10]An example is Richard E. Towey, "Money Creation and the Theory of the Banking Firm," *Journal of Finance* 29 (March 1974): 57-72.

Customer Needs Affect Objectives.   Because financial institutions provide liquidity to customers when issuing secondary securities such as demand deposits, the problems of financial institutions are different from those of nonfinancial firms, which need not honor financial liabilities on demand. Therefore, the need to provide customers with the benefits of intermediation must be considered in establishing managerial objectives for financial institutions. In addition, asset and liability decisions must be made simultaneously in financial institutions, even though joint consideration of investment and financing decisions is not necessary according to the classical theory of nonfinancial firms.[11]

Ownership Structure Affects Objectives. The ownership structure of many financial institutions is also different from that of nonfinancial firms. Instead of being owned by persons who have risked funds in order to start a business, and who are entitled to residual profits if the firm operates exceptionally well, many financial institutions are mutually owned. The *mutual form of organization* is particularly prevalent among insurance companies, savings banks, and savings and loan associations.

The implications of mutual ownership are explored in detail in Chapter 3, but for now it is enough to recognize that so-called "owners" of mutual institutions are not owners in the classical sense, because they are not entitled to personal claims on the institution's excess profits. Therefore, the classical theory—based on the idea that those who risk funds are entitled to establish the objectives of the enterprise—may not be directly relevant.

Some Evidence from Research.   In stockholder-owned institutions, empirical evidence suggests that managers *do*—whether or not they *should*—act to maximize their own, rather than owners' welfare. If so, attention to agency costs

------

[11]C. W. Sealey, "Valuation, Capital Structure, and Shareholder Unanimity for Depository Financial Intermediaries," *Journal of Finance* 38 (June 1983): 857-871.

is necessary.[12] Some researchers have argued that managers' tendencies to pursue their own goals is even stronger in mutually owned, rather than stockholder-owned, firms.[13]

Regulation Affects Objectives. Furthermore, even if owners and managers of financial institutions were the same persons, agency relationships would still exist for these owner-managers. They would arise from another agent/principal relationship: the one that exists between financial institutions and governments. This agency relationship is quite strong for some financial firms, such as commercial banks, which for many years have been expected to assist in carrying out the federal government's fiscal and monetary policies.[14]

The agency relationship with government exists for virtually all financial institutions, because most are involved in carrying out public policies such as the distribution of credit to disadvantaged borrowers. And, because governments provide insurance for many financial institutions, they regularly employ monitor-examiners, to ensure that managerial decisions do not unduly strain government insurance funds. In some instances, government agencies may actually remove managers from their positions

if they are performing their roles improperly.[15] It is unlikely, therefore, that the managers of any financial institution will, or can, pursue asset/liability management solely for the benefit of the institution's owners.

A Balancing Act

How, then, are asset/liability management objectives set? The perspective used in this book is one suggested recently in a model recognizing that owners, regulators, and managers themselves all influence managerial behavior. The model was developed specifically for banking firms, but its insight holds for other financial institutions. As the author expresses it:[16]

The banking firm is a complex organization. As a financial intermediary, it performs both a brokerage and a risk transformation function. As a business, it must yield a return to its owners. As a regulated enterprise, it must operate within the bounds specified by the supervisory agencies.

In most institutions, an individual manager or a management team is responsible for balancing the risk/return preferences of all parties. Most managers may personally wish to maximize the net interest margin because their salaries and expense accounts depend on funds remaining after interest obligations are paid. On the other hand, they also recognize that institutions must provide liquidity to customers, a requirement that may prohibit a risky plan to maximize the spread. Owners whose risk/return preferences differ from those of managers may further restrict managers' actions by imposing constraints such as salary or expense limitations or by structuring incentive plans, such as stock options, that reward managers for minimizing noninterest costs.

---

[12]See Franklin R. Edwards, "Managerial Objectives in Regulated Industries: Expense-Preference Behavior in Banking," *Journal of Political Economy* 85 (February 1977): 147-162; and Timothy H. Hannan and Ferdinand Mavinga, "Expense Preference and Managerial Control: The Case of the Banking Firm," *The Bell Journal of Economics* 11 (Autumn 1980): 671-682.

[13]See James A. Verbrugge and John S. Jahera, Jr., "Expense-Preference Behavior in the Savings and Loan Industry," *Journal of Money, Credit, and Banking* 13 (November 1981): 465-476. The evidence on this point is mixed, however. For a review of relevant research, see Walter J. Woerheide, *The Savings and Loan Industry: Current Problems and Possible Solutions* (Westport, CT: Quorum Books, 1984), Chapter 2.

[14]For a discussion of the origin of the agency relationship between governments and commercial banks, see Bernard Shull, "The Separation of Banking and Commerce: An Historical Perspective," *Proceedings of a Conference on Bank Structure and Competition* (Chicago: Federal Reserve Bank of Chicago, 1984), pp. 63-78.

---

[15]For example, the Federal Deposit Insurance Corporation exercised this power in its handling of the near-failure of Continental Illinois National Bank in 1984.

[16]Maureen O'Hara, "A Dynamic Theory of the Banking Firm," *Journal of Finance* 38 (March 1983): 140.

Finally, public policy conveyed by government regulation also influences managers, and the ultimate NIM targets set differ from those in the absence of an institution/government relationship. Thus, from a manager's point of view, the objective of asset/liability management is to maximize the NIM, subject to the constraints imposed by owners, regulators, and the intermediation function. These constraints result in the pursuit of a NIM target and a risk level that differ from the specific preferences of any single individual or group but that consider all parties.

operational definition of asset/liability management throughout the text.

Targets for the size of the NIM also involve consideration of its riskiness, or potential variability. Asset/liability objectives set by institutions must be responsive to the risk/return preferences of four important audiences: owners, regulators, customers, and managers themselves. Successful management of a financial institution means making simultaneous decisions about asset choices and sources of funds, while at the same time balancing the frequently disparate needs and preferences of those four groups.

SUMMARY

Financial institutions are a unique set of business firms whose assets and liabilities, regulatory restrictions, and economic functions establish them as an important subject of study. The vast quantity of assets controlled by institutions and the increasing freedom of deregulation have sparked a growing interest in asset/liability management techniques.

Firms classified as financial institutions hold portfolios primarily composed of financial assets, in contrast to the real asset holdings of nonfinancial firms. Institutions are designed to offer intermediary or brokerage services to assist savers in the allocation of their funds. The services provided by financial institutions reduce information, portfolio selection, risk management, monitoring, and liquidity costs to investors.

As in any other business, a key to successful management of a financial institution is earning a return on assets that exceeds the cost to the firm of acquiring those assets, including their financing costs. Because financial assets dominate the balance sheets of financial institutions, the difference between returns and costs can be measured by the net interest margin, the focus of asset/liability management. The chapters to follow examine management of the net interest margin to ensure that its level and riskiness are compatible with the institution's risk/return objectives. This is the

PLAN OF THE BOOK

Part I of the book encompasses Chapters 1 through 4. The three chapters following this one examine the environment of asset/liability management. Chapter 2 profiles the regulatory environment, and Chapter 3 provides more information on how the ownership structure of financial institutions affects asset/liability management. Chapter 4 introduces specific assets and liabilities important to virtually all institutions and illustrates how to calculate effective rates of return on these instruments.

Part II is concerned with interest rates: how they are determined in the markets; how they affect the risks to which an institution is exposed; and how to manage those risks. Chapters 5 and 6 explain the major theories of the general level and term structure of interest rates and examine ways these theories are incorporated into asset/liability management. Chapter 7 introduces the concept and measurement of "interest rate risk." Chapters 8 through 10 develop the theory and application of several major tools for managing interest rate risk, including duration, financial futures, and options. Each plays a part in the overall asset/liability management of financial institutions.

The third part of the book is about the management of assets and liabilities in depository institutions. Chapter 11 introduces, compares, and contrasts different depository institutions. Chapter 12 is concerned with liquidity and securities portfolio management in depositories, while Chapters 13 and 14 are about their lending decisions. Liability management and capital management policies are the subjects of Chapters 15 and 16.

Part IV begins with Chapters 17 and 18, integrating materials from the preceding chapters into overall asset/liability management strategies for depositories. Chapters 19 and 20 discuss the role of noninterest income and noninterest expense in asset/liability management and cover such topics as capital investment decisions and the management of fee-based services. Finally, Chapter 21 provides techniques for evaluating the effectiveness of asset/liability management in depositories.

Part V discusses asset/liability management in nondepository institutions, beginning with Chapter 22 on finance companies. Insurance companies are the subject of Chapter 23, while Chapter 24 discusses financial management in pension funds, investment companies, and securities firms. The book ends with a chapter on diversified financial services companies.

Questions

1. What forces have increased the complexity of managing financial institutions in recent years? How have these forces affected the management of financial institutions?

2. Find several newspaper and magazine articles on the crises in Ohio and Maryland thrifts during 1985. Do you think the coverage was overly sensational, or did it accurately reflect the risk to which depositors were exposed? Do you think state and federal regulators acted appropriately in these situations? Why or why not?

3. Explain the difference between real assets and financial assets. How is the asset composition of most business firms different from that of financial institutions?

4. Explain the relationship between financial assets and financial liabilities. From your personal experience, give two examples of this relationship.

5. Compare and contrast the different types of depository institutions.

6. Define the term "thrift institution." *The Wall Street Journal* recently quoted a leading marketing professional as saying that the word "thrift" is a "dirty old Depression-sounding word." Do you agree or disagree? Why?

7. Why are insurance companies and pension funds called contractual savings institutions?

8. Why have life insurers traditionally held portfolios different from those of property and casualty insurers? What types of investments would you expect each insurer to hold?

9. What is the difference between direct and indirect investment? Between primary and secondary securities?

10. Define risk. Why does owning financial assets involve risk?

11. Under what circumstances does a financial institution act as an intermediary? As a broker?

12. Suppose you have a choice between buying shares of stock in several large firms or investing $10,000 in a mutual fund. Explain how choosing indirect investment would affect your transactions costs.

13. What is the net interest margin? The spread? How is the NIM related to asset/liability management?

14. What is the classical theory of firm behavior? Is it a normative or positive theory? Is the classical theory appropriate for financial institutions? Why or why not?

15. Explain what is meant by agency costs. Give an example of an agency cost that might exist in a commercial bank today. How does agency theory relate to asset/liability management? Is agency theory a normative or positive theory? Why?

16. What important groups influence the setting of objectives by financial institution managers? Give an example of a situation in which the objectives of regulators and those of owners might conflict.

17. What is the objective of asset/liability management?

18. Find an article on a financial institution that is doing well financially and one on an institution that is doing poorly or has failed. What seem to be the causes of the differences in performance?

Selected References

Benston, George J., and Clifford W. Smith, Jr. "A Transactions Cost Approach to the Theory of Financial Intermediation." *Journal of Finance* 31 (May 1976): 215-231.

Deshmukh, Sudhakar D., Stuart I. Greenbaum, and George Kanatas. "Interest Rate Uncertainty and the Financial Intermediary's Choice of Exposure." *Journal of Finance* 38 (March 1983): 141-147.

Edwards, Franklin R. "Managerial Objectives in Regulated Industries: Expense-Preference Behavior in Banking." *Journal of Political Economy* 85 (February 1977): 147-162.

Fisher, Irving. *The Theory of Interest*. New York: Macmillan, 1930.

Hannan, Timothy H., and Ferdinand Mavinga. "Expense Preference and Managerial Control: The Case of the Banking Firm." *The Bell Journal of Economics* 11 (Autumn 1980): 671-682.

Hirschleifer, Jack. "On the Theory of Optimal Investment Decision." *Journal of Political Economy* 67 (August 1958): 329-352.

———. "Investment Decision Under Uncertainty: Choice Theoretic Approaches." *Quarterly Journal of Economics* 79 (November 1965): 509-536.

Jensen, Michael C., and William H. Meckling. "Theory of the Firm: Managerial Behavior, Agency Costs, and Ownership Structure." *Journal of Financial Economics* 3 (1976): 305-360.

O'Brian, J. A., Harold M. Sollenberger, and Ronald Olson. *Asset/Liability Management: A Model for Credit Unions*. Richmond: Robert F. Dame, 1982.

O'Hara, Maureen. "A Dynamic Theory of the Banking Firm." *Journal of Finance* 38 (March 1983): 127-140.

Santomero, Anthony M. "Modeling the Banking Firm: A Survey." *Journal of Money, Credit, and Banking* 16 (November 1984, Part 2): 526-616.

Sealey, C. W. "Valuation, Capital Structure, and Shareholder Unanimity for Depository Financial Intermediaries." *Journal of Finance* 38 (June 1983): 857-871.

Shull, Bernard. "The Separation of Banking and Commerce: An Historical Perspective." *Proceedings of a Conference on Bank Structure and Competition*. Chicago: Federal Reserve Bank of Chicago, 1984: 63-78.

Towey, Richard E. "Money Creation and the Theory of the Banking Firm." *Journal of Finance* 29 (March 1974): 57-72.

Verbrugge, James A., and John S. Jahera, Jr. "Expense-Preference Behavior in the Savings and Loan Industry." *Journal of Money, Credit, and Banking* 13 (November 1981): 465-476.

Williamson, Oliver. "Managerial Discretion and Business Behavior." *American Economic Review* 53 (December 1963): 1032-1067.

Woerheide, Walter J. *The Savings and Loan Industry: Current Problems and Possible Solutions*. Westport, CT: Quorum Books, 1984.

Chapter 2

REGULATION, TECHNOLOGY, AND FINANCIAL INNOVATION

. . . the possibility of financial services deregulation . . . is less important than the actual fact of "deregulated thinking" today . . .

Matthew M. Lind
Vice President
The Travelers Corporation (1984)

IN 1981, Marlin D. Jackson, who later became the Arkansas Commissioner of Banking, was incensed to learn that Citicorp was advertising in rural Arkansas papers, offering high interest rates on deposits in its new limited-service bank in South Dakota. Officials of the giant New York bank argued that a competitive banking industry benefits customers, but Mr. Jackson argued that expansion efforts of large banks must be controlled by laws and regulations. He believed Citicorp's campaign to lure deposits that would otherwise remain in Arkansas was not in the best interests of the state's bankers or its economy. Jackson, ever the Southern gentleman, challenged Citicorp's Chairman to "choose his weapons and meet me under the oaks at dawn."[1]

Restriction of interstate expansion is just one of many historic regulations generating controversy recently, particularly as aggressive institutions test every legal loophole they can find. Financial institutions in general, and depository institutions in particular, are among the

---

[1]Tim Carrington, "Arkansan Is Tackling Citicorp in Fight Over Bank Compacts," *The Wall Street Journal,* March 6, 1984, p. 31.

most closely regulated firms in the United States. Over the years, limitations have been imposed on the way they raise funds, on the costs that can be incurred in doing so, on asset choices, on product and geographical diversification, and more. Although the initial justification for these regulations was to protect the safety and soundness of the economic system, subsequent modifications are not necessarily aimed at that goal. In fact, regulations and motivations for them reflect an evolutionary process that responds to innovations in the financial markets and to new asset/liability management techniques.

The debate between Arkansas bankers and Citicorp exemplifies the problem of deciding whose interests are served by regulations, and whether or not the rules should be changed. The pages that follow explore the traditional regulatory structure and recent developments. A discussion such as this is never complete, because more changes are always on the horizon, many as this book was written. The possibility of continued change means that managers can never take a given set of rules and regulations for granted and that developing strategies in a fluid environment can be frustrating. To conduct successful asset/liability management, financial managers must understand not only existing regulations, but the regulatory process.

A CONCEPTUAL FRAMEWORK FOR REGULATION, INNOVATION, AND REFORM

A simple list of regulations and regulatory agencies governing financial institutions in the United States cannot capture the impact of restrictions on managerial decisions. The relationship between regulators and regulated institutions is complex, and is best described as interactive. Only through an exploration of the interaction can historical developments and potential changes be viewed in proper perspective.

The Regulatory Dialectic

The word *dialectic* refers to change occurring through a process of action and reaction by opposing forces. In his classic presentation, the philosopher Hegel described the dialectic process as: 1) an initial set of arguments or rules (the *thesis*); 2) a conflicting set of arguments or responses (the *antithesis*); and 3) a change or modification (the *synthesis*), resulting from an exchange or interaction between the opposing forces. The idea that regulation of financial institutions is a dialectic—one of cyclical interaction between opposing political and economic forces—was introduced by Professor Edward

Kane in the late 1970s.[2] Kane's *regulatory dialectic* has since been widely adopted as an insightful characterization of regulatory developments.

The Thesis: Financial Institution Regulations

Legislators and government agencies usually provide a justification for regulations when they are introduced, but experts believe that unannounced motivations often guide the decisions of regulators. Although financial institution regulations have eventually served other purposes, from the 1930s to 1980 their stated intent was to maintain stability in the nation's financial system.

_____

[2]The concept of the regulatory dialectic was introduced in Edward J. Kane, "Good Intentions and Unintended Evil: The Case Against Selective Credit Allocation," *Journal of Money, Credit and Banking* 9 (February 1977): 55-69. Kane elaborated further on this argument in "Accelerating Inflation, Technological Innovation, and the Decreasing Effectiveness of Banking Regulation," *Journal of Finance* 36 (May 1981): 355-367; and "Technology and the Regulation of Financial Markets," in *Technology and the Regulation of Financial Markets,* Anthony Saunders and Lawrence J. White, eds. (Lexington, MA: D. C. Heath and Company, 1986), pp. 187-193.

The 1930s: Safety and Soundness. The core of modern financial regulation was drafted in the aftermath of the financial crisis of the 1930s. Laws and regulations centered on prohibiting excessive competition among financial institutions, which legislators viewed as a source of unacceptable risk.

The *Banking Act of 1933,* widely known as the *Glass-Steagall Act (G-S),* is the cornerstone of restrictions applied to the commercial banking industry. Created by this act were ceil-ings on deposit interest rates, thereafter known by Federal Reserve *Regulation Q* that enforced them. G–S also attempted to separate the commercial banking and securities industries, and reinforced geographic restrictions on bank branching outlined in the *McFadden-Pepper Act of 1927.*

Additional regulation focused on thrift institutions in the *Federal Home Loan Bank Act of 1932* and the *National Housing Act of 1934.* Attention turned to credit unions in the *Na-*

Table 2.1
Thesis: Major Financial Legislation before 1980

Date	Law	Key Provisions
1863	National Currency Act	Established Office of the Comptroller of the Currency; authorized national bank notes; limited asset choices of banks issuing national bank notes; established a system of reserve requirements
1864	National Banking Act	Authorized the granting of federal bank charters; origin of dual banking system attributed to this and the 1863 law
1913	Federal Reserve Act	Established system of Federal Reserve Banks to serve as a lender of last resort to commercial banks, promote an elastic money supply, provide a nationwide payments system and closer supervision of banks
1919	Edge Act	Permitted banks to establish subsidiaries outside their home territory for the purpose of conducting international banking
1927	McFadden-Pepper Act	Permitted national banks to branch if state banks in the same state could; left interstate branching decisions to the states
1932	Federal Home Loan Bank Act	Established Federal Home Loan Bank System to serve as a lender of last resort to S&Ls
1933	Banking Act of 1933 (Glass-Steagall Act)	Prohibited the payment of interest on demand deposits; mandated ceilings on deposit interest rates; separated Fed member banks from the securities industry; established the FDIC; further restricted asset choices of national banks
1933	Home Owners' Loan Act	Authorized the granting of federal charters for S&Ls, under the supervision of the FHLBB
1933	Securities Act of 1933	Required registration of new securities and disclosure of truthful financial information on issuers
1934	Securities Exchange Act	Established the SEC
1934	National Housing Act	Established the FSLIC
1934	National Credit Union Act	Established a federal credit union regulator which later became the NCUA; authorized the granting of federal charters for CUs
1935	Banking Act of 1935	Strengthened the power and autonomy of the Federal Reserve Board; gave Comptroller more discretion in the granting of national bank charters

tional Credit Union Act of 1934. Later, geographic and product restrictions on commercial banks were extended further by the ***Bank Holding Company (BHC) Act of 1956*** and by its ***1970 Amendments. Bank holding companies*** (discussed in Chapter 3) are corporations that hold voting control over one or more commercial banks. Through these laws, the operations of depository institutions, and particularly commercial banks, were separated from other sectors of the financial markets.

Regulations restricting nondepository institutions were already in place in the 1930s, and additional ones were added then and in the decades to follow. Of particular importance were the ***Securities Act of 1933*** and the ***Securities Exchange Act of 1934,*** placing federal restrictions on brokers and investment bankers. These laws were followed by the ***Investment Company Act of 1940,*** bringing the practices of investment companies under federal control. For other firms, such as insurers and finance companies, regulations were and still are concentrated at the state level. Table 2.1 provides a chronological summary of major federal legislation pertaining to financial institutions, including these and other acts mentioned later in the chapter. Together, they are the thesis of the dialectic.

Table 2.1 *continued*

Date	Law	Key Provisions
1940	Investment Company Act	Required disclosure of financial statements and investment objectives by investment companies; specified shareholder rights
1940	Investment Advisers Act	Required individuals or firms selling investment advice to register with the SEC
1945	McCarran-Ferguson Act	Established the right of the federal government to regulate insurance companies if states fail to do so adequately
1956	Bank Holding Company Act and Douglas Amendment to the Act	Gave the Fed control over the formation, expansion, and supervision of multibank holding companies; identified factors to be used in evaluating bank holding company acquisitions; prohibited multibank holding companies from acquiring out-of-state banks
1966	Interest Rate Adjustment Act	Extended Reg Q ceilings to thrifts
1968	Consumer Credit Protection Act (Truth-In-Lending)	Required disclosure of lending terms to consumers
1970	Amendments to Bank Holding Company Act	Extended Federal Reserve authority over one-bank holding companies; limited holding company acquisitions to businesses "closely related" to banking
1970	Amendments to Federal Credit Union Act	Established NCUSIF
1974	Equal Credit Opportunity Act	Prohibited discrimination in the granting of credit
1974	Employee Retirement Income Security Act	Imposed fiduciary responsibility on pension fund managers; provided for vesting of benefits and full funding of pension funds; established the PBGC
1975	Securities Acts Amendments	Mandated the development of a national securities market
1977	Community Reinvestment Act	Required depository institutions to consider the needs of all economic groups in their communities when granting credit
1978	International Banking Act	Imposed insurance premiums and branching restrictions on foreign banks operating in the United States

1960s and Beyond: Other Intentions? In the years following the Great Depression, the economic environment changed but regulations did not. For many financial institutions, limitations remained on starting new firms, entering distant markets, and developing new products, to name a few. Kane argues that eventually the implicit thrust of regulations was to limit competition—*not* for safety reasons—but to benefit selected market participants, such as small or weak institutions, that would suffer in a more competitive environment.

The Antithesis, Part I: Regulatory Avoidance

The relationship between regulators and the regulated has been described as a cat-and-mouse game. According to Kane, the existence of operating rules that benefit a protected class provides a strong incentive for other regulated institutions to find loopholes. The desire to compete may eventually make regulatory avoidance an end unto itself, to which institutions devote energy and resources, rather than simply a means to more competitive freedom. One of management's goals becomes circumvention of restrictions in an effort to capture a portion of a market otherwise denied. Regulators look unfavorably on this "avoidance" behavior, and if institutions are too successful in circumventing the rules, regulations will be revised. The revisions inspire further avoidance efforts, and the cycle begins anew.

The Antithesis Illustrated. Good examples of the cat-and-mouse game are the activities of institutions to avoid restrictions on sources of and interest rates paid on deposits. In the 1960s, large commercial banks developed new kinds of deposits and tapped foreign markets to avoid Regulation Q ceilings on domestic deposit interest rates. As regulators observed the success of institutions at raising funds through these unconventional methods, they changed regulations to again limit institutions' ability to compete. Large banks responded to each regulatory adjustment by introducing a substitute sufficiently different to avoid the new rules. In playing this game, regulator and regulated alike expended considerable resources.[3]

Another example of economically inefficient behavior is found in the decisions by banks and thrifts to offer noninterest incentives to attract deposits. By the late 1970s, many depositories were offering small appliances, dishes, luggage, or other rewards to customers who deposited funds. Because Regulation Q prevented institutions from offering competitive rates, they offered customers tangible assets. This strategy diminished after the ***Depository Institutions Deregulation and Monetary Control Act of 1980*** ended deposit interest rate ceilings. That law, discussed in more detail later, freed institutions to offer customers a competitive interest rate on deposits.

The Antithesis, Part II: Technological Innovations and Economic Conditions

Additional elements are part of the antithesis of the regulatory dialectic. As institutions search for competitive tools that do not violate existing regulations, changes in technology and the economy cause customers to demand new products. For example, along with the efforts of regulated institutions, catalysts for change included the "computer revolution" and increased uncertainty about inflation and interest rates.[4]

Technological Innovations. Computer technology has affected many aspects of business systems and personal habits. The ability to

---

[3]Summary discussions of the economic costs of avoidance behavior are available in: Federal Reserve Bank of Chicago, "The Depository Institutions Deregulation and Monetary Control Act of 1980," *Economic Perspectives* 4 (September/October 1980): 3-23; and R. Alton Gilbert, "Requiem for Regulation Q: What It Did and Why It Passed Away," *Review,* Federal Reserve Bank of St. Louis 68 (February 1986): 22-37.

[4]The roles of technology and financial innovations in the regulatory dialectic were initially identified by Kane; more elaborate discussion has appeared in subsequent studies. See Alfred Broaddus, "Financial Innovation in the United States—Background, Current Status and Prospects," *Economic Review,* Federal Reserve Bank of Richmond 71 (January/February 1985): 2-22; and James C. Van Horne, "Of Financial Innovations and Excesses," *Journal of Finance* 40 (July 1985): 621-631.

analyze large quantities of information quickly and efficiently and to transmit it rapidly raised the expectations of customers at financial institutions. Demand has grown rapidly for services such as cash management and electronic banking.

Not all financial institutions were able to respond to these demands quickly. Depository institutions, in particular, were slowed by legal limitations. For example, the installation of electronic banking equipment at grocery stores and shopping centers was initially challenged on grounds that such facilities were the equivalent of branch banks. In states with limited-branching laws, electronic banking was delayed. Similarly, Regulation Q interfered with introduction of cash management services by depository institutions, while securities firms were free to pioneer the development of these programs.

Economic Uncertainty.   Economic uncertainty also contributes to changing customer demands. In the late 1970s and early 1980s, high inflation and record-setting interest rates stimulated demand by businesses and individuals for investments offering protection against increased risk. Even financially unsophisticated customers resisted deposit accounts paying below-market interest rates. Savers were willing to forgo the safety of insured deposits in search of higher and more flexible returns.

As with technological innovations, some financial institutions faced more severe restrictions than others in their efforts to respond to investors' desires for savings alternatives. Strategies available to depository institutions were especially limited. Depositors whose savings were too small to invest directly in higher-return but low-risk securities, such as Treasury bills, could not be served by depositories. In contrast, money market mutual funds could offer liquid accounts with flexible rates of return. Critics of existing regulations argued that it was unfair to impose below-market interest rate ceilings on deposit accounts heavily used by small savers. These developments were part of the antithesis leading to regulatory adjustments in 1978 and thereafter.

The Synthesis: Regulatory Adjustments

Regulation of financial institutions is dynamic. Forces for change arise in part from the objectives of managers and owners of regulated institutions, but change is also market-driven. After a period of delay and analysis, regulations are adjusted. As long as any regulatory restrictions remain—and it is certain that they will—the dialectic continues. Synthesis in the regulatory dialectic is only a temporary equilibrium, because legal revisions immediately provoke new avoidance behavior. One cycle's synthesis is the next cycle's thesis.

Since 1978, regulatory changes have been introduced rapidly. Between 1978 and 1980, the actions of depository regulators were tentative, consisting of incremental changes in deposit regulations. By the end of 1982, however, Congress had lightened or eliminated many of the restrictions mentioned earlier. Those changes, in turn, affect the competitive position of other financial institutions, as depositories expand product lines and market areas. The two landmark laws culminating this period of regulatory synthesis are the Depository Institutions Deregulation and Monetary Control Act of 1980 *(DIDMCA)* and the *Garn-St Germain Depository Institutions Act of 1982 (G-St G)*. They and remaining regulations from a prior era are now the new thesis.

Before these laws can be appreciated, however, it is necessary to review the regulatory structure under which financial institutions have traditionally operated. The following discussion provides an overview of decision areas addressed by financial institution regulators. More detailed treatment of specific regulations is reserved for subsequent chapters.

DEPOSITORY INSTITUTIONS

Regulations for depository institutions affect almost every aspect of operations. The complexity of the regulatory process extends beyond the quantity of regulations. Not only are the rules numerous, so are the regulators.

Who Are the Regulators?

The federal regulatory structure is so complex that one institution may be answerable to four or five different agencies.

Commercial Banking. Banks may obtain an operating charter at the federal or state level. Those in the first group are *national banks,* and the latter, *state banks.* Many regulations for national banks are made and enforced by the *Comptroller of the Currency.*

The Comptroller was created in the *National Currency Act of 1863,* and additional powers were given to the office in the *National Banking Act of 1864.*[5] Together, these laws established standards a bank had to meet before receiving a national charter. They also promoted the development of a uniform currency by authorizing national bank notes that could be issued only by banks with federal charters. Although public confidence in the notes encouraged many state-chartered banks to switch to federal charters, other state banks remained viable by popularizing demand deposit accounts and encouraging customers to accept checks as an alternative to currency for the payment of bills. The current *dual banking system,* in which both states and the federal government issue bank charters, is traced to this period.

The *Federal Reserve System (the Fed)* supervises federally chartered institutions, which must be members of the Federal Reserve System, and state-chartered banks choosing Fed membership voluntarily. The Fed was created by the *Federal Reserve Act of 1913* to ensure the existence of both a flexible payments system and a lender of last resort for troubled banks.

State-chartered banks also must comply with the regulations of banking authorities in the state. All banks are eligible to purchase deposit insurance from the *Federal Deposit Insurance Corporation (FDIC),* created in the Glass-Steagall Act. Fed member banks must be insured by the FDIC. If a bank purchases insurance, it must comply with rules set by the FDIC.

Because the three major federal banking regulators—the Comptroller, the Fed, and the FDIC—arose at different times to serve different purposes, they are independent of one another. They are not always legally required to coordinate their actions, and conflicts and even competition exist among them, adding an additional dimension to the regulatory dialectic.

Thrifts. Like commercial banks, thrifts may have either state or federal charters. The major federal regulator for thrifts is the *Federal Home Loan Bank Board (FHLBB).* The dual chartering system for thrifts dates to the *Home Owners' Loan Act of 1933,* which empowered the FHLBB, created in 1932 to be a lender of last resort for S&Ls, to grant federal thrift charters. Deposit insurance is available from either the FDIC, the *Federal Savings and Loan Insurance Corporation (FSLIC),* or nonfederal insurance funds, depending upon whether the thrift is a savings bank or savings association. The FSLIC was created in the *National Housing Act of 1934* to perform a role similar to that of the FDIC. Finally, the Federal Reserve Board is authorized to set reserve requirements on deposits held by thrift institutions.

Credit Unions. Credit unions also operate under a dual chartering system. The major federal credit union regulator is the *National Credit Union Administration (NCUA).* Credit unions may purchase deposit insurance from the *National Credit Union Share Insurance Fund (NCUSIF),* established in the 1970 Amendments to the National Credit Union Act, or from individual state funds. Reserve requirements on deposits are enforced by the Federal Reserve Board.

What Is Regulated?

Table 2.2 on page 28 provides a summary, prepared by the Federal Reserve Bank of New York, of regulated management areas and the

---

[5]There is considerable confusion in the financial and historical literature on the names of these laws and the dates they were passed. The names and dates used here were selected after a review of historical accounts.

agencies responsible for monitoring institutions' behavior in each area. That compilation provides convincing evidence of the extent of the restrictions and the complexity of the structure. For example, 12 categories of control are identified, ranging from initial entry into an industry (chartering and licensing) to customer relationships (consumer protection).[6]

Table 2.2 identifies the agencies with which a single institution interacts. Consider, for example, a state-chartered savings and loan association (row F(2) in the table). Four state and federal authorities either set the rules for its operations, enforce the rules, or do both. For instance, a state savings institution gets its charter from a state agency, but its ability to branch or acquire other institutions is under the control of both state authorities and the FHLBB. The Federal Reserve Board determines the S&L's reserve requirements on deposits, and these deposits may be insured by the FSLIC or a nonfederal insurance fund.

Are There Too Many Regulators?

Few disagree that the activities of regulatory agencies are duplicative. In 1974, Arthur Burns, then Chairman of the Board of Governors of the Federal Reserve, called the bank regulatory system "a jurisdictional tangle that boggles the mind."[7] Beginning with the Hoover Commission in 1949, considerable resources have been devoted to analyzing the system and recommending reforms. The most recent effort was the Task Group on Deregulation of Financial Services, headed by Vice-President George Bush (and more commonly known as the *Bush Task Group*), which made its recommendations to Congress in 1984.

Some studies advocate consolidating supervisory power in a single agency, while others warn against giving any single organization too much power. The Bush Task Group did not recommend complete consolidation, but instead suggested reorganizing agencies along functional lines, giving one agency the authority over federal deposit insurance, another over examination and supervision, and so forth. The Task Group envisioned a new "superagency" for banking, with the suggested name of the Federal Banking Agency, to replace the Comptroller of the Currency. The Fed would concentrate on monetary policy and international issues, but would have veto power over the new agency. Critics believe the Bush Task Group did not go far enough toward reducing duplication, but others consider the plan an improvement over the current system. As with earlier reports, however, Congress has delayed action on the proposals. Interestingly, major opponents of reorganization include some regulated institutions, which enjoy protection under existing agencies, as Kane's dialectic predicts.[8]

FINANCE COMPANIES

In contrast to depositories, the sources and uses of funds of finance companies are not heavily regulated at the federal level. These institutions raise funds in the debt markets rather than from deposits and do not have to meet federal reserve requirements or other asset restrictions.

Licensing Restrictions

Finance companies must seek permission from state authorities to open new offices. They enjoy more freedom than banks or thrifts to expand across state lines, however, because there is no federal restriction on interstate operations. In most states, a request to open a new office is evaluated by the *"convenience and advantage" rule,* which holds that expansion should occur

---

[6]Discussion of the details of these regulations is reserved for the chapters devoted to the specific management areas. For example, regulations governing expansion are covered in Chapter 3, reserve requirements in Chapter 12, deposit restrictions in Chapter 15, and so on.

[7]Cited in Verle B. Johnson, "Reorganization?" *Weekly Letter,* Federal Reserve Bank of San Francisco, March 2, 1984.

[8]For more information, see Johnson, "Reorganization?"; Gary G. Gilbert, "An Analysis of the Bush Task Group Recommendations for Bank Regulatory Reform," *Issues in Bank Regulation* 7 (Spring 1984): 11-16; Jill Andresky, "Too Many Cooks and No Recipe," *Forbes* 136 (December 16, 1985): 96.

Table 2.2
Depository Institutions and Their Regulators

	Chartering and Licensing	Branching	
		Intrastate	Interstate
A. National Banks	Comptroller	Comptroller	**(2)**
B. State Member Banks	State authority	Federal Reserve and state authority	**(2)**
C. Insured State Nonmember Banks	State authority	FDIC and state authority	**(2)**
D. Noninsured State Banks	State authority	State authority	**(3)**
E. Savings Banks			
(1) Federal Mutual	FHLBB	FHLBB	FHLBB **(4)**
(2) State Mutual	State authority	FDIC and state authority	FDIC and state authority
F. Savings and Loan Associations			
(1) Federal	FHLBB	FHLBB	FHLBB **(4)**
(2) State	State authority	FHLBB and state authority	FHLBB and state authority
G. Credit Unions			
(1) Federal	NCUAB	**(1)**	**(1)**
(2) State	State authority	State authority	State authority

(1) Federal credit unions are not required to receive approval from the NCUAB before opening a branch.
(2) While the McFadden Act prevents interstate branching by national banks, state member banks, and insured state nonmember banks, banks can provide certain services on an interstate basis.

(3) The McFadden Act's interstate branching restrictions are generally not applicable to noninsured state banks.
(4) As a matter of policy, the FHLBB has prohibited interstate branching by federal thrifts. Limited exceptions have been made in cases of failing institutions.

continued

Comptroller	Office of the Comptroller of the Currency
FDIC	Federal Deposit Insurance Corporation
FHLBB	Federal Home Loan Bank Board
Federal Reserve	Board of Governors of the Federal Reserve System/Federal Reserve Banks
FSLIC	Federal Savings and Loan Insurance Corporation
NCUAB	National Credit Union Association Board
NCUSIF	National Credit Union Share Insurance Fund
N/A	Not applicable
S&L	Savings and loan association

Source: Federal Reserve Bank of New York, "Depository Institutions and Their Regulators," 1984.

only if the community will benefit. As a result, limitations on competition within individual states or communities may exist.[9]

---

[9]Although the absence of a federal chartering agency removes one layer of regulation, it also means that if a firm is denied a charter at the state level, no recourse is available. The resulting competitive impact of this and other state restrictions is explored more fully in Richard T. Selden, "Consumer-Oriented Intermediaries," in *Financial Institutions and Markets,* 2d ed. Murray E. Polakoff and Thomas A. Durkin, eds. (Boston: Houghton Mifflin, 1981), pp. 207-212.

Table 2.2
Depository Institutions and Their Regulators *(continued)*

Mergers, Acquisitions, and Consolidations		Reserve Requirements	Access to the Discount Window	Deposit Insurance
Intrastate	**Interstate**			
Comptroller **(5)**	**(11)**	Federal Reserve **(12)**	Federal Reserve **(13)**	FDIC
Federal Reserve and state authority **(6)**	**(11)**	Federal Reserve **(12)**	Federal Reserve **(13)**	FDIC
FDIC and state authority **(7)**	**(11)**	Federal Reserve **(12)**	Federal Reserve **(13)**	FDIC
State authority **(8)**	State authority	Federal Reserve **(12)**	Federal Reserve **(13)**	None or state insurance fund **(14)**
FHLBB	**(11)**	Federal Reserve **(12)**	Federal Reserve **(13)**	FSLIC or FDIC **(15)**
FDIC and state authority **(9)**	**(11)**	Federal Reserve **(12)**	Federal Reserve **(13)**	FDIC or state insurance fund **(15)**
FHLBB	**(11)**	Federal Reserve **(12)**	Federal Home Loan Bank and Federal Reserve **(13)**	FSLIC **(16)**
FHLBB and state authority	**(11)**	Federal Reserve **(12)**	Federal Home Loan Bank and Federal Reserve **(13)**	FSLIC or state insurance fund **(16)**
NCUAB	**(11)**	Federal Reserve **(12)**	Central Liquidity Facility and Federal Reserve **(13)**	NCUSIF **(17)**
NCUAB and state authority **(10)**	**(11)**	Federal Reserve **(12)**	Central Liquidity Facility and Federal Reserve **(13)**	NCUSIF or state insurance fund **(17)**

(5) The Comptroller must approve the merger or acquisition if the resulting bank is a national bank.

(6) The Federal Reserve must approve the merger or acquisition if the resulting bank is a state member bank.

(7) The FDIC must approve the merger or acquisition if the resulting bank is an insured state nonmember bank.

(8) In addition to state authority, the FDIC must approve mergers or acquisitions between insured and noninsured banks.

(9) The FDIC must approve the merger or acquisition if the resulting bank is an insured bank other than a federal savings bank.

(10) The NCUAB must approve the merger or acquisition if the resulting credit union is federally insured.

(11) The McFadden Act prevents interstate branching by national banks, state member banks, and insured state nonmember banks. However, the Garn-St Germain Depository Institutions Act of 1982 provides a statutory framework within which the FDIC and the FSLIC may arrange interstate and interindustry acquisitions or mergers of closed or failing federally insured depository institutions. Similar authority has also been granted to the NCUAB with regard to credit unions.

(12) Under the Depository Institutions Deregulation and Monetary Control Act of 1980, the Federal Reserve is required to set a uniform system of reserve requirements (Regulation D) for virtually all depository institutions. Those requirements will be phased in by September 1987. Noninsured state banks that are eligible for deposit insurance may be subject to reserve requirements.

(13) Nearly all depository institutions in the United States, including branches and agencies of foreign banks, have access to the discount window. These depository institutions are expected to make reasonable use of their usual sources of funds before turning to Federal Reserve Banks. For example, S&Ls and credit unions should first go to the Federal Home Loan Banks and the Central Liquidity Facility, respectively.

(14) Deposits that are not insured by the FDIC may be insured by state insurance funds.

(15) Deposits in federal savings banks are insured by the FSLIC. Deposits in state savings banks are insured by the FDIC. However, under the Garn-St Germain Depository Institutions Act, state savings banks that convert to federal charters may continue to have their deposits insured by the FDIC. Deposits in savings banks that are not insured by either of these federal deposit insurance agencies may be insured by state insurance funds.

(16) Deposits in all federal S&Ls as well as in many state S&Ls are insured by the FSLIC. Deposits in nonfederally insured institutions may be insured by state insurance funds.

(17) Shares in all federal credit unions and many state credit unions are insured by the National Credit Union Share Insurance Fund, which is administered by the NCUAB. Shares in some state credit unions may be insured by state insurance funds.

Table 2.2
Depository Institutions and Their Regulators *(continued)*

	Supervision and Examination	Prudential Limits, Safety, and Soundness	Consumer Protection	
			Rulemaking	Enforcement
A. National Banks	Comptroller	Comptroller	Federal Reserve	Comptroller
B. State Member Banks	Federal Reserve and state authority	Federal Reserve and state authority	Federal Reserve and state authority	Federal Reserve and state authority
C. Insured State Nonmember Banks	FDIC and state authority	FDIC and state authority	Federal Reserve and state authority	FDIC and state authority
D. Noninsured State Banks	State authority	State authority	Federal Reserve and state authority	State authority
E. Savings Banks **(1) Federal Mutual**	FHLBB **(18)**	FHLBB	Federal Reserve and FHLBB	FHLBB
(2) State Mutual	FDIC and state authority	FDIC and state authority	Federal Reserve, FHLBB, and state authority	FDIC, state authority, or FHLBB **(20)**
F. Savings and Loan Associations **(1) Federal**	FHLBB	FHLBB	Federal Reserve and FHLBB	FHLBB
(2) State	FSLIC or state authority **(19)**	FHLBB or state authority	Federal Reserve, FHLBB, and state authority	FHLBB, FSLIC, or state authority **(21)**
G. Credit Unions **(1) Federal**	NCUAB	NCUAB	Federal Reserve and state authority	NCUAB
(2) State	State authority	State authority	Federal Reserve and state authority	State authority

(18) The FDIC has the right to examine state savings banks that have converted to federal charter but whose deposits continue to be insured by the FDIC.

(19) Federally insured S&Ls are supervised and examined by the FSLIC: nonfederally insured state S&Ls by state authority.

(20) The FHLBB may share enforcement responsibility over savings banks that are members of the Federal Home Loan Bank System.

(21) The FHLBB would not have enforcement responsibility over state S&Ls that are neither members of the Federal Home Loan Bank System nor insured by the FSLIC.

Comptroller	Office of the Comptroller of the Currency
FDIC	Federal Deposit Insurance Corporation
FHLBB	Federal Home Loan Bank Board
Federal Reserve	Board of Governors of the Federal Reserve System/Federal Reserve Banks
FSLIC	Federal Savings and Loan Insurance Corporation

NCUAB	National Credit Union Association Board
NCUSIF	National Credit Union Share Insurance Fund
N/A	Not applicable
S&L	Savings and Loan Association

Consumer Protection Legislation

Finance companies face other regulations as well. An extensive body of consumer protection legislation has accumulated since 1968 and affects the managerial decisions of finance companies and other consumer lenders. In the finance company industry, the responsibility for monitoring compliance with consumer protection laws such as the *Consumer Credit Protection (Truth-in-Lending) Act of 1968* and *Equal Credit Opportunity Act of 1974* lies with the Bureau of Consumer Protection in the Division of Credit Practices of the Federal Trade Commission.

Federal regulations have focused on equality in the availability of credit, and on the completeness, accuracy, and uniformity of information disclosed to potential borrowers. At the state level, regulations concentrate on the rate of interest charged. In recent years, attention has focused on state *usury ceilings,* which are legal limitations on lending rates. When market interest rates rise significantly above the usury ceilings, as they did in the early 1980s, severe problems for lenders are created, and the amount of available credit is restricted.

Again, in the spirit of Kane's regulatory dialectic, state regulations have been modified in the 1980s, necessitated by market conditions or by regulatory actions at the federal level. For example, in 1980, federal law removed usury ceilings from residential mortgage loans unless states overrode the action by 1983; the majority of states did not. Many states increased or removed usury ceilings on personal loans after market interest rates rose to historic highs in 1980 and 1981.

INSURANCE COMPANIES

Life insurers and property and casualty insurers have a regulatory system that falls somewhere in between those of depository institutions and finance companies. The *McCarran-Ferguson Act of 1945* gave the federal government the right to regulate insurance companies.[10] Congress agreed, however, that the right to impose federal regulations would not be exercised until 1948, and would not be exercised at all if states adequately established and enforced standards for the industry. Thus, the legal foundation for federal regulation of insurers exists, but for all practical purposes insurers operate at the direction of state agencies. Commissioners of insurance in each state wield a considerable degree of power individually, and exert influence collectively through the *National Association of Insurance Commissioners (NAIC),* an organization with no legal power but with considerable political clout.

Recent increases in the cost of property and casualty insurance have renewed calls for federal regulation of that industry, or, at a minimum, for tighter regulation at the state level. These developments are discussed in Chapter 23.

Licensing and Solvency Requirements

Regulatory structure aside, a number of similarities exist in the scope and focus of regulations with which insurers and depository institutions must comply. For example, strict standards designed to protect the solvency of insurers are applied in granting company licenses. After entry is granted, annual financial statements are closely scrutinized, and insurers are subject to frequent examinations. Finally, analogous to deposit insurance agencies, insolvency guarantee funds are established in all states to protect policyholders should an insurer go bankrupt.

Rate Regulation

A considerable amount of time is devoted to rate regulation. Generally, regulators agree that rates charged by insurers, when combined with income from investments, must be sufficient to cover the potential liabilities of the firm. At the

---

[10]Before 1945, the insurance regulatory structure was based on the ruling of the Supreme Court in *Paul v. Virginia,* 75 U. S. 168, 8 Wall 168, 19 L Ed 357 (1869), that insurance was not interstate commerce and was therefore not subject to federal regulation. Thus, no federal regulatory structure existed when the McCarran-Ferguson Act was passed.

same time, rates must not be excessive or discriminate unfairly. Although insurers must differentiate between high-risk and low-risk customers and charge accordingly, regulations attempt to prevent rate discrimination not justified by differing levels of risk. The approach state legislators and commissioners of insurance take toward achieving ideal rates differs from state to state and varies according to the category of insurer.

Generally, the policy premiums life insurers may charge are not directly controlled, but standards designed to guarantee sufficient reserves to cover future claims are imposed in most states. Thus, the regulations establish a floor for policy rates, because insurers must set rates high enough to generate the required reserves. For property and casualty insurers, state regulations on policy rates are more extensive. Most states require property and casualty insurers to obtain the approval of regulators before increasing policy rates.[11]

Product Regulation

Just as depository institutions have operated under asset and deposit restrictions for many years, insurers must comply with limitations on the types of policies they can offer. In many states, insurers must seek the approval of the insurance commissioner before they can sell new products. The close scrutiny is intended to protect customers against unfair policy provisions and to protect the insurance firm from commitments that may undermine its financial stability.

Asset Structure

Insurers' investments are also regulated. State insurance codes specify permissible categories and quality grades of assets. Many states restrict the percentage of firms' total assets that may be

invested in specific types of securities, such as common stock.

PENSION FUNDS

Pension funds operate under contractual savings agreements that obligate them to pay retirement benefits to workers. The pension plans of private corporations are subject to the *Employee Retirement Income Security Act,* passed by Congress in 1974 and more commonly known as *ERISA.*

Investment Management

ERISA covers almost all areas of pension fund management. Two provisions set standards for *vested benefits* to plan participants, and for funding a plan so that assets are equal to accrued liabilities. Vested benefits are those to which employees are entitled even if they leave the firm before retirement. ERISA requires early vesting of benefits and ensures that most employees are 100 percent vested after 15 years of service.

ERISA also sets standards for employer contributions in relation to the fund's investment income and benefit liabilities. Generally, ERISA attempts to ensure that employers work toward making pension assets equal to the fund's obligations. Pension fund managers have *fiduciary responsibility* for investment of assets, and they are required to act solely in the interests of the fund's beneficiaries.

Pension Insurance

Another ERISA provision, also designed to protect the financial interests of fund members, established an insurance fund to guarantee that benefits are paid to eligible members even if a pension plan defaults on its obligations. This federal insurance agency is called the *Pension Benefit Guaranty Corporation (PBGC)* and is funded by assessments on an employer according to the number of employees covered. To ensure the continuing financial stability of pension funds, the law imposes requirements

---

[11]For an exhaustive review of the effect of rate regulation on property and casualty firms, see Scott Harrington, "The Impact of Rate Regulation on Prices and Underwriting Results in the Property-Liability Insurance Industry: A Survey," *Journal of Risk and Insurance* 51 (December 1984): 577-623.

for extensive and frequent reporting and disclosure.

INVESTMENT COMPANIES

Investment companies act as portfolio managers for those to whom they sell ownership shares. Because investment company shares are sold publicly, and because many of their assets are publicly traded, investment companies must comply with federal securities laws. The obligations of fund managers to shareholders are also defined by federal and state laws.

Federal Securities Laws

The issuance of ownership shares by investment companies, and the frequency and accuracy of their financial reports, are monitored by the *Securities and Exchange Commission (SEC),* under the authority of the Securities Act of 1933 and the Securities Exchange Act of 1934. Many provisions affecting investment companies also apply to other firms that issue securities for sale to the public. Some provisions address investment companies specifically, however, to ensure regular and truthful disclosures to existing and potential shareholders.

The Securities Act of 1933 focuses on new issues, requiring firms to provide full and accurate information about their financial positions and about new securities offered. The Securities and Exchange Act of 1934 established the SEC as the chief regulator of the securities markets and requires regular disclosure of financial information by firms with publicly traded securities.

Securities laws are rooted in the belief that access to information is the best guarantor of the public interest. Depository institution legislation, in contrast, has produced elaborate regulatory systems for gathering information, much of which is unavailable to the public. The securities and investment company industries operate with a strong system of self-regulation through trade organizations, whereas depository trade organizations are more like political action groups, seeking to preserve existing laws

or to promote new legislation in the halls of Congress.

Regulations on Sources and Uses of Funds

The Investment Company Act of 1940 and subsequent amendments, and the *Investment Advisers Act* of the same year, are the foundation for specific regulations governing investment companies. These laws identify responsibilities of investment advisers and fund managers. For example, the use of financial leverage is limited. In addition, mutual fund managers must obtain shareholder approval of a change in investment objectives, so that shareholders are guaranteed at least some degree of control over the risk exposure and return potential of the funds.

The Investment Company Act also imposed diversification requirements to protect shareholders against the risk of total loss. Investment companies may invest no more than 5 percent of their assets in any one firm, and may hold no more than 10 percent of the outstanding voting shares of a company. These restrictions apply to 75 percent of an investment company's portfolio; the remaining 25 percent is exempted to encourage investment in smaller businesses.

Another influence on managers is the exemption of investment company income from federal taxes if at least 90 percent of net capital gain income and 97 percent of dividend and interest income is distributed to shareholders. Taxes are paid only by individual shareholders, and no taxes are assessed on the fund, an approach to taxation known as the *conduit theory.* Finally, federal regulatory and tax codes are supplemented by state codes placing additional responsibilities on fund managers.

In contrast to savings at depository institutions, pension funds, or insurance firms, funds entrusted to investment companies have no guarantee of recovery in case of fund failure. The goal of regulation is to ensure availability of truthful information. If investors make a bad choice of investment companies, however, no federal or state insurance will mitigate the loss.

SECURITIES FIRMS

Like investment companies, securities firms are subject to SEC scrutiny under the Securities and Exchange Act and its amendments. The act established maximum levels of indebtedness for securities dealers and gave the Fed the authority to set *margin requirements* governing loans by securities firms to customers for the purchase of securities. In addition, securities firms are prohibited from using inside information about firms to profit at the expense of the public. Firms selling investment advice to clients are subject to the Investment Advisers Act of 1940, which seeks to prevent fraudulent practices. The scope of a firm's operations determines additional constraints to which it is subject. For example, members of the New York Stock Exchange must conform to the self-regulating rules of the exchange.

The industry operates under Congressional objectives for a national securities market articulated in the *Securities Acts Amendments of 1975.* This legislation directed the SEC to promote a fully competitive trading system under which investors nationwide have equal and instantaneous access to information. Historic practices concentrating trades in a few locations, like New York City, would be eliminated. Although progress has been made toward this goal, it has yet to be fully achieved.

ORIGINS OF FINANCIAL INNOVATION AND REGULATORY REFORM IN THE 1980s

The discussion of the regulatory dialectic introduced forces producing regulatory reform, including financial market changes and regulatory avoidance behavior. No example of the confluence of these forces and the regulatory response is clearer than events leading to two of the most important pieces of financial legislation of the 1980s, DIDMCA and Garn-St Germain.

By 1980, the need for reforms was widely recognized. As noted, several government commissions had studied the problems of financial institutions and recommended revisions in the regulatory structure. Congress, however, failed to respond with substantive changes. As problems motivating the formation of those study groups reappeared in the late 1970s, federal legislators again turned their attention to the possibility of regulatory reform.[12] These problems stimulated antithetical forces that culminated in major regulatory revisions.

Economic Conditions

As 1980 approached, inflation and interest rates were reaching historically high levels. Uncertainty about future interest rates was great, arising from expected inflation and fears that changes in the Federal Reserve's approach to monetary policy would increase rate volatility.

When unusual uncertainty about future economic conditions exists, financial market participants respond by demanding investments that reduce their risk exposure. A rigid regulatory structure prevents financial institutions from responding to customer demands rapidly, and in some cases prevents any response at all. Regulatory restrictions may also prevent managers of financial institutions from making investment decisions necessary to protect the stability and level of the institution's income.

Interest Rate Ceilings

As mentioned earlier, by the late 1970s, Reg Q ceilings were lower than market interest rates. As a result, depositors withdrew funds to invest in instruments with the potential to earn a higher rate of return. When funds are removed

---

[12]More details on the problems that precipitated formation of these commissions, as well as a discussion of their recommendations, are available in numerous sources, including: Robert Craig West, "The Depository Institutions Deregulation Act of 1980: A Historical Perspective," *Economic Review,* Federal Reserve Bank of Kansas City 67 (February 1982): 3–13; Federal Reserve Bank of Chicago, "The Depository Institutions Deregulation and Monetary Control Act of 1980"; and Bernard Shull, "Economic Efficiency, Public Regulation, and Financial Reform: Depository Institutions," in *Financial Institutions and Markets,* 2d ed. Murray E. Polakoff and Thomas A. Durkin, eds. (Boston: Houghton Mifflin, 1981), pp. 671–702.

from financial institutions in favor of direct investments, the phenomenon is known as *disintermediation.*

Large commercial banks had developed regulation-avoidance strategies to prevent large depositors from disintermediating. Small savers, however, had few alternatives except to try other financial institutions such as mutual funds, on which returns were tied to market conditions. In other words, depositories were also subject to *cross-intermediation,* or the transfer of funds from one financial intermediary to another. In the 1970s, many investment companies had introduced money market mutual funds (MMMFs), whose assets were invested in short-term securities. MMMFs offered liquidity through check-writing privileges and a relatively low level of risk, because fund portfolios included a large proportion of U.S. government securities. More importantly, their rate of return was not controlled by Regulation Q.

The Initial Regulatory Response to Binding Ceilings.   Beginning in 1978, regulators made several "patchwork" attempts to revise regulations that had contributed to disintermediation and cross-intermediation. New types of deposit accounts (discussed in more detail in Chapter 15) were permitted, each designed to allow small savers to earn market rates of interest or to earn a modest return on checking account balances.

Although the new accounts were popular, they could not stem the tide of disintermediation as interest rates soared to unprecedented levels in late 1979. Furthermore, the right of federal regulators to introduce deposit innovations without explicit Congressional action was challenged, and eventually a Court of Appeals ruling established a January 1, 1980, deadline for eliminating the innovations unless Congress acted. Although final action was not forthcoming by that date, Congress extended the life of the new deposits temporarily, to expire March 31, 1980.[13]

Declining Fed Membership

Additional acts of regulatory avoidance in the late 1970s added to the need for reform legislation by 1980. Before then, only commercial banks that were members of the Federal Reserve System were required to keep nonearning *reserves* at regional Federal Reserve Banks. Reserve deposits are intended to provide an institution with sufficient liquid funds to meet customers' deposit withdrawals and to assist the Fed in controlling lending. Nonmember banks, thrifts, and credit unions were not subject to the same kinds of reserve requirements. As interest rates rose, the opportunity cost of nonearning reserves was more and more burdensome for member banks.

To the dismay of Federal Reserve officials, an increasingly large number of banks resigned Fed membership, and most new banks chose to obtain state charters to avoid the Fed's reserve requirements. The Fed argued that as the proportion of deposits held by member banks declined, the effectiveness of reserve requirements as a tool of monetary policy declined. Fed officials pressured Congress to introduce a more equitable system.

Declining Profitability

Some financial institutions needed more flexibility to protect against interest rate risk, just as individual and corporate investors did. Once again, however, regulations prevented them from adjusting asset portfolios quickly in response to market conditions. For example, profits in the thrift industry suffered because institutions were, to comply with regulations, heavily invested in long-term, fixed-rate mortgages. As thrifts incurred higher interest expenses on new deposit accounts, they needed to increase returns on assets. They had little ability to diversify, however, especially in comparison to commercial banks, and their profits declined at an alarming rate.[14]

---

[13]For more details on these events, see Kent W. Colton, "Financial Reform: A Review of the Past and Prospects for the Future," invited research working paper, #37, Federal Home Loan Bank Board, September 1980.

[14]A good summary of the plight of the thrift institutions before DIDMCA is available in Bronwyn Brock, "Regulatory Changes Bring New Challenges to S&Ls, Other Depository Institutions," *Voice,* Federal Reserve Bank of Dallas (September 1980): 5-9.

Insurers also had problems. Consumers no longer demanded traditional life insurance products. Property and casualty insurers suffered because inflation increased their claims expenses more rapidly than they could increase income. These pressures, too, called for regulatory changes.

Technological Innovation

The influence of technology was also great. Computers made it possible to analyze large quantities of data efficiently and revolutionized the availability of information. *Electronic funds transfers,* or movement of funds by electronic impulse rather than by paper check or other traditional method, were increasing. As a result, financial institutions could offer more services and respond more rapidly to market conditions than ever before, and their demands for the power to diversify services became increasingly forceful.

In the face of technology, regulations began to seem antiquated. As information systems enabled some participants in the financial markets, such as securities firms, to respond almost instantaneously to changes in interest rates or other market conditions, restrictive regulations on others, such as depositories, appeared anticompetitive. Said Henry Wallich, member of the Board of Governors of the Federal Reserve, "Deregulation has been driven . . . by technological innovation. Anticompetitive practices have had to be abandoned, on pain of being circumvented; bureaucratic resistance had to yield to the pressures of the market."[15]

Competitive Inequities: The Call for a "Level Playing Field"

Depository institutions saw their competitors grow in number. Investment companies, insurance companies, brokerage firms, and even diversified firms such as Sears, Roebuck introduced financial products that encroached on territory previously controlled by depositories. The latter grew more vocal in their demands for regulatory reform, arguing that they labored under restrictions not faced by competitors. For example, while Merrill Lynch and Sears were free to offer services nationwide, many depositories could not even open a branch in the next county, let alone another state. While competitors could offer a wide variety of financial products, services offered by a depository were limited. Protestors called for a "level playing field," a set of rules allowing them to compete on an equal footing.

Changing Views on Regulation: Does It Really Promote Safety?

A final catalyst for change was more subtle. As memories of the financial crisis of the 1930s faded, regulators may have modified their views on the rationale for regulation.[16] For example, recognition grew that interest rate ceilings had a destabilizing effect on the economy, provoking reevaluation of regulations intended to prevent competition among depositories. Furthermore, it was apparent that forcing specialization on institutions such as S&Ls did not ensure their stability or solvency. The deterioration of the financial position of the thrift industry was one more incentive to examine the philosophy that had traditionally guided regulators. It was no longer clear that regulations promoted institutional safety: the possibility arose that regulations might actually make institutions riskier.

DIDMCA

These factors led Congress to enact the landmark Depository Institutions Deregulation and Monetary Control legislation on March 31,

---

[15]Henry C. Wallich, "A Broad View of Deregulation," unpublished remarks at the Conference on Pacific Basin Financial Reform, Federal Reserve Bank of San Francisco, San Francisco, California, December 1984, p. 3.

[16]References to the changing regulatory philosophy are found in Thomas F. Cargill and Gillian Garcia, *Financial Reform in the 1980s* (Stanford, CA: Hoover Institution Press, 1985), pp. 55-56; and Robert Craig West, "The Depository Institutions Deregulation Act of 1980: A Historical Perspective."

1980, the day depositories' authority to offer new deposit accounts was to expire. The act is considered the most significant financial legislation since the Federal Reserve Act of 1913 and the many acts of the 1930s.

DIDMCA had two major components evident in its name: 1) deregulation of depository institutions; and 2) improved monetary control. The deregulation provisions allowed more competition among depositories, while improving financial services for small savers. The monetary control provisions improved the effectiveness of the Fed's responses to changing economic conditions and equalized the monetary policy burden among depositories.

Depository Institutions Deregulation

The deregulation part of the act did not, of course, actually deregulate depository institutions. Many experts refer to it as *"re*-regulation." Nevertheless, DIDMCA introduced important changes in sources and uses of funds for depository institutions.

The ramifications of DIDMCA are broad and are examined in detail in subsequent chapters. The following paragraphs highlight only a few of the consequences, and Table 2.3 summarizes the act. The word "Title" in the table is a legal term indicating a major section of a law.

Elimination of Deposit Interest Rate Ceilings. Title II of DIDMCA provided for the phase-out of interest rate ceilings on deposits over a six-year period ending March 31, 1986. The intent was to provide an orderly transition to market interest rates on deposits. Legislators' introductory remarks to Title II reveal the belief that the ceilings discouraged savings, created inequities for small savers, and had not achieved desired economic goals.[17]

New Sources of Funds. Title III authorized all banks and thrifts to offer interest-bearing *transactions accounts,* or accounts on which an

unlimited number of checks can be written, to individuals and nonprofit organizations. In banks and thrifts, they are called **negotiable orders of withdrawal (NOWs),** and in credit unions, **share drafts.** Interest-bearing checking had been prohibited nationwide since Glass-Steagall in 1933.

New Uses of Funds. The precarious financial position of the thrift industry was blamed on its inability to diversify asset portfolios. To provide relief, Congress allowed savings institutions to invest in a wider variety of nonmortgage instruments, such as consumer loans, commercial paper, investment company shares, and education loans. The intent of Congress was to allow thrifts to achieve a better balance between asset and liability maturities. The importance of maturity matching for institution management is discussed at many points later in this book.

To further strengthen their competitive position, the law allowed savings institutions to offer credit card and trust services. Savings banks were permitted to make commercial loans and, for the first time, to accept **demand deposits,** or noninterest-bearing checking accounts, in conjunction with corporate loan relationships. Although these provisions allowed thrifts to diversify to an unprecedented degree, their uses of funds remained more restricted than funds sources. Congress also preempted state usury ceilings on certain categories of loans, so that thrifts and credit unions could charge rates that were more closely aligned with their cost of funds.

Monetary Control

The first title of DIDMCA addressed monetary policy. The intent was to strengthen the Fed's monetary policy responses.

Universal Reserve Requirements. To arrest the decline in Fed membership, Congress extended reserve requirements to all depositories offering transaction accounts. To improve the Fed's ability to monitor the economy, Congress authorized the Board to require regular

---

[17]Federal Reserve Bank of Chicago, "The Depository Institutions Deregulation and Monetary Control Act of 1980," pp. 12-13.

Table 2.3
Provisions of the Depository Institutions Deregulation
and Monetary Control Act of 1980

Title I: Monetary Control Act of 1980

Phased in reserve requirements on transactions accounts at all depository institutions; authorized the Fed to impose supplemental interest-bearing reserve requirements if necessary; extended discount window borrowing privileges and other Fed services to any depository institution issuing transactions accounts or nonpersonal time deposits; mandated the development of a fee structure for Fed services

Title II: Depository Institutions Deregulation Act of 1980

Provided for the orderly phase-out and ultimate elimination of interest rate ceilings on deposit accounts

Title III: Consumer Checking Account Equity Act of 1980

Authorized interest-bearing transactions accounts at all depositories; increased federal deposit insurance coverage from $40,000 to $100,000

Title IV: Expanded Powers for Thrifts

Allowed federally chartered S&Ls to invest in consumer and other loans, commercial paper, corporate bonds, and mutual funds; authorized federal thrifts to issue credit cards; increased powers for savings banks, including demand deposit accounts to commercial loan customers

Title V: Preemption of State Interest Rate Ceilings

Eliminated state usury ceilings on residential mortgage loans; tied ceiling rates on business and agricultural loans of $25,000 or more to the Federal Reserve discount rate; gave states until April 1, 1983, to reinstate usury ceilings on these loan categories; overrode state laws imposing ceilings on deposit interest rates

Title VI: Truth-in-Lending Simplification

Revised the Truth-in-Lending Act to make it easier for creditors to comply with disclosure requirements; gave consumers additional rights in case of false disclosure

Title VII: Amendments to the National Banking Laws

Miscellaneous provisions on national banks and bank holding companies

Title VIII: Financial Regulation Simplification Act of 1980

Required regulators to limit regulations to those "for which a need has been established" and to minimize compliance costs

Title IX: Foreign Control of U.S. Financial Institutions

Imposed a moratorium until July 1, 1980, on foreign takeover of U.S. financial institutions

---

reports on assets and liabilities.[18] The incentive for banks to resign from the Fed disappeared because resignation no longer offered an escape from nonearning reserves.

Some relief was available to member banks, however, because the act reduced the required percentage of deposits to be kept on reserve. Recognizing the reserve management problems depositories would face, Congress set a phase-

---

[18]In practice, severe problems arose in trying to monitor the assets and liabilities of almost 40,000 depository institutions. After those data collection and analysis problems were recognized, the first $2 million in transactions deposits were exempted from required reserves. In effect, that ruling entirely exempted a large number of smaller

depositories, especially credit unions, and was made permanent by Congress in the Garn-St Germain Act of 1982. The amount of reservable liabilities subject to the 0 percent requirement is adjusted annually using a formula stipulated by Congress.

in period for the new regulations. The reserves continue to be noninterest-bearing.[19] Details on implementation of Title I are presented in Chapter 12.

Universal Access to Federal Reserve Services. Whereas holding nonearning reserves had been a major cost of Fed membership, the ability to borrow from the Fed (to use the *discount window*) and to obtain free services such as check clearing and securities safekeeping were offsetting benefits. Once reserve requirements were extended to all institutions, Congress directed the Fed to make services available to all depositories and to charge for services that had previously been free. Any depository institution now has the right to use the discount window or to purchase Fed check-clearing or other services.[20] The same fee structure applies to members and nonmembers.

AFTER DIDMCA: CONTINUING NEED FOR REFORM

The monumental changes introduced by DIDMCA produced no overnight miracles. The act included phase-in periods for several provisions, and changes in the asset structure of thrifts could not be accomplished quickly. In the context of the regulatory dialectic, DIDMCA did not produce a synthesis. Additional pressures for change began even before final passage of DIDMCA, and afterward, continued to gain momentum.[21]

Crisis in the Thrift Industry

Despite DIDMCA, thrifts' profitability continued to decline at an alarming rate. In 1981, the Federal Home Loan Bank authorized thrifts to offer adjustable-rate mortgages, hoping the industry would be able to earn interest revenues above interest expenses. But market interest rates, especially on short-term deposits, remained high well into 1982, and the cost of funds to many S&Ls remained above the rate of return on assets. Operating losses mounted, and massive failures were predicted.[22]

The prospects of a high failure rate alarmed regulators, because both they and Congress doubted whether the resources of the FSLIC were sufficient to protect insured depositors. The status of the industry reached crisis proportions, causing Congress to move more rapidly than usual toward new legislation.

Continuing Growth of Money Market Funds

Despite plans to phase out Regulation Q interest ceilings, the migration of funds from depository institutions to money market mutual funds continued. Depositories still could not compete with the high rates, convenience, and liquidity offered by MMMFs. Leaders in the bank and thrift industries continued to call for freedom to develop deposit accounts that would effectively counteract the outflow of funds.

Pressure for Geographical Expansion

DIDMCA did not address the limits on geographical expansion by banks and thrifts. But depositories' call for a level playing field included the desire to broaden geographical markets, especially as nondepository competitors moved into areas previously served primarily by depositories.

At the same time, regulators found that geographical constraints limited their ability to

---

[19]Normally, marginal reserve requirements range from 3 percent to a maximum of 12 percent. A provision allows the Federal Reserve Board to impose a supplemental requirement of up to 4 percent under specified conditions, but the Fed is required to pay interest on those supplemental reserves.

[20]In practice, the Fed has been reluctant to loan to any institutions but member commercial banks, and it encourages others to borrow from their primary regulators. More details are provided in Chapter 12.

[21]A discussion of the period between DIDMCA and the passage of the Garn–St Germain Act is provided in Chapter 5 of Cargill and Garcia, *Financial Reform in the 1980s.* The material in this section draws on their analysis.

[22]The extent of the financial crisis in the S&L industry was documented in Andrew S. Carron, *The Plight of the Thrift Institutions* (Washington, D. C.: The Brookings Institution, 1982). Carron's predictions of high failure rates in the industry were widely quoted.

deal with troubled institutions. The FSLIC had begun relying more heavily on forced mergers for failing thrifts. Instead of closing a failing thrift, the FSLIC found a stronger institution with which to merge it, thereby avoiding immediate payments to insured depositors. The FSLIC had difficulty finding merger partners located near several large institutions, raising the possibility of a need for interstate mergers. The prospect of high failure rates put regulators and the industry on the same side of the geographic expansion question. In this case, it was clear that regulation had a destabilizing effect.

THE GARN–ST GERMAIN DEPOSITORY INSTITUTIONS ACT OF 1982

The Garn–St Germain Act became law in October 1982. In a summary of the legislation, the research staff of the Federal Reserve Bank of Chicago calls Garn–St Germain "primarily a rescue operation of the S&Ls and mutual savings banks."[23] At the same time, however, it continued the deregulation of depositories and offered new alternatives for small savers. A summary is given in Table 2.4, and highlights are discussed in the following paragraphs.

Sources of Funds

Garn–St Germain allowed banks and thrifts to offer a deposit account specifically designed to compete with MMMFs. The *money market deposit account (MMDA)* has an interest rate similar to the yield on money market funds, with the advantage of FDIC, FSLIC, or NCU-SIF insurance. Other provisions made NOW accounts available to a wider clientele, although not to businesses, and allowed S&Ls to offer demand deposits to corporate borrowers.

Additional Powers for Banks and Thrifts

Some provisions were designed to strengthen thrift institutions. Federally chartered S&Ls were permitted to make commercial loans and to invest a larger proportion of assets in consumer loans than was allowed by DIDMCA. Thrifts were also allowed to invest in securities issued by state and local governments.

Garn–St Germain also gave thrifts flexibility in changing their charter and ownership form. They were permitted to convert from state to federal charter, or vice versa; to switch between S&L and savings bank charters; and to switch forms of ownership. Thrifts were also given relief from remaining limitations on adjustable-rate mortgages and were permitted to enforce due-on-sale provisions in mortgage loan contracts.[24]

Emergency Powers for Regulators

The FDIC and the FSLIC were given broad powers to assist troubled banks and thrifts. The assistance could be loans to or deposits in financially troubled institutions, or the assumption or purchase of some of their assets and liabilities.

Net Worth Certificates. The insurers were also temporarily authorized to issue a new form of support known as a *net worth certificate.* Although essentially a bookkeeping transaction, net worth certificates can prevent an institution's insolvency and outright failure. Details on their impact are provided in Chapter 16.

Arranging Emergency Acquisitions. The FDIC, FSLIC, and federal credit union regulators were authorized to arrange interstate and inter-industry mergers if suitable partners could

---

[23]Several summaries of the act's provisions are available. See Federal Reserve Bank of New York, *Capsule,* Special Issue, No. 27, January 1983; Gillian Garcia et al., "The Garn–St Germain Depository Institutions Act of 1982," *Economic Perspectives,* Federal Reserve Bank of Chicago 7 (March/April 1983): 3-31; Cargill and Garcia, *Financial Reform in the 1980s.*

[24]A due-on-sale clause requires the borrower to repay the mortgage loan in its entirety if the home is sold before the loan has been completely repaid. Without the clause, the new owner may be able to assume the remaining balance of the mortgage loan, without renegotiating the interest rate. S&Ls argued their need to enforce due-on-sale clauses, enabling them to get older loans made at low interest rates off the books.

Table 2.4
Provisions of the Garn–St Germain Depository Institutions Act of 1982

Title I: The Deposit Insurance Flexibility Act

Gave the FDIC, FSLIC, and NCUSIF expanded options to handle failing institutions; established a priority system for emergency acquisition of insolvent depositories, permitting interstate, interindustry acquisitions as a last resort

Title II: The Net Worth Certificate Act

Permitted the FSLIC and FDIC to issue net worth certificates to provide capital assistance to qualifying S&Ls and savings banks

Title III: The Thrift Institution Restructuring Act

Gave federal thrifts broader investment powers, including commercial loans up to 10 percent of total assets by 1984; increased the permissible percentage of consumer loans from 20 percent to 30 percent of total assets; authorized the creation of an account directly competitive with money market mutual funds (later named the money market deposit account) for all depositories; overrode state laws preventing the enforcement of due-on-sale clauses in mortgages; permitted S&Ls to offer demand deposits to commercial loan customers; increased chartering flexibility for thrifts

Title IV: Provisions Relating to National and Member Banks

Increased the amount that could be loaned to a single borrower; exempted small institutions from reserve requirements

Title V: Credit Union Amendments

Streamlined the regulatory process for federal credit unions; expanded CUs' real estate lending powers; increased their authority to invest in government securities

Title VI: Amendment to the Bank Holding Company Act

Prohibited bank holding companies from selling or underwriting insurance

Title VII: Miscellaneous

Authorized the issuance of NOW accounts and share drafts to state and local governments

Title VIII: The Alternative Mortgage Transaction Act of 1982

Permitted state-chartered institutions to offer the same types of adjustable-rate mortgages authorized for federally chartered institutions, unless overridden by new state laws within three years

---

not be found within the state and/or industry.[25] Regulators were first required to attempt to merge firms in the same industry in the same state. If a suitable partner could not be found, an out-of-state institution could be sought. If intraindustry efforts failed, regulators were to seek an acquiring firm within the same state, with an interstate, interindustry merger as the last resort. These emergency powers could be applied in the case of any failing thrift institution, but only in the case of faltering commercial or savings banks with assets over $500 million.[26]

---

[25]Actually, more than one emergency takeover had been arranged and approved before Garn–St Germain was passed. The first was an interstate acquisition of S&Ls in California, New York, and Florida. The most controversial decision, however, was to allow an interindustry acquisition in which Citicorp acquired Fidelity Federal Savings and Loan (California) in mid-1982.

[26]In 1986, as a result of the problems of banks heavily invested in agriculture and energy loans, federal legislation was introduced to change the asset-size test for troubled banks. See John E. Yang, "House Votes Measure to Assist FSLIC, Increase Clout of Financial Regulators," *The Wall Street Journal,* October 8, 1986.

THE YEARS SINCE 1982: THE DIALECTIC CONTINUES

As was true of DIDMCA, Garn-St Germain left important questions either partially or completely unanswered, and there is little doubt that the cat-and-mouse game will continue. Many points of controversy between institutions and regulators, and among institutions, are examined in subsequent chapters; major ones are summarized in this section.

Removal of Geographic Restrictions

Although Garn-St Germain gave the federal stamp of approval to interstate expansion in emergencies, no power was given to *healthy* institutions to broaden markets. In the years since Garn-St Germain, however, state governments have acted where Congress has not. In some states, legislators have invited out-of-state banks to enter their borders. Other states have approved reciprocal laws, allowing out-of-state banks to enter if the opportunity is reciprocated in their home states. In some areas, such as New England, the Southeast, and the Midwest, groups of states have formed *regional compacts,* or reciprocal agreements among participating states.

The desire to compete in interstate markets is a strong incentive to avoid regulations. A favorite strategy by depositories and non-depositories alike in the mid-1980s, discussed in more detail in the next chapter, was to open *limited-service banks,* also known as *nonbank banks.* These are firms that look and act like banks, but are sufficiently different to circumvent regulatory and legal definitions of a bank. Although the Fed opposed nonbank banks, the courts upheld their existence. Many experts predict full interstate operations for all financial institutions by 1990.

Diversification by Depository Institutions

Commercial banks have also been dissatisfied with their limited ability to compete in diversified product markets. In particular, Glass-Steagall prohibitions against involvement by national banks in the securities markets have been the target of bankers' ire, in light of inroads made by securities firms into banking territory. Depositories are also eager to enter the insurance business, from which they have been, for the most part, historically restricted.

At the state level, again, deregulation has moved more quickly. Several states allow state-chartered banks to sell or even to underwrite insurance. Some states allow banks to own insurance companies, and many state-chartered banks, thrifts, and credit unions engage in brokerage activities. National banks entered the securities business through the acquisition of discount brokers in the early 1980s, followed by the Fed's authorization in 1986 of full-service brokerage for institutional customers. Nevertheless, investment banking, and full-service brokerage for consumers, continue to elude most banks. Ironically, as depositories gain new markets in the securities industry to escape one set of regulations, the SEC has attempted to expand its authority over depositories. The activities of depositories in the securities and insurance markets are discussed in Chapter 20.

CONTINUING REGULATORY CONCERNS

While regulated institutions push for freedom to compete, regulators and lawmakers continue to be concerned about safety and soundness and about overlapping regulatory authority.

Controlling Risk

The gradual removal of restrictions for depository and other financial institutions does not imply that government officials believe in complete deregulation. Instead, efforts are directed toward increasing the effectiveness and fairness of regulation.

The Role of Federal Insurance.   Many observers are concerned about the fee structure for federal insurance programs, especially for deposits and pension benefits, and about the effect these programs have on the risk assumed by managers of financial institutions. Currently, depository institutions and private pension plans obtain federal insurance by paying premiums that reflect the amount of insured obligations but not the risk of loss to the insurer. Many experts advocate a system of risk-adjusted premiums as a replacement. This option is not deregulation per se, but rather a step toward synthesis in response to the activities of institutions in the 1980s.[27]

The proponents of a new pricing system argue that institutions should be charged explicitly for the risk they choose to assume, rather than being told what they can and cannot do. Difficulties in developing a new insurance plan are explored in Chapters 15 and 16.

Stronger Capital Requirements. Regulators have also debated changing the required level of capital with which institutions operate. As explained in the next chapter, an institution's capital is a cushion that absorbs temporary operating losses, and the more the institution has, the greater its protection from failure. Capital requirements for large banks were increased in 1985. Additional potential changes include more restrictive regulations on higher-risk institutions. Toward this end, in 1986, bank regulators proposed, and thrift regulators adopted, risk-adjusted capital standards. There is disagreement, however, about the extent to which capital regulations serve their intended purposes, a topic explored in Chapter 16.

Securitization. Many intermediaries are turning from a buy-and-hold management strategy, in which they collect funds from customers, then invest them in financial assets held until maturity. Instead, institutions seek flexibility to sell financial assets to other investors should operating needs or economic conditions dictate a change in strategy. Although some financial as-

sets, such as stocks, bonds, and mortgages, have well-developed resale markets, others, such as consumer and commercial loans, do not. *Securitization* is the name given to recent attempts by financial institutions to create new securities suitable for resale out of assets that would otherwise be held to maturity. As these markets emerge, institutions are exposed to new kinds of risks. Securitization is explored in Chapter 18.

Impact of Technology. The risks to which institutions are exposed change as technology changes. Traditional examinations of the safety and soundness of financial institutions focus on balance sheets and income statements, and on subjective assessments of the quality of management. Technology enables institutions to enter and leave financial markets virtually instantaneously, assuming risks on a given day that may never appear on a balance sheet or arise in an examiner's conversation with a manager. Some experts believe that measuring and controlling the risks posed by technology are the most difficult problems facing regulators of financial institutions today.[28]

Off-Balance Sheet Involvement. In addition to instantaneous risks posed by technology, institutions are exposed to ongoing risks not reported in accounting records. For example, some institutions offer as regular services advance commitments to lend or to pay the debts of customers who go into default. These *contingent liabilities* or *off-balance sheet items* may or may not require cash outflows from the institution. Under current accounting rules, these items are not reported as obligations on the balance sheet. Because some institutions have billions of dollars of contingent liabilities,

---

[27]The most widely publicized proposal for risk-based premiums was the FDIC's plan, submitted for public comment in late 1985. No change in the premium structure can be implemented, however, without action by Congress. See "FDIC Puts New Twists on Risk-Based Insurance Idea," *ABA Banking Journal* 78 (May 1986): 32.

[28]For more discussion of these points, see Laurie S. Goodman, "The Interface Between Technology and Regulation in Banking," in *Technology and the Regulation of Financial Markets,* Anthony Saunders and Lawrence J. White, eds. (Lexington, MA: D. C. Heath and Company, 1986), pp. 181-186; E. Gerald Corrigan, "Bank Supervision in a Changing Financial Environment," *Quarterly Review,* Federal Reserve Bank of New York 10 (Winter 1985-1986): 1-5.

they are of growing concern to regulators and are discussed in Chapters 16 and 21.

Changes in the Regulatory Structure

The recommendations of the Bush Task Group as recently as 1984 suggest that reform of the regulatory system itself cannot be ignored. Increasing the probability of change are the deteriorating financial conditions of the FDIC and FSLIC. The FSLIC poses the greatest concern, because the many thrift failures and assisted mergers in the 1980s have depleted its resources. In 1985, the FSLIC established a separate organization, called the *Federal Asset Disposition Association (FADA),* to manage problem assets the FSLIC acquired from failing thrifts. Observers considered FADA to be only a temporary solution for the ailing insurance fund, however, and it did nothing to alleviate potential problems of the FDIC.[29] In July 1987, Congress passed the *Competitive Equality Banking Act,* creating new sources of financing for the FSLIC to supplement the premiums of insured thrifts. (Details on this act are provided in the appendix to this chapter.)

These problems are discussed in more detail in Chapter 15. Industry crises have also led to calls for regulatory restructuring for property and casualty insurers and pension funds, discussed in later chapters.

INTERNATIONAL INFLUENCES

Technological and financial innovations spurring regulatory revisions in the United States have implications for international regulatory reform. The rapid transmission of financial information brings the financial markets of many countries closer together, and the world's financial markets may eventually become integrated. Integration means closer communication among financial institutions worldwide.

When financial institutions interact internationally, the pressure for regulatory adjustments increases. For example, one need may be for reciprocal agreements giving foreign banks in the United States the powers that U.S. banks are seeking abroad. Conversely, foreign banks in the United States must not be perceived to have special privileges prohibited to domestic banks. As early as 1919, the *Edge Act* recognized the need for competitive equality among domestic and foreign banks by permitting domestic banks to establish operations outside their home territories to conduct international banking. Additional steps toward uniform regulations were taken in the *International Banking Act of 1978,* when foreign banks operating in the United States were required to purchase deposit insurance and prohibited from opening new branches interstate. Regulators are also aware that international operations expose financial institutions to additional risks, such as foreign currency exchange and political risks discussed in later chapters.

Pressure is increasing for uniformity in institutional regulations regardless of country. Table 2.5 summarizes comparative banking regulations in six countries with which U.S. institutions are linked through the international markets. Five of the six countries impose no balance sheet constraints on commercial banks, a fact that will almost certainly be considered by U.S. regulators in years to come.

Finally, it is clear that the power to influence domestic economic conditions is no longer solely under the control of domestic regulators, because it is impossible to separate the impact of domestic and international economic events. Further, if regulators establish restrictive rules for institutions operating in the United States, there is an immediate incentive to move operations abroad to escape those restrictions. Recognizing this, in 1987, the three federal banking regulators and the Bank of England (the chief regulator of British banks) proposed unprecedented, uniform risk-adjusted capital standards for commercial banks. The regulators expressed the hope that Japanese regulators would soon follow. Regulation and economic policy in the international arena are certain to play a ma-

---

[29]"FADA to Manage FSLIC Assets, Not Buy Them, Business Plan Reveals," *Savings Institutions* 107 (February 1986): 7, 9; Beth M. Linnen, "New 406 Corporation Will Dispose of the FSLIC's Problem Assets," *Savings Institutions* 106 (November 1985): 68-71; Ann Reilly, "Banking Reform Looks More and More Likely," *Fortune* 112 (September 2, 1985): 74.

Table 2.5
Bank Regulations in Other Countries

Country	Regulation	
	Interest Rate Controls	Balance Sheet Constraints
Canada	No (ceilings on certain certificate of deposit rates, 1972-1975)	No
France	Yes (ceilings except for long-term, large-denomination time deposits)	Credit expansion ceilings (officially lifted 1985)
Germany	No	No
Italy	No	Credit expansion ceilings (officially lifted 1983)
Japan	Yes (regulated except for foreign currency deposits and certificates of deposit)	Window guidance (limits on bank lending)
United Kingdom	No (not since 1975)	No (limits on growth of interest-bearing liabilities, intermittently 1973-1980)

Source: J. David Germany and John E. Morton, "Financial Innovation and Deregulation in Foreign Industrial Countries," *Federal Reserve Bulletin* 71 (October 1985): 745.

jor role in the regulatory dialectic of the future.[30]

SUMMARY

Financial institutions have historically been tightly regulated, although specific rules evolve as part of the regulatory dialectic. According to this concept, regulators articulate a set of regulations and the rationale (thesis); regulated firms respond by attempting to avoid regulations (antithesis); and a new set of regulations emerges (synthesis) as a result of these actions, as well as technological and market forces. The dialectic is especially evident in recent years.

Depository institutions have received the most attention from regulators. Over the years,

a dual structure of regulators has emerged. Although repeated concern has been expressed about overlapping authority, Congress has not yet enacted any proposals to simplify the bureaucracy. Nondepository institutions are also regulated, but to a lesser extent. Most regulations governing finance companies are established at the state level and are less complex than those for depositories. Insurance companies are also governed by state regulators, and the scope of regulation is substantial. Pension funds, investment companies, and securities firms are regulated by major federal statutes, and by states.

The two most important regulatory reforms in the 1980s are the Depository Institutions Deregulation and Monetary Control Act and the Garn-St Germain Depository Institutions Act. These laws removed some restrictions on the asset choices of depositories and on their sources of funds, and increased similarity in the regulation of banks, thrifts, and credit unions. Regulators were also given more flexibility to handle failing institutions.

Almost immediately, however, forces for additional change were at work. Current issues

[30]See J. David Germany and John E. Morton, "Financial Innovation and Deregulation in Foreign Industrial Countries," *Federal Reserve Bulletin* 71 (October 1985): 743-753; Preston Martin and Bryon Higgins, "The World Financial Scene: Balancing Risks and Rewards," *Economic Review*, Federal Reserve Bank of Kansas City 71 (June 1986): 3-9; John E. Yang, "Regulators in Britain and U.S. Propose Joint Rule on Banks' Capital Reserves," *The Wall Street Journal*, January 9, 1987, p. 2.

include the removal of geographic restrictions; continued diversification of depository institutions' operations; better ways of measuring and controlling the risks taken by financial institutions; reform in the regulatory structure; and the regulation of institutions with international operations. Only one thing is certain: Change is inevitable.

Questions

1. Explain in your own words the meaning of the "regulatory dialectic." Describe the three stages of the dialectic.

2. Discuss at least two historical examples of each of the three stages of the regulatory dialectic. From current publications, identify a recent regulatory decision and explain the reaction of financial institutions to it.

3. What goals and objectives guided the decisions of legislators and financial institution regulators in the 1930s? In the views of some expert observers, how did those objectives change during the 1960s and subsequent decades? How have the regulated institutions responded to this perceived change in regulatory objectives?

4. During the 1980s, significant progress was made toward easing the regulatory burden of financial institutions. Discuss the rationale for revising the regulations, many of which had their origin in the postdepression years.

5. Describe some recent technological innovations in the financial system. How have these developments affected the regulation of financial institutions?

6. Since 1980, there have been wide fluctuations in interest rates, foreign exchange rates, inflation, and other economic indexes. Give some examples of the ways this economic uncertainty can affect financial markets and financial institutions. Find a current example of the markets' response to economic developments that is not discussed in the chapter.

7. Explain the statement, "The need for financial institution regulatory reform arises from both internal and external sources." Find an example of an institutional and a market development that has provided incentives for regulatory changes.

8. A noted columnist in *The Wall Street Journal* recently wrote, "Banks . . . like to shop around for the best regulation." Discuss the regulatory structure for commercial banks and thrifts in this context. What purpose does each regulator serve? In your opinion, does there appear to be unnecessary duplication or overlap? Why or why not?

9. Can you identify any areas of depository institutions' operations that are *not* regulated? If so, what are they, and why are they not regulated?

10. Briefly describe the history of efforts to reform the regulatory structure. What were the recommendations of the Bush Task Group? Do you support those recommended changes? Why or why not?

11. Compare and contrast the restrictions on establishing new offices and moving into new geographical markets faced by commercial banks, finance companies, and insurance companies.

12. What explanations can you offer for the long-standing tradition of concentrating insurance regulation at the state rather than the federal level? Do you think this is an effective way to regulate that industry? Why or why not?

13. Briefly discuss the safeguards for employees included in the Employee Retirement Income Security Act (ERISA).

14. Describe the provisions established by Congress to regulate investment companies and securities firms.

15. Give an example of a regulatory restriction that made it difficult or impossible for depository institutions to respond to changes in economic conditions in the 1980s.

16. Why did many commercial banks threaten to resign their Federal Reserve memberships in the 1970s? What dangers did this potential decline in membership pose for the Fed's implementation of monetary policy? What was the Congressional response on the issue?

17. Discuss the areas of depository institution operations that were "deregulated" by DIDMCA and by Garn-St Germain.

18. Explain the events and conditions that led to additional regulatory reform after the passage of DIDMCA. How did the deterioration in the financial position of many savings institutions serve as an incentive for rapid Congressional action?

19. What issues remain unresolved in the regulation of financial institutions?

20. What are the current concerns of regulators regarding the safety and soundness of financial institutions?

21. What factors complicate the regulation of financial institutions operating in international markets?

22. Define the following terms:

   - dual banking system
   - regulatory avoidance
   - usury ceilings
   - vested benefits
   - conduit theory of taxation
   - disintermediation
   - cross-intermediation
   - electronic funds transfers
   - "level playing field"
   - transactions accounts
   - securitization

Selected References

Broaddus, Alfred. "Financial Innovation in the United States—Background, Current Status and Prospects." *Economic Review* (Federal Reserve Bank of Richmond) 71 (January/February 1985): 2-22.

Cargill, Thomas F., and Gillian Garcia. *Financial Reform in the 1980s*. Stanford, CA: Hoover Institution Press, 1985.

Carron, Andrew S. *The Plight of the Thrift Institutions*. Washington, DC: The Brookings Institution, 1982.

Corrigan, E. Gerald. "Bank Supervision in a Changing Financial Environment." *Quarterly Review* (Federal Reserve Bank of New York) 10 (Winter 1985-1986): 1-5.

"The Depository Institutions Deregulation and Monetary Control Act of 1980." *Economic Perspectives* (Federal Reserve Bank of Chicago) 4 (September/October 1980): 3-23.

Garcia, Gillian, et al. "The Garn-St Germain Depository Institutions Act of 1982." *Economic Perspectives* (Federal Reserve Bank of Chicago) 7 (March–April 1983): 2-31.

Gart, Alan. *Banks, Thrifts and Insurance Companies: Surviving the 1980s.* Lexington, MA: Lexington Books, 1985.

Germany, J. David, and John E. Morton. "Financial Innovation and Deregulation in Foreign Industrial Countries." *Federal Reserve Bulletin* 71 (October 1985): 743-753.

Gilbert, R. Alton. "Requiem for Regulation Q: What It Did and Why It Passed Away." *Review* (Federal Reserve Bank of St. Louis) 68 (February 1986): 22-37.

Goodman, Laurie S. "The Interface Between Technology and Regulation in Banking." In *Technology and the Regulation of Financial Markets.* Edited by Anthony Saunders and Lawrence J. White. Lexington, MA: D. C. Heath and Co., 1986, pp. 181-186.

Harrington, Scott. "The Impact of Rate Regulation on Prices and Underwriting Results in the Property-Liability Insurance Industry: A Survey." *Journal of Risk and Insurance* 51 (December 1984): 577-623.

Johnson, Verle B. "Reorganization?" *Weekly Letter* (Federal Reserve Bank of San Francisco), March 2, 1984.

Kane, Edward J. "Good Intentions and Unintended Evil: The Case Against Selective Credit Allocation." *Journal of Money, Credit, and Banking* 9 (February 1977): 55-69.

————. "Accelerating Inflation, Technological Innovation, and the Decreasing Effectiveness of Banking Regulation." *Journal of Finance* 36 (May 1981): 355-367.

————. "Technology and the Regulation of Financial Markets." In *Technology and the Regulation of Financial Markets.* Edited by Anthony Saunders and Lawrence J. White. Lexington, MA: D. C. Heath and Company, 1986, pp. 187-193.

Keeley, Michael C., and Frederick T. Furlong. "Bank Regulation and the Public Interest." *Economic Review* (Federal Reserve Bank of San Francisco) (Spring 1986), pp. 55-71.

Martin, Preston, and Bryon Higgins. "The World Financial Scene: Balancing Risks and Rewards." *Economic Review* (Federal Reserve Bank of Kansas City) 71 (June 1986): 3-9.

Rhoades, Stephen A., and Donald T. Savage. "Controlling Nationwide Concentration under Interstate Banking." *Issues in Bank Regulation* 9 (Autumn 1985): 34-40.

Selden, Richard T. "Consumer-Oriented Intermediaries." In *Financial Institutions and Markets,* 2d ed. Edited by Murray E. Polakoff and Thomas A. Durkin. Boston: Houghton Mifflin, 1981, pp. 207-212.

Shull, Bernard. "Economic Efficiency, Public Regulation, and Financial Reform: Depository Institutions." In *Financial Institutions and Markets,* 2d ed. Edited by Murray E. Polakoff and Thomas A. Durkin. Boston: Houghton Mifflin, 1981, pp. 671-702.

Van Horne, James C. "Of Financial Innovations and Excesses." *Journal of Finance* 40 (July 1985): 621-631.

West, Robert Craig. "The Depository Institutions Deregulation Act of 1980: A Historical Perspective." *Economic Review* (Federal Reserve Bank of Kansas City) 67 (February 1982): 3-13.

Appendix 2A

PROVISIONS OF THE COMPETITIVE EQUALITY BANKING ACT OF 1987

Title I: Nonbank Bank and Savings and Loan Holding Company Changes

Expanded the definition of "bank" to include any institution insured by the FDIC (does not apply to 168 nonbank banks in existence on March 5, 1987); permitted nonbank banks to acquire failing savings institutions; clarified regulations applying to thrift holding companies.

Title II: Moratorium on Additional Bank Powers

Prohibited federal bank regulators from approving new securities, real estate, or insurance activities until March 1, 1988, beginning retroactively on March 5, 1987; brought state-chartered banks that are not members of the Fed under the Glass-Steagall Act with regard to affiliation with securities firms; limited the securities activities of thrifts until March 1, 1988, unless those activities were in place before March 5, 1987.

Title III: FSLIC Recapitalization Act

Authorized the Federal Home Loan Bank System to borrow up to $10.825 billion, collateralized by zero-coupon Treasury securities, to assist the FSLIC; permitted assessment of FSLIC institutions to service the authorized debt; phased out the special assessment of FSLIC-insured institutions in effect since 1985; specified circumstances under which "exit fees" can be charged to institutions departing the FSLIC; established an FSLIC oversight committee.

Title IV: Forbearance and Thrift Regulation

Required regulators to forbear in closing troubled savings institutions during the period in which FSLIC recapitalization occurs, provided an institution's problems can be attributed to economic conditions; required uniform, generally accepted accounting standards for commercial banks and savings institutions by 1993.

Title V: Emergency Acquisition Regulations

Extended the net worth certificate program for 5 years; made Garn-St Germain emergency acquisition powers permanent; equalized emergency acquisition rules for commercial banks and savings institutions.

Title VI: Check Hold Schedules

By September 1, 1990, required depositories to make funds from local deposits available to customers within one business day.

Miscellaneous

Reaffirmed that deposits up to the legally prescribed amount are backed by the "full faith and credit" of the federal government; mandated a study of "junk bonds"; required lenders to designate and disclose a cap on adjustable rate loans.

Chapter 3

THE IMPACT OF ORGANIZATIONAL STRUCTURE

Trying to prevent entry . . . by out-of-state banks in this day and age is worse than closing the barn door after the horses have gotten out; it is similar to arguing whether a red door or a green door would have been more effective in keeping the horses in the barn.

Harvey Rosenblum and Sue Gregorash
Economists, Federal Reserve Bank of Chicago (1985)

BY April 1985, Citicorp officials had become so frustrated at their inability to take their banking business nationwide that their creativity was working overtime. The resulting experiment by the giant New York-based bank holding company could give new meaning to "Don't leave home without it," the slogan of its archrival American Express. Citicorp was testing a palm-sized computer terminal that would allow customers to plug into a telephone to conduct banking activities over any phone line. A perfected system would allow each customer to carry a miniature branch bank everywhere, yet allow Citicorp to remain within the letter of the interstate banking laws in effect at the time.[1]

---

[1] Daniel Hertzberg, "Citicorp Is Testing 'A Small Portable' Banking Terminal," *The Wall Street Journal,* April 11, 1985, p. 6.

A major reason financial institutions differ from nonfinancial firms is that most of their assets are financial claims against others. But many financial institutions are also different because of the ways they raise funds, because of who benefits from the profits, because of where they can locate, and because of who they can serve. These factors have led to differences in organizational structure explored in some detail in this chapter.

EQUITY VERSUS NET WORTH

Almost all nonfinancial businesses are organized with an equity investment by one or several persons. Webster's *Ninth New Collegiate Dictionary* defines *equity* as "a risk interest or ownership right in a property." Individuals with equity in a business may be sole owners, as in a proprietorship, with full personal liability for any debt obligations of the business; may share ownership and legal liability with others, as in a partnership; or may have an ownership interest but no personal responsibility for the firm's debt obligations, as in a corporation.

Equity Is Ownership

The "ownership right" part of Webster's definition means that those with equity in a business are entitled to all **residuals,** or profits remaining after the debt of the organization is serviced. Residual profits may be paid to owners in the form of cash dividends or retained in the business to support future operations; in either case, under current tax laws, they are subject to corporate and personal income taxes. Even if earnings are retained, each owner holds claim to a proportionate amount and may realize cash if shares are sold to new owners.

The "risk interest" part of Webster's definition of equity means that residuals may not exist, as the owners of Braniff Airlines found when the firm went bankrupt in 1982. On the other hand, residuals may be larger than ever imagined, as long-term owners of IBM have learned. Because such potential variability is risk, holders of equity are subject to considerable risk. Yet their willingness to invest makes the very existence of a business possible. Not surprisingly, then, much of finance theory has been devoted to understanding and improving the risk/expected return relationship for equity-holders of nonfinancial firms.

But Not All Ownership Is Equity

Financial institutions as a group are unusual because not all of them are organized with equity ownership interests. As noted in Chapter 1, some are mutually organized, including most savings and loan associations, savings banks, and insurance companies. Thrift depositors or insurance policyholders are the "owners" of the business. Their initial deposits or policy premium payments provide the funds from which the institution begins operations. Profits earned from investment of these funds are then returned to customers of the organization in the form of interest on deposits or refunds on past premiums paid. Unlike shareholder-owned businesses, in which an owner may sell shares in order to realize capital gains, profits not distributed to owner-members of a mutual organization are available for use only by the institution itself. Profits retained are subject to corporate taxes in the year earned, but profits paid to members are taxable at the personal level.

Not-for-Profit Organizations

Still other financial institutions, such as credit unions, are organized on a **not-for-profit** basis. Not-for-profit organizations provide goods or services at below-market or no cost to specific groups of beneficiaries. The organization either distributes income earned in excess of expenses to the beneficiary group in the form of increased services and/or refunds for previous payments or else retains the income to provide a cushion against potential losses. There are no residual claimants. Because not-for-profit organizations are presumed to be charitable, they do not pay taxes, even if they retain excess income.[2]

The Concept and Measurement of Net Worth

Although financial institutions may differ because of the presence or absence of equity ownership interests, all have one thing in common: Each institution must focus attention on its *net worth,* or the difference between the market value of its assets and the market value of its liabilities. Net worth is the cushion between bankruptcy and continued existence. It is defined as the amount by which total asset value can decline before it will be exceeded by the total value of liabilities:

$$\text{Net Worth} = \text{Value of Assets} - \text{Value of Liabilities}$$

This definition simply restates the basic balance sheet identity for an organization:

$$\text{Value of Assets} = \text{Value of Liabilities} + \text{Net Worth}$$

In institutions with equity owners, managerial attention to net worth is equivalent to preserving owners' interests. In mutual and not-for-profit institutions, attention to net worth, although not directly for the benefit of a specific residual group, is necessary to ensure that the members and beneficiary groups of the institution can continue to be served. Consequently, asset/liability management techniques are designed to assist managers in achieving the institution's net worth objectives, regardless of its specific organizational form.

THE ROLE OF NET WORTH IN ASSET/LIABILITY MANAGEMENT

Specific net worth objectives guiding asset/liability management decisions usually include both a target rate of return and a desired ratio of net worth to total assets. The target rate of return is expressed as the return on net worth (RONW), or the ratio of expected net income to net worth:

$$\text{RONW} = \frac{\text{Net Income}}{\text{Net Worth}}$$

In stockholder-owned institutions, net worth is synonymous with common equity, and return on net worth is usually called return on equity (ROE).[3]

The target ratio of net worth to total assets may be expressed directly as that ratio or as its reciprocal, called the *net worth multiplier:*

$$\text{Net Worth Multiplier} = \frac{\text{Total Assets}}{\text{Net Worth}}$$

These and other important financial statement relationships are illustrated in Figure 3.1. Ideally, according to its definition, net worth should be calculated as the amount by which asset market values exceed liability market values. In practice, because market values for some assets and liabilities may be unavailable, book values are often used.

Table 3.1 illustrates that once management has established net worth targets, a target for the NIM is also implied, given values for existing assets, liabilities, and net worth. In the example, if the target RONW is 18 percent, and if the desired ratio of net worth to total assets is 7 percent (implying a net worth multiplier of 14.3), the minimum NIM necessary to achieve these targets is 1.9 percent. Daily decisions concerning asset and liability management must be made with this target in mind.

---

[2]Federal credit unions are not the only financial institutions with earnings untaxed at the institutional level. The earnings of investment companies and pension funds are treated similarly. Because investment companies and pension funds lack the charitable objectives of credit unions, however, they are not considered not-for-profit institutions, even though they receive similar tax treatment.

---

[3]For some purposes, especially to meet regulatory requirements, preferred stock is considered part of an institution's net worth. Details on the measurement of net worth by regulators are considered in Chapter 16.

Figure 3.1
Financial Statement Relationships

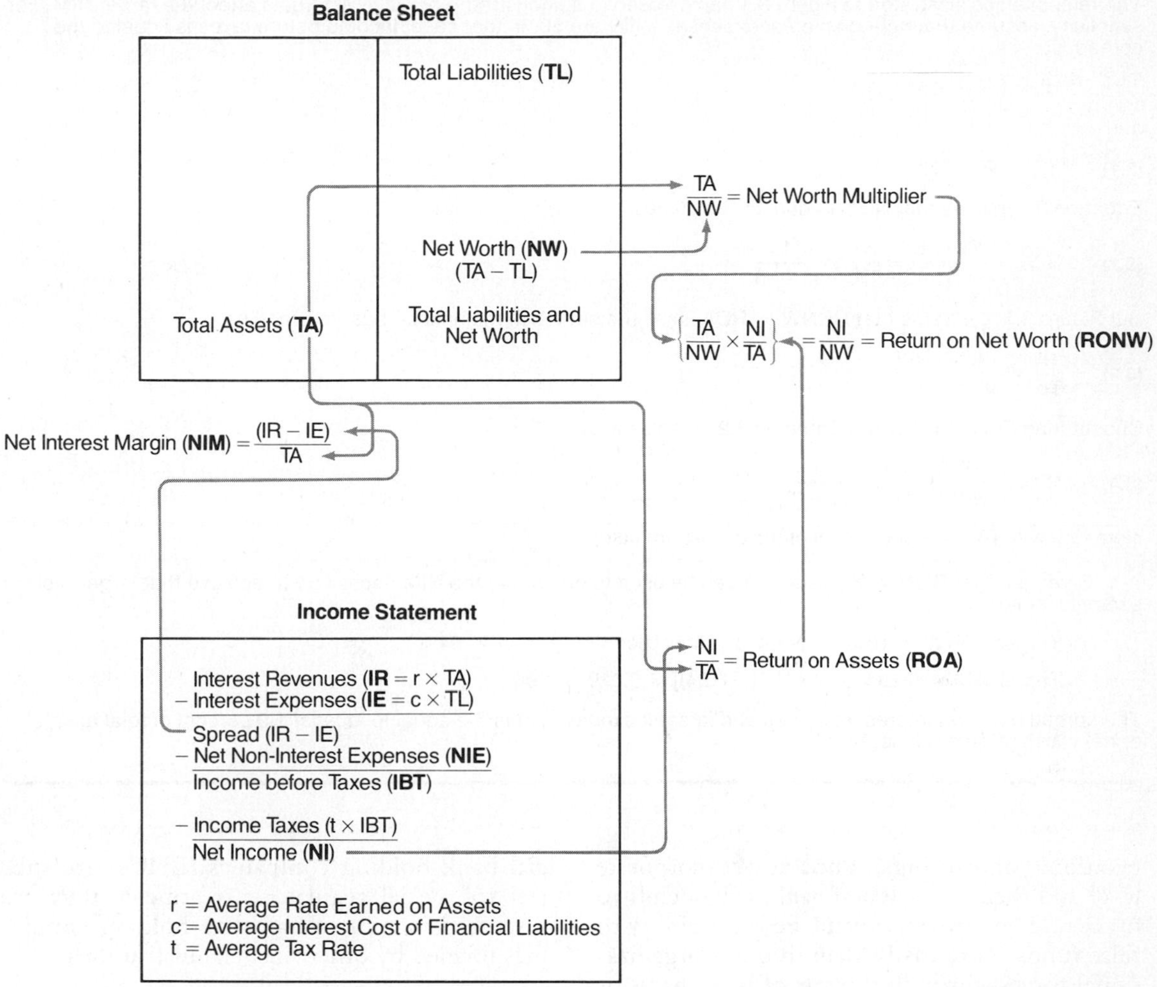

Balance Sheet

Total Liabilities (**TL**)

Net Worth (**NW**)
(TA − TL)

Total Liabilities and
Net Worth

Total Assets (**TA**)

$$\frac{TA}{NW} = \text{Net Worth Multiplier}$$

$$\left\{ \frac{TA}{NW} \times \frac{NI}{TA} \right\} = \frac{NI}{NW} = \text{Return on Net Worth (\textbf{RONW})}$$

$$\text{Net Interest Margin (\textbf{NIM})} = \frac{(IR - IE)}{TA}$$

Income Statement

Interest Revenues (**IR** = r × TA)
− Interest Expenses (**IE** = c × TL)

Spread (IR − IE)
− Net Non-Interest Expenses (**NIE**)
Income before Taxes (**IBT**)

− Income Taxes (t × IBT)
Net Income (**NI**)

r = Average Rate Earned on Assets
c = Average Interest Cost of Financial Liabilities
t = Average Tax Rate

$$\frac{NI}{TA} = \text{Return on Assets (\textbf{ROA})}$$

STOCKHOLDER-OWNED INSTITUTIONS

Although the basic organizational forms of financial institutions are stock, mutual, and not-for-profit, additional organizational arrangements arise from the basic structures. Each form and its variations have implications for financial management. In particular, the form can affect an institution's growth potential, its ability to raise capital, its opportunities to diversify operations, and its taxation.

Many financial institutions are shareholder-owned, including all commercial banks, all finance companies, many securities firms, some S&Ls and savings banks, and some insurance companies. The primary disadvantage of the corporate form of ownership is the "double

---

Table 3.1
Relationship between RONW and NIM

The relationships illustrated in Figure 3.1 can be used to demonstrate how RONW targets affect the target NIM. For simplicity, assume that net noninterest expenses (NIE) are $0. In that case, income before taxes is equal to the spread, so:

$$NI = (IR - IE) \times (1 - t)$$

and

(3.1) $(IR - IE) = NI \times 1/(1 - t)$

Equation 3.1 implies that NIM is equal to ROA times $[1/(1 - t)]$:

(3.2) $NIM = \dfrac{IR - IE}{TA} = \dfrac{NI}{TA} \times \dfrac{1}{(1 - t)}$

But Figure 3.1 illustrates that RONW = ROA times the net worth multiplier. Thus, rearranging:

(3.3) $\dfrac{NI}{TA} = \dfrac{NI}{NW} \times \dfrac{NW}{TA}$

Substituting Equation 3.3 into Equation 3.2 reveals that:

(3.4) $NIM = \dfrac{NI}{NW} \times \dfrac{NW}{TA} \times \dfrac{1}{(1 - t)}$

Note that NW/TA is the reciprocal of the net worth multiplier.

  Given a target RONW, Equation 3.4 can be used to determine the NIM necessary to achieve that target. For example, suppose:

  Target RONW = 18%   Net Worth Multiplier = 14.3   t = 34%

  Target NIM = 0.18 x 0.07 x $[1/(1 - 0.34)]$ = 0.019 = 1.9%

The spread between interest revenues and interest expenses must be equal to *at least* 1.9 percent of total assets, or net worth targets will not be met.

---

taxation" of earnings, once at the corporate level and then again when paid as dividends to owners. The primary advantage is the ability to raise funds more easily than in other organizational forms, through the sale of new shares or through access to the commercial paper and bond markets. Shareholder-owned institutions are also able to take advantage of another organizational arrangement called the ***holding company.***

Holding Companies: Commercial Banks

Holding companies are businesses formed to acquire the stock of other companies in order to control their operations. Because commer-

cial bank holding companies (BHCs) are subject to special regulatory treatment, they are discussed in more detail than holding companies formed by other financial institutions.

Growth of BHCs. In the last several decades, commercial banks have increasingly turned to the BHC form of organization, in which "controlling interest" in the stock of one or several banks—called ***subsidiaries***—is owned by a holding company. The stock of the BHC is owned by shareholders. BHCs are also permitted to own nonbank subsidiaries, provided they obtain regulatory approval.

  In the 1980s, the trend toward formation of holding companies has accelerated, encompassing small and large banks alike. Although only

177 applications to form BHCs were approved by regulators in 1977, by 1985 the number of applications approved had increased to 655. As of year-end 1985, 6,453 bank holding companies existed, compared to 1,948 as of year-end 1977, a compound annual growth rate of 16.2 percent.[4]

Regulation of BHCs.   Under current law, "controlling interest" in a bank is presumed to exist if a holding company owns 25 percent or more of the bank's voting stock. Controlling interest is presumed not to exist if less than 5 percent of the voting stock is owned. Ownership proportions of at least 5 percent but less than 25 percent are evaluated on a case-by-case basis by officials of the Federal Reserve System. If over 80 percent of the stock of a subsidiary is owned by a holding company, dividends paid by the subsidiary to the holding company are not subject to federal taxation when earned by the subsidiary. For this reason, most subsidiaries are fully owned by BHCs.

All BHC activities are regulated by the Federal Reserve System, regardless of whether the banks owned by the holding company are member banks. The Bank Holding Company Act of 1956 and its 1970 Amendments are the primary sources of existing BHC regulations. Together, they authorize the Federal Reserve Board to approve all applications for formation of BHCs and for acquisition of bank and non-bank subsidiaries. These laws also control the geographic expansion of BHCs.

The 1970 Amendments define a "bank" for the purposes of BHC regulation as an institution that accepts demand deposits *and* makes commercial loans. The Garn-St Germain Act amended the definition by stating that institutions insured by the FSLIC or chartered by the FHLBB are not banks, regardless of their activities. Although there are other definitions of *bank* in law, this meaning has been an important focus of the continuing dialectic between BHCs and their regulators.[5]

Bank holding company regulations are a separate part of the regulatory structure of banking, imposed in addition to other bank regulations. Despite this additional layer of supervision, the primary motivation for the trend toward BHCs is an attempt by banks to avoid other federal and state regulations that have historically prevented them from raising capital, diversifying their product offerings, or expanding geographically.

Raising Capital.   As noted in Chapter 2 and discussed in more detail in Chapter 16, regulators establish minimum capital standards for commercial banks, requiring that net worth be a specified minimum proportion of total assets. These standards affect the possible rate of expansion by individual banks, because for every dollar by which assets and deposits increase, net worth must also increase. For example, if a bank's equity capital must be equal to at least 6 percent of total assets, 6 cents of every dollar increase in assets must be financed by retaining earnings or by selling new stock, even though management might prefer to finance expansion solely by increasing deposits. Although BHCs are also subject to minimum capital standards, equity capital from nonbank affiliates of the BHC is currently included in the calculation of overall BHC capital. Therefore, affiliation with a BHC whose nonbank subsidiaries have relatively high capital ratios can assist a bank in expansion without jeopardizing its position with regulators.

The potential assistance provided by holding company affiliation is illustrated in Figure 3.2. If a commercial bank is owned by a holding company, the BHC may borrow money under its own name, then invest the borrowed funds as equity capital in the bank, a practice known as *downstreaming.* As long as the BHC maintains its own required capital ratio, funds borrowed by the holding company may be used to meet the bank's capital needs in an expansion. In Step 1 of the figure, a BHC borrows an additional $100 million. In Step 2, the BHC

---

[4]Board of Governors of the Federal Reserve System, *Annual Report, 1985,* p. 169.

[5]For a review of the legal history of the word *bank* since the Bank Holding Company Act of 1956, see John J.

DiClemente, "What Is a Bank?" *Economic Perspectives,* Federal Reserve Bank of Chicago 7 (January/February 1983): 20-31.

Figure 3.2
Downstreaming: BHC Leverage as a Source of Bank Equity Capital

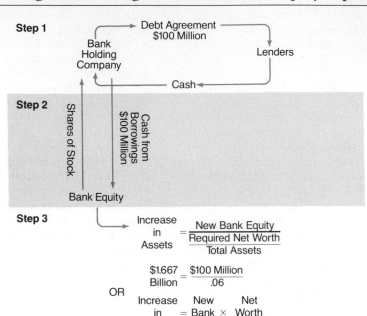

downstreams those funds as equity capital to a subsidiary bank with a 6 percent required ratio of net worth to total assets. Finally, in the third step, the bank uses the funds, as well as $1.567 billion additional deposits, to finance a $1.667 billion ($100 million divided by 0.06) increase in assets while still meeting regulatory capital standards.

This so-called *double leverage* substantially reduces the amount of equity capital required for the holding company to control a large dollar volume of bank assets. In addition, the level and riskiness of expected RONW are greatly affected by the extent to which financial institutions are leveraged.[6] An illustration of the im-

pact of leverage on RONW is provided in the appendix to this chapter.

Product Diversification. Chapter 2 explains that banks' product offerings historically have been limited by regulation. The Glass-Steagall Act, for example, prohibited Fed member banks *and* their affiliates, such as subsidiaries of the same holding company, from underwriting securities. Although Glass-Steagall restrictions have been loosened somewhat in recent years, they remain in effect against some underwriting activities.

---

[6]At least one study has concluded that the use of "prudent" leverage by BHCs is beneficial for their sharehold-

ers. See Adi S. Karna and Duane B. Graddy, "Bank Holding Company Leverage and the Return on Stockholders' Equity," *Journal of Bank Research* 13 (Spring 1982): 42-48.

Except for securities underwriting, however, legislation on whether banks should be permitted to engage in other activities besides accepting deposits and making loans has been less specific. The National Currency Act of 1863 stated that banks were allowed "all such incidental powers . . . necessary to carry on the business of banking."[7] This language is broad enough to have allowed widely varying interpretations by regulators over the years. Consequently, activities as diverse as leasing operations and the offering of travel services have been authorized as permissible "incidental powers." Still, when national banks actually engage in these incidental powers, they compete directly with other businesses, a more vulnerable position for banks than some managers and owners may wish.

A holding company gives banking organizations a way to engage in activities other than accepting deposits and making commercial loans without directly involving the bank subsidiary. For example, by operating a nonbank subsidiary in the leasing or brokerage business, the BHC gives its shareholders the benefit of the income generated by the nonbank subsidiary and also subjects them to the riskiness of that income stream. Depositors in banking subsidiaries, however, are not directly exposed to risks associated with nonbank subsidiaries. At the extreme, the failure of a nonbank subsidiary could theoretically have no effect on bank subsidiaries of the same BHC. Evidence on this point is addressed later in the chapter.

Under Federal Reserve Board **Regulation Y,** the Board may allow BHCs to form or acquire nonbank subsidiaries *if* these nonbank subsidiaries are "so closely related to banking or managing or controlling banks as to be a proper incident thereto."[8] The words *closely related* and *proper incident thereto* are subject to the same latitude in interpretation as the words *incidental powers*. Thus, the list of permissible activities has grown as different interpretations have been made.

Table 3.2 reports those nonbank activities that had been permitted and denied to BHCs as of the end of 1986. The left section includes activities that have been specifically approved under Reg Y. BHCs desiring to offer these services may do so upon approval by a regional Federal Reserve Bank. The middle section includes activities permitted by special order of the Board of Governors but not officially authorized by Reg Y. BHCs must apply directly to the Board for approval of these activities. The right section includes activities that the Board has denied to BHCs. (Some of them have been approved by the Comptroller of the Currency for national banks themselves but not by the Fed for BHCs.) For example, BHCs attempting to establish direct life or property and casualty underwriting subsidiaries have been unsuccessful, consistent with the general prohibition of banks and BHCs from underwriting "risky" ventures. In contrast, offering insurance in connection with lending activities ("credit life") has been permitted.

Geographic Expansion.   Since 1927 and the passage of the McFadden-Pepper Act, individual banks have been subject to geographic expansion laws passed by the states in which their main office is located, regardless of the type of charter the bank holds. Specifically, this has meant that individual banks could not open branch offices unless permitted by state law. Furthermore, individual banks cannot open offices outside their home states unless permitted by the laws of the other states. Although over three-quarters of the states now allow entry by "nonresident" banks, a few still prohibit the establishment of banking offices by banks domiciled in another state.

Some state laws permitting entry by out-of-state banks do so only on a regional basis, such as the Southeastern and Western compacts that emerged in 1984 and 1985. These compacts are anchored on the concept of reciprocity

---

[7]Bernard Shull, "Economic Efficiency, Public Regulation, and Financial Reform: Depository Institutions," in *Financial Institutions and Markets,* 2d ed. Murray E. Polakoff and Thomas A. Durkin, et al., eds. (Boston: Houghton Mifflin, 1981), p. 689.

[8]This phrase is from Section 4(c)8 of the 1970 BHC Amendments. Since that time, nonbank activities permitted to BHCs are often referred to as "4(c)8 activities."

Table 3.2

Permissible Nonbank Activities for Bank Holding Companies

Activities Permitted by Regulation	Activities Permitted by Order	Activities Denied by the Board
1. Extensions of credit[b]; mortgage banking; finance companies: consumer, sales, and commercial; credit cards; factoring	1. Operating a guarantee savings bank in New Hampshire	1. Insurance premium funding (combined sales of mutual funds and insurance)
2. Industrial bank, Morris Plan bank, industrial loan company	2. Buying and selling gold and silver bullion and silver coin[b,d]	2. Underwriting life insurance not related to credit extension
3. Servicing loans and other extensions of credit[b]	3. Issuing money orders and general-purpose variable-denominated payment instruments[a,b,d]	3. Sale of level-term credit life
4. Trust company[b]	4. Futures commission merchant to cover gold and silver bullion and coins[a,b]	4. Real estate brokerage (residential)
5. Investment or financial advising[b]	5. Underwriting certain federal, state, and municipal securities[a,b]	5. Armored car
6. Full-payout leasing of personal or real property[b]	6. Check verification[a,b,d]	6. Land development
7. Investment in community welfare projects[b]	7. Issuance of small-denomination debt instruments[a]	7. Real estate syndication
8. Providing bookkeeping or data-processing services[b]	8. Operating a distressed savings and loan association	8. General management consulting
9. Acting as insurance agent or broker primarily in connection with credit extensions[b]	9. Operating an Article XII Investment Company	9. Property management
10. Underwriting credit life, accident, and health insurance	10. Executing foreign banking unsolicited purchases and sales of securities	10. Computer output microfilm services
11. Providing courier services[b]	11. Engaging in commercial banking activities abroad through a limited-purpose Delaware bank	11. Underwriting mortgage guaranty insurance[c]
12. Management consulting to all depository institutions	12. Performing real estate advisory services and real estate brokerage on nonresidential properties	12. Operating a savings and loan association[a,e]
13. Sale at retail of money orders with a face value of not more than $10,000, traveler's checks, and savings bonds[a,b]	13. Operating a Pool Reserve Plan for loss reserves of banks for loans to small businesses	13. Operating a travel agency[a,b]
14. Performing appraisals of real estate[a]	14. Operating a thrift institution in Rhode Island	14. Underwriting property and casualty insurance[a]
15. Issuance and sale of traveler's checks		15. Underwriting home loan life mortgage insurance[a]
16. Arranging commercial real estate equity financing		16. Investment note issue with transactional characteristics
17. Securities brokerage		17. Real estate advisory services
18. Underwriting and dealing in government obligations and money market instruments		
19. Foreign exchange advisory and transactional services		
20. Futures commission merchant		
21. Options on financial futures		
22. Advice on options on bullion and foreign exchange		
23. Consumer financial counseling		
24. Tax planning and preparation		
25. Futures and options advisory services		
26. Check guaranty services		
27. Collection agency and credit bureau services		
28. Personal property appraisals		

[a] Added to list since January 1, 1975.
[b] Activities permissible to national banks.
[c] Board orders found these activities closely related to banking but denied proposed acquisitions as part of its "go slow" policy.
[d] To be decided on a case-by-case basis.
[e] Operating a thrift institution has been permitted by order in some states.

Sources: Federal Reserve Board and David D. Whitehead, "Interstate Banking: Probability or Reality?" Federal Reserve Bank of Atlanta *Economic Review* 70 (March 1985): 10; "Announcements," *Federal Reserve Bulletin* 72 (December 1986): 829–830.

Figure 3.3
Interstate Banking Laws as of February 1987

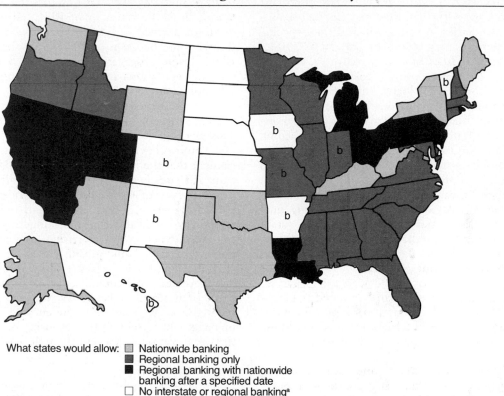

What states would allow:
- ☐ Nationwide banking
- ■ Regional banking only
- ■ Regional banking with nationwide banking after a specified date
- ☐ No interstate or regional banking[a]

[a]With possible exceptions for limited services or in case of bank failures.

[b]Legislation pending that would loosen restrictions.

Source: Larry A. Frieder, "Interstate Banking: Landscape, Policy, and Misconceptions," paper presented at the annual meeting of the Financial Management Association, October 1986; Research Department, Federal Reserve Bank of Chicago, unpublished data, February 1987.

within limited geographic areas. Their major intent has been to promote the growth and development of banks within the region while excluding the entry of large banks from states such as New York, California, and Texas. Some state laws contain a so-called **trigger provision,** automatically permitting nationwide entry after a specified time. Other laws have no triggers. Although banks in states excluded from regional compacts fought to have them declared illegal, the Supreme Court upheld the consti-

tutionality of regional banking in 1985.[9] Figure 3.3 identifies states with either regional or nationwide banking as of early 1987.

---

[9]David D. Whitehead, "Interstate Banking: Probability or Reality?" *Economic Review,* Federal Reserve Bank of Atlanta 70 (March 1985): 6-19; Robert A. Richard, "States' Interstate Banking Initiatives," *Economic Review,* Federal Reserve Bank of Atlanta 70 (March 1985): 20-22; "Supreme Court Ruling Supports Regional Banks," *The Wall Street Journal,* June 11, 1985, pp. 3, 14; G. David Wallace, "Nationwide Banking: A Welcome Mat—Not a

Bank holding companies are also subject to geographic restrictions according to the BHC Act and its Amendments, but with important differences. Although they may not have banking subsidiaries in states which do not specifically permit entry by out-of-state BHCs, BHC legislation defines *bank* very narrowly. Organizations either accepting demand deposits or making commercial loans, but not both, are not subject to BHC restrictions. It is not surprising, therefore, that thousands of out-of-state nonbank BHC subsidiaries have been established by BHCs headquartered in another state.

Besides establishing nonbank subsidiaries according to Regulation Y, BHCs have used other legal means to do so. When the BHC Act of 1956 was passed, BHCs with existing out-of-state subsidiaries were permitted to retain them under a grandfather clause. In addition, BHCs are permitted to have **loan production offices (LPOs)** out of state. Negotiations for commercial loans occur through LPOs, but no funds are dispensed. Finally, as noted in Chapter 2, BHCs may maintain banking offices out of state to pursue international business; these offices are called Edge Act subsidiaries.

BHCs and the Safety and Soundness of Commercial Banks.

Because the legal organization of BHCs makes their subsidiaries separate corporate entities, the financial problems of one theoretically should have no impact on others. It can also be argued, however, that the activities of one subsidiary may have a large effect on other affiliates. Suppose, for example, that BHC management diverts resources from a bank subsidiary to a troubled affiliate; that an affiliate provides services to a bank at a higher price than would be charged in the open market; or that public confidence in a bank is eroded because of the failure of an affiliated bank or nonbank. Federal Reserve Board regulations limit the activities of BHC subsidiaries to those deemed safe and sound and regulate transactions between affiliates of the same BHC. Some observers have argued, however, that the regulations are ineffective because they are not completely enforceable and cannot address the potential problem of a bank run caused by the failure of an affiliated subsidiary.[10]

Empirical evidence seems to support the argument that the independence of holding company affiliates is a legal theory, not reality.[11] A recent survey of **multibank holding companies (MBHCs)**—BHCs with more than one bank subsidiary—indicated that the budgeting, capital management, and portfolio management policies of their bank subsidiaries were highly centralized and that the degree of centralization has increased over time. Centralized management of nonbank subsidiaries has been documented, as well as the tendency of BHC management to rely on the resources of the entire organization to prevent the failure of an in-

Slammed Door," *Business Week,* June 24, 1985, pp. 90-91; Herbert Baer and Sue F. Gregorash, eds., *Toward Nationwide Banking: A Guide to the Issues* (Chicago: Federal Reserve Bank of Chicago, 1986).

The potential for growth among regional BHCs is discussed in Sarah Bartlett, "Banking's Balance of Power is Tilting toward the Regionals," *Business Week,* April 7, 1986, pp. 56-64; and Suzanna Andrews and John W. Milligan, "Here Come the Super-Regionals," *Institutional Investor* 19 (December 1985): 74-82.

[10]Larry D. Wall, "Insulating Banks from Non-Bank Affiliates," *Economic Review,* Federal Reserve Bank of Atlanta 69 (September 1984): 18-27.

[11]The evidence includes: Gary Whalen, "Operational Policies of Multibank Holding Companies," *Economic Review,* Federal Reserve Bank of Cleveland (Winter 1981-1982), pp. 20-31; Robert Eisenbeis, "How Should Bank Holding Companies Be Regulated?" *Economic Review,* Federal Reserve Bank of Atlanta 68 (January 1983): 43-44; Samuel B. Chase, Jr., and John J. Mingo, "The Regulation of Bank Holding Companies," *Journal of Finance* 30 (May 1975): 281-292; Anthony G. Cornyn and Samuel H. Talley, "Activity Deregulation and Bank Soundness," *Proceedings of a Conference on Bank Structure and Competition* (Chicago: Federal Reserve Bank of Chicago, 1983), pp. 28-31; and in Larry A. Frieder and Vincent P. Apilado, "Bank Holding Company Research: Classification, Synthesis, and New Directions," *Journal of Bank Research* 13 (Summer 1982): 80-95. Criticism of virtually all the BHC performance studies is provided in Donald M. Brown, "Bank Holding Company Performance Studies and the Public Interest: Normative Uses for Positive Analysis?" *Review,* Federal Reserve Bank of St. Louis 65 (March 1983): 26-34. Brown's criticisms center on the misuse and misinterpretation of financial ratios in this research.

dividual subsidiary. Affiliation with BHCs also seems to result in shifts among subsidiary banks to relatively riskier loans, lower levels of liquidity, and lower capital ratios.

Despite this evidence, there is not universal agreement that the safety and soundness of the banking system is compromised by the existence and expansion of BHCs. Some analysts argue that financial market participants view BHCs as single entities and that BHC affiliation may decrease the soundness of banks to the extent that affiliated subsidiaries engage in risky activities.[12] Others suggest that the benefits of BHC affiliation, particularly the potential for reducing risk through geographic diversification, have no negative effect or may even outweigh the potential risk increases.[13]

The one thing on which experts agree is that more research is needed into the relationship between BHC affiliation and the riskiness of banking organizations. Because the size of banking organizations increases with holding company affiliation, and because the failure of large banks is a greater shock to the financial system than the failure of smaller banks, the issue will remain critical as deregulation of the financial system proceeds.

Nonbank Banks.   By 1984, the attention of regulators, bankers, and economists alike was focused on nonbank, or limited-service, banks. Although organizations that accept deposits or make commercial loans, but not both, were formed as early as 1933, attention to this type of financial institution has heightened in the 1980s.[14] In 1980, the Comptroller of the Currency permitted Gulf and Western Industries to purchase Fidelity National Bank of Concord, California, after selling the bank's commercial loans. Several similar acquisitions were approved, but the 1983 request by Dimension Financial Corporation to charter 31 *new* nonbank banks drew nationwide attention to the phenomenon. The Fed declined to approve these requests, and Dimension sued.[15]

In early 1984, in an effort to stop the nonbank bank movement, both the Comptroller and the Federal Reserve Board imposed moratoriums on approval of pending applications. Later, however, the Comptroller resumed approval of nonbank bank applications for federally chartered banks unaffiliated with holding companies. The Fed retained a ban on nonbank banks operated by BHCs. Meanwhile, Dimension won its suit against the Fed at the appeals court level, and the Fed took the case to the Supreme Court. In January 1986, the Supreme Court ruled the Fed had exceeded its authority by attempting to halt the expansion of nonbank banks. Although the court stated there is "much to be said" for the regulation of financial institutions, including those that are the "functional equivalent" of banks, it stated that the power to do so belonged to Congress alone. The Fed subsequently recommended to Congress that an unambiguous definition of *bank* be developed, such as "any institution insured by the FDIC," so that institutions conducting similar activities are subject to the same regulations.[16]

---

[12]Cornyn and Talley, "Activity Deregulation," pp. 36-37. For an exhaustive review of this point, see Anthony Cornyn, Gerald E. Hanweck, Stephen A. Rhoades, and John T. Rose, "An Analysis of the Concept of Corporate Separateness in BHC Regulation from an Economic Perspective," *Proceedings of a Conference on Bank Structure and Competition,* (Chicago: Federal Reserve Bank of Chicago, 1986), pp. 174-212.

[13]Robert A. Eisenbeis, Robert S. Harris, and Josef Lakonishok, "Benefits of Bank Diversification: The Evidence from Shareholder Returns," *Journal of Finance* 39 (July 1984): 881-892; Larry D. Wall, "Nonbank Activities and Risk," *Economic Review,* Federal Reserve Bank of Atlanta 71 (October 1986): 19-34.

[14]Dennis Jacobe, "Nonbank Banks: A Prescription for Disaster," *Savings Institutions* 106 (March 1985): 70-76.

[15]Janice M. Moulton, "Nonbank Banks: Catalyst for Interstate Banking," *Business Review,* Federal Reserve Bank of Philadelphia (November/December 1985), pp. 3-18.

[16]Tim Carrington, "Freeze on New Consumer Banks Renewed, But Comptroller Prods Congress to Act," *The Wall Street Journal,* May 10, 1984; Monica Langley, "Rival Bank Regulators Agree Only to Disagree on Most Major Issues," *The Wall Street Journal,* January 23, 1985; Monica Langley, "Fed Puts Off, at Volcker's Insistence, Plan to End Limited-Service Bank Curb," *The Wall Street Journal,* January 10, 1985; Monica Langley, "U.S. Rejects Bank Bids Filed by 2 Companies," *The Wall Street Journal,* April

Congress finally agreed, and in the Competitive Equality Banking Act of 1987 (CEBA), defined a bank as the Fed suggested. This definition halts the formation of new nonbank banks, although 168 of them chartered before CEBA are legally exempt from the change. These nonbank banks remain as reminders of the regulatory dialectic.

Holding Companies: Nonbank Financial Institutions

Many shareholder-owned nonbank financial institutions, such as stockholder-owned savings and loans, finance companies, and insurance companies, are affiliated with holding companies. Unlike BHCs, however, laws governing nonbank holding companies are considerably less restrictive than those governing BHCs. For example, there are no federal requirements that subsidiaries of insurance holding companies engage in activities "closely related" to the insurance business. As a consequence, stockholder-owned insurers are affiliated with firms in industries unrelated to insurance, such as retailing. For example, Sears, Roebuck and Company has an insurance subsidiary that provided 46 percent of the total net income of the firm in 1985, and held 26 percent of the holding company's assets.[17] Many finance companies, too, are part of holding company organizations diversified well beyond financial services. For example, Household International, the holding company for Household Finance (one of the nation's largest) also operates affiliates in the car rental, manufacturing, grocery, and department store industries, as well as insurance, savings and loan, and nonbank bank subsidiaries.

These holding companies are entitled to many of the same taxation benefits as BHCs, such as avoidance of taxation on dividends paid by the subsidiary to the parent, but are subject to fewer regulations. In addition, some nonbank holding companies can engage in activities forbidden to BHCs, such as securities underwriting. As a result, commercial banks and BHCs have become increasingly vocal in supporting what they have termed a "level playing field" in the financial system. Competitors of commercial banks, such as thrifts, have argued that banks already have more than their fair share of advantages. For instance, S&Ls argue that there are much tighter restrictions on affiliate transactions within their holding companies than within BHCs. Final resolution of the competitive and fairness issues raised by differing legal treatment of holding companies is a matter for Congress.[18]

Chain Banking

Not all states allow MBHCs, thereby preventing the operation of several banks under one umbrella organization. The prohibition against MBHCs has not, however, prevented other ways of affiliating several banks or one-bank holding companies. One of the most common arrangements is *chain banking.* Chain banking occurs when one investor owns 5 percent of the voting stock in one or more individual banks *and* holds a managerial post in each bank; or when an individual or group owns at least 10 percent of the voting shares of two or more banks. In a few instances, chain-banking organizations have been formed by individuals with common ownership shares in two or more one-bank holding companies.

Because of the more informal structure of chain banking, the independent identity of each bank is maintained to a greater degree than in a MBHC, yet a single investor or group is able to control a substantial amount of banking assets. Furthermore, chain-banking organizations not involving holding companies are not subject to BHC geographic restrictions, so chains

1, 1985; Stephen Wermiel and Monica Langley, "Top Court Clears Limited-Service Banks and Deals Major Blow to Power of Fed," *The Wall Street Journal,* January 23, 1986, p. 4.

[17]Sears, Roebuck and Company, *1985 Annual Report,* p. 35.

[18]For more discussion of BHC advantages versus those of competitors, see Dennis Jacobe, "The New Holding Company: An Old Idea in New Guise," *Savings Institutions* 104 (August 1983): 48-56.

can cross state lines. In addition, reporting requirements are not stringent, so less is known about the performance of chain banks than about BHCs.[19]

Franchising

Another alternative to a holding company is the franchise, under which an independent financial institution leases the right to use the name and marketing programs of a larger umbrella organization. The first application of franchising to financial institutions is attributed to First Interstate Bancorp, one of the interstate banking organizations grandfathered under BHC legislation. In 1982, First Interstate began leasing the use of its name and promotional strategies to independent banks around the nation. A franchising institution must change its name to First Interstate Bank of [its town] but does not become a member of the holding company. The objective of franchisees is to obtain the benefits of association with a large banking organization, such as a wide range of marketing and other managerial talents, while still retaining operational independence.[20]

Thrift institutions also participate in franchising. The leader in the thrift franchise movement was First Nationwide Network, which leases the right to the phrase "a member of the First Nationwide Network" and makes available a host of management support systems. As with the First Interstate franchise, First Nationwide's program especially appeals to small institutions that wish to maintain operational independence.

MUTUALLY OWNED INSTITUTIONS

Unlike stockholder institutions, mutually organized firms, such as thrifts and insurers, are "owned" by their customers. Depositors, policyholders, or borrowers become "owners" when they initiate a business relationship with the institution.

Distribution of Mutual Institutions

Table 3.3 provides information on the number of shareholder versus mutually owned thrifts and insurance companies in 1985. For reasons explored later, the number of stock companies has been increasing in recent years. Nonetheless, the mutual form remains dominant among S&Ls, savings banks, and property and casualty insurers. Most life insurers are organized as stockholder-owned corporations, although the largest firms in the industry are mutually organized.

Origin and Characteristics of Mutual Ownership

The primary rationale for the mutual form of organization is that it presumably ensures that an institution will operate for the benefit of its customers, who have supplied the majority of funds and depend upon it for service and security. In the United States, this rationale dates to the early 1800s, when consumer-oriented financial institutions appeared for the first time.[21] Instead of focusing exclusively on profits, managers of mutual institutions supposedly make decisions that meet their customers' needs better.

Owners' Rights. Ownership rights in a mutual organization are considerably different from those in a stockholder-owned firm. In both instances, the owners have a right to elect

---

[19]For more information on chain banks, see Federal Reserve Bank of Kansas City, "Report on Chain Banking Organizations in Kansas, Nebraska, and Oklahoma," *Banking Studies* 1 (1983): 9-11; Anthony W. Cyrnak, "Chain Banks and Competition: The Effectiveness of Federal Reserve Policy Since 1977," *Economic Review,* Federal Reserve Bank of San Francisco (Spring 1986), pp. 5-15.

[20]See Gerald Eickhoff, "Going Interstate by Franchises or Networks," *Economic Review,* Federal Reserve Bank of Atlanta 70 (January 1985): 32-35; William J. Carner, "An Analysis of Franchising in Retail Banking," *Journal of Retail Banking* 8 (Winter 1986-87): 57-66.

[21]Martin R. Blyn, "The Evolution of the U.S. Money and Capital Markets and Financial Intermediaries," in *Financial Institutions and Markets,* 2d ed. Murray E. Polakoff and Thomas A. Durkin, et al, eds. (Boston: Houghton Mifflin, 1981), pp. 40-41.

Table 3.3
Ownership Form in the Thrift and Insurance Industries, 1985

	Federally Insured Savings and Loan Associations	
	Number	**%**
Mutual	2,159	60.4
Stock	1,087	39.6
Total	3,246	100.0

	Savings Banks	
	Number	**%**
Mutual	326	88.1
Stock	44	11.9
Total	370	100.0

	Life Insurance Companies	
	Number	**%**
Mutual	131	5.9
Stock	2,079	94.1
Total	2,210	100.0

	Property and Casualty Insurance Companies[a]	
	Number	**%**
Mutual	2,236	63.9
Stock	1,264	36.1
Total	3,500	100.0

[a]Estimated.

Sources: U. S. League of Savings Institutions, *1986 Savings Institutions Source Book*
National Council of Savings Institutions, *1986 National Fact Book of Savings Institutions*
American Council of Life Insurance, *1986 Life Insurance Fact Book*
A. M. Best and Company, *Best's Aggregates and Averages,* 1986 edition
Insurance Information Institute, *1986-87 Property and Casualty Fact Book*
Board of Governors of the Federal Reserve System, *1985 Annual Report.*

a board of directors to monitor management's performance. But potential control over management is stronger in a stockholder-owned firm. First, because ownership rights in a mutual institution cannot be sold to another party (in legal language, they are nonnegotiable), there is little chance that anyone can obtain enough influence to control the outcome of elections. Furthermore, in some thrift institutions, owners are asked to sign away their rights to vote at the time they open an account or take out a loan, in effect giving managers a permanent proxy. Some observers of thrifts have stated, in fact, that a mutual organization often results in a "self-perpetuating" board.[22] Further, while "owners" of a mutually organized company theoretically have a pro rata claim on the retained earnings of the institution, they have no way to exercise that claim. Because there are no negotiable ownership shares, no capital gains can be earned. An "owner" who cancels a policy or closes a deposit account also cancels the right to this pro rata share. Finally, mutually owned institutions are not legally required to disclose as much detail about their

[22]Walter J. Woerheide, *The Savings and Loan Industry* (Westport, CT: Quorum Books, 1984), p. 178.

financial condition as are stockholder-owned firms. Thus, depositors or policyholders may lack access to information about the safety and soundness of their institutions.

Performance of Mutual Firms.   As a result of these differences, one can argue that managers have more latitude in mutual organizations than in stockholder-held firms. Whether or not this latitude is "good" depends upon its effect on institutional performance relative to the performance of similar stockholder-owned institutions. Most of the research evidence on this point has been accumulated for savings and loan associations. Researchers have hypothesized that stock associations should be more cost-efficient and more profitable, because of managers' fear of removal by shareholders if costs are excessive and profits inferior. Agency theory, discussed in Chapter 1, suggests that mutually owned associations, in which the costs of monitoring managers are likely to be higher, may permit managers to exercise their own preferences to a greater degree than in stockholder-owned institutions. Furthermore, because of the possibility of managerial benefits from stock options in stockholder-owned associations, they should be more aggressive and willing to take more risks than managers of mutually owned firms. Finally, because mutual associations have only one source of net worth—earnings retained from profitable operations—stock associations have been hypothesized to be better capitalized than mutuals.

Tests of these hypotheses have yielded mixed results. Generally, researchers have concluded that stock associations are riskier and more aggressive because they grow at faster rates, but are not necessarily more efficient nor more profitable than their mutual counterparts.[23] Most studies were conducted during periods when the S&L industry as a whole was doing well, so performance differences based on organizational form involved profitable versus more profitable firms.

In recent years, when the thrift industry as a whole has been unprofitable, events have demonstrated that one key difference between mutuals and stocks—their ability to raise capital—is significant. When profits are negative and retained earnings are reduced, mutual associations have no way to replenish lost net worth.[24] If losses persist, mutual thrift institutions may be forced into a position of negative net worth, eventually leading to failure. Similar profitability difficulties, as well as tax considerations, have troubled mutually owned insurance companies. Increasingly, the thrift and insurance industries have turned to *conversion,* a procedure through which an institution's organizational structure changes from mutual to stock.

Conversion: The Thrifts

Between 1980 and 1984, over 200 thrifts converted from the mutual to the stock form of ownership, a rapid rate compared to the past.[25] Requirements for conversion are strictly defined by the Federal Home Loan Bank Board and were revised in late 1986. The process involves the preparation of a conversion plan by management with the approval of directors, regulators, and the majority of owner-depositors. Stock sold in a conversion is first offered to eligible depositors, none of whom may purchase over 5 percent of the new stock.

---

[23]A typical test of these hypotheses, and a review of the literature on mutual versus stock performance, can be found in W. Gary Simpson and Theodor Kohers, "The Effect of Organizational Form on Performance in the Savings and Loan Industry," *Financial Review* 14 (Fall 1979): 1–14. A more recent review of the literature can be found in Woerheide, *The Savings and Loan Industry,* pp. 29–31.

[24]This statement is not strictly true for the thrift industry, because regulators have devised proxies for net worth for thrifts with liabilities exceeding assets, but with no cash flow problems that would cause immediate failure. These proxies are discussed in Chapter 16.

[25]From 1945 to 1955, when there were few restrictions on conversion, only 30 thrifts converted. From 1955 to 1974, conversions were prohibited altogether. Even though restrictions were removed after 1974, few conversions occurred until the financial crisis in the industry beginning in 1980. See Constance Dunham, "Mutual-to-Stock Conversion by Thrifts: Implications for Soundness," *New England Economic Review,* Federal Reserve Bank of Boston (January/February 1985), pp. 31–45. For further details on policies governing conversion by thrifts, see Franklin Ornstein, *Savings Banking: An Industry in Change* (Reston, VA: Reston Publishing Co., 1985), pp. 77–94.

Depositors not interested in the stock may not sell their rights to those who are.

Before 1986, around 70 percent of the stock sold was purchased by less than 5 percent of depositors. Managers and directors ultimately bought about 20 percent of the converted shares, giving them effective control over the subsequent operations of the new organization. In periods following a conversion, management typically increased its ownership through acquisition or the exercise of stock options.

Critics frequently charged that conversion resulted in windfall benefits to a few and little, if any, return to the many depositors whose years of savings made the converting institution viable. Furthermore, studies of converted institutions indicated that they often merged with other institutions after conversion, again resulting in potential monetary gain for the few who emerged from a conversion with substantial stock ownership. As a result of these criticisms, the recently revised conversion regulations make it more difficult for converted thrifts to be acquired by other firms. In addition, the new rules encourage nonmanagement employees to buy stock in the converted institution. The FHLBB made clear its intention to promote conversions while limiting the possibility that only a few individuals can benefit at the expense of others.[26]

Conversion: The Insurers

The insurance industry, too, has faced profitability problems recently because changing consumer preferences, increasing litigation of claims, inflation, and high interest rates have required large cash outflows. Like their thrift counterparts, mutual insurers have faced pressures from reduced net worth caused by low or negative earnings. Consequently, they, too, have considered conversion as a survival strategy. Several property and casualty insurers have converted since 1984, and in 1984, the first application in 80 years for conversion of a mutual life insurer was filed by Union Mutual Life with the Maine insurance commission. The three largest life insurers, all mutually owned, have also considered conversion, although state laws governing insurers make the process somewhat more complicated than for thrifts.[27]

Motivation for conversion was further fueled by the Tax Reform Act of 1984, which lowered the amount of tax-deductible "dividends" that can be paid to policyholder-owners of mutual insurers. Because the tax-deductibility of these dividends was a major reason for the popularity of the mutual form of organization, its attractiveness has been considerably reduced. Furthermore, some experts have argued that stock option incentives available in stockholder-owned insurers will attract the talented managers needed in the industry.[28]

Because the regulation of insurers rests largely at the state, rather than federal, level, there is no uniform procedure for conversion analogous to the FHLBB's plan for thrifts. Nonetheless, evidence from recent insurance conversions suggests that the issue of windfall profits will arise in the insurance industry as well. The Union Mutual conversion involved lawsuits between the company and its employees, proxy fights over control of materials sent to policyholders, and acrimony between the state insurance commissioner and the company. Still, it has been flatly predicted that mutual insurers will "disappear" as a result of the heightened need for capital in a deregulated environment.[29] If this prediction holds, the insurance industry faces major structural change.

---

[26]Federal Home Loan Bank Board, "Conversions from Mutual to Stock Form and Acquisitions of Control of Insured Institutions," 12 CFR Parts 543, 546, 552, 562, 563, 563b, and 574, October 17, 1986.

[27]Dan Baum, "Union Mutual's Plan to Be Stock Owned Leads to Suits Against Some Agents and a Proxy Fight," *The Wall Street Journal,* February 26, 1985; Eleanor Tracy Johnson, "The Top Life Insurers Weigh Going Public," *Fortune* 109 (June 25, 1984): 96; Laura Meadows, "Minuet in Maine,"*Forbes* 136 (November 18, 1985): 208.

[28]Gregory E. Murray, "Demutualization of Insurance Companies— Advantages and Disadvantages," *Journal of the American Society of Chartered Life Underwriters* 39 (January 1985): 52-54.

[29]John Heimann, "Market-Driven Deregulation of Financial Services," *Economic Review,* Federal Reserve Bank of Atlanta 69 (December 1984): 40.

Service Corporations: The Holding Company Alternative

Stockholder-owned thrifts and insurance firms can form holding companies, but because there is no stock in mutual associations, formation of a holding company in a mutual organization is impossible. Alternative structures, however, permit thrift mutuals (and stock institutions, too, if they so desire) to diversify outside their traditional functions of accepting deposits and making mortgage loans.

Since the 1950s, S&Ls with federal charters have been permitted to form *service corporations (SCs)* to conduct diversified lines of business. An SC is formed when one or more associations purchases the stock of a new organization. The associations, as residual owners of the SC, are entitled to all profits from its operations. The amount invested in SCs is limited to 3 percent of a thrift's total assets. Although laws vary from state to state, similar arrangements exist for mutual insurance companies to form subsidiaries by using some of their assets to purchase stock in affiliated stockholder-owned organizations.

Typically, investment in SCs has been a very small proportion of the savings and loan industry's assets—only 2 percent at year-end 1985.[30] SC activities include real estate development and property management, insurance agency and brokerage services, data-processing services, and consumer lending. Little long-term evidence is available on the effect of SCs on institutional profitability, but recent data indicate that some SCs provided almost 10 percent of their parents' total income in the thrift earnings crisis of 1981-1982. Other SCs, however, lost money during that period, especially those engaged in activities closely related to mortgage lending.[31]

NOT-FOR-PROFIT INSTITUTIONS

The third organizational structure in financial institutions is the not-for-profit form. Credit unions (CUs) are currently the only major financial group with this structure. Credit unions are similar to mutually owned institutions with two major exceptions: Membership in credit unions is restricted by law to those with a "common bond," and profits retained by federal CUs to increase the net worth of the organization are not taxable.

The "common bond" requirement for membership in a CU—usually a tie formed as a result of occupational, religious, or social affiliations—is related to the cooperative motivation that theoretically underlies the formation of mutual financial institutions. Because federal CUs are exempt from taxation based on the purported strength of this cooperation, the common bond requirement is intended to ensure that the spirit of colleague helping colleague is a reality. In practice, the interpretation of the phrase *common bond* has been expanded over the years, and it is now quite liberal.[32]

CU members are "owners" of the organization. In fact, their savings are called "shares," although these shares are more like deposits than stock because they are eligible for federal deposit insurance. As in mutuals, members cannot sell shares to profit from capital gains. Also like mutuals, credit unions must maintain sufficient net worth (called "reserves") from earnings retention to withstand a potential decline in asset values; they have no other source of equity-like capital. Nevertheless, their tax exemption may enable federal CUs to charge lower loan rates, yet achieve the same additions to net worth as a comparably sized S&L or savings bank.

Service Organizations

Federal credit unions can form *credit union service organizations (CUSOs)* on a for-profit

[30]*1985 Savings Institutions Source Book* (Chicago: U.S. League of Savings Institutions, 1985), p. 54.

[31]"Service Corporations Are Ideal Diversification Tool," *Savings Institutions* 104 (October 1983): 52-55; Harold B. Olin, "Service Corporations Help the Business Diversify," *Savings Institutions* 105 (April 1984): 120-127.

[32]Douglas K. Pearce, "Recent Developments in the Credit Union Industry," *Economic Review,* Federal Reserve Bank of Kansas City 69 (June 1984): 8.

basis. As with thrift service corporations, investment in CUSOs is limited, although the restriction is expressed as a percentage of a CU's net worth, not of its assets. CUSOs enable CUs to earn income from sources that would be prohibited without the CUSO, such as insurance, brokerage, and financial-planning services. The small size of most credit unions has prevented their using CUSOs up to this point, although managers in larger CUs have found them an attractive diversification vehicle in the 1980s.[33]

COMPARATIVE TAXATION OF FINANCIAL INSTITUTIONS

Taxation of financial institutions is based largely on institutional structure. Because it is impossible to summarize all state tax laws, this section is confined to differences in federal taxation among institutions.[34] Like all entities subject to taxation, financial institutions are concerned with three types of tax provisions: tax rates, or the percentage of taxable income paid in taxes; tax deductions, or expenses that may be deducted from income before taxable income is calculated; and tax credits, or direct deductions from taxes owed. Differences in any of these areas can cause the taxation of institutions to differ substantially. As with other issues, the financial community disagrees on which institutions benefit most from the tax system.

The federal tax system has undergone several major changes since the mid-1970s, with revisions in 1976, 1978, 1981, 1982, 1984, and 1986. Until 1986, the thrust of these changes was to lower the proportion of total federal revenues generated by corporations versus individ-

uals. In the Tax Reform Act of 1986, that trend was reversed with the elimination of several provisions beneficial to business in general, and to specific financial institutions. Because tax rates were lowered in 1986, however, institutions without special privileges reducing taxable income were not harmed by the legislation and, in fact, anticipate paying lower taxes.

Clearly, taxation requires continuing attention, and managers must always consult the most recent information before making a financial decision involving taxes. Furthermore, federal taxation is so complex that volumes are required to explain the subject fully. Nonetheless, brief summaries of existing regulations are useful in illustrating the tax environment in which institutions operate.

Taxation of Depositories

Although the three types of depositories have many similarities, they are subject to strikingly different tax treatments.

Thrifts.   Before 1962, justified by the mutual organizational form and its lack of residual beneficiaries, most thrifts were not only permitted to deduct ongoing interest and operating expenses from taxable income, they were also permitted to transfer nontaxable yearly additions to their bad-debt reserves equal to 12 percent of total deposits. This 12 percent limit existed whether or not it remotely approximated the actual bad-debt losses the institution anticipated. At that time, mortgage loans were among the safest of any financial asset, so actual loan losses for the typical thrift were quite small. Thrifts paid a very small proportion of income in taxes, especially compared to commercial banks, which were not permitted such a generous bad-debt deduction.

Under prodding from the commercial banking industry, thrifts' bad-debt deductions were limited in 1962 and again in 1986, resulting in an upward drift in the percentage of taxes they have paid since the 1960s. Additional changes in tax laws in 1969 tied thrifts' bad-debt deductions to the percentage of assets in housing-related investments. Although the required

---

[33]"CUSOs Open New Service Areas," *Credit Union Magazine* 50 (November 1984): 8–14; "Leagues and Regulators Take a Hard Look," *Credit Union Magazine* 50 (December 1984): 42–45.

[34]Recently, it has been argued that the different tax treatments outlined in this section are inappropriate and that a single federal tax structure for all institutions should be enacted. See Thomas S. Neubig, "The Taxation of Financial Institutions after Deregulation," *National Tax Journal* 37 (September 1984): 351–359.

percentage of housing-related investments was lowered in 1986 from 82 percent to 60 percent, the tie-in reduces the diversification potential of thrifts wishing to take advantage of available tax deductions. In recent years, when many thrifts have experienced losses, the industry as a whole has paid few taxes. Exemption from taxes for that reason is not good news.

Commercial Banks.   The taxation of commercial banks does not differ materially from that of nonfinancial corporations, but their ability to use tax shelters for many years resulted in a relatively low proportion of income actually paid in taxes. In fact, the tax burden of commercial banks steadily declined for several decades before 1986, because they invested relatively heavily in securities on which income is tax-exempt. Although tax-exempt securities have lower pretax returns, the tax savings can easily make up the difference for many institutions. Thrifts' inability to shift asset structures away from housing-related assets has prevented their taking full advantage of tax-exempt securities.

In 1986, commercial banks were among the industries targeted for tax increases, as Congress phased out relatively generous bad-debt deductions for large banks and eliminated other deductions that encouraged banks' investments in municipal bonds. In general, income from municipal bonds remains tax-exempt to investors, including banks. However, all businesses are subject to a strictly enforced minimum tax, and banks with exceptionally large amounts of tax-exempt income may be required to pay taxes on some of it. Finally, tax deductions for taxes on income earned in foreign countries were curtailed by the 1986 legislation, increasing the taxes of banks with international operations.

Credit Unions.   During the first three years of their existence, federal CUs paid state taxes, but technical differences between CU shares and deposits meant their tax burden was quite high in some states. In 1937, Congress decided that the cooperative movement was best served by exempting federal CUs from taxation. This tax exemption has been under renewed scrutiny in recent years but survived the major tax reform of 1986. Opponents argue that the increasingly loose common bond requirements on CU membership are eroding the principal reason for their not-for-profit status, and that exemption from taxes represents a subsidy of CUs by taxpayers.[35]

Taxation of Insurance Companies

Tax provisions applying to insurers differ from those applying to depositories. In addition, different types of insurers face different tax laws.

Life Insurers.   The income of an insurance company comes from two sources: sale of policies and income from investments made by the insurer when cash inflows from sales exceed cash needed to pay claims. State regulations require insurers to estimate the rate of return they expect on their investments and to use the estimate to set policy fees, or *premiums,* under the theory that premiums charged policyholders can be lower if investment income is higher. However, conservative rules in most states allow insurers to estimate their investment income at a much lower level than has actually been earned in recent years. Consequently, a major issue in insurance company regulation is how investment income should be estimated and taxed.

The taxation of life insurers has undergone major changes since 1984.[36] Before that time, taxes were based on a 1959 law that taxed investment income actually earned *in excess* of estimated investment income. For many years, life insurer taxes were low relative to those of other financial institutions, because investment income seldom exceeded estimated income by a

---

[35]J. Carroll Moody and Gilbert C. Fite, *The Credit Union Movement* (Lincoln, NE: University of Nebraska Press, 1971), Chapter 10; Pearce, "Recent Developments," p. 18; "The 900-Pound Canary," *Forbes* (April 22, 1985), p. 118.

[36]This section draws on parts of Richard W. Kopcke, "The Federal Income Taxation of Life Insurance Companies," *New England Economic Review,* Federal Reserve Bank of Boston (March/April 1985), pp. 5-19.

large amount. As market interest rates rose, creating large discrepancies between estimates of investment income and actual earnings, life insurers paid higher and higher taxes.

By 1984, Congress decided that the 1959 law was obsolete. Therefore, a provision taxing life insurers on net income from investments was passed in the Tax Reform Act of 1984. (Net investment income is income after the deduction of portfolio management expenses.) Although the law improved the position of life insurers versus many other financial institutions, it also created some inequities between mutual and stock insurers.

To understand the source of this inequity, it is necessary to know that insurers sometimes refund a portion of premiums paid by policyholders. These premium rebates are paid in years in which investment income is especially good. Stockholder-owned life insurers may consider premium rebates as tax-deductible expenses. Because the policyholders of mutuals are "owners," however, the new law does not permit mutuals to deduct all premium rebates. Permissible deductions are governed by a complex formula based on the proportion of industry assets held by mutual firms. As a result of the 1984 law, the American Council of Life Insurance estimated that total taxes paid by the industry would increase, because most of the industry's assets are held by a few large mutuals.[37] In 1986, however, the lowering of tax rates offset the loss of deductions in the 1984 law.

Property and Casualty Insurers. Property and casualty insurers have enjoyed few of the tax benefits of their life counterparts, facing instead the same tax structure faced by nonfinancial corporations.[38] Like life insurers, their income arises from premiums and from investments. Without the favorable tax treatment historically given to life insurers, property and casualty insurers chose to invest heavily in securities providing tax-exempt income. In recent years, however, rapidly accelerating policy claims have produced losses, making investment income even more important for overall company profitability. As discussed in Chapter 23, the decline in earnings has decreased the attractiveness of tax-exempt securities. Consequently, the tax treatment of the industry has always had a strong impact on its asset/ liability management strategies.

Tax reform in 1986 was generally interpreted as unfavorable for property and casualty insurers because they lost the ability to defer some tax payments by using special accounting methods. In addition, property and casualty firms, like commercial banks, may suffer from the minimum tax provision.

Taxation of Other Financial Institutions

Federal taxation of other financial institutions also substantially affects their management strategies. Most finance companies and securities firms are taxed identically to nonfinancial firms, so the lowering of tax rates in 1986 benefited them, although finance companies lost some of their favorable bad-debt deductions. In contrast, the income of pension funds is not taxed until paid to employees upon resignation or retirement. At that time, the employee's personal tax rate is the relevant rate. Although they are not classified as not-for-profit organizations, because their beneficiaries have enforceable claims on the fund's assets, the funds' freedom from taxes makes tax-exempt securities unattractive. Other tax-related issues have little relevance for pension funds.

Mutual funds and other investment companies also enjoy favorable tax treatment at the fund level, thanks to Subchapter M of the Internal Revenue Code. Shareholders pay personal taxes on income from their shares, provided the funds pass along at least 97 percent of ordinary income and 90 percent of net capital gain income to investors. The investment company itself pays no taxes, based on the conduit theory

---

[37]*Life Insurance Fact Book* (Washington, DC: American Council of Life Insurance, 1984), p. 63.

[38]Exceptions are small insurers, which are either partially or wholly exempt from taxes if their gross income is less than $350,000. See Ernst & Whinney, *Tax Reform—1986* (Washington, DC: Ernst & Whinney, 1986): p. 193.

introduced in Chapter 2. Although other laws and regulations limit the flexibility with which mutual fund assets can be managed, taxation is not the source of major restrictions.

SUMMARY

This chapter has explored key structural issues for financial institutions, such as the way they raise funds, the beneficiaries of their profits, and their taxation. One unusual characteristic is that many institutions are mutually organized, including most thrifts and many insurance companies. As a result, customers are the "owners" of the business. Credit unions are unusual because they are organized on a not-for-profit basis and exist to provide goods or services at below-market cost to members with a common bond.

The holding company form of ownership is important for financial institutions, particularly commercial banks. Bank holding companies have become increasingly popular because they allow access to capital, potential for diversification and geographic expansion, and the benefits of financial leverage. These benefits are monitored by the Federal Reserve Board. The effect of BHCs on the safety and soundness of institutions remains controversial. Chain banking, franchising, and service corporations are also growing in popularity, but provide more limited benefits than BHCs and are not as closely regulated.

It is generally agreed that managers of mutual firms have more latitude than those of stockholder-owned firms, but profitability difficulties have troubled many mutually owned firms. Increasingly, mutuals are considering conversion, a procedure by which the ownership of an institution is transferred from customers to shareholders.

Finally, financial institutions are subject to special federal tax provisions that affect asset/liability management. Some institutions pay taxes at a relatively low rate, while others enjoy few tax privileges.

Questions

1. Identify the importance of the following terms: equity, residual claimant, net worth, net worth multiplier.

2. What is the importance of the relationship between return on net worth and net interest margin for a financial institution? How does this relationship affect the managerial planning process?

3. What is the purpose of a bank holding company? What factors have caused the number of bank holding companies to increase significantly in the past several years?

4. What are loan production offices? Edge Act subsidiaries?

5. Review some of the evidence on BHCs and the safety of the commercial banking industry. Do you support the existence of "corporate separateness?" Why or why not?

6. Recently, interest in nonbank banks has increased. What are nonbank banks? What is the objective of forming this type of organization? In your opinion, should they be regulated? If so, how?

7. In some states multibank holding companies are prohibited. For banks operating in these states, what arrangements are available to allow the operation of several banks under one organization? Compare these arrangements to the structure of a bank holding company.

8. What laws on bank branching and expansion of bank holding companies exist in your state? Have these laws changed in recent years? If so, why? Are additional changes anticipated in the future? If so, why?

9. How does a mutually owned institution differ from a stockholder-owned institution?

10. What is meant by conversion? Why have many firms in the thrift and insurance industries taken steps toward conversion? Find an article on a thrift or insurer that has converted recently. What, if any, problems arose in the process?

11. What regulations exist to govern conversions in the thrift and insurance industries? What potential controversies are regulations designed to address?

12. Compare a service corporation to a nonbank subsidiary of a bank holding company. Which organizational form do you believe is the most beneficial to an institution?

13. How does the organizational form of credit unions affect the ownership, management, and taxation of the institution? The tax-exempt status of federal credit unions has been criticized recently. Do you favor the tax-exempt status? Why or why not?

14. Compare the taxation of life insurers with that of property and casualty insurers.

15. How are investment companies taxed? Pension funds? In general, how does taxation affect their management strategies?

Problems

1. The manager of Peoples Savings and Loan needs your help. Calculate the net interest margin and before-tax interest revenues the S&L must achieve, given the following information:

Target return on net worth	24%
Target net worth multiplier	10
t	34%
Total assets	$675,000,000
Interest expense	$65,000,000
Noninterest income and expense	$0

2. Consider the following information on Community Commercial Bank:

Total assets	$550,000,000
Total liabilities	$500,000,000
RONW	21%
t	30%

   a. What level of before-tax income must the bank earn to meet its target RONW, assuming that the current net worth multiplier is considered optimal?
   b. What is the resulting target net interest margin?

3. a. If an institution earns a 2.0 percent NIM, is in the 34 percent tax bracket, and has a net worth multiplier of 12, what is its RONW? What is its ROA?
   b. If the net worth multiplier increases, will ROA and RONW increase, decrease, or remain the same? Why?

4. a. A bank affiliated with a holding company has made expansion plans. It is currently subject to a minimum ratio of net worth to total assets of 6.5 percent. Using the principle of double leverage, how much must the BHC borrow if the bank wishes to expand total assets by $200 million? By $500 million?
   b. Suppose the required net worth multiplier is 11. By how much can the bank expand total assets if the BHC borrows $300 million and uses the proceeds to purchase new shares in the bank?

5. A savings and loan association with total assets of $250 million has a ratio of net worth to total assets of 8 percent. A competitor of equal size has a ratio of 6 percent. The managers of both thrifts are uncertain of future interest revenues but believe they could range from 10 percent to 15 percent of total assets. Interest costs for both of the institutions are expected to average 11 percent of total liabilities.

   a. Graph the relationship between IR/TA and RONW for the two institutions over the forecasted range of interest revenues.

   b. Which institution's shareholders will be better off at lower levels of revenue? Which institution's owners are subjected to greater risk?

   c. If you believed interest revenues would be 14 percent of total assets, in which S&L would you prefer to own stock? Why?

Selected References

Baer, Herbert and Sue F. Gregorash. *Toward Nationwide Banking: A Guide to the Issues.* Chicago: Federal Reserve Bank of Chicago, 1986.

Blyn, Martin R. "The Evolution of the U.S. Money and Capital Markets and Financial Intermediaries." In *Financial Institutions and Markets,* 2d ed. Edited by Murray E. Polakoff and Thomas A. Durkin. Boston: Houghton Mifflin, 1981, pp. 31-45.

Boyd, John H. and Stanley L. Graham. "Risk, Regulation, and Bank Holding Company Expansion into Nonbanking." *Quarterly Review* (Federal Reserve Bank of Minneapolis) 10 (Spring 1986): 2-17.

Brown, Donald M. "Bank Holding Company Performance Studies and the Public Interest: Normative Uses for Positive Analysis?" *Review* (Federal Reserve Bank of St. Louis) 65 (March 1983): 26-34.

Chase, Samuel B. Jr., and John J. Mingo. "The Regulation of Bank Holding Companies." *Journal of Finance* 30 (May 1975): 281-292.

Cornyn, Anthony G., and Samuel H. Talley. "Activity Deregulation and Bank Soundness." *Proceedings of a Conference on Bank Structure and Competition.* Chicago: Federal Reserve Bank of Chicago, 1983: 28-31.

Cornyn, Anthony, Gerald Hanweck, Stephen Rhoades, and John Rose. "An Analysis of the Concept of Corporate Separateness in BHC Regulation from an Economic Perspective." *Proceedings of a Conference on Bank Structure and Competition.* Chicago: Federal Reserve Bank of Chicago, 1986, pp. 174-212.

DiClemente, John J. "What Is a Bank?" *Economic Perspectives* (Federal Reserve Bank of Chicago) 7 (January/February 1983): 20-31.

Dunham, Constance. "Mutual-to-Stock Conversion by Thrifts: Implications for Soundness." *New England Economic Review* (Federal Reserve Bank of Boston) (January/February 1985), pp. 31-45.

Eickhoff, Gerald. "Going Interstate by Franchises or Networks." *Economic Review* (Federal Reserve Bank of Atlanta) 70 (January 1985): 32-35.

Eisenbeis, Robert. "How Should Bank Holding Companies Be Regulated?" *Economic Review* (Federal Reserve Bank of Atlanta) 68 (January 1983): 43-44.

Eisenbeis, Robert A., Robert S. Harris, and Josef Lakonishok. "Benefits of Bank Diversification: The Evidence from Shareholder Returns." *Journal of Finance* 39 (July 1984): 881-892.

Federal Reserve Bank of Kansas City. "Report on Chain Banking Organizations in Kansas, Nebraska, and Oklahoma." *Banking Studies* 1 (1983).

Frieder, Larry A., and Vincent P. Apilado. "Bank Holding Company Research: Classification, Synthesis, and New Directions." *Journal of Bank Research* 13 (Summer 1982): 80-95.

Heimann, John. "Market-Driven Deregulation of Financial Services." *Economic Review* (Federal Reserve Bank of Atlanta) 69 (December 1984): 36-41.

Jacobe, Dennis. "Nonbank Banks: A Prescription for Disaster." *Savings Institutions* 106 (March 1985): 70-76.

Karna, Adi S., and Duane B. Graddy. "Bank Holding Company Leverage and the Return on Stockholders' Equity." *Journal of Bank Research* 13 (Spring 1982): 42-48.

Kopcke, Richard W. "The Federal Income Taxation of Life Insurance Companies." *New England Economic Review* (Federal Reserve Bank of Boston) (March/April 1985), pp. 5-19.

Moulton, Janice M. "Nonbank Banks: Catalyst for Interstate Banking." *Business Review* (Federal Reserve Bank of Philadelphia) (November/December 1985), pp. 3-18.

Neubig, Thomas S. "The Taxation of Financial Institutions after Deregulation." *National Tax Journal* 37 (September 1984): 351-359.

Ornstein, Franklin. *Savings Banking: An Industry in Change.* Reston, VA: Reston Publishing Co., 1985.

Pearce, Douglas K. "Recent Developments in the Credit Union Industry." *Economic Review* (Federal Reserve Bank of Kansas City) 69 (June 1984): 3-19.

Savage, Donald T. "Interstate Banking Developments." *Federal Reserve Bulletin* 73 (February 1987): 79-92.

Shull, Bernard. "Economic Efficiency, Public Regulation, and Financial Reform: Depository Institutions." In *Financial Institutions and Markets,* 2d ed. Edited by Murray E. Polakoff and Thomas A. Durkin. Boston: Houghton Mifflin, 1981, pp. 671-702.

Simpson, Gary W., and Theodor Kohers. "The Effects of Organizational Form on Performance in the Savings and Loan Industry." *Financial Review* 14 (Fall 1979): 1-14.

Wall, Larry D. "Insulating Banks from Non-Bank Affiliates." *Economic Review* (Federal Reserve Bank of Atlanta) 69 (September 1984): 18-27.

Wall, Larry, D. "Nonbank Activities and Risk." *Economic Review* (Federal Reserve Bank of Atlanta) 71 (October 1986): 19-34.

Whalen, Gary. "Operational Policies of Multibank Holding Companies." *Economic Review* (Federal Reserve Bank of Cleveland) (Winter 1981-1982), pp. 20-31.

Whitehead, David D. "Interstate Banking: Probability or Reality?" *Economic Review* (Federal Reserve Bank of Atlanta) 70 (March 1985): 6-19.

Woerheide, Walter J. *The Savings and Loan Industry.* Westport, CT: Quorum Books, 1984.

Appendix 3A

EFFECT OF LEVERAGE ON RETURN ON NET WORTH

Financing with borrowed funds instead of equity affects the level and variability of returns to shareholders. Because financial institutions rely heavily on liabilities, the effect of leverage is important.

Suppose a bank has assets of $10 million, with equity of $1 million. The ratio of net worth to total assets is 10 percent, so the net worth multiplier is 10. RONW can be estimated under several earnings levels. Net noninterest expenses and taxes are ignored; if included, however, they would not alter the conclusions.

Interest revenues (IR)	$670,000	$770,000	$870,000
Interest expense (IE):			
8% x TL	720,000	720,000	720,000
Net Income	−50,000	50,000	150,000
IR/Total Assets	6.7%	7.7%	8.7%
RONW (Net Income/ Net Worth)	−5.0%	5.0%	15.0%

If another bank has assets of $10 million with equity of $750,000, its ratio of net worth to total assets is 7.5 percent. Under the same levels of IR and at the same cost of borrowed funds:

Interest revenues (IR)	$670,000	$770,000	$870,000
Interest expense (IE):			
8% x TL	740,000	740,000	740,000
Net Income	−70,000	30,000	130,000
IR/Total Assets	6.7%	7.7%	8.7%
RONW	−9.33%	4.00%	17.33%

For a $10 million bank with equity of $500,000 (a ratio of net worth to total assets of 5 percent):

Interest revenues (IR)	$670,000	$770,000	$870,000
Interest expense (IE):			
8% x TL	760,000	760,000	760,000
Net Income	−90,000	10,000	110,000
IR/Total Assets	6.7%	7.7%	8.7%
RONW	−18.00%	2.00%	22.00%

The data reveal that the lower the ratio of net worth to total assets, or the more the bank is leveraged, the greater the variation in RONW as interest revenues vary. A graph makes comparison clearer. In Figure 3A.1 (on page 76), the relationship between IR/Total Assets and RONW is represented by a different line for each of the banks.

Because of the potential benefits to shareholders when earnings are positive, managers of financial institutions often choose to use leverage to its maximum possible level. Accompanying the improved expected rates of return, however, is greater risk. If earnings prospects are poor, shareholders in more highly leveraged institutions are worse off than they would be in more conservatively managed firms, because no matter what the level of earnings, interest expense must be paid. If asset returns are insufficient to pay interest, shareholders not only have no residual profits, their retained earnings are reduced by the amount of the loss.

Figure 3A.1
Leverage and RONW

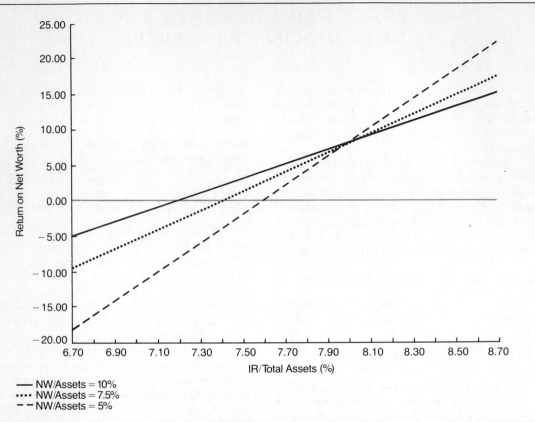

Chapter 4

FINANCIAL MARKET INSTRUMENTS AND YIELDS

Sure, there's more risk in the market these days than ever before, but you can still make a killing when you're right.

Anonymous Government Securities Dealer (1982)

EARLY in 1986, many legislators and consumers sought to focus public attention on the importance of analyzing the promised rates of return on investments. They emphasized that costs may be involved that are not obvious, but that can lower an investor's effective rate of return. Representative Charles Schumer, a Congressman from New York, investigated the results of depositing $2,000 in each of four banks in Washington, D.C., each offering a stated return of 5.25 percent per year. He found that the total accumulated after one year could differ by as much as $125, depending upon the way the banks calculated interest, set penalties, and controlled withdrawals.[1]

Across the wide spectrum of investments in primary and secondary securities are many different conventions for calculating and quoting expected rates of return. Although, as the previous chapters emphasize, regulation and legislation are important environmental influences on asset/liability management, they are by no means the only ones. Institutional managers must also be familiar with the markets for financial assets and liabilities. In particular, because asset/

---

[1]Monica Langley, "Bank Ads Trumpet Interest Rates, But Keep the Real Yields Hidden," *The Wall Street Journal,* February 10, 1986, p. 17.

liability management involves close attention to the net interest margin, managers must understand methods for calculating asset yields and liability costs accurately. As the opening story suggests, investors who take stated rates at "face value" make a serious mistake.

A discussion of financial instruments can be conceptually divided in many ways—according to their size or their cash flow characteristics, for example. By convention, however, financial instruments are most often categorized by original maturity. Securities with original maturities of one year or less are *money market,* or short-term, investments; those with original maturities in excess of one year are *capital market,* or long-term, securities. This chapter follows the tradition of emphasizing time. Because time is an important dimension, calculation of market yields requires an understanding of the time value of money. Students wishing to review the mathematics should read the appendix to this chapter before proceeding.

Although many more financial instruments exist, the major ones with which institutions are involved, and significant issues relating to their yields, are explained here.[2] More specialized instruments important to particular institutions are introduced later in the text.

ISSUES AFFECTING THE CALCULATION OF MONEY MARKET YIELDS

Dividing financial markets into categories based on original maturity might seem to reduce the necessary yield calculations to only two—one for short-term and one for long-term securities. Unfortunately, this is not the case, although many of the required formulas generalize to more than one instrument. Issues affecting calculation of money market yields are considered in this section.

Different Original Maturities

Even within one year, financial instruments have many possible original maturities. Treasury bills may be issued for 91 or 182 days, or a bank may issue a short-term deposit to a corporation for a "customized" original maturity exactly equal to the length of time the business anticipates having extra cash.

Different Holding Periods

Holders of short-term securities may sell them before the original maturity date. For example, the original investor in a 91-day Treasury bill may hold it for only 23 days, while a new purchaser anticipates its maturity in 68 days. The same bill provides a yield to both investors, but each yield is based on a different maturity.

Different Market Traditions

Even in the electronic age, traditional methods persist for calculating money market yields, dating to periods in which hand-held calculators and computers were unavailable. Some yield quotations for Treasury bills, for example, are based on a 360-day year, and investors must recognize this before using such a yield in making financial decisions.

Different Cash Flow Characteristics

Finally, short-term financial instruments may have different cash flow characteristics, even when they have the same initial maturities or holding periods. For example, a six-month loan by a life insurance company to a policyholder is an *interest-bearing security,* but commercial paper owned by the same company is a *discount*

---

[2]The definition of financial institutions in Chapter 1 stressed their activities on both the asset and liability sides of the balance sheet. They are thus concerned with both the *returns* (called yields, by convention) on institutional assets and the *costs* of institutional liabilities. For brevity, the term *yield* is used throughout this discussion. In addition, all calculations ignore transaction costs and taxes, unless specifically noted in the text.

security. In lending to a policyholder, the life insurer advances cash and expects to receive quarterly cash interest payments *and* the principal amount at maturity. When purchasing commercial paper, the life insurance company advances cash to the business issuing the paper and expects to receive a single cash payment of a higher amount at maturity. Differences in the timing of cash benefits affect the insurer's yields.

CALCULATING ANNUAL YIELDS

Yield comparisons considering these factors are facilitated by converting rates of return on instruments with different maturities, holding periods, and cash flows to *effective annual yields.* The effective annual yield (y*) on an investment is the rate of return an investor would earn, given the asset's cash flow characteristics, if the investor held it for exactly 365 days (366 days in leap years).

It is useful to separate calculations of effective annual yields on short-term securities into two categories: 1) yields for discount securities, defined as those requiring a single cash outflow from the investor, followed by a single cash inflow at a later date; and 2) yields for short-term securities with more than one cash inflow to the investor during the time the security is held.

Annual Yield with No Compounding

The equation for y, the annual yield on a discount instrument *without* considering compound interest, is:

$$(4.1) \quad y = \frac{\text{Par (or } P_1) - P_0}{P_0} \times \frac{365}{n}$$

where:

$$P_0 = \text{amount initially invested;}$$
$$\text{Par or } P_1 = \text{par value at maturity (Par) or price received if sold before maturity } (P_1);$$
$$n = \text{number of days until maturity or until sold.}$$

The equation states that the annual yield on an investment is equal to the dollars earned over the period during which the investment is held $(P_1 - P_0)$, expressed as a percentage of the dollars invested (P_0), multiplied by the number of times during the year that the amount could potentially be earned. Another way of thinking about this annual yield is as the periodic rate of return earned times the number of periods in a year.

Effective Annual Yield

Considering the additional possibility of earning interest on one period's returns during the following periods—that is, considering the possibility of compounding over a full year—the effective annual yield on a discount instrument is:

$$(4.2) \quad y^* = \left[1 + \frac{y}{(365/n)} \right]^{(365/n)} - 1$$

Equation 4.2 is a variation of the basic intrayear compounding formula from Appendix 4A—Equation 4A.2—with the number of compounding periods per year (m) expressed as 365/n.

DISCOUNT SECURITIES AND THEIR YIELDS

There are many short-term discount securities. The most important for financial institutions are Treasury bills, commercial paper, repurchase agreements (repos), bankers' acceptances, and some short-term commercial loans. A brief description of these securities and appropriate yield calculations are given in this section. Financial institutions participate in both *primary markets,* the markets for original issuance, and *secondary markets,* the markets for resale of these instruments.

Treasury Bills

Treasury bills (*T-bills* to money market participants) are short-term debt obligations of the United States government.

Characteristics of T-Bills and Their Markets. T-bills are usually issued with one of three original maturities—91 days (13 weeks), 182 days (26 weeks), or 364 days (52 weeks). Bills with irregular maturities, called *cash management bills,* are sometimes issued in minimum denominations of $1 million to raise cash in anticipation of future tax receipts.

T-bills are sold in minimum denominations of $10,000 to high bidders in weekly auctions conducted by the Federal Reserve Bank of New York. These auctions are the primary market for T-bills. Bids are expressed as a percentage of the bills' par value. For example, a discount bid of 95.556 on 26-week bills indicates the bidder's willingness to pay that percentage of par. Because bills are sold on a discount basis, purchasers' yields are based on the difference between what they pay for the bills (P_0) and the face value (Par), and on the length of time the bills are held (n). Yield calculations vary somewhat, depending upon whether or not n exceeds 182 days, but most bills are issued with 182-day or shorter maturities. Therefore, all calculations that follow pertain to bills with shorter maturities.[3]

---

[3]As of summer 1986, for example, the total volume of 91- and 182-day bills outstanding was about $279 billion, compared to about $117 billion outstanding in 52-week bills. These statistics are reported periodically in the *Treasury Bulletin* under "Public Debt Operations."

The formula for the yield on a discount security with a maturity exceeding 182 days is:

(4.1a)

$$y = \frac{\sqrt{b^2 - 4ac} - b}{2a}$$

$$a = [n/(2 \times 365)] - 0.25$$

$$b = n/365$$

$$c = \frac{P_0 - Par}{P_0}$$

For a derivation of this formula, see either Marcia Stigum, *Money Market Calculations: Yields, Break-evens, and Arbitrage* (Homewood, IL: Dow Jones-Irwin, 1981), pp. 34-35; or Richard D. C. Trainer, *The Arithmetic of Interest Rates* (New York: Federal Reserve Bank of New York, 1982), pp. 16-18, 32-33.

The equation takes into account the fact that the proceeds from "long" discount bills are not available for reinvestment at the end of six months so they are not

Figure 4.1 illustrates the major ownership characteristics of Treasury bills and other federal debt since 1950. The growth in total federal debt since the mid-1970s is apparent, as is the role of financial institutions in these markets. Although "private domestic nonfinancial" owners (a category including individual investors) hold a great deal of federal debt, commercial banks and "private nonbank financial" owners (all other financial institutions) hold more. In particular, the role of nonbank financial institutions has increased dramatically since 1980.

Markets for Treasury securities are facilitated by the activities of 40 large securities dealers who stand ready to purchase Treasury securities at every auction, and who often act as buyers and sellers in the secondary market.[4] In 1985, the New York Fed established voluntary financial guidelines for primary dealers, but many small secondary market dealers remained untouched by even voluntary standards for financial soundness. In 1986, as monthly trading volume in the secondary market for Treasury securities approached $2 trillion, Congress enacted the first comprehensive regulation of the Treasury securities markets, including the activities and financial condition of primary and secondary market dealers. Under the **Government Securities Act of 1986,** the Fed retained its authority over primary dealers. The United States Treasury was authorized to set financial standards for secondary market dealers; these standards are enforced by either the FDIC, the

---

directly equivalent to long-term securities paying interest semiannually. Because the yield in Equation 4.1 compares discount securities to interest-bearing securities that pay interest on an intrayear basis, it is not appropriate for "long" discount securities.

[4]For many years, there were 36 primary Treasury securities dealers. In June 1986, because Treasury Department officials thought it failed to generate a sufficient volume of trades, Northern Trust of Chicago was dropped. In December 1986, the Fed stunned many observers when it announced the addition of several large Japanese securities firms to the ranks of primary Treasury securities dealers. The action raised to eight the number of primary dealers controlled by foreign firms. See Michael R. Sesit and Tom Herman, "Three Big Japanese Firms Enter Ranks of Primary Dealers Despite Opposition," *The Wall Street Journal,* December 12, 1986, p. 32.

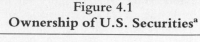

Figure 4.1
Ownership of U.S. Securities[a]

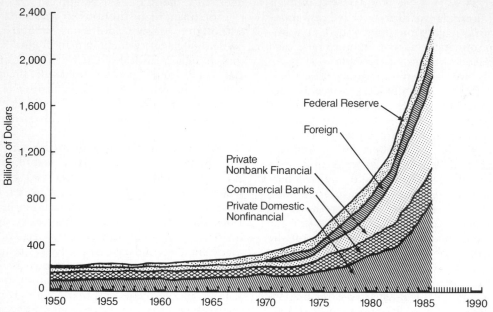

[a]Includes the dollar volume of U.S. government security issues, federally sponsored agency issues, and securities backed by mortgage pools.

Source: Board of Governors of the Federal Reserve System, *1986 Historical Chart Book.*

Comptroller of the Currency, the Fed, the FHLBB, or the SEC, depending upon the organizational structure of the dealer.[5]

[5]See "Fed Loses Oversight of Securities Dealers to Treasury," *Savings Institutions* 107 (November 1986): 161, 163. Before Congress acted, many people were unhappy about the lack of regulation. See James J. Balazsy, Jr., "The Government Securities Market and Proposed Regulation," *Economic Commentary,* Federal Reserve Bank of Cleveland, April 1, 1986; Richard Syron and Sheila L. Tschinkel, "The Government Securities Market: Playing Field for Repos," *Economic Review,* Federal Reserve Bank of Atlanta 70 (September 1985): 10-19; Sheila L. Tschinkel, "Overview," *Economic Review,* Federal Reserve Bank of Atlanta 70 (September 1985): 5-9; Eric S. Rosengren, "Is There a Need for Regulation in the Government Securities Market?" *New England Economic Review,* Federal Reserve Bank of Boston (September/October 1986), pp. 29-40.

Information from a Treasury Bill Auction. Figure 4.2 contains information on a typical group of new Treasury bill issues. The information is published on Tuesdays following regularly scheduled Monday auctions. These data are for bills auctioned on January 27, 1986. In this auction, as usual, many more bids were submitted than could be accepted, based on the volume of bills the Treasury had decided to sell.

Noncompetitive bids are applications to regional Federal Reserve Banks to purchase less than $1 million face value of bills, usually from individual investors and small institutions. Noncompetitive bidders are assured of receiving bills, but the price they pay is determined by the average competitive bid that is ultimately accepted. Winning competitive bidders are those willing to pay the highest percentage of

Figure 4.2
Results of a Typical Treasury Bill Auction

Here are the details of yesterday's Treasury bill auction:

Rates are determined by the difference between the purchase price and face value. Thus, higher bidding narrows the investor's return while lower bidding widens it. The percentage rates are calculated on a 360-day year, while the coupon equivalent yield is based on a 365-day year.

	13-Week	26-Week
Applications	$22,060,340,000	$23,213,200,000
Accepted bids	$7,212,105,000	$ 7,205,185,000
Accepted at low price	95%	80%
Accepted noncompet'ly	$1,165,955,000	$ 949,625,000
Average price (Rate)	98.251 (6.92%)	96.446 (7.03%)
High price (Rate)	98.256 (6.90%)	96.451 (7.02%)
Low price (Rate)	98.251 (6.92%)	96.446 (7.03%)
Coupon equivalent	7.14%	7.39%

Both issues are dated Jan. 30. The 13-week bills mature May 1, 1986, and the 26-week bills mature July 31, 1986.

Source: The Wall Street Journal, January 28, 1986, p. 41.

par value. Thus, noncompetitive bidders know their bids will be accepted but are unsure of the price, whereas competitive bidders know the price they will pay if they win, but have no guarantee of delivery.

Published information on T-bill auctions includes the average, high, and low prices paid for bills; the "rate," more formally called the **bank discount rate;** and the **"coupon-equivalent"** or **bond-equivalent yield;** these terms are defined later.

Effective Annual Yield on T-Bills. Suppose a small commercial bank paid the average price of 98.251 percent for a $10,000, 91-day bill. The annual yield expected if the bill is held to maturity is found from Equation 4.1:

$$y = \frac{\$10,000.00 - \$9,825.10}{\$9,825.10} \times \frac{365}{91} = 7.14\%$$

The same answer results from using percentages of par value instead of dollar values for P_0 and Par:

$$y = \frac{100 - 98.251}{98.251} \times \frac{365}{91} = 7.14\%$$

The annual yield calculated either way is reported in Figure 4.2 as the coupon-equivalent, or bond-equivalent, yield. It is the annualized rate of return to the bank, *without* considering the possibility of earning interest on reinvested profits (Par - P_0) at the end of 91 days. By definition, there is always an inverse relationship between T-bill prices and their yields, made clear in Equation 4.1.

If compounding is considered, the effective annual yield on the bill can be calculated from Equation 4.2:

$$y^* = \left[1 + \frac{0.0714}{(365/91)} \right]^{(365/91)} - 1$$

$$= 0.0733 = 7.33\%$$

If the bill is not held to maturity, but instead is sold after 7 weeks (49 days) at a price of 98.945 percent, the bond-equivalent and effective annual yields earned by the bank are:

$$y = \frac{98.945 - 98.251}{98.251} \times \frac{365}{49} = 5.26\%$$

$$y^* = \left[1 + \frac{0.0526}{(365/49)} \right]^{(365/49)} - 1$$

$$= 0.0538 = 5.38\%$$

When the effective annual yield is calculated using an initial purchase price P_0 and a known sales price P_1, the result is the annualized **holding-period yield.**

It is important to remember that whenever an institution uses information available at the time of an investment to compute an effective annual yield, the results of Equations 4.1 and 4.2 are *expected* (or *ex ante*) annual rates of return. Unless reinvestment rates at the time of a bill's maturity or sale are exactly the same as they were at the time of the original purchase, the expected annual yield will vary from the actual (or *ex post*) yield over a 365-day period. Even annualized holding-period yields, based on actual purchase and sales prices, are not guaranteed over a 365-day period. The example was based on an initial holding period of 49 days, and market conditions for the rest of the year may differ from those that prevailed during the holding period. Nonetheless, because all investment decisions are made *ex ante*, it is useful to have methods for comparing expected yields on various alternatives before deciding to commit cash.

Bank Discount Yield.   It is also important to distinguish the effective annual yield from another yield always computed on T-bills. Money market participants are familiar with bank discount yields—the "rates" given in Figure 4.2. This traditional method for quoting bill yields dates to 1929 when Treasury bills were first sold. At that time, traders found it easier to make computations considering a year as 360 days. The formula for calculating the bank discount yield (d) on T-bills is:

$$(4.3) \quad d = \frac{Par - P_0}{Par} \times \frac{360}{n}$$

The bank discount yield on a 91-day bill bought at the average price of 98.251 on January 27, 1986, and held to maturity is:

$$d = \frac{100 - 98.251}{100} \times \frac{360}{91} = 6.92\%$$

There are two major differences between Equations 4.1 and 4.2, and Equation 4.3; one is the 365- versus 360-day year. In addition, the bank discount method assumes the investor's return is calculated as a percentage of the par value, whereas Equations 4.1 and 4.2 assume the investor's yield is calculated based on the amount invested. The traditional bank discount is thus theoretically incorrect and underestimates the expected rate of return on T-bills, given market conditions at the time of a purchase.

Nonetheless, the bank discount method of quoting bill yields persists in the money markets. For this reason, it is useful to be able to convert a bank discount quotation directly into the corresponding bond-equivalent yield. A formula for making this conversion is:[6]

$$(4.4) \quad y = \frac{365d}{360 - dn}$$

Applying Equation 4.4 to the discount yield of 6.92 percent results in the bond equivalent yield found earlier for a bill selling at 98.251 percent of par:

$$y = \frac{365 (0.0692)}{360 - (0.0692 \times 91)}$$

$$= 0.0714 = 7.14\%$$

This yield can then be converted to the effective annual yield using Equation 4.2.

Using the Discount Yield to Determine a T-Bill Price.   Another reason to understand how the conventional bank discount yield is calculated is that it enables investors to determine the secondary market price for T-bills should they wish to sell or purchase bills after their original issue. Figure 4.3 shows data on Treasury bill yields in the secondary market on January 27, 1986.

In addition to the maturity date of the bills, the prices at which dealers were willing to buy (the **bid price**) and sell them (the **asked price**) are given on a bank discount basis. Asked yields

---

[6]If D equals the dollar discount from par, then $D = Par - P_0$, and $P_0 = Par - D$. Substituting for P_0 in the formula for the bond equivalent yield (Equation 4.1):

$$y = \frac{Par - (Par - D)}{Par - D} \times \frac{365}{n}$$

$$(4.1b) \quad y = \frac{D}{Par - D} \times \frac{365}{n}$$

Equation 4.3 can also be solved for D:

$$d = \frac{D}{Par} \times \frac{360}{n}, \text{ so } D = d \times Par \times \frac{n}{360}$$

Substituting for D in Equation 4.1b:

$$y = \frac{d \times Par \times (n/360)}{Par - [d \times Par \times (n/360)]} \times \frac{365}{n}$$

This expression can then be reduced to Equation 4.4.

Figure 4.3
Treasury Bills:
Secondary Market Information

U.S. Treas. Bills Mat date	Bid	Asked	Yield Discount	Mat. date	Bid	Asked	Yield Discount
				5-22	7.00	6.96	7.21
-1986-				5-29	6.99	6.95	7.21
1-30	6.56	6.38	6.47	6- 5	7.03	6.99	7.27
2- 6	6.62	6.56	6.66	6-12	6.96	6.92	7.20
2-13	6.74	6.68	6.79	6-19	7.02	6.98	7.28
2-20	6.60	6.54	6.66	6-26	7.01	6.97	7.28
2-27	6.57	6.51	6.64	7- 3	7.08	7.04	7.36
3- 6	6.74	6.70	6.84	7-10	7.10	7.06	7.39
3-13	6.84	6.80	6.95	7-17	7.10	7.06	7.40
3-20	6.93	6.89	7.05	7-24	7.07	7.05	7.40
3-27	6.91	6.87	7.04	8- 7	7.09	7.05	7.41
4- 3	6.94	6.90	7.08	9- 4	7.11	7.07	7.44
4-10	6.92	6.88	7.07	10- 2	7.12	7.08	7.47
4-17	6.99	6.95	7.15	10-30	7.12	7.10	7.52
4-86	6.95	6.93	7.14	11-28	7.13	7.09	7.53
5- T	6.92	6.88	7.10	12-26	7.13	7.09	7.56
5- 8	6.99	6.95	7.18	-1987-			
5-15	7.00	6.96	7.20	1-87	7.12	7.08	7.58

Source: The Wall Street Journal, January 28, 1986, p. 43.

are lower than bid yields. Because there is an inverse relationship between bill prices and yields, dealers were selling bills at higher prices (lower yields to buyers) than the prices at which they were willing to buy them. The spread between dealers' bid and asked prices is their anticipated profit.

Suppose that on January 27, a savings and loan association wished to purchase a Treasury bill maturing on February 27 (n = 31 days). If dealers quote buyers a discount yield of 6.51 percent, what must the S&L pay? The price is determined by solving Equation 4.3 for P_0:

$$(4.5) \quad P_0 = Par \times \left[1 - \frac{dn}{360} \right]$$

$$= 100 \times \left[1 - \frac{0.0651\,(31)}{360} \right]$$

$$= 99.439\% \text{ of par}$$

Using Equation 4.1, the bond-equivalent yield to the S&L is:

$$y = \frac{100 - 99.439}{99.439} \times \frac{365}{31} = 6.64\%$$

This is, in fact, the "yield" on this bill shown in Figure 4.3. Thus, the yields quoted in the secondary market for T-bills are coupon or bond equivalents based on the asked price.

The same equations are used to determine the current market price of commercial paper, bankers' acceptances, and other securities on which primary and secondary market yields are customarily quoted on a bank discount basis.

Repurchase/Reverse Repurchase Agreements

Repurchase agreements (repos) and *reverse repos* are money market transactions in which securities (usually Treasury securities) are sold by one party to another, with the agreement that the seller will repurchase the securities at a specified price on a specified date.

Characteristics of Repos and Their Markets. Whether the transaction is considered a repo or a reverse repo depends, by convention, upon whether an institution is the seller or the buyer in the transaction. Figure 4.4 illustrates the mechanics of several hypothetical repo/reverse repo agreements.

In Transaction 1, a large securities dealer sells Treasury securities to a commercial bank, with the agreement that the dealer will buy them back in 30 days. The dealer considers the transaction a repo; the bank considers it a reverse repo. From the bank's point of view, it is, in effect, loaning the dealer money for 30 days with the securities pledged as collateral. Transaction 3 is similar, except the counterparty to the dealer is another institution or individual. Transaction 2 illustrates an agreement in which the bank promises to repurchase securities from one of its own customers; the bank views this transaction as a repo, the customer as a reverse repo.

Repurchase agreements are commonly used by large government securities dealers to finance their inventories, and the daily volume of repurchase agreements sometimes reaches $1 trillion. Many transactions have maturities as short as one day. Therefore, financial institutions have ample opportunities to earn profits

---

Figure 4.4
Repurchase and Reverse Repurchase Agreements

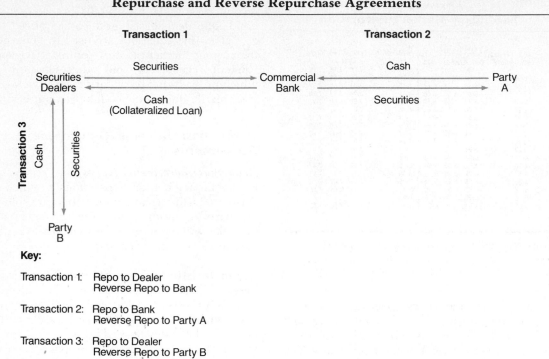

Key:

Transaction 1:   Repo to Dealer
                  Reverse Repo to Bank

Transaction 2:   Repo to Bank
                  Reverse Repo to Party A

Transaction 3:   Repo to Dealer
                  Reverse Repo to Party B

---

on temporarily idle cash by taking the other side of these transactions—that is, by advancing funds via reverse repos.

Repos are also used by the Federal Reserve to temporarily decrease the amount of reserves available in the banking system. The Fed does this by selling Treasury securities to banks with agreements to repurchase them later. Conversely, the Fed can increase bank reserves temporarily if it buys Treasury securities from banks under agreement that the banks will later repurchase them. Such transactions take place in a large and well-developed market.

The repo/reverse repo market is not without its risks. In the mid-1980s, crises in several depository institutions were precipitated by the collapse of government securities dealers with whom the depositories had large reverse repos.

Although the recent regulation of Treasury securities dealers is intended to prevent such incidents in the future, there is no guarantee that a reverse repo issuer will fulfill its obligations. In addition, no secondary market exists for reverse repos. Before an institution makes repos and reverse repos major features of its asset/liability management strategies, both the risk and return dimensions of the agreements must be fully appreciated. More information on the use of repos/reverse repos is given in Chapters 12 and 15.[7]

---

[7]For an interesting account of how the market for repos and reverse repos is organized, and a discussion of some of the risks involved in this market before Treasury securities legislation was enacted in 1986, see Chris Welles, "Drysdale: What Really Happened," *Institutional Investor* 16 (September 1982): 73-83.

Effective Annual Yield on Repos/Reverse Repos. In Figure 4.4 (Transaction 1), the bank's expected dollar return on its reverse repo is the difference between the amount initially advanced to the dealer and the price at which the dealer will repurchase the securities in 30 days. That dollar return can be converted into both an annual yield and an effective annual yield using Equations 4.1 and 4.2.

By convention, yields available on reverse repos are quoted on a bank discount basis. For example, suppose the discount yield on overnight reverse repos is quoted as 9.85 percent. The effective annual yield (y^*) to an institution engaging in repeated similar transactions is 10.50 percent, found first by converting the bank discount yield to an annual yield (y) using Equation 4.4, then using Equation 4.2. On an overnight repo, $n = 1$.

Commercial Paper

Another short-term investment of interest to many financial institutions is *commercial paper*. Commercial paper is short-term unsecured borrowing by major corporations. It has a maturity of less than 9 months, because issues of longer maturity must be registered with the Securities and Exchange Commission, increasing the borrower's cost and the time required to raise funds.

Commercial banks, savings and loan associations, insurance companies, mutual funds, and other large financial institutions are major purchasers of commercial paper. The paper is almost always bought on a discount basis and redeemed at par upon maturity. Minimum denominations are usually higher than for T-bills, ranging from $25,000 upward, depending upon whether the purchase is made through a dealer or directly from the borrowing firm.

Like other money market securities, commercial paper provides investors with short-term opportunities to invest cash. The secondary market for commercial paper is virtually nonexistent, however, compared to the secondary markets for T-bills. Therefore, most commercial paper is held to maturity. Occasionally,

the borrower is willing to repurchase its paper before maturity (that is, to repay the loan early). Securities dealers also sometimes purchase paper from initial investors. These activities maintain at least some liquidity in the commercial paper market, ensuring that it continues.

Figure 4.5 reproduces information on the money markets from the financial pages of January 28, 1986. In addition to summarizing the average bank discount yields on the Treasury auction of the day before, shown in Figure 4.1, market information is given for other important short-term instruments, including commercial paper. Two quotes are given for commercial paper, one for paper sold directly by an issuer to investors and one for paper sold through dealers.

Suppose a large life insurance firm anticipates idle cash for the next 90 days and approaches a dealer to purchase commercial paper. The dealer quote is shown as 7.70 percent on a bank discount basis. What price must the insurer pay, and what is the effective annual yield? Solving for the price using Equation 4.5, the insurance firm must pay 98.075 percent of par, for an effective annual yield (y^*) of 8.20 percent, calculated using Equations 4.1 and 4.2.

Bankers' Acceptances

Another short-term security of growing importance is the *bankers' acceptance*. Bankers' acceptances arise from international trade activities. They are short-term credit agreements, often called *time drafts*, through which international trade is financed. Because sellers often have difficulty assessing the creditworthiness of overseas customers, they may be more comfortable if the buyer's bank agrees to guarantee payment for goods ordered. The probability of banks defaulting on agreements is generally viewed as lower than the probability of default by other firms.

Creation of a Bankers' Acceptance. The complicated steps leading to the creation of a

Figure 4.5
Money Market Yield Quotations

MONEY RATES

Monday, January 27, 1986

The key U.S. and foreign annual interest rates below are a guide to general levels but don't always represent actual transactions.

PRIME RATE: 9½%. The base rate on corporate loans at large U.S. money center commercial banks.

FEDERAL FUNDS: 8¼% high; 7⅞% low; 7⅞% near closing bid. 8% offered. Reserves traded among commercial banks for overnight use in amounts of $1 million or more. Source: Prebon Money Brokers Inc., N.Y.

DISCOUNT RATE: 7½%. The charge on loans to depository institutions by the New York Federal Reserve Bank.

CALL MONEY: 8¾% to 9%. The charge on loans to brokers on stock exchange collateral.

COMMERCIAL PAPER placed directly by General Motors Acceptance Corp.: 7.75% 30 to 59 days; 7.70% 60 to 119 days; 7.65% 120 to 270 days.

COMMERCIAL PAPER: High-grade unsecured notes sold through dealers by major corporations in multiples of $1,000: 7.75% 30 days; 7.70% 60 days; 7.70% 90 days.

CERTIFICATES OF DEPOSIT: 7¾% one month; 7¾% two months; 7¾% three months; 7¾% six months; 7.80% one year. Typical rates paid by major banks on new issues of negotiable C.D.s, usually on amounts of $1 million and more. The minimum unit is $100,000.

BANKERS ACCEPTANCES: 7.74% 30 days; 7.65% 60 days; 7.61% 90 days; 7.57% 120 days; 7.57% 150 days; 7.56% 180 days. Negotiable, bank-backed business credit instruments typically financing an import order.

LONDON LATE EURODOLLARS: 8⅛% to 8% one month; 8⅛% to 8% two months; 8⅛% to 8% three months; 8⅛% to 8% four months; 8⅛% to 8% five months; 8⅛% to 8% six months.

LONDON INTERBANK OFFERED RATES (LIBOR): 8⅛% three months; 8⅛% six months; 8 5/16% one year. The average of interbank offered rates for dollar deposits in the London market based on quotations at five major banks.

FOREIGN PRIME RATES: Canada 11%; Germany 7.25%; Japan 5.69%; Switzerland 6%; Britain 12½%. These rate indications aren't directly comparable; lending practices vary widely by location. Source: Morgan Guaranty Trust Co.

TREASURY BILLS: Results of the Monday, January 27, 1986, auction of short-term U.S. government bills, sold at a discount from face value in units of $10,000 to $1 million: 6.92%, 13 weeks; 7.03%, 26 weeks.

FEDERAL HOME LOAN MORTGAGE CORP. (Freddie Mac): Posted yields on 30-year mortgage commitments for delivery within 30 days. 10.68%, standard conventional fixed-rate mortgages; 9.36%, one-year adjustable rate mortgages.

FEDERAL NATIONAL MORTGAGE ASSOCIATION (Fannie Mae): Posted yields on 30 year mortgage commitments for delivery within 30 days (priced at par). 10.45%, standard conventional fixed rate-mortgages; 9.80%, 5/2 rate capped one-year adjustable rate mortgages.

MERRILL LYNCH READY ASSETS TRUST: 7.24%. Annualized average rate of return after expenses for the past 30 days; not a forecast of future returns.

Source: The Wall Street Journal, January 28, 1986, p. 41. Reprinted by permission of *The Wall Street Journal,* © Dow Jones & Company, Inc. 1986. All Rights Reserved.

bankers' acceptance are illustrated in Figure 4.6.[8] Suppose an importer orders goods and simultaneously applies to his or her bank, Chase Manhattan, for financing (Steps 1-2). Typically, the financing request is for a letter of credit (L/C in the figure), certifying that the bank will stand behind the importer. If the financing request is approved, Chase notifies the exporter's bank that payment will be forthcoming (Steps 3-4). Upon guarantee of payment, the exporter sends the goods and forwards shipping documents and a draft (authorization for payment) with a specific payment date (hence the origin of the phrase "time draft") to his own bank. That bank in turn passes the draft and shipping information to Chase (Steps 5-7).

Upon receipt of the papers, Chase will stamp the draft "Accepted" (Step 8). At this point, the draft becomes a bankers' acceptance (B/A in the figure)—Chase has accepted unconditional responsibility for payment on the due date to whoever holds the acceptance at that time. Of course, Chase plans to collect from the importer. If Chase sends funds to the exporter's bank upon receipt of the draft, it will discount the draft, paying less than the face amount (also Step 8) in exchange for providing funds before the goods are received. The money may or may not be immediately sent to the exporter by the exporter's bank (Step 9). At this point, the acceptance remains in Chase's hands.

Bankers' Acceptances as Money Market Instruments. If Chase has already advanced funds and wants to recover them before the importer pays, it may sell the acceptance to money market investors (Steps 11-12). At this point, the purchaser of an acceptance has the promise of two parties, the importer and Chase, that the acceptance will be paid at maturity. For this rea-

---

[8]Figure 4.6 assumes that the importer and the importer's bank are in the United States, so that the U.S. bank is the "accepting" bank. Bankers' acceptances are also used when U.S. firms are exporters. Even in these cases, however, U.S. banks are most often the accepting banks, although the process by which the acceptance is created differs somewhat. See Jack L. Hervey, "Bankers' Acceptances Revisited," *Economic Perspectives,* Federal Reserve Bank of Chicago 7 (May/June 1983): 21-31.

Figure 4.6
Example of Bankers' Acceptance Financing of U.S. Imports: A Bankers' Acceptance Is Created, Discounted, Sold, and Paid at Maturity

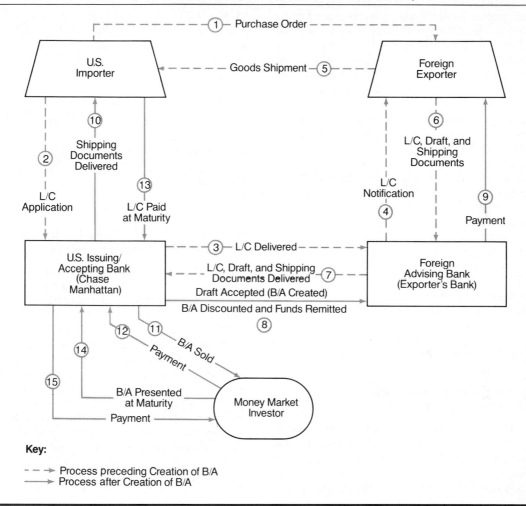

Key:

- - - ▶ Process preceding Creation of B/A
——▶ Process after Creation of B/A

Source: Adapted by the authors from Eric Hill, "Bankers' Acceptances," *Instruments of the Money Market* (Richmond, VA: Federal Reserve Bank of Richmond, 1986), p. 127.

son, the acceptance is sometimes called **"two-name" paper.**

Acceptances are sold to money market investors at a discount from the face amount. As with other discounted securities, the purchaser of the acceptance expects to receive the face amount upon maturity. Upon sale of the acceptance, Chase is no longer financing the importer's transaction; the money market investor is. When the acceptance matures, the importer pays Chase for the goods, and the funds are paid to the acceptance holder (Steps 13-15). Thus, bankers' acceptances serve not only as short-term assets to money market investors, but also as short-term sources of funds to large banks financing international transactions.

Because of the relative security of two-name paper, bankers' acceptances gained popularity in the 1970s and early 1980s. Statistics indicate, in fact, that the dollar volume of acceptances traded grew more than 1,000 percent between 1972 and 1982. By 1985, however, because importers had turned to other sources of financing and because banks had become more reluctant to accept the liability accompanying bankers' acceptances, volume in the market had declined to its 1980 level.[9]

Effective Annual Yield on Bankers' Acceptances. If the manager of a large money market mutual fund wished to purchase 60-day bankers' acceptances as part of the fund's portfolio, Figure 4.5 indicates that on January 27, 1986, a dealer would have quoted a yield of 7.65 percent. Knowing that the quotation is on a bank discount basis, the fund manager could have used Equations 4.5, 4.1, and 4.2 to determine the price of the acceptances and the effective annual yield expected on the transaction. The resulting price is 98.725 percent, with an effective annual yield (y*) of 8.12 percent.

Commercial Loans with Discounted Interest

Another short-term use of funds for some financial institutions is commercial lending, and some commercial loan yields are analogous to yields on discounted money market instruments. If lenders require interest on a loan to be paid in advance instead of at maturity, the arrangement is called a *discounted loan.* For example, suppose a small bank agrees to loan a local business $15,000 for 180 days at an annual rate of 12 percent; interest is to be paid in advance. What is the effective annual yield to the bank on this transaction?

The interest owed by the borrower is 180/365 of the annual interest, or $(180/365) \times 12\% \times \$15,000 = \$888$.[10] The bank is really advancing only $\$15,000 - \$888 = \$14,112$ to the firm, expecting repayment of the full $15,000 in 180 days. Using Equation 4.1, the annual yield (y) is:

$$y = \frac{\$15,000 - \$14,112}{\$14,112} \times \frac{365}{180} = 12.76\%$$

The effective annual yield (y*) on loans of this type would be 13.17 percent, found by using Equation 4.2.

SHORT-TERM INTEREST-BEARING SECURITIES

Although many short-term instruments are discounted, several are interest-bearing. Among the most important are negotiable CDs and Eurodollar CDs. Interest-bearing securities provide returns to investors in two ways: repayment of face value and interest earned on the face value. When interest and face value are paid simultaneously, the effective annual yield on an interest-bearing security is calculated in the same way as the effective annual yield on a discount security, because the face value and interest are, in effect, a single payment. The effective annual yield on several instruments of this type is considered in the following discussion.

Negotiable Certificates of Deposit

As Chapter 2 explains, while Regulation Q was in effect, it was often difficult for banks to retain large depositors. In times of relatively high

[9]Lynn G. Lindsay, "Bankers' Acceptances Come Into Their Own as Trade Instruments," *ABA Banking Journal* 76 (March 1984): 104, 108; Frederick H. Jensen and Patrick M. Parkinson, "Recent Developments in the Bankers Acceptance Market," *Federal Reserve Bulletin* 72 (January 1986): 1–12.

[10]Some banks calculate interest charges on the basis of a 360-day year, then multiply by 365/360. Using this method in this example, the interest charges would be: $(180/360) \times 12\% \times \$15,000 = \$900 \times 365/360 = \$912.50$. Calculating interest charges in this way increases the effective annual yield (and the borrower's cost).

interest rates, corporate depositors could earn more and obtain greater liquidity by investing directly in T-bills. In 1961, long before DIDMCA removed Reg Q ceilings, large banks, led by First National City Bank of New York (now Citibank), created a new deposit designed to please the corporate customer. Called *negotiable certificates of deposit (negotiable CDs),* they had large face values (a legal minimum of $100,000 but in practice usually over $1 million), could be sold in a secondary market in case the original depositor needed cash before maturity, and had higher ceilings than many traditional deposits. In 1973, Reg Q ceilings were removed altogether from negotiable CDs, making them even more attractive to corporate customers.

Almost without exception, negotiable CDs have original maturities of less than one year, and have a *coupon or stated rate,* which is the annual interest expressed as a percentage of par value. Interest calculations assume a 360-day year. By convention, interest and principal are both paid at maturity. Although market rates are now available on all types of deposits, negotiable CDs have retained their popularity with large investors because of the secondary market.

Innovations in the CD Market.   Recent innovations in the negotiable CD market include variable-rate CDs, on which the maturity is fixed but the interest rate varies every 30 days. In addition, Eurodollar CDs, which are dollar-denominated negotiable CDs, issued primarily by London-based branches of American, British, or other foreign banks have gained popularity.[11] The major purchasers of these CDs are large businesses or large financial institutions seeking temporary returns on idle cash.

The secondary market for Eurodollar CDs is much smaller than the secondary market for negotiable CDs issued in the United States. Because the secondary market is much smaller, giving investors less liquidity, and because the

first $100,000 of each domestic negotiable CD is eligible for federal deposit insurance, yields are usually higher on Eurodollar CDs than on domestic CDs. The volume of Eurodollar CDs was estimated at $93 billion in late 1985 versus $475 billion for the domestic negotiable CD market.[12]

Effective Annual Yield on Negotiable CDs.   Figure 4.5 indicates typical negotiable CD coupon rates prevailing in January 1986. If an investor had purchased a 90-day negotiable CD with a face value of $1 million and a coupon rate of 7.75 percent, what was the effective annual yield? Because negotiable CDs are interest-bearing but have the cash flow characteristics of discount securities, Equations 4.1 and 4.2 can be used to determine y^*. The trick is to remember that interest on negotiable CDs is paid on the basis of a 360-day year, so that in 90 days, an investor will earn interest of $7.75\%/360 \times 90$ days = 1.938% (*not* $7.75\%/365 \times 90$ days). There are still 365/90, or 4.0556, possible 90-day periods in a 365-day year, so P_1 is:

$$P_1 = \$1,000,000 + \$1,000,000 \ (0.01938)$$
$$= \$1,019,380$$

The annual yield (y) expected on the CD is 7.86 percent, and the effective annual yield (y^*) is 8.095 percent. Conventions followed for quoting interest and calculating yields in the Eurodollar CD market are identical to those in the domestic market.

Federal Funds

If depository institutions have cash reserves in excess of those required by the Fed, one possible outlet is to lend them to other institutions needing funds to meet their own reserve requirements. Excess reserves lent by one institution to another are *federal funds (fed funds)*; they are the assets of the lending institution and

---

[11]Eurodollar CDs are different from Eurodollar *time* deposits, which are deposits for which there is no secondary market. The latter are discussed in Chapter 15.

[12]Jensen and Parkinson, "Recent Developments in the Bankers Acceptance Market," p. 9; Board of Governors of the Federal Reserve System, *Flow of Funds Accounts: QIV/85 Quarterly Levels,* March 13, 1986, Table 610.

liabilities of the borrowing firm. Typically, fed funds transactions are very short-term; in fact, many are overnight, similar to repo/reverse repo agreements.

Fed funds are borrowed either through direct negotiation with the lending institution or through New York brokers. The lending institution instructs the Fed or its own bank to transfer the agreed-upon balances to the borrower. Because most fed funds transactions are overnight, the transaction is reversed the next day, including one day's interest.

Effective Annual Yield on Fed Funds.   The fed funds rate, like a negotiable CD rate, is quoted on the basis of a 360-day year, and interest is added to the principal to determine the total required repayment. For example, suppose an S&L agreed to sell a large commercial bank $100 million of fed funds overnight at a quoted rate of 8.75 percent. The amount the borrower must repay the seller on the following day is:

$$P_1 = P_0 + (i \times P_0 \times n/360)$$

$$P_1 = \$100,000,000$$
$$\quad + (0.0875 \times \$100,000,000 \times 1/360)$$
$$\quad = \$100,024,306$$

The effective annual yield (y^*) is then found from Equations 4.1 and 4.2. The annual yield is 8.87 percent; the effective annual yield is 9.28 percent.

Short-Term Interest-Bearing Loans

Many financial institutions make short-term loans to individuals or businesses requiring periodic payment of interest, with repayment of principal upon maturity. One example is a 12-month, $10,000 loan by a life insurance company to a policyholder, requiring quarterly interest payments at a 12 percent stated rate. It is easier to compare the yield on loans of this type with those on other financial assets if the effective annual yield is calculated. In doing so, the intrayear compounding equation developed in the appendix is useful.

In this example, the annual interest rate of 12 percent translates into a quarterly rate of 3 percent; because there are four quarters per year, the effective annual yield is:

(4.6) $y^* = (1 + i/m)^m - 1$

where: i = stated annual interest rate and
m = number of periods interest is earned during a year.

$$y^* = (1 + 0.12/4)^4 - 1 = 0.1255 = 12.55\%$$

Equation 4.6 is conceptually identical to Equation 4.2; differences arise only because of the terminology applied to interest-bearing versus discount securities. Thus, no matter what the investment, a financial institution manager can calculate yields that make it easy to compare a range of alternatives. Commonly quoted figures such as bank discount rates or nominal rates do not allow accurate comparisons.

CAPITAL MARKET INSTRUMENTS AND YIELDS: DEBT SECURITIES

Most financial institutions also make long-term investments. By definition, long-term assets are those with original maturities exceeding one year, a definition obviously encompassing many possible time horizons. Thus, there is a need for some standard period over which to calculate effective yields. Although any time period could in theory be chosen, one year is commonly used.

Cash returns from long-term securities come in a variety of forms: as a single payment several years after the initial investment; as a series of equal periodic payments; or as a series of unequal cash payments. This variety again causes a need for some standardization of yield calculations. Fortunately, however, there is one approach that can be used to calculate y^* on a long-term investment of any maturity and with any cash flow characteristics. Assuming annual compounding, the effective annual yield on any long-term investment can be found by solving

Equation 4.7 for y^*. Modifications are necessary when compounding occurs more than once a year; these are presented later.

$$(4.7) \quad P_0 = \sum_{t=1}^{N} \frac{C_t}{(1 + y^*)^t}$$

where: P_0 = investor's cash outflow (analogous to purchase price of a discount security);

C = periodic cash inflows (interest and/or principal);

t = sub- or superscript denoting an individual time period;

N = number of periods until maturity (or until sold).

The effective annual yield to the lender calculated from Equation 4.7 is the *internal rate of return* on the investment. It is the annualized interest rate that equates the present value of the cash outflow required to the present value of the cash inflows expected.

Unless there is a single cash inflow, or unless the cash inflows are equal or perpetual, the determination of y^* is a trial-and-error iterative process. The analyst uses successively smaller changes in y^* until a rate is found at which the present value of the cash inflows equals the cash outflow required. (See the appendix for examples.) Although formerly a tedious endeavor, the availability of financial analyst calculators and microcomputers makes determining y^* almost instantaneous. Examples of investments for which Equation 4.7 is appropriate are coupon bonds, zero-coupon bonds, mortgages, and long-term loans with add-on interest charges.

Coupon Bonds

Coupon bonds are long-term debt instruments. They are issued by the Treasury (called **T-notes** with initial maturities of ten years or less and **T-bonds** with longer maturities); by agencies such as the Federal Home Loan Banks, not directly funded by the Treasury but authorized to sell bonds to carry out their responsibilities; by

foreign governments; by states, municipalities, and counties; and by domestic and international firms of all types.

Characteristics of Bonds and Their Markets. An investor in coupon bonds pays an initial price in exchange for periodic interest payments and repayment of the par value at maturity. Most bonds have a coupon rate that does not vary, no matter how long the time to maturity. The original maturity of bonds varies greatly, although in recent years the trend is toward shorter maturities, because relatively high interest rates have made borrowers reluctant to commit themselves for long periods.

Bonds may be purchased when originally issued or at a later date in the secondary markets. The secondary market for United States Treasury notes and bonds is quite large; secondary markets for other types of bonds are smaller. As a result of the larger secondary market and the guarantee against default provided by the taxing power of Congress and the money-creation power of the Fed, Treasury notes and bonds provide lower effective yields than their non-Treasury counterparts.

Many special features are associated with bond issues, each designed to appeal to various types of investors. For example, interest on bonds of states, municipalities, and counties is not taxed at the federal level, making them attractive to investors in higher tax brackets and providing local governments with relatively low-cost funds. Still other bonds have variable coupon rates that adjust with changes in market conditions; these appeal to investors who anticipate increases in interest rates. Some corporate bonds are convertible to the common stock of the issuing corporation and are designed to appeal to investors who may wish to share in the growth prospects of the company.

In recent years, the Eurobond market has also gained prominence. Eurobonds are dollar-denominated bonds issued by United States corporations to foreign investors. Unlike most bonds issued to domestic investors, Eurobonds pay interest annually. They are attractive to international buyers who want their income in dollars. Borrowers like them because they are often issued at lower coupon rates than would prevail in the United States; in addition, they are not subject to SEC regulations. Recent research indicates, however, that higher issuance costs often negate the impact of lower coupon rates.[13]

Effective Annual Yield on Coupon Bonds.
Calculating the effective annual yield on a coupon bond paying interest annually is a straightforward application of Equation 4.7. Figure 4.7 provides data on prices of selected tax-exempt bond issues as of January 27, 1986. Most of these issues are **revenue bonds;** they will be repaid out of proceeds of the specific revenue-generating projects they were sold to finance, such as toll roads. A few of those listed are **GOs** or **general obligation bonds,** to be repaid from the general funds of the issuing entity.

Suppose that in January 1986, a property and casualty insurer purchased a State of Alabama bond and planned to hold it to maturity. Figure 4.7 indicates the bond had 15 years to maturity at that time (a maturity date of '01, or 2001) and paid an annual coupon rate of 8.375 percent (8⅜s). The asked price was 104, or 104 percent of par. Assuming a typical par value of $1,000 and annual interest payments, the effective annual yield to the insurance company is found by solving Equation 4.7 for y*:

$$\$1,040 = \sum_{t=1}^{15} \frac{\$83.75}{(1 + y^*)^t} + \frac{\$1,000}{(1 + y^*)^{15}}$$

$$y^* = 0.0791 = 7.91\%$$

Adjusting for Tax Effects.
In the case of tax-exempt bonds, an adjustment must be made to make their effective yields (y^*_{TE}) comparable to the effective annual yield on taxable investments. Because no federal tax will be paid on the cash inflows, their effective yield must be put on a **tax-equivalent basis.** Assuming the insurer is in the 34 percent marginal tax bracket

[13]David S. Kidwell, M. Wayne Marr, and G. Rodney Thompson, "Eurodollar Bonds: Alternative Financing for U.S. Companies," *Financial Management* 14 (Winter 1985): 18-27.

Figure 4.7
Secondary Market Information on Tax-Exempt Bonds

Tax-Exempt Bonds
Mon., Jan. 27, 1986
Here are current prices of several active tax-exempt revenue bonds issued by toll roads and other public authorities.

Agency	Coupon	Mat	Bid	Asked	Chg.
Alabama G.O.	8⅜s	'01	102	104	....
Bat Park City Auth NY	6⅜s	'14	75½	80½	....
Chelan Cnty PU Dist	5s	'13	74½	76½+	½
Clark Cnty Arpt Rev	10½s	'07	108	111	....
Columbia St Pwr Exch	3⅞s	'03	87	90	+ 1
Dela River Port Auth	6½s	'11	86	90	+ 1½
Douglas Cnty PU Dist	4s	'18	52½	54½+	½
Ga Mun El Auth Pwr Rev	8s	'15	91	95	....
Intermountain Pwr	7½s	'18	87½	91½	....
Intermountain Pwr	10½s	'18	117	120	....
Intermountain Pwr	14s	'21	135	138	....
Jacksonville Elec Rev	9¼s	'13	104	108	....
Loop	6½s	'08	64	68	....
MAC	7½s	'92	101	105	....
MAC	7½s	'95	100	104	....
MAC	8s	'86	99½	103½−	1
MAC	8s	'91	100	104	− 1
MAC	9.7s	'08	108½	112½	....
MAC	9¾s	'92	103	107	....
MAC	10¼s	'93	107½	111½	....
Mass Port Auth Rev	6s	'11	77½	82½+	½
Massachusetts G.O.	6½s	'00	87	90	....
Mass Wholesale	6⅜s	'15	63	67	....
Mass Wholesale	13⅜s	'17	116	120	....
Metro Transit Auth	9¼s	'15	105	109	+ 2
Michigan Public Pwr	10⅜s	'16	110	114	....

Source: The Wall Street Journal, January 28, 1986, p. 41

(tr), the tax-equivalent effective annual yield on tax-free securities is:

(4.8)

$$y^*_{TE} = \frac{y^*}{(1 - tr)}$$

$$y^*_{TE} = \frac{0.0791}{(1 - 0.34)} = 0.1198 = 11.98\%$$

Earning an effective yield of 7.91 percent on a tax-exempt security is equivalent to earning 11.98 percent on a taxable security and paying tax at 34 percent. All things equal, the higher the investor's tax bracket, the higher the tax-equivalent yield of a given tax-exempt security.

Holding-Period Yield on a Coupon Bond.
As with short-term securities, the effective annual yield (often called the **yield to maturity** on a bond) is only an expected yield. The actual

yield on a long-term investment depends upon many factors unknown at the time the investment is made, such as whether expected cash flows are actually paid or whether the investor holds the investment to maturity. If the insurer sells the Alabama bond before maturity, perhaps in 1991, the actual annualized holding-period yield earned during the 5 years can be calculated. Assuming a sales price of $1,045, Equation 4.7 can be used to determine the insurer's holding-period yield by substituting the selling price for C_N. An annualized holding-period yield of 8.13 percent results. Again, this can be converted to its tax-equivalent basis using Equation 4.8; y^*_{TE} under these assumptions is 12.32 percent.

Effect of Intrayear Interest Payments. Often the total annual interest required on bonds is paid in two equal semiannual payments, and the effective annual yield to the lender is increased because some of the cash flows are received sooner than if interest were paid annually. Under these circumstances, Equation 4.7 is first used to calculate a *periodic* yield (y_P). That periodic (semiannual in this case) rate is then converted into an effective annual rate using Equation 4.6, the intrayear compounding equation.

If the 15-year, 8.375 percent Alabama bonds paid interest semiannually, the purchaser would receive 30 (N) interest payments of $41.88 each, plus the principal repayment in 30 six-month periods.

$$\$1,040 = \sum_{t=1}^{30} \frac{\$41.88}{(1 + y_P)^t} + \frac{\$1,000}{(1 + y_P)^{30}}$$

By trial-and-error solution, $y_P = 0.0396 = 3.96\%$, and $y^* = (1 + 0.0396)^2 - 1 = 0.08077$, or 8.08%.

Again the effective yield calculations are conceptually similar, regardless of the financial instrument involved. Although notation may vary to account for the differing cash flow patterns found with money and capital market investments, in all cases the effective annual yield is found by identifying a periodic rate of return and compounding it over the number of such periods in a year.

Zero-Coupon Bonds

Zero-coupon bonds are long-term debt instruments promising a single higher cash inflow at maturity in exchange for the initial purchase price. No periodic interest payments must be made by the borrower; hence the name "zero-coupon." They are the long-term analogs of short-term discount securities. Zero-coupon bonds have recently gained popularity with borrowers anxious to avoid the periodic cash payments required to service coupon bonds.[14] From the lender's point of view, even though no interest payments are actually received, taxes must be paid as if cash returns were earned each year. "Zeros" are thus most popular with tax-exempt investors, such as pension funds or investment companies.

Applying Equation 4.7 to zero-coupon bonds is straightforward. There is but a single cash inflow, the present value of which must be equated to the investor's cash outflow. Based on data from Figure 4.8, the zero-coupon bonds of McDonald's Corporation maturing in 1994 were selling for 47 (47 percent of par) at the close of trading on January 27, 1986.[15] If the bonds have a par value of $1,000, the effective annual yield is found by direct solution of Equation 4.7 for y^*:

$$\$470 = \frac{\$1,000}{(1 + y^*)^8}$$

$$(1 + y^*)^8 = (\$1,000/\$470) = 2.1277$$

$$y^* = \sqrt[8]{2.1277} - 1$$

$$y^* = 0.09897 = 9.90\%$$

---

[14]Even the U.S. Treasury has considered zero-coupon bond issues, but at the time of this writing they had not yet been used. See Alan Murray, "Rising Interest Rates Spur Treasury to Study Debt-Financing Options," *The Wall Street Journal,* July 10, 1984; "Zero-Coupon Treasuries Are Here to Stay," *Business Week,* October 15, 1984, pp. 160-161.

[15]For illustrative purposes, the bonds are assumed to mature on January 27, 1994, exactly eight years from the calculation date. If they mature on another date, N will be slightly larger or smaller than 8.

Figure 4.8
New York Bond Exchange Quotations

NEW YORK EXCHANGE BONDS

Monday, January 27, 1986

Bonds		Cur Yld	Vol	High	Low	Close	Net Chg.
Citicp	8.45s07	10.	30	82⅜	82	82⅜	+ ⅝
Citicp	8⅛07	10.	60	80¼	80¼	80¼	....
Citicp	9.09s98t	9.4	15	97	96½	96½	− ½
Citicp	12¼93	11.	19	106⅝	106½	106⅝	− ¼
Citicp	12s90	11.	15	104¾	104¾	104¾	− ¼
Citicp	11⅞88	12.	15	103	103	103	+ ½
CitSv	6⅝99	9.4	10	70⅜	70⅜	70⅜	....
CitSv	7.65s01	10.	5	74⅜	74⅜	74⅜	....
CitSv	9¾00	11.	25	90	89	89	....
CitSv	13⅞11	13.	10	110⅛	110⅛	110⅛	....
CitSvc	zr86	..	42	93⅜	92½	93⅜	+ 7-16
CitSvc	zr87	.	44	84⅛	84⅛	84⅛	....
CitSvc	zr88	.	84	76½	76⅛	76⅛	- ⅜
CitSvc	zr89	.	170	69¼	68⅞	68⅞	- ⅜
McDnl	zr88	..	6	84⅜	84⅜	84⅜	+ 2
McDnl	zr94	..	15	47	47	47	....
McKes	6s94	cv	6	162	162	162	-- 2
McKes	9¾06	cv	10	120⅜	120⅜	120⅜	+ ⅛
McLean	12s03	15.	127	81½	81⅛	81½	+ ⅜
McLean	14¼94	15.	13	92½	91¼	92½	+ ½

Source: The Wall Street Journal, January 28, 1986, p. 44

Mortgages

Mortgages are debt instruments collateralized by real property. The property is classified as residential if it is a one- to four-family dwelling, or commercial if it is for business use or its residential capacity exceeds four families. The residential mortgage debt of individual homeowners is one of the largest single categories of private debt in the United States. Major institutional lenders in the residential mortgage market are discussed at several points later in the text.

Few financial markets have undergone such dramatic changes as have the primary mortgage markets since 1980. In general, mortgages have fixed or variable interest rates and usually carry maturities of 15 years or more.[16] Although recently many lenders have desired variable rates or shorter maturities on new mortgages, the majority of existing mortgages have fixed rates. The typical fixed-rate mortgage requires the borrower to make equal monthly payments, including interest owed for the month plus repayment on the principal balance. Repayment schedules (called ***amortization schedules***) are prepared so that both parties know the exact principal balance outstanding at any time.

Table 4.1 presents parts of the amortization schedule for a 20-year fixed-rate $100,000 mortgage with an annual interest rate of 14.5 percent, or 14.5/12 = 1.2083 percent per month. If a borrower makes each monthly payment for the entire life of the mortgage, the present value of the payments, discounted at the monthly interest rate, will equal the original principal amount of the mortgage. As shown in Appendix 4A, these monthly mortgage payments are determined by solving the present value of an annuity equation (Equation 4A.7) for the required annuity amount.

[16]Discussion of the many new mortgage instruments available is in Chapter 14. Further, the secondary market for mortgages is one of the fastest growing and most complex of all the financial markets. These markets, the mortgage-backed securities developed by market participants, and the use of secondary mortgage markets as an asset/liability management tool are discussed in Chapter 18.

Table 4.1
Mortgage Amortization Schedule

Monthly Payments: $1,280	Initial Balance: $100,000	Initial Maturity: 20 years	Points: 2½	Interest Rate: 14.5%

	(1)	(2)	(3)	(4)	(5) End-of-Month
Month	Payment	Beginning Balance	Interest (.145/12) × (2)	Principal Paid (1) − (3)	Balance (2) − (4)
1	$1,280	$100,000.00	$1,208.33	$ 71.66	$99,928.34
2	1,280	99,928.34	1,207.47	72.53	99,855.81
3	1,280	99,855.81	1,206.59	73.41	99,782.40
4	1,280	99,782.40	1,205.70	74.29	99,708.10
5	1,280	99,708.10	1,204.81	75.19	99,632.91
6	1,280	99,632.91	1,203.90	76.10	99,556.81
7	1,280	99,556.81	1,202.98	77.02	99,479.79
8	1,280	99,479.79	1,202.05	77.95	99,401.84
9	1,280	99,401.84	1,201.11	78.89	99,322.95
10	1,280	99,322.95	1,200.15	79.85	99,243.11
50	1,280	95,247.33	1,150.91	129.09	95,118.24
51	1,280	95,118.24	1,149.35	130.65	94,987.59
52	1,280	94,987.59	1,147.77	132.23	94,855.36
53	1,280	94,855.36	1,146.17	133.83	94,721.53
54	1,280	94,721.53	1,144.55	135.45	94,586.08
55	1,280	94,586.08	1,142.92	137.08	94,449.00
56	1,280	94,449.00	1,141.26	138.74	94,310.26
57	1,280	94,310.26	1,139.58	140.42	94,169.84
58	1,280	94,169.84	1,137.89	142.11	94,027.73
59	1,280	94,027.73	1,136.17	143.83	93,883.90
60	1,280	93,883.90	1,134.43	145.57	93,738.33
230	1,280	13,110.45	158.42	1,121.58	11,988.87
231	1,280	11,988.87	144.87	1,135.13	10,853.73
232	1,280	10,853.73	131.15	1,148.85	9,704.89
233	1,280	9,704.89	117.27	1,162.73	8,542.16
234	1,280	8,542.16	103.22	1,176.78	7,365.38
235	1,280	7,365.38	89.00	1,191.00	6,174.38
236	1,280	6,174.38	74.61	1,205.39	4,968.98
237	1,280	4,968.98	60.04	1,219.96	3,749.03
238	1,280	3,749.03	45.30	1,234.70	2,514.33
239	1,280	2,514.33	30.38	1,249.62	1,264.72
240	1,280	1,264.72	15.28	1,264.72	0.00

Effective Annual Yield on Mortgages. An issue of special interest is the widespread practice in the residential mortgage market of charging borrowers *mortgage points.* Each mortgage point is 1/100 of the principal balance of the loan; points must be paid in cash to the lender at the time mortgage contracts are signed. Because they reduce the net amount the lender advances to the borrower, they increase borrowers' costs and lenders' yields.

If a savings and loan association charges 2½ points on the $100,000, twenty-year mortgage with a 14.5 percent fixed interest rate, the lender actually advances a net loan of $100,000

$- (0.025 \times \$100,000) = \$97,500$, even though the borrower must repay the full $100,000. As shown in Table 4.1, monthly payments on this mortgage are $1,280. The monthly yield (y_p) is found from Equation 4.7, and Equation 4.6 is used to convert this monthly yield into an effective annual yield of 16.02 percent:

$$\$97,500 = \sum_{t=1}^{240} \frac{\$1,280}{(1 + y_p)^t}$$

$$y_p = 0.01246 = 1.246\%$$

$$y^* = (1 + 0.01246)^{12} - 1 = 16.02\%$$

Effect of Prepayments on Yields. Because most mortgages are prepaid by borrowers, institutional managers with large mortgage portfolios should estimate the effective annual yield assuming payment before maturity. Suppose the $100,000 mortgage in Table 4.1 is expected to be prepaid in five years when the borrower sells the house on which the mortgage is held. The amortization schedule indicates that after 60 monthly payments have been made, the principal balance is $93,738. Thus, the lender's anticipated cash flows when prepayment is expected consist of a monthly annuity with a lump-sum prepayment at the end. Using Equations 4.7 and 4.6:

$$\$97,500 = \sum_{t=1}^{60} \frac{\$1,280}{(1 + y_p)^t} + \frac{\$93,738}{(1 + y_p)^{60}}$$

$$y_p = 0.0127 = 1.27\%$$

$$y^* = (1 + 0.0127)^{12} - 1 = 16.35\%$$

The effective yield is higher than if the mortgage were not prepaid, because the lender receives the return of the principal balance sooner.

Add-on Loans

Some long-term loans are made with **add-on interest.** Automobile and other consumer loans by finance companies, commercial banks, credit unions, and savings and loan associations are frequently made on this basis. Add-on interest means that the total interest owed on the loan, based on the annual stated interest rate, is added to the initial principal balance *before* determining periodic payments. If, for example, an individual borrows $8,000 to purchase a car, must make monthly payments for 36 months, and is quoted a 10 percent add-on rate by a finance company, the 10 percent stated annual interest will be added to the $8,000 principal before monthly payments are calculated. In this example, $2,400 will be added on (10% × $8,000 × 3 years), for a total initial balance of $10,400. Periodic payments are then calculated by dividing the $10,400 by the number of payments to be made, resulting in cash payments of $10,400/36 = $288.89 per month. In effect, the lender is advancing $8,000 cash at the time the loan is made in exchange for 36 annuity payments of $288.89.

The effective annual yield on this loan is calculated by using Equations 4.7 and 4.6. The monthly yield (y_p) is 1.493 percent, and y^* is 19.46 percent. Unlike a mortgage, an add-on loan requires the borrower to pay interest on more than just the remaining unpaid balance of the original loan. During the first year, the borrower will pay the lender 12 × $288.89 = $3,466.68 in total payments—almost half the original amount borrowed. Even after interest owed during the first year is deducted, the borrower retains use of much less than the $8,000 originally borrowed. Yet the interest owed in both the second and third years is 10 percent of $8,000. Because interest is paid on the full principal balance after much of it has been repaid, add-on loans produce some of the biggest differences between stated and effective rates among financial assets. Federal consumer protection laws require lenders to inform borrowers of the effect of add-on interest.[17]

---

[17]Federal truth-in-lending legislation does not require the effect of compounding to be reported. To meet disclosure requirements, the monthly rate of 1.493 percent in the example would be converted to an annual rate (y) of 1.493 × 12 = 17.92%. The lender's effective yield (y*) is higher, as previously shown.

CAPITAL MARKET INSTRUMENTS AND YIELDS: EQUITY SECURITIES

Although the classification of securities into money or capital market categories is based on original maturity, two securities have no maturity date and therefore defy a strict application of this definition: preferred and common stock.[18] Both securities signify that the holder is not entitled to legal repayment of principal, but has a residual claim on the issuing firm. They are long-term claims on the firm's assets and income and are traded in capital markets.

Preferred Stock

Preferred stockholders pay an initial price for the security in exchange for expected cash dividends and/or the possibility of selling the stock at a higher price in the future. Dividends to preferred stockholders are almost always specified by the issuing firm as a dollar amount per year or as a stated percentage of the par value of the stock. The par value of preferred, however, is not an amount preferred stockholders expect to receive at a specified date, although it is the maximum per share a preferred stockholder can expect to receive if a company is liquidated. Preferred dividends are not legal obligations of the issuing firm, but they must be paid before any dividends are paid to common shareholders. Thus, unlike missing bond interest payments, failing to pay preferred dividends in a given year cannot usually force a firm into bankruptcy. Preferred stock is attractive to corporate investors, because under current tax laws, 80 percent of the dividends on preferred stock of another company are tax-exempt.

Effective Annual Yield on Preferred Stock.
Because most preferred dividends are fixed indefinitely, expected cash returns on preferred stock are perpetual annuities. Therefore, the expected annual yield on preferred stock is easily estimated from Equation 4.9, a restatement of Equation 4A.10 in the appendix.

(4.9) $y^* = \dfrac{C_1}{P_0}$

According to Figure 4.9, on January 27, 1986, the preferred stock of Xerox Corporation closed at 55⅝. Unlike bond quotes, prices on preferred and common stock are quoted as dollar figures, so this price represents $55 plus ⅝ of another dollar, or $55.63 to the nearest penny. The annual dividend was $5.45. Therefore, the expected annual yield to a purchaser who bought the stock at $55.63 and held it indefinitely was:

$$y^* = \frac{\$5.45}{\$55.63} = 9.8\%$$

Common Stock

Common stock entitles the holder to profits after employees, creditors, and preferred stockholders have been paid. In case of liquidation, all proceeds from the sale of assets go to common shareholders after the same prior claimants have been satisfied.

Returns to common shareholders are earned from cash dividends and proceeds from the resale of the stock. Like preferred stock dividends, common stock dividends are not legal requirements of issuing firms. Unlike preferred stockholders, however, common shareholders have the potential for substantial dividend increases if earnings prospects of the issuing firm are favorable. Expectations of increased earnings also increase the market value of the firm's stock, enabling a common shareholder to profit from the sale of his shares at an appreciated price in the future. Of course, a firm's prospects may decline, but most investors purchase common stock in anticipation of a positive rate of return.

Few topics in finance have received more attention in the last 20 years than the estimation of expected rates of return on common stock.

---

[18]Occasionally preferred stock is issued with stated maturity dates—usually by financial institutions—and called "limited life" preferred. These securities are classified as liabilities of the issuer, not as equity instruments.

Figure 4.9
New York Stock Exchange Quotations

NEW YORK STOCK EXCHANGE COMPOSITE TRANSACTIONS

Monday, January 27, 1986

52 Weeks High	52 Weeks Low	Stock		Div.	Yld %	P-E Ratio	Sales 100s	High	low	Close	Net Chg.
		– X–Y–Z –									
61½	41½	Xerox		3	5.1	20	3403	59⅜	58⅜	59¼	+ ⅞
56¾	49	Xerox		pf5.45	9.8	..	151	55¾	55⅝	55⅝	.....
29	20⅝	XTRA		.64	3.0	12	145	21½	21⅜	21⅜	– ⅝
34¾	26	ZaleCp		1.32	4.1	13	386	32½	32¼	32¼	– ⅜
17	6¼	Zapata		.12	1.8	48	x681	7	6¾	6¾	– ¼
66⅛	37⅞	Zayre	s	.48	.8	18	430	59½	59¼	59½	+ ⅜
25	16¼	ZenithE			..	956	2064	19½	18⅞	19⅛	+ ⅜
23⅜	17¼	Zero	s	.36	1.7	18	47	21	20¾	20⅞	– ⅛
42¾	26¾	Zurnln		1.32	3.2	15	216	42¼	41¾	41¾	– ¼

Source: *The Wall Street Journal,* January 28, 1986, p. 53. Reprinted by permission of *The Wall Street Journal,* © Dow Jones & Company, Inc. 1986. All Rights Reserved.

In the absence of universal agreement on the "best" approach for making such estimates, several widely accepted approaches are advocated in the academic literature and used in practice. Two important ones are examined in the following paragraphs.

Effective Annual Yield on Common Stock: Constant Growth Model. In theory, the effective annual yield on common stock is estimated in the same way as the return on other types of investments; it is the discount rate that equates the present value of the expected cash benefits to the purchase price. A major complication, however, is that future cash flows are more difficult to estimate for stock than for other financial assets. A way of simplifying estimation is to assume that cash benefits will grow at a constant rate, then to estimate a price at which the stock can be sold at the end of the planned holding period.

As shown in Figure 4.9, the common stock of Xerox Corporation closed at 59¼ on January 27, 1986. Suppose the manager of a pension fund planned to purchase the stock at this price and anticipated that cash dividends would grow at an annual rate of 12.5 percent over their most recent level of \$3 per share.[19] After five years, the manager plans to sell the stock and estimates the selling price will be \$65. Equation 4.7 is used to estimate the effective annual yield, based on these cash flow estimates:

$$C_1 = \$3.00\,(1.125) = \$3.38$$

$$C_2 = \$3.00\,(1.125)^2 = \$3.80$$

$$C_3 = \$3.00\,(1.125)^3 = \$4.27$$

$$C_4 = \$3.00\,(1.125)^4 = \$4.81$$

$$C_5 = \$3.00\,(1.125)^5 = \$5.41, \text{ plus the anticipated \$65 sales price} = \$70.41$$

$$\$59.25 = \sum_{t=1}^{5} \frac{C_t}{(1 + y^*)^t}$$

$$y^* = 0.0879 = 8.79\%$$

[19]This historical dividend growth rate and the beta coefficient for Xerox Corporation used later are from the January 31, 1986, report on Xerox in *Value Line Investment Survey.*

If instead the pension fund manager planned to hold Xerox shares indefinitely, the cash dividends would be a perpetually growing annuity. The effective annual yield with an indefinite holding period can be found from Equation 4A.11 in the appendix. For the Xerox stock purchased at $59.25, y^* is:

$$y^* = \frac{\$3.00\ (1.125)}{\$59.25} + 0.125$$

$$= 0.1820 = 18.20\%$$

Effective Annual Yield: Capital Asset Pricing Model. Many analysts believe that there is a better approach to estimating the expected return on common stock, particularly for investors holding large, widely diversified portfolios. This approach focuses on a firm's sensitivity to systemwide economic factors that could alter its earnings prospects, such as changes in monetary policy, fiscal policy, or the overall rate of economic growth. A measure of this sensitivity is the stock's *beta coefficient (β)*. The beta for stock j is defined in statistical terms as the covariance (cov) of its expected return (r_j) with the expected return on the *market portfolio* (r_m), divided by the variance of returns on the market portfolio (σ_m^2). The "market portfolio" is a large, diversified portfolio.

(4.10)

$$\beta_J = \frac{\text{cov}\ (r_j,\ r_m)}{\sigma_m^2}$$

Beta coefficients are estimated in several ways; the most common is regression analysis. As illustrated in Figure 4.10, the slope of a regression line between the stock's historical returns during selected periods and returns on the market portfolio during the same periods is the stock's beta (1.132 in the figure). This estimate of beta can then be adjusted for any anticipated changes.[20] The more sensitive a stock's ex-

pected returns to general market conditions, the higher the stock's beta. A beta close to 1 indicates average sensitivity.

According to the *Capital Asset Pricing Model (CAPM),* expected returns on common stocks are linearly related to their betas, as expressed in Equation 4.11:

(4.11)

$$r_j = r_f + (r_m - r_f)\ \beta_j$$

Theoretically, r_f is the expected return on an investment without risk—that is, without potential variation in expected cash inflows. The expression ($r_m - r_f$) in CAPM is the expected *market risk premium.* CAPM holds that the expected return on an investment is directly and solely proportional to its sensitivity to systematic changes in the financial markets, as measured by the beta coefficient.[21]

No investment's returns are so predictable that they are literally free of any potential vari-

---

[20]In addition to adjusting for changes in the relationship as a result of factors specific to a firm (such as a merger or divestiture), one must adjust for the tendency of betas in general to change over time. For further discussion, see Marshall Blume, "Betas and Their Regression Tendencies," *Journal of Finance* 30 (June 1975): 785-796.

[21]Initial development of CAPM is attributed to Jack Treynor in an unpublished paper; to William F. Sharpe, "Capital Asset Prices: A Theory of Market Equilibrium Under Conditions of Uncertainty," *Journal of Finance* 19 (September 1964): 425-442; and to John Lintner, "The Valuation of Risk Assets and the Selection of Risky Investments in Stock Portfolios and Capital Budgets," *Review of Economics and Statistics* 47 (February 1965): 13-37.

Since then, the theory has been subjected to voluminous empirical examination, refinement, and criticism. Thorough explication of these efforts is beyond the intent of this book. Empirical tests of CAPM are typified by Eugene F. Fama and James D. McBeth, "Risk, Return, and Equilibrium: Empirical Tests," *Journal of Political Economy* 81 (May 1973): 607-636. A comprehensive look at practical applications of the model can be found in Diana R. Harrington, *Modern Portfolio Theory and the Capital Asset Pricing Model: A User's Guide* (Englewood Cliffs, NJ: Prentice-Hall, 1983). Finally, criticisms of and alternatives to the model are found in Stephen Ross, "The Arbitrage Theory of Capital Asset Pricing," *Journal of Economic Theory* 13 (December 1976): 341-360; and in Richard Roll, "A Critique of the Asset Pricing Theory's Empirical Tests, Part I: On Past and Potential Testability of the Theory," *Journal of Financial Economics* 4 (March 1977): 129-176. A summary of criticisms written for practitioners is Anise Wallace, "Is Beta Dead?" *Institutional Investor* 14 (July 1980): 22-30.

Figure 4.10
Using Regression to Estimate Beta

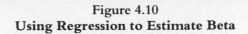

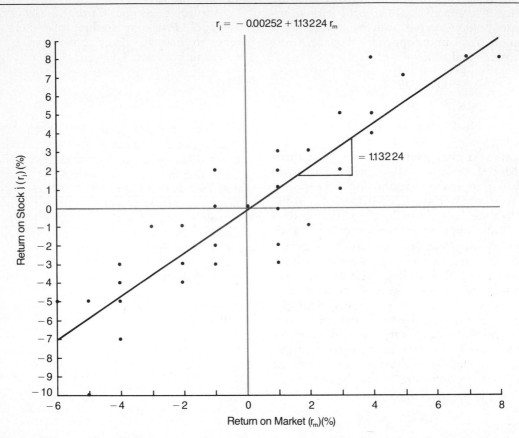

Return on Market (r_m)(%)

ation, but most managers assume that short-term Treasury securities are essentially risk-free. A user of the Capital Asset Pricing Model would estimate the expected return on Xerox common stock based on the stock's beta, the risk-free rate, and the market risk premium. Figure 4.3 indicates that as of January 27, 1986, the bond-equivalent yield on a Treasury bill maturing in 10 days (on February 6, 1986) was 6.66 percent, for an effective annual yield, using Equation 4.2, of 6.82 percent.[22] An estimate of

the expected market risk premium ($r_m − r_f$), based on 59 years of data from the financial markets is 8.3 percent.[23] *Value Line Investment*

portfolio. Carleton argues that the annualized risk-free return used in CAPM should be based on the data interval that generated the beta. This suggests that if *Value Line* betas are used, the return on a one-week Treasury security should be used to estimate the annualized risk-free rate. For this example, a ten-day maturity was used in the absence of a seven-day bill. See Willard T. Carleton, "A Highly Personal Comment on the Use of the CAPM in Public Utility Rate Cases," *Financial Management* 7 (Autumn 1978): 57-59.

[22]*Value Line* estimates stock betas by regressing weekly returns on a stock against weekly returns on a market

[23]Ibbotson Associates, *Stocks, Bonds, Bills and Inflation: 1985 Yearbook* (Chicago: Ibbotson Associates, 1985).

Survey reported in January 1986 that the beta of Xerox stock was 1.05—that is, that the stock was expected to show slightly above-average sensitivity to general market movements. Using Equation 4.11, a CAPM estimate of the expected one-year rate of return on Xerox stock, as of January 1986, is:

$$r_{Xerox} = 6.82\% + (8.3\%)\, 1.05 = 15.54\%$$

CAPM provides an alternative way to estimate the expected annual return on common stock for managers of widely diversified portfolios. Under those conditions, it can be argued that estimating individual cash flows for each stock is tedious, time-consuming, and not worth the effort required. The degree to which CAPM is an adequate replacement for individual security analysis is debatable, for not all experts agree that the sensitivity of a stock to common market factors is the only important determinant of its expected return. Nonetheless, CAPM remains a widely used alternative to other models.

WHAT DETERMINES YIELDS?

The discussion has focused thus far on the mechanics of calculating yields, stressing the importance of comparing returns on an equivalent basis. Clearly, effective annual yields depend upon the size of the cash outflows required and the size and timing of the cash inflows expected. If either the cash outflow required (the price) or the benefits to be received change, an effective yield changes. But what is the underlying factor that determines the price, given the cash flows the investor expects to receive? All else equal, it is the investment's risk.

Sources of Risk

What are some sources of potential variability? The major ones are the possibility of default, illiquidity, changes in interest rates, and market factors.

Default.   One possibility is that a borrower will *default* on a financial obligation by failing to pay interest, principal, or both. Some financial instruments are considered to be virtually free of default, although others, such as unsecured personal loans, are subject to considerable default risk. Because Treasury securities are backed by the taxing and money-creation power of the federal government, they are free of default risk, and it is in this sense that they are considered risk-free investments.

Illiquidity.   The existence of secondary markets for investments, and the size of those markets, also affect an investor's assessment of risk. An investor wishing to sell a financial asset quickly obviously needs a market in which to sell it. The larger the market, the greater the seller's opportunity to obtain cash easily without substantial loss of value—that is, the greater the *liquidity*.

Changes in Interest Rates.   Another source of potential variability is changes in market interest rates. If interest rates change, the reinvestment rate for cash received from an investment will change. In addition, as explained in Chapter 7, the price at which an investment can be sold in the future is affected by changes in market rates. The *interest rate risk* faced by an investor depends upon many features of a security, including the stated interest rate and the term to maturity.

Market Factors.   A final risk is the sensitivity of an asset's returns to factors affecting the entire financial system. This risk, emphasized in the Capital Asset Pricing Model, is *systematic or market risk*. Sources are political, legal, fiscal, and national and international economic conditions.

Effect of Risk on Yields

In general, investors, including financial institutions, are *risk-averse*. Risk aversion means that investors will pay less for the opportunity of receiving cash flows with high potential variability than for cash flows of the same expected size but lower risk. Given two investments with equal expected cash inflows, if investors pay less for the opportunity to receive the riskier flows, the expected yield on the riskier investment is higher.

For example, Figure 4.8 presents details on zero-coupon bonds issued by McDonald's Corporation and Cities Service Corporation, maturing in 1988. On January 27, 1986, the McDonald's bonds closed at 84⅜, and the Cities Service bonds closed at 76⅛. Assuming a $1,000 par value for each bond, an investor would have paid $843.75 for the McDonald's bond but only $761.25 for the Cities Service bond, yet both had the same maturity date and the same expected cash inflow. The effective annual yields on the two investments, using Equation 4.7, are 8.87 percent for the McDonald's bond and 14.61 percent on the Cities Service bond.

Although the effective annual yield on the Cities Service bond was higher than the effective annual yield on the McDonald's bond, investors did not consider the Cities Service bond "better." In fact, they were willing to pay *less* for it than for a virtually identical bond from McDonald's. Because these effective yields are *expected* yields only, the lower price for the Cities Service bond reflects the financial market's assessment that it was riskier than the McDonald's bond. Because the only cash flow expected from either bond is the par value in 1988, the lower price for the Cities Service bond was due to greater probability of default on that bond or to lower marketability. Risk-averse participants in the bond markets enforced their belief that the Cities Service bond was riskier by paying a lower price, increasing its expected annual yield.

Risk aversion does not mean that investors are unwilling to accept investments with potentially variable returns; it simply means they will pay less for them than for comparable ones with less potential variation. The principle of expecting a higher rate of return (paying a lower price) based on the riskiness of an investment is the *risk/expected return tradeoff.*

Throughout the text, the concept of risk as variability, its sources, its measurement, and its management are illustrated as asset/liability management is explored. It is important to remember that although the mechanics of yield calculations are necessary tools for the financial manager, risk assessment is equally important.

SUMMARY

Financial instruments can be categorized by their initial maturity. Securities with an initial maturity of one year or less are money market instruments, and those with longer initial maturities are capital market securities.

Care must be taken in calculating yields on money market securities, because many are traded on a discount basis, and market conventions differ. All quoted yields must be converted to effective annual yields. The equations in this chapter demonstrate similarities in yield calculations for a number of short-term securities, including Treasury bills, repurchase agreements, reverse repos, commercial paper, bankers' acceptances, negotiable CDs, federal funds, and discounted loans.

To analyze investments with more than one year to maturity, cash flows must be estimated and the internal rate of return determined. The effective yield on coupon bonds, zero-coupon bonds, mortgage loans, and add-on consumer loans are calculated similarly. A tax adjustment may be necessary because of the special characteristics of some long-term instruments, such as municipal bonds. Caution must also be taken to recognize features of mortgage and add-on loans that make effective yields higher than stated rates.

The final category of instruments is equity securities. Preferred stock returns are estimated as perpetual annuities. Returns on common stock investments are more difficult to estimate. Two ways of estimating expected yields on common stock are the constant dividend growth model and the Capital Asset Pricing Model.

Equally significant are factors affecting the level of risk, or potential variability, in returns. Sources of variability include the possibility of default, illiquidity, and exposure to interest rate and systematic (or market) risk. Investors, who are generally risk-averse, will pay less for and require higher returns on more risky investments, a relationship known as the risk/expected return tradeoff.

Questions

1. What is the difference between money market securities and capital market securities?

2. You need to compare expected returns on a number of investment alternatives: a $10,000, 26-week T-bill; $25,000, 90-day commercial paper; a $20,000, 60-day bankers' acceptance; and a $15,000, 180-day discounted commercial bank loan. What steps must you take to compare them?

3. Explain the difference between discount securities and interest-bearing securities. How does this difference affect the timing of returns and estimates of rates of return?

4. What is an annualized holding-period yield? How does it differ from an *ex ante* yield?

5. Find the results, reported in *The Wall Street Journal,* of the most recent Treasury bill auction. What was the average yield on a discount basis? The average coupon-equivalent yield? Explain the difference in the two yield quotations. If you were purchasing T-bills, which yield would you prefer as an *ex ante* estimate of return? Why?

6. Define repurchase/reverse repurchase agreements. Why are they considered money market securities?

7. What alternatives are available to an investor needing to sell commercial paper before its maturity date?

8. What are bankers' acceptances? At what point do bankers' acceptances become money market instruments? Compare their riskiness to that of other money market securities.

9. Why were negotiable certificates of deposits introduced? What are the reasons for their continued popularity?

10. Explain the difference between coupon bonds and zero-coupon bonds. How do their yield calculations differ?

11. Explain the practice of charging borrowers points on mortgage loans. How does this affect the cost to the borrower?

12. What are add-on loans? How do they differ from mortgage loans with respect to the interest paid? What effect does add-on interest have on yield to the lender and effective cost to the borrower?

13. Twenty-First Century Growth Mutual Fund is considering purchasing shares of Ameritech Co. If the mutual fund uses the constant growth model to estimate the stock's yield, what assumptions must be made about future cash flows? For what types of firms might these assumptions be reasonable? In what situations would you recommend against using the constant-growth model?

14. Suppose Twenty-First Century Growth chooses to use CAPM to estimate the yield on Ameritech. What is the importance of the beta coefficient in this model? Do you agree that emphasizing market factors may be more useful than analyzing cash flow estimates for individual securities? Why or why not?

15. The riskiness of an investment affects the price investors are willing to pay, which in turn reflects their required yield. Explain the sources of potential variability that affect required rates of return. As riskiness increases, do prices increase or decrease? Do required yields increase or decrease? Why?

Problems

1. From Figure 4.2 determine the following:
   a. The total dollar amount of 13-week Treasury bills sold at the auction
   b. The total dollar amount of 13-week T-bills sold at the low price
   c. The price noncompetitive bidders paid per $10,000, 13-week T-bill
   d. The bond-equivalent yield on 13-week T-bills.

2. A small savings and loan association placed a noncompetitive bid for a $10,000, 91-day T-bill. The high price for the auction was 96.875, the low price 96.862, and the average price 96.869.
   a. What bond-equivalent yield and what effective annual yield will the S&L earn if the bill is held to maturity?
   b. What will be the holding-period yield if the S&L sells the bill after five weeks at a price of 97.525?

3. A 26-week T-bill yields a bank discount rate of 9.65 percent. What is the bond-equivalent yield on the bill? What is the effective annual yield?

4. A 13-week T-bill yields a bank discount rate of 8.78 percent. What price will a commercial bank have to pay to purchase this T-bill from a dealer? What is the bond-equivalent yield on the bill? What is the effective annual yield?

5. If the commercial bank described in Problem 4 sells the T-bill after seven weeks at a price of 98.375, what holding-period yield will the bank realize?

6. What is the effective annual yield on a 52-week Treasury bill selling at 92.455? The bank discount yield?

7. From advertisements in your local newspaper, find as much information as possible about the rates currently being paid by financial institutions on one-year certificates of deposit. For each institution advertising the frequency of compounding, calculate the effective annual yield on a one-year CD, and compare it to the stated rate. Explain how the differences between effective and stated yields are affected by the frequency of compounding.

8. On January 27, 1986, a small commercial bank was considering the purchase of a Treasury bill maturing on March 27, 1986. Using Figure 4.3, determine the effective annual yield if the bank purchased the bill and held it until maturity.

9. The discount yield on a three-day reverse repurchase agreement is quoted in the market as 9.25 percent. Use Equation 4.4 to calculate the expected annual yield to an institution that engages in this transaction. Calculate the purchase price using Equation 4.5, and then verify your first answer using Equation 4.1. What is the effective annual yield to the institution?

10. McDouglas Corporation's pension fund manager anticipates $250,000 idle cash for the next 120 days and wishes to purchase commercial paper. She consults a commercial paper dealer who quotes her a 9⅝ percent bank-discount rate. What price must the pension fund manager pay for the commercial paper? What is the bond-equivalent yield on this investment?

11. Community Commercial Bank agrees to supply Dan Murdoch with a $25,000 discounted loan so that he may expand his restaurant's seating capacity. The loan is for one year with a stated annual rate of 11.6 percent. What is the effective annual yield to the bank?

12. World-Wide Office Supply Company has $2 million its financial manager wishes to invest in a negotiable certificate of deposit for 180 days. Metropolitan National Bank is offering a coupon rate of 13.75 percent on such a deposit. What is the effective annual yield on the CD?

13. The American Hospital Credit Union is offering short-term interest-bearing loans to its members at an annual rate of 10.5 percent. Equal monthly payments of interest and principal are required. If you take out a six-month, $10,000 loan, what will your monthly payments be?

14. Find the results of the most recent Treasury auction in *The Wall Street Journal* or other newspaper; find the most recent "Money Rates" column as well. Using that information, calculate the effective annual yields on 91-day T-bills, 3-month CDs, 90-day commercial paper, and 90-day bankers' acceptances. What factors account for the yield differences you find?

15. Rest Assured Life Insurance Company purchased a general obligation bond issued by the State of Illinois at 95 percent of par. The $1,000 par bond carries a coupon rate of 10.5 percent and matures in 15 years. Interest is paid semiannually. The marginal tax rate for Rest Assured is 34 percent. Calculate the yield to maturity for the bond (that is, the tax-equivalent yield). If Rest Assured sells the bond for $903.29 at the end of five years when the prevailing market rate for similar bonds is 12.2 percent, what is the holding-period yield to the company on its investment in the bond?

16. On January 1, 1989, Alpha Company's zero-coupon bonds, which mature on December 31, 2000, are selling for 38⅜. What is the effective annual yield to an investor who holds the bond until maturity?

17. Home Savings and Loan is currently offering certificates of deposit for an initial investment of $420. The $1,000 CDs mature in ten years. What is the effective annual yield on such an investment?

18. Federal Savings and Loan Association offers you a $50,000, 15-year mortgage with a 13.5 percent fixed interest rate. The S&L charges 3½ points on the loan. If you borrow from Federal Savings and Loan, what will your monthly loan payments be? Prepare an amortization schedule for the first five years. What is your principal balance after 60 payments?

19. Your home town bank is willing to loan you $12,000 to purchase a new car. The terms of the loan are 48 equal monthly payments at a 12.2 percent annual add-on rate of interest. What monthly payments will you be required to make? What is the effective annual yield on this loan?

20. The preferred stock of Holland Corporation is currently trading for $45 and has a par value of $100. The preferred stock carries an 8 percent dividend. What is the effective annual yield to the purchaser of this stock?

21. The preferred stock of Hamilton Company is currently trading at 36⅜. The $100 par value stock pays a 6 percent dividend.
    a. What is the effective annual yield to the purchaser of this stock?
    b. Suppose a purchaser at the current price sells the stock for $43 in five years. What is the annual holding-period yield?

22. The manager of a major pension fund is considering the purchase of American Amusement Park Company's common stock. The current market price for this company is $37.50. The annual dividend on the stock five years ago was $.75 and has grown at a constant rate to the present dividend of $1.25. This growth rate is expected to continue. If the pension fund manager has no future plans for selling the stock once it is purchased, what is the effective annual yield on a share of American Amusement Park's common stock? (Hint: Use Equation 4A.1 to find the growth rate.)

23. A major life insurance company is planning to purchase a number of shares of the Courier Corporation's common stock. The common stock currently trades at $25 per share. Common

stock dividends four years ago were $.38 per share and have grown at a rate of 7.1 percent annually. Last year, Courier Corporation paid an annual dividend of $.50.

   a. After six years, the insurance company plans to sell the stock at an estimated price of $31. What is the effective annual yield on this investment?

   b. What is the estimated annual yield if the company plans to own the stock for an indefinite period of time?

   c. What is the effective annual yield if the stock is sold for $21 in six years?

24. The manager of a major pension fund purchased a $1,000 par corporate bond at 97.75 percent of par. The bond carries a coupon rate of 11.25 percent and matures in 20 years. Interest is paid semiannually.

   a. Calculate the yield to maturity for the bond.

   b. If the pension fund manager sells the bond at the end of seven years for $925, what is the holding-period yield on the investment?

25. The Omega Savings and Loan is currently offering 20-year fixed-rate mortgages at 12.75 percent.

   a. If you borrow $175,000 to purchase the home of your dreams, the S&L will charge you 4½ points on the loan. Calculate the monthly payment required to amortize the loan and the amortization schedule for the first three years.

   b. Suppose the institution will charge only 3 points if the interest rate increases to 13.5 percent. What is the effective annual yield and the new three-year amortization schedule?

   c. If the stated interest rate is only 12 percent, how many points would Omega have to charge to earn the same effective yield as on the 13.5 percent mortgage? Would it be reasonable for the lender to charge this many points to compensate for the lower interest rate? (Hint: Find the monthly payments at the 12 percent rate, then work from there.)

26. If the beta for Admiralty Corporation is 0.84, the expected return on the market is 12 percent, and the risk-free rate is 6.5 percent, what is the expected return on Admiralty's common stock? If, instead, the expected return on Admiralty is 14 percent, what is its beta (using the same r_m and r_f estimates)?

27. Find the most recent estimate of Xerox Corporation's beta coefficient from *Value Line* or another investment publication. Using current information on Treasury security rates and an estimate of the market risk premium, calculate the expected annual return on Xerox's stock using the Capital Asset Pricing Model. Do the same for the stock of Procter and Gamble. What factors account for the difference in your answer?

Selected References

Cook, Timothy Q., and Timothy D. Rowe, eds. *Instruments of the Money Market.* 6th ed. Richmond, VA: Federal Reserve Bank of Richmond, 1986.

Fama, Eugene F., and James D. McBeth. "Risk, Return, and Equilibrium: Empirical Tests." *Journal of Political Economy* 81 (May 1973): 607-636.

Harrington, Diana R. *Modern Portfolio Theory and the Capital Asset Pricing Model: A User's Guide.* Englewood Cliffs, NJ: Prentice-Hall, 1983.

Hervey, Jack L. "Bankers' Acceptances Revisited." *Economic Perspectives* (Federal Reserve Bank of Chicago) 7 (May/June 1983): 21-31.

Ibbotson Associates. *Stocks, Bonds, Bills, and Inflation: 1985 Yearbook.* Chicago: Ibbotson Associates, 1985.

Jensen, Frederick H., and Patrick M. Parkinson. "Recent Developments in the Bankers' Acceptance Market." *Federal Reserve Bulletin* 72 (January 1986): 1-12.

Kidwell, David S., M. Wayne Marr, and G. Rodney Thompson. "Eurodollar Bonds: Alternative Financing for U.S. Companies." *Financial Management* 14 (Winter 1985): 18-27.

Roll, Richard. "A Critique of the Asset Pricing Theory's Empirical Tests, Part I: On Past and Potential Testability of the Theory." *Journal of Financial Economics* 4 (March 1977): 129-176.

Rosengren, Eric S. "Is There a Need for Regulation in the Government Securities Market?" *New England Economic Review* (Federal Reserve Bank of Boston) (September/October 1986), pp. 29-40.

Sharpe, William F. "Capital Asset Prices: A Theory of Market Equilibrium Under Conditions of Uncertainty." *Journal of Finance* 19 (September 1964): 425-442.

Stigum, Marcia. *Money Market Calculations: Yields, Break-evens, and Arbitrage.* Homewood, IL: Dow Jones-Irwin, 1981.

Syron, Richard, and Sheila L. Tschinkel. "The Government Securities Market: Playing Field for Repos." *Economic Review* (Federal Reserve Bank of Atlanta) 70 (September 1985): 10-19.

Trainer, Richard D. C. *The Arithmetic of Interest Rates.* New York: Federal Reserve Bank of New York, 1982.

Wallace, Anise. "Is Beta Dead?" *Institutional Investor* 14 (July 1980): 22-30.

Appendix 4A
THE MATHEMATICS OF COMPOUND AND PRESENT VALUE

The mathematics of compound and present value underlying effective annual yields are formal expressions of the intuitive notion that if cash is invested today and not used for consumption purposes, it should accumulate to a higher sum over time. Otherwise, postponing consumption would not be worth it, and no one would invest. The accumulation occurs through periodic interest on the initial investment.

COMPOUND (FUTURE) VALUE

If an initial amount is invested for several periods, and if subsequent interest is earned on past interest as well as on the initial amount, *compound interest,* or interest on interest, is involved. The longer the investment horizon, and the higher the rate of interest each period, the higher the accumulated sum. A less intuitive but conceptually identical expression of this idea is as follows: Given an expected rate of interest, the present value of a future cash flow is lower than the future cash flow. An even more formal mathematical expression of the same idea is the basic compound interest equation:

$$(4A.1) \quad C_N = C_0 (1 + k)^N$$

where: C_0 = initial sum invested;
C_N = future sum accumulated;
k = annual rate of interest;
N = number of years during which cash is invested.

Equation 4A.1 permits an investor to calculate the future cash benefit expected from an initial investment, given any levels of k and N. For selected levels of these two variables, tables containing values of $(1 + k)^N$ and several other time-value-of-money formulas are provided at the end of the book. Equation 4A.1 assumes that interest earned during a year is paid at the end of each year. For investments in which part of the annual interest is earned before the end of each year—for example, semiannually or quarterly—the basic compound interest equation is modified to include *intrayear compounding:*

$$(4A.2) \quad C_N = C_0 (1 + k/m)^{Nm}$$

where: m = number of compounding periods per year.

Effective annual yields in Chapter 4 consider intrayear compounding.

PRESENT VALUE

Often a different sort of problem occurs: An investor has the opportunity to receive future cash benefits whose size and timing can be estimated and must decide how much to pay for the opportunity. Here, present value is important. The present value of a future sum is the amount that must be invested initially, given an expected interest rate, to accumulate to the future sum. The expression for the present value

of a future sum is the algebraic equivalent of Equation 4A.1. The higher the expected interest rate, and the further in the future the cash benefit is expected, the lower its present value.

$$(4A.3) \quad C_0 = \frac{C_N}{(1 + k)^N}$$

If total annual interest will be divided into m payments during the year, the present value of a future cash flow is:

$$(4A.4) \quad C_0 = \frac{C_{Nm}}{(1 + k/m)^{Nm}}$$

Present Values Can Be Added

Present values are additive; that is, if several future cash flows are expected, their total present value is the sum of the present values of the individual future sums:

$$C_0 = \frac{C_1}{(1 + k)^1} + \frac{C_2}{(1 + k)^2} + \cdots + \frac{C_N}{(1 + k)^N}$$

which is simplified to:

$$(4A.5) \quad C_0 = \sum_{t=1}^{N} \frac{C_t}{(1 + k)^t}$$

where: t = sub- or superscript denoting the specific period a sum is expected.

For intrayear compounding, Equation 4A.5 is modified:

$$(4A.6) \quad C_0 = \sum_{t=1}^{Nm} \frac{C_t}{(1 + k/m)^t}$$

STREAMLINING THE CALCULATIONS: IDENTIFYING SPECIAL CASH FLOW PATTERNS

Equations 4A.5 or 4A.6 permit one to calculate the present value of a series of future benefits no matter how many individual sums are involved, no matter what their size, and no matter when they are expected. Many investment opportunities, however, return benefits in distinct patterns. Recognizing those patterns simplifies the calculation of present value.[1]

The Annuity

Among the most common special cash flow patterns is the **annuity,** a series of equal future cash flows occurring at the end of each of a finite number of periods. When an investment offers cash benefits in annuity form, its present value is:

$$(4A.7) \quad C_0 = C_1 \left[\frac{1 - (1 + k)^{-N}}{k} \right]$$

$$= C_1 \left[\frac{1 - \frac{1}{(1 + k)^N}}{k} \right]$$

Perpetual Annuities

If the equal cash inflows are expected to occur indefinitely, the cash flow stream is a **perpetual annuity,** or **perpetuity.** For a perpetuity, N approaches infinity, and $[1/(1 + k)^N]$ approaches 0. Thus, the present value of a perpetuity is equal to:

$$(4A.8) \quad C_0 = \frac{C_1}{k}$$

If the cash flows are not equal, but occur at equal time intervals and are expected to *grow* at a constant rate (g) indefinitely, the cash flow stream is a **growing perpetuity.** The present value of a growing perpetuity is:

$$(4A.9) \quad C_0 = \frac{C_1}{k - g}$$

---

[1]The derivations of formulas in this appendix are presented in many sources. Interested readers may examine a source such as Eugene F. Brigham and Louis C. Gapenski, *Intermediate Financial Management,* 2d ed. (Chicago: Dryden Press, 1987), Chapter 3 and Appendix A.

FINDING AN UNKNOWN INTEREST RATE

The problems considered so far assume that someone already knows the relevant interest rate and seeks a future or present value. Many investors, however, ask a different kind of question. They know the initial cash investment required and the benefits expected, but do not know the annual interest rate implied by the cash flows. The problem is to estimate an expected annual rate of return. Fortunately, previous formulas can be used; the proper equation must be solved for k.

Direct Solution for k

For an investment with a single cash outflow and a single cash benefit at the end of N periods, the implicit annual rate of return is found by solving Equation 4A.3 for k:

$$(4A.3) \quad C_0 = \frac{C_N}{(1 + k)^N}$$

$$(1 + k)^N = C_N/C_0$$

$$k = \sqrt[N]{C_N/C_0} - 1$$

For example, suppose that by investing $675 today, an investor expects to receive $1,000 at the end of five years. The expected annual rate of return is:

$$(1 + k)^5 = C_5/C_0$$

$$(1 + k)^5 = \$1,000/\$675 = 1.48148$$

$$k = \sqrt[5]{1.48148} - 1 = 0.08178 = 8.178\%$$

Investments with perpetual cash benefit streams also lend themselves to a direct solution for k, using either Equations 4A.8 or 4A.9. The implied annual interest rate on an investment in a perpetuity is:

$$(4A.10) \quad k = \frac{C_1}{C_0}$$

For a growing perpetuity, the implicit interest rate is:

(4A.11) $k = \dfrac{C_1}{C_0} + g$

Trial-and-Error Solution for k

Unfortunately, if neither a single cash inflow nor a perpetual series of benefits is involved, finding the implied rate of return is a trial-and-error process. The analyst must try different values for k in Equations 4A.5, 4A.6, or 4A.7, depending upon whether an annuity and/or intrayear interest payments are expected. The goal is to find an interest rate that equates the present value of the cash benefits to the cash outflow required.

To exemplify the trial-and-error process, suppose an investment of $500 today is expected to produce benefits of $200 per year at the end of each of four years:

$$C_0 = C_1 \left[\frac{1 - \dfrac{1}{(1 + k)^N}}{k} \right]$$

$$\$500 = \$200 \left[\frac{1 - \dfrac{1}{(1 + k)^4}}{k} \right]$$

Trying 20 percent (0.20) in Equation 4A.7 produces an inequality; the present value of the four $200 payments is $517.75. Because their present value is "too high" at a discount rate of 20 percent, a higher value for k should be tried; the mathematics of present value make it clear that a present value will be lower at a higher discount rate. At 21 percent, the present value of the four $200 payments is $508.09, still "too high"; and at 22 percent, it is $498.73. Thus, a precise value for k is between 21 percent and 22 percent. Further refinement results in a k of 21.86 percent.

Fortunately, financial analyst calculators and microcomputers provide a solution for k almost instantaneously. Effective interest rate calculations such as those presented in Chapter 4 are based on these principles and procedures.

Part II

Interest Rate Theories and Interest Rate Risk

Chapter 5

THE LEVEL OF INTEREST RATES: THEORIES AND FORECASTING

When you forecast, do it with great humility.

Arnold X. Moskowitz
Senior Vice President and Economist
Dean Witter Reynolds (1985)

IN July 1985, William C. Melton, Vice President of IDS Financial Services, was reading poetry to console himself because his forecast for three-month T-bill rates that year was almost 4 percent too high. He had predicted a rate of 10.6 percent, but by the second half of the year actual yields were less than 7 percent. Citing changes in the financial markets' attitudes about inflation and the federal deficit, he felt like the title character of Samuel Coleridge's "Rime of the Ancient Mariner": "A sadder and a wiser man."[1]

Preceding chapters introduced unique characteristics of financial institutions, including the predominance of financial assets and liabilities. The resulting emphasis on the net interest margin makes the interest rate environment one of the most important influences on asset/liability decisions and institutional performance. Key determinants of success are managers' abilities to understand interest rate movements, to interpret forecasts, and to develop responses.

---

[1]Edward P. Foldessy and Tom Herman, "Short-Term Interest Rates Will Edge Higher in Second Half, According to Poll of Economists," *The Wall Street Journal,* July 1, 1985, p. 2.

In an operating environment characterized by volatile interest rates, financial institution managers must respond to anticipated rate changes with a growing array of risk management strategies. But first, managers must understand theories of interest rate determination.

WHY THEORIES ARE IMPORTANT TO MANAGERS

Managers are rarely theoreticians; instead, they spend their time analyzing and making decisions critical to the future of their institutions. These decisions rely on often conflicting opinions about the direction of the economy and interest rates. To make better decisions, managers therefore must be able to evaluate available data and forecasts. Those evaluations in turn require knowledge of the principles on which forecasts are based.

For example, the manager of the investment portfolio of a life insurance company can invest in variable-coupon bonds, zero-coupon bonds, or traditional fixed-rate instruments, among many other choices. The manager's expectations about interest rate movements will certainly influence the decision. In a period of declining rates, a variable-coupon instrument will be unattractive, but a zero-coupon bond will lock in a higher rate if intermediate cash flows are not important. Similarly, raising funds also must be guided by rate forecasts.

Often economists are unable to agree about the future direction of interest rates, and managers must exercise judgment in evaluating available forecasts. This chapter and the next examine the economic, political, and behavioral factors that influence interest rates. These theories provide the foundation on which economic forecasters base their expectations about interest rate changes, which in turn affect managerial evaluation and decision making.

A HISTORICAL LOOK AT INTEREST RATES

Although interest rates are always changing, they have been particularly volatile over the last decade, reaching historically high levels in 1980

and 1981.[2] Figure 5.1 traces yields on long-term bonds in several different default risk classes over the period 1925–1986. Although an upward trend began in the late 1960s, rates rose rapidly in late 1979 and peaked about two years later, fueled by expectations of high inflation and government deficits. Even though yields declined in 1982, as inflation subsided, the volatility continued. Financial institutions find this environment a continuing challenge to their managers' skills.

Some institutions have maintained good performance records, but many firms faltered or failed. For example, in May 1981, Economy Savings and Loan Association in Chicago, a relatively small institution with assets of less than $90 million, closed its doors. Observers blamed many of Economy's problems on incorrect forecasts of interest rate movements. Managers repeatedly bet that interest rates had peaked and made commitments based on those expectations. But rates moved even higher throughout early 1981, Economy continued to lose money, and the firm's net worth plummeted. Regula-

---

[2]Based on their research at the Federal Reserve Bank of Chicago, Rosenblum and Strongin argue that, in a very long-term historical context and with a relative rather than an absolute measure of volatility, interest rates in the period following October 1979 through 1982 are not significantly more volatile than in earlier periods. They believe that, because interest rates were so much higher in the recent period, an absolute measure overstates relative volatility. It does not, however, overstate the impact on the value of financial assets and liabilities, key elements in this book. For further discussion, see Harvey Rosenblum and Steven Strongin, "Interest Rate Volatility in Historical Perspective," *Economic Perspectives,* Federal Reserve Bank of Chicago 7 (January/February 1983): 10–19. Another recent analysis of short-term rates from October 1979 to mid-1983 concluded that, in comparison to historical yields, rates in that period were significantly higher than would have been expected given previous rate levels. See Richard H. Clarida and Benjamin M. Friedman, "The Behavior of U.S. Short-Term Interest Rates since October 1979," *Journal of Finance* 39 (July 1984): 671–682.

Figure 5.1
Long-Term Bond Yields (Quarterly Averages)

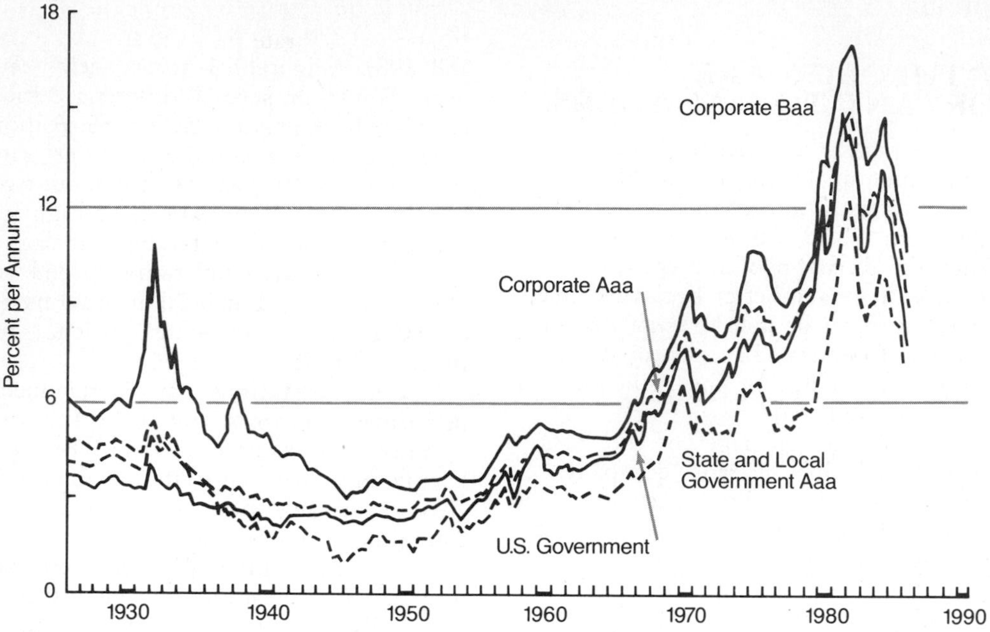

Source: Board of Governors of the Federal Reserve System, *1986 Historical Chart Book.*

---

tors closed the S&L on May 18, 1981, and began paying off insured depositors.[3]

At the same time, other institutions fared better, despite the uncertainties in their operating environment. For example, the managers of State Savings Association of Columbus, Ohio, anticipating rate increases throughout 1981, made only mortgage loans on which rates could be adjusted periodically to keep up with the institution's cost of funds. Because the forecast and management's response to it were appropriate, the institution prospered in comparison to many other thrifts that year.[4]

---

[3]Sue Shellenbarger, "Demise of an S&L in Chicago Is Linked to Belief that Interest Rates Would Fall," *The Wall Street Journal,* June 5, 1981.

[4]John N. Frank, "The Moneymakers: A Rare Bloom in 1981," *Savings and Loan News* 103 (June 1982): 54–60.

THE GENERAL LEVEL OF INTEREST RATES

Theories of interest rate determination follow several conventions. First, models usually focus on determination of the *equilibrium* level of interest. Equilibrium is a state of rest or the absence of forces for change. Actually, the financial markets are seldom if ever in equilibrium, but are in the process of approaching equilibrium as they respond to the numerous factors that cause an imbalance between supply and demand.

Second, economic models rely on a number of assumptions required to simplify the real world. The objective is to develop a useful explanation without omitting factors crucial to achieving the purpose of the model.

Finally, theories explaining the general level of interest rates do just that: they focus on *the* rate of interest. Obviously, there are numerous interest rates, as Figure 5.1 illustrates, and many other interest rates are not shown there. As discussed in Chapter 4, differences in yields reflect term to maturity, default risk, taxability, and other characteristics of the underlying security. Still, compared over time, yields on securities tend to move in the same general direction. Although the correlation is not perfect, it is strong enough that economists are justified in focusing on *one* interest rate to build a model that explains movements in *all* rates.

LOANABLE FUNDS THEORY

Several compatible theories attempt to explain interest rate movements, although they are not equally useful for forecasting changes in rates. The *loanable funds theory* focuses on the amount of funds available for investment (the supply of loanable funds) and the amount of funds borrowers want (the demand for loanable funds). It is particularly adaptable for use in forecasting and, therefore, is the one on which the discussion concentrates.

The Supply of Loanable Funds

The loanable funds theory categorizes borrowers and lenders into four distinct types: households or consumers, businesses, governments, and the foreign sector. Governments supply almost no loanable funds, but it is important to understand the forces affecting the savings decisions of individuals, businesses, and foreign investors.

The Expected Rate of Return and the Decision to Save. Economic units always have several choices for disposition of funds. They can *spend* money on consumable goods; they can *save* money by investing in financial assets; or they can choose to hold, or *hoard,* money. The motivation for consumption is self-evident. But once the amount of consumption has been determined, there is still a choice between investing and holding money.

A key motivation for saving is the expected rate of return. Because investors have a *time preference for consumption,* they will reduce current consumption to save money only if they receive some reward for doing so. That reward is the expected rate of interest, which must always be positive to induce substantial postponement of consumption. Economists have also identified several additional motivations for savings, discussed shortly, which suggest that some funds will be saved even if the expected rate of interest is zero.

Holding or hoarding cash requires postponement of consumption but, unlike saving, does not provide a positive rate of return. So why does anyone hold cash balances? Three motivations have been identified: the *transactions demand,* the *precautionary demand,* and the *speculative demand.*[5] Because individuals and businesses cannot always assume that the timing of cash inflows and cash expenditures will coincide, they usually need to maintain ready access to cash to handle transactions. In addition, some cash will be held as a precaution against unforeseen contingencies. Neither of these motivations is tied to the expected rate of interest.

The third demand for money—the speculative motivation—*is* sensitive to expected interest rates and is therefore especially important in understanding the supply of loanable funds. In the face of high expected rates on financial assets, funds suppliers will reduce cash balances as they invest; with low expected rates of return, they will hold cash in anticipation of better opportunities later. Thus, the expected rate of return is important in the decision to reduce speculative cash balances, increasing the supply of loanable funds.

Other Factors Influencing Households. These relationships lead to a better, but still incomplete, understanding of the amount of funds available for borrowing. Factors other

---

[5]See John Maynard Keynes, *The General Theory of Employment, Interest and Money* (New York: Harcourt, Brace and World, 1936).

than interest rates affect the savings decision. For example, most people voluntarily save for future needs, either because they recognize that illness or other emergencies could jeopardize their financial position, or because they will need funds to support themselves after retirement. Other people may be involved in involuntary savings programs, such as social security or required retirement programs for state and federal employees.

The income of a household is also significant. Low-income families often spend all available funds on the basic necessities of life, leaving nothing for alternative uses. At the opposite end of the spectrum, high-income families may be unable to consume all available funds even if they want to, so they must invest regardless of the expected interest rate.

Other Factors Influencing Businesses.   Although businesses are usually demanders, they also supply some loanable funds. The primary sources of these funds are the depreciation tax shield and retained earnings from profitable past operations. Expected interest rates may have some bearing on the decisions of businesses to save by investing in financial assets,

but other important factors are potential real asset investments, the nature of the business enterprise, and the philosophy of the firm's managers and owners.

The Money Supply.   The supply of loanable funds is affected by changes in the total money supply (ΔM), which are influenced by Federal Reserve policy. An increase in the money supply makes more funds available for saving after consumption is satisfied.

The Foreign Sector.   Funds available domestically are also influenced by the behavior of foreign investors. The key factor influencing funds provided by the foreign sector is not simply the expected rate of interest in the United States, but the difference between that rate and the expected rate available in other countries.

The Supply of Loanable Funds Illustrated. The combined impact of these influences on the supply of loanable funds is shown in Figure 5.2. The supply curve (S_{LF}) is positively related to the expected rate of interest; that is, the quantity supplied is larger as the interest rate in-

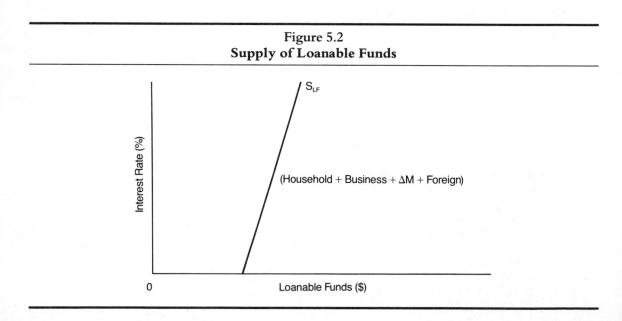

Figure 5.2
Supply of Loanable Funds

creases, but only moderately so. Even at a zero rate of interest, the supply of loanable funds exceeds zero because of nonrate factors influencing the savings decision.

The household sector is the only *net* supplier of loanable funds; that is, in a given period, households save more than they demand in the credit markets. For that reason, the borrowings of the household sector are usually netted against savings, and the S_{LF} curve is net of loanable funds demanded by households. Using this approach, households' savings equals income minus consumption minus household borrowing.

The Demand for Loanable Funds

The forces determining the demand for loanable funds—the total funds households, businesses, government units, and the foreign sector want to borrow—is tied much more closely to expected interest rates than is the supply.

The Effect of Expected Interest Rates on Borrowing. Most business borrowing is sensitive to expected interest rates. The funds raised by nonfinancial firms will depend upon their optimal budgets for investment in real assets. An optimal capital budget reflects a firm's investment opportunities. It occurs at the point where the marginal returns from investing in real assets are equal to the marginal costs of raising the funds, and the net present value of incremental investments is zero. At lower rates of interest, the capital budget will be larger, because a lower discount rate will be used for calculating net present value.[6] The investment opportunity schedule and the resulting demand

for loanable funds (D_{LF}) are inversely related to expected interest rates.

Noninterest Factors. As with the supply of loanable funds, noninterest factors motivate the demand for borrowing. For example, government units at the local, state, and federal level often must borrow regardless of interest rates. Governments borrow whenever they face budget deficits or when they need to finance major construction of roads or government buildings.[7] In fact, government demand for money is relatively inelastic with respect to interest rates.

Demand by the Foreign Sector. Foreign borrowers also seek funds in the domestic credit markets. Foreign business borrowers are motivated by the same factors affecting domestic firms, but differences between United States interest rates and those abroad will determine where borrowing actually occurs. Foreign governments also borrow in United States markets for the same reasons United States governmental units borrow. In recent years, in fact, the domestic demand for loanable funds by foreign governments has been substantial.[8]

The Demand for Loanable Funds Illustrated. The demand schedule D_{LF} for loanable funds in Figure 5.3 is for total business, government, and foreign borrowing. As noted earlier, households do borrow, but their demand is usually netted against the funds they

---

[6]The net present value (NPV) of a capital investment is defined as the discounted sum of future, after-tax cash flows less the present value of the initial cash outlay:

$$NPV = \sum_{t=1}^{N} \frac{C_t}{(1 + i)^t} - C_0$$

As i, the required rate of return, gets smaller, the NPV of a given project gets larger. Thus, at lower discount rates, more projects may be acceptable under this decision criterion. See the appendix to Chapter 4 for a more detailed discussion of discounted cash flows and Chapter 19 for more information on NPV.

[7]It can be argued that the relationship between borrowing and interest rates is not the same for state and local governments as it is for the federal government, under the assumption that the former are more flexible in spending decisions and may postpone some projects to be financed by borrowing if interest rates are high. In addition, some state or municipal statutes actually prohibit government units from borrowing if expected interest rates exceed a certain critical level. For further discussion, see Murray E. Polakoff, "Loanable Funds Theory and Interest Rate Determination," in *Financial Institutions and Markets,* 2d ed. Murray E. Polakoff and Thomas A. Durkin, eds. (Boston: Houghton Mifflin, 1981), p. 494.

[8]In recent years, the foreign sector as a whole has been a net supplier of funds to the U.S. credit market. In the past, however, it was a net borrower. See Board of Governors of the Federal Reserve System, *Flow of Funds Accounts, 1985:* QIV 1985, Tables 522-525.

Figure 5.3
Demand for Loanable Funds

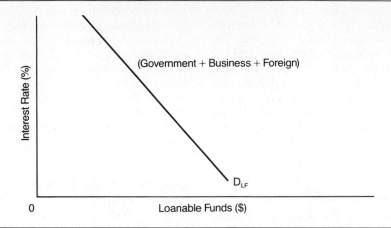

Figure 5.4
Equilibrium Rate of Interest

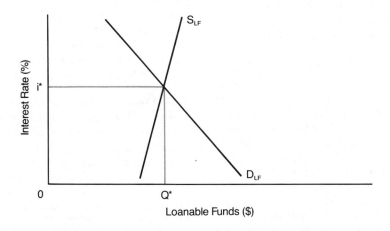

supply and is not included in the aggregate demand schedule.

The Rate of Interest

The loanable funds theory follows classical supply/demand analysis and explains the equilibrium rate of interest as the point of intersection of the supply and demand schedules. In Figure 5.4, the i* and Q* represent the equilibrium rate of interest and the equilibrium quantity of

loanable funds.[9] Many analysts use the loanable funds framework to explain and anticipate the movement of interest rates.

_____

[9]Actually, this equilibrium point may represent only temporary, rather than permanent, equilibrium. If the public needs to adjust cash balances by hoarding or dishoarding, further changes in the supply of loanable funds in the next period and a new rate of interest will result, especially if there is a shift in the money supply. However, few discussions of the loanable funds theory distinguish between temporary and permanent equilibrium.

LOANABLE FUNDS THEORY AND INTEREST RATE FORECASTING

Because the loanable funds theory explains the rate of interest as the point of intersection between supply and demand curves, political, economic, or behavioral factors shifting either curve are expected to result in a change in interest rates.

Changes in Supply or Demand

What forces could shift the supply or the demand curve? Government fiscal policy is one important force. The size of the federal budget deficit affects the demand for loanable funds. The more federal expenditures exceed federal revenues, the more frequently the government must enter the credit markets. Unless the change in government borrowing is offset by an equal and opposite change in demand for loanable funds by other sectors, the demand curve must shift, and the rate of interest will be higher. Furthermore, the supply curve may also be affected, as anticipated increases in government borrowing cause funds suppliers to increase their speculative balances in anticipation of higher interest rates.

Another fiscal policy, taxation, also has the potential for shifting the supply or demand curves. For example, an increase in corporate taxes reduces after-tax profits and thereby reduces the incentive for additional business spending. Smaller capital budgets lower the demand for borrowed funds.

Monetary policy, through its impact on the money supply, also affects interest rates. For example, an increase in the money supply relative to money demand leads to higher savings, shifting the supply curve to the right. This subsequently leads to a lower interest rate, at least in the short run.[10] Research suggests another monetary policy effect: Volatility in money growth may lead to higher interest rates because

it precipitates a reduction in the supply of loanable funds. High variability in monetary growth increases investors' uncertainty about future rates of return on financial assets. In response to that uncertainty, the suppliers of loanable funds will choose to hold more money, and the supply curve will shift to the left. Borrowers may also respond by reducing their demand for funds as they grow more uncertain about their borrowing costs.[11]

A shift in the demand curve could also result from a change in the state of the economy. As the economy moves into a recession, customer demand drops off, inventory surpluses accumulate, and expansion plans are postponed. Capital expenditures and the need for funds to support them decline.

Forecast of Future Interest Rates Illustrated

Suppose a recession is anticipated. The forecaster expects the quantity of funds required by the business community to decline in anticipation of reduced consumer demand. At the same time, estimates of lower federal tax revenues, as unemployment rises, lead to a forecast of larger deficits. The government sector, therefore, will demand more loanable funds.

In practice, an interest rate forecast requires detailed identification of all potential changes and their magnitude. As shown in Figure 5.5, if the increase in governments' demand for funds (ΔD_G) is greater than the decrease in demand by the business sector (ΔD_B), then aggregate demand will increase, the demand curve will shift to the right, and the new equilibrium interest rate (i') will be higher. If the decrease in business demand is greater than the increase in government demand ($\Delta D_B > \Delta D_G$), aggregate demand will decline, the demand curve will shift to the left, and the forecast will be for a new, lower equilibrium rate of interest. The supply curve also may shift as a result of changing conditions. This too would affect anticipated movements in interest rates.

---

[10]This effect is somewhat controversial; some analysts argue that growth in the money supply will lead to higher inflation, so that the long-term effect on interest rates is uncertain. The effects of inflation are examined in subsequent sections.

[11]Angelo Mascaro and Allan H. Meltzer, "Long and Short Term Interest Rates in a Risky World," *Journal of Monetary Economics* 12 (November 1983): 485-518.

Figure 5.5
Shifts in the Aggregate Demand Curve and Changes in the Equilibrium Rate of Interest

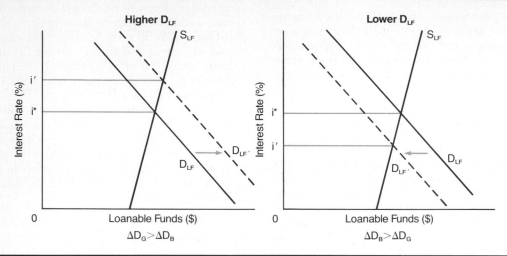

Professional Forecasts Based on the Loanable Funds Theory

The loanable funds framework is widely used by professional forecasters. They project interest rates based on an analysis of credit demand by sector and by type of security offered, as well as on the amount of loanable funds supplied and the types of securities investors will prefer. Resulting forecasts are crucial to managers who must choose what securities to issue or to purchase from among a variety with fixed and variable rates and different maturities.

Salomon Brothers' annual *Prospects for the Credit Markets* is perhaps the most widely quoted example of this approach to rate forecasting, but the American Council of Life Insurance, Morgan Guaranty Trust Company, Prudential Insurance Company, and others also make their forecasts available to financial intermediaries. Other analysts supply forecasts only on a proprietary basis. Large financial institutions often have staff economists who develop forecasts for managers. Managers of smaller firms gather information from many professional forecasters to assist in formulating asset/liability strategies appropriate for the interest rate environment.

A look at a specific forecast indicates that the loanable funds theory is the foundation for many interest rate predictions. *Fortune* magazine presents an annual forecast of a number of economic variables, including interest rates. The 1986 forecast drew several conclusions about the strength of the economy and interest rate movements during the year.[12]

Rate forecasts focused on *changes* in specific supply or demand factors, such as real business capital outlays, and the rate of personal savings. For example, the *Fortune* economists anticipated almost no change in business capital expenditures during 1986, and little growth in business inventories, except in the automobile industry. Another important influence on demand, the federal deficit, was expected to increase during

---

[12]Before 1987, a number of economic forecasts were compiled and published annually by the Federal Reserve Bank of Richmond. For more information on the *Fortune* predictions and other forecasts, see *Business Forecasts 1986* (Richmond, VA: Federal Reserve Bank of Richmond, 1986).

1986, although state and local governments were expected to maintain their previous borrowing levels.

The economists also predicted that consumer demand for loanable funds would be low, because many households had already borrowed heavily. Thus, households' supply of loanable funds was expected to remain steady or to increase. On balance, *Fortune* predicted a slight decline in interest rates for 1986. The economists, however, expected that by the end of the year, rising government deficits would stem the decline. The economists' emphasis was on forecasting changes in key economic variables, rather than actual levels, reflecting the orientation of the loanable funds theory toward *shifts* in the supply and demand functions as the key to interest rate movements.

INFLATION AND THE LEVEL OF INTEREST RATES

The rate of inflation has been of particular concern in recent years because of the volatility in and high levels of several different measures of price changes. Because anticipated changes in the purchasing power of the dollar affect investors' yields, inflation has a role in theories of the general level of interest rates.

For example, suppose a student's parents are saving for a graduation gift to be presented in one year. They are considering a one-year, $2,500 bank certificate of deposit in a federally insured institution, expected to yield 9 percent. The expected yield at the time of investment is the **nominal return.** If there is no inflation during the coming year, the *ex post* **real return** will also be 9 percent. But if the price level changes during the year, the *ex ante* yield of 9 percent will not be the *ex post* real return. Even if the depository institution pays the promised yield of 9 percent, the real rate of return will be lower because the purchasing power of the dollar has declined. The $2,500 principal repayment will not purchase the same quantity of goods as it would a year earlier, and the $225 in interest received will not be enough to make up the

difference and also provide an annual return of 9 percent.

Inflation and Financial Innovation

If inflation were uncommon, participants in the financial markets would pay relatively little attention to it in forecasting future events. Charts of historic movements in the Consumer Price Index (CPI) and the GNP Price Deflator in Figure 5.6 demonstrate, however, that neither borrowers nor lenders can afford to ignore price levels and their potential impact on returns and costs.[13] Many observers have noted, in fact, that the demand for new financial products in recent years can be attributed at least in part to expectations of inflation. Examples are adjustable-rate bonds and mortgages, zero-coupon bonds, and deposit accounts that pay variable rates of interest. An entirely new type of financial institution, the money market mutual fund, was created to allow investors to obtain yields that vary with daily changes in market conditions. Major deregulation of the financial system, via DIDMCA and the Garn-St Germain Act, permitted institutions to meet this inflation-driven demand.

More about Real and Nominal Rates

It seems reasonable to assume that if inflation is anticipated during the coming year, lenders will build in some protection against the decline in purchasing power of their dollars by increasing their required *ex ante* rate of return. The size of the premium for expected inflation and the

---

[13]There is no general agreement on how to measure inflation. The most widely used measures are the Consumer Price Index (CPI), the Producer Price Index (PPI), and the implicit GNP Price Deflator. The first two track changes in the price level of "market baskets" of goods; the third attempts to reflect price changes in all components of the GNP. A good discussion of the PPI and the GNP Price Deflator is in William H. Wallace and William E. Cullison, *Measuring Price Changes,* 4th ed. (Richmond, VA: Federal Reserve Bank, 1979). For a description of the current components of the CPI, which has been undergoing revisions since 1981, see the monthly issues of "The CPI Detailed Report," U.S. Department of Labor, Bureau of Labor Statistics.

Figure 5.6
Comprehensive Price Measures: CPI and GNP Price Deflator[a]

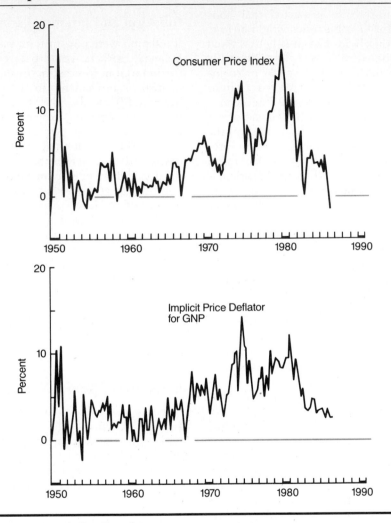

[a]Annualized quarterly rate, seasonally adjusted.

Source: Board of Governors of the Federal Reserve System, *1986 Historical Chart Book.*

way it is determined have been the subjects of much theoretical and empirical investigation. Before examining those efforts, however, the meaning of the terms real and nominal must be further clarified. The real rate of interest is the rate of exchange between present and future *goods,* while the rate of exchange between present and future *dollars* is the nominal rate of in-terest. In the absence of inflation, real and nominal rates are equal.[14]

---

[14]This discussion draws upon the work of G. J. Santoni and Courtenay C. Stone, "Navigating through the Inter-est Rate Morass: Some Basic Principles," *Economic Review,* Federal Reserve Bank of St. Louis 63 (March 1981): 11–18.

For example, suppose the real rate of interest is 12 percent. The price of a music video is $10 and is not expected to change for at least one year. An owner of 100 tapes is considering including them in a transaction. She could sell them today for $1,000 and invest the money at 12 percent, accumulating $1,120 by the end of the year. On the other hand, she could lend the 100 tapes to someone today, on the condition that she will be repaid with 112 tapes at the end of the year. The yield on the exchange of both dollars and goods would be 12 percent; in other words, the nominal and the real rates of interest would be equal. The owner of the tapes will be equally well off in one year, regardless of which arrangement she makes:

$$\frac{\$1,120 - \$1,000}{\$1,000} = \begin{array}{l} 12\% \text{ on exchange of} \\ \text{dollars for dollars} \end{array}$$

$$\frac{112 \text{ tapes} - 100 \text{ tapes}}{100 \text{ tapes}} = \begin{array}{l} 12\% \text{ on exchange of} \\ \text{goods for goods} \end{array}$$

The purchasing power of the two transactions is the same, because the dollar-for-dollar exchange permits the lender to purchase $1,120/$10 = 112 videotapes in one year, the same number she would have if she simply exchanged tapes directly.

But suppose the price of videotapes is expected to rise by 2 percent during the year, to $10.20. If this price change is accurately foreseen before any exchanges occur, a 12 percent nominal interest rate will no longer be adequate to protect lenders' purchasing power. The exchange of dollars would still result in $1,120 at the end of the year, but that amount would no longer be the equivalent to 112 videotapes, since the price of 112 tapes would be 112 × ($10 × 1.02) = $1,142 by the end of one year.

Compared to a 12 percent return on the exchange of goods, the return on the exchange of dollars will be lower. The 112 tapes received in a tape-for-tape exchange exceed the 110 tapes ($1,120/$10.20) that could be purchased in one year if dollars were exchanged for dollars at a 12 percent nominal rate. In fact, to equate the return on the two media of exchange, the nominal rate must be slightly over 14 percent:

$$\frac{\$1,142 - \$1,000}{\$1,000} = \begin{array}{l} 14.2\% \text{ nominal rate} \\ \text{required to purchase} \\ 112 \text{ tapes in one year} \end{array}$$

The nominal rate of interest must be equal to the real rate *plus* a premium for expected inflation if the lender is to be equally well off regardless of which transaction she chooses. Furthermore, if the 2 percent price change is not anticipated, and the nominal rate is not adjusted, the realized *ex post* return on a dollar-for-dollar exchange will be less than 12 percent. Because the $1,120 received at the end of the year will now purchase only 110 videotapes, the *ex post* return, adjusting for the loss of purchasing power, is 10 percent:

$$\frac{110 - 100}{100} = 10\%$$

The Fisher Effect

Although the basic principles of this real/nominal effect were first suggested in the 18th century, a 20th-century economist, Irving Fisher, is widely regarded as laying the foundation for the study of the relationship between interest rates and expected inflation.[15] That relationship, now frequently called the **Fisher effect,** is summarized as follows: The nominal rate of interest reflects the real rate of interest and a premium based on the *expected* rate of inflation.[16] Stated as an equation:

---

[15]For a discussion of the development of the theory of real and nominal rates, including Fisher's forerunners and his own contributions, see Thomas M. Humphrey, "The Early History of the Real/Nominal Interest Rate Relationship," *Economic Review,* Federal Reserve Bank of Richmond 69 (May/June 1983): 2-10.

[16]Economists have studied several relationships between yields and price levels. Fisher was interested in the relationship between security yields and *changes* in the price level. Another researcher, A. H. Gibson, studied the relationship between the actual level of prices and yields, noting that when prices are relatively high, so are interest rates, and when prices are low, yields also tend to be low. No conclusion has been reached about whether the Gibson relation is consistent or in conflict with the Fisher effect. See A. H. Gibson, "The Future Course of High Class Investment Values," *Bankers Magazine* (London) 115

(5.1) $1 + i_N = (1 + i_R)[1 + E(P)]$

$1 + i_N = 1 + i_R + E(P) + i_R E(P)$

$i_N = i_R + E(P) + i_R E(P)$

where: i_N = nominal rate;

i_R = real rate;

$E(P)$ = *expected* rate of inflation.

When the Fisher theory is applied to the problem of deciding on a nominal rate for the videotape transaction under the expectation of 2 percent inflation, the result, using Equation 5.1, is 14.2 percent, the same rate determined earlier:

$1 + i_N = (1 + 0.12)(1 + 0.02)$

$i_N = 1.142 - 1 = 14.2\%$

Usually, the convention of eliminating the cross-product term, $i_R \times E(P)$, is followed, and the nominal rate is simply expressed as the sum of the real rate and the expected rate of inflation:

(5.2) $i_N = i_R + E(P)$

$= 0.12 + 0.02 = 14\%$

The convention is justified by the argument that the cross-product term, especially for low values of i_R and $E(P)$, is so small that it does not make a material difference in the rate estimate. When the cross-product term is ignored, there is a one-to-one relationship between expected inflation and the amount by which the nominal rate exceeds the real rate.

Expected Inflation and the Loanable Funds Theory

Changes in nominal interest rates can be examined in the context of the loanable funds theory.

(January 1923): 15-34; Robert J. Shiller and Jeremy J. Siegel, "The Gibson Paradox and Historical Movements in Real Interest Rates," *Journal of Political Economy* 85 (October 1977): 891-907; and John H. Wood and Norma L. Wood, *Financial Markets* (San Diego, CA: Harcourt Brace Jovanovich, 1985): 579-586.

An anticipated increase in price levels means that savers, the suppliers of loanable funds, will require a higher nominal rate of return $[i_R + E(P)]$ at every quantity of loanable funds supplied. This change means that the original curve S_{LF} must shift to the left, to $S_{LF'}$. At the same time, however, borrowers, the demanders of loanable funds, are willing to pay the higher nominal rate, realizing that they will be repaying their loans in "cheaper dollars," so the demand curve D_{LF} shifts up to $D_{LF'}$.

The result is a new point of intersection, at a higher nominal rate of interest. The increase in nominal interest rates, or the inflationary premium, is equal to the expected rate of inflation, as shown in Figure 5.7. A key point is that the *real* rate of interest remains unchanged. The Fisher theory implicitly assumes that, even in the face of inflationary expectations, the real rate, or the rate at which goods can be exchanged for goods, is unaffected.

EVALUATION OF THE FISHER THEORY

Fisher's theory is intuitively appealing and widely cited. During the last decade, as inflation approached a modern peak of 13.6 percent in 1980 and T-bill yields were on their way to levels as high as 15.51 percent in the summer of 1981, the link between the two was emphasized even more than usual. Without actual reference to the Fisher theory, Federal Reserve officials publicly blamed high interest rates on inflation. Chairman Paul Volcker stated, "When the money supply is brought clearly under control and expectations of inflation dissipate, interest rates will tend to decline." His predecessor G. William Miller made a similar reference, stating, " . . . the recent and expected inflation also has been an extremely important factor underlying the increase in interest rates . . . "[17]

[17]William N. Cox III, "Interest Rates and Inflation: What Drives What?" *Economic Review,* Federal Reserve Bank of Atlanta 65 (May/June 1980): 20-23.

Figure 5.7
Inflation and the Equilibrium Rate of Interest

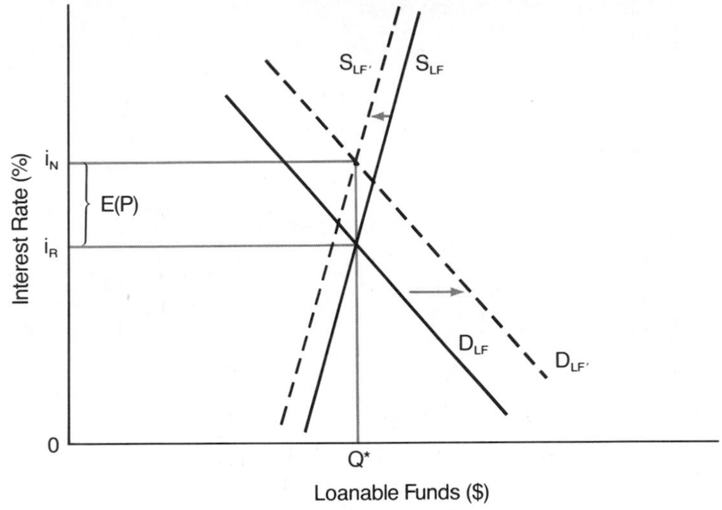

Historical Relationships

Empirical research on past interest rate movements and the rate of inflation has also been used to support the Fisher theory. Tracking historical changes in a rate of inflation measure such as the CPI against an interest rate measure almost always results in a positive correlation. For example, during the period 1966-1979, the correlation coefficient between the prime rate and the GNP Price Deflator was .70; when the commercial paper rate was used as the measure of interest rates, the correlation was .81.[18] A graphical comparison of these data over time, provided in Figure 5.8, emphasizes those findings. Although the relationship has been stronger in some periods than others, it encourages belief in the Fisher effect.

Although findings such as these are interesting, they do not prove the Fisher theory. First, observed correlation does not imply cau-

sality. Some unknown factor or factors could be affecting both interest rates and inflation in a similar fashion, so that they appear to be related to one another but are actually both related to other things. In addition, these findings focus on historical inflation rates, while the Fisher effect addresses expected inflation rates.

Measurement Problems

Efforts to validate the hypothesized relationship are confounded by several obstacles. The first is the accurate measurement of variables in the Fisher equation. Neither the real rate of interest nor the expected rate of inflation is empirically observable; both must be estimated in some manner, because one can observe only the nominal rate of interest at any time.

Proxy measurements for expected inflation have often been based on historical values. Fisher himself was the first in a long line of investigators. One of his conclusions was that investors' expectations of inflation are often in-

[18]Cox, "Interest Rates and Inflation," p. 22.

Figure 5.8
Inflation and Interest Rates: Historical Relationships

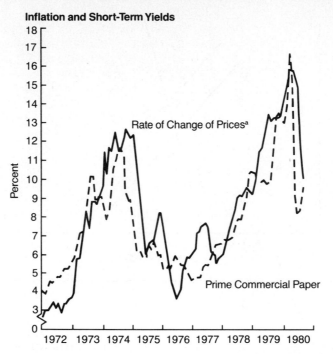

Inflation and Short-Term Yields

[a]Compounded annual rates of change in the consumer price index (seasonally adjusted) over the previous 6 months.

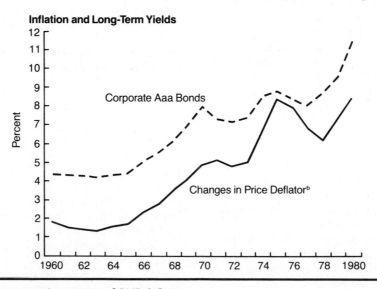

Inflation and Long-Term Yields

[b]Rate of change in 3-year moving average of GNP deflator.

Source: Norman N. Bowsher, "Rise and Fall of Interest Rates," *Review,* Federal Reserve Bank of St. Louis 62 (August/September 1980): 18–19.

accurate. Using historical data, Fisher calculated *ex post* real rates of return by subtracting *ex post* inflation rates from nominal rates:

(5.3) $I_R = i_N - P$

where: I_R = *ex post* real rate;
  P = *ex post* rate of inflation

Fisher found that *ex post* real rates were not stable. Because he believed that *ex ante* real rates were constant, he interpreted fluctuations in *ex post* real rates to mean that the markets' inflationary expectations were consistently incorrect. In later tests, he concluded that inflation premiums the markets imposed were strongly influenced by past rates of inflation, and that past price changes were inadequate estimates of future inflation.[19]

Recent *ex post* analyses confirm that, if the Fisher theory is true, inaccurate inflationary expectations persist. For example, Figure 5.9 shows that over the period 1955-1985, the *ex post* real rate was sometimes negative. This means that nominal rates were less than actual rates of inflation in some years.

Based on Fisher's early conclusions, researchers have focused on better ways of estimating the *ex ante* real rate and inflationary expectations. Estimates of real rates have included yields on Treasury bills, high-grade corporate bonds, and equity securities. Actual figures or lagged averages of one of several inflation measures such as the Consumer Price Index or the GNP Price Deflator have been used to estimate the inflationary premium. An alternative measure of inflationary expectations is a compilation of experts' forecasts of inflation, sometimes published in major newspapers. Not surprisingly, there is no uniform agreement on measurement or methodology, and the research findings are contradictory.[20]

Stability of the Real Rate

Another concern about the Fisher theory is its assumption that the real rate itself is unaffected by the expected rate of inflation and therefore remains stable. Research attention has focused increasingly on that assumption. Some economists argue that inflationary expectations affect not only the nominal rate but also the real rate. They suggest that an increase in inflationary expectations will cause people to change their asset holdings, reducing the amount of cash held because of an expected decline in its purchasing power, and increasing the amount of interest-bearing assets. This adjustment will cause the supply curve to shift to the *right* (to $S_{LF'}$), indicating more funds available. The result, shown in Figure 5.10, is that the real rate of interest falls from i_R to i_R'. This theory contrasts with the traditional result shown in Figure 5.7, where the supply of loanable funds was presumed to be reduced when inflation is expected.[21]

According to this theory, if Equation 5.1 or 5.2 is used to estimate the new nominal rate, expected inflation would be added to this lower real rate, not to the original one. The nominal rate of interest thus changes less than the rate of expected inflation, because the inflationary premium is partially offset by a lower real rate of interest.

The Tax Effect

Another complicating factor is income taxes, which are levied on nominal rather than real returns. Several researchers argue that changes in inflationary expectations cause investors to

[19]A review of Fisher's initial empirical research is provided in Humphrey, "The Early History of the Real/Nominal Interest Rate Relationship."

[20]Examples of attempts to measure inflationary expectations and/or the real rate can be found in Eugene A. Fama, "Short-Term Interest Rates as Predictors of Inflation," *American Economic Review* 65 (June 1975): 269-282;

John A. Carlson, "Short-Term Interest Rates as Predictors of Inflation: Comment," *American Economic Review* 67 (June 1977): 469-475; Donald J. Mullineaux and Aris Protopapadakis, "Revealing Real Interest Rates: Let the Market Do It," *Business Review,* Federal Reserve Bank of Philadelphia (March/April 1984), pp. 3-8; and David C. Leonard and Michael E. Solt, "Recent Evidence on the Accuracy and Rationality of Popular Inflation Forecasts," *Journal of Financial Research* 9 (Winter 1986): 281-290.

[21]Robert Mundell, "Inflation and Real Interest," *Journal of Political Economy* 71 (June 1963): 280-283; James Tobin, "Money and Economic Growth," *Econometrica* 33 (October 1965): 671-684.

Figure 5.9
Ex Post Real Interest Rates: 1955–1985

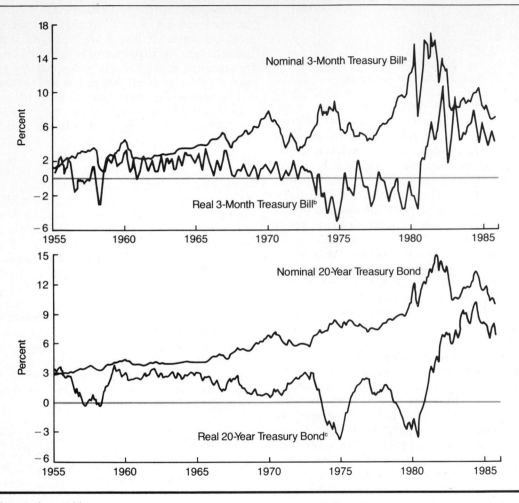

[a]Bond-equivalent yield.
[b]Real rate is a 3-month moving average estimated using the 3-month growth rate of CPI in period immediately prior.
[c]Real rate was estimated using 12-month growth rate of CPI in period immediately prior.

Source: Federal Reserve Bank of Cleveland, *Economic Trends* (January 1986), p. 20.

act to protect *after-tax* real returns.[22] For example, suppose the before-tax *ex ante* real rate is 4

---

[22]Key proponents of the tax effect are Michael R. Darby, "The Financial and Tax Effects of Monetary Policy on Interest Rates," *Economic Inquiry* 13 (June 1975): 266–276; and Martin Feldstein, "Inflation, Income Taxes and the

Rate of Interest: A Theoretical Analysis," *American Economic Review* 66 (December 1976): 809–820.

A discussion of the potential impact of changing inflationary expectations on the real rate and the subsequent tax effects is provided in A. Steven Holland, "Real Interest Rates: What Accounts for Their Recent Rise?" *Review,* Federal Reserve Bank of St. Louis 66 (December 1984): 18–29.

Figure 5.10
Inflationary Expectations and the Real Rate of Interest

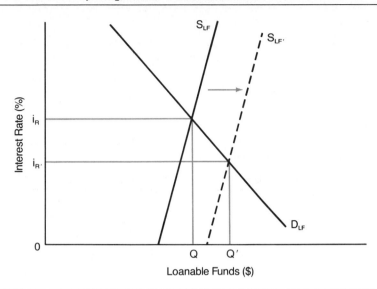

percent. For an investor in the 28 percent marginal tax bracket, an after-tax real rate of 4% × (1 − 0.28) = 2.88% would be expected in the absence of inflation.

Now suppose inflation is expected to be 4 percent. The Fisher theory would project nominal rates at 8 percent. If nominal yields rise only to that level, however, the expected real after-tax return would fall to [8% × (1 − 0.28)] − 4% = 1.76%. This tax effect exerts a new upward pressure on the nominal rate, and suggests that the change in nominal yields will actually be greater than that predicted by Fisher. To protect after-tax real returns to an investor with a 28 percent tax rate (t), the nominal yield must increase by E(P)/(1 − t):

(5.4) $i_N = i_R + [E(P)/(1 - t)]$

$i_N = 4\% + [4\%/(1 - 0.28)] = 9.56\%$

At this nominal rate, the after-tax real return would be [9.56% × (1 − 0.28)] − 4% =

2.88%, as the investor expected in the absence of inflation.[23]

The Debate Continues

Several researchers have supported the one-for-one relationship and the stable real rate of interest of the Fisher hypothesis. In contrast, other studies have concluded that inflationary expectations have a weaker impact; estimates of the effect of a one-percent change in inflationary expectations on the nominal rate range from 0.65 percent to 0.9 percent. Finally, the impact of taxes suggests that inflation has more than a one-for-one impact on nominal rates. Despite the general agreement that expected inflation affects interest rates, many questions remain

[23]Some portions of the personal tax code have been rewritten to lessen the impact of inflation. The inflation adjustments, however, are based on *ex post* rather than *ex ante* inflation rates. Thus, the problem of protecting *ex ante* after-tax yields remains.

Figure 5.11
Responses of Market Participants to Changes in Expected Inflation

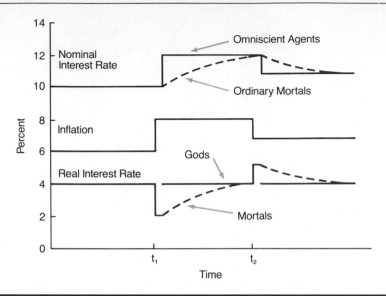

Source: John H. Wood, "Interest Rates and Inflation: An Old and Unexplained Relationship," *Economic Review,* Federal Reserve Bank of Dallas (January 1983), p. 21.

about how to measure that effect, and whether it can be estimated for forecasting purposes.[24]

One economist has provided an interesting graphical description of the problem. In a world of perfect foresight where people are "omnis-

---

[24]For further details, see Eugene F. Fama, "Short-Term Interest Rates as Predictors of Inflation"; G. J. Santoni and Courtenay Stone, "What Really Happened to Interest Rates?" *Economic Review,* Federal Reserve Bank of St. Louis 63 (November 1981): 3-14. Contrasting views are found in William P. Yohe and Denis Karnosky, "Interest Rates and Price Level Changes, 1952-1969," *Review,* Federal Reserve Bank of St. Louis 51 (December 1969): 18-39; and Benjamin Friedman, "Price Inflation, Portfolio Choice and Nominal Interest Rates," *American Economic Review* 70 (March 1980): 32-48. Reviews of several studies are found in Herbert Taylor, "Interest Rates: How Much Does Expected Inflation Matter?" *Business Review,* Federal Reserve Bank of Philadelphia (July/August 1982): 3-12; John H. Wood, "Interest Rates and Inflation," *Economic Perpectives,* Federal Reserve Bank of Chicago 5 (May/June 1981): 3-12; and James Van Horne, *Financial Market Rates and Flows* 2d ed. (Englewood Cliffs, NJ: Prentice-Hall, 1984).

cient agents" and the real rate of interest is stable, the nominal rate would exactly and immediately respond at t_1 and t_2 to changes in inflation, adjustments represented by the solid lines in Figure 5.11. But with "ordinary mortals," the adjustment is less exact and slower, as represented by the dotted lines. So nominal rates established by ordinary mortals will differ from those that would be established in markets full of omniscient agents. And, although gods would earn a constant real rate, the real rate mortals earn is not constant.

ACCURACY OF INTEREST RATE FORECASTING

As the opening paragraphs to this chapter suggest, the life of a forecaster of interest rates and inflation is difficult. Many variables must be considered before rates are predicted, and each variable is a possible source of error. Another problem is that forecasters cannot stop with a prediction of *the* rate of interest, but are expected to estimate several different rates. At commercial banks, movements in T-bill and negotiable CD rates are of great concern. At a savings institution, trends in mortgage rates are just as crucial. Managers of insurance companies are interested in long-term bond yields, as are mutual fund and pension fund managers. Finance company managers focus on interest rates on consumer credit and commercial paper.

Obtaining all relevant information and isolating supply/demand factors relevant in a particular market are ongoing challenges. Large financial institutions may have their own economics departments, while smaller firms often subscribe to professional forecasting services. Some institutions do both to compare the predictions made by internal and external forecasters.

The underlying problem with forecasting is that no matter how well someone understands the factors that cause interest rates to move, such as supply, demand, and expected inflation, predicting just when and in what magnitude those factors will change is virtually impossible. As a result, forecasts are often less than accurate.[25] For the past several years, *Institutional Investor* (*II*) has evaluated the forecasts of 50 well-known economists. After calculating the difference between the economists' predictions of various rates for a future date and actual rates as of that date, the publication ranks the economists in order of accuracy. Recent results provide excellent examples of the difficulties inherent in the profession. The forecaster who ranked number 1 on forecasts of four key rates

in 1983 was the same individual who ranked *last* on those rate predictions in 1982, and the best forecaster in 1982 fell to 36th place in 1983. The economists' difficulties continued in subsequent years; the 1986 report identified yet another forecaster for its "most-accurate" award—someone who had earned 39th place the year before.[26]

Another interesting aspect of the *II* studies is the information economists provide about the basis of their rate predictions. Their statements reveal a heavy reliance on the loanable funds and Fisher theories. For example, the top two forecasters in the 1985 survey based their prediction for lower interest rates on expectations of a noninflationary economic climate. The third-ranked economist specifically predicated his forecast on a decline in the demand for funds.

The difficulties professional forecasters experience explain why even sophisticated forecasting techniques must be accompanied by a variety of strategies for managing interest rate risk. Whether a financial institution generates its own forecasts or uses the opinions of other experts, the predictions are often wrong. This element of uncertainty presents managers with several dilemmas. First, they must decide whether to commit the entire institutional strategy to one interest rate scenario, or whether to adapt asset and liability accounts on an individual basis. For example, in response to a forecast of rising rates, should an S&L make variable-rate loans; offer long-term, fixed-rate deposits; and shorten the maturity of its securities portfolio, all at the same time? Or should the new policies affect only a certain proportion of the loan portfolio? These choices in turn suggest a second key decision—the extent to which asset/liability policies will involve hedging, or protective strategies to reduce the impact of inaccurate forecasts. This alternative for managing interest rate risk is explored in detail in chapters to follow.

---

[25]The perils of economic forecasting are discussed in more detail in Daniel T. Van Dyke, "Why Economists Make Mistakes," *Bankers Magazine* 169 (May/June 1986): 69-75. A recent study at the Federal Reserve Bank of Cleveland showed that households' forecasts of inflation are more accurate than forecasts of professional economists. See Michael F. Bryan and William T. Gavin, "Comparing Inflation Expectations of Households and Economists: Is a Little Knowledge a Dangerous Thing?" *Economic Review,* Federal Reserve Bank of Cleveland (Quarter 3 1986), pp. 14-19.

[26]Tina Aridas, "The Economists' Batting Averages," *Institutional Investor* 17 (March 1983): 251-253; Tina Aridas, "The Economists' Batting Averages," *Institutional Investor* 19 (March 1985): 299-304; Tina Aridas, "The Economists' Batting Averages," *Institutional Investor* 20 (March 1986): 253-256.

SUMMARY

Because the net interest margin is the key variable in asset/liability management, understanding the behavior of interest rates is important. This chapter discusses the general level of interest rates. Because all rates tend to move in the same direction, a forecast for the general level is a starting point for estimating future rates on specific assets and liabilities.

The most widely used explanation for movements in the general level of interest rates is the loanable funds theory, based on the motivations for saving and borrowing. Although other factors also affect the decision, the dollar amount individuals are willing to save is positively related to interest rates, and the demand for borrowing is inversely related to interest rates. The equilibrium general level of interest rates is determined by the intersection of the supply and demand curves for loanable funds.

Economists have also hypothesized that expected inflation influences the general level of interest rates. In fact, the Fisher effect suggests that nominal market rates of interest reflect a real rate of interest plus a premium equal to the expected rate of inflation. Although this theory is difficult to validate empirically, most researchers agree that inflationary expectations affect the general level of rates.

Because they attempt to predict an unknown future, interest rate forecasts, no matter how carefully made, are subject to error. So, in addition to theories, financial institution managers must be aware of techniques to minimize the impact of forecast errors on the institution's performance.

Questions

1. Characterize the interest rate environment over the last three years. In general, how have the level and volatility of interest rates affected financial institution management?

2. In what three ways can economic units use their funds? What are the motives for holding money, and how are they related to interest rates?

3. Why is the consumer sector considered a net supplier of loanable funds? What noninterest motives cause households to save?

4. Why is the federal government's demand for loanable funds relatively inelastic with respect to interest rates?

5. How is the business sector's demand for loanable funds related to interest rates? Why? What will happen to the demand curve for loanable funds if corporate taxes are lowered? Why?

6. How is the loanable funds theory used to forecast movements in interest rates? Find at least two current references to its use in a business newspaper or periodical. What aspects of the theory seem to be most important to professional forecasters?

7. Distinguish between the nominal rate and the real rate of interest. How does inflation affect the real rate of return to investors? How are real rates of return affected by taxes?

8. Could the *ex ante* real rate of return to an investor be negative? Could the *ex post* real rate be negative? Explain.

9. Explain Fisher's theory of the relationship between the nominal rate of interest and expected inflation. Is the following statement true or false? Why? A 0.9 correlation between *ex post* T-bill rates and *ex post* inflation proves that the Fisher theory is true.

10. Explain the controversy over Fisher's belief that the *ex ante* real rate of interest is constant.

11. Using the CPI as the measure of inflation, what was the *ex post* real rate of return on three-month T-bills over a recent period? Using a current forecast of inflation, determine the current *ex ante* real rate on three-month T-bills.

Problems

1. Graph the supply and demand curves for loanable funds. What is meant by the equilibrium rate of interest?

2. Using the graph from Problem 1, show what will happen if government borrowing increases while the demand for loanable funds by other sectors remains constant.

3.

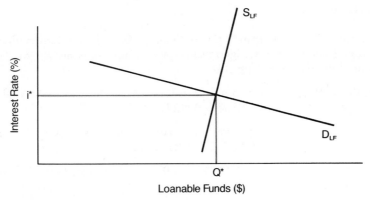

If the demand for loanable funds by the business sector decreases because of a recession, and the demand for loanable funds by the government increases, but by a smaller amount, how will the equilibrium interest rate be affected? Show the change on the graph pictured here.

4. Within the framework of the loanable funds theory, illustrate how inflation affects the equilibrium rate of interest.

5. Suppose your grandparents have just given you a gift of ten antique gold coins. The coins have a market value of $5,000 ($500 each). You have two alternatives: You could sell them, and invest the money in a bank CD earning 10 percent annually. Or a dealer has offered to take the gold coins now, in exchange for the return of 11 coins at the end of one year.
   a. Compare the rate of return on the two alternatives.
   b. Suppose you have perfect foresight, and know that the price of the coins will rise to $520 by the end of the year. Again compare the returns available on the two investments. Using the Fisher theory, explain the change in the nominal rate that should occur, given the temporary divergence in the real and nominal rates.

6. If the real rate of interest is 10 percent and investors expect a 6 percent inflation rate, what nominal rate of interest will investors demand? Use the original statement of the Fisher equation (Equation 5.1). For an investor in the 28 percent tax bracket, what will be the after-tax real return?

7. An investor requires a real return before taxes of 12 percent, anticipates an inflation rate of 3 percent, and invests in securities with a nominal rate of 15 percent. If the after-tax real return to the investor is actually only 4.5 percent, what was the *ex post* rate of inflation? Assume a 28 percent tax rate.

8.   In 1984, the First National City Bank of Houston began offering a 30-year CD with an annual return indexed to inflation. The rate offered is the annual percentage increase in the CPI, plus 4 percent. Suppose you are in the 28 percent marginal tax bracket and believe that a 3 percent real return after taxes is required. Suppose also that the annual inflation rate last year was 5 percent, so this year's annual rate on a CD investment in the Houston bank is set at 9 percent. Show the after-tax real return you would earn, assuming the inflation rate stays at 5 percent. What *ex ante* nominal rate should you require to keep your after-tax real yield at 3 percent?

Selected References

Bryan, Michael F., and William T. Gavin. "Comparing Inflation Expectations of Households and Economists: Is a Little Knowledge a Dangerous Thing?" *Economic Review* (Federal Reserve Bank of Cleveland) (Quarter 3 1986), pp. 14-19.

Clarida, Richard D., and Benjamin M. Friedman. "The Behavior of U.S. Short-Term Interest Rates since October 1979." *Journal of Finance* 39 (July 1984): 671-682.

Cox, William N. III. "Interest Rates and Inflation: What Drives What?" *Economic Review* (Federal Reserve Bank of Atlanta) 65 (May/June 1980): 20-23.

Darby, Michael R. "The Financial and Tax Effects of Monetary Policy on Interest Rates." *Economic Inquiry* 13 (June 1975): 266-276.

Fama, Eugene A. "Short-Term Interest Rates as Predictors of Inflation." *American Economic Review* 65 (June 1975): 269-282.

Feldstein, Martin. "Inflation, Income Taxes and the Rate of Interest: A Theoretical Analysis." *American Economic Review* 66 (December 1976): 809-820.

Fisher, Irving. *The Theory of Interest.* New York: Macmillan, 1930.

Friedman, Benjamin. "Price Inflation, Portfolio Choice and Nominal Interest Rates." *American Economic Review* 70 (March 1980): 32-48.

Humphrey, Thomas M. "The Early History of the Real/Nominal Interest Rate Relationship." *Economic Review* (Federal Reserve Bank of Richmond) 69 (May/June 1983): 2-10.

Keynes, John Maynard. *The General Theory of Employment, Interest, and Money.* New York: Harcourt, Brace, and World, 1936.

Mascaro, Angelo, and Allen H. Meltzer. "Long- and Short-Term Interest Rates in a Risky World." *Journal of Monetary Economics* 12 (November 1983): 485-518.

Mullineaux, Donald J., and Aris Protopapadakis. "Revealing Real Interest Rates: Let the Market Do It." *Business Review* (Federal Reserve Bank of Philadelphia) (March/April 1984), pp. 3-8.

Mundell, Robert. "Inflation and Real Interest." *Journal of Political Economy* 71 (June 1963): 280-283.

Polakoff, Murray E. "Loanable Funds Theory and Interest Rate Determination." In *Financial Institutions and Markets,* 2d ed. Edited by Murray E. Polakoff and Thomas A. Durkin. Boston: Houghton Mifflin, 1981, pp. 483-510.

Rosenblum, Harvey, and Steven Strongin. "Interest Rate Volatility in Historical Perspective." *Economic Perspectives* (Federal Reserve Bank of Chicago) 7 (January/February 1983): 10-19.

Santoni, G. J., and Courtenay C. Stone. "Navigating Through the Interest Rate Morass: Some Basic Principles." *Economic Review* (Federal Reserve Bank of St. Louis) 63 (March 1981): 11-18.

Taylor, Herbert. "Interest Rates: How Much Does Expected Inflation Matter?" *Business Review* (Federal Reserve Bank of Philadelphia) (July/August 1982), pp. 3-12.

Van Horne, James C. *Financial Market Rates and Flows*. 2d ed. Englewood Cliffs, NJ: Prentice-Hall, 1984.

Wood, John H. "Interest Rates and Inflation." *Economic Perspectives* (Federal Reserve Bank of Chicago) 5 (May/June 1981): 3-12.

Chapter 6

THE TERM STRUCTURE OF INTEREST RATES

. . . the weakest economic and financial units are unlikely to be able to withstand even the current level and structure of interest rates for more than another couple of months.

Anonymous Report in *Bank Credit Analyst* (1980)

D AVID M. Jones, Vice President and Chief Economist of Aubrey G. Lanston & Company, was called to testify before the Senate Banking Committee in April 1981. The senators were concerned about the severe profitability problems facing the savings and loan industry. They were not comforted by Mr. Jones's remarks, because he forecast an even more perilous future for many of the nation's thrifts. He cited expectations of inflation, a tight money supply, and a prevailing "inverted yield curve" as the culprits.[1]

The previous chapter points to the importance of understanding how supply and demand for credit and inflationary expectations affect the general level of interest rates. Mr. Jones's forecast for 1981, as well as the opening quotation, point to another important influence on institutional performance—the *term structure of interest rates,* often called the *yield curve.* All else equal, the term structure of interest rates is the relationship, at a specific time, between yields on securities and their maturities. For example, yields on 182-day T-bills almost always differ from those on 25-year T-bonds.

Just as there are theories explaining how the general level of interest rates is determined, there are also theories explaining the term structure. Because financial institutions simulta-

---

[1]Andrew A. Leckey, "S&Ls Squirming in a Tight Spot," *Chicago Sun-Times,* April 1981, pp. 53, 55.

neously participate in the markets for securities of many different maturities, theories of the term structure can assist managers in making decisions that commonly confront them. Some of these decisions are illustrated later in the chapter.

THE TERM STRUCTURE DEFINED: A CLOSER LOOK

As noted, the term structure of interest rates is the relationship between security yields and maturities, *all else equal.* The "all else equal" is an important qualifying phrase. To isolate the impact of maturity on yield, one must remove potential effects of other factors. Comparing a bank's existing yields on a 6-month Treasury bill and a 20-year loan to a developing nation would say little about the impact of maturity on yields but a great deal about default risk. It would also be wrong to compare a T-bill yield to the tax-exempt yield on bonds of the City of Dallas, or to compare General Motors' 90-day commercial paper rate with the yield on its preferred stock and then draw conclusions about the effect of maturity on expected return.

Identifying the Existing Term Structure

It is generally agreed that comparing yields on Treasury securities of different maturities is the best way to control for extraneous factors. Existing term structures are obtained by observing *spot rates*—current market yields—on Treasury bills, notes, and bonds. A daily listing of yields and maturities is found in the "Treasury Issues" column of major newspapers; one is shown in Figure 6.1. The few Treasury issues that are callable or have special estate tax features, called flower bonds, must be eliminated. The 3½ percent bond maturing in 1998, yielding 4.08 percent, and highlighted in the figure, is one such example. Standardized calculations must be used so that bank discount yields are not erroneously compared to bond-equivalent yields.[2]

A Historical Look at Term Structures

Just as the general level of interest rates differs over time, so does the term structure. In August 1981, for example, yields on short-term Treasury securities exceeded those on long-term Treasuries. A plot of this relationship is shown in Figure 6.2. A yield curve with this shape is often described as *downward-sloping* or *inverted,* the type forecast for all of 1981 by economist Jones in the opening paragraph. Later chapters explain why this yield curve was so ominous for thrifts.

In contrast, Figure 6.3 shows an upward-sloping relationship in June 1986, plotted from the same securities shown in Figure 6.1. Slight differences occur because Figure 6.1 yields use midafternoon prices, whereas Figure 6.3 data are based on closing prices. Figure 6.4 shows an almost constant relationship between yields and maturities in February 1982.

Figure 6.5 gives a long-term view of short- and long-term rates, showing yields on high-grade commercial paper and 30-year corporate bonds over a period of approximately 75 years.[3] Over this period, no single relationship between short- and long-term rates prevailed. Be-

---

[2]For a theoretically correct determination of the "true" term structure, the securities used should all be pure discount, zero-coupon bonds of varying maturities. In practice, this requirement is usually ignored, and coupon-bearing as well as discount security yields are used to estimate existing term structures, especially when the analyst is fitting a curve visually. In addition, bonds with different coupon rates are also usually used to construct a yield curve, causing some distortion. The relationship between coupon rate, maturity, and yield to maturity is discussed in Chapters 7 and 8.

[3]Although Figure 6.5 departs from the practice of identifying term structures using Treasury security yields, differences between the default risk and tax treatment of high-grade bonds and prime commercial paper are not substantial. Although other features, such as convertibility or callability of bonds, weigh against direct comparison with commercial paper, this discussion assumes that these factors are not material.

Figure 6.1
Treasury Bonds, Notes, and Bills

TREASURY BONDS, NOTES & BILLS

Monday, June 30, 1986

Representative mid-afternoon Over-the-Counter quotations supplied by the Federal Reserve Bank of New York City, based on transactions of $1 million or more.

Decimals in bid-and-asked and bid changes represent 32nds; 101.1 means 101 1/32. a-Plus 1/64. b-Yield to call date. d-Minus 1/64. k-Nonresident aliens exempt from withholding taxes. n-Treasury notes. p-Treasury note; nonresident aliens exempt from withholding taxes.

Treasury Bonds and Notes

Rate	Mat.	Date	Bid	Asked	Bid Chg.	Yld.
12⅝s,	1986	Jul p	100.17	100.21	− .1	4.18
8s,	1986	Aug n	100.6	100.10	.....	5.25
11⅜s,	1986	Aug n	100.19	100.23	− .1	5.20
12⅜s,	1986	Aug p	100.29	101.1	− .2	5.75
11⅞s,	1986	Sep p	101.10	101.14	− .1	5.77
12¼s,	1986	Sep n	101.12	101.16	− .1	5.88
11⅝s,	1986	Oct p	101.21	101.25	− .1	5.98
6⅛s,	1986	Nov	99.29	100.29	.....	3.61
10⅜s,	1986	Nov p	101.17	101.21	.....	6.20
11s,	1986	Nov n	101.19	101.23	− .1	6.16
13⅞s,	1986	Nov n	102.21	102.25	− .1	6.07
16⅛s,	1986	Nov n	103.18	103.22	− .1	5.81
9⅞s,	1986	Dec p	101.22	101.26	+ .2	6.10
10s,	1986	Dec n	101.23	101.27	.....	6.16
9¾s,	1987	Jan p	101.25	101.29	+ .1	6.36
9s,	1987	Feb n	101.14	101.18	.....	6.40
10s,	1987	Feb p	102.5	102.9	.....	6.44
10⅞s,	1987	Feb n	102.18	102.22	− .1	6.41
12¾s,	1987	Feb n	103.27	103.31	+ .2	6.16
10¼s,	1987	Mar n	102.20	102.24	.....	6.43
10¾s,	1987	Mar p	103	103.4	+ .1	6.40
9¾s,	1987	Apr p	102.15	102.19	.....	6.49
9⅛s,	1987	May p	102.6	102.10	+ .1	6.48
12s,	1987	May n	104.18	104.22	+ .1	6.38
12½s,	1987	May n	104.30	105.2	+ .2	6.43
14s,	1987	May n	106.6	106.10	.....	6.43
8½s,	1987	Jun p	101.26	101.30	+ .2	6.46
10½s,	1987	Jun n	103.24	103.28	+ .3	6.42
8⅞s,	1987	Jul p	102.8	102.12	+ .2	6.56
8⅞s,	1987	Aug p	102.9	102.13	+ .1	6.69
12⅜s,	1987	Aug p	106.1	106.5	− .1	6.60
13¾s,	1987	Aug n	107.18	107.22	+ .1	6.54
9s,	1987	Sep p	102.19	102.23	+ .3	6.69
11⅛s,	1987	Sep n	105.5	105.9	+ .3	6.65
8⅞s,	1987	Oct p	102.17	102.21	+ .2	6.75
7⅝s,	1987	Nov n	101.1	101.9	+ .1	6.63
8½s,	1987	Nov p	102.6	102.10	+ .1	6.76
11s,	1987	Nov p	105.9	105.13	+ .1	6.80
12⅝s,	1987	Nov n	107.15	107.19	+ .1	6.73
11¼s,	1987	Dec n	106.5	106.9	+ .1	6.76
7⅞s.	1987	Dec p	101.15	101.19	+ .2	6.74
• • •						
14⅝s,	1989	Jan n	116.28	117	+ .2	7.18
8s,	1989	Feb p	102.7	102.11	+ .3	7.01
11⅜s,	1989	Feb n	109.23	109.27	+ .2	7.19
11¼s,	1989	Mar p	109.24	110	+ .3	7.18
14⅜s,	1989	Apr n	117.18	117.26	+ .2	7.21
6⅞s,	1989	May p	99.23	99.25	+ .5	6.96
9¼s,	1989	May n	105.13	105.21	+ .5	7.04
11¾s,	1989	May n	111.11	111.15	+ .3	7.25
9⅝s,	1989	Jun p	106.11	106.15	+ .4	7.19
14½s,	1989	Jul n	119	119.4	+ .5	7.36
13⅞s,	1989	Aug n	117.22	117.26	+ .4	7.38
9⅜s,	1989	Sep p	105.27	105.31	+ .4	7.28
11⅞s,	1989	Oct n	112.25	112.29	+ .23	7.38
10¾s,	1989	Nov n	109.25	109.29	+ .4	7.38
12¾s,	1989	Nov p	115.15	115.19	+ .5	7.44
8⅜s,	1989	Dec p	103.8	103.12	+ .5	7.26
10½s,	1990	Jan n	109.9	109.13	+ .5	7.43
3½s,	1990	Feb	93.12	94.12	+ .3	5.22
11s,	1990	Feb p	110.24	110.28	.....	7.52
7¼s,	1990	Mar p	100.6	100.8	+ .4	7.17
10½s,	1990	Apr n	109.23	109.27	+ .4	7.47
8¼s,	1990	May	103.10	103.26	+ .5	7.11
11⅜s,	1990	May p	112.24	112.28	+ .6	7.48
7¼s,	1990	Jun p	100.13	100.15	+ .4	7.11
10¾s,	1990	Jul n	111	111.4	+ .2	7.50
9⅞s,	1990	Aug p	108.8	108.12	+ .5	7.48
10¾s,	1990	Aug n	111.5	111.13	+ .4	7.48
11½s,	1990	Oct n	114.4	114.8	+ .4	7.55
9⅝s,	1990	Nov k	107.22	107.26	+ .5	7.50
13s,	1990	Nov n	119.27	119.31	+ .5	7.55
• • •						
3s,	1995	Feb	93.12	94.12	− .2	3.77
10½s,	1995	Feb	117.23	117.31	+ .12	7.62
11¼s,	1995	Feb p	122.6	122.14	+ .11	7.65
10⅜s,	1995	May	117.10	117.18	+ .18	7.82
11¼s,	1995	May p	122.16	122.24	+ .12	7.67
12⅝s,	1995	May	131.6	131.14	+ .13	7.67
10½s,	1995	Aug p	118.16	118.24	+ .12	7.61
9½s,	1995	Nov p	112.27	113.3	+ .11	7.53
11½s,	1995	Nov	125.6	125.14	+ .12	7.65
8⅞s,	1996	Feb p	109.20	109.23	+ .14	7.44
7⅜s,	1996	May p	100.6	100.10	+ .8	7.33
7s,	1993-98	May	97.21	98.5	+ .6	7.23
3½s,	1998	Nov	93.12	94.12	+ .3	4.08
8½s,	1994-99	May	105.5	105.21	+ .11	7.53
7⅞s,	1995-00	Feb	101.10	101.26	+ .8	7.58
8⅜s,	1995-00	Aug	104.30	105.6	+ .10	7.58
11¾s,	2001	Feb	132.23	132.31	+ .8	7.91
13⅛s,	2001	May	144.13	144.21	+ .23	7.95
8s,	1996-01	Aug	102.18	103.2	.....	7.56
13⅜s,	2001	Aug	146.24	147.6	+ .16	7.97
15¾s,	2001	Nov	167.17	167.25	+ .19	8.01
14¼s,	2002	Feb	154.30	155.6	+ .8	8.00
11⅝s,	2002	Nov	133.2	133.10	+ .22	7.95
10¾s,	2003	Feb	125.23	125.31	+ .18	7.91
10¾s,	2003	May	125.23	125.31	+ .18	7.93
11⅛s,	2003	Aug	129.1	129.9	+ .15	7.96
11⅞s,	2003	Nov	136.5	136.13	+ .20	7.97
12⅜s,	2004	May	141.8	141.16	+ .23	7.98
13¾s,	2004	Aug	154.17	154.25	+ 1.9	7.98
11⅝s,	2004	Nov k	134.20	135.6	+ .17	7.95

U.S. Treas. Bills

Mat. date	Bid (Discount)	Asked (Discount)	Yield
-1986-			
7- 3	6.04	5.90	5.98
7-10	5.95	5.89	5.98
7-17	5.94	5.88	5.98
7-24	5.89	5.85	5.95
7-31	5.81	5.77	5.88
8- 7	6.00	5.96	6.08
8-14	5.98	5.94	6.07
8-21	5.99	5.95	6.08
8-28	5.98	5.94	6.08
9- 4	6.00	5.96	6.11
9-11	6.00	5.96	6.11
9-18	6.00	5.96	6.12
9-25	5.96	5.94	6.11
10- 2	5.99	5.95	6.13
10- 9	6.00	5.96	6.14
10-16	6.00	5.96	6.15
10-23	6.02	5.98	6.18
10-30	6.00	5.96	6.17
11- 6	6.02	5.98	6.19
11-13	6.03	5.99	6.21
11-86	6.03	5.99	6.22
11-28	6.03	5.99	6.23
12- 4	6.02	6.00	6.24
12-11	6.03	6.01	6.26
12-86	6.02	5.98	6.24
12-26	5.95	5.91	6.17
-1987-			
1-22	5.99	5.95	6.22
2-19	6.01	5.97	6.25
3-19	6.02	5.98	6.28
4-16	6.06	6.04	6.36
5-14	6.06	6.02	6.36
6-11	6.03	6.01	6.37

Source: The Wall Street Journal, June 30, 1986. Reprinted by permission of *The Wall Street Journal*, © Dow Jones & Company, Inc. 1986. All Rights Reserved.

Figure 6.2
Yields of Treasury Securities, August 31, 1981[a]

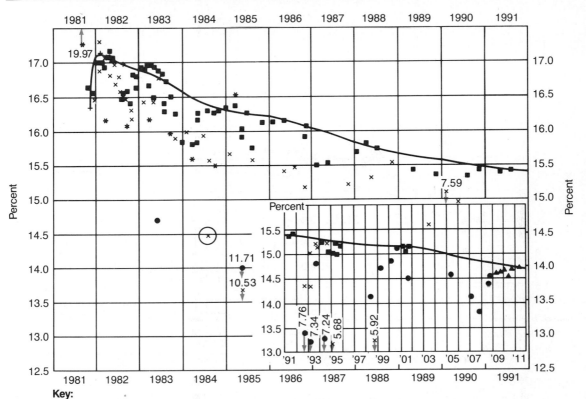

Key:
- × Fixed-Coupon Issues
- ■ High-Coupon Issues—9% and Higher Fixed-Maturity Issues
- ● Callable Issues
- ▲ High-Coupon Callable Issues—Plotted
    to Earliest Call Date When Prices Are above Par and
    to Maturity Date When Prices Are at Par or below
- ✳ 1½% Exchange Notes
- + Bills—Coupon Equivalent of 3-Months, 6-Months, and 1-Year Bills

[a]Based on closing bid quotations. The curve is fitted by eye and based only on the most actively traded issues.

Source: Treasury Bulletin, September 1981, p. 64.

fore 1960, short-term yields were less than long-term yields most of the time. Since then, the reverse has often been true, and during the 1960s, yields on bonds and commercial paper were virtually identical on several occasions. The prevalence of upward-sloping yield curves during much of the early 20th century led to

their being dubbed ***"normal" yield curves,*** which is why downward-sloping curves have been called "inverted."

A financial institution manager aware of these facts can be certain of one thing: Because short- and long-term financial markets are both part of the environment, one must understand

Figure 6.3
Yields of Treasury Securities, June 30, 1986[a]

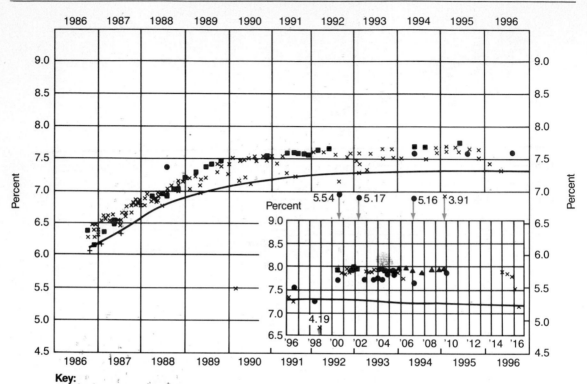

Key:
- × Fixed-Maturity Coupon Issues under 12%
- ■ Fixed-Maturity Coupon Issues of 12% or More
- ● Callable Coupon Issues under 12%
- ▲ Callable Coupon Issues of 12% or More
- + Bills—Coupon-Equivalent Yield of the Latest
  13-Week, 26-Week, and 52-Week Bills

[a]Based on closing bid quotations. The curve is fitted by eye and based only on the most actively traded issues.

Source: Treasury Bulletin, Third Quarter, Fiscal 1986, p. 36.

reasons for yield differences based on maturity and learn to anticipate changes in current relationships.

The Term Structure and the General Level of Interest Rates

Another feature of Figure 6.5 is important because it suggests a historical relationship be-

tween the general level of economic activity and the shape of the yield curve. The points marked on the graph denote peaks in the business cycle.[4] At these times, such as the late 1920s, a downward-sloping yield curve has been com-

---

[4]Peaks shown are as delineated by the National Bureau of Economic Research, U.S. Department of Commerce, *Business Conditions Digest* (February 1985), p. 104.

Figure 6.4
Yields of Treasury Securities, February 26, 1982[a]

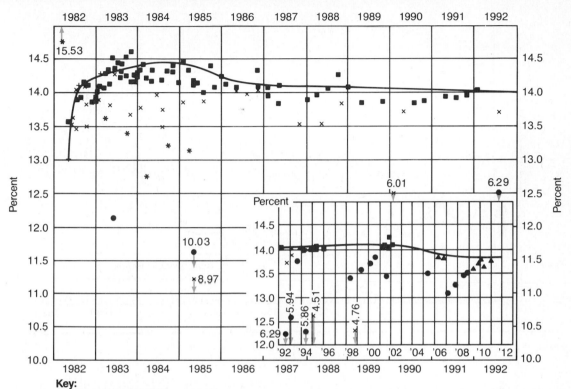

Key:

× Fixed-Coupon Issues
■ High-Coupon Issues—9% and Higher Fixed-Maturity Issues
● Callable Issues
▲ High-Coupon Callable Issues—Plotted
   to Earliest Call Date When Prices Are above Par and
   to Maturity Date When Prices Are at Par or below
∗ 1½% Exchange Notes
+ Bills—Coupon Equivalent of 3-Months, 6-Months, and 1-Year Bills

[a]Based on closing bid quotations. The curve is fitted by eye and based only on the most actively traded issues.

Source: Treasury Bulletin, March 1982, p. 63.

mon. During periods of sluggish economic performance, such as the 1930s, the yield curve is usually upward–sloping.

From the beginning of World War II until 1951, Fed policies kept the term structure independent of the level of economic activity. Although World War II caused industrial pro-

duction and demand for credit to surge, the Federal Reserve Board kept interest rates relatively low and held short-term rates below long-term rates. This policy was implemented at the request of the U.S. Treasury to keep government interest costs at a minimum. During the Korean War, however, the Fed began to ar-

Figure 6.5
Long- and Short-Term Interest Rates

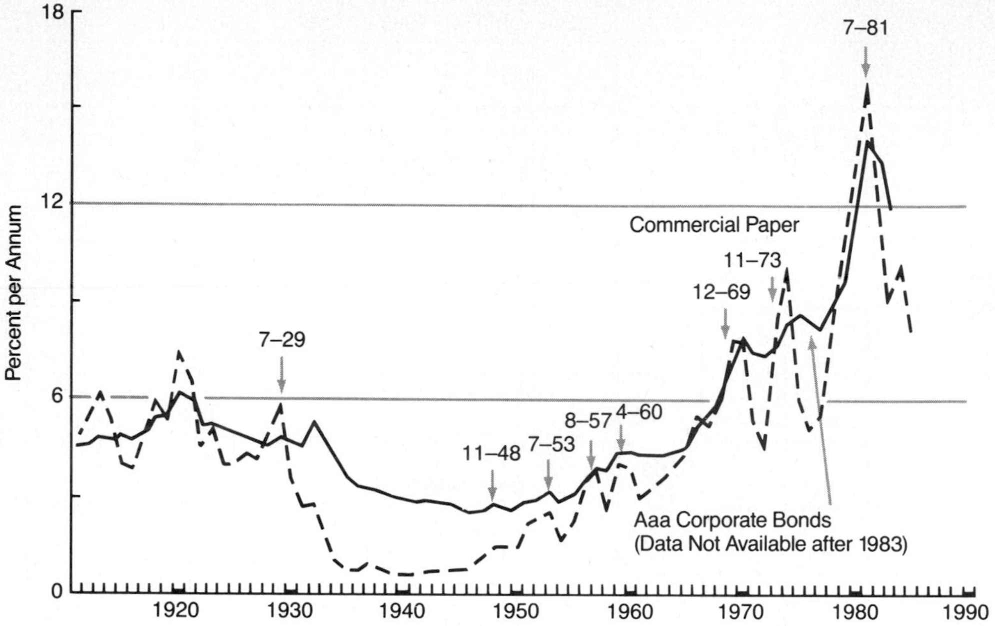

Source: Board of Governors of the Federal Reserve System, *1986 Historical Chart Book.*

gue that controlling the term structure had become, in the words of the chairman, "an engine of inflation." After long negotiations between the Fed and Treasury and with the intervention of President Harry S. Truman, controls were lifted in 1951, and rates were free to move according to the supply and demand for funds.[5] At that time, the historical pattern of downward-sloping curves at peaks and upward-sloping curves at troughs returned. The pattern can be seen most recently from the late 1970s to the early 1980s, when an inverted curve was followed by a "normal" one as the 1981-1982 recession took hold.

A different perspective on historical term structures is shown in Figure 6.6. When the general level of rates has been relatively high, term structures have tended to slope downward, and they have sloped upward when the general level has been relatively low. From 1900 to 1929, as the general level of rates drifted upward, yield curves gradually changed shape from flat to inverted. From 1930 to 1981, as rates gradually moved higher, yield curves also shifted from upward-sloping to downward-sloping. Scholars have inferred from curves such as those illustrated in Panel B that the financial markets may periodically revise their opinions of what represents a "high" general level. Before the 1930s, for example, a 7 percent short-term rate may have been considered high, although by the 1970s such a rate was considered relatively low. In this context, the 1982 "normal" curve may be an aberration from re-

---

[5]For a more detailed discussion of this policy and the "accord" that brought it to an end, see Henry C. Wallich and Peter M. Keir, "The Role of Operating Guides in U.S. Monetary Policy: A Historical Review," *Federal Reserve Bulletin* 65 (September 1979): 679-691.

Figure 6.6
Yield Curves for High-Grade Corporate Bonds, 1900–1929 and 1930–1982

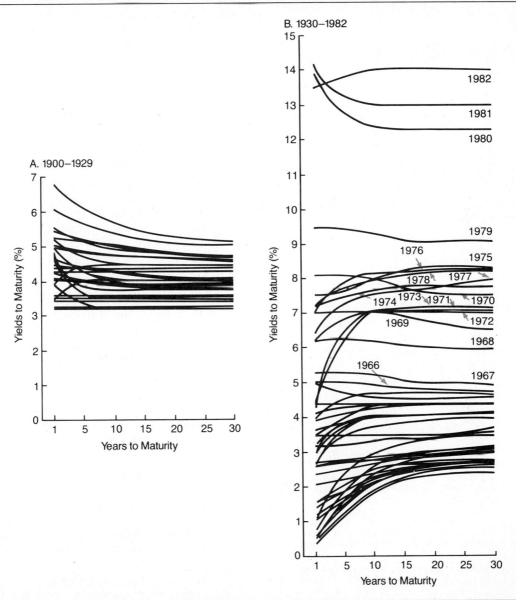

Source: John Wood, ''Do Yield Curves Normally Slope Up? The Term Structure of Interest Rates, 1862–1982,'' *Economic Perspectives,* Federal Reserve Bank of Chicago 7 (July/August 1983): 18.

cent history, or it may reflect the beginning of another revision in investors' opinions of what constitutes a low general level of interest rates.[6]

UNBIASED (PURE) EXPECTATIONS THEORY

Historical patterns and the reasons for their existence provide clues about when to expect shifts in the term structure, but they are no substitute for a theoretical understanding of the yield curve. Understanding how the term structure is determined is complicated by economists' lack of agreement on any single explanation. The existence of several theories should not be discouraging, however, since each provides insights the others lack. The body of knowledge is valuable for managers who make decisions involving assets and liabilities of different maturities.

Perhaps the most influential of the term structure theories is the *unbiased (pure) expectations theory,* which holds that observable long-term yields are the average of expected, but directly unobservable, short-term yields.[7] For example, this theory argues that the spot rate on 20-year Treasury bonds is the average of expected annual yields on short-term Treasury securities over the next 20 years. Theoretically, there is no best definition of "short-term" or "long-term." For simplicity, most of

the following examples define short-term as one year; however, the pure expectations theory also holds that the observed yield on one-year securities is the average of expected rates on shorter-maturity securities during the year. *Short-* and *long-term* can therefore be defined as the decision maker desires.

Assumptions of the Pure Expectations Theory

The pure expectations theory rests upon important assumptions about investors (lenders or demanders of securities) and markets:

1. All else equal, investors are indifferent between owning a single long-term security or a series of short-term securities over the same time period. In other words, maturity alone does not affect investors' choice of investments.

2. All investors hold common expectations about the course of short-term rates.

3. On average, investors are able to predict rates accurately. Their expectations about future rates are unbiased in the *statistical* sense—they are neither consistently low nor consistently high.

4. There are no taxes, information costs, or transaction costs in the financial markets. Investors are free to exchange securities of varying maturities quickly and without penalty.

The major implication of the pure expectations theory follows directly from these assumptions. *For a given holding period, the average expected annual yields on all combinations of maturities will be equal.*[8] For example, the theory holds that the average annual yield on a series of one-

---

[6]For more discussion, see John H. Wood, "Do Yield Curves Normally Slope Up? The Term Structure of Interest Rates, 1862-1982," *Economic Perspectives,* Federal Reserve Bank of Chicago 7 (July/August 1983): 17-23.

[7]Irving Fisher, discussed in the previous chapter in connection with inflation and the general level of rates, is often credited with the first statement of the pure expectations hypothesis in 1896. The theory was not fully developed until several decades later, however, when both J. R. Hicks, in *Value and Capital* (London: Oxford University Press, 1946), and Frederick Lutz, in "The Structure of Interest Rates," *Quarterly Journal of Economics* 30 (November 1940): 36-63, pursued it. More recent discussions are found in Burton Malkiel, *The Term Structure of Interest Rates: Theory, Empirical Evidence, and Applications* (Princeton, NJ: Princeton University Press, 1966) and David Meiselman, *The Term Structure of Interest Rates* (Englewood Cliffs, NJ: Prentice-Hall, 1962).

[8]Recently, some scholars have argued that this implication holds strictly only for a specific holding period of instantaneous duration and that it is incompatible with other versions of the expectations hypothesis, such as the statement that long-term spot rates are the average of expected short-term rates. See John C. Cox, Jonathan E. Ingersoll, Jr., and Stephen A. Ross, "A Re-Examination of Traditional Hypotheses about the Term Structure of Interest Rates," *Journal of Finance* 36 (September 1981): 769-799.

year investments over a specific five-year period will be the same as the average annual yield on a single three-year investment followed by 2 one-year investments *and* the same as the average annual yield on a single five-year security. Because investors are assumed to be indifferent about the maturity of their holdings, and because they have common and accurate predictions about future rates, they will demand securities at prices that equalize average annual yields over the period. Investors simply have no incentive to prefer one combination of maturities over another. Annual yields currently available on long-term securities will be the average of expected annual yields on shorter-term instruments.

Mathematics of the Pure Expectations Theory

Mathematically, the theory is expressed by the following formula:

(6.1)

$$1 + {}_1\bar{i}_n = \sqrt[n]{\prod_{t=1}^{n} (1 + {}_t\tilde{i}_1)}$$

$$= \sqrt[n]{(1 + {}_1\tilde{i}_1)(1 + {}_2\tilde{i}_1) \ldots (1 + {}_n\tilde{i}_1)}$$

The "average" of rates referred to earlier is not the simple arithmetic average; the symbol Π directs the user to multiply, not add, a series of expressions from $t = 1$ to $t = n$. Equation 6.1 states that the *observed* yield in period 1 (${}_1\bar{i}_n$) on an n-period security is the **geometric average** of a series of one-period *expected* yields (${}_t\tilde{i}_1$) from period 1 to period n. The geometric average is calculated by taking the n-th root of the *product* of (1 + expected one-period yields). This calculation assumes reinvestment, at rate ${}_t\tilde{i}_1$, of all proceeds throughout the holding period. In practice, the one-period yield currently observed in the securities market is used as the one-period expected yield at $t = 1$; that is, ${}_1\tilde{i}_1 = {}_1\bar{i}_1$.[9]

---

[9]The notation for pure expectations mathematics is invariably confusing. Present and compound value calculations

Table 6.1 contains investors' expectations for one-year yields over the period January 1991 to January 1995. The first three columns are used in the following examples. The fourth column of liquidity premiums is used later.

According to the unbiased expectations theory and from these expectations alone, Equation 6.1 gives the following yield to maturity on a four-year Treasury security bought in January 1991 (the beginning of period 1) and maturing in January 1995:

$$1 + {}_1\bar{i}_n = \sqrt[n]{\prod_{t=1}^{n} (1 + {}_t\tilde{i}_1)}$$

$$1 + {}_1\bar{i}_4 = \sqrt[4]{\prod_{t=1}^{4} (1 + {}_t\tilde{i}_1)}$$

$$1 + {}_1\bar{i}_4 = \sqrt[4]{(1.0850)(1.0950)(1.1100)(1.1175)}$$

$${}_1\bar{i}_4 = 1.10180 - 1 = 0.10180 = 10.180\%$$

Given the same set of expectations and again using Equation 6.1, it is possible to calculate spot yields on securities with two- and three-year maturities as of January 1991:

$$1 + {}_1\bar{i}_2 = \sqrt{(1.0850)(1.0950)}$$

$${}_1\bar{i}_2 = 1.08999 - 1 = 0.08999 = 8.999\%$$

$$1 + {}_1\bar{i}_3 = \sqrt[3]{(1.0850)(1.0950)(1.1100)}$$

$${}_1\bar{i}_3 = 1.09662 - 1 = 0.09662 = 9.662\%$$

The unbiased expectations theory implies that investors' expectations of rising short-term yields will result in an upward-sloping yield curve for Treasury securities as of January 1991, as shown in Figure 6.7.

If the pure expectations theory is correct, the average annual yield an investor could ob-

---

usually emphasize end-of-period cash flows, so $t = 1$ usually means the end of period 1 and $t = n$ means the end of period n. That usage prevails in most chapters in this book. The pure expectations theory focuses on beginning-of-period expectations, however, so $t = 1$ means the beginning of period 1 (or the end of period 0), and the notation $t = n$ means the beginning of period n.

Table 6.1
Observed and Expected One-Year Yields and Premiums as of January 1991

Bill Purchased	Bill Matures	Observed or Expected Annual Yield	Liquidity Premium
January 1991	January 1992	8.50% observed ($_1\bar{i}_1$)	0.00% (on 1-year security)
January 1992	January 1993	9.50% expected ($_2\bar{i}_1$)	0.35% (on 2-year security)
January 1993	January 1994	11.00% expected ($_3\bar{i}_1$)	0.45% (on 3-year security)
January 1994	January 1995	11.75% expected ($_4\bar{i}_1$)	0.50% (on 4-year security)

Figure 6.7
Observed Yield Curve, January 1991

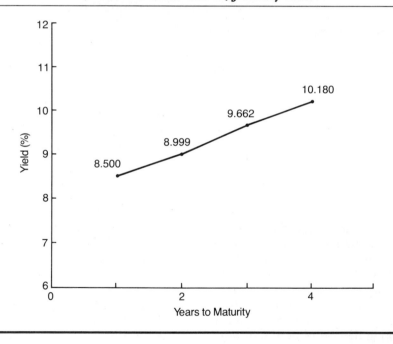

tain over the period 1991 to 1995 is the same, regardless of the investment strategy chosen. If the investor decides to buy 4 one-year securities, the average annual yield over the holding period (i_H) will be 10.180 percent. If, instead, the investments are a two-year security in January 1991 (annual yield 8.999 percent) and two successive one-year T-bills in 1993 and 1994 (expected yields of 11.000 percent and 11.750 percent, respectively), the average annual yield for this strategy is:

$$1 + i_H = \sqrt[4]{(1.08999)(1.08999)(1.11000)(1.11750)}$$

$$i_H = 1.10180 - 1 = 10.180\%$$

Or, if an investor buys a three-year T-note in 1991 (annual yield of 9.662 percent), followed by a one-year bill in 1994 (11.750 percent expected yield), the average annual yield for the holding period is:

$$1 + i_H = \sqrt[4]{(1.09662)(1.09662)(1.09662)(1.11750)}$$

$$i_H = 1.10180 - 1 = 10.180\%$$

Under the assumptions of investor indifference to maturity and unbiased expectations of future short-term rates, any combination of maturities over the period will result in an average annual yield of 10.180 percent. This will be true as long as all proceeds are reinvested and expectations of future rates remain constant during the period. In other words, the 10.180 percent average four-year yield would be expected as long as investors do not revise their one-year predictions for 1993, for example, at some point after 1991.

MODIFICATIONS OF THE UNBIASED EXPECTATIONS THEORY

The unbiased expectations theory succinctly explains the shape of any term structure: Lenders' expectations of rising short-term rates produce an observable upward-sloping yield curve; expectations of falling short-term rates produce a downward-sloping term structure; and expectations of unchanging rates produce a flat yield curve. Changes in the shape of the curve over time, such as those implied by Figures 6.5 and 6.6, can also be easily explained by changes in expectations. In addition, the theory appeals to researchers because its mathematical form provides testable hypotheses as well as the opportunity to develop models for predicting interest rates.

Criticisms of the Unbiased Expectations Theory

The theory is not without its critics, however, who focus on its restrictive assumptions as se-rious shortcomings. In particular, investors' assumed indifference between short- and long-term securities ignores the fact that a long-term investment may be riskier than a series of short-term investments. Risk, brought about by the passage of time alone, is rarely a matter of indifference. Even for two securities of the same issuer with equal initial default risk, the probability of default may increase on the long-term security over time. Furthermore, investors are never certain that personal circumstances will allow them to follow initial investment strategies throughout the holding period. If emergencies arise, they may have to sell long-term securities at a loss when forced to abandon their initial plans.[10]

A second assumption that troubles critics is that, according to the theory, issuers of securities have no influence on the term structure. This appears to contradict the negotiation process that actually occurs between borrowers and lenders in many financial markets. It is important to remember that no theory should be judged on the realism of its assumptions. The test of a theory is how well it explains "real world" relationships, and the theory enjoys some qualified empirical support. However, these criticisms have led to several theoretical modifications.

The Liquidity Premium Hypothesis

The belief that most investors find long-term securities riskier than short-term securities has led to the *liquidity premium hypothesis.* According to this theory, today's long-term rates reflect the geometric average of intervening expected short-term rates, *plus* a premium investors demand for holding long-term securities instead of a series of short-term, less risky investments. The hypothesized impact of these liquidity premiums on the term structure can

---

[10]For an investor who holds the investment throughout the planned holding period, another element of risk must be considered—the potential for *unexpected* changes in short-term yields. If such changes occur, the investor faces uncertainty from periodic reinvestment rates. This source of risk is discussed in more detail in Chapter 7.

be illustrated by considering the fourth column of Table 6.1.[11]

Using the unbiased expectations theory, spot rates of 8.99 percent, 9.66 percent, and 10.18 percent were calculated earlier for two-, three-, and four-year maturities. According to the liquidity premium hypothesis, the following yields would be observed instead, using Equation 6.1 with the premium added:

$$1 + {}_1\bar{i}_2 = \sqrt{(1.0850)(1.0950 + 0.0035)}$$

$${}_1\bar{i}_2 = 1.0917 - 1 = 0.0917 = 9.17\%$$

$$1 + {}_1\bar{i}_3 = \sqrt[3]{\begin{array}{c}(1.0850) \times (1.0950 + 0.0035) \\ \times (1.1100 + 0.0045)\end{array}}$$

$${}_1\bar{i}_3 = 1.0993 - 1 = 0.0993 = 9.93\%$$

$$1 + {}_1\bar{i}_4 = \sqrt[4]{\begin{array}{c}(1.0850) \times (1.0950 + 0.0035) \\ \times (1.1100 + 0.0045) \times (1.1175 \\ + 0.0050)\end{array}}$$

$${}_1\bar{i}_4 = 1.1050 - 1 = 0.1050 = 10.50\%$$

Because investors are no longer indifferent among maturities, the same expectations are supplemented by a premium for holding long-term securities. As shown in Figure 6.8, this term structure has a steeper slope than the term structure illustrated in Figure 6.7.

A general restatement of the term structure including liquidity premiums is provided by Equation 6.2:

(6.2)

$$(1 + {}_1\bar{i}_n) = \sqrt[n]{\prod_{t=1}^{n} (1 + {}_t\tilde{i}_1 + L_t)}$$

where:

L_t = liquidity premium for holding a t-period security instead of a one-year security. By definition, $L_1 = 0$.

The liquidity premium hypothesis does not rule out the possibility of downward-sloping yield curves, although some economists believe it explains why they are less common. If investors expect future short-term rates to fall sharply, the pure expectations theory holds that a steeply downward-sloping curve should be observed in the spot markets. If investors also demand a premium for investing long-term, the observed yield curve might still be inverted, but more gently sloped than if determined by expectations alone, as shown in Figure 6.9.

It is even possible, according to the liquidity premium hypothesis, that a yield curve reflecting expectations of falling rates could appear to be upward-sloping if investors demanded a relatively high premium on long-term issues. Such a situation is illustrated in Figure 6.10.

Incorporating the Role of Lenders

Other theories of the term structure are distinguished from the pure expectations approach because they include a role for lenders in the determination of spot rates, and they discard the assumption of indifference between maturities.

The Modified Expectations Theory. One theory is sometimes called the ***modified expectations theory*** to reflect support for the idea that expectations of future rates do, in fact, determine today's yields.[12] As this argument goes, if

---

[11]Presentations of the liquidity premium hypothesis can be found in J. R. Hicks, *Value and Capital;* and Reuben A. Kessel, *The Cyclical Behavior of the Term Structure* (New York: National Bureau of Economic Research, 1965).

Although it is easy to incorporate given liquidity premiums into the basic pure expectations equation, it is more difficult to specify the structure of liquidity premiums themselves. Scholars disagree about how to model them, but for illustrative purposes, liquidity premiums in these examples are considered to increase with time. A brief review of alternative specifications is provided later in the chapter.

[12]Warren L. Smith, *Debt Management in the United States,* Study Paper 19, Joint Economic Committee of the 86th Congress, January 1960. The modified expectations theory produces the same mathematical model as the pure expectations theory (Equation 6.1).

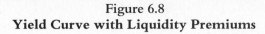

Figure 6.8
Yield Curve with Liquidity Premiums

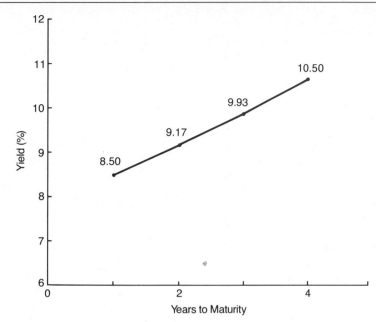

interest rates are expected to rise in the future, lenders may wish to lend short-term to avoid locking in today's lower spot rates. Such a long-term commitment would not only prevent reinvestment of principal at the expected higher rates, but also would subject lenders to capital losses should they sell their investments before maturity. On the other hand, borrowers will wish to borrow long-term to avoid expected higher interest costs.

According to the theory, the common expectations of borrowers and lenders and their conflicting maturity preferences put pressure on long-term rates, producing an upward-sloping curve. Conversely, when all parties expect interest rates to fall, lenders wish to lend long, but borrowers prefer to roll over a series of short-term loans at progressively lower expected rates. This places upward pressure on short-term rates, resulting in an inverted term structure. Thus, the conclusions of the modified expectations theory are the same as those

for the unbiased expectations theory: Expectations of rising rates produce an upward-sloping curve, while expectations of falling rates produce a downward-sloping relationship. The major difference between the theories is the motivations determining spot rates.

The Segmented Markets Theory.   The *segmented markets theory* relies heavily on the existence of market imperfections. It argues that there really is no term structure, and it has gained especially strong support among market participants.[13] The segmentation theory suggests that different spot rates on long- and short-term securities are explained not by any common set of market expectations, nor by a liquidity premium to induce lenders to switch from short- to long-term securities, but rather

---

[13]John M. Culbertson, "The Term Structure of Interest Rates," *Quarterly Journal of Economics* 71 (November 1957): 485–517.

Figure 6.9
Pure Expectations and Liquidity Premiums

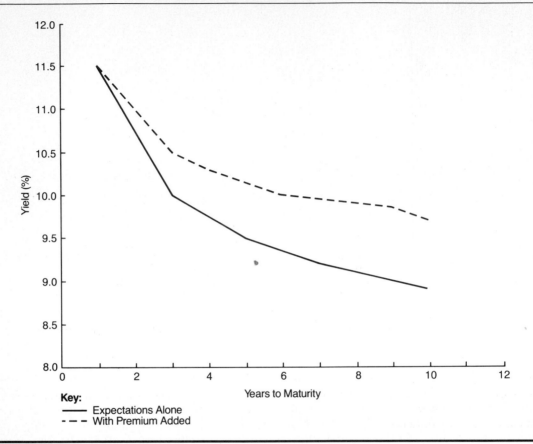

by separate supply/demand interactions in the financial markets. According to this theory, short-term yields result from interactions of individuals and institutions in the short-term market segment; the same is true of yields on long-term securities. Because laws, regulations, or institutional objectives prevent many market participants from borrowing or lending in every segment, some maturities are of little concern.

One justification for the segmented markets theory is that it reflects the preference of financial institutions to match the maturities of their assets and liabilities. Commercial banks, for example, have traditionally concentrated on lending in the short-term markets while obtaining funds from depositors in that same segment of the market. Similar segmented supply/demand factors may affect long-term rates: Life insurance firms expect long-term payment inflows from customers and invest those funds heavily in instruments with long maturities.

According to the segmented markets theory, what might seem to be a downward-sloping yield curve is really many distinct—and theoretically unrelated—market interactions, as

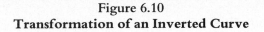

Figure 6.10
Transformation of an Inverted Curve

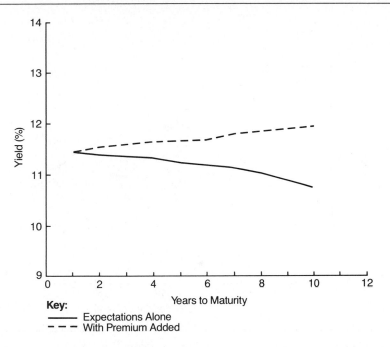

Key:
——— Expectations Alone
- - - With Premium Added

shown in Figure 6.11. Notice the similarities between this hypothetical curve and the actual term structure of interest rates shown in Figure 6.12. For example, proponents of the market segmentation theory believe the yield curve on December 31, 1969, clearly reveals distinct financial market segments. This theory has implications for interest rate forecasting that are quite distinct from those of the expectations hypothesis. It returns forecasting to supply/demand in market segments and relies on forecasting methods similar to those discussed in Chapter 5.

The Preferred Habitat Theory.   Closely related to the segmented markets theory is the *preferred habitat theory,* which assumes that although investors may strongly prefer particular segments of the market, they are not necessarily locked in to those segments. These strong pref-

erences for certain maturities arise not from legal or regulatory reasons, but rather from *consumption* preferences.[14] In other words, investors' time preferences for spending versus saving influence their choice among securities. They will lend in markets other than their preferred one, but only if a premium exists to induce them to switch. This argument differs from the liquidity premium theory in that it does not assume that all lenders prefer short-term to long-term securities. There may well be lenders who prefer to lend long, who can be

[14]See Franco Modigliani and Richard Sutch, "Innovation in Interest Rate Policy," *American Economic Review* 66 (May 1966): 178-197. Cox, Ingersoll, and Ross, "Re-Examination of Traditional Hypotheses," argue instead that risk aversion, not time-related consumption preferences, will create preferred habitats. In particular, they interpreted a habitat "as a stronger or weaker tendency to hedge against changes in the interest rate," p. 786.

Figure 6.11
Yields in Segmented Markets

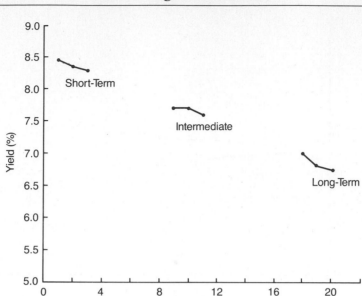

induced to lend short for a yield premium, or vice versa.

Although the preferred habitat theory recognizes that some lenders may not be persuaded to depart from their preferred habitats at any price, it holds that the markets are only partially segmented because many participants *are* willing to switch maturities if properly rewarded. Short- and long-term yield differentials are only partially explained by the expectations hypothesis; supply/demand imbalances in various markets may result in positive or negative premiums added to the pure expectations rate to induce shifts from one segment to another. Thus, the preferred habitat theory differs from the segmented markets theory in two ways:

1. It relies less on the maturity preferences of the suppliers of securities in the determination of spot rates;
2. It acknowledges that many investors con-

sider developments across the spectrum of maturities before making their decisions.

EMPIRICAL TESTS OF THE TERM STRUCTURE THEORIES

A full review of empirical tests of term structure theories would fill a book, because research interest in the subject spans almost a century. Nonetheless, no single theory has prevailed.

A Familiar Research Problem: Measuring Expectations

As the oldest of the theories, the pure expectations model has received the greatest attention. Particularly troublesome, however, is a problem also faced in tests of the Fisher effect: mea-

Figure 6.12
Yields of Treasury Securities, December 31, 1969[a]

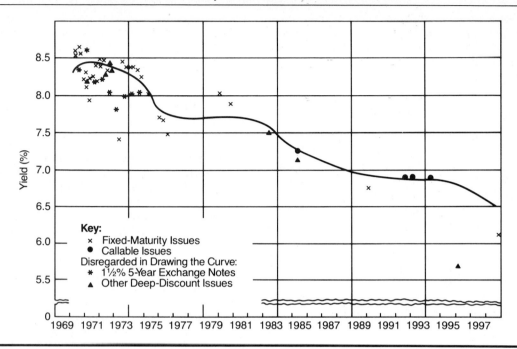

[a]Based on closing bid quotations. The curve is fitted by eye and based only on the most actively traded issues.
Source: Treasury Bulletin, January 1970, p. 83.

suring market expectations to be compared with subsequent actual rates. Researchers have used numerous alternatives. Some have used *ex post* rates as a proxy for expected rates. The conclusions are similar to those drawn by students of the Fisher theory: Even though, after the fact, expectations are not always correct, they still influence observed term structures.

For example, some researchers have developed an "error learning" model, which argues that investors continually revise their expectations in response to earlier errors. This model implies that past and present experiences affect investors' response to new information. Other researchers have argued that investors' expectations are "regressive"—that is, when the general level of rates is high, people expect them to fall, and when the general level is low, they expect rates to rise.[15]

Quite a different approach uses interest rate forecasts of professional investors and analysts as proxies for interest rate expectations.[16] Re-

[15]Examples of these studies include James Van Horne, "Interest Rate Risk and the Term Structure of Interest Rates," *Journal of Political Economy* 73 (August 1965): 344–351; Kessell, "The Cyclical Behavior of the Term Structure"; Meiselman, *The Term Structure of Interest Rates;* and John C. Wood, "Do Yield Curves Normally Slope Up?"

[16]See Edward J. Kane and Burton G. Malkiel, "The Term Structure of Interest Rates: An Analysis of a Survey of Interest Rate Expectations," *Review of Economics and Statistics* 49 (August 1967): 343–355; Benjamin M. Friedman, "Interest Rate Expectations versus Forward Rates: Evidence from an Expectations Survey," *Journal of Finance* 34 (September 1979): 965–973.

cently, researchers have recognized that the financial futures markets may provide a good method for estimating interest rate expectations and have turned to those markets for continuation of empirical tests. Regardless of the chosen measurement, most studies have concluded that expectations play a major role in determining the term structure.[17]

Evidence on Liquidity Premiums

Many researchers have concluded that investors also demand liquidity premiums, although they do not agree on the nature of these premiums. The disagreement centers on whether the premium demanded by investors is affected by the general level of interest rates (that is, whether the premium increases or decreases when rates are considered to be relatively high or low), and whether it is stable or rises monotonically with maturity. There is considerable evidence that the liquidity premium *does* vary with the general level of interest rates, but no agreement on whether the relationship is positive or negative.[18] In other words, some research indicates that when rates are higher than normal, the liquidity premium required by investors is smaller than usual, while other results suggest that it is larger.

The debate over the nature of the liquidity premium has implications for tests of the expectations hypothesis and for its usefulness as a forecasting model. Because it is difficult to determine the size and pattern of liquidity premiums, it is difficult to isolate an expected "pure" interest rate from a premium attached to it.

Some research has suggested that liquidity premiums range from 0.54 percent to 1.56 percent, but other studies have concluded that premiums are less than 0.50 percent, even for long maturities. Some researchers have even concluded that liquidity premiums decrease, not increase, with maturity.[19]

Research on Segmented Markets and Preferred Habitats

Research on the segmented markets and preferred habitat theories is extremely contradictory. Some researchers have reported findings of discontinuities in the yield curve, supporting the market segmentation theory; some have concluded that preferred habitats exist.[20] In contrast, other studies, including those supporting the expectations and liquidity premium theories, argue that the financial markets function more efficiently than the segmented markets or preferred habitat theories recognize. In other words, investors are more willing to move funds back and forth between maturities in order to maximize returns than either of these theories implies.

---

[17]It should be noted that there are serious critics. For example, one study concludes that use of the simple expectations theory " . . . to forecast the direction of future changes in the interest rate seems worthless." See Robert J. Schiller, John Y. Campbell, and Kermit L. Schoenholtz in "Forward Rates and Future Policy: Interpreting the Term Structure of Interest Rates," *Brookings Papers on Economic Activity, I: 1983* (Washington, DC: Brookings Institution, 1983), pp. 173-223.

[18]See Charles R. Nelson, *The Term Structure of Interest Rates* (New York: Basic Books, 1972); James Van Horne, "Interest Rate Risk"; and Benjamin Friedman, "Interest Rate Expectations versus Forward Rates."

[19]For further information on empirical research addressing the liquidity premium hypothesis, see J. Huston McCulloch, "An Estimation of the Liquidity Premium Hypothesis," *Journal of Political Economy* 83 (January/February 1975): 95-119; Wayne Lee, Terry S. Maness, and Donald Tuttle, "Non-Speculative Behavior and the Term Structure," *Journal of Financial and Quantitative Analysis* 15 (March 1980): 53-83; Richard Roll, *The Behavior of Interest Rates* (New York: Basic Books, 1970); and Adrian Throop, "Interest Rate Forecasts and Market Efficiency," *Economic Review,* Federal Reserve Bank of San Francisco (Spring 1981), pp. 29-43.

[20]See Modigliani and Sutch, "Innovation in Interest Rate Policy." Also see Steven W. Dobson, Richard C. Sutch, and David E. Vanderford, "An Evaluation of Alternative Empirical Models of the Term Structure of Interest Rates," *Journal of Finance* 31 (September 1976): 1,035-1,065; and Michael E. Echols and J. Walter Elliott, "Rational Expectations in a Disequilibrium Model of the Term Structure," *American Economic Review* 66 (March 1976): 28-44. Other interesting findings are discussed in V. Vance Roley, "The Determinants of the Treasury Yield Curve," *Journal of Finance* 36 (December 1981): 1,103-1,126.

APPLICATION OF TERM STRUCTURE THEORIES TO FINANCIAL INSTITUTIONS MANAGEMENT

Most managers, of course, do not personally intend to resolve these theoretical and empirical debates, but they are interested in using the fruits of research to make better decisions. Fortunately, although no one has written the definitive word on yield curves, ample insights are available from existing theory to assist a knowledgeable manager. Some of the most important problems in which term structure theories are useful are illustrated in the following discussion.

It is important to appreciate the perspective from which managers view the term structure. Instead of confronting the "raw material" of yield curves—investors' expectations, liquidity premiums, supply/demand relationships in the financial markets—managers observe the "finished products," such as the actual term structures depicted in Figures 6.2 through 6.4. Term structure theories attempt to explain how observed term structures came about. The information a manager obtains by applying theory to an existing yield curve can assist in making decisions, such as forecasting interest rates, setting a mortgage loan rate, or trading securities for the institution's portfolio.

Interest Rate Forecasting

Of particular importance to interest rate forecasting is the pure expectations theory, primarily because research on the segmented markets and preferred habitat theories is still inconclusive. Further, the mathematical expression of the pure expectations theory itself provides a forecasting model. To illustrate, suppose in June 1990, the spot Treasury yields shown in Table 6.2 for a five-year maturity horizon are observed.

Forward Rates.   According to the pure expectations theory, the two-year spot rate is the geometric average of the expected yield on a one-year Treasury security—a rate that

can be directly observed from the existing yield curve—and the expected annual yield on one-year securities as of June 1991, a rate not directly observable. That relationship was modeled mathematically in Equation 6.1:

$$1 + {_1}\tilde{i}_2 = \sqrt{(1 + {_1}\bar{i}_1)(1 + {_2}\tilde{i}_1)}$$
$$1 + 0.1185 = \sqrt{(1.1250)(1 + {_2}\tilde{i}_1)}$$

where: ${_2}\tilde{i}_1$ = unobservable expected one-year rate at the beginning of period 2.

If the pure expectations theory is correct, one can infer the expected one-year rate at the beginning of period 2 by solving Equation 6.1 for ${_2}\tilde{i}_1$:

(6.3)

$$(1 + {_1}\bar{i}_2)^2 = (1 + {_1}\bar{i}_1)(1 + {_2}\tilde{i}_1)$$

$$1 + {_2}\tilde{i}_1 = (1 + {_1}\bar{i}_2)^2/(1 + {_1}\bar{i}_1)$$

$$1 + {_2}\tilde{i}_1 = (1.1185)^2/1.1250$$

$$1 + {_2}\tilde{i}_1 = 1.1120 - 1 = 0.1120 = 11.20\%$$

An implied expected rate calculated from an existing yield curve is a **_forward rate._** The one-year forward rate at the beginning of period 2 is 11.20 percent. This rate is expected to prevail on investments made in June 1991 and maturing in June 1992. It is lower than the one-year T-bill yield in 1990, because the spot yields in Table 6.2 suggest market expectations for falling rates. If an institution's managers use the pure expectations theory, this forward rate can serve as a specific forecast for short-term Treasury bill rates in June 1992.

The general formula for a one-year forward rate as of the beginning of period t is:

(6.4) $1 + {_t}\tilde{i}_1 = (1 + {_1}\bar{i}_t)^t/(1 + {_1}\bar{i}_{t-1})^{t-1}$

Equation 6.4 allows calculation of the one-year forward rate as of the beginning of any future period (t). It is more useful than Equation 6.3,

---

Table 6.2
Hypothetical Spot Rates on Treasury Securities as of June 1990

Maturity Date	Spot Yield	Notation
June 1991	12.50%	$_1\bar{i}_1$
June 1992	11.85%	$_1\bar{i}_2$
June 1993	11.00%	$_1\bar{i}_3$
June 1994	10.90%	$_1\bar{i}_4$
June 1995	10.50%	$_1\bar{i}_5$

---

which solves only for the one-year forward rate as of the beginning of period 2.

Incorporating Liquidity Premiums. Many managers may not accept the unbiased expectations theory as the only explanation for the term structure. Fortunately, it is possible to incorporate liquidity premiums into a forecasting model. If liquidity premiums exist, spot rates for two-, three-, four-, and five-year securities in Table 6.2 are affected not only by expectations but also by premiums on long-term investments.

For example, suppose a manager believes that investors expect a premium of 0.5 percent for holding a two-year security in 1990. That belief can be incorporated into a forecast of future short-term rates by solving Equation 6.2 for the forward rate as of the beginning of period 2:

(6.5)

$$1 + {}_1\bar{i}_2 = \sqrt{(1 + {}_1\bar{i}_1)(1 + {}_2\tilde{i}_1 + L_2)}$$
$$1 + {}_2\tilde{i}_1 = [(1 + {}_1\bar{i}_2)^2/(1 + {}_1\bar{i}_1)] - L_2$$

Under the assumption of liquidity premiums, the estimate for the forward rate at the beginning of 1991 becomes:

$$(1.1185)^2 = (1.1250)(1 + {}_2\tilde{i}_1 + 0.005)$$
$$1 + {}_2\tilde{i}_1 + 0.005 = (1.1185)^2/(1.1250)$$
$$1 + {}_2\tilde{i}_1 + 0.005 = 1.1120$$
$$1 + {}_2\tilde{i}_1 = 1.1120 - 0.005 = 1.1070$$
$$_2\tilde{i}_1 = 0.1070 = 10.70\%$$

This forward rate in 1991 is lower than the forward rate of 11.20 percent calculated earlier with only the pure expectations theory as a basis for forecasting. The difference is the assumed liquidity premium required for two-year loans. If liquidity premiums exist, their effect on actual long-term rates will cause the results of Equations 6.3 or 6.4 to be biased upward. Forward rates should be lowered by the appropriate liquidity premium for the maturity involved.

Using the pure expectations theory with liquidity premiums, the general equation for calculating the one-year forward rate in period t is:

(6.6)

$$1 + {}_t\tilde{i}_1 = [(1 + {}_1\bar{i}_t)^t/(1 + {}_1\bar{i}_{t-1})^{t-1}] - L_t$$

Equation 6.6 allows estimation of the forward rate as of the beginning of any future period, adjusted for a liquidity premium. In contrast, Equation 6.5 applies only to the forward rate as of the beginning of period 2.

Setting Institutional Interest Rates

A financial institution manager frequently faces simultaneous decisions about short- and long-term interest rates. For example, if short-term deposits such as one-year CDs are to be used to finance long-term assets such as mortgages, care must be taken to establish both rates so that the cost of financing does not exceed the yield on the mortgages. Using the pure expectations theory, a manager who observes an upward-sloping Treasury security term structure can infer that most investors expect increasing short-term rates over the next several periods. The cost of one-year CDs is therefore likely to increase during the period when mortgage loans made today have a constant yield.

According to the liquidity premium theory, existing Treasury rates may also include liquidity premiums, and the manager may also believe that a premium for default risk should be required for holding mortgages instead of Treasury securities. Furthermore, the segmented markets and preferred habitat theories suggest that competitive pressures from other deposi-

tory institutions should be considered in setting both rates. For example, if there is strong competition for one-year CDs, the S&L may be forced to pay an even higher yield than the expectations hypothesis would suggest.

Estimating the Cost of Deposits.   Sample calculations and estimations involved in this decision are provided in Table 6.3. For simplicity, it is assumed that mortgages made today will mature in five years. The manager would begin by calculating a series of one-year forward rates implied in the existing yield curve, using Equation 6.4. Using Equation 6.6, liquidity premiums embedded in the current term structure

---

Table 6.3
Using Term Structure Theories to Set Institutional Interest Rates

(1) Maturity (Years)	(2) Observed Yield on Treasury Securities	(3) Unadjusted One-Year Forward Rate (from Equation 6.4)	(4) Estimated Liquidity Premium	(5) Estimated One-Year Rate with Liquidity Premium Removed (Column 3 − Column 4)
1	0.0800	0.0800	0.0000	0.0800
2	0.0825	0.0850	0.0050	0.0800
3	0.0950	0.1204	0.0100	0.1104
4	0.1025	0.1253	0.0250	0.1003
5	0.1100	0.1405	0.0350	0.1055

(6) Annual CD Cost (Column 5 + Administrative Markup of 0.25% per Year)	(7) Estimated Premium Required to Hold Mortgages	(8) Estimated Annual Required Return (Column 6 + Column 7 + Profit Markup of 0.75% per Year)
0.0825	0.0100	0.1000
0.0825	0.0250	0.1150
0.1129	0.0300	0.1504
0.1028	0.0400	0.1503
0.1080	0.0450	0.1605

(9)
Estimation of Required Annual Yield on Mortgages (Using Equation 6.1 on Data from Column 8):

$$i_m = \sqrt[5]{(1.1000)(1.1150)(1.1504)(1.1503)(1.1605)} - 1$$

$$i_m = 0.1350 = 13.50\%$$

would be removed to avoid overestimating expected one-year CD rates in future periods. Because the institution plans to issue one-year CDs each year, it would not have to offer liquidity premiums to its depositors.

The resulting series of forward rates (given in Column 5) is used to set initial and anticipated one-year CD rates. Specifically, the initial CD rate is based on the first rate in this series (8 percent), with subsequent forward rates serving as the basis for estimating the future annual interest cost of the deposits. After obtaining these costs, the manager would increase them as appropriate to account for the administrative costs of servicing deposits and for the desired profit markup (Column 6). In addition, adjustments would be made to account for premiums necessary to meet competitors' offerings. Column 6 contains estimated total interest plus noninterest costs of issuing one-year CDs each year for five years.

Setting the Mortgage Rate.   The manager would then set the five-year mortgage rate by estimating the risk premium necessary to compensate the institution for holding mortgages (Column 7). Finally, a desired profit markup of 0.75 percent per year is added to allow for a return to owners in a stockholder–owned firm or to provide for additions to net worth in a mutual institution. The resulting figures in Column 8 are the estimated annual returns required to cover all costs, including the cost of funds, noninterest costs, and a target rate of profit. Finally, the geometric average of the five rates is calculated, using Equation 6.1. This rate, 13.5 percent in Table 6.3, is the appropriate annual interest rate to charge on a mortgage made at the beginning of the five-year period. If the institution earns 13.5 percent annually for five years, and if actual costs equal estimates, the desired profit markup over the life of the mortgage will be earned. Of course, an institution's ability to charge this rate is constrained by competition, but competing institutions would also be aware of the need to recover long-term costs.

It is important to remember, of course, that even such careful forecasting and rate setting

necessarily include a great deal of uncertainty. As the review of empirical research suggested, expectations embedded in the term structure are not always fulfilled, and additional sources of error are introduced in the estimation of the liquidity premium. Such errors can be costly, because once the long-term mortgage rate has been established, it may not be subject to renegotiation, and profits will disappear if interest rates move to such a high level that costs cannot be recovered. Many thrift institutions, in particular, learned this lesson the hard way in the early 1980s. Institutions must also maintain sufficient flexibility to respond when forecasts prove to be incorrect. Increasingly sophisticated techniques for managing interest rate risk are discussed in chapters that follow.

Managing the Securities Portfolio

Term structure theories are also useful in managing the institution's securities portfolio. A common trading strategy is searching for undervalued or overvalued securities. This strategy assumes that, although the pure expectations theory applies in general, and investors price securities to make the expected annual yield the same regardless of the maturities selected over a holding period, the markets are sometimes in temporary disequilibrium. According to this line of thinking, if a security's yield exceeds those on securities of equal maturity and risk, the security is underpriced. If the institution does not own the security, it can purchase it immediately. When the market returns to equilibrium, the price of the security should rise, lowering its yield to the appropriate level. The institution can expect to profit from the capital gain.

Conversely, if a security's yield is less than those on securities of comparable maturity, the security is overpriced and should be sold. The pure expectations theory suggests that its price will fall as the market returns its yield to the level proper for its maturity. Analysts sometimes attempt to identify under- or overvalued securities in the Treasury market, for example, by studying yield curves such as those in Figures 6.2 through 6.4. In Figure 6.2, the issue circled near the center of the graph has a lower yield than securities of similar maturity. A manager who believed the market was in temporary disequilibrium would sell the issue before the anticipated drop in price increases its yield.

SUMMARY

The term structure of interest rates is the relationship at a specific time between the yields and maturities of securities of comparable default risk. Historically, this relationship has varied. The variation is related both to the general level of interest rates and to the pace of economic activity.

Economists have developed several theories to explain term structures. Researchers agree that the financial markets' expectations of future short-term rates play a large role in determining existing yields on long-term securities. Other factors, such as possible investor preferences for liquidity, their policies and attitudes, or regulation in the financial markets, appear to have less influence on the term structure.

Knowledge of term structure relationships is useful in asset/liability management. Understanding the role of expectations allows managers develop interest rate forecasts to use in institutional planning and in trading strategies for the securities portfolio. In addition, knowledge of expectations, liquidity preferences, and supply/demand interactions can help managers establish the prices of financial products such as deposits and loans.

Questions

1. What is meant by the term structure of interest rates? What factors influence the relationship between yield and maturity?

2. Historically, what relationship has existed between the shape of the yield curve and the level of economic activity? Between the shape of the yield curve and the general level of interest rates?

3. From a recent issue of *The Wall Street Journal* or other major newspaper, find yield quotations for U.S. Treasury securities. Using information for T-bills, bonds, and notes, sketch the prevailing term structure.

4. How does the pure expectations theory explain the term structure of interest rates? Briefly explain the assumptions on which the theory is based.

5. **a.** Using the pure expectations theory and the yield curve you have plotted in Question 3, what prediction would you make about the direction in which short-term interest rates will change in the future? Explain how the pure expectations theory supports your forecasts.
   b. Assuming that the yield curve currently prevailing includes liquidity premiums that gradually increase as maturity increases, roughly sketch the current *pure expectations* term structure.

6. Which of the following investment plans would an advocate of the pure expectations theory prefer over a ten-year period, assuming an expected increase in interest rates? Why?
   a. A four-year investment followed by 3 two-year investments
   b. A series of 5 two-year investments

7. Explain how the liquidity premium hypothesis differs from the pure expectations theory. With which of the pure expectations assumptions does the liquidity premium hypothesis most strongly disagree?

8. According to the modified expectations theory, how do borrowers influence interest rate levels?

9. How does the segmented markets hypothesis explain the observed term structure of interest rates? What assumptions are made about the maturity preferences of borrowers and lenders?

10. How does the preferred habitat theory characterize the maturity preferences of borrowers and lenders? Under what conditions will investors switch from one maturity to another? In your opinion, does the preferred habitat theory support the existence of a continuous yield curve? Why or why not?

11. With which theory of the term structure do you most agree? With which do you least agree? By integrating ideas from term structure theories, state briefly how you believe the term structure is determined.

Problems

1.

Treasury Bill Purchased	Treasury Bill Matures	Expected Annual Rate
August 1989	August 1990	8.32% (observed)
August 1990	August 1991	9.75
August 1991	August 1992	10.80
August 1992	August 1993	11.50
August 1993	August 1994	12.25

   a. Using the information above and the pure expectations hypothesis, calculate the yield to maturity as of August 1989 for each of the following:
   1) a two-year security
   2) a three-year security
   3) a four-year security
   4) a five-year security
   b. Calculate the expected average annual yield for each of the following investment strategies:
   1) investment in a two-year security followed by investment in a three-year security
   2) investment in a one-year security followed by investment in a four-year security
   3) investment in a series of 5 one-year securities
   c. Explain how your answers to part b support the pure expectations theory.
   d. Using your calculations in part a, sketch the term structure of interest rates that would be observed in August 1989.

2.

Treasury Bill Purchased	Treasury Bill Matures	Expected Annual Rate	Liquidity Premium as of May 1990
May 1990	May 1991	8.32% (observed)	0.0000
May 1991	May 1992	9.85	0.0020 (on 2-year security)
May 1992	May 1993	10.90	0.0030 (on 3-year security)
May 1993	May 1994	11.65	0.0035 (on 4-year security)
May 1994	May 1995	12.45	0.0040 (on 5-year security)

   a. Based on the information above and using the liquidity premium hypothesis, calculate the yield to maturity as of May 1990 for each of the following:
   1) a two-year Treasury security
   2) a three-year security
   3) a five-year security
   b. Calculate the expected annual yield for each of the following investment strategies:
   1) investment in a four-year Treasury security
   2) investment in a one-year security followed by investment in a three-year security
   3) investment in a series of 4 one-year securities

c. Using your calculations in part a, sketch the term structure of interest rates that would be observed in May 1990.

3.

Treasury Bill Purchased	Treasury Bill Matures	Expected Annual Rate
June 1988	June 1989	7.75% (observed)
June 1989	June 1990	8.90
June 1990	June 1991	10.90
June 1991	June 1992	11.25

a. Calculate the expected average annual yield for each of the following investment strategies:
  1) investment in a series of 3 one-year securities, with the investments made in June of each year from 1988 through 1990 (beginning of the month)
  2) investment in a one-year security in June 1988 followed by investment in a two-year security in June 1989

b. Calculate the expected average annual yield for each of the following investment strategies:
  1) investment in a three-year security in June 1988 followed by investment in a one-year security in June 1991
  2) investment in a series of 4 one-year securities, with the investments made in June of each year from 1988 through 1991

c. Recalculate your answers for parts a and b under the liquidity premium hypothesis, given the following liquidity premiums as of June 1988:

Maturity of Security	Liquidity Premium
1 Year	0.0000
2	0.0010
3	0.0020
4	0.0025

4.

Treasury Security Maturity Date	Spot Yield as of May 1988
May 1989	12.30%
May 1990	11.75
May 1991	11.00
May 1992	10.20
May 1993	9.50

a. Calculate the one-year forward rate as of May 1990 (the beginning of period 3).
b. Calculate the one-year forward rate as of May 1991 (the beginning of period 4).

5. For this problem, use the information on maturity dates and spot yields from Problem 4 and the liquidity premiums in the following table.
  a. Calculate the one-year forward rate with liquidity premium removed as of May 1992 (the beginning of period 5).
  b. Calculate the one-year forward rate with liquidity premium removed as of May 1991 (the beginning of period 4).

Maturity of Security	Liquidity Premium as of May 1988
1 Year	0.0000
2	0.0020
3	0.0025
4	0.0030
5	0.0035

6. A commercial bank manager must set rates for one-year CDs and four-year auto loans to be financed by the CDs. The manager observes an upward-sloping term structure for Treasury securities and wants to be confident the rate set on the auto loans is profitable because it cannot be changed over the four-year period. The following information is available. Based on this information and your knowledge of term structure theories, calculate expected rates for the one-year CDs and an appropriate rate for the four-year auto loans. Assume liquidity premiums equal 0.

Maturity	Observed Annual Yield
1 year	0.0700
2	0.0750
3	0.0850
4	0.0925

Administrative Markup   1½% per year

Premiums Required for Holding Auto Loans

Year 1	0.020
Year 2	0.025
Year 3	0.030
Year 4	0.035

7. A savings institution manager needs to set rates for mortgage loans on which the rate will be adjusted after five years, based on estimates of the cost of one-year CDs used to finance the mortgages. Use your knowledge of term structure theories to determine the rates expected for the CDs and the appropriate mortgage rate. The available information is as follows:

Maturity	Observed Yield
1 year	0.0650
2	0.0695
3	0.0725
4	0.0785
5	0.0850

Profit Markup on CDs   1¼% per year

Estimated Premiums for Holding Mortgages

Year 1	0.010
Year 2	0.020
Year 3	0.030
Year 4	0.040
Year 5	0.045

In addition to this information, the manager believes that the following liquidity premiums are included in observed long-term yields:

Maturity	Premium
1 Year	0.00000
2	0.00150
3	0.00200
4	0.00250
5	0.00275

Selected References

Cox, John C., Jonathan E. Ingersoll, Jr., and Stephen A. Ross. "A Re-Examination of Traditional Hypotheses about the Term Structure of Interest Rates." *Journal of Finance* 36 (September 1981): 769-799.

Culbertson, John M. "The Term Structure of Interest Rates." *Quarterly Journal of Economics* 71 (November 1957): 485-517.

Dobson, Steven W., Richard C. Sutch, and David E. Vanderford. "An Evaluation of Alternative Empirical Models of the Term Structure of Interest Rates." *Journal of Finance* 31 (September 1976): 1,035-1,065.

Echols, Michael E., and J. Walter Elliot. "Rational Expectations in a Disequilibrium Model of the Term Structure." *American Economic Review* 66 (March 1966): 28-44.

Friedman, Benjamin M. "Interest Rate Expectations versus Forward Rates: Evidence from an Expectations Survey." *Journal of Finance* 34 (September 1979): 965-973.

Hicks, J. R. *Value and Capital.* London: Oxford University Press, 1946.

Kane, Edward J., and Burton G. Malkiel. "The Term Structure of Interest Rates: An Analysis of a Survey of Interest Rate Expectations." *Review of Economics and Statistics* 49 (August 1967): 343-355.

Kessel, Reuben A. *The Cyclical Behavior of the Term Structure.* New York: National Bureau of Economic Research, 1965.

Lee, Wayne, Terry S. Maness, and Donald Tuttle. "Non-Speculative Behavior and the Term Structure." *Journal of Financial and Quantitative Analysis* 15 (March 1980): 53-83.

Lutz, Frederick. "The Structure of Interest Rates." *Quarterly Journal of Economics* 30 (November 1940): 36-63.

Malkiel, Burton. *The Term Structure of Interest Rates: Theory, Empirical Evidence, and Applications.* Princeton, NJ: Princeton University Press, 1966.

McCulloch, Huston J. "An Estimation of the Liquidity Premium Hypothesis." *Journal of Political Economy* 83 (January/February 1975): 95-119.

Meiselman, David. *The Term Structure of Interest Rates.* Englewood Cliffs, NJ: Prentice-Hall, 1962.

Modigliani, Franco, and Richard Sutch. "Innovation in Interest Rate Policy." *American Economic Review* 66 (May 1966): 178-197.

Nelson, Charles R. *The Term Structure of Interest Rates.* New York: Basic Books, 1972.

Roley, V. Vance. "The Determinants of the Treasury Yield Curve." *Journal of Finance* 36 (December 1981): 1,103-1,126.

Roll, Richard. *The Behavior of Interest Rates.* New York: Basic Books, 1970.

Schiller, Robert J., John Y. Campbell, and Kermit L. Schoenholtz. "Forward Rates and Future Policy: Interpreting the Term Structure of Interest Rates." In *Brookings Papers on Economic Activity, I: 1983* (Washington DC: Brookings Institution, 1983): 173-223.

Throop, Adrian. "Interest Rate Forecasts and Market Efficiency." *Economic Review* (Federal Reserve Bank of San Francisco) (Spring 1981), pp. 29–43.

Van Horne, James. "Interest Rate Risk and the Term Structure of Interest Rates." *Journal of Political Economy* 73 (August 1965): 344–351.

Wood, John H. "Do Yield Curves Normally Slope Up? The Term Structure of Interest Rates, 1862–1982." *Economic Perspectives* (Federal Reserve Bank of Chicago) 7 (July/August 1983): 17–23.

Chapter 7

INTEREST RATE RISK

Nothing on Wall Street is truly assured. But risks are more bearable if they are understood.

Robert McGough
Writer
Fortune (1984)

IN the summer of 1984, when T-bond yields exceeded 13 percent, a client with $7 million to invest approached Dale B. Krieger, a New York money manager. He asked that his funds be placed in low-risk assets, expecting to settle for a commensurately low return. Krieger chose a portfolio of T-bonds. By December 1985, when T-bond yields had fallen to about 9 percent, the portfolio's value had increased by over $700,000, a holding-period return that made the managers of some common stock portfolios envious. Because T-bonds have no default risk, the relatively high return in this instance is attributable to something else—specifically, to the steep drop in bond yields over the period. Understanding the relationship between changes in the value of financial assets and changes in their yields is the key to understanding Krieger's success as a portfolio manager.[1]

---

[1]Elizabeth Ehrlich, "The Smorgasboard of Bonds: Something for Almost Every Palate," *Business Week,* December 30, 1985, p. 122.

INTEREST RATE RISK DEFINED

Risk is a fact of life. Previous chapters have defined risk as potential variation in the returns from an investment and have briefly identified its sources in the financial markets. This chapter explains and illustrates the most significant risk faced by financial institutions: potential variation in returns caused by unexpected changes in interest rates, or **interest rate risk**.

Note the use of the word *unexpected*. As indicated in the last two chapters, investors can—and, according to empirical tests, do—incorporate *expected* changes in interest rates into their investment decisions. The risk they face, then, arises not from changes they *correctly* anticipate at the time investment decisions are made, but from changes they do not anticipate. Because even the most astute forecasters err, no investors are protected against potential variation in returns, even if forecasting is a part of their decision making.

THE PRICE/YIELD CONNECTION

Although unexpected changes in interest rates affect virtually all financial instruments, they do not affect them equally. Differences in interest rate risk occur because of the type of instrument, the maturity, the size and timing of cash inflows, and the planned holding period relative to the asset's maturity. To understand interest rate risk, however, it is first necessary to understand fundamental principles of financial asset prices.

Individual Investors Cannot Change Prices

Chapter 4 noted that most financial markets are characterized by many participants and much publicly available information. Generally, an individual investor, as only one of many buyers and sellers, is unable to influence the price of a financial asset. A manager considering the purchase of a T-bill knows that an institution must pay the going market price; it is futile to expect a lower price than other market participants are willing to pay at the time. Conversely, the manager need not fear paying more than other buyers of the same T-bill.

Supply/Demand Is Important

It is also clear, from casual observation of the financial pages of any newspaper, that market prices of financial assets change frequently. Thus, knowing the price of a Treasury bill one day does not mean that one will know it the next day or even later in the same day. A successful manager must understand factors associated with price changes.

Basic microeconomic theory establishes the influence of supply and demand in setting nonfinancial market prices. Financial assets, too, are affected by these forces. Actually, two supply/demand relationships are at work. One is the supply of and demand for a particular financial asset. Generally, the larger the quantity of a financial asset relative to similar assets, the lower its price. Thus, a corporation's sale of new stock often results in a decline in price as supply increases.

But a broader supply/demand relationship is also important, as seen in Chapter 5. For example, an increase in the total supply of loanable funds, with no increase in the demand for borrowing, will result in higher financial asset prices in general as more lenders bid for the right to hold the existing stock of financial assets instead of cash. Because new financial assets are always being created, and existing ones eliminated as borrowers repay previous liabilities, prices often change as a result of changes in overall supply and demand.

Risk Is Important, Too

There is more to the determination of prices than supply/demand relationships. As noted in Chapter 4, all else equal, the price of a riskier asset will be lower than that of a less risky one because most financial market participants are risk-averse. Risk aversion causes investors to demand higher expected rates of return from riskier investments.

Putting Them Together

The effects of these influences on security prices are incorporated in a mathematical relationship explained in Chapter 4, the general equation for the effective annual yield on a financial asset:

$$(4.7) \quad P_0 = \sum_{t=1}^{N} \frac{C_t}{(1 + y^*)^t}$$

Although this equation was used as an *implicit* formula for the effective yield, it is also an

---

Figure 7.1
Relationship between Security Prices and Market Rates

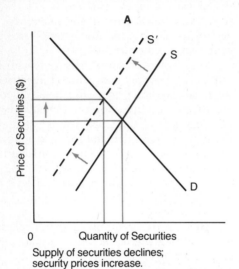

A

Supply of securities declines;
security prices increase.

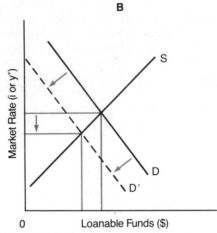

B

Demand for loanable funds declines;
market rate declines.

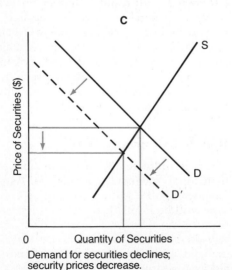

C

Demand for securities declines;
security prices decrease.

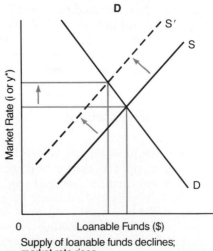

D

Supply of loanable funds declines;
market rate rises.

---

explicit expression for the price of a financial asset. Specifically, it states that the price of an asset is equal to the present value of its future cash benefits, discounted at y*, the rate of return the financial markets expect for the riskiness of the asset. This expression reveals the relationship between price and yield.

Prices and Yields Change Simultaneously.

It is evident that, all else equal, price changes must be accompanied by yield changes, and vice versa. However, one does not cause the other; they change simultaneously, both caused by changes in underlying economic conditions. For example, suppose the supply of securities declines. If there is no shift in the demand curve for securities, the price of financial assets will rise. This situation is illustrated in Panel A of Figure 7.1. A purchaser of financial assets at the new higher price expects a lower annual yield than before the price increase.

The supply of securities is also the demand for loanable funds, just as demand for securities reflects the willingness to supply loanable funds. A decrease in the supply of securities corresponds to a decrease in the demand for loanable funds. Should this occur, as shown in Panel B of Figure 7.1, the market yield will decline. Thus, both the prices of financial assets and their expected yields change simultaneously but in opposite directions. The price/yield relationship before and after a change in the supply of loanable funds, or the demand for securities, is illustrated in Panels C and D.

Including Risk in the Relationship.

Suppose increasing tension between the United States and the Soviet Union makes investors more risk-averse. If they expect the tension to lead to greater economic uncertainty, the slope of the risk/expected return relationship will change, and investors will expect greater rewards for bearing risk at all levels, as illustrated in Figure 7.2. If investors previously expected an effective annual yield of y_1* on an investment with a perceived level of risk designated by

---

Figure 7.2
Effect of a Change in Market Yields Caused by a Change in Risk Aversion

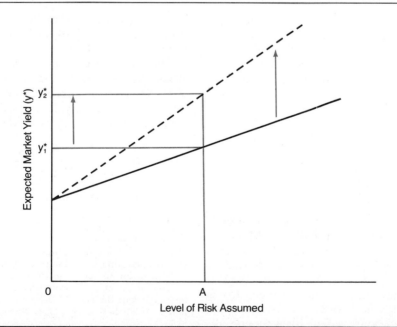

Figure 7.3
ATT Bond Prices: May 17 and May 20, 1985

NEW YORK EXCHANGE BONDS

Friday, May 17, 1985

CORPORATION BONDS
Volume, $39,110,000

Bonds	Cur Yld	Vol	High	Low	Close	Net Chg.
ABrnd 5⅞92	7.9	1	74⅛	74⅛	74⅛	....
ABrnd 11⅛89	11.	10	102	102	102	− ¼
ACan 4¾s90	6.4	25	74	74	74	+1
ACyan 7⅜01	11.	48	68⅛	68⅛	68⅛	+ ⅛
AExC 8½s86	8.6	77	99½	99⅜	99⅜	+ ⅞
AExC 11¼00	11.	2	100	100	100	.....
AmGn 11s07	cv	11	186½	186½	186½	+1¼
AmGn 11s08	cv	12	186½	186½	186½	+1
AHoist 5½93	cv	22	63¼	63¼	63¼	.....
AmMed 8¼08	cv	5	92⅞	92	92	−1
AmMed 11¾99	12.	5	97½	97½	97½	+ ½
AmMot 6s88	cv	22	80	80	80	+1
ATT 3⅞s90	4.9	41	79	78½	78⅝	+ ⅛
ATT 8¾00	11.	169	80⅞	80⅛	80¼	− ⅜
ATT 7s01	10.	51	67½	67¼	67½	− ⅛
ATT 7⅛s03	11.	66	66⅝	66¼	66½	+ ¼
ATT 8.80s05	11.	226	78⅝	78⅛	78⅜	− ⅛
ATT 8⅝s07	11.	45	76½	76	76⅜	− ⅛
ATT 10⅜90	10.	375	99⅞	99⅝	99⅞	....
ATT 13¼91	13.	845	105	104¾	105	+ ⅛
Amfac 5¼94	cv	13	80	80	80	...
Amoco 9.2s04	11.	15	84	83½	84	+ ¾
Amoco 8.9s89†	8.9	5	100	100	100	.....
Amoco 7⅞07	11.	5	73	73	73	+2
Amoco 14s91	13.	25	110	110	110	+ ¼

NEW YORK EXCHANGE BONDS

Monday, May 20, 1985

CORPORATION BONDS
Volume, $56,710,000

Bonds	Cur Yld	Vol	High	Low	Close	Net Chg.
ABrnd 4⅝90	5.8	1	79½	79½	79½	.....
ABrnd 11⅛89	11.	14	102¼	102¼	102¼	+ ¼
ACan 11⅜10	12.	25	93½	93½	93½	+1½
ACan 13¼93	12.	7	108	107	108	+1¾
ACyan 8⅜06	11.	40	75	75	75	+1
AExC 7.8s92	9.1	15	86	86	86	+5⅞
AExC 7.7s87	7.9	15	96⅞	96⅞	96⅞	+ ⅛
AExC 11¼00	11.	3	100	100	100	.....
AExC 12⅞91	12.	8	106⅜	106⅜	106⅜	+1½
AExC 11⅝92	11.	31	105⅝	103¾	105⅝	+3¾
AmGn 11s07	cv	36	196¼	189	196¼	+9¾
AmGn 11s08	cv	2	189	189	189	+2½
AmMed 9½01	cv	56	118	116¾	117	+ ½
AmMed 8¼08	cv	30	92⅛	92	92⅛	+ ⅛
AmMed 11s98	12.	5	95	95	95	+2
AmMed 11¾99	12.	11	99½	98¼	98¼	+ ¾
AmMot 6s88	cv	3	80	80	80	.....
ATT 2⅝s86	2.8	59	94⅝	94⅜	94⅜	− ⅜
ATT 2⅞s87	3.2	50	90	90	90	+ ½
ATT 3⅞s90	4.8	21	80	79	80	+1⅜
ATT 8¾00	11.	455	83⅜	81⅜	82¾	+2½
ATT 7s01	10.	259	70⅞	68¾	69¼	+1¾
ATT 7⅛s03	10.	592	68¾	67⅛	68¾	+2¼
ATT 8.80s05	11.	264	82½	79⅜	80¾	+2⅜
ATT 8⅝s07	11.	308	79	76⅞	77	+ ⅝
ATT 10⅜90	10.	584	101	100½	100⅞	+1
ATT 13¼91	13.	958	105⅜	105	105⅜	+ ⅜
Ames 10s95	12.	2	86	86	86	−1½
Ames 8½09	cv	22	139	139	139	−1
Amoco 6s91	7.3	20	81¾	81¾	81¾	+ ¼
Amoco 6s98	9.0	12	66⅞	66¾	66⅞	+ ⅛
Amoco 9.2s04	11.	11	85⅜	83¾	85⅜	+1⅜
Amoco 8.9s89†	8.9	5	100	100	100	.....

Source: The Wall Street Journal, May 20, 1985, p. 42; May 21, 1985, p. 44.

point A, but an increase in risk aversion increases the yield to y_2^*, the price of securities with that degree of risk will fall. Of course, supply/demand relationships and risk aversion can change at the same time. If so, prices and yields will still change simultaneously in opposite directions.

THE PRICE/YIELD RELATIONSHIP ILLUSTRATED

Figure 7.3 presents information about several bonds traded on Friday, May 17, and Monday, May 20, 1985. The coupon rates of American Telephone and Telegraph (ATT) bonds traded on both dates varied from 3⅞ percent to 13¼ percent, and their maturity dates ranged from 1990 to 2007; in other words, the size and timing of their cash flows varied. Even though all ATT bonds were presumably equal in default risk, they were selling at different prices and yields on Friday, May 17.

Focusing on two specific issues, the 3⅞s of 90 and the 10⅜s of 90, and assuming a par value of $1,000, annual interest payments, and exactly five years to maturity, it is possible to calculate their yields to maturity as of May 17:[2]

$$\$786.25 = \sum_{t=1}^{5} \frac{\$38.75}{(1 + y^*)^t} + \frac{\$1,000.00}{(1 + y^*)^5}$$

$$y^* = 9.43\%$$

[2]The phrase *3⅞s of 90* is standard notation in bond quotations, indicating a bond with a coupon rate of 3⅞ percent, maturing sometime in 1990. (The *s* is added to the coupon rate to facilitate pronunciation.) The specific maturity dates of the two ATT bonds are July 1 (3⅞) and June 1 (10⅜). See *Moody's Bond Record,* December 1985, p. 7.

$$\$998.75 = \sum_{t=1}^{5} \frac{\$103.75}{(1 + y^*)^t} + \frac{\$1,000.00}{(1 + y^*)^5}$$

$$y^* = 10.41\%$$

Late on May 17, the Federal Reserve Board announced it was lowering the discount rate from 8 percent to 7½ percent. Although the discount rate is an administered, not a market, rate, the Fed's message was that it was decreasing the price of loanable funds for financial institutions eligible to borrow at the discount window. On the next business day, a headline in *The Wall Street Journal* read: "Fed's Discount-Fee Cut to 7½% Is Seen Paving Way for Lower Interest Rates."[3] In fact, within minutes after the Fed's announcement, several large banks announced they were lowering their commercial loan rates.

What reaction would be predicted in the market for ATT bonds? With falling interest rates, the prices of bonds would be expected to rise. Because the maturity dates and the cash inflows expected from the two ATT bonds did not change with the Fed's announcement, the prices of these bonds would be expected to increase to bring their yields into line with new market conditions.[4] In fact, these movements

---

[3]Tom Herman and Edward Foldessy, "Fed's Discount-Fee Cut to 7½% Is Seen Paving Way for Lower Interest Rates," *The Wall Street Journal,* May 20, 1985, pp. 3, 8.

Because the discount rate is an administered rate, the relationship between market-determined rates and the discount rate is not uniform. In this instance, market rate declines and a cut in the discount rate coincided, although at other times, the Fed has, to meet monetary policy objectives, changed the discount rate in a direction opposite to that of recent changes in market rates. See John H. Wood and Norma L. Wood, *Financial Markets* (San Diego: Harcourt Brace Jovanovich, 1985), pp. 235-240.

[4]As mentioned in Chapter 4, variable-rate bonds have coupons that change over the time to maturity, usually in conjunction with the movement of a specified interest rate index. It is possible, therefore, that the expected cash benefits from some bonds could change with a change in market yields. Variable-rate bonds are the exception, however, rather than the rule. The impact of variable-rate financial assets and liabilities is explored in later chapters.

did occur, as illustrated by data from trading on Monday, May 20:

$$\$800.00 = \sum_{t=1}^{5} \frac{\$38.75}{(1 + y^*)^t} + \frac{\$1,000.00}{(1 + y^*)^5}$$

$$y^* = 9.02\%$$

$$\$1,008.75 = \sum_{t=1}^{5} \frac{\$103.75}{(1 + y^*)^t} + \frac{\$1,000.00}{(1 + y^*)^5}$$

$$y^* = 10.14\%$$

Because both bonds had five years to maturity, term structure effects did not account for yield differences. Nor did the prices of the two bonds change by the same dollar amount or by the same percentage of the May 17 price. The price of the 3⅞s bond rose by \$13.75, or 1.749 percent, whereas the price of the 10⅜s bond rose by \$10.00, or 1.001 percent.

The reason for the differences is related to the coupon rates of the two bonds relative to new market rates and is explored later. For now, the important point is that the upward movement in bond prices held for all ATT bonds shown in Figure 7.3 on May 20, 1985. This is a direct example of one of the most important economic principles in the financial markets:

> When market yields fall unexpectedly, the prices of existing financial assets rise; when market yields rise unexpectedly, the prices of existing financial assets fall.

The inverse relationship between prices and yields holds for all types of financial assets, although it is particularly important for assets with fixed future cash benefits, such as discount securities, coupon bonds, or annuities. Because both asset yields and liability costs are affected by this principle, managers cannot manage the net interest margin well without understanding it. The remainder of this chapter and the next explore the implications of the price/yield relationship for specific types of securities with different cash flow characteristics and different maturities.

THE TWO SIDES OF INTEREST RATE RISK

Another question arises from the events surrounding the change in the Fed's discount rate: To what extent did the effects of the cut represent interest rate risk to the holders of the ATT bonds? The answer depends upon the bondholder's investment planning horizon.

Effect on Investor Planning to Hold to Maturity

For an owner on May 17 planning to hold ATT bonds until maturity, the price change per se would have had no effect, because $1,000 would be expected at maturity both before and after the discount rate cut. For this investor, a significant influence on investment returns is the rate at which periodic cash flows received before maturity can be reinvested. Because market conditions changed with the discount rate cut, the rate at which periodic interest payments could be reinvested would have changed after May 17. To the extent that the change was unexpected, a bondholder was exposed to interest

rate risk. Assuming no additional market changes until the bond's maturity (a bold assumption), an investor's *realized* annual rate of return would not be the same as the *expected* y* as of May 17; it would be lower.

Table 7.1 presents the details of this situation. The May 17 price of the 3⅞s bond was $786.25, and the expected annual yield was 9.43 percent. Assuming no change in market yields until maturity, a bondholder could have expected to reinvest intermediate coupon payments at a yield of 9.43 percent. Under that assumption, the bondholder could calculate the value of each cash inflow plus earnings from reinvestment until 1990. For example, using Equation 4A.1, the basic compound interest equation, the 1986 interest payment of $38.75, reinvested at an annual rate of 9.43 percent for the four remaining years of the bond's life, would grow to $55.57 by 1990:

$$\$38.75 \times (1.0943)^4 = \$55.57$$

The total value of all reinvested cash flows plus the cash flows expected in 1990—that year's interest payment and the par value to

Table 7.1
Effect of a Change in the Reinvestment Rate on Realized Yields

Years to 1990	Cash Flow	Value of Cash Flow in 1990 if Reinvested at 9.43% (Original y*)	Value of Cash Flow in 1990 if Reinvested at 9.02% (New Market Yield)
5	($ 786.25)	—	—
4	38.75	$ 55.57	$ 54.74
3	38.75	50.78	50.21
2	38.75	46.40	46.06
1	38.75	42.40	42.25
0	1,038.75	1,038.75	1,038.75

Total Value of Cash Flows in 1990:[a]	Total Value of Cash Flows in 1990:[a]
$1,233.91	$1,232.00

Realized Annual Yield over 5 Years:	Realized Annual Yield over 5 Years:
$\sqrt[5]{\$1,233.91/\$786.25} - 1 = 9.43\%$	$\sqrt[5]{\$1,232.00/\$786.25} - 1 = 9.40\%$

[a]Does not add because of rounding.

be repaid in that year—would have been $1,233.91. As shown at the bottom of Table 7.1, the realized rate of return would have been 9.43 percent: The original $786.25 investment in May of 1985 would have had a value of $1,233.91 by 1990, a compound annual rate of return of 9.43 percent.

After the cut in the discount rate, the expected reinvestment rate was only 9.02 percent. If all intermediate cash flows were reinvested at that rate, total accumulated value would be $1,232.00 as of 1990. The realized compound annual yield on the $786.25 investment would be only 9.40 percent, lower than the expected annual yield before market conditions changed.

Reinvestment Risk and Financial Institutions.
Financial institutions have so many interest-bearing assets and liabilities that the effect of changing reinvestment rates is very important to them. Changing reinvestment rates for investors mean changing costs for financial institutions. If market yields fall unexpectedly, the interest costs of a financial institution will fall if it has incurred variable-rate liabilities. Of course, if market rates rise unexpectedly, the reverse is true. Either way, the net interest margin is subject to unexpected variation.

Effect on Investor Planning to Sell before Maturity

What about an owner who planned all along to sell the 3⅞s ATT bond at the opening of trading on May 21, expecting market conditions to remain unchanged from previous weeks? The price change *would* cause the realized return to differ from the original y*, because the sales price would be higher than anticipated. Exposure to risk does not always produce unexpected losses; risk is simply exposure to potential variability, both positive and negative. The expected return would *not* have been affected by the change in the expected rate at which interest payments from the bond could be reinvested after the discount rate cut, because the holder never planned to receive those payments in the first place.

Reinvestment versus Price Risk

Thus, interest rate risk has two facets: potential variation from unexpected changes in the rate at which intermediate cash flows can be reinvested—**reinvestment risk**—and potential variation from unexpected changes in market prices of financial assets—**market value or price risk.** For a given change in market conditions, the two types of interest rate risk have opposite effects. A decline in market rates lowers reinvestment rates but increases prices; an increase in market rates improves reinvestment rates but decreases prices. It is not surprising, then, that interest rate risk is so hard to manage successfully.

EFFECT OF INTEREST RATE CHANGES ON DEBT SECURITIES

Financial institution balance sheets have become more similar in recent years, but different types of institutions still focus on different instruments. Even though the general price/yield relationship is illustrated in graphs such as Figure 7.1, the impact of unexpected changes in interest rates varies from instrument to instrument.

Bond Theorems

In 1962, as part of an article on the term structure of interest rates, Burton Malkiel proposed and proved mathematically a series of theorems on the relationship between the yields and prices of fixed-income securities. These theorems have become known simply as "the bond theorems."[5] Malkiel differentiated a bond price

---

[5] Differences between the two major types of debt securities—discount and coupon-bearing—are examined in Chapter 4. They also have an important similarity in that the purchaser who holds them to maturity knows in advance the dollar amounts of the expected cash benefits from both types of instruments. Therefore, in this section they are discussed together under the generic term *bonds*. The bond theorems are discussed and proved on pp. 201–206 of Burton G. Malkiel, "Expectations, Bond Prices, and the Term Structure of Interest Rates," *Quarterly Journal of Economics* 76 (May 1962): 197–218.

equation, similar to Equation 4.7, with respect to yield and maturity, and drew the following conclusions.

Theorem I.   *Bond prices move inversely to bond yields.* The implications of Theorem I are explained earlier in this chapter.

Theorem II.   *Holding the coupon rate constant, for a given change in market yields, percentage changes in bond prices are greater, the longer the term to maturity.*[6] To illustrate, consider two $1,000 bonds with 12 percent coupon rates, one with 15 years to maturity and one with 5 years to maturity. If the expected yield for bonds in this risk class is 12 percent and the term structure is flat, both will sell at par because the present value of the future cash flows, discounted at 12 percent, is $1,000. If market yields rise to 14 percent, the resulting bond prices will be:

$$\$931 = \sum_{t=1}^{5} \frac{\$120}{(1.14)^t} + \frac{\$1,000}{(1.14)^5}$$

$$\$877 = \sum_{t=1}^{15} \frac{\$120}{(1.14)^t} + \frac{\$1,000}{(1.14)^{15}}$$

The price of the 5-year bond will fall to $931, while the 15-year bond will sell for only $877. The percentage change in the price of the 5-year bond is 6.9 percent; for the 15-year bond, the price decline is 12.3 percent. If market yields fall to 11 percent, the price of the 5-year bond will rise to $1,037, a 3.7 percent increase. The 15-year bond price will increase to $1,072, a change of 7.2 percent. In both instances, the price of the 15-year bond changes by a larger percentage than the price of the 5-year bond, as stated formally in Theorem II. For any given change in market yields away from 12 percent, this is true.

An interesting historical look at the implications of Theorem II is given in Figure 7.4, showing yearly rates of return—interest income plus price changes as a percentage of value at the beginning of the year—for portfolios of long-term government bonds and Treasury bills.[7] Beginning at the left side, each bar represents a realized one-year rate over the period 1926-1984. The series of annual returns is more variable for the long-term government bond portfolio than for T-bills. The figure demonstrates Theorem II's statement that, holding default risk constant, long-term bonds are more subject to market value risk than are short-term securities.

Theorem III.   *The percentage price changes described in Theorem II increase at a decreasing rate as N increases.* In other words, the longer the time to maturity, the less the difference in percentage price changes. For example, when yields change, the prices of 15-year bonds change by a greater percentage than the prices of 10-year bonds, but the difference is less than the difference between the price changes of a 5-year bond and a 10-year bond.

Figure 7.5 plots the prices of 5-, 10-, and 15-year, 12 percent coupon bonds at market yields ranging from 1 percent to 24 percent. Because the slopes of the lines are the *rates* (percentages) at which prices change as yields change, lines with similar slopes depict bonds with similar percentage price changes as yields change. The slopes of the lines for price changes of 10- and 15-year bonds are more similar than the slopes of the 5- and 10-year lines. The 15-year line is the steepest of all, as Theorem II suggests, and the 5-year line is the flattest.

Theorem IV.   *Holding N constant and starting from the same market yield, equal yield changes up or down* do not *result in equal percentage price changes. A decrease in yield increases prices more than an equal*

---

[6]Theorem II is true for bonds selling at or above par at the time of a change in market yields, but not for all discount bonds. Malkiel observed this but did not examine why it was so, as other authors have done subsequently. Chapter 8 develops a more general relationship between the prices and yields of bonds selling at all levels—below, at, and above par.

[7]These series are two of several historical portfolio returns presented in Ibbotson Associates, *Stocks, Bonds, Bills and Inflation: 1985 Yearbook* (Chicago: Ibbotson Associates, 1985).

Figure 7.4
Year-by-Year Returns on Treasury Bonds and Bills, 1926–1984

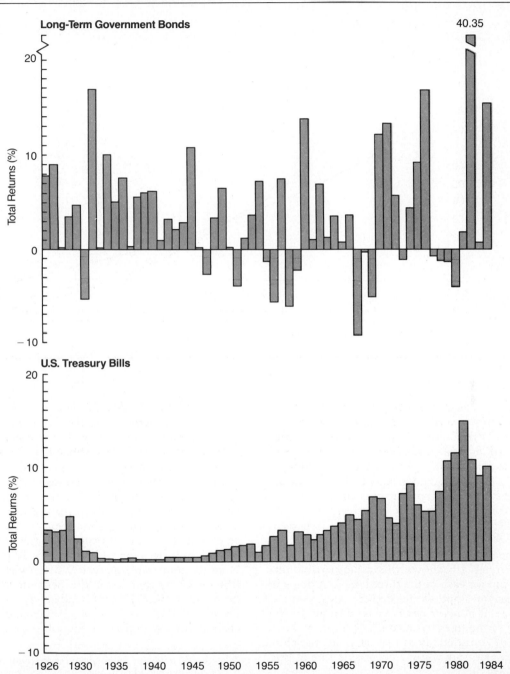

Source: Stocks, Bonds, Bills and Inflation: 1985 Yearbook, (Chicago: Ibbotson Associates, 1985), p. 11. Reprinted with permission.

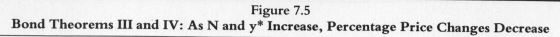

Figure 7.5
Bond Theorems III and IV: As N and y* Increase, Percentage Price Changes Decrease

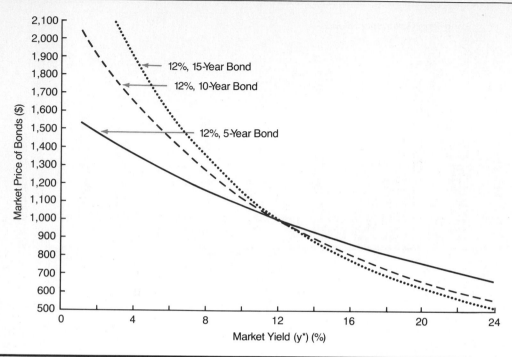

increase in yield decreases prices. In more formal terms, price changes are asymmetric with respect to changes in yield. For example, consider the effect of equal increases and decreases in market yields on the price of a 12 percent coupon, eight-year bond. If market yields start at 12 percent and increase to 14 percent, the price of the bond will fall from $1,000 to $907, a decrease of 9.3 percent. If market yields instead fall to 10 percent, the bond's price will increase to $1,107, a percentage increase of 10.7 percent.

Figure 7.5 shows this asymmetrical relationship for each of the three bonds. A line with a constant slope would depict a steady rate of change in bond prices as yields change. In fact, none of the lines has a constant slope, and each flattens considerably as market yields rise above 12 percent, indicating a decreasing rate of price changes.

Theorem V.   *Holding N constant and starting from the same market yield, the higher the coupon rate, the smaller the percentage change in price for a given change in yield.*[8] This principle is illustrated in Figure 7.6, in which the percentage price changes of three 8-year bonds are plotted against changes in yields, starting from a 12 percent base. As yields drop from a 12 percent level, percentage changes in the price of a 6 percent, 8-year bond are greater than the percentage price changes for a 12 percent or 18 percent bond of comparable maturity. When yields rise from a 12 percent level, the percentage price decreases for the 6 percent bond are greater than for the other two bonds. Percentage price changes for the 18 percent coupon bond are the

---

[8]Theorem V holds for all bonds except perpetuities and bonds with one period to maturity.

Figure 7.6
Bond Theorem V: As Coupon Increases, Percentage
Price Changes Decrease as Yields Change

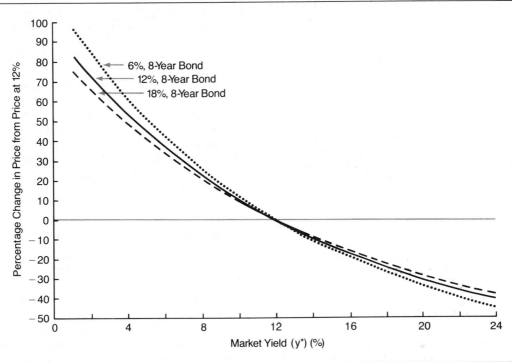

smallest of the three. This general behavior holds for any base yield from which change occurs.

A comparison of the lines in Figure 7.5 and 7.6 reveals that the coupon effect described in Theorem V has much less impact than does the maturity effect described in Theorem II. Comparison of the interest rate risk of securities considering both coupon and maturity differences is discussed in Chapter 8.

Implications for Financial Institutions

The bond theorems show that changes in market rates will not affect all bond portfolios in the same way. In periods of volatile market rates, portfolios heavily invested in long-term securities have greater price fluctuations than portfolios concentrated in money market securities. The value of portfolios heavily invested in low-coupon instruments is more changeable than portfolios of high-coupon bonds. If (a big *if*, of course) managers forecast market changes correctly and understand the bond theorems, they can position their institutions to profit from anticipated rate movements.

Throughout the rest of the book, the bond theorems enhance an understanding of the problems and opportunities confronting specific institutions. Furthermore, knowledge of the bond theorems and the related concept of "duration" enables a manager to develop a measure of interest rate risk. The development and application of such a measure are the subjects of Chapter 8.

EFFECT OF INTEREST RATE CHANGES ON COMMON STOCK

"Interest Dips, Market Flips" read the page 1 headline of the *Chicago Tribune* on Tuesday, May 21, 1985.[9] The story centered on the behavior of common stock prices after the Fed's May 17, 1985, cut in the discount rate. On Monday, May 20, the Dow Jones Industrial Average (DJIA) closed at a historical high of 1,304.88, and the following day it moved still higher. Because common stocks are financial assets, their prices behave similarly to those of bonds. As market yields fall, yields on common stock also fall and their prices rise. As market yields rise for other financial assets, the yields on common stock rise and their prices fall.

The relationship between common stock prices and changes in market yields is less clear-cut, however, than the bond theorems imply for bond prices. One simply need recall the major way in which the cash flows from stocks differ from those of bonds: The timing and amount of expected cash benefits from stock are not fixed, but are a function of the earnings of the stock issuer. Although a change in market yields seldom changes the cash flows expected by a bondholder, underlying economic events that change market yields may lead to a reassessment of the cash benefits expected by stockholders. Because the bond theorems assume fixed cash inflows, they cannot be applied to stocks.

Nonetheless, based on empirical evidence, some generalizations can be made. On an *ex post* basis, recent research indicates an inverse relationship between changes in several interest rate indexes and the market values of portfolios of common stock. This relationship, however, seems to be stronger for some firms than for others.[10]

In addition, the sensitivity of a firm's stock price to unexpected changes in interest rates is related to the amount of fixed-rate assets and liabilities held by the firm. The more fixed-rate assets (especially fixed-rate financial assets) and the longer the maturity of those assets, the greater the sensitivity of a firm's common stock to unexpected changes in interest rates.[11] In view of the bond theorems, this latter finding is not surprising. If a firm holds a large proportion of fixed-rate, long-term assets as interest rates change, the market value of the firm's assets will change more than if assets are mostly short-term. Because the market value of a firm's common stock is tied to the value of its assets, the more volatile its asset values, the more volatile the market value of its stock.

Implications for Financial Institutions

The relationship between interest rates and stock prices is important to financial institutions for two reasons. Managers of institutions with large portfolios of common stock must understand factors that affect changes in stock value in order to manage these portfolios. Managers of pension funds, insurance companies, brokerage firms, and mutual funds fall into this group. But managers of all stockholder-owned institutions must be concerned with the connection between interest rates and stock prices. For

---

[9]Charles Storch, "Interest Dips, Market Flips," *Chicago Tribune,* May 21, 1985, Section 1, p. 1.

[10]H. Russell Fogler, Kose John, and James Tipton, "Three Factors, Interest Rate Differentials and Stock Groups," *Journal of Finance* 36 (May 1981): 323-335; Andrew A. Christie, "The Stochastic Behavior of Common Stock Variances: Value, Leverage, and Interest Rate Ef-

fects," *Journal of Financial Economics* 5 (December 1981): 407-432; Mark J. Flannery and Christopher M. James, "The Effect of Interest Rate Changes on the Common Stock Returns of Financial Institutions," *Journal of Finance* 39 (September 1984): 1141-1153; Richard J. Sweeney and Arthur D. Warga, "The Pricing of Interest Rate Risk: Evidence from the Stock Market," *Journal of Finance* 41 (June 1986): 393-410.

[11]Flannery and James, "The Effect of Interest Rate Changes." Actually, Flannery and James found that the interest sensitivity of a firm's common stock is related to the *net* fixed-rate asset position of the firm, or the amount by which long-term, fixed-rate assets exceed long-term, fixed-rate liabilities. This effect was confirmed in William L. Scott and Richard L. Peterson, "Interest Rate Risk and Equity Values of Hedged and Unhedged Financial Intermediaries," *Journal of Financial Research* 9 (Winter 1986): 325-329. Maturity mismatching is discussed in Chapters 17 and 18.

example, although banks and S&Ls cannot currently own common stock as part of their asset portfolios, their own shareholders are affected by interest rate changes, based on the choices managers make within the range of available assets. For firms such as insurance companies with common stock asset holdings and their own shareholders, the lesson is doubly important.

SUMMARY

This chapter examines the dominant risk faced by financial institutions: interest rate risk. The degree of interest rate risk an institution faces is affected by a number of factors, such as asset and liability maturities, cash flow characteristics, and the magnitude and direction of changes in interest rates.

The relationship between prices and yields on financial assets is the foundation for understanding interest rate risk. Asset prices and market yields are inversely related. When the supply/demand relationship for loanable funds changes, and market yields change, the prices of financial assets also change, but in the opposite direction.

Interest rate risk can be divided into two components: reinvestment risk and market value (or price) risk. Reinvestment risk is most serious when an investor plans to hold an asset to maturity. Market value risk can be severe when an investor plans to sell an asset before maturity. Changes in market yields cause changes in market value in the opposite direction.

The bond theorems further define the impact of interest rate changes on market value. The magnitude of fluctuations in value for a given change in market yields varies with the term to maturity, the size of the coupon rate on the security, and the direction of the change in yields. The theorems hold important implications for financial institutions; the management of a given asset/liability mix must recognize varying degrees of sensitivity to shifts in market yields.

Equity securities are also sensitive to changes in interest rates, but the nature of the relationship is more difficult to identify. Recent research indicates an inverse relationship between shifts in interest rates and prices of common stock, so that even institutions primarily involved with the management of equity portfolios are susceptible to interest rate risk.

Questions

1. What is interest rate risk? Explain the two types of interest rate risk and the relationship of each to changes in market conditions. How does interest rate risk affect *ex post* returns?

2. What causes changes in the prices of financial assets? Explain these forces and give an example of each.

3. Graphically show the relationship between an increase in the supply of securities, the change in the equilibrium rate of interest, and the change in the demand for loanable funds. Repeat the analysis for an increase in the demand for securities.

4. Explain the relationship between changes in market yields and changes in prices of financial assets. Of what importance is this relationship in managing the net interest margin?

5. A bond portfolio manager has invested in five-year bonds she plans to hold until maturity. At that time, total proceeds from the bond investment will be needed to meet obligations of the institution. Explain what type of interest rate risk results from a change in market yields, and how the change may affect the returns on the investment.

6. Suppose you are a bond portfolio manager for a small insurance company, and are responsible for developing some investment strategies for the firm. You need to explain to the company's

board of directors the impact of interest rate changes on bond values and, in particular, when to buy high- versus low-coupon bonds and how to choose between long and short maturities. Given your knowledge of the bond theorems, explain to the directors the ideal composition of a bond portfolio when market yields are: a) rising; and b) falling.

7. Using the bond theorems, but without calculations, explain which bond price would fluctuate more, given a decline in market yields from 12 percent to 10 percent: 1) a 10 percent bond, 10 years to maturity; 2) a 10 percent bond, 20 years to maturity.

8. Using the bond theorems, but without calculations, explain which bond would experience the largest price change, given an increase in market yields from 14 percent to 16 percent: 1) a five-year, 10 percent bond; 2) a five-year, 13½ percent bond; 3) a five-year, 15 percent bond.

9. Given three bonds with equal years to maturity and equal market yields, will a change in market yields of 3 percent up or down result in equal percentage price changes in either direction? Explain.

10. If a bond portfolio manager expects interest rates to fall in the near future, which of the following investments should he choose today in order to benefit most from the decline in rates? Why?
    1) 12 percent, 20-year bonds
    2) 10 percent, 20-year bonds
    3) 8 percent, 20-year bonds

11. Briefly summarize the findings of empirical research on the relationship between prices of common stock and changes in market yields. Why don't the bond theorems apply to the relationship between common stock price and yield?

Problems

1. Reexamine the two bonds described in Question 7. Calculate the market values of both bonds at a 12 percent prevailing rate, and the percentage price change resulting if market rates drop from 12 percent to 10 percent. To what do you attribute the difference in the size of the price change? Assume the bonds have a par value of $1,000 with semi-annual interest payments.

2. Consider these possible bond portfolios:
    1) a portfolio of 10 percent, 5-year bonds;
    2) a portfolio of 10 percent, 20-year bonds;
    3) a portfolio of 10 percent, 25-year bonds.

    Calculate and compare the change in values of portfolios 1 and 3, and portfolios 2 and 3 if market rates drop from 10 percent to 8 percent. Which bond theorem is illustrated by these comparisons? Assume each bond has a par value of $1,000 with annual interest payments.

3. You are planning ahead for a downpayment on a new car. You want to have $2,200 on December 31, 1992, and you have set up an annuity to reach that goal. You will invest $500 on December 31 of each year from 1989 through 1992 and estimate that you will earn an average annual yield of 7%.
    a. Show that if market yields of 7 percent prevail, you will reach your investment goal of $2,200 by December 31, 1992.
    b. Suppose market yields drop to 6 percent immediately after the first $500 investment and they remain there until December 31, 1992. Calculate the accumulated funds under these market conditions. What type of risk does this problem demonstrate?

4. Graph the relationship between the percentage price changes on a 5-year, 12 percent bond as market yields change from 1 percent to 25 percent. On the same axes, graph the relationship between the percentage price changes on 20-year, 12 percent bonds and the same range of market yields. Which bond theorem does this graph illustrate? Assume the bonds have a par value of $1,000 with annual interest payments.

5. Graph the relationship between the percentage price changes on a 4 percent, five-year bond as market yields change from 1 percent to 25 percent. On the same axes, graph the relationship between the percentage price changes on an 18 percent, five-year bond and the same range of market yields. Which bond theorem does this graph illustrate? Assume the bonds have a par value of $1,000 with annual interest payments. Use 10 percent as the base market yield. (Hint: Refer to Figure 7.6.)

Selected References

Christie, Andrew A. "The Stochastic Behavior of Common Stock Variances: Value, Leverage, and Interest Rate Effects." *Journal of Financial Economics* 5 (December 1981): 407-432.

Flannery, Mark J., and Christopher M. James. "The Effect of Interest Rate Changes on the Common Stock Returns of Financial Institutions." *Journal of Finance* 39 (September 1984): 1,141-1,153.

Fogler, Russell H., Kose John, and James Tipton. "Three Factors, Interest Rate Differentials and Stock Groups." *Journal of Finance* 36 (May 1981): 323-335.

Ibbotson Associates. *Stocks, Bonds, Bills and Inflation: 1985 Yearbook.* Chicago: Ibbotson Associates, 1985.

Malkiel, Burton G. "Expectations, Bond Prices, and the Term Structure of Interest Rates." *Quarterly Journal of Economics* 76 (May 1962): 197-218.

Scott, William L., and Richard L. Peterson. "Interest Rate Risk and Equity Values of Hedged and Unhedged Financial Intermediaries." *Journal of Financial Research* 9 (Winter 1986): 325-329.

Sweeney, Richard J., and Arthur D. Warga. "The Pricing of Interest Rate Risk: Evidence from the Stock Market." *Journal of Finance* 41 (June 1986): 393-410.

Chapter 8

INTEREST RATE RISK MANAGEMENT: DURATION

A 30-year zero is probably three times as volatile as a common stock. It's like a roller coaster. You'll finish the ride with a dizzy head and woozy walk and wonder what hit you.

William H. Gross
Managing Director
Pacific Management Investment Company (1985)

IN 1984, Scudder Mutual Fund Group formed the Target Fund to capitalize on investors' growing concerns about interest rate risk. Target invests in zero-coupon instruments and was intended to help investors with problems such as sending "Junior off to college," said Bob Pruyne, a senior vice president at Scudder. By identifying specific maturity dates for certain portions of the fund and allowing investors to select their preferred date, investors' realized yields equal their expected yields at the time of investment. In other words, the potential impact of interest rate risk is neutralized.[1] Although this protection sounds too good to be true, Target is applying the concept of "immunization" discussed later in this chapter.

Understanding price/yield relationships and the effect of reinvestment rates on portfolio return provides a necessary but insufficient foundation for analyzing interest rate risk in finan-

---

[1]Robert McGough, "High-Yield Anxiety," *Forbes* 134 (September 10, 1984): 204-205.

cial institutions. Principles in Chapter 7 were often accompanied by such caveats as, "all else equal . . . this will happen," or, "given equal coupon rates (or equal terms to maturity) . . . this will occur." In reality, managers analyzing interest rate risk seldom compare financial assets or liabilities with the same coupon rates, maturities, or initial yields. Thus, it is difficult to assess the impact of unexpected economic events on an institution's total asset/liability mix without a tool that cuts across financial instruments with all types of characteristics. Fortunately, although not perfect, a measure of *interest rate elasticity*—the percentage change in the value of a financial instrument for a 1 percent change in market yields—can be estimated for almost every asset or liability. To calculate and use interest rate elasticities, however, one must first understand the concept of duration.

DURATION: AN IDEA AHEAD OF ITS TIME

It is difficult to find a recent scholarly article on financial institution management that does not mention duration. It would be easy to conclude that duration is a new idea, but in fact, it was first developed about 50 years ago by Frederick Macaulay. Similar concepts were developed shortly thereafter, but Macaulay's duration has only recently been widely appreciated for the power it brings to the management of interest rate risk.[2]

Duration Defined

Duration is the weighted average time over which the cash flows from an investment are expected, where the weights are the relative present values of the cash flows. It is an alternative to maturity for expressing the time dimension of an investment. Focusing on maturity ignores the fact that, for most securi-

ties, some cash benefits are received *before* the maturity date. Benefits received before maturity are often substantial, especially for bonds with relatively high coupon rates or annuities. It can be argued, therefore, that ignoring the time dimension of cash benefits before maturity is unwise.

The importance of the time dimension is evident in the basic expression for the market value of an investment:

$$(4.7) \quad P_0 = \sum_{t=1}^{N} \frac{C_t}{(1 + y^*)^t}$$

Because the market value of an investment equals the present value of expected benefits, and because discount factors, $(1 + y^*)^t$, are exponential functions of time, early payments are discounted less than those received later. Differences in discounted value become more pronounced as t increases. In essence, the *effective maturity*—that is, the time period over which the investor receives cash flows with relatively high present values—may differ from the *contractual*, or legally specified, maturity. Duration is a measure of this effective maturity.

Duration Calculated: Bonds

Duration is perhaps best understood through example. The following illustrations are based on the two ATT bonds introduced in the previous chapter in Figure 7.3. One had a coupon rate of 3⅞ percent, matured in 1990, and was

---

[2]Frederick R. Macaulay, *Some Theoretical Problems Suggested by the Movements of Interest Rates, Bond Yields, and Stock Prices in the U.S. since 1856* (New York: National Bureau of Economic Research, 1938).

One early work based on a property similar to duration was Paul Samuelson, "The Effects of Interest Rate Increases on the Banking System," *American Economic Review* 35 (March 1945): 16-27. In addition, several scholars have also attributed an idea virtually identical to duration to J. R. Hicks in his *Value and Capital* (Oxford: Clarendon Press, 1939). For a review of the intellectual history of duration, see Roman L. Weil, "Macaulay's Duration: An Appreciation," *Journal of Business* 46 (October 1973): 589-592.

selling for $800.00 on May 20, 1985; the other had a coupon rate of 10⅜ percent, also matured in 1990, and was selling for $1,008.75 on May 20, 1985. Although they both had five years to maturity as of 1985, their coupon rates differed substantially, so that a relatively greater *proportion* of the cash flows from the 10⅜ bond was expected earlier than from the 3⅞ bond. In other words, the effective maturity of the 10⅜ bond was less than the effective maturity of the 3⅞ bond. Duration is a measure of time that captures this difference.

Table 8.1 illustrates the calculation of the durations of the two bonds. The market prices of the bonds on May 20 were equal to the present value of their expected cash benefits, discounted at the expected market yield. Column 4 of the table shows the relative weight of each cash flow; that is, the percentage of the bond's total present value contributed by each flow. Although the par values and maturities of the bonds were equal, par was only 67.5 percent of the total value of the 10⅜ bond, but it was 84.31 percent of the total present value of the 3⅞ bond. The reason for the difference is the higher coupon payments for the 10⅜ bond.

The final column shows the calculation of duration. First, the time period in which each cash flow is to be received is multiplied by the cash flow's relative weight. The weighted time periods are summed at the bottom of the column for each bond, resulting in a duration estimate of 4.5910 years for the 3⅞ bond, and 4.1483 years for the 10⅜ bond. The weighted average time to maturity for the 3⅞ bond is longer than that of the 10⅜ bond, even though they both have five contractual years to maturity.

The Duration Equation

Although the duration of a financial asset can always be calculated in a tabular fashion, duration is usually expressed as an equation:[3]

$$(8.1) \quad DUR = \frac{\sum_{t=1}^{N} \frac{C_t(t)}{(1 + y^*)^t}}{\sum_{t=1}^{N} \frac{C_t}{(1 + y^*)^t}}$$

Examining this formula reveals that it is familiar. The denominator is Equation 4.7, the financial instrument's total present value. The numerator sums the present value of each cash flow, $C_t/(1 + y^*)^t$, times the year in which it is received, t. For example, in the case of a five-year bond, the numerator of the duration equation is the *sum* of the present value of the first year's cash flow times 1, the present value of the second year's cash flow times 2, and so on. The duration statement in Equation 8.1 expresses the procedure followed in Table 8.1 in a compact form and a slightly different order. When data from Table 8.1 are used in Equation 8.1, the result is the same duration estimate, except for rounding differences, for the 3⅞ bond:

$$DUR = \frac{\$35.54(1) + \$32.60(2) + \$29.91(3) + \$27.43(4) + \$674.52(5)}{\$800.00}$$

$$= \frac{\$3,672.79}{\$800.00} = 4.5911$$

Equation 8.1 shows that the duration of a financial instrument is based on a complex interaction of factors—cash flows, their timing, and the current market yield. If any of these changes, the duration of the instrument will change. However, because durations are denominated in numbers of periods (years in the case of Table 8.1), one can compare the dura-

---

[3]Recently, an alternative formula has been presented for the duration of investments with at least some expected cash benefits in the form of annuity payments. The formula is especially useful when the contractual maturity of the investment is lengthy, as is the case in calculating the duration of a 25-year, fixed-rate bond with semiannual interest payments. See Gary A. Benesh and Stephen E. Celec, "A Simplified Approach for Calculating Bond Duration," *Financial Review* 19 (November 1984): 394-396. Another simplified formula is presented in Jess B. Chua, "A Closed-Form Formula for Calculating Bond Duration," *Financial Analysts Journal* 40 (May-June 1984): 76-78. In practice, most professional analysts have access to microcomputers or to bond duration tables, which present durations for many combinations of yield, coupon rate, and maturity.

Table 8.1
Duration of Bonds with Equal Contractual Maturities

3⁷/₈s of 90:

(1) End of Year	(2) Cash Flows	(3) Present Value in 1985 @ 9.02%	(4) Relative Weight (% of Total Present Value)	(5) Weighted Time Period (1) × (4)
1	$ 38.75	$ 35.54	4.44%	0.0444 years
2	38.75	32.60	4.08	0.0815
3	38.75	29.91	3.74	0.1121
4	38.75	27.43	3.43	0.1372
5	1,038.75	674.52	84.31	4.2157
		$800.00	100.00%	4.5910 years (Duration)

10³/₈s of 90:

(1) End of Year	(2) Cash Flows	(3) Present Value in 1985 @ 10.14%	(4) Relative Weight (% of Total Present Value)	(5) Weighted Time Period (1) × (4)
1	$ 103.75	$ 94.20	9.34%	0.0934 years
2	103.75	85.52	8.48	0.1696
3	103.75	77.65	7.70	0.2309
4	103.75	70.49	6.99	0.2795
5	1,103.75	680.90	67.50	3.3749
		$1,008.75	100.00%	4.1483 years (Duration)

tions of several investments even if they have different yields, cash flows, or contractual maturities. It is also possible for two or more assets with very different characteristics to have the same durations.

Duration Calculated: Common Stocks

Although Macaulay originally proposed duration for bonds, others have applied the concept to common stocks.[4] An analyst must make critical assumptions to calculate a stock's duration,

but that requirement is not unique to duration. The expected cash flows from the stock, including their growth rate and timing, must be estimated. Because stocks have no maturity date, the relevant holding period must also be estimated. Finally, a method for estimating the expected annual yield must be chosen. These decisions are illustrated in Chapter 4. Once they are made, a stock's duration can be calculated.

Table 8.2 contains duration estimates for two stocks with different anticipated cash flows. Assuming that both stocks have an expected rate of return of 10 percent, the duration estimates are computed as in Table 8.1, although Equation 8.1 could also be used. Because the

[4]A history of the application of duration to common stocks is traced in Frank K. Reilly and Rupinder S. Sidhu, "The Many Uses of Bond Duration," *Financial Analysts Journal* 36 (July-August 1980): 58–72.

Table 8.2
Calculating the Duration of Two Stocks with Equal Expected Holding Periods

No Growth in Dividends:

(1) End of Year	(2) Cash Flows	(3) End of Year 0: Present Value @ 10.00%	(4) Relative Weight (% of Total Present Value)	(5) Weighted Time Period (1) × (4)
1	$ 2.00	$ 1.82	5.76%	0.0576 years
2	2.00	1.65	5.24	0.1047
3	2.00	1.50	4.76	0.1428
4	2.00	1.37	4.33	0.1731
5	2.00	1.24	3.93	0.1967
6	2.00	1.13	3.58	0.2146
7	2.00	1.03	3.25	0.2276
8	2.00	0.93	2.96	0.2365
9	2.00	0.85	2.69	0.2418
10	52.00	20.05	63.51	6.3512
		$31.57	100.00%	7.9466 years

Dividend Growth Expected:

(1) End of Year	(2) Cash Flows	(3) End of Year 0: Present Value @ 10.00%	(4) Relative Weight (% of Total Present Value)	(5) Weighted Time Period (1) × (4)
1	$ 1.00	$ 0.91	2.15%	0.0215 years
2	1.00	0.83	1.96	0.0392
3	1.40	1.05	2.49	0.0748
4	1.40	0.96	2.27	0.0907
5	1.80	1.12	2.65	0.1325
6	1.80	1.02	2.41	0.1445
7	2.40	1.23	2.92	0.2044
8	3.00	1.40	3.32	0.2654
9	3.50	1.48	3.52	0.3167
10	83.50	32.19	76.31	7.6312
		$42.19	100.00%	8.9209 years

---

anticipated price of the second stock at the end of ten years is much higher than that of the first, its relative weight is higher. Therefore, the duration of the stock with low initial dividends but anticipated growth is greater than the duration of the stock with no anticipated dividend growth.

If a stock is a good candidate for the constant growth model, and if the planned holding period is essentially perpetual, a simplified formula for calculating duration is:[5]

$$(8.2) \quad DUR_g = \frac{1 + y^*}{y^* - g}$$

---

[5] This model was presented in John A. Boquist, George A. Racette, and Gary G. Schlarbaum, "Duration and Risk Assessment for Bonds and Common Stocks," *Journal of Finance* 30 (December 1975): 1,360-1,365.

Once again, Equation 8.2 indicates that, given an expected rate of return, y*, the higher the anticipated growth in dividends, the greater the stock's estimated duration.

SOME GENERAL PROPERTIES OF DURATION

It is helpful to understand the ways duration is related to its three determinants—contractual maturity, existing market yields, and cash flow patterns. The generalizations follow from the duration equation, in much the same way the bond theorems follow from the formula for the market value of a bond.

Duration and Contractual Maturity

Duration is shorter than contractual maturity for all except one type of investment, a discount security or zero-coupon bond. Because a discount or zero-coupon instrument has but one cash inflow, with a present value equal to the asset's market value, the summation operator drops out of the formula:

$$(8.3) \quad DUR_z = \frac{\dfrac{C_N(N)}{(1 + y^*)^N}}{\dfrac{C_N}{(1 + y^*)^N}} = N$$

The duration of any instrument is positively related to maturity, except for maturities in excess of 50 years.[6] Figure 8.1 plots the du-

---

[6]The behavior of duration for bonds with very long maturities is discussed and illustrated in Lawrence Fisher and Roman Weil, "Coping with the Risk of Interest Rate Fluctuation: Returns to Bondholders from Naive and Optimal Strategies," *Journal of Business* 44 (October 1971): 418. They note that for bonds selling at or above par, duration is bounded by $(y^* + m)/(m \times y^*)$, so that the maximum duration for a bond paying interest twice a year (m = 2) with a yield of 10 percent, regardless of coupon or maturity, would be $(0.10 + 2)/(2 \times 0.10) = 2.10/0.20 = 10.5$ years. For bonds selling at a discount, duration actually decreases for maturities of more than about 50 years. The mathematical expression of the maximum duration for a discount bond is more complex and

ration of an 8 percent bond, at current market yields (y*) of 6 percent and 10 percent, against maturities of 1 to 20 years. Although the relationship is not linear, because the slopes of the lines are not constant, the duration of the bond at each market yield increases with maturity.

Duration and Current Market Yields

The relative positions of the two lines in Figure 8.1 suggest an inverse relationship between duration and current market yield, the discount rate in the duration equation. For an 8 percent coupon bond, durations at a 10 percent market yield are lower than durations at a 6 percent yield.

As y* increases, the present value of distant cash flows gets exponentially smaller. Thus, the weight given to distant time periods in the numerator of the duration equation also gets smaller, lowering duration. Figure 8.2 shows this relationship directly, by plotting the duration of a 16 percent coupon, five-year bond against market yields ranging from 0 percent to 25 percent.

Duration and Coupon Rate

Finally, duration is inversely related to coupon rate, because high-coupon bonds provide a greater proportion of their cash flows earlier than low-coupon bonds. The effect of coupon rate on duration was shown in Table 8.1, with the two ATT bonds. Figure 8.3 illustrates the relationship over a range of coupons for a five-year bond at a market yield of 10 percent. As shown by Equation 8.3, the duration of a zero-coupon bond is equal to its maturity.

---

is presented in Michael C. Hopewell and George G. Kaufman, "Bond Price Volatility and Term to Maturity: A Generalized Respecification," *American Economic Review* 63 (September 1973): 749-753, n. 2. Because, as a practical matter, few institutions have investment planning periods exceeding 50 years, and because few, if any, bonds with contractual maturities of more than 50 years are available, the limitations of this property are not considered further.

Figure 8.1
Duration versus Maturity for an 8% Bond

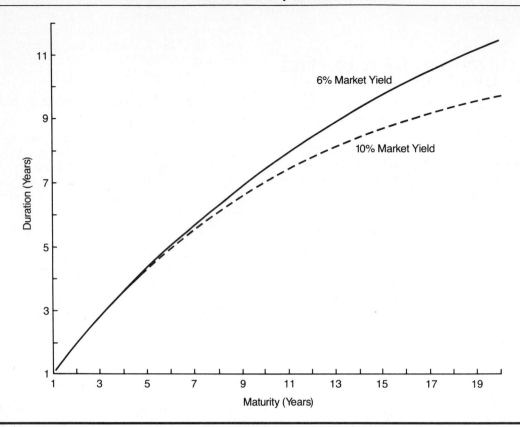

Common Stock Durations

These properties also apply in general to stocks. The duration of a stock paying no dividends is equal to the planned holding period, because the cash inflow from the sale is the only one anticipated. In addition, the longer the planned holding period, the longer a stock's duration. Further, the duration of a stock increases with decreases in the current expected yield. Finally, as was suggested in Table 8.2, the higher the interim cash dividends, the lower a stock's duration.

MEASURING INTEREST RATE RISK: THE RELATIONSHIP BETWEEN DURATION AND PRICE CHANGES

Why is duration important in assessing an institution's interest rate risk? The answer is direct: For a given change in market yields, percentage changes in asset prices are proportional to, but of opposite sign from, the asset's duration.[7]

[7]Hopewell and Kaufman, "Bond Price Volatility and Term to Maturity." This insight and the formula pre-

Figure 8.2
Duration versus Yield

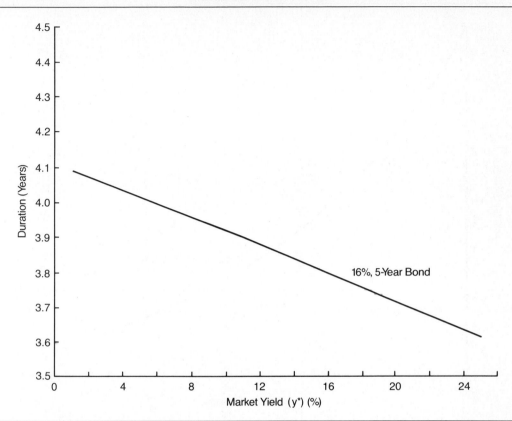

This is a powerful statement because duration is a complex variable that considers relationships among the size of cash flows, their timing, and current market expectations. Although the bond theorems allow an analyst to anticipate price changes based on one characteristic at a time, the relationship between duration and price changes considers all characteristics simultaneously.

sented as Equation 8.4 are often traced to these authors, although they acknowledge a similar derivation several years earlier in Lawrence Fisher, "An Algorithm for Finding Exact Rates of Return," *Journal of Business* 39 (January 1966): 111–118.

Estimating Percentage Price Changes

The relationship between duration and the percentage price change expected from a change in market yield is:

$$(8.4) \quad \%\Delta P_0 = \frac{\Delta P_0}{P_0} = -\text{DUR}\,\frac{\Delta y^*}{1 + y^*}$$

where Δy^* is expressed in **basis points** divided by 100. A basis point is 1/100 of a percent. For example, a positive change in market yields of 53 basis points, from 8.53 percent to 9.06 percent, would appear in Equation 8.4 as 53/100

Figure 8.3
Duration versus Coupon Rate

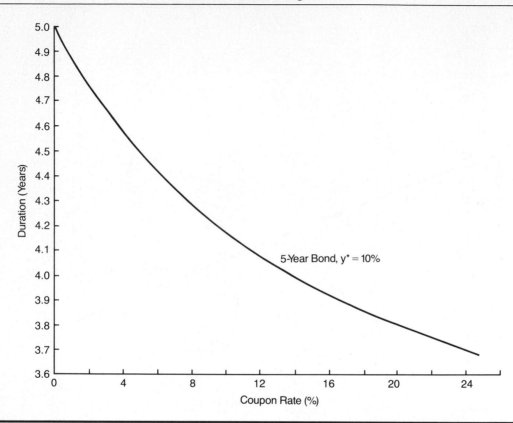

$= +0.53$; a decline of 53 basis points would appear as -0.53.

To illustrate, consider the yields and durations of the two ATT bonds as market conditions changed between May 17, 1985, and May 20, 1985. Figure 7.3 (page 172) shows that on May 17, the 3⅞ bond closed at $786.25, and the price of the 10⅜ bond was $998.75. On May 17, the bonds' durations were:

$$DUR_{3⅞} = \frac{\$3,606.37}{\$786.25} = 4.5868$$

$$DUR_{10⅜} = \frac{\$4,138.54}{\$998.75} = 4.1437$$

Table 8.3 summarizes relevant data for analyzing the relationship between duration and price changes. Yields are shown to four decimal places because rounding too soon causes the results of Equation 8.4 to vary. By substituting data from Table 8.3 into Equation 8.4, percentage price changes accompanying the change in market yields between May 17 and May 20 can be estimated:

$$\%\Delta P_{3⅞} = -4.5868 \times \frac{-0.4127}{1.094321} = +1.73\%$$

$$\%\Delta P_{10⅜} = -4.1437 \times \frac{-0.2650}{1.104083} = +0.99\%$$

Table 8.3
Duration and Bond Price Changes

	ATT 3⅞		ATT 10⅜	
	May 17	**May 20**	**May 17**	**May 20**
Yield (%)	9.4321%	9.0194%	10.4083%	10.1433%
Yield (basis points)	943.21	901.94	1040.83	1014.33
Price	$786.25	$800.00	$998.75	$1,008.75
Duration	4.5868 years	4.5910 years	4.1437 years	4.1483 years
Change in yield (basis points, May 17 to May 20)	−41.27		−26.5	
Δy^* in Equation 8.4 (basis point change ÷ 100)	−0.4127		−0.265	
Change in yield (%, May 17 to May 20)	−4.38%		−2.55%	
Estimated price change (%, May 17 to May 20, using Equation 8.4)	1.73%		0.99%	
Actual price change ($, May 17 to May 20)	$13.75		$10.00	
Actual price change (%, May 17 to May 20)	1.75%		1.00%	

Note: May 20 durations are calculated in Table 8.1.

Actual price changes for the two bonds were 1.75 percent for the 3⅞ bond and 1.00 percent for the 10⅜ bond. Considering that supply and demand for individual bonds, as well as overall market conditions, play a role in prices, the changes calculated from Equation 8.4 are good estimates.

The only data from Table 8.3 not used thus far are the durations of the two bonds on May 20, calculated earlier in Table 8.1. Because bond yields changed from May 17 to May 20, those durations are the relevant ones for analyzing the *future* expected price changes after May 20.

Estimating Interest Rate Elasticity

It is only a short step from Equation 8.4 to a measure of interest rate elasticity for a financial asset, serving as a reasonable proxy for the interest rate risk of holding the asset. Earlier, the interest rate elasticity of a financial asset was defined as the percentage price change ex-

pected for a 1 percent change in market yields. Thus:[8]

$$(8.5) \quad E = -DUR \frac{y^*}{1 + y^*}$$

---

[8]Equation 8.5 can be derived from Equation 8.4 as follows. First, note that the mathematical definition of interest rate elasticity is:

$$E = \frac{\% \Delta P_0}{\% \Delta y^*} = \frac{\frac{\Delta P_0}{P_0}}{\frac{\Delta y^*}{y^*}}$$

Therefore, Equation 8.4 can be divided by $\Delta y^*/y^*$ to obtain an expression for E:

(8.4A)

$$\frac{\frac{\Delta P_0}{P_0}}{\frac{\Delta y^*}{y^*}} = \frac{-DUR \times \frac{\Delta y^*}{1 + y^*}}{\frac{\Delta y^*}{y^*}}$$

After the right side of Equation 8.4A is simplified, and E is substituted for the left side, Equation 8.5 results.

To interpret the results of Equation 8.5, it is important to know what is meant by a "1 percent change." A 1 percent change in yields is a change equal to 1 percent of the existing yield; that is, if the present yield is 7.85 percent, a 1 percent change is an increase or decrease of 0.0785 percent (7.85 basis points), *not* an increase to 8.85 percent or a decrease to 6.85 percent (that is, *not* a 100-basis-point change). Using Equation 8.5 on data from May 17, for example, the elasticity of the 3⅞ ATT bond was:

$$E = -4.5868 \frac{0.094321}{1.094321} = -0.39534$$

At that time, for every 1 percent change in the bond's yield of 9.43 percent, the bondholder could have expected a price change of 0.39534 percent, but in the opposite direction of the yield change. Similarly, the elasticity of the 10⅜ bond on May 17 was:

$$E = -4.1437 \frac{0.104083}{1.104083} = -0.39063$$

If the bonds' interest rate elasticities are used as measures of interest rate risk, the 3⅞ bond was riskier than the 10⅜ bond as of May 17. Because yields subsequently decreased, percentage price changes for both bonds were positive, but greater for the 3⅞ bond than for the 10⅜ bond. The price change in the 3⅞ bond was beneficial in this case, but it would have been detrimental had yields increased.

As of May 20, new elasticities, based on the bonds' new durations and yields, were −0.37982 percent for the 3⅞ bond and −0.38202 percent for the 10⅜ bond. These elasticities suggest that under the new market conditions, the 10⅜ bond would be riskier than the 3⅞ bond. If a manager expected yields on the 10⅜ bond to increase shortly, to 10.35 percent, that expectation would translate to an increase of (10.35 − 10.1433)/10.1433 = 2.038%. Thus, the anticipated price decrease would be 2.038 × −0.38202 = −0.779%, or $1,008.75 × 0.00779 = $7.85 per bond.

A Comparison of Equations

Is Equation 8.4 or Equation 8.5 more helpful? Either can be used to estimate the percentage price change for an investment if a specific change in yields is anticipated. Equation 8.4 does not, however, provide a relative measure of expected price changes that can be compared across the spectrum of financial assets. Both relationships are important, but Equation 8.5 is of more general assistance to decision making.

Limitations of a Duration-Based Measure of Interest Rate Risk

As with all tools to help manage an unknown future, a duration-based risk measure has imperfections. Perhaps the most important is an assumption underlying both Equations 8.4 and 8.5: When interest rates change, there will be a parallel shift in the yield curve, so that for a given level of default risk, yields across the entire structure change equally. Only if this assumption holds can the interest rate elasticities of two investments be compared without some distortion. Some research indicates that parallel shifts in the yield curve are unusual and that relative volatility in yields, as well as duration, affect price changes.[9] Because the formula for interest rate elasticity involves both yield and duration, this conclusion is not surprising.

Other recent research on the historical relationship between duration and rates of return on Treasury securities indicates that factors besides duration are needed to explain variation in returns. In addition, the return/duration relationship is not always linear, as Equations 8.4 and 8.5 imply. Nonetheless, many experts view the benefits of duration-based interest rate risk measures as far greater than their shortcomings.[10] Most successful managers find it essential to understand duration.

[9] Jess B. Yawitz, "The Relative Importance of Duration and Yield Volatility on Bond Price Volatility," *Journal of Money, Credit and Banking* 9 (February 1977): 97–102.

[10] See, for example, Reilly and Sidhu, "The Many Uses of Bond Duration"; George Kaufman, "Measuring and Managing Interest Rate Risk: A Primer," *Economic Perspectives,* Federal Reserve Bank of Chicago 8 (January/

APPLICATIONS OF DURATION TO ASSET/LIABILITY MANAGEMENT

Duration and related measures of interest rate risk are relevant for almost every financial institution. The most common applications are discussed here, and others are mentioned in later chapters on specific institutions.

Duration and the Term Structure

Some analysts argue that the term structure of interest rates is best viewed as the relationship between yield and duration, not yield and maturity. Forward rates could be calculated from the duration-based curve for use in forecasting future yields. For example, Figure 8.4 shows two sets of yield curves for Treasury securities. The top panel plots yield against maturity, and the bottom plots yield against duration. Although the curves have similar shapes, as expected from the general duration/maturity relationship, the appropriate managerial response might be quite different.[11]

The yield/maturity panel indicates that the maximum maturity of Treasury securities increased between the two dates. The duration/yield relationship shows that the maximum duration of Treasury securities decreased instead. Because of the high general level of interest rates in 1980, new Treasury issues had high coupons and relatively short durations, even though the contractual maturities of new issues were not shortened. Using a duration measure, investors in long-term Treasury bonds were exposed to less, not more, interest rate risk in 1980 than they were in 1979; the traditional

yield/maturity relationship would have suggested otherwise. Major investors in the Treasury market may have had lower exposure to interest rate risk in 1980 than many realized.

Portfolio Immunization

Interest rate risk, both with respect to changing market values and reinvestment rates, means the realized yield on an investment will often differ from the expected yield at the time of investment. For some investors, accepting this risk may be extremely unappealing if they have financial goals or obligations that depend upon attaining a certain amount of cash at the end of a holding period. For example, a pension fund may have known obligations to retirees, and cash must be accumulated by the due date. Or an individual may retain a bank trust department, requiring that his funds attain enough by a given date to send his daughter to Harvard.

In the 1970s, a duration-based strategy for portfolio management was introduced and has since been widely adopted by financial institutions.[12] The strategy is known as ***immunization*** because it makes a portfolio "immune" to the "disease" of interest rate risk over a given holding period. Immunization is a portfolio management strategy in which the realized annual rate of return at the end of a holding period is no less than the expected annual yield at the

---

February 1984): 16-29; Martin L. Leibowitz, "How Financial Theory Evolves into the Real World—or Not: The Case of Duration and Immunization," *Financial Review* 18 (November 1983): 271-280; Alan C. Hess, "Duration Analysis for Savings and Loan Associations," *Federal Home Loan Bank Board Journal* 15 (October 1982): 12-14.

[11]These insights are provided in Joseph Bisignano and Brian Dvorak, "Risk and Duration," *San Francisco Weekly Letter,* Federal Reserve Bank of San Francisco, April 3, 1981, from which the yield curves presented in Figure 8.4 are taken.

[12]Fisher and Weil, "Coping with the Risk of Interest Rate Fluctuations." The authors acknowledge their indebtedness to the ideas of writers dating back to the 1940s (p. 409). In an interesting history of the use of immunization by institutional portfolio managers, Liebowitz notes that, regardless of its rich and lengthy academic heritage, immunization was put into practice only when the financial markets faced unprecedented events in the late 1970s. At that time, the models still widely followed were developed by practitioners. Liebowitz argues strongly, however, that theoretical interest in immunization by the academic community has immensely benefited those using the technique in the "real world." See Liebowitz, "How Financial Theory Evolves into the Real World—or Not." Applications to bond portfolios are further discussed in Martin L. Liebowitz, "Bond Immunization: A Procedure for Realizing Target Levels of Return," memorandum reprinted in John R. Brick, ed., *Financial Markets: Instruments and Concepts* (Richmond, VA: Robert F. Dame, Inc., 1981), pp. 443-454.

Figure 8.4
The Yield Curve: Duration versus Maturity as a Measure of Time

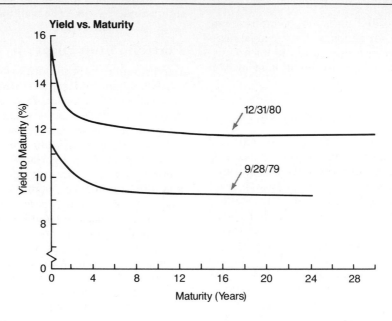

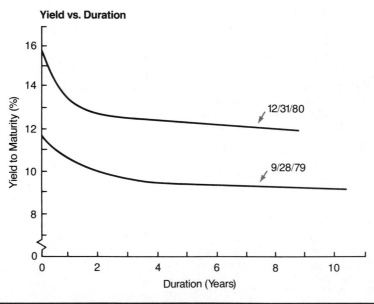

Source: Joseph Bisignano and Brian Dvorak, "Risk and Duration," *Weekly Letter,* Federal Reserve Bank of San Francisco, April 3, 1981.

beginning of the period. The Target mutual fund described in the opening paragraph is immunized; a portfolio is immunized if its duration is equal to the holding period.

Immunization Illustrated.   Suppose an individual wishes to invest over the period January 1, 1989, to October 4, 1995, at which time a loan obligation incurred some time ago must be repaid. An annual return of at least 10 percent, the market yield at the beginning of 1989, must be earned over the period. In other words, during the holding period of 6.759 years (6 years, 277 days), each $1,000 invested must grow to at least $1,000 $\times$ $(1.10)^{6.759}$ = $1,904.47. The investor asks a bank trust department to help in evaluating three alternatives, described in Table 8.4.

The first alternative is to buy a 10 percent coupon, three-year bond in January 1989, followed by a bond with 3.759 years to maturity in January 1992 and with a coupon rate equal to the market rate at that time. Under this strategy, the investor avoids incurring market value risk because both bonds would be redeemed at their par values. However, reinvestment risk is involved because the rate at which coupon payments can be reinvested is unknown, and the coupon rate on the 3.759-year bond to be purchased in January 1992 is also unknown. Another possibility is to buy a bond with a term to maturity exactly equal to the holding period—6.759 years. The investor would still incur reinvestment risk, but would know the coupon payments over the entire period and would incur no price risk. Finally, a long-term

---

Table 8.4
Duration and Portfolio Immunization

Beginning of holding period: January 1, 1989
y* = 10% on January 1, 1989; yield curve flat
End of holding period: October 4, 1995
Length of holding period: 6.759 years

Market Yield in 1992 and Beyond	Principal Value October 4, 1995	Total Coupons Received during Holding Period[a]	Interest on Coupons[b]	Total Cash October 4, 1995	Realized Annual Return
Strategy 1: 10% Bond, 3-Year Maturity on January 1, 1989; Then 3.759-Year Bond on January 1, 1992					
12.00%	$1,000.00	$751.08	$288.10	$2,039.18	11.12%
10.00	1,000.00	675.90	229.44	1,905.34	10.01
8.00	1,000.00	600.72	177.38	1,778.10	8.89
Strategy 2: 10% bond, 6.759-Year Maturity on January 1, 1989					
12.00%	$1,000.00	$675.90	$274.55	$1,950.45	10.39%
10.00	1,000.00	675.90	229.44	1,905.34	10.01
8.00	1,000.00	675.90	186.21	1,862.11	9.63
Strategy 3: 10% Bond, 10-Year Maturity on January 1, 1989; Sell on October 4, 1995					
12.00%	$ 949.77	$675.90	$274.55	$1,900.22	9.96%
10.00	1,000.56	675.90	229.44	1,905.90	10.01
8.00	1,055.88	675.90	186.21	1,917.99	10.12

[a]Assumes receipt of 75.9% of the coupon in 1995, since bond will be held for 75.9% of that year.

[b]Assumes reinvestment of coupons at 10% until 1992, then reinvestment at prevailing market yield until October 4, 1995.

bond with a ten-year maturity as of January 1989 could be chosen. This strategy is subject to both price and reinvestment risk.

Assuming a flat yield curve at 10 percent in January 1989, any one of the bonds can be purchased at its par value of $1,000. No rate changes would be anticipated from the yield curve, but unexpected rate changes could go in either direction. A trust department officer with knowledge of duration should have no trouble recommending one of the alternatives— the 10-percent coupon, ten-year bond.

Data in Table 8.4 demonstrate why this bond is the best choice. If market yields remain at 10 percent throughout the holding period, none of the bonds will be subject to either price or reinvestment risk. If rates rise unexpectedly in 1992 to 12 percent, the first strategy will provide higher coupon payments ($120 per year) for the remaining 3.759 years, plus an opportunity to reinvest them *and* the ones received before 1990 at 12 percent. If rates fall to 8 percent, the coupon rate on the 3.759-year bond will fall to 8 percent, as will the reinvestment rate. In neither case is the investor's ability to earn the required 10 percent return assured.

For the other alternatives, coupon payments will remain at $100 per year for the entire holding period, but the rate at which they can be reinvested could rise to 12 percent or fall to 8 percent. In the third strategy, the price of the bond at the end of the holding period is also uncertain. If rates rise to 12 percent by 1992 and remain there, the 10 percent, 10-year bond will have 3.241 years until maturity in 1995. If it is sold when the market yield is 12 percent, it will bring a price of $949.77, the present value of its remaining cash flows as of October 4, 1995. If rates fall to 8 percent, the bond can be sold for $1,055.88, its remaining present value at 8 percent.

An examination of the total cash accumulated shows that only the 10 percent, ten-year bond will consistently meet the investor's needs. If rates rise, the additional interest on reinvested coupons almost exactly offsets the drop in the bond's price. If rates fall, the increase in the bond's price at the time of sale almost exactly offsets the lower reinvestment

opportunities. Either way, the investor's desire for each $1,000 to accumulate to $1,904.47 by October 4, 1995, is more closely realized with the third alternative than the others. At worst, if rates rise unexpectedly to 12 percent and the bond must be sold at a discount, Equation 4A.3 can be used to find the implicit annual rate of return over the holding period:

$$y_H = \sqrt[6.759]{\frac{\$1,900.22}{\$1,000.00}} - 1 = 9.96\%$$

It is no coincidence that the duration of the 10 percent, ten-year bond as of January 1, 1989, is 6.759 years. When the duration of an investment is equal to the desired holding period, the two facets of interest rate risk almost exactly offset one another, enabling the investor to lock in an annual yield at least equal to the original expected annual yield. The investor is immunized against interest rate risk, and potential variation in returns is reduced almost to zero.

Immunization: Assumptions and Limitations.   Under certain assumptions, a bond with a duration equal to the desired holding period results in exactly offsetting market value and reinvestment risks. With a flat initial yield curve, and only *one* unexpected parallel shift in the curve immediately after the beginning of the period, the realized annual return over the holding period will *exactly* equal the expected annual yield.

The example in Table 8.4 does not conform to these assumptions; the market yield changes in the middle of the investment period, so the investor is less than perfectly immunized. In addition, interest rate changes are so common and so unpredictable that single parallel shifts in the yield curve are the exception rather that the rule.[13] Still, empirical tests of duration and maturity strategies over 44 years suggest that the

---

[13]Yawitz, "The Relative Importance of Duration and Yield Volatility on Bond Price Volatility"; and G.O. Bierwag, George G. Kaufman, and Alden Toevs, "Bond Portfolio Immunization and Stochastic Process Risk," *Journal of Bank Research* 13 (Winter 1983): 282-291.

dispersion of realized returns is consistently smaller when durations rather than maturities are matched with holding periods.

Another limitation of immunization is that it is difficult to find an investment with a duration exceeding ten years.[14] Thus, investors with lengthy desired holding periods may be unable to use the strategy. The recent advent of "stripped" securities, discussed next, has alleviated this limitation somewhat.

Immunization eliminates the possibility of unexpected gains when interest rates change. In other words, it is a *hedging,* or risk-minimization, strategy, not a profit-maximization strategy. If rates rise to 12 percent in the example in Table 8.4, the first strategy is the most desirable, but an immunizer forgoes that opportunity. Thus, immunization is appropriate for portfolio managers who wish to avoid rate forecasting, or who are willing to trade potential unexpected gains for protection from potential unexpected losses. Hedging is discussed in more detail in Chapters 9, 10, 17, and 18.

"Stripped" Securities

It follows from a discussion of the limitations of immunization that perhaps the best way to lock in a desired rate of return without reinvestment or price risk is to invest only in zero-coupon investments, whose maturities are equal to their durations. Until recently, however, it was difficult to find zero-coupon instruments with durations corresponding to a wide range of investment horizons. Furthermore, the total volume of zero-coupon issues of any duration was small, because only a few corporations had issued them.

In 1982, divisions of two major securities firms, Merrill Lynch and Salomon Brothers, introduced a new security designed to meet the potential demand for zero-coupon bonds of all durations. The generic term for these new financial assets is *"stripped" securities.* The name arose because they are created when the originators "strip" ordinary Treasury bonds of their coupon payments, then sell one or more

coupon payments or the par value separately to investors wanting single cash inflows at specified dates. The acronyms given to these securities have provoked amusement as well as interest. CATS (Certificates of Accrual on Treasury Securities) is the name for the Salomon Brothers version of a strip, while Merrill Lynch's Treasury Investment Growth Receipts are called TIGRs. Other securities firms have entered the field since 1982.[15]

In 1985, to facilitate the issuance of strips, the Treasury Department decided that each coupon payment on specified Treasury issues may be registered in a separate name.[16] The program is called Separate Trading of Registered Interest and Principal of Securities (STRIPS). Treasury issues eligible for the program are issued first to financial institutions, who may then sell each expected cash flow as if it were a separate security. This broadening and deepening of the market reduces the liquidity risk of owning strips for investors forced to sell before maturity.

Financial Institutions and Stripped Securities. If a pension fund needs a specified amount of cash in 12 years and wishes to lock in existing yields over that time, its managers can purchase a stripped security in the face amount desired, to be paid in a single sum in 12 years. The purchase price is a discount from the face amount; the cash payment to be received in 12 years will be coupon payments on a pool of Treasury securities. The pension fund manager considers the stripped security a 12-year maturity/duration, zero-coupon Treasury instrument, even though the Treasury has never issued such a bond. Because many Treasury bonds have long contractual maturities, promising the availability of coupon payments for

[14]Details are provided in Footnote 6.

[15]Kimberly Blanton, "The CATS Are out of the Bag: Salomon Brings in 3 Dealers," *Pension and Investment Age,* August 6, 1984, pp. 29-30.

[16]Alan Murray, "U.S. Is Altering Rules to Accommodate Growing Market in Zero-Coupon Bonds," *The Wall Street Journal,* January 16, 1985, p. 43. Details of the program are provided in Peter S. Nagan and Kenneth A. Kaufman, "STRIPS—An Exciting New Market for Zero-Coupons," *ABA Banking Journal* 70 (March 1985): 12, 16.

many years, stripped securities enable the creation of "synthetic" zero-coupon investments of long duration.

Stripped securities have been popular with institutions since their inception in 1982. By late 1986, more than $300 billion in Treasury securities had been stripped. The Tax Reform Act of 1986 allowed the stripping of municipal bonds for the first time, and large securities firms began doing so within minutes of the signing of the law.[17] The introduction of stripped securities provides an excellent example of the intermediation process at work. Creators of stripped securities, by issuing their own secondary securities such as CATS or TIGRs, have transformed one financial asset, the Treasury bond, into another with different risk and expected return characteristics. In so doing, they have reduced the transaction costs for owners of stripped securities. In exchange, the creators of stripped securities earn fees that enhance their own profits. The originators also accept all reinvestment risk on stripped cash flows not immediately needed for payment to strip owners.

---

[17]Ann Monroe, "Reconstituted Treasury Bonds Attract Attention as Dealers Do an About-Face," *The Wall Street Journal,* October 10, 1986, p. 31; Ann Monroe, "Goldman Sachs and Salomon Brothers Scramble for Sales of Stripped Municipal Bonds," *The Wall Street Journal,* October 23, 1986, p. 50.

SUMMARY

Duration is the foundation for analyzing an investor's exposure to interest rate risk. It is a measure superior to contractual maturity for comparing the riskiness of debt instruments because it also captures the effects of differing coupon rates and market yields. Duration can also be calculated for common stocks under certain assumptions. An important property of duration is that it is directly proportional to, but opposite in sign from, percentage changes in asset prices that result from a change in market yields. Thus, duration can be used to calculate an investment's interest rate elasticity.

Several applications of duration-based measures to financial institution management have been recognized. One of these is analysis of yield curves. Portfolio immunization is a strategy that balances reinvestment risk and market risk to protect a portfolio from the effects of an unexpected shift in interest rates. An immunized portfolio is one with a duration equal to the planned holding period for the investment. Finally, the demand for immunization through longer-duration assets has led to development of a new type of financial asset—the "stripped" security.

Questions

1. In managing interest rate risk, why is duration more useful than contractual maturity for expressing the time dimension of an investment?

2. What similarities and differences do you find between calculating duration and calculating the market price of an investment?

3. In what case are the duration of a bond and its contractual maturity the same? Why?

4. Explain interest rate elasticity and its importance in managing interest rate risk.

5. Explain the relationship between duration and price changes of financial assets.

6. Explain portfolio immunization. Is it a hedging strategy or a profit-maximization strategy? Why?

7. What are "stripped securities"? How can they be used in an immunization strategy? How are they similar to zero-coupon bonds?

Problems

1. Calculate the duration of the following bonds, each of which pays interest annually on a par value of $1,000:

   a. 6 percent coupon, 2 years to maturity, yield to maturity = 5 percent
   b. 13 percent coupon, 6 years to maturity, yield to maturity = 14 percent
   c. 13 percent coupon, 15 years to maturity, yield to maturity = 14 percent

2. You are asked to evaluate investments in two bonds: a 9½ percent bond currently trading at 87¾ and a 6⅝ percent bond trading at 62. Both bonds have eight years remaining until maturity. To estimate the interest rate risk, calculate the duration of each bond. Assume annual interest payments and a $1,000 par value. At current market prices, the annual yield to maturity of the 9½ percent bond is 11.96 percent; for the 6⅝ percent bond, the annual yield to maturity is 15.13 percent.

3. Using the format presented in Table 8.1, and May 20, 1985, data for the two ATT bonds discussed in the chapter, set up a Lotus 1-2-3 duration worksheet. Assume a yield to maturity of 9.0194 percent for the 3⅞ bond, and a yield to maturity of 10.1433 percent for the 10⅜ bond. Check your worksheet against Table 8.1. (Slight differences may occur from rounding.)

4. A bond portfolio manager is considering the purchase of two bonds, a 2⅝ percent bond trading at 77¾ and a 5½ percent bond trading for 94⅜. Both bonds have five years remaining until maturity. Using your duration worksheet from Problem 3, calculate the duration of each bond. Assume annual interest payments and a par value of $1,000 for each bond. (*Hint:* Use the @ IRR function to calculate the yield to maturity for each bond.)

5. Ms. Irving, the manager of a trust department at a local financial institution, has asked you, her assistant, to calculate the durations for two stocks she is considering. She has given you the following information:

   a. Both stocks she is considering now have an expected return of 15 percent.
   b. Ms. Irving plans to sell the stock at the end of five years.
   c. She has estimated the cash flows for the two stocks over the planned holding period as:

Year	Stock A	Stock B
1	$ 1.50	$ 1.25
2	1.50	1.50
3	1.50	1.75
4	1.50	2.00
5	61.50	82.50

   Using this information, calculate the requested durations.

6. Refer again to the information provided for the two stocks in Table 8.2. Using Equation 8.1, recalculate the duration of each stock and reconcile your answers with the results in Table 8.2.

7. You are considering a stock that currently sells for $14 and just paid a dividend of $1.25. The dividends are expected to grow at a constant rate of 6 percent indefinitely. If you purchase the stock, you have no plans to sell it in the near future. Calculate the duration for this stock. (*Hint:* Use Equation 4A.11 to find the expected rate of return on the stock.)

8. You have just begun a management training program with a regional bank and have been assigned to assist the bank's asset/liability management committee. As part of the institution's risk management strategy, durations are calculated for all assets.

a. As your first assignment, estimate duration for the following loans, which will be repaid in five equal annual installments:
1) $10,000 principal, $2,570.92 payment per year
2) $10,000 principal, $2,774.10 payment per year
   The bank's current required return (y*) for loans of this type is 6 percent.
b. Recalculate the durations at y* = 10%.
c. Compare the durations for the two loans at each discount rate. Do you find the results surprising? What explanation can you offer for your findings?

9. Use your calculations for Problem 2 and assume that the yields for the two bonds increase by 46 basis points and 64 basis points, respectively. What percentage price changes can be expected for the two bonds?

10. Using your calculations for Problem 4, assume that the prices of the bonds change by +1.8 percent and +2.24 percent, respectively. What would be the corresponding change in yields for the two bonds, expressed in basis points?

11. A bond with a yield to maturity of 10.2 percent and a coupon rate of 12 percent has ten years remaining until maturity. Calculate the duration and the interest rate elasticity for this bond, assuming annual interest payments and a par value of $1,000. If you think the required market yield on this bond will increase to 10.38 percent, what change in the bond price (in dollars) would you expect?

12. As a financial institution manager, you are comparing two bonds for possible addition to your bond portfolio. Bond A has a yield to maturity of 12 percent, a coupon rate of 11 percent, and seven years remaining until maturity. Bond B has a yield to maturity of 13.5 percent, a coupon rate of 14 percent, and five years remaining until maturity. Both bonds have a $1,000 par value and annual interest payments. You wish to invest in the bond that is less risky. Which bond should you choose? Show all calculations to support your answer.

13. A bond with a yield to maturity of 9.5 percent and a coupon rate of 10.75 percent has 15 years remaining until maturity. Assume a par value of $1,000, and annual interest payments. If you expect the required market yield on this bond to decrease by 15 basis points, use the price elasticity measure to estimate the percentage change in the bond's price.

14. You have been interviewed by a firm specializing in personal financial planning, and they may hire you as an investment counselor. The hiring decision depends upon your recommendation on the following problem that a client has brought to the firm.
    The client, Mr. Becker, wants to invest in bonds. He must choose between the following, both of which are selling at 118.9:
1) 12 percent coupon, five years to maturity (interest paid semiannually)
2) 14 percent coupon, six years to maturity (interest paid semiannually)
Mr. Becker's goal is to earn a 7.4 percent return on his investment annually, so that by the end of four years he will have accumulated $1,590 for each bond he buys. Earning that amount is crucial, because he must repay a large loan with the proceeds at the end of his four-year investment horizon. He will sell the bonds at that time.
a. Evaluate the interest rate risk exposure of the two bonds and decide which issue Mr. Becker should choose.
b. Because Mr. Becker may be skeptical, you need supporting data. Show that Mr. Becker will reach his $1,590 goal if he follows your recommendation, even if market yields drop to 6 percent immediately after he buys the bond and do not change for the next four years.

Selected References

Benesh, Gary A., and Stephen E. Celec. "A Simplified Approach for Calculating Bond Duration." *Financial Review* 19 (November 1984): 394-396.

Bierwag, G. O., George G. Kaufman, and Alden Toevs. "Bond Portfolio Immunization and Stochastic Process Risk." *Journal of Bank Research* 13 (Winter 1983): 282-291.

Boquist, John A., George A. Racette, and Gary A. Schlarbaum. "Duration and Risk Assessment for Bonds and Common Stocks." *Journal of Finance* 30 (December 1975): 1,360-1,365.

Chua, Jess B. "A Closed-Form Formula for Calculating Bond Duration." *Financial Analysts Journal* 40 (May-June 1984): 76-78.

Dietz, Peter O., H. Russell Fogler, and Anthony U. Rivers. "Duration, Non-Linearity, and Bond-Portfolio Performance." *Journal of Portfolio Management* 7 (Spring 1981): 37-41.

Fisher, Lawrence. "An Algorithm for Finding Exact Rates of Return." *Journal of Business* 39 (January 1966): 111-118.

Fisher, Lawrence, and Roman Weil. "Coping with the Risk of Interest Rate Fluctuation: Returns to Bondholders from Naive and Optimal Strategies." *Journal of Business* 44 (October 1971): 408-431.

Fogler, Russell H. "Bond Portfolio Immunization, Inflation, and the Fisher Equation." *Journal of Risk and Insurance* 51 (June 1984): 244-264.

Hess, Alan C. "Duration Analysis for Savings and Loan Associations." *Federal Home Loan Bank Board Journal* 15 (October 1982): 12-14.

Hopewell, Michael C., and George G. Kaufman. "Bond Price Volatility and Term to Maturity: A Generalized Respecification." *American Economic Review* 63 (September 1973): 749-753.

Kaufman, George G. "Measuring and Managing Interest Rate Risk: A Primer." *Economic Perspectives* (Federal Reserve Bank of Chicago) 8 (January/February 1984): 16-29.

Kaufman, George G., G. O. Bierwag, and Alden Toevs, eds. *Innovations in Bond Portfolio Management: Duration Analysis and Immunization.* Greenwich, CT: JAI Press, 1983.

Leibowitz, Martin L. "Financial Theory Evolves into the Real World—or Not: The Case of Duration and Immunization." *Financial Review* 18 (November 1983): 271-280.

Macaulay, Frederick R. *Some Theoretical Problems Suggested by the Movements of Interest Rates, Bond Yields, and Stock Prices in the U.S. since 1856.* New York: National Bureau of Economic Research, 1938.

Reilly, Frank K., and Rupinder S. Sidhu. "The Many Uses of Bond Duration." *Financial Analysts Journal* 36 (July-August 1980): 58-72.

Rosenberg, Joel L. "The Joys of Duration," *Bankers Magazine* 169 (March-April 1986): 62-67.

Samuelson, Paul. "The Effects of Interest Rate Increases on the Banking System." *American Economic Review* 35 (March 1945): 16-27.

Weil, Roman L. "Macaulay's Duration: An Appreciation." *Journal of Business* 46 (October 1973): 589-592.

Yawitz, Jess B. "The Relative Importance of Duration and Yield Volatility on Bond Price Volatility." *Journal of Money, Credit, and Banking* 9 (February 1977): 97-102.

Chapter 9

INTEREST RATE RISK MANAGEMENT: INTEREST RATE FUTURES

The banks that get hurt these days play a game called "You bet your bank." They roll the dice, try to pick a peak in rates . . . and then try to hedge away the risk in the futures market.

Owen Carney
Banking Operations Director
Office of the Comptroller of the Currency (1980)

THE managers of Pathway Financial, a Chicago S&L, forecast rising interest rates through-out 1984. Because the thrift had many short-term deposits on which rising costs were anticipated, management turned to the interest rate futures market to hedge against these increases. Unfortunately, the rate forecast was wrong. Rates went up in midyear, but by the end of the year, the general level of interest rates had fallen. Although Pathway's deposit costs actually decreased during the year, management's ill-timed venture into the futures markets resulted in a loss of over $3.9 million. Managers were happier at Broadway Bank and Trust of Paterson, New Jersey. They forecast rates correctly, and the bank benefited enough from the futures market to protect the net interest margin in 1984.[1]

---

[1] Laurie Cohen and William Gruber, "Outlook of S&Ls 'Better' Despite Some Problems," *Chicago Tribune,* October 14, 1985, Section 4, p. 3; Ford S. Worthy, "Big New Players in Financial Futures," *Fortune* 110 (September 17, 1984): 114.

In a complex economic environment, financial institutions need complex strategies. Duration is only one risk management technique. Others are explored in this and the next chapter, including financial futures contracts and options on financial futures. All are relatively new; for example, the interest rate futures contract was created in 1975 at the Chicago Board of Trade, and stock index futures began trading in 1982. Since the introduction of futures and options, financial institutions have recognized their potential for improving asset/liability management. This chapter focuses on interest rate and foreign currency futures.

As the opening quotation and paragraph indicate, futures are not without their own risks. The inherent dangers have attracted the attention of regulators and legislators, and in some cases have resulted in restrictions on their use by financial institutions. Futures have also presented some new financial reporting problems. Thus, the integration of futures into asset/liability management has, by necessity, moved somewhat slowly, with the largest institutions often serving as the trend setters.

FINANCIAL INSTITUTIONS AND FINANCIAL FUTURES

Although financial futures have received a great deal of attention, by late 1984, only 299 U.S. commercial banks out of about 14,000 actually held a position in the interest rate futures market. The relatively low level of participation can be traced to unfavorable regulatory and accounting rules for futures. Despite these rules, however, over 80 percent of the banks with assets in excess of $5 billion were using financial futures to hedge one or more aspects of their operations. Altogether, over 40 percent of banks participating in the futures markets had assets in excess of $1 billion.[2]

Other financial institutions, too, have increased their participation in the financial futures markets. Federal thrift regulators have moved quickly to make futures available to that industry. A recent survey of institutions in the western United States found that a higher percentage of responding savings institutions (30.7 percent) were using futures than were commercial bank respondents (10.4 percent) in the same region. Usage is clearly related to size; larger thrifts are more likely to trade in interest rate

futures and to recognize their potential for asset/liability management.[3]

A 1984 survey of the 53 largest life insurance firms in the United States revealed that 85 percent of respondents were legally permitted by state regulators to participate in the futures market. Of those, only 48 percent had begun to use them, but the majority of respondents who were still excluded by regulation from the futures market indicated they would get involved if permitted to do so.[4] Pension funds are also strong candidates for the futures markets; in 1984, the head of Goldman Sachs's futures division estimated that pension funds had doubled their positions in the market between 1983 and 1984.[5]

FUTURES CONTRACTS

Futures contracts on agricultural products have existed for well over a century; the first organized market for them was the Chicago Board

[2]Patrick Parkinson and Paul Spindt, "The Use of Interest Rate Futures by Commercial Banks," *Proceedings of a Conference on Bank Structure and Competition* (Chicago: Federal Reserve Bank of Chicago, 1985), pp. 457–459.

[3]James R. Booth, Richard L. Smith, and Richard W. Stolz, "Use of Interest Rate Futures by Financial Institutions," *Journal of Bank Research* 14 (Spring 1984): 15–20.

[4]Rebecca M. Hurtz and Mona J. Gardner, "Surviving in a New Environment," *Best's Review* 85 (September 1984): 152.

[5]Worthy, "Big New Players in Financial Futures," p. 118.

of Trade, also the birthplace of the financial futures contract in October 1975.

Futures Contracts Defined

A futures contract is a commitment to buy or sell a specific commodity of designated quality, at a specified price, at a specified date in the future (the **delivery date**). The specified price is an estimate of the commodity price that is *expected* to prevail at that future time. A "commodity" may fall into one of five categories, three of which are financial: agricultural products, metallurgical products, interest-bearing assets, stock and other market indexes, or foreign currencies. The last two, although not specifically focused on interest rate risk, have emerged as elements of asset/liability management for some institutions. Foreign currency futures are discussed later in this chapter, and stock index futures are described in Chapter 10.

Hedging versus Speculation

One reason for the development of futures contracts is avoidance of risk. Wheat or soybean farmers can use futures agreements to reduce uncertainty about the prices they will receive for their products. A grower, by agreeing through a futures contract to deliver a certain amount of wheat at a specified future date and price, avoids exposure to unfavorable price movements during the intervening period. Thus, futures contracts, like immunization in the previous chapter, can be used to hedge, or minimize, risk.

On the other side of the farmer's contract may be a **speculator,** someone willing to accept the risk of price fluctuations with the intention of profiting from them. The counterparty to the farmer could also be a hedger who needs the farmer's wheat at the designated time and is minimizing the risk that wheat will be in short supply at that time. Or, both parties in a futures contract could be speculators, each hoping to profit from price fluctuations.

Thus, the distinction between hedging and speculation comes not from which side of a futures contract one takes, but from the motiva-tion for entering into the contract. With few exceptions, because of regulatory limitations, financial institutions use the financial futures markets only for hedging.

Financial Futures Contracts

In a financial futures contract, the underlying commodity promised for future delivery is one of three financial commodities—an interest-bearing asset, a stock or bond index, or a foreign currency. Since 1975, contracts on many financial assets have been introduced with varying levels of success. For example, contracts on T-bills have been widely accepted, but futures contracts on commercial paper were tried without success. As of early 1987, interest-bearing assets on which contracts were written included T-bills, T-notes, T-bonds, and Eurodollar deposits, among others. The instruments span the entire yield curve, giving managers important flexibility.

Because organized futures markets exist, the original owner of a futures contract is not obligated to hold it until the delivery date. Instead, the owner may sell it to another party at any time, although the selling price will be affected by subsequent changes in the spot, or current market, price of the contracted commodity. If the commodity is an agricultural product, movements in the market price of the product affect the contract value. If the commodity is a T-bill, a change in short-term interest rates affects the price of bills in the spot market and also affects the value of a T-bill contract. Because of the way the futures markets are organized, over 98 percent of all financial futures agreements never involve a physical transfer of the underlying security from one party to another at the end of the contract period.[6]

For the markets to function efficiently, there must be some uniformity in the types of contracts written. For interest rate futures, the contract size, maturity, and (except for discount securities) the coupon rate are predetermined to facilitate efficient trading. For example, a Trea-

---

[6]*A Guide to Financial Futures at the Chicago Board of Trade,* The Chicago Board of Trade, undated, p. 29.

sury bill contract is traded in a standard size of $1 million, based only on a 90-day maturity. Treasury bond futures contracts are standardized at $100,000 with an 8 percent coupon. The contract size is the face value of the underlying securities.

Characteristics of Financial Futures Transactions

Interest rate futures contracts are traded on organized exchange markets located throughout the country.

Role of the Clearinghouse. All trading is conducted through the *clearinghouse* of each exchange. In effect, the clearinghouse acts as a buyer to every seller and a seller to every buyer; it does not simply match buy and sell orders. This procedure eliminates the need for direct contact between traders. The clearinghouse guarantees the performance of the contract and, rather than the seller, assumes responsibility for the credit worthiness of buyers. The willingness of participants to rely on the financial stability of the clearinghouse is an important characteristic of the futures markets, and the fact that the clearinghouses have so far consistently performed as promised testifies to the validity of their role. At the end of each trading day, the clearinghouse settles all accounts, paying profits earned by some traders and collecting payments due from others.

The Margin. Futures traders are required to post an initial *margin* to support their positions. The margin serves as a deposit in good faith. It may be in the form of cash, a bank letter of credit, or short-term Treasury securities. The margin required is quite small in comparison to the face value of the securities underlying the financial futures contract; the initial deposit is often no more than 5 percent of the contract face value. The margin is set by the exchange; it depends on the type of contract and whether the trader is a hedger or speculator.

At the end of each day, the clearinghouse requires a trader to settle the account; if there are losses on a given day, they are charged against the trader's margin account. If the charges reduce the account to a balance below the required minimum, the trader must immediately produce additional cash. Futures trading involves some cash flow on almost every trading day, and many observers believe the daily resettlement makes the futures markets much safer than they would be otherwise. It also is viewed as a justification for the relatively small initial cash required to trade contracts with a much higher face value. Nevertheless, managers of institutions trading futures contracts must manage cash carefully, because they must be ready each day to make deposits into their margin accounts.

Limits on Price Changes. A convention of the futures market that controls the exposure of traders is the limit on daily price changes. The exchanges set a maximum amount by which the price of a contract is allowed to change. When that limit is reached on a given day, the price cannot move further, and subsequent trades will take place only if they are within the limits. Risk exposure still exists, however. For example, the maximum price fluctuation allowed by the Chicago Board of Trade on Treasury bond and Treasury note contracts is 3 percent of par value, so the price can move by as much as $3,000 on any one day.

Because few futures contracts are carried to an actual physical transfer of assets, traders make an offsetting trade to close out their positions rather than delivering or accepting the commodity. The bookkeeping and associated transactions are handled by the exchange clearinghouse.

INTEREST RATE FUTURES

Interest rate futures contracts have interest-bearing or discount securities as the underlying commodity. Because they are an important component of asset/liability management, techniques involving interest rate futures trading are examined in detail.

Interest Rate Futures as a Hedging Device

By definition, a hedge is a position taken in the futures market to offset a potential loss in the cash or spot market. The preceding chapters stress the inverse relationship between changes in market values of interest-earning assets and changes in market yields. Because the value of a futures contract depends upon the market value of its underlying commodity, the prices of interest rate futures contracts also change inversely with interest rates. Thus, a financial institution can use futures to reduce its exposure to adverse rate changes.

For example, a decline in interest rates, lowering the reinvestment rate on an insurance company's bond portfolio, increases the price of interest rate futures contracts. Profits from the futures transactions could reduce the negative impact of the interest rate reduction on the bond portfolio. Futures can provide similar protection in times of interest rate increases.

Futures Prices and Market Yields: An Illustration

When interest rates fell in May 1985, after the Fed decided to lower the discount rate, the spot prices of bonds rose, as discussed in Chapters 7 and 8. The prices of outstanding futures contracts rose as well. Portions of *The Wall Street Journal* quotations of futures prices for Friday, May 17, and Monday, May 20, 1985, are shown in Figure 9.1.[7] The reduction in the discount rate and the money center banks' prime rate was announced late on May 17. On that date, a Treasury bond contract for September delivery had a settlement price, listed under the column heading "Settle," of 72-27.

Futures prices, like the prices of Treasury bonds and notes, are quoted in 32nds of a percent, so 72-27 means 72-27/32 percent of par,

or $72,843.75 for a contract with a par value of $100,000. Each 1/32 change is a dollar change of $31.25 ($100,000 × 1/32 × 0.01). At the close of trading May 20, the September contract settlement price was 74-13, an increase of 50/32. The dollar price change from Friday to Monday settlement was 50 × $31.25 = $1,562.50. Price changes for all other futures contracts in Figure 9.1 were positive. Traders who owned contracts for future delivery would have profited from their positions.

Long versus Short Hedges

A financial institution using futures to hedge can choose either a **long hedge** or a **short hedge.** A long hedge means the trader *buys* a futures contract. The position obligates the holder either to take delivery of securities at the preestablished price on some future date, or to sell the contract, closing out the position through the clearinghouse before the delivery date. When interest rates decline, the value of both interest-earning assets and outstanding futures contracts rises. A trader who actually takes delivery on securities can sell them at an immediate profit over the purchase price written into the futures contract. If, instead, the futures contract is sold before the delivery date, the contract selling price will be higher than the purchase price. Either way, the trader profits, so a long hedge is an appropriate strategy when a financial institution manager expects interest rates to decline.

A short hedge, in contrast, means the trader *sells* a futures contract, incurring an obligation either to deliver the underlying securities at some future point, or to close out the position before the delivery date by buying an offsetting contract. If interest rates increase in the intervening period, either obligation can be met at a profit. Suppose an institutional trader chooses to make delivery. The trader will be able to purchase securities at a lower price than would have initially been available, because market prices will decline with an increase in interest rates. It is more likely, however, that the trader will close out the position. In that case, the price of the contract purchased to close

---

[7]As noted, some types of financial futures contracts have come and gone over the years. Figure 9.1 includes two—bank CDs and GNMA certificates (a mortgage-related security discussed in Chapter 18)—that were traded infrequently by 1987.

Figure 9.1
Interest Rate Futures Prices: May 17 and May 20, 1985

FUTURES PRICES

Friday, May 17, 1985

Open Interest Reflects Previous Trading Day.

EURODOLLAR (IMM)—$1 million; pts of 100%

	Open	High	Low	Settle	Chg	Yield Settle	Chg	Open Interest
June	91.62	91.68	91.58	91.65	− .01	8.35 +	.01	44,697
Sept	90.98	91.05	90.95	91.02	− .02	8.98 +	.02	50,334
Dec	90.58	90.64	90.56	90.59	− .03	9.41 +	.03	14,360
Mr86	90.23	90.28	90.23	90.24	− .03	9.76 +	.03	4,885
June	89.94	90.00	89.94	89.96	− .03	10.04 +	.03	3,932
Sept	89.74	89.76	89.73	89.73	− .03	10.27 +	.03	2,439
Dec	89.51	89.55	89.51	89.52	− .03	10.48 +	.03	2,193
Mr87	89.34	89.36	89.31	89.33	− .02	10.67 +	.02	1,245

Est vol 31,844; vol Thurs 42,772; open int 124,085, +789.

GNMA 8% (CBT)—$100,000 prncpl; pts. 32nds of 100%

	Open	High	Low	Settle	Chg	Yield Settle	Chg	Open Interest
June	71-23	71-23	71-19	71-21	− 4	12.782 +	.027	2,281
Sept	70-31	70-31	70-28	70-28	− 7	12.952 +	.048	831
Dec	70-14	70-14	70-10	70-10	− 8	13.076 +	.055	240
Mr86	69-30	69-30	69-26	69-26	− 8	13.188 +	.056	369
June	69-14	69-14	69-12	69-12	− 9	13.287 +	.064	542
Sept	....	....	....	69-00	− 9	13.372 +	.064	91

Est vol 700; vol Thurs 472; open int 4,354, +57.

TREASURY BONDS (CBT)—$100,000; pts. 32nds of 100%

	Open	High	Low	Settle	Chg	Yield Settle	Chg	Open Interest
June	73-26	73-31	73-20	73-28	− 8	11.326 +	.040	141,331
Sept	72-25	72-30	72-18	72-27	− 8	11.496 +	.042	52,026
Dec	71-27	72-01	71-21	71-30	− 7	11.648 +	.037	13,494
Mr86	71-02	71-04	70-28	71-04	− 6	11.787 +	.033	8,727
June	70-11	70-13	70-04	70-13	− 5	11.912 +	.028	6,758
Sept	69-22	69-24	69-15	69-24	− 5	12.028 +	.028	4,590
Dec	69-03	69-05	68-28	69-05	− 5	12.135 +	.029	1,714
Mr87	....	....	....	68-20	− 4	12.231 +	.022	934
June	68-04	68-04	68-01	68-04	− 4	12.324 +	.024	1,175
Sept	....	....	....	67-22	− 4	12.405 +	.023	1,322

Est vol 105,000; vol Thurs 187,322; open int 232,081, +3383.

TREASURY NOTES (CBT)—$100,000; pts. 32nds of 100%

	Open	High	Low	Settle	Chg	Yield Settle	Chg	Open Interest
June	83-26	83-28	83-18	83-25	− 6	10.678 +	.035	29,036
Sept	82-25	82-26	82-18	82-25	− 5	10.866 +	.027	16,871
Dec	81-25	81-28	81-22	81-27	− 4	11.044 +	.024	2,261
Mr86	....	....	....	81-02	− 4	11.195 +	.024	477
June	....	....	....	80-13	− 4	11.323 +	.024	100

Est vol 10,000; vol Thurs 14,392; open int 48,745, +890.

TREASURY BILLS (IMM)—$1 mil.; pts. of 100%

	Open	High	Low	Settle	Chg	Discount Settle	Chg	Open Interest
June	92.55	92.59	92.49	92.54	− .04	7.46 +	.04	18,794
Sept	92.10	92.12	92.03	92.08	− .05	7.92 +	.05	15,525
Dec	91.74	91.78	91.72	91.74	− .05	8.26 +	.05	2,945
Mr86	91.47	91.49	91.46	91.47	− .05	8.53 +	.05	1,086
June	91.23	91.23	91.23	91.23	− .02	8.77 +	.02	1,127
Sept	91.01	91.03	91.01	91.03	− .01	8.97 +	.01	233
Dec	....	....	....	90.84	− .01	9.16 +	.01	115

Est vol 8,168; vol Thurs 13,875; open int 39,853, −777.

BANK CDs (IMM)—$1 million; pts. of 100%

	Open	High	Low	Settle	Chg	Discount Settle	Chg	Open Interest
June	91.97	92.00	91.91	91.99	− .01	8.01 +	.01	2,017
Sept	91.35	91.42	91.34	91.39	− .02	8.61 +	.02	2,072
Dec	90.93	91.02	90.93	90.98	− .02	9.02 +	.02	886
Mr86	....	....	....	90.61	− .04	9.39 +	.04	179
June	....	....	....	90.33	− .04	9.67 +	.04	157
Sept	....	....	....	90.11	− .03	9.89 +	.03	163

Est vol 298; vol Thurs 465; open int 5,510, −11.

FUTURES PRICES

Monday, May 20, 1985.

Open Interest Reflects Previous Trading Day.

EURODOLLAR (IMM)—$1 million; pts of 100%

	Open	High	Low	Settle	Chg	Yield Settle	Chg	Open Interest
June	91.90	91.96	91.87	91.91	+ .26	8.09 −	.26	43,708
Sept	91.33	91.39	91.32	91.34	+ .32	8.66 −	.32	51,159
Dec	90.93	90.99	90.92	90.93	+ .34	9.07 −	.34	14,482
Mr86	90.64	90.66	90.57	90.58	+ .34	9.42 −	.34	4,869
June	90.36	90.37	90.29	90.30	+ .34	9.70 −	.34	3,968
Sept	90.13	90.13	90.04	90.06	+ .33	9.94 −	.33	2,424
Dec	89.89	89.92	89.86	89.84	+ .32	10.16 −	.32	2,177
Mr87	89.67	89.73	89.66	89.64	+ .31	10.36 −	.31	1,245

Est vol 38,217; vol Fri 26,187; open int 124,032, −53.

GNMA 8% (CBT)—$100,000 prncpl; pts. 32nds. of 100%

	Open	High	Low	Settle	Chg	Yield Settle	Chg	Open Interest
June	72-02	72-30	72-02	72-21	− 32	12.567 −	.215	2,009
Sept	71-15	72-09	71-14	71-30	− 34	12.721 −	.231	1,107
Dec	71-03	71-21	71-03	71-12	− 34	12.843 −	.233	232
Mr86	71-00	71-02	70-24	70-28	− 34	12.952 −	.236	371
June	70-23	70-23	70-10	70-14	− 34	13.048 −	.239	542
Sept	....	....	....	70-02	− 34	13.132 −	.240	91

Est vol 600; vol Fri 827; open int 4,352, −2.

TREASURY BONDS (CBT)—$100,000; pts. 32nds of 100%

	Open	High	Low	Settle	Chg	Yield Settle	Chg	Open Interest
June	75-06	75-27	74-28	75-14	+ 50	11.077 −	.249	133,109
Sept	74-07	74-27	73-27	74-13	+ 50	11.241 −	.255	51,906
Dec	73-02	73-28	72-30	73-16	+ 50	11.387 −	.261	13,509
Mr86	72-15	73-00	72-06	72-22	+ 50	11.522 −	.265	8,743
June	71-22	72-07	71-14	71-31	+ 50	11.642 −	.270	6,775
Sept	70-25	71-18	70-25	71-09	+ 49	11.760 −	.268	4,552
Dec	70-15	71-00	70-15	70-22	+ 49	11.863 −	.272	1,623
Mr87	70-10	70-13	70-02	70-05	+ 49	11.956 −	.275	934
June	....	....	....	69-21	+ 49	12.045 −	.279	1,176
Sept	69-00	69-20	69-00	69-07	+ 49	12.123 −	.282	1,322

Est vol 200,000; vol Fri 96,378; open int 223,659, −8422.

TREASURY NOTES (CBT)—$100,000; pts. 32nds of 100%

	Open	High	Low	Settle	Chg	Yield Settle	Chg	Open Interest
June	85-02	85-19	84-26	85-06	+ 45	10.420 −	.258	31,596
Sept	84-01	84-18	83-27	84-05	+ 44	10.609 −	.257	17,047
Dec	83-02	83-20	83-02	83-07	+ 44	10.783 −	.261	2,243
Mr86	82-17	82-24	82-13	82-14	+ 44	10.931 −	.264	477
June	81-23	82-03	81-23	81-25	+ 44	11.056 −	.267	100

Est vol 15,000; vol Fri 8,245; open int 51,463, +2718.

TREASURY BILLS (IMM)—$1 mil.; pts. of 100%

	Open	High	Low	Settle	Chg	Discount Settle	Chg	Open Interest
June	92.74	92.80	92.70	92.75	+ .21	7.25 −	.21	18,133
Sept	92.33	92.40	92.28	92.35	+ .27	7.65 −	.27	16,286
Dec	91.94	92.08	91.94	92.02	+ .28	7.98 −	.28	3,048
Mr86	91.74	91.80	91.73	91.73	+ .26	8.27 −	.26	1,091
June	91.54	91.57	91.49	91.49	+ .26	8.51 −	.26	1,133
Sept	....	....	....	91.30	+ .27	8.70 −	.27	234
Dec	91.00	91.20	91.00	91.13	+ .29	8.87 −	.29	119

Est vol 9,751; vol Fri 8,241; open int 40,072, +219.

BANK CDs (IMM)—$1 million; pts. of 100%

	Open	High	Low	Settle	Chg	Discount Settle	Chg	Open Interest
June	92.24	92.29	92.19	92.26	+ .27	7.74 −	.27	1,881
Sept	91.79	91.79	91.69	91.71	+ .32	8.29 −	.32	2,115
Dec	91.38	91.38	91.29	91.30	+ .32	8.70 −	.32	781
Mr86	91.05	91.05	90.94	90.95	+ .34	9.05 −	.34	179
June	90.65	90.70	90.65	90.67	+ .34	9.33 −	.34	157
Sept	90.54	90.54	90.44	90.43	+ .32	9.57 −	.32	163

Est vol 443; vol Fri 312; open int 5,312, −198.

out the short position will be lower than the price received on the initial sale of a contract. The difference is the profit on the hedge.

Transactions costs and brokers' commissions reduce the proceeds of both long and short hedges.

The Long Hedge Illustrated

Suppose that, in June 1989, the manager of a money market portfolio expects interest rates to decline. New funds, to be received and invested in 90 days (September 1989), will suffer from the drop in yields, and the manager would like to reduce the impact on portfolio returns. The appropriate strategy under this forecast is a long hedge, because long futures positions profit from falling rates.

Gains and losses on cash and futures market transactions are summarized in Table 9.1. The money manager expects an inflow of $10 million in September. The discount yield currently available on 91-day T-bills is 10 percent, and the goal is to establish a yield of 10 percent on the anticipated funds. Because contracts on 90-day T-bills have face values of $1 million, ten contracts are needed to hedge the cash position. Assuming that the initial margin requirement is 2 percent of the contract price, the cash required in June will be slightly less than $20,000. The market value of the contracts purchased for delivery in September is $9.75 million. If the funds were available now for the T-bill investment, at a discount yield of 10 percent, the cost would be $9,747,222.

By the time the new funds arrive in September, suppose interest rates have fallen; the 91-day T-bill yield is down to 8 percent, and it now costs $9,797,778 to purchase bills with a face value of $10 million. The higher price results in an "opportunity loss" to the portfolio manager of $50,556, but the long futures hedge offsets most of that loss. With the decline in market yields, the September contracts have risen in value from $9.75 million to $9.8 million. Their sale provides a gain of $50,000, almost equaling the loss in the cash market. The effective discount yield on T-bills purchased, including the effect of the

hedge, is 9.978 percent, very close to the desired 10 percent.

By definition, a hedge is undertaken to offset potential losses in the institution's existing or planned portfolio of financial assets. Buying long futures contracts when no future investment in T-bills was planned would be speculation, not hedging, because the contract purchase would be an attempt to earn a pure profit on futures.

The Short Hedge Illustrated

If a financial institution stands to lose under forecasts of rising rates, it can undertake a short hedge. For depository institutions, many liability costs are tied to yields on short-term Treasury securities, and an increase in interest rates can raise the cost of funds significantly. Profits on a short hedge may be used to lock in a lower cost of funds.

For deposit costs pegged to the T-bill rate, Treasury bill futures provide a good vehicle for the short hedge. Suppose a savings institution in September 1990 wants to hedge $5 million in short-term CDs whose owners are expected to roll them over in 90 days. If market yields go up, the thrift must offer a higher rate on its CDs to remain competitive, reducing the net interest margin. The asset/liability manager can reduce these losses by the sale of T-bill futures contracts. With a subsequent increase in rates, the value of contracts declines, and when the position is closed out through the clearinghouse, a profit will be realized.

The short hedge illustrated in Table 9.2 is designed to offset the increase in CD rates from 7 percent to 9 percent; the interest paid on the CDs would increase by $25,000 for the three-month period. In September, the S&L sells five December contracts at a discount yield of 7 percent. To close out the position in December, after rates have risen to 9 percent, the hedger buys five T-bill contracts from the clearinghouse. They have declined in value, resulting in a $25,000 profit on the futures position. In the simplified world of this example, the institution's returns are protected from interest rate fluctuations, because the dollar interest cost for

Table 9.1
The Long Hedge
(Forecast: Falling Interest Rates)

I.

Cash Market	Futures Market

June

T-bill discount yield at 10% Price of 91-day T-bills, $10 million par: $9,747,222[a]	Buy 10 T-bill contracts for September delivery at 10% discount yield Value of contracts: $9,750,000[b]

September

T-bill discount yield at 8% Price of 91-day T-bills, $10 million par: $9,797,778	Sell 10 September T-bill contracts at 8% discount yield Value of contracts: $9,800,000

II.

Cash Market Loss		Futures Market Gain	
June cost	$9,747,222	September sale	$9,800,000
September cost	9,797,778	June purchase	9,750,000
Loss	($ 50,556)	Gain	$ 50,000

Net Loss: ($556)

III.
Effective Discount Yield with the Hedge (using Equation 4.3)

$$\frac{\$10,000,000 - (\$9,797,778 - \$50,000)}{\$10,000,000} \times \frac{360}{91} = 9.978\%$$

[a] At a discount yield of 10%, the price of a 91-day T-bill (from Equation 4.5) is:

$$P_0 = \$10,000,000\left[1 - \frac{0.1\,(91)}{360}\right] = \$9,747,222$$

[b] T-bill futures contracts are standardized at 90-day maturities, resulting in a price different from the one calculated in the cash market.

the quarter, netted against the gain on the hedge, is the desired $87,500. Again, transactions costs, brokers' fees and the opportunity cost of the margin deposit are not included.

As with the long hedge, the short hedge is undertaken only to protect an existing financial position. Attempting to gain a pure profit from rising rates would be speculation.

RISK AND THE FINANCIAL FUTURES MARKETS

The preceding scenarios are extremely simplified. For example, they assume the changes in spot and futures yields are identical. They also do not address several decisions that investors must make before entering the market, such as

---

Table 9.2
The Short Hedge
(Forecast: Rising Interest Rates)

I.

Cash Market	Futures Market
September	
Certificate of deposit rate: 7%	Sell 5 T-bill contracts for December delivery at 7% discount yield
Interest cost on $5 million in deposits (3 months): $87,500	Value of contracts: $4,912,500
December	
Certificate of deposit rate: 9%	Buy 5 December T-bill contracts at 9% discount yield
Interest cost on $5 million in deposits (3 months): $112,500	Value of contracts: $4,887,500

II.

Cash Market Loss		Futures Market Gain	
September interest	$ 87,500	September sale	$4,912,500
December interest	112,500	December purchase	4,887,500
Loss	($ 25,000)	Gain	$ 25,000
	Net Result of Hedge:	**$0**	

III.
Net Interest Cost

$112,500 − $25,000 = $87,500

---

the type and number of contracts to be purchased or sold and the length of the hedge. The examples also assume that the interest rate forecasts are accurate and timely. These more complex aspects of hedging and the risks they introduce are discussed in this section.

Incorrect Rate Forecasts

The opening paragraph illustrates that rate forecasts are an integral part of every hedge but that their accuracy determines management's satisfaction with the results. In Table 9.1, the assumption was that interest rates would fall, and funds received and invested after three months would earn a lower yield. If interest rates had not fallen, the portfolio manager could have maintained or even increased returns through the cash market position alone. The long hedge would result in a loss, because the contracts owned would decline in value. The loss on the futures hedge would reduce the otherwise favorable returns on the securities investment. The protective hedge not only limits the institution's loss from an *unfavorable* interest rate change, it also limits the potential gains from a *favorable* movement in rates. Thus, hedging is indeed a risk-minimization strategy, intended to reduce potential variation in the net interest margin.

Basis Risk

An influence on both the type and number of contracts to be traded is the **basis.** Basis is the difference between the price of a futures contract and the spot price of the underlying financial asset at time t:

(9.1) $\text{Basis} = P_{St} - P_{Ft}$

To execute a perfect hedge, one in which the cash market loss is *exactly* offset by the futures market profit, the hedger must predict the basis accurately and adjust the size of the hedge accordingly. In the simplified world of Table 9.1, the discount yield on the T-bills equaled the effective discount yield at which the T-bill contract traded. The difference in the cash and futures market results arose from the futures market convention of pricing T-bill contracts based on 90 rather than 91 days. In reality, however, although cash yields and futures market yields are closely related, they are not perfectly correlated because each market has its own supply/demand interactions. The possibility of unexpected changes in the relationship between spot and futures market prices introduces another element of risk, known as **basis risk.**

Basis Risk Illustrated.[8] When a hedger closes out cash and futures positions, the gains and losses from each are netted. These calculations are shown at the end of Tables 9.1 and 9.2. Presenting them in a different format clarifies the importance of the basis.

The results from the cash market transactions, at the close of a hedge, are determined by the number of securities bought or sold and their cost, $Q(P_{St})$. In Table 9.1, ten $1 million par value bills were bought:

$$Q(P_{S1}) = 10 \times \$979,777.80 = \$9,797,778$$

The result of the futures transaction alone is the proceeds from the sale (at t = 1), less the cost of the purchase (at t = 0):

$$Q(P_{F1}) - Q(P_{F0}) = Q(P_{F1} - P_{F0})$$

For the long hedge:

$$Q(P_{F1} - P_{F0}) = 10 \times (\$980,000 - \$975,000)$$
$$= 10 \times \$5,000$$
$$= \$50,000$$

The *net cost* of the bills purchased can be expressed as the difference between their spot price in September—the amount the institution would actually pay for the bills—and the profits from the futures trade:

(9.2)

$$\text{Net Cost} = Q(P_{S1}) - Q(P_{F1} - P_{F0})$$
$$= 10(\$979,777.80) - 10(\$980,000.00 - \$975,000.00)$$
$$= \$9,797,778 - \$50,000$$
$$= \$9,747,778$$

Rearranging, the net cost is also:

$$\text{Net Cost} = Q(P_{S1} - P_{F1}) + Q(P_{F0})$$
$$= 10(\$979,777.80 - \$980,000.00) + (10 \times \$975,000.00)$$
$$= -\$2,222 + \$9,750,000$$
$$= \$9,747,778$$

In other words, the basis at the time the position is closed out—the quantity $(P_{S1} - P_{F1})$—determines the success or failure of the hedge. If there were no uncertainty about the basis, a hedge in the futures market would involve much less risk. In reality, at the time the hedge is undertaken, the trader does not know either P_{S1} *or* P_{F1} *or* the difference between the two that will prevail in the future. As basis fluctuates, so does the potential gain or loss on the hedge.

Figure 9.2 shows prices on a popular futures instrument, Treasury bond contracts, and prices on Treasury bonds over the period December 1981-July 1982. The high positive correlation in price movements is evident from the bottom line, which is the basis over that period. Although the basis does not fluctuate greatly, it is not stable. Traders who hedge positions in the cash markets with futures incur basis risk, a fact that must be considered in the hedging decision.

---

[8]The following section draws upon James Van Horne, *Financial Market Rates and Flows,* 2d ed. (Englewood Cliffs, NJ: Prentice-Hall, 1984), pp. 154-155.

Figure 9.2
Prices of Treasury Bonds and Treasury Bond Futures, December 1981–July 1982.

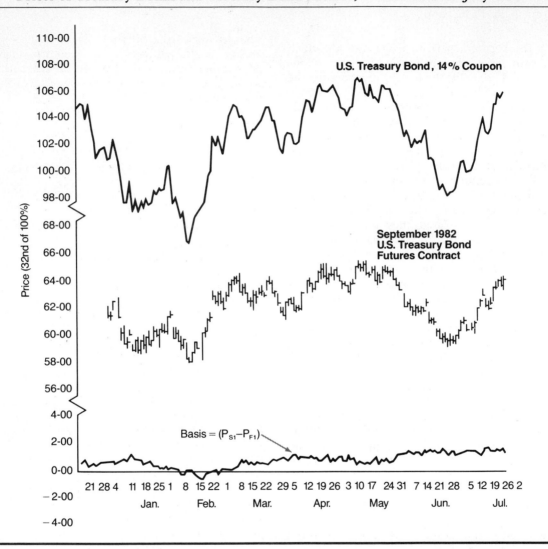

Source: Chicago Board of Trade, *Guide to Financial Futures,* p. 39. Chart reprinted with permission of Data Lab Corporation, Chicago, Illinois.

The Cross Hedge and Basis Risk

In Table 9.1, the money market portfolio manager was protecting yields on an anticipated Treasury bill investment with a T-bill futures contract. But in many hedging decisions, the limited variety of futures contracts available makes it impossible to hedge a cash instrument with a contract for future delivery of the same security. Whenever a futures hedge is constructed on an instrument other than the cash market security, as would be the case when hedging a corporate bond portfolio, the hedge is a *cross hedge.* The basis risk for these positions is even greater than when the same security is involved in both sides of the transaction; the movements in yields and prices for two different financial assets are more likely to differ.

If a short-term instrument is hedged with a futures contract on a long-term security, or vice versa, the basis risk is even greater. A change in the slope of the yield curve would produce changes of differing magnitudes for long- and short-term yields. In that case, the changes in spot and futures values would certainly diverge, and, consequently, the effectiveness of the hedge would be more uncertain.

The cross hedge exposes the hedger to basis risk for another important reason. Even if the changes in *yields* were the same on two securities, the resulting *price* changes could very well differ. The bond theorems and duration discussions in Chapters 7 and 8 demonstrate that a given basis-point change in yields will not affect the prices of securities in the same way if they have different coupon rates and/or terms to maturity, differences likely to occur in a cross hedge.

If a bond portfolio manager wants to hedge corporate bond holdings, the logical choice is Treasury bond futures. It might be possible to find a T-bond contract with the same maturity on the underlying security as on the bond portfolio, but the coupon rate would probably not match. As market interest rates fluctuate, the goal of a hedge—minimizing NIM fluctuations by realizing a profit on the futures trade that exactly offsets the cash market loss—is difficult to achieve with a cross hedge.

Choosing the Optimal Number of Contracts: The Hedge Ratio

An asset/liability manager faces additional uncertainties in determining the size of the futures position. Selecting the number of contracts to trade is particularly difficult in a cross hedge, because face value, coupon, and maturity characteristics may all differ between cash and futures instruments. The first step in structuring the hedge is to identify the assets and/or liabilities to be protected. The volume and interest rate characteristics of the instrument to be hedged are the foundation for the futures decision.[9] Once the size of the cash market position has been chosen, the **hedge ratio,** or the number of contracts to be traded, must be determined.

If the institution is not undertaking a cross hedge, it can estimate the size of the hedge with a relatively straightforward calculation:

$$(9.3) \quad HR = \frac{V}{F} \times \frac{M_C}{M_F} \times \rho$$

where:

HR = hedge ratio, the *total* number of contracts needed;

V = market value of the assets/liabilities to be hedged;

F = face value of the futures contract;

M_C = maturity of the assets/liabilities to be hedged;

M_F = maturity of the futures contract;

ρ = correlation between cash and futures interest rates.

For example, suppose a securities portfolio manager wants to protect the yield on an investment of $15 million in T-bills three months from now. The hedge ratio is:

$$HR = \frac{\$15,000,000}{\$1,000,000} \times \frac{91}{90} \times .95$$

$$= 14.408 \text{ T-bill futures contracts}$$

Several factors affect the outcome of the hedge. One is the assumption that the correlation between yields on T-bills and T-bill futures contracts during the hedge period can be accurately estimated. In this example it was assumed to be

---

[9]The development of an institutional hedging strategy is a major aspect of asset/liability management. The futures position may revolve around either a macro or micro hedge, terms referring to the magnitude of the futures position in relationship to the balance sheet of the institution. This aspect of hedging is explored in Chapter 18.

.95, but the actual correlation could be different. In addition, the hedge ratio calculated was not a whole number; the "perfect" hedge would be 14.408 contracts, but it is only possible to trade 14 or 15 contracts. So even if the assumed relationships hold, the futures market gain will not exactly equal the cash market loss. The inability to trade fractions of a contract or, for that matter, fractions of a Treasury bill, explains why the hedge results in Table 9.1 are imperfect. Although many financial theories assume "perfect divisibility" of financial assets, this seldom exists in practice.[10]

A Duration-Based Hedge Ratio.   In a cross hedge, Equation 9.3 could suggest an inappropriate hedge ratio because of the unequal price reactions in instruments with different coupons and maturities, even if yields are perfectly correlated. Including the duration of the cash and futures instruments provides a better estimate of the required hedge ratio:[11]

$$\textbf{(9.4)} \quad HR_{DUR} = \frac{R_F P_C D_C}{R_C FP_F D_F}$$

where:

HR_{DUR} = the duration-based hedge ratio—the number of contracts to be traded for *each* cash market instrument being hedged;

R_F = 1 + the rate expected to prevail on the instrument underlying the futures contract;

R_C = 1 + the expected yield to maturity on the asset to be hedged;

FP_F = the price agreed upon in the futures contract;

P_C = the expected spot price of the asset to be hedged as of the hedge termination date;

D_C = the expected duration of the asset to be hedged as of the termination date;

D_F = the expected duration of the instrument underlying the futures contract as of the termination date.

The duration-based hedge ratio adjusts the size of the futures position for potential differences in the maturity and coupon rates of the cash and futures securities. For example, consider the decision facing a bond portfolio manager in February 1989, anticipating an $8 million cash inflow in May 1989 and forecasting a decline in corporate bond yields over the intervening period. The manager is watching a bond issue maturing in 1994 and expects the yield on these bonds to be 10.14 percent in May, down from the February level of 11.14 percent. At that yield, their duration in May would be 4.148 years. If funds were available in February, 8,231 bonds ($8 million ÷ $971.83 per bond) could be purchased at the current market price. By May, however, the price is expected to have risen to $1,008.76, and $8 million will buy only 7,930 bonds.

Table 9.3 shows the calculation of a duration-based hedge ratio to fit this situation. Because there are no futures contracts on corporate bonds, a cross hedge is required. Treasury bond futures are a reasonable choice. However, because they are standardized at 8 percent coupon, with at least 15-year maturities, the duration of the cash and futures securities will differ. Constructing a hedge by simply comparing the market values of the cash and futures instruments would lead to a less than

---

[10]Equation 9.3 is presented in Mark Drabenstott and Anne O'Mara McDonley, "Futures Markets: A Primer for Financial Institutions," *Economic Review,* Federal Reserve Bank of Kansas City 69 (November 1984): 24-25. The hedging ratio has been the subject of considerable research. Recent examples are Charles T. Howard and Louis J. D'Antonio, "Treasury Bill Futures as a Hedging Tool: A Risk-Return Approach," *Journal of Financial Research* 9 (Spring 1986): 25-39; and David E. Bell and William S. Krasker, "Estimating Hedge Ratios," *Financial Management* 15 (Summer 1986): 34-39.

[11]This approach to estimating the hedge ratio was developed by Robert W. Kolb and Raymond Chiang, and its derivation is found in several sources, including "Improving Hedging Performance Using Interest Rate Futures," *Financial Management* 10 (Autumn 1981): 72-79; and Kolb and Chiang, "Duration, Immunization and Hedging with Interest Rate Futures," *Journal of Financial Research* 5 (Summer 1982): 161-170.

Table 9.3
Duration–Based Estimation of the Hedge Ratio

Expected Cash Inflow (May 1989)	$8,000,000
Cash Instrument to be Hedged	Corporate bonds: 10⅜s of 94
	Current YTM (February 1989): 11.14%
	Current price: $971.83
Number of Bonds if Purchased at Current Price	8,231
Expected Position of Cash Instrument in May 1989	Expected YTM: 10.14% (R_C = 1 + 0.1014)
	Expected market price: $1,008.76 ($P_C$)
	Duration at expected YTM: 4.148 (D_C)
February 1989 Price on T-Bond Futures (10.12% Yield)	83-24 = 83.75% of par = $83,750 ($FP_F$)
Expected Position of T-Bond Futures in May 1989	Price: 91-16 = 91.5% of par = $91,500
	Yield: 9.12% (R_F = 1 + 0.0912)
	Duration: 9.871 (D_F)

Duration-Based Hedge Ratio

(9.4)
$$HR_{DUR} = \frac{R_F P_C D_C}{R_C FP_F D_F}$$

$$HR_{DUR} = \frac{(1.0912)\,(\$1,008.76)\,(4.148)}{(1.1014)\,(\$83,750)\,(9.871)} = 0.005015$$

Number of Contracts = 0.005015 (8,231) = 41.28 = 41 contracts

---

optimal hedge. The appropriate long position for this hedge is to buy 41 T-bond contracts, which can later be sold at a profit if rates fall. The simple hedge ratio presented in Equation 9.3 would result in a ratio approximately half that size.

Table 9.4 shows the results of a long hedge with 41 T-bond contracts. Assuming the manager's expectations are perfectly fulfilled, the net gain on the hedge is $13,779, more than offsetting the opportunity loss from the decline in market yields during the period in which investment must be delayed. Nothing guarantees a perfect hedge, of course, but performance is improved if the coupon and maturity of the instrument to be hedged are matched closely to the security underlying the futures contract. As with any duration measure, the hedge protects against only one expected interest rate move-

ment, so it must be adjusted frequently as market conditions change.

Interest Rate Futures: Regulatory Restrictions and Financial Reporting

The risks accompanying the futures markets have led regulators to focus attention on policies governing institutional involvement. For state-regulated institutions, there may be as many different policies as there are state regulators. In contrast, federally chartered and/or federally insured institutions in each industry do have uniform regulations. In general, regulators disapprove of futures transactions that increase the institution's risk exposure. Instead, they expect an institution to assume a futures position that will desensitize the balance sheet to interest rate changes. Futures cannot be used as income-

Table 9.4
Results of the Duration-Based Hedge

I.

Cash Market	Futures Market
February	
Corporate bond yield: 11.14%	Buy 41 T-bond contracts for September delivery at 83-24
Price: $971.83	Yield: 10.12%
Total available if purchased in February 1989: 8,231 bonds	Cost: $3,433,750
May	
Funds received and invested: $8,000,000	Sell 41 September T-bond contracts at 91-16
Corporate bond yield: 10.14%	Yield: 9.12%
Price: $1,008.76	Price: $3,751,500
Total purchased: 7,930 bonds	

II.

Cash Market Loss		Futures Market Gain	
February cost (8,231 bonds)	$7,999,133	May sale	$3,751,500
May cost (8,231 bonds)	8,303,104	February purchase	3,433,750
Loss	($ 303,971)	Gain	$ 317,750
		Net Gain:	**$13,779**

generating instruments for speculative purposes. Regulators also expect a high-level management committee, often including members of the board of directors, to establish a hedging policy for the institution, including a set of guidelines for establishing hedges and monitoring the results.[12]

Accounting Rules.   Guidelines for reporting futures transactions have also received much attention. The accounting profession has addressed two areas of controversy: what distinguishes a hedge from a speculative trade, and how to report a futures position. Rules of the Financial Accounting Standards Board (FASB) designate a futures transaction as a hedge when two conditions are met:[13]

1.   The asset or liability to be hedged exposes the institution to interest rate risk.

2.   The futures contract chosen reduces interest rate risk, is designated as a hedge, and has price movements highly correlated with the instrument being hedged.

For reporting the results of hedges, institutions prefer to wait until a futures position is closed, and the FASB permits transactions meeting its definition to be reported at that time, after the results are known. Some regulators prefer contemporaneous reporting and re-

---

[12]For more details on the guidelines established for commercial banks and bank holding companies, see Parkinson and Spindt, ''The Use of Interest Rate Futures by Commercial Banks,'' pp. 469-474; and Gary D. Koppenhaver, ''Trimming the Hedges: Regulators, Banks and Financial Futures,'' *Economic Perspectives*, Federal Reserve Bank of Chicago 8 (November/December 1984): 3-12.

[13]Drabenstott and McDonley, ''Futures Markets: A Primer for Financial Institutions,'' p. 30. The FASB rules became effective December 31, 1984.

quire institutions to use a "mark-to-market" approach. For example, the Comptroller of the Currency requires national banks to report the market value of their futures positions before closure and thus before any gains or losses are realized. During the course of a hedge, the value of a futures contract may fluctuate significantly as financial market conditions change, although the institution's financial position is not actually affected until a contract is closed out. Thus, many bank managers believe that mark-to-market futures reporting may provide misleading information.

The Federal Home Loan Bank Board has allowed savings institutions to use deferral rather than mark-to-market for several years. Any transactions that do not meet the FASB criteria are considered speculative, and must be reported by mark-to-market. Until bank regulators revise their rules, however, banks must use different methods to report futures transactions to two different audiences.

The risks inherent in the interest rate futures markets, as well as additional regulatory and accounting standards, mean that futures strategies require careful planning and monitoring after they are implemented. The vast majority of financial institutions that are successful hedgers have established objectives and safeguards to control the additional risk exposure.

FOREIGN CURRENCY FUTURES

Financial institutions active in international markets face **exchange rate risk,** or variability in NIM caused by fluctuations in currency exchange rates. Exchange rate risk increased significantly in 1971 when the United States officially abandoned the gold standard and allowed its currency exchange rate to float. Although many other currencies had been pegged to the value of the U.S. dollar, since 1973 most have been allowed to float. As a result, institutions that have foreign branches, issue bankers' acceptances, or provide loans in the international markets are exposed to exchange rate risk.

Figure 9.3 tracks exchange rates for several foreign currencies against the U.S. dollar. The fluctuations illustrate the uncertainty faced in international finance. Foreign exchange, or currency, futures contracts provide a tool for hedging some of that uncertainty. These instruments were introduced at the International Monetary Market in 1972, so they have existed longer than interest rate futures.

Exchange Rate Risk

Exchange rate risk is present whenever a financial institution negotiates an international transaction involving a transfer of funds at a later date, so that the rate at which foreign currencies and dollars will be exchanged is unknown when the transaction is negotiated. For example, suppose a U.S. bank agreed in March 1986 to finance a U.S. importer of Swiss chocolates. The cost of the imported chocolates, in Swiss francs (SF), was 25 million; the bank did not actually have to provide the funds until June 1986. As shown in Figure 9.4, the exchange rate prevailing on March 6, 1986, was:

$$\$/SF = 0.5283$$
$$SF/\$ = 1.8930$$

In other words, one Swiss franc would buy 0.5283 U. S. dollars, the **direct rate,** or dollars per unit of foreign currency; and one U.S. dollar would buy 1.8930 Swiss francs, the **indirect rate,** or units of foreign currency per dollar. Direct and indirect rates are reciprocals.

If the funds transfer had occurred in March 1986, the bank would have loaned:

$$SF25,000,000 \div 1.893 = \$13,206,550$$

Uncertainty was introduced because the SF25,000,000 was not to be paid until June 1986. Potential exchange rate fluctuations could cause the actual dollar commitment to be more or less than $13,206,550. In fact, Figure 9.4 shows that on June 6, 1986, the direct exchange rate was 0.5455, and the indirect rate was 1.8330. The value of the dollar had declined, and SF25,000,000 cost $13,638,843. Large com-

Figure 9.3
Spot Exchange Rate Indexes, 1983–1986

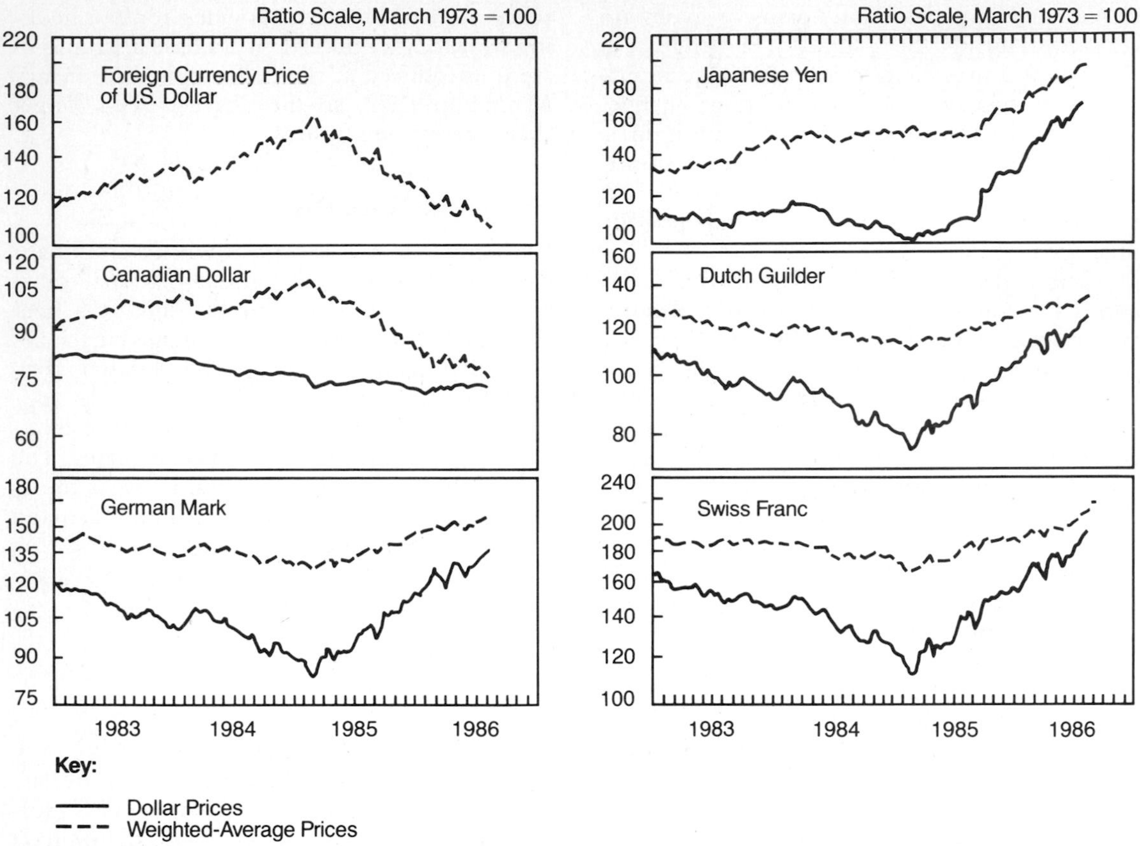

Key:

——— Dollar Prices
– – – Weighted-Average Prices

Source: Board of Governors of the Federal Reserve System, *1986 Historical Chart Book,* p. 110.

mercial banks, which maintain inventories in many currencies to meet the financial needs of customers, carry a daily exposure to such uncertainties.

Sources of Exchange Rate Risk

Exchange rate fluctuations have been the focus of much academic research. Some theories of exchange rate determination focus on supply/demand relationships for goods and services exchanged between two countries. Imbalances may lead to trade or balance-of-payments defi-

cits that eventually affect currency exchange rates.

Other theories suggest that exchange rate risk is closely tied to interest rate risk. The ***interest rate parity theorem*** asserts that interest rates and exchange rates are interdependent. If interest rates in one country differ from those in another, supply and demand for the currencies of the two countries can be affected. According to this theory, when interest rates in the United States are high relative to those in other countries, foreign investors will demand U.S. dollars so they can take advantage of more

Figure 9.4
Foreign Exchange Rates

FOREIGN EXCHANGE

Thursday, March 6, 1986

The New York foreign exchange selling rates below apply to trading among banks in amounts of $1 million and more, as quoted at 3 p.m. Eastern time by Bankers Trust Co. Retail transactions provide fewer units of foreign currency per dollar.

Country	U.S. $ equiv. Thurs.	Wed.	Currency per U.S. $ Thurs.	Wed.
Argentina (Austral) ...	1.2484	1.2484	.801	.801
Australia (Dollar) ...	.7025	.7015	1.4235	1.4255
Austria (Schilling)	.06353	.0633	15.74	15.79
Belgium (Franc)				
Commercial rate	.02178	.02182	45.92	45.84
Financial rate	.02164	.02168	46.22	46.13
Brazil (Cruzeiro)	.0007262	.0007262	13770.00	13770.00
Britain (Pound)	1.4470	1.4470	.6911	.6911
30-Day Forward	1.4413	1.4410	.6938	.6940
90-Day Forward	1.4314	1.4306	.6986	.6990
180-Day Forward	1.4189	1.4180	.7048	.7052
Canada (Dollar)	.7065	.7092	1.4155	1.1100
. . . .				
South Korea (Won)	.001131	.001131	884.50	884.50
Spain (Peseta)	.007072	.007092	141.00	141.40
Sweden (Krona)	.1383	.1381	7.2300	7.2400
Switzerland (Franc) ..	.5283	.5214	1.8930	1.9180
30-Day Forward	.5302	.5232	1.8862	1.9112
90-Day Forward	.5338	.5268	1.8733	1.8984
180-Day Forward	.5391	.5318	1.8550	1.8805
Taiwan (Dollar)	.02563	.02563	39.01	39.01
Thailand (Baht)	.03788	.03788	26.40	26.40
United Arab (Dirham) ...	.2723	.2723	3.673	3.673
Uruguay (New Peso)				
Financial	.007526	.007526	132.87	132.87
Venezuela (Bolivar)				
Official rate	.13333	.13333	7.50	7.50
Floating rate	.05650	.05450	17.70	18.35
W. Germany (Mark) ..	.4466	.4398	2.2390	2.2740
30-Day Forward	.4479	.4527	2.2326	2.2090
90-Day Forward	.4504	.4434	2.2202	2.2551
180-Day Forward	.4538	.4471	2.2037	2.2367
SDR	1.14941	1.15583	0.870013	0.865180
ECU	0.960980	0.968041	....	....

Special Drawing Rights are based on exchange rates for the U.S., West German, British, French and Japanese currencies. Source: International Monetary Fund.

ECU is based on a basket of community currencies. Source: European Community Commission.

FOREIGN EXCHANGE

Friday, June 6, 1986

The New York foreign exchange selling rates below apply to trading among banks in amounts of $1 million and more, as quoted at 3 p.m. Eastern time by Bankers Trust Co. Retail transactions provide fewer units of foreign currency per dollar.

Country	U.S. $ equiv. Fri.	Thurs.	Currency per U.S. $ Fri.	Thurs.
Argentina (Austral) ...	1.1614	1.1614	.861	.861
Australia (Dollar) ...	.6990	.6928	1.4306	1.4434
Austria (Schilling)	.06397	.06352	15.63	15.74
Belgium (Franc)				
Commercial rate	.02153	.02191	46.45	45.65
Financial rate	.02139	.02176	46.75	45.95
Brazil (Cruzado)	.07262	.07262	13.77	13.77
Britain (Pound)	1.5050	1.4950	.6645	.6689
30-Day Forward	1.5014	1.4914	.6660	.6705
90-Day Forward	1.4954	1.4856	.6687	.6731
180-Day Forward	1.4883	1.4783	.6719	.6765
Canada (Dollar)	.7158	.7184	1.3970	1.3920
. . . .				
South Korea (Won)	.001129	.001129	889.20	889.20
Spain (Peseta)	.007029	.006988	142.25	143.10
Sweden (Krona)	.1393	.1385	7.1775	7.2200
Switzerland (Franc) ..	.5455	.5427	1.8330	1.8425
30-Day Forward	.5465	.5438	1.8297	1.8388
90-Day Forward	.5488	.5462	1.8220	1.8306
180-Day Forward	.5525	.5499	1.8100	1.8185
Taiwan (Dollar)	.02614	.02614	38.25	38.25
Thailand (Baht)	.03789	.03789	26.39	26.39
Turkey (Lira)	.001451	.001451	689.00	689.00
United Arab (Dirham) ...	.2723	.2723	3.673	3.673
Uruguay (New Peso)				
Financial	.006885	.006885	145.25	145.25
Venezuela (Bolivar)				
Official rate	.1333	.1333	7.50	7.50
Floating rate	.04924	.04885	20.31	20.47
W. Germany (Mark) ..	.4494	.4458	2.2250	2.2430
30-Day Forward	.4504	.4468	2.2200	2.2881
90-Day Forward	.4523	.4380	2.2108	2.2831
180-Day Forward	.4552	.4517	2.1970	2.2140
SDR	1.16424	1.15635	0.858932	0.864789
ECU	0.962358	0.952504	....	....

Special Drawing Rights are based on exchange rates for the U.S., West German, British, French and Japanese currencies. Source: International Monetary Fund.

ECU is based on a basket of community currencies. Source: European Community Commission.
z-Not quoted.

Source: *The Wall Street Journal,* March 7, 1986, p. 28; June 9, 1986, p. 30. Reprinted by permission of *The Wall Street Journal,* © Dow Jones & Company, Inc. 1986. All Rights Reserved.

desirable rates of return. Exchange rates will then adjust to reflect the interest rate differentials. The ***purchasing power parity theorem*** ties exchange rates to differential inflation rates across countries. Under the Fisher theorem, discussed in Chapter 5, interest rates are directly related to expected inflation rates. Thus,

both "parity" theorems are consistent explanations for exchange rate relationships.[14]

[14]Further discussion of the parity theorems can be found in Roger M. Kubarych, *Foreign Exchange Markets in the United States,* 2d ed. (New York: Federal Reserve Bank of New York, 1983); Alan C. Shapiro, "What Does Pur-

As with interest rate forecasting, it is difficult to forecast future currency exchange rates accurately. Nevertheless, theories of exchange rate risk suggest that changing interest rates affect not only a financial institution's asset values but also the currency exchange transactions in which it is involved.

Foreign Currency Futures as a Hedging Tool

Foreign currency futures are instruments to hedge exchange rate risk, just as interest rate futures are for interest rate risk. Hedging strategies useful to the bank financing the chocolate transaction are similar to the choices available for hedging against interest rate fluctuations. As of early 1987, available futures contracts included the West German mark, the Japanese yen, the Swiss franc, the British pound, the French franc, the Mexican peso, and the Canadian dollar. Contract prices are quoted as direct rates, or dollars per unit of the foreign currency. When the value of the dollar declines, the values of the foreign currency and the futures contract on that currency rise.

As of March 6, 1986, the settlement price on a futures contract for September 1986 delivery of Swiss francs was 0.5395 ($/SF). To avoid the adverse effects of a decline in the value of a dollar between March and June, requiring a larger dollar commitment in June than originally planned, the bank could hedge by buying futures contracts on Swiss francs at the settlement price prevailing in March. Because the value of the dollar had declined by June, the settlement price on the contract rose to 0.5463 ($/SF) and could have been sold at a profit to offset the higher dollar cost of the chocolate transaction.[15]

A Digression: The Forward Currency Market

A discussion of exchange rate risk would be incomplete without mention of an alternative to futures contracts heavily used by major commercial banks—the *forward currency market.* The forward markets also provide a mechanism for avoiding the uncertainty of exchange rate fluctuations over a given planning period. A forward exchange is an agreement between two parties to exchange a specified amount of one currency for another, at a specified future date, at a specified rate of exchange. The forward rate agreed upon may be different from the spot rate at the time of negotiation and also from the spot rate at the time the exchange actually occurs. Forward contracts are useful hedging tools because they remove uncertainty; the institution can forecast its cash flows more precisely.

Forward rates are quoted daily along with the spot rates of exchange; for many currencies, rates for 30-, 90-, and 180-day forward exchanges are reported. In Figure 9.4, all three forward rates are quoted for the Swiss franc. As of March 6, 1986, the forward rates for the franc against the U.S. dollar were higher than the spot rate of 0.5283. If the U.S. bank, in its agreement to finance the Swiss chocolate importer, had wanted to hedge in the forward, rather than the futures, market, it could have negotiated an agreement at the 90-day forward rate. The 90-day forward rate prevailing on March 6, 1986, was:

$$\$/SF = 0.5338$$
$$SF/\$ = 1.8733$$

In other words, the bank could have guaranteed that in June, the SF25,000,000 it had to provide to the importer would represent an investment, in dollars, in the amount of:

$$SF25,000,000 \div 1.8733 = \$13,345,433$$

chasing Power Parity Mean?" *Journal of International Money and Finance* (December 1983): 295-318; and Ian H. Giddy and Gunter Dufey, "The Random Behavior of Flexible Exchange Rates," *Journal of International Business Studies* 6 (Spring 1975): 1-32.

[15]For more on the currency futures markets, see Norman S. Fieleke, "The Rise of the Foreign Currency Futures Markets," *New England Economic Review,* Federal Reserve Bank of Boston (March/April 1985), pp. 38-47; and

Henry S. Goldstein, "Foreign Currency Futures: Some Further Aspects," *Economic Perspectives,* Federal Reserve Bank of Chicago 7 (November/December 1983): 3-13.

Even though the forward rate was unfavorable compared to March's spot rate, it was a figure on which plans could be based. The uncertainty about the dollar commitment in June was eliminated. As in a futures hedge, however, the transaction could have locked the bank into an exchange rate less desirable than the spot rate that prevailed in June. The potential for a favorable movement in rates was traded for certain knowledge of the rate of exchange. In this instance, the spot rate in June was higher than the 90-day forward rate in March, so a forward contract would have helped the bank.

Differences between Forward and Futures Markets.   Forward agreements differ from futures contracts in several important ways. They are private transactions. There are no central exchanges, such as the International Monetary Market of the Chicago Mercantile Exchange, where forward agreements are traded. Because of this difference, institutions are exposed to the risk that the counterparty will default on the contract. The size of a forward contract is negotiated, while the size of futures contracts is standardized by exchanges to facilitate rapid trades and price quotations. Finally, although futures contracts, by convention, mature in only one of four months (March, June, September, and December), forward agreements can mature any business day.

SUMMARY

Tools for managing interest rate risk include two types of financial futures—interest rate and foreign currency futures. They permit managers to adopt a hedging strategy, through which expected profits on the institution's existing financial position are protected against unfavorable changes in interest or foreign exchange rates. Hedging is a risk-minimization approach; it does not allow an institution to profit from unexpected favorable changes. Futures are traded on organized exchanges, facilitating their liquidity, and the clearinghouse plays an important role in transactions.

An interest rate futures contract is an agreement between a buyer and seller to exchange a fixed quantity of a financial asset at a specified price on a specified date. The buyer has a long futures position and would purchase a contract when interest rates are expected to fall. The seller of a futures contract takes a short position in anticipation of rising rates. Because the prices of futures contracts move in the same direction as prices on underlying financial assets, falling interest rates coincide with rising prices for futures contracts, and rising rates coincide with falling futures prices. The hedger uses profits earned on futures transactions to offset losses incurred on other financial assets. Additional markets permit institutions to hedge against the risk of changes in currency exchange rates. Forward contracts are also available to hedge against exchange rate risk.

Futures contracts are not without their own risks. Among the most important is basis risk, especially prevalent in cross hedging. Management also must pay close attention to the hedging ratio, and financial institutions must be careful to follow regulatory and accounting rules governing the use of futures contracts.

Questions

1. Explain the difference between hedging in the financial futures market and using futures for speculation.

2. Explain the important differences between cash markets and futures markets.

3. What is an interest rate futures contract? Find the futures price quotations in a recent major newspaper and identify the types of financial instruments on which financial futures contracts are now written.

4. Identify situations in which each of the following is appropriate:

    a. Short hedge
    b. Long hedge
    c. Cross hedge

5. Explain the role of clearinghouses in the trading of financial futures and the reason for margin requirements by the clearinghouse.

6. What is meant by the terms basis and basis risk? What types of hedges have the greatest exposure to basis risk?

7. Why is determining the hedge ratio in a cross hedge more complicated than in an ordinary hedge? Explain why the use of duration can result in a more accurate hedge ratio.

8. What is a perfect hedge? Are perfect hedges common? Why or why not?

9. Explain how foreign exchange futures markets differ from forward currency markets.

Problems

1. In April, the manager of an S&L forecasts an increase in interest rates over the next three months. The S&L currently has $15 million in certificates of deposit costing 12 percent. The cost of the CDs is tied to Treasury bill rates. The manager wishes to hedge against the expected increase in interest rates by trading fifteen 90-day T-bill futures contracts.
    a. Should a long or short hedge be used? Why?
    b. Based on the following information, calculate the gain or loss on the hedge.

	CD Cost	T-Bill Futures Settlement Price
April	12.0%	98-24 (July delivery)
July	13.5	98-12

2. Calculate the appropriate hedge ratio in the following situations:

Hedged Instrument Value	Hedged Instrument Maturity	Futures Instrument	Futures Maturity	Correlation
$12,500,000	100 days	T-bills	90 days	.91
$40,000,000	365 days	T-bonds	360 days	.93

Refer to Figure 9.1 to determine the contract size for each futures instrument.

3. Mr. Samms, manager of the money market portfolio at Cape Cod National Bank, forecasts an increase in interest rates over the next 6 months and wants to hedge $7 million in short-term CDs. The holders of the CDs are expected to roll them over in 6 months (180 days). Mr. Samms notes that the cost of CDs is tied to the T-bill rate. Assume a correlation coefficient between the CDs and T-bill futures of .90, and the following rates and prices:

	CD Cost	T-Bill Futures Settlement Price
January	9.25%	97-30 (July delivery)
July	10.50	97-20

    a. Decide on the appropriate hedge.
    b. Calculate the hedge ratio.
    c. Calculate the gain or loss on the hedge.

4. After studying market forecasts, the manager of a money market portfolio anticipates that interest rates will decline over the next three months. She expects to receive $10 million in new funds in 90 days, which she will invest in Treasury bills. Because she wishes to avoid the adverse effect of the interest rate decline on her expected yield, she decides to hedge in the futures market.

   a. Should she assume a short or a long position?

   b. Based on the following information, calculate the resulting gain or loss on the hedge.

	T-Bill Discount Yield	T-Bill Futures Settlement Price
March	9.75%	97-17 (June delivery)
June	8.80	97-25

   c. Suppose the manager's interest rate forecast is incorrect, and interest rates increase instead. By June, the discount yield on T-bills is 10.25 percent, and the settlement price on June contracts is 97-12. What is the resulting gain or loss on the hedge?

5. Return to the duration-based hedging example in Tables 9.3 and 9.4. Suppose that the current (February 1989) price of the instrument to be hedged is $955. The expected position of the cash instrument is the same as in Table 9.3. The expected duration of T-bond futures in May 1989 is 10.06, and the expected yield on futures in May 1989 is 8.50 percent for an expected price of 96-24. Calculate the new duration-based hedge ratio and the results of the new hedge.

6. Consolidated National, a large commercial bank, regularly extends loans to importer/exporter customers. In February, management agrees to finance a shipment of cameras for an importer, who does not have to pay for the merchandise until it arrives in May. The current cost of the cameras in Japanese yen is 200 million. The prevailing exchange rate is $/yen = 0.004224 and yen/$ = 236.74. The bank's economists anticipate that the value of the dollar will fall over the next three months and recommend a hedge with foreign exchange rate futures. Using the following information, calculate the gain or loss on the hedge.

	Spot Rate ($/Yen)	May Yen Futures
February	0.004224	0.004125
May	0.004600	0.004502

   The standard size of a Japanese yen futures contract is 12.5 million yen.

7. A bank extends a loan to an importer of French wine. The wine shipment will arrive in 90 days, at which time payment is due. If the payment due is 12 million francs, and the value of the dollar is expected to fall, how could the bank use the forward currency market to hedge? What price in U.S. dollars would the bank be obligated to pay if the current 90-day forward rate is 0.1135 $/franc? What risks is the bank assuming by using the forward market?

Selected References

Booth, James R., Richard L. Smith, and Richard W. Stolz. "Use of Interest Rate Futures by Financial Institutions." *Journal of Bank Research* 14 (Spring 1984): 15–20.

Chicago Board of Trade. *Interest Rate Futures for Institutional Investors.* Chicago: Board of Trade of the City of Chicago, 1985.

Chicago Mercantile Exchange. *Trading and Hedging with Currency Futures and Options.* Chicago: Chicago Mercantile Exchange, 1985.

Drabenstott, Mark, and Anne O'Mara McDonley. "Futures Markets: A Primer for Financial Institutions." *Economic Review* (Federal Reserve Bank of Kansas City) 69 (November 1984): 17–33.

Fieleke, Norman S. "The Rise of the Foreign Currency Futures Markets." *New England Economic Review* (Federal Reserve Bank of Boston) (March/April 1985), pp. 38–47.

Giddy, Ian H., and Gunter Dufey. "The Random Behavior of Flexible Exchange Rates." *Journal of International Business Studies* 6 (Spring 1975): 1–32.

Goldstein, Henry S. "Foreign Currency Futures: Some Further Aspects." *Economic Perspectives* (Federal Reserve Bank of Chicago) 7 (November/December 1983): 3–13.

Hakkio, Craig S. "Interest Rates and Exchange Rates—What Is the Relationship?" *Economic Review* (Federal Reserve Bank of Kansas City) 71 (November 1986): 33–43.

Hieronymous, Thomas A. *Economics of Futures Trading.* New York: Commodity Research Bureau, Inc., 1971.

Howard, Charles T., and Louis J. D'Antonio. "Treasury Bill Futures as a Hedging Tool: A Risk-Return Approach." *Journal of Financial Research* 9 (Spring 1986) : 25–39.

Kolb, Robert W. *Understanding Futures Markets.* Glenview, IL: Scott, Foresman and Co., 1985.

Kolb, Robert W., and Raymond Chiang. "Improving Hedging Performance Using Interest Rate Futures." *Financial Management* 10 (Autumn 1981): 72–79.

———. "Duration, Immunization and Hedging with Interest Rate Futures." *Journal of Financial Research* 5 (Summer 1982): 161–170.

Koppenhaver, Gary D. "Futures Market Regulation." *Economic Perspectives* (Federal Reserve Bank of Chicago) 11 (January/February 1987): 3–15.

———. "Trimming the Hedges: Regulators, Banks and Financial Futures." *Economic Perspectives* (Federal Reserve Bank of Chicago) 8 (November/December 1984): 3–12.

Kubarych, Roger M. *Foreign Exchange Markets in the United States.* 2d ed. New York: Federal Reserve Bank of New York, 1983.

Parkinson, Patrick, and Paul Spindt. "The Use of Interest Rate Futures by Commercial Banks." *Proceedings of a Conference on Bank Structure and Competition* (Chicago: Federal Reserve Bank of Chicago, 1985): 457–489.

Shapiro, Alan C. "What Does Purchasing Power Parity Mean?" *Journal of International Money and Finance* (December 1983): 295–318.

Smirlock, Michael C. "Hedging Bank Borrowing Costs With Financial Futures." *Business Review* (Federal Reserve Bank of Philadelphia) (May-June 1986), pp. 13–23.

Chapter 10

INTEREST RATE RISK MANAGEMENT: INDEX FUTURES AND OPTIONS

. . . they are the Pac Man of investments. They are addictive.

Anonymous Securities Firm Executive (1983)

BANK trust departments are often considered the epitome of conservative money management. In 1983, the trust department of Security Pacific, one of the nation's ten largest
banks, was out to change that image. In a period of seven days, through a series of transactions
that involved selling stock, buying stock index futures, selling futures and buying back stock,
the institution earned a profit of 0.5 percent (a compound annual return of 29.6 percent) and
incurred, according to management, "virtually no risk."[1]

That series of transactions would not only have been unusual a year earlier, it would have
been impossible; stock index futures contracts did not exist. Today, index futures are another
of the growing array of risk management tools available to financial institutions. This chapter
continues the discussion of hedging techniques begun in Chapter 9 and compares and contrasts
the use of several major strategies for managing risk.

---

[1]"Stock Futures: A Hot New World," *Business Week,* August 22, 1983, pp. 58-66.

STOCK INDEX FUTURES

Like interest rate and currency futures, **stock index futures** are instruments for hedging exposure to changes in market values, specifically for exposure to the change of values in equity portfolios. Participants in the stock index futures markets include commercial bank trust departments, insurance companies, pension funds, and equity mutual funds. In contrast to the contracts discussed in Chapter 9, stock index futures do not protect against changes in interest rates, but instead their value is pegged to movements in one of several aggregate measures of stock market performance. Their origins in the "wild and woolly" commodities markets coupled with their appeal to conservative financial institutions have led to their nickname of "pin-striped pork bellies."[2]

As of early 1987, futures contracts were regularly traded on the Standard and Poor's (S&P) 500; the New York Stock Exchange (NYSE) Index; the Value Line Composite Index; and the Major Market Index (MMI) of 20 large firms, designed to emulate the Dow Jones Industrial Average. An attempt by the Chicago Board of Trade to offer a contract based on the Dow was met by a lawsuit from the Dow Jones Company. Because of the resulting legal battle, introduction of that futures contract has been postponed.[3]

As is true of interest rate futures, developments in the stock index futures market are rapid. New contracts come into the market and old ones leave relatively often, and the array of available contracts is likely to change with time.

Theoretical Basis of Stock Index Futures

Stock index futures are based on capital market theory, as reflected in the Capital Asset Pricing Model (CAPM) and the **efficient markets hypothesis (EMH).** As explained in Chapter 4, CAPM models the price of an individual asset or portfolio as a function of its beta coefficient, which is in turn a function of the covariance between the asset's expected returns and the expected returns on the "market portfolio." The market portfolio, with a beta of 1, is a fully diversified combination of assets that represents the standard of comparison for all others. EMH argues that, given the wide availability of information to market participants and the speed with which prices react to it, investors with well-diversified portfolios cannot consistently earn returns higher than those on the market portfolio. Investors who choose portfolios with more or less risk than the market portfolio, as measured by beta, can expect to earn a return commensurate with the risk of the portfolio they choose.

Although not perfect, many stock indexes are used as surrogates for the stock market as a whole; the portfolio of stocks underlying an index is assumed to have a beta of 1. The performance of many professional portfolio managers is evaluated through comparison to a market index, and those who earn lower returns are soundly criticized. Smaller investors, who may be prevented by brokerage fees, commissions, or funds limitations from holding a well-diversified portfolio, often use "the market" as a standard of comparison for interpreting their own results. Later examples indicate why using a stock index as a benchmark of market performance is useful to managers hedging equity portfolios.

History and Characteristics of Stock Index Futures

The first stock index futures contract, based on the Value Line Composite Index, was traded on the Kansas City Board of Trade in February 1982. Within three months, an S&P 500 contract was trading at the Chicago Mercantile Exchange, and an NYSE contract was trading on the New York Futures Exchange. The indexes are similar, in that they are composite measures of the prices of several stocks, but there are also

---

[2]Kathleen Kerwin, "Pin-Striped Pork Bellies: Why Stock Index Futures Are Red Hot," *Barron's* (February 14, 1983), pp. 14, 32–34.

[3]See Richard Zeckhauser and Victor Niederhoffer, "The Performance of Market Index Futures Contracts," *Financial Analysts' Journal* 39 (January/February 1983): 59–65; and "Stock Futures: A Hot New World."

Table 10.1
Composition of Selected Stock Market Indexes

Index	Composition
S&P 500 Index	Measures value of 500 representative stocks listed on national and regional exchanges. The index is a weighted average; the weights reflect each stock's market value.
NYSE Composite Index	Measures the value of all common stocks listed on the New York Stock Exchange (over 1,500 stocks). The index is a weighted average; the weights reflect each stock's market value.
Value Line Composite Index	Measures the value of over 1,700 stocks listed on national and regional exchanges and traded in the OTC markets. The index is a geometric average; all values are equally weighted.
Dow Jones Industrial Average (DJIA)	Measures the price of 30 blue-chip industrial stocks. The index is a simple average; all values are equally weighted.
AMEX Major Market Index	Measures the price of 20 blue-chip stocks. The index is a simple average. It had a .97 correlation with the DJIA during 1982-1985.
AMEX Market Value Index	Measures value of all stocks traded on the American Stock Exchange (approximately 850).
Pacific Stock Exchange Technology Index	Measures value of 100 technology stocks (listed and OTC issues).
S&P 100 Index	Measures value of 100 stocks, selected from and designed to mirror the S&P 500. The index is value-weighted.
S&P 250 Index	Measures value of the 250 largest OTC stocks. The index is a simple average.
NASDAQ 100 Index	Measures the value of the 100 largest nonfinancial firms traded over the counter.

---

important differences. Table 10.1 compares the composition and calculation of several indexes, including some developed expressly for use in the index futures and options markets.

Because the indexes are not identical, they do not behave identically, although their movements are similar. Table 10.2 contains correlations among four widely quoted market index measures. The correlations are all positive but less than 1. The NYSE and the S&P 500 indexes, the most similar in composition and calculation, have the highest correlation.

Impossibility of Delivery. In comparison to other futures contracts, stock index futures have a distinguishing characteristic: It is not possible to make or take physical delivery of an index. Consequently, profits or losses occur only when positions are closed out. If closure does not occur before the delivery month, the settlement level is the same as the level of the index on a given date in either March, June, September, or December, the four months during the year when index futures contracts expire.

Value of a Contract. The value of a stock index contract is calculated as the level of the index, multipled by an established amount, usually $500. The dollar multiplier for each index is given in daily price quotations in major newspapers. For example, Figure 10.1, show-

Table 10.2
Correlations among Stock Market Indexes:
January 1977–August 1982[a]

	S&P 500	Value Line	NYSE	Dow Jones
S&P 500 Index	1.000			
Value Line Composite Index	.819	1.000		
NYSE Index	.992	.844	1.000	
Dow Jones Industrial Average	.885	.758	.869	1.000

[a]Correlations are for weekly price changes.

Source: Richard Zeckhauser and Victor Niederhoffer, "The Performance of Market Index Futures Contracts," *Financial Analysts Journal* 39 (January/February 1983): 60.

ing July 28, 1986, data for index futures from *The Wall Street Journal* of the next day, indicates that the settlement price on an S&P 500 Index contract scheduled to expire in September was:

$$234.85 \times \$500 = \$117,425$$

The reported market indexes themselves are also shown in Figure 10.1. Because July 28, 1986, was not a contract expiration date, the closing settlement level on the S&P contract (234.85) was not the same as the closing level of the S&P 500 index (236.01).

Lack of Limits on Price Movements. In contrast to other financial futures instruments, stock index futures contracts have no limit on daily price movements. Most index futures do, however, have minimum price movements of $25, equal to, for most contracts, a change of 0.05 ($0.05 \times \$500 = \$25$) in the underlying index.

Greater Price Volatility. Observers of stock index futures have identified another distinguishing characteristic. The price volatility of each index futures contract, measured by the standard deviation of daily percentage price changes, is greater than the volatility of the underlying index. That relationship suggests that basis risk exposure can be significant for institutions using index futures to hedge their eq-

uity portfolios. But because index futures are so new, it is too early to draw conclusions about their long-term behavior.[4]

FINANCIAL INSTITUTIONS AND STOCK INDEX FUTURES

As a result of regulatory restrictions and unfamiliarity with index futures, institutions at first engaged in only limited trading, but usage is growing.

Hedging against a Decline in the Market

A direct use of stock index futures is as a hedge for an equity portfolio, designed to protect against swings in the market that could reduce

---

[4]Greg Kipnis and Steve Tsang, "Index Futures Track Each Other Better Than Indexes," *Commodities* (February 1983), p. 50.

Some professional investors consider stock index futures important market indicators. A 1983 study by a private commodity brokerage firm concluded that short-term market price swings appeared first in futures prices, although major cycles in the market were seldom correctly anticipated. But investors must move quickly to take advantage of these signals, because futures prices led the market movements by less than 20 minutes! See "Study Finds Stock-Index Futures Predict Stock Market Moves About 58% Correctly," *The Wall Street Journal,* May 6, 1983, p. 30.

Figure 10.1
Stock Index Futures and Stock Market Indexes

```
                                                        Open
             Open  High  Low  Settle  Chg   High  Low  Interest
S&P 500 INDEX (CME) 500 times index
Sept   240.20 240.20 234.00 234.85 − 6.05 255.20 187.00 103,413
Dec    241.60 241.85 235.60 236.50 − 6.10 257.25 209.50   5,766
  Est vol 81,762; vol Fri.; 51,508; open int 109,239, −747.
  The index: High 240.25; Low 235.23; Close 236.01 −4.22
NYSE COMPOSITE INDEX (NYFE) 500 times index
Sept   138.25 138.30 134.75 135.20 − 3.50 146.80 108.10   9,944
Dec    139.05 139.20 135.70 136.10 − 3.60 148.00 121.10   1,181
Mar87  140.05 140.05 136.70 137.05 − 3.65 148.95 136.50     421
  Est vol 11,260; vol Fri 7,397; open int 11,593, +44.
  The index: High 138.45; Low 135.82; Close 136.11 −2.30
KC VALUE LINE INDEX (KC) 500 times index
Sept   228.50 228.60 222.70 223.15 − 6.05 250.35 199.45   7,327
Dec    229.40 229.40 224.00 224.10 − 6.00 250.10 224.00     350
Mar87  225.00 225.60 225.00 225.20 − 6.00 231.20 225.00     107
  Est vol 3,400; vol Fri 2,047; open int 7,784, +193.
  The index: High 230.58; Low 227.23; Close 227.38 −3.12
MAJOR MKT INDEX (CBT) $250 times index
Aug    344.80 345.50 337.70 338.95 − 7.05 366.20 333.75   3,079
Sept   345.00 345.90 338.20 339.55 − 7.20 366.90 331.00   4,395
  Est vol 6,000; vol Fri 4,090; open int 7,479, +263.
  The index: High 346.19; Low 337.66; Close 338.67 −7.52
```

STOCK MARKET DATA BANK   July 28, 1986

Major Indexes

HIGH	LOW (12 MOS)		CLOSE	NET CH	% CH	12 MO CH	%	FROM 12/31	%
DOW JONES AVERAGES									
1909.03	1297.94	30 Industrials	x1773.90	− 36.14	− 2.00	+ 430.04	+32.00	+ 227.23	+14.69
830.84	640.57	20 Transportation	x713.63	− 6.87	− 0.95	+ 33.85	+ 4.98	+ 5.42	+ 0.77
207.45	150.08	15 Utilities	203.01	− 4.44	− 2.14	+ 47.75	+30.75	+ 28.20	+16.13
730.18	532.38	65 Composite	x685.14	− 12.22	− 1.75	+ 133.18	+24.13	+ 68.61	+11.13
NEW YORK STOCK EXCHANGE									
145.15	104.55	Composite	136.11	− 2.30	− 1.66	+ 26.31	+23.96	+ 14.53	+11.95
167.70	120.10	Industrials	154.65	− 2.73	− 1.73	+ 28.52	+22.61	+ 15.38	+11.04
76.36	54.53	Utilities	75.27	− 1.09	− 1.43	+ 18.71	+33.08	+ 12.08	+19.12
132.54	102.20	Transportation	107.04	− 0.79	− 0.73	− 3.13	− 2.84	− 6.93	− 6.08
159.45	107.17	Finance	147.55	− 2.55	1.70	32.17	27.88	16.26	−12.38
STANDARD & POOR'S INDEXES									
252.70	180.66	500 Index	236.01	− 4.21	− 1.75	+ 46.41	+24.48	+ 24.63	+11.66
282.24	201.53	400 Industrials	260.51	− 4.81	− 1.81	+ 49.25	+23.31	+ 25.95	+11.06
217.28	163.62	20 Transportation	177.82	− 2.19	− 1.22	+ 1.61	+ 0.91	− 10.90	− 5.78
115.35	79.23	40 Utilities	113.86	− 1.49	− 1.29	+ 31.24	+37.81	+ 20.69	+22.21
31.13	20.45	40 Financials	28.07	− 0.61	− 2.13	+ 5.89	+26.56	+ 2.35	+ 9.14
NASDAQ									
411.16	276.95	OTC Composite	374.78	− 5.05	− 1.33	+ 73.84	+24.54	+ 49.85	+15.34
414.15	278.04	Industrials	369.84	− 5.89	− 1.57	+ 58.98	+18.97	+ 39.67	+12.02
467.05	326.64	Insurance	427.55	− 5.67	− 1.31	+ 78.09	+22.35	+ 45.48	+11.90
457.59	293.65	Banks	433.03	− 4.57	− 1.04	+ 139.07	+47.31	+ 83.67	+23.95
174.84	117.06	Nat. Mkt. Comp.	159.23	− 2.16	− 1.34	+ 31.90	+25.05	+ 20.97	+15.17
155.55	103.47	Nat. Mkt. Indus.	138.62	− 2.24	− 1.59	+ 22.56	+19.44	+ 14.49	+11.67
OTHERS									
285.19	220.70	AMEX	263.68	− 2.63	− 0.99	+ 30.14	+12.91	+ 17.55	+ 7.13
1425.9	932.4	Fin. Times Indus.	1263.8	+ 0.1	+ 0.01	+ 331.4	+35.54	+ 132.4	+11.70
18050.59	12232.27	Nikkei Stock Avg.	18038.94	− 11.65	− 0.06	+5447.52	+43.26	+4925.62	+37.56
246.80	188.61	Value-Line	227.38	− 3.12	− 1.35	+ 25.66	+12.72	+ 12.52	+ 5.83
2598.03	1863.39	Wilshire 5000	2426.35	− 39.37	− 1.60	+ 463.78	+23.63	+ 261.66	+12.09

Source: The Wall Street Journal, July 29, 1986, pp. 40, 53. Reprinted by permission of *The Wall Street Journal,* © Dow Jones & Company, Inc. 1986. All Rights Reserved.

returns. The most obvious need for a hedge occurs when a market downturn is anticipated. The manager of a large equity position would naturally want to avoid a significant decline in portfolio value if a **bear market** is forecast—one in which prices in general are expected to fall.

One way to avoid losses is to sell large portions of the portfolio before the decline, but transactions costs could be significant. Another drawback is the time required to choose the stocks to be sold. As an alternative, the manager could hedge against market price declines with a short hedge by selling stock index futures. If the market indexes do indeed fall, so will the value of the contracts, resulting in a profit when the position is closed out, and offsetting losses in the stock portfolio.

Again, as with interest rate futures, an increase in expected market yields (decline in prices) suggests a short hedge. The small margin requirements on index futures contracts allow an institution to assume a significant position with a small amount of cash.

Importance of the Hedge Ratio

A major determinant of the effectiveness of the hedge, as in any other futures position, is the hedge ratio. In addition to the size of the portfolio, the hedge ratio is affected by the volatility of returns on the portfolio relative to the market indexes on which futures contracts are available. Beta is a relative measure of volatility. Because the portfolio of stocks underlying a market index is assumed to have a beta of 1, if the portfolio to be hedged has a beta greater or less than 1, changes in the value of the hedged portfolio will be more or less than changes in the index underlying the futures contract. Thus, the hedge ratio must be adjusted to structure an effective hedge.

The Hedge Ratio When Portfolio Beta Is 1.
Suppose a pension fund manager holds a stock portfolio of $450 million in March; the NYSE index is at 130.15. The equity market has been on the upswing, but the surge is expected to end soon. Rather than liquidating portions of the portfolio, the manager chooses to sell

NYSE stock index futures. The previous day's index settlement level on June futures was 132.75. Assuming the portfolio beta is 1, the number of contracts to sell is:

(10.1)

$$HR_p = \frac{\text{Value of Stock Portfolio}}{\text{Index Settlement Level} \times \$500} \times Beta_p$$

$$= \frac{\$450,000,000}{132.75 \times \$500} \times 1 = 6,779.66$$

$$= 6,780 \text{ contracts}$$

Now suppose that by June, the market index falls, as anticipated, to 126.9, a decline of 2.5 percent. Results of the hedge are summarized in Table 10.3. The value of the futures contracts, with a settlement level now also down by 2.5 percent to 129.43, declines to:

$$129.43 \times \$500 \times 6,780 \text{ contracts}$$

$$= \$438,767,700$$

When the position is closed out, the profits before transactions costs are $11,254,800. Because the original portfolio beta is 1, its value declines by 2.5 percent, to $438,750,000, a loss of $11,250,000.

The Hedge Ratio When Beta Is Not 1.
What are the consequences of the hedge if the price volatility of the portfolio exceeds that of the market index? Suppose the portfolio beta is 1.3. When the market index declines by 2.5 percent, the portfolio value declines by $1.3 \times 2.5\% = 3.25\%$, a dollar decline of $\$450,000,000 \times 0.0325 = \$14,625,000$. A hedge with only 6,780 NYSE Index contracts would be insufficient protection, because the gain on a hedge using that number of contracts is only $11,254,800. The net result of the hedge would be a loss of over $3 million.

A better hedge position would adjust for the beta coefficient:

$$HR_p = \frac{\$450,000,000}{132.75 \times \$500} \times 1.3$$

$$= 8,813.56 = 8,814 \text{ contracts}$$

Table 10.3
The Short Hedge: Portfolio Beta of 1.0
(Forecast: Bear Market)

Cash Market	Futures Market
May	
NYSE Index: 130.15	NYSE Index settlement level: 132.75
Stock portfolio value:	Sell 6,780 contracts:
$450,000,000	132.75 × $500 × 6,780 = $450,022,500
June	
Market decline = 2.5%	NYSE Index settlement level:
NYSE Index: 126.9	132.75 (1 − 0.025) = 129.43
Stock portfolio value:	Close out position by buying 6,780 contracts:
$450,000,000 (1 − 0.025) = $438,750,000	129.43 × $500 × 6,780 = $438,767,700

Cash Market Loss		Futures Market Gain	
June value	$438,750,000	May sale	$450,022,500
May value	450,000,000	June purchase	438,767,700
Loss	($ 11,250,000)	Gain	$ 11,254,800

Net Gain: $4,800

As shown in Table 10.4, with a short hedge of 8,814 contracts, the decline in the NYSE settlement price to 129.43 produces a gain of $14,631,240, and a net gain on the hedge of $6,240. This example assumes that price movements in the hedged portfolio and the futures contract are perfectly correlated; in practice, the correlation would not be perfect.

Hedging When an Upturn Is Anticipated

A stock index futures hedge in anticipation of a stronger equity market would be more unusual but still possible. For example, a long hedge might be undertaken when a trust department has good reason to expect a large inflow of funds at some future point, funds that can be invested only after an expected upswing. The invested funds would miss the benefits of the **bull market,** one in which price increases are anticipated. If the manager buys stock index futures contracts, they will increase in value during the bull market. When the position is later closed out by selling the contracts, the increase in value produces a profit that compensates for the higher prices at which new stock must be purchased. Once again, the effectiveness of the hedge is based on the price volatility of the stock purchased relative to the price volatility of the futures contract.

Program Trading

A controversial use of stock index futures (and index options, discussed in later sections) by some financial institutions is *program trading*. Program trading is the simultaneous trading of stock and stock index futures in order to profit from changes in the spread between the two, the strategy used by the trust department described in the opening paragraph. Managers us-

---

Table 10.4
The Short Hedge: Portfolio Beta of 1.3
(Forecast: Bear Market)

Cash Market	Futures Market
May	
NYSE Index: 130.15	NYSE Index settlement level: 132.75
Stock portfolio value:	Sell 8,814 contracts:
$450,000,000	132.75 x $500 x 8,814 = $585,029,250
June	
Market decline = 2.5%	NYSE Index settlement level:
Stock portfolio value change:	132.75 (1 − 0.025) = 129.43
−2.5% × 1.3 = −3.25%	Close out position by buying 8,814 contracts:
Stock portfolio value:	129.43 × $500 × 8,814 = $570,398,010
$450,000,000 (1 − 0.0325) = $435,375,000	

Cash Market Loss		Futures Market Gain	
June value	$435,375,000	May sale	$585,029,250
May value	450,000,000	June purchase	570,398,010
Loss	($ 14,625,000)	Gain	$ 14,631,240

Net Gain: $6,240

---

ing program trading focus only on stocks in one of the market indexes. The phrase "program trading" refers to the widespread use of computer programs to determine when to enter into this series of trades.

Table 10.5 illustrates a simple example of program trading using the Major Market Index.[5] Suppose that on February 26, a manager buys 2,000 shares of each stock in the Major Market Index (MMI), simultaneously selling 35 MMI futures contracts. The MMI is at 311.74, and the futures settlement level is 313.55 on that date. The contracts expire on March 21, and the manager knows that, as is true of all index futures, the contract settlement level and the MMI itself will converge by the expiration date, even though they differ on February 26.

On March 21, the stock portfolio will be liquidated, and the short futures position closed out. Regardless of the actual level of stock prices on that day, the manager profits. If prices rise, the value of the stock will increase more than the loss on the futures contract, resulting in a net profit. If prices fall, the value of the stock will fall less than the value of the futures contracts. This is true because both the index and the contract settlement value must be the same on March 21, but the contract settlement value is higher on February 26. The gain on the futures contracts will exceed losses on the stock portfolio, again resulting in a net profit.

Program trading differs from hedging because hedgers use futures to offset adverse changes in a portfolio held in the normal course of operations. Program traders, however, choose and manage portfolios based solely on the characteristics of available futures contracts, with the intention of profiting from fluctua-

---

[5]This example is similar to one in Jeffrey Laderman, "Those Big Swings on Wall Street," *Business Week,* April 7, 1986, pp. 32-36.

Table 10.5
Program Trading

Cash Market	Futures Market
February 26	
MMI: 311.74	MMI settlement level: 313.55
Buy 2,000 shares of each MMI stock: Value = $2,749,000	Sell 35 contracts: 313.55 × $250 × 35 = $2,743,563

Cash Market	Futures Market
If Prices Increase by March 21	
MMI increase = 5.238%	MMI settlement level: 328.07, an increase of 4.631%
MMI: 328.07	Close out position by buying 35 contracts:
Stock portfolio value: $2,893,000	328.07 × $250 × 35 = $2,870,613

Cash Market Gain		**Futures Market Loss**	
3/21 value	$2,893,000	2/26 sale	$2,743,563
2/26 value	$2,749,000	3/21 purchase	$2,870,613
Gain	$ 144,000	Loss	($ 127,050)

Net Gain: $16,950

Cash Market	Futures Market
If Prices Decrease by March 21	
MMI decrease = 5.238%	MMI settlement level: 295.41, a decrease of 5.785%
MMI: 295.41	Close out position by buying 35 contracts:
Stock portfolio value: $2,605,000	$295.41 × $250 × 35 = $2,584,838

Cash Market Loss		**Futures Market Gain**	
3/21 value	$2,605,000	2/26 sale	$2,743,563
2/26 value	$2,749,000	3/21 purchase	$2,584,838
Loss	$(144,000)	Gain	$ 158,725

Net Gain: $14,725

tions in the basis. Because program trading involves buying and selling large quantities of selected stocks, it has been blamed for wide fluctuations in the prices of those stocks in recent years. Congress and the SEC have investigated whether individual investors coincidentally trading these stocks are subject to greater risk as a result of program trading. A major academic study concluded, however, that small investors may even benefit from program trading, because they know in advance when price volatility may be high and thus can avoid the market on those days.[6]

---

[6]Hans R. Stoll and Robert E. Whaley, *Expiration Day Effects of Index Options and Futures* (New York: Salomon Brothers Center for the Study of Financial Institutions, 1986). In September 1986, program trading was blamed

OTHER INDEX FUTURES

An institution's ability to hedge against portfolio declines through index futures is not limited to stock index futures. Several other contracts have recently been introduced. The Chicago Board of Trade's Bond Buyer Municipal Bond Index futures contracts were first traded in 1985. This contract was motivated by the relatively poor historical results for cross hedges of municipal bond portfolios using T-bond futures. Using a newly created index of 40 municipal bonds, daily settlement prices are calculated as $1,000 times the index level. Institutions with diversified holdings of municipals, such as commercial banks, mutual funds, securities firms, and property and casualty insurers, have indicated that the new contracts hold much promise for protecting against broad-based declines in the bond markets.[7]

Other index futures contracts have been developed to protect investors against inflation (Consumer Price Index Futures); against exchange rate risk in general, for those not wishing to hedge against a particular currency (U.S. Dollar Index and European Currency Unit Index); and against changes in the value of precious metals (Commodity Research Bureau Index). Stock index futures for stocks traded on the London, Sydney, Tokyo, Singapore, and Hong Kong exchanges have recently been developed, and are traded on foreign stock exchanges. The popularity of these new index contracts has yet to be determined.[8]

OPTIONS ON FINANCIAL ASSETS

Another financial innovation is enjoying greater acceptance as a hedging instrument for financial institutions—*options* on stock index futures, Treasury bond futures, stock market indexes, Treasury bonds, and foreign currencies. Although options are similar to futures contracts, important differences separate the two types of hedging mechanisms. Like futures, options can be used for speculation, but this discussion emphasizes hedging.

Options on individual stocks have existed for some time. When they were concentrated in the over-the-counter markets, trading was relatively infrequent. The move in 1973 to offer standardized instruments on the organized exchanges has improved liquidity, and newer types of options have attracted a wider group of market participants.

Options Defined

An option is an agreement giving its holder the right to buy or sell a specified asset, over a limited time period, at a specified price. The option itself is created by an *option writer,* someone who stands ready to buy or sell the asset when the holder wishes to make a transaction. The price written into the option agreement is the *exercise (*or *strike) price.* Because options are traded on organized exchanges, they may also be sold to other investors before they expire.

Although options are similar to futures agreements, there are differences. As the name suggests, an option does not obligate the holder

---

for the largest single drop in the history of the Dow Jones Industrial Average, touching off a wave of calls for regulation. Later, the New York Stock Exchange and the Chicago Mercantile Exchange formed a joint task force to study intermarket trading. In December 1986, the Chicago Mercantile Exchange proposed a new rule that would end trading on expiring contracts at the close of one day, and base cash settlements on stock prices at the opening of trading the next day. See Jeffrey M. Laderman and John N. Frank, "How Chicago Zaps Wall Street," *Business Week,* September 29, 1986, pp. 92-102; Scott McMurray and Patricia Bellew Gray, "Big Board and Chicago Merc Team Up for Study of Trading and Other Links," *The Wall Street Journal,* November 7, 1986, p. 2; Scott McMurray and Sue Shellenbarger, " 'Triple-Witching' New Rules Sought by Chicago Merc," *The Wall Street Journal,* December 16, 1986, p. 43.

[7]Delia Flores, "Municipal Bond Index Futures Contract Set for Launch; Slow Start Is Predicted," *The Wall Street Journal,* June 10, 1985; John N. Frank, "You Can Keep Doing Well in the Pits—If You Have the Stomach for It," *Business Week,* December 10, 1985, pp. 131-132.

[8]Frank, "You Can Keep Doing Well in the Pits"; *An Introduction to Inflation Futures* (New York: Coffee, Sugar, and Cocoa Exchange, 1985); Scott McMurray, "Export Versions of Stock-Index Futures Gaining Popularity in U.S. and Abroad," *The Wall Street Journal,* September 10, 1986, p. 34.

to undertake the purchase or sale. Depending upon movements in the value of the underlying asset, the holder may choose not to exercise the option to buy or sell. If so, the option expires at maturity and becomes worthless. Another difference is that an option may be exercised at any point during its life, but in a futures contract the exchange of securities takes place only at the specified delivery date.

Call Options. There are two types of options. A ***call option*** is an agreement in which the option writer sells the holder the right to buy a specified asset on or before a future date. The buyer of a call option expects the price of the asset to increase over the life of the option, eventually exceeding the exercise price. If the asset price rises, the value of the option also rises, and the option holder has the additional opportunity to sell it at a profit before it expires.

Put Options. A ***put option*** is the opposite of a call. Puts give the holder the right to sell an asset at the strike price, and the option writer is obligated to buy it if the holder desires to sell. The buyer of a put option expects the asset's price to fall below the strike price. If the price falls, the put option becomes increasingly valuable.

Premiums. If market prices do not move as the option buyer forecasts, the option is allowed to expire. There is no obligation to exercise it if market conditions make it unprofitable to do so. The cost, however, is the original price (the ***premium***) of the option. If the option is not exercised, that cost cannot be recovered; the writer or seller of the option realizes a gain.

Option Values Illustrated

Over the life of an option, its value is influenced by the difference between the market and exercise prices of the underlying asset. Another influence is *potential* changes in the market/strike price relationship, as well as potential volatility in the price of the underlying asset.

Figure 10.2
Options on Treasury Securities: Price Quotations

INTEREST RATE OPTIONS

Thursday March 6, 1986

For Notes and Bonds, decimals in closing prices represent 32nds; 1.01 means 1 1/32. For Bills, decimals in closing prices represent basis points; $25 per .01

American Exchange

U.S. TREASURY NOTE—$100,000 principal value

Underlying Issue	Strike Price	Calls—Last May	Calls—Last Aug	....	Puts—Last May	Puts—Last Aug	....
8⅞ note	102	....	....	....	0.19	....	....
due 2/15/96	106	1.16	....	....	....	....	....

3 p.m. prices of underlying issues supplied by Merrill Lynch: 8⅞%105 25/32; 9½% 109 4/32; T-Bill 6.67.
Total call vol. 30 Call open int. 1,115
Total put vol. 6 Put open int. 1,877

Chicago Board Options Exchange

U.S. TREASURY BOND—$100,000 principal value

Underlying Issue	Strike Price	Calls—Last Mar	Calls—Last Jun	Calls—Last Sep	Puts—Last Mar	Puts—Last Jun	Puts—Last Sep
10⅝%	126	....	2.10	....	....	....	....
due 8/2015		....	....	....	....	....	....
		....	....	....	....	....	....
9⅞	104	....	12.00	....	....	....	....
due 10/2015	108	....	....	....	....	1.00	....
	114	2.27	....	....	0.24	....	....
	116	1.18	....	....	1.10	....	....
	118	0.24	....	3.06	....	....	....
		....	....	....	....	....	....
9¼	104	....	....	....	....	1.03	1.18
due 2/2016	106	....	6.07	....	....	....	....
	108	....	....	....	0.16	2.09	....
	110	....	3.17	....	0.23	3.00	....
	112	1.12	2.08	....	1.15	4.00	....
	114	0.20	1.28	2.22	....	5.08	....

Total call vol. 1,501 Call open int. 11,580
Total put vol. 1,411 Put open int. 27,488
3 p.m. prices of underlying issues supplied by Merrill Lynch: 11¾% 131 31/32; 11¼% 129 10/32; 10⅝% 122 16/32; 9⅞%(B) 115 16/32; 9⅞%(N) 107 15/32; 9⅝%(N) 106 27/32; 9¼% 111 19/32; 9⅛% 105 9/32; 8⅛% 101 27/32.

Source: The Wall Street Journal, March 7, 1986, p. 30. Reprinted by permission of *The Wall Street Journal,*

Figure 10.2 shows options on 9¼ percent Treasury bonds (due February 2016) with a face value of $100,000 and an expiration date of June 1986. Call options on this bond are offered with several different strike prices, ranging from 104 to 114. On March 6, 1986, the call option with a strike price of 106 traded at 6.07, or 6 7/32 percent of the face value of the underlying bond.

The T-bond itself traded at 111¹⁹/₃₂ on that same date. This option, with a strike price less than the market price, is said to be *"in the money"*; when the strike price is greater than the market price, the option is *"out of the money."* In Figure 10.2, even options that are "out of the money" have a positive value, indicating expectations that at some point during their lives it will be profitable to exercise them.

Call Option Values, Strike Prices, and Expiration Dates. Holding expiration date constant, given an underlying asset, call options with higher strike prices have lower values. For example, for strike prices ranging from 104 to 114, call options on the 9¼ T-bond decline in value from 6.07 to 1.28. The higher the strike price, the less likely the market price of the bond will rise above the strike price, so the less valuable the option.

Holding strike price constant, call options with more distant expiration dates are more valuable. For the single strike price of 114, the call option value ranges from 0.20 to 2.22 as the expiration date moves from March to September. The longer time to maturity increases the chances that the market price of the bond will eventually exceed the strike price.[9]

Put Option Values, Strike Prices, and Expiration Dates. In contrast, the value of a put option, holding expiration date constant, is higher, the higher the strike price, because the strike price is a cash outflow for the writer, not the holder, of the option. In Figure 10.2, the value of a put on a 9¼ T-bond with a June delivery date ranges from 1.03 to 5.08 at strike prices ranging from 104 to 114. As with a call option, however, holding strike price constant, the put value increases as the expiration date becomes more distant. Again, the chance that an option will eventually be profitable for the holder is greater, the longer the time to maturity.

OPTIONS AND FINANCIAL INSTITUTIONS

Options on assets other than common stock were originated in 1982. Table 10.6 lists the nonstock options traded as of early 1987. Options are written both on physical assets (such as bonds, gold, or stock) and on a variety of futures contracts. As with contracts for stock index futures, the list of options on financial instruments is in a state of flux. Based on trading volume, stock index options had attracted the largest group of traders by 1987, but this fact, too, may well change as the markets mature. Preliminary evidence indicates that individuals, rather than institutions, are the most active traders in stock index options, but that institutions dominate the trading on debt options.[10]

Regulation of Options Trading

As suggested by the earlier discussion of options, writers and holders both can use them for speculative purposes. Either party can profit by correctly forecasting price movements on the underlying asset. Some financial institutions, however, may use options only to hedge against adverse movements in the prices of existing assets. As with futures, federal bank regulators disapprove of options trading that increases risk exposure. For example, buying stock options without owning stock would increase risk and thus be disallowed. In addition, regulators may question banks that write, rather than buy, options. Thrifts are permitted broader authority both to write and to purchase options, as long as they report their positions to regulators and as long as the positions are related to financial instruments in which an institution can legally invest.[11]

---

[9]The increase in value with more distant expiration dates holds for the vast majority of options, but there are exceptions. See Laurie Goodman, "New Options Markets," *Quarterly Review,* Federal Reserve Bank of New York 8 (Autumn 1983): 42.

[10]Goodman, "New Options Markets," p. 37; G. D. Koppenhaver, "Futures Options and Their Use by Financial Intermediaries," *Economic Perspectives,* Federal Reserve Bank of Chicago 10 (January/February 1986): 18-31.

[11]Koppenhaver, "Futures Options and Their Use by Financial Intermediaries"; Federal Home Loan Bank of Chicago, "Supervisory News," May 2, 1985.

Table 10.6
Option Instruments and Markets

Options on Physical Financial Assets	Options on Financial Futures Contracts
Interest Rate Options	**Options on Interest Rate Futures**

American Stock Exchange
    Treasury bills
    Treasury notes
Chicago Board Options Exchange
    Treasury bonds
    5-year Treasury notes
	Chicago Board of Trade
	    Treasury bonds
	    Treasury notes
	Chicago Mercantile Exchange
	    Eurodollars
	    Treasury bills
	London International Financial Futures Exchange
	    Eurodollars

Stock Index Options	**Options on Stock Index Futures**

American Stock Exchange
    AMEX Major Market Index
    Computer Technology Index
    Oil Index
    Airline Index
    Institutional Index
Chicago Board Options Exchange
    S&P 100 Index
    S&P 500 Index
New York Stock Exchange
    NYSE Index
    NYSE Beta Index
Philadelphia Exchange
    Gold/Silver Index
    Value Line Index options
    National O-T-C Index options
Pacific Exchange
    Technology Index
    Financial News Index
National Association of Securities Dealers (NASD)
    NASDAQ 100 Index
	Chicago Mercantile Exchange
	    S&P 500 Index
	New York Futures Exchange
	    NYSE Composite Index

	Options on Foreign Currency Futures

	Chicago Mercantile Exchange
	    British pounds
	    West German marks
	    Swiss francs
	    Japanese yen
	    Canadian dollars
	London International Financial Futures Exchange
	    Sterling

Foreign Currency Options	

Philadelphia Exchange
    British pounds
    Canadian dollars
    West German marks
    French francs
    Japanese yen
    Swiss francs
    European Currency Units
Chicago Board Options Exchange
    British pounds
    Canadian dollars
    West German marks
    French francs
    Japanese yen
    Swiss francs	

Source: The Wall Street Journal, various issues.

Hedging with Options

The choice of options depends upon the portfolio to be hedged. The manager of an equity mutual fund might hedge with options on stock indexes or stock index futures. For managers protecting the value of interest-bearing assets, options on debt instruments or interest rate futures are a logical choice.

When Options Make a Good Hedge.   Options are a particularly good hedging choice when a financial institution faces potential declines in profitability at the discretion of its customers. For example, a commercial bank may make a commitment to lend in the future at a fixed rate negotiated today. Falling rates could cause the borrower to ignore the commitment; but if interest rates rise, the borrower is almost certain to complete the transaction, and the bank's net interest margin will decline when its deposit costs increase. Or, if mortgage rates are expected to decline, existing customers may choose to prepay their mortgages, borrowing at new lower rates and lowering a thrift's interest revenues.

A bank could hedge its commitment to lend in the future by buying a put option on a T-bond. If rates go up, bond values will fall, and the bank can exercise its right to sell bonds at the strike price. The profit on the hedge can be used to offset liability costs that will increase as market rates increase. On the other hand, if rates decline, the value of T-bonds will rise, and the bank will not exercise the put. The option premium is the price the lender pays for protecting the spread against rising rates.

A thrift could protect itself against potential mortgage prepayments in the face of falling rates by purchasing a call option on T-bonds. As rates fall and the value of bonds rises, the call option will also rise in value. Profits from selling the option can be used to offset a decline in interest revenues as mortgages are prepaid. If rates rise instead, the option premium is the price paid for attempting to protect the spread.

A Put or a Call?   As suggested by the preceding examples, the decision to buy a put or a call depends on the direction of market changes anticipated. For example, consider the alternatives faced by an equity fund manager who expects a reversal in the market. With a bear market forecast, a stock index *put* option is indicated. If the market index does in fact decline, the option value will increase as the index falls below the strike price. A put option is also the proper choice for hedging an existing portfolio of interest-bearing assets if rates are expected to rise. If the forecast is accurate, the put's value will increase, offsetting the decline in value of the existing portfolio.

An Option on an Asset or a Futures Contract?   The choice between an option on a financial asset itself or an option on a financial futures contract is influenced by whether or not the manager intends to exercise the option. To exercise an option on Treasury bonds, for example, funds must be available to purchase securities at the strike price. To exercise an option on a futures contract, however, only a relatively small margin requirement is needed to buy the contract.[12] In general, the appropriate hedge strategies, under various market forecasts, are summarized in Table 10.7.

Hedging with Options: An Illustration

Suppose that in June 1990 the bond portfolio manager for a large insurance firm forecasts a sharp decline in interest rates over the next three months. Because of several new products developed by the company, a large inflow from sales of insurance policies in September also is expected. The manager wants to hedge the opportunity loss on the investment of those premiums.

---

[12]Another reason for preferring one type of option over another is the difficulty of determining the appropriate size of the hedge. Because T-bond futures contracts are standardized with an 8 percent coupon, they sometimes trade at deep discounts, and the number of contracts (or options on contracts) must be adjusted to reflect that discount. For options on the T-bonds themselves, however, the difference between coupon and current market rates is seldom as large, because T-bond and T-note options are traded on issues with many different coupons.

Table 10.7
Market Forecasts and Options Hedges

	Hedge			
	Index or Index Futures		T-Bonds or Interest Rate Futures	
Forecast	Call	Put	Call	Put
Increase				
Stock prices	X			
Interest rates				X
Decrease				
Stock prices		X		
Interest rates			X	

On the other side of town, however, is the manager of a money market fund who holds the opposite expectation for interest rate movements and is willing to write a call option on T-bond futures contracts. T-bond futures for September delivery ($100,000 face value) are currently trading at 75.5. The call option has a strike price of 76 and a premium of $1,187.50, with an expiration date of September 1990. Table 10.8 summarizes the effect of the hedge on the position of the insurance company under three different interest rate scenarios.

First, if interest rates go up instead of down, the bond manager will not exercise the option because the market value of the futures contract is less than the strike price. The company will lose the $1,187.50 option premium. Second, if interest rates do fall, but not by a significant amount, the value of the T-bond futures, and the T-bond futures option, will increase. But the rise in value—for example, to 77—will be insufficient to recover the entire purchase premium. The bond manager will suffer an opportunity cost on the investment of the new funds received in September, and this cost will be increased by the additional loss of $187.50 on the options transactions.

Finally, suppose interest rates drop sharply. The value of the T-bond futures contract rises sharply to 81. The bond portfolio manager exercises the call at 76 and immediately resells the futures contracts at 81, for a $5,000 profit. That profit is still offset somewhat by the cost of the option, but the hedge has now provided a net gain of $3,812.50, compensating for the lower return on the newly invested funds. The larger the drop in interest rates, the higher the profits earned. The bond manager could also choose to sell the option before its expiration date, also at a profit, although that hedge would require the purchase of a larger number of options. Finally, the manager could retain ownership of the futures contracts and take delivery on the T-bonds, at a yield reflecting the higher levels that were available in June.

OPTIONS AND FUTURES HEDGING: A COMPARISON

A financial institution manager needing to hedge unfavorable market movements must evaluate the relative advantages and disadvantages offered by options and futures. The most important differences are the size and nature of the investment required and the potential size of losses and gains on the two instruments.

Table 10.8
Hedging with Options on Treasury Bond Futures Contracts

Treasury Bond Call Option (as of June 1990)

Premium: $1,187.50
Strike price: 76
Expiration date: September 1990
Security: Treasury bond futures contract
                  $100,000 face value
                  Current market value: 75.5

Scenario 1: Interest Rates Rise

T-bond futures contract market value: < 76
Call option not exercised
Results of hedge: −$1,187.50 (premium)

Scenario 2: Interest Rates Fall Slightly

T-bond futures contract market value: 77
Call option exercised: Contract purchased at 76 and sold at 77
Results of hedge:

$1,000.00	Profit on futures trade
− 1,187.50	Premium
($ 187.50)	Loss

Scenario 3: Interest Rates Fall Significantly

T-bond futures contract market value: 81
Call option exercised: Contract purchased at 76 and sold at 81
Results of hedge:

$5,000.00	Profit on futures trade
− 1,187.50	Premium
$3,812.50	Gain

Investment Required

The margin requirements on positions in the futures market are discussed in Chapter 9. They are established by the clearinghouse as a percentage of the contract value and must be maintained on a daily basis. In options trading, however, the investment required is the price of the option. It must be paid when the option is purchased, and no further payments are required unless the option is exercised.

Potential Risk and Return

A more important distinction between options and futures is the different risk exposures for an option purchaser and a futures hedger. The potential profits or losses on a futures transactions are virtually unlimited, but the loss on the purchase of an option is limited to the option price, and profits are offset by the option premium.[13] A comparison of a long hedge with T-bond futures contracts and the T-bond futures call option just illustrated should clarify the differences in risk/return exposure.

The insurance company manager with a forecast of falling rates could have assumed a long hedge in Treasury bond futures, buying at a price of 75.5. The results of the futures hedge are summarized in Table 10.9. If interest rates

---

[13]Theoretically, losses on futures contracts are halted when the value of the contract falls to $0.

Table 10.9
Hedging with Treasury Bond Futures Contracts

The Long Hedge

Treasury bond futures contract
$100,000 face value
Current market value: 75.5

Scenario 1: Interest Rates Rise

T-bond futures contract market value: 70
Position closed at loss of 5.5 per contract
Results of hedge: −$5,500

Scenario 2: Interest Rates Fall Slightly

T-bond futures contract market value: 77
Position closed at profit of 1.5 per contract
Results of hedge: $1,500 profit

Scenario 3: Interest Rates Fall Significantly

T-bond futures contract market value: 81
Position closed at profit of 5.5 per contract
Results of hedge: $5,500 profit

---

move against the manager's forecasts, his losses have no ceiling except for those imposed by the movement of interest rates. If interest rates rise sharply and the contract value falls to, for example, 70, there will be a significant loss when the position is closed out. The greater the increase in interest rates, the greater the loss on the long hedge. Losses on the hedge will offset the returns gained from investing the new funds at the higher market rates.

On the other hand, if the manager's forecasts for lower interest rates are correct, there is no purchase premium to reduce the profits from the hedge. If the value of the T-bond futures contract rises to 81, there will be a profit of $5,500 per contract, instead of the gain of $3,812.50 shown in Table 10.8.

Figure 10.3 summarizes graphically the differences in risk exposure between futures and options hedges. The top of the figure assumes a forecast of falling rates. With a call option, shown in Panel A, until the underlying asset price reaches the strike price (S), the loss is equal to the option premium (Pr). As the asset price increases, returns on the option increase,

eventually becoming positive after the premium is recovered. With a long futures contract hedge, shown in Panel B, a change in the price of the contract after purchase at P_0 is translated into a gain or loss, since no premium must be recovered. Thus, hedging with futures is riskier than hedging with options.

The lower half of the figure compares a put option and the sale of futures contracts under a forecast of rising rates. Panel C shows that the purchaser of a put suffers a loss equal to the premium until the market price of the underlying asset falls below the strike price. As the asset's price continues to fall, the option holder's position improves and becomes profitable once the cost of the premium has been earned. In contrast, any change in the price of a futures contract translates directly into a profit or loss for the contract holder, as shown in Panel D.

SUMMARY

This chapter concludes the material on tools for managing interest rate risk by discussing index futures and options. Like other financial fu-

Figure 10.3
Comparison of Risk Exposure in Futures and Options Hedges

Forecast of Rising Prices, Falling Rates

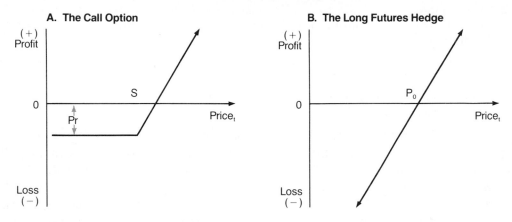

A. The Call Option

B. The Long Futures Hedge

Forecast of Falling Prices, Rising Rates

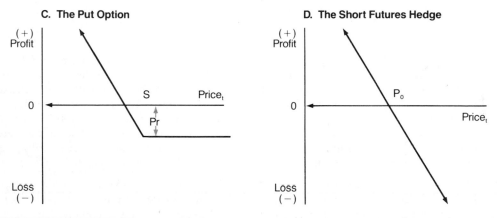

C. The Put Option

D. The Short Futures Hedge

tures, stock index futures are used to hedge against declines in existing financial positions, especially in equity portfolios. Procedures governing their use are similar to those for all futures contracts. Futures contracts have also been developed for market indexes on other financial instruments.

Options are also available for hedging. An option enables the holder to purchase or sell a physical asset or a futures contract at the strike price. A call option is purchased in anticipation of rising asset prices or falling interest rates. If the forecast is incorrect, losses are limited to the option premium. In contrast to the call option, the holder purchases a put in anticipation of falling asset prices or rising interest rates. The final section of the chapter compares hedging with futures to hedging with options. In general, financial futures present more risk to the hedger but can be more profitable.

Questions

1. What are stock index futures? How do financial institutions use them for asset/liability management? Why is the correlation between an institution's stock portfolio and the stock index used for hedging important?

2. Given a forecast of a bear market, why might an asset/liability manager hedge with stock index futures, rather than adjusting the cash portfolio? What are the advantages and disadvantages of each strategy?

3. Compare important market features, such as delivery terms and price movement limits, for stock index futures and interest rate futures.

4. What is an option? Compare a call option and a put option. Under what equity market forecast would a hedger buy a call option? A put option? Why?

5. Under what interest rate forecast would a hedger buy a call option? A put option? Why?

6. Under what circumstances should an asset/liability manager choose a financial futures hedge rather than an options hedge? When is the options hedge preferred? Compare the risk exposure of an options hedge and a futures hedge.

7. The increased use of program trading has generated concern about the influence institutional investors have in the financial markets relative to individual investors. Based on articles you find in business newspapers and periodicals, do you think this concern is legitimate? If so, what course of action, if any, should regulators take?

Problems

1. Ms. Morris, of Boston Property and Casualty Insurance Company, manages a $600 million stock portfolio. In March, she is watching the stock market carefully and anticipates a downturn in the next two months. She knows that liquidating part of the portfolio will involve transactions costs, so she instead chooses a hedge with stock index futures. The S&P stock index is currently at 189.20. Yesterday's settlement level for May S&P index futures was 190.75. Ms. Morris expects the market index to fall by 6.5 percent over the next two months. She has estimated that the company's portfolio has a beta of 1.25. Calculate the hedge ratio and the resulting gain or loss on the hedge, assuming the market index falls by 6.5 percent as predicted.

2. Mr. Samuels, Randax Corporation's pension fund manager, is expecting a $50 million cash inflow in August, two months from now, which he must invest in the equity market. Economists forecast an upswing in the stock market over the next two months. Knowing that the expected funds will miss the upswing and resulting benefits, Mr. Samuels has decided to hedge using stock index futures. The Value Line index currently stands at 198.75. Yesterday's settlement level for the Value Line futures index was 199.5. Economists predict an increase of 4.5% in the index over the next two months. The beta of the stocks in which the incoming funds will be invested is 1.5.
   a. Recommend the hedge ratio.
   b. Calculate the gain or loss on the hedge if the economists are correct.

3. Mr. Lloyd, a commercial loan officer, has made a commitment to one of his best clients to provide a fixed-rate loan for $500,000 in three months at the rate prevailing today. However, Mr. Lloyd forecasts rising rates in the interim. He recommends to the bank's portfolio manager that the position be hedged by buying a put option on Treasury bond futures contracts, written

by a manager at another bank whose economists are now forecasting falling rates. The following information is available:

T-bond futures   Face value: $100,000
                 Current price: 97-16
Put option   Strike price: 97-12
                 Premium: $4,000

Calculate the gain or loss on the hedge under the following conditions:
a. Interest rates decrease; T–bond futures rise to 98.
b. Interest rates increase; T–bond futures fall to 96–25.
c. Interest rates increase; T–bond futures fall to 95.

4. Suppose Ms. Morris, whose situation is described in Problem 1, can buy a stock index futures put option for a premium of $10,000, with a strike price of 189. Assume the option is written for the same number of contracts that would be bought or sold in Problem 1.
   a. Calculate the gain or loss on the options transaction under each of the following conditions that could prevail when the option expires:
      1) the S&P index futures continue to trade at 190.75
      2) the S&P index futures settlement level drops to 181
      3) the S&P index futures settlement level rises to 195
   b. Calculate the gain or loss on a futures hedge described in Problem 1 under each of the three scenarios in part a.
   c. Compare the futures results to the gain or loss on the options hedge, and assess the risk exposure of the two alternatives.
   Note: This problem does not require you to calculate the *net* result of the options or futures hedges; that is, no calculations are required for the stock portfolio results.

Selected References

Chicago Board of Trade. *NASDAQ-100 Index Futures*. Chicago: Board of Trade of the City of Chicago, 1986.

————. *Options on U.S. Treasury Bond Futures for Institutional Investors*. Chicago: Board of Trade of the City of Chicago, 1985.

Chicago Mercantile Exchange. *Using S&P Stock Index Futures and Options*. Chicago: Chicago Mercantile Exchange, 1985.

Goodman, Laurie. "New Options Markets." *Quarterly Review* (Federal Reserve Bank of New York) 8 (Autumn 1983): 35-47.

Koppenhaver, G. D. "Futures Options and Their Use by Financial Intermediaries." *Economic Perspectives* (Federal Reserve Bank of Chicago) 10 (January/February 1986): 18-31.

Laderman, Jeffrey M., and John N. Frank. "How Chicago Zaps Wall Street." *Business Week* (September 29, 1986), pp. 92-102.

Lee, Susan. "What's with the Casino Society?" *Forbes* 138 (September 22, 1986): 150-158.

Stoll, Hans R., and Robert E. Whaley. *Expiration Day Effects of Index Futures and Options*. New York: Salomon Brothers Center for the Study of Financial Institutions, 1986.

Zeckhauser, Richard, and Victor Niederhoffer. "The Performance of Market Index Futures Contracts." *Financial Analysts' Journal* 39 (January/February 1983): 59-65.

Part III

MANAGING ASSETS AND LIABILITIES IN DEPOSITORY INSTITUTIONS

Chapter 11

DEPOSITORY INSTITUTIONS: OVERVIEW AND COMPARISON

The thrifts are losing money. So what?

Donald T. Regan
Secretary of the Treasury (1981)

BONNIE Jean Beesley, wife of Brent Beesley—a Salt Lake City lawyer, businessman, self-made millionaire, and amateur pilot—once described her husband as a person who "seems to gravitate toward distress situations." What more fitting assignment, then, for Mr. Beesley than the one he drew from 1981 through 1983 as Director of the Federal Savings and Loan Insurance Corporation? Financial market participants quickly nicknamed him "Dr. Doom," based on his efforts to consolidate the thrift industry during his tenure in Washington. His advice for his successor: "Don't make any plans for holiday weekends."[1]

The study of depository institutions begins with this chapter. Defined earlier, they are firms for which deposits are the largest sources of funds. They include commercial banks, savings and loan associations (S&Ls), savings banks, and credit unions (CUs). The purpose of this chapter is to describe their assets, liabilities, and industry structures. In addition, their

---

[1]William D. Marbach and Christopher Ma, " 'Dr. Doom' Calling," *Business Week,* March 15, 1982, p. 55; Timothy D. Schellhardt, "FSLIC's 'Doctor Doom' Irritates Thrifts with His Big Sales Campaign for Mergers," *The Wall Street Journal,* October 29, 1981.

operations and performance in recent years are compared, including a review of the thrift industry crisis suggested by the opening quotation and paragraph. Managerial decisions in depositories are the subjects of the ten chapters that follow.

COMMERCIAL BANKS: INDUSTRY STRUCTURE

As of year-end 1985, there were 15,068 commercial banks in the United States.[2] Although the question, "What is a bank?" has no easy answer, this figure refers to institutions for which business loans are a regular and significant portion of operations and that collect deposits subsequently redeemable on demand.[3] It excludes thrifts that perform both functions but for which commercial business is not significant.

Commercial banks are not the most numerous depositories—that distinction belongs to CUs—but they hold by far the most assets. Historically, banks have played a dominant role not only in business lending, but also in payments transfers and money creation. Although they now share these functions with other depositories, and even some nondepositories, commercial banks remain at the heart of the financial system.

Size Differences

Commercial banks are not homogeneous. They differ in how they are chartered, examined, and insured, as well as in their asset and liability choices. They also differ in size. Charters and organizational structures of commercial banks are discussed in Chapters 2 and 3. In this chapter, the concern is with asset and liability structures of banks of different sizes.

Table 11.1 divides the banking industry into groups based on total assets. Although Citicorp, the largest bank holding company in

1985, had assets in excess of $173 billion, less than 6 percent of all insured banks had more than $300 million in assets in 1985. In contrast, just over 9 percent were in the smallest group. About 60 percent held under $50 million in assets.

ASSETS OF COMMERCIAL BANKS

Table 11.2 presents the asset composition of the average commercial bank in 1985, and of typical members of the smallest and largest groups.[4] Federal regulators require banks to submit financial statements, known in the industry as *"Call Reports,"* providing extensive detail on their assets, liabilities, income, and expenses. The tables include only the major categories.

Cash and Due from Depositories

The *cash and due* account includes coin and currency in vaults on the premises; reserves on deposit with the Fed; deposits with other banks; and checks deposited by customers on which funds have not yet been collected from the paying bank, the "due" part of the category. The volume of due balances in the banking system as a whole is called *"the float."* Although necessary for business, the cash and due account is a nonearning asset because vault cash is idle, and the Fed pays no interest on reserves.[5]

Cash and due for small banks is a lower percentage of assets than for large banks. Banks with deposits under about $37 million must

---

[2] Board of Governors of the Federal Reserve System, *72nd Annual Report, 1985,* p. 234.

[3] See John J. DiClemente, "What Is a Bank?" *Economic Perspectives,* Federal Reserve Bank of Chicago 7 (January/February 1983): 20-31 for more discussion of distinctions between banks and other institutions.

[4] Tables 11.2 and 11.3 were prepared from data on banks over three years old, because young banks tend to differ from their more mature counterparts.

[5] As noted in Chapter 2, the Fed must pay interest on supplemental reserves that may, at some point in its judgment, be necessary.

Table 11.1
**Size Distribution of Insured Commercial Banks
by Total Assets, Year-End 1985**

Size Category	Category Total	% of Total
Under $10 million	1,310	9.13%
$10 to under $25 million	3,909	27.23
$25 to under $50 million	3,839	26.74
$50 to under $300 million	4,497	31.32
$300 million and over	801	5.58
Total, all sizes	14,356	100.00%

Source: Prepared by the authors with data from the Board of Governors of the Federal Reserve System, Division of Research and Statistics.

keep only 3 percent of their transaction accounts on reserve with the Fed, but the requirement for larger institutions is 12 percent.[6] Reserve account management, part of a bank's liquidity management strategy, is discussed in Chapter 12.

Securities Held

Securities held consist chiefly of Treasury securities; federal agency securities; and the debt obligations of states, counties, and municipalities, which are included as part of "other securities" in Table 11.2. Securities are held primarily for investment purposes, although some must be held as collateral by institutions with government deposits. Default risk is ordinarily not a serious concern in a bank's securities portfolio, because regulations limit insured banks' investment in corporate bonds and prohibit investment in stock.[7] Management of the bank's securities portfolio is tied to liquidity,

and it, too, is discussed in Chapter 12. Securities held do not include customers' portfolios managed by the trust department, for which a bank receives fee income. These securities are the assets of the customers, not the bank.

Federal Funds Sold

By reporting custom, the asset category "federal funds sold" includes reverse repurchase agreements with other financial institutions, discussed in detail in Chapter 4. More important, however, is the asset for which the category is named. Excess reserves lent to other institutions are fed funds "sold" and are the assets of the lending institution; they earn interest at the fed funds rate, illustrated in Chapter 4. Because these transactions are short-term, they are an important part of an institution's liquidity planning. As a proportion of total assets, small banks sell more fed funds than do large banks. In fact, cash, securities, and fed funds are almost half of the typical small bank's assets, but less than one-third of a large bank's.

Loans

Loans are the single largest asset for banks of all sizes, but within the general category, small and large banks differ markedly. Real estate loans are loans secured by real property and consist primarily of commercial and residential mort-

---

[6]Reserve requirements must be held against transactions accounts. The formula is modified annually according to the growth in total system deposits over the previous year. As of 1987, the cutoff point between 3 percent and 12 percent marginal reserve requirements was $36.7 million in transaction accounts.

[7]In the 1970s, some concern for default risk was expressed by institutions with investments in the bonds issued by New York City and Cleveland.

Table 11.2

Distribution of Assets: Banks over Three Years Old, Year-End 1985

	Average Bank under $10 Million (1,040 Banks)		Average Bank over $300 Million (796 Banks)		Average Mature Bank, All Sizes (13,210 Banks)	
	Thousands	% of Total	Thousands	% of Total	Thousands	% of Total
Assets						
Cash and due	$ 699	10.10 %	$ 346,462	13.71 %	$ 25,150	12.43 %
Securities held:						
United States Treasury and federal agency	$1,764	25.49 %	$ 155,151	6.14 %	$ 18,202	8.99 %
Other securities	277	4.00	160,282	6.34	14,530	7.18
Total securities	2,041	29.49	315,433	12.48	32,732	16.17
Federal funds sold	626	9.04	108,633	4.30	9,726	4.81
Loans:						
Real estate	971	14.03	360,956	14.28	32,479	16.05
Commercial and industrial (C&I)	597	8.63	596,744	23.61	42,947	21.22
Consumer	755	10.91	267,014	10.56	22,466	11.10
All other	1,013	14.64	345,204	13.66	24,268	11.99
Less unearned income and allowance for possible loan losses	(106)	−1.53	(36,256)	−1.43	(3,025)	−1.49
Total loans	3,230	46.67	1,533,662	60.67	119,135	58.86
Other assets	325	4.70	223,539	8.84	15,655	7.73
Total Assets	$6,921	100.00%	$2,527,729	100.00%	$202,398	100.00%
Liabilities and Equity						
Liabilities:						
Deposits						
Domestic (individual, partnership, and corporation—IPC)	$5,376		$1,289,958		$118,011	
Domestic non-IPC	681		179,421		14,898	
Foreign	0		402,426		24,287	
Total deposits	$6,057	87.52 %	$1,871,805	74.05 %	$157,196	77.67 %
Federal funds purchased	12	0.17	258,899	10.24	16,342	8.07
Other liabilities for borrowed money	3	0.04	112,128	4.44	6,986	3.45
Other liabilities	95	1.37	127,438	5.04	8,351	4.13
Total liabilities	$6,167	89.11%	$2,370,270	93.77%	$188,875	93.32%
Subordinated notes and debentures	$ 1	0.01 %	$ 17,473	0.69 %	$ 1,103	0.54 %
Equity capital:						
Preferred and common stock	149	2.15	23,733	0.94	2,116	1.05
Surplus	301	4.35	47,142	1.86	4,235	2.09
Undivided profits and reserves	303	4.38	69,111	2.73	6,069	3.00
Total equity capital	$ 753	10.88%	$ 139,986	5.54%	$ 12,420	6.14%
Total Liabilities and Equity	$6,921	100.00%	$2,527,729	100.00%	$202,398	100.00%

Source: Prepared by the authors with data from the Board of Governors of the Federal Reserve System, Division of Research and Statistics.

gages. Historically, they have been less significant to banks than to other depository institutions. Small and large banks hold about equal proportions of these loans.

Commercial and industrial (C&I) loans are a different story. They are made to corporations, partnerships, and proprietorships for all purposes other than personal, family or household, or charitable uses. They are usually short-term, ranging in maturity from a few months to five or more years. Included are not only individually negotiated loans between a bank and a borrower, but also assets such as the bankers' acceptances of other banks. As a proportion of total assets, they are much more important for large banks than for small banks.

Traditionally, C&I loans have been the specialty of commercial banks. In recent years, banks have faced increasing competition from other commercial lenders, especially finance companies and insurance companies. They also face *de jure* (legally authorized) but not substantial *de facto* (actual) competition from other depositories, as shown later in this chapter.

Consumer loans are primarily installment loans to individuals for all purposes other than residential mortgages or mobile homes. Included are loans for automobiles and other vehicles, education, and travel, as well as credit extended through credit cards. Most financial institutions have entered the consumer credit market in recent years, escalating competition.

"Other loans" include a wide variety of credit-granting activities such as loans of nonfed funds to other financial institutions; loans for the purchase of securities (made to brokers, dealers, and individuals); loans to not-for-profit organizations; loans to governments; and loans not clearly falling into any of the other categories.

The category "unearned income and allowance for possible loan losses" is a deduction arising from two sources. Unearned income is interest paid in advance on discounted loans and is deducted because, as discussed in Chapter 4, it is actually income to the bank and not principal extended to the borrower. The allowance for possible loan losses is an estimate of the dollar amount of uncollectible loans. For banks with assets over $500 million, this account is being phased out, in accordance with the Tax Reform Act of 1986. More information on loan loss accounting is given in later chapters.

Perhaps the central asset management problem in a depository institution is managing the loan portfolio, including credit analysis of individual borrowers and decisions about the appropriate mix among various categories of loans. Unlike bonds and stocks, these financial assets often are not marketable if the original lender needs cash unexpectedly. Furthermore, information available to the lender before a credit-granting decision is always less than perfect. Although present in any investment decision, the problem is more significant in small, local financial markets, compared to, for example, the Treasury security markets. These problems and others in managing the loan portfolio are discussed in Chapters 13 and 14.

Other Assets

The final asset category in Table 11.2 is a catch-all. Its major component is bank premises and equipment, such as computers and electronic banking machinery, although assets acquired by repossessing the property of borrowers in default also is included. Because large institutions are more likely to have corporate headquarters buildings and extensive branch networks, this category is a substantially higher proportion of their assets than for the smallest banks. A long-term commitment of funds is clearly required for these activities.

Historically, bank premises and equipment have been considered nonearning because they do not bear an explicit rate of return as securities and loans do. But, because they provide necessary services for customers, and may increase employee productivity, they are important to the success of financial institutions. Long-term asset decisions for depository institutions are discussed in Chapter 19.

LIABILITIES OF COMMERCIAL BANKS

By definition, the major liabilities of depository institutions are deposits. The generic term "deposits" includes many types of accounts, all of which are financial liabilities of the institution and financial assets of depositors. In addition, depositories have a variety of nondeposit liabilities. Chapter 15 is devoted to liability management in depositories, and the following discussion is intended only as a brief overview.

Deposits in General

Table 11.2 divides deposits according to type of depositor. Although not reported separately, within each of the three categories are accounts with varying interest rate, transactions, and maturity characteristics. Some of these account categories are discussed in this section.

Domestic individual, partnership, and corporate *(IPC)* accounts are a large majority of deposits for banks of all sizes. Domestic non-IPC deposits are mostly those of financial institutions and governmental units. Small banks seldom have offices overseas, but for large banks, deposits in foreign offices can be important sources of funds. Among the most important types of foreign deposits is the *Eurodollar deposit,* a deposit account denominated in dollars but held outside the United States. At the time of their origination, most of these deposits were in Europe—hence the name *Eurodollars.* Today dollar-denominated deposits are held all over the world, but the term *Eurodollar* continues to be used. Eurodollar deposits are an important tool of liability management in large banks and are discussed in more detail in Chapter 15.

Deposits: Transactions Accounts

Transactions accounts—those on which checks can be written—include demand deposits and negotiable orders of withdrawal (NOWs). Reserve requirements are highest on these deposits. Some transactions accounts are interest-bearing and some are not.

Demand Deposits. Demand deposits are noninterest-bearing accounts from which the institution must provide cash upon the request of the account holder—i.e., demand deposits are traditional checking accounts. No other

transactions accounts carry this immediate legal obligation. Demand deposits are eligible for federal deposit insurance up to $100,000. Although savings banks and S&Ls are permitted to issue demand deposits, neither has given commercial banks much competition in this market.

NOWs. First defined in Chapter 2, a NOW account is an interest-bearing checking account. It differs from a demand deposit in that, technically, an institution is not required to honor NOW checks immediately, but may withhold payment for seven days or more. NOWs have no legal maturity nor any limitations on the number of checks that may be written per month. Not-for-profit organizations may have them, but businesses may not.

Time and Savings Deposits

Time and savings deposits include interest-bearing deposits customers hold for both transactions and investment purposes, and those held for investment purposes alone. *Savings deposits* have no specified period for which funds must be left on deposit to avoid an early-withdrawal penalty. *Time deposits* have a specified maturity date. Withdrawal before maturity results in the forfeiture of some interest earned before withdrawal. In some cases, even part of the principal may be forfeited. Federal Reserve regulations require depositories to hold reserves against all *nonpersonal* time and savings deposits—that is, accounts "in which a beneficial interest is held by a depositor that is not a natural person."[8] Required reserves are lower for time and savings deposits than for unlimited transactions accounts.

MMDAs. First discussed in Chapter 2, money market deposit accounts (MMDAs) are a relatively new form of hybrid transactions/savings instrument. The depositor may write a

---

[8]Board of Governors of the Federal Reserve System, "Regulation D Reserve Requirements of Depository Institutions," Section 204.2, as amended effective June 20, 1983. As of April 1, 1986, rules for withdrawal penalties were transferred from Reg Q to Reg D.

limited number of checks per month on an MMDA, but when the Fed assesses reserve requirements, it considers MMDAs savings, not transactions, accounts. The institution may require a seven-day notice for withdrawal, but few do. The yield on MMDAs exceeds that on NOWs because the depositor gives up the unlimited transactions feature. Interest rates are variable and may be adjusted once a month or even more often. Introduced in December 1982, they became, for depository institutions as a whole, the fastest growing accounts in history.

Passbook Savings Accounts.   *Passbook savings accounts* are nontransactions accounts without a maturity date. "Nontransactions" means that the account owner may not transfer funds from a savings account directly to a third party—someone besides the depositor or the depository institution. Still, passbook savings deposits (so-called because ownership is evidenced by a small account book) are quite liquid because an individual may withdraw funds on very short notice. In exchange for the liquidity, depositors accept a relatively low interest rate. Historically, however, most of these deposits have involved very few transactions per month, requiring little administrative cost to the institution. For many years, they were one of the most stable sources of funds to which a depository had access.

Until recently, the maximum rate that could be paid on passbooks was fixed well below market levels, making them among the lowest-cost of all sources of funds. However, because of the advent of MMDAs and other liquid accounts paying market rates of interest, the passbook account is a diminishing source of funds to depositories. Although not shown in Table 11.2, small banks have proportionately more passbook deposits than do large banks whose customers are primarily large corporations.

Certificates of Deposit.   The most important type of time deposit is the certificate of deposit (CD), an interest-bearing account with a specified maturity date. CDs are available in all denominations, with variable and fixed rates, across the entire spectrum of maturities. Most involve penalties to the depositor for early withdrawal. For this reason, a secondary market for negotiable CDs, previously discussed in Chapter 4, was developed to allow large depositors to sell their deposits to other investors if they need cash before the maturity date. CDs with denominations under $100,000 are nonnegotiable, and depositors wishing to avoid penalties must hold their CDs until maturity.

Individual Retirement Accounts (IRAs). *Individual retirement accounts (IRAs)* are time deposits with special tax benefits for consumer depositors. Although annual dollar deposits are limited by federal law, federal tax on contributions by eligible depositors is deferred until withdrawal of funds after age 59½. All taxpayers not covered by an employer-sponsored pension plan are eligible for the tax deferment on contributions, as are taxpayers covered by employer-sponsored pensions but with income below a specified level. All taxpayers, regardless of income or coverage by other pension plans, are eligible for deferment of interest earned on IRA accounts.

Borrowings

In addition to deposits, banks have nondeposit liabilities. Sources of nondeposit borrowing vary according to bank size.

Federal Funds Purchased.   Federal funds purchased are reserves borrowed from other depositories and are a substantially larger obligation for large banks than for small ones. Repurchase agreements that are liabilities of a bank are also included in this category. The role of these nondeposit obligations in liability management is discussed in Chapter 15.

Other Liabilities for Borrowed Money. Other liabilities for borrowed money include miscellaneous debt obligations of the bank, some of which are loans from the Federal Reserve System's discount window. Use of the discount window is a tool of bank liquidity management and is discussed in Chapter 12. In addition, bankers' acceptances to which the bank is obligated are included here. Because only large banks are involved in international finance, this liability category is considerably larger for the average bank with over $300 million in assets than for other banks.

Other Liabilities. The "other liabilities" category is comparable to accounts payable and accrued expenses for nonfinancial corporations.

Subordinated Notes and Debentures. *Subordinated notes and debentures* are long-term, unsecured debt obligations, analogous to the unsecured bonds of other corporations. Although they are legal liabilities of the institution, under certain circumstances, regulators count them when deciding whether or not the depository has adequate capital to protect depositors.

Subordinated notes and debentures are a relatively small proportion of even the largest banks' total obligations. They can usually be marketed only by institutions with a presence beyond their local communities. These instruments have an important role explored in Chapter 16.

Equity Capital (Net Worth) of Commercial Banks

As they do for all corporations, the preferred stock and common stock accounts reflect the par value of the bank's equity securities. Some net worth accounts, however, are peculiar to bank accounting. A bank's *surplus* account is the total of proceeds from the sale of equity securities in excess of their par value, *plus* earnings retained until the surplus account equals the common stock account. *Undivided profits* are earnings retained in excess of those included in the surplus account. *Reserves* are portions of retained earnings set aside to provide a cushion against losses on securities or other contingencies, such as lawsuits in which the bank is involved. For reasons apparent in Chapter 16, equity capital as a percentage of total assets is

almost twice as high for small banks as it is for large ones.

Reserves in this section of the balance sheet should not be confused with the reserves of an institution held to comply with Fed reserve requirement regulations. The latter are noninterest-bearing assets, accounted for in the cash and due account.

INCOME AND EXPENSES OF COMMERCIAL BANKS

It follows logically from a balance sheet analysis that the income and expenses of small and large banks differ. Table 11.3 presents the percentage distribution of income and expenses for small, large, and average banks in 1985.

Interest Income. The categories of interest income in Table 11.3 correspond in general to the categories of interest-earning assets on the balance sheets in Table 11.2. Because loans are a larger proportion of assets at large banks, interest and fees on loans are a more important source of their income than for smaller banks. Small banks are more dependent upon income from securities and fed funds sold, as expected from the relative size of their securities and fed funds portfolios.

Service Charges on Deposits. Service charges are a small proportion of operating income for banks of all sizes, but they are more important for small banks. Deposits are almost 90 percent of the funds sources of small banks, but less than 75 percent for large banks.

All Other Operating Income. Because of their role as *correspondent banks,* large banks derive income from nondeposit activities. In exchange for a fee, correspondent banks assist smaller institutions with check clearing, cash and portfolio management, and reserve account management, to name but a few services. In addition, large banks have led in developing new fee-based services (such as discount brokerage operations and cash management ad-

Table 11.3
Distribution of Income and Expenses: Banks over Three Years Old, 1985

	Average Bank under $10 Million (1,040 Banks)		Average Bank over $300 Million (796 Banks)		Average Mature Bank, All Sizes (13,210 Banks)	
	Thousands	% of Total	Thousands	% of Total	Thousands	% of Total
Operating Income						
Interest income:						
Interest and fees on loans	$443		$172,062		$13,624	
Interest on balances at depository institutions	23		14,981		1,029	
Income on federal funds sold	41		7,805		700	
Income on securities	211		25,456		2,814	
Total interest income	$718	90.31%	$220,304	86.00%	$18,167	87.69%
Service charges on deposits	28	3.52	5,743	2.24	545	2.63
Other operating income	49	6.16	30,108	11.75	2,006	9.68
Total Operating Income	$795	100.00%	$256,155	100.00%	$20,718	100.00%
Operating Expenses						
Interest expense:						
Interest on deposits	$394		$114,989		$9,731	
Expense of federal funds purchased	1		19,511		1,235	
Interest on other borrowed money	0		10,163		626	
Interest on subordinated notes and debentures	0		1,622		107	
Total interest expense	$395	52.11%	$146,285	61.97%	$11,699	61.37%
Provision for loan losses	73	9.63	15,318	6.49	1,285	6.74
Salaries and employee benefits	148	19.53	36,256	15.36	2,961	15.53
Other noninterest operating expense	142	18.73	38,189	16.18	3,117	16.35
Total Operating Expenses	$758	100.00%	$236,048	100.00%	$19,062	100.00%
Net Operating Income	$37	4.65%[a]	$20,107	7.85%[a]	$1,656	7.99%[a]
Less taxes	(14)		(5,349)		(418)	
Net security gains and losses (including extraordinary items)	6		1,638		138	
Net Income	$29	3.65%[a]	$16,396	6.40%[a]	$1,376	6.64%[a]

[a]Percent of total operating income.

Source: Prepared by the authors with data from the Board of Governors of the Federal Reserve System, Division of Research and Statistics.

vice), from which they earn noninterest income. Noninterest income also includes profits from trading foreign currencies. Because small banks are seldom involved in these activities, only a small portion of their operating income arises from these sources.

It is clear why attention to the net interest margin is the chief objective of financial institution management. Interest income, one of the key components of NIM, is the overriding source of profits. The next section reveals the role of another key component—interest expense.

Expenses of Commercial Banks

Small and large banks also have different expenses.

Interest Expense. Interest expenses, especially interest on deposits, dominate total expenses. Although small banks have proportionately more deposit liabilities, their interest expenses are lower as a proportion of total expenses. This difference often arises because larger banks tend to participate in more competitive markets, vying for customers within an entire geographic region or even nationally and internationally. They also have a smaller proportion of traditional savings accounts, which cost less than sources of funds such as negotiable CDs. Because small banks issue almost no subordinated notes and debentures, and purchase only minimal amounts of fed funds, other categories of interest expense are also less important to them.

Provision for Loan Losses. The provision for loan losses is analogous to the "bad debt expense" on the income statements of nonfinancial firms. It is an *estimate* of uncollectible loans, not a report of actual losses during the period. In 1985, loan loss provisions were higher for small banks than for large ones. Because small banks' business customers are heavily concentrated in retailing and farming, and because loan losses typically lag the business

cycle, the 1985 data reflect the impact of the recession of the early 1980s and of recent problems in the agricultural sector.[9]

The Tax Reform Act of 1986 revised the method used by large banks—those with assets in excess of $500 million—for reporting loan losses. (All banks controlled by a single holding company are grouped together when the $500-million asset test is applied.) Beginning in 1987, large banks or bank holding company subsidiaries may report only *actual* losses on loans made after 1986 as tax deductions on their income statements. They may continue to report *estimates* of losses on loans made before January 1, 1987. Table 11.3 is based on 1985 data and does not reflect this change in the tax code.

Salaries and Employee Benefits. The smallest banks have a higher percentage of expenses in salaries and wages, demonstrating the traditional labor-intensive nature of banking. Although larger banks have widely adopted electronic banking, the high cost of automation has slowed smaller banks' adoption of technology-driven approaches to delivering services. Hence, their employee expenses remain higher.

Other Noninterest Operating Expense. Other noninterest operating expense includes expenses incurred for bank premises, such as

---

[9]Kolari and Fraser found that banks with under $25 million in total assets became increasingly vulnerable to loan losses over a period ending in 1982, because of their greater exposure to small business loans. See James W. Kolari and Donald R. Fraser, "Size and Profitability in Banking," *Proceedings of a Conference on Bank Structure and Competition* (Chicago: Federal Reserve Bank of Chicago, 1984), pp. 289-308. In subsequent years, Wall found that higher loan losses and decreased NIM were the primary causes of declining profitability among banks, but that large banks were recovering well by the end of 1985. See Larry D. Wall, "Commercial Bank Profitability in 1983," *Economic Review,* Federal Reserve Bank of Atlanta 69 (June 1984): 18-29; Larry D. Wall, "Profitability: SE Banks Fare Better than Most," *Economic Review,* Federal Reserve Bank of Atlanta 70 (June/July 1985): 18-29; Larry D. Wall, "Profits in '85: Large Banks Gain While Others Continue to Lag," *Economic Review,* Federal Reserve Bank of Atlanta 71 (August/September 1986): 18-31.

depreciation. Supplies and advertising expenses are also included.

Profits in Commercial Banking

Several levels of profit are customarily computed and analyzed for commercial banks. The first is *net operating income,* or the difference between total operating income and total operating expense. Table 11.3 shows this amount as a dollar figure and as a percentage of total operating income. Financial institutions typically report capital gains and losses separately, because securities transactions are a significant portion of their operations but involve management strategies different from those of the loan portfolio. The *net income* of banks reflects the impact of all managerial activities on profits for the reporting period. For the average bank, net income was between 6 percent and 7 percent of each dollar of operating income in 1985. The smallest banks were much less profitable, primarily because they had high loan loss provisions and salary expenses.

SAVINGS INSTITUTIONS: INDUSTRY STRUCTURE

The second-largest group of depositories, measured by total assets, are the savings institutions. As noted earlier, savings institutions are divided into two subgroups: S&Ls and savings banks. Both types of institutions were founded to promote thrift among consumers.[10]

---

[10]For more details on the history of savings institutions see Martin R. Blyn, "The Evolution of Money and Capital Markets and Financial Institutions," in *Financial Markets and Institutions,* 2d ed. Murray E. Polakoff and Thomas A. Durkin, eds. (Boston: Houghton Mifflin, 1981), pp. 33-54; Maria Kulczycky, "The History of Associations: From a Homebuyers Club to a $600-Billion Business," *Savings and Loan News* 101 (December 1980): 70-73; Delia O'Hara, Beth M. Linnen, and Marilyn Melia, "Savings Banks' Evolution: From Different Roots, but Like Associations Today," *Savings Institutions* 104 (July 1983): 62-67; and Beth M. Linnen, "Sister Businesses Grow Together," *Savings Institutions* 104 (July 1983): 42-46.

Differences between Savings Banks and S&Ls

Savings banks arose in the 1700s because no existing institutions were willing to accept savings deposits from a growing population of workers. By the time the population moved west, commercial banks had turned their attention to individual as well as business customers, so the savings bank movement was never established outside the Northeast. Furthermore, a new type of institution with a dual interest in promoting thrift and homeownership emerged by the 1800s, the forerunner of the modern S&L. S&Ls spread nationwide with the population.

For most of their history, important regulatory and operating differences separated S&Ls and savings banks. Savings banks could issue demand deposits and make commercial loans in limited amounts. Unlike other depositories, they could also invest in corporate stock. S&Ls' asset choices were greatly restricted until 1980 because a combination of regulations and tax laws virtually assured that over 80 percent of their assets were mortgage-related. Today, both types of thrifts may invest up to 10 percent of their assets in commercial loans and may issue traditional demand deposits in limited amounts. With minor exceptions, however, S&Ls are prohibited from investing in corporate stock.

In the past, chartering and insurance regulations differed for the two types of thrifts. Until 1978, savings banks were eligible only for state charters, and until 1982, they were required to be mutually organized. Until that year also, they purchased deposit insurance only from the FDIC. S&Ls, in contrast, could have either state or federal charters, could be either mutually or stockholder-owned, and were federally insured by the FSLIC.

The Increasing Importance of Charter Selection

In 1982, as part of the Garn-St Germain legislation, increased chartering flexibility was given to savings institutions, making it easier for

Table 11.4
Size Distribution of FSLIC-Insured Savings Institutions by Total Assets, Year-End 1985

Size Category	Firms in Category	% of Total Firms	% of Industry Assets
Under $25 million	457	14.08%	0.70%
$25 to under $50 million	554	17.07	1.90
$50 to under $100 million	714	22.00	4.70
$100 to under $250 million	779	24.00	11.60
$250 to under $500 million	343	10.57	11.00
$500 million and over	399	12.29	70.10
Total, all sizes	3,246	100.00%	100.00%

Source: U.S. League of Savings Institutions, *1986 Savings Institutions Source Book,* p. 45.

S&Ls to convert to savings banks and vice versa. *Previously existing* state-chartered savings banks can now more easily convert to federal charters, resulting in a depository institution insured by the FDIC but governed in most other ways by the Federal Home Loan Bank Board. The Federal Home Loan Bank Board was also authorized to charter *new* federal savings banks, insured by the FSLIC and governed by the FHLBB. Federal savings banks can now convert from the mutual to stock form of organization. For savings institutions with state charters, conversion and other privileges depend upon state law.

This legislation has made the choice of a charter an increasingly important strategic decision. In some states, it has been advantageous for savings institutions wishing to broaden their powers to be state-chartered savings banks, because these states have identical legislation governing commercial and savings banks. In other states, federally chartered S&Ls have more powers than state-chartered savings banks.

Institutions have been willing to use these broadened options. Recently, for example, the increased cost of FSLIC insurance encouraged several S&Ls and federal savings banks to become state-chartered savings banks with FDIC insurance. In response, the regulatory dialectic proceeded as the FSLIC announced the assessment of large "exit penalties" against institutions that withdraw from the fund, and the FHLBB asserted its authority to veto proposed charter conversions.[11] Court challenges to the "exit penalties" make their future uncertain.

Size of Savings Institutions

Like commercial banking, the thrift industry is not homogeneous. Table 11.4 presents the size distribution of FSLIC-insured thrifts as of year-end 1985. The largest firms in the table, about 12 percent of the firms in the industry, have over 70 percent of the assets. Even the largest thrifts, however, are much smaller than the largest commercial banks. The largest savings institution in 1985, American Savings of Stockton, California, had total assets of under $30 billion compared to Citicorp's $173 billion.

[11]See "FHLBB Uses 'Exit Fee' in Battle Against FSLIC Conversions," *Savings Institutions* 107 (November 1986): 8-11; Janet L. Fix, "The Switch Is On," *Forbes* 137 (February 24, 1986): 33-34; Jim McTague, "League Says Special FSLIC Assessment Driving Thrifts to Convert to Banks," *American Banker,* October 13, 1986, p. 1. The circumstances surrounding the FSLIC's increased premiums are discussed in Chapter 15.

THE BALANCE SHEET OF SAVINGS INSTITUTIONS

Since 1980, it has become common for savings institutions to be viewed as quite similar to commercial banks. In fact, both types of depositories are legally permitted to engage in many of the same activities, and many of the assets and liabilities described earlier are found in thrifts. Furthermore, managerial issues in the two types of depositories are similar, because all managers must be concerned with liquidity and capital, credit analysis, and interest rate risk. Substantial differences remain, however, in the balance sheets of banks and thrifts. Reasons for these persistent differences and their impact on the recent performance of the two types of institutions are explored in the latter part of this chapter.

Table 11.5 presents the distribution of assets and liabilities for all federally insured savings institutions as of year-end 1985. Information is divided into that for FSLIC-insured thrifts, mostly S&Ls, but including a few newly chartered federal savings banks; and FDIC-insured thrifts, primarily state-chartered savings banks, but including a few that recently converted to federal charters. These data are not strictly comparable to those in Table 11.2, because the bank data are institutional averages, and thrift data are industry totals. Still, general assessments are possible.

Assets of Savings Institutions

FDIC-insured institutions have a higher proportion of assets invested in cash and securities than do FSLIC-insured institutions. Savings banks have for many years had broader authority to invest in securities than S&Ls, and the FDIC-insured group includes no S&Ls.

For the thrift industry as a whole, cash and securities are a lower percentage of total assets than for commercial banks, reflecting two factors: historic restrictions on S&Ls and the fact that thrifts as a whole issue comparatively few unlimited transactions deposits against which cash reserves must be held. In fact, as of year-end 1985, FSLIC-insured institutions issued virtually no demand deposits.

Loans. A comparison of the loan portfolios of FSLIC- and FDIC-insured institutions shows that mortgages and related assets are more important for FSLIC-insured thrifts than for those insured by the FDIC. Commercial loans are included in the "other loans" category in the table. Despite authority to make commercial loans since Garn-St Germain, the FSLIC-insured group had almost none by 1985. FDIC-insured thrifts, with the freedom to make C&I loans for a much longer period, also had very few. Consequently, although they were over 35 percent of the loan portfolio of the average commercial bank, and over 20 percent of total assets, C&I loans were less than 1 percent of thrift industry assets in 1985. Even nonmortgage consumer loans, which thrifts made to a much greater extent than commercial loans, were just over 3 percent of the assets of the industry as a whole, compared to over 10 percent for the average commercial bank.

Asset Differences between Banks and Thrifts.

Several differences between depositories emerge from the tables. One of the most important is that asset maturity for the average commercial bank is shorter than for savings institutions. From the lessons of the bond theorems and duration, it follows that thrifts' exposure to interest rate risk is greater than that of commercial banks.

In addition, commercial banks have more diversified portfolios than thrifts, especially those insured by the FSLIC, despite broadened investment powers for thrifts since 1980. Figure 11.1 illustrates the relative stability in the proportion of mortgages and mortgage-related assets in thrifts over the period 1978-1985. The major implication of this lack of diversification is that thrifts are more vulnerable to performance declines because of developments in a single financial market.

Research indicates that traditional mortgage-dominated portfolios are not simply a function of the recency with which federally chartered thrifts have been given expanded powers. Studies of S&L diversification by economists at the Federal Reserve Bank of Atlanta indicate that, even in state-chartered institutions

Table 11.5

Distribution of Assets: All Federally Insured Savings Institutions, Year-End 1985

	FSLIC-Insured (3,246 Institutions)		FDIC-Insured (370 Institutions)		All Federally Insured (3,616 Institutions)	
	Millions	% of Total	Millions	% of Total	Millions	% of Total
Assets						
Cash and securities	$ 141,721	13.25%	$ 49,160	22.68%	$ 190,881	14.84%
Loans:						
Mortgages and related assets	$772,271	72.22%	$132,343	61.05%	$ 904,614	70.33%
Consumer	33,550	3.14	11,071	5.11	44,621	3.47
Other loans	—[a]		11,089	5.12	11,089	0.86
Total loans	805,821	75.35	154,503	71.27	960,324	74.67
Other assets	121,857	11.39	13,113	6.05	134,970	10.49
Total Assets	$1,069,399	100.00%[b]	$216,776	100.00%	$1,286,175	100.00%
Liabilities and Net Worth						
Liabilities:						
Deposits:						
Savings	$141,861		$ 78,610		$220,471	
Time	702,072		103,311		805,383	
Other	—[a]		4,051		4,051	
Total deposits	$843,933	78.92%	$185,972	85.79%	$1,029,905	80.08%
Other liabilities for borrowed money	156,649	14.65	14,678	6.77	171,327	13.32
Other liabilities	21,997	2.06	3,884	1.79	25,881	2.01
Total Liabilities	$1,022,579	95.62%	$204,534	94.35%	$1,227,113	95.41%
Net Worth	$ 46,820	4.38%	$ 12,242	5.65%	$ 59,062	4.59%
Total Liabilities and Net Worth	$1,069,399	100.00%	$216,776	100.00%	$1,286,175	100.00%

[a]Less than 0.01%.
[b]Does not add to 100.00% because of rounding.

Sources: U.S. League of Savings Institutions, *1986 Savings Institutions Source Book*, p. 53; National Council of Savings Institutions, *1986 National Fact Book of Savings Institutions*, p. 7.

Figure 11.1
Mortgages as a Percentage of Thrift Assets

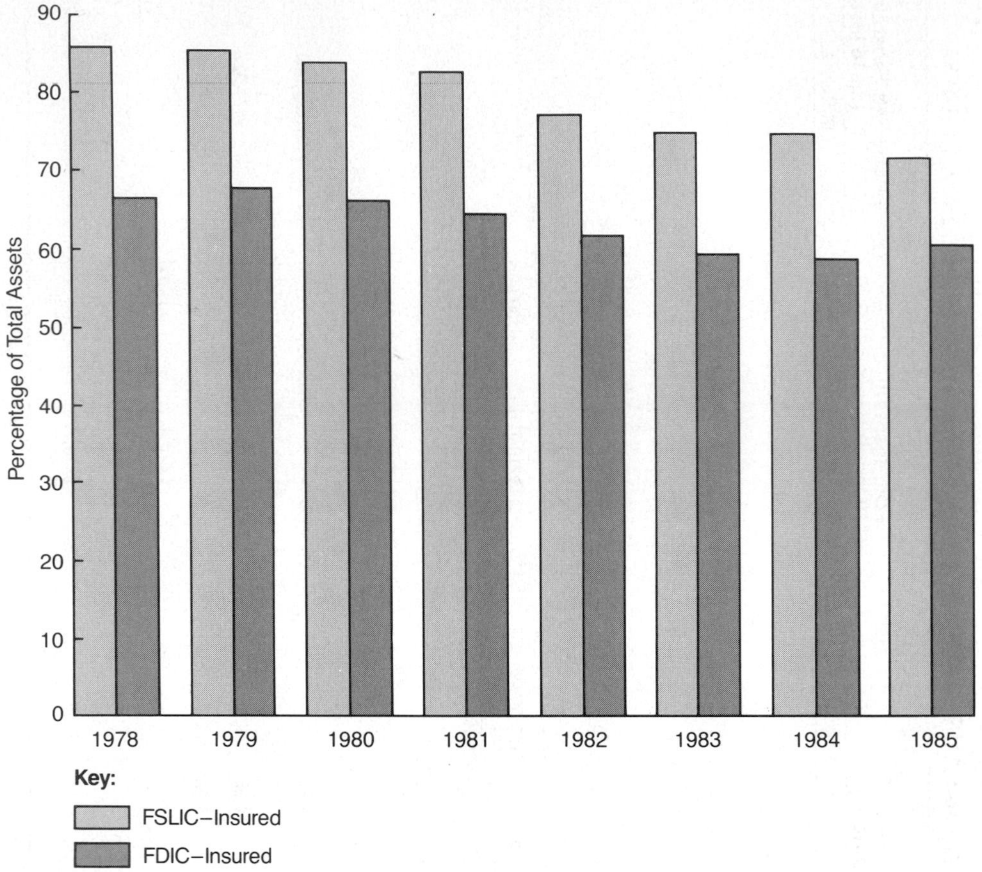

Key:

FSLIC–Insured

FDIC–Insured

Sources: Prepared by the authors with data from Patrick I. Mahoney and Alice P. White, "The Thrift Industry in Transition," *Federal Reserve Bulletin* 71 (March 1985): 142; U.S. League of Savings Institutions, *1986 Savings Institutions Source Book,* pp. 53, 55.

with expanded powers for over a decade, few nontraditional assets are held, primarily because many managers view the cost of developing expertise in those areas as prohibitive.[12]

[12]Robert E. Goudreau, "S&L Use of New Powers: A Comparative Study of State- and Federal-Chartered Associations," *Economic Review,* Federal Reserve Bank of Atlanta 69 (October 1984): 18-33; Robert E. Goudreau, "S&L Use of New Powers: Consumer and Commercial Loan Expansion," *Economic Review,* Federal Reserve Bank

Deposits of Savings Institutions

Like commercial banks, savings institutions raise funds primarily from customer deposits. Also like banks, they are authorized to issue

of Atlanta 69 (December 1984): 15-35; Robert E. Goudreau and Harold E. Ford, "Changing Thrifts: What Makes Them Choose Commercial Lending?" *Economic Review,* Federal Reserve Bank of Atlanta 71 (June/July 1986): 24-39.

traditional demand deposits (called *noninterest NOWs or NINOWs*), as well as NOWs, MMDAs, passbook accounts, and CDs of all types. NINOWs, included in the "other" deposits category in the table, are of virtually no importance to thrifts. NOWs, however, have become more significant for thrifts since their nationwide authorization in 1980. MMDAs have also greatly increased in importance since 1982, and passbook accounts have correspondingly declined with the rise in new transactions and market-rate savings vehicles.

Interest Rates and the Changing Deposit Mix. To highlight the implications of this trend for thrifts, Figure 11.2 illustrates market rates on three-month T-bills and negotiable CDs over a recent period. Figure 11.3 illustrates the deposit composition at savings institutions, with a steady decline in low-cost fixed-rate passbook savings for both types of thrifts coinciding with the period of increasing market interest rates illustrated in Figure 11.2. Because depositors abandoned passbook savings in favor of market-sensitive deposits, the cost of funds to thrifts skyrocketed during this period.

Figure 11.1 shows that thrift assets changed very little over the period when deposit structures were undergoing the most change. Thus, thrift assets remain heavily tied to long-term investments on which yields, even if variable over the life of the loan, change less often than the costs of liabilities. In addition, in the eyes of depositors, a thrift's liabilities are highly liquid,

---

Figure 11.2
Short-Term Interest Rates[a]

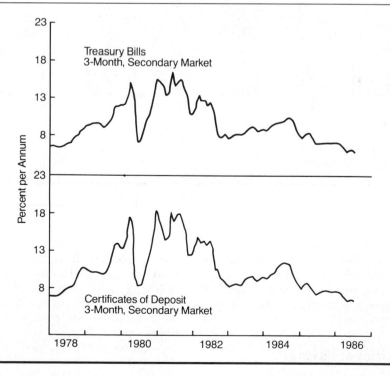

[a]Monthly averages.

Source: Board of Governors of the Federal Reserve System, *Federal Reserve Chart Book,* August 1986, p. 72.

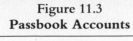

Figure 11.3
Passbook Accounts

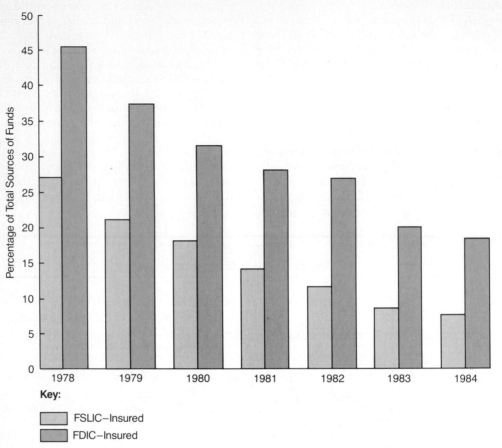

Key:

FSLIC–Insured

FDIC–Insured

Source: Patrick I. Mahoney and Alice P. White, "The Thrift Industry in Transition," *Federal Reserve Bulletin* 71 (March 1985): 142.

whereas its assets, in the eyes of homeowners whose mortgages are those assets, are quite illiquid. Managing the net interest margin of a savings institution is clearly a challenge in a deregulated environment.

Other Liabilities of Savings Institutions

In Table 11.5, the major component of liabilities for borrowed money in FSLIC-insured institu-

tions is advances from the Federal Home Loan Bank System, used to meet liquidity and other operating needs. Because FDIC-insured institutions lack access to this source of funding, other liabilities for borrowed money are less significant for them.

Further items included in the category of other liabilities for borrowed money are subordinated notes and debentures issued by stockholder-owned thrifts. Mutually owned thrifts are permitted to issue long-term debt securities called *mutual capital certificates,* quite similar to subordinated notes and debentures and described in more detail in Chapter 16. As with commercial banks, only the largest thrifts find a market for these securities, and they are a relatively small proportion of the liabilities of the industry as a whole. The last category of thrift liabilities, "other liabilities," includes items comparable to accounts payable and accrued expenses on a nonfinancial balance sheet.

Net Worth of Savings Institutions

A final element of the savings industry balance sheet is its net worth, a term that encompasses the reserves and retained earnings accounts of all institutions, as well as the common stock, preferred stock, and paid-in capital accounts of stockholder-owned institutions. Also included in the net worth of thrifts are unique regulatory sources of capital, such as net worth certificates. These items, first discussed in Chapter 2, are accounting entries that under specified conditions count as net worth for regulatory purposes. They are explained and illustrated in Chapter 16.

For the industry as a whole, net worth was about 4½ percent of total sources of funds in 1985, lower than for the largest banks and less than half that for the smallest banks. The asset/liability mismatch problems illustrated by comparing Figures 11.1 and 11.3 have caused earnings difficulties throughout the 1980s, reducing earnings available for retention. Most thrifts are mutually owned and have limited sources of equity capital, which explains the low ratio of net worth to total sources of funds.

INCOME AND EXPENSES OF SAVINGS INSTITUTIONS

Table 11.6 presents income and expense data for savings institutions in 1985. As with commercial banks, the asset composition of the industry is the major determinant of income. Interest and fees (mostly mortgage points) on mortgages are by far the largest source of operating income. Noninterest income, including service charges on deposits, accounted for more operating income for thrifts than for banks.

Expenses of Savings Institutions

Interest expense is a larger portion of total operating expenses for thrifts than for commercial banks, because thrifts have almost no noninterest-bearing deposits. Their noninterest operating expenses, such as salaries, wages, and occupancy expenses, are relatively low compared to commercial banks. In recent years, thrifts have been streamlining operations to cut costs. Because interest costs cannot be cut substantially if a thrift is to remain competitive with other depositories, noninterest operating expenses have been the place to start.

Profits of Savings Institutions

Given the potential problems in managing a thrift institution suggested by its asset and liability structure, it is not surprising that FSLIC-insured institutions, a large majority of the industry, had very low net operating income. When net nonoperating income and expense are considered, however, the result was more favorable. This item is similar to net security gains and losses on a bank's income statement. Profits on the sale of securities and mortgages accounted for over a third of the net income before tax for FSLIC-insured thrifts in 1985. Net income as a percentage of operating income remained lower for savings institutions than for the average commercial bank in 1985.

CREDIT UNIONS: INDUSTRY STRUCTURE

The third type of depository is the credit union. CUs are the most numerous of depositories, totaling 17,672 institutions in 1985, most of which are federally insured. As discussed in Chapter 3, CUs are not-for-profit organizations, with members associated through a common bond. Technically, the investments of members are called shares, not deposits, but CUs are viewed as depositories despite this difference in nomenclature.

Table 11.6
Distribution of Income and Expenses: All Federally Insured Savings Institutions, 1985

	FSLIC-Insured (3,246 Institutions)		FDIC-Insured (370 Institutions)		All Federally Insured (3,616 Institutions)	
	Millions	% of Total	Millions	% of Total	Millions	% of Total
Operating Income						
Interest income:						
Interest and fees on mortgage loans	$74,388		$13,891		$88,279	
Interest on investments	11,734		5,021		16,755	
Total interest income	$ 86,122	77.80%	$18,912	87.23%	$105,034	79.34%
Other operating income	24,575	22.20	2,768	12.77	27,343	20.66
Total Operating Income	$110,697	100.00%	$21,680	100.00%	$132,377	100.00%
Operating Expenses						
Interest expense:						
Interest on savings deposits	$73,578		$14,921[a]		$88,499	
Interest on borrowed money	14,083				14,083	
Total interest expense	$ 87,661	81.77%	$14,921	74.28%	$102,582	80.59%
Noninterest operating expenses	19,542	18.23	5,166	25.72	24,708	19.41
Total Operating Expenses	$107,203	100.00%	$20,087	100.00%	$127,290	100.00%
Net Operating Income	$ 3,494	3.16%[b]	$ 1,593	7.35%[b]	$ 5,087	3.84%[b]
Net nonoperating income and expense	2,602		166		2,768	
Net income before taxes	6,096	5.51[b]	1,759	8.11[b]	7,855	5.93[b]
Less tax	(2,126)		(500)		(2,626)	
Net Income	$ 3,970	3.59%[b]	$ 1,259	5.81%[b]	$ 5,229	3.95%[b]

[a]Includes interest on borrowed money.
[b]Percent of total operating income.

Source: U.S. League of Savings Institutions, *1986 Savings Institutions Source Book,* pp. 49-50; National Council of Savings Institutions, 1986 *National Fact Book of Savings Institutions,* p. 30.

Table 11.7
Size Distribution of Credit Unions by Total Assets, Year-End 1985

Size Category	Category Total	% of Total
$500,000 or less	5,196	29.40%
Over $500,000 to $2 million	5,107	28.90
Over $2 million to $5 million	3,057	17.30
Over $5 million to $50 million	3,746	21.20
Over $50 million	566	3.20
Total reporting CUs, all sizes	17,672	100.00%

Source: Credit Union National Association, *1985 Credit Union Report.*

Like other depositories, credit unions may choose either state or federal charters. Federally chartered CUs are regulated by the National Credit Union Administration (NCUA) and insured by the National Credit Union Share Insurance Fund (NCUSIF), a fund similar to the FDIC or FSLIC. State-chartered CUs may choose to offer share insurance through NCUSIF, and most do. The ability of CUs to offer federal share insurance is, in fact, a major reason why they are considered depository institutions.

As is true of other depositories, the CU industry is not homogeneous. Differences between small and large CUs are highlighted by Tables 11.7 and 11.8. Table 11.7 presents the percentage distribution of CUs by asset size at year-end 1985. The table shows that most credit unions are quite small; almost 80 percent have under $5 million in total assets. Many small CUs depend heavily on volunteer labor and donated facilities. Other CUs are relatively large, although small in comparison to other depositories. They offer services that rival those at many large banks, as shown in Table 11.8.

Support Systems for Credit Unions

Credit unions enjoy the benefits of strong trade organizations. Because so many CUs are small, they often need facilities and managerial exper-

tise that larger depositories develop in-house. The largest of the trade organizations is the **Credit Union National Association (CUNA)** and its affiliates. Among the most important affiliates is the **Corporate Credit Union (CCU) Network,** a group of credit unions for credit unions. Individual CUs own interest-earning shares in CCUs; the latter pool the funds of small credit unions and invest in money and capital market instruments. CCUs also function similarly to correspondent banks, offering advice, cash management, check processing, and assistance necessary for the operations of individual CUs. As of year-end 1985, total assets of CCUs were $11.9 billion.[13]

The credit union industry also enjoys the benefits of popular support. At year-end 1985, estimated total membership in credit unions in the United States exceeded 50 million. Although more citizens probably have commercial banking relationships, banks do not share the cooperative image of credit unions. A recent survey commissioned by the banking industry indicated that more CU members were satisfied with their institutions' services than were customers of other depositories. What credit

---

[13]The role and functions of trade organizations is discussed in Douglas K. Pearce, "Recent Developments in the Credit Union Industry," *Economic Review,* Federal Reserve Bank of Kansas City 69 (June 1984): 3-19; and CUNA *Annual Reports,* various years.

Table 11.8
Services Offered by Credit Unions by Size, 1985

Service	Percentage Offering Service by Size (Millions)										Total CUs
	$0–$0.2	$0.2–$0.5	$0.5–$1	$1–$2	$2–$5	$5–$10	$10–$20	$20–$50	$50–$100	$100+	
Stock or bond brokerage	0.6%	0.7%	1.1%	0.9%	4.2%	8.2%	12.9%	21.3%	20.5%	25.0%	4.6%
Auto leasing	0.3	0.8	0.4	0.6	0.9	1.2	1.9	4.0	4.0	6.2	1.0
Preauthorized payments	9.2	13.4	17.0	25.3	39.0	54.9	65.1	76.7	81.8	84.0	32.2
Direct deposit Federal recurring payments	5.5	9.9	18.9	37.5	59.3	79.5	89.3	95.3	97.8	97.4	42.1
Corporate payroll	12.0	16.1	21.9	28.1	40.1	52.9	60.4	69.9	76.4	75.8	33.3
Payroll deduction	75.9	85.8	90.7	91.0	94.7	96.9	97.3	98.4	97.4	99.5	90.3
Money orders	3.8	7.3	11.3	21.7	34.9	53.5	65.9	71.6	75.8	70.7	27.9
Safe deposit box	1.6	1.0	1.4	1.7	1.8	5.8	15.6	30.2	40.6	43.7	5.6
Remedial financial planning	5.1	8.0	9.7	13.9	19.8	25.7	30.6	35.5	39.5	40.4	16.3
Financial planning and investment	3.4	2.9	4.1	5.3	8.4	9.3	15.1	18.2	18.7	19.8	7.2
Telephone bill paying	0.6	1.5	0.9	2.0	3.1	3.7	6.5	8.2	10.8	10.2	2.8
Home banking	2.3	1.3	1.6	1.8	2.0	3.2	4.0	6.6	14.0	22.9	2.8
ATMs	0.3	0.3	0.5	2.5	7.2	19.0	36.4	58.6	79.5	85.7	11.5
Credit cards	0.0	0.1	0.1	1.1	4.9	18.3	37.6	57.3	66.7	66.3	10.2
Debit cards	0.1	0.1	0.0	0.4	0.7	2.1	5.7	10.0	19.1	15.9	1.9
Share drafts	4.8	4.6	8.0	19.5	43.2	69.1	82.1	89.3	95.5	94.8	32.3
IRAs	1.9	7.8	21.4	42.0	61.1	82.6	90.1	94.6	97.4	97.9	42.9
Traveler's checks	2.1	6.7	15.0	30.0	48.2	69.7	81.1	89.1	92.2	93.7	35.6
Wire transfers	5.9	7.7	12.7	20.1	37.9	59.2	74.4	86.9	94.0	94.8	31.2
Money market accounts	0.6	1.8	3.8	7.1	14.9	30.5	38.6	55.3	62.8	62.5	14.7

Source: Credit Union National Association, Inc., *1985 Credit Union Report.* Reprinted with permission.

unions lack in size, therefore, they make up for in customer loyalty.[14]

THE BALANCE SHEET OF CREDIT UNIONS

Table 11.9 presents the balance sheet of the credit union industry as of year-end 1985. Included are data for all federally chartered CUs, as well as for a larger group voluntarily reporting financial information to CUNA.

Assets of Credit Unions

Compared to other depositories, the asset structure of credit unions is simple. They are permitted to make loans only to members, most of which are for automobile financing. Since 1979, federal CUs have been able to offer home mortgages, but they remain a relatively small portion of the industry's total portfolio. Given the experience of thrifts after 1979, CUs have benefitted from slow progress into mortgage lending. Additional consumer credit is extended for educational purposes, and through credit cards, especially by larger credit unions. Some state-chartered CUs are permitted to make commercial loans, but few have chosen to do so.

The remainder of CU assets is concentrated in cash, investments in the Corporate Credit Union Network, Treasury and federal agency securities, and deposits in commercial banks

and savings institutions.[15] Because most are too small to fall under the Fed's reserve requirements, and because they offer no traditional demand deposits, credit unions' cash balances are modest. Since many credit unions operate in headquarters donated by an employer whose workers are credit union members, fixed assets are an even smaller proportion of assets for CUs than for other depositories.

Liabilities of Credit Unions

Members' savings were over 90 percent of the total sources of funds for CUs in 1985. Savings consist of *share drafts,* the credit union equivalent of NOW accounts; IRAs; *share certificates,* the equivalent of CDs; *money market accounts,* the equivalent of MMDAs; and regular savings, the equivalent of passbook accounts. As indicated in Table 11.8, less than 1/3 of all credit unions offered share drafts in 1985, led by those in asset size categories exceeding $2 million.

Like savings institutions, credit unions have seen a decline in the proportion of total savings held in regular savings accounts, with the percentage falling from almost 100 percent in the late 1970s to about 60 percent of total savings as of year-end 1985. In addition, the industry has liabilities to other creditors, including borrowings from the *Central Liquidity Fund (CLF),* an agency of the NCUA providing funds to meet CUs' needs for liquidity and other operating funds.

Capital of Credit Unions

Because of their not-for-profit form of organization and the common bond required, credit unions have limited access to funds except through the savings of members or retained earnings. Like other depositories, the balance

---

[14]Bill Barnhart, "Public Calling Signals as Bankers Fumble Ball," *Chicago Tribune,* October 27, 1985, Section 7, p. 1. In fact, "grass roots" support of CUs is so strong that some observers attribute the passage of the Depository Institutions Deregulation and Monetary Control Act of 1980 (DIDMCA) to the efforts of CU members to ensure the continued existence of interest-bearing checking accounts. CUs' authority to offer them was scheduled to expire on March 31, 1980, the day DIDMCA was passed, unless Congress had acted. CU members launched an "S.O.S." ("Save Our Sharedrafts") campaign, during which over 150,000 letters were written to members of Congress, urging passage of the act. See "A Blitz on Behalf of Credit Unions," *Business Week,* July 16, 1979, pp. 39–40.

[15]Unfortunately for the industry, the practice of investing in interest-bearing deposits in excess of the insured maximum ($100,000 per account holder) has led to losses. In the summer of 1982, when Penn Square Bank in Oklahoma City failed, almost half of the total $250 million in uninsured deposits was held by 150 credit unions. See "What Penn Square Taught Credit Unions," *Business Week,* July 26, 1982, pp. 19–20.

Table 11.9

Distribution of Assets: Federally Chartered and Other Reporting Credit Unions, Year-End 1985[a]

| | Federally Chartered CUs (10,125 Institutions) | | All Reporting CUs (17,672 Institutions) | |
	Millions	% of Total	Millions	% of Total
Assets				
Cash	$ 1,888	2.41%		
Securities	26,234	33.55		
Other assets	2,180	2.79		
Cash and securities			$ 52,029	37.93%
Loans:				
Mortgages and related assets			$ 7,572	5.52%
Automobile loans			30,577	22.29
Other loans			46,990	34.26
Total loans	47,903	61.25	85,139	62.07
Total Assets	$78,205	100.00%	$137,168	100.00%
Liabilities and Capital				
Shares:				
Share drafts	$ 6,819		$11,140	
Share certificates	13,588		22,096	
Individual retirement accounts (IRAs)	8,386		13,677	
Regular and other share accounts	42,824		78,599	
Total shares	$71,617	91.57%	$125,512	91.50%
Other liabilities	1,641	2.10	2,191	1.60
Total liabilities	$73,258	93.67%	$127,703	93.10%
Capital:				
Reserves	$2,884		$ 5,330	
Undivided earnings	2,063		4,135	
Total capital	$ 4,947	6.33%	$ 9,465	6.90%
Total Liabilities and Capital	$78,205	100.00%	$137,168	100.00%

[a]Reporting credit unions are all institutions voluntarily reporting financial information to CUNA.

Sources: NCUA, *1985 Annual Report,* CUNA, *1985 Credit Union Report.*

sheets of CUs contain reserve accounts, or portions of retained earnings designated to serve as cushions against which future loan and investment losses can be charged. Earnings retained in excess of those officially designated as reserves are called undivided earnings, similar to undivided profits in commercial banks. The total of reserves and undivided earnings is equal to the capital or net worth of the credit union. For the industry as a whole in 1985, capital was almost 7 percent of assets, exceeding the ratio of net worth to assets for all other depositories except small banks. The ratio was somewhat smaller for federal CUs.

INCOME, EXPENSES, AND EARNINGS OF CREDIT UNIONS

Although CUs are not-for-profit organizations, both CU trade organizations and regulators stress earnings as the most significant measure of CU performance. Table 11.10 shows 1985 income and expense data for federally chartered credit unions.

More than any other depository, CUs obtain their operating income from interest. The item "refund of interest" reflects a long-standing tradition of some CUs to refund interest to members if a year's operations are

Table 11.10
Distribution of Income and Expenses: Federal Credit Unions, Year-End 1985

	10,125 Institutions	
	Millions	% of Total
Operating Income		
Interest income:		
Interest and fees on loans	$6,135	
Interest on investments	2,120	
Less refund of interest	(27)	
Total interest income	$8,228	96.50%
Other operating income	298	3.50
Total Operating Income	$8,526	100.00%
Operating Expenses		
Interest Expense:		
Interest on savings deposits	$5,090	
Interest on borrowed money	38	
Total interest expense	$5,128	66.18%
Noninterest operating expenses	2,620	33.82
Total Operating Expenses	$7,748	100.00%
Net Operating Income	$ 778	9.13%[a]
Net nonoperating income/(expense)	43	
Less transfer to reserve accounts	(290)	
Net Income	$ 531	6.23%[a]

[a]Percent of total operating income.
Source: NCUA, *1985 Annual Report,* p. 41.

Table 11.11
Compound Annual Growth Rates in Assets of Depositories, 1960–1985

	1960–1985	1960–1965	1965–1975	1975–1980	1980–1985
Commercial banks	9.14%	8.36%	8.91%	9.68%	9.86%
S&Ls	11.44	12.25	10.09	13.30	11.50
Savings banks	6.95	7.57	7.44	7.21	5.12
Credit unions	13.09	11.88	12.87	14.18	13.69

Source: Prepared by the authors with data from Board of Governors of the Federal Reserve System, *Flow of Funds Accounts,* 1949–1978, 1961–1984, Q-IV/85.

successful. Although larger CUs offer services that generate fee income, most do not, so other sources of operating income are insignificant for the industry as a whole. Interest expenses for CUs are twice as large as any other expense, emphasizing the need for managing interest rate risk in these institutions.

Despite differences in the services offered by small and large credit unions, recent research indicates relatively few income/expense differences. A study of Georgia credit unions conducted at the Federal Reserve Bank of Atlanta noted that the largest CUs in that state were no more efficient, as measured by the average ratio of operating expenses to total assets, than were smaller credit unions.[16]

In 1985, credit unions outperformed thrifts and small banks, as measured by the ratio of net income to total operating income. CUs' tax exemption was no small factor in that comparison.

FINANCIAL STRUCTURE AND PERFORMANCE OF DEPOSITORIES: A COMPARISON

Recent balance sheets and income statements of depository institutions suggest both similarities and differences among them. Further understanding is gained from comparing the recent performance of these institutions along several dimensions.

Asset Growth

Commercial banks are, on average, the largest depositories by far. In 1985, for example, the largest commercial bank holding company had assets of over $173 billion; the largest S&L had total assets of only $27.3 billion; and the largest credit union had only about $1 billion in total assets. In fact, the entire credit union industry held only 10.6 percent of total thrift assets and 5.6 percent of total commercial bank assets as of year-end 1985.

The three types of depositories have also experienced different rates of asset growth during the recent past. Table 11.11 presents compound annual growth rates in total financial assets held by depositories from 1960 through 1985. Savings banks showed the lowest growth rates over the 25-year period. In contrast, the growth of credit unions outstripped that of other depositories over the entire period, and in three of four subperiods. Most recently, the distance between CU growth and that of competitors has widened. Of course, credit unions are also the smallest depositories, so CU growth expressed in dollars has not exceeded dollar asset increases at other depositories.

Another lesson of the table is that asset growth rates over the entire 25 years were most stable for commercial banks, changing little between the highest and lowest subperiods. In

---

[16]William N. Cox and Pamela V. Whigham, "What Distinguishes Larger and More Efficient Credit Unions?" *Economic Review,* Federal Reserve Bank of Atlanta 69 (October 1984): 34–41. This study somewhat contradicts the economies-of-scale study cited in Footnote 19, although the two studies are not directly comparable.

contrast, periodic growth rates ranged from 11.88 percent to 14.18 percent for CUs, and from 10.09 percent to 13.30 percent for S&Ls. Annual growth rates for savings banks consistently declined in each subperiod, dropping to 5.12 percent in the 1980–1985 period.

The Balance Sheets Compared

Figure 11.4 compares the balance sheets of the three depositories as of year-end 1985. In all depositories, loans are over half of total assets—nearly 75 percent for thrifts. A different type of loan dominates the portfolio for each industry,

however, with banks focusing on commercial loans, thrifts on mortgages, and CUs on non-mortgage consumer credit.

The graphs also highlight the importance of deposit taking and emphasize the high degree of financial leverage used by all institutions. In fact, all except the relatively small "slices" of net worth in the bottom panels represent debt obligations of depositories. Thrifts make the most use of financial leverage. Credit unions rely heavily on members' shares, lacking access to external sources of funds available to many banks and thrifts.

Figure 11.4
Balance Sheets of Depository Institutions, Year-End 1985

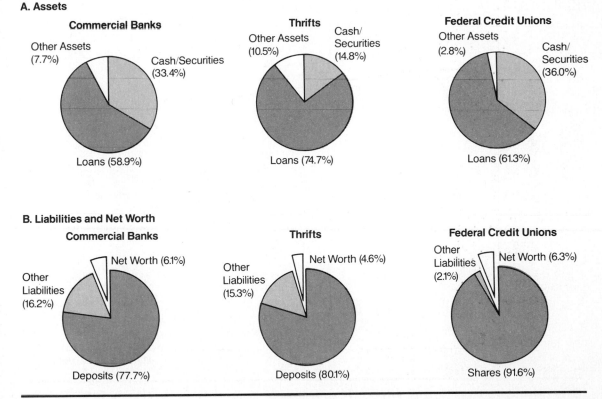

Sources: Board of Governors of the Federal Reserve System, unpublished data; National Council of Savings Institutions, *1986 National Fact Book of Savings Institutions,* p. 7; National Credit Union Administration, *1985 Annual Report,* p. 39.

Profitability

Profitability is the greatest difference among depositories.

Banks and Thrifts.   Figure 11.5 illustrates the return on assets (net income ÷ total assets) for commercial banks, S&Ls, and federal CUs over the period 1980 to 1985. Several points are clear from the graph: The profitability of S&Ls was low at best and negative at worst. In contrast, when savings institutions hit the bottom of the earnings chart, in 1981, banks managed to maintain earnings at almost their 1980 level. Bank profitability was much more stable than

were thrift earnings. Finally, federal credit unions prospered after regulatory ceilings on loan rates were lifted in 1980, freeing them to charge market rates.

Several reasons can be offered for these trends. Changes in the regulatory and economic environment of depositories have not affected the net interest margin of all institutions equally. Institutions with asset maturities substantially longer than liability maturities always have difficulty if market interest rates rise rapidly and liability costs go with them, while asset returns remain unchanged. Savings institutions found themselves in that unenviable po-

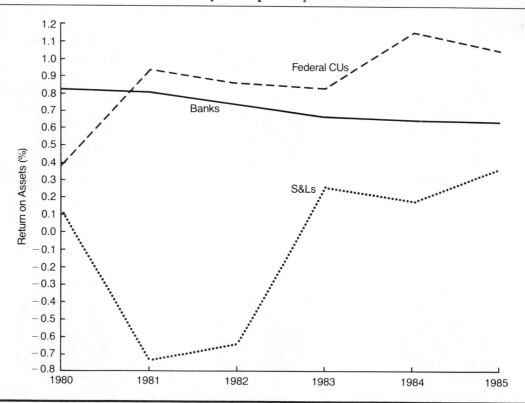

Figure 11.5
Profitability of Depository Institutions

Sources: Prepared by the authors with data from Ross Waldrop, "Commercial Bank Performance in 1985," *Banking and Economic Review,* FDIC 4 (April 1986): 21; National Credit Union Administration, *1985 Annual Report,* p. 43; U.S. League of Savings Institutions, *1986 Source Book,* p. 52.

sition by late 1980. Banks and CUs, with much shorter asset maturities, did not.

Coupled with deposit rate deregulation was the severe downturn in business activity in the early 1980s, producing the highest unemployment rate since the Great Depression. Delinquencies on residential mortgages reached unprecedented levels in the 1980s, further adding to earnings difficulties at savings institutions. Loan losses for commercial banks during this period were also high relative to historical levels, but the portfolio of the industry as a whole is more diversified than that of thrifts. So, while some industries struggled to repay bank debt, others were thriving, especially as economic recovery began.

Figure 11.5 helps to explain why the net worth of savings institutions is lower as a percentage of total assets than it is for the other depositories. The losses of the early 1980s eroded reserves and retained earnings from profitable years, leaving the industry in a comparatively weak capital position as it returned to profitability. Since then, profits have been low compared to other depositories, making it unlikely that capital will be rebuilt quickly. The managerial and regulatory implications of a weakened capital position are explored more fully in Chapter 16.

Prospects for savings institutions improved considerably by 1985 because they were able to replace maturing fixed-rate mortgages with new mortgages on which yields are more closely tied to market yields. For most of 1985 and 1986, *adjustable-rate mortgages (ARMs)* were about 50 percent of new mortgage loans.[17] Although few ARMs can be repriced as often as MMDAs, for example, on which costs can change once a month or more often, shortening asset maturities is a significant step toward improving the profitability of thrifts. In addition, thrifts continue to diversify away from mort-

gages to avoid the earnings squeeze they experienced in the early 1980s.

Some Banks Suffer, Too. Figure 11.5 makes another point: The profitability of the banking industry has declined since 1980. Several researchers have concluded that the decline is largely attributable to the difficulties of the seventeen largest banks and of banks with assets under $100 million. The largest banks, controlling almost 40 percent of the industry's assets, have faced increasing competition for business customers from nondepository lenders. On the other hand, noninterest expenses increased more for small banks than for large banks over the period 1980-1985. The decline in the industry's performance does not necessarily reflect deregulation, because loan losses from small business and agriculture have hit smaller banks hard in recent years. Because banks in the smallest and largest groups have a large share of the industry's resources, the profitability of banks as a whole has declined. Some banks, however, especially midsized regionals, have done relatively well.[18]

Credit Unions. As noted, CUs' earnings have increased since 1980. Like thrifts, CUs were less diversified than commercial banks before deregulation, although their assets were of considerably shorter maturity than those of savings institutions. Nonetheless, high interest rates drove up their deposit costs and dampened members' loan demand. During the 1981-1982 recession, occupationally based credit unions were hit hard by unemployment and experienced savings outflows and increasing delinquencies on loans. By 1984, however, loans were again on the increase. Furthermore, the

---

[17]"The Primary Mortgage Market," *Freddie Mac Reports,* various issues. The percentage of adjustable-rate mortgages originated has varied over the past several years. In fact, there appears to be a relationship between the general level of interest rates and ARM originations. When the general level is high, ARM originations have increased, perhaps because borrowers are reluctant during those times to lock themselves into fixed rates.

[18]Diana Fortier and Dave Phillis, "Bank and Thrift Performance Since DIDMCA," *Economic Perspectives,* Federal Reserve Bank of Chicago 9 (September/October 1985): 58-68; Lynn A. Nejezchleb, "Declining Profitability at Small Commercial Banks: A Temporary Development or a Secular Trend?" *Banking and Economic Review,* FDIC 4 (June 1986): 9-21; Federal Reserve Bank of New York, *Recent Trends in Commercial Bank Profitability—A Staff Study* (New York: Federal Reserve Bank of New York, 1986). In addition, articles on bank profitability in the previous year are published annually in the *Federal Reserve Bulletin.*

industry has successfully argued for changes in the definition of *common bond* so that greater diversification of borrowers and savers is now possible.

DEPOSITORY INSTITUTIONS: MERGERS AND FAILURES

In the 1980s, profitability patterns in depositories have affected the number of firms in each industry, as distressed institutions have sought merger partners or have been consolidated into other institutions at the direction of regulators. Other depositories have merged to meet deregulation's challenges as part of a larger organization. Still other institutions have ceased to exist because their net worth shrank to the point of insolvency (the value of their liabilities exceeded that of their assets). As might be expected, commercial banks, although not unscathed, have avoided drastic consolidation so far. But even they have experienced greater rates of merger and failure in the 1980s than at any point in recent history.

Economies of Scale in Depositories

Interestingly, the number of thrifts and credit unions did not begin to decrease in the 1980s, but almost a decade before that. Credit unions reached their peak at over 23,500 organizations in 1970 and have declined in number every year since then. The total number of thrifts has decreased steadily since 1960. Declines in the number of thrifts and CUs before 1980 have been linked to *economies of scale* in those institutions. Economies of scale occur when the unit cost of producing a service—for example, making a mortgage loan or opening a savings account—declines with the volume of business. Research indicates that S&Ls and CUs are both subject to economies of scale; therefore, the shrinking number of savings institutions before 1980 can in part be explained by their managers' desire to achieve cost savings and improve performance.[19]

In contrast, commercial banks have increased in number since 1960, when there were 13,484 chartered altogether, to their 1985 level of 15,068. Generally, economies of scale in the commercial banking industry have not been found to be as great as those for thrifts and CUs, and smaller banks have less incentive to combine for cost-saving reasons alone.[20] New banks continue to be chartered, so the overall number of commercial banks has not declined, despite the increased pace of mergers in the 1980s.

Merger Activity in the Banking and Thrift Industries

Figure 11.6 presents data on the number of voluntary bank mergers from 1960 through 1983. These data do not include bank mergers undertaken because one of the two partners was about to fail. Clearly, the number of mergers annually in the early 1980s was substantially greater than in the previous two decades. Research suggests that most were undertaken to enable banking organizations to expand geographically or to enable them to withstand takeovers by large out-of-state organizations in the event of interstate banking. In addition, regulators recently have taken a more permissive attitude toward bank mergers, leading to predictions that consolidation in the industry will continue.[21]

Unions," *Journal of Finance* 35 (June 1980): 769-777; James E. McNulty, "Economies of Scale in the S&L Industry: New Evidence and Implications for Profitability," *Federal Home Loan Bank Board Journal* 14 (February 1981): 2-8; and William A. Dowling, George Philippatos, and Dosoung Choi, "Economies of Scale through Mergers in the S&L Industry," *Proceedings of a Conference on Bank Structure and Competition* (Chicago: Federal Reserve Bank of Chicago, 1984), pp. 480-497.

[20]A recent look at scale economies in banking, which also reviews prior studies, is George J. Benston, Gerald A. Hanweck, and David B. Humphrey, "Scale Economies in Banking: A Restructuring and Reassessment," *Journal of Money, Credit and Banking* 14 (November 1982): 435-456.

[21]Stephen A. Rhoades, "Mergers and Acquisitions by Commercial Banks, 1960-1983," Board of Governors of the Federal Reserve System, Staff Study Number 142, January 1985.

[19]As examples of this literature, see John D. Wolken and Frank J. Navratil, "Economies of Scale in Credit

Figure 11.6
Commercial Bank Mergers, 1960–1983

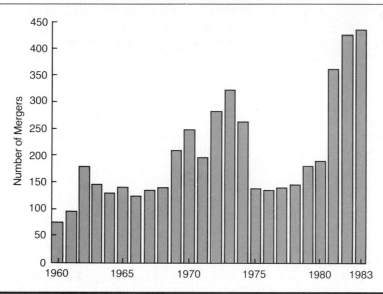

Source: Prepared by the authors with data from Stephen A. Rhoades, "Mergers and Acquisitions by Commercial Banks," Board of Governors of the Federal Reserve System, Staff Study #142, pp. 12-13, 30.

Since 1980, however, many thrifts have merged not by choice but out of necessity, because their net worth has eroded. Table 11.12 details the number of FHLB-member mergers, by type, between 1980 and 1984. Because savings banks were permitted to be FHLB members after 1982, figures for 1983 and 1984 include some savings banks as well as S&Ls. The table identifies three types of mergers: voluntary, in which two or more institutions joined without urging from the regulators; supervisory, in which mergers were directed by regulators, but without any financial assistance; and FSLIC-assisted, in which regulators not only insisted upon the merger but also provided some direct financial assistance to ensure that the resulting postmerger thrift was viable. The two recessionary years, 1981 and 1982, were those in which the merger rate—voluntary or otherwise—soared. By 1983, the merger wave had peaked, although many thrifts remain po-

tential merger candidates if earnings do not rebound strongly.

Depository Institution Failures

Figure 11.7 tracks the number of failures of FSLIC- and FDIC-insured institutions since the insurance funds were instituted in 1934. In this context, "failure" is defined as any situation in which an institution ceased to exist as a separate entity through supervisory merger into another institution or through outright closure without merger.[22] Thus, some of the supervisory and FSLIC-assisted mergers in Table 11.12 are considered failures in the bottom panel of Figure

---

[22]This definition of "failure" is that used by the researchers from which these data were drawn. See James R. Barth et al., "Thrift Institution Failures: Causes and Policy Issues," Federal Home Loan Bank Board Research Working Paper No. 117, May 1985, p. 36.

Table 11.12
Mergers of Federal Home Loan Bank System Member Institutions, 1980–1984

	Number of Mergers			
Year	Voluntary	Supervisory	FSLIC-Assisted	Total
1980	109	21	11	141
1981	217	56	23	296
1982	215	166	44	425
1983	84	31	23	138
1984	32	10	7	49

Source: Patrick I. Mahoney and Alice P. White, "The Thrift Industry in Transition," *Federal Reserve Bulletin* 71 (March 1985): 55.

11.7. The exception is the 1985 figure, which includes only outright closures of thrifts.

By historical standards, the failure rate for banks and thrifts in the 1980s has been nothing short of phenomenal. Because mortgages were formerly among the safest financial assets, thrift failure rates were lower than those for commercial banks until deregulation. In the early 1980s, however, thrift failures not only merely exceeded commercial bank failures, they were over four times as great in some years. Considering that the number of thrifts is between 20 and 25 percent of the number of commercial banks, the early period of deregulation exacted quite a toll on thrifts.

It is important to note that not all thrift failures can be blamed on bad management; in many cases, the managers of thrifts were simply unable to adjust strategies as fast as events developed. In other cases, of course, managers failed to prepare their institutions' asset and liability portfolios to cope with unexpected, or even expected, changes in the environment.

By 1985, because of regulators' concern that the FSLIC had insufficient funds to handle as many thrift failures as had occurred in the early 1980s, special programs were instituted to enable otherwise insolvent thrifts to stay in business. At the same time, economic problems in industries such as oil and farming led to an escalating number of problem banks, many of which banking regulators allowed to fail.

More on the problems of the deposit insurance funds as a result of recent failures is given in Chapter 15.

Are Depository Institution Failures Contagious? Apart from their effect on the managers and shareholders of individual institutions, failures, especially of commercial banks, are often considered undesirable for the financial system as a whole. This view arises from fears of a public run on other depository institutions when one fails, forcing solvent institutions to close, not because their net worth has vanished, but because they lack the cash to pay off all depositors on demand. Fear of runs has been especially high in the case of large bank failures.

In 1984, Continental Illinois National Bank, at that time one of the ten largest banks in the United States with assets exceeding $40 billion, teetered on the brink of failure. Rather than closing the bank, federal regulators kept it afloat by the FDIC purchase of $1 billion of Continental preferred stock to shore up the bank's net worth position. The insurance agency also purchased several billion in problem loans from Continental, enabling it to strengthen its balance sheet. This type of regulatory assistance was almost unprecedented and has been interpreted to mean that large banks will not be allowed to fail, although the same treatment would probably not be accorded to

Figure 11.7
FDIC- and FSLIC-Assisted Failures

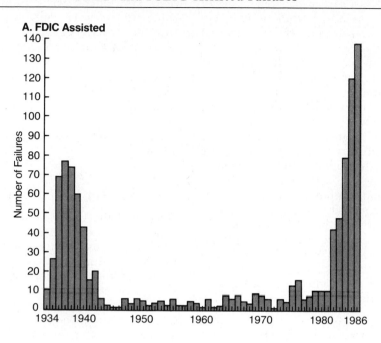

A. FDIC Assisted

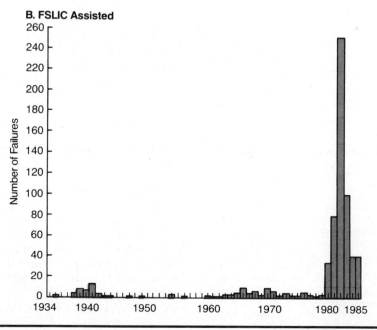

B. FSLIC Assisted

Sources: The Wall Street Journal, various issues; FDIC *Annual Reports;* James R. Barth, R. Dan Brumbaugh, Jr., Daniel Sauerhaft, and George H. K. Wang, "Thrift-Institution Failures: Causes and Policy Issues," in *Proceedings of a Conference on Bank Structure and Competition* (Chicago: Federal Reserve Bank of Chicago, 1985), p. 186.

small depositories.[23] In addition, the federal assistance was given despite widespread belief that the bank's top management, all of whom were later removed from office, were responsible for the bank's precarious financial condition.

In the Continental case, the regulators seemed to endorse the position that the failure of large institutions is more detrimental to the financial system than the failure of small ones, a belief some researchers suggest is supported by an analysis of financial market data at the time of the Continental crisis. Other experts argue, however, that federal deposit insurance, nonexistent during the bank runs of the 1930s, simply causes funds withdrawn from one institution to be redeposited in another that is perceived by the market to be safer. According to this line of reasoning, the actions of regulators in the Continental case were "incorrect and dangerous." The contagion effect of depository institution failures is another unresolved issue in depository institutions regulation.[24]

Mergers and Contraction in the Credit Union Industry

Because most CUs are small and members must have a common bond, financial problems in a single CU rarely evoke concern about spillover to other institutions. Still, the industry has contracted in recent years because deregulation and changes in the economic environment have affected CUs across the nation. Figure 11.8 shows the annual net changes in the number of federal CUs since 1960. The figures result from subtracting charter cancellations for the year from new charters granted. Although the cancellation of a charter is not synonymous with failure, many recent charter cancellations involved mergers to avoid the collapse of an individual CU. Other charter cancellations result from liquidation of troubled CUs. Figure 11.8 clearly shows that cancelled charters have greatly outnumbered new ones throughout the 1980s.

Prospects for the Future

What will the future hold for the number of depository institutions? Many experts expect continued consolidation for the remainder of the 20th century. Shrinkage is expected from continued financial problems, through voluntary mergers for economies of scale, and because the inevitable spread of interstate deposit taking encourages large institutions to purchase smaller ones to gain a foothold in a market. Still, few observers expect that only a few large depositories will dominate the nation. The classic cases used to support this point of view are California and New York State, both of which house some of the nation's largest depositories next door to some of its smallest, all with their own satisfied customers.

DEPOSITORY INSTITUTIONS: DIFFERENT, YET ALIKE

Undoubtedly, deregulation of depositories in the 1980s has led to increasing similarity among formerly distinct types of institutions. Even so, it is premature to say that all depositories are alike. Indeed, it is not clear that, even after the substantial passage of time, all depositories will *become* alike. Differences among depositories will persist because of the size, location, financial status, historical tradition, and strategic planning decisions of individual institutions, and because the current regulatory system vir-

[23]Comptroller of the Currency C. Todd Conover stated in Congressional testimony on September 9, 1984, that none of the 11 largest banks would be allowed to fail. See Tim Carrington, "U.S. Won't Let 11 Biggest Banks in Nation Fail." *The Wall Street Journal,* September 20, 1984, p. 2.

[24]Contrasting views of the contagion effect are presented in Itzhak Swary, "Continental Illinois Crisis: An Empirical Analysis of Regulatory Behavior," Salomon Brothers Center for the Study of Financial Institutions, Working Paper Number 335, January 1985; George Kaufman, "Implications of Large Bank Problems and Insolvencies for the Banking System and Economic Policy," Federal Reserve Bank of Chicago Staff Memorandum 85-3, p. 6; and Joseph Aharony and Itzhak Swary, "Contagion Effects of Bank Failures: Evidence from Capital Markets," *Journal of Business* 56 (1983): 305-321.

Figure 11.8
Net Changes in Number of Federal Credit Unions

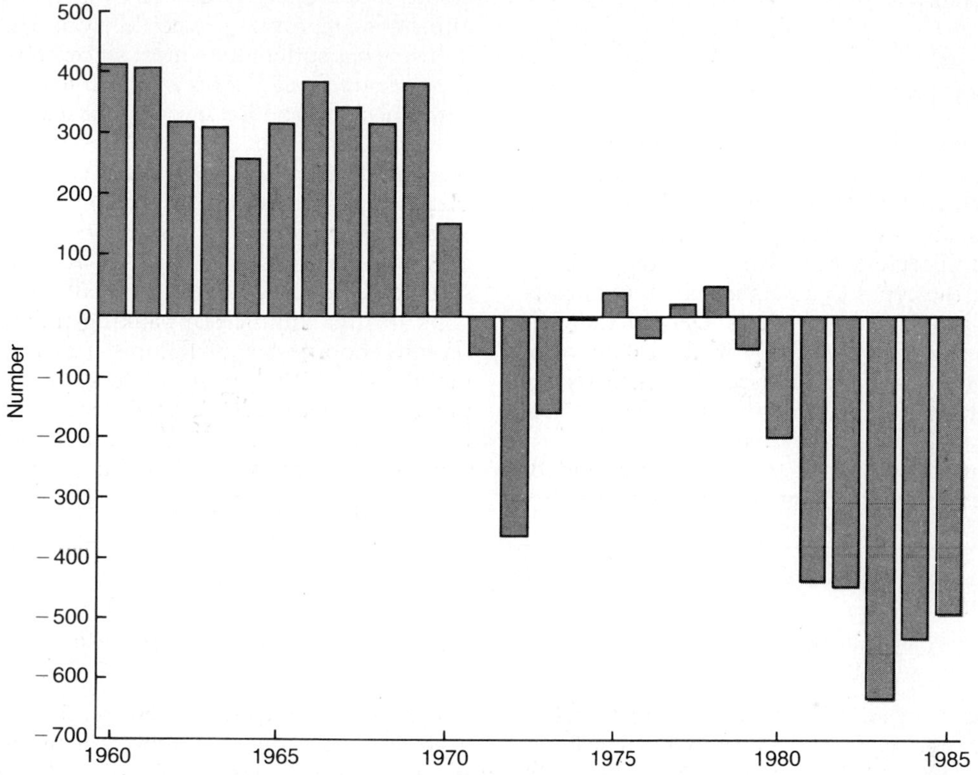

Sources: National Credit Union Administration, *Annual Reports.*

tually ensures that some traditional characteristics will remain.

Still, opportunities exist for management to shape the asset and liability structure of individual depository institutions, and to influence income and expenses, in ways that were unimaginable a decade ago. Successful managers now must set risk/return objectives, balancing their own interests and those with whom they have an agency relationship; evaluate the advantages and disadvantages of organizational and chartering alternatives; and understand and manage interest rate risk. The skills and knowledge needed to accomplish

these goals are common to all depository institutions; difference in their usage in a bank, savings institution or credit union is really one of degree, not kind.

Recognition of these needs is so strong that regulators now require all FSLIC-insured institutions to issue policy statements on interest rate risk management and on the potential effect of changing interest rates on asset values and income. Commercial banks must report asset and liability maturities, yields, costs, and net interest income to their regulators on an ongoing basis. Credit unions are increasingly turning to professional management and focusing as much on earnings performance as on service to members. The following chapters examine many of the required management skills in more detail.

SUMMARY

This chapter analyzes the asset/liability structures, income, and expenses of commercial banks, thrifts, and credit unions. Examination of the financial structures of depositories reveals some similarities, but also continuing differences in the types of assets in which each category of institution specializes. Deregulation has produced greater similarity in their sources of funds, although the assets of depositories are much less similar, despite broader powers granted to thrifts in the early 1980s.

Comparison of asset growth rates and financial performance across industries also reveals interesting differences. The commercial banking industry has enjoyed the most stable rate of asset growth and return on assets. The credit union industry has enjoyed the highest rate of asset growth. Profitability in the thrift industry has suffered the most since 1980, when deposit rate deregulation and high interest rates combined to produce several consecutive years of losses.

Finally, the chapter examines changes in the number of institutions in each industry. Failures, mergers forced by regulators, and voluntary combinations in pursuit of economies of scale have reduced the number of thrifts and CUs. In the commercial banking industry, although the number of failures has accelerated rapidly since 1980, new charters granted have prevented a decline in the total number of banking firms. Nevertheless, continued consolidation of depositories is expected in the future.

Questions

1. How does the size of a commercial bank affect its asset and liability structure? Its income and expenses?

2. Find some articles in current publications, including those of the Federal Reserve, that report on recent performance of commercial banks. Have reported earnings improved in the past few years? Why or why not? How has the performance of small banks compared to that of large banks? What reasons can you find to explain the differences?

3. Explain why the passbook savings account has become a rather insignificant source of funds for many depository institutions.

4. What are the advantages to small banks of using the services of correspondent banks? How do correspondent relationships affect the balance sheets and income statements of large banks?

5. What is a Eurodollar deposit?

6. Explain how net worth accounts differ for commercial banks, credit unions, and S&Ls.

7. Discuss the sources of income for commercial banks and explain the relative contribution of each to overall bank income.

8. Compare the proportions of various asset and liability accounts on the balance sheets of banks and thrifts. What are the most important differences?

9. Explain why the thrift industry's dependence on mortgage loans exposes the industry to greater interest rate risk than commercial banks face.

10. Compare and contrast the sources of income and expenses for commercial banks and thrifts. What explanation can you offer for significant differences?

11. Compare and contrast the roles of the Credit Union National Association and the National Credit Union Administration.

12. Compare the assets and liabilities of credit unions with those of other depositories.

13. How does the not-for-profit status of credit unions affect their performance in comparison to commercial banks and thrifts?

14. Why do you think thrifts have not moved more rapidly into commercial lending since they were given the power to do so?

15. S&L profitability was extremely poor during the 1980–1984 period, while the financial performance of banks and credit unions was stronger. What factors contributed to the differences in profitability among the three types of institutions?

16. What factors have contributed to the increasing number of thrift mergers over the past years? What factors have affected merger trends in the commercial banking industry?

17. Do you think commercial bank failures are more undesirable than the failure of nonfinancial firms? Why or why not?

18. Using information from newspapers and periodicals, compare the decisions made by banking regulators in handling the financial crises of Penn Square Bank in 1982, Continental Illinois in 1984, and Banc Oklahoma in 1986. What explanations can you offer for the regulators' decisions? What are the motivations for treating large and small banks differently?

19. Compare and contrast the regulatory responses to failing institutions in the banking and thrift industries. Do you think extreme differences are justified? Why or why not?

20. After studying the financial structure and recent performance of depository institutions, do you think there should be some consolidation among regulatory agencies, as recommended by the Bush Task Force for regulatory reform? Why or why not? (The Bush Commission report is discussed in Chapter 2.)

Selected References

Benston, George J. *An Analysis of the Causes of Savings and Loan Failures* (New York: Salomon Brothers Center for the Study of Financial Institutions, 1985).

Benston, George J., Gerald A. Hanweck, and David B. Humphrey. "Scale Economies in Banking: A Restructuring and Reassessment." *Journal of Money, Credit and Banking* 14 (November 1982): 435–456.

Blyn, Martin R. "The Evolution of Money and Capital Markets and Financial Institutions." In *Financial Institutions and Markets*. 2d ed. Murray E. Polakoff and Thomas A. Durkin, eds. Boston: Houghton Mifflin, 1981.

Cox, William N., and Pamela V. Whigham. "What Distinguishes Larger and More Efficient Credit Unions?" *Economic Review* (Federal Reserve Bank of Atlanta) 69 (October 1984): 34–41.

DiClemente, John J. "What Is a Bank?" *Economic Perspectives* (Federal Reserve Bank of Chicago) 7 (January/February 1983): 20–31.

Dowling, William A., George Philippatos, and Dosoung Choi. "Economies of Scale through Mergers in the S&L Industry." *Proceedings of a Conference on Bank Structure and Competition*. Chicago: Federal Reserve Bank of Chicago, 1984, pp. 480–497.

Federal Home Loan Bank of San Francisco. *Managing Interest Rate Risk in the Thrift Industry.* San Francisco: Federal Home Loan Bank of San Francisco, 1981.

Federal Reserve Bank of New York. *Recent Trends in Commercial Bank Profitability: A Staff Study.* New York: Federal Reserve Bank of New York, 1986.

Fortier, Diana, and David Phillis. "Bank and Thrift Performance Since DIDMCA." *Economic Perspectives* (Federal Reserve Bank of Chicago) 9 (September/October 1985): 58-68.

Goudreau, Robert E. "S&L Use of New Powers: A Comparative Study of State- and Federal-Chartered Associations." *Economic Review* (Federal Reserve Bank of Atlanta) 69 (October 1984): 18-33.

———. "S&L Use of New Powers: Consumer and Commercial Loan Expansion." *Economic Review* (Federal Reserve Bank of Atlanta) 69 (December 1984): 15-35.

Kulczycky, Maria. "The History of Associations: From a Homebuyers Club to a $600-Billion Business." *Savings and Loan News* 101 (December 1981): 70-73.

Mahoney, Patrick I., and Alice P. White. "The Thrift Industry in Transition," *Federal Reserve Bulletin* 71 (March 1985): 137-156.

McNulty, James E. "Economies of Scale in the S&L Industry: New Evidence and Implications for Profitability." *Federal Home Loan Bank Board Journal* 14 (February 1981): 2-8.

Moody, J. Carroll, and Gilbert C. Fite. *The Credit Union Movement.* Lincoln, NE: University of Nebraska Press, 1971.

Ornstein, Franklin. *Savings Banking: An Industry in Change.* Reston, VA: Reston Publishing Company, 1985.

Pearce, Douglas K. "Recent Developments in the Credit Union Industry." *Economic Review* (Federal Reserve Bank of Kansas City) 69 (June 1984): 3-19.

Rhoades, Stephen A. "Mergers and Acquisitions by Commercial Banks, 1960-1983." Board of Governors of the Federal Reserve System, Staff Study Number 142 (January 1985).

Wolken, John D., and Frank J. Navratil. "Economies of Scale in Credit Unions." *Journal of Finance* 35 (June 1980): 769-777.

Chapter 12

ASSET MANAGEMENT: LIQUIDITY RESERVES AND THE SECURITIES PORTFOLIO

Under contemporaneous reserve accounting, I don't think even God knows what excess reserves will total.

William Milton
Vice President and Senior Economist
Investors Diversified Services (1984)

BY 1985, Thomas Spiegel, President and Chief Executive Officer of Columbia Savings and Loan Association in Beverly Hills, California, had earned a reputation as an industry maverick. His innovations included providing his staff with karate and aerobics lessons at one of the S&L's two gyms. But other paths on which he led the state-chartered thrift were more controversial: 16 percent of its assets were invested in so-called *"junk" bonds,* high-yielding but low-rated corporate debt securities usually shunned by all but the bravest investors. Another 16 percent of Columbia's assets were invested in higher-grade bonds. Said one critical competitor, "S&Ls weren't put on this earth to have 33 percent of their assets in bonds." In reply, Mr. Spiegel and his supporters let Columbia's record earnings speak for themselves.[1]

---

[1]Kathleen A. Hughes, "Columbia Savings' Chief, Spiegel, Invests $1 Billion of S&L Assets in 'Junk Bonds,' " *The Wall Street Journal,* June 7, 1985, p. 7.

Earlier chapters have indicated that efforts to reduce regulation and to encourage competition have broadened market opportunities for depositories. How managers respond to these opportunities, of course, is determined by the long-term goals of the institution and is influenced by the preferences of shareholders, regulators, customers, and managers themselves. In this chapter and those to follow, major areas of decision making in depository institutions—liquidity, portfolio analysis, lending, liability and capital management—are examined. The final challenge is to coordinate decisions in separate areas into an overall asset/liability management strategy for the institution, addressing the risk and return preferences of all parties. This chapter focuses on managing liquidity and the securities portfolio. As the opening quotation and paragraph suggest, departure from tradition has been the hallmark of the 1980s.

IMPORTANCE OF LIQUIDITY IN DEPOSITORY INSTITUTIONS

First introduced in Chapter 4, liquidity is the ease with which an individual, business, or financial institution can obtain cash by selling noncash assets. In this chapter, the concept of liquidity is broadened to include the ease with which financial institutions (or others) can obtain cash by borrowing from external sources. As one expert defined it, depository institution liquidity is "the ability . . . to raise a certain amount of funds at a certain cost within a certain amount of time."[2] Access to cash is important in the financial management of all businesses, but because providing liquidity for customers is an intermediation function, a depository institution's own liquidity is even more important. Many deposits are obtained under promise of immediate or almost immediate repayment upon demand, so the investment and financing decisions for a depository are inseparable.[3] In other words, obtaining deposits and deciding how to invest them are closely intertwined.

Regulators Require Liquidity

Depository institution liquidity is emphasized by government regulatory agencies. Most depositories operate under a set of liquidity requirements established at either the state or the federal level. In addition, after DIDMCA extended Fed reserve requirements to all depository institutions, all but the smallest institutions must meet standards set by more than one regulator—the Fed's and those of their chartering or insuring agency.

Depositors Require Liquidity

In addition to the requirements of regulators, liquidity needs are affected by the expectations of depositors. The nation's largest depositories explicitly recognize this fact. A recent annual report of the First Chicago Corporation states, "The Corporation has traditionally viewed liquidity quite simply as the ability to meet all present and future financial obligations in a timely manner."[4] One of Citicorp's annual reports presents a similar view: "Citicorp defines liquidity as having sufficient available funds to fully and promptly repay all maturing liabilities or customer deposits in accordance with their terms."[5]

---

[2]Joseph E. Burns, "Bank Liquidity—A Straightforward Concept but Hard to Measure," *Business Review,* Federal Reserve Bank of Dallas (May 1971), p. 1.

[3]C.W. Sealey, Jr., "Valuation, Capital Structure, and Shareholder Unanimity for Depository Financial Intermediaries," *Journal of Finance* 38 (June 1983): 857-871. See Chapter 1 for further discussion of these concepts.

---

[4]First Chicago Corporation, *1982 Annual Report,* p. 25.

[5]Citicorp, *Citicorp Reports 1984,* p. 33.

Borrowers Require Liquidity

Depository institutions generate most of their interest income from loans and strive to develop a strong base of loan customers. To retain the loyalty of customers, a lender must be able to provide funds for all loan applications that meet its credit standards. Thus, an institution needs to maintain liquidity to support expected loan demand, in addition to meeting obligations arising from its liabilities.

Liquidity: The Risk/Return Tradeoff

With many compelling reasons to maintain liquidity, one might think that liquidity can be easily managed by keeping a large quantity of cash or marketable securities in the asset portfolio. A well-recognized tradeoff, however, is that liquid assets contribute relatively little to the firm's net interest margin, because they ordinarily offer a low rate of return. Cash and most reserve deposits earn no return at all. Under an upward-sloping yield curve, short-term, marketable securities earn a lower yield than assets with longer maturities. The conflict between the risk of illiquidity and a desire to maintain a high NIM is the heart of liquidity management. The challenge is to maintain enough liquidity to avoid a crisis, but to sacrifice no more earnings than absolutely necessary. Although the need for liquid assets arises for a variety of reasons, and all demands must be met simultaneously, each need presents a separate problem. The discussion that follows addresses the components of liquidity management individually.

ESTIMATING LIQUIDITY NEEDS: FEDERAL RESERVE BOARD REQUIREMENTS

The first reserve requirements for depository institutions were established on deposits of commercial banks with national charters in the National Currency and National Banking Acts of 1863 and 1864.[6] These reserves, established

as a percentage of deposits and other liabilities, were required as either cash or interbank deposits, depending upon the location of the bank. The rationale for reserve requirements was to protect the liquidity of the banking system in order to promote public confidence. The Federal Reserve Act of 1913 revised but continued reserve requirements. At the time of its passage, the motivation for the reserve provisions remained prevention of liquidity crises in individual institutions or geographical regions.

New Rationale

The establishment of the Federal Reserve discount window in 1913, through which member banks had access to short-term borrowed funds, provided a source of liquidity that was previously lacking. With the discount window to protect liquidity, the Fed revised its view of the purpose of reserve requirements. By 1931, they were recognized as a tool for controlling the amount of credit extended by banks, and by the 1950s they had become an important element of monetary policy. As discussed in Chapter 2, in the 1970s, the Fed argued that existing reserve requirements, applying only to Fed member commercial banks, limited the Board's ability to achieve monetary policy goals. That view finally prevailed in the passage of DIDMCA, and reserve requirements were extended to all depositories, both state and federally chartered.

Reserve Requirements since 1980

Although the rationale for imposing reserve requirements on depository institutions is no longer solely to protect the liquidity position of the financial system, meeting the requirements continues to be a key issue in individual institutions. Table 12.1 contains Fed reserve require-

---

[6]For a discussion of the history of reserve requirements, on which the historical information in this chapter is

based, see Marvin Goodfriend and Monica Hargraves, "A Historical Assessment of the Rationales and Functions of Reserve Requirements," *Economic Review,* Federal Reserve Bank of Richmond 69 (March/April 1983): 3-21. An earlier survey treatment of this topic is Robert E. Knight, "Reserve Requirements, Part I: Comparative Reserve Requirements at Member and Nonmember Banks," *Monthly Review,* Federal Reserve Bank of Kansas City 59 (April 1974): 3-20.

Table 12.1
Federal Reserve: Reserve Requirements (Percent of Deposits)[a]

Type of Deposit, and Deposit Interval	Member Bank Requirements before Implementation of the Monetary Control Act		Type of Deposit, and Deposit Interval[e]	Depository Institution Requirements after Implementation of the Monetary Control Act[f]	
	%	Effective Date		%	Effective Date
Net demand[b]			Net transaction accounts[g,h]		
$0 million-$2 million	7	12/30/76	$0-$36.7 million	3	12/30/86
$2 million-$10 million	9½	12/30/76	Over $36.7 million	12	12/30/86
$10 million-$100 million	11¾	12/30/76			
$100 million-$400 million	12¾	12/30/76	Nonpersonal time deposits[i]		
Over $400 million	16¼	12/30/76	By original maturity		
			Less than 1½ years	3	10/6/83
Time and savings[b,c]			1½ years or more	0	10/6/83
Savings	3	3/16/67			
			Eurocurrency liabilities		
Time[d]			All types	3	11/13/80
$0 million-$5 million, by maturity					
30-179 days	3	3/16/67			
180 days to 4 years	2½	1/8/76			
4 years or more	1	10/30/75			
Over $5 million, by maturity					
30-179 days	6	12/12/74			
180 days to 4 years	2½	1/8/76			
4 years or more	1	10/30/75			

[a]For changes in reserve requirements beginning 1963, see Board's *Annual Statistical Digest, 1971-1975,* and for prior changes, see Board's *Annual Report* for 1976, table 13. Under provisions of the Monetary Control Act, depository institutions include commercial banks, mutual savings banks, savings and loan associations, credit unions, agencies and branches of foreign banks, and Edge Act corporations.

[b]Requirement schedules are graduated, and each deposit interval applies to that part of the deposits of each bank. Demand deposits subject to reserve requirements were gross demand deposits minus cash items in process of collection and demand balances due from domestic banks.

The Federal Reserve Act as amended through 1978 specified different ranges of requirements for reserve city banks and for other banks. Reserve cities were designated under a criterion adopted effective November 9, 1972, by which a bank having net demand deposits of more than $400 million was considered to have the character of business of a reserve city bank. The presence of the head office of such a bank constituted designation of that place as a reserve city. Cities in which there were Federal Reserve Banks or branches were also reserve cities. Any banks having net demand deposits of $400 million or less were considered to have the character of business of banks outside of reserve cities and were permitted to maintain reserves at ratios set for banks not in reserve cities.

Effective August 24, 1978, the Regulation M reserve requirements on net balances due from domestic banks to their foreign branches and on deposits that foreign branches lend to U.S. residents were reduced to zero from 4 percent and 1 percent, respectively. The Regulation D reserve requirement of borrowings from unrelated banks abroad was also reduced to zero from 4 percent.

Effective with the reserve computation period beginning November 16, 1978, domestic deposits of Edge corporations were subject to the same reserve requirements as deposits of member banks.

[c]Negotiable order of withdrawal (NOW) accounts and time deposits such as Christmas and vacation club accounts were subject to the same requirements as savings deposits.

The average reserve requirement on savings and other time deposits before implementation of the Monetary Control Act had to be at least 3 percent, the minimum specified by law.

[d]Effective November 2, 1978, a supplementary reserve requirement of 2 percent was imposed on large time deposits of $100,000 or more, obligations of affiliates, and ineligible acceptances. This supplementary requirement was eliminated with the maintenance period beginning July 24, 1980.

(continued on next page)

Table 12.1 (continued)

Effective with the reserve maintenance period beginning October 25, 1979, a marginal reserve requirement of 8 percent was added to managed liabilities in excess of a base amount. This marginal requirement was increased to 10 percent beginning April 3, 1980, was decreased to 5 percent beginning June 12, 1980, and was eliminated beginning July 24, 1980. Managed liabilities are defined as large time deposits, Eurodollar borrowings, repurchase agreements against U.S. government and federal agency securities, federal funds borrowings from nonmember institutions, and certain other obligations. In general, the base for the marginal reserve requirement was originally the greater of (a) $100 million or (b) the average amount of the managed liabilities held by a member bank. Edge corporation, or family of U.S. branches and agencies of a foreign bank for the two reserve computation periods ending September 26, 1979. For the computation period beginning March 20, 1980, the base was lowered by (a) 7 percent or (b) the decrease in an institution's U.S. office gross loans to foreigners and gross balances due from foreign offices of other institutions between the base period (September 13-26, 1979) and the week ending March 12, 1980, whichever was greater. For the computation period beginning May 29, 1980, the base was increased by 7½ percent above the base used to calculate the marginal reserve in the statement week of May 14-21, 1980. In addition, beginning March 19, 1980, the base was reduced to the extent that foreign loans and balances declined.

[c]The Garn-St Germain Depository Institutions Act of 1982 (Public Law 97-320) provides that $2 million of reservable liabilities (transaction accounts, nonpersonal time deposits, and Eurocurrency liabilities) of each depository institution be subject to a zero percent reserve requirement. The Board is to adjust the amount of reservable liabilities subject to this zero percent reserve requirement each year for the next succeeding calendar year by 80 percent of the percentage increase in the total reservable liabilities of all depository institutions, measured on an annual basis as of June 30. No corresponding adjustment is to be made in the event of a decrease. Effective December 9, 1982, the amount of the exemption was established at $2.1 million. Effective with the reserve maintenance period beginning January 1, 1985, the amount of the exemption is $2.4 million. Effective with the reserve computation period beginning December 31, 1985, the amount of the exemption is $2.6 million. Effective with the reserve computation period beginning December 30, 1986, the amount of the exemption is $2.9 million. In determining the reserve requirements of a depository institution, the exemption shall apply in the following order: 1) nonpersonal money market deposit accounts (MMDAs) authorized under 12 CFR section 1204.122; 2) net NOW accounts (NOW accounts less allowable deductions); 3) net other transaction accounts; and 4) nonpersonal time deposits or Eurocurrency liabilities starting with those with the highest reserve ratio. With respect to NOW accounts and other transaction accounts, the exemption applies only to such accounts that would be subject to a 3 percent reserve requirement.

[f]For nonmember banks and thrift institutions that were not members of the Federal Reserve System on or after July 1, 1979, a phase-in period ends September 3, 1987. For banks that were members on or after July 1, 1979, but withdrew on or before March 31, 1980, the phase-in period established by Public Law 97-320 ends on October 24, 1985. For existing member banks the phase-in period of about three years was completed on February 2, 1984. All new institutions will have a two-year phase-in beginning with the date that they open for business, except for those institutions that have total reservable liabilities of $50 million or more.

[g]Transaction accounts include all deposits on which the account holder is permitted to make withdrawals by negotiable or transferable instruments, payment orders of withdrawal, and telephone and preauthorized transfers (in excess of three per month) for the purpose of making payments to third persons or others. However, MMDAs and similar accounts offered by institutions not subject to the rules that permit no more than six preauthorized, automatic, or other transfers per month of which no more than three can be checks—are not transaction accounts (such accounts are savings deposits subject to time deposit reserve requirements).

[h]The Monetary Control Act of 1980 requires that the amount of transaction accounts against which the 3 percent reserve requirement applies be modified annually by 80 percent of the percentage increase in transaction accounts held by all depository institutions determined as of June 30 each year. Effective December 31, 1981, the amount was increased accordingly from $25 million to $26 million; effective December 30, 1982, to $26.3 million; effective December 29, 1983, to $28.9 million; effective January 1, 1985, to $29.8 million; effective December 31, 1985, to $31.7 million; and effective December 30, 1986, to $36.7 million.

[i]In general, nonpersonal time deposits are time deposits, including savings deposits, that are not transaction accounts and in which a beneficial interest is held by a depositor that is not a natural person. Also included are certain transferable time deposits held by natural persons, and certain obligations issued to depository institution offices located outside the United States. For details, see section 204.2 of Regulation D.

Note: Required reserves must be held in the form of deposits with Federal Reserve Banks or vault cash. Nonmembers may maintain reserve balances with a Federal Reserve Bank indirectly on a pass-through basis with certain approved institutions.

Source: Federal Reserve *Bulletin,* March 1987, p. A7.

ments since 1976; for large Fed member commercial banks, the reserve burden has decreased considerably since 1980, when the maximum percentage was lowered from 16¼ to 12. For smaller member banks, and for all other depositories brought under the reserve ruling in 1980, the reserve burden has increased. Footnote h of Table 12.1 points out that in 1987, the 12 percent requirement applied to total transactions accounts in excess of $36.7 million.

At the recommendation of the Fed, a "reprieve" was granted to the smallest depository institutions in the Garn–St Germain Act of 1982. That law contained a provision that the first $2 million of reservable deposits were subject to a 0 percent reserve requirement. The amount of deposits to which this provision applies is adjusted annually, based upon the total growth of bank deposits during the year. By 1987, the 0 percent bracket was $2.9 million, as stated in Footnote e of Table 12.1.

Managing the Reserve Position

Required reserves must be held as vault cash or as deposits at a district Federal Reserve Bank. The Fed requires weekly reports from large depositories; a quarterly schedule applies to institutions with total deposits below an amount specified in Federal Reserve **Regulation D.** If an institution's reserves are below the minimum required, it is subject to a penalty imposed by the Fed. The Fed does not pay interest on reserve deposits, so reserve balances are nonearning assets for depositories.[7] Because of the penalty exacted for having too few reserves, and the loss of income from having too many, dep-

ositories must estimate their reserve requirements as accurately as possible.

Contemporaneous Reserve Accounting. From 1968 until early 1984, calculating reserve requirements was relatively straightforward. An institution knew a week in advance the amount of reserves needed, because they were based on average deposits for the week ending seven days earlier, a system called *lagged reserve accounting (LRA).* The chief problem for management was deciding the most efficient way to obtain this known quantity of funds.

The Fed, however, viewed the lagged system as an impediment to effective monetary control. In October 1979, the Fed revised its monetary control procedures, placing greater emphasis on depository reserves as a way of achieving monetary growth targets. Subsequently, on February 2, 1984, the Board of Governors instituted a procedure known as *contemporaneous reserve accounting (CRA).* As suggested by the opening quotation, the new system has complicated reserve management. CRA applies only to weekly reporting institutions; others continue to compute required reserves under a lagged system.

CRA Rules.   Under CRA, an institution's required reserves on transactions deposits are determined by deposit levels in the same period, rather than in a previous period as is the case under the lagged system. Reserves on nontransactions liabilities are still computed on a lagged basis. The *maintenance period* is the time during which reserve balances must be on deposit. It lasts 2 weeks, extending from a Thursday to a Wednesday 14 days later. The reserve *computation period* is also 2 weeks, beginning on Tuesday in the same week the maintenance period begins, and ending on the Monday 14 days later. The average daily level of reserves during the maintenance period must meet the required percentages on the average level of deposits during the computation period.[8]

---

[7]In one DIDMCA provision, Congress established a range of 8–14 percent for the marginal reserve requirements on transactions accounts. It gave the Fed the authority to set a higher percentage for monetary policy reasons, but stipulated that the Fed must pay interest on those reserves. The authority has never been exercised. For further details, see "The Depository Institutions Deregulation and Monetary Control Act of 1980," *Economic Perspectives,* Federal Reserve Bank of Chicago 4 (September/October 1980): 3–23; and J. A. Cacy and Scott Winningham, "Reserve Requirements Under the Depository Institutions Deregulation and Monetary Control Act of 1980," *Economic Review,* Federal Reserve Bank of Kansas City 65 (September/October 1980): 3–16.

---

[8]More details on the comparison between lagged reserve accounting and contemporaneous reserve accounting may be found in the following articles, which also serve as the

These rules, which sound—and are—confusing, are illustrated in Figure 12.1. The computation and maintenance periods are not strictly contemporaneous, although they overlap. On the calendar at the bottom of Figure 12.1, the computation period on transactions deposits extends from day 29 to day 42, and the maintenance period covers days 31-44. As deposits fluctuate, reserve balances must be adjusted almost simultaneously. For example, suppose deposits increase on day 42, at the end of the computation period. The depository must adjust its reserves quickly to meet the minimum required during the maintenance period ending two days later. The institution has only two days, 43 and 44, to hold higher reserve balances in order to increase the overall maintenance period average to the required level.

Figure 12.1 also illustrates that reserve balances on nontransactions liabilities continue to be computed on a lagged schedule. These liabilities include nonpersonal time deposits, such as large negotiable CDs with initial maturities less than 1½ years, and all Eurocurrency liabilities. As shown in Table 12.1, they carry a 3 percent reserve requirement.

Forms in Which Reserves Are Held.   Further complicating reserve management is the variety in acceptable forms of reserves. First, an institution may hold deposits at Federal Reserve Banks during the 14-day maintenance period. For nonmember institutions, reserve balances may be deposited at designated institutions; these balances are called "pass-through" balances. Correspondent banks often serve as holders of reserve deposits for their institutional

customers. In addition, an institution may also count average daily vault cash held during the 14-day computation period ending about a month earlier.[9]

Knowing the exact amount of cash and reserves available to meet reserve requirements is complicated by the check clearing process. As checks are cleared through the district Federal Reserve banks, the Fed transfers funds from the account of one bank to the account of another. At any time, then, an institution's total reserves contain **clearing balances,** which may be subsequently transferred as a result of customers' transactions. Conversely, reserves from other institutions may be transferred in. The Fed recognizes the difficulty of forecasting deposit balances accurately and permits a **carryover privilege.**

The carryover allows a depository to get credit in one maintenance period for excess reserves in the previous maintenance period. The amount carried over may not exceed the greater of 2 percent of the average daily minimum reserve balance in the current period, or $25,000. An institution also may carry a negative reserve position for one period without penalty, if reserves in the next period offset the shortcoming.[10]

---

sources for the description of CRA in the paragraphs that follow: Mary Susan Rosenbaum, "Contemporaneous Reserve Accounting: The New System and Its Implications for Monetary Policy," *Economic Review,* Federal Reserve Bank of Atlanta 69 (April 1984): 46-57; Kausar Hamdani, "CRR and Excess Reserves: An Early Appraisal," *Quarterly Review,* Federal Reserve Bank of New York 9 (Autumn 1984): 16-23; Vefa Tarhan, "Individual Bank Reserve Management," *Economic Perspectives,* Federal Reserve Bank of Chicago 8 (July/August 1984): 17-23. In addition, major portions of the December 1983 and January 1984 issues of *Roundup,* Federal Reserve Bank of Dallas, were devoted to the change in reserve accounting procedures.

---

[9]Average cash balances counted toward reserve requirements are based on the same computation period as that used for reserves against nontransactions balances. See Rosenbaum, "Contemporaneous Reserve Accounting."

[10]Most institutions do, in fact, hold excess reserves most of the time. Research indicates that the quantity of excess reserves held under LRA varied inversely with the size of the depository institution. Preliminary research under CRA, published by the Federal Reserve Bank of New York, has detected no change in the pattern. The largest commercial banks tend to have the lowest levels of excess reserves, while small banks and thrifts hold higher levels. A common explanation for this pattern has been suggested. If an institution wants to keep reserves at the lowest possible level, the attention of a full-time manager is usually required. For some institutions, the costs may exceed the opportunity cost of holding the extra nonearning reserves. The introduction of CRA is so recent that it is not possible to draw conclusions about whether this pattern will continue.

Difficulty in forecasting the deposit levels against which reserves must be held is considered a particularly serious component of CRA. Research conducted at the Federal Reserve Bank of St. Louis has concluded that

Figure 12.1
Reserve Requirement Computation: Contemporaneous Reserve Accounting

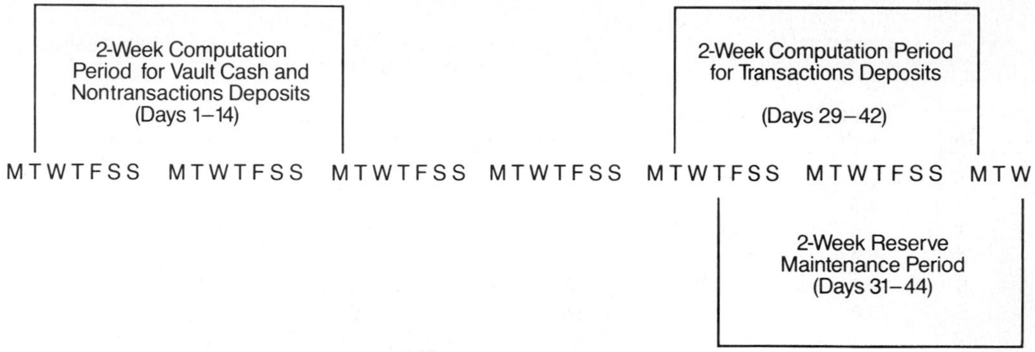

Reserve Management Calendar

M	T	W	T	F	S	S
	1	2	3	4	5	6
7	8	9	10	11	12	13
14	15	16	17	18	19	20
21	22	23	24	25	26	27
28	29	30	31	32	33	34
35	36	37	38	39	40	41
42	43	44				

Lagged Computation Period (Days 1–14)

Contemporaneous Computation Period (Days 29–42)

Maintenance Period (Days 31–44)

(Maintenance Period Is Shaded.)

Sources: Adapted from Mary Susan Rosenbaum, "Contemporaneous Reserve Accounting: The New System and Its Implications for Monetary Policy," *Economic Review,* Federal Reserve Bank of Atlanta 69 (April 1984): 47; "Contemporaneous Reserves Change Accounting Procedures," *Roundup,* Federal Reserve Bank of Dallas, December 1983.

forecasting errors could be large enough to justify an increase in the positive/negative carryover privilege to 5 percent from the present 2 percent. See R. Alton Gilbert, "Lagged Reserve Requirements: Implications for Monetary Control and Bank Reserve Management," *Review,* Federal Reserve Bank of St. Louis 62 (May 1980): 7-20 and Hamdani, "CRR and Excess Reserves."

Calculating Required Reserves

Table 12.2 provides an example of calculating required reserves under CRA. The institution is a hypothetical commercial bank, but the process would be similar for any institution subject to the CRA rules. The days correspond

Table 12.2
Reserve Balance Computation
(Millions)

Lagged Computation Period				Contemporaneous Computation Period			Maintenance Period		
Day #	Day	Vault Cash	Non-transactions Liabilities	Day #	Day	Transactions Deposits	Day #	Day	Reserve Balances
1	T	$ 9.5	$450	29	T	$ 982			
2	W	9.3	485	30	W	990			
3	T	9.6	460	31	T	955	31	T	$118
4	F	9.8	445	32	F	985	32	S	119
5	S	9.8	445	33	S	1,008	33	S	124
6	S	9.8	445	34	S	1,015	34	S	121
7	M	9.1	440	35	M	1,000	35	M	119
8	T	9.5	425	36	T	1,010	36	T	120
9	W	9.2	465	37	W	1,012	37	W	122
10	T	9.8	450	38	T	1,000	38	T	119
11	F	9.9	475	39	F	1,005	39	F	121
12	S	9.9	475	40	S	1,038	40	S	121
13	S	9.9	475	41	S	1,072	41	S	119
14	M	10.3	460	42	M	1,055	42	M	120
							43	T	
							44	W	
Average		$ 9.671	$456.786			$1,009.071	12-day average		$120.250

Required average daily reserve balance:

3% of nontransactions liabilities (lagged)	$ 13.704
+ 3% of first $31.7 in transactions deposits (contemporaneous)[a]	0.951
+ 12% of remaining transactions deposits (contemporaneous)	117.285
− Average vault cash (lagged)	(9.671)
Average daily balance required	$ 122.268[b]

Reserve adjustment required:

Cumulative total reserves required (daily average × 14)	$1,711.748
Less cumulative total achieved	1,443.000
Total amount required for last two days	$ 268.748
Average balance required last two days ($268.748/2)	$ 134.374

Maximum negative carryover allowed:

Daily requirement × 0.02	$2.445

[a]Based on 3% bracket in effect during 1986.

[b]Does not add because of rounding.

to the reserve management calendar in Figure 12.1, and all dollar amounts are in millions. The lagged computation period is a two-week span (days 1-14) that ends two weeks before the contemporaneous computation period (days 29-42) begins.

The Lagged Computation Period. Suppose the average daily level of vault cash for this bank was $9,671,000 during days 1-14, cash that will later be counted as part of required reserves. The average level of nontransactions liabilities subject to reserves was $456,786,000. Thus, the bank must hold reserves equal to 3 percent of that, or $13,704,000. Management can determine these two components of the reserve balance several weeks before the actual maintenance period.

The Contemporaneous Computation Period. The same is not true of transactions deposits subject to reserves; the average daily reserve balance will depend on average account levels for days 29-42. As a part of the planning process, management can forecast transaction deposit levels for the computation and maintenance periods, incorporating information about past deposits, seasonal trends, and other factors relevant for the period. Suppose these forecasts suggest that average reserves on transactions deposits should be $116,967,000. After adjusting for vault cash previously held and reserves on nontransactions liabilities, the target daily reserve balance during the maintenance period is $121,000,000:

(12.1)

$$\text{Target Balance} = TR + NTR - VC$$
$$= \$116,967,000 + \$13,704,000$$
$$\quad - \$9,671,000$$
$$= \$121,000,000$$

where:

  TR = transactions deposit reserves;

NTR = nontransactions liabilities reserves;

  VC = average vault cash during computation period.

Suppose deposits rise unexpectedly on the last two days of the computation period. For this bank, as shown in Table 12.2, the unanticipated deposit changes result in a higher actual required average daily reserve balance of $122,268,000. For the first 12 days of the maintenance period, the bank has held an average balance of only $120,250,000—below the minimum requirement. To meet the Fed's standards, the bank must significantly increase reserve holdings for the last two days.

The calculations for the additional amount needed are shown at the bottom of Table 12.2. At the average requirement of $122,268,000, cumulative total reserves over the period must be $1,711,748,000, but the total held for the previous 12-day period is only $1,443,000,000. The average balance for the last two days of the maintenance period, then, must be $134,374,000.

If the bank has held excess reserves in the previous maintenance period, management would use the positive carryover privilege to cover some of the current required balances. In addition, the bank may take advantage of the negative carryover privilege and end the maintenance period with slightly less than the total required ($2,445,000 would be allowed in this case). Still, the bank's managers must make some quick decisions if they want to avoid a Fed-imposed penalty. Alternative actions are discussed later in the chapter.

RESERVE REQUIREMENTS OF OTHER REGULATORS

Many depositories are affected by the reserve requirements of other regulators. Because state rules vary considerably, the following discussion encompasses only federal regulations.

The Federal Home Loan Bank Board

The FHLBB first established liquidity requirements for federal S&Ls in 1950. They have been revised frequently since 1968. Instead of setting minimum cash levels or requiring reserve deposits, the FHLBB views liquidity much more broadly. It defines liquid assets to include a variety of investments, such as federal funds sold and even municipal bonds, in addition to cash and short-term government securities.

Minimum liquidity requirements for federal thrifts are set as a percentage of transactions accounts, MMDAs, passbook accounts and short-term CDs, plus borrowings repayable on demand or within one year. The most recent revision, in April 1980, set the minimum amount of liquid assets at 5 percent of qualifying liabilities. The FHLBB may vary the requirement within the range of 4 to 10 percent; 20 percent of the required liquid assets must be in cash or short-term securities.[11]

Reflecting traditional concerns for safety and soundness, liquidity provisions are intended to ensure that savings institutions can meet the demands of deposit withdrawals. They are also designed to allow regulators to influence the volume of lending in a given period, because assets that must be held in cash or securities cannot be used for new loans. There is some question, however, about the degree to which liquidity requirements can control mortgage activity.[12]

National Credit Union Administration

The NCUA has the authority to impose liquidity requirements, but does not always exercise it. Between 1979 and 1982, federal credit unions offering share drafts or those with assets in excess of $2 million were required to hold liquid assets equal to 5 percent of member accounts plus notes payable. The additional liquidity standards were discontinued after the extension of Fed reserve requirements to these institutions.[13] Nevertheless, the lack of specific regulatory requirements does not eliminate concern for liquidity. Several decisions involved in credit union liquidity management are addressed in later sections.

ESTIMATING NONRESERVE LIQUIDITY NEEDS

In addition to meeting standards set by government regulators, depository institutions need liquid funds to meet customer loan demand and deposit withdrawals. Commercial banks, having offered transaction accounts and short-term commercial loans longer than other depositories, have traditionally been more concerned with liquidity needs arising from operations, but changes in nonbank depositories now require increased attention to their liquidity positions.

Discretionary and Nondiscretionary Factors

The balance sheet of a depository can be divided into discretionary and nondiscretionary items.[14] Discretionary items include those over which management can exert considerable influence, such as the use of repurchase agreements. Nondiscretionary items are those beyond the short-run control of an institution, such as deposit fluctuations, loan demand, and reserve requirements. Some nondiscretionary items—such as deposit increases or maturing loans—are sources of liquidity, but others are drains on liquidity.

Managers must understand the implications of nondiscretionary items for their institutions. A depository that derives the majority of its revenues from loans does not really wish to deny loans to good customers based on liquidity shortages. Such actions would undermine customer relationships built over long years of service and damage profit potential. Refusing

[11]*1985 Savings Institutions Source Book* (Chicago: United States League of Savings Institutions, 1985): 12, 52.

[12]Walter J. Woerheide, *The Savings and Loan Industry: Current Problems and Possible Solutions* (Westport, CT: Quorum Books, 1984), pp. 10–14.

[13]Douglas K. Pearce, "Recent Developments in the Credit Union Industry," *Economic Review,* Federal Reserve Bank of Kansas City 69 (June 1984): 10–12.

[14]This dichotomy was proposed in Dudley G. Luckett, "Approaches to Bank Liquidity Management," *Economic Review,* Federal Reserve Bank of Kansas City 65 (March 1980): 12–13.

to honor customer requests for deposit withdrawal would obviously have even more severe consequences. These operations-based liquidity demands are an important part of the planning process.

Estimating Liquidity Needs for Operations: An Example

The estimation of liquidity needs arising from anticipated volatility in deposits and expected loan demand involves a number of techniques, ranging from managerial judgment to quantitative models. Table 12.3 presents a simplified example of estimating a liquidity surplus or deficit over a single planning period.[15] The first step is to estimate total balances in each major asset and funding source category.

Liquid and Illiquid Assets.   Asset categories are then divided into liquid or illiquid components; liquid assets in this context are those available to meet operational needs. For example, at the top of Table 12.3, the institution's total cash balances during the next period are estimated at almost $210 million. But because of reserve requirements and daily transactions, total cash balances are never entirely available to meet deposit withdrawals or increased loan demand. In fact, management has estimated that only $21 million could be used to fulfill these needs. Within the investments category, liquid investments are those that can be sold easily without great loss of value during the planning period. More about managing the securities portfolio to allow for operational liquidity appears later in the chapter.

Volatile and Nonvolatile Sources of Funds.   Drains on liquidity can be estimated by examining funds sources. In this institution, most deposits are considered relatively stable, so only $130 million are judged to be volatile. In contrast, other liabilities for borrowed

money, including negotiable CDs, repurchase agreements, and federal funds purchased, are quite volatile. Management assumes that most could be withdrawn or become unavailable on short notice. The equity of the institution is entirely nonvolatile in the short-run.

A liquidity deficit is projected for the upcoming period because liquid assets are less than volatile funds sources by $34.3 million. If management's estimates are correct, the institution must somehow generate additional cash in that amount.

Additional Drains on Liquidity.   The top of Table 12.3 assumes that next period's loan demand can be completely met by maturing loans or stable deposits—that is, the loan portfolio is viewed neither as a source of liquidity nor as a drain on liquidity. A more conservative approach would build in coverage for unexpected loan demand by assigning a *negative* balance to the liquid loan category. Suppose management wishes to allow for additional loan demand equal to 1 percent of that already forecast, or a total of $12.1 million. The liquidity deficit from operations would rise to $46.4 million in that case, shown in the bottom panel of Table 12.3.

Incorporating Quantitative Models.   A more quantitative method of estimating liquidity needs is to forecast from a regression analysis of past data. For example, in the analysis of expected loan demand, management could use a model relating past loan demand, D, to time, t: $D = f(t)$. The resulting regression equation can serve as a basis for projecting a range of future demand, incorporating past volatility and knowledge of other economic or seasonal factors that may cause a change from past trends. An even better forecast might be generated with multiple regression, because loan demand is also affected by factors such as economic conditions, interest rates, and competition from other institutions, to name just a few. Similar analyses can be done for all nondiscretionary items affecting liquidity.

Sophistication in forecasting techniques is positively related to the size of depository insti-

---

[15]This example is similar to one in Daniel J. Kaufman, Jr. and David R. Lee, "Planning Liquidity: A Practical Approach," *Magazine of Bank Administration* 53 (November 1977): 55-63.

Table 12.3
Estimating Liquidity Needs for Operations

	Total (Millions)	Liquid (%)	Liquid	Illiquid
I. Original Assumptions				
Assets:				
Cash	$ 209.7	10%	$ 21.0	$ 188.7
Investments	1,037.6	59	609.4	428.2
Loans	1,214.4	0	0.0	1,214.4
Other assets	171.0	9	15.0	156.0
Total	$2,632.7		$645.4	$1,987.3

		Volatile (%)	Volatile	Nonvolatile
Funds sources:				
Deposits	$1,755.0	7%	$130.0	$1,625.0
Other liabilities	674.0	82	549.7	124.3
Equity	203.7	0	0.0	203.7
Total	$2,632.7		$679.7	$1,953.0

Liquidity deficit (liquid assets − volatile funds):

$645.4 − $679.7 = ($34.3)

	Total (Millions)	Liquid (%)	Liquid	Illiquid
II. Additional Loan Demand				
Assets:				
Cash	$ 209.7	10%	$ 21.0	$ 188.7
Investments	1,037.6	59	609.4	428.2
Loans	1,214.4	−1	(12.1)	1,226.5
Other assets	171.0	9	15.0	156.0
Total	$2,632.7		$633.3	$1,999.4

Liquidity deficit (liquid assets − volatile funds):

$633.3 − $679.7 = ($46.4)

tutions; this is not surprising because it is expensive to employ forecasting specialists.[16]

[16]A recent survey of forecasting techniques revealed that the percentage of the large banks (deposits in excess of $400 million) using sophisticated forecasting techniques such as multiple regression, time series forecasting, and simulation, was higher than among smaller banks. A large number of institutions of all sizes, however, relied on managerial judgment—either alone or in combination with quantitative methods—for estimating future deposit levels and loan demand. See Gary Giroux, "A Survey of Forecasting Techniques Used by Commercial Banks," *Journal of Bank Research* 11 (Spring 1980): 51-53.

Regardless of how forecasts are generated, they are an important part of the liquidity management solution. These estimates combine with estimates of required reserves to represent a target level of liquid funds for the planning period.

MANAGING THE LIQUIDITY POSITION

Table 12.2 presents a bank's reserve dilemma; the bank had a potential reserve deficiency and needed immediate access to liquid funds to bring the two-week daily average balance in line with the Fed requirements.[17] The institution in Table 12.3 needed liquidity as a result of operational factors. Whatever the reason, managers must act.

Borrowing versus Selling Securities

Two general liquidity management strategies are available. First, management can borrow funds, either from the regulators or from nondeposit creditors in the financial markets. Obtaining nondeposit sources of cash, a technique used more often by large commercial banks than by other depositories, is called *liability management.* Because the use of nondeposit funds, such as federal funds and Euromarket borrowing, has implications far beyond liquidity management, full discussion of liability management is deferred until Chapter 15. This chapter discusses borrowing from regulators as a source of liquidity.

A second strategy is to liquidate assets from the securities portfolio. High market interest rates can make this approach undesirable. In addition, depositories hold securities for purposes other than liquidity, so tradeoffs are involved in this approach to liquidity management. Some of them are discussed later in the chapter.

---

[17]Of course, management of the reserve position is not limited to the problem of covering reserve deficiencies. Depositories may also find themselves with *excess* reserves toward the end of the maintenance period. When the institution has excess reserves, management may choose to loan them in the federal funds market. The asset thus created is defined in Chapter 11 as "federal funds sold." Calculating the effective yield on federal funds sold is illustrated in Chapter 4.

Factors Influencing Liquidity Management

The choice between borrowing or selling securities is influenced by a number of factors, including the size of the institution, its financial stability, its industry, and the risk/return preferences of managers and owners.

Size and Financial Stability.   Small or financially weak institutions are especially likely to look to the securities portfolio, not to liability management, for generating liquidity. Within the asset portfolio, too, liquidity is influenced by institutional size. As discussed more fully later, active portfolio management is expensive; thus, a smaller institution is likely to keep larger proportions of readily marketable short-term securities and higher excess reserve balances.

Industry Membership.   Another influence over which a depository institution usually has little control is its industry. Regulatory policies governing an industry limit its operations—including the composition of its securities portfolio, the proportion of liquid assets held, and the sources of short-term loans for liquidity purposes. Recently, however, regulators have provided depository institutions with more freedom to change from one industry to another by simplifying the process of applying for new charters.

Risk/Return Preferences.   Managers' and owners' risk preferences also influence liquidity management. For a variety of reasons explored in Chapter 15, liability management exposes an institution to greater risks than does a strategy of selling securities when cash is needed. Furthermore, some strategies for managing the securities portfolio are riskier than others, as discussed later in this chapter.

Borrowing from Regulators as a Source of Liquidity

The carryover privilege on Fed reserve requirements is useful in meeting small deficiencies in liquid assets. For example, if deposits fluctuate unexpectedly toward the end of the maintenance period, an institution can postpone major reserve adjustments until the next period, as long as the fluctuations are not too large. However, if deficiencies are large or frequent, the institution can turn to federal regulators for other sources of cash for liquidity management.

The Discount Window.   The Fed discount window was originally available only to member commercial banks, but DIDMCA opened it to all depositories subject to Fed reserve requirements. Commercial banks remain by far the largest users because Fed policy requires other depositories to exhaust traditional sources of regulatory borrowing before turning to the discount window.

The interest cost and availability of these borrowings are major factors in the decision to use the window. Ordinarily, discount-window borrowings are very short-term, used only to meet genuine liquidity emergencies and not as additional funds for expanding the loan portfolio. Officials at the Fed monitor an institution's use of the window and may ask management to discontinue borrowing should norms for the amount and frequency of borrowing be exceeded. Thus, frequent borrowing at the window has negative connotations that managers are careful to avoid.[18]

FHLBB Advances.   Federal savings institutions facing a shortage of qualifying liquid assets may apply for advances from the Federal Home Loan Bank System. This FHLBB lending program was originated in the Federal Home Loan Bank Act of 1932 and modeled after that of the Federal Reserve System. Advances differ from discount-window loans in that they tend to be longer-term and the interest

rate is often adjusted to promote compliance with policies other than liquidity standards. In fact, the FHLBB has at times offered advances at rates below current market levels to encourage thrifts to make certain types of mortgage loans considered key elements of national economic policy.[19] The role of advances in promoting FHLBB policies, combined with the longer maturities of these loans, means that they play a less regular role in the liquidity management of individual thrifts than does discount-window borrowing for commercial banks.

Sources of Borrowing for Credit Unions.   For credit unions, three sources of short-term funds are available, two of these from regulatory sources. One source of liquidity was authorized by Congress in 1978, when it approved the creation of the Central Liquidity Facility (CLF), mentioned in Chapter 11 as an arm of the NCUA. The CLF functions as the lender of last resort for credit unions voluntarily choosing to join it. In contrast to FHLBB advances, CLF loans are made for liquidity purposes only. The interest rate charged is administered as a "penalty rate"; that is, the rate charged is higher than prevailing market rates. Fed discount-window loans are also available to credit unions offering transactions deposits or nonpersonal time deposits. Finally, a CU that is a member of a Corporate Credit Union (CCU) may borrow from the CCU.[20]

The Securities Portfolio as a Source of Liquidity

Managing the securities portfolio—in particular, choosing an optimal combination of liquid versus higher-yielding assets—is an integral part of liquidity management for depository

---

[18]Details on the administration of the window can be found in James Parthemos and Walter Varvel, "The Discount Window," in *Instruments of the Money Market,* 5th ed. Timothy Q. Cook and Bruce J. Summers, eds. (Richmond, VA: Federal Reserve Bank of Richmond, 1981), pp. 59-72; David Mengle, "The Discount Window," *Economic Review,* Federal Reserve Bank of Richmond 72 (May/June 1986): 2-10.

[19]Woerheide, *The Savings and Loan Industry,* pp. 4, 11-15. During parts of 1983 and 1984, for instance, the monthly average rate on advances from the FHLBB was *lower* than the monthly average cost to the FHLBB of raising new funds.

[20]Pearce, "Recent Developments in the Credit Union Industry"; Credit Union National Association, *Credit Union Report 1981,* p. 3.

institutions. Because commercial banks have carried the highest reserve requirements and the shortest-term liabilities, most research on liquidity management has focused on banks. With the acceleration of deregulation, these issues are of increasing concern to all depositories.

The Relative Liquidity of Securities. Assets central to liquidity planning are often categorized according to their relative liquidity. Cash balances held over and above required reserves are known as *primary reserves.* Securities held to protect short-term liquidity are called *secondary reserves,* consisting of short-term marketable securities, such as Treasury bills, that can be readily sold without extreme exposure to market value risk.

Not all highly marketable securities are considered secondary reserves. Some must be held as collateral for repurchase agreements or borrowings from regulators, and others as "pledges" against government deposits. These requirements restrict the securities portfolio as a source of liquidity. For example, institutions receiving deposits from the U.S. government in excess of the FDIC insurance ceiling are required to pledge collateral against these deposits. Only certain assets, such as U.S. government, state, or local securities, qualify as collateral. Most states also have laws requiring backing for public deposits. In addition, institutions serving as major dealers in money market assets must keep an inventory of *trading account securities* from which to make trades with customers.

Finally, other investments providing potential liquidity over a longer-term planning horizon are designated as *tertiary reserves.* These securities have longer maturities, but are still marketable if cash is needed to meet unexpected changes in deposit withdrawals or loan demand. Beyond the three categories are securities viewed as investment assets, which may fulfill different objectives, such as the generation of income. A key problem in management of liquidity through the securities portfolio is determining the proportionate investment across these categories.

Matching Cash Flows. One school of thought for protecting liquidity argues that a depository institution should carefully analyze its deposit structure and loan demand to forecast the timing and quantity of cash needs. Maturities of the investment portfolio should then be chosen to coincide with those forecasts. In other words, investments should mature, providing a cash inflow, at just the time an institution needs liquid funds. The relative proportion of primary, secondary, and tertiary sources of asset liquidity would be determined by cash flow forecasts. A problem with this policy is that forecasts contain errors, so there could still be a liquidity crisis.

Ladder of Maturities. An alternative investment strategy is the *ladder of maturities,* which spreads the maturity of securities held for liquidity purposes evenly across a given period. For example, suppose a savings bank decided the maximum maturity of its tertiary reserves should be five years. In the ladder-of-maturities strategy, an equal proportion of the portfolio would mature each planning period. Cash received at maturity would be reinvested in assets with a five-year term to maturity. One way of conceptualizing the ladder of maturities is as a conveyor belt. Assets move along the belt for five years toward their maturity date; when they reach the end of the line (maturity), the funds are placed back at the beginning through reinvestment if not immediately needed for liquidity purposes.

Perhaps the most serious criticism of the ladder portfolio is that it does not attempt to optimize investment returns for the institution. It is a relatively passive approach to investment management; no real effort is made to distinguish between secondary and tertiary reserves. Consequently, the institution may forgo investments that could increase returns without also incurring unacceptable liquidity risks. But for institutions without personnel to manage the securities portfolio, it may be a viable strategy.

Barbell Strategy. An alternative to the ladder-of-maturities strategy is to invest funds at either end of the yield curve, but not in the middle, a strategy called the **barbell** or **split-maturity** portfolio. This approach retains some very liquid assets as secondary reserves, but (assuming an upward-sloping yield curve) allows a larger investment in higher-return, long-term securities. To manage a barbell portfolio efficiently, however, the institution must devote resources to interest rate forecasting, because the anticipated direction of rate movements plays an important role in the proportionate investments at either end of the yield curve.

For example, under expectations of falling rates, the portfolio manager would want to increase the investment at the long end of the portfolio. The manager would be locking in current high rates, and the market value of the securities would benefit from the declining rates if long-term tertiary reserves must be liquidated. With the opposite interest rate scenario, more funds would be invested in short-term assets. Consequently, knowledge of interest rate theories, the bond theorems, and duration, discussed in Chapters 5 through 8, would play an integral role in the management of liquidity reserves.

Choosing a Strategy.   The choice between a ladder-of-maturities or barbell strategy depends upon the institution's risk/expected return objectives. Risk arises from several sources. The risk of illiquidity is obviously the primary concern. But exposure to interest rate risk under a ladder-of-maturities portfolio is also quite different from that of the barbell. A ladder-of-maturities portfolio, with its regular reinvestment schedule, poses extreme exposure to reinvestment risk, but little or no risk from fluctuations in market value, because securities are held to maturity. In the barbell portfolio, the exposure to market value risk could be severe, especially if the portfolio is heavily invested at the long end of the term structure. As interest rates change, returns could fluctuate significantly if it becomes necessary to liquidate securities. But if managers correctly anticipate interest rate movements, adjusting portfolio maturities in advance of rate changes can allow them to take advantage of favorable price changes. Of course, such regular monitoring of

the portfolio and interest rate forecasts requires a larger commitment of resources.[21]

IMPACT OF REGULATION ON PORTFOLIO MANAGEMENT

Historically, the focus of asset management in depository institutions has been the loan portfolio, but the importance of the securities portfolio is gaining recognition. In addition to liquidity, institutions hope to gain other benefits from their investment in securities. In pursuing these objectives, management's policies must conform to federal and state regulations governing more than just liquidity planning. These regulations, and nonliquidity objectives discussed in subsequent sections of the chapter, have resulted in somewhat different portfolio characteristics among depositories.

Depository Institutions Compared

Figure 12.2 presents recent data on the cash and securities portfolios of depository institutions. The key feature of the pie chart for commercial banks is the importance of Treasury and tax-exempt securities. The latter group consists of debt issues of state, municipal, and county governments. "Other" securities, primarily foreign and corporate bonds, are a small portion of commercial banks' portfolios.

The portfolio of S&Ls is quite different. Federal agency securities are prominent, especially securities issued by government agencies involved in housing finance, such as the Government National Mortgage Association (GNMA). Also important are "other" securi-

---

[21]An early discussion of the split-maturity portfolio (but called spaced maturity) was included in Roland I. Robinson, *The Management of Bank Funds* (New York: McGraw-Hill, 1962), pp. 370-375. Another good source on alternatives for managing liquidity through the investment portfolio is Ronald D. Watson, "Bank Bond Management: The Maturity Dilemma," *Business Review,* Federal Reserve Bank of Philadelphia (March 1972), pp. 23-29. The descriptions of the ladder-of-maturities and barbell portfolios also draw on Watson.

Figure 12.2
Cash and Securities Portfolios of Depository Institutions, Year-End 1985

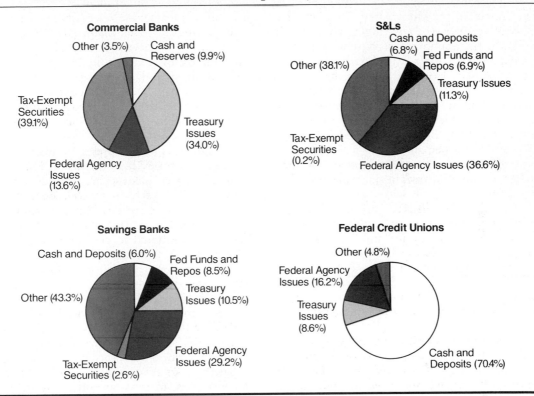

Commercial Banks

Other (3.5%)
Cash and Reserves (9.9%)
Tax-Exempt Securities (39.1%)
Treasury Issues (34.0%)
Federal Agency Issues (13.6%)

S&Ls

Cash and Deposits (6.8%)
Fed Funds and Repos (6.9%)
Other (38.1%)
Treasury Issues (11.3%)
Tax-Exempt Securities (0.2%)
Federal Agency Issues (36.6%)

Savings Banks

Cash and Deposits (6.0%)
Fed Funds and Repos (8.5%)
Treasury Issues (10.5%)
Other (43.3%)
Federal Agency Issues (29.2%)
Tax-Exempt Securities (2.6%)

Federal Credit Unions

Other (4.8%)
Federal Agency Issues (16.2%)
Treasury Issues (8.6%)
Cash and Deposits (70.4%)

Source: Prepared by the authors with data from the Board of Governors of the Federal Reserve System, *Flow of Funds,* QIV/1985; National Credit Union Administration, *1985 Annual Report,* p. 39.

ties, which in the S&L graph are mortgage-related securities, such as mortgage-backed bonds, discussed in more detail in later chapters. Portfolios of savings banks are similar. The major difference is in "other" securities, which for savings banks include corporate stocks and bonds as well as mortgage-related securities. Finally, the cash and securities portfolio of federal credit unions is heavily invested in other depositories, especially in commercial banks and S&Ls. Because of their concentration in insured deposits, CUs' direct holdings of Treasury securities are smaller than those of other depositories.

Regulatory Restrictions on the Investment Portfolio

Regulators have established specific categories of assets in which investment by federally chartered or federally insured institutions is either limited or prohibited entirely. Although they vary across industries, promoting the safety and soundness of depositories is the stated rationale for all these policies. To that end, investment in Treasury and federal agency securities is unrestricted. Portfolio managers are expected to act prudently in their selection of other securities, carefully weighing risk exposure against potentially higher yields.

Restrictions on Commercial Banks.   With a few minor exceptions, national banks may not invest in corporate equity securities. Banks are also limited in the amount they may invest in the debt securities of any single private issuer; generally, the maximum in any one issuer is 10 percent of the bank's capital and surplus. No limits are placed on the amount that may be invested in municipal securities, even though concentration in the debt of a single issuer may pose considerable threat to individual institutions, as holders of Cleveland and New York City bonds learned in the 1970s. The lack of limitation on municipals is considered by some to be a major oversight in bank portfolio regulation.

Recently, Fed officials have urged that restrictions be placed on the ability of federally insured banks to invest in "junk" bonds. These bonds carry ratings of BB or lower, because they are judged to be of above-average default risk. In the 1980s, they have been issued by many companies to finance corporate acquisitions or to repay previous debt obligations.

Restrictions on Thrifts.   Similar regulations apply to the investment portfolios of federally chartered or federally insured thrifts. Federally chartered thrifts may not invest in equity securities at all, except through service corporations. In 1985, however, the Federal Home Loan Bank Board ruled that state-chartered but FSLIC-insured institutions could invest the greater of 10 percent of assets or twice their net worth in equities, and that federal approval could be sought in cases where additional investment was desired.[22] Because many managers believe the ruling gives an advantage to state-chartered institutions, it emphasizes the strategic importance of charter selection.

DIDMCA first permitted federally chartered S&Ls to invest in corporate bonds, although important limitations are imposed. Total investment in bonds, commercial paper, and consumer loans may not exceed 30 percent

of assets. In addition, the average maturity of corporate debt in the portfolio may not exceed six years. Finally, investment in bonds is limited to "investment-grade" securities—bonds carrying ratings no lower than BBB.[23] Some state-chartered thrifts have more flexibility, including the opportunity to invest in the junk bond market, as illustrated in the opening paragraph. Regulators have expressed concern, however, about the involvement of thrifts in this market and have considered prohibitions on their inclusion in portfolios.

Regulators have expressed similar concerns about depositories' investments in reverse repos issued by government securities dealers. In 1984 and 1985, several dealers collapsed. No one could find the securities that had supposedly been pledged as collateral. As a result, many institutions suffered severe losses, and in 1985, Home State Savings in Ohio failed, destroying the system of private deposit insurance in that state. Shortly thereafter, a similar crisis occurred in Maryland.

Although no formal restrictions have been established on investment in reverse repos, the Treasury is responsible for standards to which securities dealers are expected to adhere in arranging repos/reverse repos with customers. Depositories, in turn, are urged by regulators to monitor the capital of any party whose reverse repo they hold, to take possession of the securities involved, and to monitor the value of the collateral as market conditions change.[24]

Restrictions on Credit Unions.   Federal CUs may make unlimited investment in Treasury and agency securities, and in insured accounts at other depositories. In 1984, additional

---

[22]Beth Linnen, "State and Federal Regulators Tangle in a Showdown for Control," *Savings Institutions* 106 (October 1985): 54-60.

[23]U. S. League of Savings Institutions, "Developing an Investment Policy," *Special Management Bulletin,* August 23, 1985.

[24]Shiela S. Tschinkel, "Overview," *Economic Review,* Federal Reserve Bank of Atlanta 70 (September 1985): 5-9; Gary Haberman and Catherine Piche, "Controlling Credit Risk Associated with Repos: Know Your Counterparty," *Economic Review,* Federal Reserve Bank of Atlanta 70 (September 1985): 28-34; "Fed Loses Oversight of Securities Dealers to Treasury," *Savings Institutions* 107 (November 1986): 161-163.

authority was granted for investment in Euro-dollar deposits and bankers acceptances. Federal CUs may also invest in municipal securities, although holdings from any one issuer may not exceed 10 percent of capital plus surplus. Beyond this, federal CUs may invest only in the securities of organizations providing services "associated with the routine operations of credit unions"; even then, the amount invested may not exceed 1 percent of capital plus surplus.[25]

PORTFOLIO MANAGEMENT STRATEGIES

Once liquidity and other regulatory concerns have been addressed, managers must turn their attention to additional objectives for the securities portfolio. As the opening paragraph to the chapter suggests, securities are increasingly viewed as income-producing investments, so their potential contribution to the net interest margin is a consideration in portfolio management. For example, special tax provisions apply to certain types of securities. Bond-trading strategies to increase yields in periods of market disequilibrium have also been developed.

In addition, the securities portfolio can be managed to reduce exposure to interest rate risk. Although it is difficult to immunize the loan portfolio, parts of the securities portfolio can be immunized to shelter part of the institution's balance sheet from reinvestment and market value risk. Finally, securities are vehicles for diversifying the total portfolio. Each of these objectives and strategies is discussed in this section.

Managing for Income: Influence of Tax Policies

As mentioned earlier, federal tax policies are a major influence on portfolio management in depository institutions.

[25]"The Federal Credit Union Act as Amended January 12, 1983" (Washington, DC: National Credit Union Administration), pp. 5-6; National Credit Union Administration, *1984 Annual Report*, pp. 5, 28.

Deductions for Housing-Related Activities.   Federal law allows a tax deduction for additions to bad-debt reserves, for which an institution can qualify only if it meets certain asset composition standards. To be eligible for the deduction, a thrift must invest 60 percent of assets in housing-related investments or Treasury securities. This provision is a strong incentive against large holdings of other securities.

Tax-Exempt Securities.   Other federal tax codes address interest income from investment in state, municipal, and county government securities. This income is not taxed at the federal level, and some states also do not tax interest income earned from investments in securities issued by governmental units within the state. There are tradeoffs, of course. The interest costs of funds raised to purchase most tax-exempt securities are not tax-deductible at the federal level. In addition, as discussed in Chapter 4, stated yields on tax-exempt securities are lower than those on taxable securities, although they are competitive on a tax-adjusted basis. Finally, even some portions of normally tax-exempt income may be taxed to ensure that each business pays at least a minimum level of federal tax.

Interest rate and default risk also must be considered. Most municipals are long-term and expose an institution to considerable interest rate risk. Furthermore, Moody's bond rating service reduced the credit ratings of more issues between 1978 and 1983 than it increased, and fear of greater default risk on municipals has discouraged institutional investment since then.[26]

[26]Allen J. Proctor and Kathleen K. Donahoo, "Commercial Bank Investment in Municipal Securities," *Quarterly Review*, Federal Reserve Bank of New York 8 (Winter 1983-1984): 35. To address the increased concern for default risk, some insurance companies have been willing to insure municipals. In 1985, in fact, about 25 percent of all long-term municipals were insured, compared to only 3 percent in 1980. Insured municipals sell at lower yields than comparable uninsured issues. Elaine Johnson, "Insured Municipal Bonds Offer Investors Slightly Lower Yields but Greater Safety," *The Wall Street Journal*, January 14, 1986.

Figure 12.2 shows that, among depositories, commercial banks hold by far the largest proportion of tax-exempt securities. Because the Tax Reform Act of 1986 eliminated many benefits to banks of holding municipals, most experts predict that banks will reduce their investments in tax-exempt securities in the future. Savings institutions, with the special tax benefits offered for mortgages, have not needed the municipal-bond tax exemption as much and have not been major participants in the market. Credit unions, with their tax-exempt status, have no reason at all to invest in municipals.

Managing for Income: Bond Portfolio "Swaps"

A bond "swap" is the sale of one bond and purchase of another to increase portfolio yield in the short run. Four types of swaps have been devised to take advantage of temporary market disequilibriums.[27] Swaps require a willingness to engage in active management of the bond portfolio.

Substitution Swap. Suppose a manager observes a bond with coupon rate, maturity, quality, and other features identical to one already in the institution's portfolio, but selling at a lower price/higher yield. This disequilibrium cannot persist indefinitely, because demand for the higher-yielding bond will eventually increase its price. But an immediate sale of the higher-priced bond and purchase of the other—a *substitution swap*—may enable a manager to increase portfolio yield in the short run by taking advantage of the expected capital gain on the lower-priced bond.

Intermarket Spread Swap. An *intermarket spread swap* involves two bonds similar in all

respects but one (such as maturity, quality, coupon). Some price/yield differences between bonds differing according to a single feature are expected, and the portfolio manager must track the difference over time and execute a swap if it seems larger than "normal." As in the substitution swap, the manager sells a bond with a relatively high price and buys one with a relatively low price. Presumably, profits will result when the price of the latter increases as the spread returns to its "normal" level.

Rate Anticipation Swap. As discussed in Chapters 7 and 8, bond prices change with interest rate changes, but bonds with different characteristics respond differently to the same rate change. A *rate anticipation swap* is designed to earn short-run profits by altering the portfolio to take advantage of anticipated changes in interest rates. For example, if rates are expected to decrease, shorter-maturity bonds can be swapped for longer-maturity bonds with the same coupon. If interest rate expectations are correct, portfolio value will increase beyond its preswap level. Naturally, because of the hazards of interest rate forecasting, this swap is riskier than swaps that rely only upon the assumption that markets are in temporary disequilibrium.

Pure Yield Pickup Swap. The *pure yield pickup swap* is designed solely to earn a short-term increase in income. A lower-yielding bond is sold and a higher-yielding bond purchased. No attempt is made to forecast interest rates or to track spreads between bond prices/yields in various segments of the market. Instead, this swap implies a willingness to change the fundamental characteristics of the portfolio and to accept the additional risk associated with the higher-yielding bond.

Reducing Exposure to Interest Rate Risk

Financial managers have become increasingly concerned about exposure to interest rate risk, and the securities portfolio is now viewed as a vehicle through which that exposure can be reduced. Two strategies to achieve this objective

[27]The classic discussion of bond swaps is found in Sidney Homer and Martin Liebowitz, *Inside the Yield Book* (New York: Prentice-Hall and the New York Institute of Finance, 1972), pp. 79-108. Other discussions are found in Peter O. Dietz, H. Russell Fogler, and Donald J. Hardy, "The Challenge of Analyzing Bond Portfolio Returns," *Journal of Portfolio Management* 6 (Spring 1980): 53-58; and Calvin M. Boardman and Stephen E. Celec, "Bond Swaps and the Application of Duration," *Business Economics* 15 (September 1980): 49-54.

are matching the maturity of securities with that of selected liabilities and immunizing part of the securities portfolio.

Matching Maturities.   Although they may seem restrictive, many of the federal regulations outlined earlier have been designed to increase the flexibility with which securities portfolios can be managed. Thrift institutions have gained access to many shorter-term loan markets, but the transition to different forms of lending takes time. Thus, through the investment portfolio, they have found a more immediate ability to bring asset maturities in line with their deposit structures. Credit unions, too, have enjoyed increased flexibility. Techniques for managing mismatched asset and liability structures, including the role the securities portfolio can play, are discussed extensively in Chapter 17.

Immunization.   The benefits of using duration to immunize returns against unexpected changes in interest rates have already been introduced. Recall that an immunized investment protects the investor from both reinvestment and market risk arising from an unexpected change in interest rates. Immunization is achieved by setting the duration of the investment equal to the desired holding period. For a depository institution with many sources of funds, immunization involves matching the weighted average duration of assets with the weighted average duration of funds sources.

Parts of the asset portfolio, including securities held as investments, are especially helpful in achieving the institution's desired asset duration. Investment securities offer a wider selection of maturities and yields than are ordinarily available from originating new loans. This is particularly true for thrifts, where long-term mortgages continue to dominate the asset side of many balance sheets. An example of using duration to immunize a balance sheet is presented in Chapter 18.

Diversifying the Portfolio to Reduce Risk

Students of financial management and investments are familiar with the term *diversifica-*

tion, or reducing variability in returns on a portfolio by selecting a variety of assets, rather than concentrating on investments with similar characteristics. Over several decades, in fact, finance theorists have developed a quantitative approach to measuring the benefits of diversification. A major conclusion of the theory of diversification is that the risk of a portfolio is reduced by choosing assets whose returns are not highly correlated with returns on the existing portfolio. Students wishing to review the statistics used to measure and manage portfolio risk through diversification are encouraged to read the appendix to this chapter.

Depository institutions can diversify in many ways—by changing the maturity, the geographic orientation, or simply the types of assets held. These changes can often be accomplished through the securities portfolio. As a depository institution adds securities with expected returns that are less than perfectly correlated with expected returns on existing assets, it reduces its overall exposure to risk. The lower the correlation, the greater the risk reduction.

For example, many small and medium-sized institutions concentrate their lending in a relatively narrow geographic region. As the local economy prospers or declines, so does the performance of the loan portfolio. Among its assets, an institution can easily include securities from issuers in many locations, offsetting the effects of the locally concentrated loan portfolio. Similarly, the institution can use securities to lengthen or shorten the average maturity of the total asset portfolio, depending upon its lending orientation. As long as expected returns on added securities are not perfectly correlated with expected returns on other assets, the overall variability of asset returns should be reduced.

SUMMARY

Liquidity, or the ability to obtain cash with little risk of financial loss, is one of the most important concerns of depository institutions. Sufficient liquidity is necessary for two reasons: to meet regulatory requirements, and to assure uninterrupted operations in the face of unexpected loan demand or deposit withdrawals.

The Federal Reserve Board influences institutional liquidity through reserve requirements on transactions accounts and time deposits. Because deposit levels fluctuate constantly, estimating liquidity needs is a challenge for management. Recently, large institutions have been required to use contemporaneous reserve accounting, accelerating the need for forecasting tools in depository institutions management. In addition to meeting Federal Reserve specifications, some depositories must comply with liquidity requirements set by states or other federal regulators.

Depositories also require liquidity in order to meet unexpected loan demand or deposit withdrawals. To avoid selling assets at a loss when these needs arise, management should maintain liquid assets in excess of those required by regulators. Because liquid assets are often low-yielding, however, liquidity needs must be balanced against profitability. Several strategies are available, varying according to risk/return characteristics and appropriateness for large versus small institutions.

The securities portfolio also fulfills other institutional objectives. The generation of income and risk management are examples of objectives that can be achieved in part through the securities portfolio. Techniques include selecting securities with particular tax features, executing bond swaps, matching maturities, immunizing, and diversifying.

Questions

1. How does the role of depository institutions as financial intermediaries affect their need for liquidity?

2. Explain the difference between lagged reserve accounting and contemporaneous reserve accounting. How have changes in reserve accounting affected liquidity management for depositories? What was the Fed's motivation for making the change in policy?

3. What is the purpose of Federal Reserve reserve requirements for depository institutions? What purposes do the liquidity requirements of the Federal Home Loan Bank Board serve?

4. Explain the functions of the Federal Reserve discount window. Contrast the use of the window to FHLBB advances and to sources of credit union liquidity.

5. In what forms may depository institutions hold required reserves? In general, what options are available for managing their reserve positions?

6. Identify and explain the factors that influence the choice of liquidity management tools by depository institutions.

7. A key problem for depository managers is to estimate accurately their liquidity needs for operations. How is this effort affected by the relative proportion of volatile and nonvolatile funds? By changes in economic conditions and return to depositors on alternative investments?

8. The cash and securities portfolios of depository institutions are often characterized by their relative liquidity. Explain the four categories usually used and identify the types of assets included in each. How does this categorization assist depositories in managing for liquidity and earnings?

9. Why are accurate interest rate forecasts important when using a barbell portfolio investment strategy? How does exposure to interest rate risk differ for the ladder-of-maturities and the barbell portfolio investment strategies? Compare the relative rates of return managers might expect from the two strategies, under upward-sloping, flat, and downward-sloping yield curves.

10. How do tax policies for municipal securities affect investment by commercial banks, thrifts, and credit unions?

11. What is a "junk" bond? Do you think junk bonds are appropriate investments for depositories? Why or why not?

12. What is the purpose of a bond swap? Explain the differences among the four commonly used swap techniques.

13. What is meant by portfolio diversification? What is its purpose in portfolio management? What strategies might a depository use to diversify its total asset portfolio?

Problems

1. You have just been placed in charge of managing your bank's reserve position. It is now the morning of day 43 of the maintenance period. Your immediate responsibility is to set reserve deposit levels for days 43 and 44. You have been given the following information:

Days 1-14	Average vault cash	$ 3,500,000
	Average nontransactions liabilities	200,000,000
Days 29-42	Average transactions balances	550,000,000
Days 31-42	Average reserve balances	70,000,000

   a. Compute the average reserve balances required for the maintenance period (days 31–44). Assume a 3 percent reserve bracket of $36.7 million for transactions balances.
   b. Compute average balances required for the last two days if the carryover privilege is *not* used.
   c. Compute the average balance needed for the final two days of the maintenance period, assuming the bank uses its carryover privilege.

2. One of your major responsibilities at the Desert City National Bank is calculating the Federal Reserve reserve requirements for the bank. Your supervisor has provided the following data for your bank and for another subsidiary of the holding company. Calculate the average daily reserve target balance and the minimum reserve balances required for the final two days of the maintenance period. Assume a 3 percent reserve bracket of $36.7 million for transactions balances.

Bank 1: Forecast for average reserves on transaction deposits—$93,500,000:

Day #	Day	Vault Cash	Nontransactions Liabilities
1	T	$6.5	$340
2	W	6.4	360
3	Th	6.6	360
4	F	6.6	335
5	Sat	6.7	350
6	S	6.7	345
7	M	6.2	345
8	T	6.4	345
9	W	6.3	380
10	Th	6.6	375
11	F	6.2	390
12	Sat	6.1	390
13	S	6.1	350
14	M	6.7	340

Contemporaneous Computation Period				Maintenance Period		
Day #	Day	Transactions Deposits		Day #	Day	Reserve Balances
29	T	$760				
30	W	764				
31	Th	775		31	Th	$100
32	F	776		32	F	94
33	Sat	775		33	Sat	92
34	S	740		34	S	92
35	M	750		35	M	98
36	T	750		36	T	100
37	W	762		37	W	102
38	Th	765		38	Th	98
39	F	820		39	F	95
40	Sat	840		40	Sat	94
41	S	840		41	S	94
42	M	880		42	M	98
				43	T	
				44	W	

Bank 2: Forecast for average reserves on transactions deposits—$45,775,000:

Day #	Day	Vault Cash	Nontransactions Liabilities
1	T	$2.10	$150
2	W	2.40	140
3	Th	2.25	135
4	F	2.30	160
5	Sat	2.40	155
6	S	2.40	155
7	M	2.50	130
8	T	2.20	135
9	W	2.30	150
10	Th	2.30	145
11	F	2.60	160
12	Sat	2.75	135
13	S	2.10	135
14	M	2.10	140

Contemporaneous Computation Period				Maintenance Period		
Day #	Day	Transactions Deposits		Day #	Day	Reserve Balances
29	T	$350				
30	W	355				
31	Th	370		31	Th	$45
32	F	364		32	F	40
33	Sat	340		33	Sat	42
34	S	340		34	S	42
35	M	370		35	M	50
36	T	380		36	T	47
37	W	320		37	W	45

Contemporaneous Computation Period			Maintenance Period		
Day #	Day	Transactions Deposits	Day #	Day	Reserve Balances
38	Th	322	38	Th	41
39	F	335	39	F	41
40	Sat	345	40	Sat	45
41	S	345	41	S	45
42	M	390	42	M	50
			43	T	
			44	W	

3. **a.** West Coast Bank must estimate its liquidity needs over the next four months. Using the following information given for that period, estimate the bank's liquidity surplus or deficit:

Assets	Millions	% Liquid
Cash	$ 266.25	12%
Commercial loans	1,002.27	0
Consumer loans	539.68	0
Investments	1,317.45	55
Other assets	217.15	17
Total	$3,342.80	

Sources of Funds	Millions	% Volatile
Deposits	$2,228.38	10%
Other liabilities	855.79	79
Equity	258.63	0
Total	$3,342.80	

b. Assume that West Coast Bank wants to be prepared for an increase in commercial loan demand of 2 percent and an increase in consumer loan demand of 1 percent over the next four months. Recalculate the bank's liquidity surplus or deficit under these assumptions.

The following problems are based on material presented in Appendix 12A.

4.

Investment A		Investment B	
Probability	Possible Outcome	Probability	Possible Outcome
.15	10%	.10	6%
.20	12	.20	10
.25	16	.30	15
.40	20	.40	22

a. Calculate the expected return and standard deviation for each investment. Which investment is riskier? Why?

b. Calculate the expected return and standard deviation for a two-security portfolio composed of 75 percent investment A and 25 percent investment B. Use correlation coefficients of:

1) $\rho_{ab} = 1$
2) $\rho_{ab} = .4$
3) $\rho_{ab} = -.6$

How does the correlation between the expected returns on the two investments affect the total risk of the portfolio?

5.

Asset X		Asset Y	
Probability	Possible Outcome	Probability	Possible Outcome
.1	0%	.2	0%
.3	3	.6	3
.4	8	.1	10
.2	12	.1	12

a. Calculate the expected value and standard deviation for asset X and asset Y. Which asset is riskier?

b. Calculate the expected value and the standard deviation for an investment plan in which half of the allocated funds are invested in asset X and half of the funds are invested in asset Y. Assume a correlation coefficient between the expected returns on the two assets of .45.

Selected References

Cacy, J. A., and Scott Winningham. "Reserve Requirements under the Depository Institutions Deregulation and Monetary Control Act of 1980." *Economic Review* (Federal Reserve Bank of Kansas City) 65 (September/October 1980): 3–16.

"The Depository Institutions Deregulation and Monetary Control Act of 1980." *Economic Perspectives* (Federal Reserve Bank of Chicago) 4 (September/October 1980): 3–23.

Gilbert, R. Alton. "Lagged Reserve Requirements: Implications for Monetary Control and Bank Reserve Management." *Review* (Federal Reserve Bank of St. Louis) 62 (May 1980): 7–20.

Giroux, Gary. "A Survey of Forecasting Techniques Used by Commercial Banks." *Journal of Bank Research* 11 (Spring 1980): 51–53.

Goodfriend, Marvin, and Monica Hargraves. "A Historic Assessment of the Rationales and Functions of Reserve Requirements." *Economic Review* (Federal Reserve Bank of Richmond) 69 (March/April 1983): 3–21.

Haberman, Gary, and Catherine Piche. "Controlling Credit Risk Associated with Repos: Know Your Counterparty." *Economic Review* (Federal Reserve Bank of Atlanta) 70 (September 1985): 28–34.

Hamdani, Kausar. "CRR and Excess Reserves: An Early Appraisal." *Quarterly Review* (Federal Reserve Bank of New York) 9 (Autumn 1984): 16–23.

Luckett, Dudley G. "Approaches to Bank Liquidity Management." *Economic Review* (Federal Reserve Bank of Kansas City) 65 (March 1980): 11–27.

Mengle, David L. "The Discount Window." *Instruments of the Money Market,* 6th ed. Edited by Timothy Q. Cook and Timothy D. Rowe. Richmond, VA: Federal Reserve Bank of Richmond, 1986.

Proctor, Allen J., and Kathleen K. Donahoo. "Commercial Bank Investment in Municipal Securities." *Quarterly Review* (Federal Reserve Bank of New York) 8 (Winter 1983–1984): 26–37.

Rosenbaum, Mary Susan. "Contemporaneous Reserve Accounting: The New System and Its Implications for Monetary Policy." *Economic Review* (Federal Reserve Bank of Atlanta) 69 (April 1984): 46–57.

Tarhan, Vefa. "Individual Bank Reserve Management." *Economic Perspectives* (Federal Reserve Bank of Chicago) 8 (July/August 1984): 17-23.

Watson, Ronald D. "Bank Bond Management: The Maturity Dilemma." *Business Review* (Federal Reserve Bank of Philadelphia) (March 1972), pp. 23-29.

Woerheide, Walter J. *The Savings and Loan Industry: Current Problems and Possible Solutions.* Westport, CT: Quorum Books, 1984.

Appendix 12A

REDUCING PORTFOLIO RISK THROUGH DIVERSIFICATION

Standard tools of investment management are the statistical measures of **expected value** and **standard deviation.** To calculate the expected value of an investment, one begins with an estimate of the distribution of potential outcomes—the rates of return possible and the probability of occurrence for each. Although realistically such a distribution is continuous, a reasonable approximation results from a finite number of possible outcomes. Suppose a portfolio manager estimates the set of potential outcomes shown in Table 12A.1, and for each one-period yield, r_i, the probability, Pr_i, that it will occur.

The expected value, $E(r)$, is the average of the potential outcomes, weighted by their probability of occurrence. Stated formally, the expected value of a series of possible outcomes is:

(12A.1)

$$E(r) = \sum_{i=1}^{n} r_i \, Pr_i$$

$$= r_1 \, Pr_1 + r_2 \, Pr_2 + \cdots + r_n \, Pr_n$$

As shown in Table 12A.1, for this asset, $E(r) = 8.8\%$.

The investment's risk is the potential variability of its returns. The same data used in measuring expected return are needed to calcu-

late the variance and the standard deviation, which serve as measures of risk because they are statistical measures of variation. The variance is the sum of the squared deviations from the expected value, found as follows:

(12A.2)

$$\sigma_A^2 = \sum_{i=1}^{n} [r_i - E(r)]^2 \, Pr_i$$

$$= [r_1 - E(r)]^2 \, (Pr_1) + \cdots$$

$$+ [r_n - E(r)]^2 \, (Pr_n)$$

The standard deviation is the square root of the variance:

$$\sigma_A = \sqrt{\sigma_A^2}$$

In the example, the variance and standard deviation are 2.126 percent squared, and 14.579 percent, respectively. The standard deviation is more frequently used because it is measured in percentages.

Portfolio Risk, Return, and Diversification

In addition to risk/return measures for a single asset, similar estimates are needed for the portfolio as a whole. The expected return of a port-

---

Table 12A.1
Measuring Risk and Return for a Single Asset (A)

Proposed Investment Asset

Possible Outcomes (r_i)	Probability of Occurrence (Pr_i)
−25%	.1
1	.2
10	.4
18	.2
35	.1

Expected Return

(12A.1) $\displaystyle E(r) = \sum_{i=1}^{n} r_i \, Pr_i$

$= -25(.1) + 1(.2) + 10(.4) + 18(.2) + 35(.1)$

$= 8.8\%$

Variance

(12A.2) $\displaystyle \sigma_A^2 = \sum_{i=1}^{n} [r_i - E(r)]^2 \, Pr_i$

$= (-25 - 8.8)^2 \,(.1) + (1 - 8.8)^2 \,(.2) + (10 - 8.8)^2 \,(.4)$

$+ (18 - 8.8)^2 \,(.2) + (35 - 8.8)^2 \,(.1)$

$= 2.126 \text{ (measured in percent squared)}$

Standard Deviation (Square Root of Variance)

$$\sigma_A = \sqrt{\sigma_A^2}$$

$$= 14.579\%$$

---

folio of securities is the weighted average of the expected rates of return of its components:

(12A.3)

$$E(r_p) = \sum_{i=1}^{n} W_i \, E(r_i)$$

where:

W_i = the proportion of total funds invested in asset i;

$E(r_i)$ = the expected return on asset i.

Suppose the portfolio manager evaluating the asset in Table 12A.1 (designated asset A) has selected another investment (asset B), with estimated one-period return and risk of $E(r_B) = 8.8\%$ and $\sigma_B = 14.579\%$, the same as for asset A. If funds are to be split equally between these two securities, $W_A = W_B = .5$. The expected return on the portfolio, shown in Table 12A.2, is also 8.8 percent.

In addition to the risk of the individual assets, portfolio risk is affected by the correlation, or by the way in which the potential outcomes of the two investments are expected to change in response to similar sources of risk. Portfolio

---

Table 12A.2
Measuring Risk and Return for a Two–Asset Portfolio

The portfolio is composed of two assets, equally weighted, with expected returns and standard deviations as follows:

$$E(r_A) = 8.8\% \qquad \sigma_A = 14.579\%$$

$$E(r_B) = 8.8\% \qquad \sigma_B = 14.579\%$$

$$W_A = W_B = .5$$

Expected Return

(12A.3) $$E(r_p) = \sum_{i=1}^{n} W_i\, E(r_i)$$

$$= (8.8\%)(.5) + (8.8\%)(.5)$$

$$= 8.8\%$$

Variance

(12A.4) $$\sigma_P^2 = W_A^2\, \sigma_A^2 + W_B^2\, \sigma_B^2 + 2\, W_A W_B\, \sigma_A\, \sigma_B\, \rho_{AB}$$

$$= (.5)^2\, (14.579)^2 + (.5)^2\, (14.579)^2 + 2(.5)(.5)(14.579)(14.579)(.35)$$

$$= 1.43 \text{ (measured in percent squared)}$$

Standard Deviation (Square Root of Variance)

$$\sigma_P = 11.978\%$$

---

variability is determined partly by the weighted standard deviations of its components, and partly by the correlation of expected returns on each pair of assets in the portfolio. The equation for the variance of a two-asset portfolio is:

(12A.4)

$$\sigma_P^2 = W_A^2\, \sigma_A^2 + W_B^2\, \sigma_B^2 + 2W_A W_B(\rho_{AB}\sigma_A\sigma_B)$$

where:

ρ_{AB} = correlation coefficient.

The quantity $(\rho_{AB}\, \sigma_A\, \sigma_B)$ is the covariance between assets A and B.

The formula for the variance of an n–asset portfolio is:

(12A.5)

$$\sigma_P^2 = \sum_{i=1}^{n} \sum_{j=1}^{n} W_i\, W_j\, \rho_{ij}\, \sigma_i\, \sigma_j$$

Effect of the Correlation between Assets

The correlation coefficient is a statistical measure with a range of -1 to $+1$. If estimated returns on two assets are uncorrelated, they have a correlation coefficient close to 0 and are expected to exhibit little similarity in response to similar sources of risk. On the other hand, if ρ_{AB} is close to $+1$, expected returns are positively correlated and expected movements are in the same direction and of similar proportions. With ρ_{AB} close to -1, expected move-

---

Table 12A.3
Effect of the Correlation Coefficient on Portfolio Risk

Standard deviations for an equally weighted two-asset portfolio, assuming different correlation coefficients:

ρ_{AB}	σ_P
1.0	14.579%
.6	13.040
.3	11.754
0	10.309
−.3	8.625
−.6	6.520
−1.0	0.000

---

ments are in opposite direction, but of similar proportions.

To examine the impact of correlation on portfolio risk, assume initially that $\rho_{AB} = .35$. The variance of the portfolio, using Equation 12A.4 and the data in Table 12A.2, is 1.43 percent squared, and σ_p is 11.978 percent. It is possible to combine two equally risky assets ($\sigma_A = \sigma_B = 14.579\%$) into a portfolio that has *lower* risk. Thus, diversification can reduce variability in expected return without sacrificing the level.

Portfolio risk is positively related to the correlation coefficient. If the expected returns

of assets A and B had an even lower correlation, the portfolio standard deviation would also be lower. If it were possible to find two assets that were perfectly negatively correlated ($\rho_{AB} = -1$), they could be combined with a particular weighting in a two-asset portfolio that would produce a variance of 0. Table 12A.3 demonstrates changes in portfolio risk as the correlation coefficient for assets A and B varies. Unless they are perfectly positively correlated, in fact, portfolio variance and standard deviation are always less than the risk of the individual assets.

Chapter 13

ASSET MANAGEMENT: COMMERCIAL, AGRICULTURAL, AND INTERNATIONAL LENDING

Never take collateral that eats.

Old banker's saying as quoted in
Forbes (1986)

THE tables have been turned recently for some commercial banks accustomed to dictating loan terms on a "Take it or leave it" basis. For small businesses, "taking it" often meant borrowing and then, as Naval Mehra, a Maryland pub owner recently put it, "just crying the blues about high interest rates." Mehra and two other small business owners joined forces and confronted their local bank, threatening to move their checking accounts if the bank did not provide loans at rates they felt were affordable. The strategy worked, and Mehra was able to refinance a 20 percent loan at 11.5 percent interest, a move he said "made all the difference between making and losing money."[1]

Lending traditionally has been considered the most important and profitable use of funds for depository institutions. Today, although not all depositories face customers as "rebellious"

---

[1]Steven P. Galante, "Companies Join Forces to Get Reduced Rates on Bank Loans," *The Wall Street Journal,* February 10, 1986, p. 17.

as Mehra and his friends, most have found that deregulation and increased competition have changed the way their customers view lending relationships. Nevertheless, lending remains a focal point in the management of depository institutions, and the loan portfolio comprises over half the assets of depositories in general. This chapter initially considers important policy issues in loan portfolio management and continues with applications to commercial, agricultural, and international lending. The next chapter considers consumer and residential mortgage lending.

LOAN PORTFOLIOS OF DEPOSITORY INSTITUTIONS

Depositories offer loans for many purposes and to many types of borrowers. The types of loans in which each industry specializes have similarities and differences.

Commercial Banks

Figure 13.1 provides information on the loan portfolios of all depository institutions as of year-end 1985. Of the total loans outstanding— a volume of almost $1.5 trillion—the largest category for commercial banks was commercial

---

Figure 13.1
Loan Portfolios of Depository Institutions, Year-End 1985

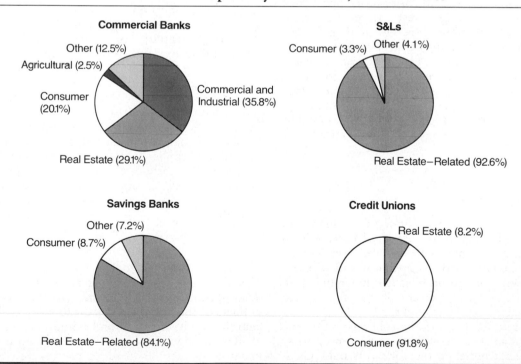

Sources: Prepared by the authors with data from the *Federal Reserve Bulletin* 72 (December 1986); National Council of Savings Institutions, *1986 National Fact Book of Savings Institutions;* and Board of Governors of the Federal Reserve System, *Flow of Funds,* QIV/1985, Table 552.

and industrial (C&I) loans, followed by real estate and consumer loans. Banks do not restrict their mortgage lending to the residential markets, and commercial mortgage loans are included in the real estate category. Thus, the total volume of loans to businesses is actually larger than the C&I figure alone.

Agricultural loans are less than 3 percent of total loans for the banking industry as a whole, but for some banks they represent a much larger proportion. The "Other" loan category includes loans to foreign governments, state and local governments, and other financial institutions. None of these is more than 5 percent of the loan portfolio for the banking industry as a whole, although they, too, are more significant for some banks.

Savings Institutions

For thrifts, the vast majority of lending is real estate-related. S&Ls invest a larger proportion of the loan portfolio in real estate than do savings banks. At savings banks, consumer loans are more important. These differences reflect the relatively recent authorization of consumer and commercial loans at S&Ls. Consumer loans made by both types of thrifts include those to finance educational expenditures, automobiles, and other borrowings repaid on an installment basis.

Credit Unions

Little detail is available about credit union loan portfolios. Data from the Federal Reserve indicate that consumer loans equaled over 90 percent of CUs' portfolios. Almost half of these loans were for automobiles. As shown in Figure 13.1, less than 10 percent of loan funds were invested in real estate credit.

Figure 13.1 shows the continuation of traditional areas of concentration by depositories, despite expanded powers for thrifts and CUs in recent years. Nonetheless, issues in establishing loan policies and procedures span industry lines.

INSTITUTIONAL POLICIES AND OBJECTIVES

In administering the loan portfolio, lenders must address numerous areas, either regularly or infrequently. Although the formality may vary according to the size of the institution and the scope of its operations, every lender establishes lending objectives, reflecting the risk/return preferences of managers and owners through the target net interest margin and its expected variability. Institutional objectives must also meet regulatory requirements. These objectives set the guidelines for evaluating every loan application and identify the lines of authority used in the loan approval process.

Credit policies must be based on a plan for the overall asset portfolio, and managers must set general guidelines for the size of the loan portfolio, its composition, and the maximum acceptable level of default risk. For example, in a commercial bank, decisions must be made about the proportion of loan funds to be invested in C&I loans, the proportion earmarked for agricultural purposes, or the relative level of consumer loans. A thrift institution must decide whether to confine itself to the mortgage markets or to enter the commercial and consumer markets. These decisions influence the way a depository advertises its services, the customers whose loan applications will be given preference, and many other aspects of lending. Major credit policy issues are outlined and discussed in this section. An official credit policy is rarely specific in any one area, but instead reflects the institution's long-term strategic planning.

Size

The first decision to be made is the size of the loan portfolio as a proportion of total assets. It influences the quantity of loan funds available and the emphasis placed on lending in comparison to other investments. For most depository institutions, the standard practice is to view lending as the primary function, although the size of the loan portfolio is not always under the institution's control. Demand for loans may decrease under poor economic conditions. Even when demand is strong, the institution may lack funds to lend in a rapidly growing economy where competition for funds is keen. In addition, regulators look closely at the size of the loan portfolio relative to an institution's net worth, so regulatory standards may influence the choice between expanding the loan portfolio or investing in securities.

Composition

Other important strategic decisions for depository institutions are what type of loan customers to serve and how funds will be allocated across many potential loan categories. One consideration is the institution's deposit structure and its other sources of funds. Their maturities may affect management's loan maturity preferences, and thus the types of loans granted. In addition, the choices an institution makes reflect its operating environment. A farm community may have few business applicants. In a suburb, demand is high for consumer loans and home mortgages. Banks must also decide whether to confine lending to a local geographic area or whether to seek loan applicants from farther away. For many banks, whether to specialize or to diversify is a major strategic choice.[2]

For savings institutions and CUs, the composition of the loan portfolio is a major decision as well, because diversification beyond traditional lending areas requires a significant commitment of resources. Each type of lending requires different areas of expertise, so the movement into new arenas must be preceded by careful planning.[3] Lending strategies have im-

plications for other aspects of thrift financial management as well, because the Garn-St Germain Act allows thrifts to accept commercial demand deposits only from their commercial loan customers. A case analysis on the composition of the loan portfolio is included at the end of the book.

Maturity

Closely tied to the types of loans in the portfolio is the decision about average loan maturity. If mortgages are the majority of an institution's loans, the portfolio maturity will be relatively long. Most nonmortgage commercial loans have initial maturities of five years or less, so an institution heavily oriented toward business lending will have a portfolio with a shorter average maturity. Within those general guidelines, however, managers can exercise much discretion, with important ramifications for overall asset/liability performance.

The relative maturities of an institution's assets and sources of funds influence the stability of the NIM. Rate volatility is not equal for short- and long-term securities, and, except under a flat yield curve, neither are rates. In fact, the need to shorten average asset maturities to bring them closer to liability maturities was an argument used to support DIDMCA provisions allowing broader lending powers for savings institutions.[4]

Managing Default Risk

Every lender faces the possibility that a borrower will default, although the degree of default risk faced is, to a certain extent, under the

---

[2]Some large commercial banks have specialized to an extreme. For example, Bankers Trust several years ago decided to abandon the consumer market entirely and to serve only large business customers. An institution choosing that route is known as a "wholesale" bank. One that attracts few funds from businesses, and does little commercial lending, is often called a "retail" bank. More information about the choice between wholesale and retail strategies is provided in Chapter 15.

[3]A number of articles have addressed the challenges thrifts face as they move into new lending areas. For further discussion of these issues, see Dixie Mills and Guerry

Suggs, "Developing a Commercial Lending Strategy: Key Issues for Savings Institutions," *Federal Home Loan Bank Board Journal* 15 (May/June 1983): 26-31; Douglas Hughes, "Planning Can Cushion the Jump into Commercial Lending," *Savings Institutions* 105 (October 1984): 103-108; and Pat Allen, "Commercial Loans Transform a 'Traditional' Portfolio," *Savings Institutions* 106 (October 1985): 120-126.

[4]Robert Craig West, "The Depository Institutions Deregulation Act of 1980: A Historical Perspective," *Economic Review,* Federal Reserve Bank of Kansas City 67 (February 1982): 10-13.

institution's control. It is determined by the thoroughness with which the financial position of a borrower is analyzed and the standards set for accepting or rejecting loan applicants based on the analysis.

Estimating an Applicant's Default Risk. Standards for evaluating the financial stability of a prospective borrower are reflected in information collected at the time of application and in the subsequent analysis. Credit analysis varies according to the type of loan and the type of borrower. In commercial lending, loan officers and credit analysts must be proficient in interpreting financial statements. For consumer loans, credit bureau reports provide a guide to the likelihood of default.

The complexity of risk assessment varies with the size of the institution, the risk aversion of its owners or managers, and their willingness to devote resources to preliminary screening of applicants. Large institutions often have a credit department responsible for screening financial ratios and cash flows according to pre-established minimums. Final interpretation of the data, however, is the responsibility of the loan officer.

Many institutions establish a risk-rating system used by loan officers to assign each application to a risk category reflecting the probability of default. Such a classification scheme is not foolproof and is not always purely quantitative. In commercial banking, for example, a subjective assessment of an applicant's attitude toward financial obligations is widely recognized as an element in the lending decision.

Establishing Credit Standards. Regardless of how credit risk is estimated, standards for maximum exposure must be established to guide the recommendations of loan officers and the subsequent actions of senior officers. These standards affect both the volume of lending and the variability in earnings. If a depository decides to accept borrowers with relatively poor financial ratings, it will have more qualified applicants and greater opportunities for growth in earnings from the loan portfolio. On the other hand, lower-quality loans have a higher proba-

bility of default. If a lender adopts a policy of greater selectivity, it may lose customers to competing lenders but may avoid high losses. The risk/return tradeoff is once again evident.

ESTABLISHING LOAN TERMS

Equally important to the financial performance of a lender are guidelines governing the terms of individual loans.

Establishing the Base Lending Rate

The size of the loan portfolio as a proportion of total assets suggests that keeping loan rates at appropriate levels is a prerequisite to earning the target NIM and target rate of return on net worth (RONW). *Base lending rates* are established at the institutional level and used as benchmarks for determining specific loan rates. Very good customers may be offered a lower rate, and higher-risk customers are charged a higher rate. But the base sets the boundaries within which the loan officer can exercise discretion.[5]

Adjusting for Net Noninterest Expenses. In Chapter 3, Table 3.1 (see page 54) introduces the relationship between the target RONW and the target NIM. In that table, the unrealistic assumption was made that net noninterest expenses (NIE) were $0, so that the only important expense to be considered in profit planning was interest expense (IE). Given a target RONW and net worth multiplier (TA/NW), the target NIM was determined using Equation 3.4. For the hypothetical institution in that table, with a target after-tax RONW of 18 percent, a net worth multiplier of 14.3, and a tax rate of 34 percent, the target NIM was 1.9 percent.

This NIM will not, however, recover net noninterest expenses (noninterest expenses net-

---

[5]Historically, the base rate at commercial banks was known as the "prime" lending rate. For reasons explained later in the chapter, the terms *base rate* and *prime rate* are no longer always synonymous.

ted against noninterest revenues). In evaluating the total cost of operations, managers must consider salaries, the opportunity cost of holding reserve requirements on transactions deposits, the cost of facilities, computer support and other supplies, in addition to the interest cost of raising funds. Net income is really defined as the after-tax difference between the spread (IR − IE) and net noninterest expenses:

$$NI = [(IR − IE) − NIE] \times (1 − t)$$

This means that Equation 3.2 must be restated as:

(13.1)

$$\frac{IR − IE}{TA} − \frac{NIE}{TA} = \frac{NI}{TA} \times \frac{1}{1 − t}$$

In addition, Equation 3.4 must be restated as:

(13.2)

$$\frac{[IR − IE]}{TA} = \left(\frac{NI}{NW} \times \frac{NW}{TA} \times \frac{1}{1 − t} \right) + \frac{NIE}{TA}$$

Equation 13.2 shows that the target NIM—the left-hand side of the expression—is equal to the desired before-tax RONW, times the reciprocal of the net worth multiplier, plus net noninterest expenses as a proportion of total assets. If, for the hypothetical institution in Table 3.1, NIE averages 1 percent of total assets, the target NIM increases to 2.9 percent.

Calculating the Base Loan Rate. In establishing loan rates, it is important to remember that loans are not the only asset contributing to the target NIM. Suppose the hypothetical institution illustrated in Table 3.1 and reintroduced in Table 13.1 has nonearning assets equal to 10 percent of total assets. In addition, suppose that 30 percent of the institution's total assets are invested in securities, on which the before-tax average rate of return is 10.5 percent. The remaining 60 percent of total assets are invested in loans. The mix of assets, including the fact that some are nonearning, must be considered in planning for the total spread, because differ-

ent spreads will be earned on different categories of assets:

(13.3)

$$IR − IE = \left[\sum_{i=1}^{n} r_i \times A_i \right] − (c \times TL)$$

where:

r_i = the interest rate earned on asset category i;

A_i = total dollar investment in asset category i;

c = average interest cost of financial liabilities; and

TL = total liabilities.

Note that $\sum_{i=1}^{n} r_i \times A_i$ equals total interest revenues (IR) and c × TL equals total interest expense (IE). Equation 13.3 can be used to solve for the base loan rate, r_L.

Table 13.1 notes that the average cost of liabilities is 9 percent, and that liabilities total $93 million. If the target NIM—a calculation based on *total* assets—is 2.9 percent, the necessary spread between interest revenues and the interest cost of liabilities is $2.9 million. Using Equation 13.3, the target spread is expressed in millions as:

$$Spread = [(0\% \times \$10) + (10.5\% \times \$30)$$
$$+ (r_L \times \$60)] − (9\% \times \$93)$$
$$\$2.9 = [\$0 + \$3.15 + (r_L \times \$60)] − \$8.37$$
$$r_L \times \$60 = \$8.12$$
$$r_L = \$8.12/\$60 = 13.53\%$$

Because nonearning assets and securities both contribute to the target NIM at a lower rate than do loans, interest earned on loans must provide a higher than average return for the institution's financial objectives to be achieved. The **pro forma** (projected) income statement at the bottom of Table 13.1 illustrates

Table 13.1
The Base Lending Rate and Meeting Target Rates of Return

I. Balance Sheet and Planning Assumptions

Assets		Liabilities and Net Worth	
Securities	$ 30	Liabilities	$ 93
Loans	60		
Nonearning assets	10	Net worth	7
Total	$100	Total	$100

Return on securities: 10.5%
Return on nonearning assets: 0%
Target NIM: 2.9%
t = 34%
Base loan rate: 13.53% (as calculated in text)

Average cost of liabilities: 9%
Net worth multiplier: 14.3
Target RONW: 18%

II. Pro Forma Income Statement

Interest revenues:
   10.50% × $30 = $3.150
   13.53% × $60 = 8.118
    0.00% × $10 = 0.000
    Total $11.268

Interest expense:
   9.00% × $93 =   (8.370)
Spread $ 2.898

Less net noninterest expenses:
   1.00% × $100 =   (1.000)
Income before taxes $ 1.898
Less income taxes (.34)   (0.645)
Net income $ 1.253

NIM = $2.9/$100 = 2.9%
RONW = $1.253/$7 = 18%

---

this point. The base rate of 13.53 percent is appropriate for customers of average cost and average risk; it is a starting point for loan officers in setting loan terms for individual customers.

Fixed-Rate versus Variable-Rate Lending

In addition to establishing the base rate, in a volatile interest rate environment lenders emphasize whether rates offered should be adjusted as market rates change or be fixed for the term of the loan. Adjustable-rate lending passes the lender's exposure to interest rate risk to the borrower; as the cost of raising funds changes, so does the lender's rate of return. In periods of rising interest rates, depository institutions may emphasize variable-rate loans to protect the level and stability of the NIM. In that case, the base rate is used only to establish the initial interest rate. As with many risk-reduction strategies, however, variable-rate lending limits growth in the NIM, because when interest expense decreases, so do interest revenues. These advantages and disadvantages are explored in detail as specific categories of lending are discussed in this and the next chapter.

Other Loan Terms

Another decision is whether to require a more risky applicant to pledge assets as collateral. As the opening quotation suggests, not all forms of collateral are desirable to the lender. Other terms used either to increase the lender's rate of return or to reduce risk include requiring borrowers to keep a given amount, known as a **compensating balance,** on deposit over the life of the loan; requiring borrowers to apply for credit insurance; and requiring regular principal and interest payments versus issuing a **term loan,** where interest and principal are repaid at maturity. Use of these loan features is at the option of the lender, and their ramifications are explored as each type of loan is discussed.

ADDITIONAL POLICY AREAS

Carefully establishing institutional objectives and setting individual loan terms to fit those objectives are insufficient to ensure a successful lending operation. Control and monitoring of loan procedures also are necessary.

Procedures for Loan Authorization

Loan approval becomes more formal as the size of an institution and its staff grow. If loan officers are also executives of a depository institution, they are directly responsible to the board of directors, owners, and regulators for their decisions. But in larger organizations, the personnel having direct contact with loan applicants are not also the executives, so a review procedure by those who will bear ultimate responsibility must be established. Often, there is a dollar amount below which a loan officer may grant a loan without approval from higher authorities. The maximum amount is positively related to the loan officer's experience and qualifications.

When the maximum loan amount is exceeded, the officer must present all relevant data, along with a recommendation for loan terms, to a higher-ranking loan officer or to a loan committee consisting of the executives of the loan department. Final decisions are reviewed by the board of directors. The review is a control to guard against mismanagement of loan funds and to ensure that management's and/or owners' risk preferences are applied. Because of time constraints, however, the loan officer's analysis and recommendations are given great weight.

Monitoring Loans after Approval

Once a loan is granted, a lender cannot simply forget it. The quality of a loan relies upon the borrower's continued financial stability; if the borrower's financial position is deteriorating, the lender needs to know before the maturity date. In an installment loan, when a regular payment plan is set in advance, deterioration in the borrower's position is evident as soon as an installment payment is missed. Before the situation gets too bad, the lender can contact the borrower.

In a term loan, the lender must take a more active role in checking the borrower's compliance. For a commercial loan, for example, the account officer may require that interim financial statements be provided. Loans assigned a relatively high risk rating at the time of their approval need to be reviewed more frequently than less risky agreements. Early detection of problems may enable the lender to intervene and prevent further deterioration, reducing potential variability in the NIM.

Loan Monitoring and Financial Reporting. Loan monitoring also has important ramifications for financial reporting to the public and to regulatory agencies. As explained in Chapter 11, small institutions identify problem loans and report them in the Allowance for Possible Loan Losses account on their balance sheets. Table 13.2 shows a typical report of a small bank's loss allowance for consumer loans. From the ending balance for the previous year, actual loan losses, called **loan chargeoffs,** are deducted. If any loans previously written off as losses were subsequently collected, they are added back to the allowance. Finally, the allowance is increased by current estimates of anticipated loan losses. Thus, the allowance account is always an estimate of future loan losses, not a record of past losses.

Table 13.2
Calculating the Loan Loss Allowance at Small Banks and Thrifts

	1989 (Thousands)	1988 (Thousands)
Balance at beginning of year	$226	$190
Deductions:		
Loan losses	$386	$283
Less loan recoveries	(100)	(87)
Net loan losses	$286	$196
Additions:		
Consumer credit loss expense	$346	$227
Other additions	34	5
	$380	$232
Balance at end of year	$320	$226

As noted in Chapter 11, large banks (those with assets exceeding $500 million) are prohibited from using the "allowance" method on their balance sheets, and instead account for loan losses by deducting actual chargeoffs as expenses on the income statement each year. This system, arising from the Tax Reform Act of 1986, is being gradually phased in, and existing allowances for loan losses phased out.

Regardless of the accounting method used, estimating future loan losses for planning purposes is of considerable concern to depositories. To estimate losses with a reasonable degree of accuracy, lenders develop procedures to identify when a borrower moves into the "questionable" category. Regulators expect these policies to accomplish their purpose; when they do not, disciplinary actions may be taken. For example, in 1985, First City Bancorp of Texas disclosed that the Comptroller of the Currency had declared its loan-monitoring policies inadequate. The bank was forced to set up special loan review committees as a deterrent against similar shortcomings in the future, and regulators could have taken even more severe actions.[6]

---
[6]"First City Bancorp Discloses that U.S. Calls 3 Banks' Loan Policies Inadequate," *The Wall Street Journal,* March 21, 1985, p. 34.

Delinquent Loans.   Regardless of the care with which loan applications are scrutinized, some borrowers inevitably will be unable or unwilling to meet their repayment schedules. When a borrower is seriously delinquent, management of the loan moves from the loan officer to those responsible for collection. In all cases, collection personnel want to avoid legal action, because it consumes resources and time. For example, a savings institution doesn't really want to foreclose on a mortgage loan; the legal expenses are large, and the institution must sell the repossessed property or maintain it until sold. Lenders will usually work closely with borrowers to set up revised repayment plans, suggest general financial counseling, or provide advice on financial management. Such efforts are often termed *workouts*.

Monitoring collateral can be difficult in some cases. When vehicle loans become delinquent, the lender must move quickly—because the collateral is mobile! As with other aspects of loan management, the more resources committed to the collection effort, the greater the protection against instability in the NIM, but the greater the additions to net noninterest expenses.

Competitive Lending Strategies

The competitive strategy an institution chooses is reflected in many aspects of its lending policy, including the types of customers served, the interest rates charged, other loan terms offered, and the riskiness of approved borrowers. But the competitive strategy affects other activities as well. Depository institutions are increasingly undertaking formal marketing campaigns preceded by extensive research to identify potentially profitable market segments. For example, Wachovia Bank in North Carolina has been recognized as setting a standard for service in the retail banking market through its "personal banking" program; by building on individual relationships with customers, it is strengthening its consumer loan market.[7] An increasing number of institutions are seeking to broaden the geographic area they serve, taking advantage of statewide, regional, or national expansion allowed by state and federal laws.

Recently, a major change from historical practice has occurred as lending officers have been required to undertake "selling" activities. These programs contrast with the traditional idea of waiting for loan customers to come to them. Today, loan officers may research potential customers, visit prospects to explain how the institution's services can meet their needs, and report the results in regular meetings. More aggressive competitive strategies, however, may involve higher expenses and greater risk exposure as the institution moves into markets where it lacks historical experience to serve as a guide.

RECENT TRENDS IN COMMERCIAL LENDING

The remainder of this chapter and the next apply general principles of lending to several types of loans, beginning with commercial loans, a category that actually includes quite a variety of investments. The definition of a commercial loan has important implications for regulatory decisions, as discussed in Chapter 3, because the Bank Holding Company Act defines a commercial bank as one that both accepts demand deposits and makes commercial loans. In applying the law to BHCs, the Fed traditionally defined commercial loans broadly as "all loans to a company or individual, secured or unsecured, other than a loan the proceeds of which are used to acquire property or services used by the borrower for his own personal, family or household purposes, or for charitable purposes." In 1982, the Board expanded this definition to include indirect lending through the purchase of commercial paper, bankers' acceptances, certificates of deposit, and the sale of federal funds.[8] The discussion in this chapter is confined to direct lending.

Because C&I loans are so heavily concentrated in the commercial banking industry, most of the data on C&I loan volume and maturities are limited to that industry. Information is available for other depository institutions, but the detail is not comparable.

Commercial Banks

As would be expected, the volume of commercial lending is highly influenced by general economic conditions. Figure 13.2 tracks commercial lending volume at commercial banks over the period 1978–1986. The top panel indicates that total loans outstanding grew from slightly over $200 billion to about $500 billion over the period, but the bottom illustrates that annualized rates of growth were by no means constant. At times, such as parts of 1980, 1983, and 1985, growth rates in commercial lending were negative; at other times, such as parts of 1984, growth exceeded 30 percent. The shaded periods denote recessions, accompanied by declines in lending volume; the brisk growth in late 1983 and early 1984 reflects economic recovery. Patterns illustrated for this period are typical.

---

[7]"Retail Banking with a Personal Touch," *ABA Banking Journal* 77 (April 1985): 40, 43.

[8]Joseph A. Gagnon, "What Is a Commercial Loan?" *New England Economic Review,* Federal Reserve Bank of Boston (July/August 1983), p. 37.

Figure 13.2
Commercial and Industrial Loan Volume in Commercial Banks[a]

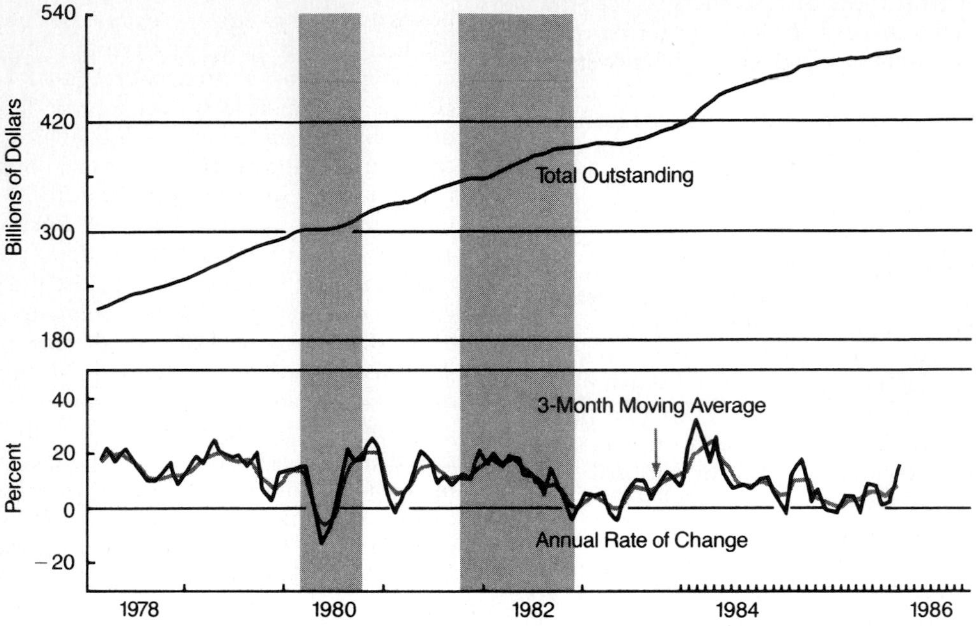

[a]Monthly averages, seasonally adjusted.

Source: Board of Governors of the Federal Reserve System, *Federal Reserve Chart Book,* August 1986, p. 48.

Periodic surveys of commercial lending practices conducted by the Fed indicate that short-term loans are the vast majority of business lending agreements.[9] Table 13.3 tracks the proportions of long- and short-term loans by total dollar volume, and the average maturities of each category, from 1982 through mid-1986. In no period were long-term loans more than 16 percent of the total. The average maturity of short-term loans ranged from 1 to 1.6 months, with maturities of long-term agreements rang-

ing from slightly over 46 to 55.6 months. The maturities reported are for all commercial banks and are weighted by loan size. Thus, because big banks make larger loans, reported data are highly influenced by the practices at the largest institutions. In fact, additional Fed data for this period reveal that short-term commercial loans by small banks had average maturities of two to three months, while those by very large banks averaged under one month.

Savings Institutions

Except for savings banks, which have had commercial lending authority for many years, thrifts do not have a high profile in the market for commercial loans. Data collected through June of 1986 indicate that thrifts have not moved

[9]Surveys are conducted regularly by the Federal Reserve, including the Survey of Terms of Bank Lending and the Senior Loan Officer Opinion Survey of Bank Lending Practices. For a discussion of the results of one set of surveys, see Thomas F. Brady, "Changes in Loan Pricing and Business Lending at Commercial Banks," *Federal Reserve Bulletin* 71 (January 1985): 1-13.

Table 13.3
Maturities of Commercial and Industrial Loans

Quarter	Year	% Short-Term	Average Maturity (Months)	% Long-Term	Average Maturity (Months)
1	1982	89.92%	1.4	10.08%	51.6
2	1982	90.81	1.2	9.19	49.8
3	1982	90.58	1.2	9.42	46.5
4	1982	90.42	1.2	9.58	46.2
1	1983	92.14	1.0	7.86	52.5
2	1983	90.09	1.4	9.91	55.6
3	1983	89.13	1.2	10.87	55.3
4	1983	90.47	1.3	9.53	50.8
1	1984	91.18	1.1	8.82	48.0
2	1984	90.37	1.4	9.63	47.9
3	1984	90.28	1.2	9.72	49.4
4	1984	88.35	1.3	11.65	51.4
1	1985	87.84	1.3	12.16	50.0
2	1985	88.87	1.4	11.13	55.0
3	1985	86.53	1.6	13.47	52.0
4	1985	84.63	1.5	15.37	50.0
1	1986	89.72	1.5	10.28	54.0
2	1986	88.48	1.4	11.52	50.0
3	1986	89.56	1.3	10.44	55.0

Source: Federal Reserve Bulletin, various issues, 1982-1986.

quickly to take advantage of new lending powers, with only 1.7 percent of assets invested in commercial loans. Not even New England savings banks, the largest commercial lenders among thrifts, devote large proportions of their portfolios to business loans. As of year-end 1984, fewer than ten of these institutions had even 10 percent of their assets in commercial loans, and about half made no commercial loans at all. At the same time, however, evidence suggested that among those thrifts making commercial loans, the volume of business was increasing. By the end of 1984, savings banks held 6.6 percent of all commercial loans in New England, compared to only 0.7 percent at the end of 1980.[10]

Factors Influencing Thrift Entry into Commercial Lending. Recent studies of savings banks and S&Ls provide insight into factors influencing their loan portfolio decisions. Researchers have examined how commercial lending strategies are affected by institutional size, market conditions, and experience with commercial customers and nonmortgage consumer lending. Larger thrifts are

---

[10]R. Lamar Brantley, "Portions of the Business Sample Diversification," *Savings Institutions* 108 (February 1987):

131, 133; Robert E. Goudreau, "S&L Use of New Powers: Consumer and Commercial Loan Expansion," *Economic Review,* Federal Reserve Bank of Atlanta 69 (December 1984): 15-33; Janice M. Moulton, "Antitrust Implications of Thrifts' Expanded Commercial Loan Powers," *Business Review,* Federal Reserve Bank of Philadelphia (September/October 1984), pp. 11-21; and Constance Dunham, "Recent Developments in Thrift Commercial Lending," *New England Economic Review,* Federal Reserve Bank of Boston (November/December 1985), pp. 41-48.

more likely to move into the business loan market. A related factor is the degree of expertise the institution's employees have with commercial customers, evidenced by participation in commercial real estate lending, or with non-mortgage consumer lending. The more experience in nonmortgage lending, the more likely the move to commercial lending, because errors in the learning process can be very expensive. To avoid the costly errors of learning the hard way, some thrifts have hired experienced personnel from the banking industry, but unless an entire lending department is purchased, errors from inexperience are unavoidable. Researchers have also found support for the hypothesis that thrifts are more likely to serve the small business market. Finally, if commercial bank services in the community are highly concentrated in a few banks, with the attendant possibility of higher loan rates, thrifts see opportunities to capture a competitive edge.[11]

COMMERCIAL LOAN CREDIT ANALYSIS

Assessing the credit worthiness of a commercial loan applicant involves collecting, analyzing, and interpreting financial and personal data.

The Cs of Credit

Over the years, a framework called the "*Cs of Credit*" has become common for describing the lending decision. At first only three Cs were used: *character, capacity,* and *capital.* Then two more were added: *conditions* and *collateral.* This framework helps the decision maker group information gathered into a small number of categories in order to assess borrower risk.[12]

Perhaps the most difficult C to evaluate is the applicant's character, because the term is supposed to capture many personal qualities, such as integrity—in short, the intention to repay any financial obligations. Information about the individual's involvement in the business community or charitable efforts is used, and particular weight is given to previous credit records. The character rating is certainly the most subjective part of the credit analysis.

Determining capacity relies on financial statements to assess the borrower's ability to repay the loan through income generated by the business.

Capital also refers to the ability to repay, but focuses more on the soundness of financial position and whether the borrower has nonborrowed sources of funds sufficient to withstand a temporary setback.

The effect of potential changes in the level of economic activity—national, local, or both—is the purpose of the conditions category. A business may be doing well at the time of the loan application, but the analyst must consider what could happen to the borrower's financial position as conditions change. This factor is especially important under certain loan terms, such as a variable interest rate. The borrower may be able to service the loan at prevailing interest rates, but might not be able to do so at higher rates, as became painfully evident under the extremely high lending rates in 1980-1982.

The final C, collateral, is self-explanatory; it involves the availability of collateral and the quality (and eating habits) of the assets involved. Commercial lenders have traditionally expressed dislike for collateralized lending, now often called *asset-based lending,* but the practice is becoming more common. Although quality

[11]Constance Dunham and Margaret Guerin-Calvert, "How Quickly Can Thrifts Move into Commercial Lending?" *New England Economic Review,* Federal Reserve Bank of Boston (November/December 1983), pp. 43–54; Christine Pavel and Dave Phillis, "Cautious Play Marks S&L Approach to Commercial Lending," *Economic Perspectives,* Federal Reserve Bank of Chicago 9 (May/June 1985): 18–27; Robert E. Goudreau and Harold D. Ford, "Changing Thrifts: What Makes Them Choose Commercial Lending?" *Economic Review,* Federal Reserve Bank of Atlanta 71 (June/July 1986): 24–39.

[12]The three or five or more Cs of credit are discussed in many sources; three of these sources are Edward G. Gill, *Commercial Lending Basics* (Reston, VA: Reston Publishing Co., 1983), pp. 203–214; Jack R. Crigger, "An Ocean of C's," *Journal of Commercial Bank Lending* 58 (December 1975): 2–8; and Eric N. Compton, "Credit Analysis *Is* Risk Analysis," *The Bankers Magazine* 168 (March/April 1985): 49–54.

of collateral is important, the real hope is that the lender never needs to take possession of the collateral.

Types of Information Required

The evaluation of a loan application is based on information from a number of sources. If the applicant is not a new customer, the loan officer already has a good base from which to work, including the borrower's previous payment record, past financial statements, and personal contacts. For new applicants, the credit analyst-loan officer will need some or all of the following:

- Past financial statements for the firm;
- Personal financial information from the applicant if the firm is not large, with diversified ownership;
- Projections of the future financial position, defined above as *pro forma* statements;
- A credit report;
- Financial performance measures for similar firms as a basis of comparison;
- Personal contact with the potential borrower and a personal visit to the business; and
- Economic projections.

Financial Analysis

Analysis of the applicant's financial position begins with calculating and interpreting standard balance sheet and income statement ratios, but may go beyond that depending upon the size of the loan and the size of the lending institution.

Information Provided by the Borrower. There are, of course, hundreds of financial ratios, but not all are necessary for credit analysis. The more ratios, the more difficult it is to interpret them and to draw conclusions about the borrower's financial standing. In fact, a significant body of research suggests that it is possible to capture all dimensions of financial performance with a relatively small number of measures; the research also indicates that the same ratios should not be used for all industries, be-

cause certain ratios provide more accurate signals for some types of firms than for others.[13]

A recent survey of loan officers at the nation's 100 largest commercial banks attempted to identify the financial ratios considered most useful in analyzing the credit risk of borrowers.[14] Respondents were asked to rank the usefulness of 59 ratios, then to identity which aspect of financial performance they believed each measured best. The three ratios on which there was greatest agreement were the debt/equity and current ratios, and the ratio of cash flow to current maturities of long-term debt. Table 13.4 lists the 15 most significant ratios and the primary area of performance they are used to measure.

Two of the important ratios involve cash flow. The cash position of the borrower and its importance in evaluating loan quality are gaining more attention among analysts. Although cash flow projections are not part of standard financial statements, a lender can request them as part of the loan application. A growing number of analysts believe that cash position provides as much or more insight into the borrower's ability to repay as do traditional accounting earnings measures. The accounting profession itself has emphasized cash flow reporting recently, at least on a historical basis.[15]

External Sources of Information.   A number of other sources of information supplement that provided by the applicant. For example, other creditors of the firm, such as suppliers, may be willing to discuss its payment record. The lender can also purchase a Dun and Bradstreet Business Information Report, which in-

---

[13]A good summary of this research is available in Kung H. Chen and Thomas A. Shimerda, "An Empirical Analysis of Useful Financial Ratios," *Financial Management* 10 (Spring 1981): 51-60. Subsequent support is offered in Michael J. Gombola and J. Edward Ketz, "Financial Ratio Patterns in Retail and Manufacturing Organizations," *Financial Management* 12 (Summer 1983): 45-56.

[14]Charles Gibson, "Financial Ratios as Perceived by Commercial Loan Officers," *Akron Business and Economic Review* 14 (Summer 1983): 23-27.

[15]Financial Accounting Standards Board, "Statement of Cash Flows," Exposure Draft, July 1986.

Table 13.4
Financial Ratios Perceived as Important by Loan Officers

Ratio	Significance Rating	Primary Measure
Debt/equity	8.71	Debt
Current ratio	8.25	Liquidity
Cash flow/current maturities of long-term debt	8.08	Debt
Fixed charge coverage	7.58	Debt
Net profit margin after tax	7.56	Profitability
Times interest earned	7.50	Debt
Net profit margin before tax	7.43	Profitability
Degree of financial leverage	7.33	Debt
Inventory turnover days	7.25	Liquidity
Accounts receivable turnover in days	7.08	Liquidity
Quick ratio	6.79	Liquidity
Cash flow/total debt	6.71	Debt
Return on assets after tax	6.69	Profitability
Accounts receivable turnover times	6.58	Liquidity
Return on equity after tax	6.30	Profitability

Significance:
  0-2   Low Importance
  7-9   High Importance

Source: Charles Gibson, "Financial Ratios As Perceived By Commercial Loan Officers," *Akron Business & Economic Review,* Vol. 14, No. 2, Summer, 1983, pp. 23-27. Reprinted with permission.

cludes D&B's own assessment of a firm's credit worthiness, and other details about its operations, owners, and management.

If the firm has a credit relationship with another commercial lender, information can be requested from that institution. Robert Morris Associates (RMA), the national trade organization for commercial loan officers, has developed a code of ethics to guide the exchange of information among lenders.[16] RMA also publishes *Annual Statement Studies* containing standard performance measures for over 300 lines of business. Other industry average ratios are found in Dun and Bradstreet's *Key Business Ratios,* the *Quarterly Financial Report for U.S. Manufacturing Corporations* (FTC and SEC), *Financial Studies of Small Business* (Financial Research As-

sociates), and the *Almanac of Business and Industrial Ratios* (Prentice-Hall). In all cases, industry averages must be interpreted with care, because an individual loan applicant is likely to have unique characteristics requiring the lending officer's judgment.[17]

Evaluating Risk

Evaluating credit worthiness requires more than financial analysis. Commercial loan officers should learn as much as possible about a business and the way it is managed. Some ex-

---

[16]The Code of Ethics is available from Robert Morris Associates, RMA National Office, 1616 Philadelphia National Bank Building, Philadelphia, PA 19107.

[17]There are literally hundreds of sources of information on interpreting and using financial ratios and industry averages. Two comprehensive treatments are George Foster, *Financial Statement Analysis* (Englewood Cliffs, NJ: Prentice-Hall, 1978); and Robert C. Higgins, *Analysis for Financial Management* (Homewood, IL: Richard D. Irwin, 1984).

perts suggest that good risk analysis asks, "What could go wrong?" and investigates all aspects of the business in an attempt to find out. Careful investigation serves another purpose as well. The more complete and accurate the information collected on a loan, the better the lender's position when regulatory examiners review the institution's loan portfolio. Maintaining accurate records, known as **loan documentation,** is important when examiners are assessing the quality of outstanding loans.

After a lending officer has tapped available information sources, the hardest task is ahead—organizing the data, rating the applicant on each dimension of the institution's risk-rating system, and recommending approval or denial. Some lenders use quantitative credit-scoring models to integrate information from a variety of sources. Data on an applicant are weighted according to predetermined standards, and a score for credit worthiness is calculated. Applicants falling below a predetermined minimum acceptable score are rejected.[18] A credit-scoring model is illustrated in Chapter 14.

If the loan is approved, the risk category to which the borrower is assigned has important ramifications for other aspects of the lending decision, including the interest rate, whether collateral is required, and whether financial standards such as minimum working capital ratios are imposed on the firm over the life of the loan. A case analysis on evaluating a commercial loan application is included at the end of the book.

INTEREST RATES ON COMMERCIAL LOANS

Commercial loan officers can tailor the terms of a loan to fit the customer's needs and those of the lending institution. Among the most important, of course, is the interest rate. In recent

years, public attention has focused on commercial loan interest rates, and the **prime rate** has become a controversial subject. For reasons explained later, it is now virtually impossible to provide a precise definition of the phrase *prime rate*. Historically, it was used to identify the interest rate charged on short-term loans to a bank's most credit-worthy commercial customers. All other borrowers, businesses or individuals, could expect to pay more. These simple rules no longer apply.

A Historical Look at the Prime

The idea of the prime was born in the depressed economy of the 1930s, when loan demand was so low that commercial lending rates approached 0 percent. The prime was introduced to establish a floor below which rates would not be allowed to fall. Although the prime was an administered, not a market-determined, rate until the early 1970s, regulators and legislators viewed it as an economic indicator of business activity.

As financial managers in large corporations became more sophisticated, however, they found other sources of short-term credit. Many turned to the commercial paper market or even to overseas sources of funds. Figure 13.3 suggests why: Before 1970, the commercial paper rate was usually lower than the prime. In addition, the commercial paper rate—which is market-determined, not administered—rose and fell with economic conditions, while the prime remained unchanged. The flight of large business borrowers from commercial banks to money markets had begun.

In response, most **money center banks**—large banks located in metropolitan financial centers such as New York, Chicago, Los Angeles, and San Francisco—formally began to link their prime rates to the commercial paper rate. This linkage is evident in Figure 13.3 by the early 1970s. But the flight by large borrowers to other credit markets accelerated, spurred by the convenience, flexibility, and lower administrative costs in those markets. Because linking the prime to money market rates had failed to serve its purpose, most large banks had

---

[18]Most credit-scoring models used in commercial lending stem from the work of Edward I. Altman, "Financial Ratios, Discriminant Analysis, and the Prediction of Corporate Bankruptcy," *Journal of Finance* 23 (September 1968): 589–609.

Figure 13.3
The Prime Rate and the Commercial Paper Rate

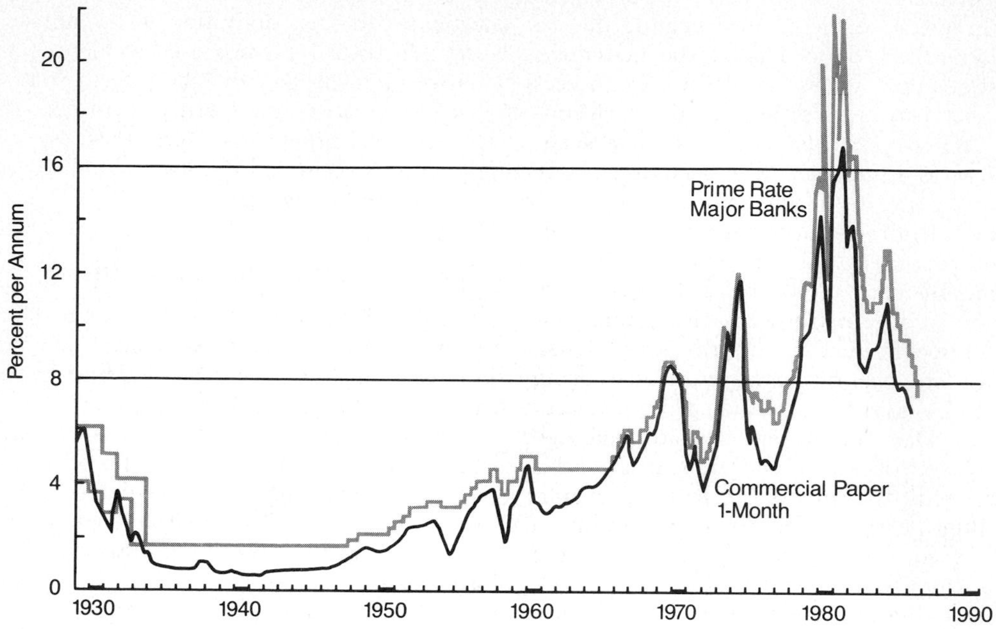

Source: Board of Governors of the Federal Reserve System, *1986 Historical Chart Book,* p. 99.

discontinued this practice by 1980, returning the prime to its administered status.

Today, money center banks tend to keep their prime rates closely in line with one another. The prime at smaller regional and community banks may be quite different, because their access to money markets is limited and their operating characteristics are different. The prime is, therefore, an administered rate that is also sensitive to market conditions.

Development of the "Two-Tiered" Market

In place of a market-determined prime as the basis for interest charges to preferred customers, large banks use the practice of *"below-prime" pricing*—lending at rates below the announced prime rate. These loan rates are tied to

federal funds or negotiable CD rates, that is, to a bank's *marginal* cost of funds. Data from the Fed's quarterly surveys on bank lending, reproduced in Table 13.5, indicate how widespread below-prime pricing has become at large banks, normally exceeding 80 percent of the dollar volume of all short-term loans.

Smaller banks use this pricing approach less frequently. An important implication of these data is that below-prime loans are concentrated in a few banks and are available primarily to large borrowers whose credit ratings are strong enough to give them access to the commercial paper market. Loans to those in poorer financial condition, or to smaller businesses (concentrated at smaller institutions), are still priced at or above the prime rate. Thus, there are now two distinct pricing strategies used for two distinct markets.

Table 13.5
Percentage[a] of Short-Term C&I Loans Made at Rates below Prime by Commercial Banks

Quarter	Year	48 Large Banks	Other Banks
3	1982	91.0%	38.0%
4	1982	92.2	40.4
1	1983	93.7	44.7
2	1983	89.2	43.6
3	1983	72.0	40.7
4	1983	89.0	46.0
1	1984	88.9	42.7
2	1984	88.2	52.2
3	1984	89.6	48.2
4	1984	94.0	55.6
1	1985	88.0	51.1
2	1985	86.1	44.4
3	1985	85.6	51.7
4	1985	81.2	49.1
1	1986	85.8	47.2
2	1986	84.7	54.6
3	1986	81.5	55.7

[a]Dollar volume of below-prime loans as a proportion of the total dollar volume of short-term loans.

Source: Federal Reserve Bulletin, various issues, 1982-1986.

What, Then, *Is* the Prime?

The prime retains importance in commercial lending, although its meaning as the rate available to the best commercial customers no longer holds. The practice of below-prime pricing initially provoked a strong reaction from borrowers who were not getting preferred treatment, beginning in 1980 when a suit was filed against the First National Bank of Atlanta by a small business customer.[19] Litigation against many other banks has followed. As a result, institutions have redefined the prime—or perhaps, more accurately, have given it a "nondefinition." For example, Morgan Guaranty Trust announced, "The bank's prime shall mean the rate of interest publicly announced by banks, and the definition of the prime has been carefully re-evaluated. In March 1984, First Atlanta proposed a settlement to avoid the cost of further litigation. Under that settlement, all plaintiffs were given the opportunity to negotiate loans at preferable rates.

For more discussion, see "The Prime Is Anything but Prime," *Time* May 18, 1981, p. 165; Susan Harrigan, "Suit Attacking Prime-Rate Practice Could Trigger Legal Assault on Banks," *The Wall Street Journal,* November 7, 1980; Tom Birsky, "A Look at Lessons in 'Kleiner v. First Atlanta,'" *ABA Banking Journal* 76 (June 1984): 59-62; Gerald D. Fischer, "The Prime Rate Controversy: There Is Light at the End of the Tunnel," *Journal of Commercial Bank Lending* 67 (November 1984): 13-22.

[19]The customer had borrowed from the bank at a rate 1 percent over prime. But the "prime" was identified in the loan contract as the "rate available to the bank's best commercial customers." When the news media reported that the bank routinely offered large commercial customers loans at rates below prime, the eventual litigant, Jackie Kleiner, requested that his rate be lowered also. When First Atlanta refused, he sued. In the years that followed, more than 40 suits were filed against other commercial

the bank in New York from time to time as the prime rate," a definition described by *Time* magazine as "sounding as if it were drafted by committee."

At many institutions, the terms *base rate* or *reference rate* are replacing the phrase *prime rate* as the basis for commercial loan pricing. In a single institution, there may be a reference rate for one category of customer and another reference rate for another category. As noted earlier, for below-prime loans, the reference rate is often tied to the marginal cost of funds to the bank. As an alternative, below-prime loans may have rates tied to **LIBOR,** an acronym for the "London Interbank Offered Rate." LIBOR is a European market rate, used when European banks negotiate loan agreements. Large borrowers, with access to funds in the international as well as domestic markets, at times may prefer to have the market-determined LIBOR as the reference rate for their loans, rather than the administered prime or a domestic market rate.

The reference rate for smaller customers may be the bank's announced prime plus a risk premium. Although researchers disagree about exactly how prime rates are set today, many experts believe that rates designated as "prime" reflect the *average* cost of funds to the lender. Because it reflects the average, not the marginal, cost of funds, the prime is more stable than rates to which below-prime loans are tied. This characteristic benefits small borrowers who may be unable to bear the risk associated with highly volatile interest costs. In addition, it benefits lenders who avoid the administrative costs of frequent rate changes and can maintain higher loan yields for a longer period of time when market rates begin to fall.[20]

Variable-Rate Commercial Lending

The previous discussion of below-prime pricing implies that another recent trend in C&I lending is variable- or *floating-rate loans.* The decision to offer a floating rate is influenced by the maturity of the loan and expectations about interest rate movements until maturity. The tendency toward variable-rate lending reflects deregulation of interest rates on deposits, with subsequent attempts by lenders to protect their spread.

Given the uncertainty about changes in interest rates over a loan period, many borrowers prefer fixed-rate loans. In fact, rapid growth in financial futures trading brought expectations that lenders would avoid adverse customer reaction by hedging in the futures market rather than transferring interest rate risk to borrowers. If, for example, deposit costs are expected to rise, lenders can make variable-rate loans, or they can offer fixed-rate loans and hedge their interest costs by selling futures contracts.[21] But in a 1984 Fed survey, responding banks reported that availability of futures hedges did not increase their willingness to make fixed-rate loans. They still preferred to hedge against rising rates with variable-rate loans.[22]

The survey results indicated another aspect of interest rate risk management in which banks did take advantage of futures hedges. Borrowers who plan their financing needs well in advance may negotiate with a lender weeks or months before they actually plan to borrow. Those negotiations often include the interest rate to be

[20]Research on determinants and use of the prime includes Myron B. Slovin and Marie Elizabeth Sushka, "A Model of the Commercial Loan Rate," *Journal of Finance* 38 (December 1983): 1,583-1,596; Michael A. Goldberg, "The Sensitivity of the Prime Rate to Money Market Conditions," *Journal of Financial Research* 7 (Winter 1984): 269-280; George Benston, "Interest on Deposits and Survival of Chartered Depository Institutions," *Economic Review,* Federal Reserve Bank of Atlanta 69 (October 1984): 42-56; and Thomas F. Brady, "The Role of the Prime Rate in the Pricing of Business Loans by Commercial Banks, 1977-1984," Board of Governors of the Federal Reserve System, Staff Study No. 146, November 1985.

[21]An interesting approach has been proposed for allocating interest rate risk between borrower and lender. A commercial lender could offer a floating-rate loan indexed to a market rate on which interest rate futures were traded; the ability to trade in futures contracts would allow the borrower to hedge the uncertainty of future interest costs. By using an index such as the T-bill rate, the lender would not be forcing the borrower to use a cross-hedge; in return, the depository institution would avoid the costs and regulatory restrictions associated with the futures markets. The resulting arrangement has been called a "synthetic" fixed-rate loan. See Oliver Abel IV, "Fixed-Rate Loans Using Variable-Rate Funds—A New Lending Instrument," *Journal of Commercial Bank Lending* 65 (August 1983): 36-43.

[22]Brady, "Changes in Loan Pricing and Business Lending," pp. 12-13.

charged, a fact borrowers need to know in order to complete other financial planning. For the lender, of course, committing to an interest rate before knowing the cost of funds is risky. For competitive reasons, however, about two-thirds of the large banks in the Fed's survey were willing to make *forward commitments,* and 40 percent of them indicated they hedged their resulting interest rate risk in the futures markets.[23]

Setting the Stated Rate on a Commercial Loan

For loan rates tied to an institution's base rate, the starting point on an individual loan is the calculation of the base rate from Equation 13.3. Adjustments are made to that base rate to reflect the condition of each borrower. A borrower with higher than average default risk would have a premium added. This system is commonly known as "base plus" pricing, or "prime plus" pricing when the institution's prime is the base. Some institutions use "prime times" pricing, determining the loan rate as the product, rather than the sum, of the base or prime rate and a risk adjustment. For example, a risky borrower might be quoted a rate of $1\frac{1}{2}$ times prime.

COMMERCIAL LENDING: NONINTEREST TERMS AND CONDITIONS

Commercial lenders use more than the interest rate to determine the effective yield on loans. A term commonly used to describe the evaluation of the total institutional relationship with a loan customer is *customer profitability analysis.* It involves examining the funds received from and the nonlending services provided to a customer, as well as a specific loan application. For example, a customer voluntarily keeping large demand deposit balances is a valuable one, because no explicit interest is paid on those balances. Customers using the institution's cash management services or those whose pension fund bal-

ances are managed by the bank's trust department are also valuable. This reasoning suggests that lenders should consider these factors in setting noninterest loan terms and conditions, the most common of which are compensating balances, commitments and commitment fees, discounting, and collateral.

Compensating Balances

A *compensating-balance requirement* obligates a borrower to maintain a stated minimum deposit at the lending institution, normally a demand deposit account. Because the borrower earns nothing on those compensating balances, the effective cost of the loan and the effective return to the lender are increased. The lender reduces the variability of the institution's deposits, and has guaranteed access to inexpensive funds. Compensating balances also reduce the lender's risk exposure, because, should the borrower default, the funds on deposit may be applicable against the liability to the lender.

Some recent analyses have suggested that the compensating-balance requirement is becoming less widespread. A 1985 survey of lending officers at the 400 largest U.S. banks, however, indicates these reports are premature. Almost all respondents (97.3 percent) said their institutions imposed compensating balances on some borrowers, and only 13.9 percent indicated that the importance of these balances had decreased over the preceding five years. Usually, compensating balances are set at 10 to 20 percent of the credit agreement and held in demand deposit accounts. Some institutions permit the use of low-interest time deposits for some of these balances, to avoid reserve requirements against demand deposits and to increase the profitability of the total loan agreement.[24]

Lines of Credit and Commitments

Lines of credit and *commitments* are agreements by the lender to extend funds to the borrower over some prearranged time period.

---

[23]Ibid.

[24]Thomas A. Ulrich, "Are Compensating Balance Practices Declining?" *Magazine of Bank Administration* 61 (January 1985): 48–52.

Because lines and commitments give valuable flexibility to the borrower, they are very popular. The difference between the two is based on the formality of the agreement. In a line of credit, a lender agrees to stand ready to quote a price for a fixed-rate loan in an amount and maturity requested by the borrower. Neither the loan rate nor the amount is agreed upon in advance, and, if a loan request is made, the rate is influenced by current market conditions. Should loan demand be high at the time of a request, the lender can ration credit by quoting a high rate to less-valued customers.

A commitment is more formal, because the maximum loan amount and the spread over the reference or base rate are agreed upon in advance. The customer can, over the credit period, choose to borrow all, some, or none of the authorized funds. When funds are borrowed, they are said to be "taken down." The terms of a commitment usually require the borrower to pay a *commitment fee* based on any amount of unused credit over the life of the agreement, and to pay interest on funds actually taken down. The fee compensates the lender for the additional complications in liquidity management produced by the agreement and is analogous to an insurance premium for the borrower. Recent data indicate that large borrowers are quite willing to pay the premium; about 70 percent of short-term commercial loans in excess of $500,000 were made as a result of a prior commitment by the lender.[25]

The most common type of commitment is a *revolving commitment,* guaranteeing that funds can be borrowed, repaid, and borrowed again over an extended period, perhaps as long as three years. The interest rate, negotiated in advance, may be fixed, or it may be pegged to a reference rate such as the prime or a market rate. The lender assumes considerable risk in a guarantee of this type, because of the potential financial deterioration of the borrower over the period, so the commitment fee will be higher than arrangements giving the lender more flexibility.

It is not uncommon for commitments to require a compensating balance in addition to the commitment fee. Both conditions increase the lender's returns, and the borrower's costs: The fee income supplements interest revenues, and the guaranteed deposit funds reduce the amount the lender must raise from other sources.

Effect of Commitment Fees Illustrated. An example of the combined effect of interest and noninterest terms on the lender's total return from a loan commitment is provided in Table 13.6.[26] The base rate plus the appropriate risk premium is 11.5 percent. A commitment fee of 0.25 percent of the credit agreement is imposed, along with compensating balances of 8 percent on the entire commitment and an additional 4 percent on funds actually borrowed. To estimate the effective rate of return on this agreement, the lending institution must project what portion of the line will actually be taken down, on average, over the commitment period. The assumption here is that the borrower will use only 60 percent of the $2 million commitment over the next one-year period.

The commitment fee of 0.25 percent will be paid on $800,000 (the 40 percent of the commitment expected to be unused), and the interest rate of 11.5 percent will be paid on the portion taken down, or $1,200,000. The lender earns total interest and fee revenues of $140,000. Net funds extended, however, are less than $1,200,000, because of compensating balances in demand deposit accounts. After adjusting for a 12 percent marginal reserve requirement, the borrower is providing $183,040 for use by the lender, funds that do not have to be raised from other sources. The depository institution is investing only $1,016,960, and the expected yield is 13.77 percent. The lending institution also incurs implicit costs not included here, such as additional uncertainty about the timing and quantity of funds demanded. No one knows when, or in what quantity, the borrower will actually request the committed funds.

[25]Mitchell Berlin, "Loan Commitments: Insurance Contracts in a Risky World," *Business Review,* Federal Reserve Bank of Philadelphia (May/June 1986), pp. 3-12.

[26]This example draws on a presentation in John R. Brick, "Pricing Commercial Loans," *Journal of Commercial Bank Lending* 66 (January 1984): 49-52.

Table 13.6
Effect of Noninterest Terms on the Lender's Expected Return

Stated interest rate	11.5% (base rate plus risk premium)
Commitment fee	0.25% on unused portion of the commitment
Term	1 year
Compensating balances	8% of commitment plus 4% of borrowed funds
Estimated average loan balance	60% of commitment
Maximum line of credit	$2,000,000

Loan Interest and Noninterest Revenues

Interest [$2,000,000(0.6)(0.115)]		$138,000
Fees [$2,000,000(0.4)(0.0025)]		2,000
Total revenues		$140,000

Net Funds Invested

Average loan balance		$1,200,000
Portion offset by compensating demand deposit balances:		
$2,000,000(0.08)	$(160,000)	
$1,200,000(0.04)	(48,000)	
Deduct reserve requirements [12% × ($160,000 + $48,000)]	24,960	
Total offsetting funds		(183,040)
Net invested funds		$1,016,960

Total Expected Return

$$\frac{\text{Interest and Noninterest Revenues}}{\text{Net Invested Funds}} = \frac{\$140,000}{\$1,016,960} = 13.77\%$$

Discounting

A lending practice that also increases the return to the lender beyond the stated interest rate is discounting. A discounted loan, illustrated in Chapter 4, is one in which interest is paid at the beginning of the loan period; that is, interest is deducted before loan funds are made available to the borrower. Because the lender never commits funds equal to the entire face amount of the loan, the discounted arrangement increases the lender's yield and the borrower's cost.

Prepayment Penalties

The development of a two-tiered market for commercial lending has produced additional contrasts between prime-based lending and loans set at lower market-based rates. Below-prime loans sometimes allow prepayment only with a substantial penalty, and require the borrower to take the funds in one lump sum, rather than allowing the flexibility of taking down the approved amount gradually. Instead, the borrower pays interest on the entire loan amount for the entire loan period. This is one way banks compensate for the relatively low interest rates they charge on below-prime loans.

Requiring Collateral

Traditionally, commercial lenders in depository institutions have preferred to make unsecured loans against which the borrower pledges no assets. Asset-based lending was left to commercial finance companies. As the largest commercial borrowers have turned to other sources of credit, depositories wishing to remain competitive and profitable in the current lending environment are offering secured financing to their commercial customers in increasing numbers. By requiring collateral, a lender can service customers who would ordinarily be considered too risky. But collateral cannot be considered a sufficient condition for lending to just any customer. The institution does not want to be forced to take possession of the borrower's assets, and credit analysis is just as important—if not more so—for a secured loan agreement as for an unsecured one.

Asset-based lending adds several important dimensions to loan analysis:

1. Determining the value of the assets to be pledged as collateral;

2. Meeting all legal requirements for securing those assets; and

3. Monitoring the condition of the collateral during the loan period.

Assets pledged in C&I loan agreements are usually tangible inventory or financial assets such as accounts receivable. The legal agreement assigning the assets as collateral is called the *security agreement.* The Uniform Commercial Code, a body of law adopted individually by states but containing many common provisions across states, establishes guidelines under which these agreements are drawn.

A *floating lien* is the most general type of security agreement; it gives the lender recourse to the borrower's entire inventory, even those portions acquired after the loan is made. *Warehouse receipts* place the specific inventory items assigned as collateral under the control of a third party, and the goods are often physically transferred to a bonded public warehouse for safekeeping. *Floor planning* allows the borrower to retain possession of the collateral; it is an agreement often used to finance expensive retail items such as major appliances or heavy equipment that can be distinguished by serial number or description.[27]

In the case of accounts receivable financing, the collateral may be either pledged or actually sold to the lender. The latter arrangement is called *factoring.* Whether pledged or factored, the loan amount is always less than the face value of the receivables to allow for potential default.

Loan Participations

A *loan participation* is an arrangement by two or more lenders to share a loan in some agreed-upon proportion. A lead institution initiates the loan agreement and usually has most of the contacts with the borrower. Participations are often necessary in large loans because of the limitations placed upon the amount a commercial bank may loan to a single borrower, limitations established as a percentage of the depository's capital.[28] Participations not only allow the lead institution to share responsibility for providing the funds, they also allow the leader to share the risk.

Loan participations are a good way for smaller institutions to increase the size of their loan portfolios, especially if they lack ready access to a business community large enough to support a direct lending program. Such agreements also allow a lender to diversify geographically. But they can lead to severe problems, especially if the participants do not make an active effort to perform their own credit analysis. Publicity recently surrounded the heavy losses incurred by Continental Illinois, Chase Manhattan, and other commercial lenders on loan participations with Penn Square Bank of Oklahoma City, which failed in 1982 when most of its loans to energy-related companies went into default.

---

[27]A more detailed discussion of terms used in asset-based lending is provided in Gill, *Commercial Lending Basics,* pp. 58-62.

[28]For commercial banks with federal charters, these limitations were revised in the Garn-St Germain Act of 1982. A bank may lend to one borrower an unsecured amount not to exceed 15 percent of capital and surplus. If "readily marketable collateral" is pledged as security, the limit rises to 25 percent of capital and surplus. The FHLBB and FSLIC have applied similar rules to commercial lending at federally insured thrifts. For more information, see Gillian Garcia et al., "The Garn-St Germain Depository Institutions Act of 1982," *Economic Perspectives,* Federal Reserve Bank of Chicago 7 (March/April 1983): 3-31; Federal Home Loan Bank Board Memorandum No. T-73a, "Loans to One Borrower," January 1, 1985.

Loan Monitoring and Review

Despite even the best credit analysis and loan policies, problems occur. Procedures for loan review are designed to identify problems early enough to circumvent the need for legal action later. As previously noted, many lending institutions assign a special group of personnel to the effort of avoiding default, a procedure referred to as workout. Workout specialists know that most of the financial problems of borrowers are traced to mismanagement, arising from inadequate training and experience or perhaps even fraud.

Problems are accelerated by the state of the local or national economy, or the condition of a particular industry, such as the effect of declining oil prices on energy-related industries throughout the 1980s. Similarly, overbuilding of commercial properties in many of the nation's largest cities has posed severe problems for thrifts who lent to the developers of these properties. Unfortunately for lenders, even secured loans provide little protection under those conditions, because the property obtained upon default has usually declined in value.[29]

MANAGEMENT OF AGRICULTURAL LOANS

Agricultural loans are really just a special category of commercial lending. As a result, credit analysis and other aspects of the loan decision are much the same for a farm loan as for other business loans. Important issues, however, are the special terms under which agricultural loans are made, the role of federal farm policies, and

the risk exposure of lenders whose loan portfolios are dominated by "ag" loans. Recent economic difficulties in the farm sector have generated increased concern about the stability of so-called "ag banks," in which agricultural lending is a major activity.

Trends in Agricultural Lending

Recently, observers have widely recognized the poor financial condition and even poorer prospects of the farming sector. Farmers had used debt financing, secured by land, aggressively in the 1970s, but the strategy backfired in the 1980s. As seen in Figure 13.4, in the early 1970s, farm debt was about three times annual farm income; by 1984, debt was eight times larger. In the early 1980s, the volume of farm exports declined drastically because of competition from foreign producers and the relative expensiveness of American products. Huge surpluses from record-setting harvests dropped prices domestically, leading to a decline in land values and producing severe repercussions for agricultural lenders with loans secured by farmland.

The impact of these problems on depository institutions as a whole must be put into perspective. Over half of all farm lending is done by federal agencies, such as the Federal Land Bank and the Farmers Home Administration. Nationwide, commercial banks held about 23 percent of the dollar volume of farm loans at the end of 1985, and agricultural loans were less than 5 percent of total commercial loans outstanding. Furthermore, Fed statistics indicate that the financial problems of farmers are not universal. In fact, farmers in serious financial stress in 1984 held only about 15 percent of all farm assets; this group, however, held about one-half of all farm debt.[30]

---

[29]For some recent examples of experiences with problem loans, see G. Christian Hill, "Smaller Banks Have Difficulty Coping with Increasing Number of Bad Loans," *The Wall Street Journal,* February 5, 1985, p. 4; Matt Moffett and Bryan Burrough, "Texas Banks Are Battered Again on Their Oil, Real Estate Loans," *The Wall Street Journal,* March 25, 1985, p. 4; Linda Sandler and Daniel Hertzberg, "Foreclosures Take Banks to Uncharted Territory of Racehorses, Gold Mines and a Golfing Resort," *The Wall Street Journal,* March 14, 1985, p. 4; Monica Langley, "Many Thrifts Ordered to Raise Reserves for Any Commercial-Realty Loan Losses," *The Wall Street Journal,* October 1, 1985.

[30]Gary L. Benjamin, "The Financial Stress in Agriculture," *Economic Perspectives,* Federal Reserve Bank of Chicago 9 (November/December 1985): 3-16; George M. Gregorash and James Morrison, "Lean Years in Agricultural Banking," *Economic Perspectives,* Federal Reserve Bank of Chicago 9 (November/December 1985): 17-21; "Agricultural Conditions and the Prospects for Farm Banks," *Banking and Economic Review,* Federal Deposit Insurance Corp. 4 (March 1986): 3-10.

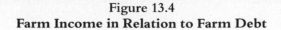

Figure 13.4
Farm Income in Relation to Farm Debt

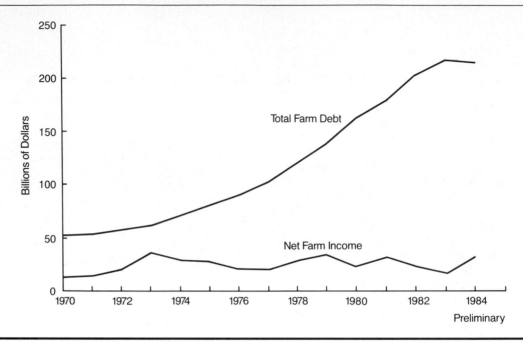

Source: Mark Drabenstott and Marvin Duncan, "Farm Credit Problems: The Policy Choices," *Economic Review,* Federal Reserve Bank of Kansas City 70 (March 1985): 4.

Because over half of those loans were provided by ag banks, defined as banks with more than one-fourth of their loans invested in agriculture, ag banks were exposed to substantial default risk. The drastic reduction in collateral value led to a significant increase in loan losses; this increase is apparent in Figure 13.5, which compares the relative sizes of net loan charge-offs for agricultural and nonagricultural banks. By 1985, net chargeoffs as a percentage of total loans for ag banks were more than twice as high as for nonagricultural banks. Between 1982 and 1986, the number of ag banks on the FDIC's "problem bank" list—a list of institutions requiring more than normal supervision—rose from less than 100 to over 600. The Federal Reserve Board responded with more lenient capital standards and discount window policies for ag banks.

One might wonder why some lenders have invested so heavily in the farm sector. There are two good reasons. Some institutions are located in rural communities and really have no other business sector to serve. They also have had no strong incentive to look for alternatives, because farm lending has generally been a good line of business. From 1970 until 1982, for example, the loan loss ratio at agricultural banks was lower than that of other comparably sized banks, and the return on equity was higher even through the end of 1982.[31]

---

[31]Emanual Melichar, "A Financial Perspective on Agriculture," *Federal Reserve Bulletin* 70 (January 1984): 10-11.

Figure 13.5
Net Loan Chargeoffs as a Percentage of Total Loans,[a] Agricultural and
Other Small Banks

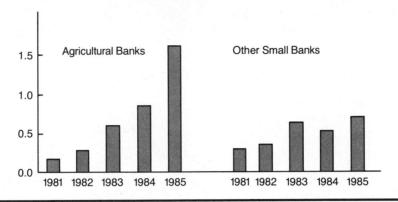

[a]Net chargeoffs during the first half of the year as a percentage of midyear loans on an annualized basis.

Source: Federal Deposit Insurance Corporation, "Agricultural Conditions and the Prospects for Farm Banks," *Banking and Economic Review,* FDIC 4 (March 1986): 7.

Major Issues in Farm Lending

Most farm loans are secured. If farmers borrow to purchase farm implements and equipment, these will be pledged as collateral. For working capital and other loans, banks usually accept farm real estate as security. The use of collateral imposes additional complications in the loan evaluation because the loan officer, although primarily concerned with the borrower's cash flow position, must also be able to estimate the value of the farm assets with reasonable accuracy. Monitoring the condition and market value of the collateral becomes an important element in the loan review process.

As with other commercial loans, the practice of requiring collateral on farm loans is designed to lessen the lender's risk exposure.[32]

But in a period of economic decline in the agricultural sector, collateral does not accomplish that purpose, because it tends to decline in value along with the financial prospects of farmers. Figure 13.6 shows the decline in the value of a nationwide index of farmland values, compared to an index of farm debt, over the period 1972–1985. As the graph suggests, if some lenders had taken possession of farm collateral during the early 1980s, they would have held tangible assets with market values below the amount owed to them.

The Farmers Home Administration and the Small Business Administration offer lenders alternatives for reducing their risk exposure. These government agencies provide guarantees on loans to high-risk borrowers denied credit through traditional lending channels. Agricultural banks also face a major competitor for high-quality loans, the Farm Credit System (FCS), a cooperatively owned organization. Two of its components, the Production Credit Agencies and the Federal Land Banks, make direct short-and intermediate-term loans available

_____

[32]Farm lenders must also adjust their standard commercial-credit risk evaluation to recognize the special characteristics of farming. A discussion highlighting potential adaptations is provided in Kathleen W. Alcott, "An Agricultural Loan Rating System," *Journal of Commercial Bank Lending* 67 (February 1985): 29-38.

Figure 13.6
Farm Land Values and Farm Debt

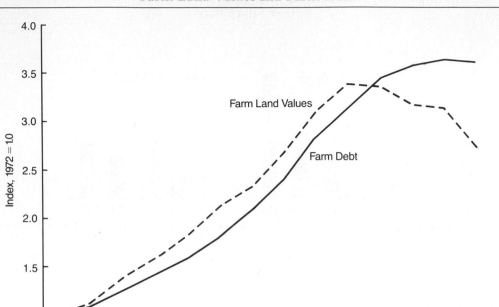

Source: Michael T. Belongia and R. Alton Gilbert, "The Farm Credit Crisis: Will It Hurt the Whole Economy?" *Review,* Federal Reserve Bank of St. Louis 67 (December 1985): 6.

to farmers. Because FCS lenders are not depository institutions, they have direct access to the national credit markets and usually offer loans at interest rates below those available from most ag banks.[33]

Ultimately, of course, the fate of many agricultural lenders is tied to the health of the farm sector. Many experts believe federal farm policies must be completely overhauled. Others believe the key to an improved agricultural outlook is to increase world markets for U. S. farm products.[34]

MANAGEMENT OF INTERNATIONAL LOANS

International lending, another special category of commercial loans, is confined to large commercial banks for several reasons. Gaining ac-

[33]For more information about recent conditions in the Farm Credit System, see Benjamin, "The Financial Stress in Agriculture"; Richard M. Todd, "Taking Stock of the Farm Credit System: Riskier for Farm Borrowers," *Quarterly Review,* Federal Reserve Bank of Minneapolis 9 (Fall 1985): 14-24; Frederick Furlong and Randall Pozdena, "Farm Credit System," *Weekly Letter,* Federal Reserve Bank of San Francisco, December 20, 1985; and "Farm Crisis May Provide FSLIC Recapitalization Solutions," *Savings Institutions* 107 (November 1986): 39-43.

[34]Many policy options are discussed in Michael D. Boehlje, "Policy Options for Agriculture," *Economic Perspectives,* Federal Reserve Bank of Chicago 9 (November/December 1985): 29-35; Marvin Duncan, Mark Drabenstott, and Kim Norris, "Farm Prosperity: Policies for the Future," *Economic Review,* Federal Reserve Bank of Kansas City 70 (September/October 1985): 25-38.

cess to international markets is difficult and usually requires special facilities. Also, lenders bear added regulatory burdens because of separate provisions applying to international loans. Finally, the additional risk that accompanies international lending acts as a deterrent. Nevertheless, the volume of international loans, even in the more risky categories, has increased throughout the 1980s.

Access to International Lending

Banks gain access to international markets in several ways. The simplest is through loan participations in which another bank acts as the lead institution. A bank just beginning to expand beyond the domestic market might choose this route while developing the necessary expertise. Just as in the domestic markets, however, loan participations expose banks to significant risks, so even nonlead banks must proceed carefully and perform conscientious credit analysis.

IBFs.   A more extensive commitment to foreign lending involves a larger investment and greater risk exposure. Since 1981, banks have been allowed to establish *international banking facilities (IBFs),* located in the United States but serving international customers exclusively. An IBF is often referred to as a "shell branch" because it does not require physical facilities apart from the parent organization, and is instead just a separate bookkeeping facility. Deposits gathered through IBFs do not qualify for deposit insurance and are not subject to reserve requirements or many other regulations applied to domestic operations.[35]

Edge Act Corporations.   Another alternative for originating international loans is through Edge Act subsidiaries, defined in Chapter 2 as

branches of the parent institution serving international customers. Unlike IBFs, Edge Act offices operate as full-service branches and are subject to regulation. By year-end 1985, there were 540 IBFs and 120 Edge Act subsidiaries, the vast majority of which were located in New York, California, and Florida. In addition, large banks operate offices or full-service branches abroad, providing more convenient service to foreign borrowers.

Growth and Regulation of International Lending

One category of foreign lending has received special attention in recent years as regulators have become painfully aware of the potentially serious level of risk exposure. Loans to borrowers in lesser-developed countries *(LDCs)* are seriously affected by changes in world economic conditions and the price level of energy products. The volume of loans from large U.S. banks to countries in this category grew rapidly after the mid-1970s. For example, the 24 largest banks in the United States provided over 80 percent of the loans to nonoil-exporting LDCs in 1982 and 1983. By mid-1985, 204 large U.S. banks had $130 billion in loans to LDCs, an amount equal to 133 percent of their combined net worth.[36]

Unfortunately, 32 foreign governments were in arrears on international payments as early as 1981. Even worse fears were realized in 1982 when Mexico and other borrowers announced they were unable to service their debt agreements. Congress responded to the crisis in 1983 by passing the *International Lending Supervision Act (ILSA)* in an attempt to control the magnitude of future problems. The act established special examination procedures for international loan portfolios; granted power to supervisory agencies to set minimum capital guidelines to ensure adequate support in the case of loan losses; and required a special allocation to loan loss reserves by institutions en-

---

[35]International banking facilities were approved by the Federal Reserve Board in 1981; federal legislation that year approved their exemption from reserve requirements and other domestic regulations. For more details, see K. Alec Chrystal, "International Banking Facilities," *Review,* Federal Reserve Bank of St. Louis 66 (April 1984): 5-11.

[36]Gerald H. Anderson, "Solutions to the International Debt Problem," *Economic Commentary,* Federal Reserve Bank of Cleveland, August 1, 1985.

gaged in foreign lending. A final deterrent to excessive international exposure came in the form of a requirement that income from loan origination fees be amortized over the life of the loan, rather than recognized as income in the year negotiated, greatly diluting the importance of these fees to bank earnings.[37]

Since 1982, the ratio of bank capital to international loans has increased. Federal banking regulators carefully monitor the financial position of foreign governments that borrow heavily from U.S. banks, and have at times issued special directives for reporting interest income and reserves for loans to specific countries deemed highly risky. Thus, the decision to participate in the international loan markets has managerial implications extending far beyond the loan portfolio itself.

Risk Analysis in International Lending

Along with the usual concerns about the financial stability of a borrower, institutions competing in the international markets face other sources of risk. One of these, exchange rate risk, arises from floating currency exchange rates and is explained in Chapter 9. Others are addressed in this section.

Country Risk.   Several related sources of variability are grouped together under the term *country risk,* also known as *transfer risk* or *sovereign risk.* Country risk includes any political, economic, social, cultural, or legal circumstances in the home country of the borrower that could prevent the timely fulfillment of debt obligations. This uncertainty can arise from many sources, such as social unrest, civil or international wars, economic decline, or a change in political ideology. A slightly different problem is one that occurs when a country's economic condition weakens, and a foreign borrower's government prohibits a currency exchange for repayment of debts (hence the term *transfer risk*). Even cultural attitudes toward indebtedness can affect borrowers' timely repayment of obligations.[38] In short, country risk includes any source of uncertainty specific to international rather than domestic lending.

As a result of the proliferation of problem foreign loans, regulators have struggled with methods of measuring and predicting country risk. The ILSA requires special procedures for rating the country risk of a bank's international loan portfolio. These ratings are, of course, *ex post* assessments that reflect the repayment record of a borrower once a loan has been granted. Finding reliable signals for *ex ante* risk is difficult because it depends upon a country's future economic and political stability. Measuring that with any degree of confidence is indeed difficult, yet necessary if the institution expects to earn a rate of return sufficient to compensate for the additional risk.

Diversification.   Although exchange rate and country risk can increase variability in an institution's NIM, international loans also provide an avenue for diversification. International lending offers access to different geographical regions and economic climates. If expected returns on international loans have low correlations with expected returns on domestic loans, the overall riskiness of the institution's loan portfolio can be reduced.

---

[37]Extensive details on the 1982 crisis and related trends in LDC lending are provided in John E. Young, "Supervision of Bank Foreign Lending," *Economic Review,* Federal Reserve Bank of Kansas City 70 (May 1985): 31-39; Norman S. Fieleke, "International Lending on Trial," *New England Economic Review,* Federal Reserve Bank of Boston (May/June 1983), pp. 5-13; Henry S. Terrell, "Bank Lending to Developing Countries: Recent Developments and Some Considerations for the Future," *Federal Reserve Bulletin* 70 (October 1984): 755-763.

[38]An interesting example of country risk occurred after the price of crude oil fell dramatically in 1986. Many Islamic borrowers with significant indebtedness to United States banks invoked the doctrine of *sharia,* which holds that the payment of interest is against the teachings of the Koran. Although they had avoided earlier conflict with the doctrine by encouraging banks to call interest charges "administrative fees," when oil prices fell, some borrowers again began viewing the so-called fees as interest and decided it was against their religion to pay charges previously incurred. In early 1986, in Saudi Arabia alone, the debt in arrears as a result of *sharia* was estimated at between $8 and $9 billion. See Bill Powell, "The Sheiks Rediscover Religion," *Newsweek,* May 12, 1986, pp. 62-63.

Banks have responded to risks in international lending in a variety of ways. Citicorp negotiated a controversial insurance policy with Cigna Corporation for the bank's foreign loans, but the policy was subsequently cancelled. Concerns expressed by regulators over the effect of such agreements on the financial stability of the insurance industry suggest that insurance may not be a viable risk-reduction strategy for international lenders.

Smaller institutions have become significantly more reluctant to enter the foreign loan market. Regional banks wanting to pursue the diversification potential of foreign markets are turning to trade financing through **letters of credit,** financial instruments through which a bank guarantees payment on imported goods, substituting its financial strength for that of the importing firm. Although less risky than direct loans to LDCs, letters of credit expose the lender to default risk if the client firm cannot make payments. Regulators' concern over risk exposure from letters of credit is discussed in Chapter 16. Finally, some institutions use overseas offices to pursue European markets, where country risk is much lower than in LDC lending.[39]

SUMMARY

Loans are the largest category of assets in depository institutions. Although commercial banks, thrifts, and credit unions tend to specialize in different types of loans, important elements of successful lending are shared by all depositories. Lending policies must incorporate specific objectives for the size, composition, maturity, interest rate characteristics, and default risk of the loan portfolio.

Procedures for evaluating and approving loan applications must then be devised to achieve those objectives. A major step is to establish a base lending rate, from which individual loan-pricing decisions follow. The process of evaluating and approving a loan includes decisions regarding what rate to charge a given customer, how often it will change, and whether special terms and conditions should be attached. Finally, procedures must be developed to monitor the performance of a loan to avoid borrower default.

Commercial lending, domestic and international, is the focus of the remainder of the chapter. Loans to businesses are of particular interest to commercial banks, although thrifts have begun to enter the market in small numbers in recent years. Of special importance in commercial lending is an analysis of the borrower's financial condition. Applicants must be categorized according to the level of default risk to which the institution is exposed.

Specific loan terms must then be determined. In the past, the standard pricing practice was to charge the institution's best customers the prime rate, and to scale other loan rates upward from there. Recently, a two-tiered pricing system has emerged for large and small borrowers. Further decisions involve compensating balances, commitments, discounting, prepayment penalties, and collateral. The expected yield to the depository will reflect all these decisions. Some institutions choose to invest in loan participation agreements originated by a lead bank instead of, or in addition to, direct lending.

Two special types of commercial loans are agricultural and international lending. Each poses unique risks and is centered only in relatively small segments of the banking industry. Agricultural lending is often secured by the value of the borrower's land. When farm prices fall, the lending institution may be left with a loan in default on which the collateral is worth less than the loan. International loans, especially those to developing countries, have been common in very large commercial banks since the 1970s. They expose the institution to country risk. Because of the large risk exposure presented by these loans, special regulations apply to international lenders.

---

[39]Edwin A. Finn, Jr., "Many Regional Banks Reduce Foreign Loans, Raise Tough Problems," *The Wall Street Journal,* November 19, 1984, p. 1.; Matthew Winkler, "U. S. Financial Firms Grab Growing Share of European Markets," *The Wall Street Journal,* February 2, 1985, p. 1.

Questions

1. How do institutional policies and objectives guide the management of the loan portfolio?

2. What areas must commercial loan officers analyze to evaluate the risk of a commercial borrower? From what sources do they obtain this information?

3. What is a base lending rate? How do lending institutions use it in setting commercial loan rates?

4. What is the traditional definition of the prime rate? Why have the definition and purpose of the prime rate changed in recent years?

5. What factors affect the choice between offering fixed-rate loans and variable-rate loans?

6. What factors affect thrifts' decisions to enter commercial lending?

7. Why has a two-tiered market developed in commercial lending?

8. Distinguish between a loan commitment and a line of credit.

9. Compare the costs and benefits to the depository of asset-based versus unsecured lending.

10. What are the benefits of loan participations for financial institutions?

11. Find some articles on the current performance of agricultural lenders. Has their financial condition improved or deteriorated since 1986? To what is the change, if any, attributed?

12. Explain the risks unique to international lending.

13. Why was the International Lending Supervision Act passed in 1983? What procedures did the act establish for international lenders?

14. In early 1987, Mexico's financial problems were particularly severe, and lenders with extensive investment in Mexico were anticipating major losses. Find information on the handling of Mexico's financial problems during that period. What lessons for international lenders can you identify from this situation?

Problems

1. Redbird Savings Bank is considering a loan application from Jan Peterson, who wants to purchase a clothing store and needs $50,000. The bank considers the loan to be of above-average risk and will add a 2 percent premium to the base rate. The bank's total assets are $100 million; interest expense is $7 million; net noninterest expense is $1 million; and the marginal tax rate is 34 percent. The target NIM is 2.6 percent, and the bank's asset structure is as follows:

   • Securities: $25 million, average yield 6.5 percent
   • Loans: $68 million
   • Nonearning assets: $7 million

   a. What rate will Jan be offered?
   b. Prepare a pro forma income statement, assuming the bank earns, on average, the base loan rate on its loan portfolio. Calculate the NIM under this assumption.
   c. What RONW is expected if the net worth multiplier is 12?

2. United Federal has total assets of $50 million, a net worth multiplier of 15, and net noninterest expense of $450,000. Its target NIM is 1.9 percent, and liability costs average 10 percent annually. Assets are distributed as follows:

- Securities: $5 million, average yield 8.25 percent
- Mortgages: $43 million
- Nonearning assets: $2 million

a. What is the base mortgage rate United must earn to achieve its target NIM?

b. Prepare a pro forma income statement, assuming United earns the base rate on its mortgages. Show that this rate will allow the S&L to earn its desired NIM.

c. What RONW is expected if the marginal tax rate is 34 percent?

3. Suppose the management of United Federal in Problem 2 raises the target NIM to 2.1 percent. What base rate must be earned to achieve this target?

4. Clyde Jefferson is negotiating a $3 million line of credit with State Bank of America. The one-year agreement requires a 0.20 percent commitment fee, with a 10 percent compensating balance on the entire commitment, and an additional 5 percent on funds actually borrowed. The stated rate of interest is 13 percent, and the loan officer estimates that Clyde will use, on average, 75 percent of the line. Calculate the total expected dollar and rate of return for the bank, assuming a 12 percent marginal reserve requirement.

5. Suppose that Clyde Jefferson in Problem 4 is offered a $3 million line of credit from First National Bank, with a stated rate of 11 percent. The compensating balance requirement is 11 percent on the total line, with an additional 5 percent on the amount borrowed. If other terms remain the same, does First National expect to earn more or less on the agreement than State Bank of America?

6. Your bank is willing to offer a $500,000 line of credit for one year to help you establish your own consulting firm. The agreement requires a 0.15 percent commitment fee, a 12 percent compensating balance on the entire commitment, and 4 percent more on funds actually borrowed. The stated rate of interest is 10 percent, and you have told the bank that you probably will not need more than an average of 60 percent of the line. Calculate the total expected dollar return and rate of return for the bank, assuming a 12 percent marginal reserve requirement.

7. What is the annual yield on a one-year loan if interest is discounted and the stated rate is 10 percent? If it is 13 percent? If it is 9.6 percent? (Discounted loan yields are calculated in Chapter 4.)

Selected References

Benjamin, Gary L. "The Financial Stress in Agriculture." *Economic Perspectives* (Federal Reserve Bank of Chicago) 9 (November/ December 1985): 3-16.

Berlin, Mitchell. "Loan Commitments: Insurance Contracts in a Risky World." *Business Review* (Federal Reserve Bank of Philadelphia) (May/June 1986), pp. 3-12.

Boehlje, Michael D. "Policy Options for Agriculture." *Economic Perspectives* (Federal Reserve Bank of Chicago) 9 (November/ December 1985): 29-35.

Brady, Thomas F. "Changes in Loan Pricing and Business Lending at Commercial Banks." *Federal Reserve Bulletin* 71 (January 1985): 1-13.

Chrystal, Alec K. "International Banking Facilities." *Review* (Federal Reserve Bank of St. Louis) 66 (April 1984): 5-11.

Cramer, Robert H., and William E. Sterk. "The Present Value Approach to Commercial Loan Pricing." *Journal of Bank Research* 12 (Winter 1982): 207-217.

Duncan, Marvin, Mark Drabenstott, and Kim Norris. "Farm Prosperity: Policies for the Future." *Economic Review* (Federal Reserve Bank of Kansas City) 70 (September/October 1985): 25-38.

Dunham, Constance. "Recent Developments in Thrift Commercial Lending." *New England Economic Review* (Federal Reserve Bank of Boston) (November/December 1985), pp. 41-48.

Dunham, Constance, and Margaret Guerin-Calvert. "How Quickly Can Thrifts Move into Commercial Lending?" *New England Economic Review* (Federal Reserve Bank of Boston) (November/December 1983), pp. 43-54.

Fieleke, Norman S. "International Lending on Trial." *New England Economic Review* (Federal Reserve Bank of Boston) (May/June 1983), pp. 5-13.

Fite, Benjamin Jones. "Prime Rate Litigation: Beyond RICO." *Banking Law Journal* 103 (September-October 1986): 450-485.

Gagnon, Joseph A. "What Is a Commercial Loan?" *New England Economic Review* (Federal Reserve Bank of Boston) (July/August 1983), pp. 36-41.

Goldberg, Michael A. "The Sensitivity of the Prime Rate to Money Market Conditions." *Journal of Financial Research* 7 (Winter 1984): 269-280.

Goudreau, Robert E. "S&L Use of New Powers: Consumer and Commercial Loan Expansion." *Economic Review* (Federal Reserve Bank of Atlanta) 69 (December 1984): 15-33.

Gregorash, George M., and James Morrison. "Lean Years in Agricultural Banking." *Economic Perspectives* (Federal Reserve Bank of Chicago) 9 (November/December 1985): 17-21.

Melichar, Emanual. "Agricultural Banks Under Stress." *Federal Reserve Bulletin* 72 (July 1986): 437-448.

Mills, Dixie, and Guerry Suggs. "Developing a Commercial Lending Strategy: Key Issues for Savings Institutions." *Federal Home Loan Bank Board Journal* 15 (May/June 1983): 26-31.

Moulton, Janice M. "Antitrust Implications of Thrifts' Expanded Commercial Loan Powers." *Business Review* (Federal Reserve Bank of Philadelphia) (September/October 1984), pp. 11-21.

Pavel, Christine, and Dave Phillis. "Cautious Play Marks S&L Approach to Commercial Lending." *Economic Perspectives* (Federal Reserve Bank of Chicago) 9 (May/June 1985): 18-27.

Slovin, Myron B., and Marie Elizabeth Sushka. "A Model of the Commercial Loan Rate." *Journal of Finance* 38 (December 1983): 1,583-1,596.

Terrell, Henry S. "Bank Lending to Developing Countries: Recent Developments and Some Considerations for the Future." *Federal Reserve Bulletin* 70 (October 1984): 755-763.

Todd, Richard M. "Taking Stock of the Farm Credit System: Riskier for Farm Borrowers." *Quarterly Review* (Federal Reserve Bank of Minneapolis) 9 (Fall 1985): 14-24.

Young, John E. "Supervision of Bank Foreign Lending." *Economic Review* (Federal Reserve Bank of Kansas City) 70 (May 1985): 31-39.

Chapter 14

ASSET MANAGEMENT: CONSUMER AND MORTGAGE LENDING

Bankers will act as good bartenders. They'll stop serving credit when people have had enough.

Mack Ruxton
United Bank of Denver (1986)

COPO Federal Credit Union loaned Wanda F. Holden $3,229 and established a 60-month repayment schedule. Holden became delinquent, however, and the CU sued to recover the money. Imagine management's surprise when, instead, the CU was accused of violating a Louisiana state usury law prohibiting interest charges in excess of 1 percent per month. The accusation arose because the CU had rounded Holden's required monthly loan payment from $62.427 to $62.43. Fortunately for the credit union, the practice of rounding to the nearest penny was upheld by the court.[1]

Consumer and residential mortgage loans fit the lending framework in the initial portions of Chapter 13. But just as there are distinct issues in commercial lending, loans to consumers have special characteristics. One distinguishing feature is that many are ***installment loans*** on which the borrower repays both principal and interest on a regular schedule. Credit evaluation, loan monitoring, and customer relations differ as well. As the opening paragraph suggests,

---

[1]"CUs in Court," *Credit Union Magazine* 49 (November 1983): 39.

consumer credit is heavily regulated, complicating the lending process. And even within the realm of consumer lending, terms and conditions of residential mortgages differ from those of other types of consumer loans.

CONSUMER CREDIT: AN OVERVIEW

American households have been increasing their debt since the end of World War II. In the last few years, however, the pace of consumer borrowing has accelerated. Figure 14.1 shows the volume of consumer credit outstanding as a proportion of disposable personal income from 1975 through mid-1986. The majority of debt is mortgage debt, held by 37 percent of all households. Installment borrowing is the second largest category, including automobile loans and the use of credit cards. The ratio of debt to income rose from less than 60 percent in 1975 to over 70 percent in 1986. Data gathered in a 1983 survey by federal regulatory agencies indicated that 62 percent of American families had credit obligations, a larger proportion than ever before.[2]

The growth in consumer credit is attributed to a variety of factors, such as changing societal attitudes toward personal indebtedness; increased willingness of lenders to service consumer credit needs; and increased demands for consumer goods, as items once considered luxuries are now viewed as necessities. Although the Tax Reform Act of 1986, which eliminated the tax deductibility of interest on nonmortgage consumer debt, is expected to dampen demand in the future, other factors point to consumers' continued need for credit. These include the maturing of the "baby boom" generation; easier access to credit through credit cards and other financial innovations; increased need for student loans to finance higher education; and the relatively low proportion of households with existing mortgage debt.

Researchers do not interpret the recent rise in consumer credit as evidence that households are overextended.[3] Although the ratio of consumer debt to income has risen, the ratio of debt to household assets has not changed significantly. In addition, the ratio of installment payments to monthly income is not alarming. Thus, the provision of credit to consumers is a service with great potential for depositories.

Who Lends to Consumers?

Depository institutions, particularly commercial banks and credit unions, are already major suppliers of consumer credit. As shown in Figure 14.2, at year-end 1985, banks held almost half of outstanding consumer installment credit, and credit unions, over 10 percent.[4] Although not shown in the chart, automobile loans are the largest category of consumer installment debt (almost 40 percent). Commercial banks lead in the provision of autombile credit, with credit unions ranking third behind finance companies.

Fed statistics indicate that the percentage of families with outstanding debt obligations to depository institutions is larger than the percentage having obligations to other lenders. Nonetheless, other suppliers of financial services are increasingly strong competitors; in 1983, eight of the ten largest individual suppliers of consumer installment credit, by dollar

---

[2]Robert B. Avery et al., "Survey of Consumer Finances, 1983: A Second Report," *Federal Reserve Bulletin* 70 (December 1984): 858, 866.

[3]Studies include Douglas K. Pearce, "Rising Household Debt in Perspective," *Economic Review,* Federal Reserve Bank of Kansas City 70 (July/August 1985): 3-17; Charles A. Luckett and James D. August, "The Growth of Consumer Debt," *Federal Reserve Bulletin* 71 (June 1985): 389-402.

[4]Even though some forms of nonmortgage consumer credit are not repaid on an installment basis, the Federal Reserve Board follows the convention of referring to all consumer, nonmortgage debt as installment credit. That convention has been followed in Figure 14.3 and the rest of the chapter.

Figure 14.1
Ratio of Personal Debt to Personal Income, 1975–1986

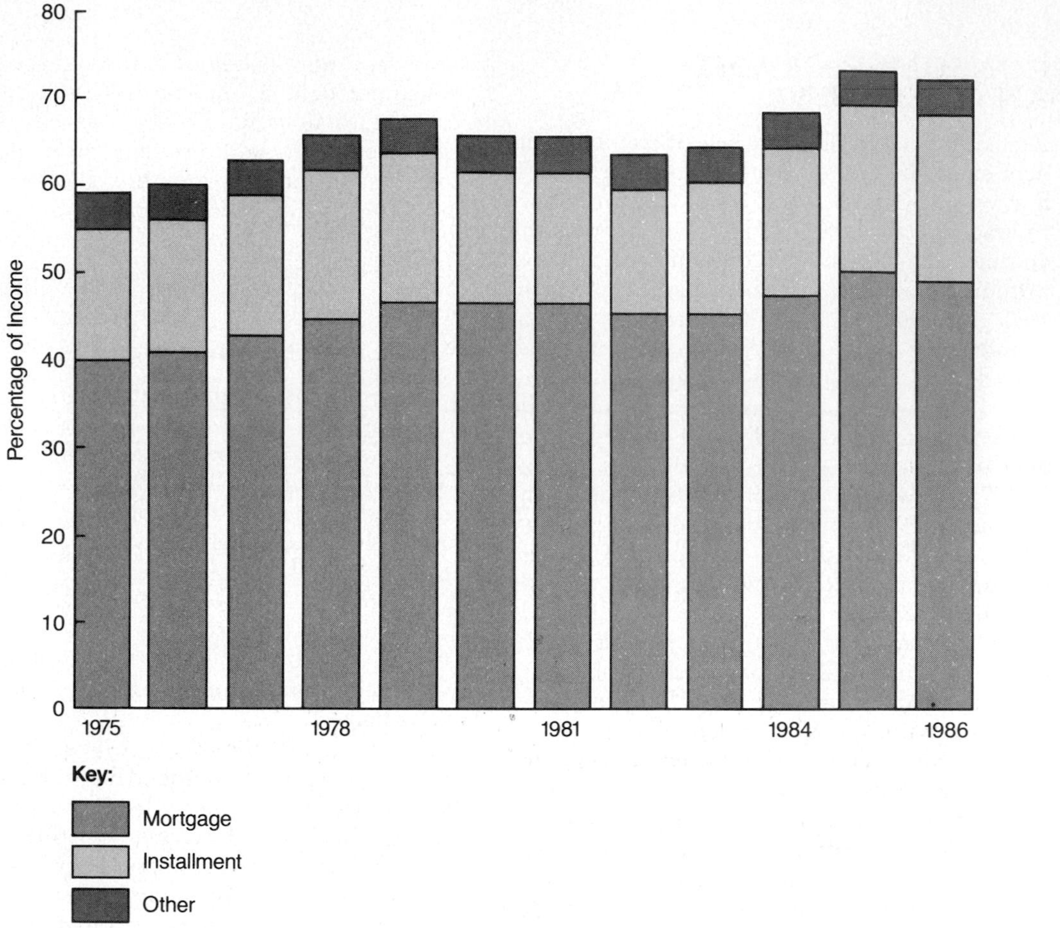

Key:
- Mortgage
- Installment
- Other

Source: Prepared by the authors with data from Lynn Paquette, "Estimating Household Debt Service Payments," *Quarterly Review,* Federal Reserve Bank of New York 11 (Summer 1986): 13.

volume, were nondepository institutions.[5] In 1986, in fact, finance companies affiliated with

[5]Avery et al., "Survey of Consumer Finances, 1983"; Christine Pavel and Harvey Rosenblum, "Banks and Nonbanks: The Horse Race Continues," *Economic Perspectives,* Federal Reserve Bank of Chicago 9 (May/June 1985): 3–17.

automobile manufacturers engaged in aggressive attempts to make car loans, offering interest rates on some loans as low as 0 percent! Thus, policies that depositories develop for managing consumer lending have a significant impact on their competitive position and financial performance.

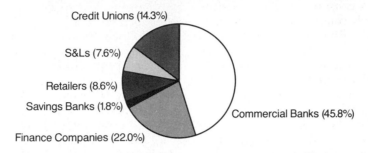

Figure 14.2
Suppliers of Consumer Credit, Year-End 1985

Credit Unions (14.3%)

S&Ls (7.6%)

Retailers (8.6%)

Savings Banks (1.8%)

Finance Companies (22.0%)

Commercial Banks (45.8%)

Source: Federal Reserve Bulletin, December 1986, p. A40.

Two recent studies of consumers indicate that prospective borrowers shop among competing lenders before signing a loan agreement, and the focus of their attention is usually the interest rate.[6] Although finance company customers have often been characterized as higher-risk, that stereotype was not confirmed; one study found that fewer than 25 percent of a sample of finance company borrowers would not have met typical bank credit standards. Instead, the majority of finance company borrowers had deliberately chosen the finance company over competing depository institutions.

Previous experience or customer relationship with a lender is important, especially if the association has been positive. Generally, research indicates that depository institutions must convince potential customers that they offer competitive rates, and must make the process of applying for a loan relatively easy and fast. They may also find that their current depositors represent an important pool of potential borrowers.

---

[6]Both studies were conducted through the Credit Research Center at Purdue University. See Richard L. Peterson and Dan A. Black, "Consumer Credit Shopping," *Journal of Retail Banking* 4 (Fall 1982): 50–61; and Robert W. Johnson and A. Charlene Sullivan, "Segmentation of the Consumer Loan Market," *Journal of Retail Banking* 3 (September 1981): 1-7.

REGULATION OF CONSUMER CREDIT

Among the most heavily regulated operations in financial institutions are the financial services they offer to consumers.

Truth-in-Lending and Equal Credit Opportunity

As noted in Chapter 2, beginning in 1968, a layer of federal consumer protection legislation was added to that already provided at the state level with the passage of the Consumer Credit Protection Act (Truth-in-Lending, or TIL). The goal of that legislation was to ensure that consumers receive accurate information about the cost of credit to facilitate comparison of different lenders' credit terms.

Numerous other acts have been passed since then; of particular interest to consumer lenders are the Equal Credit Opportunity Act of 1974, passed to control discrimination in credit evaluation, and the Truth-in-Lending Simplification and Reform Act of 1980, designed to simplify the disclosure of credit terms for the benefit of both lenders and consumers. The Federal Reserve Board enforces the provisions of TIL through *Regulation Z,* and the Equal Credit Act, through *Regulation B.* Institutions must comply with both state and federal legislation; if there are any contradictions between the two, federal statutes prevail.

Reg Z sets standards for disclosing the terms and costs of a consumer credit agreement *before* the borrower becomes obligated. It establishes a period during which a consumer may cancel a transaction, as well as procedures through which a consumer can challenge billing errors on revolving credit agreements. Reg B prohibits discrimination based on sex, age, race, marital status, color, religion, and national origin; it establishes the rights of loan applicants, including the right to receive an explanation if a credit request is denied.

Impact of Bankruptcy Laws on Default Risk

Another law that has influenced consumer credit analysis is the **Bankruptcy Reform Act,** passed by Congress in November 1978 and effective as of October 1980. The nation's bankruptcy laws had not been revised for 40 years, and the old code allowed most standards for the declaration of personal bankruptcy to be set at the state level. Of particular concern to debtors was the maximum dollar amount of assets that could be protected from liquidation when an individual filed for bankruptcy. Many state codes specified low amounts considered incompatible with current price levels. The revision established federal standards preempting state provisions unless a state revised its code after 1978.

Many lenders considered the 1978 federal guidelines to be overly generous to individuals with credit problems. For example, an individual was allowed to protect from creditors $7,500 in real and/or personal property used as a personal place of residence; up to $1,200 for a motor vehicle; up to $500 for jewelry; and future income from certain sources. For debtors who were not homeowners, the $7,500 housing exemption could be used to protect other assets. Thus, the ability of a lender to foreclose against the property of a borrower in default was limited if the borrower chose to file for personal bankruptcy.[7] In reaction to federal provisions,

most states passed new codes after 1978. Although some new state codes are more restrictive than the federal guidelines, in all cases they are more lenient to debtors than standards in effect before 1978.[8]

The new leniency in bankruptcy provisions led to a surge in personal bankruptcy filings in 1980 and 1981, although a concurrent economic recession certainly contributed. Filings increased by 60 percent in 1980 and by over 40 percent in 1981, when nearly 600,000 debtors declared bankruptcy.[9] In response to increasing loan losses, consumer lenders set higher standards for loan approvals. The availability of tangible assets in excess of prevailing exemptions became a key variable, serving as the lender's recourse if the borrower defaulted and then declared bankruptcy. Some consumer lenders ar-

---

Chapter 7 of the bankruptcy code, seeks complete absolution from indebtedness. Another form, through Chapter 13 of the code, seeks protection from creditors while the debtor works under a court-approved plan to repay obligations. Chapter 7 filings present greater potential for loss to creditors than do Chapter 13 filings. Fortunately for lenders, Chapter 13 filings are more numerous.

Research has identified borrower characteristics most often associated with the inability to repay debts versus those associated with the possibility of making at least partial repayment over time. Results of the research can provide judges with information in determining whether Chapter 7 or Chapter 13 proceedings are more appropriate for a given debtor. See, for example, Richard L. Peterson and Margaret Woo, "Bankrupt Debtors: Who Can Repay?" *Journal of Retail Banking* 6 (Fall 1984): 42-51.

[8]Bob Gatty, "Failings of Our Bankruptcy Law," *Nation's Business* 70 (May 1982): 44-46; Philip Shuchman and Thomas L. Rhorer, "Personal Bankruptcy Data for Opt-Out Hearings and Other Purposes," *American Bankruptcy Law Journal* 56 (Winter 1982): 1-28.

[9]The research staff at the Federal Reserve Bank of Atlanta estimated that from 72 percent to 82 percent of the 1980 and 1981 increases was attributable to the bankruptcy code revision, rather than to economic conditions. For further discussion, see Charlie Carter, "The Surge in Bankruptcies: Is the New Law Responsible?" *Economic Review,* Federal Reserve Bank of Atlanta 67 (January 1982): 20-30. Subsequent researchers concurred that the increase in personal bankruptcies could not be attributed to changed economic conditions alone, and concluded that their findings were "consistent with the notion that the federal law increased bankruptcy filing rates." See Richard L. Peterson and Kiyomi Aoki, "Bankruptcy Filings before and after Implementation of the Bankruptcy Reform Act," *Journal of Economics and Business* 36 (February 1984): 95-105.

---

[7]An individual declaring bankruptcy can seek two forms of protection from creditors. One form, pursuant to

gued that the more lenient bankruptcy codes hurt lower- and middle-income families, who no longer qualified for loans under the higher standards.

The protests of lenders were addressed when Congress passed the Bankruptcy Amendments and Federal Judgeship Act of 1984.[10] The amendments were designed to prevent abuses of the bankruptcy provisions that had occurred since 1978. They set lower limits on the amount of property protected from creditors and improved the monitoring system. If a federal bankruptcy judge believes an individual is abusing the law (that is, if someone actually capable of meeting financial obligations attempts to declare bankruptcy), the case can be dismissed. One provision particularly welcomed by consumer lenders requires debtors to be responsible for debts incurred shortly before bankruptcy, discouraging an individual from increasing debt with no intention of repaying it.

Usury Ceilings

In addition to disclosure and bankruptcy laws, some states restrict the rate of interest that may be charged on certain categories of loans—primarily consumer loans, but also some agricultural and small business loans. First mentioned in Chapter 2, usury laws establish rate ceilings a lender may not exceed, regardless of the lender's costs. Usury ceilings apply to lenders of all types, not just to depository institutions.

Rationale for Usury Ceilings.   Usury laws have a long history. They developed from a perceived need to protect individual borrowers, presumably less sophisticated than business borrowers, from unscrupulous lenders. During periods of low market interest rates, when the usury ceilings are above lenders' base lending rates, usury laws are not controversial. When economic conditions change, however, as they did in the late 1970s, usury laws attract attention. Congress included a provision in DIDMCA suspending state usury ceilings on some categories of loans at banks and thrifts—residential mortgages, business and agricultural loans, but not nonmortgage consumer debt. This provision preempted state regulations unless a state passed revised legislation before April 1, 1983. A separate provision of DIDMCA covered loan rate ceilings at federally chartered credit unions.[11]

Do Usury Ceilings Accomplish Their Objectives?   Although usury laws were designed to benefit consumers, a significant body of research questions their benefits. Regulatory ceilings requiring loan rates below those dictated by market conditions ("binding" ceilings) led lenders to reduce the quantity of credit they supplied. The credit-reduction effect of binding ceilings can be shown in the framework of the loanable funds theory. In Figure 14.3, the market determined rate is y^*, and the quantity of credit supplied is Q^*. If the usury ceiling is binding ($y_U < y^*$), supply and demand for credit will be out of balance. Lenders will divert loan funds to other investments. The amount of credit available falls to Q_s, significantly below Q_d, the quantity demanded.[12]

---

[10]Congress took action only after the labor movement joined the protests against the bankruptcy reforms. For a discussion of the provisions of the new amendments, see James A. Chatz and Brooke Schumm II, "Bankruptcy Changes Bode Well for Banks," *ABA Banking Journal* 76 (September 1984): 85-90; "Reform Strengthens Creditors' Rights," *Credit Union Magazine* 50 (September 1984): 10-16.

[11]Details on DIDMCA usury provisions, including the responses of state legislatures, are discussed in Donna C. Vandenbrink, "Usury Ceilings and DIDMCA," *Economic Perspectives,* Federal Reserve Bank of Chicago 9 (September/October 1985): 25-30. Federal CUs are governed by the Federal Credit Union Act of 1934, as amended by a portion of DIDMCA. The statutory ceiling rate on loans of all types at federal CUs is 15 percent; however, the NCUA has the authority to change the ceiling if economic conditions warrant it. In recent years, the NCUA has imposed a limit of 21 percent.

[12]Some researchers argue that only installment loans are restricted. Credit offered by retailers continues to be available, because merchants tend to increase the price of the merchandise to offset the loss in interest income on credit sales. Thus consumers who are denied credit by installment lenders may be able to obtain it elsewhere. See Richard L. Peterson, "Usury Laws and Consumer Credit: A Note," *Journal of Finance* 33 (September 1983): 1,299-1,304.

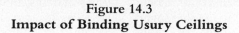

Figure 14.3
Impact of Binding Usury Ceilings

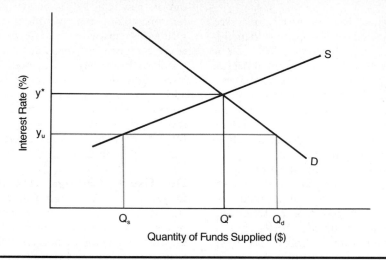

Source: Adapted from Donna M. Vandenbrink, "The Effects of Usury Ceilings," *Economic Perspectives,* Federal Reserve Bank of Chicago (Midyear 1982): 44.

When credit is restricted, the burden of reduced funds does not fall equally on all consumers. Instead, only the least risky applicants are approved. Consequently, while some consumers may receive loans at below-market rates, others are denied credit, an inequity difficult to justify. Furthermore, if retailers raise prices to compensate for low interest on credit sales, even cash customers bear the burden of usury ceilings.[13]

A second negative result of binding usury ceilings is an increase in noninterest costs to borrowers. Lenders will do whatever they can to reduce loan-processing costs and protect available profits. They may shorten loan maturities, forcing borrowers to repay funds more quickly, or they may increase the minimum

loan size to reduce administrative costs per dollar invested. They may also charge higher fees for transaction deposits and related services, in an effort to substitute noninterest income for loan revenues.

Institutional Response to Usury Ceilings. In the early 1980s, some depository institutions took an innovative approach to binding ceilings on consumer loans. Historically, large discrepancies have existed in the maximum allowable interest rates in different states. On credit granted through credit cards, the U.S. Supreme Court ruled that a bank may charge customers the rate allowed by the *bank's* home state, regardless of the *customer's* state of residence. As a result, consumers in the same state could pay different borrowing rates for the same type of credit, depending upon the legal domicile of their creditors. The ruling also opened up unimagined possibilities for innovative creditors.

In 1980, Citicorp announced it would move its credit card operations from New York to South Dakota, a state that had removed all ceil-

---

[13]Several recent articles document such inequities, including John D. Wolken and Frank J. Navratil, "The Economic Impact of the Federal Credit Union Usury Ceiling," *Journal of Finance* 36 (December 1981): 1,157-1,168; and Donna Vandenbrink, "The Effects of Usury Ceilings," *Economic Perspectives* 6 (Midyear 1982): 44-55.

ings from credit card interest rates.[14] Other lenders announced similar plans. Citicorp's strategy stimulated reform activity in many state legislatures, including New York, but Citicorp and others enacted their plans.

In addition, many lenders announced new pricing strategies in response to binding usury ceilings. They increased noninterest fees for bank credit cards, imposing an annual fee for the privilege of receiving a card, whether it was used or not. Before that time, the only cost on most credit cards was interest on the unpaid monthly balance.

Renewed Legislative Action.   In response to the actions of consumer lenders and at the urging of federal regulators, most states have revised their consumer protection legislation since 1981. In 1983, the American Bankers Association surveyed lending institutions in states that had previously had binding usury ceilings. Results indicated that several undesirable effects of the ceilings had been reversed. Lenders stated that more credit was available, credit standards had been relaxed, and procedures were more flexible. The rates charged on personal loans were higher than in the past, but, according to the ABA, were never out of line with the prime rate.[15]

In the revisions, some states removed ceilings altogether for consumer and credit card lending, and some adopted a sliding scale dependent on the size or type of loan. Other states set an adjustable ceiling pegged to a market interest rate, such as T-bill yields. Still others retain a fixed usury ceiling, higher than before DIDMCA. Thus, usury regulations remain an important influence on depository lending decisions.[16]

CONSUMER CREDIT ANALYSIS

Depository institutions offer loans to consumers for a wide variety of purposes. Loans to purchase automobiles, to finance education, or to support other personal needs are usually on installment terms. Noninstallment credit is available, too, in the form of short-term personal loans and credit cards such as MasterCard or Visa. As with commercial lending, the credit decision requires estimating an applicant's default risk category and setting appropriate loan terms for approved applications.

Personal Financial Data

Evaluating the financial position of an applicant for a consumer loan requires information similar to that needed in commercial lending, but the form in which it is received is usually quite different. Individuals, of course, do not have financial statements prepared periodically, but lenders request detailed information on the assets, liabilities, and net worth of a household. Current and anticipated income are also important. In collecting the information, the institution must comply with Regulation B. For example, for certain types of nonmortgage loans, an applicant may not be required to provide information on marital status, race, or religion.[17]

---

[14]Several years earlier, Citicorp had moved aggressively to enter the consumer credit market on a national scale, soliciting credit card customers through mass mailings nationwide. Thus the binding usury ceilings were particularly onerous to that institution. Further information on the legislation permitting Citicorp's move to South Dakota is provided in the *Federal Reserve Bulletin* 67 (February 1981): 181–183.

[15]The ABA survey was reported in William J. Stanley, Jr., "Far from Doomsday, State Usury Relief Really Helps Consumers," *ABA Banking Journal* 75 (April 1983): 75–76.

[16]For a summary of some of the new state laws, see William R. Reichenstein and Frank J. Bonello, "Usury Laws: Today and Tomorrow," *Issues in Bank Regulation* 7 (Winter 1984): 25–31; and Susan B. Kramer and Glenn B. Canner, "The Current Status of Usury Legislation in the United States," *Issues in Bank Regulation* 6 (Summer 1982): 11–23. An analysis of the complexity of balancing federal and state statutes for lenders operating in more than one state is provided in Carl D. Lobell and Howard J. Finkelstein, "Bank Interest Rate Ceilings: 'Borrowing,' 'Exporting,' and 'Importing' Rates," *Journal of Retail Banking* 6 (Winter 1984): 45–49.

[17]Not surprisingly, Reg B is complicated. For a good summary, see Dolores S. Smith, "Revision of the Board's

To verify information provided and to obtain further data, consumer lenders use the services of credit bureaus, which collect information on the credit history and financial position of individuals. The credit report indicates whether the applicant has been delinquent on previous repayment obligations; what other debts are outstanding; where checking and savings accounts are kept and their average balances; and employment information.

Assessing Information: Credit Scoring

Major problems in credit analysis include assessing all important factors about an applicant simultaneously and evaluating all applicants objectively and by the same standards. *Credit-scoring models* are quantitative efforts to ensure that both these problems are addressed. As noted in Chapter 13, credit-scoring models are available for analyzing commercial loan applications, but they are more widely used by consumer lenders.

Calculating a Score for Each Applicant.
The first step in developing a model is to determine, from past data, borrower characteristics most often associated with "bad" and "good" loans, where "bad" is defined as slow-paying, delinquent, or in default. Typical characteristics include how long the applicant has been employed at his or her current job; whether the credit history is good; number of dependents; whether the applicant rents or owns a home; and his or her income and occupation. "Points" are assigned to new applicants based on these characteristics. For example, a borrower with a higher income would be assigned more points on that characteristic than one with a lower income.

Table 14.1 illustrates a typical scoring system. In the table, some characteristics are assigned negative points because they are so often associated with default risk. Some characteristics have higher points and thus count more heavily in an applicant's final score. The relative

importance of each characteristic in overall loan quality is determined by statistical analysis of historical data, most often using a technique called discriminant analysis.[18]

The Accept/Reject Decision. Once all characteristics have been assigned points, a total score for the applicant is determined. Suppose, for example, that an applicant under the scoring system illustrated in Table 14.1 has a phone (36); owns a home (34); has a loan from another finance company (-12) and no bank credit card (0); owns a business (-3); has both a checking and savings account (19); is 37 years old (11); and has been on the job for 16 years (18). The total score is 103. This total is compared to a predetermined minimum acceptable score. The lower the minimum, the more acceptable applicants and the greater the default risk exposure; the higher the minimum, the more rejected applicants and the greater the potential loss of revenue. Ideally, the minimum should be established in an attempt to balance these costs.

Limitations of Credit-Scoring Models.
Like all models, credit-scoring schemes have limitations. They focus only on default risk, and may ignore such information as deposit or other service relationships with the customer. They also must be carefully structured to comply with Reg B: Applicant characteristics included in a model must be "demonstrably and statistically sound," as defined by the Fed.[19] But despite these limitations, major consumer lenders, especially retailers, regularly use the models, as do many depositories offering credit cards.

---

[18]A thorough review of the theory, history, and statistical properties of credit-scoring models can be found in Edward I. Altman et al., *Application of Classification Techniques in Business, Banking, and Finance* (Greenwich, CT: JAI Press, 1981), Chapter 4, pp. 167-198. Another good source is Noel Capon, "Credit Scoring Systems: A Critical Analysis," *Journal of Marketing* 46 (Spring 1982): 82-91.

[19]Smith, "Revision of the Board's Equal Credit Regulation," p. 915; Board of Governors of the Federal Reserve System, "Revision of Regulation B: Official Staff Commentary," November 13, 1985.

Equal Credit Regulation: An Overview," *Federal Reserve Bulletin* 71 (December 1985): 913-923.

Table 14.1
Hypothetical Credit-Scoring System

Applicant Characteristics	Allotted Points	Applicant Characteristics	Allotted Points
Home phone		*Checking or savings account*	
Yes	36	Neither	0
No	0	Either	13
Own or rent		Both	19
Own	34	*Applicant age*	
Rent	0	30 or less	6
Other finance company		30 + to 40	11
Yes	− 12	40 + to 50	8
No	0	Over 50	16
Bank credit card		*Years on job*	
Yes	29	5 or less	0
No	0	5 + to 15	6
Applicant occupation		Over 15	18
Professional and officials	27		
Technical and managers	5		
Proprietor	− 3		
Clerical and sales	12		
Craftsman and nonfarm-laborer	0		
Foreman and operative	26		
Service worker	14		
Farm worker	3		

Source: Gilbert A. Churchill, Jr., et al., "The Role of Credit Scoring in the Loan Decision," *The Credit World* 65 (March 1977): p. 7. *The Credit World* is the official publication of the International Credit Association, headquartered in St. Louis, MO. Reprinted with permission.

TERMS ON CONSUMER INSTALLMENT LOANS

Because consumer loans are made on an installment basis, borrowers and lenders both must understand installment terms.

Add-on Loans

Chapter 4 introduces the differences between installment loan terms and those of other loans. In an installment agreement, the borrower makes equal periodic payments. In addition, many automobile and other consumer loans use the add-on interest method: The interest on the full amount borrowed must be paid for each year of the loan term, even though the entire balance is not outstanding for the full term.

Calculating the Annual Percentage Rate

Suppose a couple decides to buy a new car, priced at $12,000. After making a $2,000 down payment, they approach their credit union for a $10,000 loan, and are quoted an add-on rate of 9 percent for four years. They will repay a total of:

$$\$10,000(0.09)(4) + \$10,000 = \$13,600$$

The repayment schedule will be $13,600/48 = $283.33 per month, resulting in a monthly interest rate of 1.3322 percent and an *annual percentage rate (APR)* of just under 16 percent, based on Equation 4.7:

$$\$10,000 = \sum_{t=1}^{48} \frac{\$283.33}{(1 + y_p)^t}$$

$$y_p = 0.013322\% = 1.3322\%$$

$$APR = 1.3322\% \times 12 = 15.9864\%$$

Regulation Z requires lenders to disclose the APR to borrowers. The Fed defines the APR as the periodic rate multiplied by, not compounded by, the number of periods in a year. Thus, the APR is a legal definition of an interest rate and is not the effective annual yield to the lender, an economic concept based on the mathematics of interest rates. Specific limitations are permitted for rounding, and the rate disclosed can vary from the exact APR by a maximum of 1/8 of 1 percent.[20]

An amortization schedule demonstrating the meaning of the APR is provided in Table 14.2. The lender earns 15.9864 percent on the outstanding principal over the life of the loan, but monthly payments are not allocated to principal and interest equally each month. Early in the loan term, a higher proportion is interest because the principal balance is large. In the last payment, only $3.72 is interest. The monthly allocation to interest is always 15.9864% ÷ 12 of the outstanding loan balance.

The Rule of 78s

When a borrower repays an installment loan before the original maturity date, lenders often apply the *rule of 78s* to calculate the remaining principal balance. This approach, also called the *sum-of-digits method,* involves adding together the digits for the number of payments to be made. The *78* in the name is derived from the sum of digits for a 12-month loan:

$$12 + 11 + 10 + 9 + 8 + 7 + 6 + 5$$
$$+ 4 + 3 + 2 + 1 = 78$$

For the example of a four-year automobile loan, the sum of digits is 1,176.[21] According to the rule of 78s, were the borrowers to pay the loan off early, they would receive credit for 48/1,176 of their total interest obligation in the first month, 47/1,176 in the second month, and so on.

Suppose the borrowers repay the loan after one year. After 12 payments of $283.33, they have paid a total of $3,399.96. Under the rule of 78s, they would be credited with (510/1,176) × $3,600 = $1,561.22 in interest. The numerator, 510, is the sum of 48, 47, 46, and so on through 37. Thus, $1,838.74 of the principal balance ($3,399.96 − $1,561.22) would be considered repaid. To discharge their obligation, the borrowers would have to pay the credit union $10,000 − $1,838.74, or $8,161.26.

The Rule as a Prepayment Penalty.   The rule of 78s is controversial because it specifies a balance for repayment higher than the balance indicated by an amortization schedule based on the APR, shown in Table 14.2. After 12 payments at an APR of 15.9864 percent, the borrowers owe $8,060.61. In most states, however, lenders are permitted to use the rule of 78s, although a few states have adopted laws specifically prohibiting it. The discrepancy is more significant for loans with higher initial balances, longer initial maturities, and higher APRs. It is essentially a prepayment penalty. Lenders argue that it is justified because it helps them recover fixed lending costs, although consumer advocates argue that the rule of 78s is unfair to borrowers.[22]

Loan Maturities

An important factor contributing to growth in consumer debt in the 1980s is the trend toward

---

[20]Board of Governors of the Federal Reserve System, "Official Staff Commentary on Regulation Z Truth-in-Lending as Amended October 16, 1984," November 1984, Section 226.14, p. 56.

[21]A shortcut for calculating the sum of the digits is $(N/2) \times (N + 1)$, where N is the number of payments.

[22]An examination of the size of the prepayment penalty in relationship to maturity, loan size, and APR is provided in Susan Kramer, "An Analysis of the Rule of 78s," *Journal of Retail Banking* 3 (September 1981): 46-55.

Table 14.2
Installment Loan Amortization Schedule

Monthly Payments: $283.33   Initial Balance: $10,000   Initial Maturity: 4 years   APR: 15.9864%

Month	(1) Payment	(2) Beginning Balance	(3) Interest .159864/12 × (2)	(4) Principal Paid (1) − (3)	(5) End-of-Month Balance (2) − (4)
1	$283.33	$10,000.00	$133.22	$150.11	$9,849.89
2	283.33	9,849.89	131.22	152.11	9,697.77
3	283.33	9,697.77	129.19	154.14	9,543.63
4	283.33	9,543.63	127.14	156.19	9,387.44
5	283.33	9,387.44	125.06	158.27	9,229.17
6	283.33	9,229.17	122.95	160.38	9,068.79
7	283.33	9,068.79	120.81	162.52	8,906.27
8	283.33	8,906.27	118.65	164.68	8,741.58
9	283.33	8,741.58	116.46	166.88	8,574.71
10	283.33	8,574.71	114.23	169.10	8,405.60
11	283.33	8,405.60	111.98	171.35	8,234.25
12	283.33	8,234.25	109.70	173.64	8,060.61
20	283.33	6,778.63	90.30	193.03	6,585.61
21	283.33	6,585.61	87.73	195.60	6,390.01
22	283.33	6,390.01	85.13	198.21	6,191.80
23	283.33	6,191.80	82.49	200.85	5,990.96
24	283.33	5,990.96	79.81	203.52	5,787.43
25	283.33	5,787.43	77.10	206.23	5,581.20
26	283.33	5,581.20	74.35	208.98	5,372.22
27	283.33	5,372.22	71.57	211.76	5,160.46
28	283.33	5,160.46	68.75	214.59	4,945.87
29	283.33	4,945.87	65.89	217.44	4,728.43
30	283.33	4,728.43	62.99	220.34	4,508.09
40	283.33	2,388.12	31.81	251.52	2,136.60
41	283.33	2,136.60	28.46	254.87	1,881.73
42	283.33	1,881.73	25.07	258.26	1,623.47
43	283.33	1,623.47	21.63	261.71	1,361.76
44	283.33	1,361.76	18.14	265.19	1,096.57
45	283.33	1,096.57	14.61	268.72	827.85
46	283.33	827.85	11.03	272.30	555.54
47	283.33	555.54	7.40	275.93	279.61
48	283.33	279.61	3.72	279.61	0.00

loans with longer maturities. As prices of consumer goods purchased on credit have increased, loan terms have been adjusted so goods will still be affordable. For example, through 1983, at commercial banks the standard maturity on a loan for a new car was 36 months. As of 1984, 48-month loans predominated. For all auto lenders, the average maturity on loans issued in August 1986 was 50.4 months. The principal amount of a new-car loan increased 22.4 percent from 1983 to 1986, to $10,756.[23]

Variable-Rate Installment Loans

Variable interest rates are a relatively new development in consumer installment lending. In some states, usury laws still prevent variable-rate consumer loans, but where permitted to do so, many lenders are using them. The use of variable-rate consumer loans differs by institutional size. A 1985 nationwide survey revealed that 45 percent of large banks and thrifts were offering them; a similar survey a year earlier showed that only 25 percent of smaller institutions were involved in this market.[24]

When the interest rate on a consumer loan changes, lenders may offer borrowers two options:

1. An adjustment in the monthly payment so that the loan is still amortized over the initial loan period; or

2. An adjustment in the loan maturity without changing the monthly payment.

Under the second option, the loan period is extended if interest rates increase or shortened if rates decline. In 1985, almost 80 percent of institutions with variable-rate consumer loans offered the maturity-change option, while less than 35 percent offered the payment-change option. As the percentages suggest, some institutions offer both.

Changing the Monthly Payment. Table 14.3 provides a standard amortization schedule for a four-year, $8,000 loan with an initial annual interest rate of 13 percent, or a monthly rate of 13% $\div$ 12 = 1.083 percent. Using Equation 4A.7 for the present value of an annuity, the monthly payment (C_1) is $214.62 in each of the 48 months if the interest rate does not change:

$$C_0 = C_1 \left[\frac{1 - (1 + k)^{-n}}{k} \right]$$

$$\$8,000 = C_1 \times 37.275$$

$$C_1 = \$214.62$$

Table 14.3 shows the effect of an increase in the interest rate, from 13 percent to 14 percent, after the 12th payment has been made. The monthly payment rises to $217.70 for the last 36 months, and the amortization schedule reflects the change as of payment 13.

Changing the Loan Term. The other alternative is to keep the monthly payment constant, but to adjust the loan maturity. The effect is demonstrated in Table 14.4. After 12 payments, the interest rate again increases to 14 percent; if the monthly payment remains at $214.62, a partial payment of $138.46 is owed in the 49th month. When a borrower believes a payment increase would unacceptably strain the monthly budget, this option may be desirable. Under neither option, however, does a 100-basis-point increase in the interest rate greatly change the borrower's obligations. If a variable-rate loan also carries a lower initial interest rate than a comparable fixed-rate loan—and most do—the impact of a payment increase may seem even less severe.

Lenders pioneering in variable-rate loans believe that transferring interest rate risk to borrowers ensures that consumer credit will continue to be available, regardless of the interest rate environment. Because such loans are new, there is little evidence about consumer response to them. One study of consumers with automobile loans from a commercial bank found that the choice between fixed and variable rates was affected by borrowers' expectations about future interest rates and inflation. Borrowers taking adjustable rates were more optimistic about economic trends and more confident that their incomes would increase, enabling them to meet potentially higher payments.[25]

[23]"Terms of Consumer Installment Credit," *Federal Reserve Bulletin* 72 (December 1986): A41.

[24]John L. Goodman, Jr., and Charles A. Luckett, "Adjustable Rate Financing in Mortgage and Consumer Credit Markets," *Federal Reserve Bulletin* 71 (November 1985): 832–833.

[25]A. Charlene Sullivan, "Consumers' Choice of Consumer Loan Contract Terms," Working Paper No. 51, Credit Research Center, Purdue University, 1985.

Table 14.3
Installment Loan Amortization Schedule: Adjustable Rate, Adjustable Payment

Initial Monthly Payment:
$214.62

Initial Balance:
$8,000

Initial Maturity:
4 years

Initial Rate:
13.00%

Adjusted Rate:
14% after month 12

Payment after
Rate Adjustment:
$217.70

Month	(1) Payment	(2) Beginning Balance	(3) Interest .13/12 × (2) or .14/12 × (2)	(4) Principal Paid (1) − (3)	(5) End-of-Month Balance (2) − (4)
1	$214.62	$8,000.00	$86.67	$127.95	$7,872.05
2	214.62	7,872.05	85.28	129.34	7,742.71
3	214.62	7,742.71	83.88	130.74	7,611.97
4	214.62	7,611.97	82.46	132.16	7,479.81
5	214.62	7,479.81	81.03	133.59	7,346.22
6	214.62	7,346.22	79.58	135.04	7,211.19
7	214.62	7,211.19	78.12	136.50	7,074.69
8	214.62	7,074.69	76.64	137.98	6,936.71
9	214.62	6,936.71	75.15	139.47	6,797.24
10	214.62	6,797.24	73.64	140.98	6,656.25
11	214.62	6,656.25	72.11	142.51	6,513.74
12	214.62	6,513.74	70.57	144.05	6,369.69
13	217.70	6,369.69	74.31	143.39	6,226.30
14	217.70	6,226.30	72.64	145.06	6,081.24
15	217.70	6,081.24	70.95	146.75	5,934.49
40	217.70	1,849.74	21.58	196.12	1,653.62
41	217.70	1,653.62	19.29	198.41	1,455.21
42	217.70	1,455.21	16.98	200.72	1,254.48
43	217.70	1,254.48	14.64	203.07	1,051.42
44	217.70	1,051.42	12.27	205.43	845.98
45	217.70	845.98	9.87	207.83	638.15
46	217.70	638.15	7.45	210.26	427.90
47	217.70	427.90	4.99	212.71	215.19
48	217.70	215.19	2.51	215.19	0.00

CONSUMER CREDIT THROUGH CREDIT CARDS

Credit cards allow consumer credit to be extended on a prearranged basis, similar to formal commercial loan commitments discussed in the previous chapter. Credit issued through cards is *revolving credit,* on which the lender designates a prearranged interest rate and maximum line of credit. The cardholder chooses when and whether to borrow, repaying the lender par-

tially or in full upon receipt of a monthly statement. The annual fee most borrowers pay for the privilege of carrying a card is analogous to a commitment fee in commercial lending.

A Brief History

Retailers were the first firms to offer credit cards. In 1951, however, Franklin National Bank of New York recognized untapped profit

Table 14.4
Installment Loan Amortization Schedule: Adjustable Rate, Fixed Payment

Initial Monthly Payment: $214.62	Initial Balance: $8,000	Initial Maturity: 48 months
Initial Rate: 13.00%	Adjusted Rate: 14% after month 12	Maturity after Rate Adjustment: 36.64 months

Month	(1) Payment	(2) Beginning Balance	(3) Interest .13/12 × (2) or .14/12 × (2)	(4) Principal Paid (1) − (3)	(5) End-of-Month Balance (2) − (4)
1	$214.62	$8,000.00	$86.67	$127.95	$7,872.05
2	214.62	7,872.05	85.28	129.34	7,742.71
3	214.62	7,742.71	83.88	130.74	7,611.97
4	214.62	7,611.97	82.46	132.16	7,479.81
5	214.62	7,479.81	81.03	133.59	7,346.22
6	214.62	7,346.22	79.58	135.04	7,211.19
7	214.62	7,211.19	78.12	136.50	7,074.69
8	214.62	7,074.69	76.64	137.98	6,936.71
9	214.62	6,936.71	75.15	139.47	6,797.24
10	214.62	6,797.24	73.64	140.98	6,656.25
11	214.62	6,656.25	72.11	142.51	6,513.74
12	214.62	6,513.74	70.57	144.05	6,369.69
13	214.62	6,369.69	74.31	140.31	6,229.38
14	214.62	6,229.38	72.68	141.94	6,087.44
15	214.62	6,087.44	71.02	143.60	5,943.84
40	214.62	1,946.85	22.71	191.91	1,754.95
41	214.62	1,754.95	20.47	194.15	1,560.80
42	214.62	1,560.80	18.21	196.41	1,364.39
43	214.62	1,364.39	15.92	198.70	1,165.69
44	214.62	1,165.69	13.60	201.02	964.67
45	214.62	964.67	11.25	203.37	761.30
46	214.62	761.30	8.88	205.74	555.57
47	214.62	555.57	6.48	208.14	347.43
48	214.62	347.43	4.05	210.57	136.86
49	138.46	136.86	1.60	136.86	0.00

potential, and the "bank card" was born. ("Bank card" is used in this chapter to refer to cards issued by all depositories.) In the late 1950s, larger banks began to participate. The depository most closely identified with bank cards is BankAmerica, which promoted its card nationwide starting in 1966; this was the origin of the current Visa system. By 1968, because of prohibitive marketing expenses, many banks dropped their private cards and joined cooper-

ative marketing organizations, the largest of which are Visa and MasterCard.[26]

Because of regulation, thrifts and CUs entered the credit card business later than banks. In 1977, federal CUs were permitted to offer lines of credit for the first time; this authority

---

[26]Details on the early history of bank credit cards are provided in Thomas Russell. *The Economics of Bank Credit Cards* (New York: Praeger Publishers, 1975).

paved the way for their entry into the bank card business, although by 1985, only 10.2 percent of all CUs had done so. Still, over 60 percent of the largest CUs were involved. DIDMCA gave federal thrifts authority to issue credit cards, and many have done so. A Fed survey showed that in 1983, 42 percent of all American families had bank credit cards. In 1985, over 93 million Visa cards and 68 million MasterCards were outstanding.[27]

The Risks and Returns from Credit Cards

Like other financial products, credit cards offer their issuers both benefits and risks.

Sources of Profit.   Annual fees, originated when many state usury ceilings were binding, are standard practice among depositories issuing credit cards. Now that usury ceilings are less burdensome, the fees are a welcome source of income not really dependent upon economic conditions. Because many current usury ceilings were set in the early 1980s, in a period of extremely high interest rates, depositories have been able to charge very profitable rates of interest on credit cards throughout most of the decade. For example, in November 1986, interest rates on bank cards averaged nearly 20 percent nationwide, while the prime rate at major banks averaged 7.5 percent.[28] As Figure 14.4 illustrates, this situation has been common for several years.

Institutions that process credit transactions and bill customers for other depositories are able to earn additional revenues. Finally, the issuing bank charges merchants accepting bank cards fees ranging from 2 percent to 5 percent of a transaction.

Sources of Risk.   Because credit cards carry preestablished lines of credit, consumers may accumulate substantial borrowings before the card issuer knows financial problems have developed. The problem is compounded because many consumers carry more than one bank card, a situation perpetuated when institutions conduct "mass mailings" to solicit new cardholders. The mass-mailing strategy has hit some snags. For example, the Bank of New Orleans sent unsolicited credit cards to a group identified by the bank's computers as having steady employment and noteworthy credit records. The mailing list consisted of inmates at a state prison.[29]

In addition, credit card issuance may lead to heavy reliance on credit-scoring models. Card applications lend themselves to use in statistical models, but the borrower's condition may change so rapidly that the results of the model do not reflect the risk to which the lender is exposed when the card is issued. Because the lender may have had no personal contact with the borrower, credit decisions are often made on no other basis.

Finally, because bank cards involve so many consumers (read "voters"), Congress is quite interested in them. In early 1987, bills to regulate interest rates on bank cards were pending in Congress. The controversy was fueled by the emergence of so-called *affinity cards*—bank cards issued to members of special interest groups. Banks' decisions to share profits with organizations such as labor unions that help market the affinity cards to members brought new charges that if profits were not already excessive, banks would not share them. Because 60 percent of the revenues from bank cards are derived from interest, federal ceilings could significantly reduce their profitability.[30]

[27]CUNA, *1985 Credit Union Report;* Avery et al., "Survey of Consumer Finances, 1983," p. 866; Monci Jo Williams, "The Great Plastic Card Fight Begins," *Fortune* 111 (February 4, 1985): 21.

[28]Christopher Farrell, "Credit Card Wars: Profits Are Taking a Direct Hit," *Business Week,* November 17, 1986, pp. 166-167.

[29]Charles F. McCoy, "Losses on Credit Cards, Other Consumer Debt Are Climbing Rapidly," *The Wall Street Journal,* December 2, 1985, pp. 1, 12.

[30]An analysis of the economic impact of proposed legislation is given in Glenn B. Canner and James T. Fergus, "The Economic Effects of Proposed Ceilings on Credit Card Interest Rates," *Federal Reserve Bulletin* 73 (January 1987): 1-13.

Figure 14.4
Bank Credit Card and Other Interest Rates

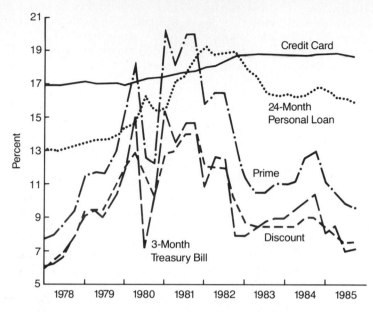

Source: Anthony Cyrnak, "Credit Card Controversy," *Weekly Letter,* Federal Reserve Bank of San Francisco, December 27, 1985.

MORTGAGE LENDING: AN OVERVIEW

Because home ownership is such an important goal in the United States, the demand for mortgage loans is expected to continue. Volume, however, is seasonal and strongly affected by the economy and interest rates. As inflation drove up housing prices in the late 1970s, accompanied by interest rate increases, home ownership seemed out of reach for many. Since that time, innovations have ensured the viability of the housing finance market. The Tax Reform Act of 1986 retained the tax deduction for mortgage interest, continuing the national commitment to home ownership.

A mortgage is a legal agreement assigning property as collateral on a loan. Although the homebuyer technically holds the title to the property, the lender may take action to obtain it if the borrower defaults. When a home purchase

is financed, the buyer signs a note stipulating the interest rate and repayment schedule for a loan to purchase the home, and a mortgage agreement designating the property as collateral on the loan.

Lenders' Market Shares

As noted, home financing accounts for the majority of consumer debt. Figure 14.5 provides recent data on the share of funds provided by depository institutions and other lenders to finance residential real estate. Although the proportion of mortgage debt held by S&Ls has declined in the 1980s, they continue to hold a larger share than other depositories. Commercial banks hold only about half as much, and credit unions, included in the "Other" slice of the pie, have relatively small amounts. For reasons discussed in later chapters, federal agencies and institutions such as pension funds and in-

Figure 14.5
Holders of Home Mortgage Debt, Year-End 1985

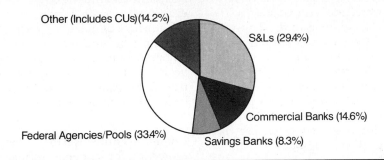

Other (Includes CUs) (14.2%)

S&Ls (29.4%)

Commercial Banks (14.6%)

Federal Agencies/Pools (33.4%)

Savings Banks (8.3%)

Source: Federal Reserve Bulletin, December 1986, p. A39.

surance companies play increasingly large roles in the mortgage market.

The Mortgage Menu

The most publicized features of housing finance in the 1980s are the new types of mortgages offered to consumers. In fact, so many different features have been introduced, collectively called the "mortgage menu," that some experts believe even financially sophisticated homebuyers are unable to evaluate them adequately.[31] Buyers are offered mortgages with variable interest rates and loan maturities; plans with lower payments in the early years of the loan; agreements refinanced periodically, with renegotiated interest rates; and many more arrangements. For a number of reasons, consumer acceptance of adjustable-rate mortgages has grown, and in recent years, the proportion of home loans originated with variable rates has ranged from around 30 percent to over 70 percent.[32]

Lenders Want Flexibility.   Mortgage lenders have good reason to offer variable-rate instruments. With the increased level and volatility of deposit interest costs, lenders are less willing to offer long-term loans carrying a fixed rate of interest. Furthermore, regulatory changes since 1981 have given mortgage lenders more flexibility to develop new mortgage instruments.

Borrowers Want Choice.   High interest rates have made consumers willing to accept the uncertainty of a variable-rate mortgage (VRM). For example, the average interest rate charged on a new mortgage in December 1978 was under 10 percent, but it had risen to over 15 percent by the end of 1981 and exceeded 13 percent in 1984. Because lenders usually offer initial interest rate discounts on VRMs, many borrowers find them more affordable than fixed-rate mortgages. Research indicates, in fact, that the initial rate discount is the most important factor in a borrower's decision to choose a variable-rate mortgage. It also shows that borrowers like a variety of home financing alternatives, because choice tends to make home ownership more affordable for many types of homebuyers.[33]

[31]For an interesting discussion of the dilemma facing homebuyers, see Jack Guttentag, "Solving the Mortgage Menu Problem," *Housing Finance Review* 3 (July 1983): 227-252.

[32]*Freddie Mac Reports,* various issues.

[33]These and other conclusions were drawn by authors of the following studies: Kent W. Colton, Donald R. Lessard, David Modest, and Arthur P. Solomon, "National Survey of Borrowers' Housing Characteristics, Attitudes and Preferences," in *Alternative Mortgage Instruments Research Study,* Volume I (Washington, DC: Federal Home Loan Bank Board, November 1977); Gerald Albaum and

Government Regulations and Mortgage Lending

The attention of regulators and legislatures to consumer credit protection has extended to the mortgage markets. In addition to the Truth-in-Lending and Equal Credit acts, mortgage lenders must comply with the Fair Housing Act of 1968, the Home Mortgage Disclosure Act of 1975, and the Community Reinvestment Act of 1979. These laws were designed to prevent discrimination on the basis of borrower race or neighborhood location, and to ensure that credit is available in all communities.

Federal regulations also control specific loan terms. Until 1981, the ability of federal thrifts to offer VRMs was severely limited. In April of that year the FHLBB approved regulations for a very flexible instrument, originally called the "adjustable mortgage loan," but now more frequently known as an **adjustable-rate mortgage (ARM).** These federal regulations overrode state laws that were more restrictive. Regulations for national banks, set by the Comptroller of the Currency, give bankers less freedom in developing new mortgage plans. Federal credit union mortgage regulations were revised in 1982, also allowing terms more attractive to lenders. These regulations are discussed more fully later in the chapter.

CREDIT RISK AND MORTGAGE LENDING

When evaluating the credit risk of a mortgage loan application, lenders rely on much of the same information used for other consumer loans, but they must consider additional factors.

Important Variables in Assessing Credit Risk

A significant amount of research has been conducted to identify factors related to mortgage delinquency or default.[34] Even though the loans are secured, foreclosure is a lengthy and expensive procedure. Furthermore, the property may be in poor condition by the time the lender takes possession of it, and its resale value may be less than the outstanding loan balance.

Loan-to-Value Ratio. One form of self-protection for lenders is to make sure the value of the property at the time of application exceeds the loan amount by enough to protect them in case of default. Research indicates that the initial **loan-to-value ratio** is positively related to both delinquency and default. The difference between the outstanding loan balance and the value of the property is the borrower's equity in the home. When the loan-to-value ratio is high—the maximum allowed initially by most lenders is 95 percent—the borrower has a small personal investment. If the borrower encounters financial difficulty early in the loan term, defaulting on the agreement may be the least painful course of action. If the market value of the home declines as a result of economic conditions or neighborhood deterioration, the reduction in the borrower's equity may contribute to default even several years after the loan agreement is made.

To estimate property values, lenders hire trained real estate appraisers and base the loan amount on the appraisal report. Recently, concern has been expressed about the quality of appraisals. In an environment of relatively low inflation, lenders must be confident that the initial appraisal does not exaggerate the value of

George Kaufman, "The Variable Rate Residential Mortgage: Implications for Borrowers," in *Alternative Mortgage Instruments Research Study,* Volume I (Washington, DC: Federal Home Loan Bank Board, November 1977); *Buying a Home in the 1980s: A Poll of American Attitudes,* (Washington, DC: Federal National Mortgage Association, September 14, 1982); Dixie L. Mills and Mona J. Gardner, "Consumer Response to Adjustable Rate Mortgages: Implications of the Evidence from Illinois and Wisconsin," *Journal of Consumer Affairs* 20 (Summer 1986): 77-105.

[34]Among the numerous studies on this topic are: John P. Herzog and James B. Earley, *Home Mortgage Delinquency and Foreclosure* (New York: National Bureau of Economics and Research, 1970); George von Furstenberg and R. Jeffrey Green, "Estimation of Delinquency Risk for Home Mortgage Portfolios," *AREUEA Journal* 2 (Fall 1974): 101-112; Tim S. Campbell and J. Kimball Dietrich, "Determinants of Default on Insured Conventional Residential Mortgage Loans," *Journal of Finance* 38 (December 1983): 1,569-1,581.

the property. One study in 1985 attributed 10 percent of the financial problems at federally insured S&Ls to faulty or fraudulent appraisals. These and other findings have led to calls for closer scrutiny of appraisal practices and even regulation of the appraisal industry.[35]

Borrower Income.   Another key variable is the expected growth and stability of the borrower's future income. The more fluctuations in income, the more difficult it may be to meet monthly payments, because a mortgage payment is usually the largest single debt obligation for a household. Again, with an adjustable-rate loan, potential income variability may be even more problematic.

The *payment-to-income ratio,* comparing the borrower's gross monthly income to the monthly loan payment, is widely used to assess the burden on the borrower. The payment is sometimes adjusted to include homeowners' insurance and property taxes. Because the *future* debt burden is of interest, however, research indicates that the initial payment-to-income ratio is not as good a predictor of delinquency or default as one might expect.

Economic Conditions

Another important influence on credit risk is outside the lender's control. The economy's general strength is negatively correlated with loan default. In a recession, for example, the unemployment rate rises. At the same time, property values may level off or even decline, putting pressure on the payment-to-income and the loan-to-value ratios. A borrower may lack the incentive to sell the home to discharge the loan, and may choose to simply walk away, leaving the lender with financial losses.

Recent delinquency and default rates illustrate the impact of economic conditions. During the double-digit inflation years of the late 1970s, homebuyers expected the value of their

houses to rise rapidly. When inflation was brought under control, followed by an economic recession, those expectations were not fulfilled. Mortgage delinquencies soared, and by the first quarter of 1985, exceeded all previous levels. Potential losses so seriously hurt the nation's thrift institutions that the long-term viability of the FSLIC was threatened, a development discussed in more detail in the next chapter.[36]

Adjustable-Rate Lending and Credit Risk

Because ARMs have been issued on a wide scale only during the 1980s, little is known about whether adjustable-rate loans increase the lender's exposure to default risk. Lacking empirical data, researchers have simulated the potential for borrower default under a variety of assumptions about interest rates and borrower income. Although VRMs permit a lender to transfer interest rate risk to the borrower, financial institutions may be more able to bear the uncertainty of rate changes than are individuals. The question is whether or when too much risk is shifted. Unfortunately, research is as yet inconclusive and often contradictory. Many agree that upwardly mobile borrowers are not high default risks, but beyond that there is little consensus.[37] Resolution of the issue awaits collec-

---

[35]Kathleen A. Hughes, "Real-Estate Appraisals Sometimes Are High, Hurting Banks, S&Ls," *The Wall Street Journal,* July 17, 1985, pp. 1, 20; Laurie Cohen, "Appraisals Tied to S&L Failures," *Chicago Tribune,* December 12, 1985, Section 2, pp. 1, 8.

[36]Robert Guenther, "More Homeowners in Financial Trouble Opt for Foreclosure," *The Wall Street Journal,* February 7, 1985, pp. 1, 22; Teresa Carson, Blanca Riemer, and G. David Wallace, "Now Bad Loans Are the Thrifts' Big Enemy," *Business Week,* March 25, 1985, pp. 63, 66; and Richard L. Stern and Mark Clifford, "Trouble at Home," *Forbes* 136 (August 12, 1985): 31-34.

[37]A representative sampling of this research includes: Thomas P. Boehm and Joseph McKenzie, "The Affordability of Alternative Mortgage Instruments: A Household Analysis," *Housing Finance Review* 2 (October 1983): 287-294; Robert M. Buckley and Kevin Villani, "Problems with the Adjustable-Rate Mortgage Regulations," *Housing Finance Review* 2 (July 1983): 183-190; Peggy Crawford and Charles P. Harper, "The Effect of the AML Index on the Borrower," *Housing Finance Review* 2 (October 1983): 309-320; Kerry D. Vandell, "Default Risk under Alternative Mortgage Instruments," *Journal of Finance* 33 (December 1978): 1,279-1,296; Bruce Webb, "Borrower Risk under Alternative Mortgage Instruments," *Journal of Finance* 37 (March 1982): 169-183.

tion and analysis of data on the incidence of default under ARMs.

Mortgage Insurance

Offsetting some of the default risk faced by lenders is mortgage insurance. Lenders may require borrowers to pay the premiums for insurance policies, naming the lender as the beneficiary in case of borrower default. Insurance is offered by federal agencies such as the *Federal Housing Administration (FHA)* and by private mortgage insurance companies. FHA insurance was mandated by the National Housing Act of 1934 as an encouragement to lenders to make housing loans in an unfavorable economic environment. Since that time, other federal mortgage-guarantee programs have been introduced, including those offered by the Veterans Administration (VA).[38] FHA and VA programs have restrictions on interest rates and other terms that make them relatively unattractive to depository institution lenders. They also may require several weeks for approval or denial. As a result, the vast majority of FHA- and VA-insured mortgages are originated by *mortgage bankers,* specialized financial institutions that originate mortgages, then sell them to other investors.

Mortgages not VA-guaranteed or FHA-insured are known as *conventional mortgages.* The unattractive features of government programs left an opening for private insurers, who insure conventional mortgages with a loan-to-value ratio as high as 95 percent. Their coverage is widely used by depository institutions. Borrowers with down payments below a specified amount may be required to apply for insurance, paying an annual premium based on the principal balance. The insurance does not remove all a lender's credit risk, however, because it protects only a portion, usually up to 25 percent, of the funds invested in the loan.[39]

ADJUSTABLE-RATE MORTGAGE TERMS

As discussed later in the chapter, mortgage innovations are not limited to interest rate characteristics, although these have been the focus of consumers and regulators. Major issues in adjustable-rate mortgage lending are presented in this section.

Regulation of ARMs

The greatest step forward in variable-rate mortgage lending occurred in 1981, when regulations for national banks and federally chartered thrifts were revised. Both types of lenders gained more freedom to tailor mortgages to fit their own asset/liability management targets. The federal regulations give thrifts more flexibility than banks, as Table 14.5 shows.

Interest Rate Index.   A widely debated issue in ARM lending is the choice of the index on which interest rate adjustments are based. National banks have only three choices: indexes of long-term mortgage rates, T-bill rates, or T-bond rates. Thrifts may use any interest rate series that is widely published, verifiable by the borrower, and not in the direct control of an individual lender. The lender must explain to the borrower exactly how the loan interest

---

[38]Technically, FHA mortgages are *insured* against default; the borrower pays a modest insurance premium for protection up to a specified maximum amount. In contrast, VA mortgages are *guaranteed.* The VA establishes a maximum dollar amount the lender is guaranteed to receive at no cost to the borrower. This guarantee may allow a borrower to obtain a loan without a down payment, because it reduces the amount the lender has at risk.

[39]Competition in the private mortgage insurance industry has led in the past to more lenient underwriting standards. See Jack M. Guttentag, "Recent Changes in the Primary Home Mortgage Market," *Housing Finance Review* 3 (July 1984): 221-254; and Claude E. Pope, "Private Mortgage Insurers Stake New Claims," *Secondary Mortgage Markets* 1 (February 1984): 18-23. A more conservative trend may be appearing among private mortgage insurers in response to higher delinquency and foreclosure rates. See William Celis III, "Mortgage Rates Are Lower, but Insurers Make It Harder for Buyers to Get Loans," *The Wall Street Journal,* June 20, 1985, p. 27; and Steven P. Doehler, "Mortgage Insurance Companies Predict a Strong Future," *Savings Institutions* 106 (November 1985): 92-98.

Table 14.5
Major Characteristics of Recent Federal Regulations Governing Adjustable–Rate Home Mortgage Lending

Major Characteristics	Federal Savings and Loan Associations and Mutual Savings Banks	National Banks
Requirement to offer fixed-rate mortgage instrument to borrower	None	None
Limit on amount of ARMs that may be held	None	None
Indexes governing mortgage rate adjustments	Any interest rate index that is readily verifiable by the borrower and not under the control of the lender, including national or regional cost-of-funds indexes for S&Ls	1 of 3 national rate indexes—a long-term mortgage rate, a Treasury bill rate, or a 3-year Treasury bond rate.
Limit on frequency of rate adjustments	None	Not more often than every 6 months.
Limit on size of periodic rate adjustments	None	1 percentage point for each 6-month period between rate adjustments, and no single rate adjustment may exceed 5 percentage points
Limit on size of total rate adjustment over life of mortgage	Must be disclosed[1]	Must be disclosed[1]
Allowable methods of adjustment to rate changes	Any combination of changes in monthly payment, loan term, or principal balance	Changes in monthly payment or rate of amortization
Limit on amount of negative amortization	No limit, but monthly payments must be adjusted periodically to fully amortize the loan over the remaining term	Limits are set, and monthly payments must be adjusted periodically to fully amortize the loan over the remaining term
Advance notice of rate adjustments	30 to 45 days before scheduled adjustment	30 to 45 days before scheduled adjustments
Prepayment restrictions or charges	None	Prepayment without penalty permitted after notification of first scheduled rate adjustment
Disclosure requirements	Full disclosure of ARM characteristics no later than time of loan application	Full disclosure of ARM characteristics no later than time of loan application

Source: Adapted from David F. Seiders, "Changing Patterns of Housing Finance," *Federal Reserve Bulletin* 67 (June 1981): 468.

[1]The Competitive Equality Banking Act of 1987 requires an overall rate cap, but does not specify what the cap must be.

rate is related to the index, and how it will be adjusted as the index changes. Recent data indicate that the one-year Treasury rate is by far the most common index.[40]

The index choice is a central part of an institution's asset/liability management strategy because of its influence on the size and stability

[40]Results of recent surveys are reported in Noel Fahey, "Consumers and Lenders Blend Needs to Shape Sound ARMs," *Savings Institutions* 106 (August 1985): 49–55; Michael Lea, "ARM Pricing Reflects Cap and Discount Costs," *Savings Institutions* 106 (February 1985): 60–65; and Federal Home Loan Bank of Chicago, "Adjustable Rate Mortgage Study," an unpublished research study prepared for the Conference of Presidents of Federal Home Loan Banks, July 1984.

Figure 14.6
Cost of Funds versus One-Year Treasury Indexes, February 1980–August 1985

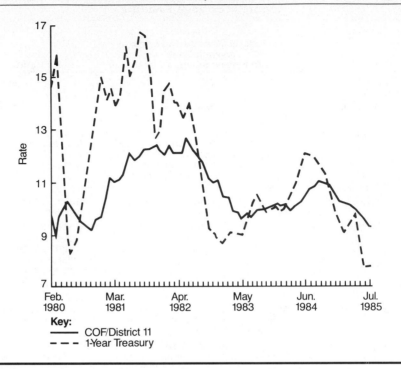

Key:
—— COF/District 11
- - - 1-Year Treasury

Source: Michael R. Asay, "How ARMs Move," *Secondary Mortgage Markets* 2 (Winter 1985/1986): 9. © 1986 by the Federal Home Loan Mortgage Corporation. All rights reserved. Used by permission.

of the NIM. ARMs provide opportunities to protect the spread between interest costs and interest revenues. Ideally, the choice of an index should depend upon the marginal cost of funds used to finance mortgage loans. Figure 14.6 shows why the one-year Treasury index is more popular with lenders in achieving that purpose than a typical average cost of funds index. The average cost index is more stable because it reflects historical as well as current rates, whereas the Treasury index reflects only current market conditions.

Interest Rate and Payment Adjustments. Federal regulations allow thrift institutions to offer ARM plans with any frequency of rate adjustments, but national banks may not change the mortgage interest rate more than once every six months. Banks also have limits,

called *caps,* on the size of the periodic rate adjustment. An overall rate cap is required by federal law, and many lenders have attempted to overcome borrower resistance to ARMs by offering a cap on each periodic interest rate adjustment, which limits the borrower's interest rate risk. Recent data indicate that over 95 percent of all ARMs originated have either rate or payment caps or both. In fact, research indicates that some type of interest rate cap is the most influential factor in gaining borrower acceptance of ARMs.[41]

Loan Term Extension and Negative Amortization.   A lender has several ways of protecting the borrower from "payment shock," a

---

[41]Mills and Gardner, "Consumer Response to Adjustable Rate Mortgages."

large increase in the monthly payment. Thrifts, but not banks, can extend the loan maturity, illustrated in Table 14.4 for an installment loan. Thrifts are allowed to increase a mortgage loan term up to a maximum of 40 years, keeping the mortgage payment in a more affordable range.

When an ARM has a periodic payment cap, but no periodic rate cap, there is potential for *negative amortization.* Negative amortization occurs whenever the interest rate increases but the payment does not increase enough to cover the additional interest charges. In that case, the unpaid interest in any one month is added to the outstanding loan balance. Instead of amortiz-

ing, or reducing, the principal, the borrower's obligation increases, and equity in the home is reduced. Plans allowing negative amortization are unpopular with consumers. A good reason for consumer resistance is that under negative amortization, the borrower actually pays compound interest, or interest on interest. A normal amortization schedule involves simple interest only.

Table 14.6 provides an example of negative amortization, using the first 2 years of a $100,000, 30-year mortgage with an initial rate of 13 percent. The monthly payment at that rate is $1,106.20. The example assumes that the payment cannot change during the first two years

Table 14.6
Mortgage Loan with Negative Amortization: Adjustable Rate, Fixed Payments

Initial Monthly Payment: $1,106.20	Initial Balance: $100,000	Initial Maturity: 30 years	Initial Rate: 13.00%	Adjusted Rate: 16% after month 12	

Month	(1) Payment to Fully Amortize	(2) Fixed Payment	(3) Beginning Balance	(4) Interest .13/12 × (3) or .16/12 × (3)	(5) Principal Paid (2) − (4)	(6) End-of-Month Balance (3) − (5)
1	$1,106.20	$1,106.20	$100,000.00	$1,083.33	$22.87	$ 99,977.13
2	1,106.20	1,106.20	99,977.13	1,083.09	23.11	99,954.02
3	1,106.20	1,106.20	99,954.02	1,082.84	23.36	99,930.66
4	1,106.20	1,106.20	99,930.66	1,082.58	23.62	99,907.04
5	1,106.20	1,106.20	99,907.04	1,082.33	23.87	99,883.16
6	1,106.20	1,106.20	99,883.16	1,082.07	24.13	99,859.03
7	1,106.20	1,106.20	99,859.03	1,081.81	24.39	99,834.64
8	1,106.20	1,106.20	99,834.64	1,081.54	24.66	99,809.98
9	1,106.20	1,106.20	99,809.98	1,081.27	24.92	99,785.06
10	1,106.20	1,106.20	99,785.06	1,081.00	25.19	99,759.86
11	1,106.20	1,106.20	99,759.86	1,080.73	25.47	99,734.39
12	1,106.20	1,106.20	99,734.39	1,080.46	25.74	99,708.65
13	1,342.82	1,106.20	99,708.65	1,329.45	(223.25)	**99,931.90**
14	1,342.82	1,106.20	99,931.90	1,332.43	(226.23)	100,158.13
15	1,342.82	1,106.20	100,158.13	1,335.44	(229.24)	100,387.37
16	1,342.82	1,106.20	100,387.37	1,338.50	(232.30)	100,619.67
17	1,342.82	1,106.20	100,619.67	1,341.60	(235.40)	100,855.06
18	1,342.82	1,106.20	100,855.06	1,344.73	(238.53)	101,093.60
19	1,342.82	1,106.20	101,093.60	1,347.91	(241.72)	101,335.31
20	1,342.82	1,106.20	101,335.31	1,351.14	(244.94)	101,580.25
21	1,342.82	1,106.20	101,580.25	1,354.40	(248.20)	101,828.45
22	1,342.82	1,106.20	101,828.45	1,357.71	(251.51)	102,079.97
23	1,342.82	1,106.20	102,079.97	1,361.07	(254.87)	102,334.83
24	1,342.82	1,106.20	102,334.83	1,364.46	(258.26)	102,593.10

of the loan but that the interest rate can be adjusted annually. If, after the first year, the interest rate is increased to 16 percent, the payment to fully amortize the mortgage over the remaining 29 years would be $1,343.82 per month. After the interest rate rises in period 13, the interest due is higher than the payment. The difference is added to the outstanding balance, and from that point, the end-of-month balance rises rather than declines. The borrower begins paying interest on the unpaid interest due in the previous month, as well as on the original loan principal. Negative amortization would continue until the payment goes up or the interest rate goes down. Eventually, one or the other must occur to protect both the borrower and the lender. Thus, federal thrift regulations require that at some point the payment be adjusted to fully amortize the loan.

Negative amortization exposes the lender to additional risk because the borrower's equity position influences the likelihood of default. A mortgage plan that deliberately reduces the homeowner's equity increases the lender's credit risk, a fact to be considered when offering ARM plans that allow negative amortization.

Setting the Initial Interest Rate

Lenders gain customer acceptance of ARMs by offering an interest rate discount that makes the initial cost of an ARM less than that of a fixed-rate mortgage.[42] Nevertheless, the lender must proceed cautiously. The importance of identifying a base rate required by the institution was emphasized in the previous chapter. That base rate must be earned, on average, if financial objectives are to be achieved.

With a low initial rate and a periodic rate cap, the lender may not be able to earn a market rate of return if interest rates rise significantly.

---

[42]The prevalence of initial rate discounts helps to explain why the national average mortgage contract rate has been a sluggish index for ARM rate adjustments. In periods in which ARMs are a high proportion of mortgages originated, the average contract rate is less representative of prevailing market conditions.

For example, suppose a lender offers a loan permitting annual rate adjustments with a periodic rate cap of 200 basis points and an initial rate discount 250 basis points below the rate that would be charged on a fixed-rate loan. Under a rising-rate scenario, it could take more than two years for the lender to bring the rate on that loan in line with other assets and liabilities. For this reason, lenders offering caps almost always offer a relatively small discount on ARMs, and the lower the cap, the smaller the discount.

MORTGAGES WITHOUT ADJUSTABLE RATES

Innovations in mortgage finance are not limited to variable-rate plans. Loans with nontraditional features have been designed to meet the needs of many different categories of borrowers. It is not hard to see why modern mortgage finance has been compared with alphabet soup.

Graduated Payment Mortgages

One of the earliest alternatives to the standard fixed-rate mortgage (FRM) was designed to make housing more affordable for first-time homebuyers. As inflated home prices and high interest rates drove up mortgage payments, many who dreamed of owning a home were priced out of the market. The *graduated payment mortgage (GPM)* was designed to enable those who anticipated higher future incomes to buy a home earlier that the FRM would allow.

Under a GPM, monthly payments are set at an artificially low level in the earliest years—that is, a level below the payment required to amortize the mortgage. Thus, in the first few years, the GPM relies on negative amortization. In each of the first three to five years, monthly payments are increased, according to a schedule known in advance, until they finally become stable at a level above the payment required had the borrowers originally had an FRM. If a borrower's income keeps pace, the higher GPM payments will not be unbearable. There is also no uncertainty, because borrowers know in advance exactly what the payments will be over the life of the mortgage. For lenders, however, the low initial payments mean lower cash flows in the early years, making them less desirable than an FRM. Thus, depositories seldom encourage borrowers to choose GPMs.

Reverse Annuity Mortgages

A *reverse annuity mortgage (RAM)* is another program for a specialized clientele—the elderly who own their homes but face cash shortages. Rather than a homeowner paying the institution, the opposite occurs: The lender makes regular payments to the homeowner over a contracted annuity period. The homeowner borrows on the basis of the value of the home, and receives the borrowed funds monthly to meet living expenses, rather than in a lump sum. When the homeowner with a RAM moves or dies, the property is sold, and the lender is repaid, with interest, from the proceeds.

RAMs have been offered sporadically since the mid-1970s and were authorized nationwide in the Garn-St Germain Act unless states passed legislation after 1982 prohibiting them. Little information is available on the terms commonly offered, but lenders appear to prefer to establish an annuity contract with a specified term, rather than a lifetime annuity for the homeowner.[43] Lenders are reluctant to offer a lifetime plan because no one knows how long the annuitant will live. The homeowner is likely to prefer a lifetime contract, however, because at the end of the RAM contract a settlement must be made. Should the homeowner outlive a preestablished contract period, difficulties could ensue if the lender attempted to claim the home while the elderly homeowner was still in residence. As is true for GPM plans, a lender offering a RAM must be willing to wait a number of years before realizing its investment returns.

Quick-Pay Mortgages

A trend in the 1980s has been borrower preference for shorter mortgage maturities. In 1985, 14 percent of all new mortgages, including FRMs and ARMs, had a 15-year maturity.[44] Sometimes called *quick-pay mortgages,* these instruments allow borrowers to build equity more quickly and to reduce total interest payments. The monthly payment for the 15-year plan is higher than for its 30-year counterpart, although the difference is less than one might expect. For example, on a $100,000 mortgage with an 11 percent interest rate, the monthly payment is $952 over a 30-year amortization period, and $1,137 for a 15-year period, an increase of less than 20 percent.

Growing Equity Mortgages

The *growing equity mortgage (GEM)* offers a fixed interest rate and a relatively short amortization period. The GEM, however, does not have fixed payments over the entire term, but rather has a predetermined schedule of payment increases over the life of the mortgage. Initial payments are set at the level that would amortize the mortgage over 30 years, but scheduled increases result in a shorter actual maturity.

The popularity of shorter-term mortgages is traced to several factors. Lending institutions, especially thrifts, are anxious to shorten the average maturities of their loan portfolios. Thus, lenders have offered interest rate discounts to borrowers who agree to the shorter mortgages, making them more appealing. Homeowners also see increased opportunities to borrow against the equity value of their homes, loans traditionally known as *second mortgages.* If homebuyers wish to take advantage of this opportunity, it is in their best interests to build the equity position as rapidly as possible. Quick-pay mortgages and GEMs offer an attractive means for doing so.

---

[43]A description of several plans offered in the Baltimore area, and an analysis of their effects on borrowers and lenders, was reported in Alexander Chen, "Alternative Reverse Mortgages: A Simulation Analysis of Initial Benefits in Baltimore," *Housing Finance Review* 2 (October 1983): 295-308.

[44]James W. Christian, "Homeownership Returns to the Basics," *Savings Institutions* 107 (February 1986): 48-54.

Price Level Adjusted Mortgages

A mortgage plan highly touted but not widely implemented is the *price level adjusted mortgage (PLAM)*. The PLAM has an adjustable interest rate tied to an inflation index rather than an interest rate index. The theoretical foundation for the PLAM is Fisher's theory on inflationary expectations and interest rates, introduced in Chapter 5. Fisher argued that the nominal rate of interest is composed of two factors: the real rate and a premium for expected inflation. In the PLAM, the initial interest rate is the real rate; the lender does not charge the borrower the inflationary premium in advance because inflationary expectations may be incorrect.

The traditional FRM has been criticized because borrowers pay in advance for anticipated future inflation, incorporated in the nominal rate quoted by the lender, whereas only after inflation occurs does borrower income rise to reduce the mortgage burden. This imbalance is known as *tilt.* Under the PLAM, a borrower pays for *actual* inflation (an adjustment made after the fact), avoids tilt, and benefits from lower initial interest costs.

For example, if the real rate is estimated as 4 percent at the time of the loan, the amortization schedule is based on that rate. If inflation is 6 percent during the first year, the unpaid balance is increased by 6 percent, and new monthly payments based on amortizing the new balance at 4 percent are required. In the following year, if inflation is 3 percent, the unpaid balance is increased by 3 percent, and so forth. An illustration of a PLAM under these conditions is presented in Table 14.7. Ideally, cost-of-living wage increases would keep real income in a stable ratio to housing payments. The lender, meanwhile, is theoretically protected from inflation-induced interest rate shocks. PLAMs offer no protection, however, from unexpected rate increases caused by other economic factors.

Despite the theoretical benefits, implementation of the PLAM has moved slowly. Several operational factors have interfered, including the problem of estimating the real rate of interest. Moderation in the inflation rate since 1981 also has reduced the attention paid to the PLAM. Furthermore, the borrower's income may not keep pace with inflation, increasing the lender's exposure to default risk. But perhaps the greatest drawback is the imbalance between the lender's cost of funds and the rate charged on the PLAM. Depository institutions must pay the nominal, not the real, rate to obtain funds, and could face liquidity and profitability problems in the early portion of the mortgage term if they earned only the real rate on their mortgage assets. In effect, the PLAM transfers the tilt from borrowers to lenders, who must raise funds by paying in advance for expected inflation.[45]

OTHER TERMS OF MORTGAGE LOANS

Several other characteristics are common to both fixed- and adjustable-rate mortgage loans.

Points

Mortgage lenders customarily charge initial service fees, known as points, at the time of the loan origination. First discussed in Chapter 4, a point is 1 percent of the principal of the loan. Points increase the effective cost for the borrower and the effective return to the lender. Under binding usury ceilings, lenders used these service charges to compensate for a below-market rate of interest. Although mortgage usury ceilings were eliminated in most states after DIDMCA, points still influence the pricing of mortgages of all types.

Prepayment Penalties

Prepayment penalties, designed to compensate lenders for the uncertainty in asset management caused by a prepayment, are used less and less.

---

[45]An excellent discussion of several alternative mortgages, including the PLAM, from which some of the preceding comments were adapted, is provided in Eleanor Erdevig and George Kaufman, "Improving Housing Finance in an Inflationary Environment: Alternative Residential Mortgage Instruments," *Economic Perspectives,* Federal Reserve Bank of Chicago 5 (July/August 1981): 3–23.

Table 14.7
Price Level Adjusted Mortgage (PLAM)

Initial Monthly Payment: $477.42	Initial Balance: $100,000	Initial Maturity: 30 years	Initial Rate (Real Rate): 4.00%	Inflation Rates: Year 1: 6% Year 2: 3% 0% thereafter

Month	(1) Monthly Payment	(2) Beginning Balance	(3) Interest .04/12 × (2)	(4) Principal Paid (1) − (3)	(5) End-of-Month Balance (2) − (4)
1	$477.42	$100,000.00	$333.33	$144.08	$ 99,855.92
2	477.42	99,855.92	332.85	144.56	99,711.36
3	477.42	99,711.36	332.37	145.04	99,566.31
4	477.42	99,566.31	331.89	145.53	99,420,78
5	477.42	99,420.78	331.40	146.01	99,274.77
6	477.42	99,274.77	330.92	146.50	99,128.27
7	477.42	99,128.27	330.43	146.99	98,981.28
8	477.42	98,981.28	329.94	147.48	98,833.81
9	477.42	98,833.81	329.45	147.97	98,685.84
10	477.42	98,685.84	328.95	148.46	98,537.37
11	477.42	98,537.37	328.46	148.96	98,388.42
12	477.42	98,388.42	327.96	149.45	98,238.96
13	506.06	**104,133.30**	347.11	158.95	103,974.35
14	506.06	103,974.35	346.58	159.48	103,814.87
15	506.06	103,814.87	346.05	160.01	103,654.86
16	506.06	103,654.86	345.52	160.54	103,494.32
17	506.06	103,494.32	344.98	161.08	103,333.24
18	506.06	103,333.24	344.44	161.62	103,171.62
19	506.06	103,171.62	343.91	162.15	103,009.47
20	506.06	103,009.47	343.36	162.70	102,846.77
21	506.06	102,846.77	342.82	163.24	102,683.54
22	506.06	102,683.54	342.28	163.78	102,519.75
23	506.06	102,519.75	341.73	164.33	102,355.43
24	506.06	102,355.43	341.18	164.88	102,190.55
25	521.24	**105,256.27**	350.85	170.39	105,085.88
26	521.24	105,085.88	350.29	170.96	104,914.92
27	521.24	104,914.92	349.72	171.53	104,743.40
28	521.24	104,743.40	349.14	172.10	104,571.30
29	521.24	104,571.30	348.57	172.67	104,398.63
30	521.24	104,398.63	348.00	173.25	104,225.38
31	521.24	104,225.38	347.42	173.82	104,051.56
32	521.24	104,051.56	346.84	174.40	103,877.16
33	521.24	103,877.16	346.26	174.98	103,702.17
34	521.24	103,702.17	345.67	175.57	103,526.60
35	521.24	103,526.60	345.09	176.15	103,350.45
36	521.24	103,350.45	344.50	176.74	103,173.71

Lenders face potentially large volumes of pre-payments if market yields fall and borrowers with fixed mortgage rates refinance their homes at lower rates. In the early 1980s, as market rates rose and most lenders were locked into low yields on outstanding mortgages, many be-gan to waive existing prepayment penalties, hoping to remove old loans from their portfo-lios. To attract new borrowers at the higher rates, however, lenders had to make loans with-out prepayment penalties. When rates fell sub-stantially in 1985 and 1986, and borrowers with mortgages originated a few years earlier refi-nanced in droves, there were no prepayment penalties for lenders to enforce.

Also leading to the virtual demise of the prepayment penalty is the fact that, as compen-sation to borrowers for additional risk expo-sure, federal regulations prohibit prepayment penalties on ARMs.

Assumptions

Increasingly common is the *due-on-sale clause,* in which the lender can require the borrower to repay the outstanding loan balance when the mortgaged property is sold. Mortgages without due-on-sale clauses are *assumable* by the new homeowner.[46]

Due-on-sale clauses protect the lender in two ways:

1. The lender may evaluate the financial posi-tion of the new owner and choose whether to continue the loan.

2. When the new owner applies for a loan, the lender can increase the interest rate if necessary.

The Garn-St Germain Act of 1982 established the ability of lenders to enforce due-on-sale

---

[46]Federal agency policies require that VA and FHA mort-gages be assumable; conventional mortgages usually have a due-on-sale clause. Federal regulations carefully define sale for purposes of enforcement of due-on-sale clauses. For a review of the technicalities, see Beth Priess, "The Garn-St Germain Act and Due-on-Sale-Clause Enforce-ment," *Housing Finance Review* 2 (October 1983): 369-377.

clauses in all mortgage agreements originated thereafter.

SECONDARY MARKET PURCHASES AND SALES

The sale or purchase of mortgages, two impor-tant alternatives to originating and holding them, deserve brief mention.

The Influence of Secondary Markets

Although secondary markets exist for other loans, the *secondary mortgage market* is the largest and most active one. Detailed discussion of market participants and use of the markets is deferred until Chapter 18, however, because of their importance to a depository's overall asset/liability management strategy. The relevant point now is that secondary market investors exert influence on loans made in the primary market. If management wants to have the op-tion to sell portions of the portfolio to other investors, it must be sensitive to the types of instruments that are salable in the secondary markets.

In fact, government or quasi-governmental agencies operating in the secondary mortgage markets have led the way toward standardiza-tion of mortgage terms. As suggested by the abundance of mortgage alternatives, investors as well as borrowers find it difficult to evaluate all possibilities. When large secondary investors publicly announce they will buy only mort-gages with certain characteristics, depository institutions must respond if they plan to deal with those investors.

Expanding the Portfolio through Purchases

Depository institutions can purchase loans originated elsewhere. For example, mortgage bankers frequently sell loans to other lenders. Usually, the originator attempts to ensure that the borrower meets the credit standards of the depository institution purchasing the loan. By acquiring loans originated elsewhere, a depository institution may geographically diversify its portfolio, an especially important benefit because of the sensitivity of mortgage delinquency and default rates to local economic conditions.

SUMMARY

This chapter continues the discussion of lending, with emphasis on consumer installment and mortgage loans. Traditionally, credit unions and thrifts, respectively, have been major lenders in these markets, although commercial banks also are active participants. One of the major differences between consumer and commercial lending is the degree of legal and regulatory protection afforded to consumer borrowers.

As with commercial lending, analysis of financial statements and credit bureau reports is important when granting consumer installment loans and issuing credit cards. Credit-scoring models assist in this task. The lender must also be alert to applicable bankruptcy laws and the influence of usury laws. In addition, creditors must decide what loan terms are appropriate; how payments will be calculated; whether the rate will be variable or fixed; and whether prepayment penalties will be attached.

Many similar decisions must be made in the granting of mortgage loans, although special emphasis is placed on the value of the mortgaged property and on the expected pattern of the borrower's income. These considerations are especially important in variable-rate lending or when economic conditions are uncertain.

Adjustable-rate mortgages are increasingly popular with lenders because of the protection they offer in stabilizing the NIM. Borrowers are willing to accept them if lenders share the interest rate risk by including rate/payment caps and offering initial rate discounts. Other important issues include how often rates or payments can be adjusted; to what index rate changes will be tied; whether the maturity of the mortgage contract can be extended; and whether negative amortization will be permitted.

Lenders and borrowers who want other special features may prefer any one of several alternatives, such as the GPM, the RAM, the quick-pay, the GEM, or the PLAM. Each of these instruments is designed either to appeal to a special demographic segment of borrowers or to meet special economic needs of borrowers and lenders. Finally, loan portfolio managers may sell and purchase loans in secondary markets. These opportunities permit additional flexibility for achieving institutional objectives.

Questions

1. What is an installment loan? Why are the majority of consumer loans made on an installment basis?

2. Why has the volume of consumer credit increased since the 1970s? Based on information you find in current publications, has the Tax Reform Act of 1986 affected the volume of consumer borrowing in recent months? If so, why and in what ways?

3. What motivated passage of the Truth-in-Lending Act in 1968? What are the major provisions of Regulation Z? What justification is there for the close regulation of consumer lending?

4. How have the bankruptcy law reforms of 1978 and 1984 influenced the risk exposure and profitability of consumer lenders?

5. What are usury laws, and why do they exist? Under what circumstances do consumers benefit from usury laws, and when do they not benefit? What are the typical responses of financial institutions to binding usury ceilings?

6. What types of information about loan applicants do financial institutions use in consumer credit analysis (excluding mortgage loans)? Compare procedures used to analyze consumer borrowers to those used to evaluate commercial loan applicants. What additional information about loan applicants must be considered in mortgage lending? Why?

7. What are credit-scoring models? What benefits do they offer? What are the drawbacks to using only credit-scoring models for loan evaluation?

8. Briefly explain the rule of 78s. How can it be disadvantageous to consumer borrowers?

9. Why has the volume of variable-rate consumer lending increased? What are its costs and benefits to institutions? To borrowers?

10. Why did financial institutions enter the credit card market? How do they profit from issuing bank cards? What risks do bank card lenders face?

11. How do typical bank card interest rates compare to the current prime rate? Why do you think interest rates on bank cards remained high long after other interest rates fell in the mid-1980s? Do you think the high rates were justified? Why or why not?

12. Compare and contrast FHA-insured and VA-guaranteed mortgages. What characteristics make them unpopular with depository institution lenders?

13. Discuss the factors that influence a lending institution's choice of ARM terms, including the interest rate index and rate/payment caps.

14. What is negative amortization? Explain the mortgage terms that could lead to negative amortization when interest rates rise. What are the advantages and disadvantages to borrowers? To lenders?

15. Compare and contrast graduated payment and quick-pay mortgages. What type of borrower would prefer each one?

16. What is a reverse annuity mortgage? What type of borrower would prefer a RAM? What problems could face an institution with a large volume of RAMs?

17. Explain the theoretical foundation for the price level adjusted mortgage. Despite theoretical support, why has the PLAM not been widely accepted among mortgage lenders?

18. What benefits do lenders receive from including a due-on-sale clause in the mortgage agreement?

Problems

1. You are purchasing a new van priced at $20,000 and have saved enough money to make a 25 percent down payment. Your local savings and loan association will finance the remaining balance at a 12.4 percent add-on rate for 4 years (48 months). Calculate the annual percentage rate.

2. Mr. and Mrs. Wilson have decided to purchase a recreational vehicle to use for family vacations and weekend trips. The RV costs $24,000, and the Wilsons are able to make a $4,000 down payment. Their bank has quoted an add-on rate of 11.5 percent, with 48 months to finance the remaining balance.
   a. Based on this information, calculate the Wilsons' monthly payments.
   b. Suppose that after 15 months, the Wilsons win $25,000 in the state lottery. Using the rule of 78s, how much would they need to pay off the loan?

3. Your brother is buying his first car. After extensive negotiations, he has agreed on a price of $10,600. He can afford a $2,000 down payment and will finance the remaining balance over a 48-month period. The bank has offered an add-on rate of 6 percent, which sounds reasonable to your brother. But the car manufacturer's subsidiary is offering four-year loans at an annual percentage rate of 6¾ percent. Compare the APRs on the two loans and decide which one your brother should accept.

4. Your bank offers you a five-year, $10,000 loan with an annual interest rate of 12 percent. The loan has an adjustable rate on which monthly payments are changed to reflect changes in the interest rate. After you make six payments, rates rise and your interest rate is adjusted to 12.5 percent. Prepare an amortization schedule reflecting the required monthly payments for the first two years of the loan.

5. First Federal Savings and Loan is offering an 18-month loan with an annual interest rate of 13 percent. The loan has an adjustable rate with fixed payments; the loan term is changed to reflect changes in the interest rate. You borrow $5,000, and ten months later the interest rate on the loan is adjusted to 13.75 percent. Prepare an amortization schedule that reflects the change in the loan term. The new interest rate goes into effect with the 11th payment.

6. You have found a nice "starter home" for $65,000. You plan to borrow $55,000 from your credit union at a 10 percent interest rate. The CU offers a choice of a standard 30-year fixed-rate loan or a 15-year fixed-rate, quick-pay loan.
   a. Calculate the monthly payments under each loan.
   b. How much total interest do you pay under each loan?
   c. Assuming you can comfortably meet either monthly payment, which loan would you choose? Why?

7. Suppose the $55,000 mortgage in Problem 6 is a thirty-year adjustable-rate mortgage on which the interest rate can change every six months but on which the payment cannot change for one year. After six months, the interest rate rises to 14 percent. Prepare an amortization schedule for the first year of the loan. What feature of ARMs is illustrated by this mortgage?

8. Mary and Edward Jones are negotiating a $75,000 mortgage loan. The Joneses are offered a price level adjusted mortgage. The loan has an initial maturity of 30 years, and the real rate is estimated at 5 percent. Assume that during the first year, inflation is 7 percent. Calculate the principal balance for the Joneses' loan at the beginning of year 2.

Selected References

Albaum, Gerald, and George Kaufman. "The Variable Rate Residential Mortgage: Implications for Borrowers." In *Alternative Mortgage Instruments Research Study,* Vol. I. Washington, DC: Federal Home Loan Bank Board, November 1977.

Altman, Edward I., et al. *Application of Classification Techniques in Business, Banking, and Finance.* Greenwich, CT: JAI Press, 1981.

Avery, Robert B., et al. "Survey of Consumer Finances, 1983: A Second Report." *Federal Reserve Bulletin* 70 (December 1984): 857-868.

Buying a Home in the 1980s: A Poll of American Attitudes. Washington, DC: Federal National Mortgage Association, September 1982.

Campbell, Tim S., and J. Kimball Dietrich. "Determinants of Default on Insured Conventional Residential Mortgage Loans." *Journal of Finance* 38 (December 1983): 1,569-1,581.

Colton, Kent W., Donald R. Lessard, David Modest, and Arthur P. Solomon. "National Survey of Borrowers' Housing Characteristics, Attitudes and Preferences." In *Alternative Mortgage Instruments Research Study,* Vol. I. Washington, DC: Federal Home Loan Bank Board, November 1977.

Erdevig, Eleanor, and George Kaufman. "Improving Housing Finance in an Inflationary Environment: Alternative Residential Mortgage Instruments." *Economic Perspectives* (Federal Reserve Bank of Chicago) 5 (July/August 1981): 3-23.

Goodman, John L., Jr., and Charles A. Luckett. "Adjustable Rate Financing in Mortgage and Consumer Credit Markets." *Federal Reserve Bulletin* 71 (November 1985): 823-835.

Guttentag, Jack. "Solving the Mortgage Menu Problem." *Housing Finance Review* 3 (July 1983): 227-252.

Herzog, John P., and James B. Earley. *Home Mortgage Delinquency and Foreclosure.* New York: National Bureau of Economics and Research, 1970.

Kramer, Susan B., and Glenn B. Canner. "The Current Status of Usury Legislation in the United States." *Issues in Bank Regulation* 6 (Summer 1982): 11-23.

Luckett, Charles A., and James D. August. "The Growth of Consumer Debt." *Federal Reserve Bulletin* 71 (June 1985): 389-402.

Mills, Dixie L., and Mona J. Gardner. "Consumer Response to Adjustable Rate Mortgages: Implications of the Evidence from Illinois and Wisconsin." *Journal of Consumer Affairs* (Summer 1986): 77-105.

Pavel, Christine, and Paula Binkley. "Costs and Competition in Bank Credit Cards." *Economic Perspectives* (Federal Reserve Bank of Chicago) 11 (March/April 1987): 3-13.

Pearce, Douglas K. "Rising Household Debt in Perspective." *Economic Review* (Federal Reserve Bank of Kansas City) 70 (July/August 1985): 3-17.

Peterson, Richard L., and Kiyomi Aoki. "Bankruptcy Filings before and after Implementation of the Bankruptcy Reform Act." *Journal of Economics and Business* 36 (February 1984): 95-105.

Peterson, Richard L., and Margaret Woo. "Bankrupt Debtors: Who Can Repay?" *Journal of Retail Banking* 6 (Fall 1984): 42-51.

Reichenstein, William R., and Frank J. Bonello. "Usury Laws: Today and Tomorrow." *Issues in Bank Regulation* 7 (Winter 1984): 25-31.

Russell, Thomas. *The Economics of Bank Credit Cards.* New York: Praeger Publishers, 1975.

Vandell, Kerry D. "Default Risk under Alternative Mortgage Instruments." *Journal of Finance* 33 (December 1978): 1,279-1,296.

Vandenbrink, Donna C. "The Effects of Usury Ceilings." *Economic Perspectives* (Federal Reserve Bank of Chicago) 6 (Midyear 1982): 44-55.

———. "Usury Ceilings and DIDMCA." *Economic Perspectives* (Federal Reserve Bank of Chicago) 9 (September/October 1985): 25-30.

Wolken, John D., and Frank J. Navratil. "The Economic Impact of the Federal Credit Union Usury Ceiling." *Journal of Finance* 36 (December 1981): 1,157-1,168.

Chapter 15

DEPOSIT AND LIABILITY MANAGEMENT

Once banks started competing for deposits, there were people who had been trained for 50 years to walk on land who were now thrown into the water, and they really don't know how to swim.

Charles Schumer
Congressman from New York (1985)

SOME depositories, including the Manhattan Savings Bank in New York City, will do anything to differentiate themselves from the crowd. In a deregulated environment, rather than luring depositors with gifts, management decided to provide free entertainment, ranging from musicals to dog shows, during lunch hours and on weekends. Even that approach to competition is risky. As befit one Mother's Day wildlife exhibit, a skunk gave birth to quintuplets in the bank lobby.[1]

The three previous chapters have examined uses of funds in depository institutions, but managers must also make important decisions about sources of funds. In this and the next chapter, those decisions are in the spotlight, beginning with a history lesson about two restrictions on managing the deposit-taking function: 1) the prohibition of interest on demand deposits; and 2) Regulation Q, the Federal Reserve rule that for half a century determined the maximum interest rates that could be paid on deposits.

---

[1]Tamalyn Miller, "Eschewing Gifts, This Bank Offers Dogs, Cats and Ice Shows," *The Wall Street Journal*, March 6, 1984.

Because regulation breeds innovation by the regulated— remember the regulatory dialectic from Chapter 2—these restrictions led to responses from depository institutions that shape the environment of today: liability management, noninterest competition, and new deposit instruments. These innovations, in turn, have led to concern about institutional safety and soundness under deregulated deposit and liability structures and to questions about the role of federal deposit insurance.

INTEREST RATE RESTRICTIONS: A HISTORY

The number of bank runs in the early 1930s convinced the federal government that the financial system would best be served by a federal deposit insurance program.[2] After January 1, 1934, banks could advertise their membership in the FDIC by paying a set percentage, originally ½ of 1 percent of *total* deposits, as an annual fee to the FDIC. Thus, the vast majority of FDIC financing was initially provided by large institutions, although a substantial portion of their deposits exceeded the initial insurance limit of $2,500 per account. These banks argued that they were paying for protection their depositors were not receiving. To obtain large banks' support of the FDIC, and because some politicians believed paying interest on demand deposits drained funds from rural areas to cities where rates were higher, the Banking Act of 1933 (the Glass-Steagall Act) prohibited that practice. Because they were the only financial institutions permitted to offer demand deposits, banks enjoyed lower interest costs without losing checking account customers.[3]

Congress believed that competition among commercial banks should be limited if banks were to receive the benefits of federal deposit insurance, so Glass-Steagall also gave the Fed authority to control maximum interest rates on time and savings deposits at national banks. Similar authority was granted to the FDIC over nonmember commercial banks in the Banking Act of 1935. In 1966, the FDIC and the Federal Home Loan Bank Board (FHLBB) were instructed to control deposit interest rates at thrifts as part of the Interest Rate Adjustment Act. Congress required all regulators to coordinate their efforts. As a result, Reg Q, although technically a Fed policy, became a generic term for all regulations on deposit rate ceilings.

Reg Q and Market Rates: The Early Years

Figure 15.1 traces the history of deposit interest rates from 1927 to 1986. The top panel shows that from 1933 until 1954, the Reg Q ceiling rate on time and savings deposits was well above yields on three-month T-bills. Thus, risk-averse depositors were unlikely to find other short-term investments more attractive. Because all banks faced the same rate ceilings, price competition was virtually nonexistent. Banks tended to focus on nonprice factors, such as customer service. Thrifts could, and usually did, offer higher rates on savings deposits than did banks, but were prohibited from offering transaction accounts and nonmortgage loans. Thus, banks were able to obtain customers by

---

[2]Recently, some experts have concluded that bank failures during the period 1929-1933 were so atypical of bank failures that it is inappropriate to base public policy on that period. Nevertheless, those years have been the predominant influence on depository institution regulation for nearly 60 years. See George J. Benston and George G. Kaufman, "Risks and Failures in Banking: Overview, History, and Evaluation," Staff Memorandum 86-1, Federal Reserve Bank of Chicago, 1986.

[3]Analyses of the reasons for and effects of interest rate restrictions are given in George Benston, "Interest on Deposits and the Survival of Chartered Depository Institutions," *Economic Review*, Federal Reserve Bank of Atlanta 69 (October 1984): 42-56; and Bryon Higgins, "Interest Payments on Demand Deposits: Historical Ev-

olution and the Current Controversy," *Monthly Review*, Federal Reserve Bank of Kansas City 62 (July-August 1977): 3-11.

Figure 15.1
Regulation Q and Market Interest Rates

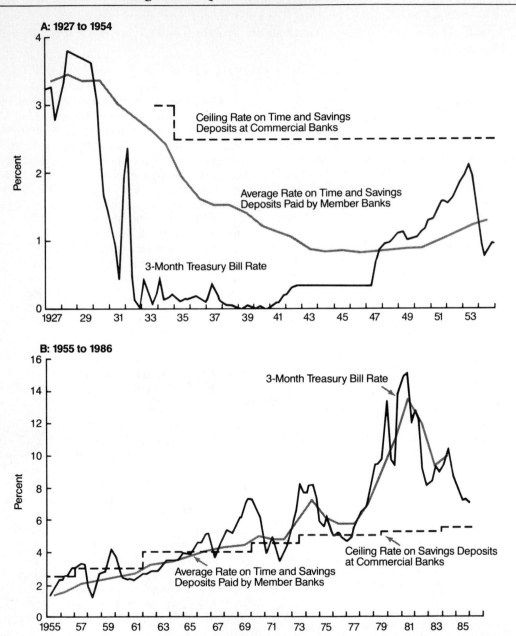

Source: R. Alton Gilbert, "Requiem for Regulation Q: What It Did and Why It Passed Away," *Review,* Federal Reserve Bank of St. Louis 68 (February 1986): 25, 29.

requiring them to maintain deposit accounts in order to receive the services they desired.

As market rates increased, regulators gradually increased Reg Q ceilings so that by 1962 they were again above prevailing market yields. Shortly thereafter, Congress sought to encourage home ownership by extending interest rate ceilings to thrifts, presumably permitting them to lower mortgage rates. To prevent banks from competing with thrifts, slightly higher ceilings (¼ percent to ½ percent) were permitted for thrifts. The ceiling structure also became more complicated after 1965, with separate ceilings for different types and sizes of deposits.[4]

The Later Years

The extension of Reg Q to thrifts coincided with other important economic and political events, such as escalated spending for domestic social programs and increased involvement in the Vietnam War. These developments led to greater government borrowing, which accelerated expectations of inflation and drove market rates higher. The relationship between market yields and the Reg Q ceiling on passbook savings deposits from 1955 to 1986 is depicted at the bottom of Figure 15.1. After 1966, the ceiling seldom equaled, much less exceeded, yields on T-bills.

Table 15.1 presents these developments in a different way. The average annual yield on several investments is shown from 1950 until 1985. Yields on deposits at banks and S&Ls are the averages for all types of deposits and thus do not coincide with the ceiling rate on any one instrument. In the periods 1965-1966, 1968-1970, 1973-1974, and 1978-1981, depositors wishing to avoid default risk could have earned more by investing in T-bills than by holding deposits at banks and thrifts. Had they wished to assume the low default risk expected on

AAA-rated bonds, depositors could have done still better.

Credit unions enjoyed higher Reg Q ceilings than other depositories. Until 1973, there was a 6 percent limit on dividends on regular share accounts at federal CUs. In 1973, the NCUA increased the maximum rate to 7 percent. The common-bond requirement was presumed to prevent adverse competition within the industry and with other depositories. Furthermore, the CU goal of providing low loan rates to members was expected to inhibit the payment of excessively high rates on shares. Still, the ceiling for federal CUs, though higher than that for banks and thrifts, was not competitive with market rates as the 1970s progressed.

Depositors Respond.   These facts did not go unnoticed by depositors, regulators, or politicians. During each of the periods highlighted in Table 15.1, banks and thrifts experienced disintermediation, cross-intermediation, or both. As discussed in Chapter 2, disintermediation is the switch by investors from indirect investment via intermediaries to direct investment in money and capital market instruments. Cross-intermediation occurs when investors switch from one financial institution to another. When either occurs, banks and thrifts can have liquidity problems because they may be unable to convert their assets to cash or to attract enough new funds to pay off departing depositors. At these times, regulators and legislators are reminded that regulations have both intended and unintended consequences.

The authorities sought to counteract the unintended consequences of Reg Q through a series of actions ultimately leading to its elimination. These actions are noted in Table 15.1. In 1965-1966 and 1968-1970, depositors withdrew funds to invest directly in Treasury securities. Banks, thrifts, and CUs were hit hard, but none appeared to gain or lose at the others' expense. Furthermore, housing starts declined by 26 percent or more in each period, events blamed on the unavailability of funds at thrifts.[5]

---

[4]For more details on the history of Regulation Q, see Scott Winningham and Donald G. Hagan, "Regulation Q: An Historical Perspective," *Economic Review*, Federal Reserve Bank of Kansas City 65 (April 1980): 3-17; R. Alton Gilbert, "Requiem for Regulation Q: What It Did and Why It Passed Away," *Review*, Federal Reserve Bank of St. Louis 68 (February 1986): 22-37.

[5]Bronwyn Brock, "Regulatory Changes Bring New Challenge to S&Ls, Other Depository Institutions," *Voice*, Federal Reserve Bank of Dallas (September 1980), pp. 5-9.

Table 15.1
Average Annual Yield on Selected Investments

Year	Savings Deposits at S&Ls	Savings Deposits at Commercial Banks	3-Month T-Bills	10-Year T-Bonds	AAA-Rated Corporate Bonds	Regulatory Response
1950	2.52%	0.94%	N/A	2.32%	2.62%	
1955	2.94	1.38	N/A	2.82	3.06	
1960	3.86	2.56	N/A	4.12	4.41	
→ 1965	4.23	3.69	3.95%	4.28	4.49	
→ 1966	4.45	4.04	4.88	4.92	5.13	Friend Study commissioned
1967	5.67	4.24	4.29	5.07	5.51	
→ 1968	4.68	4.48	5.34	5.65	6.18	Friend Study published
→ 1969	4.80	4.87	6.67	6.67	7.03	
→ 1970	5.06	4.95	6.39	7.35	8.04	Hunt Commission formed
1971	5.33	4.78	4.33	6.16	7.39	Hunt Commission reports
1972	5.39	4.66	4.07	6.21	7.21	
→ 1973	5.55	5.71	7.03	6.84	7.44	"Wild Card" experiment
→ 1974	5.98	6.93	7.84	7.56	8.57	FINE Study commissioned
1975	6.24	5.92	5.80	7.99	8.83	FINE Study reports
1976	6.32	5.53	4.98	7.61	8.43	
1977	6.41	5.50	5.27	7.42	8.02	
→ 1978	6.52	6.02	7.19	8.41	8.73	Share drafts, MMCs authorized
→ 1979	7.31	7.48	10.07	9.44	9.63	
→ 1980	8.69	9.08	11.43	11.46	11.94	DIDMCA
→ 1981	10.70	11.31	14.03	13.91	14.17	
1982	11.03	10.46	10.61	13.00	13.79	Garn-St Germain Act
1983	10.03	8.43	8.61	11.10	12.04	
1984	9.93	8.90	9.52	12.44	12.71	
1985	9.03	7.87	7.48	10.62	11.37	

Key:
→ Year in which T-bill rate exceeded the average yield at banks or S&Ls by more than 25 basis points.
N/A Not available.

Sources: Yield data are from various issues of U.S. League of Savings and Loans, *Savings and Loan Fact Book;* U.S. League of Savings Institutions, *Savings Institutions Source Book;* Board of Governors of the Federal Reserve System, *Federal Reserve Bulletin.*

The official response to these problems was to appoint national commissions to study, among other things, the effect of Reg Q. One was the Friend Study on the S&L industry, and the other was the Commission on Financial Structure and Regulation, or the Hunt Commission. The Hunt Commission recommended that Reg Q be eliminated but that the prohibition of interest on demand deposits be retained.[6] By the

time each study was made public, market yields were below Reg Q ceilings, and the need to remove it seemed less pressing.

New Financial Instruments. The 1973–1974 period began with disintermediation and ended with cross-intermediation too. In 1973,

---

[6]The report of the Hunt Commission, in particular, is one of the most important on the financial system before

1980. For more details, see Clifford B. Luttrell, "The Hunt Commission Report—An Economic View," *Review,* Federal Reserve Bank of St. Louis 54 (June 1972): 8-12.

federal regulators permitted banks and thrifts to offer "Wild Card" certificates—four-year, $1,000-minimum CDs with no rate ceilings. The experiment lasted only four months, because commercial banks immediately offered rates higher than thrifts, which were locked into fixed-rate mortgages, could offer.[7]

Elimination of the "Wild Card" did not prevent the outflow of funds from thrifts, however, because of the concurrent development of money market mutual funds (MMMFs). As noted in earlier chapters, MMMFs are nondepository financial intermediaries that invest their shareholders' funds in money market instruments. With no regulatory ceilings on returns to their shareholders, MMMFs are consistently able to offer yields that match or exceed those on short-term Treasury securities. Since their origination in the mid-1970s, MMMFs have provided substantial competition for savings.[8]

Arrival of Interest-Bearing Checking.

The interest-bearing transaction account arose during this period. Led by savings banks in Massachusetts, the NOW account was introduced in 1972. To distinguish them from demand deposits, institutions offering NOWs held to the technicality that they could refuse to honor transactions for 14 days, although few did so. NOWs quickly proved popular in New England, but Congress was reluctant to allow them nationwide and passed a law in 1976 restricting NOWs to banks and thrifts in New England, New York, and New Jersey.

The Final Chapters

The tradition of a national commission on the problem of disintermediation continued with the Financial Institutions and the Nation's Economy (FINE) report, submitted to a Congressional committee in 1975.[9] It recommended that Reg Q be eliminated and that interest be paid on demand deposits. Also in keeping with tradition, Congress took no action because market yields fell below Reg Q ceilings soon after the report. In 1978, however, interest rates began to climb, fueled by unprecedented inflation. For once, disintermediation did not go away, and yields remained above their pre-1978 level until 1985.

Share Drafts.

In 1978, federal regulators took two significant actions. The NCUA authorized the offering of share drafts by credit unions nationwide. Although experimental use of share drafts by some CUs had been permitted since 1974, the 1978 rule was the first allowing an entire class of depositories to have interest-bearing checking. A federal judge later determined that regulators had exceeded their bounds because only Congress had the authority to permit interest on transaction accounts. As noted in Chapter 11, however, the popularity of share drafts was enormous, leading to a national letter-writing campaign by CU members to retain them. Congress responded by including permanent authority for share drafts *and* NOW accounts in DIDMCA.

The Money Market Certificate.

In 1978, federal regulators also created the money market certificate (MMC), called the money market share certificate at CUs. The MMC was a six-month, $10,000-minimum CD with a rate ceiling tied to the six-month T-bill rate. The floating ceiling, with a ¼ percent advantage given to thrifts and CUs over commercial banks, was designed to stem disintermediation while protecting thrifts from a recurrence of the "Wild

---

[7]For more information and an evaluation of the "Wild Card" experiment, see Edward J. Kane, "All for the Best: The Federal Reserve Board's 60th Annual Report," in Thomas Havrilesky and John T. Boorman, eds., *Current Perspectives in Banking* (Arlington Heights, IL: AHM Publishing Corporation, 1976), pp. 523-532.

[8]During this period, MMMF managers invested a substantial portion of their funds in the negotiable CDs of large banks, thus returning some of the cross-intermediated funds to the banking system. Of course, large banks benefited more than small banks or thrifts. For more information, see Constance Dunham, "The Growth of Money Market Funds," *New England Economic Review,* Federal Reserve Bank of Boston (September/October 1980), pp. 20-34.

[9]U. S. Congress, House Committee on Banking, Currency, and Housing, *Financial Institutions and the Nation's Economy (FINE): Discussion Principles,* 94th Congress, November 1975.

Table 15.2
Household Acquisition of Deposits by Type of Institution
(Percentage Distribution)

	1971	1972	1973	1974	1975	1976	1977	1978	1979	1980	1981
Demand deposits and currency	15.2	15.5	17.9	11.0	4.4	12.0	17.1	14.0	10.9	1.8	Negative
Time deposits at commercial banks	35.1	32.9	45.4	52.1	27.5	32.3	30.5	33.8	27.8	46.9	39.5
Time deposits at thrifts	49.6	51.5	36.4	33.3	66.5	55.6	52.3	46.9	34.8	33.7	4.7
Money market funds	—	—	—	3.7	1.5	—	0.2	5.3	26.6	17.5	58.7

Source: Kenneth T. Rosen, "Deposit Deregulation and Risk Management in an Era of Transition," in *Managing Interest Rate Risk in the Thrift Industry* (San Francisco: Federal Home Loan Bank of San Francisco, 1981), p. 26. Reprinted with permission.

Card" experience.[10] The MMC was extremely popular with depositors. But again, the regulations creating it had unintended consequences. The short maturity and floating ceiling of the MMC greatly increased the cost of funds for depositories. Thrifts, with their long-term, fixed-rate mortgage portfolios were hit especially hard. As illustrated in Chapter 11, the collision of short-term, market-rate sources of funds and long-term, fixed-rate uses of funds, set in motion by the introduction of the MMC, resulted in severe earnings problems for thrifts in the 1980s.

Impact of the New Instruments.   Even the MMC could not prevent the flow of funds from depositories. The six-month maturity of the MMC seemed too long to some depositors, given the rapid increase in market rates from October 1979 through early 1980. Money market mutual funds continued to grow, financed by depositors who abandoned their banks, thrifts, and CUs for yields that could increase daily. Added to the thrifts' profitability woes were liquidity problems resulting from cross-intermediation.

Table 15.2 shows the annual percentage of *new* short-term savings captured by banks, thrifts, and MMMFs from 1971 through 1981. Beginning in 1979, banks and thrifts rapidly lost ground to MMMFs. By March 1980, Congress concluded that a permanent solution to disintermediation and cross-intermediation was essential, and the phase-out of Reg Q was mandated as part of DIDMCA.

The six-year phase-out was to ease the way for small banks and thrifts, who argued they would be unable to compete for deposits in a deregulated environment. Administration of the phase-out was assigned to the **Depository Institutions Deregulation Committee (DIDC),** composed of the heads of six federal regulatory agencies. Because members could not agree on steps for the removal of Reg Q, the committee did little during its first two years.

Credit unions were the only beneficiaries of this arrangement. Although the chairman of the NCUA sat on the DIDC, CU rate ceilings were not under the DIDC's jurisdiction. In 1981, the NCUA increased the maximum rate on share accounts to 12 percent, well above savings rates at banks and thrifts. Technically, the National Credit Union Act specifies a 6 percent maximum on regular shares, but the NCUA may override this ceiling, with Congressional approval. The 6 percent ceiling has not been enforced since the mid-1970s, and no ceiling at all has been imposed since 1982.

[10]Regulations governing the MMC were actually much more complex than this by the time they were fully in place. The bank/thrift differential varied according to actual T-bill yields, and the certificates had floor, as well as ceiling, rates attached.

The Money Market Deposit Account. The promise of Reg Q's elimination did not keep depositors from defecting from banks and thrifts following the passage of DIDMCA. Between 1978 and 1981, depositories continued to lose market share to MMMFs. Congress, realizing that speedy DIDC action was unlikely, took action to permit a deposit account competitive with MMMFs. In October 1982, the Garn–St Germain Act effectively ended the reign of Reg Q as a factor in depository institutions management by creating the money market deposit account (MMDA).[11] As explained in Chapter 11, the MMDA is a short-term deposit with a variable interest rate on which a limited number of third-party transactions is permitted. Garn–St Germain also authorized an account called the *"Super NOW,"* which was an interest-bearing, unlimited transactions account with a high minimum balance and no interest ceilings.

The effect of the MMDA on depositories was immediate and astounding, as Figure 15.2 illustrates. The volume of MMDAs grew from $0 in December 1982 to nearly $400 billion only a few months later. The dollar volume of MMMF shares, labeled MMF in the figure, dropped markedly at the same time. Experts believe that the attraction of FDIC, FSLIC, or NCUSIF insurance explains investors' preference for MMDAs over MMMFs. Within depository institutions, dollars flowed rapidly from small time deposits (MMCs, for example) and savings accounts into MMDAs.

The Current Situation

Table 15.3 shows characteristics of deposit accounts, which vary according to maturity, interest rate sensitivity, liquidity, and other features. The relatively simple deposit structure of the 1930s has been transformed into an array of choices, and each institution theoretically can offer as many unique accounts as it has customers. The table does not include Super NOWs, because after April 1, 1986, regulatory distinctions between NOWs and Super NOWs disappeared. An ironic footnote to Reg Q history is that the first major change in the passbook rate following complete deregulation was a decrease, from 5½ percent to 5 percent, by Security Pacific National Bank of Los Angeles in August 1986.

One of the few remaining regulatory issues is whether to allow interest on demand deposits, giving businesses access to interest-bearing checking.[12] This change is opposed by small commercial banks but supported by thrifts as a competitive tool to gain commercial customers.

Depositors Like Competition. What managerial lessons arise from this history of interest rate restrictions? Perhaps one of the most important is that depositors like competition for their business and are willing to switch institutional relationships for a "better deal." They also like the safety of deposit insurance and are eager to do business with institutions that offer it. Third, deposit taking is no longer a passive activity for any depository. Fourth, each deposit category and its relative proportion in an institution's financial structure affect interest and noninterest costs, and the expected level and variation in the net interest margin. The target mix and pricing structure for these accounts are explored later in the chapter.

Change Is Permanent. It is also clear that regulators and legislators are willing to alter major policies, so planning for change has become a necessity. Further, management must anticipate the unintended as well as the intended consequences of regulations. Finally, as long as managers and investors are creative, they will

---

[11]Minor elements of the Reg Q phase-out remained after 1982. In particular, ceilings remained on passbook accounts until April 1, 1986. By that time, however, remaining passbook balances at depositories were held in small accounts and/or by persons not generally sensitive to changes in market rates. Minimum denominations remained in effect for certain types of accounts until 1986, having been gradually phased down from minimums as high as $10,000 in earlier years. Interest ceilings also remained on NOW accounts until April 1, 1986, because their unlimited transactions benefits to customers were believed to justify such a limitation.

[12]For details, see Michael C. Keeley, "Interest on Business Checking Accounts?" *Weekly Letter,* Federal Reserve Bank of San Francisco, May 2, 1986.

Figure 15.2
Money Market Funds versus Components of Total Deposits
(Combined Bank and Thrift Total)

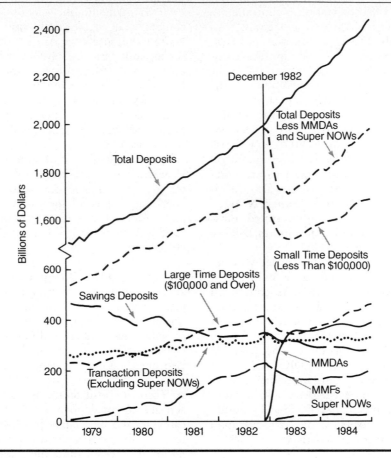

Source: Michael C. Keeley and Gary C. Zimmerman, "Competition for Money Market Deposit Accounts," *Proceedings of a Conference on Bank Structure and Competition* (Chicago: Federal Reserve Bank of Chicago, 1985), p. 615.

find a way to circumvent regulatory controls. The dialectic will continue.

LIABILITY MANAGEMENT

As managers of depositories watched regulators and Congress respond to a changing economy, few sat idly by awaiting the final removal of rate restrictions. As early as 1961, in fact, money center banks began to develop alternatives to traditional deposits. The active search for non-deposit funds to meet liquidity needs, enhance profits, or achieve growth is defined in Chapter 12 as liability management. Although liability management arose primarily because large institutions wished to grow more quickly than traditional strategies allowed, it accelerated in the late 1960s because of constraints imposed by Regulation Q and the absence of interest-

Table 15.3
Characteristics of Deposit Accounts

Account	Minimum Maturity	Interest Rate Characteristics	Reserve Requirements	Special Features
Demand deposits (NINOWs at thrifts)	None; payable on demand of the depositor	No explicit interest permitted	3% on first ≈ $37 million total of demand deposits and NOW accounts; 12% on total thereafter	May not be offered by federal CUs; may be offered by most thrifts to businesses only in connection with a commercial lending relationship
NOW accounts (share drafts at CUs)	Institution must reserve the right to require 7 days' advance notice before withdrawal	Fixed or variable; no restrictions at banks and thrifts[a]	Same as demand deposits	Unlimited number of transactions; may not be offered to businesses
Money market deposit accounts (MMDAs)	Same as NOWs	Fixed or variable; no restrictions	3% on accounts held by businesses; none on personal accounts	Pre-authorized transfers to and from account limited to 6 per month, including 3 by check; unlimited in-person, mail, or automatic teller transactions
Passbook savings (savings shares at CUs)	Same as NOWs	Same as MMDAs	Same as MMDAs	No check-writing privileges
Nonnegotiable certificates of deposit (CDs, or share certificates at CUs)	7 days	Same as MMDAs	Same as MMDAs	Forfeiture penalties imposed on withdrawals within the first 6 days; additional penalties may be imposed on nonpersonal accounts with original maturities of 18 months or more
Individual retirement accounts (IRAs)	Depends upon type of plan; MMDA-type plan has no legal minimum; CD-type plan has minimum based on maturity	Depends on plan selected	None	Depositors with income below specified levels may make tax-deferred additions to these accounts up to a maximum of $2,000 per year per individual; interest earned on accounts is tax-deferred, regardless of depositor income; penalties for withdrawal before age 59½
Negotiable certificates of deposit (Jumbos)	7 days	Same as MMDAs	Same as MMDAs	$100,000 minimum denomination; depositor can sell the deposit to a buyer before maturity, price is market-determined; no federal insurance on amount over $100,000

[a]Federal law sets a 6% ceiling for credit union interest on deposits, but the NCUA may override it. As of 1987, the NCUA had imposed no interest ceiling for CU deposits.

Source: Prepared by the authors from information in Board of Governors of the Federal Reserve System, "Regulation Q: Interest on Deposits," as amended effective January 1, 1984; Amendments to Regulations Q and D as cited in the *Federal Reserve Bulletin,* May 1986.

bearing demand deposits. Even without Reg Q, liability management is a vital part of the strategies of many institutions.

History of Liability Management[13]

Commercial banks ended World War II with about 75 percent of their assets in cash and Treasury bills; thus, it took considerable time—in fact, until the late 1950s—for them to run out of assets to liquidate to meet postwar loan demand. By the early 1960s, however, money center banks needed additional loanable funds. The shortage of funds was exacerbated by improvements in corporate cash management that caused large firms to reduce demand deposit balances to the bare minimum, investing surplus cash in T-bills and commercial paper.

Precipitating Events.   As explained in Chapter 4, First National City Bank of New York (now Citibank) developed the negotiable CD in response to changed customer preferences. Although large CDs had been sold by major banks before this time, the key to First National City's success was an agreement by securities dealers to create a secondary market, permitting corporations to invest in the CDs yet maintain liquidity. The negotiable CD became a tool for keeping current depositors as well as attracting new ones, allowing a bank's loan portfolio to grow. Soon, other nondeposit funds were used for the same purposes. Large banks so actively sought cash in the financial markets, rather than liquidating assets, that managed liabilities went from 0 percent of new funds at large banks in 1960 to almost 30 percent by 1974. In the 1970s, a few large savings institutions also began to use the technique.

Expanded Objectives.   Today, liability management serves several purposes. A common way of categorizing institutional objectives is

according to those related to managing the reserve position and those related to meeting loan demand.[14] These two motivations, the tools used to achieve them, and the risks and rewards are discussed in this section.

Using Liabilities to Cover Reserve Deficiencies

One of the motivations for liability management is to maintain liquidity, an issue explored in Chapter 12 from the asset side of the balance sheet. As explained in that chapter, for many years depository institutions looked for liquidity solely in their asset portfolios. But that approach to liquidity management may not coincide with the risk/expected return preference of managers and owners, so institutions have increasingly turned to nontraditional deposits and other liabilities as sources of liquidity.[15] If one categorizes funds as either discretionary or nondiscretionary, nontraditional deposits and other liabilities, along with short-term investment securities, are discretionary items. They can be actively employed to adjust a depository's liquidity position.

The major categories of discretionary liabilities are the Fed's discount window and borrowings from other regulators; the fed funds market; and the issuance of repurchase agreements, large certificates of deposit, and Eurodollar deposits. Because borrowing from regulators is ordinarily used only to cover reserve deficiencies and not to expand assets, those sources are discussed in the sections on reserve position management in Chapter 12.

---

[13]Parts of this section are based on Stuart A. Schweitzer, "Bank Liability Management: For Better or for Worse?" *Business Review,* Federal Reserve Bank of Philadelphia (December 1974), p. 4.

[14]Edward J. Kane, "The Three Faces of Commercial Bank Liability Management," in *The Political Economy of Policy-Making,* ed. M. J. Dooley (Beverly Hills, CA: Sage Publications, 1979), pp. 149-174. Note that these are the same reasons for liquidity identified in Chapter 12.

[15]For more discussion of the choice between asset liquidity and liability liquidity, see George W. McKinney, "Liability Management: Its Costs and Uses," in *Financial Institutions and Markets in a Changing World,* eds. Donald R. Fraser and Peter S. Rose (Dallas: Business Publications, 1980), pp. 90-104.

Remaining tools of liability management are discussed in the following paragraphs.[16]

Federal Funds Purchased.   Unlike the discount window, regular use of which is discouraged by the Fed, the federal funds market, first discussed in Chapter 4, is used by many depositories, some on a daily basis. As early as 1970, over 60 percent of all member banks were reportedly involved; by 1977, nearly 35 percent of the funds supplied in the market came from nonbank depositories.[17]

Like discount-window borrowings, federal funds are not considered deposits, so no reserves must be held against them. The lending institution instructs the Fed or its correspondent bank to transfer agreed-upon balances to the borrower instantaneously through Fedwire, the Fed's communication system. Because most fed funds transactions are *"overnight loans,"* the transaction is usually reversed the next day, including one day's interest calculated at the fed funds rate. The yield on these transactions is illustrated in Chapter 4.

Because the fed funds rate changes daily, a major problem with fed funds as a regular source of financing is estimating the cost. This problem has escalated since late 1979, when the Fed began placing less emphasis on the fed funds rate as an instrument of monetary policy. Empirical evidence from the period immediately following the Fed's policy change suggests that the rate became significantly more variable

after October 1979 than it had been since 1973.[18] As seen in Figure 15.3, fed funds have usually been more expensive than discount-window borrowings, although the spread between the two is not constant. When the differential becomes too great, institutions sometimes try to substitute one source of funds for the other, complicating the Fed's efforts to manage the discount window.

Although fed funds are readily available, the cost is difficult to forecast. An institution borrowing fed funds and investing them in assets on which yields do not change daily increases potential variability in its net interest margin. For this reason, the number of *"term" fed funds* transactions, with maturities of a week or more, or sometimes even several years, has increased recently. These transactions remain the exception, however, rather than the rule.

Using Liabilities to Meet Loan Demand or Pursue Growth

Institutions can also use liability management to obtain cash when a valued customer has an unplanned need to borrow, or when a customer withdraws a large deposit unexpectedly. Customers who might disintermediate may be persuaded not to if the institution can offer an attractive alternative. An institution can also bid aggressively for funds in the financial markets to expand its size and customer base, even when disintermediation of existing customers is not a problem. The characteristics of discount-window borrowing and fed funds make them inappropriate for these purposes, so alternative ways of raising funds have been developed.

Negotiable Certificates of Deposit.   Negotiable CDs, called *"jumbos"* by thrifts, are large-denomination (greater than $100,000) time deposits with a minimum maturity of seven days, for which there is a secondary market. They can be marketed aggressively when

---

[16]The following discussion relies on Marcia Stigum, *The Money Market,* 3d ed. (Homewood, IL: Dow Jones-Irwin, 1983); and Elijah Brewer, "Bank Funds Management Comes of Age—A Balance Sheet Analysis," *Economic Perspectives,* Federal Reserve Bank of Chicago 4 (May/June 1980): 13-18.

[17]Seth P. Maerowitz, "Federal Funds," in *Instruments of the Money Market,* 5th ed. (Richmond, VA: Federal Reserve Bank of Richmond, 1981), pp. 42-51. Research on reserve position management has suggested that managers are risk-averse and borrow fed funds early in a maintenance period to avoid emergency borrowing at the end. Thus, excess supplies may be accumulated by the end of a period, and the funds rate may be lower than at earlier points. For a review of this literature, see John H. Wood and Norma L. Wood, *Financial Markets* (San Diego: Harcourt Brace Jovanovich, 1985), Chapter 9.

[18]Michael G. Vogt and R. S. Hanna, "Variations of the Federal Funds Rate and Bank Reserve Management," *Journal of Bank Research* 15 (Autumn 1984): 188-192.

Figure 15.3
The Federal Funds Rate versus the Discount Rate, 1978–1986

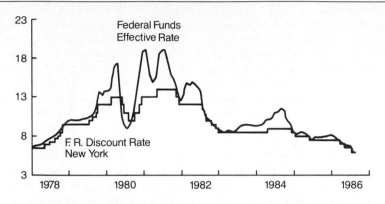

Source: Board of Governors of the Federal Reserve System, *Federal Reserve Chart Book,* August 1986, p. 72.

---

an institution needs cash. As noted, when first created, they helped stem the flow of corporate deposits from large banks and enabled the banks to meet new loan demand. But after the mid-1960s, because Reg Q ceilings were below market rates more often than not, negotiable CDs were not competitive with T-bills, and the loss of these deposits contributed to disintermediation at money center banks. In a move sympathetic to large institutions, the Fed temporarily suspended ceilings on negotiable CDs in 1970, and finally removed them altogether in 1973. Thus, for many years, they have been a tool for aggressive liability managers.

Most negotiable CDs are issued directly to customers, although some large institutions issue them to dealers, who then sell them to other investors. Dealer participation allows institutions to obtain funds with fewer delays. The high face value of the CDs means that the portion in excess of $100,000 is not federally insured. Consequently, institutions in financial difficulty find that this source of funds evaporates quickly, a particular problem if CDs are habitually used to fund reserve deficiencies or are invested in long-term loans to customers.

Continental Illinois, at the time among the ten largest banks in the country, serves as an extreme example. In the spring of 1984, the bank's financial problems surfaced as a result of large loan losses. Large CDs were almost 75 percent of its deposits worldwide, and depositors reacted quickly by withdrawing large volumes of these uninsured deposits. Only an unprecedented pledge by the FDIC to guarantee all deposits, regardless of size, stemmed the outflow. Continental was able to meet its daily liquidity requirements only through loans from the Fed and other large commercial banks. Although this experience is the exception, not the rule, it demonstrates that acquisition of liquidity or the pursuit of growth through liability management is more risky than "storing" liquidity in the asset portfolio or tailoring growth to traditional deposit flows.[19]

Eurodollar Deposits. Eurodollar deposits *(Eurodeposits)* are time deposits denominated

---

[19]Frederick T. Furlong, "Market Responses to Continental Illinois," *Weekly Letter,* Federal Reserve Bank of San Francisco, August 31, 1984; Jeff Bailey and G. Christian Hill, "Continental Illinois Gets Full U.S. Support," *The Wall Street Journal,* May 18, 1984, p. 3.

In reaction to increased concern in the financial markets caused by the Continental crisis and the recent large number of depository failures, some savings institutions have begun to offer "collateralized" CDs to appeal to large investors reluctant to commit funds in excess of the federal deposit insurance ceiling. See Lisa Spooner, "Cut from the Last Regulatory Ties, Savings Rates Fly Free," *Savings Institutions* 106 (December 1985): 45.

Figure 15.4
Creation of a Eurodollar Deposit

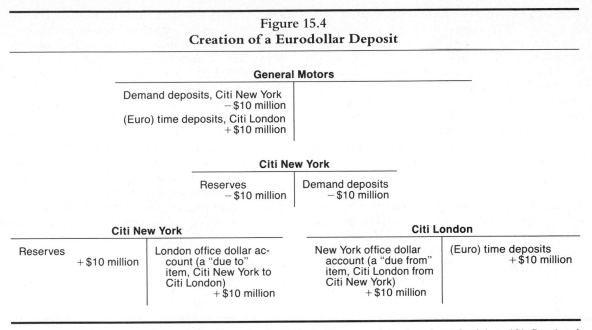

General Motors

Demand deposits, Citi New York − $10 million	
(Euro) time deposits, Citi London + $10 million	

Citi New York

Reserves − $10 million	Demand deposits − $10 million

Citi New York		**Citi London**	
Reserves + $10 million	London office dollar account (a "due to" item, Citi New York to Citi London) + $10 million	New York office dollar account (a "due from" item, Citi London from Citi New York) + $10 million	(Euro) time deposits + $10 million

Source: Adapted from Marcia Stigum, *The Money Market,* 2nd ed. (Homewood, IL: Dow Jones-Irwin), p. 131. Reprinted with permission.

in dollars but held in banks outside the United States, including foreign branches of U.S. banks. Eurodeposits are created in several ways, but the most straightforward is when a domestic customer transfers funds on deposit in the United States to a foreign bank or branch. The motivation is usually to obtain a higher rate of interest, and the depositor faces no currency exchange risk because the deposits remain in dollars. For many years, in fact, Eurodeposits were the only time deposits on which Reg Q ceilings were not binding, because they did not apply to funds held outside the United States. Therefore, when Reg Q became binding at home, domestic banks encouraged their customers to transfer funds to foreign branches where they could pay a competitive rate to prevent disintermediation.

Eurodeposits become a source of funds to domestic institutions when they borrow from foreign banks or branches, creating a liability reported on the domestic bank's balance sheet as "Due to Foreign Banks or Branches." Eurodeposits may range in maturity from as short as overnight to as long as five years, but the ma-

jority have maturities of six months or less. They are nonnegotiable and all funds obtained through Eurodeposits are subject to Fed reserve requirements. The 3 percent requirement is applied to *net* Eurodollar borrowings, or the difference between funds loaned and borrowed in this market.[20]

How Eurodollar Deposits Are Created. Figure 15.4 traces the creation of a typical Eurodeposit. If a large corporation like General Motors wishes to withdraw funds from its domestic demand deposit account in order to earn interest, it may notify one of its New York banks—Citibank, for example. To avoid losing the funds, Citibank can encourage GM to make a Eurodollar deposit at a London branch, where the going rate of interest may be higher than on

---

[20]As noted in Chapter 4, there are also *negotiable* Eurodollar CDs, for which there is a secondary market centered in London. This market is relatively small, however, and few institutions are able to raise funds by issuing them. Nonnegotiable Eurodeposits, the subject of the current discussion, are much more common sources of funds to U.S. banks.

deposits of similar maturity in the United States. Citibank's London branch will then deposit the funds received in an account at its parent bank in New York. The New York branch now has a "due to" liability on its books, and the London branch has a "due from" asset. By tradition, all transactions are carried out electronically over **CHIPS,** the *Clearing House Interbank Payments System,* a privately owned funds transfer system in New York. GM keeps $10 million on deposit with Citibank and earns a competitive rate of return. Citibank not only retains the deposit, but gains loanable funds, because reserve requirements are lower on "due to" liabilities to branches than on demand deposits.

Citibank could use the same approach to obtain GM's business from a competing bank. If GM has demand deposits in Chemical Bank,

for example, Citibank may offer to pay a relatively high rate of return on Eurodollar deposits in its London branch. If GM withdraws its funds from Chemical to hold a Eurodeposit in Citibank's London office, the London branch would again show a "due from" asset in the amount of the deposit, while Citibank New York would show a "due to" liability.

An important point about both examples is that *at no time does a Eurodeposit actually leave the home country.* Funds that start out in the United States end up there as well. Eurodeposits are really nothing more than a series of accounting entries, resulting in the customer's holding a time deposit and the domestic bank's incurring a liability, on which reserves must be held.

Cost of Eurodeposits.   Figure 15.5 illustrates the relationship between the cost of Eurodollar

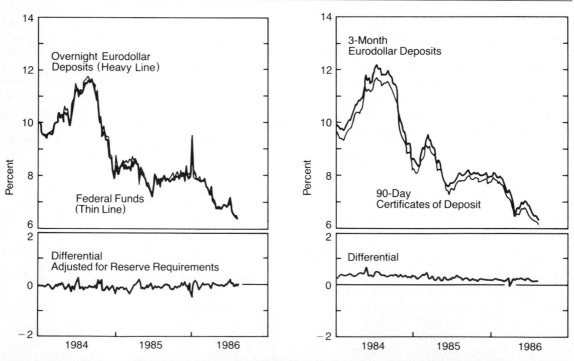

Figure 15.5
Eurodollar and U.S. Money Market Rates

Source: Board of Governors of the Federal Reserve System, *Federal Reserve Chart Book,* August 1986, p. 84.

liabilities and alternative sources of funds. The cost of overnight Eurodollars is very close to the federal funds rate. After adjustment for the lack of reserve requirements on fed funds purchased, Eurodollars often, but not always, cost slightly more than fed funds. A larger difference exists between three-month Eurodollar deposits and domestic CDs with similar maturities. Because most Eurodeposits are held by U. S. investors, a premium is demanded as protection against the lack of deposit insurance and against country risk, or potential loss caused by unanticipated problems in a foreign country. A depository must weigh the additional costs of Eurodollars against the benefits, such as the potential for growth, their relatively low reserve requirements, and the fact that no deposit insurance premiums are paid on them.[21]

Repurchase Agreements.   Repurchase agreements ("repos"), explained and illustrated in Chapter 4, are another tool of liability management. Repos are the "sale" of marketable securities by an institution, with an agreement to repurchase at a specified future date. The seller obtains use of cash for other purposes. Buyers are seeking liquid, short-term investments as an alternative to nonearning demand deposits; they consider the transactions "reverse repos."

The depository institution secures the funds obtained by pledging some of its own investment securities as collateral. As long as securities pledged against repos are U.S. government or government agency securities, repos are not subject to reserve requirements. The cost of issuing repos is ordinarily lower than the rate paid on similar maturities in the Fed funds or CD markets. Because repos are backed by high-quality securities, default risk is lower.

If the investor insists that the institution transfer the collateral elsewhere for safekeeping, the rate paid on the repo may be even lower, because of the increased cost to the depository and lower risk to the investor.

Repo maturities range from overnight to 30 days or longer. Transactions can occur between institutions and individuals, in which case they are called "retail repos," or between financial institutions. Because they involve collateral, they are not considered deposits and are therefore ineligible for deposit insurance. This further lowers the cost to the institution issuing them.

Mortgage-Backed Securities.[22]   The growth of the repo market in recent years has encouraged depository institutions to envision other ways to use existing assets as collateral to obtain new funds. For mortgage lenders, using mortgages to back new securities is a logical step, and in the 1980s, several types of mortgage-backed securities have been developed. They enable an institution to raise funds for new mortgage loans at current rates without having to sell existing mortgages, which may have declined in value. Among the most popular of the new securities are *mortgage-backed bonds* and *collateralized mortgage obligations (CMOs)*. As their names suggest, they are long-term nondeposit liabilities. A mortgage-backed bond is the debt obligation of an institution backed by expected cash flows from its general mortgage portfolio. A CMO is a special kind of *pay-through bond.*[23] A pay-through bond is one for which cash flows from specific existing mort-

---

[21]It is difficult to assess the riskiness of Eurodeposits versus domestic deposits accurately. The elements of risk previously discussed are given from the viewpoint of an American deposit holder. An Iranian, in contrast, might consider Eurodeposits less risky than dollar-denominated deposits in a bank in the United States. For more discussion of the problems involved in evaluating Eurodollar risk, see Marvin Goodfriend, "Eurodollars," in *Instruments of the Money Market* 6th ed. (Richmond, VA: Federal Reserve Bank of Richmond, 1986), pp. 53-64.

[22]Except as noted, information in this section was obtained from *Freddie Mac Reports,* various issues.

[23]Another type of mortgage-backed security, the pass-through, is also one on which borrowers' monthly payments on a package of mortgages are passed directly each month to the mortgage-backed security holder. They are discussed in more detail in Chapter 18. A pay-through bond is similar, although there are differences in the tax treatment of returns on the two types of bonds. Pay-throughs are designed to appeal to tax-exempt investors. See Donald J. Puglisi and Joseph A. McKenzie, "Capital Market Strategies for Thrift Institutions," *Federal Home Loan Bank Board Journal* 16 (November 1983): 2-8.

gages are designated to repay bond principal and interest. CMOs are issued with a staggered maturity schedule, allowing an institution to attract buyers with different investment criteria to a single issue. Each maturity class is paid off sequentially; all obligations from one class are paid before any payment is made on the next class.

Because mortgages are high-quality collateral, institutions issuing mortgage-backed securities often do so at only a slight premium over the T-bond rate. Initially, only fixed-rate mortgages were believed to be suitable collateral. The variety of ARM plans discussed in the preceding chapter made it difficult to assemble a pool of similar loans, and uncertainty about their future cash flows exposed the purchaser of an ARM-backed bond to additional risk. By 1985, however, standardization of ARMs and increasing familiarity with mortgage-backed securities encouraged issuance of ARM-backed securities. This development is important to mortgage lenders, who can use ARMs to shorten the interest sensitivity of asset portfolios while retaining access to the mortgage-backed bond market as a source of nondeposit funds.

Because of administrative and flotation costs, mortgage-backed bonds are usually issued with minimum face values of $100 million. To make it easier for small depositories to use mortgage-backed securities, methods have been developed by which several firms working together can pool collateral and issue bonds. Pooling has increased the participation of small thrift institutions in this form of liability management.[24]

Brokered Deposits. *Brokered deposits* are obtained when a depository engages a broker to raise funds. The broker receives a commission and may solicit money on a national or even international basis, usually assigning the total funds raised to individual accounts in fully insured portions of up to $100,000 each. Institutions raising funds in this way are often small and unable to sell uninsured negotiable CDs because they lack the necessary financial reputation. Through the use of brokered deposits, they can attract funds from a wide geographic area and expose depositors to no default risk. Some institutions using brokered deposits have achieved much greater than normal growth, paying yields higher than the "going rate" and advertising features seldom offered on deposits. For example, in 1984, a California S&L with assets of only $22 million paid E. F. Hutton to raise $60 million in additional deposits. The CDs had a maturity of 12 years and an interest rate tied to the institution's rate of return on a package of commercial mortgage loans not yet made.[25]

There are several motivations for such a strategy. A financially weak institution may view insured, brokered deposits as a good source of liquidity if it faces a potential drain of funds from uninsured sources. Institutions in low-growth areas may be unable to diversify or restructure their assets if they depend solely on local deposit growth for new cash. Nevertheless, an institution using brokered deposits is faced with the task of finding investment outlets for the funds raised. Ordinarily, it would be difficult to quadruple a firm's assets quickly without a substantial increase in riskiness. If management is unskilled in risk assessment, or if it is venturing into uncharted territory, it is unlikely to succeed. Failure of an institution heavily dependent upon brokered deposits could require substantial assistance from the federal insurance funds. As a consequence, the FHLBB has restricted the percentage of brokered deposits used by FSLIC-insured savings institutions with weak net worth positions.[26]

---

[24]Further information on recent developments in the CMO market is provided in "ARM-Backed Securities Evolve," *ABA Banking Journal* 75 (May 1985): 66; and Pat Allen, "CMO Conduit Participants Use Proceeds to Boost Profits," *Savings Institutions* 106 (October 1986): 76–79.

[25]Further discussion is available in Caroline T. Harless, "Brokered Deposits," *Economic Review,* Federal Reserve Bank of Atlanta 69 (March 1984): 14–25; and Mary Kuntz, "Proceed at Your Own Risk," *Forbes,* 134 (December 31, 1984): 94.

[26]The FDIC and the FSLIC both initially attempted to limit insurance coverage on brokered deposits, but that policy was struck down in federal court in 1984 after a suit by the Securities Industry Association.

Factors Influencing the Use of Liability Management

"Confidence-sensitive" money is any source of funds sensitive to a loss of confidence either in a particular institution or in the banking system in general. Many tools of liability management are confidence-sensitive. Further, even when an institution is not the object of a loss of confidence, major investors in the instruments of liability management are willing to move funds from one institution to another to gain a few basis points. Funds that move quickly in response to yield differences are often called *"hot money"* or *"money at a price."*[27]

Institutions relying heavily on either confidence-sensitive or hot money adopt an aggressive strategy; as financial conditions change, they can lose access to those funds. In contrast, managers who prefer to rely on their own resources for immediate liquidity needs, and "store" those resources in the asset portfolio, are adopting a more conservative stance, as are those institutions which plan their asset growth at the same pace as expected growth in deposits and net worth. Several general factors are associated with a depository's choice between these management styles.

Size and Industry Membership. The smaller an institution, the less likely that it will issue large CDs, repurchase agreements, or Eurodollar liabilities, simply because it lacks a large enough capital base or securities portfolio to support those operations. In addition, the customers may be individuals or small local businesses lacking the funds to make these investments. Further, access to the Eurodollar markets is difficult for nonmoney center banks or for those without foreign branches. Thus, liability management continues to remain in the realm of very large commercial banks and a few savings institutions.

In the past, thrifts using liability management have issued large-denomination CDs through New York dealers, but the volume is small. Recently, thrifts have also increased their use of mortgage-backed bonds, CMOs, and brokered deposits. Credit unions, with the common-bond requirement, are greatly restricted in the use of liability management tools such as brokered deposits. They can use repurchase agreements, federal funds, or borrowings from federal regulators, and some have done so. But because one of their objectives is to offer relatively low loan rates to members, CUs' aggressive use of high-cost nonshare sources of funds is not great.

Financial Strength. The firm's financial position affects its access to uninsured liabilities. When an institution issues liabilities beyond the protective umbrella of federal insurance, all funds suppliers assess their exposure to default risk. Increasing depository failure rates have made prospective investors and uninsured depositors more cautious. When an institution's financial performance deteriorates, investors require a larger risk premium, and they may eventually withdraw all funds regardless of the premium the institution is willing to pay. In mid-1984, the nation's largest thrift institution, American Savings, faced just such a scenario; uninsured depositors withdrew significant sums when its financial condition worsened. Eventually, the chief executive officer, architect of American's aggressive liability management strategy, was forced to resign.[28]

The aggressive use of fully insured tools of liability management, such as brokered deposits, has also been associated with weak institutions. The chairman of the FDIC reported that 16 percent of the total deposits in the 72 banks

---

[27]The term *confidence-sensitive* was introduced in Dudley Luckett, "Approaches to Bank Liquidity Management," *Economic Review*, Federal Reserve Bank of Kansas City, 65 (March 1980): 15-16. Other references to these issues include Howard D. Crosse, "Bank Liquidity Revisited," *The Bankers Magazine* 158 (Spring 1975): 37-41; and Joseph E. Burns, "Bank Liquidity—A Straightforward Concept but Hard to Measure," *Business Review*, Federal Reserve Bank of Dallas (May 1971), pp. 1-4.

[28]Frederick M. Muir and Tim Carrington, "Knapp Resigns from Financial Corporation of America," *The Wall Street Journal*, August 28, 1984; and Frederick M. Muir and Tim Carrington, "Financial Corporation of America May Get a Federal Guarantee for All Deposits," *The Wall Street Journal*, August 30, 1984.

that failed between February 1982 and October 1983 were brokered. Empire Savings and Loan of Mesquite, Texas, used brokered deposits to grow more than 1,500 percent in less than two years. In March 1984, the speculative construction loans it had made went into default, and the institution failed, draining over $150 million from the FSLIC insurance fund.[29]

CHANGING SOURCES OF FUNDS: A SUMMARY

Figure 15.6 shows the impact of new deposits and liability management tools on depositories over a 23-year period. Demand and savings deposits plummeted as investors sought to escape interest rate restrictions. Milestones in the removal of those restrictions are evident, as is the increased use of major liability management tools. For example, the removal of Reg Q ceilings on large time deposits (included in managed liabilities) is evident after 1970, as is the impact of the MMC on small CDs after 1975. NOWs, share drafts, and MMDAs became more significant after 1980. Finally, the recent growth in all managed liabilities, including negotiable CDs, repos, and Eurodollars is also shown. The figure summarizes the changing nature of funds sources at depositories and suggests the need for careful management attention to potential changes in the future.

NONINTEREST COMPETITION AMONG DEPOSITORIES

New deposit instruments and liability management are not the only consequences of historical restrictions on deposit taking. Both Reg Q and the prohibition of interest on demand deposits led to the use of *implicit interest payments,* or services provided to depositors in lieu of explicit interest. Implicit interest permits depository institutions to compete when explicit interest competition is prohibited, or when managers believe implicit interest competition is less costly or more desirable to customers than increasing explicit interest. Over the years, implicit interest has taken many forms, ranging from pots and pans for new account holders, to entertainment such as that described in the opening paragraph of the chapter, to opening branch offices or drive-through windows to increase convenience. Depositories also offer a wide range of account-related services such as free checking, automatic transfer of funds from savings to checking, pre-authorized bill payments, automatic payroll deposits, or preferential treatment on loans.

Economic Efficiency of Noninterest Competition

An important question for individual institutions, and for the financial system as a whole, is whether or not implicit interest payments benefit financial market participants. Most experts conclude that they do not.

The Institution's Point of View.   Before the removal of Reg Q, small depositories, in particular, argued that they could not afford to pay market rates on so-called *"core" deposits*—transaction accounts, passbook savings, and small consumer CDs. Research indicates, however, that savings in explicit interest costs under Reg Q did not result in increased profits, but were redirected toward increased operating expenses. Estimates of implicit annual interest rates paid to demand depositors through the provision of services range from under 1 percent in 1954 to nearly 5 percent in the late 1960s.[30]

---

[29]David Pyle, "Some Implications of Deposit Deregulation," *Weekly Letter,* Federal Reserve Bank of San Francisco, February 10, 1984; G. Christian Hill, "Agencies that Insure Bank, Thrift Deposits Face Major Problems," *The Wall Street Journal,* May 23, 1984, pp. 1, 18.

[30]Lawrence J. White, "Price Regulation and Quality Rivalry in a Profit Maximizing Model: The Case of Bank Branching," *Journal of Money, Credit and Banking* 8 (February 1976): 97-106; Robert A. Taggart, Jr., "Effects of Deposit Rate Ceilings: The Evidence from Massachusetts Savings Banks," *Journal of Money, Credit and Banking* 10 (May 1978): 139-157; Michael Dotsey, "An Examination of Implicit Interest Rates on Demand Deposits," *Economic Review,* Federal Reserve Bank of Richmond 69 (September/October 1983): 3-11.

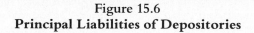

Figure 15.6
Principal Liabilities of Depositories

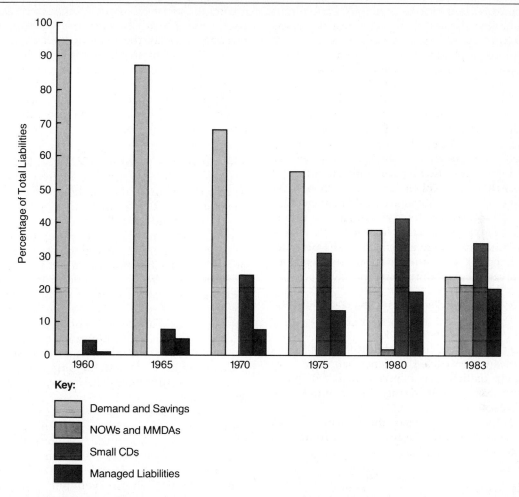

Key:

- Demand and Savings
- NOWs and MMDAs
- Small CDs
- Managed Liabilities

Source: Adapted from data provided in Alfred Broaddus, "Financial Innovations in the U.S.: Background, Current Status and Prospects," *Economic Review,* Federal Reserve Bank of Richmond 71 (January/February 1985): 11.

It is easy to see how these costs arise. Suppose a bank offers "free" checking to demand deposit customers, who then have no economic incentive to restrict the number of checks they write. To the extent that the institution's resources are tied to check processing rather than to income-producing activities, the cost of providing services to depositors may equal or even exceed what the bank saves by not paying interest on the deposits. Of course, if profits are significantly less variable as a result of implicit rather than explicit interest, institutions and their owners may not be harmed even if operating expenses increase. Evidence indicates, however, that explicit interest costs are unrelated to systematic risk and negatively related to total risk for banks. This evidence implies that institutions would not be more risky, and might even be less risky, if explicit interest payments *increased* as a percentage of total expenses.[31]

Some implicit interest payments, such as building additional branches or hiring additional staff, are analogous to fixed costs in industrial firms. Although the analogy is not perfect, it is useful for examining why implicit interest payments may be financially undesirable for a depository. The costs of operating a branch or employing a new staff member are harder to adjust downward with revenue decreases than are explicit interest payments. As students of corporate financial management know, a high level of fixed costs in a firm means a high **degree of operating leverage**. The degree of operating leverage is defined as the percentage change in operating profits resulting from a 1 percent change in total revenues (TR):

$$DOL_{TR} = \frac{\%\Delta \text{ Operating Income}}{\%\Delta \text{ Revenues}}$$

A degree of operating leverage of 3, for example, means that each 1 percent change in revenues, up or down, is expected to result in a 3 percent change in operating income in the same direction.

DOL is a function of the variable- versus fixed-cost structure of a firm at its current level of revenue, calculated as:[32]

$$(15.1) \quad DOL_{TR} = \frac{TR - VC}{TR - VC - FC}$$

where:

VC = total variable costs; and

FC = total fixed costs.

The higher the level of fixed costs, the higher the degree of operating leverage. The higher the degree of operating leverage, the greater the variation in operating income as revenue varies. In a depository institution, total revenues vary as the general level of interest rates or the term structure changes. It follows that a higher level of implicit interest payments, which are usually fixed costs, results in greater variation in the operating income of a depository than if the institution paid more in explicit interest, a variable cost.

The Customer's Point of View.   The use of implicit rather than explicit interest may not benefit depositors either, although the issue is less clear-cut than it is for financial institutions. On the one hand, an individual may not want a new toaster from a bank, preferring to earn the equivalent amount in cash. Regulations permitting the toaster but not the cash are not to the customer's benefit. Some economists also argue that interest rate controls, forcing implicit interest competition, increase loan rates at depositories. Without rate controls, the quantity of deposits should increase, increasing the availability of loanable funds and simultaneously reducing wasteful implicit interest costs. The result should be lower, not higher, lending rates.[33]

There are reasons, however, why some customers prefer implicit to explicit interest. Implicit interest is not taxed, whereas for most recipients, explicit interest is. To the extent that a customer actually desires the "free" services provided by the depository, implicit interest, or at least some combination of explicit and implicit interest, is preferable. The higher the personal tax bracket, the more likely this is to be true. This argument suggests that even if interest were paid on demand deposits, some forms of implicit interest would remain.

---

[31]This research is examined in Benston, "Interest on Deposits and the Survival of Chartered Depository Institutions," p. 51.

[32]The derivation and assumptions underlying Equation 15.1 are given in many good financial management texts. One example can be found in Eugene F. Brigham and Louis C. Gapenski *Intermediate Financial Management,* 2d ed. (Chicago: Dryden Press, 1987), Chapter 6.

[33]For arguments supporting the benefits of explicit interest to customers, see Milton Friedman, "Controls on Interest Rates Paid by Banks," *Journal of Money, Credit and Banking* 2 (February 1970): 15-32; and Michael C. Keeley, "Interest-Rate Deregulation," *Weekly Letter,* Federal Reserve Bank of San Francisco, January 13, 1984.

Figure 15.7
Implicit Interest Expenses at Banks and Thrifts

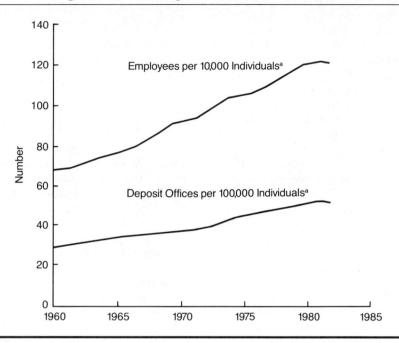

[a]20 Years and Over

Source: David Pyle, "Some Implications of Deposit Deregulation," *Weekly Letter,* Federal Reserve Bank of San Francisco, February 10, 1984.

Implicit Interest after the Removal of Reg Q

Based on this analysis, one would expect to find changes in the behavior of depositories following the removal of Reg Q. The evidence so far is consistent with expectations. Figure 15.7 traces two elements of implicit interest—deposit offices and employees compared to the adult population—from 1960 to the mid-1980s. When interest rate controls were especially binding, from the early 1970s to 1981, the slopes of these trend lines were their greatest. Depositories substituted convenience and service for the inability to provide market yields to customers. After the introduction of the MMDA in 1982, both trend lines turned down for the first time, as depositories recognized that the level of implicit interest they had been

providing was suboptimal. By late 1986, 70% of transactions balances were in interest-bearing checking accounts, suggesting that most customers prefer explicit to implicit interest.[34] The Tax Reform Act of 1986, which lowered considerably the highest personal tax bracket, is likely to accelerate this trend.

Increased Use of Deposit Service Charges

Another recent development is the imposition of deposit service charges where none existed, or the increase in charges at institutions that had

---

[34]Gary C. Zimmerman and Michael C. Keeley. "Interest Checking," *Weekly Letter,* Federal Reserve Bank of San Francisco, November 14, 1986.

previously had them. At many institutions, customers with high balances are given "free" checking and other implicit interest benefits. Less affluent customers are charged explicitly for each deposit or withdrawal, and in some cases for simply using a teller. A study conducted for the House Banking Committee estimated that the average U.S. household faced an increase of 104 percent in the cost of basic banking services from 1979 to 1983—from $91.94 per year to $187.59. A study by economists at the Federal Reserve Board concluded that the overall profitability of personal checking accounts did not increase, however, and that banks were simply charging fees necessary to cover their costs.[35]

Nonetheless, because new pricing systems permit those with high balances to receive "free" or low-cost banking services, they are consistent with the idea that wealthy customers benefit from the nontaxable implicit interest. Concern has been raised about the ability of low-income households to afford services formerly offered as a substitute for market interest rates. The Massachusetts legislature passed a law in 1984 preventing state-chartered banks from imposing service charges on persons under 18 or over 65. Recently, proposals requiring the existence of minimum-cost "lifeline" deposit accounts surfaced in several states and in the U.S. Congress.

ACQUISITION OF FUNDS IN A DEREGULATED ENVIRONMENT

The managers of depository institutions are faced with a complex set of decisions when planning how to raise and retain funds. Although no models are available for a mechanical analysis of these problems, certain issues must

---

[35]Daniel Hertzberg, "Smaller Customers Get Less Service at Banks and Pay More Charges," *The Wall Street Journal,* October 18, 1984, p. 16; Glenn B. Canner and Robert D. Kurtz, "Service Charges as a Source of Bank Income and Their Impact on Consumers," Federal Reserve Board Staff Study No. 145, August 1985.

be considered systematically. They can be classified into three categories:

1. The broad choice between wholesale and retail funds sources;

2. The mix of deposit and nondeposit liabilities; and

3. The pricing of accounts and services.

Wholesale versus Retail Funds

The first major decision is whether to seek wholesale or retail funds. *Wholesale funds* are those provided by nonfinancial businesses and other financial institutions; *retail funds* are provided by households. This decision is part of strategic planning, because it determines many operating policies thereafter. Managers must evaluate several points in making the decision.

Availability.   Chapter 5 notes that only the household sector is a net supplier of funds, and businesses and governments are net borrowers. Thus, in the financial system as a whole, more retail funds are available than wholesale funds, and few depository institutions can afford to ignore the retail market altogether. Still, in some areas—midtown Manhattan, for example—wholesale funds may be more plentiful. In 1980, Bankers Trust of New York, one of the nation's ten largest banks, abandoned retail business completely by selling the few branches it operated. Management believed that the long-run profit potential was greater from that course of action. The bank already had a solid base of corporate customers, and its prime New York location positioned it well to pursue additional wholesale funds.

The discussion of liability management noted other factors that influence an institution's decision to use nontraditional funds sources: size, industry membership, and financial condition. Because the tools of liability management are largely wholesale, those characteristics also play a role in a depository's strategic choice between wholesale and retail funds. Yet even large banks on solid financial ground do not always depend solely on wholesale funds just because they can get them. At the same time Bankers Trust became a wholesaler, Citibank, with its extensive branch network, renewed its commitment to retail banking by expanding credit card operations and other consumer services. Neither Bankers Trust's nor Citicorp's decision was made lightly, because the commitment to wholesale or retail funds affects the entire range of products and services offered.

Funds Volatility.   Retail and wholesale funds can both be volatile, but wholesale funds ineligible for deposit insurance are especially rate- and confidence-sensitive, as the cases of Continental Illinois and American Savings indicate. Institutions relying heavily on wholesale funds must be prepared to bid aggressively to keep them when rates increase, and to have alternative funds sources in case of emergencies.

In contrast, retail deposits may involve commitments to depositories on the part of the consumer. Households choose institutions based not only on their rates and reputations, but also their locations and convenience. Although consumers did not hesitate to switch to other forms of investment in the mid- to late 1970s, they returned to depositories quickly when given a reasonable opportunity to do so in 1982. Even though MMDA yields were below money fund rates from 1983 through early 1985, MMDAs did not show a loss of volume to MMMFs. A recent survey reported that over 40 percent of households with interest-bearing checking accounts said they would not move an account to an equally convenient depository on the basis of interest rate differentials. Another 30 percent said only a rate differential of at least 2 percent would induce them to move.[36] Al-

though respondents reported they would be more likely to move MMDAs among depositories because of rate differences, the evidence suggests that consumers are less rate-sensitive than was believed before the removal of Reg Q.

Cost.   Many managers argue that the cost of retail funds is higher, because retail banking requires a branch network and/or a large staff, but the pursuit of wholesale funds is also costly. Nonpersonal time deposits, for example, carry a 3 percent reserve requirement, whereas personal time deposits do not. For small institutions, or for thrifts only recently involved with commercial customers, the cost of locating sources of corporate and institutional money can be substantial. Some depositories have turned to brokers, but they lack loyalty to individual institutions and will not hesitate to move clients' money on short notice. Other depositories have turned to techniques such as "800 banking," soliciting large deposits through toll-free numbers advertised in national business publications. As respondents call, in-house personnel are available to answer questions and open accounts. But employees must be trained in the subjects important to wholesale customers, such as financial market conditions, and training is expensive.

Anticipated Uses of Funds.   For many institutions, the decision to pursue particular types of liabilities depends upon planned uses of the funds. Although the relationship between asset and liability strategies is the subject of Chapters 17 and 18 and is not discussed in detail here, plans to make ten-year mortgage loans, for example, will be complicated considerably if they are funded by hot money in times of rising rates. Conversely, if funds are needed temporarily to meet a shortfall of required reserves, raising the money through three- to five-year retail CDs would be inappropriate. Further, if the planned use of funds is commercial loans, management may wish to develop a customer base by first obtaining wholesale deposits. If consumer credit is the desired investment, it may be appropriate to seek retail deposits.

---

[36]Mark Flannery has argued that retail deposits can be considered quasi-fixed sources of funds, since the depositor is required to incur both search and set-up costs when choosing an individual institution. Still, there is likely to be some threshold yield on alternate investments that will cause the depositor to switch to another institution, even though additional costs will be incurred. See Mark Flannery, "Retail Bank Deposits as Quasi-Fixed Factors of Production," *American Economic Review* 72 (June 1982): 527-536.

Mix of Funds Sources

In the past, the rule of thumb for choosing the deposit mix was simple: Attract as many core deposits as possible. They were relatively cheap, plentiful, and uncomplicated. Because explicit interest was not a competitive tool and geographic expansion was limited by law and technology, core deposits flowed into institutions according to the convenience of their locations. Today, even if an institution pursues retail deposits exclusively, it cannot follow that rule of thumb blindly. The relative cost of core deposits versus others, their maturity, and the sensitivity of their costs to interest rate changes must be considered. Low-balance core deposits, for example, may cost more to administer than MMDAs, when the cost of reserve requirements is included, even though the explicit MMDA rate is higher than the explicit rate paid on NOWs or the implicit rate on demand deposits.

Pricing

Establishing goals for the types of funds to be raised is of little use unless pricing strategies are geared to attract them. The pricing of deposit accounts involves three separate but related decisions: the explicit interest rate to be offered, the division of returns between explicit and implicit interest, and fees to be charged for each account.

Setting Explicit Interest Rates.   The opening quotation to the chapter suggests that, until recently, most depository institution managers had no experience in setting rates to attract funds. The negotiable CD, fed funds, and Eurodollar markets are national or international in scope, so even managers practicing liability management faced limited discretion in rate setting. Today, managers of all depositories are required to use judgment. One course of action is simply to follow the crowd—to establish interest rates similar to those offered by key competitors, especially ones viewed as market leaders. For many years, some depositories have used this strategy to establish loan rates.

Some managers may wish to take more control over the explicit prices they pay for deposits, requiring data collection and analysis. This is especially important for accounts such as MMDAs, on which depositors are more interest-sensitive. By collecting data on an institution's MMDA balances over time, management can use regression analysis to relate those balances to the interest paid by the institution itself, by rival depositories, or by MMMFs. The resulting regression coefficients can assist in estimating how the institution's MMDA balances vary as rates vary. The same approach could be used for any source of funds for which explicit interest rates must be set. Given the accessibility of microcomputers, almost any depository can use quantitative models that can be easily updated as more data become available or conditions change.[37]

Wealthier customers may be more rate-sensitive than customers with lower incomes. Accordingly, many depositories have established *tiered pricing systems,* under which the explicit rate increases as a customer's balance increases beyond threshold levels. For example, one rate may be paid on MMDA balances below $500, and successively higher rates as an account balance exceeds $1,000, $2,500, $10,000, and so forth. In fact, by 1985, nearly 40 percent of thrifts were using tiered systems for MMDAs, with smaller numbers using them for other accounts.[38]

Explicit versus Implicit Pricing.   As noted, some depositors prefer to be compensated entirely with explicit interest, while others prefer

---

[37]This approach is illustrated by Neil B. Murphy and Richard H. Kraas, who used weekly deposit data from a small bank, in "Measuring the Interest Sensitivity of Money Market Accounts," *Magazine of Bank Administration* 60 (May 1984): 70-74. Two researchers at the Federal Reserve Bank of Atlanta used a similar approach to assess the rate-sensitivity of MMDA balances and concluded that long-run rather than weekly data were more useful. See Larry D. Wall and Harold D. Ford, "Money Market Account Competition," *Economic Review,* Federal Reserve Bank of Atlanta 69 (December 1984): 4-14.

[38]See U.S. League of Savings Institutions, Management Report MR-11, October 9, 1985, p. 15.

implicit interest to avoid taxation. Thus, setting an explicit rate is not enough to ensure that the desired deposit structure will be attained. Because some customers may prefer one combination while others prefer another, a pricing approach that allows consumer choice is likely to be most satisfactory.

Two general explicit/implicit pricing strategies have been suggested. One is based on the New England experience with NOW accounts in the 1970s. A *"conditionally free" account* is, as the name implies, one for which no service charges are imposed under certain conditions—usually, that the depositor keeps a specified minimum balance in the account. If the balance falls below the minimum, a service charge is imposed, as a flat fee, a price per service rendered, or both. The customer determines the mix of implicit and explicit interest by the way the account is managed.

An alternative to the "conditionally free" account is the *"interest buydown" account.* With this approach, each service associated with an account is priced on a markdown basis from the explicit interest rate. Table 15.4 illustrates such a strategy. Suppose through regression analysis, or from watching a market leader, management sets the explicit interest rate on a NOW account at 10 percent, with no implicit interest included. In addition, suppose the services listed in Table 15.4 are available to account holders. With the interest buydown pricing strategy, the customer selects the desired services in exchange for a lower explicit rate of interest. Should the customers wish to use services not initially "bought," fees can be charged as services are used. In this example, the explicit interest is bought down to 2 percent, because the account holder has selected services considered equivalent to an 8 percent annual return.[39]

Setting Fees for Specific Account-Related Services

Fee-based services, whether specifically related to deposits or offered as supplements to traditional depository services, have become so important that Chapter 20 is entirely devoted to them. The foregoing discussion indicates, however, that deposit-account pricing has become more complicated. Managers must now identify prices for each type of service formerly included in a deposit-related package. Pricing theorists refer to this development as the *"unbundling"* of services.

Ideally, prices should be related to the costs incurred by the institution, so cost analysis, a relatively new activity for depositories, is attracting more attention. The Federal Reserve System has for several years provided a Functional Cost Analysis service, through which it calculates the unit costs of key services for institutions providing the necessary data.[40] Many depositories have recently instituted cost accounting systems for the first time, using the data to price products. Trade groups in each industry have been active in assisting small institutions with cost accounting problems.

In addition to estimating the cost of providing a service, some institutions estimate the value of that service to customers. If the cost of providing it exceeds the value to the recipient, the service is eliminated. For example, preauthorized bill payment services are offered by some depositories as part of a transaction account package. Through this service, a depository automatically transfers funds from a customer's account to pay regular household expenditures such as insurance and utilities. The value of this service to a customer is unlikely to exceed the sum of the costs of a stamp, an envelope, and the time necessary to write and record a check, probably no more than $.40

---

[39]Further discussion of pricing strategies is provided in Robert J. Rogowski, "Pricing the Money Market Deposit and Super-NOW Accounts in 1983," *Journal of Bank Research* 15 (Summer 1984): 72-81; Peter J. Elmer, "Developing Service-Oriented Deposit Accounts," *Bankers Magazine* 168 (March-April 1985): 60-63; and Tom Parliment, "Not Paying Market Is an Option," *Savings Institutions* 106 (April 1985): S12-S17.

[40]For more details on Functional Cost Analysis, see Carla M. Warberg, "Functional Cost Analysis—A New System Approach to Gauging Profitability, *Business Review,* Federal Reserve Bank of Dallas (August 1971), pp. 7-11; Alan R. Winger, "On the Importance of Functional Cost Data to Thrift Institutions," *Federal Home Loan Bank Board Journal* 16 (December 1983): 4-7.

Table 15.4
The "Interest Buydown" Pricing Strategy

Service	Cost	Desired by Customer
Unlimited transactions	3.00%	Yes
Use of automatic teller machines	1.00	Yes
Use of teller window	1.00	Yes
Free travelers checks	0.50	No
Free safe deposit box	0.50	No
Preauthorized bill payments for:		
Mortgage	0.50	Yes
Car	0.50	No
Insurance	0.50	No
Credit life insurance for:		
Mortgage	1.00	Yes
Car	1.00	No
Personal computer linkage with:		
Stock market data	1.50	No
Bond market data	1.50	Yes

Base explicit interest rate: 10%
Total cost of "bought" services: 8%
Explicit interest rate: 2%

Source: Adapted from Peter J. Elmer, "Developing Service-Oriented Deposit Accounts," *The Bankers Magazine* 168 (March–April 1985): 60-63.

to $.50 for most persons. If the institution can provide the service and make a profit for less than that, both parties will benefit. If not, the service is not worth its cost.[41]

Pricing Strategies in Practice

Depository managers have approached pricing problems in a variety of ways in recent years.

Use of Conditionally Free Accounts. A 1983 survey of banks and thrifts indicated that conditionally free pricing strategies dominated both MMDAs and Super NOWs; within states, thrifts imposed fewer fees than banks and offered slightly higher explicit rates on both accounts. By 1985, the use of conditionally free

accounts was common, with minimums to avoid service charges ranging from over $1,000 to over $3,300.

In response to concern about the inability of lower-income households to afford basic checking services, both the Comptroller of the Currency and trade organizations have urged depositories to develop "no frills" accounts on which fees are minimized. The American Bankers Association, a major trade organization, recently reported that 45 percent of all large banks and 60 percent of smaller banks offer or plan to offer these accounts. In exchange for the low cost, the number of transactions is limited and no interest is earned by the accountholder.[42]

[41]James A. Logue, "Pricing Strategies for the 1980s," *Magazine of Bank Administration* 59 (September 1983): 28-34.

[42]Rogowski, "Pricing the Money Market Deposit and Super-NOW Account in 1983"; Leon E. Wynter, "Too High a Price: Consumers Feel Ripped Off by Bank Deregulation," *The Wall Street Journal,* October 9, 1985, p. 33; Gary C. Zimmerman, "Shopping Pays," *Weekly Letter,* Federal Reserve Bank of San Francisco, November 8, 1985.

Other Pricing Strategies.   A 1983 survey at the Federal Reserve Bank of Cleveland provided additional evidence of depositories' account pricing and served as a leading indicator of strategies in subsequent years. Some institutions were using a tiered system for setting explicit interest rates, although tiering was more common for CDs than for more liquid accounts. On interest-bearing accounts, required minimum balances varied negatively with the liquidity of the account. In all cases, however, minimum balances needed to earn interest exceeded regulatory minimums in effect at the time of the survey, and were as high as $20,000 in some institutions. Later national surveys of banks and thrifts revealed most did not, in fact, lower minimum balance requirements on interest-bearing accounts after regulations first permitted it. These data suggest that minimum balance requirements will remain in the absence of regulation.[43]

As account pricing has become more complex, regulators are under increasing pressure to require institutions to disclose the full cost of deposit accounts in a standard format. Such a requirement would be analogous to the APR disclosure on consumer loans. Laws to this effect have been considered at both the state and federal levels. Despite the concern, some experts praise the economic efficiency of new pricing strategies allowing customers to choose the accounts they want while bearing the costs of their choices. Ideally, when in place at every depository, cost-based pricing strategies should allow customers to pay no more, but no less, than their fair share of the cost of receiving deposit services.

DEREGULATION AND FEDERAL DEPOSIT INSURANCE

A discussion of deposit taking and liability management in a deregulated world is incomplete without examining the relationship between depository institution management and the federal deposit and share insurance funds.

Moral Hazard

Economists argue that liability management increases the efficiency by which scarce capital is allocated. If institutions with profitable lending opportunities obtain funds by bidding in a competitive marketplace, the potential for funds to flow to the most efficient users is enhanced. Deposit deregulation, and the resulting competition for funds among intermediaries, should have a similar impact on economic efficiency. Unfortunately, most experts also believe that these benefits are reduced considerably, and perhaps even outweighed, by allocational inefficiencies caused by the federal deposit and share insurance programs.

The basis for this conclusion is that the current system produces a **moral hazard** for the insurers—that is, it increases the likelihood that institution managers will take excessive risks with depositors' funds and, therefore, that the insurer will be required to pay claims. To understand this argument, one must understand how the deposit insurance system operates.

Financing the Insurance Funds

To advertise themselves as federally insured, depository institutions must pay premiums to the federal agencies insuring them. The premium structure differs by type of institution, but all have one thing in common: Unlike other insurance policies, the insured is *not* charged a premium based on the estimated risk posed for the insurer. No matter how risky the assets of a depository, its insurance premium is proportionately no more than that of an institution whose only assets are T-bills.

Bank and Thrift Insurance.   Commercial and savings banks insured by the FDIC are assessed a premium of $\frac{1}{12}$ of 1 percent per year on average total domestic deposits, payable in

---

[43]Paul R. Watro, "Deregulation and Deposit Pricing," *Economic Commentary*, Federal Reserve Bank of Cleveland, April 23, 1984; Spooner, "Cut from the Last Regulatory Ties, Savings Rates Fly Free," pp. 44–45; and Zimmerman and Keeley, "Interest Checking."

advance on a semiannual basis.[44] By law, the FDIC must rebate premiums to member banks in July following an assessed calendar year. The rebate formula was established in DIDMCA and is designed to maintain the fund's level at between 1.25 percent and 1.40 percent of insured deposits.[45] FSLIC premiums are assessed the same way. The FDIC and the FSLIC are both authorized to make special assessments when necessary, but only the FSLIC has done so. In 1985, an additional 1/32 of 1 percent per quarter was imposed on FSLIC-insured thrifts, although Congress mandated the phase-out of this assessment in the Competitive Equality Banking Act of 1987.

Credit Union Insurance. The National Credit Union Share Insurance Fund (NCUSIF) is financed quite differently, as established by the Deficit Reduction Act of 1984. That law requires federally insured credit unions to maintain a deposit in NCUSIF equal to 1 percent of their insured shares. Interest earned on NCUSIF investments made with these deposits adds to the fund each year, although NCUSIF's assets may not exceed 1.3 percent of total insured shares in any year. Accumulations in excess of that amount are returned to CUs. Unlike FSLIC and FDIC regulations, special assessments are prohibited, although annual premiums of $1/12$ of 1 percent of insured shares can

be reinstituted in the future if conditions warrant.[46]

Insurance Fund Resources. None of the three funds has, nor is intended to have, resources equal to the total amount of deposits for which insurance coverage is provided. This point is often misunderstood. The best insurance any depositor has—indeed, any creditor of any business firm has—is the quality of the firm's assets. The creditors of most depositories have no need of the guarantee, because returns on the firm's assets are used to pay interest and repay principal to funds suppliers. Even if every depository were closed today, the liquidation of assets at most institutions would provide cash to pay off liabilities in full.

Federal deposit insurance has a great psychological impact, however, because it prevents a recurrence of the debilitating runs on depositories that occurred in the 1930s. Furthermore, all three insurance funds have a line of credit with the Treasury, assuring them of cash should funds be depleted in an emergency. This arrangement further enhances public confidence in the banking system. The public appears to value these lines of credit, even if unused. In 1985, runs on nonfederally insured thrifts in Ohio and Maryland forced the failure of some and the temporary closure of others, but the runs did not extend to federally insured institutions. Confidence in federal insurance is more important than the insurance itself.

Coverage Provided

Because of insurance coverage rules and because the financial resources of consumers and businesses differ, the impact of federal insurance varies according to type of depositor.

Effect on Consumer Depositors. A common description of federal insurance coverage is that depositors are insured up to a maximum of $100,000, exclusive of IRA accounts, at each depository in which they have funds. Additional coverage of up to $100,000 is provided for IRAs at the same institution. As Table 15.5 demonstrates, however, the possibilities for coverage beyond these amounts are consider-

---

[44]The assessment for domestic deposits only is a bone of contention among bankers. Although large banks do not pay insurance premiums on their foreign deposits, foreign depositors have been the beneficiaries of the American insurance system. In the last FDIC assessment before it failed, Continental Illinois paid on the basis of its $13.7 billion in domestic deposits. When the FDIC later announced full insurance coverage for the bank, $16.6 billion in foreign deposits were included in the guarantee. See Leon E. Wynter, "Big Banks Said to Escape Fees on Some Deposits," *The Wall Street Journal,* June 7, 1985, p. 3. For an examination of the arguments concerning insurance coverage of foreign deposits, see Christine M. Cumming, "Federal Deposit Insurance and Deposits at Foreign Branches of U.S. Banks," *Quarterly Review,* Federal Reserve Bank of New York 10 (Autumn 1985): 30-38.

[45]"Notes to Financial Statements," Federal Deposit Insurance Corporation, *1985 Annual Report,* p. 40.

[46]National Credit Union Administration, *1985 Annual Report,* pp. 21-22.

Table 15.5
Extending Deposit Insurance Coverage

Husband, Wife, and Two Children:
Insured accounts totaling $1,400,000

Individual Accounts

Husband	$100,000
Wife	100,000
Child number 1	100,000
Child number 2	100,000

Joint Accounts[a]

Husband and wife	$100,000
Husband and child number 1	100,000
Wife and child number 2	100,000
Child number 1 and child number 2	100,000

Revocable Trust Accounts

Husband as trustee for wife	$100,000
Husband as trustee for child number 1	100,000
Husband as trustee for child number 2	100,000
Wife as trustee for husband	100,000
Wife as trustee for child number 1	100,000
Wife as trustee for child number 2	100,000

[a]Joint account with right of survivorship

Source: The Wall Street Journal, May 21, 1985, p. 37. Reprinted by permission of *The Wall Street Journal,* © Dow Jones & Company, Inc., 1985. All Rights Reserved.

able. A family of four could have deposit insurance of up to $1.4 million *at each institution* with which it had a relationship. The key is identifying the ownership of various accounts in such a way that no more than $100,000 is claimed by any one legal owner. In this example, for instance, "revocable trust accounts" are shown for all family members. These are accounts established for the benefit of one person but administered by another; they are legally separate from other accounts owned by either individual.

Although this example is deliberately ex-

treme, it makes an important point: Under the current system, most consumers can have full insurance coverage for all their deposits. For this reason, consumer depositors, even though they are creditors, have little reason to examine the credit worthiness of institutions. Thus, insured depositors exert little influence on management's decisions about how deposits will be invested.

Effect on Business Depositors. Commercial and institutional investors are different. Establishing insured accounts in many different names would usually be legally impossible and too costly. Consequently, many corporate and institutional deposits exceed the federally insurable limit. In theory, these large depositors should be prime sources of *market discipline,* which is the possibility that creditors and/or owners will react negatively to management's decisions and subsequently refuse to entrust funds to the institution. With market discipline, bank, thrift, or CU managers facing the loss of confidence-sensitive money should think twice before investing funds in excessively risky loans or securities.

Impact on Market Discipline. In practice, large depositors have little reason to exercise market discipline. Except for the failure of Penn Square Bank in 1982, it has been the apparent, if not stated, policy of federal insurers to prevent even uninsured depositors from losing money when an institution fails. The insurers' approach to institutional failures has almost always been to merge a failed depository into a healthy one, so that creditors, insured and uninsured, simply become creditors of another, healthier firm. This approach reduces the incentive of uninsured creditors to monitor the risk-taking activities of the depositories with which they do business.

In the Penn Square case, the bank had a high proportion of energy-related loans and was poorly diversified. Its credit-granting standards were extremely low, and many of the loans were in default. After the bank was closed on July 5, 1982, the deposits of fully insured depositors were assumed by an FDIC-created bank, which opened for business the next morning. More than half of Penn Square's deposit accounts exceeded the insurance limit, however, and the FDIC gave unprecedented notice that it did not intend to guarantee them. This action was widely interpreted to mean that federal insurers were embarking upon a new approach to handling failures, invoking market discipline as a substitute for federal bailouts. Shortly thereafter, in fact, the FDIC announced a "modified payout" plan under which it would cover deposits over the insured limit only when there was a high probability

that a liquidated bank's assets would provide the cash to do so.[47]

Only months later, the course was diverted by FDIC actions in the crisis at Continental Illinois, a $40 billion institution. All creditors were notified that FDIC guarantees were completely in force, regardless of the size or nature of Continental's liabilities. When the FDIC was unable to find a suitable merger partner for Continental, it arranged for the bank to remain open under new management. Not a penny was lost by any creditor.[48]

Need for Reform

Neither internal managerial discipline, to avoid higher insurance premiums, nor market discipline is promoted by the current federal insurance system. When asset choices and deposit interest rates were constrained by regulation, moral hazard existed, but consequences for the insurance funds were not as great. Now that managerial discretion is much broader, the moral hazard built into the system is considerable.

The increased number of depository failures in the 1980s is documented in Chapter 11. Not only does the current system threaten to drain federal resources, should the Treasury be forced to support any or all of the insurance funds, but it promotes inefficiency and inequity in the allocation of resources. Some managers are encouraged to make investments unjustified by their riskiness and to bid for funding at much higher than market rates, while more prudent institutions subsidize these actions through their insurance premiums.

---

[47]An analysis of the FDIC's modified payout plan is given in Frederick T. Furlong, "A View on Deposit Insurance Coverage," *Economic Review,* Federal Reserve Bank of San Francisco (Spring 1984), pp. 31-38.

[48]Accounts of the handling of Penn Square and Continental are found in many newspaper and magazine articles at the time these events unfolded. The information on FDIC policies followed in the two cases is taken from the FDIC *Annual Reports* for 1982 and 1984. It should be noted that the FDIC does not consider Continental Illinois a failed bank, since it continues to operate under its original name; many observers believe otherwise.

As a result of increased failures, the FDIC and the FSLIC have faced financial pressures in recent years. In late 1985, the FDIC began a program of selling loans it had acquired from failed banks in order to generate necessary operating cash. In 1986, the agency had no excess premiums to rebate to insured institutions for the first time in almost 40 years. At the same time, cash flow problems at the FSLIC became so great that the Federal Asset Disposition Agency (FADA), first discussed in Chapter 2, was formed to manage and liquidate the assets of failed thrifts. When the activities of FADA and the special insurance assessments mentioned earlier were not enough, the Bank Board won Congressional approval of a complicated plan to refinance the FSLIC. The plan was necessary because the FSLIC's needs for cash exceeded $20 billion, but its assets totalled only $6 billion.[49] The plan is outlined in more detail in the appendix to Chapter 2 (p. 49).

Legislators are keenly aware of these problems. The Garn-St Germain Act required each insurance agency to submit proposals for reform of the system. The 1984 task force on regulatory reform headed by Vice President George Bush also studied deposit insurance. In 1987, Congress debated proposals to give the FSLIC access to cash above and beyond premium income, but declined to undertake major deposit insurance reforms. Congress is stalled because it lacks general agreement on the best way to proceed. Some of the thorniest issues are outlined in the following paragraphs.[50]

Amount of Coverage.   Some argue that the financial system is weakened by less than 100 percent coverage on all depository liabilities, particularly those of short maturity. Pointing to Continental, they note that the crisis occurred because uninsured creditors fled the bank, precipitating a liquidity crisis. Others argue that protecting the small depositor is the objective of the system, and large depositors, presumably more sophisticated, are better able to protect themselves. This argument implies that the $100,000 limit is too high, not too low, and that lower limits would encourage vigilance and expose the insurers to fewer losses. If federal insurance has dual objectives, however— protecting the financial system from runs as well as protecting small depositors—then lower coverage will not prevent runs.

Premium Structure.   Problems with the insurance program involve not only the amount of coverage but also the flat-premium system. As a consequence, many experts advocate risk-sensitive premiums. Obvious questions are raised: What are the relevant risks? How should they be measured? One reform proposal includes an index of risk using a duration-based calculation of interest rate risk, combined with measures of default risk and the risk of an undiversified portfolio. An alternative proposal advocates calculating the probability of institutional failure, based on historical data, and as-

[49]Details on these actions can be found in Leon E. Wynter and Phillip L. Zweig, "FDIC Taps the Securities Market to Sell Assets It Acquired from Failed Banks," *The Wall Street Journal,* December 24, 1985, p. 3; Leon E. Wynter, "FDIC Sets Aside '85 Loss Reserve of $2.3 Billion," *The Wall Street Journal,* March 10, 1986, p. 8; and "Senate Banking Approves FSLIC Recap, Emergency Powers," *Savings Institutions* 107 (September 1986): 9.

[50]The literature on insurance reform is both interesting and extensive. Reviewing it would fill a book. Students are encouraged to consult some of the many good examples of this literature such as Mark Flannery, "Deposit Insurance Creates a Need for Bank Regulation," *Business Review,* Federal Reserve Bank of Philadelphia (January/February 1982), pp. 17-24; "Research on Federal Deposit Insurance," a series of ten articles in Section II of *Proceedings of a Conference on Bank Structure and Competition* (Chi-

cago: Federal Reserve Bank of Chicago, 1983), pp. 196-298; Edward J. Kane, "A Six-Point Program for Deposit Insurance Reform," *Housing Finance Review* 2 (July 1983): 269-278; and Tim S. Campbell and David Glenn, "Deposit Insurance in a Deregulated Environment," *Journal of Finance* 39 (July 1984): 775-787.

Also of interest are the regulators' position papers prepared to comply with the Garn-St Germain Act: FDIC, *Deposit Insurance in a Changing Environment,* 1983; FHLBB, *Agenda for Reform,* 1983; and NCUA, *Credit Union Share Insurance,* 1983; Herbert Baer, "Private Prices, Public Insurance: The Pricing of Federal Deposit Insurance," *Economic Perspectives,* Federal Reserve Bank of Chicago 9 (September/October 1985): 45-57; Allan Sloan and Howard Rudnitsky, "What Will the Bank Dicks Do Now?" *Forbes* 136 (July 1, 1985): 86-90; and Gerald A. Hanweck, "Federal Deposit Insurance: A Critical Review of Some Proposals for Reform," *Issues in Bank Regulation* 9 (Winter 1986): 25-29.

signing premiums accordingly. The FDIC itself has proposed dual risk assessment based on **CAMEL ratings** and selected financial ratios. (CAMEL ratings are composite ratings of Capital Adequacy, Asset Quality, Management, Earnings, and Liquidity prepared by depository institution examiners.) None of these methods, however, prevents possible manipulation of accounting records or measures the risk of failure because of fraud, the leading cause in the past. Even if a consensus system is found for assigning risk-based premiums, other questions remain. For example, when and how often should premiums be assessed? How large should they be? How should they be publicized?[51]

Private versus Governmental Providers.
A third issue in the reform of deposit insurance is who should provide the insurance. Some experts advocate private-sector solutions for almost all economic problems, and deposit insurance is no exception. They argue that competition among potential providers of insurance will encourage efficiency and effectiveness, removing institutions from the tangles of the federal bureaucracy.

Opponents question the ability of the private sector to protect both individual depositors and the financial system as a whole. For example, are private firms large enough? Would they act in the public interest, or would they simply

cancel the insurance of an institution they believe is too risky? If federal monitoring and intervention are needed, is it better to simply keep the federal insurance agencies? Finally, would the public trust private insurance? A number of observers, including depository institution managers, doubt that it would. Nearly 500 credit unions sought federal insurance after the S&L insurance crises in Ohio and Maryland in 1985, even though no credit unions were involved in those incidents. As the President of the Federal Reserve Bank of Cleveland stated of the events in Ohio, "My most lasting impression of the crisis is how quickly depositors' confidence plummeted at the privately insured institutions . . . . Without depositors' confidence, even the best capitalized financial institution can be severely affected."[52]

Necessary Regulation and Supervision.
Continuation of federal insurance raises questions about the need to regulate and supervise depository institutions. Many argue that the tools needed to prevent excessive risk taking are already in place, but that regulators and examiners should enforce and publicize them more zealously. To this end, all federal bank and thrift regulators are studying a policy of disclosing "enforcement actions," or requirements imposed on managers to cease undesirable practices. A system of disclosure was to have taken effect in 1986, but was postponed after depositories howled in protest. Stronger capital regulations, discussed in the next chapter, have also been adopted recently. An additional alternative is fully insuring, but imposing a rate ceiling, on all unlimited transaction accounts to prevent depositories from bidding for demand deposits that could be withdrawn at the first rumor of trouble.

Congressional decisions on each of these issues will affect depository institution management for years to come. The more information a manager has about the alternatives being considered and their consequences, the better.

[51]For discussion of these proposals, see G. O. Bierwag and George G. Kaufman, "A Proposal for Federal Deposit Insurance with Risk-Sensitive Premiums," Working Paper 83-3, Federal Reserve Bank of Chicago, March 16, 1983, which was the basis for a final paper in *Agenda for Reform,* the FHLBB's study of deposit insurance reform mandated in the Garn-St Germain Act; Robert B. Avery, Gerald A. Hanweck, and Myron L. Kwast in "An Analysis of Risk-Based Deposit Insurance for Commercial Banks," *Proceedings of the Conference on Bank Structure and Competition* (Chicago: Federal Reserve Bank of Chicago, 1985), pp. 217-250; Eric Hirschhorn, "Developing a Proposal for Risk-Related Deposit Insurance," *Banking and Economic Review,* Federal Deposit Insurance Corporation 4 (September/October 1986): 3-10; and Arthur J. Murton, "A Survey of the Issues and the Literature Concerning Risk-Related Deposit Insurance," *Banking and Economic Review,* Federal Deposit Insurance Corporation 4 (September/October 1986): 11-20.

[52]Statement by Karen N. Horn, *1985 Annual Report,* Federal Reserve Bank of Cleveland, p. 3.

SUMMARY

Deposit and nondeposit liabilities for depository institutions, and regulations governing their management, are the subjects of this chapter. The phase-out of Regulation Q, officially completed on April 1, 1986, has given institutions new freedom to offer a wide variety of accounts with different maturities and interest rate characteristics. Larger and more aggressive institutions also rely heavily on managed liabilities, including negotiable CDs, Eurodollar deposits, repurchase agreements, mortgage-backed securities, and brokered deposits.

The elimination of restrictions on institutions' access to funds has given managers new challenges. Institutions formerly relying on implicit interest payments as the only allowable form of competition must now analyze pricing strategies, and the choice between explicit and implicit interest affects the volatility of returns. Many firms are evaluating flexible pricing mechanisms that provide more choices to customers and to management. In conjunction with pricing decisions, management must set goals for the mix of funds the firm will seek.

Federal deposit insurance continues to influence management decisions. Insurance reduces the risk borne by depositors and therefore reduces the potential volatility of funds to insured institutions. But because insurance premiums are not adjusted to reflect the relative riskiness of an institution, the program encourages some institutions to take excessive risks. Several recommendations for reform have been considered, but there is no doubt that some form of deposit insurance will continue to provide a buffer against loss of confidence in the financial system.

Questions

1. What was the rationale for including ceilings on deposit interest rates (Regulation Q) in the Glass-Steagall Act of 1933? Contrast Reg Q's impact on depository institutions before 1966, and between 1966 and 1980. Why was Reg Q finally abolished?

2. How did the introduction of money market mutual funds in the 1970s affect sources of funds to depository institutions? What instruments were depository institutions allowed to introduce at that time to compete with MMMFs, and what were the effects of these new instruments?

3. Compare the characteristics of the money market certificate created in 1978 to those of money market deposit accounts created through the Garn-St Germain Act. How did each affect the performance of depository institutions and the returns to their customers?

4. What was the "Wild Card" certificate? Why was the experiment abandoned after only four months? What changes have occurred in regulations and economic conditions that give deposits like Wild Card certificates, considered unacceptable in the 1970s, a major role in today's financial system?

5. What is liability management? Explain its purposes, and the types of funds used for each purpose. Compare and contrast the risks of each liability source with those of traditional deposit sources of funds.

6. IEC Incorporated is a large corporate customer of First City Bank. IEC cash managers have just contacted the bank to arrange a withdrawal of $50 million from the corporate checking account, for reinvestment in interest-bearing marketable securities. Bank management suggests, as an alternative, that the corporation consider a Eurodollar deposit in its branch in Zurich. Illustrate with T-accounts the creation of the Eurodollar deposit and its effect on the assets and liabilities of both the domestic and foreign branches of the bank.

7. Explain how mortgage lenders use mortgage-backed bonds and collateralized mortgage obligations to obtain new funds.

8. What are brokered deposits? What are the advantages to financial institutions of hiring a broker to raise funds? What are the risks involved? Do you think brokered deposits should be regulated? Why or why not?

9. Explain the difference between confidence-sensitive money and hot money. What factors influence a depository institution manager's choice between aggressive and conservative strategies for funds management?

10. What are implicit interest payments? Why have depositories used them, and why do some depositors prefer them? How do implicit-interest pricing strategies affect the stability of earnings as interest revenues change?

11. Compare the cost and volatility of retail and wholesale funds. What additional factors affect a depository's decision to specialize in one source of funds or the other?

12. Several options are available for setting explicit interest rates, including conditionally free accounts and interest buydowns. Compare and contrast these strategies, and the benefits and costs of each for depositors.

13. In early 1986, a thrift in Skokie, Illinois, offered a one-year CD with an interest rate tied to the score of the 1986 Super Bowl game. The thrift agreed to raise its interest rate by 0.01% for every point by which the Chicago Bears outscored the New England Patriots, and the marketing ploy attracted over $13 million. Sports fans will recall that the Bears beat the Patriots 46-10, increasing the cost of those deposits by 36 basis points. What potential positive and negative effects can such marketing strategies have on a depository institution's financial performance?

14. Discuss the concept of "moral hazard" and its impact on the effectiveness of federal deposit and share insurance programs.

15. In recent years, concern has been expressed about the viability of the federal deposit insurance systems. Briefly discuss the sources of the insurers' financial problems. How have increasing numbers of failures among depository institutions affected the funds?

16. Briefly discuss the alternatives that have been suggested for reforming the deposit insurance system. What are the advantages and disadvantages of risk-adjusted insurance premiums? Do you think a private insurance system is a viable alternative for some institutions? Why or why not?

17. Could the financial system survive without federal deposit insurance? Why or why not? Would your answer change if you were retired and living on Social Security? If you were on *Forbes* magazine's annual list of the 400 richest Americans? In your opinion, whom should the ideal federal insurance program protect? How much protection should be available? Who should pay the cost? What responsibilities should be placed on depository institution managers under the ideal system?

Problems

1. Community Savings and Loan has agreed to sell Commercial National Bank $10 million in federal funds for two days at a quoted rate of 9.5 percent. How much must Commercial National repay to Community? What is the effective annual yield to the S&L? (Fed funds yields are illustrated in Chapter 4.)

2. Washington Bank is purchasing $5 million in fed funds overnight, at a rate of 7.75 percent. How much must the bank repay the next day? What is the effective annual cost of the transaction?

3. Hartford Savings sells a jumbo CD to Westland Corporation in a face amount of $2 million. The stated annual rate is 8.25 percent, and the maturity is 180 days. How much must Hartford provide to Westland upon maturity? What is the effective annual cost of the CD? (Yields on negotiable CDs are illustrated in Chapter 4.)

4. Suppose, instead, that the maturity of the CD in Problem 3 were 182 days. How much must Hartford repay, and what is the effective annual cost?

5. Calculate the degree of operating leverage for First National Bank if total revenues are $250 million, variable costs are $150 million, and fixed costs are $75 million. If revenues increase by 5 percent, by how much will operating income increase?

6. The management of Lincoln Credit Union is analyzing its cost structure. You have been asked to evaluate the impact of implicit interest payments on operating income; approximately 30 percent of fixed costs is traced to implicit interest. The following information is provided:

   - Total revenues: $67 million
   - Total variable costs: 80 percent of total revenues
   - Total fixed costs: $8.5 million

   a. If explicit interest were substituted for implicit interest, what percentage of total revenues would variable costs be? What would total fixed costs be?
   b. Calculate the degree of operating leverage with and without implicit interest payments (that is, both under the current structure and under the one described in a).
   c. If revenues increase by 10 percent, by how much would you expect operating income to change under the current cost structure? Under the alternative structure?
   d. If revenues decrease by 10 percent, what would operating income be under the current and alternative cost structures?
   e. What risk/return tradeoff is involved with implicit versus explicit interest?

7. Return to Table 15.4. Suppose a customer wanted to add a safe deposit box and preauthorized car payments to the services desired, and to remove automatic mortgage payments and mortgage credit life insurance. What explicit interest would be paid to the customer?

Selected References

Avery, Robert B., Gerald A. Hanweck, and Myron L. Kwast. "An Analysis of Risk-Based Deposit Insurance for Commercial Banks." *Proceedings of a Conference on Bank Structure and Competition.* Chicago: Federal Reserve Bank of Chicago, 1985: 217-250.

Baer, Herbert. "Private Prices, Public Insurance: The Pricing of Federal Deposit Insurance." *Economic Perspectives* (Federal Reserve Bank of Chicago) 9 (September/October 1985): 45-57.

Baer, Herbert, and Elijah Brewer, "Uninsured Deposits as a Source of Market Discipline." *Economic Perspectives* (Federal Reserve Bank of Chicago) 10 (September/October 1986): 23-31.

Benston, George. "Interest on Deposits and the Survival of Chartered Depository Institutions." *Economic Review* (Federal Reserve Bank of Atlanta) 69 (October 1984): 42-56.

Brewer, Elijah. "Bank Funds Management Comes of Age—A Balance Sheet Analysis." *Economic Perspectives* (Federal Reserve Bank of Chicago) 4 (May/June 1980): 13-18.

Brock, Bronwyn. "Regulation Changes Bring New Challenges to S&Ls, Other Depository Institutions." *Voice* (Federal Reserve Bank of Dallas) (September 1980), pp. 5-9.

Campbell, Tim S., and David Glenn. "Deposit Insurance in a Deregulated Environment." *Journal of Finance* 39 (July 1984): 775-787.

Carraro, Kenneth C., and Daniel L. Thornton. "The Cost of Checkable Deposits in the United States." *Review* (Federal Reserve Bank of St. Louis) 68 (April 1986): 19-27.

Cumming, Christine M. "Federal Deposit Insurance and Deposits at Foreign Branches of U.S. Banks." *Quarterly Review* (Federal Reserve Bank of New York) 10 (Autumn 1985): 30-38.

Davis, Richard G., and Leon Korobow. "The Pricing of Consumer Deposit Products—The Non-rate Dimensions." *Quarterly Review* (Federal Reserve Bank of New York) 11 (Winter 1986-87): 14-18.

Davis, Richard G., Leon Korobow, and John Wenninger. "Bankers on Pricing Consumer Deposits." *Quarterly Review* (Federal Reserve Bank of New York) 11 (Winter 1986-87): 6-13.

Dotsey, Michael. "An Examination of Implicit Interest Rates on Demand Deposits." *Economic Review* (Federal Reserve Bank of Richmond) 69 (September/October 1983): 3-11.

Flannery, Mark. "Deposit Insurance Creates a Need for Bank Regulation." *Business Review* (Federal Reserve Bank of Philadelphia) (January/February 1982), pp. 17-24.

———. "Retail Bank Deposits as Quasi-Fixed Factors of Production." *American Economic Review* 72 (June 1982): 527-536.

Friedman, Milton. "Controls on Interest Rates Paid by Banks." *Journal of Money, Credit, and Banking* 2 (February 1970): 15-32.

Furlong, Frederick. "A View on Deposit Insurance Coverage." *Economic Review* (Federal Reserve Bank of San Francisco) (Spring 1984), pp. 31-38.

Goodfriend, Marvin. "Eurodollars." In *Instruments of the Money Market,* 6th ed. Richmond, VA: Federal Reserve Bank of Richmond, 1986, pp. 53-64.

Goodfriend, Marvin, and William Whelpley. "Federal Funds." In *Instruments of the Money Market,* 6th ed. Richmond, VA: Federal Reserve Bank of Richmond, 1986, pp. 8-22.

Hanweck, Gerald A. "Federal Deposit Insurance: A Critical Review of Some Proposals for Reform." *Issues in Bank Regulation* 9 (Winter 1986): 25-29.

Harless, Caroline T. "Brokered Deposits." *Economic Review* (Federal Reserve Bank of Atlanta) 69 (March 1984): 14-25.

Higgins, Bryon. "Interest Payments on Demand Deposits: Historical Evolution and the Current Controversy." *Monthly Review* (Federal Reserve Bank of Kansas City) 62 (July-August 1977): 3-11.

Hirschhorn, Eric. "Developing a Proposal for Risk-Related Deposit Insurance." *Banking and Economic Review* (Federal Deposit Insurance Corporation) 4 (September/October 1986): 3-10.

Kane, Edward J. "The Three Faces of Commercial Bank Liability Management." In *The Political Economy of Policy-Making,* edited by M. J. Dooley. Beverly Hills, CA: Sage Publications, 1979.

————. "A Six-Point Program for Deposit Insurance Reform." *Housing Finance Review* 2 (July 1983): 269-278.

————. *The Gathering Crisis in Federal Deposit Insurance*. (Cambridge, MA: The MIT Press, 1985).

Keeley, Michael C., and Gary C. Zimmerman. "Competition for Money Market Deposit Accounts." *Economic Review* (Federal Reserve Bank of San Francisco) (Spring 1985), pp. 5-27.

Luckett, Dudley. "Approaches to Bank Liquidity Management." *Economic Review* (Federal Reserve Bank of Kansas City) 65 (March 1980): 11-27.

Luttrell, Clifford B. "The Hunt Commission Report—An Economic View." *Review* (Federal Reserve Bank of St. Louis) 54 (June 1972): 8-12.

Murton, Arthur J. "A Survey of the Issues and the Literature Concerning Risk-Related Deposit Insurance." *Banking and Economic Review* (Federal Deposit Insurance Corporation) 4 (September/October 1986): 11-20.

Puglisi, Donald J., and Joseph A. McKenzie. "Capital Market Strategies for Thrift Institutions." *Federal Home Loan Bank Board Journal* 16 (November 1983): 2-8.

Schweitzer, Stuart A. "Bank Liability Management: For Better or for Worse?" *Business Review* (Federal Reserve Bank of Philadelphia) (December 1974), pp. 3-16.

U.S. Congress. House Committee on Banking, Currency, and Housing. *Financial Institutions and the Nation's Economy: Discussion Principles*. 94th Congress, 1975.

Wall, Larry D., and Harold D. Ford. "Money Market Account Competition." *Economic Review* (Federal Reserve Bank of Atlanta) 69 (December 1984): 4-14.

Winningham, Scott, and Donald G. Hagan. "Regulation Q: An Historical Perspective." *Economic Review* (Federal Reserve Bank of Kansas City) 65 (April 1980): 3-17.

Chapter 16

THE ROLE OF CAPITAL

. . . we wouldn't have any capital if I charged off even half of the loans I should.

Robert Hadland
President, Farmers and Merchants Bank
of Lamberton, Minnesota (1986)

THE year 1985 brought the Live Aid concert for African famine relief and the Farm Aid concert to assist needy farmers. Considering the financial crisis at the FSLIC, it is no wonder that staff members with a sense of humor wore T-shirts with "FSLIC Aid" on the front at the Christmas party that year. On the back, the shirts read "We do it with mirrors," a message referring to the unusual accounting system used by the agency to support thrift institutions that would otherwise have no capital, and legible only when held to a mirror.[1]

Although depository institutions rely heavily on deposits and other liabilities, they could not operate without *capital.* Capital consists of all long-term, nondeposit funds subordinate to deposits in claims on the firm's income and assets. Major sources of capital are long-term debt, common and preferred stock, and retained earnings. All businesses need capital, but only financial institutions have minimum capital requirements specifically identified by regulators. That fact indicates the importance of capital in the financial management of depositories.

The initial question addressed is: Why is capital so important? Next, more precise definitions of capital than the one in the preceding paragraph are examined. Regulators' *capital adequacy* standards are also discussed. The standards are their attempts to answer the question, How much capital is enough? Finally, problems in determining and attaining the desired level of capital in an individual depository are outlined.

---

[1] "Washington Wire: Laughing Lenders," *The Wall Street Journal,* December 27, 1985, p. 1.

WHY CAPITAL?

Capital fulfills several functions, but their relative importance is a subject of debate.

Capital Provides Support for Fixed Investment

Everyone agrees on one reason for capital. The long-term commitment of funds by investors willing to put money at risk enables a business to begin operations. Initial capital is used to purchase or rent premises, to hire employees, and to obtain other assets necessary to begin taking deposits and making loans. In the early stages, cash contributed by initial capital suppliers may be critically important until a profitable operating plan can be developed. Once a depository is firmly established, expansions requiring additional fixed assets are usually financed with capital rather than deposits. Because these assets are permanent additions to the institution's operations, paying for them with short-term liabilities would be unwise.

Capital Promotes Confidence

The preceding chapter emphasizes the significance of depositor confidence in an institution. Federal deposit insurance plays a major role in transmitting that confidence to many who require it, but uninsured depositors and other short-term creditors require additional evidence to justify placing confidence-sensitive money in an institution. Because capital suppliers have a subordinate claim on the depository's income and assets, their investment helps to reassure uninsured creditors. Even if the institution has financial difficulty, uninsured depositors know the extent to which the value of assets can shrink before they are in danger of not recovering all their funds; that amount is equal to the total capital of the institution. The more capital, the more protection afforded to uninsured depositors and other short-term creditors.

The Role of Capital Illustrated.   Suppose a savings bank has assets with a market value of $100 million and deposits of $92 million, of which $80 million qualify for full federal insurance. Total capital in the institution is $8 million:

Majestic Savings Bank Balance Sheet

Assets		Deposits and Capital	
$ 30,000,000	T-Bills	$ 92,000,000	Deposits ($80,000,000 Insured)
70,000,000	Loans (Including $55,000,000 in Mortgages)	8,000,000	Capital
$100,000,000	Total	$100,000,000	Total

Suppose a major employer in town announces it is transferring its headquarters out of state. Many of the firm's employees are to lose their jobs, and Majestic has made mortgage loans to some of them. If delinquent payments reduce mortgage income, Majestic's uninsured depositors may begin to evaluate whether the institution could fail. Any mortgages on which payments are not being made will decline in value, determined as the present value of the remaining cash flows expected from the loans.

The $8 million in capital, however, means that the value of the firm's assets must decline by $8 million before uninsured deposits are endangered. Because that amount would represent an immediate deterioration of about 14.5 percent ($8/$55) in the mortgage portfolio, many uninsured depositors may conclude that such a sharp decline is unlikely and leave their money on deposit. Obviously, that decision will greatly assist Majestic as it copes with the delinquencies, because a liquidity crisis may be averted. Were capital low—for example, only $2 million—the decline in the mortgage portfolio would have to be only 3.6 percent ($2/$55) for capital to be exhausted, a much more probable occurrence. Large depositors would be more likely to withdraw funds, impeding the institution's ability to resolve its financial problems in time to avoid failure.

Capital Supports Growth

Capital also assists depositories in achieving growth objectives. Although an institution may actively seek a deposit volume and mix based on a strategic plan, it faces unknown responses from customers and competitors. If specific investment goals are to be attained, they must wait if deposit growth takes longer to materialize than anticipated. Capital is an alternative source of funding. If an institution sells new stock or bonds, or retains profits from previous periods, it can acquire new assets. It can also pursue opportunities without delays that may result from sluggish deposit growth or the risks that may be incurred from using confidence-sensitive money.

This does not imply that depository institution managers are eager to use capital. Suppliers of capital must be compensated for their investment, so managers must make a convincing case for the funds, and investors must have prospects for earning an expected return commensurate with the risk they take. If capital is raised by issuing common stock, existing shareholders may be concerned that additional shares will dilute their claims to residual income and assets. Nonetheless, capital may sometimes be the most appropriate source of funds for achieving growth.

Capital Reduces Moral Hazard

The previous chapter discusses the moral hazard produced by the federal deposit insurance system. The premium structure, the scope of coverage, and the agencies' handling of failures all encourage depository managers to take excessive risks. Some economists also argue that the less capital the institution has, the greater the moral hazard. Conversely, the more capital, the greater the protection for the insurance funds.[2]

Consider an institution that begins with assets of $5 million in cash; the source of the cash is $5 million of capital. The cash can be used to make loans with a 50 percent probability of default (that is, the entire initial $5 million will be lost) and a 50 percent probability of producing a $5 million profit after all expenses are paid. The expected dollar return on the investment is:

$$0.5(-\$5,000,000) + 0.5(\$5,000,000) = \$0$$

The expected rate of return to capital suppliers is 0 percent, and they would probably encourage management to seek better investments.

On the other hand, suppose the institution is funded by $4 million in insured deposits at a cost of 10 percent, and $1 million in capital. The most capital suppliers can lose is $1 million, and *their* expected dollar profit if the depository makes the loans is now:

$$0.5(-\$1,000,000) + \\ 0.5(\$5,000,000 - \$400,000) = \$1,800,000$$

Their expected rate of return is 180 percent, not 0 percent, even though the firm's potential investments are the same. The lower the amount of capital, the less incentive capital suppliers have to monitor the actions of management to prevent excessive risk taking. They have less to lose if things go poorly, and more to gain if things go well.

This example recalls a principle discussed in Chapter 3: the impact of leverage on expected return to the residual claimants. In most businesses, creditors would step in to prevent a firm from using so much leverage that their own funds were in jeopardy.[3] But when the creditors are insured by an outside agency, as is the case of federally insured depositors, their monitoring incentive is removed. All things equal, then, a federally insured depository with more capital will have fewer reasons to take excessive risks than one with less.

---

[2]The following example is similar to one used by Frederick T. Furlong and Michael W. Keran in "The Federal Safety Net for Commercial Banks: Part II," *Weekly Letter,* Federal Reserve Bank of San Francisco, August 3, 1984.

[3]This conclusion derives from the agency theory literature in corporate finance, introduced in Chapter 1. See Michael C. Jensen and William H. Meckling, "Theory of the Firm: Managerial Behavior, Agency Costs, and Ownership Structure," *Journal of Financial Economics* 3 (1976): 305-360.

COMPONENTS OF CAPITAL

Because capital serves different purposes and because the relative importance of those purposes may differ among customers, managers, owners, and regulators, complete agreement is lacking on exactly how capital should be defined. The arguments are not simply hair splitting. The reasons for capital suggest that regulators are likely to favor more capital for an institution than its managers and capital suppliers might like. Viewed in this context, exactly what should be considered capital takes on added importance. The discussion is furthered by partitioning capital into two broad categories—net worth and debt capital.

Net Worth: Traditional Sources

As discussed in Chapter 3, net worth is the amount by which the value of the institution's assets exceeds the value of its liabilities, whether short- or long-term, insured or uninsured. Controversy exists over whether net worth should be measured in market values or accounting (book) values, a controversy explored in more detail later. Here, book-value definitions are assumed.

Common Equity.   In shareholder-owned institutions, "net worth" and "equity capital" are synonymous, where equity capital is the claim on the business by common and preferred shareholders. Common equity—the sum of funds initially contributed by common shareholders plus retained earnings—is the owners' claim on shareholder-owned financial institutions. Owners are entitled to all residual profits but also must absorb losses. Thus, common equity fulfills all the purposes capital is intended to have: It is a long-term source of funds, with a claim on the institution's income and assets subordinate to deposits. It provides the initial funding by which a shareholder-owned depository begins operations; promotes confidence on the part of uninsured depositors; supports growth; and reduces moral hazard. It is one component of capital on which everyone can agree.

Of course, not all depositories are shareholder-owned. In mutually owned or not-for-profit depositories, the only permanently invested funds are earnings retained from profitable operations. As noted in Chapter 3, however, retained earnings (or undivided profits or reserves, as they are sometimes called) in a mutual or not-for-profit institution serve a function identical to common equity in a shareholder-owned firm. Thus, everyone agrees that they also fulfill the purposes of capital.

Preferred Stock.   The classification of preferred stock, another long-term source of funds for depositories, is less clear-cut. Some preferred stock is issued with a maturity date; most is not. Some is convertible into common stock at the option of the preferred stockholder; some is not. Thus, the permanence with which preferred stockholders view their holdings may differ, depending upon the specific issue of stock they have purchased. On the other hand, preferred stock has a claim on income and assets subordinate to the claims of depositors and other creditors. So with some exceptions, preferred stock fulfills the purposes of capital. In shareholder-owned institutions, the sum of common equity and preferred stock is the firm's total equity capital, or its net worth.

Although preferred stock issues have historically been more popular for banks than for thrifts, the FHLBB has recently enabled mutual as well as stockholder-owned S&Ls to sell preferred stock through affiliated service corporations, and many have done so. In addition, to meet regulators' increasingly stringent capital requirements discussed later in the chapter, many bank holding companies have issued preferred stock in the last several years.[4]

Mutual Capital Certificates.   Similar to preferred stock, but designed for direct issuance by

---

[4]"Finance Subsidiary Rule Boosts Use of Preferred Stock," *Savings Institutions* 105 (October 1984): 135-137; Martin H. Wolfson, "Financial Developments of Bank Holding Companies in 1984," *Federal Reserve Bulletin* 71 (December 1985): 932.

mutual institutions, are **mutual capital certificates (MCCs),** first authorized in DIDMCA. MCCs are securities with a minimum denomination of $100,000 and a minimum maturity of at least ten years. Their claim on income and assets is subordinate to that of depositors and other creditors. MCCs are intended to supplement undivided profits and reserves as a source of net worth for a mutually owned institution.

MCCs have not proved very useful, however, because regulatory requirements for the certificates have not coincided with market preferences. For example, it is difficult for institutions to sell fixed-rate MCCs with minimum maturities as long as the required 10 years. Although variable-rate MCCs could be issued to attract investors, they would not assist thrifts in correcting their maturity mismatch problems. Sometimes fixed-rate securities can be made more attractive to the market if they are convertible to common stock at the option of the purchaser. Obviously, however, convertible MCCs cannot be issued, because there is no common stock in mutual institutions. Thus, they remain a little-used source of funds.[5]

Net Worth: Regulatory Sources

Recently, federal regulators have created nontraditional sources of net worth to support institutions with earnings or liquidity problems. These sources are controversial, for many financial market participants do not believe they fulfill the intended purposes of capital. For the most part, federal regulators intend them to be temporary solutions to the problems of the thrift industry. In at least one major case, however, regulatory net worth sources have been used in the banking industry.

Net Worth Certificates.   Authorized in the Garn-St Germain Act and first defined in Chapter 2, net worth certificates (NWCs) are a form of capital assistance. They can be offered by the

FDIC or the FSLIC to thrifts considered viable in the long run but with earnings squeezes that endanger traditional net worth in the short run. No cash changes hands in an NWC issue, so a participating institution receives no additional funds. Nonetheless, capital is increased.

Figure 16.1 illustrates the mechanics of NWCs for First Federal S&L, an FSLIC-insured institution. An institution meeting established guidelines is permitted to issue certificates in exchange for a promissory note from the agency. The NWC then counts as capital, and the promissory note from the insurer serves as the offsetting increase in assets. The FSLIC pays cash interest on the note to the thrift. The thrift is obligated on paper to pay the FSLIC dividends on the net worth certificates, but no cash dividends are actually paid until and unless the thrift returns to profitability.

In Panel A of the figure, an institution has net worth equal to 0.5 percent of total assets. After issuing NWCs, as shown in Panel B, it now has substantially more capital, even though it has received no real injection of funds. Presumably, the additional "paper" net worth will enable the S&L to avoid insolvency—to avoid being forced to close because the value of its assets no longer equals or exceeds the value of legal claims against them.

When the institution recovers, it must remove the certificates from its books as income permits, offsetting any decrease in NWCs by writing down the value of the promissory note. This effect is shown in Panel C. Suppose the institution is able to add $100,000 to retained earnings and expects a profitable future. It decides to "repay" $50,000 in NWCs, writing down the promissory note by an equivalent amount. If, instead, the thrift fails, the promissory note from the FSLIC is considered an asset to be liquidated to meet liabilities.[6]

---

[5]More details about MCCs can be found in Donald J. Puglisi and Joseph A. McKenzie, "Capital Market Strategies for Thrift Institutions," *Federal Home Loan Bank Board Journal* 16 (November 1983): 2-8.

[6]The accounting provisions for net worth certificates are actually much more complicated than Figure 16.1 indicates. For more information on this regulatory program, see Herbert Baer, "The Garn-St Germain Depository Institutions Act of 1982: The Act's Impact on S&Ls," *Economic Perspectives* 7 (March-April 1983): 14-15; and Thomas P. Vartanian, "The Garn-St Germain Depository Institutions Act of 1982: The Impact on Thrifts," *Housing Finance Review* 2 (April 1983): 169-171.

Figure 16.1
Capital Injection through Net Worth Certificates

First Federal Savings and Loan Balance Sheet

A.   Before the Issuance of Net Worth Certificates:

Assets		Liabilities and Net Worth	
$ 9,900,000	Securities	$ 99,500,000	Liabilities
90,000,000	Loans	500,000	Net Worth
100,000	Premises		
$100,000,000	Total	$100,000,000	Total

Net Worth/Total Assets = 0.50%

B.   After the Issuance of Net Worth Certificates:

Assets		Liabilities and Net Worth	
$ 9,900,000	Securities	$ 99,500,000	Liabilities
90,000,000	Loans	500,000	Net Worth
100,000	Premises		
1,500,000	FSLIC Note	1,500,000	Net Worth Certificate
$101,500,000	Total	$101,500,000	Total

Net Worth/Total Assets = 1.97%

C.   After a Profitable Period:

Assets		Liabilities and Net Worth	
$ 10,000,000	Securities	$ 99,500,000	Liabilities
90,000,000	Loans	600,000	Net Worth
100,000	Premises		
1,450,000	FSLIC Note	1,450,000	Net Worth Certificate
$101,550,000	Total	$101,550,000	Total

Net Worth/Total Assets = 2.02%

Accountants, among others, compare this method of creating net worth to the "smoke and mirrors" tricks of magicians; hence, the "We do it with mirrors" T-shirts mentioned at the outset of the chapter. The program has been defended on several bases. Regulators established strict guidelines governing institutions eligible to receive aid and exclude those thought to have no chance to recover. Well-managed institutions, however, have been given an opportunity to recover from adverse financial circumstances largely beyond their control. In addition, some experts view the the closure of all thrifts with financial difficulties as a threat to the competitive balance among depositories. Initial supporters argued that the NWC program would make it possible for a large number of thrifts to remain open, while confining actual cash outlays by the insurance agencies to only the most severe cases.

In fact, the impact of the NWC program on the industry has been far smaller than many anticipated. Immediately after the passage of Garn-St Germain, the chairman of the Federal Home Loan Bank Board predicted that 1,018 S&Ls would participate by year-end. A year later, only 51 associations had used the program.[7] The stringent requirements for eligibility, as well as the regulatory scrutiny of managers in qualifying institutions may be responsible for the lack of participation. The NWC program originally was to expire in October 1985, but legislation to extend it was subsequently enacted. Whenever the program is terminated, however, NWCs will affect the management of capital in the thrift industry for years to come.

Appraised Equity Capital.   Another controversial source of net worth for S&Ls in the 1980s is *appraised equity capital,* or the amount by which the market value of the institution's land and office buildings exceeds their book value. Figure 16.2 shows how this source of net worth, in addition to NWCs, would affect First Federal S&L. In fact, institutions using NWCs are required by the FHLBB to count appraised equity capital as net worth. Estimates are that this *regulatory accounting principle (RAP)* added $1 billion to the net worth of the industry in 1983.

Because generally accepted accounting principles (GAAP), established by the accounting profession itself, do not permit the historical cost of land and real estate to be written up to reflect current market conditions, accountants in general do not approve of this regulatory convention. The FHLBB has defended the practice as allowing struggling institutions to remain solvent with an opportunity to return to health. In addition, the regulators argue that appraised equity capital gives the FSLIC a better idea of the extent to which the insurance fund

may be required to provide cash should the institution fail.[8]

Open Bank Assistance. Although the FHLBB's use of RAP instead of GAAP has been severely criticized by accountants and officials of other depository institutions, it is not the only nontraditional source of net worth in recent years. In 1984, the FDIC purchased, for cash, $1 billion of preferred stock from Continental Illinois Corporation, the holding company for Continental Illinois National Bank and Trust. Some of the preferred stock was convertible into common stock; according to the FDIC's own estimate, if converted, its initial investment would have equaled 80 percent ownership of the holding company.[9] This financing plan was undertaken to avoid the closure of Continental Illinois Bank and its default on nearly $30 billion in uninsured deposits. At the time, 2,300 small banks had uninsured deposits at Continental, many with amounts equal to 50 percent or more of their own total capital.

To be sure, the parallels between the FDIC action in the case of Continental and the FHLBB's use of RAP instead of GAAP to solve the net worth crisis of thrifts in the 1980s are imperfect. The FDIC actually paid cash in the Continental rescue, whereas the FSLIC promises to pay cash only if necessary under the net worth certificate program. Continental needed immediate cash to stay in business, whereas many thrifts using NWCs, though technically insolvent, do not have liquidity crises. In addition, the FDIC plan for Continental, which has

---

[7]"Net Worth Aid Coming Soon," *Savings and Loan News* 103 (November 1982): 42; Puglisi and McKenzie, "Capital Market Strategies," p. 11.

[8]Barbara Bennett, "S&L Accounting," *Weekly Letter,* Federal Reserve Bank of San Francisco, December 21, 1984. Additional discussion of GAAP versus RAP is given in "Capital Assistance: Big Decisions Face Management," *Savings and Loan News* 104 (January 1983): 92-93; Lee Berton, "Accounting at Thrifts Provokes Controversy as Gimmickry Mounts," *The Wall Street Journal,* March 29, 1985, pp. 1, 13; Ronald P. Auerbach and Alan S. McCall, "Permissive Accounting Practices Inflate Savings and Loan Industry Earnings and Net Worth," *Issues in Bank Regulation* 9 (Summer 1985): 17-21. For more details on the FHLBB's position on appraised equity capital, see Federal Home Loan Bank Board, "Appraised Equity Capital," 12 CFR Part 563, October 24, 1985.

[9]FDIC, *1984 Annual Report,* pp. 4-5.

Figure 16.2
Appraised Equity Capital

First Federal Savings and Loan Balance Sheet

After the Issuance of Net Worth Certificates and Appraisal of the Market Value of
the Premises:

Assets		Liabilities and Net Worth	
$ 9,900,000	Securities	$ 99,500,000	Liabilities
90,000,000	Loans	500,000	Net Worth
130,000	Premises	30,000	Appraised Equity Capital
1,500,000	FSLIC Note	1,500,000	Net Worth Certificate
$101,530,000	Total	$101,530,000	Total

Net Worth/Total Assets = 2.00%

been termed **open bank assistance** and used after 1984 to keep other commercial banks from
closing, provides the potential for the FDIC to
recover its funds when a bank's financial condition improves.[10]

Still, there are conceptual similarities between the forms of regulatory assistance. In
particular, the programs have been developed
to prevent the potential insolvency of a large
number of depositories in a short period and to
minimize the cash outflow required by the federal insurers in order to maintain the stability
of the financial system. Each program has also
brought new meaning to the term *net worth*.

Debt Capital

In addition to net worth, depositories have access to long-term debt as a source of capital.
Because all debt has a maturity date, whether it
really fulfills the role of capital can be questioned. Long-term debt carries a repayment obligation that is just as real as an uninsured
deposit, so it is not really a permanent source
of funds. On the other hand, long-term debt,
when legally subordinate to deposits, is a
source of funds that does not place an immediate repayment burden on the institution and offers some protection to depositors; thus, it
offers a quasipermanence similar to capital.[11]

The consensus on long-term debt is a compromise position. Most observers, including
federal regulators, consider subordinated notes
and debentures with carefully specified characteristics as part of a depository's capital. Subordinated notes and debentures qualify as
capital under three conditions:

1. They must have an original maturity of
   seven years or more.

[10]Monica Langley and Francis C. Brown III, "Bank Oklahoma Unit in Oklahoma City to Get $130 Million in
FDIC Assistance," *The Wall Street Journal*, August 18,
1986, p. 2. In November 1986, the FDIC sold about 25
percent of its Continental stock and recovered some of
its funds. See Jeff Bailey, "Continental Illinois Raises Rescue Estimate," *The Wall Street Journal*, December 30,
1986, p. 2.

[11]For further development of these arguments, see Ronald
D. Watson, "Banking's Capital Shortage: The Malaise
and the Myth," *Business Review*, Federal Reserve Bank of
Philadelphia (September 1975), pp. 3-13. Before 1985,
the FDIC adopted the position that long-term debt
should not be considered capital, while other federal bank
and thrift regulators supported the view that limited
amounts of long-term debt were suitable capital components. In 1985, the three federal banking regulators came
to an agreement, described later in the chapter.

2. They must be clearly identified at the time of issuance as subordinate to deposits.

3. They must be uninsured.

Debt securities with those features satisfy the arguments of both sides.

HOW IS CAPITAL MEASURED?

It should not be surprising that no consensus exists on how capital, once defined, should be measured. Issues relating to the appropriate measurement of capital revolve around the accounting (book-value) versus market-value approach, the relative importance of specific capital components, and the other firm-specific financial variables to which capital should be related.

Book versus Market Values

Finance and accounting theorists have debated for years whether the periodic results of the financial activities of a business should be reported at book or market value. Although most experts acknowledge the distortions produced by book-value measures, based on historical events, many also believe that reporting the value of balance sheet items at estimated current market value is too imprecise to be justified. They reason that unless something is sold, its potential market value is subject to rapid change. Indeed, for some financial assets and liabilities, there is no secondary market in which value can be determined. On the other hand, supporters of market-value measurements argue that market values are the only relevant ones if a firm is forced to liquidate its assets, and any measure of capital that does not consider market values is severely distorted.

This debate is important for the measurement of capital because of capital's role as a cushion between the value of the firm's assets and the value of its outstanding liabilities. While the book-versus-market question is relevant for all businesses, it is especially significant to depository institutions because of their high degree of financial leverage. The greater the proportion of financing from debt obligations, the less the value of assets can shrink before insolvency.

Market Value Capital and Interest Rates. In a financial institution, the difference between book and market values is primarily related to changes in interest rates between the time an asset is acquired and a subsequent period. The difference between using book and market values to measure an institution's capital is illustrated in Figure 16.3. For simplicity, this "generic" depository institution is assumed to have only three assets: cash and due from other depositories, three-month Treasury bills, and 10 percent automobile loans with a four-year remaining maturity. All deposits are assumed to be variable-rate so that depositors always earn current market rates. (If some deposits were fixed-rate, long-term CDs, their value to depositors would change with market conditions.)

In Panel A of the figure, capital is measured as the difference between the book value of assets and the book value of liabilities. Alternately, the book value of capital could be obtained by simply adding the book values of all the capital components on an institution's balance sheet, such as the common stock, preferred stock, and retained earnings accounts.

Suppose that after the loans were made, the market rate for auto loans rose to 13 percent. The market value of the 10 percent loans will no longer be as high as the book value, should the institution wish to sell them. The current value of the deposit liabilities will not drop, however, because the institution is obligated to repay them at their full face value. As shown in Panel B of Figure 16.3, the capital of the institution, calculated by subtracting the current value of liabilities from the current value of assets, is considerably lower than its book value.

Of course, changes in interest rates can increase as well as decrease market values. In Panel C, market rates for automobile loans are assumed to fall to 7.5 percent. Measuring net worth at market instead of book value improves the institution's capital position.

Figure 16.3
The Book Value versus the Market Value of Capital

A.   Book-Value Accounting:

Assets		Liabilities and Net Worth	
$ 1,000,000	Cash	$65,800,000	Deposits
19,000,000	T-Bills	4,200,000	Net Worth
50,000,000	10% Loans[a]		
$70,000,000	Total	$70,000,000	Total

Net Worth/Total Assets = 6.00%

[a]Amortizing these loans over 48 months, at a monthly rate of 10%/12 = 0.833%, results in total expected monthly payments of $1,268,129.20. That is, the present value of $1,268,129.20, discounted at 0.833% for 48 months, is $50,000,000.

B.   Market-Value Accounting (loan rates rise to 13%):

Assets		Liabilities and Net Worth	
$ 1,000,000	Cash	$65,800,000	Deposits
19,000,000	T-Bills	1,469,757	Net Worth
47,269,757	10% Loans[b]		
$67,269,757	Total	$67,269,757	Total

Net Worth/Total Assets = 2.18%

[b]The present value of the monthly payments discounted at 13%/12 = 1.0833%.

C.   Market-Value Accounting (loan rates fall to 7.5%):

Assets		Liabilities and Net Worth	
$ 1,000,000	Cash	$65,800,000	Deposits
19,000,000	T-Bills	6,647,757	Net Worth
52,447,757	10% Loans[c]		
$72,447,757	Total	$72,447,757	Total

Net Worth/Total Assets = 9.18%

[c]The present value of the monthly payments discounted at 7.5%/12 = 0.625%.

The divergence between book and market values is shown in Figure 16.4, plotting book- and market-value capital to asset ratios for 14 publicly traded thrift institutions over the period December 1979–January 1986. Although book-value ratios declined fairly steadily until 1985, reflecting losses that decreased retained earnings, market-value ratios fluctuated above and below book value, reflecting changes in interest rates.

Calculating Market–Value Capital. Measures of capital now used by regulators are based on book values. Because of the problems

---

Figure 16.4
Capital-to-Asset Ratios for Savings and Loans: December 1979–January 1986

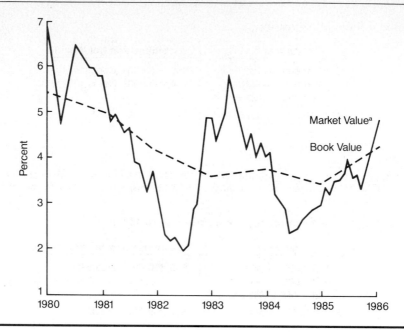

---

[a]Market Value Capital-to-Asset Ratio = Market Value of Capital ÷ (Market Value of Capital + Book Value of Liabilities).

Source: Michael C. Keeley, "The Health of Banks and Thrifts," *Weekly Letter,* Federal Reserve Bank of San Francisco, February 21, 1986.

of identifying current values for marketable assets, and because there are no markets for some assets, difficulties in calculating market-value measures are seen as outweighing their benefits. For a stockholder-owned institution with publicly traded stock, however, the difference between the market value of its assets and liabilities can be estimated by calculating the total market value of common and preferred stock. This simply requires multiplying the number of shares of each type of stock outstanding by the current price. Theoretically, the financial markets are evaluating the shares based on participants' estimate of the value of shareholders' residual claims on the institution's assets. This total market value will be either less than, or greater than, the book value of net

worth, depending upon the markets' assessment of the value of the firm's assets.

In most depository institutions, however, either no stock is outstanding or the stock is not publicly traded, so market assessments are unavailable. From time to time, regulators have proposed plans such as the "mark-to-market" system for valuing assets advocated by the FHLBB in the early 1980s, but none has yet been implemented.[12] Nevertheless, managers should understand the difference between the two measurement systems, because in a severe financial crisis, asset market values may deter-

---

[12]"Mark to Market Will Move the Business into a New World," *Savings and Loan News* 103 (October 1982): 102-103.

mine the extent to which the institution can service its obligations.

Relative Importance of Capital Components

Capital measurement problems are not confined to book versus market values; also at issue is whether the various components are equally important. Because specific numerical standards for depository capital are set by federal regulators, the relative significance of each component plays a role in determining how well an institution meets its capital standards.

View of Federal Banking Regulators. Federal banking regulators categorize components as primary or secondary capital. *Primary capital* consists of items the regulators believe truly serve as a cushion against unexpected or abnormally large losses—capital components with no maturity or redemption dates. *Secondary capital* includes other items, such as redeemable preferred stock or subordinated notes and debentures, with some of the characteristics of a cushion, but not all. Details on this division are given in Table 16.1. Most of the table is self-explanatory, based on earlier discussions and the descriptions in the table, although a few clarifications are in order.

Only traditional sources of equity capital are considered primary capital with no strings attached. An item that is at any time something other than equity, such as convertible debt, is counted partially as primary and partially as secondary capital (see footnotes a and d of the table). In addition, from the sum of capital components, deductions are made for the book value of intangible assets.

By far the largest intangible asset in most financial institutions is *goodwill.* Goodwill, illustrated in Figure 16.5, arises when one institution purchases another. It represents dollar values that may not be realized should the institution be forced to liquidate, so federal banking regulators deduct goodwill from capital calculations.

In Figure 16.5, the depository institution in Figure 16.3 is purchased by another depository

when market rates on auto loans are 13 percent. The market value of the acquired firm's loans is less than book value, and the combined balance sheet reflects that market value as part of the Loans account for the combined firm. The difference between market and book value is goodwill. In the eyes of bank regulators, the capital of the combined institution would not include goodwill, because it could not be liquidated to pay off liabilities. The net worth remaining after deduction of goodwill is *tangible net worth.*

View of Federal Thrift Regulators. The Federal Home Loan Bank Board makes no distinction between primary and secondary capital. Instead, it has identified *regulatory net worth,* the total of all retained earnings, reserves, common stock, preferred stock, mutual capital certificates, net worth certificates, appraised equity capital, and subordinated notes and debentures with an original maturity of seven years or more. Unlike the restrictions placed on the amount of subordinated notes and debentures that count as capital in commercial banks (see footnote c of Table 16.1), the FHLBB considers 100 percent of these debt instruments as regulatory net worth, as long as they have at least seven years until maturity. A similar policy holds for some preferred stock issues. Over time, as the redemption date of these instruments approaches, smaller and smaller proportions can be counted. No deduction is required for goodwill or other intangibles.[13]

This definition permits the FHLBB to consider many institutions solvent that might otherwise not be. Figure 16.6 shows three views of the total net worth of FHLBB-regulated thrifts from year-end 1979 to early 1984. The top line reflects regulatory net worth, which exceeded its 1979 levels by 1984. Net worth as measured by GAAP (which, like RAP, creates a goodwill

---

[13]Federal Home Loan Bank Board, "Amendments Relating to the Issuance and Use of Subordinated Debt Securities," 12 CFR Parts 561 and 563, April 18, 1985; and "Preferred Stock as Regulatory Net Worth," 12 CFR Parts 561 and 563.7-5, June 21, 1985.

Table 16.1

Components of Bank Capital as Measured by the Federal Bank Regulatory Agencies

Item		Description
Primary Capital Measure		
	Common stock	Aggregate par or stated value of outstanding common stock.
	Perpetual preferred stock	Aggregate par or stated value of outstanding perpetual preferred stock. Preferred stock is a form of ownership interest in a bank or other company which entitles its holders to some preference or priority over the owners of common stock, usually with respect to dividends or asset distributions in a liquidation. Perpetual preferred stock does not have a stated maturity date and cannot be redeemed at the option of the holder. It includes those issues that are automatically converted into common stock at a stated date.
Equity capital	Surplus	Amount received from the sale of common or perpetual preferred stock in excess of its par or stated value.
	Undivided profits	Accumulated dollar value of profits after taxes that have not been distributed to shareholders of common and preferred stock as dividends.
	Capital reserves	Contingency and other capital reserves. Reserves for contingencies include amounts set aside for possible unforeseen or indeterminate liabilities not otherwise reflected on the bank's books and not covered by insurance. Capital reserves include amounts set aside for cash dividends on common and preferred stock not yet declared and amounts allocated for retirement of limited-life preferred stock and debentures subordinated to deposits.
Plus:	Mandatory convertible instruments[a]	Debt issues that mandate conversion to common or perpetual preferred stock at some future date. They must meet the following conditions to be included in primary capital: 1. The securities must mature (convert to common or preferred stock) in 12 years or less. 2. The aggregate amount of mandatory convertible securities counted as primary capital may not exceed 20% of primary capital net of mandatory convertible securities. 3. The issuer may redeem the securities before maturity only with the proceeds of the sale of common or perpetual preferred stock. 4. The holder of the security cannot accelerate the payment of principal except in the event of bankruptcy, insolvency or reorganization. 5. The security must be subordinated in right of payment to all senior indebtedness of the issuer.
	Reserves for loan and lease losses	Amount set aside to absorb anticipated losses. All chargeoffs of loans and leases are charged to this capital account, and recoveries on loans and leases previously charged off are credited to this capital account.
	Minority interest in consolidated subsidiaries	The sum of the equity capital of the subsidiaries in which the bank has minority interest multiplied by the percentage ownership of the bank in the subsidiaries.
Minus:	Equity commitment notes	Debt obligations which the issuer must repay only from the proceeds of the sale of common or perpetual preferred stock. These notes are included in mandatory convertible instruments, but excluded from primary capital.
	Intangible assets[b]	Generally these assets represent the purchase price of firms that have been acquired in excess of their book value.

---

[a]Only up to 20% of primary capital excluding mandatory convertible instruments.

[b]The FDIC and OCC subtract *all* intangible assets except for purchased mortgage servicing rights. The Fed subtracts only the "goodwill" portion of intangible asets.

Table 16.1
(*Continued*)

Item	Description
Secondary Capital Measure	
Limited-life preferred stock[c]	Preferred stock with a maturity date.
Plus: Subordinated notes and debentures[c]	Debt obligations of issuer, with fixed maturity dates, that are subordinated to depositors in case of insolvency. Subordinated notes and debentures issued by depository institutions are not insured by the federal deposit insurance agencies.
Mandatory convertible instruments not eligible for primary capital[d]	See the definition of mandatory convertible instruments under Primary Capital Measure.

[c]The limited-life preferred stock and subordinated notes and debentures included in secondary capital must have an original weighted average maturity of at least 7 years. All 3 federal banking agencies limit the aggregate amount of secondary capital to less than 50% of the amount of a bank's primary capital.

[d]The amount that exceeds 20% of primary capital excluding mandatory convertible instruments; equity commitment notes excluded from primary capital.

Source: R. Alton Gilbert, Courtenay C. Stone, and Michael E. Trebing, "The New Bank Capital Adequacy Standards," *Review*, Federal Reserve Bank of St. Louis 67 (May 1985): 14-15.

asset in case of mergers) is lower, because net worth certificates and appraised equity capital are excluded. After goodwill is removed, tangible net worth, depicted by the bottom line, is considerably lower. By January 1985, in fact, tangible net worth of FHLBB-regulated institutions was reported to be just 0.04 percent of total assets![14] It must be emphasized, however, that technically insolvent businesses can operate on a day-to-day basis, as long they experience no severe liquidity crises that force the sale of assets.

FDIC-regulated savings banks are governed by many of the capital measures in Table 16.1, although mutually owned savings banks have no common stock accounts. Savings banks are permitted to have net worth certificates, whereas commercial banks are not, but only 21 savings banks were using the net worth certificate program at year-end 1985. Unlike S&Ls, savings banks may not recognize appraised equity capital.[15]

View of Federal Credit Union Regulators. In the credit union industry, measuring capital is considerably simpler than for other depositories, because CUs have not-for-profit status. Because they may not sell securities to the general public, CU capital consists entirely of undivided earnings and reserves from past operations. Reserves are amounts set aside from earnings each year to cover future losses on investments or loans; undivided earnings are those retained in excess of reserves.

CAPITAL COMPARED TO WHAT?

A final problem in capital measurement is deciding what comparisons should be made to de-

---

[14]"FHLBB Tightens Net Worth Rules Despite Opposition," *Savings Institutions* 106 (January 1985): 6. Auerbach and McCall, in "Permissive Accounting Practices Inflate Savings and Loan Industry Earnings and Net Worth," report that tangible net worth declined 92 percent from the end of 1979 to the end of 1983.

[15]FDIC, *1985 Annual Report*, p. 31.

Figure 16.5
The Effect of Goodwill on Capital Measurement

Book Value before Purchase (Acquired Firm):

Assets		Liabilities and Net Worth	
$ 1,000,000	Cash	$65,800,000	Deposits
19,000,000	T-Bills	4,200,000	Net Worth
50,000,000	10% Loans[a]		
$70,000,000	Total	$70,000,000	Total

[a]The current market rate is 13%, giving these loans a market value of $47,269,757 ($2,730,243 less than the book value).

Book Value Accounting (Acquiring Firm):

Assets		Liabilities and Net Worth	
$ 25,000,000	Cash	$211,500,000	Deposits
		13,500,000	Net Worth
200,000,000	Loans		
$225,000,000	Total	$225,000,000	Total

Net Worth/Total Assets = 6.00%

Book Value Accounting (Combined Firm):

Assets		Liabilities and Net Worth	
$ 26,000,000	Cash	$277,300,000	Deposits
19,000,000	T-Bills	17,700,000	Net Worth
247,269,757	Loans		
2,730,243	Goodwill		
$295,000,000	Total	$295,000,000	Total

Tangible Net Worth: $17,700,000 − $2,730,243 = $14,969,757
Tangible Net Worth/Total Assets = 5.07%

---

termine how an institution's capital "stacks up" against its own internal standards or those of regulators. Like all financial data, dollar figures alone are not sufficient for decision making. It would mean very little, for example, to say that a bank had $1 million in capital. Unless the value of its assets, or its uninsured deposits, or its loans are also known, the raw figure has no significance.

Balance Sheet Measures

Federal regulators have a long history of comparing an institution's capital to balance sheet items, although specific measures have varied.

Traditional Bases of Comparison.   In 1914, the Comptroller of the Currency decided that commercial banks should have equity capital

Figure 16.6
Three Views of the Net Worth of Thrifts

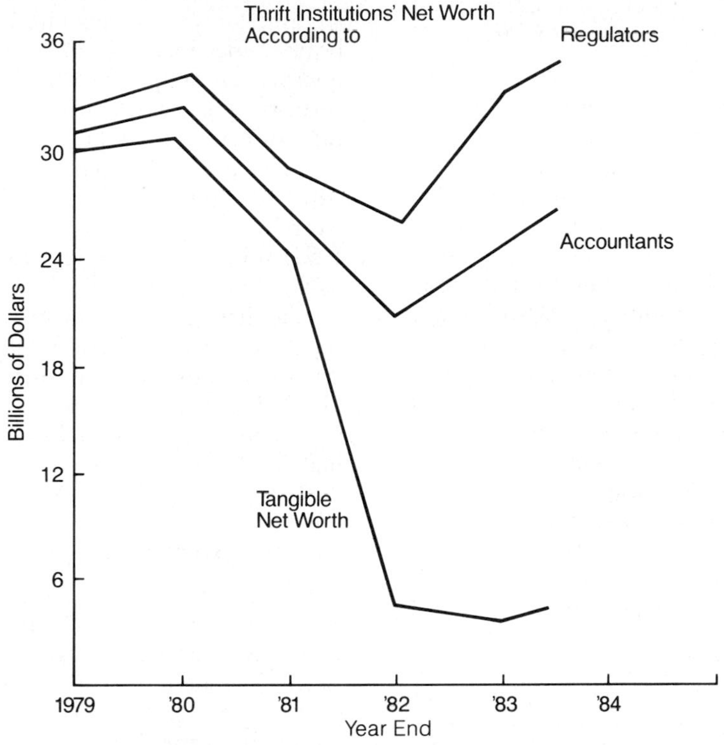

Source: Gary Hector, "The Thrift Industry Is Under Siege Again," *FORTUNE* 110 (October 15, 1984): 175. Reprinted with permission.

equal to 10 percent of deposits. In the 1930s, the FDIC emphasized a capital/assets ratio instead. However, when banks' assets were dominated by risk-free Treasury securities purchased to help finance World War II, that measure became less useful, and the ratio of capital to **risk assets** (then defined as total assets less cash and Treasury securities) emerged.[16]

Today, in deregulated markets, the capital/total assets ratio has regained favor in regula-tors' eyes. Such a ratio answers the question, By how much could the book value of assets decline before it falls below liabilities? Federal thrift regulators look to both the net worth/total assets and net worth/total liabilities ratios as signals of capital adequacy. Regulators of federal credit unions focus on still another balance sheet comparison, the reserves/risk assets ratio.

A New Concept. In 1986, federal bank regulators proposed an additional measure of capital adequacy, the **supplemental adjusted capital measure.** This measure differs from previous capital adequacy ratios in two ways:

---

[16]More information on the history and use of specific capital measures in banking before 1985 is found in Karlyn Mitchell, "Capital Adequacy at Commercial Banks," *Economic Review,* Federal Reserve Bank of Kansas City 69 (September/October 1984): 17-30.

1. It recognizes that the traditional definition of risk assets fails to consider degrees of risk among those assets.

2. It recognizes that some risks against which capital must protect depositors are not on the balance sheet.

As first noted in Chapter 2, the risk reflected in an institution's off-balance sheet items may be significant, especially in large depositories. Off-balance sheet items include obligations, such as loan commitments and lines of credit discussed in Chapter 13, arising in the ordinary course of business but not reflected in traditional financial statements. Also included are *standby letters of credit,* or fee-based agreements obligating an institution to pay some of a customer's debts if the customer defaults. For some banks, off-balance sheet items are a significant potential commitment, estimated at *$1.5 trillion* for the 25 largest banks in 1985. Standby letters alone were estimated at 11 to 12 percent of assets in some institutions.[17]

A sample calculation of a supplemental adjusted capital measure is shown in Table 16.2. The institution is assumed to have total assets of $100,000 and off-balance sheet items of $50,000. Primary capital totals $7,000. Assets and off-balance sheet items are divided into four risk categories, each assigned a weight that increases with riskiness, shown in Column 3. The weights range from 0 percent for cash and short-term Treasury securities to 100 percent for "standard risk" assets such as commercial and consumer loans and corporate securities. Money market risk assets are those with little or no default risk and high liquidity, such as long-term Treasury securities. Moderate risk assets are those with some credit and liquidity risk, such as municipal securities. Off-balance sheet items are assigned to one of the two highest-risk categories, using rules specified by the regulators. The dollar volume of assets or off-balance sheet items in each category is multiplied by the risk weight, and a weighted risk

asset total (shown at the bottom of Column 4) is calculated.

In this example, because of the large number of off-balance sheet items, the total of weighted risk assets is higher than a simple book-value measure of total assets. Consequently, the supplemental adjusted capital measure is 6.45 percent, lower than the 7 percent ratio of primary capital to total assets.

The FHLBB recently approved new risk-adjusted capital standards, although bank regulators' proposals had not been finalized in early 1987. While bank standards would focus on off-balance sheet items, the FHLBB policy focuses on liability growth and on the proportion of fixed-rate loans and real estate investments in a thrift's portfolio as indicators of riskiness. The FHLBB rules permit lower capital standards for an institution with long-term liabilities to match its fixed-rate assets.[18]

Income Measures

Not everyone agrees that balance sheet ratios are the best way to evaluate capital, and some argue that measuring capital against expected earnings is better. They reason that the major purpose of capital is to absorb temporary losses, and capital ratios are useful only if they compare an institution's capital to anticipated profits or losses. Losses from many sources can be estimated—because of default, changes in interest rates, fluctuating exchange rates, even fraud.[19] Although this argument is conceptually appealing, it suffers from many of the same implementation difficulties as market value accounting. Thus, regulators have not yet adopted anticipated earnings tests as official capital measures, although estimates of earnings quality are used by examiners in developing CAMEL ratings.

---

[17]Patricia Brannon, "Off-Balance Sheet Activities: Coming Out of Hiding," *Trends and Topics,* Federal Home Loan Bank of Chicago 3 (Summer 1986): 9–12.

[18]Brian P. Smith, "The FHLBB Crafts New, but Workable, Capital Rules," *Savings Institutions* 107 (October 1986): 197–199.

[19]This approach is outlined and illustrated in detail in George J. Vojta, *Bank Capital Adequacy* (New York: Citicorp, 1973).

Table 16.2
Supplemental Adjusted Capital Measure: A Sample Calculation

(1) Risk Category	(2) Amount of On- and Off-Balance Sheet Items in Category	(3) Risk Weight	(4) Weighted Risk Assets and Off- Balance Sheet Items
Cash and equivalents	$ 5,000	0.00	$ 0
Money market risk	35,000	0.30	10,500
Moderate risk	30,000	0.60	18,000
Standard risk	80,000	1.00	80,000
Total (including $100,000 in total assets and $50,000 in off-balance sheet items)	$150,000		$108,500
Primary capital	$7,000		
Primary capital/total assets ratio (as defined under existing guidelines)	$\dfrac{\$7,000}{\$100,000} = 7.00\%$		
Supplemental adjusted capital measure (as proposed)	$\dfrac{\$7,000}{\$108,500} = 6.45\%$		

Source: Federal Reserve Board, Press Release, January 24, 1986, p. 4.

HOW MUCH CAPITAL IS ENOUGH?

Assuming that ratios of capital to balance sheet or off-balance sheet accounts, despite measurement flaws, remain the most carefully watched indicators of capital adequacy, how high should those ratios be? This question raises another one: Who should decide?

Should the Market Decide?

Some economists advocate complete deregulation of depositories' capital ratios, or at least those of large institutions. They argue that the financial markets are equipped to evaluate whether existing capital provides a sufficient cushion. Institutions with too little capital will be unable to attract funds from uninsured depositors and will be forced to rein in their risk-taking activities. Shareholders, too, will put pressure on managers if they take too many risks; excessive riskiness will be reflected in a lowered price for the institution's stock. Conversely, managers of institutions with too much capital will be pressured to use more leverage to increase investors' expected returns. A costly layer of bureaucracy will be removed if markets, not regulators, determine capital standards.

Are Market Solutions Feasible?   Opponents of this view argue that many institutions are not exposed to market discipline. The stock of most small banks and thrifts is not traded publicly, and most mutual institutions have no public securities of any kind. In addition, as discussions of the federal deposit insurance system in Chapter 15 suggest, the financial markets may lack sufficient incentives to exert the discipline required.[20]

If market solutions are used, more public disclosure of the activities of depository institutions is required. Currently, much information regulators collect on individual firms is unavailable to the public. Commercial banks are now required to disclose more details about their loan portfolios than in the past, and the debate over additional disclosure continues. The evidence on whether the markets would assess new information correctly is mixed. Generally, the equity and subordinated debt markets appear to monitor and respond to changes in an institution's financial condition more rapidly than do uninsured depositors.[21]

Are Market Solutions Optimal?   Some experts note that the appropriate capital/assets ratio depends upon for whose benefit the standard is set—an individual institution or the financial system as a whole.[22] Too little capital in a depository can result in its failure; too little capital in the banking system as a whole could result

in a chain of failures, with disruptive social consequences. Too much capital also has negative consequences. For individual institutions, excess capital reduces the expected return to capital suppliers. For society as a whole, too much capital in depository institutions means less available for industries in which it might be invested more profitably.

For an individual institution, the ideal amount of capital is one at which the marginal costs and marginal benefits to its capital suppliers are equal. For society as a whole, the ideal level of capital is one at which the marginal cost of reduced investment in other industries is balanced against the marginal return from preventing the failure of additional depositories, a relationship demonstrated in Figure 16.7. The optimum capital/assets ratio (c^*) for the system as a whole is determined at the intersection of the social marginal cost and marginal return functions.

There is no guarantee, however, that the optimal capital ratio from the point of view of an individual institution will be the same as c^*. It may or may not be, depending upon the relationship between the specific marginal costs and benefits of more capital in an institution versus their relationship for society as a whole.

Should the Regulators Decide?

If public costs are to be explicitly considered in all cases, capital ratios must be regulated. Although some experts have argued that regulators will err on the high side of the optimum, because they tend to weigh the social costs of undercapitalization more heavily than the costs of overcapitalization, research suggests that regulators' capital standards in recent years may actually have been less than optimal from a societal viewpoint.[23]

Empirical research also indicates that, when no specific capital requirements exist, capital/

[20]The argument is further developed in Arnold A. Heggestad and B. Frank King, "Regulation of Bank Capital: An Evaluation," *Economic Review,* Federal Reserve Bank of Atlanta 67 (March 1982): 35-43; Mitchell, "Capital Adequacy Measures at Commercial Banks"; and Robert P. Forrestal, "Bank Safety: Risks and Responsibilities," *Economic Review,* Federal Reserve Bank of Atlanta 70 (August 1985): 4-12.

[21]Some major banks began disclosing information on off-balance sheet activities in their 1985 annual reports, based on what they viewed as investor concern that has been "blown out of proportion" in recent years. See Phillip L. Zweig, "Major Banks Tell More about Risks on Investor Pleas," *The Wall Street Journal,* March 6, 1986, p. 9. For a review and analysis of the literature on disclosure and market discipline, see Gary G. Gilbert, "Disclosure and Market Discipline: Issues and Evidence," *Economic Review,* Federal Reserve Bank of Atlanta 68 (November 1983): 70-76; and Elijah Brewer III and Cheng Few Lee, "How the Market Judges Bank Risk," *Economic Perspectives,* Federal Reserve Bank of Chicago 10 (November/December 1986): 25-31.

[22]Anthony M. Santomero and Ronald D. Watson, "Determining an Optimal Capital Standard for the Banking Industry," *Journal of Finance* 32 (September 1977): 1,267-1,282; Larry D. Wall, "Regulation of Banks' Equity Capital," *Economic Review,* Federal Reserve Bank of Atlanta 70 (November 1985): 4-18.

[23]Santomero and Watson, "Determining an Optimal Capital Standard for the Banking Industry"; Dilip K. Shome, Stephen D. Smith, and Arnold A. Heggestad, "Capital Adequacy and the Valuation of Large Commercial Banking Organizations," *Journal of Financial Research* 9 (Winter 1986): 331-341.

Figure 16.7
The Socially Optimal Capital Ratio

At low levels of capital/assets, the marginal benefit of increasing the ratio is high, and the marginal cost of increasing the ratio is low. At high capital/assets ratios, the marginal cost of more capital in depositories is high, and the marginal benefit of more capital is low. The ideal capital/assets ratio is the one at which marginal costs and benefits are equal.

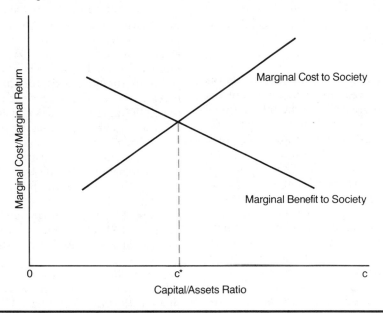

Source: Adapted from Anthony M. Santomero and Ronald J. Watson, "Determining an Optimal Capital Standard for the Banking Industry," *Journal of Finance* 32 (September 1977): 1278. Reprinted with permission.

assets ratios in commercial banks vary inversely with interest rates. Because periods of high rates are those in which bank capital may be most needed, this evidence further suggests a need for required minimum capital ratios.[24] Thus, federal regulators have been charged with the responsibility for determining capital adequacy standards. But just as they have disagreed on the components of capital, regulators have come to different conclusions about how much capital is enough.

Capital Regulations in Commercial Banks before 1985. Historically, the three federal bank regulators avoided setting specific required ratios of capital to assets. Each agency reserved the right to analyze capital adequacy on a case-by-case basis. In fact, some experts argue that scrutiny of capital ratios, and accompanying pressure to increase them if examiners found them deficient, served as an implicit risk adjustment in the absence of risk-based deposit insurance.[25]

[24]Alan J. Marcus, "The Bank Capital Decision: A Time Series-Cross Section Analysis," *Journal of Finance* 38 (September 1983): 1,217-1,232.

[25]Stephen A. Buser, Andrew H. Chen, and Edward J. Kane, "Federal Deposit Insurance, Regulatory Policy, and Optimal Bank Capital," *Journal of Finance* 36 (March 1981): 51-60.

Under this flexible system, an institution was evaluated primarily in relation to its peers. Thus, if an entire group of banks were under-capitalized according to some optimal standard, regulators took no action against any one of them. Similarly, an entire group of banks could be overcapitalized. The result of this system was that large banks operated with much less capital than small banks, and the capital/assets ratio of the industry as a whole declined, as illustrated in Figure 16.8.

Capital Regulations in Commercial Banks since 1985.

Congressional concern about the decline became so great that in the International Lending Supervision Act of 1983, Congress required federal banking regulators to enforce minimum capital ratios. All three agencies established specific standards in 1985. All insured commercial banks and their holding companies are subject to the same minimum capital/assets ratios: The primary capital/assets ratio must be at least 5.5 percent and total capital (primary plus secondary capital) must be at least 6 percent of total assets. Most banks are expected to exceed the minimums. In addition, the agencies may require higher minimums for individual institutions if justified by the riskiness of the bank's operations.[26] Supplemental adjusted capital measures, such as the one illustrated earlier, would not replace the 1985 guidelines but are intended to provide a "second opinion" on capital adequacy.

Capital Standards for Thrift Institutions.

Thrift regulators first tightened capital requirements in 1985 in response to criticisms of lax regulation in the early 1980s and the deterioration of net worth to assets in the industry. The deterioration coincided with changes in the industry's asset structure. Although it is not clear that asset changes have increased thrift riskiness, and indeed they may have decreased riskiness in the long run, the severe capital decline evoked concern that capital was below prudent levels. Accordingly, in 1985 the FDIC announced capital standards for savings banks equal to the standards for commercial banks it regulates. At the request of industry groups, the FDIC agreed to consider any savings bank with a primary capital/assets ratio equal to at least 3 percent as in initial compliance with the standards, if the bank submitted a plan for increasing capital by 0.5 percent per year until it reaches the 5.5 percent minimum standard.[27]

The FHLBB took a much more unusual path for FSLIC-insured institutions. Wary of the problems caused by risky management strategies, especially those relying on brokered deposits, the agency tied its net worth/total liability requirements to marginal rates of growth in an institution's liabilities. The higher the rate of growth, the larger the capital requirement. Under these guidelines, however, many FSLIC-insured thrifts could have regulatory net worth totaling less than 3 percent of assets.[28]

In 1986, responding to continuing criticism that its standards were too lax, the FHLBB increased capital requirements for thrifts, regardless of growth rates. The required ratio of net worth to liabilities was increased to 6 percent, to be phased in gradually based on the industry's performance over a period of 6 to 12 years. Although the requirements are less stringent than those for banks, they are closer than they have been for many years. The FHLBB also re-

---

[26]The three banking agencies disagree about how the requirements should be enforced. The FDIC and the Comptroller of the Currency view them as fixed standards, whereas the Federal Reserve uses a "zone" system, under which institutions with 7 percent or more capital are considered adequately capitalized, those with 6 to 7 percent considered marginally capitalized, and those with less than 6 percent undercapitalized. The zone system thus applies to state-chartered Fed-member banks and to bank holding companies. Definitions of primary and secondary capital differ slightly for BHCs. For further discussion of capital definitions for banks, see R. Alton Gilbert, Courtenay C. Stone, and Michael E. Trebing, "The New Bank Capital Adequacy Standards," *Review,* Federal Reserve Bank of St. Louis 67 (May 1985): 12–20.

---

[27]National Council of Savings Institutions, *1984-85 Annual Report of the President,* p. 15.

[28]Thomas J. Parliment, "The Net Worth Regulations Force Institutions to Find an Affordable Growth Rate," *Savings Institutions* 106 (June 1985): 62–69.

Figure 16.8
Capital Ratios of Commercial Banks, 1900–1984

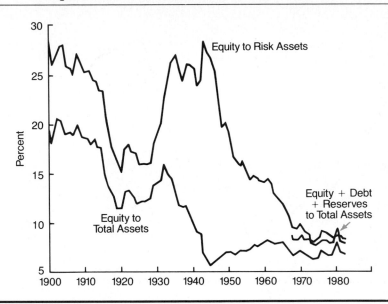

Source: Karlyn Mitchell, "Capital Adequacy at Commercial Banks," *Economic Review,* Federal Reserve Bank of Kansas City 69 (September/October 1984): 22.

quired thrifts with below-average net worth as of the first quarter of 1987 to increase it at a faster rate than those with above-average capital ratios. Additional capital can be required for institutions with direct investments in real estate and other designated assets.[29]

Capital Standards for Credit Unions. Figure 16.9 shows that in the late 1970s federal credit unions experienced a deterioration in the ratio of reserves plus undivided earnings to total assets. At that time, a 12 percent usury ceiling on loans, in effect since the 1930s, and rapidly escalating interest costs on CU shares made it

difficult for CU income to exceed expenses. In addition, as noted in Chapter 14, revisions in federal bankruptcy law escalated default rates on consumer loans, the major assets of CUs. By 1984, the decline in capital ratios for the industry as a whole had been reversed. Helping this were improved economic conditions, an increase in the loan rate ceiling to 21 percent, and a tightening of bankruptcy laws. No special capital regulations, other than those historically in effect, have been imposed on the industry.

The NCUA approach differs from the plans of both banking and thrift regulators because it is based on size and age. In general, federal CUs are expected to focus on the ratio of reserves to risk assets. Risk assets are defined by the NCUA to be total assets less cash, Treasury securities, and loans not considered subject to default risk, such as federally guaranteed student loans and loans to members backed by

[29]"FHLBB Moves for Increase in Net Worth Requirements," *Savings Institutions* 107 (September 1986): 13; Smith, "The FHLBB Crafts New, but Workable, Capital Rules."

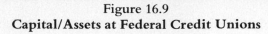

Figure 16.9
Capital/Assets at Federal Credit Unions

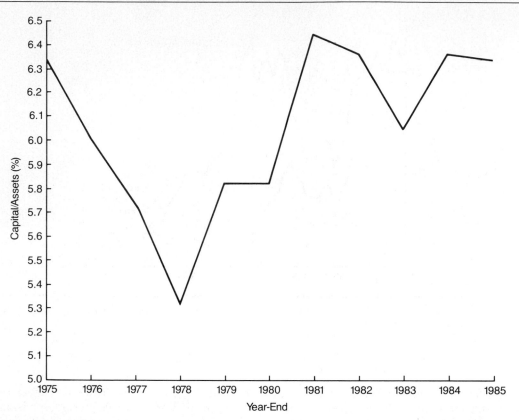

Source: Prepared by the authors with data from National Credit Union Administration, *1985 Annual Report,* pp. 42-43.

their personal share accounts. Institutions four years old or older with over $500,000 in total assets are required to have reserves/risk assets ratios equal to 6 percent. CUs with less than $500,000 in assets or those less than four years old must have a ratio of 10 percent. Special restrictions are placed on very small CUs not meeting the 10 percent requirement.

In addition, the NCUA uses the *Early Warning System (EWS)* to work with individual institutions before capital ratios reach the point of insolvency. Under EWS, examiners

classify CUs into one of five safety and soundness categories, based in part on capital adequacy. Many of the "problem" institutions identified through the Early Warning System are small—in 1985 almost half of them had assets of less than $1 million. For the most part, regulators attempt to handle insolvencies through merger with larger institutions. In addition, they have issued warnings against excessive growth attained by paying above-market rates to attract savings. Because those funds must be reinvested at even higher rates, the

NCUA is concerned that CUs will select high-risk assets, resulting in excessive losses.[30]

Are Capital Standards Equitable?

An unresolved issue is whether different capital requirements for different types of depositories are fair. Commercial banks, on which the highest standards are imposed, argue that they are not. Savings institutions and CUs counter that their assets are less subject to default risk than those of banks, and therefore the lower capital requirements are justified. That argument ignores the fact that there are other sources of capital erosion besides loan losses. Until these questions of fairness are resolved to the satisfaction of regulators and depositories alike, proposals to consolidate the federal regulatory agencies, such as those mentioned in Chapter 2, are unlikely to progress.

MANAGEMENT OF CAPITAL: GROWTH

For operational as well as for regulatory reasons, no manager can ignore capital requirements. The rest of the chapter discusses several specific management problems. They include estimating the rate at which capital can be generated from operations without need of external sources; estimating the cost of capital in long-term planning; and, for stockholder-owned firms, evaluating the impact of dividend policy.

Estimating the Rate of Capital Growth from Operations

It may be difficult to generate capital externally because the reception of the financial markets may be uncertain (or even nonexistent in the case of CUs) and existing shareholders may object to a dilution of their claims on the institution. To be sure of meeting capital requirements, managers often prefer to generate capital by increasing net worth through retained

earnings. That requires an understanding of some fundamental financial relationships between growth, the net interest margin, and the return on net worth.

What Is Growth in Net Worth?   Assuming the use of book values, the rate of growth in net worth (g_{NW}) from one period to the next can be defined as $\Delta NW/NW$. (NW represents net worth.) If no funds are raised externally, any additions (ΔNW) must come from net income for the period, less any dividends (DIV) that are paid:

(16.1) $\Delta NW = NI - DIV$

Thus, the rate of growth in net worth is tied to dividend policy in shareholder-owned firms, a topic considered later.

From the definition of return on net worth (NI/NW), another relationship emerges:

(16.2) $NW = NI/RONW$

Substituting Equations 16.1 and 16.2 in the definition of g_{NW} ($\Delta NW/NW$) and simplifying:

(16.3) $g_{NW} = \Delta NW/NW$
$= RONW \times (NI - DIV)/NI$

The ratio $(NI - DIV)/NI$ is the percentage of net income retained in the institution, or the *retention rate*. Internally generated growth in net worth is a function of the expected RONW and the expected retention rate. The higher the expected return, or the greater the proportion of earnings retained, the greater the growth of internally generated capital. If return on net worth is expected to be 16 percent, and if 60 percent of net earnings will be retained, g_{NW} will be $16\% \times 0.60 = 9.6\%$. A more difficult task is setting and achieving targets for the two decision variables—RONW and the rate of retention.

Growth and the Net Interest Margin.   In Chapter 13, it is shown that a depository's target NIM is a function of its target RONW, its

---

[30]NCUA, *1984 Annual Report*, pp. 16, 30.

capital position (as measured by the reciprocal of the equity multiplier), and net noninterest expenses:

(13.2)

$$\frac{IR - IE}{TA} = \left(\frac{NI}{NW} \times \frac{NW}{TA} \times \frac{1}{1 - t} \right) + \frac{NIE}{TA}$$

Although Equation 13.2 was used as a planning tool to set *ex ante* targets, the relationships also hold *ex post:* if the target NIM is not achieved, neither RONW nor capital adequacy targets will be achieved. And, because growth in net worth is related to RONW (Equation 16.3), if NIM is not managed skillfully, the institution's net worth position may fail to grow as planned.

Importance of the Rate of Internal Capital Growth

Planning for g_{NW} is important because if external sources of capital are unavailable or undesirable, the rate of growth in net worth determines how much the depository's liabilities and assets can grow without violating capital adequacy standards. It does little good to plan an ambitious campaign to increase deposits or loans by 25 percent if the expected rate of capital growth is too low to support such a program. In fact, if existing ratios of capital to assets or capital to liabilities are exactly equal to required ratios, asset and liability growth must be no greater than the expected rate of capital growth. Otherwise, capital standards will be violated. If existing ratios exceed requirements, the institution can support a higher level of asset and liability growth. If the institution is approaching required capital standards from a deficient position, asset and liability growth must be lower than growth in net worth.

Limitations placed on the institution by the expected rate of growth in net worth are especially significant in depositories because they have less control over growth in their liabilities, and thus the offsetting growth in assets, than many other businesses. The interest institutions pay on many deposit accounts is automatically reinvested by account holders. Thus, if an S&L paid an average of 10.5 percent annually on deposits, and if all depositors reinvested their interest, deposits would grow by 10.5 percent even if the institution made no effort to attract new funds. Assets would automatically grow by a slightly lower percentage, depending upon the total assets/deposits ratio. Unless net worth is expected to grow by at least 10.5 percent, the capital ratios of the S&L would deteriorate over time. Because g_{NW} depends upon the rate the institution earns on existing net worth, which depends upon the net interest margin, managing the NIM is the key.

Growth and Capital Adequacy: An Example

Table 16.3 presents a condensed balance sheet and income statement for Giantcorp; data are simplified from a recent annual report of one of the largest BHCs. Table 16.4 uses data from Table 16.3 and the growth relationships discussed earlier. All calculations assume that the RONW and dividend payout of the institution will remain unchanged from current levels, so these data are used to estimate growth for the next year.

Because the institution has issued redeemable preferred stock, which is not considered a permanent source of net worth, the numerator of RONW is earnings available to common shareholders, measured as net income less preferred dividends ($890,000,000 − $56,000,000), not net income. Of that amount, $263,000,000 was paid to common shareholders, for a retention rate of 68.47 percent. Assuming those rates will continue, g_{NW} can be projected, using Equation 16.3, as 9.87 percent.

Before the dollar growth rate in assets can be calculated, a growth rate in liabilities is estimated. Suppose it is 10.25 percent for Giantcorp, resulting in projected growth in liabilities of $14,842,000,000. The total dollar growth in assets is $15,413,000,000—the sum of expected increases in liabilities and net worth. Because the growth rate in assets (10.24 percent) exceeds the expected growth rate in net worth, the capital position of Giantcorp de-

Table 16.3
Selected Financial Information for Giantcorp
(Millions)

Assets		Liabilities and Equity	
Cash and deposits at other banks	$ 14,285	Deposits	$ 90,349
Securities and federal funds	16,808	Other liabilities and long-term debt	52,110
Loans and leases	102,707	Convertible notes	12
Other assets	14,646	Subordinated debt	1,649
Premises	2,140	Redeemable preferred stock	680
		Total liabilities	$144,800
		Common stock (par and surplus)	$ 1,514
		Retained earnings	4,637
		Less Treasury stock	(365)
		Total equity	$ 5,786
Total assets	$150,586	Total liabilities and equity	$150,586

Income and Dividends

Interest revenue	$18,194
Interest expense	(13,875)
NIM	$ 4,319
Loan loss expense	(619)
NIM after loan losses	$ 3,700
Net nonoperating income and expense	(2,156)
Income before taxes	$ 1,544
Taxes	(654)
Net income	$ 890
Preferred stock dividends	56
Earnings available to common shareholders	$ 834
Common stock dividends	$ 263

clines. The reason is that the growth in liabilities is expected to exceed the growth in net worth. Because the institution is highly leveraged, the growth rate in assets is greatly influenced by the expected growth in liabilities.

The asset growth rate could also be calculated directly as a weighted average of the growth rates of liabilities and net worth:

(16.4) $g_A = w_L g_L + w_{NW} g_{NW}$

where:

w_L = percentage of assets financed by liabilities; and

w_{NW} = percentage of assets financed by net worth.

In this example:

$$g_A = 0.9616(10.25\%) + 0.0384(9.87\%)$$
$$= 10.24\%$$

Table 16.4
Expected Growth in Net Worth and Capital Adequacy (Millions)

Return on net worth: ($890 − $56)/$5,786	14.41%
Retention rate: ($834 − $263)/$834	68.47%
Net worth/assets ratio: $5,786/$150,586	3.84%
Net worth/liabilities ratio: $5,786/$144,800	4.00%
Liabilities/assets ratio: $144,800/$150,586	96.16%

Projections for Next Year:

Expected rate of growth in net worth: (g = RONW × Retention Rate)	9.87%
Expected dollar growth in net worth: 0.0987 × $5,786	$ 571
Total net worth, year-end	$ 6,357
Growth in liabilities (assumed at a rate of 10.25%):	
Expected dollar growth in liabilities: 0.1025 × $144,800	$ 14,842
Total liabilities, year-end	$159,642
Growth in assets:	
Expected dollar growth in assets: $571 + $14,842	$ 15,413
Expected growth rate in assets: $15,413/$150,586	10.24%
Total assets, year-end	$165,999
Expected net worth/assets ratio	3.83%
Expected net worth/liabilities ratio	3.98%
Expected liabilities/assets ratio	96.17%

Planning for Growth

The expected decrease in an already low capital/assets ratio can be prevented in several ways, if it is anticipated.

Increase the Retention Rate. Managers can try to increase the rate of internal growth. Because g_{NW} is determined by RONW and by the rate of retention, the firm could retain a greater proportion of earnings. This may displease shareholders, who may have come to expect a certain level of dividends, but it may be less painful than other alternatives.

Increase Earnings or Decrease Deposit and Loan Growth. Managers can try to increase RONW. Increased asset yields, reduced interest expense, or better control of noninterest costs could result in a higher RONW. Of course, these strategies carry risks. Pursuing higher asset yields usually means accepting greater risk. Reducing interest costs may be a more promising strategy; a decision to pay lower rates on deposits might lead some depositors to defect to competitors. If so, not only will interest costs be reduced, but the rate of growth in assets and liabilities will be slowed as funds are withdrawn. Together, these developments could result in improved capital ratios by the end of the next year.

The risk with this strategy would be to force such a high proportion of withdrawals that a liquidity crisis is provoked, although lowering rates on only the least interest-sensitive accounts would probably prevent this. Further, if the institution does not actively plan for growth, some borrowers may be denied loan funds. To avoid the potential clash between capital adequacy and growth, some institutions have used fees generated by off-balance sheet liabilities to increase income without increasing liabilities and assets, a strategy addressed by banking regulators' supplemental capital measures.

Raise External Capital. Finally, capital could be raised externally to supplement the expected $571 million increase in retained earnings during the next year. This approach has its risks, too, because market reception is uncertain. Existing shareholders might object to the sale of additional stock, especially in small, closely held institutions. For mutual institutions, of course, mutual capital certificates or subordinated notes and debentures are the only types of securities available. Some mutual organizations, concerned about their limited access to external capital, have converted to stock ownership. As discussed in Chapter 3, however, conversion is part of a long-run strategic plan, not a short-run adjustment, as is needed in the Giantcorp example.

Growth and Capital Adequacy: A Revised Plan

Specific actions would be based on the risk/return preferences of managers and owners; in cases such as Giantcorp, when capital ratios are relatively low already, the regulators might have a suggestion or two. In any case, a range of options is available to managers who understand the relationship between growth and capital adequacy. Suppose managers decide to lower the rate paid on MMDAs, and to limit common stock dividends to 20 percent of earn-ings available next year. The lower MMDA rate is expected to increase RONW to 15 percent, and to decrease the growth in liabilities to 9 percent. Table 16.5 presents estimates of expected capital ratios under these new assumptions.

The revised plan should result in a higher net worth/assets ratio. If the increase is insufficient to satisfy managers, owners, or regulators, plans to raise capital externally can be made, or further changes in operating plans can be considered.

MANAGEMENT OF CAPITAL: COST OF CAPITAL

Another capital-related concept of concern to many managers is the **cost of capital,** or the weighted average rate of return expected by suppliers of new long-term funds. Because their expected return is a cost to the institution, the phrase *cost of capital* connotes an insider's look at the issue. As the phrase is defined here, it is distinguished from the **cost of funds,** or the weighted average cost of *all* sources of funds in a depository, including deposits, nondeposit liabilities, and capital.

Cost of Capital versus Cost of Funds

For an institution to operate successfully in the long run, the average yield on its total asset portfolio must equal or exceed the average cost of all funds. Some theorists, therefore, do not distinguish between the cost of capital and the overall cost of funds, arguing that the latter is the only relevant cost. It is certainly true that overall funds costs are important, and discussions of the NIM throughout the book emphasize that asset returns must exceed the cost of deposits and liabilities *and* provide a target return on net worth.

Nonetheless, many argue for the need to identify the cost of long-term funds, or capital, separately. In some institutions, the cost of capital is an important consideration in decisions concerning long-term nonfinancial assets, such as new office buildings, computer hardware, or

---

Table 16.5
Expected Growth in Net Worth and Capital Adequacy: Revised Plan

Net worth/assets ratio:	
$5,786/$150,586	3.84%
Net worth/liabilities ratio:	
$5,786/$144,800	4.00%
Liabilities/assets ratio:	
$144,800/$150,586	96.16%

New Projections:

Expected rate of growth in net worth:	
(g = RONW × Retention Rate)	
(15% × 80%)	12.00%
Expected dollar growth in net worth:	
0.12 × $5,786	$ 694
Total net worth, year-end	$ 6,480
Growth in liabilities (assumed at 9.00%):	
Expected dollar growth in liabilities:	
0.09 × $144,800	$ 13,032
Total liabilities, year-end	$157,832
Growth in assets:	
Expected dollar growth in assets:	
$694 + $13,032	$ 13,726
Expected growth rate in assets:	
$13,726/$150,586	9.12%
Total assets, year-end	$164,312
Expected net worth/assets ratio	3.94%
Expected net worth/liabilities ratio	4.11%
Expected liabilities/assets ratio	96.06%

---

electronic funds transfer equipment—decisions that are the subject of Chapter 19. According to this belief, the need to identify a cost of capital is based on the first function of capital: to serve as the source of funds for fixed, noninterest-bearing assets required to operate and expand over time.[31] The depository must therefore estimate the yield current investors require to justify continued investment and new investors

require to supply additional funds. Although its use is controversial, managers should understand how the cost of capital is calculated and applied in some institutions.

Conceptual Issues

Calculating the cost of capital requires assimilating concepts already discussed at several points in the book.

Expected Yields.   The first is the concept of expected annual yields, illustrated at length in Chapter 4. Because there are several sources of capital, each with different characteristics, it would be wrong to use the expected annual

---

[31]For a practitioner's discussion of the importance of identifying the cost of capital, see Robert D. Perry, "The Cost of Capital," *Magazine of Bank Administration* 58 (February 1982): 26-31. For a theoretical treatment of the cost of capital versus the overall cost of funds, see John M. Mason, *Financial Management of Commercial Banks* (Boston: Warren, Gorham, and Lamont, 1979), pp. 228-232.

yield of preferred shareholders, for example, as *the* cost of capital to the institution. Instead, a weighted average annual yield expected by all sources of capital is more appropriate. Management can estimate the yields current bondholders, preferred stockholders, and common stockholders expect, using the same data investors themselves use. Suppliers of new capital will certainly be unwilling to accept yields lower than those on existing capital, so existing yields are good starting points for estimating the marginal cost of new long-term funds.

Effect of Taxes.   Taxation must also be considered. Banks and S&Ls can deduct interest paid to bondholders from income *before* taxes, effectively reducing the required cash outflow. As a result, the cost of long-term borrowed funds is lower than the expected yield to bondholders, a fact to be considered in estimating the weighted average cost of capital. The issue is irrelevant for credit unions, because they pay no taxes. In addition, CUs do not consider long-term borrowings as capital.

Effect of Capital Structure.   A third factor in the cost of capital is the institution's *capital structure,* the mix of long-term debt, preferred and common equity that compose total capital. The existence of an *optimal capital structure*— one that maximizes the value of the institution's publicly traded securities—is controversial among finance theorists and practitioners.[32] On the one hand, the tax deductibility of interest on debt makes debt relatively cheap. Shareholders benefit from the cash saved and may value the firm's stock more highly. On the other hand, using too much debt exposes the institution to potential insolvency. Shareholders and bondholders may both consider their securities less valuable as the risk of insolvency becomes too great.

The concept of an optimal capital structure implies that there is a judicious mix of debt and equity capital that allows a firm to avoid the hazards associated with either extreme, as illustrated in Figure 16.10. The total value of the firm's capital is lower when the ratio of debt to total capital is either too low or too high. Within a certain range, however, the value of the firm's securities is maximized.

Depositories Are Different.   In theory, if an optimal capital structure exists, managers should attempt to find it by changing the capital structure and observing market response to incremental changes. In practice, capital structure decisions in many depositories are decided on less theoretical grounds. For one thing, regulatory requirements constrain the capital mix within certain ranges, and regulators' decisions may or may not be optimal from an individual depository's point of view. In addition, lack of access to financial markets renders market-directed attempts to find an optimal capital structure impossible for many depositories. Preferences of managers, owners, and regulators are likely to be the deciding factors. Thus, an institution may achieve a *target capital structure* (one that is an established managerial objective) but not a theoretically optimal capital structure (one that maximizes the value of the firm's capital).

Even so, whether an optimal capital structure exists for depositories is not an irrelevant question. The search for an answer may lead regulators to make better decisions about capital adequacy and lead managers to make better operating decisions. Given current knowledge and regulatory policies, however, the search for an optimal capital structure in many depositories may not be fruitful.

[32]A substantial portion of many corporate finance courses is spent on capital structure analysis, including conflicting theories on the existence of an optimal capital structure. Not only is the conflict unresolved after several decades, there is additional controversy about the applicability of these theories to regulated financial institutions. This material will not be reviewed here. Three good treatments of the capital structure decision in non-financial corporations can be found in Richard Brealey and Stewart Myers, *Principles of Corporate Finance,* 2d ed. (New York: McGraw-Hill, 1984), Chapters 17 and 18; Eugene F. Brigham and Louis C. Gapenski, *Intermediate Financial Management,* 2d ed. (Hinsdale, IL: The Dryden Press, 1987), Chapters 5 and 6; James C. Van Horne, *Financial Management and Policy,* 7th ed. (Englewood Cliffs, NJ: Prentice-Hall, Inc., 1986), Chapters 9 and 10. Each of these texts provides numerous references to original research.

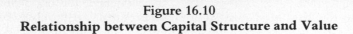

Figure 16.10
Relationship between Capital Structure and Value

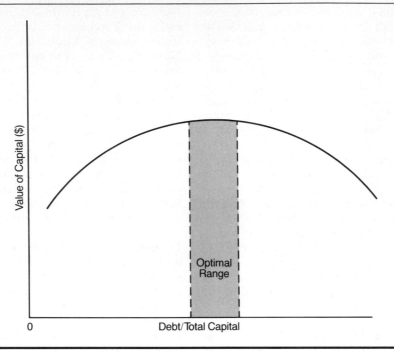

Effect of Mutual Ownership. Finally, a question arises about the relevance of calculating a "cost" of capital in mutually owned or not-for-profit depositories. Because new capital arises primarily from additions to retained earnings, it is tempting to think that retaining earnings is costless. In a deregulated environment, however, it is a mistake to consider earnings retained as having no marginal cost to the institution's owners-depositors or members. Every dollar retained in the institution is a dollar unavailable to depositors or members, on which they could earn at least the "going rate" on MMDAs or CDs. Thus, raising new funds by retaining earnings has an opportunity cost that management cannot ignore.

Calculating the Cost of Capital

The definition of the cost of capital implicitly contains its formula. Because the cost of capital is the weighted average cost of long-term sources of funds, its calculation is a weighted average of the yields expected by suppliers of capital, adjusted for tax differences between the institution and investors. The weights assigned to each yield are the proportions of the target-capital structure devoted to a particular source of funds:

(16.5) $\quad k_A = \sum_{i=1}^{n} w_i k_i$

The w_i are the weights of each source of capital, and the k_i, the costs. Because of tax-deductible interest costs in banks and thrifts, the expected return to investors (y^*) must be reduced to estimate k_D, the marginal after-tax cost of debt capital:

(16.6) $\quad k_D = y_D^*(1 - t)$

Table 16.6 contains a sample calculation for Giantcorp, for which financial data are given in Table 16.3. It is assumed that effective annual yields on each source of capital (y_i^*) have been determined using formulas from Chapter 4. In addition, the institution's existing capital structure is assumed to be its target capital structure. If the mix of capital changes, future weights should be used to calculate the marginal cost of capital.

The first step is to identify the institution's sources of capital and to determine their weight in the total capital structure. Expected annual yields (y_i^*) for the various sources of funds are then estimated; the input data are not shown here. Next, factors causing the depository's costs to differ from investors' expected yields, such as the tax deductibility of interest on debt, must be considered. Finally, the costs are weighted and summed to obtain the weighted average marginal cost of capital, or the expected annual cost to the firm of raising new capital. If, in the future, investors' expected yields change because the riskiness of the institution changes, or if the target capital structure changes, k_A must be reestimated.

In mutual or not-for-profit firms, the major cost to be considered is the cost of net worth. As suggested earlier, the opportunity cost (analogous to y^*) of the institution's decision to retain earnings would be, at a minimum, the market rate on long-term risk free investments such as T-bonds or CDs. The appropriate weight would be the weight of reserves and undivided earnings in the institution's total capital structure. To estimate k_A, that weighted cost would then be summed along with the cost of mutual capital certificates, preferred stock, subordinated notes and debentures, or other sources of capital in the target capital structure.

MANAGEMENT OF CAPITAL: DIVIDEND POLICY

The final issues addressed in this chapter are those surrounding the payment of dividends by stockholder-owned depositories. No policy decision is required for preferred stock dividends. They must be paid as scheduled, or no dividends can be declared for common shareholders. Dividend policy decisions, then, really revolve around what proportion of earnings available to common shareholders should be retained versus paid in dividends.

Table 16.6
Calculating the Weighted Average Marginal Cost of Capital for Giantcorp

Source of Capital	Amount (Millions)	w_i	y^*	k_i	Weighted Cost
Convertible notes	$ 12	0.15%	11.50%	7.59%	0.01%
Subordinated debt	1,649	20.29	12.50	8.25	1.67
Redeemable preferred stock	680	8.37	14.00	14.00	1.17
Common equity	5,786	71.19	18.50	18.50	13.17
Total capital	$8,127	100.00%			16.03% ⟶ k_A

Notes:
1. The current capital structure is the target capital structure.

2. Giantcorp's marginal tax rate is 34%; thus, the after-tax annual cost of debt capital is $y^* \times (1 - t)$, where t is the institution's marginal tax rate. For example:

$$k_D = y_D^*(1 - t) = 11.50\%(1 - .34) = 7.59\%$$

3. $k_A = \sum_{i=1}^{n} w_i k_i$

Dividend Decisions as Financing Decisions

A full examination of the controversy on common stock dividend policy is beyond the scope of this text. The academic literature is full of theoretical and empirical analyses, although no consensus has been reached on the optimal policy. At issue is whether some dividend policies are favored by the financial markets, leading to increases in the value of the firm's stock. One theory holds that investors prefer cash dividends to capital gains after a firm reinvests earnings. An opposing view holds that investors are concerned with returns on the firm's assets and are indifferent between receiving benefits from these earnings as current cash dividends or future capital gains.[33]

Regardless of the resolution of the controversy, an important point holds. Every dollar paid in dividends is a dollar unavailable to meet capital requirements and support growth. The division of net income between dividends and retained earnings is really a decision about how to finance the institution.

Dividends as Residuals

Because paying dividends reduces cash available for investment in additional assets, one principle managers sometimes use in setting dividend policy is whether the institution has reinvestment opportunities superior to those available to individual shareholders. If so, earnings should be retained; if not, cash dividends should be paid. This principle implies that dividends are a residual of asset portfolio decisions. If strictly followed, a *residual dividend policy* could result in an erratic stream of dividends over time, depending upon the firm's investment opportunities from year to year. The concept of dividends as a residual must be balanced against other factors.

---

[33]Discussions of the dividend policy controversy can be found in Brealey and Myers, *Principles of Corporate Finance,* Chapter 16; Brigham and Gapenski, *Intermediate Financial Management,* Chapter 11; and Van Horne, *Financial Management and Policy,* Chapter 11. Again, many references to original research are provided.

Information Content of Dividends

In recommending a dividend policy to the board of directors, which legally authorizes dividend payments, managers must understand another key point. Current dividends have *information content*: Changes in dividends often signal changes in the firm's future earnings prospects. Unexpected dividend changes from quarter to quarter and year to year, the likely result of following a residual dividend policy exclusively, are undesirable.

To avoid conveying unintended messages to shareholders, many managers prefer to compromise between paying out cash only if there are no investments to be made, and paying out so much cash that future earnings of the firm are impaired. The results of the compromise are seen in *increasing-stream dividend policies.* Under these policies, stable or gently rising dividends per share are observed over time. The pattern is interrupted only if long-term changes are anticipated in the firm's prospects.

Regulation and Dividend Policy

In addition to considering the institution's investment opportunities and the information content of dividends, managers of depository institutions know that the payment of cash dividends is constrained by capital adequacy requirements and other regulatory pressures. Recently, for example, federal banking regulators publicly warned against the payment of high cash dividends in certain economic environments and threatened enforcement actions against institutions defying their advice.[34] Because there are over 14,000 commercial banks, it is likely that statements such as these influence some banks to retain earnings even if they cannot be invested to earn a marginal return as high as shareholders could earn by investing cash dividends. In addition, management's ability to use dividends as a signal about a firm's future prospects is impaired. This incident em-

---

[34]Leon E. Wynter, "Regulators Warn Banks on Dividends, Urge Use of Profits to Shore Up Capital," *The Wall Street Journal,* November 4, 1985, p. 8.

phasizes the fact that policies regulators believe are socially optimal may not be optimal for an individual depository and its shareholders.

Dividend Policies in Commercial Banks

Several studies of the dividend policies of commercial banks have been published. According to a recent survey, the most important influence on bank managers was the desire to maintain stable or increasing dividend streams. The idea that dividends are residuals was not supported by statements of respondents. Researchers noted, however, that dividends were lower in regions with high economic growth rates, suggesting that the residual principle was implicitly influencing dividend decisions. No evidence is available on the dividend policies of stockholder-owned thrifts.[35]

SUMMARY

Capital is the permanent financing of a depository. Controversies exist about what should be considered capital, how much a depository

should have, and its role in asset/liability management. Most experts agree, however, that capital supports confidence in the financial stability of a business organization, supports growth, and reduces moral hazard.

Sources of capital to depository institutions include traditional ones, such as common or preferred stock, retained earnings, and long-term debt. Recent regulatory policies have introduced nontraditional sources, such as mutual capital certificates, net worth certificates, and appraised equity capital. Controversy continues over standards for capital adequacy. Two topics of debate are whether capital should be measured at book or market value, and whether it should be compared to balance sheet measures or income/loss measures. Generally, regulators across depository institution industries have agreed to disagree; different standards exist for FDIC- and FSLIC-insured institutions, and for credit unions. The variations in requirements across industries have led some to question whether the regulatory system is equitable.

There is no question, however, that managers must meet the standards explicitly imposed by regulators and implicitly influenced by owners. Managing the net worth position is closely tied to other targets, such as the net interest margin. In addition, as managers plan for growth in assets and liabilities, they must also plan for growth in net worth. Finally, managing capital involves understanding its cost, as well as its relationship to the firm's dividend policy.

[35]James C. Van Horne and Raymond C. Helwig, "Patterns in Bank Dividend Policy," *Bankers Magazine* 150 (Spring 1967): 61-65; Manak C. Gupta and David A. Walker, "Dividend Dispersal Practices in Commercial Banking," *Journal of Financial and Quantitative Analysis* 10 (September 1975): 515-529; William F. Kennedy and David F. Scott, Jr., "Some Observations on the Dividend Policies of Large Commercial Banks," *Journal of Bank Research* 13 (Winter 1983): 292-296.

Questions

1. What needs of depository institutions does capital fulfill? How does capital promote confidence in an institution?

2. Explain why a positive relationship exists between the amount of an institution's capital and the degree of protection for the deposit or share insurance funds.

3. What are mutual capital certificates (MCCs)? How effective have they been in improving capital positions of mutual institutions?

4. Under what circumstances do the FSLIC and FDIC offer net worth certificates to thrifts? Explain the mechanics of a net worth certificate. Do you think regulators and Congress were correct to permit this form of net worth? If so, why? If not, what alternatives would you suggest to improve the capital position of the thrift industry?

5. Define appraised equity capital. Explain why accountants do not approve of it. Why does the FHLBB permit its use? Do you think it is appropriate? Why or why not?

6. For thrifts, what are the components of regulatory net worth? Of tangible net worth? What advantages are offered to thrifts through regulatory net worth?

7. Should regulators and professional accountants have different accounting standards? Why or why not? Should commercial bank accounting standards differ from thrift or credit union accounting methods? Why or why not?

8. Theoretically, is book value or market value a better measure of capital? Why? Which is used more often in practice? Why?

9. Under what conditions does a depository institution's long-term debt qualify as capital? Do you agree that subordinated debt fulfills the functions of capital? Why or why not?

10. Explain the difference between primary capital and secondary capital as defined by commercial bank regulators. How do federal bank regulators treat goodwill in the definition of capital? What is the rationale for this treatment?

11. Compare the balance sheet measures used by banks, thrifts, and credit union regulators to assess capital adequacy. Should they be different? If so, why? If not, which measures should all institutions use?

12. Explain the idea behind supplemental risk-adjusted capital measures. How do they differ from traditional measures of capital adequacy? Identify several off-balance sheet items and explain why federal regulators believe they pose risks from which depositors must be protected.

13. Discuss advantages and disadvantages of allowing the financial markets to determine adequate capital for an institution. Is it a feasible process? An optimal one? Why do you think many managers of depository institutions have opposed additional disclosure of information, especially information discussed in routine regulatory examinations?

14. In 1985 and 1986, *The Wall Street Journal* and *Business Week* reported that some commercial banks were responding to increased capital requirements by reducing asset size rather than increasing capital. As a result, higher-risk borrowers were denied loans. Are higher capital standards for all institutions unfair to some segments of society? Why or why not?

15. How can a depository institution internally generate increases in net worth? If a decrease in the capital/assets ratio is expected, what options are available to prevent the decline? What risks, if any, are there in each strategy?

16. Distinguish between the terms *cost of capital* and *cost of funds*. Why must financial managers understand both terms? Do mutually owned and not-for-profit institutions have a cost of capital? Explain.

17. What factors affect capital structure decisions for depository institutions?

18. Explain why the dividend policy decision of a financial institution is a financing decision. What is a residual dividend policy? If dividends are treated as a pure residual, what other dividend considerations are ignored?

Problems

1. Based on the following information, measure the capital adequacy of Jefferson Bank using both the ratio of primary capital to total assets and the supplemental adjusted capital ratio illustrated in Table 16.2. Primary capital is $60,000,000.

Assets (Thousands)	
Cash	$ 10,000
Short-term Treasury securities	28,000
Long-term Treasury securities	243,500
Municipal bonds	123,000
Other long-term securities	50,000
Consumer loans	200,000
Commercial loans	320,000

Risk Category	Off-Balance Sheet Items in Category
Cash and equivalents	$ 2,000
Money market risk	75,000
Moderate risk	150,000
Standard risk	157,500

2. Consider the balance sheet of Home Town Federal before application to the regulators for net worth assistance:

Home Town Federal Savings and Loan Balance Sheet

Assets		Liabilities and Net Worth	
$ 55,000,000	Securities	$246,250,000	Liabilities
195,000,000	Loans	5,250,000	Net Worth
1,500,000	Premises		
$251,500,000	Total	$251,500,000	Total

a. Illustrate Home Town's balance sheet after the issuance of $3,750,000 of net worth certificates from the FSLIC. Calculate the ratio of net worth to total assets before and after the transaction.

b. Suppose that, in addition, premises are reappraised at $2,500,000. Illustrate the new balance sheet and calculate the ratio of net worth to total assets.

3. The following book value balance sheet is available for Metropolitan Credit Union:

Assets		Liabilities and Net Worth	
$ 500,000	Cash	$40,500,000	Deposits
9,000,000	T-Bills	4,000,000	Net Worth
35,000,000	12% Loans		
$44,500,000	Total	$44,500,000	Total

All loans are consumer installment agreements, with an average maturity of 24 months; the credit union receives monthly payments on all of them.

a. If the current market rate on consumer loans is 10 percent, illustrate Metropolitan's balance sheet on a market-value basis. Compare market-value and book-value capital ratios.

b. Suppose, instead, that current market rates on consumer loans average 15 percent. Show the market-value balance sheet and the capital/assets ratio under this situation.

4. University National Bank is being purchased by an out-of-state bank. The balance sheets of University and the acquiring bank are presented here:

Book Value before Purchase:
University National Bank

Assets		Liabilities and Net Worth	
$ 5,000,000	Cash	$85,000,000	Deposits
21,000,000	Securities		
65,000,000	Loans	6,000,000	Net Worth
$91,000,000	Total	$91,000,000	Total

Acquiring Bank

Assets		Liabilities and Net Worth	
$ 15,000,000	Cash	$272,000,000	Deposits
50,000,000	Securities		
225,000,000	Loans	18,000,000	Net Worth
$290,000,000	Total	$290,000,000	Total

University's loans now have a market value of $54,000,000 because of an increase in the general level of interest rates. Prepare a balance sheet for the combined firm, showing the effect of goodwill. What is the ratio of net worth to total assets? What is the ratio of tangible net worth to total assets?

5. Butterfield National Bank, with total assets of $750 million and a net worth multiplier of 13, last year earned a RONW of 12 percent. Dividends were 45 percent of net income.
   a. What growth in net worth is expected?
   b. If deposits increase by 8.5 percent, what asset growth rate can be expected?
   c. If these projections materialize, will the net worth multiplier be higher or lower than 13 at the end of next year?

6. The management of First Federal S&L forecasts 20 percent growth in assets for the coming year, and 18 percent growth in liabilities. If the net worth/total assets ratio is now 5 percent, what rate of growth in net worth is anticipated for next year? Will the net worth multiplier increase, decrease, or remain the same?

7. American Banking Corporation is concerned about its capital adequacy. To better assess the position, management plans to estimate the rate of growth in assets for the coming year. An 11.2 percent growth in liabilities is projected, and the bank plans to maintain a stable dividend payout ratio. Last year, the firm earned net income of $15.6 million and paid dividends of $8.5 million. The following additional information is available:

   - Total assets: $1,370,000,000
   - Total liabilities: $1,281,000,000
   - Total net worth: $89,000,000

   a. Calculate the expected growth in net worth and assets.
   b. What ratio of capital to assets is expected by the end of the next year?
   c. If this ratio is unacceptably low to management, suggest ways to improve it.

8. The partial balance sheet of Bay City Bank and Trust is shown below (in thousands), along with other information:

Liabilities and Equity		Before-Tax Cost
Deposits	$1,336,393	8.08%
Fed funds	359,807	8.70
Long-term debt	54,350	9.70
Common equity	161,653	15.50
Total	$1,912,203	

Bay City is in the 34 percent marginal tax bracket.

a. Assuming the current capital structure is optimal, calculate Bay City's marginal cost of capital.

b. Calculate Bay City's cost of funds.

Selected References

Auerbach, Ronald P., and Alan S. McCall. "Permissive Accounting Practices Inflate Savings and Loan Industry Earnings and Net Worth." *Issues in Bank Regulation* 9 (Summer 1985): 17-21.

Brewer, Elijah III, and Cheng Few Lee. "How the Market Judges Bank Risk." *Economic Perspectives* (Federal Reserve Bank of Chicago) 10 (November/December 1986): 25-31.

Buser, Stephen A., Andrew H. Chen, and Edward J. Kane. "Federal Deposit Insurance, Regulatory Policy, and Optimal Bank Capital." *Journal of Finance* 36 (March 1981): 51-60.

Chessen, James. "Regulatory Proposals for a Supplemental-Adjusted-Capital Measure." *Banking and Economic Review* (Federal Deposit Insurance Corporation) 4 (March 1986): 11-17.

Eisenbeis, Robert A., and Gary G. Gilbert. "Market Discipline and the Prevention of Bank Problems and Failures." *Issues in Bank Regulation* 8 (Winter 1985): 16-23.

Forrestal, Robert P. "Bank Safety: Risks and Responsibilities." *Economic Review* (Federal Reserve Bank of Atlanta) 70 (August 1985): 4-12.

Gilbert, Gary G. "Disclosures and Market Discipline: Issues and Evidence." *Economic Review* 68 (Federal Reserve Bank of Atlanta) (November 1983): 70-76.

Gilbert, R. Alton, Courtenay C. Stone, and Michael E. Trebing. "The New Bank Capital Adequacy Standards." *Review* (Federal Reserve Bank of St. Louis) 67 (May 1985): 12-20.

Heggestad, Arnold A., and B. Frank King. "Regulation of Bank Capital: An Evaluation." *Economic Review* (Federal Reserve Bank of Atlanta) 67 (March 1982): 35-43.

Marcus, Alan J. "The Bank Capital Decision: A Time Series-Cross Section Analysis." *Journal of Finance* 38 (September 1983): 1217-32.

Mitchell, Karlyn. "Capital Adequacy at Commercial Banks." *Economic Review* (Federal Reserve Bank of Kansas City) 69 (September/October 1984): 17-30.

Perry, Robert D. "The Cost of Capital." *Magazine of Bank Administration* 58 (February 1982): 26-31.

Puglisi, Donald J., and Joseph A. McKenzie. "Capital Market Strategies for Thrift Institutions." *Federal Home Loan Bank Board Journal* 16 (November 1983): 2-8.

Santomero, Anthony M., and Ronald D. Watson. "Determining an Optimal Capital Standard for the Banking Industry." *Journal of Finance* 32 (September 1977): 1,267-1,282.

Shome, Dilip K., Stephen D. Smith, and Arnold A. Heggestad, "Capital Adequacy and the Valuation of Large Commercial Banking Organizations." *Journal of Financial Research* 9 (Winter 1986): 331-431.

Vojta, George J. *Bank Capital Adequacy.* New York: Citicorp, 1973.

Wall, Larry D. "Regulation of Banks' Equity Capital." *Economic Review* (Federal Reserve Bank of Atlanta) 70 (November 1985): 4-18.

Part IV

ASSET/LIABILITY MANAGEMENT IN DEPOSITORY INSTITUTIONS

Chapter 17

ASSET/LIABILITY MANAGEMENT: GAP ANALYSIS

It is terribly important that savings institutions begin to think match!

Edwin J. Gray, Chairman
Federal Home Loan Bank Board (1983)

IN the early 1980s, as interest rates hovered near record levels and changed almost daily, the wife of the chief economist of Philadelphia National Bank gave him a crystal ball for his desk. It symbolized his transition from author of an occasional economic newsletter for the bank's customers to a central player in its profitability plans. From that point, his chief responsibilities were forecasting the direction and magnitude of interest rate changes and advising management on the proper "GAP" to achieve in light of his forecasts.[1] What is a GAP? That is the major question addressed in this chapter.

Preceding chapters have established that individual decisions about investment in assets, types of funds sought, and capital position clearly affect a depository's performance. What has not yet been considered, however, is how asset and liability decisions combine to affect financial objectives.

---

[1]Richard F. Janssen, "Hedged Interest Rate Gap Is Strategy of Heebner at Philadelphia National," *The Wall Street Journal,* March 17, 1981, p. 6.

THE NEED FOR AN INTEGRATED POLICY

The net interest margin reflects the joint impact of asset and liability decisions because its numerator, the spread (IR − IE), is affected by both sides of the balance sheet. The targeted level for NIM and RONW cannot be achieved if management makes investment decisions without being sensitive to the nature of funds sources, or if deposits and other liabilities are acquired without some assurance that they can be invested profitably. Managers must simultaneously consider credit risk, which affects asset yields and liability costs, and interest rate risk, which is related to the relative maturities of assets and liabilities and affects the variability of returns.

High-Cost Funds and Credit Risk

Suppose an institution adopts a growth strategy based on an aggressive liability management policy of raising funds in the negotiable CD market. If the institution is smaller than competitors, uninsured depositors may perceive it as more risky and require it to offer a higher rate of interest. Recognizing this, managers face a major difficulty: Investment choices must reflect an acceptable level of risk exposure, but must contribute enough to the spread to enable the institution to achieve its NIM and RONW targets. Obviously, then, a liability management policy must be consistent with the firm's investment policies.

Unfortunately, recent financial history is littered with stories of depositories whose managers ignored the relationships between institutional risk, yields on assets, and liability costs. The failure of Oklahoma City's Penn Square Bank in 1982 provides an excellent example of the perils involved. In an effort to increase its asset size rapidly, the bank's chief lending officers garnered funds at increasingly higher costs in the negotiable CD market. These funds were then placed almost entirely in supposedly high-yielding energy-related loans—loans on which high rates were charged because, in many cases, the borrowers' capacities to repay were ques-

tionable. As the institution's loan losses mounted, wary depositors withdrew funds from Penn Square in numbers sufficient to create a liquidity crisis for the bank. The FDIC closed the bank, and uninsured depositors faced substantial losses.[2]

A similar example in the thrift industry is the failure of Beverly Hills Savings and Loan in 1985. The S&L undertook an aggressive growth strategy, relied heavily on high-cost brokered deposits, and selected risky real estate investments and junk bonds to boost asset returns. Representatives of the Federal Home Loan Bank Board described the institution's investment policies as "questionable" when combined with management's decisions to depend on purchased money as a major source of funds.[3]

Relative Asset and Liability Maturities

Severe maturity mismatches can undermine NIM and RONW performance just as readily as mismanaging default risk in the asset/liability portfolio, as many S&Ls discovered during recent periods of high interest rates and high volatility. Although successful for many years, the traditional S&L practice of holding long-term mortgages financed by short-term funds was not viable as short-term rates increased in the late 1970s. S&Ls, protected by government regulations, had ignored a longstanding tenet of financial management, **the hedging principle.**

The hedging principle suggests that a firm should finance long-term or permanent assets with long-term sources of funds, and short-term or temporary assets with short-term

---

[2]The causes of the Penn Square failure should not be oversimplified; after its failure, Penn Square's executives were accused of questionable practices that extended beyond their poor asset/liability management decisions. An assessment of the costs of the Penn Square failure was presented in G. Christian Hill, "Losses from Penn Square Bank's Failure Total $1.22 Billion and Are Still Growing," The Wall Street Journal, April 12, 1984.

[3]See Bruce Ingersoll and Edward Pound, "Regulators Didn't Heed Signs of Trouble at Beverly Hills S&L, Probe Indicates," The Wall Street Journal, June 19, 1985, p. 14.

sources of funds. One objective of this principle is to protect against illiquidity by ensuring that a firm invests in assets that will provide cash when it is needed to retire liabilities. Another objective, particularly applicable to financial institutions, is to protect against insolvency, which occurs when the value of assets falls below the value of liabilities.

In the early 1980s, savings institutions, relying on passbook or other short-term deposits to finance investments in long-term mortgages, fell victim to negative spreads when liability costs increased much more rapidly than asset returns. Of course, at the time, many thrifts operated under such inflexible portfolio regulations that it would have been virtually impossible to match maturities. But even under regulations permitting greater use of short-term assets, savings institutions have moved cautiously toward balance sheet restructuring and still face risks produced by their maturity mismatches.

Commercial banks and credit unions, on the other hand, have traditionally had more closely matched asset/liability portfolio maturities. Their emphasis on shorter-term commercial and consumer loans limited their exposure to interest rate risk arising from maturity mismatches. Still, the balance sheets of banks and CUs are by no means perfectly matched, and their managers, too, must understand the consequences of mismatching on risk and financial performance.

the maturity of available funds sources may not be wise either, because such adjustments might result in the acquisition of assets that are unacceptably risky. For example, a mortgage lender with most of its deposits in NOWs and MMDAs would not find many borrowers if it offered only short-term mortgages. Even if it did, requiring all borrowers to repay mortgages rapidly might subject the institution to excessive loan losses. Although management can exercise some discretion in adjusting the composition of assets and liabilities, there are limits to the degree to which the hedging principle can serve as an absolute guide to asset/liability concerns.

Fortunately, in recent years several complementary strategies for addressing the problems of asset/liability management have been developed. One of these strategies requires actively managing the composition of both asset and liability portfolios. Following this approach, managers adjust portfolios in response to economic conditions and interest rate forecasts to prevent undesirable imbalances between asset and liability maturities. Other strategies rely on tools for managing interest rate risk (introduced in earlier chapters), such as duration analysis, financial futures, and options, as alternatives to balance sheet restructuring. In fact, many managers use all of these strategies at one time or another. The remainder of this chapter focuses on principles of balance sheet restructuring. Chapter 18 considers risk management tools to supplement that restructuring.

ALTERNATIVES FOR ASSET/LIABILITY MANAGEMENT

What strategies do depository institutions have to control their exposure to these dangers? Would it be feasible, for example, for an S&L to find enough long-term funds to support all of its mortgage investments? Could a credit union always sell three-month CDs to support its three-month loans, or four-year CDs to fund all of its four-year automobile loans?

It is unlikely that funds with the preferred maturity will always be available on acceptable terms. Adjusting the loan portfolio to match

MONITORING THE BALANCE SHEET: GAP ANALYSIS

The first step in restructuring the balance sheet to manage interest rate risk is to focus attention on the *interest rate characteristics* of an institution's sources and uses of funds. If a depository selects assets and liabilities that are repriced on a similar schedule, even if their contractual maturities differ, it should be possible to earn a positive spread and maintain a reasonably stable NIM and RONW despite interest rate variability. For example, variable-rate mortgages are designed to keep asset returns in line with the cost of funds, even though the mortgages themselves have long-term contractual maturities. Monitoring the interest rate sensitivities and maturities of an institution's assets and liabilities is called **GAP management,** a technique defined and examined in the sections to follow.[4]

The Concept of Interest Rate Sensitivity

GAP management begins with analysis of the interest rate characteristics of the earning assets and the liabilities on the existing balance sheet. That evaluation reveals relative interest rate sensitivities and, in turn, the extent of current exposure to risks arising from changing interest rates.

Table 17.1 shows the average asset and liability balances and average returns and costs of a large commercial bank. All costs and yields are adjusted to reflect noninterest expenses and revenues, such as check-processing costs or loan origination fees. For example, demand deposits with no explicit interest expense have an average total cost of 7.55 percent. In addition, all yields and costs, including the target return on net worth, are expressed on a *pretax* basis. The balance sheet is representative of the asset/liability mix of many of the nation's largest banks in the 1980s. Although the example is complex, it is used to illustrate asset/liability management realistically.

From the data in the table, the degree of interest rate sensitivity on both sides of the balance sheet can be determined. A *rate-sensitive asset or liability* is defined as one on which the interest rate can change with market conditions during the institution's planning period. The definition of rate sensitivity varies from institution to institution depending on the planning horizon, which is heavily influenced by sources of funds. A small savings institution or credit union that extensively relies on nonnegotiable CDs may view a rate-sensitive asset or liability as one that can be repriced at least once a year. Many larger institutions reduce the rate-sensitive time horizon over which they make strategic plans to a much shorter period—perhaps even a day—because they rely more heavily on negotiable CDs, repurchase agreements, or federal funds purchased. Some institutions have a series of planning periods over which they monitor the interest rate sensitivity of their assets and liabilities.

Identifying Interest Rate Sensitivity

Assume that ABC Bank uses a three-month definition of sensitivity. Given that definition, what is its profile of rate-sensitive assets and liabilities? The results of an analysis are shown in Table 17.2.

Rate-Sensitive Assets.   The asset portfolio contains several items that are rate-sensitive:

- Securities (including fed funds) with remaining maturities of less than three months;
- Fixed-rate loans with remaining maturities of less than three months;
- Floating-rate loans that can be repriced within three months, regardless of contractual maturity.

The total dollar volume of rate-sensitive assets (RSAs)—assets that can be repriced during the planning period—is $17.306 billion.

Rate-Sensitive Liabilities.   On the liability side are the following rate-sensitive balances:

- Transactions balances such as MMDAs;
- Consumer time deposits with remaining maturities of less than three months;
- Other time deposits with remaining maturities of less than three months;

---

[4]The professional literature includes many articles on GAP management. Examples are a series of five articles in *Banking* (now the *ABA Banking Journal*) by James V. Baker, monthly from June through October 1978; a series of three articles by Barrett F. Binder in the *Magazine of Bank Administration* from November 1980 through January 1981; and Mona J. Gardner and Dixie L. Mills, "Asset/Liability Management: Current Perspectives for Small Banks," *Journal of Commercial Bank Lending* 64 (December 1981): 14-31. The example in this chapter incorporates many of the approaches suggested in these and other articles.

Table 17.1
ABC Bank Balance Sheet

	Average Balances (Millions)	Average Annual Rate of Return
Assets		
Cash and due (floating-rate)	$ 4,743	11.500%
Cash and due (fixed-rate)	2,554	10.850
Total cash and due (interest-bearing)	$ 7,297	
Short-term Treasury securities	$ 1,105	8.900
Other Treasury and agency securities	248	9.750
State and municipal securities	514	7.500
Other securities:		
Floating-rate	798	10.950
Fixed-rate	638	12.000
Matched with liabilities	160	12.700
Total securities	3,463	
Commercial loans:		
Floating-rate	$11,500	12.000
Short-term (more than 3 months)	4,040	12.750
Long-term (more than 1 year)	4,300	13.240
Consumer loans:		
Fixed-rate	2,360	14.700
Floating-rate	690	14.150
Other loans:		
Fixed-rate	476	14.200
Floating-rate	3,213	14.000
Lease financing	359	14.960
Gross loans and leases	26,938	
Total earning assets	$37,698	
Cash and due (noninterest-bearing)	$ 1,640	
Credit loss provision	(202)	
Other assets	1,497	
Total assets	$40,633	

- Foreign deposits that can be repriced within three months;
- Borrowed funds, including some fed funds purchased and repurchase agreements.

The volume of rate-sensitive liabilities (RSLs) is $15.310 billion.

Fixed-Rate Assets and Liabilities. The returns or costs of *fixed-rate assets (FRAs)* and *fixed-rate liabilities (FRLs)* will remain constant over the three-month period. Assets that do not earn an explicit rate of return are not considered in analyzing interest rate sensitivity,

Table 17.1
(continued)

	Average Balances (Millions)	Average Total Cost	Interest Expense
Liabilities and Equity			
Domestic demand deposits	$ 4,008	7.550%	0.000%
NOW balances	1,789	10.550	5.250
Other transactions balances	811	11.100	10.550
Time deposits:			
Savings	$1,320	8.550	5.500
Consumer time (fixed-rate)	1,339	12.350	11.950
Consumer time (floating-rate)	236	11.750	11.550
Other time (fixed-rate)	2,844	13.400	12.500
Other time (floating-rate)	4,809	11.600	11.150
Other time (matched)	1,336	10.200	9.850
Total domestic time deposits	11,884		
Foreign deposits:			
Fixed-rate	$3,800	13.050	12.340
Floating-rate	6,806	11.970	11.150
Total foreign deposits	10,606		
Total deposits	$29,098		
Borrowed funds	$ 6,215	11.500	11.400
Long-term debt	1,230	11.000	11.000
Other liabilities (accrued expenses, etc.)	2,248	7.150	0.000
Total deposits and liabilities	$38,791		
Capital stock and paid-in capital	$ 899		
Retained earnings	943		
Total equity capital	$ 1,842	25.000	
Total liabilities and equity	$40,633		

although their totals are shown at the bottom of Table 17.2.[5]

---

[5]In practice, of course, costs are associated with nonearning assets (such as facilities maintenance and repair) that must be considered in profitability analyses. Because these costs are relatively small for the average depository institution, they are ignored in this example. Their impact is discussed in other chapters.

Identifying and Measuring the GAP

Segregating balance sheet items by interest rate sensitivity rather than by traditional accounting categories permits managers to examine several distinct asset/liability groupings:

- The dollar volume of RSAs financed by RSLs. Because RSAs exceed RSLs, this fig-

Table 17.2
Balance Sheet Sensitivity Analysis

Rate-Sensitive Assets (RSAs)		Rate of Return	Rate-Sensitive Liabilities (RSLs)			Cost	
Short-term Treasury securities	$ 1,105	8.900%	Other transactions balances	$	811	11.100%	
Floating-rate commercial loans	11,500	12.000	Consumer time deposits (floating)		236	11.750	
Other securities (floating-rate)	798	10.950	Other time deposits (floating)		4,809	11.600	
Consumer loans (floating-rate)	690	14.150	Foreign (floating-rate)		4,306	11.970	
Other loans (floating-rate)	3,213	14.000	Borrowed funds		5,148	11.500	
Total rate-sensitive assets	$17,306		Total rate-sensitive liabilities	$15,310			**Rate Differential** (12.211 − 11.646) = 0.564%
Average return on RSAs		12.211%	Average cost of RSLs			11.646%	

Matched-Rate Assets (MRAs)		Rate of Return	Matched-Rate Liabilities (MRLs)		Cost	
Cash and due from (floating)	$ 4,743	11.500%	Other time deposits (matched)	$ 1,336	10.200%	
Other securities (matched)	160	12.700	Foreign (floating but matched)	2,500	11.970	
			Borrowed funds (matched)	1,067	11.500	
Total matched-rate assets	$ 4,903		Total matched-rate liabilities	$ 4,903		**Rate Differential** (11.539 − 11.385) = 0.154%
Average return on MRAs		11.539%	Average cost of MRLs		11.385%	

ure is $15.310 billion, equal to the total amount of RSLs.

- The dollar volume of FRAs financed by FRLs. This amount is $15.489 billion, the full amount of FRAs.
- *Matched assets and liabilities,* including sources and uses of funds with a predetermined rate spread and identical maturities. For example, a repurchase agreement with a three-month maturity may be issued to a customer and the proceeds invested in a reverse repo of the same maturity and dollar volume. The matched category totals $4.903 billion for ABC.
- The dollar volume of RSAs financed

with FRLs—the category known in asset/liability management parlance as *the GAP:*

(17.1)

$$GAP = RSAs - RSLs$$

ABC's GAP is $1.996 billion, calculated as $17.306 − $15.310. In other words, $1.996 billion of the bank's rate-sensitive investments are not financed with rate-sensitive or matched funds sources; consequently, they are financed with fixed-rate funds.

Another way of comparing RSAs and RSLs is the **GAP ratio,** defined as:

Table 17.2
(continued)

Fixed-rate Earning Assets (FRAs)		Rate of Return	Fixed-Rate Liabilities (FRLs)		Cost	
Cash and due (fixed-rate)	$ 2,554	10.850%	Domestic demand deposits	$ 4,008	7.550%	
Other Treasury and agency securities	248	9.750	NOW balances	1,789	10.550	
State and municipal securities	514	7.500	Savings deposits	1,320	8.550	
Other securities (fixed-rate)	638	12.000	Consumer time deposits (fixed-rate)	1,339	12.350	
Short-term commercial loans (3 months to 1 year)	4,040	12.750	Other time deposits (fixed-rate)	2,844	13.400	
Long-term commercial loans (more than 1 year)	4,300	13.240	Foreign (fixed-rate and noninterest-bearing)	3,800	13.050	
Consumer loans (fixed-rate)	2,360	14.700	Long-term debt	1,230	11.000	
Other loans (fixed-rate)	476	14.200	Other liabilities	2,248	7.150	
Lease financing	359	14.960				
Total fixed-rate earning assets	$15,489		Total fixed-rate liabilities	$18,578		**Rate Differential**
Average return on FRAs		12.712%	Average cost of FRLs		10.456%	(12.712 − 10.456) = 2.256%
Nonearning assets (including nonearning cash and due)	$ 2,935		Equity capital	$ 1,842		
Total assets	$40,633		Total liabilities and equity	$40,633		

(17.2)

$$\text{GAP Ratio} = \frac{\text{RSAs}}{\text{RSLs}}$$

For ABC Bank, the GAP ratio is:

$$\frac{\$17,306}{\$15,310} = 1.13$$

In other words, ABC Bank has $1.13 of rate-sensitive assets for every $1 of rate-sensitive funds during the next 90-day period.

Like other ratios, the GAP ratio permits comparison of the relative interest rate sensitivity of an institution to other depositories or to the institution's previous positions, allowing for differences in institutional size. The GAP expressed as a dollar amount, although used in estimating expected profits, is not useful for making comparisons.

Positive and Negative GAPs. A GAP ratio of 1 means the rate sensitivity of earning assets and liabilities is perfectly matched; as interest rates rise, returns on assets should rise to protect the margin over funding costs. Although the perfect match is unobtainable, many risk-averse managers using GAP management strive to achieve as small a GAP as possible—or a GAP ratio close to 1—over the planning horizon.

A positive GAP, such as ABC Bank's, means there are more rate-sensitive assets than there are rate-sensitive liabilities. If interest rates increase, institutions with large positive GAPs should find their asset returns increasing faster than their liability costs. Negative GAPs are also possible, indicating that the amount of rate-sensitive liabilities exceeds the volume of rate-sensitive assets. If interest rates fall, liability costs for firms with large negative GAPs should fall faster than asset yields. Few institutions are so confident of their interest rate forecasts, however, that they are willing to risk the potentially dangerous consequences of a large GAP, either positive or negative.[6] Among S&Ls, in fact, minimizing the GAP has become a common objective since April 1987, when the FHLBB's new rules became effective, permitting lower capital ratios for institutions with lower GAPs.

The GAP and the Planning Horizon

It is important to emphasize that evaluation and management of the GAP and the GAP ratio depend on the planning period. For example, a savings institution with adjustable-rate mortgages may have a positive GAP if measured over a five-year horizon, but a negative GAP in the short run if it has substantial funding in the form of MMDAs. Both GAP measurements are important for long-range planning and for regulatory assessments of an institution's viability. In the short run, a substantial rate increase could produce a liquidity crisis for the institution, although in the long run, its chances of insolvency might be small. An illustration of GAP measurement over several planning periods is shown in the appendix to this chapter.

---

[6]Summary statistics on the GAP positions of depository institutions are difficult to find. A study of approximately 100 banks in the seventh Federal Reserve district over the period 1975-1980 found that only the largest banks, defined as those with assets in excess of $300 million, had GAP ratios of less than 1. Generally, the smaller the institution, the larger the GAP ratio, regardless of the interest rate environment. See Duane B. Graddy and Adi S. Karma, "Net Interest Margin Sensitivity among Banks of Different Sizes," *Journal of Bank Research* 14 (Winter 1984): 283-290.

IMPACT OF THE GAP ON RONW

Rate-sensitivity analysis is important for analyzing the effect of an institution's current position on RONW. Table 17.3 shows an estimate of pretax profits and RONW for ABC Bank at the interest rate and cost levels identified in Tables 17.1 and 17.2.

Calculating Rate Differentials.   The first step in developing a GAP profitability analysis is identifying the *rate differentials* on each of the four asset/liability groupings from data in Table 17.2. These differentials are simply the weighted average expected return on the assets in a particular category less the weighted average cost of their funding sources. To calculate the weighted average return or cost of a category, each account must be expressed as a percentage of the total in that category and multiplied by the account's rate of return or cost. For example, the average return on matched assets is 11.539 percent:

$$[(\$4{,}743/\$4{,}903) \times 11.50\%]$$
$$+ [(\$160/\$4{,}903) \times 12.70\%]$$
$$= 11.539\%$$

The average cost of matched liabilities is 11.385 percent, so the rate differential for the matched category is 0.154 percent. On average, the return on a dollar of matched assets exceeds the cost of matched liabilities by just over 15 basis points. This differential, calculated net of noninterest expenses, is smaller than the net difference in interest rates alone. In other words, the differential, expressed in dollars, is smaller than the spread, IR − IE, expressed in dollars.

In Table 17.3, all average costs and rate differentials are rounded to three decimal places, causing small discrepancies in some of the subsequent calculations.

Estimating Pretax Profits.   The dollar amount in each category of rate sensitivity is identified in Table 17.2. As shown in Table 17.3, anticipated annual pretax profits for ABC Bank are estimated by multiplying the rate differential for each category by the corresponding

Table 17.3
Profitability Analysis

GAP = Rate-Sensitive Assets − Rate-Sensitive Liabilities = $1,996

Rate Differential (Annual)

On rate-sensitive assets and liabilities	0.564%
On matched assets and liabilities	0.154
On fixed-rate assets and liabilities	2.256
On the GAP	
Return on RSAs − Cost of FRLs	1.754

Sensitivity Category	Amount	Rate Differential	Expected Profit
Matched assets and liabilities	$ 4,903	0.154%	$ 7.538
FRAs financed by FRLs	15,489	2.256	349.439
RSAs financed by RSLs	15,310	0.564	86.412
The GAP	1,996	1.754	35.016
Total pretax profits			$478.404
Pretax RONW (Annualized)			25.97%

dollar amount of assets. Total pretax profits, projecting the quarterly performance to an annual basis without compounding, are estimated as approximately $478 million, giving a pretax RONW of $478/$1,842 = 25.97%. If management's target pretax RONW is 25 percent, the current GAP should allow that goal to be achieved if interest rates remain the same during the year *and* if maturing assets and liabilities are replaced with similar ones. If the bank pays an average of 40 percent of its pretax income in state and federal taxes, the target pretax RONW translates into an after-tax RONW of 25% × (1 − 0.4) = 15%. The profitability analysis projects an after-tax RONW of 15.58 percent.

MANAGING THE GAP IN RESPONSE TO INTEREST RATE FORECASTS

As students of interest rates recognize, the assumption that rates will remain unchanged is seldom appropriate. Suppose the bank's economists forecast declining rates over the next 90

to 180 days. The preceding GAP analysis allows managers to reestimate annual pretax RONW if they make no attempt to "manage the GAP" in light of this forecast.

Results of Inactivity

If returns and costs for rate-sensitive assets and liabilities decline to the levels shown in Table 17.4, the bank's returns on short-term investments and floating-rate loans will fall. The interest expense and total cost of short-term deposits and liabilities will also go down. For example, note in Table 17.4 that the rate on short-term Treasury securities drops from 8.9 percent to 7.6 percent, and on floating-rate commercial loans from 12.0 percent to 11.2 percent. The total cost of short-term consumer time deposits falls from 11.75 percent to 11.05 percent.

Although rate-sensitive accounts move in the same direction, it is usually impossible to hold the rate differential between RSAs and RSLs constant. A major reason, introduced in Chapter 15 in the discussion of operating lever-

Table 17.4
Balance Sheet Sensitivity Analysis
under Lower Interest Rates with No Balance Sheet Revisions

Rate-Sensitive Assets (RSAs)		Rate of Return	Rate-Sensitive Liabilities (RSLs)		Cost	
Short-term Treasury securities	$ 1,105	7.600%	Other transactions balances	$ 811	10.850%	
Floating-rate commercial loans	11,500	11.200	Consumer time deposits (floating)	236	11.050	
Other securities (floating-rate)	798	9.950	Other time deposits (floating)	4,809	10.950	
Consumer loans (floating-rate)	690	13.750	Foreign (floating-rate)	4,306	11.450	
Other loans (floating-rate)	3,213	13.100	Borrowed funds	5,148	11.000	
Total rate-sensitive assets	$17,306		Total rate-sensitive liabilities	$15,310		Rate Differential
Average return on RSAs		11.367%	Average cost of RSLs		11.104%	11.367 − 11.104 = 0.263%

Matched-Rate Assets (MRAs)		Rate of Return	Matched-Rate Liabilities (MRLs)		Cost	
Cash and due from (floating)	$ 4,743	10.770%	Other time deposits (matched)	$ 1,336	9.700%	
Other securities (matched)	160	11.900	Foreign (floating but matched)	2,500	11.050	
			Borrowed funds (matched)	1,067	11.000	
Total matched-rate assets	$ 4,903		Total matched-rate liabilities	$ 4,903		Rate Differential
Average return on MRAs		10.807%	Average cost of MRLs		10.671%	10.807 − 10.671 = 0.136%

age, is that implicit interest expenses will probably not change as the general level of interest rates falls. Consequently, the total cost of liabilities will change less than the expected return on assets.

A revised profitability analysis shown in Table 17.5 indicates that the differential on rate-sensitive categories declines from 0.564 percent to 0.263 percent. The key figure that has affected profit estimates, however, is the differential on the GAP, down from 1.754 percent to 0.910 percent. Average returns on RSAs drop with the general decline in interest rates, but the cost of funding those assets remains the same because they are financed through fixed-rate liabilities. The estimate of the annualized

pretax profit falls to $414.562 million. The pretax RONW of 22.51 percent and the after-tax RONW projection of only 13.51 percent [22.51% × (1 − 0.4)] are below management's targets.

Active GAP Management

An active GAP management strategy could mitigate some of the negative impact of falling rates. Active GAP management requires managers to monitor all the markets in which the institution customarily operates. It also requires a willingness to use interest rate forecasts as the basis for restructuring the institution's balance

Table 17.4
(continued)

Fixed-Rate Earning Assets (FRAs)		Rate of Return	Fixed-Rate Liabilities (FRLs)		Cost	
Cash and due (fixed-rate)	$ 2,554	10.850%	Domestic demand deposits	$ 4,008	7.550%	
Other Treasury and federal agency securities	248	9.750	NOW balances	1,789	10.550	
State and municipal securities	514	7.500	Savings deposits	1,320	8.550	
Other securities (fixed-rate)	638	12.000	Consumer time deposits (fixed)	1,339	12.350	
Short-term commercial loans (3 months to 1 year)	4,040	12.750	Other time deposits (fixed)	2,844	13.400	
Long-term commercial loans (more than 1 year)	4,300	13.240	Foreign (fixed-rate and noninterest-bearing)	3,800	13.050	
Consumer loans (fixed-rate)	2,360	14.700	Long-term debt	1,230	11.000	
Other loans (fixed-rate)	476	14.200	Other liabilities	2,248	7.150	
Lease financing	359	14.960				
Total fixed-rate earning assets	$15,489		Total fixed-rate liabilities	$18,578		**Rate Differential**
Average return on FRAs		12.712%	Average cost of FRLs		10.456%	12.712 − 10.456 = 2.256%
Nonearning assets (including nonearning cash and due)	$ 2,935		Equity capital	$ 1,842		
Total assets	$40,633		Total liabilities and equity	$40,633		

sheet. These requirements mean that active GAP management has its drawbacks, discussed later in the chapter.

Under ABC's forecast of declining rates, an active GAP manager would attempt to narrow the GAP *before* rates fall, so that the proportion of rate-sensitive assets supported by fixed-rate liabilities would be reduced. Personnel throughout the bank would become involved, because both the loan and the securities portfolios would be affected by this GAP management goal.

Asset Restructuring. Initially, the bank's managers could attempt to reduce the total volume of rate-sensitive assets. As commercial or individual customers come to discuss new loans or to renegotiate maturing loans, they could be encouraged to accept fixed-rate rather than floating-rate alternatives. In that way, the bank could lock in existing higher returns and reduce exposure to the impact of falling rates. Most fixed-rate loans would also have to include prepayment penalties to discourage borrowers from taking advantage of future rate declines. The securities portfolio could also be reallocated, within liquidity constraints limiting transfers of funds from short-term to longer-term securities.

Liability Restructuring. On the liability side, little restructuring could occur without new deposit inflows. Ideally, managers would prefer to increase the bank's rate-sensitive sources of funds to take advantage of anticipated declining costs, but customers with long-term

---

Table 17.5
Profitability Analysis with Lower Rates, No Balance Sheet Revisions

GAP = Rate Sensitive Assets − Rate Sensitive Liabilities = $1,996

Rate Differentials (Annual)

On rate-sensitive assets and liabilities	0.263%
On matched assets and liabilities	0.136
On fixed-rate assets and liabilities	2.256
On the GAP	
Return on RSAs − Cost of FRLs	0.910

Sensitivity Category	Amount	Rate Differential	Expected Profit
Matched assets and liabilities	$ 4,903	0.136%	$ 6.649
FRAs financed by FRLs	15,489	2.256	349.439
RSAs financed by RSLs	15,310	0.263	40.301
The GAP	1,996	0.910	18.174
Total pretax profits			$414.562
Pretax RONW (annualized)			22.51%

CDs cannot be forced to transfer funds to floating-rate deposits. Only if total deposits increase can active liability restructuring be practiced. If new deposits materialize, the liability maturity mix can be adjusted in the opposite direction from that of asset restructuring. This, too, would narrow the GAP. Competitive pricing strategies might be necessary to convince customers to make the desired selections.

Results of Active GAP Management

An example of a rate-sensitivity analysis after asset restructuring, but assuming no immediate increase in deposits and thus no change in liability structure, is shown in Table 17.6. The total dollar volume of floating-rate loans has been reduced by about $1.75 billion, and the securities portfolio has also been adjusted to lower the proportion of short-term securities.

Figure 17.1 presents a graphical comparison of the rate sensitivity of ABC's balance sheet before and after the restructuring. Management's efforts have almost eliminated the GAP, which falls from $1.996 billion to $53

million. As shown in Table 17.7, expected profits under an active asset/liability policy are better than they would be without one. The amount of fixed-rate assets financed by fixed-rate liabilities has been increased to take advantage of the higher differential, and the GAP has been reduced to lessen the impact of its lower return. The pretax performance is better than under a passive strategy: Profits are $458.388 million, and pretax RONW is 24.89 percent. Although returns are still lower than expected before the decline in interest rates, and the projected RONW is slightly lower than management's target return, the forecast in Table 17.7 is much better than the estimates in Table 17.5. The after-tax RONW is held above 14 percent by restructuring the balance sheet.

PRINCIPLES OF GAP MANAGEMENT

While most institutions cannot eliminate the GAP, those that choose to keep the GAP as close to $0 as possible in all interest rate envi-

Table 17.6
Balance Sheet Sensitivity Analysis
under Lower Interest Rates after Balance Sheet Revisions

Rate-Sensitive Assets (RSAs)		Rate of Return	Rate-Sensitive Liabilities (RSLs)		Cost	
Short-term Treasury securities	$ 915	7.600%	Other transactions balances	$ 811	10.850%	
Floating-rate commercial loans	10,200	11.200	Consumer time deposits (floating)	236	11.050	
Other securities (floating-rate)	798	9.950	Other time deposits (floating)	4,809	10.950	
Consumer loans (floating-rate)	690	13.750	Foreign floating-rate	4,306	11.450	
Other loans (floating-rate)	2,760	13.100	Borrowed funds	5,148	11.000	
Total rate-sensitive assets	$15,363		Total rate-sensitive liabilities	$15,310		**Rate Differential**
Average return on RSAs		11.377%	Average cost of RSLs		11.104%	11.377 − 11.104 = 0.273%

Matched-Rate Assets (MRAs)		Rate of Return	Matched-Rate Liabilities (MRLs)		Cost	
Cash and due from (floating)	$ 4,743	10.770%	Other time deposits (matched)	$ 1,336	9.700%	
Other securities (matched)	160	11.900	Foreign (floating but matched)	2,500	11.050	
			Borrowed funds (matched)	1,067	11.000	
Total matched-rate assets	$ 4,903		Total matched-rate liabilities	$ 4,903		**Rate Differential**
Average return on MRAs		10.807%	Average cost of MRLs		10.671%	10.807 − 10.671 = 0.136%

continued

ronments emphasize stability of returns. Those that are willing to adjust the GAP in anticipation of interest rate changes, as ABC Bank did, are willing to risk potential variability in exchange for higher expected rates of return. The risk preferences of managers and owners, and the resources available for balance sheet adjustments, often are a function of the size of the institution and affect the choice of a GAP strategy. If an active approach is chosen, several important principles apply.

GAP Management and Interest Rate Forecasts

The ABC Bank example illustrated a narrowing of the GAP in anticipation of rate declines.

Under a forecast of rising rates, the appropriate strategy under active GAP management would be to increase the size of the GAP, because the spread on the GAP would widen as the returns on rate-sensitive assets rose while fixed-rate funding costs remained stable. In fact, a general principle of GAP management is to increase the GAP under forecasts of rising rates, and to narrow the GAP under forecasts of falling interest rates. Figure 17.2 shows appropriate management goals for the GAP in relation to changing interest rate expectations.

The GAP management strategies chosen will depend not only on the direction of but also on the degree of uncertainty about future interest rates. In periods of high interest rate volatility, confidence in interest rate forecasts

Table 17.6 (*continued*)
Balance Sheet Sensitivity Analysis
under Lower Interest Rates after Balance Sheet Revisions

Fixed-Rate Earning Assets (FRAs)		Rate of Return	Fixed-Rate Liabilities (FRLs)		Cost	
Cash and due (fixed-rate)	$ 2,554	10.850%	Domestic demand deposits	$ 4,008	7.550%	
Other Treasury and federal agency securities	263	9.750	NOW balances	1,789	10.550	
			Savings deposits	1,320	8.550	
State and municipal securities	514	7.500	Consumer time deposits (fixed)	1,339	12.350	
Other securities (fixed-rate)	663	12.000	Other time deposits (fixed)	2,844	13.400	
Short-term commercial loans (3 months to 1 year)	4,440	12.750	Foreign (fixed-rate and noninterest-bearing)	3,800	13.050	
Long-term commercial loans (more than 1 year)	5,100	13.240	Long-term debt	1,230	11.000	
Consumer loans (fixed-rate)	2,760	14.700	Other liabilities	2,248	7.150	
Other loans (fixed-rate)	779	14.200				
Lease financing	359	14.960				
Total fixed-rate earning assets	$17,432		Total fixed-rate liabilities	$18,578		Rate Differential
Average return on FRAs		12.805%	Average cost of FRLs		10.456%	12.805 − 10.456 = 2.349%
Nonearning assets (including nonearning cash and due)	$ 2,935		Total equity capital	$ 1,842		
Total assets	$40,633		Total liabilities and equity	$40,633		

may be low, and managers may choose to adopt a more closely matched position.[7] If managers revise a balance sheet based on a forecast that

proves to be incorrect, the result will be poorer financial performance than if no active GAP management were undertaken.

GAP Management and the Proportion of Rate–Sensitive Assets

The success of a GAP management strategy is affected by a number of institutional, as well as market, factors, one of which is the proportion of rate-sensitive assets and liabilities to total earning assets. For the ABC Bank in Table 17.1, rate-sensitive assets are over 40 percent of

[7]A theoretical development of this argument was presented in Sudhakar D. Deshmukh, Stuart I. Greenbaum, and George Kanatas, "Interest Rate Uncertainty and the Financial Intermediary's Choice of Exposure," *Journal of Finance* 38 (March 1983): 141–147. The authors characterize the well-matched portfolio as a managerial decision to perform brokerage functions instead of intermediation. The brokerage strategy is more conservative than engaging in asset transformations, which necessarily require more significant and deliberate mismatching.

Figure 17.1
Results of Active GAP Management

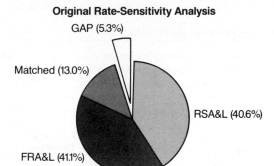

Original Rate-Sensitivity Analysis

GAP (5.3%)

Matched (13.0%)

RSA&L (40.6%)

FRA&L (41.1%)

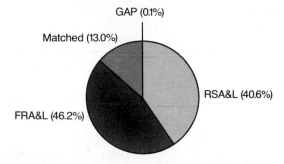

Revised Rate-Sensitivity Analysis

GAP (0.1%)

Matched (13.0%)

RSA&L (40.6%)

FRA&L (46.2%)

the institution's total asset portfolio. Thus, a fairly large proportion of total assets was available for repricing during the next planning period, enhancing the restructuring of the balance sheet. If this proportion were smaller, however, even an active GAP management effort would offer less potential to protect profits than the bank achieved in this example.

LIMITATIONS OF GAP MANAGEMENT

Unfortunately, the desired GAP is probably impossible to achieve. Many market and institutional factors interfere with adjustments of the asset/liability mix.

GAP Management and Customers

Some of the strongest obstacles to desired GAP adjustments can be the institution's customers. The objectives of those customers, in light of generally held interest rate expectations, would be the opposite of the institution's objectives. If interest rates are expected to fall, a depositor would want to move funds quickly into a fixed-rate certificate so that today's higher rate could be locked in. At the same time, the institution is trying to move funds *out* of fixed-rate and into floating-rate deposits to narrow the GAP. If the forecast is for rising interest rates, a depository would be urging borrowers to take floating-rate loans. But prospective borrowers approach variable rate loans warily if interest

Table 17.7
Profitability Analysis after Balance Sheet Revisions

GAP = Rate Sensitive Assets − Rate Sensitive Liabilities = $53

Rate Differentials (Annual)

On rate-sensitive assets and liabilities	0.273%
On matched assets and liabilities	0.136
On fixed-rate assets and liabilities	2.349
On the GAP	
Return on RSAs − Cost of FRLs	0.920

Sensitivity Category	Amount	Rate Differential	Expected Profit
Matched assets and liabilities	$ 4,903	0.136%	$ 6.649
FRAs financed by FRLs	17,432	2.349	409.479
RSAs financed by RSLs	15,310	0.273	41.772
The GAP	53	0.920	0.488
Total pretax profits			$458.388
Pretax RONW (annualized)			24.89%

rate increases are expected, so a manager may find GAP adjustment strategies thwarted by customer resistance. Because of potential conflicts between institutions and customers, supplements to GAP management, such as those presented in the next chapter, have been developed.

Balancing Interest Rate Risk and Default Risk

In addition, managers' efforts to reduce the institution's exposure to interest rate risk simultaneously pass that exposure on to customers. If rates rise after borrowers have been induced to take variable-rate loans, loan losses may increase if some borrowers cannot make their higher interest payments. Similarly, if rates are expected to fall and customers have been encouraged to borrow at high fixed rates, the potential for default risk is increased if borrowers have difficulty meeting the higher required loan payments. GAP management requires a recognition that a lower exposure to interest rate risk may increase default risk, a concept first introduced in Chapters 13 and 14.

GAP Management Uses Resources

GAP management may also lead to higher costs, even if it does not increase the institution's exposure to default risk. To obtain the desired interest-sensitivity profile, a bank may have to offer premium rates on deposits with the interest rate characteristics it wishes to attract, or discounts on the loan categories into which it wants to direct borrowers. These costs may reduce the profitability of active GAP management.

The Two Sides of Interest Rate Risk Revisited

Finally, GAP management as illustrated in this chapter concentrates only on funds flows—that is, variability in revenues and costs and, subsequently, the NIM and RONW. No attention has yet been given to the effect of interest rate

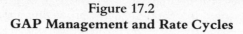

Figure 17.2
GAP Management and Rate Cycles

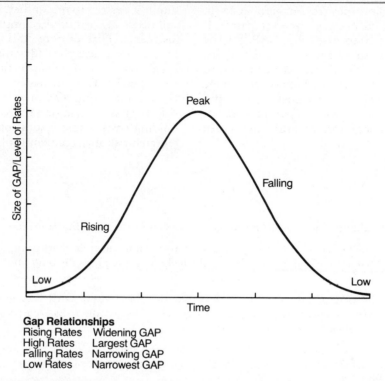

Gap Relationships

Rising Rates	Widening GAP
High Rates	Largest GAP
Falling Rates	Narrowing GAP
Low Rates	Narrowest GAP

movements on the *value* of an institution's assets and liabilities over the longer term.[8] Earlier discussions, beginning in Chapters 7 and 8, emphasize that interest rate risk has two sides—the risks of changing reinvestment rates and of changing market values. Although GAP management is important, supplemental risk management techniques must be part of every manager's plans if the goals of asset/liability management are to be achieved. The additional tools are used when active GAP management is infeasible or undesirable, or when it fails to provide enough protection from earnings variability.

[8]This point is argued and amplified in Donald G. Simonson and George H. Hempel, "Improving Gap Management for Controlling Interest Rate Risk," *Journal of Bank Research* 13 (Summer 1982): 109–115.

SUMMARY

Techniques for managing individual assets and liabilities are of limited usefulness unless they are part of an integrated strategy for achieving a target net interest margin and return on net worth. This chapter explores one of the most commonly used integrated financial management strategies: GAP management.

GAP management involves frequently monitoring the interest rate characteristics of a depository institution's assets and liabilities. Managers must identify the volume and mix of rate-sensitive, matched, and fixed-rate assets and liabilities. Once assets and liabilities are classified, the GAP—the dollar amount of rate-sensitive assets financed by fixed-rate liabilities—can be identified.

Maintaining a GAP as close to $0 as possible is a risk-minimization strategy. In contrast, active GAP management adjusts the size of the GAP to achieve desired financial goals in anticipation of changes in interest rates. If rates are expected to rise, the GAP can be widened to take advantage of anticipated increases in asset yields. If rates are expected to fall, the GAP can be narrowed to take advantage of anticipated lower liability costs. Successful GAP management allows an institution to attain the targeted net interest margin and return on net worth.

GAP management has limitations as a tool for protecting a depository against adverse developments in the financial markets. The institution's desires may conflict with the desires and needs of customers, complicating GAP adjustments. Furthermore, if interest rate forecasts prove inaccurate, adjusting the GAP may harm, rather than enhance, financial performance. Finally, GAP management is designed to assist in managing only one facet of interest rate risk, the risk of changing reinvestment rates and funding costs. Most institutions need other integrated risk management tools as well.

Questions

1. Why should depository institutions use an integrated asset/liability management strategy?

2. Explain the hedging principle. How does it assist an institution in achieving its financial objectives? What are the limitations of using the hedging principle as the only guide for asset/liability decisions?

3. Define the GAP and the GAP ratio. What are the objectives of GAP management? Explain the difference between a positive and a negative GAP. Discuss the risks each presents to a financial institution when interest rates change.

4. Explain what is meant by rate-sensitive assets and liabilities. Give an example of each. What institutional factors must be considered when identifying rate-sensitive versus fixed-rate assets and liabilities?

5. What are matched assets and liabilities? Give an example.

6. Explain the difference between an active GAP management strategy and a risk-minimization strategy. What factors influence an institution's choice between the two?

7. Discuss the options available to managers for restructuring the balance sheet under active GAP management. What are the advantages and disadvantages of each? As interest rates change, why is it usually impossible to maintain a stable rate differential between rate-sensitive assets and rate-sensitive liabilities?

8. For an institution following an active GAP management strategy, what adjustments should managers make under expectations of declining interest rates? Under expectations of rising rates?

9. Why do managers supplement GAP management with other risk management techniques?

Problems

1. Following is a simplified balance sheet for State Bank of San Jose. Annual average rates of return or average costs are provided for each asset and liability category.

Balance Sheet
(Millions)

Interest-bearing Assets		Interest-bearing Funds Sources	
Matched	$100 (12.0%)	Matched	$100 (11.0%)
Rate-sensitive	450 (12.5%)	Rate-sensitive	400 (11.0%)
Fixed-rate	150 (8.0%)	Fixed-rate	200 (6.0%)
Total assets	$700	Total funds sources	$700

a. Calculate the bank's GAP and its GAP ratio.

b. Estimate the annual pretax profits.

c. If interest rates are expected to fall in the near future, should bank management widen or narrow the GAP? Explain.

2. Consider the financial data for Cathay Savings and Loan:

Balance Sheet
(Millions)

Interest-bearing Assets		Interest-bearing Funds Sources	
Matched	$ 5 (8.0%)	Matched	$ 5 (7.0%)
Rate-sensitive	20 (7.0%)	Rate-sensitive	35 (5.5%)
Fixed-rate	40 (9.5%)	Fixed-rate	25 (7.5%)
Total assets	$65	Total funds sources	$65

a. Calculate Cathay's GAP and GAP ratio.

b. Estimate annual pretax profits.

c. Recalculate profits assuming there is an upward shift in the yield curve of 200 basis points with no GAP management.

d. What active GAP management strategy would be indicated if the increase in interest rates were anticipated? Explain why Cathay may not be able to stabilize profits even if its managers use an active GAP management strategy.

3. The year-end 1988 balance sheet for the Hamilton National Bank follows. A second table provides the average yields and costs for the bank's assets and liabilities as of January 1, 1989. Assume that the bank uses a six-month planning horizon for defining a rate-sensitive asset or liability.

Hamilton National Bank
Balance Sheet as of Year Ending
December 31, 1988
(Millions)

Cash and due	$ 97.056	Demand deposits	$ 250.722
Interest-bearing deposits	0.068	MMDAs	263.275
Fed funds sold	245.387	Time deposits	424.789
Investments	290.739	Fed funds purchased	214.018
Loans		Long-term debt	40.775
Commercial	445.508	Other liabilities	26.583
Real estate	140.532	Net worth	100.781
Other assets	101.653		
Total assets	$1,320.943	Total liabilities and net worth	$1,320.943

Hamilton National Bank
Asset/Liability Yields and Costs
as of January 1, 1989
(Millions)

Investments:		Yield	Deposits:		Cost
Short-term Treasury*	$ 150.497	9.60%	Noninterest-bearing	$ 250.722	7.50%
Fed funds sold	245.387	10.45	MMDAs	263.275	8.90
Other Treasury securities	85.000	11.30	Time (less than 6 months)	150.497	10.50
State and municipal	55.242	11.45	Time (1 year)	92.958	10.85
Interest-bearing deposits	0.068	7.00	Time (more than 1 year)	181.334	11.15

Loans:		Yield	Purchased Liabilities:		Cost
Floating-rate commercial*	$ 173.652	12.40%	Fed funds purchased	$ 214.018	9.90%
Short-term commercial*	190.838	12.95	Long-term debt	40.775	11.50
Long-term commercial	81.018	13.21			
Floating-rate real estate*	82.395	11.50			
Fixed-rate real estate	58.137	12.15			

Other:			Other:		
Cash	$ 97.056	0.00%	Other liabilities	$ 26.583	7.05%
Other assets	101.653	0.00	Capital	100.781	
Total assets	$1,320.943		Total liabilities and equity	$1,320.943	

*Maturity or interest rate change in 6 months or less.

a. Categorize Hamilton's balance sheet according to the rate sensitivity of its assets and liabilities. (**Note:** Hamilton has no matched assets and liabilities.)

b. Using the results of the balance sheet analysis, calculate the following:
   1) RSAs financed by RSLs
   2) FRAs financed by FRLs
   3) the GAP

c. Calculate the rate differentials for each of the asset/liability categories in b, and the bank's estimated annual pretax profits at current interest yields/costs.

d. Assume that the economic forecasters whose services are purchased by the bank are predicting an interest rate decline. To help the bank's managers develop some pro forma forecasts, assume the yield curve will shift downward by 100 basis points. Revise your estimates of the bank's annual pretax profits, assuming managers are unable to make any balance sheet adjustments before rates fall.

e. If managers are able to restructure the balance sheet before the yields and costs change, what adjustments should they make if they want to stabilize profits? What actions should they take if they wish to maximize potential profit? What risks are associated with a maximization strategy?

4. Hometown Federal Savings and Loan is under new management, after its recent acquisition by a large S&L with statewide operations. The institution will operate as an autonomous unit, and you have been brought in as a consultant.

The thrift has been operated rather conservatively in the past, and its customers usually resist change, particularly when it is in the form of adjustable-rate mortgages or other variable-rate loans. The management personnel who were retained after the takeover are also rather conservative, and have expressed some skepticism toward suggestions that the S&L's asset/liability mix may need adjustment.

Hometown's financial data follow. The balance sheet as of December 31, 1990, and asset/liability yields and costs as of January 1, 1991, are also available. The planning period is 6 months.

Hometown Federal Savings and Loan
Balance Sheet as of Year Ending
December 31, 1990
(Millions)

Cash	$ 29.9	Passbook deposits	$ 377.0
Investments	256.1	Time deposits	1,541.8
Loans		Borrowed funds	456.3
Real estate	2,067.0	Other liabilities	117.0
Other loans	106.6	Net worth	122.2
Other assets	154.7		
Total assets	$2,614.3	Total liabilities and net worth	$2,614.3

Hometown Federal Savings and Loan
Asset/Liability Yields and Costs
as of January 1, 1991
(Millions)

Investments:		Yield	Deposits:		Cost
Less than 6 months	$ 101.4	8.70%	Less than 6 months	$ 405.6	8.60%
6 months-1 year	68.9	8.70	Passbook	377.0	7.50
1-2 years	62.4	10.00	6 months-1 year	653.9	8.70
2-3 years	20.8	10.50	1-2 years	215.8	9.15
3-4 years	2.6	10.75	2-3 years	115.7	9.40
			3-4 years	68.9	10.00
			Over 4 years	81.9	10.25

Loans:		Yield	Purchased Liabilities:		Cost
Less than 6 months	$ 68.9	8.90%	Less than 6 months	$ 306.8	8.95%
6 months-1 year	68.9	9.00	6 months-1 year	80.6	8.75
1-2 years	130.0	10.15	1-2 years		
2-3 years	136.5	10.90	2-3 years	41.6	10.95
3-4 years	145.6	11.15	3-4 years	27.3	11.05
Over 4 years	1,623.7	11.50			

Other:			Other:		Cost
Cash	$ 29.9	0.00%	Other liabilities	$ 117.0	10.00%
Other assets	154.7	0.00	Net worth	122.2	
Total assets	$2,614.3		Total liabilities and net worth	$2,614.3	

a. Before you recommend any actions, complete an analysis of balance sheet sensitivity, compute rate differentials for each category, and estimate the thrift's pretax profits and RONW under the current rate levels. (Hometown has no matched assets and liabilities.)

b. To convince both old and new managers of the risk the thrift is facing under its current balance sheet structure, prepare new estimates of pretax earnings and RONW in the following scenarios:
1) a parallel upward shift in the yield curve of 150 basis points
2) a parallel downward shift in the yield curve of 200 basis points

c. Using this information, prepare recommendations for Hometown's managers. Discuss how they should adjust the balance sheet under different interest rate forecasts if they wish to stabilize profits and if they wish to maximize profits.

d. What problems might the thrift encounter if it implements these strategies?

5. From the following information, calculate the periodic and cumulative GAPs for each time period designated. Base your analysis on the appendix to this chapter.

	Repricing in:			
	0-180 Days	181-365 Days	1-2 Years	Over 2 Years
Interest-Earning Assets				
Loans	$980	$230	$ 50	$ 30
Investments	250	190	250	60
Fed funds sold	200	—	—	—
Other	10	5	—	—
Interest-Bearing Liabilities				
Deposits	$800	$450	$260	$100
Funds purchased	300	20	—	—
Long-term debt	—	—	10	20

Selected References

Baker, James V., Jr. "Why You Need a Formal Asset/Liability Management Policy." *Banking* 70 (June 1978): 33-43. The first of a five-part series. *Banking* is now the *ABA Banking Journal.*

Binder, Barrett S. "Asset/Liability Management: Part 1." *Magazine of Bank Administration* 56 (November 1980): 42-48. The first of a three-part series.

Gardner, Mona J., and Dixie L. Mills. "Asset/Liability Management: Current Perspectives for Small Banks." *Journal of Commercial Bank Lending* 64 (December 1981): 14-31.

Graddy, Duane B., and Adi S. Karma. "Net Interest Margin Sensitivity among Banks of Different Sizes." *Journal of Bank Research* 14 (Winter 1984): 283-290.

Greenbaum, Stuart I., and George Kanatas. "Interest Rate Uncertainty and the Financial Intermediary's Choice of Exposure." *Journal of Finance* 38 (March 1983): 141-147.

Simonson, Donald G., and George H. Hempel. "Improving Gap Management for Controlling Interest Rate Risk." *Journal of Bank Research* 13 (Summer 1982): 109-115.

Appendix 17A

MEASURING THE GAP OVER SEVERAL PLANNING HORIZONS

As noted in the chapter, the sizes of an institution's GAP and GAP ratio depend upon the time period over which they are measured. Table 17A.1 shows both the periodic and cumulative GAPs for a regional commercial bank as presented in a recent annual report.

The first column of numbers in the table shows total interest-earning assets and liabilities for the institution as of the date of the report. The second column shows that within 90 days, $1.54 billion in interest-earning assets and $1.315 billion in interest-bearing liabilities can be repriced. Because $13 million of long-term debt will be maturing within 90 days and will be renewed at a current market rate, it is considered interest-sensitive for purposes of the report.

The third column shows that during a period 91 to 180 days from the date of the report, an additional $172 million in interest-earning assets and $179 million in interest-bearing liabilities are subject to repricing. For this period, the institution has a negative GAP—that is, more liabilities than assets are rate-sensitive. Cumulatively, however, in the first 180 days following the report, the institution's GAP is a positive $218 million—more assets than liabilities will be repriced within six months. The same interpretation can be given to both the "Total GAP" and "Cumulative GAP" rows throughout the table. Thus, the size of the GAP changes with the planning horizon.

Table 17A.1
The Rate-Sensitivity GAP over Multiple Periods

	Total (Millions)	0-90 Days	91-180 Days	181-365 Days	1-2 Years	Over 2 Years
Interest-Earning Assets						
Loans	$1,968	$1,020	$113	$191	$187	$457
Investments:						
Taxable	441	56	53	76	132	124
Nontaxable	121	10	5	20	19	67
Funds sold	452	451	1	—	—	—
Interest-bearing deposits in banks	3	3	—	—	—	—
Total interest-earning assets	$2,985	$1,540	$172	$287	$338	$648
Interest-Bearing Liabilities						
Deposits						
Savings and NOW accounts	$ 398	$ 58	$ —	$ —	$ —	$340
Other interest-bearing deposits	1,492	838	179	152	176	147
Funds purchased	406	406	—	—	—	—
Long-term debt	55	13	—	1	6	35
Total interest-bearing liabilities	$2,351	$1,315	$179	$153	$182	$522
Total GAP	$ 634	$ 225	$ (7)	$134	$156	$126
Cumulative GAP		$ 225	$218	$352	$508	$634

Chapter 18

ASSET/LIABILITY MANAGEMENT: BEYOND GAP ANALYSIS

No single asset/liability tool is perfect.

Alden Toevs, Vice President
Morgan Stanley and Company (1985)

IN early 1984, *Fortune* magazine spotlighted the impressive profitability of Bankers Trust Corporation. The article focused on the role of the bank's President, Charles S. Sanford, Jr., who holds degrees in history and philosophy from the University of Georgia and in business from the Wharton School of the University of Pennsylvania. Mr. Sanford, whose grandfather was Chancellor at the University of Georgia and for whom the school's Sanford Stadium is named, chose banking as a profession because it was one in which his performance could be measured. In the opinion of the *Fortune* writers, Mr. Sanford measured up quite well. At the time, he was improving the bank's asset/liability management by introducing sophisticated analytical tools such as duration analysis, described by *Fortune* as "a powerful technique for measuring interest rate risk," and was exploring new ways to increase the flexibility of the bank's asset portfolio.[1]

Many decision makers at depository institutions recognize that managing the rate-sensitivity GAP does not always completely protect earnings, just as it did not for the ABC

---

[1]Gary Hector, "Bankers Trust Takes on Wall Street," *Fortune* 109 (January 9, 1984): 104-107.

Bank example in Chapter 17. This chapter discusses several techniques introduced earlier, such as duration analysis, interest rate futures, and secondary asset markets, along with a new one, interest rate swaps. These tools provide asset/liability managers with flexibility in structuring an institution's risk exposure, flexibility that is lost if only one technique is used.

WHY GAP MANAGEMENT IS INSUFFICIENT

The GAP management efforts of ABC Bank were reasonably successful but did not prevent the institution's expected profits from falling. In addition to GAP management's less than perfect effectiveness, several factors have led institutions to implement other techniques.

Limited Flexibility

The ability of managers to widen or to narrow the GAP depends to a certain extent on the response of depositors and loan customers. For the ABC Bank, the rate sensitivity of deposits could not be "managed" unless new funds flowed into the institution. Thus, the volume of any GAP adjustment is limited, as is the speed with which managers can change the rate-sensitivity balance. Market instruments allowing managers to avoid potentially resistant customers while hedging interest rate risk increase the viability of asset/liability management.

Illiquidity versus Insolvency

The rate-sensitivity GAP model presented in Chapter 17 focuses on an institution's net interest position. A perfectly matched balance sheet theoretically matches changes in interest revenues and costs, so that pretax returns remain stable despite fluctuations in market rates. But for depositories with the long-run goal of protecting owners or members by preserving the value of net worth, stable pretax income is insufficient.

Management of the rate-sensitivity GAP may protect an institution from illiquidity, but it does not necessarily protect against insolvency. Even under matched cash flows, chang-

ing interest rate conditions can alter the value of a depository institution's assets and liabilities so that the value of liabilities may exceed the present value of assets.

Insolvency versus Illiquidity: An Example. Table 18.1 clarifies the distinction between these two financial concerns.[2] Data are provided for a hypothetical savings institution assumed to have nonearning assets of $50,000,000; net worth of $50,000,000; a single category of earning assets, three-month variable-rate loans; and a single category of rate-sensitive liabilities, three-month CDs.

The initial stated interest rate on the three-month loans is 9.645 percent, which translates into an expected annual yield of 10 percent, assuming quarterly reinvestment of principal and interest. The initial stated rate on the CD is 7.77 percent; thus, a depositor reinvesting principal and interest every 90 days for a year (assuming a 360-day year) expects to earn an effective annual yield of 8 percent. The rate-sensitivity GAP for this institution is $0 (and the GAP ratio is 1) for every 90-day period over the course of a year because the rate sensitivity of assets and liabilities is identical. This example ignores noninterest income, noninterest expenses, and taxes.

The figures in the top panel of Table 18.1 are generated under the assumption that interest rates remain constant over a one-year period. Loans made on day 0 are repaid, with interest, at the end of each quarter; those inflows are reinvested in new loans. The CDs are also rolled over, with interest reinvested by deposi-

---

[2]For additional discussion of liquidity versus value hedging see Michael T. Belongia and G. J. Santoni, "Cash Flow or Present Value: What's Lurking Behind That Hedge?" *Review*, Federal Reserve Bank of St. Louis 67 (January 1985): 5-13.

Table 18.1
GAP Management:
Protecting Present Value versus Matching Rate Sensitivity

Interest Rates Stable	Day 0	Day 90	Day 180	Day 270	Day 360
Assets (loans)					
Cash outflows	($500,000.00)	($512,056.84)	($524,404.42)	($537,049.75)	
Cash receipts (9.645% stated rate, adjusted quarterly)		512,056.84	524,404.42	537,049.75	$550,000.00
Interest revenues		$ 12,056.84	$ 12,347.58	$ 12,645.33	$ 12,950.25
Liabilities (CDs)					
Cash inflows	$500,000.00	$509,713.27	$519,615.24	$529,709.57	
Cash outflows (7.77% stated rate, adjusted quarterly)		(509,713.27)	(519,615.24)	(529,709.57)	(540,000.00)
Interest costs		$ 9,713.27	$ 9,901.97	$ 10,094.33	$ 10,290.43
Net interest (interest revenues − interest expense)		$ 2,343.57	$ 2,445.61	$ 2,551.00	$ 2,659.82
Present value of change in net worth: $\sum_{t=1}^{4} [C_t/(1 + 0.05)^t]$					$ 8,842.10

Effective Annual Yields Increase by 50 Basis Points	Day 0	Day 90	Day 180	Day 270	Day 360
Assets (loans)					
Cash outflows	($500,000.00)	($512,056.84)	($524,999.33)	($538,268.93)	
Cash receipts (9.645% stated rate, adjusted to 10.11% at day 90)		512,056.84	524,999.33	538,268.93	$551,873.94
Interest revenues		$ 12,056.84	$ 12,942.48	$ 13,269.61	$ 13,605.00
Liabilities (CDs)					
Cash inflows	$500,000.00	$509,713.27	$520,209.61	$530,928.22	
Cash outflows (7.77% stated rate, adjusted to 8.24% at day 90)		(509,713.27)	(520,209.61)	(530,928.22)	(541,867.67)
Interest costs		$ 9,713.27	$ 10,496.34	$ 10,718.60	$ 10,939.46
Net interest		$ 2,343.57	$ 2,446.14	$ 2,551.00	$ 2,665.55
Present value of change in net worth: $\dfrac{C_1}{1.05} + \sum_{t=2}^{4} \dfrac{C_t}{1.05125^t}$					$ 8,823.76

Note: Amounts are in thousands. Some do not add because of rounding.

tors, every three months. The spread (IR − IE) for each quarter is shown in the row labeled "Net interest." Because noninterest expenses and taxes are ignored, this amount each quarter is available to be added to net worth. The total present value of these additions, calculated at a 20 percent annual required return on net worth (5 percent quarterly), is $8,842,100.

In the lower panel, the assumption is made that expected annual yields increase by 50 basis points at the end of the first quarter. Thus the stated interest rate on 90-day loans rises to 10.11 percent at the end of the first quarter (an expected annual yield of 10.50 percent), and the CD rate goes to 8.24 percent at the same time (an expected cost to the institution of 8.50 percent annually). Because the GAP ratio is still 1, quarterly net interest is protected from deterioration; in every quarter the spread is equal to or even better than under stable economic conditions.

What has not been protected is the present value of additions to the institution's net worth. With the change in market rates, the required return on net worth increases to 20.50 percent, and the present value of additions to net worth falls by over $18,000. If that seems like a minor amount, consider the impact of such changes over long periods of time under interest rate conditions more volatile than those used in the example. Even in the simplified world of Table 18.1, the S&L has been protected from reinvestment risk, but it has not been protected from market value risk. Fortunately, however, the concept of duration is useful for managing this risk exposure.

DURATION AS AN ASSET/LIABILITY MANAGEMENT TOOL

Chapter 8 presents the concept and mathematics of duration, its potential as a measure of interest rate risk, and its use in several isolated situations. As defined in that chapter, the duration of an asset or liability is the weighted average time over which cash flows are expected, where the weights are the relative present values of the cash flows. Mathematically, the duration of security j is defined as:

$$(8.1) \qquad DUR_j = \frac{\displaystyle\sum_{t=1}^{n} \frac{C_t(t)}{(1 + y^*)^t}}{\displaystyle\sum_{t=1}^{n} \frac{C_t}{(1 + y^*)^t}}$$

where:

$$C_t = \text{cash flow of security j in period t;}$$

$$y^* = \text{current market yield; and}$$

$$\sum_{t=1}^{n} \frac{C_t}{(1 + y^*)^t} = \text{market value of the security.}$$

Duration can play a major role in an integrated asset/liability management strategy as an alternative measure of the time dimension of a financial asset or liability. Consequently, matching the durations of assets and liabilities, instead of matching time until repricing, is another way to approach GAP management. In fact, a number of experts argue that measuring and managing the *duration GAP* is a more effective way to protect the value of an institution from interest rate risk than traditional GAP management.[3] The merits of those arguments are examined after the mechanics of duration GAP are illustrated.

The Duration GAP: Data Collection

Measuring the duration GAP is more complex than measuring the rate-sensitivity GAP because the dollar amounts and the timing of cash flows for both assets and liabilities must be identified. For fixed-rate assets and liabilities, this task is not too difficult, although prepay-

---

[3]See, for example, Harvey Rosenblum, "Liability Strategies for Minimizing Interest Rate Risk," in *Managing Interest Rate Risk in the Thrift Industry* (San Francisco: Federal Home Loan Bank of San Francisco, 1981), pp. 157–180; George Kaufman, "Measuring and Managing Interest Rate Risk: A Primer," *Economic Perspectives,* Federal Reserve Bank of Chicago 8 (January/February 1984): 16–29; Alden L. Toevs, "Proper Tools Are Needed to Build a Good Risk Shelter," *Savings Institutions* 106 (April 1985): S75–S78; Charles W. Haley, "Interest Rate Risk in Financial Intermediaries: Prospects for Immunization," in *Proceedings of a Conference on Bank Structure and Competition* (Chicago: Federal Reserve Bank of Chicago, 1982), pp. 309–317; Donald G. Simonson and Dennis E. Bennett, "How Much Is Your Balance Sheet Worth?" *Trends and Topics,* Federal Home Loan Bank of Chicago 4 (Winter 1985): 9–11; Joel L. Rosenberg, "The Joys of Duration," *Bankers Magazine* 169 (March–April 1986): 62–67.

Table 18.2
Heartland Credit Union (HCU) Balance Sheet
(Millions)

Assets	Amount	%	Liabilities and Ownership	Amount	%
Cash and equivalents	$ 0.5	a	Regular shares	$108.3	39
CDs owned	27.0	10	Share drafts	15.8	6
Investments	30.0	11	Share certificates	132.8	47
Consumer loans	162.0	58	Notes payable	9.9	3
Mortgage loans	51.0	18	Other liabilities	2.6	1
Land and buildings	5.8	2	Reserves and undivided earnings	10.4	4
Other assets	3.5	1			
Total assets	$279.8	100%	Total liabilities and members' ownership	$279.8	100%

[a]Less than 1%.

ments on long-term loans must be estimated. For assets and liabilities with variable rates, interest to be received or paid over entire contractual maturities must be projected.[4] Forward rates on Treasury securities, illustrated in Chapter 6, can be used as forecasts of risk-free rates to which appropriate risk premiums can be added. Other data needed to calculate a duration GAP are current market yields on assets and liabilities.

Asset Maturities and Returns.
Table 18.2 provides year-end balance sheet data adapted from the financial statements of one of the ten largest credit unions in the United States, hypothetically named Heartland Credit Union (HCU). The data are used to illustrate the calculation of a duration GAP.

The first step is to estimate the maturities and yields for assets, shown in Table 18.3. Most consumer loans at CUs are 3- to 5-year personal or automobile installment loans to members, so

it is reasonable to assume an average maturity of 3.5 years for HCU's consumer loans. The average rate of return is assumed to be 10 percent. Because most mortgages are prepaid, an *effective* average maturity of 10 years is estimated for the mortgage loan portfolio, even though the initial contractual maturity is 30 years. They have an estimated average rate of return of 9.6 percent.

The CDs and investments, primarily Treasury securities, owned by the credit union are almost entirely short-term. The example assumes an average maturity of three months for these assets. Because these data were collected when market rates were quite high, the average rate of return was around 15.75 percent for three-month CDs and 13.25 percent for Treasury securities.

Liability Maturities and Costs.
The maturities of HCU's shares and share drafts are subject to depositor wishes and are difficult to determine. Estimating the maturity and/or duration of these accounts is a subject of some debate. Should they be considered as having an instantaneous maturity because they can be withdrawn at will? Depositors certainly can reclaim their funds, but their loyalty, as well as their cash flow needs, make it highly unlikely that the shortest-case scenario will actually oc-

---

[4]Some argue that variable-rate instruments can be treated as zero-coupon instruments maturing at the time of repricing. In that case, their durations would always be equal to the length of time until repricing. See Rosenberg, "The Joys of Duration." Others, such as Kaufman in "Measuring and Managing Interest Rate Risk," base duration on expected cash flows until contractual maturity.

Table 18.3
HCU Assets and Liabilities:
Estimated Maturities and Yields/Costs

Category	Estimated Average Maturity	Average Annual Yield/Cost	Current Market Yield/Cost
Cash	0 months	0.00%	0.00%
CDs owned	3	15.75	17.20
Investments	3	13.25	14.80
Consumer loans	42[a]	10.00	18.00
Mortgage loans	120[b]	9.60	13.50
Land and buildings	—	0.00	0.00
Other assets	—	0.00	0.00
Regular shares	3	6.50	6.50
Share drafts	0.5	6.50	6.50
Share certificates	3	10.05	15.30
Notes payable	6	17.50	17.50
Other liabilities	0	0.00	0.00

[a]The assumption of a 3½-year (42-month) maturity for consumer installment loans, and an annual rate of 10% (0.833% per month), results in estimated monthly cash flow to the credit union of $4.587 million, based on amortization of the $162 million in consumer loans outstanding at the end of the year.

[b]The assumption of an existing annual mortgage rate of 9.6% (0.80% per month) results in estimated total monthly mortgage payments to HCU of $433,000 when payments on the $51 million of mortgages outstanding are amortized over a 30-year contractual maturity. Under the assumption that mortgages will be prepaid at the end of the 10th year, a single cash flow of $46.1 million would be received at that time.

cur. In fact, many institutions count on a core volume of transactions or passbook deposits that remain relatively stable. Thus, a depository must examine the behavior of its deposits under various interest rate conditions and use that information to estimate deposit maturity.[5] Because share drafts are transaction accounts, their average maturity is estimated at a relatively short two weeks, and the average maturity of regular shares, at three months. The average interest cost for both those accounts is assumed to be approximately 6.5 percent.

The vast majority of share certificates have an original maturity of six months. If they mature at an even pace, the average maturity of the total volume of CDs is three months, and their average cost is about 10.05 percent. Notes payable are short-term floating-rate loans secured by property and costing 17.5 percent on average. The other liabilities are accruals, which bear no interest cost. The credit union follows a policy of adding to reserves and undivided earnings each year at a target rate of 20 percent. At a minimum, management desires to maintain these accounts at their current levels—in other words, avoiding erosion in net worth is a major objective.

Market Data.   Additional data needed to calculate the duration GAP for HCU are estimates of current market yields for the various categories of assets and liabilities. It is assumed that market conditions have changed since many of the CU's assets were acquired; the yield to CUs on new consumer loans is now about 18 per-

[5]George Kaufman, in "Measuring and Managing Interest Rate Risk: A Primer," concludes (page 26) that the correct duration for transactions deposits "awaits additional research," and that the price behavior of an individual institution's deposits must guide the duration estimate.

cent.[6] Conventional mortgages with a ten-year effective maturity are yielding 13.50 percent, and the average yield on new three-month Treasury securities is about 14.80 percent. The estimated average cost of new short-term CDs tied to Treasury securities is 0.5 percent higher, or 15.30 percent. The cost of shares and share drafts is unchanged from previous levels. These assumptions are summarized in Table 18.3.

The Duration GAP: Calculating Durations

Once data are collected, weighted average durations of assets and liabilities are estimated and the duration GAP calculated.

Assets and Liabilities.   Determining the duration of HCU's assets and liabilities is easier than it may seem in view of the data that must be estimated. A careful examination of the CU's assets and liabilities shows that many are very similar to zero-coupon instruments, for which duration is equal to maturity. Short-term CDs on both sides of the balance sheet, T-bills, regular shares, and share drafts fall into this group because they do not involve interim cash flows. Although shares and share drafts are interest-bearing, the interest earned during their assumed short maturity would not have a large impact on a duration calculation; in any case, it does not resemble coupon payments. These facts make it possible to estimate the durations of many instruments by using their maturities.

The two largest categories of assets, however, are not similar to zero-coupon securities, and their durations must be calculated using Equation 8.1.

For HCU's 3.5-year (or 42-month) installment loans, duration is:

$$DUR_j = \frac{\sum\limits_{t=1}^{42} \dfrac{C_t(t)}{(1 + 0.015)^t}}{\sum\limits_{t=1}^{42} \dfrac{C_t}{(1 + 0.015)^t}}$$

For these loans, each monthly cash flow (C_1 through C_{42}) is equal to \$4.587 million. The relevant monthly market rate with which these cash flows are discounted is 18% ÷ 12 = 1.5%, and the total present value is \$142.17 million. This figure is also the estimated current market value of the loans; it is below book value because market rates increased after most of the loans were made. The numerator of the duration equation, in which each cash flow is weighted by the time period in which it is to be received, is \$2,747.68 million (\$2.748 billion). The estimated duration of HCU's installment loans is \$2,747.68 ÷ \$142.17 = 19.3 months, or 1.61 years, lower than their maturity of 42 months.

For mortgage loans, each monthly cash flow (C_1 through C_{119}) is \$433,000 (\$.433 million), with a final cash flow (C_{120}) of \$46.1 million. Again using Equation 8.1, the duration is \$2,781.1 ÷ \$40.3 = 68.9 months, or 5.74 years, almost half the estimated effective maturity, and less than one-fourth of their contractual maturity of 30 years.

Duration GAP.   The last step is to estimate the weighted average duration of the credit union's assets and liabilities. This calculation is shown in Table 18.4. Each asset and liability is expressed as a percentage of total assets or liabilities; the duration of each account is weighted by its percentage; and weighted durations are summed to obtain the weighted average asset and liability durations. For HCU, the weighted average asset duration is 24.23 months, or 2.02 years; the weighted average liability duration is 2.79 months, or 0.23 years.

The duration GAP can be calculated after the weighted average liability duration is adjusted to reflect the percentage of liabilities to total assets on the balance sheet. Reserves and undivided earnings are 4 percent of the credit

---

[6]The difference between the relatively low yields to maturity on HCU's existing assets and assumed current market rates may seem large, but it was realistic in the early 1980s. After interest rates fell in the latter part of the decade, existing asset yields were often higher than prevailing market rates. Unless interest rates remain stable for an extended period, differences of varying magnitudes and directions will occur.

Table 18.4
Heartland Credit Union:
Duration and Weighted Average Duration of Assets and Liabilities

Assets	Duration	%	Weighted Duration
Cash	0 months	a	a
CDs owned	3	10[c]	0.30 months
Investments	3	11	0.33
Consumer loans	19.3	58	11.19
Mortgage loans	68.9	18	12.41
Land and buildings	NA[b]	2	—
Other assets	NA[b]	1	—

Weighted average duration[d]: 24.23 months
(2.02 years)

Total value of assets = $279.8

Liabilities and ownership	Duration	%	Weighted Duration
Regular shares	3 months	39	1.17 months
Share drafts	0.5	6	0.03
Share certificates	3	47	1.41
Notes payable	6	3	0.18
Other liabilities	0	1	0.00
Reserves and undivided earnings	NA[b]	4	—

Weighted average duration[d]: 2.79 months
(0.23 years)

Total value of liabilities and members' ownership = $279.8

[a]Less than 1%.

[b]Not Applicable.

[c]Technically, the weights applied to individual durations in order to determine the weighted average duration of assets should be market value weights. In this case, however, the difference between book value and market value weights would be quite small, so the recalculation is ignored.

[d]The weighted average duration is calculated by summing the weighted durations of the assets or liabilities.

union's sources of funds, so liabilities are 96 percent. The duration GAP is:

(18.1) $\quad DUR_{GAP} = DUR_A - w_L DUR_L$

where w_L is the percentage of assets financed by liabilities.

For HCU:

$DUR_{GAP} = 2.02 - (0.96)(0.23) = 1.80$ years.

Because duration is a measure of time, the duration GAP has a time dimension and is not a dollar figure like the rate-sensitivity GAP.

Interpreting the Duration GAP

In view of the extensive calculations necessary to measure a duration GAP, why would a depository institution wish to do so? The answer lies in the property of duration introduced in Chapter 8: The duration of an asset or liability is directly related to the change in its market value as interest rates change. Recall that Δy^* in Equation 8.4 is the change expressed in basis points and divided by 100:

$$(8.4) \qquad \%\Delta P_0 = \frac{\Delta P_0}{P_0} = -\text{DUR}\,\frac{\Delta y^*}{1 + y^*}$$

Suppose there is an immediate 50-basis-point increase in market interest rates. What would be the expected percentage change in the market value of HCU's mortgage loans, currently at $40.3 million? Using Equation 8.4:

$$\%\Delta P_0 = -5.74\,\frac{0.50}{1 + 0.135} = -2.53\%$$

The new market value of the mortgages is estimated as $40.3 - (0.0253 \times \$40.3) = \$39.2$ million after the increase in interest rates. For consumer loans, the estimated percentage change in value is $-1.61 \times (0.50/1.18) = -0.68\%$. Their market value, previously $140 million, would decline to $139.05 million.

Duration directly measures the potential variation in the value of assets because of interest rate changes. If interest rates rise substantially, asset values could decline enough to threaten capital adequacy or even endanger solvency. Financial institution managers aware of this risk exposure could try to reduce it before interest rates change.

Duration GAP and Changes in Net Worth.
The duration GAP directly indicates the exposure of the institution's net worth accounts to a change in interest rates. As noted, the Heartland Credit Union, like most depositories, desires at a minimum to protect reserves and undivided earnings at their current levels. With a slightly modified Equation 8.4, the duration GAP can be used to estimate the percentage change in the institution's net worth account that would occur if interest rates change and assets and liabilities are restated at their new market values. Again, suppose yields increase by 0.5 percent[7]:

$$(18.2)$$

$$\frac{\Delta NW_j}{NW_j} = -\text{DUR}_{\text{GAP}}\,\frac{\Delta y^*}{1 + y^*}$$

$$\frac{\Delta NW_j}{NW_j} = -1.80 \times \frac{0.5}{1 + 0.20} = -0.75\%$$

The projected increase in interest rates would result in a 0.75 percent decline in the value of capital. The greater the increase in interest rates, the larger the decline in the value of reserves and undivided earnings. In addition, the larger the duration GAP, the greater the potential erosion of net worth, given an increase in interest rates.

But if an institution's managers know the duration GAP, they can take steps to manage it actively. For HCU, managing the duration GAP would involve lengthening liability durations and/or shortening asset durations, strategies similar to those undertaken in managing the rate-sensitivity GAP. Characteristics of securities that would reduce the duration GAP, however, are not necessarily the same as those that would reduce maturity GAP, because durations are affected not only by maturity, but also by an asset or liability's interest rate characteristics (such as coupon-bearing versus discount) and by the existing level of market rates.

Active duration GAP management might result in the development of a different mix of products than under active maturity GAP management, and these products might be more appealing to customers than those involving maturity adjustments alone. Still, active duration GAP management as a strategy for integrated asset/liability management is likely to encounter some of the same hurdles that active

---

[7]This equation shows the impact of the duration GAP assuming that management's goal is to preserve the level of net worth. If the focus is the capital/assets ratio, the duration GAP is measured as $\text{DUR}_A - \text{DUR}_L$. Toevs also presents a use of duration GAP to protect net income. These alternatives are discussed in Kaufman, "Measuring and Managing Interest Rate Risk"; Alden Toevs, "Gap Management: Managing Interest Rate Risk in Banks and Thrifts," *Economic Review,* Federal Reserve Bank of San Francisco (Spring 1983), pp. 20-35; and Elijah Brewer, "Bank Gap Management and the Use of Financial Futures," *Economic Perspectives,* Federal Reserve Bank of Chicago 9 (March/April 1985): 12-22.

rate-sensitivity GAP management encounters. However, duration more accurately estimates the impact of rate changes on the institution.[8]

Immunization: A Partial Duration GAP Strategy

Active duration GAP management presents another complication: The duration GAP is subject to frequent changes, because durations change with each interest rate change. For this reason, and to avoid the marketing problems introduced by active GAP management, some institutions make only limited use of a duration-based management strategy. Matching the duration of designated deposits and assets causes the duration GAP on a portion of the balance sheet to be 0. That part of the balance sheet is then "immunized" against unexpected changes in interest rates. Immunization is introduced in Chapter 8 to illustrate how an investor could select a security of a specified duration to lock in a current market yield over a predetermined holding period. A depository can use the same strategy to lock in a specific asset/liability spread. Enhancing the potential use of this strategy is the removal of virtually all restrictions on the types of accounts that institutions can offer.

Suppose because of the current interest rate environment, managers of an S&L believe it is desirable to make fixed-rate mortgages with a contractual maturity of fifteen years and a duration of four years. A partial duration GAP strategy would fund those mortgages only with deposits of equal duration, possibly four-year CDs sold at a discount with no intervening interest payments. No mortgages with a four-year duration would be issued unless matched deposits were available to fund them. This is a very different strategy from matching maturities, and a four-year deposit is likely to be much more palatable to depositors than a fifteen-year

CD. Although the duration of the liabilities cannot be guaranteed, because customers are free to withdraw before maturity, the institution can reduce that likelihood by imposing withdrawal penalties. Thus, a particular portion of the balance sheet would be immunized against interest rate changes, and the interest rate risk to which the institution is exposed would be limited to that of the remaining asset/liability mix.

This strategy has one further advantage: If the institution is uncomfortable with making interest rate forecasts on which its entire profitability depends, immunization provides relief from that problem. Once the spread between particular assets and liabilities has been immunized, it is essentially fixed, regardless of the next rate change. Although the chance to profit unexpectedly is minimized, so is the chance for unanticipated losses. All or parts of the remaining asset/liability mix can then be managed using techniques requiring active rate forecasting. Nevertheless, managers using immunization must remember the assumptions on which the technique is based, discussed in Chapter 8.

FINANCIAL FUTURES AS AN ASSET/LIABILITY TOOL

It is clearly impossible to achieve a desired level of exposure to interest rate risk, as measured by either the rate-sensitivity or duration GAP. Something other than balance sheet restructuring is needed. One effective supplement to GAP management that is gaining popularity is futures hedging. As the discussion in Chapter 9 emphasizes, futures provide a powerful method for reducing exposure to interest rate risk.

Futures Increase Flexibility

One benefit of the futures hedge as an asset/liability management tool is that it allows a depository institution to offer a wide range of financial products and services to attract as broad a customer base as its objectives dictate.

---

[8]Despite the difficulties of active duration GAP management, there is strong support for its use. Haley concludes, for example, that "value immunization is sufficient to protect financial intermediaries from failure." See Haley, "Interest Rate Risk in Financial Intermediaries: Prospects for Immunization," p. 317.

The potential costs of an interest rate sensitivity mismatch are avoided by taking the appropriate position in the futures market, rather than by forcing customers to choose deposit accounts or loans that may displease them or even cause them to patronize a competitor.

Perhaps a more important advantage of the futures markets is that they allow management to "unbundle" asset and liability decision making. A bank or thrift can pursue investment choices that management hopes will provide the highest rates of return in a particular interest rate environment. At the same time, it can pursue sources of funds that carry the lowest costs, even if the asset/liability mix produces a rate-sensitivity mismatch. Hedging in the futures market offers managers enough flexibility to fulfill one of the intermediation functions—offering loans and deposits tailored to individual maturity preferences—without exposing their institutions to excessive interest rate risk.[9]

Futures as a Supplement to GAP Management

An example will clarify the benefits contributed by futures instruments. The top panel of Table 18.5 presents a rate-sensitivity and duration analysis for a hypothetical bank. The bank has a rate-sensitivity GAP ratio of 1.06, and a duration GAP of 0.95 years. The target return on net worth is 11.5 percent. The profitability analysis at the bottom of the table indicates expected profits of $4.82 million, and an expected return on net worth of slightly over 12 percent, in excess of the target.

Active GAP Management. If the bank's managers expect a 75-basis-point increase in interest rates, they might want to maintain or

even increase the positive rate-sensitivity GAP before rates rise. In managing the GAP, the emphasis would be on increasing rate-sensitive assets whose returns will rise with market rates as the cost of fixed-rate funding sources remains unchanged. Table 18.6 analyzes the results of bank management's efforts. The GAP ratio has been increased to 1.1, and the duration GAP is shortened to 0.80 years. Earnings are down slightly, although results are still above the target RONW.

Potential damage remains, however, from the bank's positive duration GAP. Despite the balance sheet restructuring, which reduced the weighted average duration of assets, the DUR_{GAP} is still a positive 0.80 years. If interest rates increase, the present value of the bank's assets will fall more than the value of its liabilities, eroding the present value of net worth. A 75-basis-point increase reduces the value of the bank's net worth by about ½ of 1 percent, from $40 million to $39.78 million.

$$\frac{\Delta NW_j}{NW_j} = -0.80 \times \frac{0.75}{1 + 0.115} = -0.538\%$$

Using Futures to Offset the GAP.   To overcome some of the difficulties in bringing the duration GAP to its optimal level, the bank's managers can use futures to protect the value of the firm. For this bank, the need to increase the variable-rate portion of the loan portfolio would be reduced if GAP strategies were augmented by futures trading. In this case, the bank managers should sell futures contracts, or assume a short position. The institution does not receive cash initially, but each day cash will be deposited to or deducted from the institution's margin account, consistent with the daily settlement practices of futures trading.

If interest rates increase, the value of the contracts sold will decline, and the value of the margin account will increase. If the proper number of contracts is sold, the increase in cash will offset the decline in the value of other assets when the short position is closed out. Ideally, the net change in asset value will equal the

[9]This point is made in Dwight Jaffee, "Interest Rate Hedging Strategies for Savings and Loan Associations." Other support is offered in Reid Nagle, "The Use of Financial Futures in Asset/Liability Management," in *Managing Interest Rate Risk in the Thrift Industry*, (San Francisco: Federal Home Loan Bank of San Francisco, 1981), pp. 83-132.

Table 18.5
Rate–Sensitivity, Duration, and GAP Analysis
(Millions)

Rate-sensitive assets (RSAs)	$275	Rate-sensitive liabilities (RSLs)	$260
Fixed-rate earning assets (FRAs)	205	Fixed-rate liabilities (FRLs)	245
		Net worth	40
Weighted average duration of assets	1.56 years	Weighted average duration of liabilities	0.66 years
Interest-sensitivity (maturity) GAP ($275 − $260)	$15		
GAP ratio ($275/$260)	1.06		
Duration GAP [1.56 − (0.927)(0.66)]	0.95 years		

Profitability Analysis

Sensitivity Category	Amount	Rate Differential	Expected Profit
FRAs funded by FRLs	$205.00	1.05%	$2.15
RSAs funded by RSLs	260.00	0.95	2.47
GAP	15.00	1.30	0.19
Total			$4.82
Expected RONW	12.04%		
Target RONW	11.50%		

Table 18.6
Rate–Sensitivity, Duration, and GAP Analysis: Revised
(Millions)

Rate-sensitive assets (RSAs)	$285	Rate-sensitive liabilities (RSLs)	$260
Fixed-rate earning assets (FRAs)	195	Fixed-rate liabilities (FRLs)	245
		Net worth	40
Weighted average duration of assets	1.41 years	Weighted average duration of liabilities	0.66 years
Interest-sensitivity (maturity) GAP ($285 − $260)	$25		
GAP ratio ($285/$260)	1.10		
Duration GAP [1.41 − (0.927)(0.66)]	0.80 years		

Profitability Analysis: Revised

Sensitivity Category	Amount	Rate Differential	Expected Profit
FRAs funded by FRLs	$195.00	1.05%	$2.05
RSAs funded by RSLs	260.00	0.91	2.37
GAP	25.00	1.45	0.36
Total			$4.78
Expected RONW	11.94%		

change in the value of liabilities, and net worth value will remain stable.[10]

Macro Hedges versus Micro Hedges

The hedging strategy just described is a *macro hedge* because it was designed to hedge the bank's *net* duration position to bring the entire asset/liability portfolio into balance. The macro hedge requires detailed knowledge of the bank's total exposure to interest rate risk. It requires a relatively large transaction in the futures market because it is designed to protect the value of the entire asset portfolio. The institution makes a significant commitment to its interest rate forecast.

In contrast, a *micro hedge* ties the futures position to a specific category of assets or liabilities rather than to the institution's net interest rate exposure. Although macro hedges are theoretically more effective for protecting net worth, micro hedges are a more realistic alternative for several reasons.[11]

---

[10]The number of futures contracts necessary to offset a forecast decline in existing asset values can be estimated by solving for N_f in the following equation:

$$(18.3) \quad DUR_p = DUR_a + DUR_f \frac{N_f \times FP_f}{P_a}$$

where:

> DUR_p = the desired duration of a combined asset/futures portfolio;
> DUR_a = the duration of existing assets;
> DUR_f = the duration of the security underlying the futures contract;
> FP_f = the price agreed upon in the futures contract;
> N_f = the number of futures contracts to be bought or sold; and
> P_a = the market value of existing assets.

If N_f is negative, contracts should be sold; if it is positive, a long futures position is indicated. See Toevs, "GAP Management: Managing Interest Rate Risk in Banks and Thrifts," p. 28; Brewer, "Bank GAP Management and the Use of Financial Futures," p. 19.

[11]More detailed analysis of the choice between macro and micro hedging strategies is provided in Robert W. Kolb, Stephen G. Timme, and Gerald D. Gay, "Macro versus Micro Futures Hedges at Commercial Banks," *Journal of the Futures Markets* 4 (1984): 47–54; and George M. McCabe and Robert W. McLeod, "The Use of Financial

Information Requirements.   First, the amount of information required to monitor the depository institution's total GAP position continuously may be prohibitive. Managers often find it more feasible to select a group of assets or liabilities, such as fixed-rate loans or CDs of a given dollar volume and average maturity, that will be adversely affected by changes in interest rates. A futures trade is then chosen to hedge that specific category of accounts. Under both micro and macro strategies, of course, the futures position must be closely monitored and adjusted as interest rate expectations change.

Accounting Standards.   The Financial Accounting Standards Board recommends more favorable accounting methods for futures hedges linked to an identifiable cash market instrument (micro hedges) than for more general hedges (macro hedges). In other words, hedging a portfolio of six-month adjustable rate mortgages with T-bill futures contracts, a micro hedge, qualifies for more favorable reporting than a macro hedge that shortens the duration GAP but cannot be linked to a specific asset category.

Unless an institution can identify a specific asset or liability for which a hedge has been selected, accounting rules require the results of the hedge to be reported as gains or losses on the income statement *before* the final futures position is closed out. Because changes in interest rates during the course of a hedge may produce temporary losses that are ultimately recovered, reporting hedging results before the position is closed can increase variability in reported earnings. The results of micro hedges, in contrast, must be reported only when closed out, and can be amortized over the remaining life of a hedged asset or liability. Not surprisingly, then, managers often favor micro hedges for accounting reasons alone.[12]

Futures in Banking," *Journal of Commercial Bank Lending* 65 (August 1983): 6–22; *Interest Rate Futures for Institutional Investors* (Chicago: Chicago Board of Trade, 1985), pp. 42–50.

[12]A good explanation of the impact of accounting standards on the macro and micro strategies is provided in Brewer, "Bank Gap Management and the Use of Financial Futures," p. 21; further discussion is contained in

Managerial Flexibility. The micro hedge is also espoused by some managers who feel it gives them flexibility to structure bank or thrift services to meet the needs of particularly desirable customers. For example, a bank may have a large commercial borrower who expects to borrow at fixed rates and whose business the bank wants to keep. The lender can accommodate the wishes of the borrower and at the same time limit its own exposure to interest rate risk by structuring a futures position properly. Because the lender's profits will be hurt if rates rise, a short position in the futures market can be used to hedge against this possibility.[13]

Some institutions have devised a twist on this strategy, offering customers variable-rate loans indexed to an instrument on which futures contracts are traded. They then assist the borrower in structuring a futures position that hedges against changes in the loan rate. Such an arrangement is called a *synthetic fixed-rate loan.* It gives both the borrower and lender the advantages of reduced risk exposure while avoiding potentially undesirable futures accounting treatment for the depository.[14]

Limitations of Futures in Asset/Liability Management

As discussed in Chapter 9, setting the appropriate hedge ratio and selecting the most effective futures instrument are difficult problems for

any type of hedge. For many assets held by depositories, no futures contracts exist, forcing institutions to cross hedge and increasing basis risk. These decisions are less complex for a micro hedge, however, because only one instrument and one maturity are involved. Monitoring the institution's futures position is also time-consuming, especially in a micro strategy that may involve a large number of individual hedges. Finally, the daily cash settlements required for futures trading place additional liquidity demands on the institution, especially if rate forecasts prove to be incorrect. The disadvantages must be weighed against the additional flexibility futures provide.

INTEREST RATE SWAPS

One of the newest tools in asset/liability management is an *interest rate swap,* or a transaction in which each of two parties agrees to pay the interest rate obligations on a specified debt obligation of the other party. Usually, one party exchanges a fixed-rate obligation for a floating-rate one, while the other, called the *counterparty,* exchanges floating for fixed.[15]

Motivations for Swaps

A government agency introduced swaps to the United States, although the technique had previously appeared in the Eurobond market. The Student Loan Marketing Association, known as

Gary Koppenhaver, "Trimming the Hedges: Regulators, Banks, and Financial Futures," *Economic Perspectives,* Federal Reserve Bank of Chicago 8 (November/December 1984): 3-12.

[13]A number of articles advocate hedging to allow more flexibility in lending terms to meet the needs of individual customers. See, for example, Mark L. Laudeman, "An Application of Financial Futures to Fixed Rate Lending," *Journal of Commercial Bank Lending* 65 (August 1983): 23-35; Jeffrey M. Walters, "The Futures Alternative to Fixed-Rate Financing," *Journal of Commercial Bank Lending* 67 (February 1985): 39-46; Rodney L. Jacobs, "Fixed-Rate Lending and Interest Rate Futures Hedging," *Journal of Bank Research* 13 (Autumn 1983): 193-202; and George W. Gau and Michael A. Goldberg, "Interest Rate Risk, Residential Mortgages and Financial Futures Markets," *AREUEA Journal* 11 (1983): 445-461.

[14]Oliver Abel IV, "Fixed Rate Loans Using Variable Rate Funds—A New Lending Instrument," *Journal of Commercial Bank Lending* 65 (August 1983): 36-43.

[15]Further discussion of interest rate swaps is provided in James Bicksler and Andrew H. Chen, "An Economic Analysis of Interest Rate Swaps," *Journal of Finance* 41 (July 1986): 645-655; David Lereah, "The Growth of Interest Rate Swaps," *Bankers Magazine* 169 (May-June 1986): 36-41; Jan G. Loeys, "Interest Rate Swaps: A New Tool for Managing Risk," *Business Review,* Federal Reserve Bank of Philadelphia (May/June 1985), pp. 17-25; Michael M. Hutchinson, "Swaps," *Weekly Letter,* Federal Reserve Bank of San Francisco, May 3, 1985; Lawrence M. Backes, "Interest Rate Swaps and Capped Rate Programs," *Trends and Topics,* Federal Home Loan Bank of Chicago 2 (Winter 1985): 12-14; Clifford W. Smith, Jr., Charles W. Smithson, and Lee Macdonald Wakeman, "The Evolving Market for Swaps," *Midland Corporate Finance Journal* 4 (Winter 1986): 20-32; and Robert Baldoni and Gerhard Isele, "A Simple Guide to Choosing Between Futures and Swaps," *Intermarket* 3 (October 1986): 15-22.

Sallie Mae, pioneered swap programs in the United States in 1982, because of an asset structure heavily dominated by floating-rate student loans and advances. Investors supplying funds to Sallie Mae preferred to lock in the high rates prevailing at that time. The agency, of course, preferred to fund its rate-sensitive assets with sources of funds of a similar nature. Hence, Sallie Mae sought a swap to meet both its and its investors' needs. In the intervening years, the popularity of rate swaps has increased at a phenomenal rate. By the end of 1986, the entire market, including non-financial corporations and financial institutions, was estimated to involve liabilities with principal values of almost $400 billion.[16]

For a financial institution, the objective of a swap is to trade one form of rate sensitivity on liabilities for another that better matches its asset structure. Federal S&Ls, for example, are permitted by regulation to seek swaps only in order to trade rate-sensitive deposit costs for fixed costs, and not the reverse. A swap allows a thrift to reduce its rate-sensitivity GAP and to lock in a spread on long-term, fixed-rate assets. Conversely, a multinational commercial bank that borrows in the long-term Eurodollar market may prefer to swap fixed-rate interest obligations on Eurodollar deposits for floating-rate payments, if most of its assets are rate-sensitive.

Nonfinancial firms are also participants in the swap market. They gain the ability to tailor interest obligations to suit their cash flow patterns without having to restructure existing balance sheets. This flexibility may save substantial transaction costs. At times, a nonfinancial counterparty may even be able to reduce its interest costs because the depository may pay lower rates reflecting the impact of deposit insurance.

Swaps as a Hedging Tool

An example of the mechanics of a swap is presented in Tables 18.7 through 18.9. The exam-

ple involves both a savings institution, with interest rate risk exposure from substantial long-term mortgage commitments, and a large bank with more ready access to the Eurobond and other long-term fixed-rate funding markets.

Southwest Savings and Loan has a negative GAP when estimated over the next two-year planning period; that is, a large portion of its fixed-rate mortgages are funded by rate-sensitive liabilities to be repriced within two years. Under a forecast of rising rates, sufficient GAP adjustments are not feasible, and the thrift's asset/liability committee is considering an interest rate swap. The first step in structuring an agreement is estimating the average cost of short- and long-term funding sources and the expected yield on long-term fixed-rate assets. Table 18.7 shows the results of this evaluation; the current return on the thrift's RSAs is 10.5 percent, and on FRAs, 13.5 percent.

The earnings projections for Southwest S&L, also shown in Table 18.7, are positive, but the firm has a negative GAP of $37 million. It is exposed if interest rates increase. The thrift's managers decide to reduce the GAP by finding an interest rate swap partner willing to assume some of the floating-rate liability costs. In exchange, the S&L will accept some of the counterparty's fixed-rate obligations. In effect, the swap reduces the S&L's volume of RSLs, and thereby reduces the GAP.

Terms of the Interest Rate Swap

Suppose the association finds a multinational bank willing to negotiate an agreement covering debt with a principal value of $15 million. The swap reduces Southwest's GAP to −$22 million. The terms of the agreement require Southwest to pay the interest costs on $15 million of the bank's debt, which carries an interest rate of 11.50 percent. The bank will make payments to the S&L at a floating rate, set at 25 basis points above the LIBOR rate, currently at 10.35 percent. Thus the S&L will receive payments at a rate of 10.60 percent, 80 basis points higher than its current cost of rate-sensitive liabilities. It will pay interest at a cost that pro-

---

[16]Sarah Bartlett, "They Swapped—and They're Sorry," *Business Week,* May 26, 1986, p. 111; J. Gregg Whittaker, "Interest Rate Swaps: Risk and Regulation," *Economic Review,* Federal Reserve Bank of St. Louis 72 (March 1987): 7.

Table 18.7
Southwest Savings Association Financial Data
(Millions)

Assets		Liabilities and Net Worth	

Short-term securities and adjustable-rate loans
   Average return: 10.50%
	$25.5	Short-term and floating-rate funds
		   Average cost: 9.80%
			$62.5

Fixed-rate loans
   Average return: 13.50%
	65.8	Fixed-rate funds
		   Average cost: 11.85%
			28.8

Nonearning assets	4.5	Net worth	4.5
Total assets	$95.8	Total liabilities and net worth	$95.8

GAP = $25.5 − $62.5 = −$37.0

Projected Pretax Earnings

Revenues:		
Rate-sensitive assets	$2.678	
Fixed-rate assets	8.883	
		$11.561
Interest expense:		
Rate-sensitive liabilities	($6.125)	
Fixed-rate liabilities	(3.413)	
		($9.538)
Pretax earnings		$2.023

---

vides a rate differential on fixed-rate assets of 13.50% − 11.50% = 2.00%.

The diagram in Figure 18.1 indicates the flow of funds in this agreement. The S&L initially exchanges lower- for higher–cost funds as it switches from floating to fixed rates. The added cost is the price of the "insurance" against interest rate increases. The bank counterparty is exposed to the risk that the floating rate will rise above its current fixed-rate obligation of 11.50 percent.

Costs and Benefits of a Swap Agreement

Initially, before any interest rate shifts, the swap agreement appears costly to the S&L. As shown in Table 18.8, the swap interest inflows initially are less than the S&L's outflows in the agreement. But this is a hedging technique; the agreement was sought to protect against future rate increases.

What happens if rates do increase, and the S&L's costs of rate-sensitive liabilities rise significantly? Assume that average returns on rate-sensitive assets rise to 12.30 percent, and rate-sensitive liability costs rise to 11.10 percent. The LIBOR rate goes up to 11.95 percent, increasing the rate at which payments are received from the banking counterparty to 12.20 percent (11.95 percent plus 25 basis points). Without the swap, as shown at the top of Table 18.9, pretax earnings would fall to $1.669 million. But the swap protects returns, and the earnings decline is smaller, to $1.774 million, as shown at the bottom of Table 18.9. The S&L could have increased protection by agreeing to a larger swap, but the "insurance" cost would also have been greater.

Important Factors in a Swap

Managers face many decisions in a swap agreement.

Figure 18.1
Exchange of Obligations in an Interest Rate Swap

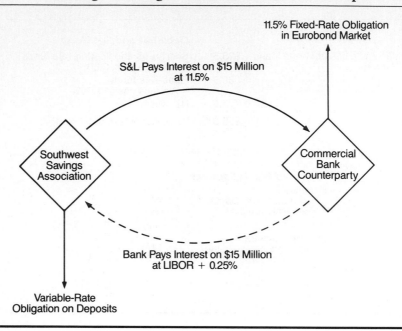

Table 18.8
Southwest Savings Association Projected Pretax Earnings with Swap
(Millions)

Revenues:		
Rate-sensitive assets	$2.678	
Fixed-rate assets	8.883	
Swap interest income ($15 at 10.60%)	1.590	
		$13.151
Interest expense:		
Rate-sensitive liabilities	($6.125)	
Fixed-rate liabilities	(3.413)	
Swap payments ($15 at 11.50%)	(1.725)	
		(11.263)
Pretax earnings		$ 1.888

Table 18.9
Southwest Savings Association
Projected Pretax Earnings
after Interest Rate Increase

Without Swap

Revenues:

Rate-sensitive assets (at 12.30%)	$3.137	
Fixed-rate assets (at 13.50%)	8.883	
		$12.020

Interest expense:

Rate-sensitive liabilities (at 11.10%)	($6.938)	
Fixed-rate liabilities (at 11.85%)	(3.413)	
		($10.351)
Pretax earnings		$ 1.669

With Swap

Revenues:

Rate-sensitive assets (at 12.30%)	$3.137	
Fixed-rate assets (at 13.50%)	8.883	
Swap interest income ($15 at 12.20%)	1.830	
		$13.850

Interest expense:

Rate-sensitive liabilities (at 11.10%)	($6.938)	
Fixed-rate liabilities (at 11.85%)	(3.413)	
Swap payments ($15 at 11.50%)	(1.725)	
		($12.076)
Pretax earnings		$ 1.774

Maturity. The maturity of the interest rate exchange can vary from a relatively short period to as long as 20 years. The longer maturities available in the swap market make swaps suitable hedges when futures contracts are not. If interest rate forecasts underlying the swap prove to be incorrect, however, five or ten years is a long time to pay for one's mistakes.[17] For

this reason, shorter swaps are becoming more popular, and termination clauses are usually included in the original agreement. The party that "unwinds" (the swap market term for ending a swap early) must pay a penalty, but that may be cheaper than the consequences of con-

---

[17]Details on swap agreements are difficult to obtain because they are off-balance sheet items. In early 1986, as market rates dropped, there was speculation that many

thrifts were unable to take advantage of this otherwise favorable development because they were locked into fixed-rate obligations made under swap agreements in previous years. See Bartlett, "They Swapped—and They're Sorry."

tinuing the swap under an unfavorable interest rate scenario.

Interest Rate Index.   Another important issue for negotiation is the index by which floating-rate interest payments will be adjusted. In the example, the S&L would seek assurance that this payment stream is positively correlated with the rate on its short-term deposits and at least equal to the average deposit cost. There is no guarantee, of course, that the anticipated relationship will materialize.

In the earliest swap agreements, the LIBOR rate was the predominant index, but as the technique has gained popularity, the T-bill has gained favor. Increased competition for deposits may change the effectiveness of a given index, and as deregulation continues, it may become even more difficult to predict whether the desired relationship will prevail.

The Role of the Broker.   Interest rate swaps are often arranged through a broker. Although it is possible for a small depository to find a swap partner on its own, the process is time-consuming; that may change, of course, as swaps become more common.

In 1984, the FHLBB formally recognized the potential benefits of swaps for thrift institutions and allowed the district Federal Home Loan Banks to serve as brokers and counterparties to member institutions. Thus, member associations can take advantage of reduced transactions costs if they work through the FHLB system. Many large commercial banks and investment bankers have entered the market both as brokers and as counterparties, and earn substantial fee income from arranging swaps for others. Some brokers, rather than matching other swap partners, become the counterparty to each member of a group of swap customers.

Credit Risk.   A financial institution must evaluate the credit position of the counterparty, because some confidence is needed that there will be no default. When a broker actually becomes a principal in an agreement and guarantees the payment streams, the financial position of the broker is the most important issue.

Concern about controlling credit risk escalated when Beverly Hills Savings and Loan failed in 1985. It had previously made a swap with one of the subsidiaries of Renault, the French automaker. When the thrift failed, the FSLIC and Renault disagreed about who had claim to the $2 million in collateral pledged by Beverly Hills to secure the swap. Although counterparties with weak financial positions had become accustomed to pledging collateral to improve their chances of finding swap partners, the Beverly Hills incident provoked concern from stronger market participants and regulators about access to assets pledged.

Recently, federal bank regulators have questioned whether balance sheet assets should be used to bolster off-balance sheet activities such as swaps and have sought to limit the exposure of national banks to the risk of swaps with weak counterparties. Because of financial problems in the thrift industry, the Federal Home Loan Banks can issue standby letters of credit on behalf of S&Ls wishing to enter the swap market. In essence, these standby letters substitute the FHLBB's credit rating for that of the participating thrift and may lower the thrift's interest costs.[18]

Swaps versus Futures Hedging

Table 18.10 summarizes important differences between hedging with futures and hedging with interest rate swaps. In general, the swap market is less complex, and agreements do not require the daily monitoring needed in futures trading. Swaps allow management more flexibility in negotiating the initial size and maturity of a hedge, but futures hedges are easier and less costly to reverse once in place. Currently, the futures markets are larger, more liquid, and more competitive, although experts predict eventual standardization—and even exchange trading—of interest rate swaps. Thus, the choice between futures and swaps as tools of

---

[18]Owen Carney, "Interest Rate Swaps," *Proceedings of a Conference on Bank Structure and Competition* (Chicago: Federal Reserve Bank of Chicago, 1986), pp. 457–466; Backes, "Interest Rate Swaps and Capped Rate Programs."

Table 18.10
Comparing Interest Rate Futures and Interest Rate Swaps

Feature	Futures	Swaps
Maturities available	1½ to 2 years	1 month to 20 years
Costs	Margins and commissions	Brokers' fees
Size of hedges available	Standardized contract values	Any amount over $10 million
Contract expiration dates	Fixed quarterly cycle	Any dates
Difficulty of management	Complex	Simple
Termination of positions	Closed out with opposite contract	Unwound or reversed
Transactions completed through	Organized exchanges	Commercial, investment banks

Source: Adapted from Robert Baldoni and Gerhard Isele, "A Simple Guide to Choosing Between Futures and Swaps," Intermarket 3 (October 1986): 16.

asset/liability management depends upon the expertise of managers and the regularity with which hedges will be managed.

THE SECONDARY MORTGAGE MARKET AS AN ASSET/LIABILITY TOOL

Another asset/liability management alternative is of special interest to mortgage lenders, because it is an opportunity to alter the structure of the asset portfolio by selling mortgages to secondary investors or trading mortgages for securities that can be either held or sold. These transactions are part of the secondary mortgage market, mentioned briefly in Chapter 14. This market has grown rapidly since 1980, a trend attributed to the innovative securities offered and the increasing number of investors responding to interest rate uncertainty.

A detailed description of all participants and instruments in the secondary mortgage markets could fill several chapters. This discussion is a brief overview of the market and the managerial objectives determining an institution's involvement.[19]

Development of the Secondary Mortgage Market

In the 1930s, when Congress authorized the creation of what is now the *Federal National Mortgage Association (Fannie Mae or FNMA),* it envisioned the secondary mortgage market as facilitating the flow of capital to residential housing. Today, a nationwide secondary market continues to fulfill the original purposes: alleviating geographic mismatches in supply and demand for mortgages; smoothing out cyclical fluctuations in the housing market; and providing mortgage lenders with access to liquidity.

In 1968, Congress transformed Fannie Mae into a semiprivate corporation, now stockholder-owned and profit-oriented. It no longer receives direct funding from the U.S. Treasury, but it enjoys the status of a government agency when issuing debt securities in the credit markets, reducing its borrowing costs.[20] Also in

---

Are, What They Do and How to Measure Them," *Secondary Mortgage Markets* 1 (February 1984): 24-44; and "The Secondary Mortgage Market Is a Key to the Future," *Savings Institutions* 105 (January 1984): S1-S105. Special alternatives for credit unions are discussed in Gary Smuckler, "The Secondary Mortgage Market," *Credit Union Executive* (Winter 1984), pp. 12-19.

[20]The favored borrowing status of Fannie Mae, leading many investors to believe that the federal government would not allow the corporation to default, has been sharply criticized by some experts. According to this view, the quasi-public status of FNMA produces a moral

---

[19]For further information on the history and operations of the secondary mortgage market, numerous references are available. Sources include Dall Bennewitz, *Introduction to the Secondary Mortgage Market: A Primer,* rev. ed. (Chicago: U. S. League of Savings Institutions, 1984); Kevin Villani, "The Secondary Mortgage Markets: What They

1968, Congress created the *Government National Mortgage Association (Ginnie Mae or GNMA)* to continue government involvement in the secondary mortgage market.

Finally, in 1970, the *Federal Home Loan Mortgage Corporation (Freddie Mac or FHLMC)* was formed as a subsidiary of the Federal Home Loan Bank System. Freddie Mac was initially intended to serve only FHLB members, but now services a broader audience.

Together, Fannie Mae, Ginnie Mae, and Freddie Mac have accounted for over 50 percent of the dollar volume of purchases in the secondary mortgage market in recent years, leading many observers to question whether the federal government should be so extensively involved in a private market.[21] Although other investors such as pension funds, life insurance companies, mortgage bankers, and depositories also purchase mortgages from originators, the dominance of the three government-related organizations requires that managers understand their activities.

Restructuring Assets through the Secondary Mortgage Market

Each of the organizations offers a slightly different mix of alternatives to managers of mortgage lending institutions, and the complexity of tools offered is growing at a rapid pace.

Selling Mortgage Loans.   The simplest secondary market transaction is a straightforward sale of mortgage loans, either new or old. Institutions may adopt this strategy to obtain cash to make new loans in times of heavy demand. Until recently, many mortgage lenders had

limited ability to sell mortgages, because secondary market investors would not accept adjustable-rate loans. Now, however, all three major participants in the secondary market have adjustable-mortgage programs.

Some mortgage lenders, wary of the risk of holding long-term assets, adopt a regular policy of selling mortgages as soon as they are originated. For a fee, these institutions continue to collect monthly payments from borrowers, passing them along to new mortgage investors. Fee income generated from *servicing* mortgages can be substantial.[22]

Sometimes the sale of old mortgages is designed to increase the average rate of return on the entire portfolio in an environment of rising interest rates. If the lender wishes to continue to hold mortgages, proceeds from a sale can be reinvested in higher-yielding assets. The drawback, however, is that the market value of the older loans sold will be below their book value, requiring the institution to recognize a loss on its financial statements that might be postponed otherwise. Lenders may believe this is an acceptable price to pay, especially since the loss is a tax-deductible expense that may be used to shelter future earnings or recover taxes paid previously. Management must also consider transactions costs involved in secondary market sales.[23]

Fannie Mae, Ginnie Mae, and Freddie Mac are all engaged in the purchase of mortgages from originating institutions, as are private investors, such as pension funds. But private investors often buy only in large volumes, so

hazard for the Treasury similar to the one produced for deposit insurers by fixed-rate deposit insurance: FNMA's managers have little reason to avoid excessive risk taking. See Edward J. Kane and Chester Foster, "Valuing Conjectural Government Guarantees of FNMA Liabilities," *Proceedings of a Conference on Bank Structure and Competition* (Chicago: Federal Reserve Bank of Chicago, 1986), pp. 347-368.

[21]Joann S. Lublin, "Panel Says Freddie Mac Should Split into Government Firm, Private Entity," *The Wall Street Journal,* October 10, 1986, p. 33.

[22]It is also possible to sell the rights to service mortgages to companies specializing in that operation or even to other depositories. In fact, this practice is growing, although it is often confusing to borrowers who have loans from one institution but make payments to another. See Carrie Dolan, "Rising Sales of Mortgage-Servicing Rights Cause Headaches for Many Homeowners," *The Wall Street Journal,* October 24, 1985, p. 33.

[23]FHLBB-regulated thrifts are permitted to amortize losses on the sale of mortgages in the secondary markets. This accounting rule was enacted to enable them to restructure their portfolios without threatening solvency in the process. See Federal Home Loan Bank Board, "Assets Qualifying for the Deferral and Amortization of Gains and Losses," 12 CFR Part 563C, April 18, 1985.

small lenders, such as CUs, usually sell only to agencies such as Ginnie Mae and Freddie Mac. To facilitate the growth of mortgage trading, Fannie Mae took the first step toward organizing a national mortgage exchange in 1986. In April 1987, after securities firms and thrifts objected to FNMA's expanding role in the mortgage markets, Fannie Mae abandoned these plans, citing improvements in existing mortgage trading systems.[24]

Mortgage Swaps.   Freddie Mac and Fannie Mae have programs that allow a mortgage lender to alter its asset composition by exchanging mortgage loans for securities issued by the secondary market agency. The objective of the lending institution is to change the liquidity and expected return on its existing investments by swapping conventional, fixed-rate mortgages for securities that can then be resold to investors, used as collateral for borrowing, or held for repurchase agreements. In contrast to an outright sale, a swap of mortgages for other securities allows the lender to avoid reporting a loss of value on the mortgages if rates have risen since their issue.

The first program of this type, called the *Guarantor Program,* was introduced by Freddie Mac in 1981. In exchange for mortgages, lenders receive a security issued by FHLMC called a *participation certificate (PC),* which can be used to change the rate sensitivity or duration of the asset portfolio. Details on PCs are given later; for accounting and tax purposes, they are considered real estate investments, just like mortgages, but are much more liquid. FNMA instituted a similar program after FHLMC's.[25]

If mortgage rates and loan demand are high, the lender might sell the PCs obtained through the mortgage swap to other investors,

thereby raising cash that can be reinvested in new variable-rate or shorter-term mortgages. If a firm wants to attract new liabilities, it might use the securities in repurchase agreements. Thrifts, the FHLMC, and the FNMA continue to experiment with a variety of alternative uses for mortgage swaps.

A typical series of transactions involving a mortgage swap is illustrated in Figure 18.2. In step 1, the lender designates a package of mortgages to be assigned to FHLMC. In exchange, FHLMC issues PCs to the lender. Step 2 illustrates the choices now available to the lender. On the one hand, the PCs can be sold to other investors for cash. As an alternative, the PCs can be used as collateral for repurchase agreements or mortgage-backed bonds, enabling the lender to obtain cash for new investments.

Characteristics of Guaranteed Mortgage Securities

The two choices available in the secondary mortgage market—sell or swap—are better appreciated after examining characteristics of secondary market securities.

The GNMA Pass-Through Program.   One security arising from secondary mortgage market transactions is called a *pass-through (PT).* PTs are guaranteed by GNMA but are actually issued by mortgage lenders. If the issuer defaults, there are back-up guarantees.

Figure 18.3 illustrates the process by which GNMA pass-throughs are created. In step 1, a lender deposits a pool of FHA-insured or VA-guaranteed mortgages with a trustee, usually a commercial bank commissioned by GNMA; no conventional mortgages may be used in the GNMA program. Both the trustee and GNMA examine the designated pool, and, if it is satisfactory, GNMA agrees to provide subsequent guarantees against default on these mortgages.

With the benefit of the GNMA guarantee, the original lender sells securities to investors for cash. This cash can then be used to make additional investments, a process not shown in Figure 18.3. The GNMA securities have maturities equal to the remaining maturity of the

---

[24]Michel McQueen, "Fannie Mae Drops Plans for Exchange for Mortgages," *The Wall Street Journal,* April 27, 1987, p. 27.

[25]Further discussion on mortgage swap programs is available in "Rate Volatility Points to Increase in Mortgage Swaps," *Freddie Mac Reports* 2 (August 1984): 1-2; and Kevin Villani, "Liquidity, Flexibility Spur the Market," *Savings Institutions* 106 (January 1985): S33-S36.

Figure 18.2
Results of a Mortgage Swap

Step 1: The Swap Occurs

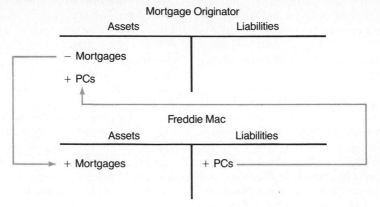

Step 2: PCs Are Used to Generate New Funds

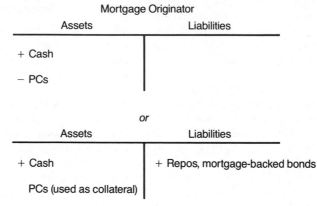

mortgage pool. Unlike ordinary bonds, on which no principal is due until maturity, GNMA securities are amortized like mortgages; that is, monthly payments include both principal and interest. Furthermore, as mortgages in the pool are prepaid, investors in GNMAs receive these prepayments.

In step 2 of the figure, borrowers continue to make payments on the pool of FHA or VA mortgages as usual. As lenders receive these cash payments, they pass them through to GNMA investors. Should any borrower

default, GNMA guarantees assure investors they will continue to receive their promised payments.

Participation Certificates. A participation certificate (PC) is a security issued and guaranteed against default by FHLMC. As illustrated earlier in Figure 18.2, PCs are collateralized by mortgages FHLMC has received from mortgage lenders in a purchase or swap. FNMA issues similar securities called "mortgage-backed securities" (MBS). Subsequent discussions

Figure 18.3
The GNMA Pass-Through Program

Step 1: GNMAs Are Issued

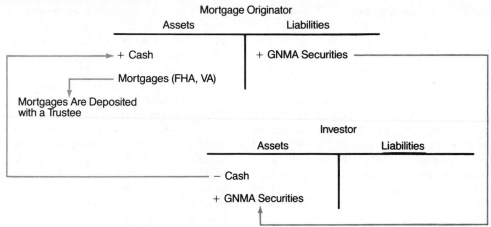

Step 2: Mortgage Payments Are Passed through to Investors

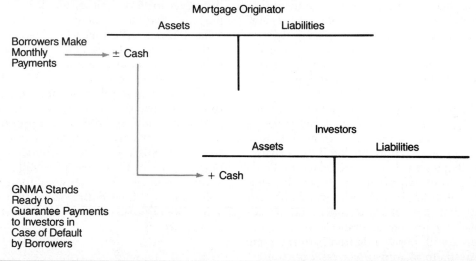

use PC to refer to both FHLMC and FNMA issues.

Like PTs, PCs pass returns through to investors in the form of monthly principal and interest payments from a specified pool of mortgage loans. Unlike PTs, however, the mortgage pool backing PCs is owned by the secondary market agency rather than the original lender. FNMA and FHLMC reduce the risk to the security holder by promising to continue payments even if the borrower defaults on an underlying mortgage. This guarantee makes the securities more marketable than the mortgages themselves. This factor explains why, in

Figure 18.2, the mortgage originator can use PCs as collateral against a repo or mortgage-backed bond issue when the mortgages themselves might not have qualified.

PTs and PCs as Investments.   PCs and PTs are not used by depositories solely as ways of raising new funds. They also serve as investments for mortgage lenders with excess funds. When mortgage demand in a market is low, holding PCs or PTs allows the lender to continue the desired level of involvement in the real estate market, but as a secondary rather than a primary market investor. The willingness of traditional mortgage lenders to buy PCs and PTs allows mortgage funds to be efficiently redistributed among geographic regions. In fact, savings institutions are the largest category of investors in the PC market, holding almost half of the PCs outstanding in recent years.

A major drawback of PTs and PCs to the secondary market investor is the uncertainty of cash flows, because there are no assurances that the underlying mortgage will not be prepaid. This possibility exposes the security holder to reinvestment risk. To address this problem, Fannie Mae began selling stripped pass-throughs in 1986, similar to the stripped Treasury securities discussed in Chapter 8.

Another security that attempts to circumvent the reinvestment problem is the collateralized mortgage obligation (CMO), first described in the section on liability management in Chapter 15. CMOs are issued by Freddie Mac as well as primary mortgage lenders. Because CMOs are issued with several different classes of cash flow characteristics, and are accompanied by greater assurances to investors that returns will follow a desired pattern, some thrifts buy them to adjust their asset portfolios. CMOs can be purchased with short, intermediate, or long maturities, depending on the desired change in the weighted average duration of assets.

Restructuring Liabilities through the Secondary Market

Although the greatest attraction of the secondary mortgage market is to reposition the asset portfolio, there are a few avenues for restructuring liabilities as well. One alternative illustrated earlier is to use the PCs obtained through mortgage sales or swaps to obtain new funds through mortgage-backed bonds. In fact, if the goal is to better match longer-term assets with longer-term liabilities, this could be an attractive strategy. Although investors would require a risk premium for buying uninsured debt from depositories, those pledging PCs as collateral can find interested buyers at affordable rates.

Some lending institutions have begun to set aside portions of their mortgage portfolio to secure long-term debt, a strategy that can reduce both the rate-sensitivity and duration GAP. Mortgage-backed bonds also provide cash flow flexibility, because the interest and principal payments on the collateral are received monthly, but returns are paid only semi-annually to investors in the bonds backed by the mortgages.

Although increasing liability duration is desirable to most mortgage lenders, accomplishing that adjustment through mortgage-backed bonds has drawbacks. The most serious is the volume of loans that must be pledged as collateral. In an environment of rising interest rates, the market value of loans will decline, and the principal value of mortgages required to collateralize the debt could exceed the bond principal significantly. A related problem is that mortgage loans are repaid on an amortized basis, but bonds are not. The bond principal is outstanding for the entire time, and a very large volume of mortgages is required to produce full collateral over their entire maturity. Finally, issuing bonds involves transaction costs, which reduce profits.

SECURITIZATION: DEVELOPMENT OF OTHER SECONDARY LOAN MARKETS

Also increasing the flexibility of depositories' asset portfolios is the development of secondary markets for loans other than mortgages. First defined in Chapter 2, the process of converting nonmarketable assets into forms acceptable to secondary market purchasers is called securitization.

An early effort was the creation of a security backed by automobile loans, marketed in 1985 by Marine Midland Bank of New York with help from Salomon Brothers investment bankers. The securities were aptly named *Certificates for Automobile Receivables (CARs).*[26] These securities were followed by others backed by loans on cars, trucks, and computers. Thus far, finance companies have been the largest issuers. Additional types of consumer and commercial loans are currently candidates for securitization, and using accounts receivable as collateral for new securities is being explored by nonfinancial firms.

The new secondary market instruments, generically called *asset-backed securities,* are similar to mortgage pass-throughs; a financial institution passes through monthly loan payments to security holders. In some cases, a third party, such as an insurance company or a large bank, promises to continue payment on the loans should original borrowers default. In other cases, the issuer provides its own limited guarantee or pledges collateral in excess of the security principal.

Asset-backed securities promise improvements in asset management. They offer ways for commercial banks and credit unions, for example, to sell loans to increase liquidity. Thrifts with difficulty building a clientele of consumer borrowers may be able to diversify asset portfolios more quickly by investing in asset-backed securities than by originating loans themselves. In addition, institutions with loan demand but without sufficient capital to support growth can benefit from selling their loans to other investors.

However, regulators and investors have expressed concern about securitization. A market for asset-backed securities with low-quality loans as collateral is not likely to arise. Consequently, institutions desiring to issue asset-backed securities may be pressured to pledge their highest-quality loans, exposing existing creditors to increased risk. Further regulatory scrutiny is guaranteed as the market develops.

SUMMARY

Traditional GAP management has limitations that have led to the development of supplementary tools for asset/liability management. One is the use of duration-based GAP management. Duration GAP measurements are more closely related to potential changes in the value of net worth than are rate-sensitivity GAP measurements. The disadvantage is the somewhat complex calculations required to manage duration GAPs properly.

Additional techniques are available for hedging GAPs rather than restructuring them. Two prominent ones are the markets for interest rate futures and interest rate swaps. Their advantage is the avoidance of the active balance sheet restructuring required in GAP management. Their disadvantages are that they require considerable management expertise and, as hedging tools, do not permit an institution to increase profits from unexpected but favorable shifts in interest rates.

Finally, secondary markets exist for some assets, especially mortgages. These markets present additional opportunities for balance sheet restructuring. Managers must familiarize themselves with these tools in order to meet their goals for the net interest margin and return on net worth.

[26]"CARS Program Leads the Way to New Types of Securities," *Savings Institutions* 106 (June 1985): 109, 111; Wayne Olson, "Securitization Comes to Other Assets," *Savings Institutions* 107 (May 1986): 81-85; Christopher Farrell and Maralyn Edid, "Rolling Consumer Debt into Reams of New Paper," *Business Week,* January 13, 1986, pp. 110-111; Harvey D. Shapiro, "The Securitization of Practically Everything," *Institutional Investor* 19 (May 1985): 196-202; Randall J. Pozdena, "Securitization and Banking," Federal Reserve Bank of San Francisco *Weekly Letter,* July 4, 1986; Christopher Farrell, "Making More Debt Do Double Duty," *Business Week*, March 30, 1987, pp. 67-68.

Questions

1. Explain how a depository could become insolvent even with perfectly matched asset and liability maturities.

2. What are the advantages of duration GAP measurements? What data are used to calculate a duration GAP? Why do some financial institutions immunize only portions of the balance sheet when using a duration GAP management strategy?

3. Compare and contrast strategies for managing the rate-sensitivity GAP and the duration GAP under expectations of rising rates and under expectations of falling rates.

4. What advantages are offered by futures hedges that are not provided by GAP management? Explain the difference between a macro hedge and a micro hedge. Which type is more realistic for most institutions? Why? How do accounting and regulatory standards affect hedging strategies?

5. Explain how futures can be used to create loan terms that meet the interest rate risk preferences of both borrowers and lenders.

6. Explain the problems faced by depository institution managers who use futures in asset/liability management.

7. What is an interest rate swap? What are the motivations for participating in swaps? Explain the factors financial institutions must consider in negotiating swaps.

8. Compare and contrast the advantages and disadvantages of using interest rate futures and interest rate swaps as supplements to GAP management.

9. Explain how mortgage lenders can use the secondary mortgage market as an asset/liability management tool. In particular, identify differences in the effects of selling versus swapping mortgages.

10. Explain the federal government's role in developing the secondary mortgage market. Do you think that the debt of private firms such as Fannie Mae should continue to carry government agency status and thereby receive favorable borrowing rates? Why or why not?

11. What are participation certificates? How do financial institutions use them in asset/liability management? Explain differences in the ownership of the mortgage pool backing pass-throughs and participation certificates.

12. Briefly explain the GNMA pass-through program.

13. Under what circumstances do mortgage lenders use pass-throughs and participation certificates as investments? For secondary market investors, what risks are associated with holding pass-throughs and participation certificates?

14. How can the secondary mortgage markets be used to adjust the liability structure of a depository institution?

15. What is securitization? Of what advantage is securitization to commercial banks? To credit unions? How does securitization change the traditional operating characteristics of lending institutions? Do you think depositories' participation in emerging secondary asset markets should be regulated? Why or why not?

Problems

1. Return to the Heartland Credit Union example in the chapter. Assume the consumer loans have an average maturity of 60 months (10 percent annual rate); the mortgages are expected to be prepaid in 12 years (9.6 percent annual rate); and the share certificates have an average maturity of two months. Current market yields/costs are as shown in Table 18.3.

   a. Under these new assumptions, calculate the duration GAP. (Hint: The amount to be received in 12 years when the mortgages are prepaid is the remaining principal balance at that time. You can prepare an amortization schedule for the mortgages to determine that amount.)

   b. Estimate the percentage by which net worth would change, given the following changes in market rates:

   1) an increase of 100 basis points
   2) a decrease of 75 basis points

2. The balance sheet of Landmark Savings Bank follows, along with the average duration of each account.

Landmark Savings Bank
Balance Sheet Analysis
(Millions)

Assets		Liabilities and Net Worth	
Short-term securities and adjustable-rate loans	$250	Short-term and floating-rate funds	$600
Duration: 3 months		Duration: 1 month	
Fixed-rate loans	650	Fixed-rate funds	280
Duration: 8 years		Duration: 35 months	
Nonearning assets	40	Net worth	60
Duration: NA		Duration: NA	
Total assets	$940	Total liabilities and net worth	$940

   a. Calculate Landmark's duration GAP.

   b. If return on net worth is now 16 percent, and if the general level of interest rates increases by 60 basis points, by how much will Landmark's net worth change?

   c. Suppose the expected change in net worth is unacceptable to management. Suggest several actions that could be taken to counteract it. What are the advantages and disadvantages of each action?

3. Return to the example of the Southwest Savings and Loan Association interest rate swap in the chapter. Suppose that Southwest agrees to swap interest on $35 million principal value of short-term liabilities under the same terms as described in the chapter—paying interest of 11.50 percent on the bank's debt while receiving 25 basis points above the LIBOR rate, currently at 10.35 percent.

   a. What is the dollar cost of the "insurance" the swap provides if there is no rate increase after the swap?

   b. What would pretax earnings be if rates increase after the $35 million swap, as described in the chapter—that is, if the yield on rate-sensitive assets increases to 12.30 percent, the cost of rate-sensitive liabilities increases to 11.10 percent, and the LIBOR rate increases to 11.95 percent?

4. The management of Mercantile Bank and Trust has conducted an interest-rate sensitivity analysis of the bank's balance sheet. The result is given below:

Mercantile Bank and Trust
Balance Sheet Analysis
(Millions)

Assets		*Liabilities and Equity*	
Cash	$ 10.0		
Average return: 0%			
Short-term securities and floating-rate loans	65.0	Short-term and floating-rate funds	$ 43.0
Average return: 8.5%		Average cost: 7.2%	
Fixed-rate loans	20.0	Fixed-rate funds	50.0
Average return: 10.0%		Average cost: 9.0%	
Nonearning assets	8.0	Equity	10.0
Total assets	$103.0	Total liabilities and equity	$103.0

Management expects interest rates to decline but is reluctant to force customers into fixed-rate loans or to encourage depositors into floating-rate deposits, for fear of alienating them. A broker has found an S&L forecasting higher interest rates that is willing to serve as a counterparty to an interest rate swap. The S&L will assume interest payments on $30 million of fixed-rate deposits at an average rate of 8.8 percent. Mercantile agrees to pay interest on $30 million at a floating rate 1 percent higher than the one-year T–bill index. The initial rate Mercantile will pay is 7.4 percent.

a. Calculate Mercantile's expected pretax profits before the swap.

b. Suppose Mercantile is right, and rates begin to fall. The T–bill index drops to 6 percent, the return on rate-sensitive assets falls to 8.0 percent, and the cost of rate-sensitive liabilities falls to 6.8 percent. Recompute Mercantile's expected pretax profits after the swap.

c. Suppose the S&L is right, and rates increase. The T–bill index rises to 7.2 percent, the return on rate-sensitive assets rises to 9.0 percent, and the cost of rate-sensitive liabilities rises to 8.1 percent. Calculate Mercantile's expected profits under this scenario.

d. Besides the risk of incorrect interest rate forecasts, to what other risks does the swap expose Mercantile?

Selected References

Belongia, Michael T., and G. J. Santoni. "Cash Flow or Present Value: What's Lurking Behind the Hedge?" *Review* (Federal Reserve Bank of St. Louis) 67 (January 1985): 5-13.

Bennewitz, Dall. *Introduction to the Secondary Mortgage Market: A Primer.* Revised ed. Chicago: U.S. League of Savings Institutions, 1984.

Bicksler, James, and Andrew H. Chen. "An Economic Analysis of Interest Rate Swaps." *Journal of Finance* 41 (July 1986): 645-655.

Brewer, Elijah. "Bank GAP Management and the Use of Financial Futures." *Economic Perspectives* (Federal Reserve Bank of Chicago) 9 (March/April 1985): 12-22.

Chicago Board of Trade. *Interest Rate Futures for Institutional Investors.* Chicago: Board of Trade of the City of Chicago, 1985.

Gau, George W., and Michael A. Goldberg. "Interest Rate Risk, Residential Mortgages and Financial Futures Markets." *AREUEA Journal* 11 (1983): 445-461.

Haley, Charles W. "Interest Rate Risk in Financial Intermediaries: Prospects for Immunization." In *Proceedings of a Conference on Bank Structure and Competition*. Chicago: Federal Reserve Bank of Chicago, 1982, pp. 309-317.

Jacobs, Rodney L. "Fixed-Rate Lending and Interest Rate Futures Hedging." *Journal of Bank Research* 13 (Autumn 1983): 193-202.

Kane, Edward J., and Chester Foster. "Valuing Conjectural Government Guarantees of FNMA Liabilities," *Proceedings of a Conference on Bank Structure and Competition*. Chicago: Federal Reserve Bank of Chicago, 1986, pp. 347-368.

Kaufman, George. "Measuring and Managing Interest Rate Risk: A Primer." *Economic Perspectives* (Federal Reserve Bank of Chicago) 8 (January/February 1984): 16-29.

Kolb, Robert W., Stephen G. Timme, and Gerald D. Gay. "Macro versus Micro Futures Hedges at Commercial Banks." *Journal of the Futures Markets* 4 (1984): 47-54.

Koppenhaver, Gary. "Trimming the Hedges: Regulators, Banks, and Financial Futures." *Economic Perspectives* (Federal Reserve Bank of Chicago) 8 (November/December 1984): 3-12.

Lereah, David. "The Growth of Interest Rate Swaps." *Bankers Magazine* 169 (May-June 1986): 36-44.

Loeys, Jan G. "Interest Rate Swaps: A New Tool for Managing Risk." *Business Review* (Federal Reserve Bank of Philadelphia) (May/June 1985), pp. 17-25.

Nagle, Reid. "The Use of Financial Futures in Asset/Liability Management." In *Managing Interest Rate Risk in the Thrift Industry*. San Francisco: Federal Home Loan Bank of San Francisco, 1981, pp. 109-132.

Olson, Wayne. "Securitization Comes to Other Assets." *Savings Institutions* 107 (May 1986): 81-85.

Rosenblum, Harvey. "Liability Strategies for Minimizing Interest Rate Risk." In *Managing Interest Rate Risk in the Thrift Industry*. San Francisco: Federal Home Loan Bank of San Francisco, 1981, pp. 157-180.

Shapiro, Harvey D. "The Securitization of Practically Everything." *Institutional Investor* 19 (May 1985): 196-202.

Smith, Clifford W., Jr., Charles W. Smithson, and Lee Macdonald Wakeman. "The Evolving Market for Swaps." *Midland Corporate Finance Journal* 4 (Winter 1986): 20-32.

Toevs, Alden L. "Gap Management: Managing Interest Rate Risk in Banks and Thrifts." *Economic Review* (Federal Reserve Bank of San Francisco) (Spring 1983), pp. 20-35.

Turnbull, Stuart M. "Swaps: A Zero Sum Game?" *Financial Management* 16 (Spring 1987): 15-21.

Villani, Kevin. "The Secondary Mortgage Markets: What They Are, What They Do and How to Measure Them." *Secondary Mortgage Markets* 1 (February 1984): 24-44.

Walters, Jeffrey M. "The Futures Alternative to Fixed Rate Financing." *Journal of Commercial Bank Lending* 67 (February 1985): 39-46.

Whittaker, J. Gregg. "Interest Rate Swaps: Risk and Regulation." *Economic Review* (Federal Reserve Bank of St. Louis) 72 (March 1987): 3-13.

Chapter 19

LONG-TERM ASSET/ LIABILITY MANAGEMENT DECISIONS

Checks are like dead bodies. They are not a lot of use to you anymore, but you want to know they are taken care of and you don't really want them around the house.

Fred L. Stadler, Industry Development
Specialist for IBM (1980)

GERARD Marrotte of Middletown, Connecticut, had an unusual experience in February 1985. In a contest open to those who conducted their banking through automated teller machines (ATMs), his depository institution, Liberty Bank for Savings, let him keep all the $10 bills he could withdraw from an ATM in three minutes. He left with $1,000. At the same time, customers of Norwest Bank in Minneapolis were enjoying meals at McDonald's, courtesy of the bank, because they had used its ATMs.[1]

These institutions made the free offers because their managers had decided, as part of a long-term plan, to invest in electronic banking equipment. The equipment is expensive, and over time its benefits must exceed its costs. But unless customers use the equipment, there are no benefits. Thus, decisions with long-run implications must be analyzed especially carefully, and once undertaken must be managed properly to increase the probability that expected

---

[1]Daniel Hertzberg, "If Carrots Don't Persuade People to Use ATMs, Banks Go for Sticks," *The Wall Street Journal,* February 21, 1985, p. 33.

benefits will materialize. The Liberty and Norwest offers were a small part of the follow-up to an important long-term investment decision.

SHORT-RUN VERSUS LONG-RUN DECISIONS

A major portion of the material in Chapters 12-18 focuses on decisions that restructure a depository's balance sheet in response to expected changes in interest rates or to actions of competitors and regulators. Many of those decisions are intended to be relatively short-term adjustments. Even if they are not, they can usually be reversed, should conditions dictate, through the natural passage of time. For example, the periodic maturing of loans and deposits provides managers with opportunities to alter the asset and liability mix, "undoing" past decisions if necessary. Thus, even though costs are associated with making the wrong portfolio decisions, few such decisions are irreversible.

Other decisions that restructure the balance sheet may be harder to undo. Implementing a plan to computerize lending and deposit taking, which substantially increases investment in fixed assets, may take months or even years. Once the equipment is in place, only as it wears out are there automatic opportunities to reverse the course, so management must be prepared to monitor decisions and to take action necessary to secure their success. If not, the consequences of a bad decision may be costly. Frequently, as in this example, decisions that are difficult to undo involve investment in real, instead of financial, assets.

This chapter examines long-term asset/liability planning in depository institutions, beginning with a decision framework for long-term investments. The framework is applied to two of the most important types of long-term decisions made by depositories: 1) whether to invest in electronic funds transfer equipment; and 2) whether to merge by acquiring another financial institution. Although the information in the chapter is limited to those two issues, the process illustrated applies to any long-term commitment of funds by the institution, such as opening a new branch office or remodeling headquarters.

THE MODEL FOR LONG-TERM INVESTMENT DECISIONS

Students of corporate finance need not look far for a model of long-term investment in depositories, because *net present value (NPV)* is relevant for both nonfinancial and financial firms.

General Formula

The net present value of a decision is the present value of the after-tax cash inflows expected during a planning period (N) netted against the present value of the expected after-tax cash outflows required. This concept is reflected in the formula below, in which i is used in a general sense to reflect the interest rate, discount rate, or required rate of return. This is the same sense in which i is used to reflect the general level of market yields in earlier chapters.

$$(19.1) \quad NPV = \sum_{t=0}^{N} \frac{C_t}{(1 + i)^t}$$

Periodic cash flows (C_t) can be positive or negative, depending upon whether they are inflows or outflows. The only relevant after-tax cash benefits and costs are *incremental* ones—those cash flows specifically resulting from the proposed decision, *not* those expected whether or not the decision is made.

Modifications of the General Formula

Of course, no single interest or discount rate applies to all present-value decisions. The discount rate used to calculate an NPV should reflect the riskiness of the decision. For long-term decisions considered to be of average risk compared to the ongoing operations of the business, the weighted average cost of capital (k_A) is often suggested as the appropriate discount rate. Introduced in Chapter 16, k_A represents the average yield expected by the institution's suppliers of long-term funds. Thus, the NPV model for projects of average risk is:

$$(19.2) \quad NPV = \sum_{t=0}^{N} \frac{C_t}{(1 + k_A)^t}$$

Investments of above- or below-average risk should be discounted at a rate lower or higher than the cost of capital.[2]

If cash outflows are expected only when the decision is made, the NPV equation is often written as:

$$(19.3) \quad NPV = \sum_{t=1}^{N} \frac{C_t}{(1 + k_A)^t} - C_0$$

In Equation 19.3, C_0 is the after-tax cash cost of a project.

Objective of NPV Analysis

Once cash flows have been estimated, calculating the NPV is a mechanical task that acquires meaning only with proper interpretation. Fortunately, interpretation is straightforward: If the NPV of a decision is positive, the institution expects to earn more than its minimum required rate of return; the PV of benefits outweighs the PV of costs, including the opportunity cost reflected in the discount rate. If the NPV is negative, the opposite is true. If the NPV is $0, the decision is expected to have a neutral long-term financial effect on the institution.

A positive NPV is economically desirable; value will be added to the existing value of the institution. A negative-NPV decision will decrease the value of the institution, and a $0-NPV decision will leave value unchanged. Thus, institutions avoid negative-NPV decisions unless required for legal or regulatory reasons.

NPV analysis has another desirable characteristic from a decision-making standpoint. The NPVs of investments can be compared directly with one another because each NPV calculation implicitly considers the size and riskiness of the project involved. Thus, if one decision has an NPV of $50,000, while another has an NPV of only $40,000, a manager knows that the higher-NPV project is expected to add more value to the institution, even if it costs more initially and is riskier. Although both projects are acceptable, the $50,000-NPV project is better.

NPV Analysis and the Net Interest Margin

An institution's long-term investment decisions can affect interest revenues and expenses, non-interest revenues and expenses, or both. Thus, on a year-by-year basis, they affect NIM and return on net worth, just as other management decisions do. But because projects most suitable for NPV analysis are often relatively small compared to the institution's overall portfolio, their impact on the firm from start to finish can get lost in the short run. NPV analysis attempts

---

[2]Selecting the proper discount rate for decisions that are not of average risk is not a "cut-and-dried" matter. Some scholars advocate using a CAPM-determined rate reflecting the yield the financial markets require on financial assets that are equivalent in risk to the project at hand. This approach requires estimating the beta coefficient of the project, a difficult process for investments without a large body of data. Others suggest selecting the discount rate based on different measures of risk, such as the standard deviation or coefficient of variation of the investment's cash flows. Practitioners often suggest a subjective assessment, adjusting the discount rate up or down from the cost of capital, depending upon management's personal assessment of project risk.

There are many discussions of these alternatives and other NPV issues, among which are Richard Brealey and Stuart Myers, *Principles of Corporate Finance* (New York: McGraw-Hill, 1984), Chapters 5, 6, and 9; Haim Levy

and Marshall Sarnatt, *Capital Investment and Financial Decisions,* 3d ed. (Englewood Cliffs, NJ: Prentice-Hall, 1986); and Allen H. Seed III, "Structuring Capital Spending Hurdle Rates," *Financial Executive* (February 1982): 20-28.

to isolate the effect of a single decision on the long-run value of the depository. Thus, it is complementary to, not in conflict with, strategies for short-run asset/liability management.

ELECTRONIC FUNDS TRANSFER SYSTEMS

Analyzing potential investments in electronic funds transfer (EFT) systems is an important application of NPV models. First defined in Chapter 2, EFTs are methods of transmitting funds from one party to another by electronically encoded impulses, rather than by paper check, money order, currency and coin, or other physical means. Although nonphysical methods of transferring funds date at least to the establishment of the Fed's wire transfer system in 1915, emphasis on EFTs has grown in recent years.

For example, the federal government promotes the "direct deposit" of Social Security payments. Television messages encourage citizens to forgo Postal Service delivery of checks in favor of electronic communications. In a direct deposit transaction, the Social Security Administration encodes a magnetic tape with instructions, which are then processed by computer at a regional Federal Reserve Bank. The Fed increases the account of the recipient's institution and in turn notifies the institution to credit the recipient's account.

Advantages and Disadvantages of EFT

The advantages of direct deposit—one of the applications of EFT—are many. A great number of transactions can be completed almost instantaneously. Record keeping is streamlined, enabling large users to reduce personnel costs. Checks cannot get lost in the mail, destroyed, or stolen. Funds are deposited even when the recipient is hospitalized or immobile. Finally, the mountain of paper processed by the government, the depository institution, and the recipient is reduced.

There are disadvantages, too. The equipment for processing transactions electronically is expensive. Transactions can be executed incorrectly, creating difficulty in tracing the source of the error once funds have been transferred. Further, there is a small risk of loss through fraud or damaged equipment.

Most depository institutions have concluded in recent years that the benefits of EFTs far outweigh their disadvantages. A recent staff study for the Board of Governors of the Federal Reserve System concluded, in fact, that as early as 1981, the present value of the savings to the federal government and financial institutions from direct deposit of Social Security benefits in lieu of paper checks ranged from \$4.11 to \$51.62 *per account,* depending upon how a check recipient actually deposited his check.[3] Because there are millions of Social Security accounts, the potential savings is substantial, and direct deposit is only one of many possible ways EFT can replace checks.

An American Bankers Association study found that the average check is handled a minimum of 10.2 times during processing. With EFT, the transactions costs can be cut substantially, from an average of \$.59 by mail or \$.24 by teller to \$.07 by EFT.[4] Thus, institutions use promotions like those described in the opening paragraph to encourage customers to use EFT. Before applying the NPV framework to an EFT decision, however, it is useful to know more about the range of EFT applications available. As with all computer technology, options increase rapidly, but the following are the most common forms of EFT in the 1980s.

---

[3]William Dudley, "A Comparison of Direct Deposit and Check Payment Costs," Board of Governors of the Federal Reserve System, Staff Study No. 141, November 1984. Dudley's estimates do not include the costs of fraud with either check or direct deposit payments, nor do they include estimates of the relative costs and benefits of both systems to the payment recipients.

[4]Judy Wenzel, "Electronic Buying to Come, in TYME," *Milwaukee Journal,* March 6, 1983, Business and Finance Section, p. 1; Paul Cox, "Direct Deposit of U.S. Checks Gains Popularity," *The Wall Street Journal,* April 21, 1986, p. 21.

Automated Clearinghouses

A clearinghouse is a system through which a depository institution receives information about payments to and from its customers' accounts. Since its creation, the Federal Reserve System has played a major role in clearing services as part of its mandate to provide the nation with a stable payments system. Typically, regional Federal Reserve Banks serve as clearing locations where institutions' accounts are debited or credited as necessary, and checks are sorted, bundled, and returned to participating depositories. Often the Fed's clearing services are supplemented by privately operated systems, such as the New York Clearing House Association, which arose to assist institutions with large numbers of daily transactions drawn on one another.

By the 1970s, population growth and prosperity had pushed estimates of the annual volume of paper checks in the 1980s to astronomical levels, beyond the capabilities of existing processing systems.[5] This concern led to the formation of *automated clearinghouses (ACHs),* processing systems established by private institutions agreeing to exchange information by magnetic tape. In 1986, regional ACH systems numbered 31, serving 16,000 financial institutions and 34,000 nonfinancial corporations. The Federal Reserve and four private processing organizations handle transactions, with the Fed processing by far the largest volume.[6]

The federal government is currently the largest user of ACHs. Not only does it encourage Social Security recipients to use direct deposit, it also encourages federal employees to accept salaries, wages, and pension payments that way. As a result of the government's emphasis on EFT, 299 million federal transactions were processed through ACHs in 1985. Other major users include life insurance companies, many of which encourage customers to preauthorize electronic transfer of premium payments from their accounts to the insurers'. Over 278 million commercial transactions were processed through ACHs in 1985.

ACHs in the Future.   Resistance to EFT from large corporations is perhaps the single biggest reason why ACH usage has not reached the level forecast by early proponents. The traditional method of meeting a payroll allows corporations to use the float. If payday is on a Friday, and an employee cashes or deposits his check on the way home from work, the corporation has the use of the funds at least until Monday when the check is physically cleared at the nearest Fed or other clearinghouse. Float is also available on other types of corporate funds transfers, such as the payment of accounts payable.[7]

---

[5]Based on the annual growth rate in check volume from 1960 to 1973, an estimate of 1985 check volume was 54 billion items, made in the 1970s, in Robert E. Knight, "The Changing Payments Mechanism: Electronic Funds Transfer Arrangements," *Monthly Review,* Federal Reserve Bank of Kansas City 60 (July-August 1974): 10. Actually, in 1985, only 45 billion checks were written. See William Gruber, "Checks Get Credit for Longevity," *Chicago Tribune,* June 25, 1986, Section 3, pp. 1, 6; Pamela S. Frisbee, "The ACH: An Elusive Dream," *Economic Review,* Federal Reserve Bank of Atlanta 71 (March 1986): 7.

[6]The role of the Federal Reserve in ACH operations is controversial. On the one hand, some argue that the cost of establishing an ACH is so great that only the Fed can afford it. If promoting EFTs is in the nation's best interests, Fed involvement is indicated. On the other hand, it

can be argued that federal presence in the development of ACHs prevents private initiative and innovation. Congress was influenced by the latter view in 1980, when DIDMCA included a requirement that the Fed price its own clearing services so as not to stifle private entry into the market.

For further discussion, see Bernard Shull, "Economic Efficiency, Public Regulation, and Financial Reform: Depository Institutions," in *Financial Institutions and Markets,* 2d ed. Murray E. Polakoff and Thomas A. Durkin, eds. (Boston: Houghton Mifflin, 1981), p. 696; Theodore E. Allison, "The Federal Reserve's Role in the Payments Mechanism and Its Communication Plans," *Economic Review,* Federal Reserve Bank of Richmond, 68 (March/April 1982): 21-25; and Bernell K. Stone, "Electronic Payment Basics," *Economic Review,* Federal Reserve Bank of Atlanta 71 (March 1986): 9-18; James N. Duprey, "A Visible Hand: The Fed's Involvement in the Check Payments System," *Quarterly Review,* Federal Reserve Bank of Minneapolis 10 (Spring 1986): 18-29.

[7]In 1983, for example, the Westinghouse Electric Corporation estimated that it would have a net loss of approxi-

Historical opposition to EFT from large corporations is likely to change in the future. DIDMCA's mandate to the Fed to lower or eliminate the float has resulted in attempts to speed check processing of all types and to charge interest to depositories on any float remaining. Depositories have responded by charging customers greater fees for paper transactions.[8] In addition, the loss of payment float is offset by the speed with which funds can be collected with EFT. Finally, corporations are increasingly automating all routine functions in order to obtain the greatest productivity from investment in computers. EFT is another way of making sure in-house systems are used to capacity.

For a financial institution to participate in ACH activities, it must have the equipment to receive and send electronic messages. In addition, its customers must be willing to send and receive funds in nontraditional ways. Because change in both these areas is gradual, the vast majority of payment processing continues to be through nonelectronic means; by 1985, ACH volume was only 1.5 percent of total check-processing volume.[9] Still, the decreasing cost of electronic equipment and changing customer attitudes increase the likelihood that ACH vol-

ume will grow through the 1990s. To encourage growth, the Fed embarked on a major upgrade of its electronic communication systems in the early 1980s. Objectives of this project are, among others, to create nationwide ACH capabilities and to enhance both the technical and economic feasibility of ACHs for all institutions.

Automated Teller Machines

Automated teller machines (ATMs) are what their name suggests—machines that perform the functions of tellers using electronic instructions from a customer. ATMs verify account balances, dispense cash, accept deposits, receive bill payments, and even make loans. They are available 24 hours a day. Of all the EFT applications, ATMs are by far the most commonly used by consumers. In 1985, slightly over 60,000 ATMs were installed in the United States, involving over 300 million transactions monthly.[10]

Customer Attitudes toward ATMs. Because of their dominant role, ATMs provide the basis for most research into consumer attitudes toward EFT. Early surveys indicated that consumers did not like the substitution of machines for human beings, and that they were apprehensive about the safety and security of ATM transactions. In recent years, however, data on transactions volumes suggest increasing approval of ATMs. The Federal Reserve Bank of Atlanta reported that from 1974 to 1981, usage per ATM per month increased at a compound annual rate of 29.2 percent. Considering that the number of ATMs increased at an annual rate of 34.8 percent over the same period, the sixfold increase in average transactions per machine is impressive evidence that customers will accept

---

mately $2.7 million per year if it used EFT rather than checks for accounts payable; although substantial savings in banking fees and administrative costs could be achieved, the loss of the float pushed the overall result into the red. See Robert L. Caruso, "New Look at ACH Cost/Benefit Details," *ABA Banking Journal* 75 (April 1983): 44-45. For other sources of corporate resistance, see Bernell K. Stone, "Corporate Trade Payments: Hard Lessons in Product Design," *Economic Review,* Federal Reserve Bank of Atlanta 71 (April 1986): 9-21.

[8]It is important to recognize that no customer is entitled to the use of float; it simply arises as a function of check-processing time. Although float is attractive, its demise was probably inevitable even without DIDMCA, as technology has increased efficiency in all parts of the payments system.

[9]Bernell K. Stone, "Electronic Payments at the Crossroads," *Economic Review,* Federal Reserve Bank of Atlanta 71 (March 1986): 20. As small as this percentage seems, ACH volume was only 1 percent of total check volume in 1982, so substantial growth occurred in only three years. See "Electronic Banking," *Business Week,* January 18, 1982, p. 74.

[10]"League Study Offers Check on the Status of Payment Systems," *Savings Institutions* 106 (October 1985): 165-167; Linda Fenner Zimmer, "The Future of ATM Products and Services," *Magazine of Bank Administration* 62 (May 1986): 24; Steven D. Felgran and R. Edward Ferguson, "The Evolution of Retail EFT Networks," *New England Economic Review,* Federal Reserve Bank of Boston (July/August 1986): 40-56.

substitutes for paper checks. In a 1985 survey, 22 percent of the respondents said they actually preferred to use ATMs to conduct their transactions, and another 28 percent expressed no preference between an ATM and a human teller. ATMs were most popular with younger people and city dwellers.[11]

Customer acceptance of EFT has been modeled according to the theory of *innovation adoption.* According to this theory, the proportion of individuals accepting a particular innovation follows an S-curve, such as the one projected for ATMs by researchers at the Federal Reserve Bank of Atlanta, shown in Figure 19.1. When an innovation appears, the proportion of people willing to try it grows slowly, as occurred with the ATM from 1977 to 1980. Then a point is reached at which popularity increases rapidly, and the slope of the adoption curve becomes much steeper, as depicted for the period 1980-1984. Finally, the rate of adoption slows, because most people willing to try the innovation have already done so. That phase is illustrated by the 1984-1986 period in Figure 19.1. In 1983, the time of the Atlanta Fed study, the ATM was expected to plateau at an adoption level of 65 percent by 1987. Some researchers believe the adoption of other EFT systems will follow a similar pattern, beginning in the late 1980s and reaching a saturation point in the 1990s.[12]

ATMs in the Future.   Some evidence suggests that usage of ATMs may have plateaued before 1987 and that the number of ATMs may not increase substantially in the future. Not only have depository institutions invested in them, but retailers, especially grocers and gas stations, have installed them on premises. With a large volume of transactions per machine needed to recover the cost of purchase and installation, and with few ATMs currently used to that point, an increase in the number of ATMs nationwide may not be economically justified.[13]

Even if this conclusion is correct, individual institutions cannot ignore ATMs in the future. The fact that average ATM volume for the system as a whole is below cost-effective levels does not mean that every firm's ATMs share this characteristic. For example, although national averages indicate that most ATM transactions are conducted by only 33 percent of all depository customers, between 70 percent and 80 percent of Citibank's retail customers regularly use its ATMs. Other financial institutions have also been successful in generating high volumes on strategically located machines, such as one on the University of Pennsylvania campus generating 47,000 to 60,000 transactions per month.[14] Furthermore, the technology of ATMs is constantly changing. Improvements in speed, cost, and efficiency may cause a depository to consider ATMs for the first time in the future or to replace existing ATMs with better models. Either way, managers must know how to analyze the alternatives.

Home Banking

Perhaps the most unusual EFT application is *home banking,* in which a customer directs the transfer of funds from his checking account using an in-home video terminal. Although the novelty of this application attracted considerable attention in the early 1980s, including predictions that it would be in use by 30 percent to 40 percent of all American homes by 1990, home banking is not likely to be a major force

---

[11]Examples of the results of research on consumers and EFT include Peter Mears, Daniel E. McCarty, and Robert Osborn, "An Empirical Investigation of Banking Customers' Perception of Bank Machines," *Journal of Bank Research* 9 (Summer 1978): 112-115; Donna M. Gist, "Effective EFT Strategies Demand Consumer Acceptance," *Savings Institutions* 107 (April 1986): 86-87.

[12]William N. Cox and Paul F. Metzker, "Special Issue: Displacing the Check." *Economic Review,* Federal Reserve Bank of Atlanta 68 (August 1983).

[13]See Bernell Stone, "The Revolution in Retail Payments: A Synthesis," *Economic Review,* Federal Reserve Bank of Atlanta 69 (July/August 1984): 46, 54; Zimmer, "The Future of ATM Products and Services"; Paul Duke, Jr., "Bank Machine Makers Rethink Strategy," *The Wall Street Journal,* June 5, 1986, p. 6.

[14]Linda Fenner Zimmer, "A Time for Opportunity," *Magazine of Bank Administration* 61 (May 1985): 20-32.

Figure 19.1
Innovation–Adoption Curve for ATMs

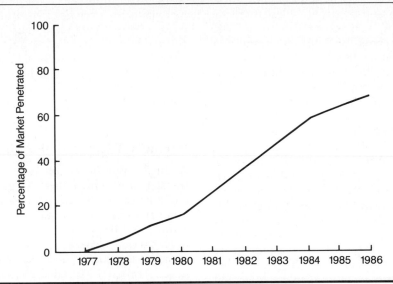

Source: William N. Cox and Paul F. Metzker, "Special Issue: Displacing the Check," *Economic Review,* Federal Reserve Bank of Atlanta 68 (August 1983): 33.

in EFT for many years, if at all. Its potential is limited for two reasons: 1) It is costly for customers, who must have a computer terminal or microcomputer and modem at home; and 2) the most popular EFT transactions, withdrawing cash and making deposits, are not possible with home banking. By 1986, only 38 institutions had home-banking programs, with only 75,000 subscribers nationwide. Few observers predict significant market penetration in the near future unless improved technology allows the service to be priced more attractively.[15]

---

[15]BankAmerica was an innovator in home banking, but usage has fallen short of the institution's early projections. In 1985, it joined with Chemical Bank, AT&T, and Time, Incorporated, in a joint venture offering electronic services to households. Some observers interpreted the joint venture as a "tacit admission" that the payoff from home banking is not likely to be great for an individual firm. See Felgran and Ferguson, "The Evolution of Retail EFT Networks," p. 52.

Point-of-Sale Terminals and Debit Cards

An EFT application with more growth potential is the *point-of-sale (POS) terminal* and the accompanying use of *debit cards.* POS terminals are in-store machines to transfer funds from a buyer's to a seller's account when the buyer uses an electronically encoded debit card. The debit card is used with a number known only to the buyer (his *personal identification number* or *PIN*) and is a substitute for a checkbook. PINs are also used with ATMs, and the plastic cards required to access many ATMs are a type of debit card because they permit the immediate withdrawal of funds from a customer's account.

One difference between paying by check and paying by debit card at a POS terminal is that the buyer loses use of the float. A 1984 survey by the Bank Administration Institute, however, found that consumers objected more to the loss of cancelled checks and the possibility of computer error than to the loss of the float.[16] Thus, debit transactions do not automatically appeal to purchasers, unless there are other cost-saving reasons to use them over checks or credit cards. With the increasing cost of checking accounts, however, and with recent increases in fees and interest on credit cards, the loss of the float may become less costly than other methods of payment.

POS/Debit Cards in the Future. An increasing number of consumers carry debit cards—the total number of debit cards of all types was estimated to be 33 million in 1984. By 1986, 7,500 POS terminals were in commercial use in the United States, up from only 600 in 1984. Although usage of the cards is low compared to credit cards, growth rates into the 1990s for the three major means of payment are forecast to be quite different: 36 percent per year for debit cards, versus 2 percent for credit cards and 2.8 percent for checks. In 1985, fewer than 15 million POS transactions were made, but one research group projected the 1990 volume at between 10 and 20 *billion*. Although such rapid growth seems unlikely, increased acceptance of ATMs will no doubt spur the use of debit cards, because the same card and PIN are often used for both types of EFT transactions.[17]

The use of POS and debit cards also depends on the attitude of sellers. For POS to work, EFT equipment must be available to both merchants and financial institutions, and they must be somehow linked. The question of how costs will be allocated among financial and nonfinancial firms is unresolved, and the answer will be determined when both sides are better able to quantify the costs and benefits of POS systems.

Partially Electronic Funds Transfers

A final application of nontraditional funds transfers for which there is growth potential could be called "PEFT," for partially electronic funds transfers. The best example is *check truncation.* With check truncation, an account holder writes a check, and the payee deposits or cashes it as usual. The check writer, however, never receives a cancelled check upon completion of the transaction. The "paper trail" may stop at either the clearinghouse or the payee's bank. The check itself may be put into storage, or filmed and destroyed. Information on the check is electronically encoded and included as part of the account holder's regular monthly statement.

Credit unions were pioneers in check truncation, and many share drafts are truncated. The motivation for shortening the paper trail is that the issuing institution reduces processing costs. Although early speculation held that customers would oppose truncation, CUs and thrifts, for whose customers checking accounts are relatively new anyway, have not faced great resistance. Banks, which have historically provided full check processing, have had a more difficult time introducing truncation, because their customers have perceived it as a decrease in service. Recently, however, the acceptance of check truncation has increased even among commercial bank customers.[18]

---

[16]The debit does not have to be instantaneous. Because of the expense of equipment permitting instantaneous ("real time") debiting, many POS terminals employ batch processing. With a batch system, all sales via debit card for a particular seller may be accumulated during the day, then sent at one time to an ACH for subsequent execution. The user survey results are reported in Marjolijn van der Velde, "Point of Sale: Attitudes and Perceptions of Financial Institutions, Merchants and Customers," *Magazine of Bank Administration* 60 (April 1985): 42-48

[17]These data are drawn from Janet Bamford, "Perils in Plastic," *Forbes* 134 (December 17, 1984): 200-204; Edwin A. Finn, Jr., "Customers Are Cool to Debit Cards Despite Growing Presence in Stores," *The Wall Street Journal,* August 20, 1985, p. 27; Felgran and Ferguson, "The Evolution of Retail EFT Networks," p. 49; Gist, "The EFT-Check Tussle Outlasts the Predictions," p. 89; and Ronald Osterberg, "POS Is on Its Way," *Economic Review,* Federal Reserve Bank of Atlanta 69 (July/August 1984): 32.

---

[18]D. William Hume, Otto P. Trostel, and Eleanor M. Kruk, "Implementing Check Truncation," *Bankers Magazine* 168 (November/ December 1985): 36-42.

Shared EFT Systems

An important decision individual institutions must make about EFT is whether to invest in equipment that only their customers can use—*proprietary systems*—or whether to initiate or join *shared systems.* Because of high start-up costs, many small institutions participate in shared ATM and POS systems. Institutions investing in electronic equipment can also benefit from shared systems by earning fee income from participating depositories.

The NPV example in the next section focuses on the decision of an individual institution to install a particular type of EFT equipment, and it does not touch upon the issues involved in shared systems. In contrast, a case analysis at the end of the book focuses specifically on the advantages and disadvantages of shared systems, including regulatory, financial, and competitive considerations.

Regulation of EFT

As with most operations of depository institutions, EFT is regulated. In the Electronic Funds Transfer Act of 1974, Congress instructed each of the major depository institution regulators to enforce provisions guaranteeing consumers the right of redress in case of electronic errors, the right to receive receipts for EFT transactions, limited liability for fraudulent use of a debit card or PIN, and other protections. These regulations were codified by the Federal Reserve in *Regulation E,* which serves as a model for other regulators.

Initially, depositories expressed concern about the cost of compliance with Reg E, which first took effect in 1980. In 1985, however, a study for the Board of Governors of the Federal Reserve System indicated that large institutions enjoy substantial economies of scale in compliance costs. Although small institutions offering a full line of proprietary EFT services may be at a cost disadvantage, those wishing to join shared systems can benefit from scale economies. Further, the Fed has recently amended Reg E to exempt depositories with under $25 million in assets. The study also found "negligible" fraud and error with EFT, suggesting that consumers will not be jeopardized as EFT displaces traditional methods of funds delivery.[19]

APPLICATION OF NPV ANALYSIS TO EFT

The analysis to follow focuses on one of the simplest and most common long-term decisions facing depositories: whether to invest in ATMs for dispensing cash, the EFT transaction most popular with customers. A systematic plan should be followed. The first step is to determine the time frame. Then, expected cash inflows and cash outflows—on an incremental, after-tax basis—are estimated. Next, a discount rate is selected, based on the relative riskiness of the decision. Finally, the NPV is calculated. If it is positive, the decision should be undertaken. If the NPV is negative, the plan should be rejected. If it is $0, it is a matter of indifference.

Estimating the Time Frame

There are few rules for estimating a planning horizon. Sometimes, a long-term decision has a known horizon, such as the termination date on a lease. In other situations, the planning period is a matter of judgment. For example, if the decision involves EFT with the possibility of technological obsolescence, the physical life of the equipment may be quite different from its economic life. In any case, the mathematics of present value mean that planning periods of great length are usually unnecessary. The present value of a cash flow expected at a point far in the future is virtually nil anyway.

Suppose that in 1990, a thrift is considering the installation of four cash-dispensing machines at strategic locations in the community,

---

[19]Frederick J. Schroeder, "Compliance Costs and Consumer Benefits of the Electronic Funds Transfer Act: Recent Survey Evidence," Board of Governors of the Federal Reserve System, Staff Study No. 143, April 1985; and Frederick J. Schroeder, "Developments in Consumer Electronic Fund Transfers," *Federal Reserve Bulletin* 69 (June 1983): 395-403.

such as shopping malls and grocery stores. The proposed machines are "state of the art" and are not anticipated to become obsolete for ten years; their physical life is likely to be longer. Because the present value of cash flows expected in later years, especially at relatively high discount rates, is quite small, management decides that the period from the beginning of 1990 to the end of the year 2000, an 11-year horizon, is most appropriate.

Estimating the Cash Flows

The next step in the NPV analysis is estimating incremental cash costs and benefits.[20]

Net Cash Outflows.   The thrift currently has several ATMs it plans to continue operating. Thus, the cost of the four new machines will be entirely incremental; there is no salvage value in 1990 from selling existing machines. Furthermore, no large cash outflows are expected after time 0. The price of a single ATM is estimated at $40,000, but when four are purchased at once, they can be obtained for $35,000 apiece. Installation will add another $35,000 total to the cost in 1990. These figures are certain, because they are based on firm quotations from the ATM vendor. Thus, total cash outflows are $175,000.[21]

Net Cash Inflows.   The cash benefits expected from the new ATMs are much less certain. Both the per-transaction cash savings to

the institution over the next ten years and the volume of transactions are subject to variation. Based on figures available to management, the per-transaction savings expected when a customer uses an ATM instead of writing a check for cash ranges from $0.15 to $2.50, depending upon what happens to a check during processing. The most likely savings is $0.45.

A manager can make a better decision if probabilities are attached to several possible outcomes, and the expected cash savings is based on those probabilities. Suppose there is only a 1 percent chance that the per-transaction savings will be $2.50, a 26 percent chance that the savings will be $0.15, and a 73 percent chance that the cash benefit will be $0.45. The expected per transaction savings is:

$$.01(\$2.50) + .26(\$.15) + .73(\$.45) = \$.39.$$

For simplicity, the manager also assumes that the costs of ATM and paper transactions will increase by approximately equal amounts, so that year-to-year per-transaction savings will remain the same over the ten-year period. If this were not the case, separate savings could be estimated for each year.

Estimating volume is a bit trickier, but clues are available. Using 1979 as the base year, when 18 billion personal payments were made, research in the mid-1980s forecast a 4 percent growth in personal funds transfers of all types into the 1990s. Other studies have indicated that a relatively stable 12 percent of all personal transactions are for cash. As noted earlier, about 65 percent of all cash transactions are projected to occur via ATM when the market becomes fully saturated. If this point is reached by 1990, it is possible to estimate systemwide ATM transactions volume for the period 1990 to 2000. Based on the 80,000 ATMs assumed to be in operation in 1990, it is then possible to estimate per-machine volume for use in the NPV calculation.

Estimates of per-machine volume for the planning period are shown in Table 19.1. The annual transactions per machine are estimated at 27,000 in 1990, growing to 40,000 by the end of the planning period.

---

[20]Because long-term investments may change revenues and expenses of the firm, they have tax implications for most institutions. Discussion of specific tax issues is beyond the scope of this text. In practice, managers of banks and thrifts pay careful attention to taxation, since the tax savings involved in an investment may substantially affect the estimate of value.

[21]In this section, most of the estimates of cash flow and volume are based on actual and projected published data. Major sources for these estimates are Cox and Metzker, "Special Issue: Displacing the Check"; "Electronic Banking," *Business Week,* January 18, 1982, 80-90; Wenzel, "Electronic Buying to Come"; and Marjolijn van der Velde, "Two New Models Tell How Much an ATM Transaction *Really* Costs," *Magazine of Bank Administration* 59 (June 1983): 34-40.

Table 19.1
Volume Estimates for Transactions per ATM, 1990–2000

Assumptions

Base year (1979) volume of personal payments transactions: 18 billion
Estimated annual growth in personal payments: 4%
Percentage of all transactions made to obtain cash: 12%
Percentage of cash transactions made via ATMs: 65%
Total ATMs in operation at saturation point: 80,000
Yearly total personal transactions volume in millions = $18,000 (1.04)^t$, where t = the number of years since 1979 (for example, for 1990, t = 11)

(1) Year	(2) Total Transactions (Millions)	(3) Total Cash Transactions .12 × (2)	(4) Total ATM Cash Transactions .65 × (3)	(5) Transactions per ATM (Millions) (4) ÷ 80,000
1990	27,710.17	3,325.22	2,161.39	0.027
1991	28,818.58	3,458.23	2,247.85	0.028
1992	29,971.32	3,596.56	2,337.76	0.029
1993	31,170.18	3,740.42	2,431.27	0.030
1994	32,416.98	3,890.04	2,528.52	0.032
1995	33,713.66	4,045.64	2,629.67	0.033
1996	35,062.21	4,207.47	2,734.85	0.034
1997	36,464.70	4,376.76	2,844.25	0.036
1998	37,923.29	4,550.79	2,958.02	0.037
1999	39,440.22	4,732.83	3,076.34	0.038
2000	41,017.83	4,922.14	3,199.39	0.040

Selecting a Discount Rate

The thrift has used EFT for many years, and nothing about the proposed ATMs makes them either more or less acceptable to customers than other similar machines. Thus, management views the decision to add these cash dispensers as one of average risk to the institution. The weighted average cost of capital (k_A), 18.5 percent, is selected as the appropriate discount rate.

Calculating the NPV

Using these data, the NPV of the decision is calculated in Table 19.2. The positive NPV of $46,166 indicates that installation of the four ATMs is expected to be economically feasible and will add value to the thrift. The same NPV approach would be used for any other EFT decision, or for any potential expenditure for fixed assets, such as the opening of a new branch office.[22]

MERGER ANALYSIS: ANOTHER USE OF NPV

The discussion of depository institutions in Chapter 11 ends with a look at the increasing number of mergers in recent years. Many mergers have been involuntary, especially among thrifts forced by federal regulators to consolidate. But many have also been voluntary—the result of conscious decisions by man-

---

[22]For example, an illustration of NPV analysis applied to point-of-sale is presented in Russell D. Morris, "An Empirical Analysis of Costs and Revenue Requirements for Point-of-Sale EFTS," *Journal of Bank Research* 9 (Autumn 1978): 136-145.

Table 19.2
Calculating the NPV of the ATM Decision

Assumptions

Initial cash cost plus installation = $175,000, to be paid at the beginning of 1990
Cash savings realized at the end of each year, including 1990
k_A = 18.5% for a project of average risk
Cash Inflow per Year = Per-ATM Volume × 4 ATMs × $.39

End of Year	Volume per ATM (Thousands)	Total Annual Volume	Cash Inflow	Present Value at 18.5%
1990	27,000	108,000	$42,120	$ 35,544
1991	28,000	112,000	43,680	31,106
1992	29,000	116,000	45,240	27,187
1993	30,000	120,000	46,800	23,734
1994	32,000	128,000	49,920	21,364
1995	33,000	132,000	51,480	18,592
1996	34,000	136,000	53,040	16,165
1997	36,000	144,000	56,160	14,444
1998	37,000	148,000	57,720	12,527
1999	38,000	152,000	59,280	10,857
2000	40,000	160,000	62,400	9,645

$221,166 Total present value

Net present value = $221,166 − $175,000 = $46,166 (acceptable)

---

agers and/or owners to join with other institutions. Although NPV analysis is used in involuntary mergers, as regulators and acquiring firms haggle over how much the assets of an insolvent institution are *really* worth, it is essential in analyzing the economic aspects of voluntary mergers.

Merger analysis is an extremely complicated subject, with legal, regulatory, marketing, accounting, and financial dimensions that must be fully explored before a merger is undertaken. Merger analysis also differs depending upon whether a depository is the acquired or the acquiring firm, and this chapter cannot treat the subject fully from both sides. The following discussion focuses on the financial implications of a voluntary decision by an institution or a holding company to acquire another institution. Students wishing a more comprehensive treatment of merger analysis

should consult sources listed at the end of the chapter.

Economic Objectives of Mergers

Like the analysis of EFT decisions, the economic objective of a merger is to acquire ownership rights to assets whose future benefits exceed their costs. It is important to understand what an institution is buying when it acquires another. Essentially, the acquiring institution is buying the net worth of the acquired institution—the amount by which the value of the acquired institution's assets exceed its liabilities, the latter of which become the liabilities of the acquiring firm. Thus, in stockholder-owned firms, the acquirer offers to buy the common stock of the acquired firm. For mutual firms, the merger process involves conversion of one or both to the stock form of ownership first, followed by the acquisition of one institution's stock by another.[23] Either way, the objective is for the acquirer to obtain rights to assets whose present value exceeds their cost.

Upon first thought, this objective may seem impossible. If the acquired firm's stock is publicly traded, wouldn't the acquiring firm simply pay the market price of the stock? If the price reflects the present value of the benefits of owning the stock, how could the acquiring firm expect to buy the stock in anything other than a $0-NPV transaction? That is, wouldn't the firm expect to pay what the stock is worth, no more and no less? If the acquired firm's stock is not publicly traded, wouldn't the acquiring firm simply pay the book value of net worth plus or minus a discount or premium to reflect current market values for the firm's assets? Shouldn't that price, too, reflect the true value of the acquired firm's net worth, no more and no less?

Research into recent bank mergers provides what may be surprising answers to those questions.[24] Because most acquired banks are small, and because stocks of most small banks are not publicly traded, much available data compare merger prices to book, not market, value. According to information collected from 1968 to 1985, most acquiring banks pay *more* than book value for acquired firms' stock—from 110 percent to 280 percent of book value. From October 1983 to September 1984, data on larger institutions indicate that an average premium of 33 percent *above* market prices was paid to the stockholders of acquired banks.

Is it possible that most of these mergers were actually negative-NPV transactions from the acquirers' point of view? Some observers have, in fact, argued that bank merger prices are often too high, based on the real value of the acquired institution. It is unlikely, however, that all acquiring institutions made bad investment decisions year after year. There is more to the economics of mergers than has been seen so far.

The Mathematics of Mergers: 2 + 2 = 5

Synergy occurs when the combined value of two institutions exceeds their total value as independent entities; it is often expressed more simply as 2 + 2 = 5. If the acquiring institution expects synergy from a merger, its management believes that the present value of the combined operations of two firms will exceed the cost of executing the merger, including the cost of acquiring the other firm's stock. In other words, the acquiring firm believes it can increase total cash inflows from the assets of the two firms by managing them as one. There are several major sources of these expectations.

Economies of Scale.   Some firms acquire others because they believe they can reap the benefits of economies of scale. If an S&L doubles the number of NOW accounts serviced as a result of a merger, its managers may expect check-processing costs to increase by less than

[23]A detailed look at merger-conversions is given in William M. Moore, Jr., and Richard G. Marcis, "Merger-Conversions Link Financial Gains and Management Strength," *Savings Institutions* 106 (August 1985): 98-102. Merger-conversions have for the first time made it possible for mutual and stock institutions to merge. In the past, thrift mergers involved mutuals with mutuals and stocks with stocks.

[24]Historical information on mergers is provided in Jerome C. Darnell, "Bank Mergers: Prices Paid to Marriage Partners," *Business Review,* Federal Reserve Bank of Philadelphia (July 1973), pp. 16-25; Robert A. Bullington and Arnold E. Jensen, "Pricing a Bank," *Bankers Magazine* 164 (May-June 1981): 94-98; Paul Nadler, "Bank Acquisitions Seen from Both Sides," *Bankers Monthly Magazine* 99 (September 1982): 8-23; and David Cates, "Banks Are Paying Too Much to Merge," *Fortune* 112 (December 23, 1985): 151, 154; David C. Cates, "Prices Paid for Banks," *Economic Review,* Federal Reserve Bank of Atlanta 70 (January 1985): 36-41.

Rhoades examined 4,383 bank acquisitions from 1960 through 1983. He showed that small banks (under $50 million) accounted for 84 percent of the acquisitions during this period. See Stephen Rhoades, "Mergers and Acquisitions by Commercial Banks," Board of Governors of the Federal Reserve System, Staff Study No. 142 (January 1985), Table 5. Voluntary thrift mergers have also historically involved the acquisition of small firms by much larger ones. See Walter J. Woerheide, *The Savings and Loan Industry* (Westport, CT: Quorum Books, 1984), Chapter 9.

100 percent, reducing the cost per account. Because economies of scale occur when unit costs decline with volume (recall the discussion in Chapter 11), the net cash saved may increase total cash benefits available to owners.

Combinations of Strength.   Merging firms may also believe their assets "fit" well together. For example, in 1985, when Wachovia Corporation of North Carolina and First Atlanta Corporation of Georgia announced plans to merge into an institution called First Wachovia, financial analysts pronounced the merger a "good fit" because it combined First Atlanta's $870 million credit card operations with Wachovia's large consumer lending portfolio. Opportunities for geographic expansion of both operations, and the possibility of "cross-selling" (selling credit cards to consumer borrowers and consumer loans to credit card holders) led to expectations of increases in total cash benefits to the owners of the combined firm.

Better Management.   Another potential source of synergy is improved management of the acquired bank's existing assets. For example, some small depositories have been founded, owned, and managed by a single family throughout their history. Managers and officers may be hired more for their family relationships than for their managerial skills. The acquiring depository may believe that under its management, the assets of the acquired firm can be more profitable. If so, the expected cash inflows of the combined institution will exceed those of the institutions operated separately, increasing value. A study conducted at the Federal Reserve Bank of Chicago concluded that the potential to improve income from fee-generating services was a major motivation behind premiums paid in several recent interstate mergers.[25]

Survival.   Perhaps the reason most often cited recently for depository institution mergers is survival—to avoid either merger partner's being subsequently taken over by one of the nation's financial giants. Said one Missouri banker, "Before being thrown against Citicorp . . . , we should be permitted to reach a certain fighting weight."[26] Although continuity is no guarantee of increased institutional value, this statement implies at least some belief in synergy. If a combined institution can be operated to maximize value, a financial giant is less likely to find opportunities to improve that value via a takeover attempt and may turn its attention to other targets.

These objectives for financial institution mergers were reflected in the responses of bank holding company executives to a recent survey about the process of merger decision making. As shown in Table 19.3, survey participants indicated a variety of possible objectives for an acquisition; although not stated in identical terms, key factors included the concern for enhancing management, increasing growth and profitability, and reaching an optimal size.

ESTIMATING VALUE IN A MERGER

The most critical estimate required before a merger is the present value of the acquired institution's net worth, and the previous discussion suggests that *current* market or book value may not always reflect that value. In fact, the cash flow analysis used in all NPV decisions is needed. The present value of estimated cash flows can then be compared to the price demanded by the acquired institution's current owners, usually a multiple of current book or

---

[25]Dave Phillis and Christine Pavel, "Interstate Banking Game Plans: Implications for the Midwest," *Economic Perspectives,* Federal Reserve Bank of Chicago 10 (March/April 1986): 23–39. The authors also found that institutions with high spreads (IR − IE) and low loan chargeoffs were especially attractive.

[26]Felix Kessler, "Here Come the Regional Superbanks," *Fortune* 110 (December 10, 1984): 138. This comment is typical of bankers' sentiments as reported in other sources. See, for example, Scott Scredon, "Bank Mergers Start to Sizzle in the South," *Business Week,* July 1, 1985, pp. 25-26, in which $20 billion in assets was suggested as the minimum necessary "fighting weight"; and Daniel Hertzberg, "Competition Spurs Mergers of U.S. Banks," *The Wall Street Journal,* October 2, 1984.

Table 19.3
Potential Objectives for Acquisition of Another Financial Institution

To maximize profit
To maximize shareholder wealth
To increase management prestige
To minimize risk (to diversify)
To become the largest holding company in state
To maintain holding company's market position
To achieve profit rate targets
To achieve growth rate targets
To achieve a "critical" mass
To achieve commercial strength
To complement existing subsidiaries
To enter new markets

Source: Jan R. Squires, "An Acquisitions Checklist for Bank Holding Company Managers," *Bankers Magazine* 176 (January/February 1984): 72.

market value. If the estimated present value exceeds what must be paid to obtain the stock, the merger is economically feasible. If not, the merger should be reconsidered.

Estimating Present Value: An Illustration

Suppose a bank is considering acquiring another institution with a book value of $100 per share. Before the acquisition, the candidate's average return on net worth has been 12 percent. For the first ten years after the merger, RONW is expected to increase to 18 percent because it is believed that management of the acquired firm's assets can be improved substantially without increasing risk. After the initial period, when opportunities for superior profits have dissipated, RONW is expected to fall to 15 percent. For the first ten years, growth in assets and net worth are expected to be 8 percent, but after that, the growth rate will drop to a more normal 5 percent indefinitely. The acquiring firm's required rate of return on long-term investments is 15 percent.

The acquiring firm's objective is to estimate the cash flows to owners of the acquired firm under these assumptions. Because $g_{NW} =$ RONW × Retention Rate (Equation 16.3), estimates of an 18 percent RONW and a growth of 8 percent annually imply a planned retention rate of 8% ÷ 18% = 44%. Therefore, cash available for dividends to the firm's owners will be 56 percent of earnings each year. Resulting cash flows for the first ten years are given in Table 19.4. The present value of these cash flows totals $67.15.[27]

The bottom of Table 19.4 shows estimates of the present value of the cash flows from year 11 onward. Because the acquisition is expected to provide annual cash flows growing at a rate of 5 percent from that point, their present value is estimated, using the constant-growth model, at $53.61. Adding $53.61 to the total present value of the first ten years' cash flows ($67.15) gives an estimate of the stock's per-share value of $120.77, a 21 percent premium over the current $100.00 book value. This analysis follows the pattern used in the earlier EFT decision: identification of the time frame, estimation of the periodic cash flows, selection of a discount rate, and calculation of total present value.

---

[27]This example is partially based on one in Bullington and Jensen, "Pricing a Bank."

Table 19.4
Estimating the Present Value of an Acquisition Candidate

(1) Year	(2) Book Value at Beginning of Year	(3) Book Value at End of Year (g = 8%)	(4) Net Income Per Share 18% × (2)	(5) Earnings Retained 44% × (4)	(6) Cash Available (4) − (5)	(7) Present Value of Cash at 15%
0		$100.00				
1	$100.00	108.00	$18.00	$ 7.92	$10.08	$ 8.77
2	108.00	116.64	19.44	8.55	10.89	8.23
3	116.64	125.97	21.00	9.24	11.76	7.73
4	125.97	136.05	22.67	9.98	12.70	7.26
5	136.05	146.93	24.49	10.78	13.71	6.82
6	146.93	158.69	26.45	11.64	14.81	6.40
7	158.69	171.38	28.56	12.57	16.00	6.01
8	171.38	185.09	30.85	13.57	17.28	5.65
9	185.09	199.90	33.32	14.66	18.66	5.30
10	199.90	215.89	35.98	15.83	20.15	4.98
						$67.15 Total

At the end of year 10, RONW is expected to drop to 15%. This implies a retention rate of 5% ÷ 15% = 33% from year 11 on. Thus, in year 11, earnings will be 15% × $215.89 = $32.38, and cash available to owners will be 67% × $32.38 = $21.69.

Since the stock is expected to conform to the constant-growth model from that point on, the value of all future cash flows from the end of year 11 on, as of the end of year 10, is:

$$V_{10} = \frac{C_{11}}{k - g} = \frac{\$21.69}{0.15 - 0.05} = \$216.90$$

As of year 0, its present value is $216.90/1.15^{10} = $53.61

Thus, the total per-share value of the acquisition is estimated as:

$$\begin{array}{r} \$ \ 67.15 \\ +53.61 \\ \hline \$120.77 \end{array}$$

The Merger Decision

Existing owners of the proposed acquisition will have their own ideas about its worth. Because most acquirers have paid a hefty premium over book value to obtain an acquisition candidate, the latter's owners will no doubt attempt to obtain a price considerably higher than $100.

Even if the full potential of the institution's assets cannot be realized under current management, selling owners will attempt to capitalize on the desire of the acquiring firm to close the deal. The present value analysis indicates, however, that from an economic standpoint the acquirer should pay no more than $120.77 per share. Otherwise, the NPV of the transaction to the acquirer would be negative, decreasing the long-run value of the institution.[28]

OTHER ESTIMATES OF ACQUISITION VALUE

Because estimating the present value of the benefits from an acquisition is difficult and uncertain, many managers and owners are accustomed to thinking of merger values in other terms. Because these measures are often cited in reports of institutional mergers, a brief review is in order. Each of them, however, has limitations compared to NPV analysis.

Merger Market Value (Cash-to-Book Ratio)

The *merger market value,* or cash-to-book ratio, of an institution is simply its value based on cash prices recently paid in merger transactions involving similar institutions:

(19.4)

Merger Market Value =
        Average Cash-to-Book Ratio
        × Candidate's Book Value

If the average ratio of cash/book value for recent mergers in a state were 1.75, the per-share merger market value of an acquisition with book value of $50 per share is $1.75 \times \$50 = \$87.50$. Use of this measure to determine the value of an acquisition ignores special institutional circumstances that make its economic value greater or less than average.

Book Value to Book Value

In many mergers, transactions are completed by exchanging stock for stock, rather than by pay-

ing cash to the acquired firm's current owners. It is possible, therefore, to estimate the value of a potential acquiree's stock by examining the average ratio of book values exchanged in similar mergers. Suppose an acquiring firm knows that recent mergers in the region have resulted in an average book value-to-book value exchange ratio of 1.58. If the book value of a candidate's stock is $95, the book value of shares that might be offered by the acquiring firm is:

(19.5)

Merger   Average   Candidate's
Book   =   Book-to-Book ×   Book
Value   Ratio   Value

   $150 = 1.58 \times \$95$

If the current book value of the acquiring firm's stock is $75, two shares with a total book value of $150 would be offered for one share of the acquiree's stock. A major problem with evaluating merger terms on this basis is that book values may have little relationship to the economic value exchanged by either party.

Value Based on Earnings

Some analysts argue that assessing the value of an acquisition according to earnings is superior to measuring it based on book value. Thus, examining the ratio of purchase price to earnings per share (EPS) is sometimes suggested. Suppose an S&L knows that the average ratio of price paid to acquiree's EPS has been 11.58 recently. If a candidate's EPS were $9.50 last year, the value of the acquiree's stock could be estimated as:

(19.6)

Price/Earnings Value =
        Average Price/Earnings Ratio
        × Candidate's EPS

        $110 = 11.58 \times \$9.50$

The problem with this measure is that the acquiring institution is buying, and the selling owners are giving up, future earnings. Unless future earnings remain similar to current fig-

---

[28]In practice, administrative costs of executing the merger must be included in NPV analysis. Since consultation with accountants and attorneys is essential to a successful merger, their fees must also be added to the total price paid to the acquired firm's owners; these total costs would then be compared to the present value of the benefits from the merger.

ures—an unlikely expectation if a merger is synergistic—values based on historical earnings ratios are unlikely to equal economic values.

DILUTION: IS NPV BEST IN THE SHORT RUN?

A major concern of owners and managers in an acquiring institution is **dilution,** or a reduction in per-share earnings caused by the issuance of new shares. A well-known bank analyst noted recently that fear of dilution is one of the two "driving forces" behind agreed-upon bank merger prices.[29] If he is correct, then in stock-for-stock mergers, acquirers attempt to avoid issuing so many shares to obtain the acquired firm that EPS falls after the merger, regardless of whether the long-run economic value exchanged would justify the decision.

A simplified example of dilution after a merger is illustrated in Table 19.5.[30] Suppose, based on NPV analysis, a large bank acquires a small one and issues 1.08 million new shares, equal in total to 1.62 times the book value of the acquired bank. If the synergistic benefits of increased earnings do not occur immediately, the table shows that from the acquiring shareholders' point of view, EPS will fall from $2.00 to $1.85 the first year after the merger. This is a percentage dilution of 7.5 percent, exceeding the 5 percent level some analysts believe is acceptable.[31]

Should the NPV criterion be ignored if dilution is expected? Not at all. In the short run,

decisions based on NPV sometimes conflict with other standards. In this example, the acquired firm has a higher book value ratio of capital to assets than the acquiring firm, so the resulting book value capital/assets ratio in the combined institution will be larger than the acquiring firm's. As explained in Chapter 16, the higher capital ratio means a higher potential growth rate in assets and earnings than would have been possible before the merger. That possibility, combined with synergy expected from combining administrative operations, for example, may result in a long-run earnings stream that exceeds the acquiring firm's earnings before the merger. In addition, the acquired firm, even if not more highly capitalized, may have assets with greater growth prospects after the merger than those of the acquiring firm. Any or all of these three factors may work to add long-run value that is not instantly captured in short-run accounting earnings figures.

Based on the merger in Table 19.5, Table 19.6 illustrates future EPS possibilities for ten years, assuming no synergy occurs until year 2. The EPS figures for the combined firm in the first year are $1.85, but in the second year earnings are expected to increase an *additional* 8 percent over and above the increase caused by growth without the merger. For the acquiring firm, earnings are expected to increase annually by 5 percent.

The point at which EPS for the combined firm exceeds the EPS the acquiring firm could achieve without the merger depends on three factors: 1) the expected growth rate in EPS of the acquired institution; 2) the synergistic effect, which here is the one-time boost in year 2; and 3) the relative size of the two institutions. In this example, the smaller firm is only one-eighth the size of the larger firm, so it is one-ninth of the combined firm. Its effect is less dramatic than if two firms of relatively equal size but different expected earnings growth were to combine.

The EPS estimates in Table 19.6 are based on growth rates for the smaller firm ranging from 3 percent to 20 percent. The long-term growth rates for the combined banks are estimated as the weighted average of the two sepa-

---

[29]Cates, "Prices Paid for Banks," p. 38; Cates's other driving force was the market value-to-market value ratio, which is relevant only for institutions with frequently traded stock.

[30]This example is based, in part, on one in Peter C. Eisemann and George A. Budd, "Acquisition and Dilution," *Magazine of Bank Administration* 58 (November 1982): 34-38.

[31]The 5 percent figure is cited by Cates as a rule of thumb of investment bankers and professional investors. See Cates, "Prices Paid for Banks," p. 37. In other work, he has called larger percentage dilutions "dilutions of grandeur." See Cates, "Banks Are Paying Too Much to Merge."

Table 19.5
Dilution Resulting from a Merger

	Acquiring Institution	Acquired Institution
Total assets	$800 million	$100 million
Total net worth (book)	$40 million	$8 million
Net worth/total assets	5.0%	8.0%
Net income	$10 million	$1.25 million
Shares outstanding	5 million	
Stock price (per share)	$12	
Earnings per share (EPS)	$2.00	

A purchase price of 1.62 times the book value of the acquired firm is:

$$1.62 \times \$8 \text{ million} = \$12.96 \text{ million}$$

That requires the issuance of $12.96 ÷ $12 = 1.08 million new shares.

If earnings do not increase at first, EPS for year 1 will be:

$$(\$10 \text{ million} + \$1.25 \text{ million}) \div (5 + 1.08) = \$1.85$$

rate institutions, and range from 4.78 percent to 6.65 percent. For example, if the acquired firm's expected growth rate is 10 percent, the estimated growth rate of the combined firms would be $1/9(10\%) + 8/9(5\%) = 5.55\%$. In year 2, recall that synergy makes the growth rate 8 percent higher. For all but one possible growth rate, combined EPS will exceed the nonmerger level by the second year. Only if the acquired firm's postmerger growth prospects are disappointing—3 percent in this case—will postmerger EPS continue to show the effects of dilution after one year.

REGULATION OF DEPOSITORY INSTITUTIONS MERGERS

It should come as no surprise that the merger activities of depository institutions are regulated. Regulatory authority over mergers follows the same pattern as regulation of other activities. The Fed is the chief regulator of mergers involving BHCs or state member banks; the Comptroller of the Currency must approve national bank mergers; the FDIC oversees state-chartered, insured banks and FDIC-insured thrifts; the FHLBB must approve FSLIC-insured depository mergers; and the NCUA must sanction the mergers of federal CUs. State authorities must also approve the merger of all state-chartered institutions.

Because they may reduce competition, especially if institutions within relative geographical proximity wish to combine, mergers are closely watched by regulators and by the U.S. Department of Justice, which is responsible for antitrust actions against financial as well as nonfinancial firms. The history of merger regulation and legislation in depository institutions is long and rich and is not reviewed in detail here. Rather, the purpose of this discussion is to outline major issues that could affect depository mergers in the future.

Since the inception of federal antitrust legislation, its thrust has been to prevent business combinations that decrease competition. To de-

Table 19.6
Dilution and Growth

	Without Merger Growth = 5%	Acquiree Growth = 3%	Acquiree Growth = 10%	Acquiree Growth = 15%	Acquiree Growth = 20%
Year 1 EPS	$2.00	$1.85	$1.85	$1.85	$1.85
Combined growth rate (weighted average)	5.00%	4.78%	5.55%	6.10%	6.65%
Future EPS of combined firm					
Year					
2[a]	$2.10[b]	$2.09	$2.11	$2.12	$2.13
3	2.21	2.19	2.23	2.25	2.27
4	2.32	2.30	2.35	2.39	2.42
5	2.43	2.41	2.48	2.53	2.58
6	2.55	2.52	2.62	2.69	2.76
7	2.68	2.64	2.76	2.85	2.94
8	2.81	2.77	2.92	3.02	3.14
9	2.95	2.90	3.08	3.21	3.34
10	3.10	3.04	3.25	3.40	3.57

[a]In year 2, a one-time earnings increase of 8% occurs for the combined firm as a result of synergy. Then the expected growth path resumes.

[b]Reflects only the 5% annual growth expected for the original firm without the merger.

termine whether a merger will have an adverse competitive effect, the regulators must answer several critical questions. The answers influence whether a merger is approved or not, and each of the questions involves a gray area. An illustrative example of the Federal Reserve Board's answers to the questions is presented in Figure 19.2, announcing the approval of the 1985 merger of First Atlanta Corporation of Atlanta, Georgia, with First Gwinnett Bancshares, Inc., of Lawrenceville, Georgia. Key passages are highlighted.

Figure 19.2
Approval of a Merger Application by Federal Regulators

First Atlanta Corporation
Atlanta, Georgia

Order Approving the Merger of Bank Holding Companies

First Atlanta Corporation, Atlanta, Georgia, a bank holding company within the meaning of the Bank Holding Company Act ("Act"), has applied for the Board's approval under section 3(a)(5) of the Act (12 U.S.C. § 1842(a)(5)) to merge with First Gwinnett Bancshares, Inc., Lawrenceville, Georgia ("First Gwinnett") and thereby acquire its subsidiary bank, First National Bank of Gwinnett County.

Notice of the application, affording opportunity for interested persons to submit comments, has been given in accordance with section 3(b) of the Act. The time for filing comments has expired, and the Board has considered the application and all comments received in light of the factors set forth in section 3(c) of the Act (12 U.S.C. § 1842(c)).

Applicant is the third largest banking organization in Georgia with three subsidiary banks that control aggregate deposits of approximately $4.0 billion, representing 14.4 percent of the total deposits in commercial banks in the state.[1] First Gwinnett is the 27th largest banking organization in Georgia, with one banking subsidiary that con-

Figure 19.2 (*continued*)

trols deposits of $121.8 million, representing 0.4 percent of the total deposits in commercial banks in the state. **Upon consummation of the proposed acquisition, Applicant's share of the total deposits in commercial banks in the state would increase to 14.8 percent,** and Applicant would become the second largest commercial banking organization in the state. **The Board has considered the effect of the proposal on the structure of banking in Georgia and has concluded that consummation of this transaction would not significantly increase the concentration of banking resources in the state.**

Applicant and First Gwinnett compete directly in only one market, the Atlanta metropolitan banking market.[2] Applicant is the largest of 24 commercial banking organizations in the market, controlling 25.2 percent of the total deposits in commercial banks in the market. First Gwinnett is the eighth largest commercial banking organization in the relevant banking market, controlling slightly less than 1.0 percent of the total deposits in commercial banks therein. Upon consummation of this proposal, Applicant would remain the largest commercial banking organization in the market, controlling approximately 26.2 percent of the total deposits in commercial banks in the market.

While consummation of the proposal would eliminate some existing competition in the Atlanta metropolitan banking market, the Board believes that certain factors substantially mitigate the anticompetitive effects of the proposal. **Upon consummation, Applicant's share of the total deposits in commercial banks in the market would increase by only 1.0 percentage point to 26.2 percent, and the Herfindahl-Hirschman Index ("HHI") would increase by only 49 points to 1839.[3]** Twenty-three commercial banking alternatives would remain in the market after consummation of the transaction.

The Board also has considered the influence of thrift institutions in evaluating the competitive effects of this proposal.[4] In this case, the small increase in concentration in the Atlanta metropolitan

banking market is alleviated by the presence of 16 thrift institutions in the market, controlling $5.1 billion in deposits, which represents 33 percent of the total deposits in commercial banks and thrift institutions in the market. The thrift institutions offer a full range of consumer services and transaction accounts and some are engaged in commercial lending. Consequently, the Board has determined that consummation of this proposal would not have a significantly adverse effect on existing competition in the Atlanta metropolitan banking market.[5]

The financial and managerial resources of Applicant, First Gwinnett, and their subsidiaries are satisfactory and their prospects appear favorable. Thus, banking factors are consistent with approval of the application. Upon consummation of this proposal, First Gwinnett's customers would have access to Applicant's larger system of automated teller machines. Consequently, considerations relating to the convenience and needs of the community to be served lend weight toward approval of the application. Accordingly, the Board has determined that consummation of the transaction would be consistent with the public interest and that the application should be approved.

On the basis of the record, this application is approved for the reasons summarized above. The transaction shall not be consummated before the thirtieth calendar day following the effective date of this Order, or later than three months after the effective date of this Order, unless such period is extended for good cause by the Board or by the Federal Reserve Bank of Atlanta, acting pursuant to delegated authority.

By order of the Board of Governors, effective June 27, 1985.

Voting for this action: Vice Chairman Martin and Governors Wallich, Partee, Rice, Gramley, and Seger. Absent and not voting: Chairman Volcker.

[SEAL]

JAMES MCAFEE
Associate Secretary of the Board

---

[1]Unless otherwise indicated, all banking data are as of June 30, 1984.

[2]The Atlanta metropolitan banking market is approximated by Clayton, Cobb, DeKalb, Douglas, Fulton, Gwinnett, Henry, and Rockdale Counties, in Georgia.

[3]Under the United States Justice Department Merger Guidelines, a market in which the post-merger HHI is above 1800 is considered highly concentrated. In such markets, the Department is not likely to challenge a merger that produces an increase in the HHI of less than 50 points, as in this case.

[4]The Board has previously determined that thrift institutions have become, or at least have the potential to become, major competitors of commercial banks. *E.g., Midlantic Banks, Inc.,* 71 FEDERAL RESERVE BULLETIN 458 (1985); *NCNB Corporation (Ellis),* 70 FEDERAL RESERVE BULLETIN 225 (1984); *Comerica (Pontiac State Bank),* 69 FEDERAL RESERVE BULLETIN 911 (1983); *First Tennessee National Corporation,* 69 FEDERAL RESERVE BULLETIN 298 (1983).

[5]**If 50 percent of the deposits of the thrift institutions were taken into account in computing market shares, Applicant's market share would be 20.2 percent, First Gwinnett's market share would be 0.5 percent, and the HHI would be 1215. Upon consummation of this proposal, Applicant's market share would increase to approximately 20.7 percent, and the HHI would increase by only 20 points to 1235, a level considered only moderately concentrated under the U.S. Department of Justice Merger Guidelines.**

Source: Federal Reserve Bulletin 71 (August 1985): 635–636.

What Is the Relevant Market Area?

One competitive question is how the relevant geographic market for the merger is to be defined. If the only two banks in a small town ask to merge, and if neither one serves customers outside the community, identifying the relevant market is easy. But rarely is the question so clear-cut.

Ideally, a market should be defined in economic terms—that is, the geographic area in which deposits will be taken and loans made after the merger should be identified, regardless of whether it conforms to legal boundaries such as city, county, or state lines.[32] In practice, legal boundaries are most often used.

In the First Atlanta-First Gwinnett merger, the Federal Reserve Board first examined the Georgia banking market, then turned its attention to the Atlanta metropolitan area. It apparently did not consider regional or national markets to be relevant. In the First Atlanta-Wachovia merger mentioned earlier, however, regional and even national market areas would be more appropriate.

How Should the Degree of Competition Be Measured?

After the relevant market is defined, regulators must measure competition in that market. Currently, two measures of competition are used. One is a simple market concentration ratio, in which the percentage of total market deposits held by merger candidates before and after the merger is examined. The Fed's recent policy has been to refrain from challenging a merger unless the three largest firms in the market have a combined deposit concentration ratio exceeding 75 percent after the merger.[33]

A more complex measure of competition is the *Herfindahl-Hirschman Index (HHI),* which is the sum of the squares of the market shares of all competitors in a market. It is calculated before and after a potential merger. In 1982, the Justice Department established new guidelines for merger approvals based on the HHI, believed by many economists and legal scholars to be more theoretically sound than simple concentration ratios.[34] The Justice Department defines a market as unconcentrated if the HHI is 1,000 or less, moderately concentrated if it is 1,000-1,800, and highly concentrated if it is greater than 1,800. Generally, a merger in a market with an HHI of 1,000 or less will go unchallenged by the Justice Department, but those in markets with higher HHIs may be questioned, depending upon the effect of the merger on the market's HHI. For clarification, Table 19.7 shows measures of competition for a hypothetical market before and after a merger of the first and fourth largest institutions.[35]

In the First Atlanta-First Gwinnett merger, the Fed calculated both the HHI and deposit concentration measures for the Atlanta metropolitan banking market and deposit concentration ratios for the state of Georgia. It noted that, because the Atlanta area was already quite concentrated according to the HHI, an increase of only 49 points as a result of the proposed

---

[32]Economists have made many attempts to define markets in general and banking markets in particular. A review and synthesis of this research is provided in John D. Wolken, "Geographic Market Delineation: A Review of the Literature," Board of Governors of the Federal Reserve System, Staff Study No. 140, October 1984.

[33]There are other criteria, primarily related to the size of the banks involved, that also govern whether the Fed will challenge a merger. For more details, see Michael J. Stutzer, "Probable Future Competition in Banking An-

titrust Determination: Research Findings," *Quarterly Review,* Federal Reserve Bank of Minneapolis 8 (Summer 1984): 9-17.

[34]Rhoades has argued, based on a review of recent literature, that the three-firm concentration ratio is as good a measure of banking market structure as is the HHI. See Stephen Rhoades, "Structure-Performance Studies in Banking: An Updated Summary and Evaluation," Board of Governors of the Federal Reserve System, Staff Study No. 119, August 1982.

[35]Of course, the *real* concern is the effect of the merger on future competition, something static measures like the deposit concentration ratio or the HHI do not capture. Will the merger cause the candidates or their remaining competitors to act in ways they would not have acted without the merger? There is obviously no easy answer to that question. For further analysis, see Stutzer, "Probable Future Competition in Banking Antitrust Determination."

Table 19.7
Measures of Competition in a Geographic Market

Institution	Total Deposits (Millions)	Concentration Ratio (% of Total)	% Squared
A	$1,200	26.45%	699.56[a]
B	975	21.49	461.82
C	800	17.63	310.92
D	650	14.33	205.25
E	200	4.41	19.43
F	175	3.86	14.88
G	160	3.53	12.44
H	120	2.64	7.00
I	98	2.16	4.67
J	75	1.65	2.73
K	43	0.95	0.90
L	27	0.60	0.35
M	14	0.31	0.10
Totals	$4,537	100.00%	1,740.04 = HHI

Market Competition Measures Assuming Institutions A and D Merge

Institution	Total Deposits (Millions)	Concentration Ratio (% of Total)	% Squared
A + D	$1,850	40.78%	1,662.67
B	975	21.49	461.82
C	800	17.63	310.92
E	200	4.41	19.43
F	175	3.86	14.88
G	160	3.53	12.44
H	120	2.64	7.00
I	98	2.16	4.67
J	75	1.65	2.73
K	43	0.95	0.90
L	27	0.60	0.35
M	14	0.31	0.10
Totals	$4,537	100.00%	2,497.89 = HHI

[a]Calculated as 26.45 × 26.45, not 0.2645 × 0.2645.

merger was likely to go unchallenged by the Justice Department.

With Whom Are the Merger Candidates Potentially Competing?

A final issue in depository institution mergers is identifying with whom the proposed merger candidates are competing. On the one hand, increasing similarity in products offered by depositories suggests that competitive measures such as the deposit concentration ratio or the HHI should be calculated using all depositories in the defined market. On the other hand, evidence in earlier chapters suggests many areas in which thrifts, CUs, and banks do not yet compete. It is not surprising, therefore, that both state and federal regulators have only recently widened the scope of competitive measures to include other depositories besides those undertaking a merger. For example, some analysts believe that the 1986 merger of two giant California banks, Wells Fargo and Crocker National, was permitted only because thrifts were viewed as "capable competitors" of commercial banks in the state.[36]

The inclusion of thrifts in bank merger analysis is illustrated in the First Atlanta-First Gwinnett decision. Market concentration ratios and HHIs are substantially reduced when more potential competitors are included, as shown in note 5 of the Fed's decision. A remaining unresolved issue is whether nondepository institutions, such as finance companies and mutual funds, are also significant competitors and should be included in evaluating the competitive effect of depository mergers.

SUMMARY

This chapter focuses on techniques for analyzing long-term financial decisions. Generally, these decisions require net present value analy-

sis, comparing the cost of an investment with the present value of future benefits. They also require an awareness of special legal and/or regulatory issues that may affect the results of the investment. For each investment, the NPV technique requires: 1) choice of a planning period; 2) estimation of incremental costs and benefits; 3) identification of a risk-adjusted required rate of return; and 4) comparison of the discounted values of costs and benefits.

NPV is presented in the context of two important categories of long-term investments: electronic funds transfer systems (EFTs) and acquisitions of other depository institutions. EFT systems include automated clearinghouses, automated teller machines, point-of-sale systems, and home-banking equipment. Cash flow estimates for any of these investments must consider potential response of individual and institutional customers and costs imposed by regulations. Because customer acceptance of this technology is still in the growth stage, future cash flows are subject to considerable variability.

Whether to acquire another depository institution is a decision faced by many asset/liability managers. Again, the NPV of the acquisition is the best decision technique. Because acquisitions involve payment to the owners of the target institution, an important aspect of the decision is the offering price. That choice must reflect the potential synergistic effects of the combination, over and above the normal profits of the two separate institutions. Although other techniques are sometimes suggested for analyzing mergers, NPV is advocated, even with short-run earnings dilution. Any merger of financial institutions may be prohibited if the resulting combination is anticompetitive.

---

[36]Frederick T. Furlong, "The Wells Fargo-Crocker Acquisition," *Weekly Letter,* Federal Reserve Bank of San Francisco, November 28, 1986. Rhoades notes that few of the studies of market structure and performance that he reviewed before the Wells Fargo-Crocker merger found evidence of significant competition among banks, thrifts, and CUs. See Rhoades, "Structure-Performance Studies in Banking." In contrast, Hannan found significant competitive interactions among banks and thrifts in Pennsylvania, even before substantial deregulation. See Timothy H. Hannan, "Competition between Commercial Bank and Thrift Institutions: An Empirical Examination," *Journal of Bank Research* 15 (Spring 1984): 8-14.

Questions

1. How do NPV techniques assist an institution in reaching its financial objectives? Are decisions made on the basis of NPV compatible with achieving net interest margin and RONW targets? Why or why not?

2. What types of cash flows are used in an NPV analysis? What discount rate should be used to calculate the NPV of investments of average risk? Should the same rate be used for long-term decisions of above- or below-average risk? Why or why not?

3. What are electronic funds transfer systems? Give examples of three EFT systems and explain how they are used by institutions and/or their customers.

4. Some customers object to direct payroll deposit because they like to see their paychecks. What arguments can depository institutions use to overcome this objection? What marketing strategies for direct deposit would you suggest?

5. What are automated clearinghouses, and what role do they play in EFTs? Why have some corporations resisted the use of electronic funds transfers? What arguments can depositories use to overcome this resistance?

6. Do you think the Fed's involvement in EFTs, particularly in the development and expansion of automated clearinghouses, poses unfair competition for the private sector? Why or why not?

7. How does the theory of innovation adoption explain the public's response to ATMs? Based on this theory, do you expect extensive growth in ATM networks in the next decade? Why or why not? Do you expect that home banking will follow the same adoption pattern? Why or why not?

8. Compare the advantages and disadvantages of debit versus credit cards from the points of view of merchants, customers, and depositories.

9. What is check truncation? Why have customers of credit unions and thrifts accepted this form of EFT more readily than bank customers?

10. What problems was Regulation E designed to prevent? What requirements are placed on depositories as a result of this regulation?

11. Explain why NPV analysis is relevant for merger decisions.

12. Define synergy. Why is it important? What are some potential sources of synergy in financial institution mergers?

13. As noted in the chapter, in 1986, Wells Fargo Bank acquired Crocker National Bank, both domiciled in California. Immediately, 1,600 Crocker employees were fired. In the first quarter after the merger, Wells Fargo reported an increase in profits of 39 percent over the previous year, and analysts were predicting further improvements by 1988. Find information on the recent performance of Wells Fargo. Has the merger proven to be synergistic? To what areas of the bank's operations can the results of the merger be traced?

14. Other than PV estimates, what alternatives are available for estimating the value of a potential acquisition? What are the advantages and disadvantages of each?

15. Explain why an emphasis on the potential for short-run dilution after a merger may lead to a decision that conflicts with NPV. What factors affect earnings per share for a combined firm after a merger?

16. What questions do regulators consider when evaluating whether a proposed merger will have an adverse effect on competition? Do you think bank mergers should be evaluated by looking at competition from thrifts and credit unions in the market area? Why or why not?

17. Discuss the alternatives for measuring a proposed merger's impact on market competition.

Problems

1. The management of Sunbelt Bank is contemplating the purchase of a new computer to reduce costs associated with its growing number of transactions accounts. The new computer will cost $85,000 plus $7,500 for installation. Management estimates an after-tax cost savings of $2 per year per account. The current volume of transaction accounts is 15,000, although a 5 percent growth in the number of accounts is expected each year for the next five years. Sunbelt's required rate of return on long-term investments is 13 percent annually.

   a. Using projections over the next five years, should the computer be purchased?

   b. What is the maximum amount Sunbelt should invest in a new computer system, considering the expected benefits of such a system?

2. The Avocado Growers and Workers Credit Union is considering whether to open a branch office close to one of the largest avocado groves in California. Cash start-up costs, including architectural and construction expenses, are estimated at $100,000. Because of the convenience of the new location, management expects additional business from workers in the grove who are not currently members. Based on the anticipated volume of consumer lending, interest revenues in each of the next 20 years are expected to be $350,000 higher than the current level. Interest and operating costs as a result of new share accounts are expected to be $339,000 higher each year.

   a. If the credit union requires a 10 percent annual return on all long-term investments, should the new branch be opened?

   b. Suppose management is uncertain about the proper discount rate and thinks that the branch expansion decision is of lower than average risk. If it is reevaluated at a risk-adjusted rate, will it be more or less desirable than at a 10 percent discount rate? Why?

   c. At what discount rate will the NPV of the branch be equal to $0?

3. The Black Hills National Bank is analyzing the purchase of Badlands State Bank. The acquiree's shares have a current book value of $130, with an average RONW of 10 percent. The management of Black Hills believes the merger could increase RONW to 16 percent for eight years after the acquisition. After that time, RONW is expected to stabilize at 13 percent. During the first eight years, growth in assets and net worth for Badlands is expected to be 6 percent, falling to a constant rate of 4 percent thereafter. Black Hills' required rate of return on the investment is 12 percent.

   a. Calculate the expected retention rate for Badlands during the first eight years.

   b. Using the retention rate found in a, estimate the earnings that will be retained each year for eight years and the cash available each year.

   c. Calculate the retention rate for the period of constant growth beginning in the ninth year after the merger, and the cash available at the end of the ninth year.

   d. Calculate the total present value of the cash available to Black Hills as a result of the merger. What is the most that should be paid for each share of Badlands's stock?

4. Suppose that the management of Black Hills National Bank in Problem 3 wants to estimate the value of a share of Badlands's stock using data from other mergers recently completed in the region. Black Hills's stock currently has a book value of $85.

   a. If recent mergers have resulted in an average cash-to-book value ratio of 1.6, what price is suggested for Badlands?

   b. If recent mergers have resulted in an average book-to-book exchange ratio of 1.1, how many shares of Black Hills stock would be exchanged for one share of Badlands?

   c. If the ratio of price to acquiree's EPS has averaged 10.7 recently, what is your estimate of the per-share price for Black Hills to offer Badlands's shareholders?

   d. What limitations do these measures have compared to NPV analysis?

5. Using NPV analysis, Jersey S&L has recently agreed to pay 1.55 times the book value of Northeast Savings' net worth in an upcoming merger. Stock will be sold to obtain the cash to acquire Northeast. Assume no change in net income during the first year.

	Jersey	Northeast
Total assets	$600 million	$75 million
Net worth (book)	$27 million	$6 million
Net income	$7.5 million	$937,500
Shares outstanding	4 million	
Market price/share	$10	

   a. Based on the information shown, determine whether EPS will be diluted in the first year as a result of the merger. Can you conclude that the merger is a mistake from the point of view of Jersey's shareholders?

   b. Suppose that the management of Jersey S&L anticipates a 12 percent synergistic increase in earnings in the second year after the merger. What EPS can Jersey's shareholders anticipate during that year? Is the merger a mistake?

6. First National has applied to acquire Citizens National. The regulators require a competitive analysis using both the market concentration ratio and HHI. The relevant market is the Southern third of the state, and the following information is available:

Institutions	Deposits (Millions)
First National	$1,050
Kendall State	960
Hampton Bank	875
United Security S&L	700
DeSoto National	650
King Federal	300
Citizens National	175
Newport State	92
Palm Beach Federal	55
Walnut Grove National	37
Golden East State	22
Logansport Savings	11

   a. Measure the degree of competition before and after the merger, using the market concentration ratio.

   b. Measure the degree of competition before and after the merger, using the HHI. Is the Justice Department likely to challenge the proposed merger? Why or why not?

Selected References

Allison, Theodore E. "The Federal Reserve's Role in the Payments Mechanism and Its Communication Plans." *Economic Review* (Federal Reserve Bank of Richmond) 68 (March/April 1982): 21-25.

"The Automated Clearinghouse Alternative: How Do We Get There from Here?" *Economic Review* (Federal Reserve Bank of Atlanta) 71 (April 1986): entire issue.

Bullington, Robert A., and Arnold E. Jensen. "Pricing a Bank." *Bankers Magazine* 164 (May-June 1981): 94-98.

Cates, David C. "Prices Paid for Banks." *Economic Review* (Federal Reserve Bank of Atlanta) 70 (January 1985): 36-41.

Cox, William N., and Paul F. Metzker. "Special Issue: Displacing the Check." *Economic Review* (Federal Reserve Bank of Atlanta) 68 (August 1983): entire issue.

Darnell, Jerome C. "Bank Mergers: Prices Paid to Marriage Partners." *Business Review* (Federal Reserve Bank of Philadelphia) (July 1973), pp. 16-25.

Dunham, Constance R. "Regional Banking Competition." *New England Economic Review* (Federal Reserve Bank of Boston) (July/August 1986), pp. 3-19.

Eisemann, Peter C., and George A. Budd. "Acquisitions and Dilution." *Magazine of Bank Administration* 58 (November 1982): 34-38.

Felgran, Steven D., and R. Edward Ferguson. "The Evolution of Retail EFT Networks." *New England Economic Review* (Federal Reserve Bank of Boston) (July/August 1986), pp. 41-56.

Frisbee, Pamela S. "The ACH: An Elusive Dream." *Economic Review* (Federal Reserve Bank of Atlanta) 71 (March 1986): 4-8.

Gist, Donna M. "The EFT-Check Tussle Outlasts the Predictions." *Savings Institutions* 105 (November 1984): 86-90.

Hannan, Timothy H. "Competition between Commercial Bank and Thrift Institutions: An Empirical Examination." *Journal of Bank Research* 15 (Spring 1984): 8-14.

Mitchell, George W., and Raymond F. Hodgdon. "Federal Reserve and the Payments System." *Federal Reserve Bulletin* 67 (February 1981): 109-116.

Morris, Russell D. "An Empirical Analysis of Costs and Revenue Requirements for Point-of-Sale EFTS." *Journal of Bank Research* 9 (Autumn 1978): 136-145.

Murdock, Gene W., and Lori Franz. "Habit and Perceived Risk as Factors in the Resistance to Use of ATMs." *Journal of Retail Banking* 5 (Summer 1983): 20-29.

Nadler, Paul. "Bank Acquisitions Seen from Both Sides." *Bankers Magazine* 99 (September 1982): 8-23.

Osterberg, Ronald. "POS Is on Its Way." *Economic Review* (Federal Reserve Bank of Atlanta) 69 (July/August 1984): 32-35.

Phillis, Dave, and Christine Pavel. "Interstate Banking Game Plans: Implications for the Midwest." *Economic Perspectives* (Federal Reserve Bank of Chicago) 10 (March/April 1986): 23-39.

Schroeder, Frederick. "Developments in Consumer Electronic Fund Transfers." *Federal Reserve Bulletin* 69 (June 1983): 395-403.

Stanley, Thomas J., and George P. Moschis. "The ATM-Prone Consumer: A Profile and Implications." *Journal of Retail Banking* 5 (Spring 1983): 45-51.

Stone, Bernell K. "Electronic Payments at the Crossroads." *Economic Review* (Federal Reserve Bank of Atlanta) 71 (March 1986): 20-33.

————. "The Revolution in Retail Payments: A Synthesis." *Economic Review* (Federal Reserve Bank of Atlanta) 69 (July/August 1984): 46-55.

Stutzer, Michael J. "Probable Future Competition in Banking Antitrust Determination: Research Findings." *Quarterly Review* (Federal Reserve Bank of Minneapolis) 8 (Summer 1984): 9–17.

van der Velde, Marjolijn. "Point of Sale: Attitudes and Perceptions of Financial Institutions, Merchants and Customers." *Magazine of Bank Administration* 60 (April 1985): 42–48.

Welker, Donald L. "Thrift Competition: Does It Matter?" *Economic Review* (Federal Reserve Bank of Richmond) 72 (January–February 1986), pp. 2–10.

Chapter 20

FEE-BASED SERVICES

*We're always looking at the vast frontiers of this society to find a place
to build a log cabin.*

Anonymous Citicorp Official (1985)

CUSTOMERS entering the door of a retail establishment in Upper Arlington, Ohio, pass under an elegant arched canopy. Inside they find an insurance agency in one corner, a travel agency and a discount broker in others, and a real estate office nearby. Across the way are an ATM and several desks at which personnel sit ready to help. Although it may sound like a shopping mall, the "store" is actually a branch of Bank One. In 1986, to attract new customers and keep old ones, the bank hired consultants usually employed by department stores. Said one consultant, "What we're doing . . . is merchandising banks to the level of the Neiman-Marcuses, the Bonwit Tellers, and the Bergdorf Goodmans."[1] In addition, the new services offered will presumably provide an important source of noninterest income to the bank.

Bank One's emphasis on nontraditional services is not unique. Institutions of all types are not only developing new fee-based services, such as discount brokerage and insurance, but emphasizing old ones, such as trust management. The purpose of this chapter is to trace the rise of these phenomena and how they relate to other facets of asset/liability management.

---

[1]Steve Weiner, "Banks Hire Retailing Consultant for Help in Becoming Financial Products 'Stores,' " *The Wall Street Journal,* May 20, 1986, p. 33.

THE ROLE OF FEE-BASED SERVICES

If a growing number of depository institutions are discovering lines of business somewhat removed from deposit taking and lending, there must be reasons. The primary ones are financial.

Benefits of Fee Income

The vast majority of depositories' revenues continues to come from interest-earning assets, and the majority of expenses from interest-bearing liabilities. In the increasingly competitive environment, however, rate differentials between various categories of assets and their funding sources are narrower than in the past. This narrowing puts downward pressure on net income, the institution's capital position, internal growth, and possible dividend payments—unless noninterest sources of revenue, such as service fees, can be found.

Fee income is also more stable than other revenue sources because it is less likely to rise and fall with the general level of interest rates or with shifts in the term structure. It also is independent of unpredictable day-to-day deposit inflows and outflows. In other words, fee income rarely is highly positively correlated with other cash flows, so it provides diversification benefits by reducing variability in cash flows.

Growth of Fee Income

As with other changes, the recent emphasis on fee-based services is often traced to money center banks. As explained in Chapter 13, by the late 1970s, most large banks faced the possibility of losing their best commercial lending customers to the commercial paper market. As a result, some banks, notably Bankers Trust of New York, began replacing lost interest income with fees from offering cash management services to corporate customers.[2]

Nevertheless, evidence from depository institutions of all sizes and types indicates that this view of the rise of fee-based income is too narrow. The increasing importance of fees is not confined to traditional "financial powers." From 1977 to 1981, for example, noninterest income as a contributor to net income actually grew for banks of all sizes, and especially for midsized banks (those with $750 million to $1 billion in assets). The growth coincided with declines in the spread that have accelerated with deregulation.[3]

Statistics from the thrift and CU industries also show the growing importance of noninterest income. From 1977 to 1985, fee income unrelated to mortgages (fee income in excess of mortgage points) grew from 7.4 percent to 22.2 percent of operating income at FSLIC-insured institutions. Among federal credit unions, noninterest income grew more than 40 percent *per year* between 1982 and 1985, the largest single change in any income or expense category during those years. Indications are that these trends mark the beginning of an era in which fee-based activities will assume a major role in the management of depository institutions.[4]

TRADITIONAL FEE-BASED SERVICES

Some sources of fee income have been available to depositories for many years but only recently have received greater attention as part of an overall financial management strategy. Several traditional sources of fee income, such as deposit service charges and credit card fees, are discussed in earlier chapters. Two other important traditional services are trust departments and correspondent banking. Although growth in fee income may occur primarily from nontraditional lines of business, the evolving nature of the two traditional services is of interest.

---

[2]For more details, see "Wholesale Banking's New Hard Sell," *Business Week,* April 13, 1981, pp. 82-86.

[3]Carol T. Karkut, "The Growing Importance of Fee Income in Strategic Planning," *Magazine of Bank Administration* 59 (January 1983): 21, 22.

[4]*1986 Savings Institutions Source Book* (Chicago: U.S. League of Savings Institutions, 1986), p. 50; National Credit Union Administration, various annual reports.

TRUST DEPARTMENT OPERATIONS

Trust departments are responsible for managing the investments of individuals or institutional clients such as pension funds. These monies are the assets of clients, separate from the depository institution's assets, and are managed according to clients' risk/return preferences. In addition to investment management, many trust departments offer related services, such as estate planning and tax preparation.

Trust departments have historically been most important in large institutions, although smaller institutions have become more active in recent years. Insured commercial and savings banks must receive the approval both of state regulators and the FDIC before engaging in trust management. As of year-end 1985, 2,552 commercial bank trust departments and 48 savings bank trust departments were operating under FDIC supervision, with total assets under trust management in excess of $82 billion. Similar data on FSLIC-insured institutions is difficult to obtain, although industry publications indicate an increasing interest in trust services. Although credit unions seldom offer formal trust departments, by 1985 7.2 percent of all CUs were providing fee-based investment advice for members.[5]

In the past, trust services were offered to wealthy customers at no explicit charge, in exchange for the client's agreement to keep low-cost deposit balances with the institution. Trust departments were "loss leaders," rarely profitable but operated because they enabled the institution to attract desirable customers. Consequently, trust department managers were under minimal pressure to earn high rates of return on trust assets. Many customers viewed the trust department as an added convenience of doing business with a particular institution and not as the source of high investment returns.

These conditions are reflected in available data on trust operations in the past. In one survey of trust officers in the early 1970s, 60 percent believed that maximizing service was their chief objective. Only 19 percent indicated that maximizing portfolio profitability was the goal, and only 3 percent indicated that fee income generated by the department was an important measure of success. Another study of 300 bank trust departments over the period 1972-1981 indicated they provided customers with only a 4 percent average annual return, compared to 4.9 percent for other money managers.[6]

New Directions

It is understandable that when yields on most investments were relatively low, the performance of trust departments was not considered important to an institution's success. Customers with conservative investment preferences might not have been able to do much better anywhere else. But higher market rates and deregulation have changed that. Few high-balance customers are now willing to keep their money in low- or no-interest accounts, and few are willing to settle for lower risk-adjusted rates of return on trust assets than they can receive elsewhere. In addition, corporations seeking managers for their employees' pension funds will not settle for below-market returns, because an employer's contributions to the fund depend upon how much investment income is earned on existing fund assets.

In response to new pressures to contribute fee income to the depository and to satisfy customers, trust departments are changing. Most now charge explicit fees for trust services, often based on the principal value of the client's assets. New marketing strategies are aimed at newly affluent individuals and families, instead of traditional "old money" clients. Some depositories continue to offer in-house trust departments, but assign the management of the portfolio to outside managers. This strategy

[5]Federal Deposit Insurance Corporation, *1985 Annual Report,* p. 16; *1986 Savings Institutions Source Book,* p. 8; Credit Union National Association, *1985 Credit Union Report,* p. 2.

[6]Keith V. Smith and Maurice B. Goudzwaard, "The Profitability of Commercial Bank Trust Management," *Journal of Bank Research* 3 (Autumn 1972): 166-177; and Daniel Hertzberg, "In Big Shift, Bankers Start Hiring Outsiders for Money Management," *The Wall Street Journal,* December 6, 1982.

can result in the hiring of a competitor, such as a mutual fund, to manage clients' money.

Other institutions retain internal management of trust portfolios, but place new emphasis on portfolio management results. This may require managers who are schooled in sophisticated investment techniques illustrated in earlier chapters, such as duration, options, and futures.[7] The new emphasis is paying off, according to a recent study covering the decade from 1974 to 1984. For the entire period, average annual yields on stock portfolios managed by bank trust departments trailed those supervised by other money managers (13.7 percent versus over 14 percent), but they exceeded their competitors' returns over the last three years of the study (16.3 percent for bank trust departments versus 15.9 percent for portfolios managed by insurance companies and less than 15 percent for other competitors). Despite improved performance, however, bank trust departments continued to lose market share, whether measured by the number of equity funds or by the total dollar amount of assets managed.[8]

A Related Service: Personal Financial Planning

New emphasis on fee income has generated interest in another service that is a natural outgrowth of trust departments: personal financial planning. Financial planners assist individuals with decisions on budgeting, taxes, investments, retirement and estate planning, and other financial matters. Institutions emphasizing this service know it can be costly: If truly individualized advice is given, the expense of training and maintaining a staff is considerable. Fees must therefore be commensurate with the cost of producing the service. For this reason, some institutions have developed general financial plans that can be quickly generated by computer, using basic information about the client (such as age, income, family size, and assets). Financial planning of this type is a low-fee, low-cost service, dependent upon high volume for profitability.

CORRESPONDENT BANKING

First defined in Chapter 11, correspondent banks sell management and administrative services such as check clearing, securities safekeeping, and federal funds trading, to smaller institutions (*respondents*). Like trust operations, correspondent banking is now very different from its earlier days. A particularly interesting change is the unusual competition for fee income between large commercial banks and federal regulators.

Major Services Offered

In the past, services were usually offered to respondents at less than full cost in exchange for their keeping relatively high demand deposit balances with the correspondent bank. Like trust customers, respondents were willing to forgo interest income in exchange for convenience and management expertise. Often, correspondents offered a bundle of services for a single fee and/or deposit balance requirement. In fact, a complete list of all correspondent services would require several pages and might be misleading.

Although literally dozens of functions could be "hired out," the bulk of correspondent banking was centered on just a few activities. Over 80 percent of the correspondents surveyed in the late 1970s considered check collection their most important service, followed by securities safekeeping, fed funds trading, wire

---

[7]For a discussion of the application of some of these techniques to trust management, see George M. Bollenbacher, "Using Stock Index Products in Trust Banking," *Bankers Magazine* 167 (July–August 1984): 57–61.

[8]Michael C. Baker, "Equity Performance Study Shows Banks Coming on Strong," *Trusts and Estates* 125 (May 1985): 19–20; Donald Korytowski and Carolyn Mainguene, "Banks versus Counselors: The Race Continues," *Trusts and Estates* 124 (September 1985):45–48; and Dexter Hutchins, "Banks Shine at Managing Money," *Fortune* 112 (1986 Investors Guide), p. 161. Not all recent performance studies have favored banks, however. For an opposing view, see William B. Madden, "New Figures Show Bank Investing Slips," *Trusts and Estates* 124 (November 1985): 53–55.

transfer, and securities transfer and clearance. The importance of a service was based on the volume of respondent balances the service attracted. A more recent survey supported the continued importance of these five functions, as well as of loan participations offered to respondents by their correspondents.[9]

DIDMCA and the Fed's Entry into Correspondent Banking

Before DIDMCA, parties in a correspondent banking relationship had few reasons to complain because each side believed it had something to gain. DIDMCA, however, contained several provisions that "upset the apple cart." The most important were those mandating universal reserve requirements, access to Fed services for all depositories, the explicit pricing of Fed services, and the authorization of transactions accounts for thrifts and CUs.

Pricing Fed Services. Before DIDMCA, the Fed charged member banks no explicit fees for check clearing and other services as compensation for required noninterest-bearing reserves. Because most correspondent banks were large, and most large banks were Fed members, they would use the Fed's "free" services and charge their smaller nonmember respondents explicit fees for the same services. Now, however, with universal reserve requirements, access by all to Fed services, and explicit Fed pricing, all institutions are motivated to shop for the services they need.

Now included among the price lists to be checked is the Fed's, and because the Fed publishes an unbundled list, in which each service is priced separately, traditional correspondents have also gone to unbundled explicit pricing. Respondents pay only for the services they need and feel no obligation to keep excess low-earning balances with correspondents. A recent study found, for example, that between 1981 and 1984, percentage declines in correspondent balances at the six largest correspondents ranged from 11 percent to nearly 45 percent.[10]

Data collected by the American Bankers Association indicate that large correspondent commercial banks now consider the Fed their strongest competitor. Although smaller correspondent banks consider large banks their most formidable competitors, correspondents of all sizes believe the Fed's explicit pricing of services has hurt profitability.[11]

Competitive Outlook for the Fed. According to a study of the Fed's impact on correspondent banking over the five-year period following the passage of DIDMCA, the Fed initially lost customers to private correspondents and clearinghouses. Upon recognizing the loss of market share, however, the Fed revised services and pricing and began to recapture lost customers. Despite protests that the Fed is an unfair competitor, Congress supports an expanded Fed role in correspondent services. In fact, some observers argue that the Fed's entry into traditional correspondent banking has produced more efficient markets for these services. The conclusion of the 1985 study was that the Fed is committed to the market for correspondent services, and that its influence is likely to grow, not diminish.[12]

[9]Constance Dunham, "Commercial Bank Costs and Correspondent Banking," *New England Economic Review,* Federal Reserve Bank of Boston (September/October 1981), Table 2, p. 29. Thomas P. Rideout and Susan Seidler, "Special Report: Correspondent Banking," *ABA Banking Journal* 73 (November 1981): 67-72.

[10]Merrill O. Burns, "The Future of Correspondent Banking," *Magazine of Bank Administration* 62 (May 1986): 54-64.

[11]As cited in Peter Merrill, "Correspondent Banking and the Payments System," *Economic Review,* Federal Reserve Bank of Atlanta 68 (June 1983), Table 3.

Congress mandated that Fed prices incorporate a private sector markup, reflecting the cost of capital, to allow private correspondents to compete. Determining what that cost should be, however, is controversial. See Anatoli Kuprianov, "An Analysis of Federal Reserve Pricing," *Economic Review,* Federal Reserve Bank of Richmond 72 (March/April 1986): 3-19.

[12]Douglas D. Evanoff, "Priced Services: The Fed's Impact on Correspondent Banking," *Economic Perspectives,* Federal Reserve Bank of Chicago 9 (September/October 1985): 31-44. Although many bankers argue that the Fed is unfair competition, given its size and the fact that it makes the rules by which banks must abide, not all ex-

Figure 20.1
Importance and Profitability of Correspondent Services
to Small and Large Correspondents

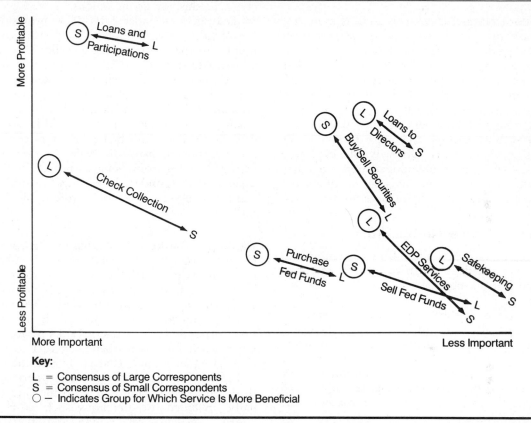

Key:
L = Consensus of Large Correspondents
S = Consensus of Small Correspondents
○ − Indicates Group for Which Service Is More Beneficial

Source: Peter Merrill, "Correspondent Banking and the Payments System," *Economic Review,* Federal Reserve Bank of Atlanta 68 (June 1983): 37.

perts agree. Some argue that the Fed's activities have been procompetitive, not anticompetitive, and that the Fed is not likely to end up a monopolist in the provision of correspondent services. See, for example, Alan K. Reichert, "The Role of the Federal Reserve in the Provision of Correspondent Financial Services," *Proceedings of a Conference on Bank Structure and Competition* (Chicago: Federal Reserve Bank of Chicago, 1981), pp. 231-240; Merrill, "Correspondent Banking and the Payments System"; and Joanna Frodin, "Fed Pricing and the Check Collection Business: The Private Sector Response," *Business Review,* Federal Reserve Bank of Philadelphia (January/February 1984), pp. 13-21.

Relative Benefits of Correspondent Services. With the trend toward unbundled pricing has come the recognition that not all services are equally profitable. Figure 20.1 shows the relative importance and profitability of several major correspondent services to both small and large correspondents. It also reveals whether a service is viewed more favorably (that is, as more profitable) by larger or smaller correspondent banks. The services appearing closer to the left side of the figure are viewed as more important, and those toward the right are relatively less important. The letter circled for each service (S or L) indicates the size group (small or large) for which the service is more beneficial.

For example, check collection is more important than other services to correspondent banks, and more profitable for large institutions. Selling fed funds for respondents is a less important correspondent activity than check clearing, but is relatively more profitable for small correspondents. Offering loans and participations to respondents is viewed as important by both groups and more profitable for small correspondents. On the whole, the figure suggests that some correspondent activities may be subject to economies of scale, making those services more profitable for large institutions.

Entry of Other Competitors

The entry of thrifts and CUs into transactions accounts added a layer of complexity to correspondent banking.

The FHLB System.   Because they were relatively small, few thrifts or CUs established their own check-clearing systems, but many sought to speed their entry into the market by offering truncated checks. Traditional check clearing by correspondent banks seldom offered a truncation feature, however, encouraging the Federal Home Loan Bank system to offer check-clearing services, including truncation, for interested thrifts. As a consequence, the FHLB system has captured a greater share of thrifts' check-clearing business than have correspondent commercial banks.[13]

Corporate Credit Unions.   Correspondent banking has also been changed by the introduction of transaction accounts in the credit union industry. The changes are welcomed by CUs

because most are small enough to escape post-DIDMCA reserve requirements, although they remain eligible to purchase Fed services.

Corporate CUs, defined in Chapter 11 as credit unions for credit unions, gained access to Fed services under DIDMCA provisions. Using this access, corporate CUs have grown rapidly in the 1980s, offering technology and expertise to small CUs. For example, corporate credit unions provide securities safekeeping for member CUs by establishing a corporate CU account at the Fed. The cost to a small CU of having its securities safeguarded this way is often lower than if it obtained the service from a correspondent bank. In 1985, the estimated savings to CUs from using corporate CUs instead of correspondent banks was $72 million; annual savings by 1990 were projected at $200 million.[14]

Bankers' Banks.   Analogous to corporate credit unions are *bankers' banks*. Bankers' banks are what their name suggests: banks for banks. The first was formed in Minnesota in 1975, and by 1984, an estimated 1,300 small banks nationwide were using their services. Like corporate CUs, bankers' banks are formed when small institutions band together to purchase stock in a newly chartered bank; the new institution performs functions for owner-banks that would be more costly if performed individually. Included are functions such as check clearing, securities safekeeping, and other correspondent services. Also like corporate CUs, bankers' banks have access to Fed services. Like the FHLB system and corporate credit unions, bankers' banks provide increasing competition for the traditional suppliers of correspondent services.[15]

As a result of these developments, several possible changes loom on the correspondent

---

[13]Ronald R. Morphew, "Correspondent Financial Services—The Federal Home Loan Bank System Reacts to Title III Consumer Checking Account Equity Act of 1980," *Proceedings of a Conference on Bank Structure and Competition* (Chicago: Federal Reserve Bank of Chicago, 1981), p. 243.

[14]Credit Union National Association, *1985 Annual Report,* pp. 20–21.

[15]For more information on the functions of and laws governing bankers' banks, see Pamela Frisbee, "Bankers' Banks: An Institution Whose Time Has Come?" *Economic Review,* Federal Reserve Bank of Atlanta 69 (April 1984): 31–35.

banking horizon. Because some services are profitable only on a large scale, smaller institutions may be unable to maintain a full range of services. In addition, institutions that continue to offer correspondent banking must expand their markets to include not only smaller banks, but thrifts, CUs, and even nondepository institutions. Finally, correspondents must be aware of technological developments affecting the cost and profitability of operations and be prepared to make substantial expenditures to remain competitive.[16]

A Related Service: Corporate Cash Management

Several fee-based services closely related to correspondent banking are developing. Of particular importance are cash management services for nonfinancial corporations, offered by commercial banks with which businesses maintain close financial relationships. Cash management services include assisting customers with collecting accounts, disbursing expenditures, forecasting cash balances, and investing temporarily idle cash in money market instruments.

Although traditionally the province of large banks, the field is promising for small institutions. A recent survey indicated that over 60 percent of small business managers responding named cash management as their greatest concern. Profitable entry into cash management, however, requires careful attention to the choice of services offered, their costs and their prices, and the target customers to whom marketing efforts will be addressed.[17]

---

[16]For more discussion of these and other points, see Peter Merrill and John H. Neely, "A Shaking Out Is Shaping Up for Correspondents," *ABA Banking Journal* 75 (March 1983): 43-46; "Correspondent Banks Set New Courses," *ABA Banking Journal* 77 (March 1985): 48-49; Alan K. Reichert, "Correspondent Banking: Services in Transition," *Magazine of Bank Administration* 61 (August 1985): 16-18; and Burns, "The Future of Correspondent Banking."

[17]James R. Pastorell, "Cash Management for Community Banks," *Magazine of Bank Administration* 59 (July 1983): 46-48. Another good source on cash management is Brett

EMERGING FEE-BASED SERVICES

Although trust and correspondent services have enjoyed renewed attention recently, depositories have shown even greater interest in expanding the range of fee-based services. The type, legal and regulatory status, and perceived financial benefits of new services vary substantially.

Table 20.1 shows the results of a recent survey of bankers on two categories of products: those they believed would enhance income, and those they would probably offer, whether profitable or not. Many of the products and services are discussed at earlier points in this book, including EFT-based products, credit cards, personal financial planning, consumer lending, and money market accounts. The surveyed bankers ranked most of these low in profitability. Among items of high or medium attractiveness, many relate to two product areas: insurance and securities. Unfortunately for survey respondents, direct participation of depositories in some aspects of these businesses is restricted.

As later chapters indicate, recent financial conditions in segments of the insurance and securities industries cause one to wonder whether the survey results in Table 20.1 reflect the "grass is always greener" syndrome. Indeed, many insurers and securities firms seek to enter deposit taking and lending, while depositories bemoan the profitability of these traditional functions. Barriers to entry on both sides are being eroded rapidly, however, and depository managers must understand the issues and opportunities involved.

SECURITIES ACTIVITIES: BHCs AND MEMBER BANKS

In its broadest form, the phrase *securities activities* means underwriting, distributing, investing in, advising about, and trading government and corporate debt instruments and corporate

---

Hart Brockman, "Planning and Marketing Cash Management Services," *Magazine of Bank Administration* 61 (May 1985): 74-86.

Table 20.1
Banker Attitudes toward Sources of Fee Income

Probability of Adding or Expanding	Product Attractiveness[a]		
	High	**Medium**	**Low**
High	Credit life insurance Fee-generating lending services Increased fees on current products	Shared ATM network	Money market funds
Medium	Leasing Life and health insurance brokerage Mortgage banking	Consumer finance Property and casualty insurance Real estate development	Card-based services Discount brokerage Financial planning Home banking Point-of-sale systems Proprietary ATMs
Low	Securities brokerage	Property management Real estate brokerage Travel agency (full-service)	Insurance underwriting Real estate appraisals

[a]Product attractiveness is the potential for substantially increasing income.

Source: Bank Administration Institute, *Banking Issues and Innovations,* Sample Issue, 1984, p. 3. Also from Survey of Texas Bankers conducted by The MAC Group for the Texas Bankers Association, *The Impact of Deregulation on Small and Medium Sized Texas Banks,* 1983. Reprinted with permission of The MAC Group.

stock. Restrictions on depository institutions' involvement in these activities is discussed at several points earlier in the book, such as investment portfolio restrictions in Chapter 12. Most managers view other types of securities regulations, especially those on underwriting and brokerage services, as more onerous. Like many regulations, specific restrictions depend upon an institution's charter type.

Securities Underwriting

Because of their size and influence in the financial system, Fed member banks have been particularly active in attempting to enter the securities business. They have also been subject to the tightest restrictions. Activities of BHCs with member bank subsidiaries are governed by Federal Reserve Regulation Y, discussed in Chapter 3. That regulation is based on the premise that nonbank affiliates of BHCs must be "closely related" to banking. Separate re-

straints on Fed member banks, in addition to their parent holding companies, were imposed by post-Depression legislation.

Prohibitions on Underwriting of Corporate Securities. Of particular concern to Fed member banks are prohibitions against underwriting corporate securities. In performing this intermediation activity, which involves assisting in the transfer of securities and cash between a seller and an initial buyer, the underwriter usually assumes temporary ownership of the securities. Although underwriters earn income from fees charged for these transfer services, underwriting profits (or losses) also result from price changes in the securities in the brief time the underwriter owns them.

As noted in Chapters 2 and 3, opposition to securities underwriting originated after the banking crisis of the 1930s. Opposition was based on the belief that underwriting could expose a depository to market, default, and interest rate risk over and above the riskiness of the institution's primary assets. At that time, Congress believed that banks involved in underwriting were more likely to fail than others, a belief that led to the passage of the Glass-Steagall Act. Glass-Steagall prohibited the affiliation of a Fed member bank with any other firm "engaged principally in the issue, flotation, underwriting, public sale, or distribution" of securities, except those securities specifically exempted in the act.[18] The next section of the law prohibited underwriters from accepting deposits. Henceforth, commercial banking, in theory at least, was legally separated from investment banking. In practice, however, the issues are not at all clear-cut.

Outlook for Underwriting Activities.

Glass-Steagall exemptions and later legal interpretations have permitted Fed member banks to underwrite Treasury securities, federal agency securities, Eurobonds, and certain types of state and municipal securities. In December 1986, BHCs won a battle ongoing since 1979, when a federal appeals court ruled that their subsidiaries may act as advisors and agents in the sale of commercial paper, although they may not take an independent financial stake in a transaction. This ruling and Fed guidelines issued after the court's decision technically prohibited "underwriting," but for the first time since Glass-Steagall the door was opened for BHC involvement in the sale of corporate securities.[19]

Immediately following these events, both the Fed and Congress began considering proposals to allow BHCs to underwrite municipal revenue bonds and asset-backed securities, such as CARs and CMOs. Although securities firms expressed strong opposition, the Fed approved these activities for BHCs in April 1987.

Underwriting corporate bonds and stocks is still prohibited, however, and many Fed members see this activity as a desirable source of noninterest income. They have relationships with corporations whose securities they would like to underwrite. In addition, banks argue that large underwriting firms have invaded commercial bank territory through their affiliation with brokerage firms offering deposit-type accounts. Some securities firms have even been allowed by the Comptroller of the Currency to obtain federal charters to establish commercial bank affiliates, although the Fed has subsequently refused to grant Fed membership to the applicant banks. Because national banks must be Fed members, the Fed's actions have caused securities firms wishing to establish banks to use nonbank banks, a development discussed in Chapter 3.[20]

In addition to arguments raised by banks, many economists believe that allowing banks into corporate underwriting would have positive consequences. Existing underwriters appear to have charged unnecessarily high fees for underwriting the securities of small firms; with competition from commercial banks, some experts argue that underwriting services would be more competitively priced and that the benefits would outweigh the costs of potential abuses by banks. Indirect support for allowing greater

---

[18]This phrase is from Section 20 of the Act and is cited in many sources, among them Thomas G. Fischer, William H. Gram, George G. Kaufman, and Larry R. Mote, "The Securities Activities of Commercial Banks: A Legal and Economic Analysis," *Tennessee Law Review* 51 (1984): 467–518.

[19]In 1979, Bankers Trust Company acted as an agent in the sale of commercial paper, which the Fed ruled was enough like a short-term commercial loan to be exempt from the definition of "security" in the Glass-Steagall Act. The Supreme Court held that commercial paper *was* a security, and ordered a lower court to decide whether Bankers Trust's commercial paper activities were underwriting and thus violated the G-S Act. Bankers Trust lost in the lower court, but won on appeal when the court ruled that the extent of the bank's involvement was not underwriting as meant in G-S. See Fischer et al., "The

Securities Activities of Commercial Banks," pp. 492–496; Gary Hector, "Bankers Trust Takes on Wall Street," *Fortune,* 107 (January 9, 1984): 104–107; Joseph Diamond, "How Banks Cope with Glass-Steagall," *Bankers Magazine* 169 (September/October 1986): 18–23; John E. Yang and Phillip L. Zweig, "Bank's Sales of Commercial Paper Approved," *The Wall Street Journal,* December 24, 1986, p. 2; John E. Yang and Phillip L. Zweig, "Bankers Trust Gets Additional Fed Clearance," *The Wall Street Journal,* December 26, 1986, p. 2;

[20]Fischer et al., "The Securities Activities of Commercial Banks," pp. 498–502.

competition among underwriters is provided by events following the recent implementation of **Rule 415** of the Securities and Exchange Commission (SEC). Discussed in more detail in Chapter 24, Rule 415 permits firms to obtain permission to issue securities up to two years in advance instead of contracting with an underwriter at the time of a security issue. Firms using Rule 415 have found underwriters competing for their business, often resulting in lower fees than they would have paid otherwise.[21]

Currently, however, Congress sees underwriting of corporate stocks and bonds by commercial banks as incompatible with deposit insurance and the "moral hazard" problem introduced in Chapters 15 and 16. Until Congress acts, the controversy will remain unresolved.

Private Placement versus Underwriting. The status of member banks and the private placement of corporate securities is clearer. A financial intermediary's role in private placements is much more limited than in underwriting. Usually, the private placement of new issues involves bringing together the securities issuer and one or several large buyers. The intermediary earns a "finder's fee" of sorts, but does not take even brief possession of the securities. Both the Fed and Comptroller have ruled that private placement is not underwriting under Glass-Steagall and have permitted commercial banks to earn private placement fees.[22]

Securities Brokerage Services

Fed member banks also view securities brokerage services as potential sources of lucrative fee income, and they have enjoyed more success in pursuing them than in underwriting. Regulators and the courts have interpreted Glass-Steagall prohibitions against the "public sale" of securities by banks to mean underwriting, not simply arranging the purchase or sale of securities for members of the public.

Ironically, member banks and BHCs themselves may be responsible for continuing litigation on securities brokerage, even though some experts believe there is really no serious legal question. Until quite recently, banks and BHCs showed almost no interest in establishing brokerage functions. In 1982, both Security Pacific Bank and the BHC of which BankAmerica is a subsidiary filed applications with their principal regulators to establish discount brokerage services. As noted in Chapter 1, discount brokers arrange the purchase and sale of securities for customers but do not offer investment advice, in contrast to full-service brokers, who do both.

A point made by both Security Pacific and BankAmerica Corporation was that the services they proposed did not include investment advice. Consequently, they argued, the affiliated banks did not have even a remote interest in the success or failure of any company or security and would be insulated from any alleged increase in riskiness caused by a close relationship between securities activities and commercial banking. Both applications were approved, and after challenge by the securities industry, were upheld in court. In 1987, the Supreme Court ruled that BHCs and national banks may operate discount brokerage offices nationwide without violating interstate banking laws.[23]

Regulatory Interpretation. In 1984, the Fed added discount brokerage to the list of permissible BHC subsidiaries under Reg Y, but

[21]Anthony Saunders, "Securities Activities of Commercial Banks: The Problem of Conflicts of Interest," *Business Review*, Federal Reserve Bank of Philadelphia (July-August 1985), pp. 17-27; Robert J. Rogowski and Eric H. Sorenson, "Deregulation in Investment Banking: Shelf Registrations, Structure, and Performance," *Financial Management* 14 (Spring 1985): 5-15.

[22]Fischer et al., "The Securities Activities of Commercial Banks," pp. 496-498; and Hector, "Bankers Trust Takes on Wall Street."

[23]Accounts of these events are found in several places. See, for example, "Bankers as Brokers," *Business Week,* April 11, 1983, pp. 70-74; Gary Hector, "The Banks Invade Wall Street," *Fortune* 105 (February 7, 1983): 44-48; Fischer et al., "The Securities Activities of Commercial Banks," pp. 484-490; and Stephen Wermeil and John E. Yang, "Supreme Court Widens Banks' Brokerage Role," *The Wall Street Journal,* January 15, 1987, p. 2. In 1987, financially troubled BankAmerica sold its discount brokerage subsidiary back to the founder, Charles Schwab.

explicitly noted that full-service brokerage services were not permitted. In contrast, the Comptroller's office has permitted national banks to offer both discount brokerage and investment advice as part of their securities activities, stating that it finds nothing in Glass-Steagall to prohibit it. Naturally, the securities industry sued, and the Supreme Court announced its intention to rule on the matter in 1987.[24]

The SEC and Bank Securities Brokerage. The most recent regulatory challenge to the securities activities of member banks comes from the SEC. In 1985, the SEC ruled that banks soliciting any kind of brokerage business must register with the SEC or transfer all securities operations to a separate subsidiary. Banking industry leaders stated the rule would cost millions of dollars and challenged the SEC's authority in court. In November 1986, a federal appeals court agreed that the SEC lacked authority to regulate depository institutions, but the SEC asked the court to reconsider because the case was "of exceptional importance." As of early 1987, a decision was pending.[25]

SECURITIES ACTIVITIES OF OTHER DEPOSITORY INSTITUTIONS

Unlike Fed member banks, state nonmember banks, thrifts, and CUs are not bound by the specific language of the Glass-Steagall Act.

Limits on their securities activities are thus somewhat different from those of member banks and BHCs.

FDIC–Insured Nonmember Institutions

FDIC-insured institutions, regardless of charter type, must abide by FDIC regulations. In 1984, the FDIC released an official policy statement that FDIC-insured institutions, both banks and thrifts, were *not* prohibited from engaging in securities activities. The insurer also noted, however, that "some risk may be associated with those activities," and that restrictions may apply on specific activities or on transactions between nonmember depositories and their securities affiliates.[26]

The securities activities of nonmember commercial and savings banks are determined by state laws; as a result, some state-chartered institutions can engage in underwriting or full-service brokerage activities. Some states, such as South Dakota and Delaware, have used their authority to lure nonresident institutions to establish local state-chartered securities subsidiaries. BHC regulations must still be met in any case, however, so money center banks affiliated with BHCs have not yet succeeded in entering corporate underwriting through the back door.

Many nonmember depositories are quite small, and underwriting, in particular, is likely to be incompatible with existing customer bases. Discount brokerage operations are relatively common, however; over 600 banks had established them within 18 months of the Security Pacific and BankAmerica decisions, and an estimated 3,000 depositories had done so by late 1986. Full-service brokerage activities, though more costly to operate, are attractive to some. The financial implications of offering these services are discussed later in the chapter.

FSLIC–Insured Institutions

Although not prohibited from securities activities by Glass-Steagall, FSLIC-insured institu-

[24]"Brokerage Services Approved by Board," *DallasFed,* Federal Reserve Bank of Dallas, October 1983, p. 1; Christopher Conte, "Comptroller Allows Texas Bank to Start Investment Adviser," *The Wall Street Journal,* September 8, 1983; and "Court to Decide If Banks Can Set Up Brokerages," *Chicago Tribune,* March 4, 1986, Section 3, p. 6.

[25]Monica Langley, "SEC Extends Brokerage Rules to Banks; Industry Strongly Opposes Regulation," *The Wall Street Journal,* July 2, 1985, p. 3; Nick Gilbert, "The Early Bureau Gets the Worm," *Forbes* 136 (September 16, 1985): 48; Bruce Ingersoll, "SEC Extends Its Regulatory Reach over Banks and Thrifts, Aggravating Many in the Industry," *The Wall Street Journal,* January 3, 1986, p. 28; and Bruce Ingersoll, "SEC Asks Court Review of Ruling Ending Its Regulation of Banks with Brokerage," *The Wall Street Journal,* December 23, 1986, p. 44.

[26]Federal Deposit Insurance Corporation, *1984 Annual Report,* p. 39.

tions have only recently moved aggressively into the securities business. Because they presently have few corporate customers, underwriting corporate securities is not a feasible source of fee-based income. Brokerage services, however, are another matter.

In 1986, over 650 savings institutions were involved in discount or full-service brokerage activities. Many thrifts offering brokerage services have entered via collectively owned service corporations. The largest of these organizations is Invest of Tampa, Florida. Invest establishes booths in S&L offices, from which personnel provide advice and execute securities trades for the thrift's customers. Recommendations to clients are not based on original research, but are taken from standard sources such as Value Line. As a result, fees charged are between those of discount and full-service brokers. Participating thrifts provide space, salaries, and advertising, and they split commission fees with Invest. Thrifts not wishing to participate in Invest-type programs have elected to affiliate with discount or full-service brokers or to develop in-house brokerage facilities.[27]

Credit Unions

As of year-end 1985, only 4.6 percent of CUs had moved into the brokerage business, and most had total assets in excess of $20 million.[28] Similar to the thrift industry, brokerage services are offered through credit union service organizations (CUSOs). Credit unions of all sizes are assisted by CUNA Brokerage, a division of the industry's major trade organization, the Credit Union National Association. CUNA Brokerage enables participating CUs to offer retail brokerage services to members without employing in-house personnel trained in the se-

curities business. CUNA Brokerage executes trades for individual members of affiliated CUs; because of its not-for-profit status, fees can be lower than those charged by competing brokers.

FINANCIAL IMPLICATIONS OF BROKERAGE ACTIVITIES

As with other fee-based services, one motivation for depositories' entry into brokerage services is increased profitability. Data on the brokerage industry in general suggest that discount brokerage operations can be quite lucrative. During the period 1977-1983, the after-tax return on net worth of brokerage firms exceeded after-tax RONW for BHCs, and the profitability of discount brokers exceeded that of full-service brokers each year.[29]

Securities Activities and Portfolio Risk

Although securities activities can increase fee income, they cannot be undertaken without careful analysis of all ramifications. Discount brokerage firms have proportionately more fixed costs than do full-service brokers, because the former have large investments in computers and other electronic equipment and fewer personnel. Because of operating leverage, profits of discount brokers are more volatile as revenues vary than are profits of firms with smaller fixed costs. In 1983, for example, quarterly RONW for discount brokers ranged from 39 percent in the first quarter to 2 percent in the fourth quarter; profits for full-service brokers ranged between 31 percent and 6 percent.[30]

There is no reason to assume that the discount brokerage activities of depositories differ. Thus, institutions considering a heavy commitment to discount brokerage must consider

[27]John N. Frank, "Stock Brokerage Joins the Growing List of Association Offerings," *Savings Institutions* 104 (February 1983): 38-43; and Mitchell Gordon, "The Invasion of Wall Street—II: Here Come the Savings and Loans," *Barron's,* September 27, 1982, pp. 7, 38; Katherine Morrall, "New Strategies and Stronger Management Role Trigger Profits," *Savings Institutions* 107 (November 1986): 110-116.

[28]CUNA, *1985 Credit Union Report,* p. 2.

[29]Steven D. Felgran, "Bank Entry into Securities Brokerage: Competitive and Legal Aspects," *New England Economic Review,* Federal Reserve Bank of Boston (November/December 1984): 14.

[30]Ibid., pp. 14-15.

Table 20.2
Selected Statistics: Banks and Other Financial Institutions, 1970–1980

	Coefficient of Variation for Return on Assets	Correlation with Return on Assets for Banks
Banks	0.2115	—
Savings banks	0.2961	−0.4345
Savings and loan associations	0.3373	−0.2078
Security brokers and dealers	0.4066	−0.1782
Insurance firms:		
Life insurance underwriters	0.1010	0.1636
Other insurance underwriters	0.4272	0.2023
Insurance agents and brokers	0.1186	0.4874

Source: Adapted from Robert A. Eisenbeis and Larry D. Wall, "Bank Holding Company Nonbanking Activities and Risk," *Proceedings of a Conference on Bank Structure and Competition* (Chicago: Federal Reserve Bank of Chicago, 1984), p. 345.

whether the higher potential returns may be accompanied by higher risk. Portfolio theory, discussed in Chapter 12, suggests that before drawing conclusions, the institution must also consider the covariability of revenues from securities operations with the institution's other sources of income.

Table 20.2 presents evidence on this question from a recent study. Column 1 shows the *coefficient of variation* of return on assets for several industries over the period 1970–1980; the coefficient of variation is the standard deviation of returns over the period divided by the average return for the industry. Because it provides a measure of risk per unit of return, the higher the measure, the more variable the profits of the industry. Column 2 presents the correlation of returns for each industry with those for bank holding companies. The authors found that return on asset figures for securities firms were negatively correlated with return on asset figures for BHCs.

This finding implies that BHCs may obtain diversification benefits from securities activities, even though, taken alone, securities activities may be riskier than "mainstream" banking. On the other hand, the evidence suggests indirectly that the activities of thrifts and securities

firms may be positively correlated with each other, because they were both negatively correlated with commercial banking. If so, thrifts pursuing brokerage activities may reduce risk only a little. Although historical patterns may not be repeated, depositories seeking to diversify must consider potential correlation of securities services with those on lending and other activities.[31]

---

[31]The data in Table 20.2 are among the most recent available. Previous research covering different time periods has suggested other relationships between returns on the various industries listed in the table. For a review, see Robert A. Eisenbeis and Larry D. Wall, "Bank Holding Company Nonbanking Activities and Risk," *Proceedings of a Conference on Bank Structure and Competition* (Chicago: Federal Reserve Bank of Chicago, 1984): 345. Table 20.2 and the related discussion merely illustrate the need to consider correlations and are not intended to represent definitive conclusions.

More recently, Saunders and Smirlock found that the announcement of BHC intent to engage in securities activities has no effect on the value of BHC stock and that, in any case, securities activities are only a small proportion of total BHC returns. See Anthony Saunders and Michael Smirlock, "Intra- and Interindustry Effects of Bank Securities Market Activities: The Case of Discount Brokerage," unpublished working paper, No. 352, Salomon Brothers Center for the Study of Financial Institutions, 1985.

No Guarantees of Success

To date, brokerage activities of depositories have yet to provide substantial profits. Although estimates vary, some experts believe it takes an average of 100 trades a day for a full-service brokerage operation to be profitable for a depository, and an average of 35 trades a day for a profitable discount brokerage. In reply to a 1985 survey conducted for the American Bankers Association, most respondents offering brokerage services for more than six months stated that few customers actually used the brokerage accounts they had opened. Consequently, brokerage services in the early years have been quite costly to administer while providing few revenues, a situation the researchers said could be be an "embarrassing flop" for bankers.[32] Others argue, however, that brokerage services have kept customers who want a full-service financial institution from abandoning their depository in favor of a competitor that offers a greater range of services. Bank One, profiled in the opening paragraph, is an institution holding the latter belief.

Although no firm conclusions can be drawn, the assumption of automatic success from depositories' diversification beyond traditional activities is not warranted. Managers considering the potential benefits of securities activities must also recognize the costs, and thorough analysis must replace the "herd instinct" to offer a service just because another institution is doing it. In particular, institutions with low capital ratios must be cautious in pursuing activities that may expose them to additional risk without additional profits.

INSURANCE ACTIVITIES AS SOURCES OF FEE-BASED INCOME

Insurance is another area of increasing interest to depositories. Like securities activities, insurance activities consist of both underwriting and brokerage.

---

[32]Frank, "Stock Brokerage Joins the Growing List of Association Offerings," p. 39; Edmon W. Blount and Louise Glass, "Will Banks Pass the Brokerage Test?" *ABA Banking Journal* 77 (February 1985): 61-71.

Basic Principles

Insurance underwriters agree to bear, for a fee, the financial risk against which the insured seeks protection. An automobile insurance underwriter agrees to bear potential costs resulting from a car accident in exchange for a premium paid by the car owner. If no accident occurs, the insurer profits from the premium and from earnings on investment of the premium, less the administrative costs of providing insurance services. If there is an accident, the insurer suffers a loss in an amount unknown at the time the policy is written. Thus, insurance underwriters act as intermediaries, transforming the unknown financial risk to which the insured is exposed to a fixed dollar amount consisting of the policy premium.

Insurance brokers, on the other hand, sell insurance policies for a fee, without bearing risks. Insurance brokerage is a marketing function, bringing together underwriters and policy seekers. Local insurance agents are brokers; for a commission, they sell policies underwritten by others. Like other financial institutions, insurance agencies reduce transactions costs for both parties, especially search costs that underwriter and policyholder might otherwise bear.

Until recently, these distinctions were somewhat academic for depository institutions, because most of them acted neither as underwriters nor as brokers. The exception to this general rule, mentioned in Chapter 3, was the offering of *credit life insurance* to borrowers. In a credit life policy, the insurer, usually also the lender, agrees to pay the borrower's loan in case of death; fees are levied at the time the loan contract is signed. Now, however, the legal status of insurance activities in depositories is no longer clearly defined, and changes are occurring as rapidly as they are in securities underwriting and brokerage. The current status of insurance activities depends on the size and type of institution.

Insurance Activities of Fed Member Banks and Their BHCs

Federal legislation on national banks, BHCs, and insurance spans the period 1933-1982. Initially, as part of Congress's intent to reduce the risks to which banks were exposed, the Glass-Steagall Act prohibited national banks from selling insurance in towns with populations in excess of 5,000. This provision prevented money center banks—those most likely to want to do so—from pursuing insurance. Subsequent BHC laws gave the Fed the right to apply the "closely related" test to potential insurance subsidiaries of BHCs, and the Fed determined that the underwriting and sale of credit life *were* closely related to banking.

In the Garn-St Germain Act, however, Congress decided to limit the scope of large BHCs' insurance activities. That law holds that BHCs with total assets under $50 million have unlimited rights to engage in insurance activities, but other BHCs are prohibited from acting as underwriters or brokers of all insurance products except credit life, accident, health, or unemployment insurance. The result of five decades of legislation has been to prevent large banks from engaging in insurance activities.[33]

Insurance Activities of Other Depository Institutions

Like securities activities, the insurance activities of non-Fed member depositories are subject to more varied rules and regulations than those of Fed member institutions or BHCs.[34]

FDIC-Insured Nonmember Institutions.
The insurance activities of state-chartered commercial and savings banks are left to state laws, and many states see no conflict between banking and insurance. In fact, savings banks and some state-chartered commercial banks have engaged in various aspects of the insurance business for several years. In general, state-chartered commercial banks in states prohibiting bank branching face fewer restrictions on their insurance activities than those in states permitting geographic expansion of banks. The reason for this difference is that unit banks provide less competition for existing insurers than do banks with extensive branch networks. Thus, state legislators are able to offer something to both types of institutions while alienating neither.

Some states have been particularly creative in their banking/insurance laws. In a 1983 law soon nicknamed the ***"South Dakota loophole,"*** the state invited out-of-state depository institutions to set up insurance operations by purchasing state-chartered banks in South Dakota. According to the law, insurance could then be marketed by these organizations in every state *but* South Dakota, thus protecting existing insurance agents in the state! The Fed was not amused, however, and, invoking its BHC authority, subsequently refused to permit any non-South Dakota banks to enter insurance through the "loophole" route.[35]

Some states restricting commercial bank entry into insurance, however, give savings banks considerable authority to pursue insurance. Savings banks in Massachusetts, Connecticut, and New York have a long and successful involvement in life insurance, rooted in their origin as depositories for the urban working class. By eliminating agent commissions, the nearly 300 savings banks in these states offer customers life insurance at a lower cost than comparable policies marketed by insurance companies.

FSLIC-Insured Institutions.
Since 1967, federally chartered S&Ls have been permitted to broker all types of insurance except private mortgage insurance, and to engage in limited underwriting, through affiliated service corpo-

---

[33]Garn-St Germain also contained a "grandfather clause," permitting large BHCs with any other kind of insurance services allowed by the Fed before May 1, 1982, to retain them. For more details on Garn-St Germain insurance provisions, see Steven D. Felgran, "Banks as Insurance Agencies: Legal Constraints and Competitive Advances," *New England Economic Review,* Federal Reserve Bank of Boston (September/October 1985), pp. 34-49.

[34]A good summary and comparison of the regulations governing insurance activities of depositories, by charter type, as of 1986 is William C. Crum, "Banking in Insurance: A Guide to Chaos," *Bankers Magazine* 169 (January/February 1986): 51-58.

[35]William Gruber, "Fed Blocks Citicorp on Insurance," *Chicago Tribune,* August 2, 1985, Sec. 2, p. 1; and Felgran, "Banks as Insurance Agencies," pp. 44-45.

rations.[36] During 1982, the most recent data available, insurance was the second most important type of S&L service corporation activity (behind real estate–related operations), accounting for 13.6 percent of activities nationwide. The latitude permitted to state-chartered S&Ls in their insurance activities varies considerably.

Credit Unions. Many credit unions have offered insurance similar to credit life for a number of years. Unlike banks and thrifts, however, the loan protection insurance offered by CUs was often paid for by CUs, not by members themselves. These programs were offered as part of the service objectives of the CU movement. But CUs have found their net interest margins squeezed and are seeking sources of fee-based income to protect earnings. As a result, many are now selling member-paid credit life insurance, as well as other types of life and casualty insurance policies.

State-chartered CUs are governed by state laws. Federal CUs are subject to the NCUA's regulations, currently requiring that insurance be offered through credit union service organizations (CUSOs), the industry's equivalent of S&L service corporations. CUSOs may offer policies underwritten by other insurance providers. Among the largest underwriters with which CUSOs deal is the CUNA Mutual Insurance Group, affiliated with the Credit Union National Association. CUNA Mutual, founded by CUs for CUs, is a major national provider of credit life insurance, based on dollar volume of coverage in force. It also underwrites a variety of other insurance products for CU members nationwide.[37]

Rationale for Excluding Depositories from Insurance Activities

It is useful to understand the rationale for federal legislation keeping large depositories out of the insurance business. Most objections to mixing banking and insurance fall into two categories: those related to safety and soundness and those related to potential coercion of borrowers.

Safety and Soundness. As with securities underwriting, insurance underwriting was viewed as riskier than normal banking activities by the framers of post-Depression financial legislation. Discussed in more detail in Chapter 23, the risks to which insurers are exposed are different from those faced by depositories in their day-to-day operations. Congress, concerned about the problem of moral hazard, has chosen to view these risks as incompatible with a depository's ability to offer deposit insurance to customers. Interestingly enough, the FDIC and the Comptroller of the Currency have not shared this perspective recently. In 1984, the FDIC proposed to allow a subsidiary of any insured bank to underwrite insurance and to permit insured institutions themselves to act as insurance brokers. The proposed policy was directly opposed by the insurance industry, however, and indirectly opposed by the Federal Reserve in its August 1985 ruling against Citicorp's bid to enter insurance underwriting via a South Dakota subsidiary. Thus, it was still in the proposal stage in 1987. The Comptroller of the Currency has also held that national banks can sell insurance anywhere in the United States from small branch offices. The insurance industry has sued to halt implementation of the ruling.[38]

Coercion of Borrowers. A second argument used by opponents of mixing depositories and insurance is that depositories, if permitted to underwrite and sell insurance, would make lending contingent upon the purchase of insurance from the lender. Although few data are available, a recent study by one consumer interest group concluded that fees for credit life insurance at savings institutions were "excessive"

---

[36]Pat Allen, "Treasures in Insurance: Many Paths Lead to Profitability," *Savings Institutions* 106 (October 1984): 84; and Crum, "Banking in Insurance: A Guide to Chaos."

[37]For a 50-year history of insurance services in the credit union industry, see CUNA Mutual Insurance Group, *1984 Annual Report*.

[38]Federal Deposit Insurance Corporation, *1984 Annual Report*, p. 41; Crum, "Banking in Insurance: A Guide to Chaos"; Monica Langley, "U.S. Regulators Move to Let Banks Enter Several New Businesses," *The Wall Street Journal*, December 29, 1986, pp. 1, 15.

and that the number of policies sold exceeded the normal expected level of market penetration. In contrast, a 1979 Federal Reserve study of the insurance activities of major lenders found little evidence of coercion.[39] Depositories defend their credit life practices on the basis of the increased convenience offered to consumers who need not shop for what is essentially an inexpensive product anyway. Despite the lack of concrete evidence, the potential for coercion has been argued repeatedly by influential Congressional lobbyists working for the nation's independent insurance agents.

FINANCIAL IMPLICATIONS OF INSURANCE ACTIVITIES

Because widespread insurance involvement is new, few data about its impact on depositories are available. It is possible, however, to identify the expected financial impact.

Insurance Activities and Portfolio Risk

Insurance activities are attractive to depositories because they require few fixed costs and have a low degree of operating leverage. Often, no new facilities or personnel are needed, and the opportunities to cross-sell insurance and other depository products are considerable. Of course, riskiness also must be considered. Table 20.2 shows that the coefficients of variation for life insurers and insurance agents were less than those of depositories from 1970 to 1980, reflecting their lower operating leverage. In contrast, however, the coefficient of variation for property and casualty insurers was greater than those of banks and thrifts. For reasons explained in Chapter 23, property and casualty earnings are especially subject to cyclical economic variations from which life insurers have been exempt.

The profitability of insurance also seems alluring—at least at times. During the period 1970-1980, the average return on assets of insurance underwriters and agencies exceeded that of banks and thrifts. From 1976 through 1983, the return on equity for insurance agencies and brokers, though declining over the period, substantially exceeded that of savings institutions each year. From 1979 through 1983, the returns on equity for life and property/casualty underwriters also exceeded those for thrifts.[40] More recently, however, insurers have suffered profitability downturns that make the business seem less than a sure thing.

Diversification Potential.   During the period depicted in Table 20.2, returns on assets for all types of insurance operations were positively correlated with banking. Because thrift profitability was negatively correlated with banking returns, the data suggest the possibility of negative correlation between insurers and thrifts. Taken together, these data imply that life insurance may prove more beneficial to depositories than property and casualty insurance operations. In addition, if historical patterns persist, the diversification benefits of insurance may be greater for some depositories than for others.

Exposure to New Risks.   It is also important for banks and thrifts considering underwriting to recognize the differences between assessing credit risk or interest rate risk and assessing underwriting risks. Techniques such as financial statement analysis and GAP management are central to successful depository institutions, but they do not necessarily develop the skills required to evaluate life expectancies or to estimate the probabilities that property damage will occur. For most depositories, especially small ones, entering insurance via the brokerage route is probably more appropriate. In addition, institutions with low capital ratios should be especially careful.

---

[39]See Pat Allen, "Treasures in Insurance: Regulators and Market Forces Make the Gold Hard to Get," *Savings Institutions* 105 (November 1984): 99; Robert M. Shafton and Donald D. Gabay, "The Banking Outlook for Diversification into Insurance," *Bankers Magazine* 168 (January/February 1985): 23.

[40]Eisenbeis and Wall, "Bank Holding Company Nonbanking Activities and Risk," p. 345; Allen, "Treasures in Insurance: Many Paths Lead to Profitability," p. 81; Allen, "Treasures in Insurance: Regulators and Market Forces Make the Gold Hard to Get," p. 100.

Expected Volume of Business

Depositories have learned from their securities activities that no avenue of fee income is beneficial without sufficient volume. Some evidence suggests greater potential for insurance volume in depositories than for brokerage operations. For example, recent surveys indicate that the public has a more favorable impression of depository institutions than of insurance companies in areas such as quality of service, reliability, and trustworthiness. Consequently, many depositories hope to capitalize on this perceived advantage to take insurance business from insurers and insurance agencies.[41]

In addition to image, depositories also have an edge in convenience. A 1980 study indicated that the average consumer had 38 contacts per year with a bank and 20 with a thrift, but only 6 with a property/casualty insurer and 5 with a life insurer.[42] Many purposes for which consumers visit depositories— for example, to obtain financing for a car or a house—also lead to the purchase of insurance. Opportunities for depositories to cross-sell loan and insurance products are especially attractive.

In addition to convenience, the branch networks established by depositories may allow them to offer insurance at a cost advantage over traditional insurers. Because the average depository already has the necessary personnel, equipment, and facilities through which to sell insurance policies, most institutions would simply be using existing facilities to greater capacity. A recent national survey of bank and thrift executives indicated that 75 percent had formal plans to enter insurance, primarily through establishing agencies in existing facilities.[43] In

contrast, most independent insurance agencies do not have data-processing capabilities, so they must hire outsiders to process policies, increasing their costs and the commissions they charge.

OTHER EMERGING FEE-BASED SERVICES

The previous discussions of securities and insurance illustrate some of the reasons why new sources of fee income are both attractive and risky for depositories. They also indicate the controversy arising when one group of financial institutions attempts to enter territory other firms have previously considered to be theirs alone. Securities and insurance, although getting the most attention recently, are not the only controversial activities. This section briefly describes a few others. Although not all these areas provide income in the form of fees alone, they are all somewhat removed from the traditional lending and deposit-taking functions of banks, thrifts, and CUs.

Real Estate-Related Activities

All depository institutions can loan money secured by real property, but few can invest in real estate directly. Many depositories believe that the potential profitability of real estate investments is quite high, however, because greater price appreciation on real estate is possible than on typical depository institution assets. In addition, real estate-related activities such as fee-generating property management, real estate brokerage, and title certification services, are attractive to depositories but not yet universally available to them. As always, both state and federal regulations apply. Historically, most national banks and their BHCs have been prohibited from owning real property either directly or through subsidiaries, although in early 1987, the Fed proposed revisions in Regulation Y that would permit BHCs to own real estate subsidiaries, with limitations tied to a BHC's capital ratios. National banks and their BHCs are prohibited from operating subsidiaries for either property management or residential real

---

[41]These surveys, conducted by insurance industry representatives, private consulting groups, and depository institutions representatives, are cited in Allen, "Treasures in Insurance: Many Paths Lead to Profitability"; Shafton and Gabay, "The Banking Outlook for Diversification into Insurance"; and "Survey Finds Large Market for Personal Lines in Banks," *National Underwriter,* Property and Casualty Edition, December 28, 1984.

[42]Allen, "Treasures in Insurance: Many Paths Lead to Profitability," p. 80.

[43]Ronald K. Randall, "Insurance: A Survey of Bankers' Plans," *Magazine of Bank Administration* 61 (September 1985): 20-26.

estate brokerage. The laws governing state institutions vary.[44]

Thrifts, more closely allied to mortgage lending than other depositories, face fewer restrictions on real estate-related activities than do commercial banks. As a consequence, some S&Ls are engaged in property management, appraisal, and even direct real estate development through service corporations. In fact, by year-end 1982, the most recent data available, real estate-related business accounted for about 50 percent of all S&L service corporation activities. As of year-end 1985, slightly over 35 percent of all savings banks were involved in real estate development.[45]

Recent rulings of federal regulators, however, have not encouraged the expansion of thrifts' real estate authority. In 1984, the FHLBB restricted FSLIC-insured institutions' investments in real estate through service corporations to specified percentages of their net worth. A revision effective April 1987 made it more difficult for thrifts with low net worth to invest in real estate, but loosened restrictions on those with stronger capital positions.[46] Recently, both the FDIC and the Fed restricted the conditions under which FDIC-insured savings banks can engage in real estate development. In these cases, the regulators reflected concerns about the illiquidity and highly uncertain value of real estate. Although the thrift industry was opposed to these and other rules, concern about the failure rate of thrifts may influence the extent to which additional real estate powers will be granted in the immediate future.

---

[44]Some depositories may own real estate not of their own choosing because mortgage defaults may result in the lenders acquiring the mortgaged property. Real estate owned for this reason does not violate laws prohibiting equity positions in real property, although limits are placed on the length of time the property can be held before sale.

[45]Jacobe, "Service Corporations Are Ideal Diversification Tool," pp. 52-53; National Council of Savings Institutions, *1986 National Fact Book of Savings Institutions*, p. 41.

[46]Federal Home Loan Bank Board, "Regulation of Equity Risk Investments by Insured Institutions," 12 CFR Part 563, February 27, 1987.

And the List Goes On

Additional areas in which depository institutions have experimented in recent years include services as diverse as travel agencies and *venture capital* subsidiaries. Venture capital operations are those in which an institution takes a temporary equity position in a young or brand-new company. This relationship contrasts considerably with traditional commercial relationships in which the depository acts as creditor to a business after careful financial analysis of past performance. Although potential growth in the value of a venture capital investment may be attractive, the risks are high.

Other institutions do not offer nontraditional services themselves but cash in on the trend toward fee-based income by leasing space to direct providers of the services. These depositories benefit from the lease income while offering their customers the on-premises convenience of a wider range of services.

At this point, it is worth rereading the quotation with which this chapter begins, because it suggests an appropriate closing note as well. Given the creativity of managers and the pace at which the financial system has changed recently, the list of potential fee-based sources of income is in a constant state of flux, as the regulatory dialectic predicts. Today's list will no doubt be incomplete or obsolete tomorrow. Regardless of the services considered by a depository, however, the need to supplement interest income to remain profitable and competitive will continue, as will the need to assess the risks involved in building each new "log cabin."

SUMMARY

The focus of this chapter is the increasingly important role of fee-based services in depository institution management. Fee-based products include traditional ones, such as trust departments and correspondent banking, and new ones, such as securities brokerage and insurance. Experience suggests that some sources of fee income may be less volatile than traditional income sources.

Trust departments are changing in response to customer preferences. An emphasis on improved performance has made such operations more competitive. The services offered by correspondent institutions also face greater competition. With regulatory changes, the Fed, the FHLB System and corporate credit unions all compete in the correspondent services markets.

Some depository institutions are interested in expanding securities activities. Although restrictions against full underwriting powers remain, depositories have made inroads. Regulators agree that institutions can offer discount brokerage services, although the status of full-service brokers is uncertain. In response to these developments, managers must move cautiously; brokerage income tends to be volatile, although it may offer a source of diversification.

Another new service alternative is insurance. Federal regulations prevent BHCs and national banks from extensive involvement in insurance brokering and underwriting, based on concerns that insurance activities may threaten institutional safety or lead to coercion of customers. State regulators, however, have been more permissive, as have the thrift and credit union regulators. Both thrift and credit union service organizations actively broker insurance policies, but underwriting activity is limited.

Additional service areas emerge regularly as depository institutions seek to diversify their sources of funds and to capitalize on opportunities for increasing income and profitability. Each opportunity also poses additional risks.

Questions

1. Why is fee income increasingly important to depository institutions?

2. Compare the past profitability of trust departments to their current performance. What conditions prompted the shift in emphasis on profitability?

3. Compare correspondent banks' past and present pricing techniques. What factors influenced the change?

4. Do you think the Fed and other regulators provide unfair competition to privately operated financial institutions in the market for correspondent banking services? Explain. Why do you think economies of scale exist for some correspondent services?

5. Explain the major restrictions on the securities activities of Fed member banks. What is the rationale for the restrictions? Considering the operating advantages and disadvantages of being a member bank, do you think current securities regulations are unfair to them relative to their competitors? Explain.

6. Do you think corporations would benefit if commercial banks were allowed to underwrite all corporate securities? Why or why not?

7. Compare the regulation of securities activities for FSLIC-insured institutions, FDIC-insured nonmember banks, and credit unions. Do they have advantages or disadvantages compared to Fed member banks?

8. What are the financial implications of securities activities for depository institutions? Are there benefits? Are there additional risks?

9. Contrast the regulation of insurance activities for Fed member banks, FDIC-insured nonmember banks, FSLIC-insured institutions, and credit unions. What rationale exists for the regulations?

10. Discuss the financial implications of insurance activities for depositories. Are there risks? Do you expect growth in insurance activities by depositories? Why or why not?

11. Would you choose a depository institution based on whether it offers brokerage services or can sell insurance? If your current depository began offering these services, would you use them if needed, or would you choose a firm specializing in securities brokerage or insurance? Why?

12. Should depository institutions be prohibited from taking direct ownership positions in real estate, small businesses, and other nontraditional investments? Why or why not? Do these activities have implications for the deposit insurance system? Explain.

Selected References

Bollenbacher, George M. "Using Stock Index Products in Trust Banking." *Bankers Magazine* 167 (July-August 1984): 57-61.

Burns, Merrill O. "The Future of Correspondent Banking." *Magazine of Bank Administration* 62 (May 1986): 54-64.

Crum, William C. "Banking in Insurance: A Guide to Chaos." *Bankers Magazine* 169 (January/February 1986): 51-58.

Dunham, Constance. "Commercial Bank Costs and Correspondent Banking." *New England Economic Review* (Federal Reserve Bank of Boston) (September/October 1981), pp. 22-36.

Eisenbeis, Robert A., and Larry D. Wall. "Bank Holding Company Nonbanking Activities and Risk." *Proceedings of a Conference on Bank Structure and Competition*. Chicago: Federal Reserve Bank of Chicago, 1984: 340-357.

Evanoff, Douglas D. "Priced Services: The Fed's Impact on Correspondent Banking." *Economic Perspectives* (Federal Reserve Bank of Chicago) 9 (September/October 1985): 31-44.

Felgran, Steven D. "Bank Entry into Securities Brokerage: Competitive and Legal Aspects." *New England Economic Review* (Federal Reserve Bank of Boston) (November/December 1984), pp. 12-33.

———. "Banks as Insurance Agencies: Legal Constraints and Competitive Advances." *New England Economic Review* (Federal Reserve Bank of Boston) (September/October 1985), pp. 34-49.

Fischer, Thomas G., William H. Gram, George G. Kaufman, and Larry R. Mote. "The Securities Activities of Commercial Banks: A Legal and Economic Analysis." *Tennessee Law Review* 51 (1984): 467-518.

Frisbee, Pamela. "Bankers' Banks: An Institution Whose Time Has Come?" *Economic Review* (Federal Reserve Bank of Atlanta) 69 (April 1984): 31-35.

Frodin, Joanna. "Fed Pricing and the Check Collection Business: The Private Sector Response." *Business Review* (Federal Reserve Bank of Philadelphia) (January/February 1984), pp. 13-21.

Hayes, Samuel H. III. "Commercial Banking Inroads into Investment Banking." *Issues in Bank Regulation* 8 (Autumn 1984): 21-31.

Kuprianov, Anatoli. "An Analysis of Federal Reserve Pricing." *Economic Review* (Federal Reserve Bank of Richmond) 72 (March/April 1986): 3-19.

Merrill, Peter. "Correspondent Banking and the Payments System." *Economic Review* (Federal Reserve Bank of Atlanta) 68 (June 1983): 33-39.

Reichert, Alan K. "Correspondent Banking: Services in Transition." *Magazine of Bank Administration* 61 (August 1985): 16-18.

Rogowski, Robert J., and Eric H. Sorenson. "Deregulation in Investment Banking: Shelf Registrations, Structure, and Performance." *Financial Management* 14 (Spring 1985): 5-15.

Saunders, Anthony. "Securities Activities of Commercial Banks: The Problem of Conflicts of Interest." *Business Review* (Federal Reserve Bank of Philadelphia) (July-August 1985), pp. 17-27.

Shafton, Robert M., and Donald D. Gabay. "The Banking Outlook for Diversification into Insurance." *Bankers Magazine* 168 (January/February 1985): 22-26.

Chapter 21

PERFORMANCE EVALUATION

It's not how much money you make,
it's how much you don't lose.

Robert Boyd
Director of Research
Mercantile-Safe Deposit and Trust Company
Baltimore, Maryland (1986)

MARK Taper, former CEO of American Savings in Los Angeles, had a reputation for urging cost efficiency on his employees. In fact, he was so concerned about cost reduction that he reportedly ordered personnel to save all the paper clips they received on incoming mail for reuse. In contrast, Centennial Savings in Guerneville, California, kept a chef on its payroll, at an annual cost of $48,000.[1] Managerial decisions such as these may seem unimportant compared to establishing and implementing lending policies or managing the GAP, but non-interest expenses have a big impact on performance. Ultimately, the results of decisions, large and small, find their way to the balance sheet and income statement. This final chapter on depository institution management explores how reported financial data, covering all aspects of management, are used to evaluate institutional performance.

---

[1]Maria Kulczycky, "Institutions Trim Costs for Bigger Profits," *Savings Institutions* 106 (September 1985): 47-53.

GENERAL GUIDELINES

A continuing theme throughout this book is the importance of the net interest margin and the return on net worth. In performance evaluation of depositories, however, as in any financial analysis, many additional measures are used to determine the success of institutions and to explain why one did or did not perform at acceptable levels. Although external observers, such as investors, regulators, and security analysts, are major users of financial statement data, managers of depositories must know how the results of their activities are interpreted. Not only must they know how others view their work, they also rely on financial analysis to revise and improve asset/liability decisions.

Performance: More than Profitability

The organizational scheme for preceding chapters provides a convenient framework for financial analysis: Liquidity management, investment policies, the loan portfolio, liability and capital management, and overall interest rate sensitivity are the decision areas affecting an institution's risk and return. Ratio analysis of each area helps to explain the bottom line.

A Profit by Another Name May Not Smell as Sweet. Looking beyond (or, more accurately, above) the bottom line is important for other purposes as well. Because of differing regulatory and accounting standards for reporting financial data, managers of banks, thrifts, and credit unions may exercise a great deal of discretion in reporting performance. For example, the dramatic difference in net worth according to regulatory accounting principles (RAP) versus generally accepted accounting principles (GAAP) is illustrated in Chapter 16. Digging beyond the "showcased" numbers is necessary, as suggested in the opening quotation. For example, in 1983, the thrift with the highest RONW (an amazing 82 percent) was Financial Corporation of America, whose position deteriorated so rapidly from loan losses that its CEO was removed by federal regulators in 1984. By 1986, Wall Street pundits jokingly

referred to the S&L as "Financial Corpse of America."[2] The moral to the story: One or two reported performance indicators seldom provide a complete picture of an institution's financial position.

Common Size Statements

In addition to financial ratios, useful information is gleaned by expressing balance sheet accounts as a percentage of total assets and income statement items as a percentage of total revenues. The resulting *common-size statements* allow comparison among firms and help managers or external analysts to identify performance areas that are out of line with those of competitors.[3]

Interpreting the Numbers

Performance evaluation is more complicated than simply calculating ratios and common-size statements; the hard part is interpreting the numbers. One calculation, viewed in isolation, means little. It is only informative when compared either to a standard for the industry or industry subgroup, or to the firm's recent past performance.

Sources of Industry Information. Industry standards providing a perspective for interpreting the performance of an individual firm are available from several sources. A comprehensive source of operating statistics for the banking industry, entitled *Uniform Bank Performance Reports,* is available from the Federal Financial

---

[2]For accounts of the institution's rise and fall, see "How Charles Knapp Pushed Financial Corp. into a Class by Itself," *Business Week,* February 13, 1984, pp. 114-115; Jennifer Bingham Hull, "Financial Corp. of America's Auditor Questions Its Future as a Going Concern," *The Wall Street Journal,* January 2, 1985, p. 2; Teresa Carson, "FCA Still Has to Live up to Its Stock Price," *Business Week,* March 10, 1986, p. 34.

[3]A third financial statement once required by the Financial Accounting Standards Board (FASB) is the Statement of Changes in Financial Position, but it is scheduled to be replaced by a statement of cash flows. The FASB's final rules on the new statement were expected by mid-1987.

Table 21.1

First National Corporation and Subsidiaries, Consolidated Statements of Condition as of December 31, 1983-1985
(Thousands)

	1985		1984		1983	
Assets						
Cash and due from banks	$ 244,079	7.14%	$ 215,830	7.76%	$ 209,700	7.97%
Investment securities:						
U.S. Treasury and agencies	$ 437,225		$ 334,429		$ 378,095	
States and political subdivisions	121,191		122,759		134,128	
Other securities	4,069		3,903		3,907	
Total investment securities	562,485	16.45	461,091	16.59	516,130	19.60
Federal funds sold and reverse repos	452,475	13.23	545,305	19.61	521,530	19.81
Loans:						
Commercial and agricultural	$ 740,798		$ 452,258		$ 488,960	
Real estate—construction	68,583		39,408		27,924	
Real estate—mortgage	368,242		324,203		275,493	
Installment and credit card	622,935		453,502		325,455	
Other	214,358		181,910		149,763	
Total loans	$2,014,916		$1,451,281		$1,267,595	
Less unearned interest	(47,001)		(37,841)		(39,776)	
Less allowance for possible loan losses	(23,325)		(16,734)		(13,440)	
Net loans	1,944,590	56.88	1,396,706	50.24	1,214,379	46.13
Premises and equipment	63,697	1.86	56,589	2.04	57,565	2.19
Acceptances, customers' liability	49,297	1.44	36,797	1.32	43,111	1.64
Other assets	102,232	2.99	67,813	2.44	70,332	2.67
Total assets	$3,418,855	100.00%	$2,780,131	100.00%	$2,632,747	100.00%

Liabilities and Net Worth

	Amount	%	Amount	%	Amount	%
Deposits:						
Noninterest-bearing deposits	$ 692,392		$ 557,159		$ 540,736	
Interest-bearing deposits:						
Savings	804,788		585,056		555,157	
Time	1,085,157		810,641		659,151	
Total deposits	$2,582,337	75.53%	$1,952,856	70.24%	$1,755,044	66.66%
Short-term borrowings (primarily fed funds purchased and repos)	405,693	11.87	476,595	17.14	533,783	20.27
Long-term debt	54,807	1.60	45,166	1.62	52,242	1.98
Acceptances executed	49,297	1.44	36,797	1.32	43,111	1.64
Other liabilities	66,836	1.95	47,962	1.73	44,924	1.71
Total liabilities	$3,158,970		$2,559,376		$2,429,104	
Preferred stock	$ 0	0.00	$ 0	0.00	$ 0	0.00
Common stock	52,824	1.55	24,750	0.89	22,500	0.85
Surplus	54,349	1.59	66,625	2.40	52,000	1.98
Undivided profits	152,712	4.47	129,380	4.65	129,143	4.91
Total net worth	$ 259,885		$ 220,755		$ 203,643	
Total liabilities and net worth	$3,418,855	100.00%	$2,780,131	100.00%	$2,632,747	100.00%
Market value of securities at year-end	$ 568,208		$ 458,777		$ 508,723	

Table 21.2

First National Corporation and Subsidiaries, Consolidated Statements of Earnings for Years Ending December 31, 1983-1985
(Thousands)

	1985	% of Total Operating Income[a]	1984	% of Total Operating Income	1983	% of Total Operating Income
Interest income:						
Interest and fees on loans	$187,405	60.05%	$162,417	54.81%	$128,255	50.57%
Interest on federal funds sold	33,307	10.67	51,032	17.22	46,142	18.19
Interest on investment securities:						
Taxable	43,614	13.98	39,511	13.33	37,462	14.77
Nontaxable	7,045	2.26	7,220	2.44	7,754	3.06
Other interest income	629	0.20	1,033	0.35	2,897	1.14
Total interest income	$272,000		$261,213		$222,510	
Noninterest income:						
Trust income	$ 13,064	4.19	$ 11,460	3.87	$ 9,855	3.89
Service charges and fees	22,390	7.17	17,802	6.01	16,173	6.38
Other operating income	4,612	1.48	5,866	1.98	5,088	2.01
Total noninterest income	40,066		35,128		31,116	
Interest expense:						
Interest on savings deposits	$ 19,086	6.12	$ 16,035	5.41	$ 13,120	5.17
Interest on time deposits	113,524	36.38	100,476	33.91	82,213	32.42
Interest on short-term borrowings	28,740	9.21	50,420	17.01	43,632	17.20
Interest on long-term debt	5,531	1.77	5,023	1.70	4,846	1.91
Total interest expense	166,881		171,954		143,811	
Provision for possible loan losses	9,083	2.91	6,543	2.21	5,915	2.33

Noninterest expense:						
Salaries	$ 38,419	12.31	$ 32,966	11.12	$ 30,264	11.93
Pension and other employee benefits	6,612	2.12	5,951	2.01	5,142	2.03
Equipment expense	9,693	3.11	8,160	2.75	7,603	3.00
Occupancy expense	5,692	1.82	4,609	1.56	4,550	1.79
State taxes	4,102	1.31	3,887	1.31	3,719	1.47
Other operating expense	30,516	9.78	25,144	8.48	21,380	8.43
Total noninterest expense	95,034		80,717		72,658	
Net operating income before tax	$ 41,068	13.16	$ 37,127	12.53	$ 31,242	12.32
Taxes	9,843	3.15	7,539	2.54	5,712	2.25
Income before securities gains or losses (IBSGL)	$ 31,225	10.01	$ 29,588	9.98	$ 25,530	10.07
Other income (primarily security gains or losses)	2,906	0.93	101	0.03	102	0.04
Net income	$ 34,131	10.94	$ 29,689	10.02	$ 25,632	10.11
Per share:						
Net income	$3.31		$3.00		$2.59	
Dividends	$1.40		$1.27		$1.18	

aTotal Operating Income = Total Interest Income + Total Noninterest Income

579

Institutions Examination Council. Average ratios are provided for asset size groups and states in the *Peer Groups Report* and the *State Average Report,* respectively. Less detailed annual summaries on the performance of commercial banks and BHCs are published in the *Federal Reserve Bulletin* and the FDIC's *Banking and Economic Review.* The Federal Reserve Banks also compile statistics on performance within their districts; these reports concentrate on selected size groups or a limited number of performance measures. The U.S. Bureau of the Census publishes time series data, including performance ratios, on all types of depository institutions in its *Statistical Abstract of the United States.* Finally, several private consulting groups, the best known of which is Sheshunoff and Company of Austin, Texas, analyze industry performance.

The Economic and Research Division of the Credit Union National Association regularly publishes summaries of CU data, entitled "Credit Union Operating Ratios and Spreads." Selected data are available every month in *Credit Union Magazine.* The complete, detailed reports are available from CUNA. For the thrift industry, the district Federal Home Loan Banks, the Federal Home Loan Bank Board, the U.S. League of Savings Institutions, and the National Council of Savings Institutions are sources of aggregate performance data for comparison purposes.

Beware: Ratio Definitions Are Not Standard. Before choosing from among many possible ratio or common-size calculations, an analyst is well advised to select the industry standards to be used for comparison. The publishers of aggregate performance data often use different definitions for a given ratio. Unless ratios are calculated in the same way as industry comparison data, conclusions are suspect.

Categories of Performance Evaluation

Ratios should be categorized according to the area of performance with which they are most closely connected. For every area of performance evaluation, many ratio measures are available. Each can contribute something, but using too many may cause confusion. Consequently, the following discussion includes only a representative group of ratios. Alternative specifications of these measures, along with additional ratios, are provided in Appendix 21A. Although their interpretation is similar to that of the ratios discussed in the text, data availability, the source of industry data, or a special purpose may cause an analyst to choose one measure over another.

Performance Evaluation Illustrated

The financial statements of a regional bank holding company are used to provide a framework for calculating and interpreting financial ratios and other performance data. The statements of condition and earnings for this unidentified BHC for the years 1983 through 1985 are provided in Tables 21.1 and 21.2 (see pages 576–579). In addition to raw data, common-size statements are shown. In Table 21.1, asset, liability, and net worth accounts are expressed as a percentage of total assets; in the second table, income and expense figures are expressed as a percentage of total operating income (that is, the sum of interest and noninterest income).

Useful information is also provided in the notes and tables accompanying the financial statements in the annual reports of publicly held institutions. Examples of these data are shown in Appendix 21B. Obtaining this information enhances the accuracy of performance evaluation.

LIQUIDITY AND PORTFOLIO MANAGEMENT

The first management areas examined for First National are the institution's cash and securities portfolio holdings.

Liquidity Position

The liquidity of a depository is harder to measure than it might appear at first glance. The objective is to determine the institution's ability to respond to unexpected changes in asset or liability accounts. Difficulty arises because institutions have access to liquidity from two distinct sources: 1) cash and near-cash assets; and 2) funds that can be purchased in the form of short-term liabilities.

On the asset side, it is not readily apparent to an external analyst what portion of liquid assets is held to meet reserve requirements, and what portion is available to meet unexpected operating liquidity needs. On the liability side, it is possible to identify the extent to which a firm has already relied on purchased liabilities, but even management cannot be sure of the *additional* liquidity that could be purchased quickly if needed.

Asset Liquidity.   To measure the liquidity of the asset portfolio, the firm's shortest-term assets—cash, deposits at other institutions, short-term securities, and federal funds sold—are compared with other balance sheet accounts. The resulting ratios (Ratios 21.1 and 21.2 in Table 21.3) indicate the proportion of total assets held in cash and securities (Ratio 21.1), and the amount of these assets relative to average deposits (Ratio 21.2). Calculations for Ratios 21.1 and 21.2 rely on the maturity schedule of the investment portfolio, found in the BHC's annual report and shown in Appendix 21B for 1985 only. The source of comparison peer group data is the *Uniform Bank Performance Report*.

A complication in financial analysis should be noted at this point. Annual reports for BHCs aggregate data for all bank subsidiaries, so First National's ratios reflect the operations of the lead bank (with assets of $2.2 billion) and of nine smaller institutions. In examining a BHC, analysts must sometimes choose which peer group figures to use for comparison—those for banks the size of the lead bank, or those for banks the size of the BHC ($3.4 billion in the case of First National). Because First National's ratios are calculated from the annual report of the BHC, peer group comparisons are based on banks with $3 to $10 billion in assets. Other analysts, recognizing the lead bank as the most influential on BHC performance, might select a peer group in the range of $1 to $3 billion.

Ratio 21.1 provides a general assessment of the institution's asset maturity mix. Ratio 21.2 compares liquid or near-liquid assets to depos-

its, many of which are short-term. Ideally, analysts and managers would like to know what portion of deposits are expected to turn over in the short run. Unfortunately, account titles on balance sheets do not provide that information. For example, the core level of transactions deposits is obscured. In addition, some accounts classified as time deposits may have relatively short maturities.

The ratios in Table 21.3, and those introduced later, use an *average* rather than a *total* balance for most balance sheet accounts. When evaluating performance, an analyst would like to know the ongoing position of the firm, rather than the year-end position. That information is usually unavailable externally and may be costly to obtain internally. By averaging beginning and ending balances, an external analyst roughly estimates average levels during the year.

As shown by Ratio 21.1, from 1983 to 1985, over 30 percent of First National's assets were in the shortest-term category.[4] For the

---

[4]To conserve space, specifics on the calculation of every ratio are not given. For clarification, details on the calculation of Ratio 21.1 for 1985 are as follows:

- Year-end short-term assets, 1985:

Cash and due	$244,079	(from Table 21.1)
Short-term securities maturing within 1 year:		
U.S. Treasury and agency	185,364	(from Appendix 21B)
States and political subdivisions	35,222	
Other bonds, notes, debentures	77	
Federal funds sold	452,475	(from Table 21.1)
Total	$917,217	

- Year-end short-term assets, 1984 (from Table 21.1 and from footnotes of 1984 financial statements, not shown here): $966,570
- Average short-term assets, 1985:

  [$966,570 (year-end 1984) + $917,217 (year-end 1985)]/2 = $941,893.50

- Average total assets:

  ($3,418,855 + $2,780,131)/2 = $3,099,493

Ratio 21.1 for 1985 (as shown in Table 21.3):

$$\frac{\text{Average Short-Term Assets}}{\text{Average Total Assets}} = \frac{\$941,893.50}{\$3,099,493}$$
$$= 0.3039$$
$$= 30.39\%$$

Table 21.3
**Measures of Liquidity and Portfolio Management
in Depository Institutions**

Ratio		First National 1985	First National 1984	First National 1983	Peer Group Averages[b] 1985
Liquidity Ratios[a]					
21.1	Average Cash and Short-Term Securities[c] / Average Total Assets	30.39%	34.97%	37.18%	23.89%
21.2	Average Cash and Short-Term Securities / Average Deposits	41.54	51.05	56.59	32.36
21.3	Average Net Loans / Average Deposits	73.67	70.42	64.78	81.33
21.4	Average Purchased Liabilities[d] / Average Total Assets	23.16	27.76	29.51	36.68
Portfolio Management Ratio					**Taxable** / **Nontaxable**
21.5	Market Value of Securities / Book Value of Securities	100.33%	99.01%	88.52%	101.36% / 96.36%

[a]The average balance for these and all subsequent calculations is defined as:

> (Beginning Balance + Ending Balance)/2

[b]Source of peer group averages is *Uniform Bank Performance Report,* Peer Group Report, December 31, 1985, published by the Federal Financial Institutions Examination Council.

[c]Cash + Short-Term Securities + Due from Depositories + Federal Funds Sold

Data from the Investment Maturity Schedule, shown in Appendix 21B for 1985 only, were used to identify average short-term assets.

[d]Purchased Liabilities = Negotiable CDs + Foreign Deposits + Acceptances Executed + Short-Term Borrowings

The latter two items are shown on the balance sheet; negotiable CDs are taken from the Maturity of Time Deposits table in Appendix 21B. First National has no foreign deposits.

first two years, Ratio 21.2 shows that more than 50 cents of short-term assets were held for every dollar of deposits. By 1985, the ratio had dropped. Still, it is unlikely that over 40 percent of the institution's deposits would be withdrawn at once, and the BHC's asset liquidity during this period seems adequate. In comparison to banks of similar size, First National has a strong liquidity position, despite the decline in 1985.

Purchased Liquidity.   Other liquidity measures indicate an institution's reliance on purchased liabilities. Ratio 21.3 in Table 21.3 reveals the relative sizes of net loan and total deposit accounts; if the ratio is greater than 1, a depository may be using purchased liabilities to support loans. Given the volatility in the liability markets, an institution is exposed to more risk than if the ratio is 1 or less. The final liquidity measure (Ratio 21.4) focuses directly on the proportion of assets funded by purchased liabilities. Balance sheets of depository institutions may not identify negotiable CDs as a separate account category, so external analysts may have to obtain the information elsewhere. Appendix 21B presents First National's 1985 deposit mix and maturity of large time deposits, from which some of the data used in Ratio 21.4 are taken.

For First National, Ratio 21.3 indicates that the loan/deposit ratio was less than 80 percent in all three years, although it increased each year. Ratio 21.4 shows that the proportion of purchased funds to total assets declined over the same period, however, suggesting that the bank has not relied on potentially volatile funds sources to make new loans. A comparison to its peer group shows that First National is managed conservatively. Its loan/deposit ratio is relatively low, as is its reliance on more volatile purchased liabilities.

Investment Performance

Because the maturity of the investment portfolio is used to assess liquidity, liquidity ratios also evaluate one aspect of portfolio management. Portfolio composition by type of issuer, such as the U.S. Treasury, government agencies, municipalities, or private corporations, provides additional information on investment management. To external observers, these data may reveal whether liquidity and safety are primary goals, or whether expected yields or tax considerations are more influential.

Examining Tax Effects.   In the banking industry, income statement details on gains and losses from securities transactions (SGL) have become obscure, thanks to a change in reporting methods introduced by the Securities Exchange Commission in 1984.[5] Before then, commercial banks with publicly traded stock were required to report income before and after

securities gains and losses, separating the effects of operating and investment decisions. Under the new standards, both need not be directly reported. In Table 21.2, the data for First National have been rearranged somewhat from their original format to isolate net operating income; the tax effect of securities gains or losses cannot be isolated, however, because it is aggregated in the "Taxes" data item.

To ensure comparability when evaluating *rates* of return on investments, dollar returns from investment in nontaxable municipal bonds must be evaluated on a tax-equivalent basis, as explained in Chapters 4 and 12. Returns on tax-exempt securities must be multiplied by the factor $1/(1 - t)$, where t is the depository's tax rate, to convert them to a pretax basis. Some institutions make the adjustment in their financial reports, and external analysts should look for this information.

Yields and Riskiness.   Often, even after adjustments for tax effects, the average yield earned on the investment portfolio is difficult to determine. Some depositories now provide that information in annual reports. In First National's schedule of investment maturities, for example, shown in Appendix 21B, yields are given for various investment categories, and all are provided on a tax-equivalent basis.

Equally important is assessing the risk of the securities. The relative weight given to Treasury and federal agency securities is a clue, of course. But for an external analyst, information on the default risk of nonfederal securities is difficult to obtain, as are estimates of the correlations between returns on various categories of securities. Because these elements of portfolio analysis are important, the skills of portfolio managers cannot be assessed from financial statements alone.

Market versus Book Values.   Finally, a comparison of market and book values of securities owned (Ratio 21.5 in Table 21.3) provides information about the response of the portfolio to changing market conditions. The market value of the portfolio is found on the report of condition or in an accompanying note. Data for

---

[5]The concern over the new SEC rules has been discussed in several forums. See, for example, Daniel Hertzberg, "Bank Profit Reports Are Distorted by New SEC Rules, Other Changes," *The Wall Street Journal*, January 2, 1984.

First National for 1985 are given at the bottom of the balance sheet in Table 21.1. The market value of First National's portfolio increased significantly in relation to book value from 1983 to 1985, rising from 88.5 percent to slightly over 100 percent. During this period of declining market yields, the market value of the bank's securities rose. The peer group performance measures are separated into taxable and nontaxable securities, so the information available in First National's annual report is not directly comparable, but First National appears to be generally in line with other institutions.

THE LOAN PORTFOLIO

Loan portfolio analysis includes an examination of both returns and credit risk exposure.

Analyzing Loan Losses

The analyst cannot directly identify the *ex ante* level of loan portfolio risk. But for banks or BHCs with less than $500 million in total assets, and for all thrifts, the provision for loan losses on the income statement and the allowance for loan losses on the balance sheet can be informative. Each institution may identify, based on past experience, an annual provision for loan losses, which is charged against current earnings. Although not equal to actual loan losses for the year, the provision reflects management's estimate of the additions to the allowance for loan losses on the balance sheet necessary to reflect total exposure to credit risk. Thrifts choosing not to use this experience-based method may simply deduct 8 percent of taxable income as a provision for loan losses each year, as long as they have 60 percent or more of assets in mortgage-related investments.

Analysts have recognized that loan loss provisions and allowances may be overstated because of errors in judgment, or deliberately underestimated to disguise risky lending policies. Because these measures may be misleading, the Tax Reform Act of 1986 disallowed them for banks and BHCs with assets exceeding $500 million, beginning in 1987. These institutions may now deduct only actual loan losses from income before calculating taxes. Previously accumulated allowances are being removed from the balance sheets of these banks over a period of four years.[6]

Net Chargeoffs.   *Ex post* credit risk is easier to determine than *ex ante* risk. For large banks, losses are reported in the year in which they occur. For smaller banks and thrifts, analysts can examine net chargeoffs, or the difference between loans actually written off as uncollectible and recoveries on loans previously classified as uncollectible. Net chargeoffs are reported to regulatory authorities and are available in supplementary data in publicly held institutions' annual reports. As an example, the 1985 chargeoff experience of First National is presented in Appendix 21B. Because of its size, First National is now unable to use the "allowance for possible loan loss" account, but its 1985 report is typical of the format used by eligible institutions.

Losses on International Lending.   Although First National had no international investments as of 1985, questions have been raised about the default risk exposure of commercial banks heavily invested in loans to foreign borrowers, especially borrowers in developing countries. In recognition of the higher risk, regulators have required banks to set up special "allocated transfer risk reserves"; the amounts required are determined as a percentage of funds invested in certain countries, such as Nicaragua, Poland, and others.[7] Charging off these special amounts lowers net income for institutions lending heavily to countries on the list. The list is influenced by a desire not to offend close allies of the United States, so the debate

---

[6]Details on the changes are available in Staff of Joint Committee on Taxation, "Title IX. Financial Institutions," *Summary of Conference Agreement on HR 3838 (Tax Reform Act of 1986)* (Washington, DC: U.S. Government Printing Office, August 29, 1986), p. 31.

[7]Suzanna Andrews, "Accounting for LDC Debt," *Institutional Investor* 18 (August 1984): 189–194. Recall from Chapter 13 that *transfer risk* is a synonym for country risk.

continues over adequacy of loss reserves for international lenders.

Credit Risk Ratios

Ratios commonly used to measure credit risk are listed in Table 21.4. Ratios 21.6 through 21.8 express the loan loss provision, the allowance for loan losses, and net chargeoffs as a percentage of average net loans. A trend analysis of these figures, examining changes over time, is particularly revealing. If the trends reveal a significant change, it is important to determine whether riskier lending policies have been implemented, or whether management has changed its opinion on the credit risk of loans made in past years. Finally, a loss coverage ratio (Ratio 21.9) compares net income or income before securities gains and losses (IBSGL) to the loan loss provision or to actual loan losses. The higher this ratio, the more earnings are protected.

For First National, all credit risk ratios in Table 21.4 indicate a decline in credit risk from 1983 to 1984 but an increase from 1984 to 1985. Managers allocated more to the allowance for loan losses in years when actual loan losses, re-flected in net chargeoffs, were higher. This suggests they used actual experience as a guide to the future, adjusting their estimates of future credit risk accordingly. First National's credit risk exposure was lower than that of peer banks, with its loan loss coverage more than twice as great as the comparison figure.

MANAGEMENT OF LIABILITIES AND CAPITAL

A major concern to all observers of financial institutions is the adequacy of the net worth cushion. Many ratios are available for evaluating the safety of a depository institution; the measurement is complicated by the numerous and contradictory definitions of capital presented in Chapter 16.

Comparing Net Worth to Assets

Two widely quoted ratios compare an institution's net worth to average total assets (Ratio 21.10 in Table 21.5) or to average risk assets (Ratio 21.11), defined as total assets less those not subject to default risk. The first comparison

---

Table 21.4
Measures of Credit Risk in Depository Institutions

Ratio		First National			Peer Group Averages
		1985	1984	1983	1985
21.6	$\dfrac{\text{Loan Loss Provision}}{\text{Average Net Loans}}$	0.54%	0.50%	0.57%	0.77%
21.7	$\dfrac{\text{Allowance for Loan Losses}}{\text{Average Net Loans}}$	1.20	1.16	1.24	1.35
21.8	$\dfrac{\text{Net Loan Chargeoffs}^{a}}{\text{Average Net Loans}}$	0.32	0.25	0.52	0.56
21.9	$\dfrac{\text{Net Income}^{b}}{\text{Loan Loss Provision}}$	3.76	4.54	4.33	1.80

[a]Net loan chargeoff data are given in the Summary of Loan Loss Experience, shown in Appendix 21B.
[b]Income before securities gains or losses (IBSGL) may be substituted.

Table 21.5
Measures of Leverage in Depository Institutions

Ratio		First National			Peer Group Averages
		1985	1984	1983	1985
21.10	Average Net Worth / Average Total Assets	7.75%	7.84%	8.07%	5.72%
21.11	Average Net Worth / Average Risk Assets	10.18	10.56	11.03	NA
21.12	Average Net Worth / Average Net Loans	14.38	16.25	18.97	9.45
21.13	Average Net Worth / Average Deposits	10.60	11.45	12.29	7.79

---

indicates the maximum amount by which the book value of the institution's assets can decline before falling below the value of total liabilities. Many analysts prefer the second ratio, because it focuses on assets that are subject to potential default risk. Another ratio, Ratio 21.12, compares net worth to net loans, which for many institutions is the largest and most risky asset category.

First National has no preferred stock outstanding. If it did, preferred stock would be added to common equity (the sum of the common stock, surplus, and undivided profits accounts) to determine total net worth. As explained in Chapter 16, net worth would then be different from common equity.

Comparing Net Worth to Liabilities

It is also possible to assess the institution's capital adequacy by comparing net worth to liabilities. For smaller institutions, deposits are the shortest-term liabilities, and the ratio of capital to deposits is an important measure, shown as Ratio 21.13 in Table 21.5. First National's leverage ratios indicate that its net worth position has declined slightly, regardless of the ratio used. Despite that decline, however, the figures still indicate a conservative position compared to the peer group.

A Reminder on Defining *Capital* for Performance Analysis

Chapter 16 indicates that bank and thrift regulators include long-term debt in the regulatory definition of capital. For evaluative purposes, however, some analysts use only net worth to assess solvency. Even then complications remain, such as the treatment of intangible assets and the existence of regulatory net worth in the thrift industry. Credit unions, with no access to external capital, allow a more straightforward analysis, because net worth consists solely of undivided earnings and reserves. These industry differences must be considered in measuring the performance of individual institutions.

EFFICIENCY AND PRODUCTIVITY

The introductory paragraph to this chapter suggests the importance of monitoring noninterest expenses. In fact, many researchers have identified the ability of managers to control noninterest expenses while generating target levels of interest and noninterest revenues as a distinguishing characteristic of outstanding performers among depositories. Thus, no "report card" on asset/liability management would be complete without measures of efficiency and productivity.

Noninterest Expenses

One way to measure efficiency is to compare noninterest expenses—such as personnel costs, occupancy expense, and equipment expense—to total operating expenses, including interest expense. Noninterest expenses may also be compared to total operating income for the period. These two efficiency ratios are Ratios 21.14 and 21.15 in Table 21.6.

Trend analysis of these ratios gives conflicting signals for First National. Ratios 21.14 and 21.15 suggest increased efficiency from 1983 to 1984, when noninterest expenses declined in relationship to other operating figures. In 1985, however, both ratios increased. First National's

noninterest expenses are lower than those of its peer institutions, however, regardless of the measure used, suggesting higher efficiency.

Noninterest Income

As discussed in Chapter 20, to supplement revenues from investments in loans and securities, institutions generate income by charging fees for both traditional and nontraditional products and services. Offering services efficiently, so that they can be priced competitively, has become increasingly important in the current operating environment.

The contribution of noninterest income to institutional performance can be measured by comparing it to total operating income—Ratio 21.16 in Table 21.6. If a separate figure is available for fee income from originating and serv-

Table 21.6
Measures of Efficiency and Productivity in Depository Institutions

Ratio		First National 1985	1984	1983	Peer Group Averages 1985
Noninterest Expenses					
21.14	Noninterest Expenses / Total Operating Expenses	35.07%	31.14%	32.67%	39.88%
21.15	Noninterest Expenses / Total Operating Income[a]	30.45	27.24	28.65	34.99
Noninterest income					
21.16	Noninterest Income / Total Operating Income	12.84%	11.85%	12.27%	12.25%
21.17	Loan Fee Income / Average Net Loans	NA	NA	NA	NA
21.18	Noninterest Income / Average Total Assets	1.29%	1.30%	1.28%	1.36%
Productivity (Asset Utilization)					
21.19	Total Operating Income / Average Total Assets	10.07%	10.95%	10.41%	11.10%

[a]Total Operating Income = Interest Income + Noninterest Income.

icing loans, it may be compared to total average net loans (Ratio 21.17); this measure is especially important for thrift institutions charging mortgage points. If the institution reports only a combined figure for loan fees and service charges, as is the case for First National, total noninterest income can be compared to total assets, shown as Ratio 21.18. As a percentage of total operating income, First National exceeds comparable institutions in its ability to generate fee income, but is slightly below peer group banks when the amount of noninterest income is compared to total assets. In other words, First National generates a relatively high proportion of its income from noninterest sources, but that amount is still slightly low compared to banks of comparable size.

Productivity (Asset Utilization)

Productivity measures focus on the firm's ability to generate revenues compared to the asset base on which revenues can be earned. The most common measure, called *asset turnover* in industrial firms and *asset utilization* in financial institutions, compares total operating income to average total assets (Ratio 21.19 in Table 21.6). First National's asset utilization improved from 1983 to 1984; in the latter year, almost 11 cents of revenue were generated for every dollar of assets. In 1985, that figure decreased to slightly over 10 cents. First National's annual report for 1985 described the acquisition of two smaller banks during the year, along with ten branches of a failed thrift in the same state. As discussed in Chapter 19, when an institution's assets are changed by merger or acquisition, a period of adjustment is expected, and the eventual efficiency by which combined assets are managed may not immediately appear. Good analysts and managers observing First National's asset utilization in 1985 would keep this point in mind.

PROFITABILITY

Profitability ratios include the figures most often quoted in evaluating asset/liability management. All profitability measures compare income to another financial statement figure. The proper definition of income, however, is subject to debate.

Measuring Income

Previous discussion distinguished net income from income before securities gains and losses (IBSGL). When IBSGL is available, some analysts believe it best reflects the management of traditional loan and deposit activities. The final net income figure, in contrast, reflects more than the results of an institution's "core" operations. If it is used alone to assess performance, conclusions may be distorted.

For example, an institution anticipating poor IBSGL performance may be able to boost net income by selling parts of the securities portfolio, or by liquidating real estate or other assets acquired from borrowers in financial difficulty. In 1985, BankAmerica actually sold its corporate headquarters in what was described as "obviously an earnings-driven deal."[8] The financial giant had experienced highly publicized profitability problems for several years and added $580 million to reported earnings in subsequent years as a result of the sale. Because such transactions are one-time occurrences, however, it would be unwise to use them to judge an institution's past performance or future potential. When possible, it is worthwhile to isolate income generated by basic operations.

Profitability Ratios

Two common profitability ratios compare a measure of income to revenues and average total assets (Ratios 21.20 and 21.21 in Table 21.7). The first measure, the *profit margin,* reflects the percentage of each dollar of revenue remaining after all costs and expenses are paid. An institution with a relatively high cost structure has a lower profit margin than a more efficient institution. The second ratio, known as return on assets (ROA), is viewed as a comprehensive

[8]Patricia Bellew Gray, "BankAmerica Agrees to Sell Headquarters," *The Wall Street Journal,* September 16, 1985, p. 8.

Table 21.7
Measures of Profitability in Depository Institutions

Ratio		First National			Peer Group Averages
		1985	1984	1983	1985
21.20	Profit Margin = $\dfrac{\text{Net Income}^a}{\text{Total Operating Income}}$	10.94%	10.02%	10.11%	7.93%
21.21	Return on Assets = $\dfrac{\text{Net Income}}{\text{Average Total Assets}}$	1.10%	1.10%	1.05%	0.88%
21.22	$\dfrac{\text{Net Income} - \text{Preferred Dividends}^b}{\text{Average Net Worth}}$	14.20%	13.99%	13.03%	15.38%
21.23	Earnings per Share = $\dfrac{\text{Net Income}}{\text{Number of Common Shares Outstanding}}$	$3.31	$3.00	$2.59	
21.24	Net Interest Margin = $\dfrac{\text{Interest Revenues} - \text{Interest Expense}}{\text{Average Total Assets}}$	3.39%	3.30%	3.23%	3.94%

[a]IBSGL (income before securities gains or losses) could be substituted for net income.

[b]With no preferred stock outstanding, as in the case of First National, this ratio is calculated as:

$$\frac{\text{Net Income}}{\text{Net Worth}} = \text{Return on Net Worth}$$

measure of profitability, indicating the dollar return per dollar of assets held by the firm.

A third profitability ratio (Ratio 21.22) is the rate of return to common shareholders. The ratio compares after-tax income to common equity and is equal to return on net worth (RONW) when no preferred stock is outstanding. If preferred stock has been issued, income after preferred dividends is divided by common equity to determine the rate of return to common shareholders; income before preferred dividends is divided by preferred stock plus common equity to determine return on net worth.

First National's profitability calculations are based on net income, because in two of the three years income from securities trading was quite small. In addition, the industry average source selected uses net income. Ratios 21.20 and 21.21 increased slightly, but not steadily, over the period. Profit margin and ROA are strong in comparison to peer group banks. First National's RONW, Ratio 21.22, went up steadily. The fact that First National uses less lever-age than comparable banks explains why its RONW is low in comparison to peers. The rising trend in First National's RONW, despite the relatively stable ROA, is explained by a steady increase in the use of financial leverage over the period. More is said later about the relationship between asset and equity returns.

Another profitability measure that equity investors watch closely is performance on a *per-share* basis. The earnings per share (EPS) ratio is Ratio 21.23 in Table 21.7. As illustrated in Chapter 19, trends in EPS can be used to identify potential earnings dilution on a per-share basis, which may occur even when aggregate earnings increase. In most instances, EPS is included in reported financial data and need not be calculated.

Finally, the net interest margin (Ratio 21.24), is a comprehensive measure of management's ability to control the spread between interest revenues and interest costs. (This ratio, of course, is identical to Equation 1.1.) The NIM for First National increased over the period, but remained below that of comparable banks. The

BHC made up for this shortfall, however, by its relatively low noninterest expenses, and its overall return on assets exceeded that of the peer group.

An Integrated Model of Profitability

A helpful model for measuring, evaluating, and explaining profitability is the ***Dupont system.*** The Dupont model illustrates the joint impact of efficiency and productivity on ROA; and the ability of financial leverage to boost the RONW above ROA.

A Model of Return on Assets.   The Dupont system recognizes that ROA is determined by asset utilization and profit margin:

(21.25)

$$ROA = \frac{Total\ Revenues}{Average\ Total\ Assets} \times \frac{Net\ Income}{Total\ Revenues}$$

This formulation focuses attention on the source of either particularly good or particularly bad performance. For example, a thrift reporting a return on assets above the industry average may have reached that enviable position either by being more cost-efficient (reflected in a high profit margin), by using its assets better (reflected in high asset utilization), or by excelling in both areas. On the other hand, relatively poor performance could arise from problems in one of the two areas or both. The areas deserving closer examination by managers or analysts are pinpointed more easily within the Dupont framework.

The Dupont ROA calculation for First National is, of course, numerically consistent with the calculation shown in Table 21.7, because the Dupont method is merely a different way of looking at the same data. For 1985, for example, using Ratio 21.25:

$$ROA = 0.1007 \times 10.94\% = 1.10\%$$

As noted earlier, the ROA exceeds industry averages. Although First National's asset utilization is below average, its profit margin is quite a bit higher, resulting in a return on average assets that exceeds that of peer institutions. Thus, the BHC's efficiency compensates for the shortfall in productivity. The interaction of these effects is not evident in the simple ROA calculation given in Ratio 21.21. As the bank's managers seek to raise ROA to even higher levels, the Dupont method indicates that asset utilization is an area to examine. In particular, the BHC's high level of liquid assets may be the reason for the lower revenues relative to total assets.

A Model of RONW.   The second contribution of the Dupont model is to explain the relationship between ROA and RONW. The difference between the two arises from the use of financial leverage. By multiplying ROA by the net worth multiplier—the ratio of total assets to net worth—an analyst can also calculate RONW.[9]

(21.26)

$$RONW = \frac{Total\ Revenues}{Average\ Total\ Assets} \times \frac{Net\ Income}{Total\ Revenues} \times \frac{Average\ Total\ Assets}{Average\ Net\ Worth}$$

The benefit of this formulation is that it better explains performance. If an institution reports RONW either above or below industry standards, it is possible to trace that performance to either the ROA or to leverage, or both. If high financial leverage results in a high RONW, analysts and shareholders recognize

---

[9]Another way of expressing this same relationship is:

(21.26a)

$$RONW = \frac{ROA}{1 - (Total\ Liabilities/Total\ Assets)}$$

Note that the denominator of this expression is equal to Ratio 21.10 and is the reciprocal of the net worth multiplier.

the risk incurred in achieving the reported level of performance. If, in contrast, a high RONW is achieved through superior asset management, itself a product of productivity and efficiency as seen in Ratio 21.25, quite a different message is conveyed about managerial practices.

Using Ratio 21.26 for First National in 1985:

$$RONW = 0.1007 \times 10.94\% \times 12.90$$
$$= 14.21\%$$

The Dupont RONW model clarifies the fact that the bank's RONW was below that of peer institutions because of lower asset utilization and lower leverage. Thus, the lower return to shareholders was accompanied by lower risk.

In the thrift industry, the Dupont formulation is particularly informative in explaining RONW. Aggregate data for FSLIC-insured thrift institutions for 1984 and 1985 indicate net worth multipliers of 26.25 and 24.03 for those two years. For 1985, for example, average RONW was 9.37 percent, but average ROA was only 0.39 percent.[10] Leverage ratios were slightly lower for FDIC-insured savings banks, but still much higher than those in the banking industry.

TREND ANALYSIS

Another dimension to performance analysis compares an institution to its own past history. An institution may currently look profitable compared to industry averages but still be in the midst of a decline that is revealed only through trend analysis. To illustrate the process, Figures 21.1 through 21.3 depict information on three important ratios for First National over the

period from year-end 1976 through year-end 1985.

The figures should be examined together, because they depict a time series of Dupont relationships. Figure 21.1 shows that ROA for First National declined from 1979 through 1983, with an upturn in 1984. At the same time, Figure 21.2 shows that the ratio of net worth to total assets increased from 1977 through 1981, then decreased sharply after 1982. Finally, Figure 21.3 shows that RONW followed a trend similar to ROA, declining through 1983 but rising in each of the next two years.

During the period 1978-1982, the initial years of banking deregulation, First National's managers appear to have taken a relatively low-risk approach by decreasing reliance on borrowed funds even though ROA was declining. They could have attempted to boost RONW through aggressive liability management during this period, but did not do so. Only after ROA continued to decline in 1983 does management appear to have responded by increasing leverage. By 1984, ROA had also turned upward, and the increase in RONW that year can be attributed both to liability management strategies and to increased asset returns. A pattern of low-risk liability and capital management emerges, less so toward the end of the period.

The complete analysis of First National reveals a conservative institution that, like most depositories, experienced earnings pressures during the early 1980s. Although the institution had declining capital ratios by the end of the period, it was more highly capitalized than similar institutions and easily exceeded even the most rigorous regulatory standards for capital. In addition, the institution maintained a high level of asset liquidity, a hallmark of a conservative management philosophy. Barring a change in the bank's management, an analyst would probably project continued conservatism, along with profitability similar to institutions in its peer group. Sudden or spectacular growth, however, would require a more aggressive management approach than owners and managers seem willing to take.

---

[10]U.S. League of Savings Institutions, *1986 Savings Institution Source Book* (Chicago: U. S. League of Savings Institutions, 1986), p. 52. A good article on integrating the Dupont system into asset/liability management in thrifts is David W. Cole, "Profitability: The Key to Success," *Trends and Topics,* Federal Home Loan Bank of Chicago 2 (Fall 1985): 13-21.

Figure 21.1
First National Bank: Return on Assets

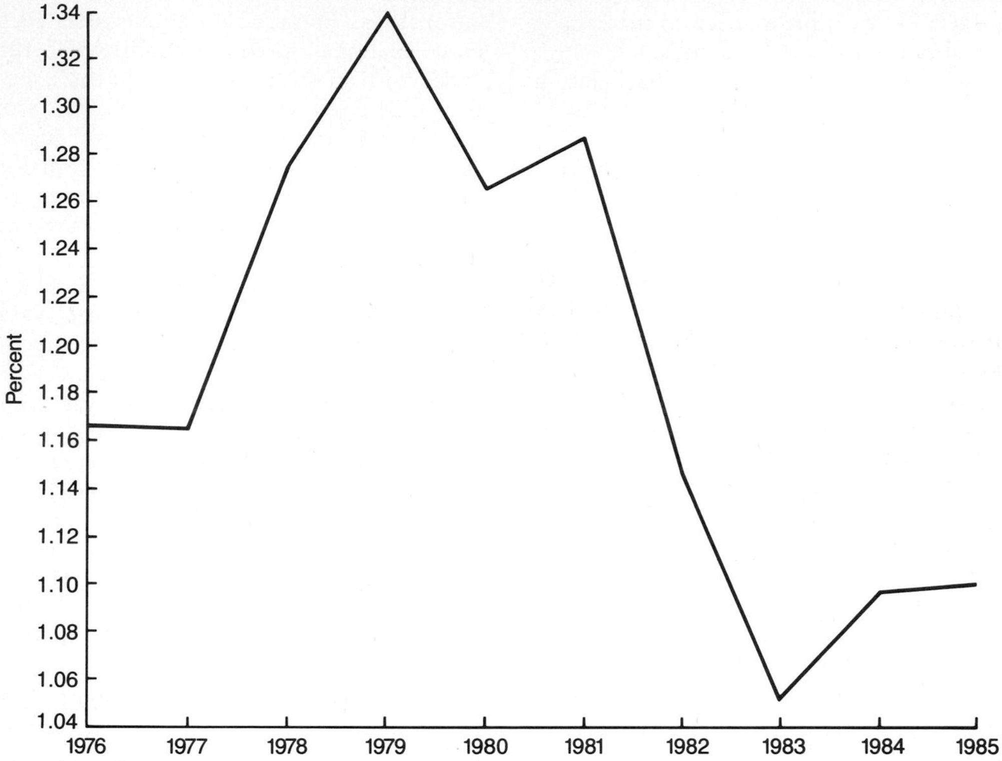

DETERMINANTS OF EXCEPTIONAL PERFORMANCE IN DEPOSITORIES

Many studies have attempted to identify performance areas that distinguish exceptional institutions from others. Here, "exceptional" refers both to very good and very bad institutions; failed institutions have received as much attention as profitable firms. This research focuses the attention of managers on key operating characteristics. Although some critical factors are qualitative, not quantitative, such as the innovativeness of managers or the ability to

assess market needs, many determinants of success are evident in reported financial data.

Commercial Banks

More research on performance has been conducted for banks than for other depository institutions. Several representative studies summarize the conclusions of this body of research.

High–Performance Banks in the 1970s. Widely quoted conclusions are based on the results of a multiyear analysis of high-performance banks conducted by William Ford

Figure 21.2
First National Bank: Net Worth/Total Assets

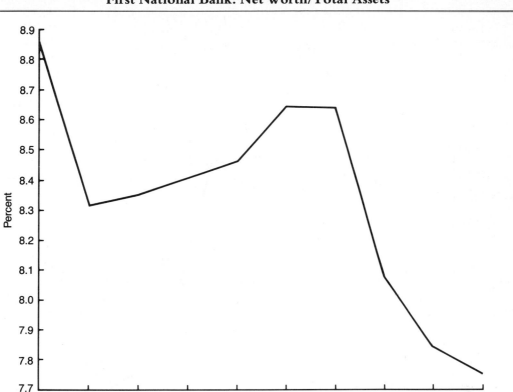

and Dennis Olson during the mid-1970s.[11] Using a sample of high-performance banks (high ROA and RONW) over the period 1972-1977, they compared key operating statistics for this group to those of other banks. Although the

[11]William F. Ford and Dennis A. Olson, "How 1,000 High-Performance Banks Weathered the Recent Recession," *Banking* 70 (April 1978): 36-48. Other studies in the series include: William F. Ford, "Profitability: Why Do Some Banks Perform Better than Average?" *Banking* 66 (October 1974): 29-33; Dennis A. Olson, "How High-Profit Banks Get That Way," *Banking* 67 (May 1975): 46-58; William F. Ford, "Using 'High-Performance' Data to Plan Your Bank's Future." *Banking* 70 (October 1978): 40-48, 162.

authors found some performance determinants to be outside management's control, such as the level of competition in their markets, they also identified important operating characteristics that reflected managerial decisions. For example, high performers had higher loan revenues relative to total loans, achieved through strategic pricing decisions. Flexibility in the asset portfolio was also a key factor, a characteristic perhaps even more important under deregulation because it allows management to respond to a changing interest rate environment.

Superior performers had lower overhead and occupancy expenses, lower personnel expenses per employee, and lower ratios of fixed

Figure 21.3
First National Bank: Return on Net Worth

assets to total assets. Ford and Olson concluded that although high revenues are important, proper control of noninterest expenses is even more important.

In 1982, two economists at the Fed analyzed ROA for banks with more than $500 million in assets during the period 1970–1977. Their conclusions were somewhat different from those of Ford and Olson. They concluded that pricing policies and cost efficiencies were *not* significantly different between high- and low-performance banks, and that regional and local economic conditions, portfolio and risk preferences, and "some aspect of managerial ability not captured here" accounted for profit-

ability differences.[12] Their study called attention to the need for more research into performance differences among depository institutions, particularly as deregulation of the financial system progresses.

Lessons from Failed Banks.   Other studies have focused on the lowest end of the profitability spectrum. In a comparison of failed and nonfailed banks over the period 1970–1975, Sinkey concluded that the distinguishing factor

---

[12]Myron L. Kwast and John T. Rose, "Pricing, Operating Efficiency, and Profitability among Large Commercial Banks," *Journal of Banking and Finance* 6 (1982): 233–254.

was management of costs. Costs that seemed most important were: 1) poor loan quality, measured by the provision for loan losses; 2) the cost of liability management, measured by the expense of federal funds purchased; and 3) poor expense control, measured by the size of non-interest operating expenses.[13]

Banking Profitability in the 1980s. More recently, studies by Larry Wall at the Federal Reserve Bank of Atlanta have drawn similar conclusions, despite changes in the regulatory and economic environment since the 1970s.[14] Wall agreed that control of noninterest expenses was a key determinant of profitability. He also found that the most profitable banks held a proportionately larger investment portfolio, earning additional revenues without the high expenses associated with lending. Stronger performers also used lower-cost sources of borrowed funds and relied more heavily on equity capital. He concluded that "the road to consistently high bank profitability (as measured by banks' return on assets) has not changed in recent years." The relatively high ROA of First National during the period 1983-1985 reflected many of these characteristics.

In the past, many investigators have noted that small banks were more profitable than large ones. In the mid-1980s, however, analysts noted that small banks' profits were suffering. Although it is too early to draw definitive conclusions, problems in the energy and agricultural sectors, rather than deregulation or general operating conditions in the industry, may be responsible for the decline.[15]

Thrift Institutions

Studies of the performance of thrift institutions are more difficult to interpret in light of the many changes in the industry in recent years. Two studies were published in the late 1970s. One concluded that competitive and regulatory conditions and institutional size were important influences on performance. Managerial decision making was also crucial, however, especially efforts to control costs and the choice of loan portfolio composition.[16]

The second study found that high-performance S&Ls relied more heavily on borrowed funds relative to deposits, maintained lower liquidity, and had a stronger net worth position. The more profitable institutions also generated more income from fees and returns on the securities portfolio. Control of noninterest expenses was again a characteristic distinguishing the better performers.[17] Another conclusion drawn by several investigators is that high-performance thrifts follow a strategy of rapid turnover of the mortgage loan portfolio through frequent sales in the secondary mortgage market.[18]

[13]Joseph F. Sinkey, Jr., *Problem and Failed Institutions in the Commercial Banking Industry* (Greenwich, CT: JAI Press, 1979).

[14]Larry D. Wall, "Why Are Some Banks More Profitable?" *Economic Review,* Federal Reserve Bank of Atlanta 48 (September 1983): 42-47. Wall controlled for several factors not considered by Ford and Olson, such as holding-company affiliation and changes in the economic environment. He also found that factors beyond managerial control, such as market concentration (competition), did not appear to affect profitability.
Cates Consulting Analysts, Inc. is developing a long-term data base on high-performing retail banks. In 1986, the project was in its infancy. See Raymond T. Garea and Gail Triner, "What's the Secret of Profitable Retail Banking?" *ABA Banking Journal* 78 (April 1986): 41-43.

[15]Stephen A. Rhoades and Donald T. Savage, "The Viability of the Small Bank: Can Small Banks Compete?" *Bankers Magazine* 168 (July/August 1985): 66-72; Lynn A. Nejezchleb, "Declining Profitability at Small Commercial Banks: A Temporary Development or a Secular Trend?", *Banking and Economic Review,* Federal Deposit Insurance Corporation 4 (June 1986): 9-21; Larry D. Wall, "Profits in '85: Large Banks Gain While Others Continue to Lag," *Economic Review,* Federal Reserve Bank of Atlanta 71 (September/October 1986): 18-31.

[16]James A. Verbrugge, Richard A. Schick, and Kenneth J. Thygerson, "An Analysis of Savings and Loan Profit Performance," *Journal of Finance* 31 (December 1976): 1,427-1,442.

[17]David L. Smith, Donald M. Kaplan, and William F. Ford, "Why Some Associations Perform Far above Average," *Federal Home Loan Bank Board Journal* 10 (November 1977): 7-13.

[18]An excellent summary and discussion of this body of literature is provided in Walter J. Woerheide, *The Savings and Loan Industry: Current Problems and Possible Solutions* (Westport, CT: Quorum Press, 1984), pp. 28-48.

Credit Unions

Research on performance in the credit union industry is more descriptive than analytical. An obvious explanation, of course, is that, in the alleged absence of a profitability goal, it is difficult to define "high performance." Researchers at the Federal Reserve Bank of Atlanta published a study of CUs in 1984; they focused on *efficiency,* attempting to identify distinguishing characteristics of the more efficient organizations.[19]

Two definitions of efficiency were applied; each focused on the level of noninterest expenses and were similar to Ratios 21.15 and 21.16 in Table 21.6. Although the study was limited to large credit unions in Georgia, so that conclusions should be interpreted with care, the findings offer the only available analysis of "superior" performance. More efficient organizations had significantly fewer loans, emphasizing investment in securities, which is cheaper to administer. This management strategy, of course, may conflict with the service-to-members goal often suggested for credit unions. The high-performance group also managed to attract a higher proportion of deposits through less expensive regular share and share draft accounts. Again, however, reducing interest expenses is not necessarily consistent with the presumed orientation of CUs. The researchers expected better performers to be more aggressive in generating service charges and fee income as sources of revenue, but found that less efficient organizations had higher proportions of noninterest income.

Generally, the benefits of more efficient operations were passed on to customers, in the form of lower rates on loans and higher rates on some deposits. Thus, although the more effi-

cient institutions made fewer loans, those that were granted were at favorable rates. In addition, although they had relatively fewer interest-bearing share accounts, their interest-bearing accounts paid higher rates than those at less efficient credit unions. The higher returns were not used to boost net worth to a relatively larger proportion of assets.

OFF-BALANCE SHEET ACTIVITIES AND PERFORMANCE EVALUATION

Several references have been made to data not directly included on the balance sheet or income statement. The investment maturity schedule, for example, is used to evaluate the liquidity position. Other off-balance sheet data also deserve analysts' attention.

Standby Letters of Credit

Chapter 16 explains and illustrates the growing importance of off-balance sheet items in determining capital adequacy. In particular, attention has been focused on standby letters of credit. A commercial letter of credit is often used in international trade, when a lender agrees to provide a customer financing to purchase specific goods. Upon documentation of the completion of a transaction between the customer and a third party, the bank fully expects to advance funds. A standby letter of credit is a similar idea with an important difference: Rather than a definite commitment to finance a transaction, a standby letter is an obligation of the bank to pay a third party *only if* the bank's customer defaults. Standby letters are used not only in commercial transactions but also to enhance the marketability of municipal bonds or to guarantee performance on construction contracts. They act as insurance for a risk-averse third party in a transaction.

Ideally, banks provide this insurance only for the obligations of customers on which there is little likelihood of nonperformance. The bank charges a fee for the commitment, and, most importantly, assumes that the standby let-

---

[19]William N. Cox and Pamela V. Whigham, "What Distinguishes Larger and More Efficient Credit Unions?" *Economic Review,* Federal Reserve Bank of Atlanta 49 (October 1984): 34-41. A subsequent article provided credit union industry aggregate data in a comparison of black-controlled credit unions with other organizations, but did not investigate the sources of performance differences. See Harold A. Black and Robert L. Schweitzer, "Black-Controlled Credit Unions: A Comparative Analysis," *Journal of Financial Research* 8 (Fall 1985): 193-202.

ter will expire unused. Because they require no advance commitment of funds, standby letters are not included as liabilities on the balance sheets of issuing depository institutions, but are considered contingent liabilities.

The volume of commitments made with standby letters more than tripled between 1980 and 1985. Although concentrated in the 25 largest banks, 50 percent of all commercial banks reported standby letters outstanding by 1985. The rapid growth has led to concern about the degree of risk exposure, concern heightened by the failure of a large issuer of standby letters—Penn Square Bank in Oklahoma City. A study at the Federal Reserve Board concluded that banks with assets over $100 million do not have higher capital ratios to accompany their higher levels of standby letters of credit.[20] This concern led to the concept of the supplemental adjusted capital ratio illustrated in Chapter 16.

Incorporating Standby Letters into Financial Analysis.   Regulatory examiners have access to detailed data on standby letters, but external analysts can identify only the total vol-

ume of an institution's contingent liabilities, and then only in the notes to financial statements. First National's 1985 annual report, for example, revealed that contingent liabilities totaled almost $43 million, up from about $35 million in 1983. An accompanying statement said no significant losses were expected from these commitments (see Appendix 21B). External analysts have only this limited information with which to evaluate risk.

Loan Commitments

Loan commitments—including revolving lines of credit; lines backing the commercial paper of large corporations; and note issuance facilities, in which the bank agrees to buy short-term notes if a borrower is unable to sell them elsewhere—are other off-balance sheet liabilities. In 1985, loan commitments at commercial banks were estimated at over $530 billion, greatly exceeding the estimated volume of standby letters of credit ($175 billion). Like standby letters, loan commitments are often activated only if a borrower's financial condition deteriorates. Ideally, they, too, should be considered by external analysts in assessing the total risk to which an institution is exposed. Again, however, information is limited.

Hedging Strategies: Financial Futures and Swaps

Although banks and thrifts are allowed to engage in financial futures transactions for hedging purposes only, hedges are accompanied by exposure to basis risk. It is never easy, and may even be impossible, to assess the degree of a depository's involvement by looking at published financial statements. Ordinarily, it is necessary to consult regulatory sources to get this information.

Since 1983, large commercial banks have been required to report their total obligations for future delivery of securities on quarterly call reports. That information, however, is not reported separately on the balance sheet, nor are the results of hedges isolated on the income statement. Although the number of banks and

---

[20]Michael A. Goldberg and Peter R. Lloyd-Davies, "Standby Letters of Credit: Are Banks Overextending Themselves?" *Journal of Bank Research* 16 (Spring 1985): 28-39. Barbara Bennett, "Off-Balance Sheet Risk in Banking: The Case of Standby Letters of Credit," *Economic Review,* Federal Reserve Bank of San Francisco (Winter 1986), pp. 19-29; Barbara Bennett, "Standby Letters of Credit," *Weekly Letter,* Federal Reserve Bank of San Francisco, May 23, 1986; G. D. Koppenhaver, "A Logit Analysis of U.S. Commercial Bank Off-Balance Sheet Activities," unpublished paper presented at the annual meeting of the Midwest Finance Association, Chicago, Illinois, March 1986; Suzanna Andrews and Henny Sender, "Off Balance Sheet Risk: Where Is It Leading the Banks?" *Institutional Investor* 20 (January 1986): 75-84; James Chessen, "Off-Balance-Sheet Activity: A Growing Concern? *Proceedings of a Conference on Bank Structure and Competition* (Chicago: Federal Reserve Bank of Chicago, 1986), pp. 369-386; Lawrence M. Benveniste and Allen N. Berger, "An Empirical Analysis of Standby Letters of Credit," *Proceedings of a Conference on Bank Structure and Competition* (Chicago: Federal Reserve Bank of Chicago, 1986), pp. 387-412.

Figures cited in these and other articles suggest that among the largest banks, off-balance sheet commitments ranged from 166 percent to nearly 300 percent of total bank assets in 1985.

thrifts actively engaged in futures trading is still relatively small, forecasts for growing participation suggest that questions about hedging should be asked as a part of performance assessment. The problem does not arise for federal CUs, of course, which are currently prohibited by regulation from involvement in the futures markets.

Interest rate swaps are also off-balance sheet commitments. Although swap activity is reported to federal regulators, standard financial statement analysis will not reflect the true exposure of institutions with high profiles in the market. Analysts must be aware that there is considerable risk involved if an institution's counterparty defaults.

PERFORMANCE RATING SERVICES

Just as well-known agencies provide risk ratings for debt issues of nonfinancial corporations, risk-rating services for depository institutions are becoming increasingly important to potential investors and depositors—especially to those with accounts in excess of the FDIC- and FSLIC-insured maximum. As these rating agencies have become better known, they have generated controversy. Institutions receiving more risky ratings are critical of procedures used to arrive at the rankings.

Most rating agencies sell their analyses on a proprietary basis and are reluctant to reveal the data on which conclusions are based. One rating service for the S&L industry drew the criticism of the U. S. League of Savings Institutions recently for "nondisclosure of methodology."[21] Other observers have noted, however, that institution executives are often willing to provide these services with data not generally available

to other analysts, in hopes of maintaining or improving their ratings.[22] Thus, the opinions of professional risk raters may reflect better information than that available to the average analyst.

SUMMARY

Financial performance evaluation of a depository institution is a multifaceted procedure, involving ratio analysis, common-size statements, trend analysis, and consideration of additional data not always found in published financial reports. Analysts look behind the reported numbers because financial statements are prepared using accounting rules that may disguise important developments. Relationships among various financial ratios and between financial and nonfinancial data must also be considered.

It is convenient to analyze the results of a depository institution's operations using several performance dimensions: liquidity, credit risk exposure, financial leverage, efficiency or productivity, and profitability. Many ratios are available to capture each dimension. Integrated models such as the Dupont system show how various dimensions of performance interact to produce a given level of ROA or RONW.

Trend analysis shows whether the depository's performance has changed over time and is as important as knowing the current position of the institution. Finally, the footnotes to financial statements may highlight the presence of off-balance sheet items that may affect projections of future performance.

---

[21]"Performance Rating Focuses Debate on Use of FHLBB Data," *Savings Institutions* 106 (September 1985): 7–10.

[22]Jeff Bailey and G. Christian Hill, "Bank-Rating Service's Influence Grows," *The Wall Street Journal,* August 6, 1985, p. 6. The authors reported that First Chicago CEO Barry Sullivan traveled to New York in June 1985, to lobby analysts of the Keefe, Bruyette and Woods agency in an effort to avoid further downgrading of the bank's rating.

Questions

1. What areas of a depository's activities can be analyzed through financial ratios and common-size statements? For proper interpretation of financial information, what comparisons should be made?

2. What sources of industry performance are available to depository institution analysts?

3. What problems do analysts face when using financial ratios to assess the liquidity of a depository?

4. In evaluating portfolio management, what factors should be considered and why?

5. What differences exist between loan loss reporting for large banks and other depositories? Why is trend analysis especially important in the evaluation of credit risk ratios? What complications in loan portfolio analysis are introduced by international lending?

6. What conclusions have researchers drawn about the importance of efficiency and productivity measures in depository performance?

7. Explain the benefits of the Dupont system for analyzing return on assets, RONW, and the management of capital.

8. What important information is typically provided in the notes and tables that accompany financial statements?

9. What are standby letters of credit? Why is the examination of these and other off-balance sheet items essential to the financial analysis of depositories?

Problems

1. You have been hired by First Security Corporation, the largest bank holding company in the state. Your first project is to complete an analysis of First Security's performance over the past year. That analysis involves calculating performance ratios and comparing them to those for similar banks.

Problem 21.1

**First Security Corporation and Subsidiaries,
Consolidated Statements of Condition
as of December 31, 1988 and 1989
(Thousands)**

	1989		1988	
Assets				
Cash and due from banks		$ 220,185		$ 173,303
Investment securities:				
U.S. Treasury and agencies	$397,000		$268,604	
States and political subdivisions	140,834		142,588	
Other securities	4,102		114,417	
Total investment securities		541,936		525,609
Federal funds sold and reverse repos		547,607		563,610

---

continued

Problem 21.1 (*continued*)

First Security Corporation and Subsidiaries, Consolidated Statements of Condition as of December 31, 1988 and 1989 (Thousands)

	1989	1988
Loans:		
Commercial and agricultural	$513,408	$399,185
Real estate—construction	29,320	14,452
Real estate—mortgage	289,268	253,657
Installment and credit card	341,728	242,948
Other	157,251	
Less unearned interest	(41,765)	(39,099)
Less allowance for possible loan losses	(14,112)	(12,264)
Net loans	1,275,098	858,879
Premises and equipment	60,443	57,339
Acceptances, customers' liability	45,267	
Other assets	73,849	60,146
Total Assets	$2,764,385	$2,238,886
Liabilities and Net Worth		
Deposits:		
Noninterest-bearing deposits	$567,773	$459,404
Interest-bearing deposits:		
Savings	582,915	378,394
Time	692,109	607,743
Total deposits	$1,842,797	$1,445,541
Short-term borrowings		
(primarily federal funds purchased and repos)	$560,472	$522,476
Long-term debt	65,036	42,529
Acceptances executed	45,267	
Other liabilities	47,170	38,629
Total nondeposit liabilities	717,945	603,634
Preferred stock	$ 0	$ 0
Common stock	22,500	22,500
Surplus	52,000	52,000
Undivided profits	129,143	115,211
Total net worth	203,643	189,711
Liabilities and Net Worth	$2,764,385	$2,238,886
Market value of securities at year-end	$ 534,159	$ 413,405

Problem 21.1 (*continued*)

First Security Corporation and Subsidiaries, Consolidated Statements of Earnings for Years Ending December 31, 1988 and 1989 (Thousands)

	1989		1988	
Interest income:				
Interest and fees on loans	$136,820		$113,935	
Interest on federal funds sold	47,065		57,378	
Interest on investment securities:				
Taxable	39,211		28,836	
Nontaxable	7,909		17,376	
Other interest income	3,101		3,888	
Total interest income		$234,106		$221,413
Noninterest income:				
Trust income	$ 10,052		$ 8,677	
Service charges and fees	16,496		13,220	
Other operating income	6,185		2,470	
Total noninterest income		32,733		24,367
Interest expense:				
Interest on savings deposits	$ 13,250		$ 15,359	
Interest on time deposits	86,357		76,557	
Interest on short-term borrowings	42,405		55,016	
Interest on long-term debt	4,943		4,311	
Total interest expense		146,955		151,243
Provision for possible loan losses		6,033		2,152
Noninterest expense:				
Salaries	$ 36,869		$ 27,091	
Pension and other employee benefits	5,245		4,786	
Equipment expense	7,755		6,258	
Occupancy expense	6,042		4,215	
Supplies	3,793		2,829	
Other operating expense	20,808		17,313	
Total noninterest expense		80,512		62,492
Net operating income before tax		$ 33,339		$ 29,893
Taxes		5,826		5,141
Income before securities gains or losses (IBSGL)		$ 27,513		$ 24,752
Other income (primarily security gains and losses)		104		(458)
Net income		$ 27,617		$ 24,294
Per share:				
Net income		$6.14		$5.40
Dividends		$2.95		$2.45

continued

Problem 21.1 (*continued*)
First Security Corporation, Peer Group Ratios

Ratio		Peer Group Averages, 1989
Liquidity		
21.1	Average Cash and Short-Term Securities / Average Total Assets	28.20%
21.2	Average Cash and Short-Term Securities / Average Deposits	38.90%
21.3	Average Net Loans / Average Deposits	71.88%
21.4	Average Purchased Liabilities / Average Total Assets	44.54%

Ratio		**Taxable**	**Nontaxable**
Portfolio Management			
21.5	Market Value of Securities / Book Value of Securities	97.55%	90.31%

Ratio		Peer Group Averages, 1989
Credit Risk		
21.6	Loan Loss Provision / Average Net Loans	0.75%
21.7	Allowance for Loan Losses / Average Net Loans	1.32%
21.8	Net Loan Chargeoffs / Average Net Loans	0.58%
21.9	Net Income / Loan Loss Provision	1.78 times
Leverage		
21.10	Average Net Worth / Average Total Assets	5.35%
21.12	Average Net Worth / Average Net Loans	10.27%
21.13	Average Net Worth / Average Deposits	7.38%
Efficiency: Noninterest Expenses		
21.14	Noninterest Expenses / Total Operating Expenses	36.57%
21.15	Noninterest Expenses / Total Operating Income	32.48%

Problem 21.1 (*continued*)
First Security Corporation,
Peer Group Ratios

Ratio		Peer Group Averages, 1989
Efficiency: Noninterest Income		
21.16	$\dfrac{\text{Noninterest Income}}{\text{Total Operating Income}}$	10.44%
21.18	$\dfrac{\text{Noninterest Income}}{\text{Average Total Assets}}$	1.15%
Productivity (Asset Utilization)		
21.19	$\dfrac{\text{Total Operating Income}}{\text{Average Total Assets}}$	11.02%
Profitability		
21.20	$\dfrac{\text{Net Income}}{\text{Total Operating Income}}$	6.44%
21.21	$\dfrac{\text{Net Income}}{\text{Average Total Assets}}$	0.71%
21.22	$\dfrac{\text{Net Income} - \text{Preferred Dividends}}{\text{Average Net Worth}}$	13.27%
21.23	$\dfrac{\text{Net Income}}{\text{Number of Common Shares Outstanding}}$	
21.24	$\dfrac{\text{Interest Revenues} - \text{Interest Expense}}{\text{Average Total Assets}}$	3.64%

To assist you in completing the evaluation, your supervisor has provided comparative figures from the Uniform Bank Performance Reports, Peer Group Averages, for 1989. The statements of income and condition for 1989 and 1988 are also provided for your use. In addition, the following figures from the tables and footnotes in the bank's annual report may be useful:

	1989	1988
Short-term securities	$195,025	$147,990
Negotiable CDs	171,003	167,318
Net loan chargeoffs	5,391	2,383

Prepare a report of First Security's performance. Evaluate the bank holding company's strengths and weaknesses in each of the following areas:

a. Liquidity
b. Credit risk
c. Leverage
d. Efficiency
e. Productivity
f. Profitability

2. **a.** Using the information in Problem 1, recalculate First Security's ROA and RONW using the Dupont ratios.
    b. What information does the Dupont method provide for interpreting the bank's return on assets that is not provided by the ratios used in Problem 1? What recommendation would you give to First Security's managers for improving performance?
    c. How has the bank's use of leverage affected its return to shareholders, especially in comparison to peer banks?

3. The summary of loan loss experience for First Bank and Trust Company from 1990 through 1992 is provided in the following table. Using that information and appropriate ratios, answer the following questions about the bank's credit risk.

Problem 21.3
First Bank & Trust,
Summary of Changes in the Allowance
for Possible Loan Losses, 1990–1992
(Thousands)

	1992	1991	1990
1. Balance at beginning of period	$1,115	$999	$950
Deductions:			
2. Loan chargeoffs	720	694	668
3. Less loan loss recoveries	180	135	128
4. Net chargeoffs [(2) − (3)]	540	559	601
Additions:			
5. Provision for possible loan losses	700	675	650
6. Balance at end of period [(1) − (4) + (5)]	$1,275	$1,115	$999
Net income	$1,602	$1,548	$1,301
Average net loans	$120,619	$115,751	$111,053
Average net worth	$12,197	$10,586	$9,515
Average total assets	$178,276	$165,408	$155,825

Ratios	Peer Group Averages		
21.6	0.67%	0.66%	0.61%
21.7	1.18%	1.16%	1.07%
21.8	0.54%	0.52%	0.52%
21.9	2.13	2.15	2.20
21.10	6.50%	6.30%	6.30%

---

a. What trend is apparent in the bank's *actual* loan loss experience? Which of the ratios help to assess *ex post* risk?
b. What trend is evident in management's estimate of potential loan losses? On which ratio(s) do you base your response?
c. What is your assessment of the bank's overall ability to handle its current level of credit risk?

4. Mary Garcia is a financial analyst for one of the nation's largest S&Ls. Her institution has followed an aggressive growth strategy over the last four years, and is now considering acquiring the Surfside Federal Savings and Loan, a thrift operating in the same state but in a different metropolitan area. She has Surfside's financial statements for the past two years, and has been asked to provide an opinion of the institution's financial performance.

Problem 21.4

Surfside Federal
Savings and Loan Association,
Statement of Condition
as of December 31, 1991 and 1992
(Millions)

	1992		1991	
Assets				
Cash		$ 16.677		$ 15.883
Short-term securities		39.579		39.706
Loans:				
Mortgages	$340.205		$336.711	
Home improvement	61.148		58.766	
Education	2.224		1.588	
Other consumer	14.898		9.000	
Total loans		418.475		406.065
Long-term securities		23.903		19.589
Real estate owned		5.559		4.235
Building and equipment		7.227		7.412
Other assets		44.471		36.531
Total Assets		$555.891		$529.421
Liabilities and Net Worth				
Deposits:				
NOWs, passbooks, MMDAs	$110.622		$131.825	
CDs	335.202		302.298	
Total deposits		$445.824		$434.123
FHLBB advances	40.580		37.059	
Other borrowed money	37.245		26.471	
All other liabilities	10.562		10.591	
Total nondeposit liabilities		88.387		74.121
Net worth		$ 21.680		$ 21.177
Total Liabilities and Net Worth		$555.891		$529.421
Market value of securities		$ 60.064		$ 59.782

continued

Problem 21.4 (*continued*)

Surfside Federal
Savings and Loan Association,
Income and Expenses
for Years Ending December 31, 1991 and 1992
(Millions)

	1992		1991	
Interest income:				
Interest on loans	$38.545		$36.627	
Interest on investment securities	7.594		6.377	
Loan fees and discounts	2.999		3.330	
Other operating income	14.678		10.102	
Total operating income		$63.816		$56.436
Interest expense:				
Interest on deposits	$43.009		$37.475	
Interest on borrowed money	7.331		6.207	
Salaries and employee benefits	3.788		3.407	
Other expenses	6.965		5.503	
Total operating expenses		61.093		52.412
Net operating income before tax		$ 2.723		$ 4.024
Nonoperating income (expense)		(1.001)		(1.800)
Income before taxes		$ 1.722		$ 2.224
Taxes		0.500		0.424
Net income		$ 1.222		$ 1.800
Earnings per share		$0.23		$0.29

Problem 21.4 (*continued*)
Surfside Federal Savings and Loan Association
Peer Group Ratios

Ratio		Peer Group Averages 1992	Surfside Federal Performance Ratios 1991	Surfside Federal Performance Ratios 1990
Liquidity				
21.1	Average Cash and Short-Term Securities / Average Total Assets	6.95%	7.05%	6.95%
21.2	Average Cash and Short-Term Securities / Average Deposits	8.75%	8.50%	8.10%
21.3	Average Net Loans / Average Deposits	94.88%	92.65%	91.85%
21.4	Average Purchased Liabilities / Average Total Assets	10.95%	12.75%	11.95%

Problem 21.4 (*continued*)
Surfside Federal Savings and Loan Association
Peer Group Ratios

Ratio	Peer Group Averages 1992	Surfside Federal Performance Ratios 1991	Surfside Federal Performance Ratios 1990
Portfolio Management			
21.5 $\dfrac{\text{Market Value of Securities}}{\text{Book Value of Securities}}$	97.95%	100.8%	99.00%
Leverage			
21.10 $\dfrac{\text{Average Net Worth}}{\text{Average Total Assets}}$	4.35%	4.10%	4.16%
21.12 $\dfrac{\text{Average Net Worth}}{\text{Average Net Loans}}$	6.01%	5.35%	5.50%
21.13 $\dfrac{\text{Average Net Worth}}{\text{Average Deposits}}$	5.95%	4.89%	5.03%
Efficiency: Noninterest Expenses			
21.14 $\dfrac{\text{Noninterest Expenses}}{\text{Total Operating Expenses}}$	16.75%	16.99%	16.80%
21.15 $\dfrac{\text{Noninterest Expenses}}{\text{Total Operating Income}}$	14.65%	15.79%	14.95%
Efficiency: Noninterest Income			
21.16 $\dfrac{\text{Noninterest Income}}{\text{Total Operating Income}}$	22.75%	23.80%	22.50%
21.17 $\dfrac{\text{Loan Fee Income}}{\text{Average Net Loans}}$	0.85%	0.84%	0.86%
21.18 $\dfrac{\text{Noninterest Income}}{\text{Average Total Assets}}$	2.25%	2.47%	2.35%
Productivity (Asset Utilization)			
21.19 $\dfrac{\text{Total Operating Income}}{\text{Average Total Assets}}$	11.65%	10.75%	10.95%
Profitability			
21.20 $\dfrac{\text{Net Income}}{\text{Total Operating Income}}$	3.95%	3.19%	3.85%
21.21 $\dfrac{\text{Net Income}}{\text{Average Total Assets}}$	0.56%	0.45%	0.50%
21.22 $\dfrac{\text{Net Income} - \text{Preferred Dividends}}{\text{Average Net Worth}}$	9.25%	8.75%	8.80%
21.23 $\dfrac{\text{Net Income}}{\text{Number of Common Shares Outstanding}}$		$.29	$.32
21.24 $\dfrac{\text{Interest Revenues} - \text{Interest Expense}}{\text{Average Total Assets}}$	0.98%	0.15%	0.18%

a. Using the balance sheet and income statement data in the table, along with the industry comparative data and ratios for previous years, evaluate Surfside's financial strengths and weaknesses.

b. Based on the analysis in a, should Mary recommend proceeding with the acquisition? Why or why not?

5. The River City Federal Credit Union is one of the state's largest credit unions. The chairman of the asset/liability management committee is evaluating River City's financial strength.

Statements of condition and income for the CU are given in the following tables. The institution's net loan losses for the period are: $277,950 (for 1992) and $230,036 (for 1991). Evaluate River City Federal's financial position.

Problem 21.5

River City Federal Credit Union, Statement of Condition as of December 31, 1991 and 1992 (Millions)

	1992		1991	
Assets				
Cash		$ 2.142		$ 1.646
Short-term securities		3.980		8.789
Loans:				
Consumer	$139.305		$106.798	
Mortgages	38.320		26.082	
Home improvement	2.013		2.300	
Less allowance for loan losses	(0.300)		(0.300)	
Net loans		179.338		134.880
Long-term securities		11.471		15.170
Real estate owned		0.480		0.000
Building and equipment		2.363		2.406
Other assets		1.890		0.847
Total Assets		$201.664		$163.738
Liabilities and Net Worth				
Deposits:				
Share accounts and share drafts	$118.813		$107.353	
Share certificates	69.142		44.865	
Total deposits		$187.955		$152.218
All other liabilities		2.374		1.711
Reserves and undivided earnings		$ 11.335		$ 9.809
Total Liabilities and Net Worth		$201.664		$163.738
Market value of securities		$ 14.080		$ 23.446

Problem 21.5 (*continued*)

River City Federal Credit Union,
Income and Expenses
for Years Ending December 31, 1991 and 1992
(Millions)

	1992		1991	
Interest income:				
Interest on loans	$15.602		$11.744	
Interest on investment securities	1.851		1.988	
Loan fees and discounts	0.290		0.201	
Other operating income	0.008		0.005	
Total operating income		$17.751		$13.938
Interest expense:				
Interest on shares	$ 8.148		$ 5.920	
Interest on borrowed money	2.254		2.331	
Salaries and employee benefits	3.332		2.538	
Other expenses	2.372		1.562	
Total operating expenses		16.106		12.351
Net operating income		$ 1.645		$ 1.587
Nonoperating income (expense)		(0.086)		0.142
Net income		$ 1.559		$ 1.729

Problem 21.5 (*continued*)
River City Federal Credit Union,
Peer Group Ratios

Ratio		Peer Group Averages 1992
Liquidity		
21.1	$\dfrac{\text{Average Cash and Short-Term Securities}}{\text{Average Total Assets}}$	4.60%
21.2	$\dfrac{\text{Average Cash and Short-Term Securities}}{\text{Average Deposits}}$	4.90%
21.3	$\dfrac{\text{Average Net Loans}}{\text{Average Deposits}}$	79.52%
Portfolio Management		
21.5	$\dfrac{\text{Market Value of Securities}}{\text{Book Value of Securities}}$	94.89%

continued

Problem 21.5 (*continued*)
River City Federal Credit Union,
Peer Group Ratios

Ratio	Peer Group Averages 1992
Credit Risk	
21.7 $\dfrac{\text{Allowance for Loan Losses}}{\text{Average Net Loans}}$	3.45%
21.8 $\dfrac{\text{Net Loan Chargeoffs}}{\text{Average Net Loans}}$	0.38%
Leverage	
21.10 $\dfrac{\text{Average Net Worth}}{\text{Average Total Assets}}$	6.00%
21.12 $\dfrac{\text{Average Net Worth}}{\text{Average Net Loans}}$	9.86%
21.13 $\dfrac{\text{Average Net Worth}}{\text{Average Deposits}}$	6.45%
Efficiency: Noninterest Expenses	
21.14 $\dfrac{\text{Noninterest Expenses}}{\text{Total Operating Expenses}}$	35.95%
21.15 $\dfrac{\text{Noninterest Expenses}}{\text{Total Operating Income}}$	24.85%
Efficiency: Noninterest Income	
21.16 $\dfrac{\text{Noninterest Income}}{\text{Total Operating Income}}$	1.58%
21.18 $\dfrac{\text{Noninterest Income}}{\text{Average Total Assets}}$	0.17%
Productivity (Asset Utilization)	
21.19 $\dfrac{\text{Total Operating Income}}{\text{Average Total Assets}}$	9.35%
Profitability	
21.20 $\dfrac{\text{Net Income}}{\text{Total Operating Income}}$	6.10%
21.21 $\dfrac{\text{Net Income}}{\text{Average Total Assets}}$	0.93%
21.24 $\dfrac{\text{Interest Revenues} - \text{Interest Expense}}{\text{Average Total Assets}}$	3.55%

6. The Second National Bank and Trust company has year-end financial data for the most recent period as follows:

ROA	1.45%
RONW	15.95%
Net income	$10,895,900

a. Calculate the bank's net worth multiplier and its ratio of net worth to total assets.

b. Calculate the institution's total assets and net worth.

c. Suppose the bank increases total liabilities by $10,000,000 and reduces net worth by the same amount. Assuming no change in net income, what will be the new ROA and RONW ratios? What do these changes reveal about the impact of financial leverage?

Selected References

Andrews, Suzanna. "Accounting for LDC Debt." *Institutional Investor* 18 (August 1984): 189-194.

Andrews, Suzanna, and Henny Sender. "Off Balance Sheet Risk: Where Is It Leading the Banks?" *Institutional Investor* 20 (January 1986): 75-84.

Bennett, Barbara. "Off-Balance Sheet Risk in Banking: The Case of Standby Letters of Credit." *Economic Review* (Federal Reserve Bank of San Francisco) (Winter 1986), pp. 19-29.

Chessen, James. "Off-Balance-Sheet Activity: A Growing Concern?" *Proceedings of a Conference on Bank Structure and Competition.* (Chicago: Federal Reserve Bank of Chicago, 1986), pp. 369-386.

Cox, William N., and Pamela V. Whigham. "What Distinguishes Larger and More Efficient Credit Unions?" *Economic Review* (Federal Reserve Bank of Atlanta) 49 (October 1984): 34-41.

Federal Financial Institutions Examination Council. *Uniform Bank Performance Report.* Annual.

Federal Reserve Bank of New York. *Recent Trends in Commercial Bank Profitability.* (New York: Federal Reserve Bank of New York, 1986.)

Ford, William F. "Profitability: Why Do Some Banks Perform Better Than Average?" *Banking* 66 (October 1974): 29-33. The first of a series between 1974 and 1978.

Goldberg, Michael A., and Peter R. Lloyd-Davies. "Standby Letters of Credit: Are Banks Overextending Themselves?" *Journal of Bank Research* 16 (Spring 1985): 28-39.

Kwast, Myron L., and John T. Rose. "Pricing, Operating Efficiency, and Profitability among Large Commercial Banks." *Journal of Banking and Finance* 6 (1982): 233-254.

Nejezchleb, Lynn A. "Declining Profitability at Small Commercial Banks: A Temporary Development or a Secular Trend?" *Banking and Economic Review* (Federal Deposit Insurance Corporation) 4 (June 1986): 9-21.

Rhoades, Stephen A., and Donald T. Savage. "The Viability of the Small Bank: Can Small Banks Compete?" *Bankers Magazine* 168 (July/August 1985): 66-72.

Sinkey, Joseph F., Jr. *Problem and Failed Institutions in the Commercial Banking Industry.* Greenwich, CT: JAI Press, 1979.

Smith, David L., Donald M. Kaplan, and William F. Ford. "Why Some Associations Perform Far above Average." *Federal Home Loan Bank Board Journal* 10 (November 1977): 7-13.

U.S. League of Savings Institutions. *Savings Institution Source Book*. Chicago: U.S. League of Savings Institutions. Annual.

Verbrugge, James A., Richard A. Schick, and Kenneth J. Thygerson. "An Analysis of Savings and Loan Profit Performance." *Journal of Finance* 31 (December 1976): 1,427-1,442.

Wall, Larry A. "Why Are Some Banks More Profitable?" *Economic Review* (Federal Reserve Bank of Atlanta) 48 (September 1983): 42-47.

Woerheide, Walter J. *The Savings and Loan Industry: Current Problems and Possible Solutions*. Westport, CT: Quorum Press, 1984.

Appendix 21A

ALTERNATIVE RATIOS FOR EVALUATING PERFORMANCE

Liquidity

Cash and Due From Depositories/Average Demand Deposits

Short-Term Assets/Demand Deposits

Short-Term Securities/Average Assets

Short-Term Liabilities/Total Liabilities

Average Net Loans/Average Assets

Short-Term Loans/Net Loans

Average Short-Term Assets/Average Net Loans

Credit Risk

Loan Recoveries/Average Net Loans

(Loan Recoveries − Loan Chargeoffs)/Average Net Loans

Loan Loss Provision/Average Assets

Loan Loss Provision/Net Chargeoffs

Allowance for Loan Losses/Loan Loss Provision

Net Loan Chargeoffs/Net Income

Leverage

Total Liabilities/Net Worth

(Net Worth − Intangible Assets)/Average Total Assets

(Net Worth + Long-Term Debt)/Average Total Assets

Net Worth/Average Short-Term Liabilities

Efficiency

Personnel Expenses/Number of Employees

Number of Employees/Average Total Assets

Occupancy Expense/Average Total Assets

Occupancy Expense/Total Revenues

Personnel Expenses/Total Revenues

Noninterest Expenses/Net Income

Loan Fee Income/Net Income

Noninterest Income/Net Income

Appendix 21B

SUPPLEMENTARY FINANCIAL INFORMATION FOR FIRST NATIONAL CORPORATION

Maturities of Selected Investment Securities as of December 31, 1985
(Thousands)

	Book Value	Market Value	Average Maturity	Weighted Average Yield*
U.S. Treasury and agencies:				
Within 1 year	$185,364	$188,632	0.5 yrs.	10.86%
1-5 years	250,188	256,320	1.8	9.65
5-10 years	6	6	8.7	5.32
Over 10 years	1,667	1,698	18.8	9.54
Total	$437,225	$446,656	1.3 yrs.	10.16%
States and political subdivisions:				
Within 1 year	$ 35,222	$ 34,988	0.6 yrs.	10.38%
1-5 years	64,945	63,154	2.8	9.71
5-10 years	18,573	16,671	8.7	10.55
Over 10 years	2,451	2,207	18.9	13.18
Total	$121,191	$117,020	2.8 yrs.	10.10%
Other bonds, notes and debentures:				
Within 1 year	$ 77	$ 187	0.6 yrs.	11.17%
1-5 years	—	—	—	—
5-10 years	—	—	—	—
Over 10 years	266	266	13.7	3.30
Total	$ 343	$ 453	7.1 yrs.	3.84%

*Yields on nontaxable investment securities have been computed on a fully taxable equivalent basis.

Deposit Mix as of December 31
(Thousands)

	1985	1984	1983
Noninterest-Bearing Demand Deposits			
Individual, business and other	$ 640,468	$ 514,220	$ 449,375
Commercial banks	28,323	14,314	15,483
Public funds	23,601	28,625	25,878
Total noninterest-bearing deposits	$ 692,392	$ 557,159	$ 540,736

continued

Deposit Mix as of December 31 (continued)
(Thousands)

	1985	1984	1983
Interest-Bearing Deposits			
Savings	$ 208,243	$ 168,868	$ 185,786
NOW	131,289	118,803	112,829
Super NOW	57,983	34,296	27,419
Money market savings	407,273	263,089	229,123
Time deposits $100,000 and over	257,492	267,655	177,759
All other time deposits	827,665	542,986	481,392
Total interest-bearing deposits	$1,889,945	$1,395,697	$1,214,308
Total deposits	$2,582,337	$1,952,856	$1,755,044

Maturity of Time Deposits $100,000 and Over
as of December 31, 1985
(Thousands)

	Certificates of Deposit	Other Time Deposits	Total
3 months or less	$175,794	$1,761	$177,555
Over 3 months through 6 months	31,290	403	31,693
Over 6 months through 12 months	18,964	206	19,170
Over 12 months	28,773	301	29,074
Total	$254,821	$2,671	$257,492

Summary of Loan Loss Experience
for the Years Ended December 31
(Thousands)

	1985	1984	1983
Average loans—net of unearned interest	$1,699,148	$1,341,416	$1,086,585
Allowance for possible loan losses:			
Balance—beginning of period	$ 16,734	$ 13,440	$ 12,264
Chargeoffs:			
Commercial	(3,955)	(2,629)	(5,397)
Real estate	(71)	(215)	(245)
Retail	(4,125)	(2,504)	(2,171)
Total chargeoffs	(8,151)	(5,348)	(7,813)
Recoveries:			
Commercial	1,634	1,129	1,477
Real estate	16	83	27
Retail	1,155	887	918
Total recoveries	2,805	2,099	2,422
Net chargeoffs	(5,346)	(3,249)	(5,391)
Provision charged to earnings	9,083	6,543	5,915
Allowances of banks acquired	2,854	—	652
Balance—end of period	$ 23,325	$ 16,734	$ 13,440

Commitments and Contingent Liabilities

The Corporation has various commitments and contingent liabilities outstanding, such as guarantees and commitments to extend credit made in the normal course of business, that are not reflected in the consolidated financial statements. No significant losses are anticipated as a result of these commitments. The aggregate amount of outstanding standby letters of credit was $42,963,000 at December 31, 1985, and $34,861,000 at December 31, 1984.

Part V

ASSET/LIABILITY MANAGEMENT IN NONDEPOSITORY INSTITUTIONS

Chapter 22

FINANCE COMPANIES

Household International does not fit the image of the finance company of yesteryear . . . .
Household is engaged in pilot programs that make insurance, ATMs, equity lines of
credit, and safe deposit boxes available at its consumer finance offices. Such offices
could become the one-stop financial center for a substantial portion of our population.

Donald Koch
Senior Vice President
Federal Reserve Bank of Atlanta (1984)

WHAT commercial lender would rank 25th on *Fortune* magazine's list of the largest banking organizations in 1985 and would be 7th most profitable—*if it were a bank*? The answer is General Electric Credit Corporation, the most successful and fastest growing of GE's lines of business. According to *Fortune,* GE Credit's nonperforming loans, none of which were agricultural or foreign, were less than 1 percent of its total portfolio, compared to 3.7 percent for some large banks. One admiring rival, describing the management group at GE Credit, said, "They're like the 1927 Yankees," a team viewed by many baseball fans as the greatest of all time.[1] GE Credit is a finance company, and one of the many nondepository institutions muscling into territory formerly dominated by banks, thrifts, and CUs. The management strategies propelling GE Credit and other finance companies into the spotlight are the subject of this chapter.

---

[1]Gary Hector, "GE Credit Corp. Braces for the Tax Reformers," *Fortune* 112 (August 5, 1985): 66.

NONDEPOSITORY INSTITUTIONS: WHAT ARE THEY?

For the rest of the book, the focus is nondepository financial institutions: finance companies, insurance companies, investment companies, securities firms, pension funds, and diversified financial services firms.

Nondepositories Are Intermediaries

These institutions do what depositories do: accept funds on which investors expect a rate of return, and reinvest those funds in financial assets—in other words, they are intermediaries. Consequently, many management tools explained earlier are useful in asset/liability management of nondepository firms. What separates nondepositories from depositories is that the former cannot offer transaction accounts insured by federal agencies. The problem of moral hazard is less likely to arise, and the financial assets in which they can invest are less restricted than the assets of depositories.

Not all nondepositories are alike, however. Laws and regulations dating back decades separate the activities of some nondepositories, such as insurers, from others, such as investment companies.

Growing Competition

Deregulation of depositories has brought increasing competition between them and nondepositories, and changing business and consumer behavior has increased competition among nondepositories. Thus, it is somewhat artificial to make fine distinctions between what a finance company, an insurance company, a securities firm, or even a bank can do that other firms cannot. Nonetheless, enough differences remain that this book's discussion of asset/liability management in nondepositories is divided by type of institution.

FINANCE COMPANIES: WHAT ARE THEY?

The opening quotation suggests that finance companies have undergone a transformation that makes them hard to define. Actually, although finance companies have changed in the last decade, they have always been hard to define. Only two things characterize firms that are traditionally considered finance companies:

1. Their lending practices are regulated almost entirely at the state level.

2. Their funds sources are not deposits.

Their origins help to identify finance companies more clearly.

Brief History

Finance companies are 20th-century creations. They arose mainly to serve the unmet credit needs of consumers, although they now serve broader purposes. Traditionally, the industry consisted of three distinct types of companies, based on primary clientele. Although the distinctions are now blurred, this historical material follows the traditional lines.

Sales Finance Companies. A *sales finance company* provides credit, usually on an installment basis, to buyers making specific purchases. The first sales finance company was formed in 1904 by a piano manufacturer, which extended installment contracts to consumers who otherwise could not afford such an expensive item. The idea was rapidly adopted by automobile manufacturers rising to prominence at the time. By 1922, over 1,000 sales finance firms operated in the United States.

Their credit practices were virtually unregulated because a principle of British common law was in effect, holding that the difference between the cash price of a good and the total sum of the installment payments required to purchase it was not defined as "interest." Therefore, installment contracts offered by these firms were exempt from state usury laws.[2] This legal principle has since fallen from favor, and sales finance companies are now subject to state and federal laws governing the provision of credit, including usury statutes and Truth-in-Lending regulations.

As they grew in number, sales finance companies were distinguished by whether or not they were operated as subsidiaries of major manufacturers. Subsidiaries of industrials came to be known as *captive finance companies,* while others were termed *independent finance companies.* Automobile and appliance manufacturers led the development of captive finance companies, and General Motors Acceptance Corporation and General Electric Credit Corporation are now familiar names to most consumers. The distinction between captive and independent continues to influence the financial strategies of finance companies, discussed in more detail later in the chapter.

Consumer Finance Companies.   About the same time sales finance companies emerged, the Russell Sage Foundation, a not-for-profit philanthropic organization based in New York, became concerned about the scarcity of consumer credit. Commercial banks were interested in business lending, and thrifts were interested in financing homes. Sometimes desperate consumers had few opportunities to obtain emergency cash except through loan sharks, who might demand "an arm and a leg" (literally and figuratively) in interest charges. The Russell Sage Foundation waged a nationwide campaign to reform state laws on consumer credit. The intent was to make consumer lending attractive to legitimate lenders, by permitting them to charge relatively high, but state-regulated, interest rates. *Consumer finance companies* arose in this new environment as providers of small, unsecured personal loans.

In recent years, the distinction between sales finance and consumer finance companies

has virtually disappeared. Most finance companies, captive or independent, make both unsecured and secured personal loans. Secured lending today includes residential mortgages and second mortgages (sometimes called *junior liens* to indicate their subordinate claim on mortgaged property).

Commercial Finance Companies.   As suggested by the opening comments on GE Credit, a third market in which finance companies have become active in recent years is commercial lending. In fact, in late 1986, business loans accounted for over 45 percent of the dollar volume of credit outstanding at finance companies, and at times recently business lending has approached 50 percent of total finance company lending.[3] Chapter 13 notes that, until recently, commercial banks shunned asset-based lending, or business loans collateralized by the borrower's inventory or receivables. *Commercial finance companies* arose to fill the need for this type of credit.

These companies are traced to the incorporation of the Mercantile Credit Company in Chicago in 1905. Its founders were encyclopedia salesmen who had suffered cash shortages but found no lenders interested in borrowers whose only assets were inventory and installment receivables. They left the encyclopedia business to found a specialized financial institution making cash loans collateralized by receivables. After 1954, states' widespread adoption of the Uniform Commercial Code clarified the rights of asset-based lenders and provided strong impetus for growth of commercial finance companies. Today, many such companies continue to provide short-term asset-based loans, but they also offer long-term commercial financing and leasing.[4]

At Last, a Definition.   The previous discussion explains why Fed economists define a finance company as

---

[2]Richard T. Selden, "Consumer-Oriented Intermediaries," in *Financial Institutions and Markets,* 2d ed. Murray Polakoff and Thomas A. Durkin, eds. (Boston: Houghton Mifflin, 1981), pp. 205-206.

[3]"Domestic Finance Companies, Assets and Liabilities," *Federal Reserve Bulletin* 73 (March 1987): A37.

[4]Doreen Wolchik, "History of Asset-Based Lending," unpublished paper, Citicorp Industrial Credit, 1984.

any company (. . . excluding banks, credit unions, savings and loan associations . . . and mutual savings banks) the largest portion of whose assets is in one or more of the following kinds of receivables . . . sales finance receivables, personal cash loans to individuals and families, short- and intermediate-term business credit, junior liens on real estate . . . . [5]

(No one claims economists are persons of few words.) Firms meeting this definition are profiled in the following paragraphs.

Current Industry Structure

All finance companies are stockholder-owned, but their ownership structures are not homogeneous. Some, like Household International, are independent, publicly held companies. Some, including (but not limited to) captive finance companies, are owned by nonfinancial firms. For example, Control Data Corporation, a computer firm, owns Commercial Credit. Others are operated as subsidiaries of financial institutions. In fact, because the Fed has determined that finance company activities are "closely related" to banking, some BHCs, especially those of money center banks, operate finance subsidiaries.

The number of finance companies has declined in recent years, down from nearly 3,400 in 1975 to fewer than 1,800 in 1985.[6] Reasons for the decline are familiar: Competition and changing laws and regulations have resulted in merger or failure, as is the case with depository institutions. The financial management problems of finance companies are discussed more fully later.

The finance company industry is similar to depositories in another way, too: It consists of

many relatively small firms and a few very large institutions. Table 22.1 provides data on the number and size of finance companies as of 1985. About 75 percent of the firms in the industry had under $5 million in total loans outstanding; fewer than 5 percent of the firms were in the largest category. In fact, firms with receivables of $25 million or more accounted for more than 99 percent of total finance company assets in the industry, signifying a high degree of economic concentration.

As noted in Chapter 2, most states require finance companies to demonstrate to authorities that a new branch office will provide "convenience and advantage" to customers. Unlike depositories, however, finance companies are free from restrictions on interstate expansion. In the past, this relative freedom gave finance companies a competitive edge over depositories in reaching customers, and, consequently, the largest finance companies built extensive nationwide branch networks. Recently, the cost of operating "brick and mortar" branches has risen, and finance companies have turned to less expensive ways, such as mail solicitations, to attract customers and deliver services. The result is that the number of branch offices operated by finance companies declined about 25 percent between 1977 and 1985.[7]

ASSETS AND LIABILITIES OF FINANCE COMPANIES

The industry's asset and liability structure differs according to firm size. Data on the year-end 1985 balance sheets of finance companies are given in Table 22.2.

Assets of Finance Companies

Finance company portfolios, even more than those of depositories, are dominated by loans.

---

[5]Evelyn M. Hurley, "Survey of Finance Companies, 1980," *Federal Reserve Bulletin* 67 (May 1981): 402-403.

[6]These data, and many others cited in the chapter, are drawn from a series of quinquennial (occurring every five years) surveys conducted by the staff of the Board of Governors of the Federal Reserve System. The most recent industry figures were generalized from those obtained from a systematic random sampling of firms in 1985. The sample included all finance companies with assets in excess of $25 million and selected smaller institutions. See

Hurley, "Survey of Finance Companies, 1980," for methodological details of typical surveys. Between these quinquennial studies, the Fed publishes quarterly updates of certain balance sheet data in the *Federal Reserve Bulletin.*

[7]Thomas A. Durkin, "Finance Companies 1977-1985," *Finance Facts,* May-June 1986.

Table 22.1
Distribution of Finance Companies
by Size of Loan Portfolio, June 1985

Size Category	Number of Firms in Category	% of Total Firms	Assets of Firms in Category (Millions)	% of Total Assets
Under $5 million	1,287	74.09%	$ 857	0.29%
$5 to $24 million	161	9.27	2,028	0.70
$25 to $99 million	96	5.53	5,639	1.94
$100 to $499 million	115	6.62	25,530	8.78
$500 million and over	78	4.49	256,652	88.29
Total, all sizes	1,737	100.00%	$290,706	100.00%

Source: Board of Governors of the Federal Reserve System, unpublished data, 1987.

Table 22.2
Balance Sheet of Finance Companies, Year-End 1985

	Billions		% of Total	
Assets				
Consumer receivables		$120.8		39.62%
Business receivables		152.8		50.11
Wholesale paper	$34.9		11.44%	
Retail paper	34.9		11.45	
Lease paper	55.4		18.16	
Other business credit	27.6		9.06	
Real estate loans		30.4		9.97
Total receivables, gross		$304.0		
Less unearned income and allowance for losses		(45.9)		−15.05
Total receivables, net		$258.1		84.65%
Other assets		46.8		15.35
Total assets		$304.9		100.00%
Liabilities and Net Worth				
Bank loans		$ 21.0		6.89%
Commercial paper		96.9		31.78
Other short-term debt		17.2		5.64
Long-term debt		93.1		30.53
Other liabilities		39.6		12.99
Total liabilities		$267.8		87.83%
Net worth		37.1		12.17
Total liabilities and net worth		$304.9		100.00%

Source: Prepared by the authors with data from the *Federal Reserve Bulletin* 73 (February 1987), p. A37.

The importance of different types of receivables, however, has changed over time.

Consumer Lending. The industry originated to supply consumer loans, and finance companies of all sizes are active in this market. Although not shown in the table, for small firms, consumer lending comprises over 50 percent of total assets. Within consumer lending, personal cash loans are more important for small companies, but automobile loans are more important for large firms. Sometime car loans are made directly by a finance company; at other times, a car dealer originates the transaction and sells the loan contract to a finance company. Finance companies also finance mobile homes and consumer goods as diverse as furniture, appliances, boats, and private planes.

Business Lending. Although business receivables are held by most finance companies, large firms hold more. As with depositories, large companies are able to offer a wider variety of services. Small institutions, with fewer personnel and facilities, can often offer only the basics. Large finance companies make larger loans, too, for reasons that become clear as sources of funds are considered. Historically, regardless of size, most finance companies have served small and medium-sized businesses.[8]

Wholesale paper includes manufacturers' loans to dealers, later purchased by finance companies. A typical transaction involves a loan by a large manufacturer, such as John Deere, to a rural farm implement dealer. If a finance company later purchases the loan from Deere, it appears as a receivable on the finance company's books. Because the dealer is not the ultimate user of the goods, the financial transaction is termed a wholesale one. In contrast, the category *retail paper* under the business receivables heading includes credit arising from the final sale of goods to business firms, such as the purchase by IBM of cars for its executives. Because IBM is the ultimate user of the cars, the transaction is a retail one, although it is business lending because household consumers are not involved.

Business lending by finance companies also includes leasing, which more than doubled from 1980 to 1985. Finally, asset-based lending (under "other business credit") accounts for most business loans at small finance companies.

Real Estate Loans. Real estate lending is a relatively recent addition for finance companies. In the early 1980s, they showed a decided preference for second mortgages because yields on junior liens are higher than on first mortgages, to compensate for the subordinate claim on the property in case of default. Still, even a secondary claim on real property is less risky for the lender than a personal cash loan to a consumer. For the borrower, the cost of a second mortgage loan may be lower than that of a personal cash loan, because collateral is involved. In the high-interest environment of the early 1980s, finance company customers took note of the lower-cost borrowing opportunity, and second mortgage financing grew.

As interest rates fell in the mid-1980s, borrowers lost interest in second mortages. In addition, high delinquency rates on first mortgages made second mortgages seem even riskier to lenders, so the growth of junior lien financing plummeted. Tax reform measures passed in 1986, eliminating interest deductions on many consumer loans but not on second mortgages, may renew demand.

Unearned Income and Allowance for Losses. The account called unearned income and allowance for losses is the sum of interest on discounted loans and the allowance for expected loan losses. The 1985 figure in Table 22.2 is the total for all loans; amounts for each category were unavailable. As with large commercial banks, the Tax Reform Act of 1986 requires finance companies to eliminate loan loss allowances over a four-year period that began in 1987.

---

[8]For more information on historical trends in business lending by finance companies, see Maury Harris, "Finance Companies as Business Lenders," *Quarterly Review,* Federal Reserve Bank of New York 4 (Summer 1979): 35-39.

Other Assets. The miscellaneous category called other assets includes premises, cash, investments in subsidiary companies, and securities. The securities holdings of finance companies are conspicuous by their absence, providing one of the major differences between depositories and finance companies.

Liabilities and Net Worth of Finance Companies

The sources of funds for finance companies differ somewhat from those of depositories.

Bank Loans. Most bank borrowing is by small finance companies. The reason will become clear in the discussion of other funding sources.

Commercial Paper. Almost one-third of the funds of finance companies are raised through commercial paper. Because only large, nationally known firms raise money in this market, commercial paper is inaccessible to the small firms that make up most of the industry. Further, because commercial paper is sold only in large denominations, small firms do not need the quantity of funds that typically must be raised in a commercial paper issue. In 1985, for example, only 78 finance companies accounted for 93 percent of the industry's outstanding commercial paper.[9] As noted, small finance companies rely more heavily on commercial bank financing.

Other Liabilities. The remaining liability categories—other short-term debt, long-term debt, and other liabilities—represent a variety of sources.[10] Large firms have greater access to

the bond markets, so they rely more heavily on long-term borrowings than do small finance companies. In addition, large firms are more heavily involved in mortgage lending and leasing, two activities contributing to longer asset portfolio maturities. From a maturity-matching perspective, long-term funds are more attractive to large firms than to small finance companies whose assets are concentrated in relatively short-term consumer cash loans.

Net Worth. For the industry as a whole, net worth is just over 12 percent of total sources of funds. Large firms are more highly leveraged, however, and small finance companies rely on equity for almost half of their financing. Clearly, returns to shareholders of large finance companies are potentially much more variable. The industry profile is consistent with that of depository institutions, because large depositories are more highly leveraged than small ones. The limited access of small institutions to the money and capital markets helps to account for their more conservative financial structures. But even the largest finance companies use less leverage than small depositories, for reasons explained later.

INCOME, EXPENSES, AND PROFITABILITY OF FINANCE COMPANIES

Little information is available on the income, expenses, and profitability of finance companies, because Fed surveys, on which previous asset and liability data are based, do not include income statement information. Fortunately, the American Financial Services Association, a trade organization for finance companies, annually collects data from voluntarily reporting finance companies. Table 22.3 contains selected information from a subsample of consistently reporting firms over the period 1977-1985.

---

[9]Board of Governors of the Federal Reserve System, unpublished data, 1987.

[10]A small proportion of these liabilities is savings deposits and saving certificates that are deposit-type liabilities of "industrial" or "Morris plan" banks. These financial institutions, of which there were over 1,000 in 1984, are small state-chartered finance companies authorized to make installment loans to consumers and small businesses. They are concentrated in only a few states, and are not considered commercial banks because they do not

accept demand deposits. For more details, see Ysabel M. Burns and Thomas A. Durkin, "Industrial Banking Companies," *Finance Facts,* February 1984.

Table 22.3
Selected Income and Expense Data for Finance Companies, 1977-1985

	1977	1978	1979	1980	1981	1982	1983	1984	1985
Gross income/total assets	11.4%	12.0%	13.1%	15.0%	15.4%	16.0%	14.3%	14.2%	13.0%
Operating expenses/total assets	4.6	4.5	4.6	5.3	4.5	4.6	4.5	4.6	4.5
Cost of borrowed funds/total assets	4.7	5.4	6.8	8.0	9.4	8.9	6.8	7.2	6.2
Net income/total assets (ROA)	1.3	1.3	1.2	1.2	1.0	1.5	1.9	1.6	1.4
Net income/net worth (RONW)	11.2	11.3	10.6	9.6	8.6	12.2	18.3	15.4	16.1

Source: Thomas A. Durkin, "Finance Companies 1977-1985," *Finance Facts,* May-June 1986.

As the table shows, return on assets improved, as did return on net worth, following a periodic low in 1981. Reasons for the trends are seen in the first and third rows of the table. Between 1977 and 1981, interest costs increased more relative to total assets than did gross income, or interest revenues. As interest rates began to fall in 1982, interest costs as a percentage of assets declined more than gross income as a percentage of assets. In other words, finance company managers controlled the spread well enough between 1982 and 1985 to earn higher ROA and RONW than in the early part of the period.

A study by economists at the Federal Reserve Bank of New York found that from 1975-1984 large finance companies had higher ROAs and RONWs on a pretax basis than did commercial banks, although on an after-tax basis, banks had higher RONWs. During the last part of the period, however, the profitability of large finance companies improved considerably, and their ROA was more than twice as high as the ROA for banks (1.68 percent versus 0.71 percent). The researchers attributed the superior performance of finance companies to managers' ability to manage the spread and to the larger proportion of higher-yielding consumer loans in finance companies' portfolios.[11]

As in depositories, then, finance company managers must understand what affects the amount and stability of net interest income, or they cannot achieve the target level of RONW. The NIM is affected by the interest rate sensitivity of the company's assets and liabilities, and managers must pay attention to relative asset/liability maturities and to interest rate forecasts that may dictate a shift in maturity composition. In addition, because many large finance companies are highly leveraged but have no insured liabilities, asset quality—especially the default risk exposure of receivables—is a significant management concern. Not only does poor asset quality depress earnings in a single period, through loan losses charged off, it affects expected future earnings. If a finance company's investors believe its assets have deteriorated, they will demand higher yields to compensate for the additional risk, squeezing NIM in later periods. Ultimately, investors may refuse to provide funds at any price. These issues are addressed in the discussion of asset/liability management topics in the next sections.

ASSET MANAGEMENT

Because finance companies do not offer transactions accounts, they are not subject to reserve requirements or to unanticipated withdrawal of funds by investors. Maturity dates on bank notes, commercial paper, and long-term debt are known in advance, so liquidity planning is

---

[11]Federal Reserve Bank of New York, *Recent Trends in Commercial Bank Profitability* (New York: Federal Reserve Bank of New York, 1986), pp. 277-281.

easier for finance companies than it is for depositories. This explains finance companies' relatively low holdings of cash and securities. Of course, loan demand cannot be completely anticipated, and maturing liabilities must be repaid or rolled over, so cash flow planning cannot be ignored. Generally, however, default risk and interest sensitivity are more important managerial considerations.

Default Risk

Like depositories, finance companies must assess the credit worthiness of businesses and/or consumers. Issues central to credit analysis, presented in Chapters 13 and 14, apply to the management of finance companies. In addition, finance companies face special credit analysis problems because of the types of loans on which they concentrate.

Unsecured Personal Loans.   For the industry as a whole, and especially for its many small companies, personal cash loans are major assets. These loans are relatively small, and the cost of administering each one is high as a proportion of loan size.[12] Personal cash loans are also unsecured. Together, these factors allow the lender to charge a higher interest rate than on automobile or other collateralized loans.

With the expected higher yield to the lender comes greater default risk. Relatively high interest rates not only dissuade applicants who can get more favorable terms elsewhere, they increase the borrower's repayment requirements. Thus, assessing the borrower's willingness and ability to repay—or his character and capacity, two of the "Cs of credit" mentioned in Chapter 13—is particularly important. Because individuals do not supply audited financial statements, accurate assessment is often more difficult than with business borrowers. Information such as past credit history, occupation, age, income, and existing assets and liabilities are critical proxies for character and capacity.

Second Mortgage Loans.   Second mortgage loans are riskier than first mortgages, because if a borrower defaults, the second mortgage holder's position is subordinate to that of the first mortgage lender. Since 1979, the availability of private mortgage insurance on second mortgages has diminished that risk somewhat. Nonetheless, default risk remains. A recent study by the National Second Mortgage Association showed that delinquency rates on second mortgages were highest at finance companies and lowest at commercial banks, thrifts, and mortgage banks. Uncertainty in finance company cash flows is further increased by growth in the proportion of second mortgage loans with variable rates.[13]

Riskiness of Finance Company Borrowers. Complicating credit analysis is the fact that finance company borrowers often have no previous financial relationship with the lender. In contrast, borrowers from depositories usually have a deposit account. Thus, managers of finance companies cannot directly examine how the potential borrower handles finances. It is often alleged, in fact, that consumers who borrow from finance companies would not do so if they qualified for loans at depositories. This allegation implies that consumer lending is riskier for finance companies than for other suppliers of consumer credit.

It is interesting to examine the direct and indirect evidence for that contention. A recent study of borrowers at commercial banks and finance companies found that about 75 percent of the finance company borrowers would also have qualified for loans using typical commercial bank credit standards. Finance company borrowers, however, *perceived themselves* as less credit worthy than bank borrowers and believed they were more likely to receive credit at a fi-

---

[12]An analysis of operating costs relative to loan size in finance companies is provided in George J. Benston, "Rate Ceiling Implications of the Cost Structure of Consumer Finance Companies," *Journal of Finance* 21 (September 1977): 1,169-1,194.

[13]Dru Johnston Bergman, "Second Mortgages Build Image as First Class Investment," *Freddie Mac Reports* 3 (November 1985): 1-2.

nance company than at a bank. The authors concluded that the market for consumer credit was not segmented because of lenders' views of credit risk, but because of consumer choice.[14]

The same authors found evidence, however, that some financial characteristics of finance company borrowers differ significantly from those of depository institution borrowers. For example, borrowers from banks had significantly higher average monthly incomes and greater average total assets, conditions confirmed in a later survey by researchers at the Fed. Selected results from the Fed survey are shown in Table 22.4, which compares non-mortgage borrowers from four financial institutions.

Much of the financial data are median figures, so 50 percent of the borrowers from a particular lender ranked above the relevant number in the table and 50 percent ranked below. Depository institution borrowers had higher median incomes and accumulated financial assets than finance company borrowers, even though the mean age of borrowers was about the same. The results suggest that most families who used finance company credit had lower incomes and fewer assets on which to draw in case of emergencies than did borrowers from depository institutions. Finance company borrowers, however, had less consumer debt outstanding. They were also less likely to be homeowners or to have credit cards, so they were less able to tap equity accumulated in a home or a line of credit on a bank card than were depository borrowers.

Although these data do not prove that finance company borrowers are greater credit risks than depository institution borrowers, they do show that, on average, finance companies lend to consumers with fewer financial resources. Careful personal credit analysis is an essential element of finance company manage-

ment, and credit-scoring models have been developed for this purpose. Managers must also establish systems to monitor the payment performance of individual loans, as well as policies for collecting on delinquent receivables.

Effect of Bankruptcy Legislation on Consumer Credit. The impact on depositories of recent changes in personal bankruptcy laws is discussed in Chapter 14, but no financial institutions have been more affected than finance companies. The first year the 1978 Bankruptcy Reform Act went into effect, making it easier for consumers to declare bankruptcy while retaining many of their assets, loan losses at finance companies more than doubled. In fact, the bankruptcy law changes explain the large increase in operating expenses of finance companies in 1980, shown in Table 22.3. Another bad year was 1981; profits for the industry as a whole fell 20 percent. GE Credit, for example, estimated that by 1982, 3,085 consumer borrowers *per month* were declaring bankruptcy.[15]

Finance companies' responses to these events are a good illustration of the regulatory dialectic. They reacted to soaring bankruptcies in two ways. The first was to diversify away from unsecured consumer lending. Some firms virtually shut down traditional personal cash-lending operations. Large firms' move into second mortgage lending, already evident by 1980, accelerated. By 1981, they had an estimated 40 percent share of the market for second mortgage loans.

On a second front, the industry worked to change bankruptcy laws at the state level. The 1978 federal bankruptcy law preempted state bankruptcy statutes unless states specifically passed new ones. Armed with an industry-financed study by researchers at Purdue University, demonstrating that almost 30 percent of

---

[14]Robert W. Johnson and A. Charlene Sullivan, "Segmentation of the Consumer Loan Market," *Journal of Retail Banking* 3 (September 1981): 1-7. Similar findings were reported by Gregory E. Boczar using data from 1970 in "Competition between Banks and Finance Companies: A Cross Section Study of Personal Loan Debtors," *Journal of Finance* 33 (March 1978): 245-258.

[15]Some of the information in this and the following paragraphs is drawn from "A New Source of Mortgage Money," *Business Week,* March 23, 1981, p. 95; "Finance Companies Show the Strain," *Business Week,* March 22, 1982, pp. 80-81; "The Allure of Second Mortgages," *Business Week,* March 16, 1981, p. 126; "Turning Back a Tide of Personal Bankruptcy," *Business Week,* June 14, 1982, p. 32.

Table 22.4
Comparison of Characteristics among Finance Company and
Depository Institution Borrowers, 1983

Borrower Characteristic	Lender			
	Commercial Bank	Thrift	Credit Union	Finance Company
Average age of family head (years)	40	41	39	39
Median 1982 family income	$24,200	$26,800	$32,200	$23,080
Median checking account balance	$300	$300	$300	$200
Median liquid assets	$1,398	$3,863	$2,453	$950
Median financial assets	$1,800	$4,300	$2,815	$1,000
Median consumer debt outstanding	$4,430	$4,365	$4,705	$4,183
Percentage of homeowners	68	74	74	62
Percentage with bank credit card	54	56	60	44

Source: Prepared by the authors with data from Robert B. Avery et al., "Survey of Consumer Finances, 1983: A Second Report," *Federal Reserve Bulletin* 70 (December 1984): 866-867.

those declaring bankruptcy under the 1978 law could have repaid their debts from future income, finance companies began lobbying in earnest. By mid-1982, 33 states had enacted new bankruptcy legislation, in most cases less lenient than the 1978 federal law, although still more generous to debtors than before 1978. In June 1984, a new federal bankruptcy law was passed, making it more difficult for debtors to abuse their credit privileges by declaring bankruptcy. The new law has encouraged the reentry of finance companies into the market for personal cash loans, although many observers believe the losses of the early 1980s were so severe that the largest firms will never return to their former prominence in that market.

Credit Risk and Business Lending.   Finance companies also face special problems in granting business credit, because the majority of their commercial borrowers are small to medium-sized. The failure rate among small businesses is higher than for large ones, and in times of economic hardship, small businesses' financial difficulties are especially severe. In 1981, for example, when many finance companies were turning away from consumer credit for reasons previously discussed, the business failure rate

jumped 45 percent, putting further pressure on finance company earnings during that difficult time.

In addition, the effects of a recession on creditors are often felt long after an economic upturn, as lenders write off loans that went sour during the slump. Commercial loan losses continued to be high for finance companies into the mid-1980s, even though most economists view that period as one of economic expansion. Thus, finance company managers must not only conduct a thorough credit analysis of individual borrowers, they must also keep a watchful eye on the overall level of credit risk to which the company is exposed in case of an economic downturn.

Additional Influences on the Extension of Credit

Like other consumer lenders, finance companies are affected by state usury laws. Chapter 14 notes that one impact of binding usury ceilings is to make less credit available to borrowers at depository institutions. The same effect has been observed for finance company borrowers. One study of finance company lending noted that the ratio of consumer installment loans to total loans held by finance companies declined from 50 percent to 39 percent over the period 1965-1974, a period characterized by increasing interest rates but static usury ceilings in most states.[16] A similar decrease in available credit has occurred more recently. For example, as the general level of interest rates reached its historical high in 1981, Beneficial Corporation, the nation's second-largest consumer finance company, closed 400 of its 1,900 offices. The states in which offices were closed were those with the lowest usury ceilings. Because many state usury laws have been rewritten in the 1980s to permit higher ceilings, future problems they pose for finance companies will be less severe.

Other regulations affecting the consumer-lending operations of finance companies concern disclosure of terms and equal access to credit. Finance companies are required to comply with federal Truth-in-Lending legislation and with regulations governing nondiscriminatory credit-granting practices. Although these regulations benefit many borrowers, they add to finance companies' costs of offering consumer loans.

Interest Sensitivity of Assets

Because finance companies of all sizes rely on short-term sources of funds, their managers must be alert to the relationship between asset and liability maturities. The average maturity of commercial and consumer nonmortgage loans is shorter than for mortgages, so finance companies have never faced the large negative maturity GAP that thrifts face. But large finance companies, more dependent upon short-term financing than smaller, highly capitalized firms, now offer variable-rate consumer loans pegged to commercial paper or other short-term market rates. As in depositories, the objective of minimizing the GAP by matching maturities is to lock in a spread, reducing potential variability in NIM and RONW.

The attention given to rate sensitivity, however, varies based on whether the finance com-

pany is of the captive sales type. Many captive sales companies use credit terms to attract buyers for the parent company's products. This tactic was clearly seen in 1985 and 1986, when the captive finance subsidiaries of General Motors, Ford, Chrysler, and American Motors offered widely publicized below-market (as low as 0 percent in some cases!), fixed-rate financing to spur flagging automobile sales. The campaigns succeeded in increasing car sales, although they locked the captive finance companies into low returns on a portion of their asset portfolios for several years to come. Despite the pressure on captive finance company profits, some observers believe the campaigns may have succeeded in permanently attracting some borrowers away from depositories.[17]

New Directions in Asset Management

Like depositories, finance companies are expanding the scope of operations. New directions involve finance companies in financial markets they have previously ignored, creating opportunities and challenges both for them and for their competitors.

Secondary Mortgage Markets. As finance companies continue their activity in residential mortgages, they will no doubt become participants in the secondary mortgage markets. As noted in Chapter 18, the secondary markets provide opportunities for mortgage lenders to update yields by selling older mortgages and lending the proceeds at current market rates.

To add to the confusion, there is even a secondary market for second mortgages, important for finance companies because of their heavy investment in these loans. The secondary market for second mortgage loans is small but growing; Freddie Mac began purchasing selected types of second mortgages in 1981, and

---

[16]Benston, "Rate Ceiling Implications of the Cost Structure of Consumer Finance Companies," p. 1,193.

[17]Details on the interest rate reduction programs of auto manufacturers' captive finance companies are discussed in Charles A. Luckett, "Recent Developments in Automobile Finance," *Federal Reserve Bulletin* 72 (June 1986): 355-365.

participation by other institutions had broadened significantly by 1985.[18]

The secondary mortgage markets are complex, however, and participants must appreciate the effect of interest rate risk on the market value of financial assets. Because finance company managers are more accustomed to analyzing credit risk, entry into the mortgage markets requires development of new expertise in risk analysis.

Secondary Markets for Automobile Loans.

An additional development of special interest to finance companies is securitization, especially of automobile loans. Described in Chapters 14 and 18, organized trading in car loans is one of the newest financial markets. Although depository institutions have access to these markets, it was actually the cooperation of finance companies and securities firms that first led to their development. In February 1985, the securities firm of Salomon Brothers bought $10 million in automobile loans from the Lloyd Anderson Group of finance companies. This transaction resulted in the first Certificates for Automobile Receivables, or CARs.

Like Ginnie Mae and Freddie Mac pass-throughs, borrowers' payments of principal and interest on automobile loans are passed through to investors in CARs. Shortly after the Lloyd Anderson Group transaction, Marine Midland Bank joined Salomon Brothers in the program, as did other securities firms and lenders throughout 1985. The size of the secondary market for automobile loans—and its credibility, according to many observers—was increased dramatically when GMAC, General Motors' captive finance company, packaged almost $1 billion in car and truck loans for sale in late 1985 and early 1986.[19]

Because finance companies recently have increased their share of the automobile loan market, developments in the market for CARs and related securities are important to them. Some observers are optimistic that CAR-type securities will be popular with investors because of their relatively short maturity, but others are less certain. Unlike Ginnie Mae or Freddie Mac pass-throughs, these securities lack government agency protection of investors against default by the automobile purchaser. In addition, some finance companies fear their images could be weakened by the sale of auto loans. This belief stems from the 1970s, when Chrysler's finance company subsidiary attempted to sell auto loans because it was perceived as so weak financially that it could not obtain cash elsewhere.[20]

Increasing Interest in the Primary Mortgage Market.

In 1986, GMAC purchased the mortgage lending and servicing units of a major commercial bank and a mortgage banker. In an effort to counteract cycles in automobile lending, the giant finance company launched a pilot program to offer home mortgages in Michigan to "better credit risks" among its existing borrowers. If the program succeeds, GMAC plans to expand it to its 250 offices nationwide, competing directly with local depositories.[21]

Issuance of Credit Cards.

Consumer finance companies are increasingly issuing credit cards instead of making personal cash loans. Not only are national cards such as Visa and MasterCard available from finance companies, but some large companies have issued "private label" credit cards as well. As noted earlier, branch networks have become more expensive, and lending via credit cards is a cheaper alternative. In addition, major card issuers have found that the loss rate on credit card loans is less than that on personal cash loans, because

---

[18]Bergman, "Second Mortgages Build Image as First Class Investment."

[19]"Receivables Are Receivables," *Financial World* 154 (March 6-19, 1985): 27; Harvey D. Shapiro, "Securitizing Corporate Assets," *Institutional Investor* 19 (December 1985): 225, 229; Wayne Olson, "Securitization Comes to Other Assets," *Savings Institutions* 107 (May 1986): 81-85.

[20]Ann Monroe, "Sales of Receivables by Big Firms Gain Respect in Public Offerings," *The Wall Street Journal,* December 2, 1985.

[21]Melinda Grenier Guiles, "GM to Begin Michigan Test of Home Loans," *The Wall Street Journal,* May 12, 1986, p. 5; Beth McGoldrick, "The Carmakers That Would Be Bankers," *Institutional Investor* 20 (February 1986): 175-177.

borrowers are anxious to avoid losing the convenience and prestige associated with the card.

Loan Participations with Commercial Banks. Now that commercial banks are more interested in asset-based lending, it is not unusual to see cooperative lending agreements between them and commercial finance companies. Because commercial finance companies are leaders in asset-based lending, banks, more accustomed to monitoring unsecured loans, depend on the expertise of finance companies for monitoring the receivables and inventory of firms to whom credit has been extended.

In a typical deal, a commercial finance company sells participations in an asset-based loan to banks in exchange for cash. Proceeds from the loan are then divided between the finance company and the banks according to their relative shares in the participation. Although some participations are actually arranged by banks, then sold to finance companies, most participations require the finance company to remain active in tracking the performance of the assets pledged as collateral. Often, because bank lending rates are lower than finance company rates, the borrower is given a "blended" rate reflecting the relative shares of the two lenders.[22]

LIABILITY AND CAPITAL MANAGEMENT

Although finance companies lack the benefits of deposit insurance, many finance companies, especially the largest ones, have a degree of flexibility in financing not shared by depositories. Finance companies are not directly subject to capital requirements, nor are they participants in the implicit and explicit interest competition that pervades the consumer deposit market. Thus, the specific liability management issues

they face differ from those faced by depositories. Still, managers of finance companies confront the same question facing managers of depository institutions: What financial structure will allow the institution to achieve its risk/expected return objectives?

Raising Funds Externally: Bond and Commercial Paper Markets

Because of the size of commercial paper issues and the methods of issuance, most commercial paper is held by institutional investors. Certainly that is true of finance company paper. Many long-term bonds issued by large finance companies are also held by large institutional investors. Through skillful negotiation with funds suppliers, large finance companies with access to both the commercial paper and long-term bond markets have opportunities to tailor the terms of their financing to conform to interest rate forecasts or to match the maturities of their planned asset structures.

Market Discipline. In exercising these opportunities, finance companies are subject to the market discipline from which depositories have thus far been largely exempt. One source of market discipline for finance companies is publicly disclosed risk ratings on their bonds and commercial paper. All the major rating agencies—Standard and Poor's Corporation, Moody's Investors Service, Duff & Phelps, Inc., and Fitch Investors Service, Inc.—focus heavily on asset quality, the primary determinant of future earnings. The views of the rating agencies can profoundly affect finance company performance. During finance companies' peak period of loan losses in the early 1980s, net earnings of the largest companies were further depressed by high interest costs, the result not only of an increase in interest rates but also of lowered bond and commercial paper ratings.

A watchful eye on the ratings keeps many large finance companies from using as much leverage as depositories because financial structure plays a role in the rating agencies' risk assessments. In 1985, for example, GE Credit had $1 of net worth for every $12 of assets, compared to about $1 of net worth to $16 of assets

---

[22]For more information on participations, see John Logan and Richard J. Dorgan, "Asset-Based Lending: You're Doing It, but Are You Doing It Right?" *Journal of Commercial Bank Lending* 67 (June 1984): 9-16; Richard J. Dorgan, "Banks Keen to Make Asset-Based Loans," *NCFA Journal* 40 (September 1984): 5-14.

at commercial banks. GE Credit's managers cited their desire to maintain high bond ratings as the major reason for maintaining the relatively high ratio.

Indirect Regulation.   In some states, regulators indirectly control finance company capital structures through their direct control of institutional investors such as insurance companies. Some regulated institutions can purchase bonds only if the issuing companies maintain minimum capital levels. A finance company needing access to these investors may be forced to limit its use of leverage, even in the absence of specific capital requirements.

Raising Funds Externally: Are Banks Allies or Competitors?

The discussion of finance company balance sheets indicates that some companies depend on bank financing as a major source of funds. At the same time, finance companies compete with banks for access to business and consumer borrowers. This cooperative/competitive relationship with banks is especially true for small finance companies, which depend much more on commercial bank financing than do large finance companies. Small companies are less likely, therefore, to price their loans aggressively to take business away from their funds suppliers, the banks.

Not so for large finance companies. Their access to the bond and commercial paper markets gives them more freedom to compete with commercial banks. Nowhere is this more evident than in the market for automobile loans. Figure 22.1 presents data on the market shares of automobile loans for finance companies and commercial banks over more than a decade. Although banks led finance companies in overall share in 1986, finance companies had clearly gained over the period, primarily because of the pricing policies of the largest finance companies.[23]

Depositories and finance companies continue to compete on other fronts as well. In 1986, Household International, the subject of the chapter's opening quotation, launched a nationwide banking operation under the name Household Bank, through its savings banks in Illinois, Maryland, and Ohio. Added to its 1,100 finance company offices, the firm expects to make major inroads into consumer banking on both the lending and deposit side by the end of the decade. At the same time, BankAmerica sold its consumer finance subsidiary to Chrysler, giving the automaker's captive finance arm an additional 267 branches. In 1985, Ford Motor Company bought First Nationwide Savings, a pioneer in interstate banking and franchising. Although the two were not formally combined, the president of First Nationwide reports to the president of Ford's finance subsidiary. In 1987, the two presidents announced that First Nationwide was launching a five-year campaign to open as many as 1,000 branch offices in K mart stores, hoping to become a major provider of financial services to middle-income households. Each of these developments suggests that finance companies intend to be major participants in the deregulated financial markets for years to come.[24]

USE OF OVERALL ASSET/ LIABILITY TECHNIQUES

In addition to specific management issues, finance company managers must consider integrated asset/liability management strategies.

---

[23]Credit unions are major participants in the automobile loan market, too, but their share of the market has been steadily declining since 1980. According to Federal Reserve statistics, at year-end 1980, CUs held 18 percent of automobile loans outstanding; by the end of 1985, their share had fallen to 14.8 percent. They have increased investments in other types of consumer loans, however, because they have maintained approximately 14% of the total volume of consumer loans. See Mark Tatge, "Banks in Tough Battle to Regain Car Loans," *Denver Post,* October 13, 1985, Section G, p. 1.; Board of Governors of the Federal Reserve, *Federal Reserve Bulletin,* various issues; National Credit Union Administration, *1985 Annual Report.*

[24]William Gruber, "Banking Is Latest Household Object," *Chicago Tribune,* March 7, 1986; McGoldrick, "The Carmakers That Would Be Bankers"; Jonathan B. Levine, "Attention, Savers! K mart Wants You," *Business Week,* January 19, 1987, pp. 81–82.

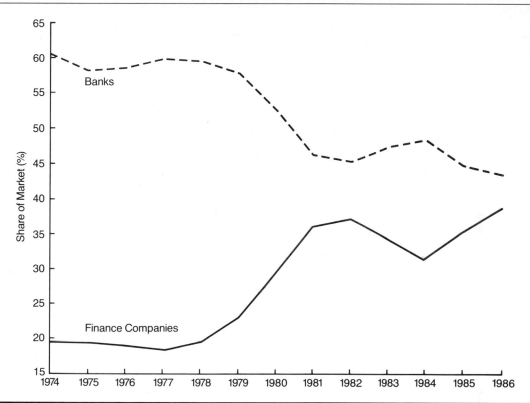

Figure 22.1
Percentage of Automobile Loans Held

Source: *Federal Reserve Bulletin,* various issues.

Many techniques discussed earlier in the text, such as the use of secondary asset markets to restructure portfolios and the use of variable-rate lending, are already in place in finance companies. In addition, approaches such as GAP management, on both a maturity and duration basis, and the use of financial futures to lock in borrowing costs in a rising-rate environment are as applicable to finance companies as they are to depositories. The risks and rewards of using these techniques are similar regardless of the type of institution, although finance companies enjoy fewer legal restrictions on their use of futures and options than do depositories. At present, however, there are no data indicating the extent to which finance companies use these tools for asset/liability management.

PERFORMANCE MEASUREMENT IN FINANCE COMPANIES

Potential creditors and stockholders, as well as finance company managers, are interested in assessing the performance of individual firms. The process is similar in most ways to analyzing the performance of an individual depository institution. Financial ratios are calculated, then compared to the firm's past history and to financial data for similar firms. Using these comparisons in conjunction with other information about the company, such as off-balance sheet commitments, the analyst draws inferences about the firm's prospects.

Sources of Industry Financial Information

Because a wide variety of firms are defined as finance companies, it is more difficult to identify a peer group to which to compare an individual company than it is to identify peer group depositories. With the use of careful judgment, however, several sources of financial data on finance companies are available.

One publicly available data base on finance company performance is compiled by the First National Bank of Chicago and summarized annually in the *Journal of Commercial Bank Lending,* a publication of Robert Morris Associates, a trade organization for commercial lenders. Separate data are shown for consumer finance companies and diversified (both commercial and consumer) finance companies. Although the primary purpose of these data is to assist bankers who lend to finance companies, they also contain ratios of interest to shareholders.

The American Financial Services Association (AFSA) conducts an annual survey of finance companies, including information on year-end balance sheets and income statements of participating institutions. A document entitled *Research Report on Finance Companies* is published annually and is available from the AFSA. The National Commercial Finance Association, a trade organization for asset-based lenders, compiles financial ratios annually; information is available to members only. Finally, economists at the Fed, besides conducting comprehensive studies of finance company balance sheets every five years, provide monthly updates of key balance sheet accounts for the industry in the *Federal Reserve Bulletin.*

All of these sources, however, provide only aggregate data for groups of firms; information on the "best" or "worst" performing companies is not presented. For information on finance companies given by quartiles, Dun and Bradstreet's *Key Business Ratios* is a source. Un-

fortunately, the ratios given by D&B are not necessarily the areas of greatest interest to the analyst.

Important Financial Ratios for Finance Companies

The important dimensions of finance company performance are similar to those used to assess depository institution performance: liquidity and portfolio management, leverage, efficiency and productivity, and profitability. Table 22.5 contains a representative set of ratios for the financial analysis of a finance company, as well as industry averages for two broad subgroups in the industry. Except as noted in the following discussion, data used to construct these ratios, and their interpretation, are similar enough to the presentation in Chapter 21 that they are not repeated here.

Liquidity.   Because finance companies have few investments in securities, asset liquidity is best measured by the amount of actual cash on hand relative to the short-term obligations of the firm. Another view of liquidity is the proportion of receivables to be repaid within one year. Thus, Ratios 22.1 and 22.2 assist the analyst in estimating how easily the company's assets can be converted to cash.

Like depositories, however, finance companies may also meet liquidity needs through liability management. The dollar amount of unused credit lines arranged through commercial banks, compared to the amount of debt already outstanding (Ratio 22.3) provides an indication of the company's ability to generate cash from additional borrowing. Information on unused credit lines is found in footnotes to the company's annual report.

Credit Risk.   Because personal cash loans are among the riskiest made by finance companies, the ratio of those loans to total credit extended by the company (Ratio 22.4) suggests the overall riskiness of the portfolio. In addition, a measure of credit risk using net chargeoffs is relevant (Ratio 22.5). As with depository institutions, however, the analyst must recognize

Table 22.5
Selected Performance Measures for Finance Companies

Ratio		Consumer Finance Industry Averages 1985	Diversified Finance Industry Averages 1985
Liquidity			
22.1	Cash/Short-Term Debt	1.53%	2.05%
22.2	Receivables Maturing in 12 Months/ Total Receivables	—	38.36%
22.3	Unused Credit Lines/Total Debt	—	—
Credit Risk			
22.4	Direct Cash Loans/Gross Receivables	47.87%	9.58%
22.5	Net Chargeoffs/Average Net Receivables	1.48%	—
Leverage			
22.6	Total Debt/Net Worth	5.56 times	6.98 times
22.7	Interest Expense/Average Net Receivables	9.12%	8.20%
Efficiency/Productivity			
22.8	Operating Expenses (Exclusive of Loan Loss Expense)/Average Net Receivables	8.83%	4.20%
22.9	Average Monthly Principal Collections/ Average Net Monthly Receivables	5.20%	—
22.10	Annual Gross Finance Revenues/ Average Net Receivables	26.15%	17.37%
Profitability			
22.11	Net Finance Profit/Average Net Receivables	3.24%	2.19%
22.12	Net Interest Margin = (Gross Finance Revenue − Interest Expense)/ Average Net Receivables	17.03%	9.17%
22.13	Return on Net Worth = Net Income/ Average Net Worth	18.24%	14.78%

Source: Raymond M. Neihengen, Jr., and Mark L. McClure, "Analysis of Finance Company Ratios in 1985," *Journal of Commercial Bank Lending* 69 (September 1986): 47–56.

that this is an *ex post,* not an *ex ante,* measure of risk.

Leverage.   In addition to familiar measures of leverage, such as total debt to net worth (Ratio 22.6), it is useful to compare interest expense to receivables (which for most finance companies are approximately equal to total earning assets).

Not only when compared to the figure for other firms, but also when used as part of a trend analysis of a single company, this ratio (Ratio 22.7) provides a good indication of a firm's debt service burden.

Efficiency/Productivity.   As with depositories, how well a finance company controls its nonlending operating expenses affects its performance. Ratio 22.8, which compares these expenses to average net receivables, is one measure of operating efficiency. Additional measures of productivity are Ratios 22.9 and 22.10. Ratio 22.9 is average monthly principal collections to average monthly net receivables. When calculated over a period of time, this ratio may indicate the thoroughness of the firm's collection and loan-monitoring policies. A declining trend indicates either that the firm is increasing the maturity of its loan portfolio and, as a result, a smaller amount of principal is collected on loans made recently, or that efforts to collect are more lax than in the past. Either way, questions should be asked. One cautionary note: The schedule of collections can be difficult to obtain. A firm may include some of this information in footnotes to the financial statements, but if not, unpublished information is necessary.

The last ratio in this category, Ratio 22.10, compares total revenue from finance operations to average receivables, and is analogous to asset utilization for depositories. It reveals how much revenue was generated per dollar loaned during the period. For example, Table 22.5 shows that for consumer finance companies as a whole in 1985, 26.15 cents of finance revenue was returned to the firm for every dollar of credit extended. Because some finance companies have nonfinance subsidiaries, the intent of this ratio is to focus only on the firm's financial operations. For finance companies that have not diversified beyond lending, the numerator of Ratio 22.10 would be total revenues.

Profitability.   Ratio 22.11, comparing the net profit on financial operations to average net receivables, is analogous to measuring the net rate of return on earning assets in other firms. Similarly, Ratio 22.12 is a measure of the net interest margin. Finally, Ratio 22.13 is a standard measure of RONW.

SUMMARY

Finance companies are diverse financial institutions grouped together under one industry classification. They share an emphasis on consumer and business lending, and they differ from depositories in their lack of deposits as a source of funds. The industry was historically grouped into sales, personal, and commercial finance companies, although these distinctions are now blurred.

The vast majority of assets in the industry is invested in loans, although proportions invested in different loan categories vary by firm size and type. Large finance companies raise funds in the money and capital markets, and finance companies of all sizes borrow from commercial banks.

A significant issue in asset management of finance companies is default risk. Unsecured personal loans and second mortgage loans have a great potential for loss. Lending policies are governed by federal and state consumer protection laws. Like depositories, finance companies must also consider the maturities of funds sources when selecting asset maturities.

In response to recent operating difficulties, finance companies have introduced new products or techniques, many of which are part of an integrated asset/liability strategy. Sales of real estate and automobile loans in the secondary markets; issuance of credit cards; entry into the primary mortgage market; and asset-based loan participations all provide managerial flexibility. Entry into these markets makes finance companies more competitive with depositories, and analysis of finance company performance uses ratios similar to those used for depositories.

Questions

1. What two characteristics do all finance companies have in common? Into what three categories have finance companies traditionally been divided? Why?

2. Explain how the size of a finance company affects its asset and liability structure.

3. Why have some finance companies shown more interest in second mortgages than first mortgages? What risks are associated with junior liens?

4. Compare the major issues in the asset management of finance companies with those in depository institutions. What reasons can you give for the differences?

5. Based on research findings comparing finance company and commercial bank borrowers, what characteristics do each possess? Do finance companies face greater credit risks? What are the implications for credit analysis of finance company applicants?

6. What actions did finance companies take to combat bankruptcy legislation enacted in 1978? Explain them in the context of the regulatory dialectic. What were the results of these actions?

7. Finance companies are becoming increasingly involved in the secondary mortgage markets, credit cards, and securitization. What are the financial benefits and risks of each area?

8. Explain the competitive/cooperative relationship between finance companies and commercial banks. How does the size of a finance company affect this relationship?

9. At a recent speech attended by the authors, the chairman of Chrysler Corporation's captive finance company said he "felt sorry" for banks. What do you think he meant? If you were a banker, what would be your reaction to such a comment?

10. As noted in the chapter, in the mid-1980s several large manufacturers offered low-interest-rate loans through their captive finance companies. Some commercial banks charged that these low rates were deceptive, because the manufacturers compensated for the financing costs by raising prices on the cars. Do you agree with the bankers, or with the finance companies? Do such special offers violate the spirit of Truth-in-Lending legislation if they are accompanied by higher prices? Why or why not?

11. Explain how financial analysis of finance companies resembles that of depository institutions. How is it different? What sources of industry performance information are available for finance companies?

Problem

1. The financial statements for the American Credit Corporation for the year ending December 31, 19XX, are provided in the following tables. American Credit is a subsidiary of a large, diversified firm that your company may acquire. As a member of the financial analysis staff, you have been asked to assess the financial position of the finance subsidiary. The notes to American Credit's financial statements indicate that the firm has lines of credit with various financial institutions totaling $5.5 million.

   a. Use the ratios and industry average data provided in Table 22.5 to evaluate the liquidity, leverage, and efficiency of American Credit.

   b. Is American Credit's profitability at an acceptable level? Its level of risk? Why or why not?

   c. Based on these ratios, would you consider American Credit a desirable acquisition? Why or why not?

   d. If American Credit were a consumer finance company, what differences would you expect to find in its financial statements? Why? In your opinion, would those differences be associated with more or less exposure to credit risk? Why?

Problem 22.1

**American Credit Corporation
Statement of Financial Position
as of December 31, 19xx
(Thousands)**

Assets

Cash and short-term investments		$ 78.1
Marketable securities		308.3
Financing receivables		
Installment credit	$ 883.1	
Retailer financing	898.5	
Commercial loans	685.8	
Equipment sales financing	407.4	
Real estate loans	610.3	
Leases	1,973.9	
Other	320.2	
Total receivables, gross	5,779.2	
Less unearned income and allowance for losses	(553.1)	
Total receivables, net		5,226.1
Buildings and equipment		355.7
Other assets		187.5
Total Assets		$6,155.7

Liabilities and Net Worth

Notes payable within one year	$2,808.2	
Notes payable after one year	1,353.0	
Total notes payable	$4,161.2	
Accounts payable	167.1	
Other liabilities	804.9	
Total liabilities		$5,133.2
Preferred stock	$ 30.2	
Common stock	223.7	
Additional paid-in capital	130.4	
Retained earnings	638.2	
Total net worth		1,022.5
Total Liabilities and Net Worth		$6,155.7

Problem 22.1 (*continued*)

**American Credit Corporation
Statement of Earnings
for Year Ending December 31, 19xx
(Thousands)**

Earned income		
Interest income	$507.9	
Lease income	228.2	
Other income	101.3	
Total earned income		$837.4
Expenses		
Interest expense	$358.6	
Operating and administrative expense	171.1	
Loan losses	37.0	
Other expense	144.6	
Total expenses		711.3
Income before taxes		$126.1
Taxes		19.5
Net income		$106.6
Cash dividends paid		$100.0

Selected References

American Financial Services Association. *Finance Facts*. Various issues.

Benston, George J. "Rate Ceiling Implications of the Cost Structure of Consumer Finance Companies." *Journal of Finance* 21 (September 1977): 1,169-1,194.

Boczar, Gregory E. "Competition between Banks and Finance Companies: A Cross Section Study of Personal Loan Debtors." *Journal of Finance* 33 (March 1978): 245-258.

Fooladi, Iraj, Gordon Roberts, and Jerry Viscione. "Captive Finance Subsidiaries: Overview and Synthesis." *Financial Review* 21 (May 1986): 259-275.

Harris, Maury. "Finance Companies as Business Lenders." *Quarterly Review* (Federal Reserve Bank of New York) 4 (Summer 1979): 35-39.

Hurley, Evelyn M. "Survey of Finance Companies, 1980." *Federal Reserve Bulletin* 67 (May 1981): 398-409.

Johnson, Robert W., and A. Charlene Sullivan. "Segmentation of the Consumer Loan Market." *Journal of Retail Banking* 3 (September 1981): 1-7.

Luckett, Charles A. "Recent Developments in Automobile Finance." *Federal Reserve Bulletin* 72 (June 1986): 355-365.

McGoldrick, Beth. "The Carmakers That Would Be Bankers." *Institutional Investor* 20 (February 1986): 175-177.

Neihengen, R. M., Jr. and Mark L. McClure. "Analysis of Finance Company Ratios in 1985." *Journal of Commercial Bank Lending* 69 (September 1986): 47-56.

Olson, Wayne. "Securitization Comes to Other Assets." *Savings Institutions* 107 (May 1986): 81-85.

Selden, Richard T. "Consumer-Oriented Intermediaries." In *Financial Institutions and Markets,* 2d ed. Edited by Murray Polakoff and Thomas A. Durkin. Boston: Houghton Mifflin, 1981, pp. 202-215.

Swift, John R. "Consumer Finance Companies: A Step Back and a Look Forward." *Journal of Commercial Bank Lending* 65 (January 1982): 53-54.

Chapter 23

INSURANCE COMPANIES

It is unlikely that the insurance industry ever again will return to simpler times when interest rate risk could be ignored. That is why asset/liability matching techniques are so important today.

Joseph M. Fitzgerald
Vice President
CIGNA Reinsurance (1984)

IN the summer of 1985, the life of an eight-pound poodle was saved by a pacemaker surgically implanted to regulate its heart. The poodle's owner paid only half the $1,500 bill because he had previously purchased a policy underwritten by the Veterinary Pet Insurance Company. For an annual premium ranging from $25 to $99, people could insure their canines or felines against the cost of "cat"-astrophic illness. As of 1985, 45,000 devoted pet owners, mostly Californians, had chosen to do so.[1]

Although Veterinary Pet is not an ordinary insurance company, it functions like more traditional insurance underwriters. For a fee, the company agrees to bear the financial risk of unforeseen events that adversely affect policyholders. Fees, called premiums, not needed for immediate payment of claims are invested by the firm to earn additional income. To the extent that premiums plus investment income earned in a period exceed the costs of claims and operating expenses during the same period, a company's owners benefit.

The financial opportunities and problems insurers face are both similar to and different from those faced by the institutions discussed in previous chapters. Similarities arise because

---

[1]Walt Bogdanich, "Coverage Provided by Specialty Insurance Is Relatively Expensive, Seldom Necessary," *The Wall Street Journal,* August 28, 1985, p. 19.

most assets of insurers are financial and subject to interest rate and other risks in the financial markets. Differences occur because most liabilities of insurers are neither deposits, commercial paper, nor bonds, but potential claims against the company by policyholders or their beneficiaries. Another difference between insurers and depositories, mentioned in Chapter 2, is that the McCarran-Ferguson Act of 1945 leaves the regulation of insurers to states. Examination of these similarities and differences is the objective of this chapter.[2]

AN INDUSTRY FOUNDED ON PROBABILITIES

The financial problems against which insurance companies provide risk protection span a broad spectrum, from the traumatic to the merely inconvenient. Most Americans are protected from multiple risks by a variety of insurance policies. According to a 1983 study, heading the list of insurance coverage is that for automobiles, held by 84 percent of the American public. Two-thirds of the population had purchased life insurance policies, and 50 percent had another life insurance policy provided by their employers. Duplicate health insurance policies are also common. Further, 65 percent of the population had homeowners' insurance, and these data do not reflect the many policies purchased each year by businesses and not-for-profit organizations.[3]

Policyholders Assess Probabilities

The public's ownership of insurance does not necessarily correspond to its estimate of the probability that it will actually need protection. Some people have insurance because an employer provides it or it is required with another financial transaction, such as a mortgage loan. More often, however, people buy insurance because they believe that the risk of loss without the policy is too great. In making a decision, the prospective policyholder considers not only the probability of loss but also the dollar amount of protection required if loss occurs. More formally, a person buys insurance if the expected value of a policy's benefits—emotional and financial—exceeds the present value of premiums required to obtain it.[4]

And So Do Insurers, but Differently

The insurer also must consider probabilities, but the insurer's task is different from the policyholder's. The policyholder asks, "What is the probability that a given loss will occur to *me*, and how much protection do I need if it does?"; the insurer asks, "Out of all the firm's policyholders, what proportion will make claims during the period, and how much will they cost?" The insurance company also must evaluate the probability of loss, but its real concern is with a statistical principle called the *"law of large numbers."* According to this law, one cannot determine the probability that an individual will die (or become disabled, or have an automobile accident, or lose a home in a fire) in a given period. However, the number of persons among a large group who will die or face other losses in a period is more predictable, especially when relevant demographic and other data are available on that group.

---

[2]As discussed initially in the context of depositories in Chapter 20, there are two major types of insurance activities: underwriting and brokerage. The management strategies discussed in this chapter are geared to firms acting primarily as underwriters. Firms operating as agencies, selling policies underwritten by others, are not discussed in the text, because their financial management problems are not particularly adaptable to the asset/liability framework.

[3]Louis Harris and Associates, "Public Attitudes toward Risk," Study No. 837008, August 1983, p. 59.

[4]For an analysis of the problem facing an individual purchasing an insurance policy, see Robert I. Meir and Sandra G. Gustavson, *Life Insurance: Theory and Practice* (Plano, TX: Business Publications, Inc., 1984), Chapter 2, pp. 25–29.

Ex ante loss prediction among a group of policyholders is usually based on analysis of *ex post* data from a similar group of insureds. Estimating the probability of losses of a certain type and size among a group of policyholders during a designated period is the business of **actuaries.** The difficulty of estimating probabilities differs, depending upon the event involved. For example, actuarial calculations of the mortality rate among a group of individuals are more reliable than estimates of the probability of property damage to their houses. The difference arises because random factors such as tornadoes, earthquakes, and vandalism play a large role in property damage, whereas a single nonrandom factor, age, is highly correlated with mortality.

This actuarial difference explains the traditional division of the insurance industry into the two major subgroups discussed at several points earlier in the book: life insurers and property and casualty (P&C) insurers. Underwriters of health insurance policies are usually grouped with life insurers because serious illness is correlated with age, although to a lesser extent than death.

Insurers use actuarial calculations not only to estimate probable cash outflows during a period but also to establish the premium payments necessary for cash inflows to be equal to or greater than expected cash outflows. An example of premium estimation is provided in the appendix to this chapter.

OWNERSHIP STRUCTURE OF THE INSURANCE INDUSTRY

Premiums on the many insurance policies Americans hold add up to big business. In 1985, the over 5,700 domestically chartered life and P&C insurance companies held more assets in total than any other financial institutions except commercial banks and thrifts. Insurers are both mutually and stockholder-owned. Table 3.3 indicates that in 1985, less than 6 percent of all life insurance companies were mutually owned. These firms, however, accounted for the majority of assets in the industry. In contrast, over 60 percent of P&C companies were mutually owned, although the majority of assets was concentrated in a few stock P&C insurers.[5]

The trend is away from mutual ownership, for the same reason as in the thrift industry: difficulty in generating net worth from internal sources alone. Chapter 2 notes that states impose minimum capital requirements on insurers selling policies in the state. Financial problems among both life and P&C companies have increasingly complicated the generation of capital through retained earnings. A solution short of failure is conversion to the stock form of organization. In addition to offering access to external sources of capital, conversion provides flexibility for financing future acquisitions and greater potential for diversification into other financial services. In addition, federal tax laws favorable to the mutual form of organization were revised in 1984, and the stock form is now financially more attractive than in the past.

Procedures by which mutual insurers may convert, and the consequences of doing so, are less clear than for mutually owned thrifts because the absence of federal regulation leaves conversion rules up to individual states. As a result, the number of mutuals actually converting during the 1980s has been lower than once anticipated, although many managers continue to publicly express their desire to do so.[6]

---

[5]American Council of Life Insurance, *1986 Life Insurance Fact Book,* p. 90; Insurance Information Institute, *1986-87 Property/Casualty Fact Book,* p. 11.

[6]Many large mutual insurers have home offices in New York, so New York regulations are often used as models for laws in other states. As of this writing, New York had not established firm guidelines for conversion, although several large mutual insurers in that state had expressed an interest in doing so. The National Association of Insurance Commissioners, a group of state regulators, is working on a model conversion law. See Laura Meadows, "Minuet in Maine," *Forbes* 136 (November 18, 1985): 208; and Ben Weberman, "The Stock Answer," *Forbes* 134 (December 3, 1984): 146, 151.

Meanwhile, the two largest mutuals, Prudential and Metropolitan Life, have discarded the idea of converting as a result of internal task force reports. Nevertheless, an Ernst and Whinney study found recently that over 50 percent of mutual life companies and 22 percent of P&C firms were considering demutualization. See Raymond A. Matison, "Bypassing Conversion," *Best's Review* 87

Apart from ownership structures, life and P&C insurers differ somewhat, so they are discussed separately.

ASSETS OF LIFE INSURERS

Like those of other financial institutions, the balance sheets of life insurers have changed in recent years. Some changes are responses to the deregulation of competitors, and others reflect changes in the economic environment.

Table 23.1 presents data on the assets of life insurers as of year-end 1985. Although all states permit the general types of investments outlined in this section, many states limit the *percentage* of the total portfolio that can be invested in specific categories, especially common stock and real estate.

Government Securities

Insurers hold substantial amounts of Treasury and federal agency securities, but have only small investments in state, local, and foreign government issues. Since 1973, when state, local, and foreign issues were more than 60 percent of all the governmental securities held by life insurers, the relative importance of various types of government securities has changed completely.[7]

Like finance companies, life insurers do not face unexpected deposit withdrawals, so their government securities portfolios are held primarily for purposes of investment, not liquidity. In recent years, however, life insurers have increased their holdings of Treasury bonds relative to long-term corporate obligations because T-bonds are much more marketable, should cash be required unexpectedly. Later in this chapter, the changing portfolio management strategies of life insurers is discussed further.

Corporate Securities

Life insurers are not bound by the same portfolio restrictions as are depositories, so their corporate holdings include common and preferred stock as well as bonds. Because of their low need for liquidity, insurers hold relatively few money market securities such as commercial paper and bankers acceptances, although the percentage has increased slightly in recent years.

Importance of Private Placements. Investment in corporate bonds is not new for life insurers; they have been the largest holders of corporate bonds since the 1930s. As of year-end 1985, in fact, they held about 50 percent of the domestic corporate bonds outstanding. Most are obtained through *private or direct placement,* involving face-to-face negotiation between a life insurer and a bond issuer. Although private placement has substantial advantages, because issues can be tailored to suit both borrower and lender, it also has risks. Of particular relevance to life insurers is the lack of a secondary market for privately placed bonds. Because private placements are not accompanied by the financial disclosure required in a public issue, they cannot be resold to the public. Consequently, privately placed bonds are some of the least liquid assets a financial institution can hold. As their liquidity needs have increased, life insurers have reduced somewhat the proportion of new funds they are willing to invest in private placements.[8]

Corporate Stock. Investment in corporate stock has increased in recent years for two reasons:

1. State laws have been liberalized to permit insurers to hold stock.

(May 1986): 40-48; and Mary Rowland, "Insurance," *Forbes* (Special Advertising Supplement) 136 (October 21, 1985): 12.

[7]Unless otherwise noted, the statistics cited here and later in the life insurance section of the chapter are drawn from various issues of the *Life Insurance Fact Book.*

[8]Timothy Curry and Mark Warshawsky, "Life Insurance Companies in a Changing Environment," *Federal Reserve Bulletin* 72 (July 1986): 449-460.

Table 23.1
Assets and Obligations of Life Insurance Companies, Year–End 1985 (2,260 Firmsª)

	Millions		% of Total	
Assets				
Government securities (includes Treasury, federal agency, state, local, and foreign governments)		$124,598		15.09%
Corporate securities		374,344		45.33
Bonds	$296,848		35.94%	
Stock	77,496		9.38	
Real estate loans		171,797		20.80
Farm mortgages	$ 11,852		1.44%	
Nonfarm conventional	159,945		19.37	
Real estate investments		28,822		3.49
Loans to policyholders		54,369		6.58
Other assets		71,971		8.71
Total Assets		$825,901		100.00%
Obligations and Net Worth				
Policy reserves		$665,302		80.55%
Life insurance	$235,854		28.56%	
Health insurance	18,805		2.28	
Annuities	405,931		49.15	
Other	4,712		0.57	
Policy dividend obligations		26,348		3.19
Accumulations	$ 14,638		1.77%	
Payable during the year	11,710		1.42	
Other obligations		77,471		9.38
Total obligations		$769,121		93.13%
Surplus	$54,039		6.54%	
Common stock	2,741		0.33	
Total net worth (surplus and common stock)		56,780		6.87
Total Obligations and Net Worth		$825,901		100.00%

ªThe total number of firms at year-end 1985 differs from the number shown in Table 3.3 because figures for stock and mutual firms in Table 3.3 are reported at mid-year.

Source: Prepared by the authors with data from the American Council of Life Insurance, *1986 Life Insurance Fact Book*.

2. The variable cash flows expected from stock are now more attractive because insurers' financial obligations have become less predictable.

More details are given later about the changing nature of these obligations.

Real Estate Loans and Investments

Because their liquidity needs are less than those of depositories, life insurers are well suited to make mortgage loans. In fact, mortgages are the second-largest category of life insurance assets. In the 1960s, almost 60 percent of the mortgages held by insurers were for 1- to 4-family homes, but the attractiveness decreased in the 1970s as interest rates rose and residential mortgage rates were held down by state usury laws. Today, the vast majority of insurers' mortgages are nonfarm conventional loans, made primarily to finance commercial properties or apartment buildings.

Unlike some depositories, life insurers are permitted to invest directly in real estate. Most of their real estate holdings are apartment buildings, shopping centers, and office complexes, on which they receive periodic cash inflows from rental or lease payments.[9] Direct real estate investment has increased as a proportion of assets over the last three decades, as firms have sought to increase the average return on assets. This category also includes investment in premises, a small proportion of total assets, as is common in financial institutions.

Loans to Policyholders

Loans to policyholders are personal cash loans to customers who have borrowed against the **cash values** of certain types of life insurance policies. The accumulated cash value of a policy is the total amount paid in premiums since the inception of the policy, less the cost of providing insurance protection over that period, plus interest or other benefits accruing on previously paid premiums.[10] Policies that accumulate a cash value permit the insured to borrow against that value on terms specified when the policy is written. The proportion of insurer assets devoted to policy loans has been higher in the 1980s than at any time since the 1930s. This

---

[9]For more details on the direct real estate investments and mortgage holdings of life insurers, see James R. Webb, "Real Estate Investment Acquisition Rules for Life Insurance Companies and Pension Funds: A Survey," *AREUEA Journal* 12 (Winter 1984): 495-520.

[10]The cash value of a policy is a complicated function of the face value of the policy, the period over which the premiums are to be paid, the interest rate paid on premiums not needed to provide death protection, and something actuaries call "survivorship benefits." There are many good, detailed treatments of the economics of life insurance policies. See, for example, Gustavson and Meir, *Life Insurance: Theory and Practice,* Chapter 3.

phenomenon is discussed in greater depth later in the chapter.

Other Assets

Liquidity differences between depositories and insurers are underscored by the fact that insurers have only 1 percent of their assets in cash. The miscellaneous category "other assets" also includes premiums due but not yet paid, and bond interest accrued but not received.

OBLIGATIONS OF LIFE INSURERS

Life insurers issue a large volume of financial liabilities, but these obligations are unlike those associated with deposits, bonds, or commercial paper.

Policy Reserves

By far the largest category of life insurance liabilities is **policy reserves.** Because the word *reserves* is used so often in financial institutions, it is easy to confuse its meaning in a given context. In depositories, cash held to meet regulators' reserve requirements is an asset of the institution. In thrifts and credit unions, the term *reserves* may be synonymous with capital or net worth. The policy reserves of insurance companies are liabilities, however, not assets or capital. Insurers' reserves are analogous to the deposits of a depository.

Estimation of Reserves.   The dollar amount of reserves is an estimate of the total present value of future financial obligations—that is, the total present value of expected death, medical, or lifetime income benefits the company may be required to pay to current policyholders. The amount, determined actuarially, considers the following information:

1. Mortality and morbidity (disease) rates, reflecting the reasons future claims will be made
2. The present value of future premium payments to be received from those currently insured

3. The expected rate of return on the company's investments

In sum, the reserves on a life insurer's balance sheet are the present value of expected claims, *net* of the present value of estimated receipts of premium and investment incomes.

Reserves for Annuities.

Table 23.1 indicates that the largest single category of reserves is not for outstanding life insurance policies, but for **annuity policies.** In addition to providing death benefits, life insurers sell protection against the risk of outliving one's accumulated financial resources. In exchange for a lump sum payment or a series of smaller payments relatively early in a policyholder's life, insurers provide a predetermined postretirement monthly income, either fixed or variable, and usually lasting for the life of the policyholder.

Actuaries project the cash outflows expected under an annuity policy, based on how long the policyholder may live after annuity payments begin. The amount the customer must pay before receiving the first annuity payment is set equal to the present value of the insurer's anticipated cash outflows. Although individual annuity policies can be purchased, most of the annuity obligations of life insurers are from group pension plans established by employers for employees.

Policy Dividend Obligations

Like *reserves, dividend* has an ambiguous meaning. Typically, a dividend is a benefit paid to common stockholders of a firm after all other operating and financial obligations have been fulfilled. These benefits are taxable to the recipient under current federal tax law.

In the case of mutual insurance companies, however, the meaning of *dividend* is somewhat different, closer to the meaning of *refund.* Policy dividends are features of **participating insurance policies.** A participating policyholder receives a rebate on premiums paid during the year, if the loss experience, operating expenses, and investment income of the insurer are better than expected at the beginning of the year. In

practice, to maximize the probability that dividends can be paid regularly, premiums on participating policies are higher than premiums on **nonparticipating policies** providing similar coverage. Holders of nonparticipating policies are not entitled to dividends.

In Table 23.1, policy dividend "accumulations" are past dividends that policyholders have reinvested in interest-bearing accounts; dividend obligations "payable" are policy dividends declared during the current year but not yet paid to policyholders. Because policy dividends are considered refunds of previous payments, they are not taxable to the insured when paid.

Other Obligations

The miscellaneous category called "other obligations" includes accrued expenses and prepaid premiums.

Surplus and Common Stock

Surplus and common stock are the net worth or capital of the life insurance industry. The surplus account is analogous to retained earnings in other firms. The common stock shown is for shareholder-owned insurers. The book value of an insurer's surplus plus common stock shows how much the book value of assets can shrink before estimated claims on the insurer exceed asset values.

Protecting policyholders from the risk of insurer insolvency is the objective of minimum capital standards set by state insurance commissions. In mutual firms, in particular, capital increases only when premium and investment income exceeds claims and expenses. In attempting to maintain or exceed capital adequacy standards, financial managers of life insurance companies face problems similar to those of depositories.

INCOME AND EXPENSES OF LIFE INSURERS

The income statement for the industry is shown in Table 23.2.

Table 23.2
Income and Expenses of Life Insurers, 1985 (Millions)

Revenues:				
Premium payments		$153,420	68.60%	
Net investment earnings and other income		70,224	31.40	
Total Revenues				$223,644	100.00%
Expenses:				
Benefit payments		$102,205	45.70%	
Additions to policy reserves		74,697	33.40	
Operating expenses				
Commission to agents	$13,195	5.90%		
Office expenses	20,128	9.00		
Total operating expenses		33,323	14.90	
Total Expenses				$210,225	94.00%
Taxes				6,038	2.70
Net Income				$ 7,381	3.30%
Dividends to stockholders of shareholder-owned firms				$ 3,131	1.40%
Additions to surplus				$ 4,250	1.90%

Source: Adapted from the American Council of Life Insurance, 1986 Life Insurance Fact Book, p. 65.

Revenues

In 1985, over twice as many dollars were received from premium payments as from investment income. Investment income is stated on a *net* basis, and portfolio management costs are deducted before a total is reported. The proportions of premium and investment income vary with conditions in the financial markets, although premium income is consistently greater. Large firms spend more on portfolio management and rely more heavily on investment income than do small insurers.

Expenses

The two major expense categories are obligations to policyholders or their beneficiaries and operating expenses. As noted, policy obligations include both current disbursements and reserves against expected future claims. Operating expenses include payments to sales agents and costs such as depreciation, rent, and managerial salaries. Altogether, 1985 expenses

equaled 94 percent of the industry's net revenues. The remaining 6 percent of net revenues was consumed by taxes, dividends to stockholders, and additions to surplus.

THE NIM MODIFIED

The net interest margin, defined as (Interest Revenues − Interest Expenses)/Total Assets, applies to every financial institution discussed thus far. In the insurance industry, however, the basic NIM concept is modified to reflect the nature of the industry's major source of funds and expenses—insurance policies. For all types of insurers, a managerial target analogous to the NIM in other institutions is:

(23.1)

$$\text{Net Underwriting Margin} = \frac{\text{Premium Income} - \text{Policy Expenses}}{\text{Total Assets}}$$

Despite the different focus, the basic nature of asset/liability management is the same in the insurance industry.[11] Management must earn a sufficient margin after all policy-related costs to pay operating expenses and to earn an acceptable return on net worth. Otherwise, neither policyholders, stockholders, nor regulators will be satisfied, and in extreme situations, the insurer may become insolvent. Important risk/return characteristics of premium income and premium expenses for insurers are discussed later in the chapter.

To achieve financial objectives, insurers usually need additional income from investments. In fact, the difference between an insurer's and a depository's central financial management problem is one of emphasis: Depositories use fee income to supplement interest revenues to attain their financial objectives, and insurers use interest income to supplement fees to achieve theirs. Because insurers' assets and liabilities differ from those of other institutions, they also require differences in risk management tools, as discussed later.

TYPES OF LIFE INSURANCE POLICIES

Because the unusual nature of life insurers' liabilities influences their financial management strategies, it is important to distinguish among the types of policies from which those obligations arise. Little more than a decade ago, a list of the major life insurance policies would have been as uncomplicated as a list of deposits then available at an S&L. However, the regulatory and economic changes that caused depositories to broaden their product lines have affected life insurers as well, and the range of insurance products has expanded. Although Table 23.1 shows that annuity policies are an important part of insurers' business, the most significant changes have occurred in life insurance products, the focus of much of the remaining discussion.

Whole Life

The traditional "best-seller" in the life insurance industry is the *whole life policy*. A whole life policyholder pays fixed annual premiums in exchange for a known death benefit, the *face amount* of the policy. The annual premium is established when a policy is written, and, for an equivalent face amount and medical history, is inversely related to the policyholder's age. Because the probability of dying increases with age, the policyholder pays more than is actuarially needed to protect his beneficiaries during the early years a policy is in force, and less than is actuarially needed during the later years.

A whole life policy is so named because it provides death protection for the policyholder's entire life. The insured's beneficiary receives the full face amount, regardless of the date of death. As a consequence of the premium payment system, whole life policies accumulate cash values the insured may take in lieu of maintaining the full death protection. In any year in which the policyholder does not die, the portion of the premium exceeding the cost of providing death protection adds to the cash value of the policy. A fixed annual rate of return, established at the time the policy is written, is earned on the cash value.

In some states, the minimum yield that insurers must guarantee to policyholders on the cash buildup of their policies is about 4 percent. Because this yield is not taxable to the policyholder unless the policy is surrendered, the tax equivalent of 4 percent to someone in the 28 percent tax bracket is $4\%/(1 - 0.28) = 5.56\%$, or about what could be earned on passbook savings accounts before March 31, 1986. Policy-

---

[11]This statement is somewhat simplistic. Because policy premiums are actuarially determined based on expected policy expenses, an excess of income over expenses may result from conservative assumptions that set premiums higher than necessary to cover expenses. If all firms in a state make assumptions based on conservative insurance codes in the state, an excess of premium income over expenses may not reflect good management but may simply be a function of assumptions. For an individual firm, however, using more conservative assumptions solely to increase premiums could reduce total income as policyholders choose other firms. The role of assumptions in setting premiums is explained in greater depth later in the chapter.

holders with participating policies may also receive dividends if the company's earnings are good.

Term Insurance

Whole life policies have both death protection and savings features, but **term insurance policies** offer only death protection for a specified period.[12] The probability of the insured's dying increases with age, so the annual premium increases with age. Term policies are frequently offered as part of employee benefits packages. Until recently, term and whole life were virtually the only two types of life insurance policies available.

Variable Life

First introduced in 1976, **variable life policies** gained popularity after 1980. Like whole life policies, variable life policies require level premium payments throughout the policyholder's life, but there are important differences. For example, excess premiums that add to cash value earn variable, not fixed, rates of return, based on the insurer's yield on assets of the *policyholder's* choice. If the selected assets perform well, cash value and death benefits both increase. If not, the cash value may be zero, so the insured bears the entire investment risk. A minimum death benefit is specified in the policy, although there is no maximum. The actual payment to beneficiaries depends on yields earned on excess premiums.

Universal Life

The most flexible of all policies, **universal life,** was introduced in 1979. It combines the death protection features of term insurance with the opportunity to earn market rates of return on excess premiums. Unlike variable life, with its level premium structure, premiums on univer-

---

[12]Some term policies contracted for a long period may build up cash value, but these are the exception, not the rule.

sal life policies can be changed. The policyholder can pay as high a "premium" as desired, instructing the insurer to invest the excess over that required for death protection in the *insurer's* choice of assets. Later, if the policyholder wishes to pay no premium at all, the insurer can deduct the cost of providing death protection for the year from the cash value accumulated in previous years. With other types of policies, skipping a premium would cause the policy to lapse.

Unlike whole or variable life policies, the face amount of guaranteed death protection in a universal life policy can be changed at the policyholder's option. Also unlike other policies, policyholders can make withdrawals from the cash value. Holders of variable or whole life policies can obtain access to cash values only by borrowing against the policy or terminating it.

COMPARISON OF POLICY CASH FLOWS

The four policy types result in different premiums, and a comparison of the cash flows is important to financial managers. The following examples consider a 35-year-old male seeking a policy in a face amount of $100,000.

Role of Mortality Tables

Regardless of the policy, the insurer begins calculating the premium by examining a mortality table. Table 23.3 presents excerpts from a typical mortality table. This one was published in 1980, based on mortality from 1970 through 1975. It is called the Commissioners Standard Ordinary (CSO) Table because it was recommended as a basis for calculating required insurer reserves by the National Association of Insurance Commissioners (NAIC), an organization of insurance regulators. Death rates per 1,000 are calculated conservatively, according to the number of insured men actually dying during the 1970–1975 period, with an increase to allow for a margin of error. When setting premiums, an insurer uses actuarial estimates re-

Table 23.3
Excerpts from Commissioners 1980 Standard Ordinary Mortality Table
(Based on Death Rates of Males, 1970–1975)

(1) Age	(2) Number Living	(3) Number Dying	(4) Deaths per 1,000 [(3)/(2)] × 1,000
0	10,000,000	41,800	4.18
1	9,958,200	10,655	1.07
2	9,947,545	9,848	0.99
3	9,937,697	9,739	0.98
4	9,927,958	9,531	0.96
5	9,918,427	8,927	0.90
6	9,909,500	8,522	0.86
7	9,900,978	7,921	0.80
8	9,893,057	7,519	0.76
9	9,885,539	7,315	0.74
10	9,878,223	7,211	0.73
.	.	.	.
.	.	.	.
.	.	.	.
35	9,491,617	20,027	2.11
36	9,471,590	21,216	2.24
37	9,450,374	22,681	2.40
38	9,427,693	24,323	2.58
39	9,403,369	26,235	2.79
.	.	.	.
.	.	.	.
.	.	.	.
70	6,274,100	247,890	39.51
71	6,026,210	260,935	43.30
72	5,765,275	274,715	47.65
73	5,490,560	289,023	52.64
74	5,201,537	302,677	58.19
75	4,898,859	314,458	64.19
.	.	.	.
.	.	.	.
.	.	.	.
95	146,720	48,412	329.96
96	98,308	37,804	384.55
97	60,504	29,054	480.20
98	31,450	20,693	657.97
99	10,756	10,756	1,000.00

flecting the most recent information available, including new causes of death such as AIDS, or new treatments for formerly fatal diseases. For illustrative purposes, however, the 1980 Commissioners Table is used.[13]

According to the conservative estimates in the table, of any 10,000,000 men, 9,491,617 are expected to reach age 35, and 146,720 are expected to reach age 95. Of those reaching 35, 20,027 are expected to die before age 36, a rate of 2.11 men per 1,000. The probability that an individual claim will be made during the year a policyholder is 35 can be estimated as:

$$20,027 \div 9,491,617 = 0.00211 = 0.211\%$$

Other Assumptions

To set premiums, an insurer assumes when during the year death claims will be made and when premium payments will be received. In this example, the assumption is that claims are not paid until the end of the year for which insurance is purchased, although premium payments are assumed to occur at the beginning of a policy year. The insurer also estimates the rate of return to be earned on premium payments made in advance of claims. Because most states require insurers to use conservative assumptions about the rate they will earn on invested premiums, this example assumes a rate of 4 percent.

---

[13]Because mortality rates for men and women differ, life insurers use separate tables to calculate premiums for each sex. In addition, P&C companies use separate premium schedules for men and women drivers, for example, since women have had better driving records. Recently, these practices have been challenged in court as being discriminatory against both sexes. Most insurers object vigorously to so-called "unisex" pricing, believing that premium and benefit differences between the sexes are justified. The issue may well be decided in Congress, which has considered several unisex insurance bills in the 1980s. See Daniel Seligman, "Insurance and the Price of Sex," *Fortune* 107 (February 21, 1983): 84-85; "Unisex Pricing Splinters the Industry," *Business Week,* April 18, 1983, pp. 107-108; and Andrea Bennett, "Setting the Unisex Pace," *Best's Review* (Life/Health Edition) 86 (January 1986): 22-24, 106-108.

Premium on a One-Year Term Policy

Suppose a 35-year-old male seeks a $100,000 term policy for only 1 year. The expected value of the cash outflow required by the insurer at the *end* of the year is the face amount of the policy times the probability that a claim will be made:

(23.2)

$$\text{One-Year Term premium} = \text{Face Amount} \times \text{Probability of Claim}$$

$$\$100,000 \times 0.00211 = \$211.00$$

The $211 can also be viewed in another way. Suppose the insurer has 9,491,617 35-year-old male policyholders, each with $100,000 policies. According to the CSO table, 20,027 will die during the year. If they do, the total cost to the insurer would be $2,002,700,000. Because, at the beginning of the year, no one know which individuals will die, the insurance industry operates on the principle that the cost of providing death protection should be shared by everyone. Each person's equal share is:

$$\frac{\$2,002,700,000}{9,491,617} = \$210.99, \text{ or } \$211$$

The present value of this amount at the *beginning* of the year, when premiums are assumed to be paid, is the required or **pure premium.** It will be increased by a **loading** to cover operating expenses and profit for shareholders. Using a discount rate of 4 percent, the pure premium is:

$$\$211.00 \div 1.04 = \$202.88$$

If someone were 70 and wished to purchase one-year term insurance with a face value of $100,000, the cost to the insurer at the end of the year, using Equation 23.2, would be:

$$\$100,000 \times (247,890 \div 6,274,100) = \$3,951$$

The pure premium would be $3,951 ÷ 1.04 = $3,799, a charge reflecting the higher expected cost of providing death protection.[14]

Role of the Discount Rate.   The low 4 percent rate assumed on the insurer's investments produces a higher premium than if a higher discount rate were used. Throughout the 1980s, life insurers' net (after management expenses) return on investments has exceeded 8 percent, and in 1984 and 1985, it exceeded 9 percent. Insurers and state regulators justify the continued use of low rates in the interests of conservatism. If a higher discount rate were used in premium calculations, and if *ex post* investment income failed to reach that rate, some argue that insurers' solvency would be threatened and that policyholders would face the risk that their claims could not be met. As seen later, policyholders in the early 1980s were reluctant to accept this argument.

Annual Premium on a Whole Life Policy

The calculation of the annual premium on a $100,000 whole life policy for a 35-year-old male is based on the same principles used for term insurance. An adjustment is made, however, because death protection is being purchased for the rest of the insured's life. Although the premium is fixed, the probability of death changes each year, a fact considered at the time the policy is written. An illustration is given in the appendix to the chapter, resulting in an annual pure premium of $1,260.43.

Cash Values and Death Benefits.   The beginning-of-year cost of providing death protec-

tion for a male at age 35 was estimated earlier to be only $202.88, but the pure whole life premium is $1,260.43. If the policyholder does not die, the insurer invests premiums in excess of those actually required to provide death protection. The $1,260.43 would be collected each year, but the cost of death protection would increase as the policyholder ages, with less added to the cash value. Cash value also increases based on the assumed interest rate. Regardless of the insurer's actual investment earnings, nonparticipating whole life policyholders earn a fixed rate, and their beneficiaries receive a fixed death benefit. In contrast, participating policyholders may receive dividends in good years.

Universal and Variable Life Premiums

The basic concepts involved in calculating term and whole life policy premiums hold for variable and universal life policies. In both types of policies, a 35-year-old male seeking $100,000 of coverage would be quoted a pure annual premium of $1,260.43 plus a markup for operating costs and profit margin. The amount required for death protection each year would be deducted, and the rest invested in market-rate instruments. The interest rate actually earned on the cash value is not determined in advance. As noted, universal life policies give the holder great flexibility. The insured may pay more or less than the quoted level premium; the difference between what is paid and the cost of death protection is added to or subtracted from the cash value.

THE EVOLVING LIFE INSURANCE PRODUCT MIX: CAUSES AND RESULTS

When disintermediation and/or cross-intermediation occur, financial institutions face unexpected withdrawals of funds as customers seek more attractive yields from direct investments or from other financial institutions. Consider the situation facing life insurers in the early 1980s. Whole life customers were earning rela-

---

[14]Not every insurer would charge the pure premium plus the same loading. Individual insurance underwriters must decide what types of risks they are willing to bear. In some cases, if a company prefers to deal with one type of client (say, nonsmokers) it may undercharge them and overcharge smokers to make up the difference. As a result, policies with identical features may be priced differently, depending upon the underwriter's risk preferences. For an example of the range of premiums on a given term policy, see Richard Morais, "Double Idemnity," *Forbes* 136 (November 18, 1985): 280.

tively low rates on the cash buildup of their policies. Although not subject to income tax, the tax-equivalent yield simply was intolerably low. Many policyholders dissatisfied with the low return on the "forced" savings in the early years of a whole life policy did one of three things: They switched to term insurance; borrowed against the accumulated cash value of existing whole life policies; or stopped paying premiums, allowing policies to lapse. The collective effects of these actions changed the life insurance business permanently.

The Switch to Term Insurance

Between 1972 and 1982, the face value of new whole life policies as a percentage of "ordinary" insurance purchased declined steadily from 53 percent to 40 percent, and term insurance rose from 41 percent to 60 percent of new insurance in force. (Variable and universal life policies are not defined as "ordinary" policies by the industry.) This development was critical to the financial management of life insurance companies. Steady, predictable cash flows declined, and, because premiums from term policies vary from year to year, uncertainty in insurers' cash inflows increased. The increased riskiness affected the investment choices of life insurers, as discussed later in the chapter. Although whole life regained market share as interest rates fell between 1983 and 1985, changes in insurers' investment practices remain, as the opening quotation to the chapter suggests.

The Increase in Policy Loans

Figure 23.1 illustrates the second way whole life policyholders have responded to the changing economic environment. It tracks the dollar volume borrowed against the cash value of whole life policies since 1960. In the past, the rate at which a policyholder could borrow was usually established at a rate prevailing at the time the policy was written. During periods in which market rates remained relatively stable, there was no systematic incentive for a large number of policyholders to borrow against accumulated cash values at one time.

In the late 1970s and early 1980s, however, as market rates reached historical highs, the ability to borrow against one's life insurance policy at, for example, 5 percent, and to reinvest loan proceeds in Treasury bills at 16.5 percent, proved irresistible to many policyholders.[15] Although insurers lobbied successfully to persuade regulators to increase permissible policy loan rates (up to 8 percent or more in some states) or to permit variable-rate policy loans, some states still prohibit current market rates.

Growth in policyholder loans has added to the riskiness of insurers' cash flows. The insurer is legally obligated to provide policy loans on the terms established in the policy, so cash must be obtained somewhere. Because high demand for policy loans coincided with the switch to term insurance, some insurers were forced to liquidate assets, sometimes at a loss in value. In 1980, in fact, the industry was forced to use over 22 percent of total funds available for investment to make new policy loans.[16] Some insurers had to borrow at rates higher than they earned on the policy loans they made with the borrowed money. The increased demand for policy loans placed them in the unaccustomed position of considering new sources of funds such as bank loans and commercial paper.

Policy Lapses

Perhaps the most serious effect on insurer cash flows has come from cancellation of life insurance policies as customers rely on "self-

---

[15]For insurers, perhaps the "unkindest cut of all" came in 1982, when a former insurance agent founded a company called Idle Assets. Idle Assets trained bank and S&L employees to call their own customers, encouraging them to bring their life insurance policies into the depository. If a customer complied, the employee would then explain how to borrow against the policy and encourage the policyholder to reinvest his policy loan in a high-yielding bank or S&L CD. Idle Assets collected a modest fee from the bank or S&L for services rendered. David P. Garino, "Life Insurers Irked by Reinvestment Plan that Hurts Them but Aids Holders, Banks," *The Wall Street Journal,* March 5, 1982.

[16]Curry and Warshawsky, "Life Insurance Companies in a Changing Environment," p. 449.

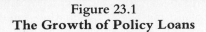

Figure 23.1
The Growth of Policy Loans

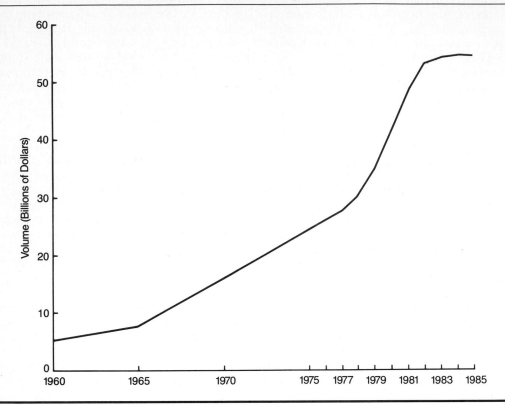

Source: American Council of Life Insurance, *1986 Life Insurance Fact Book,* p. 72.

insurance" from savings or on term insurance available through employers. Between 1960 and 1985, voluntary policy terminations per year more than doubled, from about 5 percent to over 12 percent of policies in force. Policy lapses are especially likely to occur among customers with the least need for insurance protection. The result of continued cancellations could be to skew insurers' customer base toward more risky customers than those on which mortality tables are based. A declining customer base threatens not only the profitability of insurers in the short run, as shown by a decrease in premium income and the net underwriting margin, but can affect their long-run solvency.

Introduction of Variable and Universal Life

Variable and universal life policies are designed to attract customers who fled whole life policies, but they have also affected the financial management of insurers.

Impact on Cash Flows.   Because customers' satisfaction with new policies depends on the performance of the insurer's investment portfolio, emphasis on that aspect of management has intensified. Further, servicing the new policies costs more, because market rates are paid on the cash buildup portion of premiums. The increased cost is reflected in the reserves required to provide for future policy obligations, considerably squeezing the net underwriting margin. The cash inflows and outflows for the new policies are also much less predictable than for traditional whole life, creating a need for asset liquidity that had not been significant for insurers. Liquidity pressures made many insurers reluctant to offer the new products at first; they have done so only after extensive cancellations taught the bitter lesson that a return to the old days is unlikely.[17]

Impact on Operating Costs.   The new policies have also caused the management of operating costs to change. Historically, because the yield paid on whole life policies was so low, insurers could keep a large force of sales agents and pay them huge commissions on the sale of new policies, often up to 100 percent of the first year's premium. With underwriting margins on variable and universal life policies squeezed to a minimum, the compensation system must be overhauled. Some insurers are reducing their sales force and finding new ways to market policies, such as renting space in local depositories or selling through the mail. Remaining agents must be trained in the complex details of the new policies. Furthermore, sophisticated computer systems are needed to maintain necessary records. These expenses put further pressure on insurer earnings as their product mix changes.

New Policies in Force

The initial popularity of variable and universal life policies exceeded the estimates of even the most optimistic observers, as illustrated in Figure 23.2. Because the growth in the number of these policies has been so rapid, the scale on the graph is not linear, but logarithmic. That means that the distances between points on the vertical scale reflect equal rates of change, not equal amounts. In the figure, the equal distances between points labeled 1, 100, 1,000, and 10,000 all represent a tenfold increase in policies from the previous point. Between 1981 and 1983, and again between 1982 and 1985, the amount of universal life in force increased almost tenfold!

In addition to universal and variable life, innovations are emerging that make whole life more appealing to consumers who want both the death protection and stable forced savings features of that type of policy.[18] Other new products, such as *variable/universal life,* combine the flexible premium structure of universal life with the investment options of variable life. Figure 23.2 shows that variable/universal life got off to a good start in 1985, the first year it was introduced. The days of predictable cash obligations of insurers are gone forever. Financial managers in insurance companies need to understand how asset management is affected.

LIFE INSURERS: ASSET MANAGEMENT

Because the assets of life insurers are mostly stocks and bonds, many management tools in previous chapters are relevant for insurers. It is important for them to carefully analyze the default risk to which bond portfolios are exposed. In fact, because so many of the corporate bonds held by life insurers are privately placed, assessment of default risk is paramount.

Assessment of interest rate risk is also critical, now more than ever, because increasing needs for liquidity mean insurers may have to sell assets before maturity. Insurers must have knowledge of portfolio diversification using correlations between expected returns on individual investments, as well as the ability to

---

[17]For example, the second-largest life insurer did not introduce universal life policies until 1983. When it did, premiums on universal life policies grew rapidly to 47 percent of all new premiums written. See "Upheaval in Life Insurance," *Business Week,* June 24, 1984, pp. 58-66.

[18]The traditional whole life policy continues to provide a package of options for the policyholder provided by no other insurance product, so it is likely to remain a viable product regardless of its interest rate features. For an analysis and empirical support, see Michael L. Smith, "The Life Insurance Policy as an Options Package," *Journal of Risk and Insurance* 49 (December 1982): 583-601; and Michael L. Walden, "The Whole Life Insurance Policy as an Options Package: An Empirical Investigation," *Journal of Risk and Insurance* 52 (March 1985): 44-58.

Figure 23.2
Growth of Variable and Universal Life

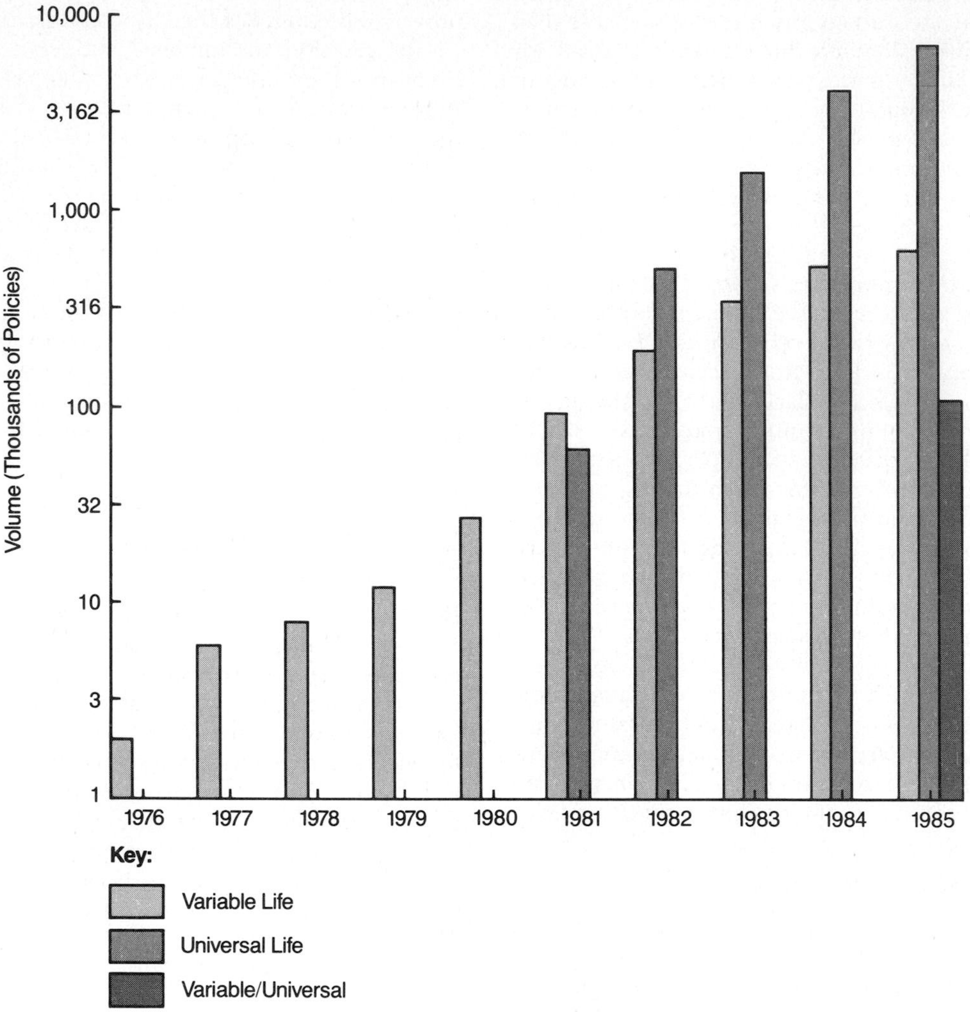

Source: American Council of Life Insurance, *1986 Life Insurance Fact Book,* p. 29.

assess the market risk of a common stock portfolio. These issues are explored in Chapters 4, 7, 8, and 12.

Investment in a third category of life insurer assets, real estate, requires a somewhat different approach, also discussed earlier in the text. These investments are significant long-term commitments by insurers to the development and management of real property. Thus, they are particularly suited to net present value analysis, illustrated in Chapter 19. Recent evidence indicates that life insurers are increasingly employing NPV techniques for this purpose. By 1983, about 50 percent of a sample of life insurance executives indicated that their firms used NPV to assess after-tax cash flows from real estate investments, compared to less than 10 percent a decade earlier.[19] The trend toward more sophisticated real estate investment analysis will undoubtedly continue.

New Directions in Asset Management

Although basic asset management issues are of continuing importance to life insurers, their greatest challenge is determining the best asset portfolio in a competitive environment in which interest rate risk management has become critical. In the past, a buy-and-hold strategy was common among insurers; yields on assets exceeding the yield paid on whole life policies were "gravy." Now, asset portfolios must be structured to earn competitive yields, but must be flexible enough to change as insurers' cash obligations change. One adjustment to new conditions is the increase in short-term U.S. government securities held in case of increased policy loan demand.[20]

Earnings pressures have raised concerns both in and outside the industry. Just as some depositories have been tempted to invest in riskier than normal assets to attract depositors to above-average yields, some insurers have been accused of taking excessive risks to attract buyers of variable and universal life policies. The mortality and morbidity risks that actuaries assess are different from risks in the financial markets. Fortunately for insurers, however, most integrated asset/liability management tools available to depositories are suitable for insurers, too.

---

[19]Webb, "Real Estate Investment Acquisition Rules," pp. 501, 503.

[20]For more discussion of these points, see Anthony Saunders, "The Effect of Changing Regulation on Investment Policy of Life Insurance Companies," in *The Emerging Financial Industry,* Arnold W. Sametz, ed. (Lexington, MA: Lexington Books, 1984), pp. 85-94. Other evidence on integrated balance sheet structures is provided in John D. Stowe and Collin J. Watson, "A Multivariate Analysis of the Composition of Life Insurer Balance Sheets," *Journal of Risk and Insurance* 52 (June 1985): 222-240.

LIFE INSURERS: TECHNIQUES FOR INTEGRATED ASSET/ LIABILITY MANAGEMENT

The sections below illustrate the use of several integrated asset/liability management tools in life insurance firms.

Maturity and Duration Matching

As the opening quotation suggests, matching is as legitimate a risk management tool for insurers as it is for depositories. Contrary to what the quotation suggests, the idea is not a new one. In 1942, an economist at a Philadelphia life insurance company stressed the importance of matching the cash flows from assets and liabilities to lock in an overall rate of profit. A 1952 article in an actuarial science journal developed a measure of the "mean term" of insurer asset and liability cash flows. The measure was virtually identical to the duration measure Macaulay developed 15 years earlier. Insurers were encouraged to match the mean term of assets and liabilities to stabilize profits in an environment of changing rates.[21]

Although insurance companies were among the first institutions for which matching maturities or durations was suggested, many small and medium-sized companies have not yet embraced the suggestion. As in small depositories, the major reason is the extensive data collection and analyses required in establishing a GAP management system. Nonetheless, industry insiders increasingly encourage life insurers of all sizes to practice matching to reduce the adverse impact of interest rate risk.[22]

Duration and the Immunization of Separate Accounts

For duration to be a useful tool, managers of life insurance companies need not manage the overall duration GAP. Segments of the asset portfolio can be immunized to lock in yields,

---

[21]These papers are cited in Roman Weil, "Macaulay's Duration," *Journal of Business* 46 (October 1973): 590-591.

[22]Joseph M. Fitzgerald, "Myth or Management Tool?" *Best's Review* (Life/Health Edition) 85 (May 1984): 16-20.

even if the total portfolio is not. Immunization is especially appropriate for insurers with substantial *separate accounts,* defined as groups of assets designated as backing for specific obligations. If an insurer manages pension fund obligations for an employer, separate accounts are often used to support these obligations. In addition, reserves for variable and universal life policies are often backed by separate accounts.

To immunize yields on separate accounts, the insurer must estimate the holding period over which a given yield is desired. A logical holding period is the estimated duration of the obligations for which a separate account has been established. The average duration of the designated assets is then set equal to that holding period. As explained in Chapter 8, immunization balances the reinvestment risk of the assets with their exposure to price risk. Whether rates increase or decrease, the initial yield is protected. Immunization strategies for separate accounts are similar to those used in pension fund management, and an example is included in Chapter 24.[23]

Financial Futures and Options

Life insurers' substantial investments in bonds make them ideal candidates for using financial futures. For example, if a manager expects interest rates to increase within six months and expects the demand for policy loans to increase, long-term bonds may have to be sold to obtain the cash. By acting on this forecast in advance, the manager can use profits on a short position in the futures market to offset losses on the sale of bonds that decline in value.

Insurance companies can potentially benefit more from long futures positions than can depositories. Insurers often agree to purchase corporate bonds under *forward commitments.* In a forward commitment, the insurer agrees to buy bonds before the actual transaction. If management commits the firm to buying bonds in three months, but fears that yields will drift downward before then, profits on a long futures position can help to offset the "opportunity loss" of investing at the lower anticipated rate.[24]

Finally, the stock portfolios of insurers suggest the use of stock index futures and options. Although not all states permit life insurers to use these more "exotic" management strategies, many insurers are lobbying state regulators for changes.

BALANCE SHEET OF PROPERTY AND CASUALTY INSURERS

P&C companies face problems that are similar to yet distinct from those of life insurers. But before a discusssion of special problems, an examination of the balance sheet, income, and expenses of P&C companies is appropriate.

Statutory versus GAAP Accounting

Interpreting available financial data on P&C insurers is somewhat more difficult than for other financial institutions. Insurance companies, like thrifts, are subject to two sets of accounting rules: regulatory principles, which insurers call *statutory accounting,* and GAAP. Statutory accounting rules are prescribed by laws in each state, but most states have adopted a uniform set recommended by the National Association of Insurance Commissioners.

Statutory accounting is a combination of cash–based and accrual accounting; expenses are recognized when paid, but revenues are not recognized until earned. In general, it is a more conservative way of reporting financial results than GAAP. Statutory accounting affects bal-

---

[23]The need for immunization and other new financial management techniques is discussed in Stephen W. Forbes, "The Revolution in Life Insurance Financial Management," *Journal of the American Society of CLU and ChFC* 41 (January 1987): 70-73.

[24]Recent evidence indicates that large insurers are using both long and short futures positions. See Jeff Bailey, "Insurers Plan to Use Futures Trades as Tool against Interest Rate Rises," *The Wall Street Journal,* February 7, 1984; and Rebecca M. Hurtz and Mona J. Gardner, "Surviving in a New Environment," *Best's Review* (Life/Health Edition) 85 (September/October 1984): 152-153.

ance sheets and income statements for all insurers, although differences between statutory accounting and GAAP are greater for P&C insurers than for life insurers. Virtually all data on life insurers presented earlier are consistent with GAAP. However, the same cannot be said for data on the P&C industry; this discussion notes significant differences between statutory and GAAP figures as they are relevant.

Assets of P&C Insurers

Like life insurers, P&C companies invest heavily in bonds and stock, but in different proportions. Table 23.4 presents the balance sheet of P&C insurers at the end of 1985.

Bonds.   The bond portfolios of P&C companies are dominated by government securities, especially state and local issues, including spe-

cial revenue bonds, the largest category of P&C assets. Like commercial banks, P&C insurers choose these investments because interest earned is exempt from federal taxes.

Unfortunately for P&C insurers, their relatively large investment in state, local, and revenue bonds has been a two-edged sword. If underwriting profits are good, the tax shelter provided by municipal bonds is desirable. If underwriting losses occur, the lower yield on municipals hurts profitability. In the mid-1980s, the latter situation was common.

Preferred and Common Stock.   P&C insurers devote more of their portfolios to stock than do life insurers because of differences in the cash flows of the two types of insurers. More is said later about the premium income and expenses of P&C insurers, but their cash inflows are less stable than those of life insurers,

---

Table 23.4
Assets and Obligations of Property and Casualty Companies, Year-End 1985
(Approximately 3,500 Firms)

	Millions		% of Total	
Assets				
Bonds		$170,610		54.79%
U.S. Treasury	$49,331		15.84%	
State and local	28,336		9.10	
Special revenue	64,173		20.61	
Other	28,770		9.24	
Common stock		44,002		14.13
Preferred stock		8,736		2.81
Mortgages and other loans		5,329		1.71
Other assets		82,688		26.56
Total Assets		$311,365		100.00%
Liabilities and Net Worth				
Total loss and unearned premium reserves		$235,854		75.75%
Total surplus and common stock		75,511		24.25
Total Liabilities and Net Worth		$311,365		100.00%

Source: Prepared by the authors with data from the Insurance Information Institute, *1986-87 Property/Casualty Fact Book,* pp. 18, 23.

and their cash outflows are more strongly affected by inflation. Common stock, with the possibility of substantial price appreciation, is a more suitable investment choice for P&C companies than for life insurers, at least until recently.

Statutory accounting requires that unrealized gains or losses on the stock holdings of insurers be reflected on the balance sheet, directly affecting both reported asset holdings and insurers' net worth. In years in which stock market values increase, asset and net worth accounts are both written up; in bad years, they are written down. This procedure is inconsistent with GAAP, which requires the reporting of securities holdings as the lower of either cost or market value. Consequently, statutory values for assets and net worth often differ from those reported under GAAP.

Mortgages and Other Loans. The fully taxable income from mortgage loans and less potential price appreciation has made mortgages relatively unattractive to P&C insurers.

Other Assets. The category "other assets" includes all assets, such as cash, not held as investments. It does not, however, include premises of property and casualty insurers. Statutory accounting rules require P&C insurers to report only *admitted assets,* those that could be liquidated should the insurer face a financial emergency. Premises of insurers are not considered admitted assets. Thus, the reported net worth of P&C insurers is understated by nonadmitted assets not shown on the balance sheet.[25]

Liabilities and Policyholders' Surplus of P&C Insurers

Like life insurers, P&C companies estimate expected future claims on existing policies; these estimates are called *loss reserves.* Loss reserves are the sum of claims made but not yet paid and estimates of claims that will be made; they are

the largest portion of the industry's liabilities. Because P&C insurers do not rely on mortality and morbidity tables, estimated losses are often based on past experience, with adjustments to reflect increased costs due to inflation or other factors. Unlike life insurers, P&C insurers seldom report their liabilities as the discounted value of a series of future cash outflows. In fact, statutory accounting for P&C insurers virtually ignores the time value of money.

For the unexpired terms of outstanding policies, P&C insurers have obligations to policyholders who have paid premiums in advance. These *unearned premium reserves* are often calculated under the assumption that services have been rendered for only one-half the amount of premiums paid during the year. For example, assume an insurer has $2 million in total premiums during a calendar year, received evenly at a rate of $166,667 per month. Obligations on policies written in January would have almost expired by the end of December; those written in February would have about one month's obligation remaining; those written in December would have about eleven months left, and so on. On average, the insurer would have obligations remaining on six months' worth of premium payments, and the unearned premium reserve for the year would be valued at $1 million.

P&C insurers must also maintain sufficient net worth to absorb net losses in years in which income is insufficient to meet expenses. The net worth of the industry consists of common stock, a relatively small proportion of industry capital, and *policyholders' surplus,* the P&C term for retained earnings. This total does not reflect the value of nonadmitted assets. As in all financial institutions, net worth is viewed as a measure of financial strength and affects the insurer's capacity to write additional policies. In general, state regulations discourage insurers from writing an annual dollar volume of premiums that exceeds three times the surplus account.

Figure 23.3 compares the balance sheets of life and P&C insurers and highlights the differences between them. Although they select similar assets, the proportions differ noticeably, as highlighted by P&Cs' extensive investment in

---

[25]Statutory accounting rules for life insurers also require that they report only admitted assets. The data in Table 23.1, however, were restated by the American Council of Life Insurance to reflect nonadmitted assets such as premises.

Figure 23.3
Life Insurers and P&C Insurers: A Comparison of Assets, Obligations, and Net Worth

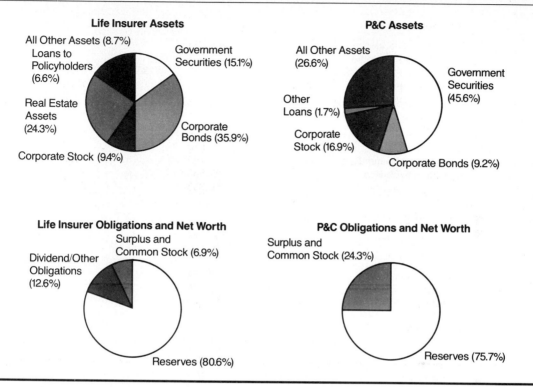

Life Insurer Assets

All Other Assets (8.7%)
Loans to Policyholders (6.6%)
Government Securities (15.1%)
Real Estate Assets (24.3%)
Corporate Bonds (35.9%)
Corporate Stock (9.4%)

P&C Assets

All Other Assets (26.6%)
Government Securities (45.6%)
Other Loans (1.7%)
Corporate Stock (16.9%)
Corporate Bonds (9.2%)

Life Insurer Obligations and Net Worth

Surplus and Common Stock (6.9%)
Dividend/Other Obligations (12.6%)
Reserves (80.6%)

P&C Obligations and Net Worth

Surplus and Common Stock (24.3%)
Reserves (75.7%)

Source: American Council of Life Insurance, *1986 Life Insurance Fact Book;* Insurance Information Institute, *1986-87 Property/Casualty Fact Book.*

government securities, mostly municipals. In addition, P&C insurers do not loan to policyholders.

The major liabilities of both groups are reserves, but the P&C industry has proportionately much more net worth than life insurers. The additional buffer is required because reserves necessary to meet P&Cs' policy obligations are much less predictable.

INCOME AND EXPENSES OF P&C INSURERS

The statutory practice of reporting income using accrual accounting and expenses using cash accounting prevents meaningful presentation of a complete income statement for the P&C industry. Therefore, major components of P&C income and expenses are discussed separately.

Revenues

Like life insurers, P&C insurers derive their revenues from two sources, premiums and investments. As the top portion of Table 23.5 indicates, premiums are by far the largest proportion of P&C revenues, arising from the sale of risk protection both to businesses and individuals. Many types of property can be protected, although automobile insurance was by far the largest single source of total P&C premium revenues in 1985. Other important cate-

Table 23.5
Earnings of Property and Casualty Insurers, 1985 (Billions)

Revenues

Total premiums written	$144.859		
Less unearned premiums	11.517		
Total earned premiums		$133.342	87.24%
Net investment earnings and other income		19.508	12.76
Total Revenues		$152.850	100.00%

Expenses

Loss expenses	$118.572	74.88%
Policyholder dividends	2.196	1.39
Operating expenses	37.585	23.73
Total Expenses	$158.353	100.00%

Underwriting Results

Earned premiums	$133.342
Less:	
Loss expenses	118.572
Operating expenses	37.585
Statutory underwriting gain (loss)	($ 22.815)
Less dividends to policyholders	2.196
Net Underwriting Gain (Loss)	($ 25.011)

Source: Insurance Information Institute, *1986-87 Property/Casualty Fact Book,* pp. 20, inside cover.

gories of protection (called *lines* in the industry) include workers' compensation, homeowners' insurance, and general liability insurance for businesses and professionals.

Premium Income. The $144.859 billion "total premiums written" in the top panel of Table 23.5 is referred to in the industry as "net premiums written." It is premiums collected before deducting those paid but not yet earned. The $133.342 billion is earned premiums, determined according to statutory accounting rules. Accounting rules for unearned premiums on the income statement differ from the method discussed earlier for determining unearned premium reserves on the balance sheet. As a result, unearned premium reserves on the balance sheet are often overstated, and net

worth understated, for the industry. Some experts estimate the extent of reserve overstatement to be as much as 35 percent.[26]

Investment Income. As with life insurers, investment income is reported net of portfolio management expenses, but before taxes. Annual investment income for the industry tripled between 1975 and 1985, providing an important source of funds to supplement premiums.[27] As

[26]Emmett J. Vaughan, *Fundamentals of Risk and Insurance* (New York: John Wiley and Sons, 1982), p. 109, n. 7. Many observers believe that the overly conservative statutory rules hurt the industry, because they overstate its liabilities relative to its net worth. See Robert I. Meir, *Fundamentals of Insurance* (Homewood, IL: Richard D. Irwin, 1983), pp. 470-471.

[27]*1986-87 Property/Casualty Fact Book,* p. 20.

illustrated later, however, this growth has not always been enough to guarantee profitability in the industry.

Expenses

Expenses of offering insurance protection are the largest category for the industry, totaling almost three-quarters of the total expenses shown in the middle panel of Table 23.5. Refunds, or dividends, to policyholders in profitable lines of business are a small proportion of expenses, and the remainder is normal operating expenses, including salaries and commissions to agents.

The commission structure in the P&C industry differs from that of the life insurance industry. Whereas a life insurance agent might earn up to 100 percent of the first year's premium as commission and relatively little thereafter on the same policy, a P&C agent might earn only 20 percent of the first year's premium on an automobile policy. Because an automobile policy is usually renewed year after year, however, the agent earns subsequent years' commissions with little effort.

Underwriting Gains (Losses) and the Impact of Investment Income

The importance of both income and expenses from underwriting makes it natural to focus on underwriting results. Regulatory accounting rules require insurers to present two levels of underwriting results, statutory and net underwriting gain (loss). As shown at the bottom of Table 23.5, the difference between the two is that the latter computation includes a deduction for policy dividends. In 1985, the industry reported a net underwriting loss, using statutory accounting rules, in excess of $25 billion. This loss was the largest in a long series of underwriting results dating back almost two decades, although underwriting results have been especially unfavorable in the 1980s.

Of course, P&C insurers can and do use investment income to supplement underwriting results. Figure 23.4 shows that investment and underwriting income have moved in different directions over the last two decades. Despite the tripling of investment income, combined income before taxes declined steadily from 1975 through 1985, as is shown in Figure 23.4. Reasons for this decline and the resulting changes in the financial management of the industry are discussed in the next section.[28]

CHANGES IN THE P&C INDUSTRY: CAUSES AND RESULTS

The decline in the fortunes of P&C firms in the 1980s results from a coincidence of usual events in the industry and unusual regulatory and economic developments.

The Underwriting Cycle

The P&C business has always been subject to the *underwriting cycle*. Because premiums received are invested in financial assets, increases in the general level of interest rates give insurers an incentive to write more policies in order to increase investment income. Frequently, the desire to increase premium income in order to increase investment income results in price wars in which one company undercuts premiums charged by competitors. If rate wars continue long enough, premium income may be insufficient to cover underwriting expenses and policy claims during the year, resulting in a net underwriting loss. This is the "down" part of the cycle.

When insurers raise rates to compensate for the losses, they encounter resistance from customers who like the lower rates, and this resistance postpones insurers' financial recovery. If

---

[28]Ideally, underwriting results reported under GAAP would be the basis of comparison. Unfortunately, there are virtually no data to permit such an analysis because many large P&C firms are mutually owned and report only on a statutory basis. Statutory profits are often lower than they would be if reported on a GAAP basis, so the pattern in Figure 23.4 may exaggerate the financial plight of the industry in the 1980s. Nevertheless, the downward trend would doubtless remain even under GAAP.

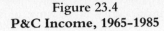

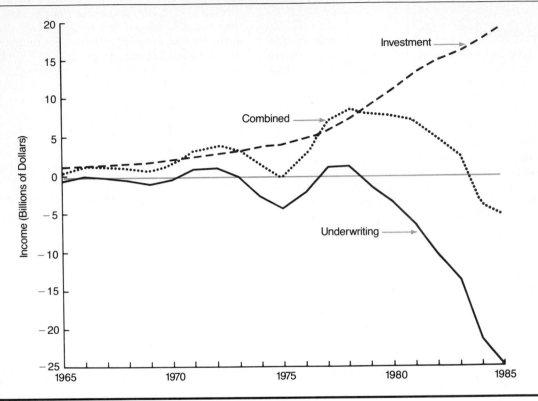

Figure 23.4
P&C Income, 1965–1985

Source: Insurance Information Institute, *1986-87 Property/Casualty Fact Book,* pp. 19-20.

interest rates have fallen, investment income may not make up for continued underwriting losses. Eventually, however, the cycle turns back up as the balance between premium and investment income is restored and the industry regains profitability.

The cyclical nature of underwriting losses is seen in Figure 23.4. Underwriting profits turned to losses in the late 1960s, the mid-1970s, and again in the 1980s, all periods of historically high interest rates. In the 1980s, however, the underwriting cycle was accompanied by unprecedented social, economic, and regulatory forces, making recovery from the down part of the cycle more difficult than before.

Social Forces

Since the 1960s, Americans have been increasingly prone to sue one another, and courts have awarded large amounts to successful plaintiffs. Escalating malpractice awards against physicians and the growing volume of product liability suits against manufacturers have received considerable publicity as examples of these social trends.[29]

---

[29]Statistics on the number of lawsuits, and the damages awarded as a result, are found in the *1986-87 Property/Casualty Fact Book.* Other discussion is provided in Marlys Harris, "Crisis in the Courts," *Insurance Review* 47 (April 1986): 52-57; and Thomas S. Healey, "Insurers under Siege," *Insurance Review* 47 (May 1986): 50-57.

Not only have defendants in these cases felt the effects, so have insurance companies. Premiums collected for insurance protection have grossly understated required cash outflows when claims are made. To protect itself, the P&C industry often turns to *reinsurers*— insurance companies for insurance companies. Reinsurers agree, in exchange for a share of premium income, to assume responsibility for claims on policies written by other companies. In the 1980s, however, damage awards resulting from products such as Agent Orange and asbestos have taken a toll on even reinsurers' capacity to function profitably.[30]

P&C companies and reinsurers responded to severe losses in key lines of insurance either by raising premiums so high that many customers can no longer afford them, or by dropping lines of protection altogether. For example, some public school systems and municipal governments with stable or declining tax revenues found liability insurance policies unaffordable. Some physicians in high-risk specialties were forced to discontinue practice. Many analysts believe that, in the long run, changes in P&C operations caused by recent developments are not in the public interest, because desired levels of risk protection may no longer be available at affordable prices.

Economic and Regulatory Forces

At the same time, accelerating inflation affected claims on many lines of insurance. Escalating costs of claims require insurers to increase premium income, investment income, or both. Difficulties are compounded if cost increases occur during the downside of an underwriting cycle, a circumstance facing the industry in the mid-1980s. Adding to the challenge are increases in competition, such as that from depositories, which further limit premium increases to compensate for losses.

In 1984-1985, these forces collided. As shown in Figure 23.4, underwriting losses

among P&C firms set a new record each year. Many mutually owned insurers teetered on the brink of failure, their financial difficulties increased by an inability to raise external capital.[31] By raising premiums an average of 25 percent in 1986, the industry improved underwriting income so much that it reported an operating profit. P&C insurers were immediately criticized by consumer groups and politicians for bringing the so-called "insurance crisis" on themselves with the rate wars of the early 1980s.

Solutions to such "crises" that are fair to both policyholders and insurers are being sought at the state and federal level. For example, as of early 1987, 30 states had revised the way damages are awarded in civil lawsuits. The most publicized revision occurred in Florida in 1986, when the legislature limited liability awards for "pain and suffering" but tied the limits to a 40 percent rollback in premiums on commercial liability insurance. In keeping with the regulatory dialectic, several P&C firms announced they would no longer write commercial policies in Florida.[32]

Despite recent improvements in profitability for the industry as a whole, many small firms may have been "mortally wounded" by the events of 1984-1985. Analysts point to small firms' limited access to capital and to their poorly diversified product lines as the reasons for their continuing difficulties, and increased numbers of failures in the industry are predicted.

---

[30]"Now Even Insurers Have a Hard Time Getting Coverage," *Business Week,* December 2, 1985, pp. 128-129; and David B. Hilder, "Uncollectable Reinsurance Hurts Firms," *The Wall Street Journal,* April 1, 1986, p. 6.

[31]For more discussion, see "Insurance: Now It's a Risky Business," *Newsweek* 106 (November 4, 1985): 48-49; Rowland, "Insurance," pp. 1-10; "Business Struggles to Adapt as Insurance Crisis Spreads," *The Wall Street Journal,* January 21, 1986, p. 37; Harry Bacas, "Liability: Trying Times," *Nation's Business* 74 (February 1986): 22-27; and Stephen Taub, "Elephants Can Remember," *Financial World* 155 (March 18, 1986): 14-17.

[32]Roger Lowenstein, "Florida Legislature Votes 'Tort Reform' Aimed at Cutting Insurance Rates 40%," *The Wall Street Journal,* June 9, 1986, p. 2; Roger Lowenstein, "More Insurers Set Florida Cutbacks on New Coverage," *The Wall Street Journal,* June 11, 1986, p. 7; Robert E. Norton, "Tort Laws under Fire," *Fortune* 114 (July 7, 1986): 85-86; Albert J. Millus, "Tort Reform: Cure or Curse?" *Best's Review* (Property/Casualty Edition) 87 (November 1986): 28-34, 98-100.

P&C INSURERS: TECHNIQUES FOR INTEGRATED ASSET/ LIABILITY MANAGEMENT

Increasingly, the use of asset/liability management tools such as duration, futures, and options are mentioned as the keys to effective financial management in the new environment.

For example, industry publications stress the importance of estimating a firm's anticipated cash outflows resulting from policy claims, many of which may not actually occur until months or even years after a policy is written. If estimates are carefully made, asset portfolios can be selected with cash inflows to match the anticipated series of outflows. Thus, insurers can attempt to immunize at least portions of the balance sheet.[33] This strategy is quite a contrast to traditional management approaches, which use a lump sum estimate of claims based on past experience, then select asset portfolios to maximize investment income as a supplement to premium income.

Also stressed are interest rate or stock index futures and options as hedges against changes in the value of bond or stock portfolios.[34] The usual cautions involved in futures and options trading apply to insurers. In addition, the NAIC requires that gains and losses on futures positions be directly reflected in additions or reductions of net worth, rather than amortized over time. Still, in an environment of rising rates, profitable hedges can protect insurers against the shrinkage of net worth caused by a decline in portfolio values, which also must be directly written off against net worth. The emphasis on duration, interest rate futures, and options underscores the similarity of the principles of interest rate risk management and asset/liability management among financial institutions.

---

[33]Jeffrey B. Pantages, "Negating the Interest Rate Risk," *Best's Review* (Property/Casualty Edition) 85 (May 1984): 24-28, 120.

[34]Charles P. Edmonds, John S. Jahera, Jr., and Terry Rose, "Hedging the Future," *Best's Review* (Property/ Casualty Edition) 84 (September 1983): 30-32, 118; David J. Nye and Robert W. Kolb, "Inflation, Interest Rates, and Property-Liability Insurer Risk," *Journal of Risk and Insurance* 53 (March 1986): 144-154.

PERFORMANCE EVALUATION OF INSURANCE COMPANIES

Never has there been greater interest in evaluating the financial performance of individual life and P&C insurance companies. Managers, financial analysts, regulators, and investors are concerned with underwriting margins, operating costs, and investment portfolio earnings. Many financial ratios presented for depositories, especially those measuring portfolio performance, are appropriate for insurers and are not reviewed here. In addition, performance measures such as before- and after-tax return on assets and return on net worth are relevant for insurers. The special nature of insurer liabilities and the use of statutory accounting create a need for other performance measures, several of which are discussed in the following paragraphs.

The Combined Ratio

Because of the unique nature of insurer liabilities, no accurate measure of underwriting profits or losses exists. Nevertheless, P&C analysts have developed measures approximating the separate aspects of underwriting operations: claims losses and ordinary operating expenses. One widely used measure examines claims losses relative to earned premiums:

(23.3)

$$\text{Loss Ratio} = \frac{\text{Loss Expenses}}{\text{Total Earned Premiums}}$$

Another widely used measure is the expense ratio, calculated as:

(23.4)

$$\text{Expense Ratio} = \frac{\text{Operating Expenses}}{\text{Total Premiums Written}}$$

A third ratio closely followed for the P&C industry is the **combined ratio,** which is the *sum* of the loss and expense ratios, and is intended to measure the total relationship between premium income and premium expenses:

(23.5)

$$\frac{\text{Combined}}{\text{Ratio}} = \frac{\text{Loss}}{\text{Ratio}} + \frac{\text{Expense}}{\text{Ratio}}$$

Managers and analysts must be familiar with this performance measure because it is so widely cited. However, it is subject to interpretation problems because, as shown in Equations 23.3 and 23.4, the premiums used in the denominators of the loss ratio and the expense ratio are different. This difficulty increases the greater the difference between premiums written and premiums earned, a difference magnified during times of rapidly increasing policy sales. The use of the combined ratio is justified, however, by the fact that losses incurred are related to premiums earned during the period, while operating expenses, most of which are agents' commissions, are related to premiums written during the same period.

The Combined Ratio Illustrated.   Data in Table 23.5 are used in the following illustration of the combined ratio for the industry in 1985:

$$\text{Loss Ratio} = \frac{\text{Loss and Adjustment Expenses}}{\text{Total Earned Premiums}}$$

$$= \frac{\$118.572}{\$133.342} = 0.889$$

$$\text{Expense Ratio} = \frac{\text{Operating Expenses}}{\text{Total Premiums Written}}$$

$$= \frac{\$37.585}{\$144.859} = 0.259$$

$$\text{Combined Ratio} = 0.889 + 0.259 = 1.148$$
$$= 114.8\%$$

This figure is usually interpreted to mean that underwriting expenses exceeded underwriting income by almost 15 percent. A combined ratio of less than 1 indicates an underwriting profit.

Net Underwriting Margin as a Performance Measure

The net underwriting margin (Equation 23.1) examines both premium and expense data as a percentage of assets. It is a different way of measuring underwriting results. Because P&C insurers report expenses on a cash basis, the use of total premiums written may be the best choice in the ratio if it is available.

The net underwriting margin indicates the extent to which underwriting gains or losses contribute to overall profitability, and can be used for both life insurers and P&C insurers, although only a calculation for P&C insurers is shown here. Using data from Tables 23.4 and 23.5, the net underwriting margin for the P&C industry as a whole in 1985 was:

$$\frac{\text{Net}}{\text{Underwriting}} = \frac{\frac{\text{Premium}}{\text{Income}} - \frac{\text{Policy}}{\text{Expenses}}}{\text{Total Assets}}$$

$$\frac{\$144.859 - \$158.353}{\$311.365} = -0.043 = -4.3\%$$

In the P&C industry in 1985, for each dollar of admitted assets, 4.3 cents were lost. Of course, net investment income of $19.508 billion was available to offset some of the shortfall. Because underwriting accounts for the vast majority of insurers' cash inflows and outflows, individual firms are unlikely to meet targets for ROA and RONW unless they carefully watch the margin between premium income and policy expenses. In recent years, this has meant reducing operating expenses, especially commissions, and pricing insurance to better reflect the financial risk the insurer assumes, rather than engaging in rate wars to increase market share. Insurers will continue to emphasize cost management and proper pricing of risks.

Sources of Industry Information

A problem faced by insurance industry analysts is the shortage of performance standards against which to compare individual firms. Aggregate industry data are available in the annual *Fact Books* for both life and P&C insurers, cited throughout this chapter, but the information sheds little light on the performance of individual companies or subgroups. Because conditions in different lines of insurance may differ markedly, aggregate comparison information may mislead the analyst of a particular insurer.

A. M. Best Publications.   The A. M. Best Company of Oldwick, New Jersey, publishes *Best's Aggregates and Averages,* a compilation of statistical information on P&C insurers, with breakdowns by line of insurance. Emphasis in these reports, and in periodic issues of *Best's Review* (a monthly trade publication with editions for both life and P&C insurers), is on larger insurers.

Best also publishes *Best's Insurance Reports* annually for both life and P&C companies. These large volumes present condensed balance sheets and income statements for all active insurers, along with Best's own rating of a firm's financial condition. Best's ratings are based on analysis of liquidity, profitability, and leverage ratios, and on information such as policy volume and cancellations. These ratings have been considered authoritative by investors and industry observers for many years. Rating methods were revised in 1986 in the wake of increasing criticism that they were not sufficiently sensitive to changing financial conditions in a firm.[35]

Because of the difficulty in obtaining averages reflecting comparable groups of firms, it is helpful to prepare comparative analyses for several similar insurers rather than to rely solely on available sources of industry information. The data required for such analyses are available in Best publications.

---

[35]Arthur Snyder, "Best's Ratings: A New Look," *Best's Review,* (Property/Casualty Edition) 87 (April 1986): 14-16, 122-128; Fredric Dannen, "How Good Are A. M. Best's Ratings?" *Institutional Investor* 19 (December 1985): 153, 156, 160.

SUMMARY

Insurance companies are founded on probability estimation, better known to insurers as actuarial science. Premiums and reported obligations are based on estimates of the amount and timing of claims a firm will pay in the future. Successful financial management involves balancing premium income and investment income against benefits paid to policyholders. Life and P&C insurers have different financial characteristics, arising from the types of policies they write. They have structural characteristics in common, however, and all have experienced earnings pressures in the 1980s.

Life insurers have traditionally enjoyed predictable cash flows, thanks to the popularity of traditional whole life insurance. Higher interest rates and changing consumer preferences, however, have forced insurers to develop alternate products, making premium income and obligations to policyholders subject to market conditions and policyholder preferences. Changes in operating conditions have made asset/liability management strategies increasingly important for life insurers.

Property and casualty insurers have faced a similar need to adapt management strategies to changing market and economic conditions, although incentives for change are different. In recent years, the major influences on earnings of P&C insurers have been inflation and larger litigation awards. These factors, along with the traditional underwriting cycle, depressed underwriting income so strongly in the mid-1980s that even rapidly rising investment income could not protect earnings. As with life insurers, these operating changes require P&C insurers to adjust asset/liability management strategies.

Questions

1. Compare and contrast the asset and liability structures of life insurers and P&C insurers. What explanations can you offer for the differences? For the similarities?

2. Compare the assets and liabilities of both life insurers and P&C insurers to those of depository institutions. How do services offered and sources of funds result in balance sheet differences across the three industries?

3. How is the insurance industry regulated? How does the structure of insurance regulation compare to that of depository institution regulation? Which approach do you consider more efficient and effective? Why?

4. Why have life insurers traditionally invested heavily in long-term Treasury securities and privately placed bonds? Why have life insurers recently adopted new portfolio strategies?

5. What are policy reserves? How is the amount of policy reserves on a life insurer's balance sheet related to the law of large numbers? To the estimates of actuaries? To the estimates of premium and investment income?

6. What are the two major sources of revenues for life insurers? Explain how actuarial estimates and anticipated investment income affect the level of premiums set by insurers.

7. What is the net underwriting margin? How does it differ from the net interest margin emphasized in the management of depository institutions?

8. Compare and contrast the major types of life insurance policies. If you were managing a life insurance firm, which type would you prefer to offer? If you were the customer, what policy characteristics would you prefer to purchase? Why? How have new types of policies forced insurers to focus on asset/liability management?

9. How were high interest rates in the early 1980s related to consumer demand for new types of life insurance policies? To the increase in policy loans on life insurers' balance sheets?

10. How have new life insurance policies, such as variable life and universal life, affected cash flows, operating costs, and investment policies of life insurance companies?

11. What are separate asset accounts? Why do some insurance managers view these assets as good candidates for immunization? What are the advantages and disadvantages of immunizing these accounts?

12. Explain the basic differences between statutory accounting and generally accepted accounting principles. Do you agree that regulators' and professional accountants' reporting standards should differ? Why or why not?

13. What is the underwriting cycle in the property and casualty insurance business? Explain the forces in the mid-1980s that joined with the underwriting cycle to cause severe problems for P&C insurers.

14. Find recent articles about interest rates and policy premiums for P&C insurance, and identify whether the industry is currently in the up or down phase of the underwriting cycle.

15. What is the function of reinsurers?

16. What problems are encountered in analyzing the performance of insurers through trend analysis and comparison to industry standards? How are these problems different from those encountered in performance analysis of other financial institutions? Of nonfinancial firms?

17. As noted in the chapter, to solve the recent insurance "crisis," politicians in some states placed limits on insurance premiums and/or damage awards to which plaintiffs are entitled in civil suits. From recent publications, such as *Best's Review,* find information on the current status of regulatory efforts and insurers' responses, particularly in your state.

18. What are the potential problems with placing regulatory ceilings on liability insurance premiums? The potential benefits? What types of solutions to the problem might you offer to your legislative representatives? Do you think everyone has a right to be insured at an affordable cost? Why or why not?

Problems

1. Use information from the Commissioners Standard Ordinary Table abbreviated in Table 23.3, and an assumed rate of return on invested premiums of 6 percent, to answer the following questions.
   a. What is the probability that a policyholder who is 38 years old will live to be 39?
   b. What is the pure premium on a $75,000 one-year term policy for a 38-year-old man? Show two ways to calculate it.
   c. If the assumed rate of return on invested premiums were 9 percent, what would the pure premium be for the policy described in b? What if the assumed rate were 3 percent?
   d. If, instead, the policyholder wished to take out a whole life policy with a face amount of $75,000, identify the additional steps taken to calculate the premium. (No calculations are necessary, but consult the appendix to this chapter for information.) Would the first year's premium on the whole life policy be higher or lower than the premium you calculated in b? Why?

2. a. Using information from the Commissioners Standard Ordinary Table abbreviated in Table 23.3, and an assumed rate of return on invested premiums of 8 percent, calculate the pure premium on a $250,000 one-year term policy for a four-year-old boy. If you were the parent of a four-year-old boy, what factors might influence you to take out a life insurance policy on him? What type of policy would you prefer? Why?
   b. Calculate the pure premium on a $250,000 one-year term policy for a 70-year-old man. If you were 70 and had no life insurance, what type of policy, if any, would you choose? Why?

3. Use the data given on Gibraltar Life Insurance Company to answer the following questions.

Problem 23.3
Gibraltar Life Insurance Company, Year-End 1984 and 1985 (Millions)

	1984		1985	
Assets				
Government securities		$ 1,677		$ 3,741
Corporate securities		12,510		17,051
Bonds	$11,216		$13,836	
Stock	1,294		3,215	
Real estate loans		10,989		12,411
Real estate investments		971		1,678
Loans to policyholders		1,322		1,953
Other assets		1,665		2,475
Total Assets		$29,134		$39,309
Obligations and Net Worth				
Policy reserves	$24,622		$33,534	
Policy dividend obligations	595		781	
Other obligations	1,898		2,907	
Total obligations		$27,115		$37,222
Total net worth (surplus and common stock)		2,019		2,087
Total Obligations and Net Worth		$29,134		$39,309

a. Compare Gibraltar's financial condition and performance in 1985 to that of the industry as a whole, shown in Tables 23.1 and 23.2. What similarities and differences in financial management between Gibraltar and the industry do you find? Can you suggest areas in which Gibraltar should improve?

b. What trends, if any, appear in Gibraltar's financial condition and performance over the two years? In your analysis, be sure to consider the net underwriting margin and RONW.

Problem 23.3
Gilbraltar Life Insurance Company, Income and Expenses for 1984 and 1985 (Millions)

	1984		1985	
Revenues:				
Premium payments	$3,930		$5,760	
Net investment earnings and other income	1,463		2,924	
Total Revenues		$5,393		$8,684
Expenses:				
Benefit payments	$3,091		$4,666	
Additions to policy reserves	1,258		2,509	
Operating expenses	703		1,043	
Total Expenses		5,052		8,218
Net Operating Income		$ 341		$ 466
Taxes		262		372
Net Income		$ 79		$ 94

Problem 23.4
Town and Country Mutual Automobile Insurance Company, Year-End 1984 and 1985 (Millions)

	1984		1985	
Assets				
Bonds		$ 8,109		$ 9,165
U.S. Treasury	$1,169		$1,106	
State and local	2,779		3,505	
Special revenue	4,097		4,497	
Other	64		57	
Common and preferred stock		3,192		3,260
Mortgages and other loans		2,422		2,501
Other assets		1,652		1,745
Total Assets		$15,375		$16,671
Liabilities and Net Worth				
Total loss and unearned premium reserves		$ 7,185		$ 7,879
Total surplus and common stock		8,190		8,792
Total Liabilities and Net Worth		$15,375		$16,671

Problem 23.4
Town and Country Mutual Automobile Insurance Company,
Income and Expenses for 1984 and 1985 (Millions)

	1984		1985	
Revenues				
Total premiums written	$8,011		$8,975	
Less unearned premiums	375		473	
Total earned premiums		$7,636		$8,502
Net investment earnings and other income		682		1,022
Total Revenues		$8,318		$9,524
Expenses				
Loss expenses	$6,077		$7,276	
Policyholder dividends	136		4	
Operating expenses	1,355		1,511	
Total Expenses	$7,568		$8,791	
Underwriting Results				
Earned premiums	$7,636		$8,502	
Less:				
Loss expenses	6,077		7,276	
Operating expenses	1,355		1,511	
Statutory underwriting gain (loss)	$ 204		($ 285)	
Less dividends to policyholders	136		4	
Net Underwriting Gain (Loss)	$ 68		($ 289)	

---

  c. What other information about Gibraltar would you like to have before assessing the quality of its financial management?

4. Using the data for Town and Country Mutual Automobile Insurance Company, answer the following questions:

  a. Compare Town and Country's financial condition and performance in 1985 to that of the industry as a whole, shown in Tables 23.4 and 23.5. What similarities and differences in financial management do you find between Town and Country and the industry? Can you suggest areas for improvement?

  b. What major differences do you find between Town and Country's 1984 and 1985 operating results? To what do you think the differences can probably be attributed? In your analysis, be sure to consider the net underwriting margin, RONW, and the combined ratio.

Selected References

American Council of Life Insurance. *Life Insurance Fact Book*. Various issues.

Curry, Timothy, and Mark Warshawsky. "Life Insurance Companies in a Changing Environment." *Federal Reserve Bulletin* 72 (July 1986): 449-460.

Insurance Information Institute. *Property and Casualty Fact Book*. Various issues.

Kopcke, Richard W. "The Federal Income Taxation of Life Insurance Companies." *New England Economic Review* (Federal Reserve Bank of Boston) (March/April 1985), pp. 5-19.

McGee, Robert T. "The Cycle in Property/Casualty Insurance." *Quarterly Review* (Federal Reserve Bank of New York) 11 (Autumn 1986): 22-30.

Meir, Robert I., and Sandra G. Gustavson. *Life Insurance: Theory and Practice*. Plano, TX: Business Publications, Inc., 1984.

Nye, David J., and Robert W. Kolb. "Inflation, Interest Rates, and Property-Liability Insurer Risk." *Journal of Risk and Insurance* 53 (March 1986): 144-154.

Pesando, James E. "The Interest Sensitivity of the Flow of Funds through Life Insurance Companies: An Econometric Analysis." *Journal of Finance* 29 (September 1974): 1,105-1,121.

Saunders, Anthony. "The Effect of Changing Regulation on Investment Policy of Life Insurance Companies." In *The Emerging Financial Industry*. Edited by Arnold W. Sametz. Lexington, MA: Lexington Books, 1984, pp. 85-94.

Smith, Michael L. "The Life Insurance Policy as an Options Package." *Journal of Risk and Insurance* 49 (December 1982): 583-601.

Snyder, Arthur. "Best's Ratings: A New Look." *Best's Review* (Property/Casualty Edition) 87 (April 1986): 14-16, 122-128.

Stowe, John D., and Collin J. Watson. "A Multivariate Analysis of the Composition of Life Insurer Balance Sheets." *Journal of Risk and Insurance* 52 (June 1985): 222-240.

Walden, Michael L. "The Whole Life Insurance Policy as an Options Package: An Empirical Investigation." *Journal of Risk and Insurance* 52 (March 1985): 44-58.

Webb, James R. "Real Estate Investment Acquisition Rules for Life Insurance Companies and Pension Funds: A Survey." *AREUEA Journal* 12 (Winter 1984): 495-520.

Appendix 23A

CALCULATION OF THE PREMIUM ON A WHOLE LIFE POLICY

If a 35-year-old male seeks a $100,000 whole life policy, the insurer estimates the expected cash outflow, based on the odds of the purchaser's dying, for each year up to age 100. (Most mortality tables assume a 100 percent probability of death between the ages of 99 and 100.) Table 23A.1 shows the calculation for selected years between age 35 and age 100, using data from the Commissioners Standard Ordinary Mortality Table (Table 23.3) and a 4 percent discount rate for present value calculations.

Probability of Claims

Because a man taking out a policy at age 35 is expected to be 1 of 9,491,617 who have survived to that point, that number becomes the base against which the probability of claims in subsequent years is measured. For example, of those living until age 36, 21,216 are expected to die before age 37; that is, of 9,491,617 persons insured as of age 35, 21,216 ÷ 9,491,617 = 0.002235 = 0.2235% are expected to die between the ages of 36 and 37. There is, consequently, a .002235 probability that his beneficiaries under a policy originated at age 35 will make a claim during the second year of the policy. Several of these probabilities are shown in Column 5 of Table 23A.1.

If the insurer does not pay until the *end* of the year, the present value of each year's expected claims is calculated as of the time the policy is sold, as shown in Column 7. For example, the present value of $223.53, the expected cash outflow to the insurer at the *end* of policy year 2, is $206.66 as of the origination date of the policy (*beginning* of policy year 1):

$$\$223.53 \div (1.04)^2 = \$206.66$$

Lump Sum Premium Required

Because insurance protection will be provided until age 100, the total present value of the insurer's cash outflows is the sum over 65 years, or $24,682.38. The total includes some yearly amounts not shown in the table. It is possible for a 35-year-old to buy a $100,000 whole life policy at age 35 by paying this single sum plus loading, but few people choose this option. Not only does it require considerable cash at one time, but some premiums may never be needed. If the insured dies at age 40 and has prepaid for protection until age 100, the prepayment would be nothing but lost money to his beneficiaries, who would receive $100,000 in death benefits regardless of when he dies.

Converting the Lump Sum into a Level Premium

Most whole life customers elect to pay a level premium. Table 23A.1 assumes the payment of premiums as long as the insured lives. The level premium is based on data in Columns 8 and 9. Insurers count on receiving premiums from some policyholders at the beginning of each policy year in order to meet the claims of others. But policyholders who die during a year will not be around to pay the next year's premium, so not only will the insurance company not get their premium payments, it will not earn interest on them either. Insurers would be ignoring these facts if they simply divided the total lump sum premium required to insure a 35-year-old (as previously calculated) by the number of years until age 100, and charged that amount each year.

To take these factors into account, the insurer calculates the probability of someone's surviving to pay his premium at the beginning of each policy year. Shown in Column 8, the

Table 23A.1
Calculation of Level Annual Premium on $100,000 Whole Life Policy for a 35-Year-Old Male

(1) Policy Year	(2) Age	(3) Number Living	(4) Number Dying	(5) Probability of Claims by Those Living at Age 35 (4) ÷ 9,491,617	(6) Insurer's Annual Expected Cash Outflow at End of Year (5) × $100,000	(7) Present Value of Cash Outflow as of the Beginning of Year 1 (6) discounted at 4%	(8) Of Those Alive at Age 35, Proportion That Will Pay Premium at Beginning of Year (3) ÷ 9,491,617	(9) Discounted Value of Column 8 as of Beginning of Year 1
1	35	9,491,617	20,027	.002110	$211.00	$202.88	1.000000	1.000000
2	36	9,471,590	21,216	.002235	223.53	206.66	0.997890	0.959510
3	37	9,450,374	22,681	.002390	238.96	212.43	0.995655	0.920539
4	38	9,427,693	24,323	.002563	256.26	219.05	0.993265	0.883009
5	39	9,403,369	26,235	.002764	276.41	227.19	0.990703	0.846857
6	40	9,377,134	28,319	.002984	298.36	235.80	0.987938	0.812013
.	.	.	.	.	.	.	.	.
.	.	.	.	.	.	.	.	.
61	95	146,720	48,412	.005100	510.05	46.62	0.0154578273	0.001469
62	96	98,308	37,804	.003983	398.29	35.01	0.0103573626	0.000947
63	97	60,504	29,054	.003061	306.10	25.87	0.0063744388	0.000560
64	98	31,450	20,693	.002180	218.02	17.72	0.0033134333	0.000280
65	99	10,756	10,756	.001133	113.33	8.85	0.0011332605	0.000092

Total premium due: $24,682.38   Column (9) Total: 19.582582

Annual premium due: $24,682.38 ÷ 19.582582 = $1,260.43

677

number of policyholders expected to reach a given age is divided by the number who reached 35, the base year in the example. For instance, the 9,471,590 men expected to be alive at age 36 are 9,471,590 ÷ 9,491,617 = 0.99789 = 99.789% of those who lived until age 35. Thus, there is a probability in excess of 99 percent that someone taking out a policy at age 35 will be around to pay the premium at age 36, but only a 0.11 percent probability that the same policyholder will be around to pay his premium when he is 99.

Column 9 further reduces the probability that a premium payment will actually be received by considering the interest lost by the insurer from not receiving the lump-sum premium in advance, or from not receiving the interest on lost premium payments from those who die. Because premium payments are assumed to be received at the *beginning* of a year

for which protection is purchased, the probability that someone will pay the initial premium is, of course, 100 percent—life insurance policies are not issued to dead people. The probability that the second year's policy premium will be made is discounted back only one period, because it is assumed to be made at the beginning of that year—in other words, the end of the first policy year:

$$.99789 \div 1.04 = .95951$$

The sum of the values in Column 9 is the weighted number of premium payments expected, considering the probability of death and the impact of lost interest. When divided into the expected cost of insuring a 35-year-old for life, the level annual pure premium is $1,260.43, without considering operating costs.

Chapter 24

PENSION FUNDS, INVESTMENT COMPANIES, AND SECURITIES FIRMS

Nobody's ashamed anymore to admit at a cocktail party that he's into mutual funds.

David Silver
President
Investment Company Institute (1986)

ONE Monday morning in 1979, a visitor walked into an Atlanta bank and requested a $50,000 cash advance on his Visa card. When informed that an advance of this size was unheard of, he asked the bank to validate the transaction with the processing bank, Bank One in Columbus, Ohio. Bank One approved the advance without question, and later approved two more for the same customer, who was in town to attend an auction. The stranger's Visa card was a debit card and was not issued by a bank at all, but by the securities firm of Merrill Lynch. It entitled the customer to borrow against securities held in his Merrill Lynch Cash Management Account (CMA).[1] Essentially, the securities firm was making a secured loan to its CMA customer, as a bank might do.

Statistics in Chapter 1 indicate the importance of pension funds, investment companies, and securities firms—the institutions discussed in this chapter. Private pension funds held assets

---

[1]Martin Mayer, "Merrill Lynch Quacks Like a Bank," *Fortune* 102 (October 20, 1980): 134-144.

in excess of $1 *trillion* by year-end 1985. Money market and other mutual funds, only one segment of the investment company industry, controlled about $500 billion in financial assets.[2]

Not only does their size make these institutions important, their role in the flow of funds across economic sectors is significant. Pension funds offer financial security for the retired population. Investment companies provide professional investment management and diversified portfolios to small savers at reasonable costs. Many securities firms, particularly through the investment banking function, bear the risk for firms raising funds in the capital markets.

The managers of these institutions face just as many challenges as do those of depositories, finance companies, and insurance firms in the current economic environment. Management techniques in these three types of nondepositories are examined in the pages that follow.

TYPES AND GROWTH OF PENSION FUNDS

A pension plan is a program established by an employer to provide retirement and disability benefits to employees. An organization called a pension fund administers the program and manages assets purchased with the contributions of employers and employees.[3]

Types of Pension Funds

There are three broad categories of pension funds: federal government, state and local government, and private. Only private funds are covered in this chapter. Federal plans, the largest of which is the Old Age, Survivors, and Disability Insurance System (Social Security), do not rely heavily on asset accumulation to fund benefits. Instead, they collect from those currently employed to pay retirement benefits, and assets under management are quite small in comparison to the number of workers covered. The Social Security system, for example, which in 1984 paid benefits of over $175 billion to approximately 36 million people, had year-end assets of only $31 billion.[4] Although state and local retirement systems accumulate a larger volume of assets, they also differ in many ways from private funds. Most importantly, they are not regulated by the same federal laws that govern private plans. Management differs from state to state, depending upon regulations and objectives.

There are even two categories of private pension funds, insured and noninsured. An insured plan operates under a service arrangement with a life insurance company, giving the insurer responsibility for collecting receipts, paying benefits, and/or administering the fund's assets. Noninsured plans are twice as large as insured plans. Because of their size and importance, the discussion that follows is confined to managerial issues affecting noninsured private pension plans.

Pension Fund Growth

The lifespan of Americans has increased in the 20th century, from an average of about 47 years in 1900 to about 75 years in the 1980s. The extended lifespan means that employees must plan for retirement income, and pension fund contributions and asset accumulation have

---

[2]Board of Governors of the Federal Reserve System, *Flow of Funds Accounts, Year-End 1962-1985,* September 1986, p. 28.

[3]The pension plan is technically considered to be the formal arrangement under which benefits will be accumulated and distributed, and the fund is the organization for administering the plan. The Employee Retirement Income Security Act of 1974 (ERISA), however, did not distinguish the two, so for accounting purposes the Financial Accounting Standards Board considers the *plan* to be the reporting entity. See Richard M. Steinberg and Harold Dankner, *Pensions: An ERISA Accounting and Management Guide* (New York: John Wiley and Sons, 1983). In this chapter, the terms are used interchangeably.

[4]American Council of Life Insurance, *1986 Pension Facts Update,* pp. 9-10.

grown accordingly. Support from labor unions also contributed to the growth of pensions. In 1949, the Supreme Court ruled that pension benefits could be included in collective bargaining agreements, and the nation's largest unions took advantage of the ruling. The period 1950–1960 was one of strong growth for pension funds; the number of private plan participants more than doubled, and fund assets grew at a similar rate. Private pension fund growth continued at an average annual rate of over 13 percent between 1970 and the mid-1980s.[5]

INFLUENCE OF ERISA

As pension plans grew, so did the possibility that some of the funds and/or sponsoring corporations would fail to meet obligations to participants. Probably the most widely publicized failure occurred when the Studebaker automobile company in South Bend, Indiana, went out of business in 1964. Inadequacies in the Studebaker pension fund left most of the firm's employees with fewer benefits than promised, or none at all. Ten years later, Congress passed the Employee Retirement Income Security Act (ERISA), with the intention of preventing pension fund insolvencies. ERISA, introduced in Chapter 2, affected many aspects of the management of privately sponsored pension plans.[6]

Benefit Vesting and Full Funding

As noted in Chapter 2, ERISA set standards for 100 percent vesting of benefits for most employees after 15 or fewer years of service; employees are entitled to vested benefits even if they leave the employer before retirement. The law also attempted to ensure that employers worked toward full funding, or the equality of pension assets and accrued liabilities.

Defined Contributions versus Defined Benefits. The funding obligations of the employer are affected by whether the plan is a *defined benefit* program or a *defined contribution* program. A defined benefit plan promises in advance to pay employees a specified level of benefits. The total amount of the fund's liabilities and the date incurred are not known with certainty and depend on the characteristics (such as age and sex) of the company's work force. The fund's liabilities are estimated using actuarial methods, and the employer's contributions are based on those calculations. A major question in the management and regulation of defined benefit plans is whether an employer's contribution to the fund is sufficient to meet future pension liabilities.

In a defined contribution plan, the per employee contributions made by the employer are specified, but benefits paid during retirement are not promised in advance. Instead, they depend upon contributions and earnings accumulated over time. Because employees are not promised specific benefits, the question of funding adequacy does not arise.

Pension Benefits Guaranty Corporation

ERISA established the Pension Benefits Guaranty Corporation (PBGC) to assure, within limits, the payment of up to 85 percent of vested benefits if a defined benefit pension fund fails. The PBGC is supported by annual premiums paid by private pension funds and is based on the number of participants covered. If a plan is terminated, the PBGC takes control of the fund's assets and uses them to pay as large a portion of the benefits as possible. The sponsoring company of a terminated plan may be held liable for unfunded benefits based on a formula established by Congress in the Single Employer Pension Plan Amendment Act of 1986.[7]

In recent years, the PBGC has faced problems similar to those of the FDIC and especially of the FSLIC. The PBGC must insure all private defined benefit plans, so it faces moral haz-

---

[5]Steinberg and Dankner, *Pensions*, p. 4 and *1986 Pension Facts Update*, p. 3.

[6]In addition to ERISA, the Multiemployer Pension Plan Amendments Act of 1980 affects plans jointly sponsored by more than one employer.

[7]Joel Chernoff, "Premium to PBGC Triples under New Law," *Pensions and Investment Age,* March 31, 1986, p. 3.

ard from the actions of poor fund managers. In addition, firms with financial problems and unfunded liabilities in excess of a specified percentage of net worth can turn their obligations over to the PBGC. Unlike the deposit insurers, however, the PBGC has a very limited line of credit with the Treasury.

By 1987, the agency's net worth was estimated at a *negative* $4 billion (that is, it was insolvent), thanks to the financial difficulties of several large firms that sought to transfer to the PBGC their unfunded liabilities. These developments may affect healthy pension plans as well. For example, in 1986, a law was passed that more than tripled the required per-participant insurance premium sponsors must pay. Risk-related insurance premiums also have been considered, similar to proposals for deposit insurance.[8]

Fiduciary Responsibilities

ERISA also addressed the fiduciary responsibilities of pension fund managers. Investment decisions are generally based on the **prudent man rule,** which requires a manager to make decisions with the same care and judgment that a prudent individual (man *or* woman) would use in handling personal investments.

The ERISA guidelines modified this traditional interpretation. ERISA stated that the pension fund fiduciary should emulate investment principles that a person "acting in like capacity and familiar with such matters would use in the conduct of an enterprise of like character with like aims."[9] Some observers believe

ERISA applies a "prudent expert" rule to pension fund management, opening the door to more sophisticated investment techniques. In particular, earlier trust law focuses on individual securities, rather than a portfolio, and does not recognize the importance of diversification in risk management.

The impact of ERISA on strategies for managing pension funds has been a subject of great interest. Evidence on that relationship is examined later in the chapter. At this point, however, two provisions that ERISA did *not* include should be emphasized. No requirements are placed on the level of benefits promised by an employer or on the dollar amount of employer contributions. Nor does ERISA require employers to establish pension plans. Rather, the intent is to protect employee interests once a plan has been established and benefits defined.

PENSION FUNDS: DESCRIPTIVE DATA

Asset Structure

Noninsured private pension funds invest the largest proportion of their assets in corporate stock. Under ERISA's encouragement to diversify portfolios, however, other assets are a bit more important than in 1975, when equities were more than 54 percent of total assets. As expected under changing market conditions and as seen in Table 24.1, private pension fund portfolios are not stable. Corporate equities, U.S. government securities, and corporate and foreign bonds are large asset categories. Smaller holdings include deposits, mortgages, commercial ("open market") paper, and miscellaneous assets.

Sources of Funds

Pension funds, unlike some institutions, have no liabilities with face amounts or maturity dates in the traditional sense. They have obligations to covered employees, but most obligations are difficult to quantify and must be estimated by actuaries. Instead of considering pension fund obligations in the traditional bal-

---

[8]The financial viability of the PBGC is discussed in Diane Hal Gropper, "Propping up the PBGC," *Institutional Investor* 20 (September 1986): 161-170; James F. Siekmeier, "Can We Count on Private Pensions?" *Economic Commentary,* Federal Reserve Bank of Cleveland, February 15, 1986; "Pension Insurance Fund Suffers from FSLIC-Like Woes," *Savings Institutions* 106 (December 1985): 124-125; and Alicia H. Munnell, "Guaranteeing Private Pension Benefits: A Potentially Expensive Business," *New England Economic Review,* Federal Reserve Bank of Boston (March/April 1982), pp. 24-47.

[9]Interpretation of ERISA's fiduciary requirements is discussed in Robert C. Pozen, "The Prudent Person Rule and ERISA: A Legal Perspective," *Financial Analysts Journal* 33 (March/April 1977): 30-35.

Table 24.1
Assets of Private Noninsured Pension Funds (Millions)

	1981		1982		1983		1984		1985	
Demand deposits and currency	$ 3,300	0.69%	$ 3,500	0.64%	$ 4,100	0.63%	$ 4,500	0.68%	$ 4,500	0.59%
Time deposits	26,700	5.59	27,600	5.03	32,400	5.00	35,400	5.37	35,300	4.66
Corporate equities	210,000	43.98	258,100	47.00	311,300	48.00	297,200	45.09	383,000	50.57
U.S. government securities	73,000	15.29	79,400	14.46	92,400	14.25	99,700	15.13	106,500	14.06
Corporate and foreign bonds	85,100	17.82	91,600	16.68	103,300	15.93	113,700	17.25	119,400	15.76
Mortgages	3,900	0.82	4,200	0.76	4,200	0.65	4,500	0.68	4,800	0.63
Open market paper	21,800	4.57	23,000	4.19	27,800	4.29	31,200	4.73	31,200	4.12
Miscellaneous assets	53,700	11.25	61,700	11.24	73,100	11.27	72,900	11.06	72,700	9.60
Total Assets	$477,500	100.00%	$549,100	100.00%	$648,600	100.00%	$659,100	100.00%	$757,400	100.00%

Source: Board of Governors of the Federal Reserve System, *Flow of Funds Accounts, Financial Assets and Liabilities Year-End, 1962-1985.*

ance sheet sense, the ensuing focus is on sources of funds to private pension funds.

Corporations with employees covered by pension plans provide the majority of funds with which assets are purchased. While employees may also contribute, in many cases they do not. Thus, corporate decisions determine whether the plan is adequately funded, **overfunded,** or **underfunded.** If a plan is overfunded, the value of its assets exceeds that of its estimated obligations, and the fund accumulates net worth, or an excess of assets over liabilities. When a fund is underfunded, it has negative net worth because assets are less than the value of estimated obligations. Adequately funded plans have no net worth, and asset values equal the value of estimated future obligations.

Because corporate contributions to pension funds reduce the corporation's after-tax profits, firms face conflicting influences on the contribution decision. On the one hand, ERISA guidelines require eventual full funding; on the other, reductions in pension contributions improve profitability. The problem is further complicated by the fact that asset and obligation values for pension funds change with market conditions.

Actuarial Assumptions. The adequacy of contributions also depends upon actuarial assumptions. Most obligations depend on future occurrences, such as the retirement age of covered employees and how long they live after retirement. To be *fully funded,* a pension fund's assets must equal the *present value* of future obligations less the *present value* of future contributions, an amount known as the *funding target.* The funding target depends on actuarial assumptions about future obligations and the yield on the fund's assets over time. These assumptions resemble those used to establish reserves in the life insurance industry, illustrated in the previous chapter. Like life insurance actuaries, pension actuaries are cautious, preferring to err by overestimating future obligations rather than by underestimating them.

Effects of Changing Actuarial Assumptions. The impact on pension plans of changing even one actuarial assumption has been the

subject of research. The assumptions affect new funds the employer contributes, and thus funds available for investment each year, as well as the plan's standing with regulatory authorities.

Because each pension plan operates under its own set of actuarial assumptions, it is impossible to assess the funding adequacy and net worth, if any, of the pension system as a whole. A recent study of large Canadian pension funds concluded, however, that under uniform, reasonable actuarial assumptions, the majority of plans were overfunded, and that managers would benefit from public, explicit, and uniform actuarial assumptions.[10]

When pension fund actuaries notify the corporate sponsor that a plan is overfunded, contributions may decrease, subsequently affecting pension fund management. For example, the stock market surge and falling interest rates between 1982 and 1986 increased the value of pension fund assets. Actuarial assumptions in some plans were changed, increasing the expected rate of return on assets in the future. Because this rate is used to discount future obligations, estimates of the present value of obligations decreased, and some corporations reduced contributions. Some firms even terminated their pension plans to capture the excess assets. The Tax Reform Act of 1986 discourages terminations, however, by imposing a 10 percent excise tax on recaptured excess pension fund assets.[11]

MANAGING PENSION FUND ASSETS

The assets and sources of funds for private pension funds suggest that their management is

[10]D. Don Ezra and Keith P. Ambachtsheer, "Pension Funds: Rich or Poor?" *Financial Analysts Journal* 41 (March/April 1985): 43-56.

[11]"Pension Funding: An Irksome Piece of the Savings Puzzle," *Business Week,* July 8, 1985, p. 16; Christopher Farrell and Resa W. King, "Not Everybody's Happy about Low Interest Rates," *Business Week,* April 14, 1986, p. 82; Lynn Asinof, "Excess Pension Assets Lure Corporate Raiders," *The Wall Street Journal,* September 11, 1985, p. 6; Stuart Weiss, "Fat Pension Funds Can Make Companies Tempting Targets," *Business Week,* November 10, 1986, pp. 106-108.

more like that of insurance firms than management of other financial institutions.

Liquidity

Pensions need not consider explicit reserve requirements, but as insurers must protect cash flows to ensure payments to policyholders, pension funds must have cash for benefit payments. Outflows for pension funds and life insurers are much more predictable than for depositories. Furthermore, for new or growing plans, corporate contributions usually exceed payments to covered employees in the same period, so liquidity considerations are not managers' foremost concern.

Taxability

Taxation is an important influence. Earnings on pension fund assets are not taxable at the fund level. For all practical purposes, this removes tax-exempt securities from investment consideration because of their inferior yields.

Corporate Sponsor Preferences

One of the unusual aspects of pension fund management is the potential division of control among several parties. The pension fund itself must operate in the best interests of covered employees but depends upon the sponsoring firm for its sources of funds. The plan's administrators may make investment decisions themselves, or they may entrust the responsibility for investing all or a portion of fund assets to professional portfolio managers. The sponsoring firm, the administrators, and the managers may at times have conflicting interests.

Earnings Level and Sponsor Contributions.   As noted, the better the earnings performance of the fund's assets, the more likely that corporate contributions will be reduced. That possibility introduces a potential conflict between investment performance and access to new funds, because corporate sponsors may wish to substitute the fund's current earnings for some of their pension fund expenses, in order to meet funding targets.

Financial Position of the Corporate Sponsor.   The financial strength of the sponsor also affects asset management. For example, in 1982, U.S. Steel decided not to make its pension contribution in cash. Instead, the firm printed a new issue of preferred stock, assigned it a value of $100 per share, and contributed it to the pension plan. The market value of the securities was unknown at the time, because the stock had never been publicly traded. Through this paper transaction, U.S. Steel added over $300 million to the equity portion of its own balance sheet and avoided borrowing to meet its pension obligation. That same year, a difficult one for many industrial firms, several companies used the same approach to financing pension obligations.[12]

The sponsor's decision to contribute stock is out of the control of pension fund managers, yet it may strongly affect their discretion. If the securities are publicly traded, as was the case for a contribution of three million shares of common stock made by Kodak in 1982, the fund can choose to sell or hold. But in cases like the U.S. Steel preferred stock, financial problems of corporate sponsors may make it difficult for the fund to sell the securities at a price similar to the assigned value.

The corporate sponsor's financial strength may further affect pension fund management. A recent study of over 500 private pension funds argued that corporations tend to view management of the pension fund they sponsor as an extended part of corporate financial policy. Any plan surplus or deficit accrues to the firm's shareholders because it affects the firm's payment obligations. If a firm is financially sound and its pension fund invests in taxable bonds, the tax benefits of the fund are passed to the firm's shareholders in the form of lower future contributions.[13]

On the other hand, a firm in poor financial condition may prefer to have its pension fund invested in risky assets like common stock. If

---

[12]William Harris, "Let Them Eat Stock," *Forbes* 130 (November 22, 1982): 41-42.

[13]Zvi Bodie et al., "Corporate Pension Policy: An Empirical Investigation," *Financial Analysts Journal* 41 (September/October 1985): 10-16.

successful, the pension plan earns a high rate of return; if unsuccessful, the fund's liabilities can be shifted to the PBGC. Research has not confirmed or denied these potential influences, but underfunded plans are indeed more heavily invested in common stocks. The impact of corporate sponsor preferences on management of fund assets is an area of continuing study.

Investment Policy and Choice of Investment Managers

A pension fund's trustees set investment policies for the fund's assets, including standards for risk and return and selection of the investment manager. As noted, many pension funds are not managed by in-house managers. Instead, plan trustees designate external professional managers to make investment decisions. Often, trust departments of commercial banks are selected, but securities firms or other investment advisers also may be used.

Some pension funds spread the management of assets among several external investment advisers. Surveys indicate that the vast majority of plans use outside management for at least part of the asset portfolio. ERISA has influenced pension plan trustees to develop written statements of investment objectives and to establish formal guidelines for investment managers.[14]

Inflation

Two obvious effects of inflation on pension funds are its impact on benefit payments and on the return on fund assets.

Effect on Retiree Benefits.   Two methods are commonly used to determine a retiree's benefit payments. One, the *career-average plan,* bases retirement income on an employee's average salary over his or her entire career. The other, called a *final-average plan,* weighs income just before retirement more heavily in computing benefits. Under the latter method, inflation strongly affects pension obligations, because employees' cost-of-living raises are directly translated into higher pension fund obligations. Under a career-average plan, even several years of high inflation toward the end of an employee's career may not increase retirement benefits significantly. Between 1950 and 1975, there was a shift toward the final-average method. In 1950, 72 percent of pension plans used the career-average method, but by 1975, 52 percent were using the final-average approach.[15]

Effect on Investment Income.   The impact of inflation on interest rates is explored in Chapter 5. That discussion indicates that nominal yields do not always keep up with the rate of inflation. Similar conclusions have been drawn about equity returns. Although traditional wisdom views stocks as good inflation hedges, research shows that stock returns during the 1970s were *negatively* correlated with inflation. One would expect, then, that pension fund managers would have had difficulty protecting returns on their funds' assets from inflation.

A study of pension funds in the mid-1970s showed that few kept up with inflation. Even after adjusting for risk, most funds performed worse than the markets in general, and actively managed funds performed worst.[16] Strategies for avoiding inflation's negative impact are explored in later sections.

International Diversification

ERISA has increased the availability of modern portfolio management techniques, including diversification. Recently, pension funds have

---

[14]J. David Cummins et al., "Effects of ERISA on the Investment Policies of Private Pension Plans: Survey Evidence," *Journal of Risk and Insurance* 47 (September 1980): 447-476. A model of optimal pension fund portfolios is developed in Fred W. McKenna and Yong H. Kim, "Managerial Risk Preferences, Real Pension Costs and Long-Run Corporate Pension Fund Investment Policy," *Journal of Risk and Insurance* 53 (March 1986): 29-48.

[15]Dennis E. Logue and Richard J. Rogalski, *Managing Corporate Pension Plans: The Impact of Inflation* (Washington, DC: American Enterprise Institute, 1984), p. 7.

[16]An overview of these findings is provided in Logue and Rogalski, *Managing Corporate Pension Plans,* pp. 15-30.

turned to international diversification.[17] One motive is a desire to reduce variability in total returns by holding assets with low correlation in expected returns. A second is a desire to improve the risk-adjusted return on the portfolio by investing in rapidly growing foreign firms with abundant raw materials and lower labor costs. Of course, managers must be aware of additional risks, such as exchange rate uncertainty, transfer risk, and limited access to market information.

Emerging Issues in Asset Management

Although the issues discussed so far are likely to remain the most significant for pension fund managers, additional concerns have arisen in recent years.

Real Estate Investments. As emphasis on portfolio diversification has grown after ERISA, a new category of assets for pension funds has received significant attention: real estate-related investments. Table 24.1 showed that less than 1 percent of private pension fund assets has been invested in mortgages recently. Some observers attribute pension funds' tardiness in tapping real estate markets to their managers' lack of expertise. For example, because bank trust departments are familiar with bonds and stocks, they may not give mortgages extensive consideration. Others point to widely publicized problems in real estate-related investments in the 1970s that may deter fund managers. Nevertheless, potential benefits to housing could result from increased pension fund participation, and the issue interests public policymakers.[18]

---

[17]For more discussion on international diversification, see Edna E. Ehrlich, "International Diversification by United States Pension Funds," *Quarterly Review,* Federal Reserve Bank of New York 6 (Autumn 1981): 1-14.

[18]This opinion is found in a variety of sources, along with the argument that corporate sponsors should give new direction to trust department investment managers. See, for example, Kenneth T. Rosen, "The Role of Pension Funds in Housing Finance," *Housing Finance Review* 1 (April 1982): 147-177.

Social Responsibility. At times, pension funds receive pressure to avoid investing in certain companies or countries, such as recent protests against investing in firms doing business in the Republic of South Africa. Managers argue that, with this "interference," the most efficient portfolio for the pension fund may be unobtainable. Some observers question whether ERISA's prudence rule prohibits social investing, but as yet there is no direct answer. According to ERISA, however, decisions must clearly be in the best interests of the covered employees, must not interfere with diversification, and must coincide with the fund's investment objectives.[19]

INTEGRATED MANAGEMENT STRATEGIES

Because pension funds as a whole lack identifiable net worth, it may seem unusual to discuss integrated asset/liability models. At any one time, however, an individual fund has assets and obligations with present values that may or may not be equal. When they are not equal, the fund has either positive or negative net worth that can be affected by changes in market yields. Thus, risk management techniques introduced in previous chapters can be applied to pension fund management. Because of the long-term nature of pension fund assets and liabilities, particular attention has been given to duration-based techniques.

Immunization

A pension fund is immunized if its net worth at the end of a holding period is at least equal to its net worth at the beginning of the holding period. The value of a pension fund's assets is affected by changing market yields. Because a pension fund's future obligations are estimated using present-value techniques, their value is also affected by market conditions reflected in

---

[19]These issues are discussed more fully in *Investment Policy Guidebook for Corporate Pension Plan Trustees* (Brookfield, WI: International Foundation of Employee Benefit Plans, 1984), pp. 121-129.

Table 24.2
Immunizing the Net Worth of a Pension Fund

Beginning Balance Sheet (Market Rate = 5%)

Cash	$ 65.65	Obligations	$432.95
Bonds	515.23	Net worth	147.93
Total Assets	$580.88	Total Obligations and Net Worth	$580.88

Duration of assets = 2.163 years
Duration of obligations = 2.903 years

$$(24.1) \quad D_A \times V_A = D_L \times V_L = \$1{,}256$$

Revised Balance Sheet (Market Rate = 6%)

Cash	$ 65.65	Obligations	$421.24
Bonds	503.48	Net worth	147.89
Total Assets	$569.13	Total Obligations and Net Worth	$569.13

---

the discount rate. The net worth of a fund will change if, for a given change in market yields, changes in asset values differ from changes in the present value of future obligations. As illustrated in Table 24.2, to be immunized, a fund must hold assets whose duration multipled by their beginning market value equals the duration of obligations times their total present value.[20]

The top panel shows the market values of assets and obligations, assuming that beginning market yields are 5 percent. Obligations of the fund are assumed to be $100 per year for five years, with a total present value at 5 percent of $432.95. The duration of the obligations, calculated from Equation 8.1, is 2.903 years. The total value of obligations times the duration is $1,256.

To immunize the fund against increases in market yields, the manager selects assets whose total present value, $580.88, times their duration, equals $1,256. This example assumes that the bonds selected are pass-through securities,

paying $145.30 per year for 4 years. The weighted duration of the asset portfolio, including cash on hand, is 2.163 years, and asset value times asset duration is $1,256. The excess of asset values over obligations—the fund's net worth—is $147.93.

If market rates increase, for example, to 6 percent, the present value of both assets and liabilities will decrease, as shown in the bottom panel of the table. Because the fund is immunized, however, the decline in value is proportionate and net worth is $147.89. If interest rates had fallen, the increase in asset and liability values would also be proportionate, and net worth would also be unchanged.

Special Problems in Calculating Duration for Pension Funds.   The nature of pension fund liabilities introduces some unusual problems in immunizing a fund's net worth. First, the present value of liabilities is sensitive to actuarial assumptions about mortality. In addition, whether liabilities should include only those to employees with vested benefits or should consider potential obligations for all employees is another point of controversy. The assumptions affect the estimates of future cash flows, which are prerequisites to the duration calculation.

---

[20]This discussion and example relies on the work of Richard J. Kientz and Clyde P. Stickney, "Immunization of Pension Funds and Sensitivity to Actuarial Assumptions," *Journal of Risk and Insurance* 47 (June 1980): 223-239.

A third problem arises from the ongoing nature of pension fund liabilities. The lack of a maturity date for liabilities, and the fact that new employees may be regularly joining the sponsoring firm, mean that the fund's obligations may stretch far into the future. As a result, the duration of a fund's liabilities will be long. If plans are underfunded, asset values are smaller than the present value of liabilities, and the duration of assets must be quite large to achieve immunization. Because it is often difficult to find securities with extremely long durations, full immunization may be unattainable.

PERFORMANCE EVALUATION OF PENSION FUNDS

Because of the nature of the funds sources and obligations of pension funds, performance measures discussed previously have little meaning for them. Although they are subject to interest rate and other risks, pension funds cannot be said to have an interest or underwriting "margin," nor are typical leverage or liquidity measures significant. Instead, performance appraisals focus on the yields on a fund's assets.

Even then, evaluating the performance of pension fund managers is difficult because appropriate comparative data are scarce, and because responsibility for managing the assets of a fund may be divided among several management groups. Some data on funds administered by the trust departments of major commercial banks are available through surveys and from Wilshire Associates, a California-based financial information firm. Fund performance is usually compared to overall market indexes for the same period, such as the S&P 500 or a bond market index.

Internal versus External Management

A recent survey of pension funds reported in *Institutional Investor* revealed that only about 25 percent of the responding funds managed assets internally, and those that did retained management of 10 percent or less of their assets. Those funds managing a significant portion of assets internally reported that the performance of internal managers, both in equities and in bonds, exceeded the returns achieved by external professional managers. They also reported that internal management was accompanied by significant cost savings. Despite these findings, reliance on external management continues.[21]

Desirability of Active Management

Regardless of whether a pension fund chooses internal or external managers, a significant performance issue is whether active portfolio management can achieve greater returns than a simple buy-and-hold strategy. Wilshire Associates data on over 1,000 funds is reported periodically in *Forbes* magazine. Over the period 1980-1986, the Wilshire data show that the median return on pension funds' equity portfolios was slightly lower than the return on the S&P 500. The median return on fixed-income investments was slightly lower than the Shearson-Lehman bond index over most of the same period.[22]

A study commissioned by the U.S. Department of Labor and completed in 1986 reported that, as pension funds become larger, their portfolios inevitably mirror the market portfolio. Even so, annual turnover in fund portfolios increased dramatically from 1979 to 1983. For example, annual turnover in fixed-income securities rose from 46 percent of total assets in 1979 to 134 percent in 1983, greatly increasing transactions costs. Ironically, as active management increases, the huge volume of assets held by pension funds makes it hard to find trades of comparable size except with other pension funds, and funds often simply trade assets with one another. As pension funds continue to grow under the funding provisions of ERISA, many observers believe that their sheer size may make general market conditions, not individual

---

[21]"In-House Management Continues to Thrive," *Institutional Investor* 19 (July 1985): 141-142.

[22]Robert A. G. Monks, "How to Earn More on $1 Trillion," *Fortune* 112 (September 1985): 98-99; "The Forbes/TUCS Institutional Portfolio Report," *Forbes* 139 (February 23, 1987): 156-157.

management decisions, the major determinant of performance.[23]

The implication of these findings is that active management of pension funds is not worthwhile, and that investment in a portfolio that approximates a market index could offer results as good as, if not superior to, those achieved by managers in the 1980s. The explanation offered by many observers is that pension funds cannot beat the market because they *are* the market. In 1986, in fact, the three largest pension funds—managed by Wells Fargo Bank, Bankers Trust, and the College Retirement Equities Fund—were so-called *index funds,* with portfolios deliberately selected to mirror the market as a whole. These three funds alone accounted for almost $90 billion in total assets.[24]

An alternative to active management is the use of *guaranteed investment contracts (GICs),* by which a pension fund contracts with a life insurer to earn a fixed rate of return over a specified period. The fund pays a lump sum to the insurer and receives annuity payments in return. The insurer provides the payments from earnings on its own bond portfolio. Although GICs are designed to reduce uncertainty in pension fund earnings, they are not risk-free. The "guarantee" is only as sound as the financial condition of the life insurer. In addition, if interest rates rise, pensions with large amounts of funds in GICs are unable to profit from higher market yields.[25]

Emerging Issues in Performance Measurement

The accumulating evidence that it is difficult for pension fund managers to "beat the market" has encouraged some state and local government sponsors to change the way they compensate fund managers. Instead of paying managers a flat percentage of assets managed, *performance fees* tie compensation to managers' ability to outperform market indexes. If managers are then reluctant to accept the challenge that performance fees present, they are encouraged to manage the fund as an index fund. As of early 1987, regulators had not given final approval for the use of performance fees in ERISA-governed private pension plans, although they were expected to do so. Thus, many observers believe the trend toward indexation and passive fund management will accelerate.

INVESTMENT COMPANIES: AN OVERVIEW

Investment companies raise funds by selling ownership shares to investors, many of whom are small savers. The money is then invested in a variety of assets under the direction of professional managers. Investment companies perform the intermediation functions outlined in Chapter 1, but in a manner different from other institutions.

How Investment Companies Operate

Investment company shareholders obtain benefits unavailable from direct investment or other financial intermediaries. They get greater diversification, lower transactions costs, and expert investment opinion at a lower cost than if they invested directly in the financial markets. Most investment companies rely on the sale of shares

[23]In fact, the volume of corporate securities under pension fund control has led some to suggest that funds should go beyond investment management and become involved to some extent in the management of the corporations whose securities they own. In other words, pension funds should try to increase asset values by increasing the value of the underlying firm, rather than attempting to accomplish that through portfolio restructuring and market trading. More evidence on the size of pension funds is available in Berkowitz, Logue, and Associates, "Pension Plan Performance: How Do We Know?" paper presented at the Midwest Finance Association annual meeting, Chicago, March 21, 1986.

[24]George Anders, "Managers Fail to Equal Rise of Benchmarks in Stocks, Bonds," *The Wall Street Journal,* January 2, 1987, p. 24B. Recent surveys report that 89.9 percent of pension fund managers believe they can beat the market, regardless of evidence to the contrary. See "The Abiding Faith in Active Management," *Institutional Investor* 20 (May 1986): 97, 100.

[25]Robert L. Rose, "GICs: Popular, Safe—But Are They Smart?" *The Wall Street Journal,* March 5, 1986, p. 33.

and do not use financial leverage, so the investor avoids the added risk of owning stock in an intermediary with large liabilities. In contrast to depository institutions, however, investment companies promise no guaranteed return to savers. Returns depend upon managers' investment decisions and market conditions, with no insurance to protect the saver against loss of principal.

Management Companies.   Investment companies are separate from management companies hired to make investment decisions and to market new shares of the investment company. Management companies earn fees for their services, usually a percentage of investment company assets. Along with transactions costs, fees are subtracted from returns on investment company assets before benefits are distributed to shareholders. Because management companies also have shareholders, investment managers must earn profits for them and for the investment company. Thus, a conflict may arise between the two groups of shareholders as fees and transactions costs increase. Management fees must be disclosed in the prospectus, and investment companies' annual reports give information about expenses. Public disclosure is intended to ensure that fund managers price their services competitively.

Open-End Companies: Mutual Funds

The investment company industry is divided into two broad categories: *open-end* and *closed-end* companies. An open-end fund is always willing to sell new shares to prospective investors, or to redeem shares held by investors, at the fund's current *net asset value.* The net asset value is the difference between the value of the investment company's assets and its liabilities, stated on a per-share basis. Although the phrase *net asset value* is customary in the investment company industry and is used in this discussion, it is conceptually identical to a fund's net worth per share.

Open-end companies are better known as mutual funds; they are the most popular type of investment company and, as noted, control the vast majority of industry assets.

Load and No-Load Companies.   An important distinction exists between load and no-load mutual funds. A *load* is a sales charge assessed to the investor when mutual fund shares are purchased or sold. A *front-end load* is charged when shares are purchased; a *back-end load* (a newer feature) is a charge assessed when the investor redeems shares.

When a front-end load is charged, it is added to the price at purchase. Loads usually range from 4 percent to 8.5 percent, although they can be as low as ½ of 1 percent. Often, load funds are marketed to investors through securities brokers or by the management company's sales force, who receive the load as a sales commission. The choice between a load and a no-load fund is an important one for investors. With a front-end load, as little as 91.5 cents of every dollar saved could actually be invested by the fund. Back-end loads, usually in the 5 percent range, also reduce returns. In recent years, sales of no-load funds have increased, although a large majority of mutual fund sales are for load funds. In 1985, for example, no-load funds, exclusive of money market funds, accounted for only 24 percent of total mutual fund sales.[26]

12b-1 Plans.   A 1980 ruling by the SEC allowed mutual funds to cover sales charges differently. The SEC's *Rule 12b-1* now permits mutual funds to charge advertising and selling expenses, including sales commissions to brokers, as an annual operating cost against the fund's assets, rather than by assessing new purchasers. Brokers who sell shares for the mutual fund still earn a commission, but it is charged against the fund's total assets so that all shareholders in the fund bear the burden, not just new investors. Funds that use the 12b-1 plans can call themselves no-load, but many industry observers view the annual 12b-1 charge as just a load by another name. Some funds use 12b-1 plans and also charge front-end loads to new investors. The way a fund chooses to handle selling and advertising expenses must be dis-

---

[26]Unless otherwise noted, statistics cited in this section are drawn from the Investment Company Institute, *1986 Mutual Fund Fact Book.*

closed in the prospectus issued in compliance with SEC regulations.

Closed-End Companies: REITs and Unit Trusts

A closed-end investment company will not automatically redeem shares when a current investor wants to liquidate them. The shareholder must usually find another investor willing to buy out the position. Because the price of shares is affected by supply and demand, as well as by fund performance, the seller has no guarantee of receiving the net asset value. New closed-end shares are not necessarily issued at net asset value, but at market value. If market value is less than net asset value, new shares cannot be issued without diluting the current investors' position, and the company is essentially closed to new investment.

REITs.   The most widely known type of closed-end fund is the *real estate investment trust,* or *REIT.* (The acronym rhymes with feet.) As the name implies, REITs specialize in real estate-related assets. Closed-end funds are a small part of the investment company industry; REITs, for example, held assets of under $15 billion at the end of 1985, compared to about $500 billion for all types of open-end funds.[27]

Unit Trusts.   A *unit trust* is a closed-end fund specializing in one type of investment; it is similar to a REIT but is not confined to real estate. The assets chosen determine the return potential and the tax benefits of the trust. A unit trust differs from other funds because a portfolio of assets is purchased when the trust is formed. When fixed-income securities are chosen, they are held to maturity. Consequently, there are no ongoing management fees, although large initial fees may be charged when the trust is formed. Fixed-income trusts offer low liquidity

---

[27]Board of Governors of the Federal Reserve System, *Flow of Funds Year-End 1962-1985,* p. 28.

because shares cannot be redeemed before the portfolio matures.

Recently, unit trusts in equity securities have been offered by national securities firms. A date at which the portfolio will be liquidated is established when the trust is formed. In the interim, the portfolio is not actively managed. Equity trusts allow investors to redeem shares at market value before the trust expires and are more liquid than fixed-income trusts. Even so, investors are still exposed to market risk.

INVESTMENT COMPANIES: REGULATORY INFLUENCES

Investment companies in the United States have gone through several boom-and-bust periods in their relatively short history. They were introduced in the United States by British investors who pooled funds to finance economic development after the Civil War. Closed-end firms were established domestically late in the 19th century, and the first mutual fund was founded in the mid-1920s. The performance of many investment companies suffered after the 1929 stock market crash, and the industry lost popularity. Investment losses led to regulatory scrutiny, and new legislation addressed some of the problems encountered by shareholders. By the end of 1940, the year the Investment Company Act was passed, mutual funds had total assets of only about $400 million.

The Investment Company Act of 1940

The Investment Company Act of 1940, first introduced in Chapter 2, has exerted more direct influence on the industry than any other single law. It regulates the composition and selection of the board of directors, and the agreement between the company and its investment managers. The act requires investment company managers to clarify investment objectives and makes the objectives subject to the approval of shareholders. For example, some mutual funds concentrate on income-producing investments, while some seek long-term capital gains, and others offer a balance between the two.

The act set standards for capital structure, severely limiting mutual funds' use of financial leverage. The act also imposed diversification requirements on investment company portfolios. In addition, managers have a fiduciary duty with respect to compensation. Because the language of the law is interpreted broadly, even when fees are disclosed, shareholders may argue that they are excessive. Although lawsuits have been filed against investment companies, seeking reduced management compensation, the courts have never ruled against the industry. Still, the possibility of further legal action always exists. Finally, the Investment Advisors Act, also passed in 1940, sets standards for the activities of investment managers.

Although regulated for decades, investment companies express little desire to modify the current structure. As competition with depositories increases, many industry leaders believe that regulation gives shareholders confidence in the absence of federal deposit insurance.

Taxation and Other Regulations

Federal tax laws applying to the public sale of securities have important effects on the operations of investment companies. Federal tax policy for investment companies is based on the conduit theory, introduced in Chapter 2. As long as an investment company distributes at least 97 percent of dividend or interest income and 90 percent of capital gains to shareholders, the fund itself is not taxed. Earnings are taxed at the individual investor's personal tax rate. To qualify for tax benefits, the firm must meet the Internal Revenue Service's minimum standards for diversification.

Because they sell ownership shares publicly, investment companies must adhere to the securities laws passed in 1933 and 1934. Investment companies must regularly disclose their financial position and other managerial and investment policies, and meet the SEC requirements imposed on all publicly traded firms. Some states impose requirements on investment companies selling shares within the state.

GROWTH OF INVESTMENT COMPANIES SINCE 1970

Although regulation promotes the viability of the industry, it does not assure stability. Since 1970, the assets of mutual funds and REITs have fluctuated significantly. By 1969, mutual fund assets had reached almost $60 billion, but poor returns and investors' loss of confidence eroded that growth; by 1974, asset holdings had declined to $34 billion. REIT assets peaked at $21.8 billion in 1974, declining after reversals in the real estate market caused numerous losses and even fund failures. The problems of investment companies were so widespread during this period that many viewed the industry as moribund.

Such reports were premature, however, because the industry revived in the years preceding the phase-out of Reg Q at depository institutions. Savers turned to money market mutual funds because they offered market rates and desirable liquidity features. Money market fund assets grew from $3.9 billion at year-end 1978 to over $200 billion only four years later.

Mutual fund managers recognized that investor trust was returning and developed the *family of funds* concept, making it easy for investors to switch from a stock fund to a bond fund, for example, under the management of the same parent organization. Research has indicated that marketing effectiveness significantly influences mutual fund growth, as reflected in the sale of new shares. Many in the industry share the belief that the financial performance of funds is not nearly as important to shareholders as the convenience and service they provide.[28]

These factors are reflected in Figure 24.1. The industry's renewed popularity is also evident in the number of mutual funds, which rose from 564 in 1980 to 1,531 by the end of 1985.

---

[28]Walt Woerheide, "Investor Response to Suggested Criteria for the Selection of Mutual Funds," *Journal of Financial and Quantitative Analysis* 17 (March 1982): 129-137; and Jeffrey M. Laderman et al., "The People's Choice: Mutual Funds," *Business Week,* February 24, 1986, pp. 54-57.

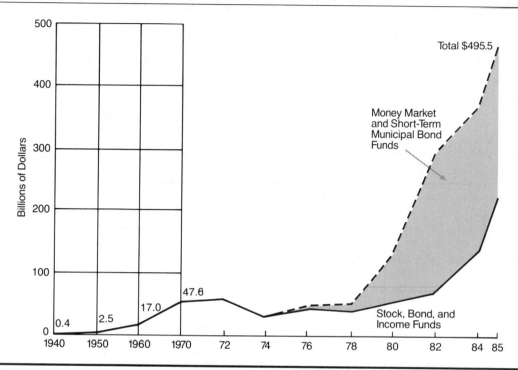

Figure 24.1
Assets of Mutual Funds, 1940–1985

Source: Investment Company Institute, *1986 Mutual Fund Fact Book*, p. 14. Reprinted with permission.

INVESTMENT COMPANIES: DESCRIPTIVE DATA

With the exception of REITs, noted later, most investment companies use minimal financial leverage. Consequently, for mutual funds, only asset composition is examined.

Assets of Mutual Funds

The assets of a mutual fund reflect the fund's stated investment objectives. Broad fund categories for the industry include equity, bond-income, short-term municipals, and money market funds.[29] The distribution of assets across these four types of funds at the end of 1975 and again in 1985 is shown in Figure 24.2. The phenomenal growth of money funds over this decade is clear; they are now the largest type of mutual fund.

Assets of Money Market Funds. Money market funds hold only short-term assets. At year-end 1985, over 40 percent of MMMF assets was invested in commercial paper; other large categories were repurchase agreements, Eurodollar CDs, and Treasury bills. The portfolio composition of money market funds is provided in Table 24.3.

Assets of Nonmoney Market Funds. The majority of assets of nonmoney market mutual funds is invested in common stock. The next largest categories of investment include long-

[29]There are many ways to categorize the objectives of the over 1,500 mutual funds. These four were chosen because they are highlighted by the Investment Company Institute, the industry's most important trade organization.

Figure 24.2
Percentage Distribution of Mutual Fund Assets

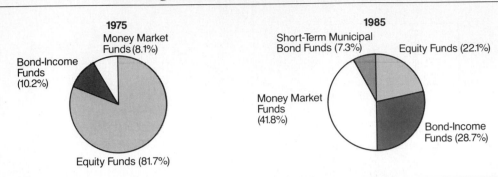

Source: Investment Company Institute, *1986 Mutual Fund Fact Book,* p. 12. Reprinted with permission.

Table 24.3
Assets of Money Market Mutual Funds, Year-End 1985—348 Firms
(Millions)

Commercial paper	$ 87,555.4	42.19%
Repurchase agreements	26,068.6	12.56
Eurodollar CDs	19,027.0	9.17
Treasury bills	20,391.5	9.83
Bankers' acceptances	11,573.3	5.58
Commercial bank CDs	13,255.8	6.39
Other federal securities	4,206.6	2.03
Other domestic CDs	3,579.0	1.72
Other Treasury securities	18,108.4	8.73
Other	3,764.7	1.81
Total assets	$207,530.3	100.00%
Average asset maturity (days)	37	

Source: Investment Company Institute, *1986 Mutual Fund Fact Book,* p. 83.

term Treasury securities, municipal bonds, and corporate bonds. Aggregate holdings of equity, bond, and income funds, by asset category, are provided in Table 24.4.

Balance Sheet of REITs

Of the closed-end firms, REITs are the largest, and the only category for which the Federal Reserve reports data. They have a short and unstable history, but enjoyed new growth in the mid–1980s. As shown in Table 24.5, at the end of 1985, REITs were invested more heavily in financial than in physical assets. The table also reveals an important contrast between REITs and open-end investment companies—liabilities. REITs rely heavily on financial leverage; liabilities financed over 40 percent of total assets at year-end 1985. Almost half of the liabilities were mortgage loans on physical structures owned by REITs.

Table 24.4
Assets of Nonmoney Market Mutual Funds, Year-End 1985
(Millions)

Common stock	$119,698	47.56%
Municipal bonds	38,339	15.23
Corporate bonds	24,961	9.92
Liquid assets	9,207	3.66
Long-term Treasury securities	43,472	17.27
Short-term government securities	11,400	4.53
Preferred stock	3,773	1.50
Other	846	0.34
Total assets	$251,696	100.00%

Source: Investment Company Institute, *1986 Mutual Fund Fact Book,* pp. 21, 61.

Table 24.5
Real Estate Investment Trusts, Assets and Liabilities, Year-End
(Millions)

	1983		1984		1985	
Assets						
Physical:						
Multifamily structures	$1,300	17.33%	$ 1,600	15.69%	$ 2,100	14.58%
Nonresidential structures	2,700	36.00	3,200	31.37	4,200	29.17
Financial:						
Home mortgages	200	2.67	200	1.96	300	2.08
Commercial mortgages	1,500	20.00	1,900	18.63	3,800	26.39
Multifamily mortgages	900	12.00	1,300	12.75	1,800	12.50
Miscellaneous assets	900	12.00	2,000	19.61	2,200	15.28
Total Assets	$7,500	100.00%	$10,200	100.00%	$14,400	100.00%
Liabilities and Equity						
Mortgages on physical assets	$2,100	28.00%	$ 2,500	24.51	$ 2,700	18.75%
Corporate bonds	700	9.33	800	7.84	1,500	10.42
Other bank loans	300	4.00	500	4.90	700	4.86
Open market paper	400	5.33	600	5.88	700	4.86
Miscellaneous	400	5.33	500	4.90	500	3.47
Equity	3,600	48.00	5,300	51.96	8,300	57.64
Total Liabilities and Equity	$7,500	100.00%	$10,200	100.00%	$14,400	100.00%

Source: Board of Governors of the Federal Reserve System, *Flow of Funds Accounts, Financial Assets and Liabilities Year-End 1962-1985.*

MANAGING MUTUAL FUND ASSETS

The management of mutual fund assets is very much influenced by the fund's investment objectives. Factors discussed under pension fund management, such as taxability, inflation, and diversification, are important influences in the investment company industry and are not repeated here. Additional influences and recent evidence about the ways mutual fund managers fulfill their responsibilities are reviewed in the following sections.

Timing and Security Selection

Timing refers to the coordination of investment decisions with anticipated market movements. Industry observers have debated the ability of mutual fund managers to time their decisions to achieve superior investment returns. Recent evidence indicates that fund managers' most common approach to timing is to shift cash or other liquid assets into bonds or stocks, or vice versa. For example, when an upswing in the equity market is anticipated, managers use liquid assets to purchase stocks. When a downturn is forecast, they sell stock and hold the proceeds in cash in anticipation of another market movement. Few managers report that they are likely to shift assets from bonds to stocks, or vice versa, based on their expectations.[30]

Fund managers report that the identification of over- or undervalued securities has a more significant impact on fund performance than attempts to anticipate market changes and make portfolio adjustments. This belief was confirmed by studies of mutual funds over the period 1973-1983. The researchers found that few managers correctly anticipated market movements, but were better at identifying undervalued securities.[31]

Managers of money market funds place more emphasis on timing. In contrast to other mutual funds, research indicates that, over the period 1975-1980, MMMF managers had a fairly consistent record of timing yield changes accurately. They succeeded in shortening portfolio maturities before rates increased, giving them the ability to invest maturing assets at higher yields, and in lengthening portfolio maturities before a decline in yields.[32]

Diversification

Many mutual fund managers set diversification standards for funds beyond those required by the Investment Company Act of 1940 or other regulations. The measures of diversification reported are quite different from those advocated in portfolio theory, such as correlation between individual assets or portfolio variance. Instead, many managers use guidelines such as limiting the amount invested in a single industry, or limiting the proportion of the portfolio invested in certain securities.

Fund Size

Researchers have also examined the effects of asset growth in the mutual fund industry. They agree that a large fund cannot use the same investment strategy as a small fund, but not that one is better than the other. For example, a large fund has less flexibility to make portfolio adjustments, because trades must necessarily be in large volume. Some mutual fund managers, including those with excellent performance records, have recently decided to control asset growth by closing the funds to new investors after reaching a certain size. On the other hand, large funds may provide more safety and diver-

---

[30]E. Theodore Veit and John M. Cheney, "Managing Investment Portfolios: A Survey of Mutual Funds," *Financial Review* 19 (November 1984): 321-338.

[31]Carl R. Chen and Steve Stockum, "Selectivity, Market Timing, and Random Beta Behavior of Mutual Funds: A Generalized Model," *Journal of Financial Research* 9 (Spring

1986): 87-96; Jess H. Chua and Richard S. Woodward, *Gains from Stock Market Timing* (New York: Salomon Brothers Center for the Study of Financial Institutions, 1986).

[32]Michael G. Ferri and H. Dennis Oberhelman, "A Study of the Management of Money Market Mutual Funds: 1975-1980," *Financial Management* 10 (Autumn 1981): 24-29.

sification than those with fewer assets. They may also be able to afford a larger and better-trained investment staff, and may command volume discounts to reduce transactions costs. In the opinion of some observers, the appropriate fund size is based on investment objectives, and no general guidelines govern growth.[33]

Specialization

The degree to which a mutual fund should specialize is also subject to debate. Some funds choose goals more specific than "growth" or "income." For example, some choose securities of the health care industry, service industries, Ginnie Mae certificates, "junk" bonds, socially concerned companies, or new firms. These funds are known as *sector funds.* Many large mutual fund families offer at least one sector fund.

The decision to invest in a sector fund is a decision to forgo the potential benefits of diversification. Yet sector funds have attracted many new investors in the 1980s. International investments have been especially popular, and the top-performing mutual funds in 1985 and 1986 included several exclusively international portfolios. Some more highly specialized firms invest in the securities of a single foreign country, such as France or Germany. Such specialization, of course, carries added risks.

Some investors have shown interest in a type of mutual fund at the opposite end of the spectrum. Known as a "fund of funds," such a fund affords the maximum degree of diversification by investing in the shares of other mutual funds! A potential problem is excessive diversification, which increases management costs with little reduction in portfolio risk. Most experts argue that any large mutual fund provides sufficient diversification, and little benefit is received from paying managers to select shares of other mutual funds.

MANAGING REIT ASSETS

For two reasons, REITs have attracted the attention of investors in the 1980s: tax benefits and flexibility.[34]

Taxation

Under tax policies established many years ago and modified in the Tax Reform Act of 1986, REIT earnings are exempt from taxation at the fund level if at least 75 percent of assets is invested in real estate and at least 85 percent of ordinary income is distributed to the fund's shareholders.[35] Earnings are taxed at the investor's personal tax rate, as with mutual fund returns. Federal tax reform in the 1980s has eliminated most tax shelters on direct investment in limited real estate partnerships, and many wealthy investors have turned to REITs as an alternative. Tax-exempt investors, such as pension funds, or holders of tax–exempt retirement plans, such as IRAs, also find REITs attractive.

Flexibility

A second important development is new flexibility in real estate-related investments. REIT investors can now choose from among a wide array of assets. For example, equity REITs specialize in owning real estate, and investors can profit from increases in the value of the physical assets held. Other REITs specialize in holding

---

[33]The opinions of many industry experts are summarized in Laura Walbert, "Bigness and Badness," *Forbes* 136 (July 29, 1985): 70-71.

---

[34]The discussion of REITs that follows draws heavily upon information in the following articles: Terri Thompson, "What's Powering the REITs Rocket," *Business Week,* August 12, 1985, p. 66; Terri Thompson, "It May Be Time to Rediscover REITs," *Business Week,* October 14, 1985, pp. 162-166; Joanne Lipman, "Real Estate Investment Trusts Cultivate Fresh Image and New Crop of Investors," *The Wall Street Journal,* June 18, 1985, p. 13; James R. Webb and Willard McIntosh, "Real Estate Investment Rules for REITs: A Survey," *The Journal of Real Estate Research* 1 (Fall 1986): 77-91.

[35]To avoid taxation, REITs must also distribute 95 percent of capital gains income to shareholders. The Tax Reform Act of 1986 eased some rules applied to REITs. In particular, they may hold equity or debt securities temporarily after receiving new equity capital.

mortgages. Investor returns are generated by the interest payments made by borrowers and are subject to the risk of borrower default.

Another type of REIT combines features of both equity and mortgage REITs. Known as "participating" mortgage REITs, they hold mortgages on real estate, but also have the right to a portion of the increase in property value. Many REITs not only invest in real estate, but also actively manage it. For example, a REIT may buy properties and renovate them, or invest in commercial real estate and control management and tenant relationships. Recent research indicates that many REIT managers use NPV techniques to select new properties and that most recognize the importance of portfolio diversification.

Additional flexibility is offered through self-liquidating funds, known as finite-life REITs (FREITs). FREITs are similar to unit trusts, but they specialize in real estate. Investors are not forced to sell shares to terminate their interest in the fund, because the funds themselves have a maturity date. Managers argue that FREIT shares are less likely than REIT shares to sell at a discount from net asset value, because market value approaches net asset value as the liquidation date approaches.

PERFORMANCE EVALUATION OF INVESTMENT COMPANIES

Traditional ratio analysis is inappropriate for evaluating most investment companies, but there is considerable interest in other measures of the industry's performance, especially that of mutual funds. Over the past two decades, numerous academic studies have attempted to establish guidelines for managing fund assets. The four asset management issues discussed earlier have been addressed: 1) timing and security selection; 2) diversification and risk management; 3) fund size; and 4) specialization. Generally, the research questions whether managers successfully evaluate securities and time portfolio adjustments, whether they achieve appropriate portfolio diversification, and whether

they earn rates of return commensurate with the risk assumed.[36]

Evaluating Rates of Return

A key question in evaluating investment companies is whether they offer shareholders a rate of return higher than could be obtained through direct investment. For mutual funds, research has attempted to ascertain whether an investor could adopt a simple buy-and-hold strategy and earn a better return than is achieved by the typically active investment style of a mutual fund's professional managers—and the associated costs. Two approaches are used for evaluating rates of return.

Ex Post versus Ex Ante Returns.   The academic literature compares *ex post* risk-adjusted rates of return to those that would be expected *ex ante,* using performance measures based on capital market theory and the efficient-markets hypothesis. Many studies have concluded that the efforts of professional managers do not achieve results superior to buy-and-hold strategies.

The findings are consistent with the efficient-markets hypothesis in that even professional investment managers seem unable to outperform the market. Many experts have recommended an approach to mutual fund management similar to that for large pension funds: Invest in a market or index portfolio, and attempt to earn a return equal to the market as a whole. In the 1980s, in fact, bond index funds have grown in popularity, as investors seemed to recognize that interest rate forecasting is, at best, an inexact science. The trend may prove

---

[36]There is a large body of research on this topic. Some representative studies include Irwin Friend, Marshall Blume, and Jean Crockett, *Mutual Funds and Other Institutional Investors* (New York: McGraw-Hill, 1970), pp. 50-68; Michael C. Jensen, "The Performance of Mutual Funds in the Period 1945-1964," *Journal of Finance* 23 (May 1968): 389-416; William F. Sharpe, "Mutual Fund Performance," *Journal of Business* 39 (January 1966): 119-138; Stanley Kon and Frank C. Jen, "The Investment Performance of Mutual Funds: An Empirical Investigation of Timing, Selectivity and Market Efficiency," *Journal of Business* 42 (April 1979): 263-289.

to be profitable. A recent study indicated that between 1981 and 1984, few managers of fixed-income portfolios earned a return as high as the Shearson-Lehman bond index, and in 1985 and 1986, not even half did as well as the index.[37]

Relative Performance Evaluation.   Practitioners tend to evaluate performance by comparing an individual fund to funds with similar investment objectives or to some market index. Surveys of mutual fund managers reveal that they do not consider risk-adjusted performance measures useful, and that they tend to use comparative techniques instead.[38]

Performance comparison for managers and investors is facilitated by several regularly published reports on the industry. Arthur Weisenberger Services publishes an annual volume entitled *Investment Companies,* including not only performance information but also a fund's history, management, and other pertinent data. Quarterly and monthly reports of performance are also available from Weisenberger. *Barron's* publishes a quarterly report on mutual funds prepared by Lipper Analytical Services. *Forbes* and *Business Week* prepare annual reports on mutual funds, including short- and long-term records. Updates on selected funds are provided more frequently. All sources categorize funds by objective and identify load fees and management expenses. They often include a qualitative risk rating and indicate a fund's performance in both up and down markets.

Size and Performance

Some comparative studies have concluded that small funds have outperformed large mutual funds in recent years. These results should not be interpreted as blanket support for small funds, however, because smaller funds have less diversification potential and may expose investors to higher risk. Unless risk-adjusted returns are considered, one cannot conclude that size is instrumental to fund performance.

SECURITIES FIRMS: AN OVERVIEW

Securities firms perform several different but related financial functions. Since 1975, as a result of two separate regulatory rulings, the securities industry has changed significantly, challenging even its largest firms and most capable managers. Changes include mergers of established securities firms, acquisitions of securities companies by firms outside the industry, heightened competition, the development of creative financial services and instruments, and more elusive profits.

The services offered by securities firms include investment banking; brokerage services and securities trading; merchant banking; and services such as asset management accounts, financial advisory services, and mutual fund sponsorship.

Investment Banking

Experts define investment banking as a "business which has as its function the flotation of new securities, both debt and equity, to the general public . . . for the purpose of raising funds for clients . . . ."[39] Their role in the issuance of securities makes investment bankers dominant in the primary securities markets.

Creating New Securities.   Investment bankers assist both private firms and public entities in selecting securities to issue and their characteristics (coupon rates, maturities, offering prices, and so on). In recent years, investment bankers have been influential in adding new twists to financial instruments. In 1982, Salomon Brothers created stripped zero-coupon issues from existing Treasury securities, a

---

[37]George Anders, "Returns Seesaw for Managers Seeking to Top Index on Bonds," *The Wall Street Journal,* April 21, 1986, p. 33; Anders, "Managers Fail to Equal Rise of Benchmarks."

[38]Veit and Cheney, "Managing Investment Portfolios."

[39]This definition appears in the comprehensive study of the investment banking industry by Irwin Friend et al., *Investment Banking and the New Issues Market* (Cleveland: World Publishing Company, 1967), p. 80.

development first discussed in Chapter 8. In the uncertain interest rate environment of 1984, Merrill Lynch and Company and other investment bankers advised clients to issue bonds with put options, giving the holder the right to redeem the bond at par before maturity. The investor is protected against interest rate risk because the bonds can be liquidated without a loss even if interest rates have risen. Salomon Brothers, in late 1984, introduced securities backed by automobile loans (CARs), discussed in earlier chapters. Investment bankers have also led the development of mortgage-backed securities.[40]

Underwriting.   Also important is the underwriting function, in which investment bankers assume the risk of adverse price movements immediately after the issuance of new securities. An underwriter purchases new securities from a client for a price negotiated in advance, then resells them. The difference between the price paid by the underwriter and the price at which the securities are sold to the public (the "spread") is a source of profit in the underwriting business—and a source of risk as well. Capital advanced to the issuer may be provided by a group of investment bankers, known as a *syndicate*.[41]

Alternatives to Underwriting.   The relationship between investment bankers and their clients depends on the financial position of the client and the breadth of the market for its securities. Sometimes investment bankers, unwilling to bear the risk of underwriting a new issue, sell it on a *best efforts* basis. In best efforts deals, the investment banker does not buy the securities from the issuing firm, but merely assists in distribution, profiting from fees for services. An alternative that clients sometimes choose is private placement, for which investment bankers earn fees for bringing buyers and sellers together.

Brokerage and Trading

Brokerage and trading services involve handling securities transactions for individual or institutional customers and managing the firm's own securities inventory. Securities firms also act as investment advisers for mutual and pension funds. Full-service brokerage firms conduct security analysis and provide investment advice to clients, and both full-service and discount brokers complete securities transactions.

Merchant Banking

Merchant banking is the name given to a group of activities such as investing in real estate, taking an equity position in new firms (extending venture capital), providing financing for mergers and acquisitions, or other endeavors that securities firms make on their own behalf. Larger firms in the industry are diversifying into these activities to smooth out the income variability inherent in investment banking and brokerage.

Other Financial Services

As competition has heightened, securities firms have introduced a variety of financial services to meet the needs of individual and institutional customers. Some firms, such as First Boston, serve only institutional clients, selling their expertise at arranging interest rate swaps and other hedging techniques.

Other industry members emphasize services to retail clients. Merrill Lynch's trademarked Cash Management Account (CMA) is a pioneering effort in the marketing of personal financial services. As the introductory story in this chapter suggests, Merrill Lynch, through the CMA introduced in 1977, offers customers financial services that compete directly with depository institutions. Other firms introduced similar **asset management accounts** shortly thereafter, enabling brokers to attract additional

[40]For further discussion of these innovations, see Robert McGough, "Bonds in Many Flavors," *Forbes* 134 (December 17, 1984): 133-134; and Anthony Bianco, "The King of Wall Street," *Business Week,* December 9, 1985, pp. 98-104

[41]The role of the syndicate in the issuance of new securities is diminishing. For details, see Beth Selby, "The Twilight of the Syndicate," *Institutional Investor* 19 (August 1985): 205-209.

funds from their clients. In turn, they provide investment advice and counsel, regular statements of account, easy access to cash through check-writing privileges in cooperation with participating banks, and the ability to borrow against securities holdings, such as the Visa cash advance drawn by the visitor in Atlanta. Any funds "deposited" by an investor earn market rates while under the securities firm's management.

Asset management accounts provide depositories with one of the strongest arguments for more rapid deregulation. In March 1980, Walter Wriston, then Chairman of Citicorp, argued that his "dream bank" already existed. He said, "Don Regan runs it, and it's called Merrill Lynch Pierce Fenner and Smith."[42]

SECURITIES FIRMS: REGULATORY INFLUENCES

As indicated in Chapter 2, the securities industry is regulated, primarily by the SEC. In contrast to depository institutions, securities firms have faced no restrictions on geographical expansion. However, their involvement in issuing and trading securities is closely monitored. Two important rulings by the SEC since 1975 exert strong influence on the industry.

The End of Fixed Brokerage Commissions

On May 1, 1975, an SEC ruling ended the New York Stock Exchange's (NYSE) system of fixed brokerage commissions. NYSE rules had established the same fee structure for all member firms, effectively eliminating price competition among securities firms. Industry members predicted that the **May Day ruling,** as it came to be called, would wreak havoc in the industry.

Impact on Fee Structures.   Although some firms did fail in the aftermath of May Day, their numbers were relatively small, and the securities industry adjusted. But things have never been the same. Once customers recognized their ability to negotiate fees, institutional traders managed to reduce transactions costs on large volume trades. In contrast, individual investors, whose average trades are much smaller, face higher transactions costs. The pattern in commission fees at full-service brokerage houses in the decade following May Day is evident in Figure 24.3.

Rise of Discount Brokers.   An industry development that can also be traced directly to the May Day ruling is the entry of discount brokers. First defined in Chapter 1, discount brokers offer limited investment advice and services, and charge lower fees than firms offering a full line of services. By 1985, over 600 discount brokerage firms were in operation. Discount firms provide an alternative for small investors willing to manage their own accounts to minimize transactions costs. By 1985, discount brokers handled about 20 percent of individuals' stock trades. Because about 40 percent of their business comes from investors under the age of 50, discount firms are expected to enjoy increased market share as current customers gain wealth.[43]

Diversification.   An additional change in the industry commonly traced to the May Day ruling is the trend toward diversification. Because brokers anticipated declining revenues from traditional services, they began experimenting with other opportunities to replace or even enhance profits. Asset management accounts, merchant banking endeavors, and mutual fund

---

[42]This story is related in Mayer, "Merrill Lynch Quacks Like a Bank," p. 135. Donald Regan, who was chairman of Merrill Lynch in 1980, left shortly thereafter to become Secretary of the Treasury and later Chief of Staff to President Ronald Reagan, until he was forced to resign in February 1987. More on the head-to-head confrontations between Citicorp and Merrill Lynch is presented in Chapter 25.

[43]See Scott McMurray and Randall Smith, "Wall Street Is Finding, after 10 Years, that It Enjoys Unfixed Rates," *The Wall Street Journal,* April 22, 1985, p. 1; and "Discount Brokers Attract a Growing Number," *The Wall Street Journal,* December 26, 1985, p. 1.

Figure 24.3
Brokerage Commission Rates, May 1, 1975–December 31, 1984

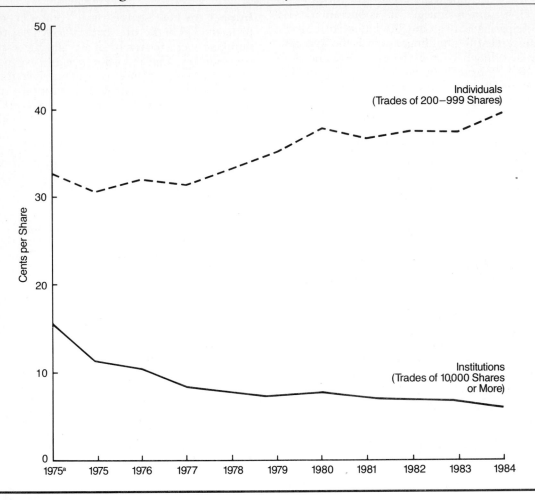

---

sponsorship are examples of these efforts to diversify.

Rule 415: Shelf Registration

In March 1982, the SEC approved another policy change that has significantly affected the securities industry. The policy, known as Rule 415 and first discussed in Chapter 20, changed the procedures by which firms can issue new securities. Before Rule 415, firms had to seek SEC approval for each new issue. Under the new rule, a procedure known as *shelf registration* was approved. Shelf registration allows a firm to file its intention to issue new securities with the SEC up to two years in advance. Once the

SEC approves, the firm has the flexibility to choose how many securities to sell and when to sell them "off the shelf." The new policy was intended to eliminate barriers to firms seeking new capital and to lower regulatory costs.

Opponents of the rule made dire predictions for the new issues markets. Concerns were raised that competition and reduced profits would drive smaller, regional investment banking houses out of business, causing the industry to consolidate and become dominated by a few large firms. Critics also feared that investors would lack access to sufficient current information under the advance registration procedures.

Underwriting Spreads. The impact on underwriters' spreads on new issues is still inconclusive. A study of new bond issues during the first months of Rule 415 found lower underwriter fees with shelf registrations. But a longer-term analysis of the period January 1981-October 1983 found no significant change in underwriter spreads on new bond issues with Rule 415. A study sponsored by the SEC, analyzing new equity issues between March and December of 1983, found that, on average, firms reduced issuing costs by using shelf registrations.[44]

Competitive Effects. It is also difficult to conclude how Rule 415 has affected concentration in the securities industry. The number of regional firms was already declining before Rule 415. Whether the new policy has exacerbated the decline is unclear, but Rule 415 has undoubtedly heightened competition among investment bankers. When a company files a registration statement, it announces its intention to issue new securities. Often, before the firm has decided which investment banker to approach, it may be contacted by one or more

potential underwriters, an occurrence practically unheard of before 1982.

Another clear result is that investment bankers are more creative in the financing alternatives they present to prospective clients, and more aggressive in seeking and maintaining customer relationships. For example, a technique originated since Rule 415 is the *bought deal.* Under this strategy, the underwriter purchases an entire issue using only its own capital, instead of including other underwriters in a syndicate. Risk exposure is greater, but profits are not shared. Because bought deals can be negotiated and completed more quickly than syndications, they are a useful competitive tool.

Investment bankers must now be marketers. They contact prospective clients and propose creative financing tailored to individual needs. Swaps, futures, options, and other hedging techniques are often included in these alternatives.

Limitations on Insider Trading

Attempts by brokers and investment bankers to profit from inside information have been illegal for many years, having been scrutinized by Congress most recently in the 1984 Insider Trading Sanctions Act. Recently, however, widespread publicity has been given to several investment bankers convicted of *insider trading.* Although the SEC attempts to track trading in the stock of a firm that is a takeover target or on which there is unusual trading volume, prevention of illegal insider trading profits lies largely with the securities industry itself.

A special focus of concern is maintaining the so-called *Chinese wall,* an imaginary barrier between the investment banking arm of a securities firm and its brokerage and trading arm. Theoretically, the firm may not profit on trades for its own inventory using information obtained through investment bankers' contacts with clients. Enforcement is difficult, however, and the issue is sure to receive considerable attention in the future.[45]

---

[44]See David S. Kidwell et al., "SEC Rule 415: The Ultimate Competitive Bid," *Journal of Financial and Quantitative Analysis* 19 (June 1984): 183-196; Robert J. Rogowski and Eric H. Sorenson, "Deregulation in Investment Banking: Shelf Registrations, Structure and Performance," *Financial Management* 14 (Spring 1985): 5-15; and Leon E. Wynter, "SEC Study Reports Shelf Registration Is Boon for Issuers," *The Wall Street Journal,* September 17, 1984.

[45]James B. Stewart, "Levine Pleads Guilty, Agrees to Cooperate," *The Wall Street Journal,* June 6, 1986, p. 3; Anthony Bianco, "Wall Street's Frantic Push to Clean Up Its

Emerging Issues

As investment banks have increased their merchant banking activities, some clients have questioned whether investment banks are becoming more concerned with their own investments than with their traditional functions of advising clients and arranging financing for others. And, because depository institutions are prohibited from underwriting bonds and stock, disgruntled clients of investment bankers have few alternatives. The compatibility of merchant banking and investment banking is sure to be an issue regulators consider in the future.[46]

SECURITIES FIRMS: DESCRIPTIVE DATA

Many securities firms are not publicly held, but function as partnerships. Consequently, financial data are limited to reports required by the SEC, with aggregate figures published in SEC annual reports. Recent data reveal that assets for the industry as a whole, nearly 7,000 firms, exceed $300 billion.[47] The Securities Industry Association (SIA), a trade organization, also periodically publishes *Securities Industry Trends*. But because not all securities firms participate in all activities, aggregate data do not reflect individual managerial choices, even those for firms of similar type and size.

Table 24.6 provides income and expense data for 400 large securities firms from 1981 through 1985, compiled by the SIA. The two largest sources of industry revenues are securities commissions and gains on securities trading for the firms' own portfolios. Revenues from underwriting and selling vary proportionately over time, but throughout the 1980s they have exceeded the 1979 figure of less than 7 percent of total revenues.[48]

As in other financial institutions, fee and interest income are both important to the securities industry. The firms' exposure to interest rate and market risk is shown by the importance of trading and underwriting as sources of income. The sensitivity of operations to economic conditions is revealed by differences in the relative importance of income categories from year to year.

Interest expense, incurred on borrowings to purchase securities inventories, is a major expense category, and profitability is greatly affected by changes in interest rates. The industry is labor-intensive, reflected by compensation for "registered representatives" (brokers) and other personnel. Because interest costs are determined by the financial markets and not by an individual firm, management of personnel expenses is extremely important.

Despite changes introduced by the competitive environment and Rule 415, earnings for the industry have not suffered recently, although they have varied. Revenue components are sensitive to market conditions, but total revenues have increased steadily since 1980, as shown in Figure 24.4. Profits dropped in 1984, because of the proportionate increase in interest costs shown in Table 24.6, but earnings rebounded again in 1985.

SECURITIES FIRMS: MANAGING ASSETS AND LIABILITIES

Important aspects of asset/liability management in the securities industry have already been introduced.

Act," *Business Week,* June 9, 1986, pp. 82-83; Ford S. Worthy, "Wall Street's Spreading Scandal, *Fortune* 114 (December 22, 1986): 27-37; Chris Welles, "Who'll Be the Next to Fall?" *Business Week,* December 1, 1986, pp. 28-35; Peter Fuhrman, "The Securities Act of 1988?" *Forbes* 139 (March 9, 1987): 40-41.

[46]For more discussion of the potential conflict of interest, see Anthony Bianco, "American Business Has a New Kingpin: The Investment Banker," *Business Week,* November 24, 1986, pp. 77-83.

[47]*Annual Report of the Securities and Exchange Commission, 1985,* Appendix.

[48]*Annual Report of the Securities and Exchange Commission, 1985,* Appendix; Securities Industry Association, "Charting a Course for the Future: How Different Firm Categories Navigated a Profitable 1985," *Securities Industry Trends* 12 (May 30, 1986).

Table 24.6
Selected Financial Data, Securities Brokers and Dealers—400 Firms, 1981-1985
(Millions)

	1981		1982		1983		1984		1985	
Revenues										
Securities commissions	$ 5,340	27.0%	$ 6,012	25.9%	$ 8,350	28.2%	$ 7,095	22.7%	$ 8,238	21.3%
Gains/losses in trading and investment accounts	4,811	24.3	6,558	28.3	7,577	25.6	8,278	26.5	11,034	28.6
Gains/losses from underwriting and selling	1,690	8.5	2,604	11.2	4,494	15.2	3,457	11.1	5,893	15.3
Other securities-related revenue	3,837	19.4	4,970	21.4	5,799	19.6	7,727	24.8	9,125	23.6
Margin interest	2,890	14.6	2,011	8.7	2,130	7.2	2,868	9.2	2,578	6.7
Other revenue	1,229	6.2	1,056	4.5	1,217	4.1	1,792	5.7	1,758	4.6
Total revenues	$19,797	100.0%	$23,211	100.0%	$29,566	100.0%	$31,217	100.0%	$38,625	100.0%
Expenses										
Registered representatives compensation	$ 3,334	18.9%	$ 4,104	20.3%	$ 5,750	22.3%	$ 5,249	17.7%	$ 6,903	20.0%
Other employee compensation	3,925	22.2	4,714	23.4	6,320	24.6	6,478	21.9	7,670	22.2
Floor expenses	725	4.1	864	4.3	1,143	4.4	1,163	3.9	1,310	3.8
Interest expense	5,685	32.2	5,481	27.2	6,058	23.5	9,505	32.1	10,128	29.4
Other expenses	3,986	22.6	5,012	24.8	6,471	25.1	7,215	24.4	8,479	24.6
Total expenses	$17,655	100.0%	$20,175	100.0%	$25,742	100.0%	$29,610	100.0%	$34,490	100.0%
Pretax Income	$ 2,142		$ 3,036		$ 3,824		$ 1,607		$ 4,135	
Pretax Return on Equity	35.9%		40.5%		36.6%		13.3%		29.4%	

Source: Securities Industry Association, *Securities Industry Trends*, May 1986.

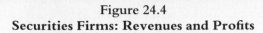

Figure 24.4
Securities Firms: Revenues and Profits

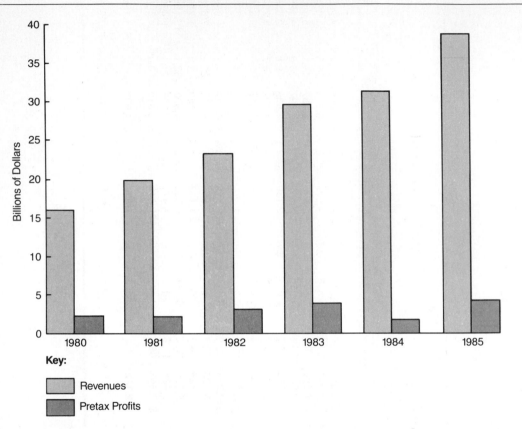

Key:

Revenues

Pretax Profits

Source: Prepared by the authors with data from "Charting a Course for the Future: How Different Firm Categories Navigated a Profitable 1985," *Securities Industry Trends* 12 (May 30, 1986): 4.

Diversification to Protect Income

Securities firms have diversified not only to respond to competition, but also to protect against swings in commission income resulting from changes in market conditions. Diversification is prominently discussed in the annual reports of many leading securities firms. It has contributed to the increase in revenues in recent years, despite the wide variety of economic and regulatory conditions the industry has faced.

Use of Risk Management Tools

Securities firms are not only developing hedging techniques for their clients, they are themselves relying on sophisticated hedging strategies to manage interest rate risk. One of the earliest and most widely publicized examples of hedging in the industry came in 1979 when Salomon Brothers underwrote an IBM bond issue. Just after the underwriting agreement was completed and the coupon rate was established, interest rates jumped sharply. The increase in market rates caused the bonds' market value to drop below Salomon's original estimates, wiping out expected profits. Industry observers assumed Salomon had taken a big loss, but soon learned that the deal had been hedged in the futures market, so the firm's losses were limited. In the increasingly competitive environment of Rule 415, where underwriting spreads have been pared, hedges are commonplace. In addition, the SEC has recognized the importance of integrated asset/liability management in the industry by permitting lower capital requirements for securities firms whose corporate bond holdings are hedged.[49]

PERFORMANCE EVALUATION OF SECURITIES FIRMS

Because many securities firms are privately owned, available financial data are limited. Aggregate data are available from several sources such as Dun and Bradstreet financial ratios; SEC annual reports; Securities Industry Association publications, with information on industry subgroups; annual rankings of large brokers by *Institutional Investor;* and industry outlooks in *Forbes* and *Fortune.* These sources of data must be used carefully when drawing conclusions about individual firms.

In the absence of good comparative data, a trend analysis of expense and income ratios sheds light on a firm's efficiency and productivity. As with other institutions, a clear result of deregulation in the industry is the need for managers to control operating costs carefully.

A measure sometimes used to evaluate performance of the investment banking function is the volume of securities for which the firm served as the sole underwriter or the leader in a syndicate. The quantity of issues is viewed as a

sign of a firm's competence and creativity. A final performance guideline is return on equity. Because of the prominence of partnerships in the industry, pretax ROE is usually the focus because taxes are paid at partners' personal tax rates. For firms included in Table 24.6, pretax ROE ranged from a low of 13.3 percent in 1984, to a high of over 40 percent in 1982.

Studies at the Federal Reserve Bank of New York indicate that ROEs in the securities industry have been much more variable than those of commercial banks in recent years. Interestingly, ROEs for the most diversified firms have been lower than those for firms specializing in brokerage services—either full-service or discount—or in investment banking. The poorer performance of diversified firms may result from their higher operating costs.[50]

SUMMARY

This chapter considers asset/liability management in three nondepository intermediaries: pension funds, investment companies, and securities firms. Each industry faces unique regulations and problems in the management of interest rate and other financial market risks. Each also shares the challenges of increasing competition in the financial markets.

Private pension funds are responsible for investing monies to be used later to pay retirement benefits. ERISA establishes fiduciary responsibilities of managers, funding standards, methods for guaranteeing benefits, and other important issues. Most pension fund assets are invested in common stock and corporate bonds, and the funds' obligations are determined actuarially. The major sources of funds to pension plans are employer contributions and earnings on assets. Especially important to pension funds are taxation, inflation, diversification, and the financial condition of the corporate sponsor. In recent years, pension funds have applied new techniques for manag-

[49]"How Salomon Brothers Hedged the IBM Deal," *Business Week,* October 29, 1979, p. 50; Cynthia S. Grisdella, "Capital Rules Eased for Securities Firms that Hedge Corporate Bond Holdings," *The Wall Street Journal,* November 5, 1986, p. 4.

[50]Federal Reserve Bank of New York, *Recent Trends in Commercial Bank Profitability* (New York: Federal Reserve Bank of New York, 1986), pp. 286-294.

ing portfolio and interest rate risk. Because of the large size of many pension funds, however, active portfolio management is not always advisable.

Investment companies are financial intermediaries that sell shares to the public and reinvest proceeds in the financial markets. Open-end companies, called mutual funds, are by far the largest type. Investment companies are regulated by the SEC, according to the Investment Company and Investment Advisors Acts of 1940. The industry has grown rapidly in the last decade. The majority of the industry's assets are in money market instruments, followed by common stock, Treasury securities, and bonds. Many of the portfolio management issues facing pension funds also apply to investment companies. Research on evaluating the performance of investment companies has not favored the industry, although there is not universal agreement with this conclusion.

Securities firms are financial institutions providing brokerage, trading, underwriting, and other financial services to wholesale and retail customers. The industry has faced competitive pressures from deregulation, particularly from competitive fee structures and Rule 415. Securities firms have met these competitive challenges successfully. They have introduced new financial instruments and techniques and, although earnings have varied, they have been consistently profitable in recent years.

Questions

1. What is the difference between defined benefit pension plans and defined contribution plans? Between insured and noninsured funds? Which types of plans do you think employees would prefer? Why?

2. Discuss how the fiduciary responsibilities of pension fund managers have changed because of ERISA guidelines. What is the impact of the PBGC? Briefly explain the reasons for the PBGC's recent financial problems.

3. Why does ERISA place emphasis on full funding of pension liabilities? What are some of the difficulties in measuring whether or not a plan is fully funded? How does the funding target change over time?

4. Discuss the impact of the financial position of the corporate sponsor on the financial management of pension funds. If you had been employed by U. S. Steel (now USX) in 1982, would you have been disturbed by the company's contribution of preferred stock instead of cash? Why or why not?

5. Social activists have placed increasing pressure on pension fund managers to add social objectives to traditional financial objectives. What are the potential problems with a social investment strategy? The potential benefits? What balance between the two types of objectives is optimal?

6. Briefly discuss researchers' conclusions about the financial performance of pension funds. Why have managers emphasized real estate and international investments in recent years? What additional risk/return tradeoffs do these new types of assets present?

7. Explain the unique problems faced when applying immunization to pension fund management.

8. Do you think active portfolio management is feasible and desirable for pension funds? Does your answer depend upon the size of the fund? Are guaranteed investment contracts a viable alternative to active management? What are their advantages and disadvantages?

9. What benefits do investment companies offer to shareholders that are not provided by direct or other indirect investment alternatives?

10. Distinguish between open-end and closed-end investment companies. What advantages and disadvantages do each offer shareholders? What is the function of management companies in the investment company industry?

11. What is a load mutual fund? How do loads affect returns to shareholders? Explain the difference between a front-end load and a back-end load. How has SEC Rule 12b-1 changed the way some mutual funds charge shareholders for advertising, selling expenses, and brokers' commissions? Would you categorize a 12b-1 plan as a load or a no-load fund?

12. Explain the similarities and differences between real estate investment trusts and unit trusts. How do they differ from other types of investment companies?

13. What are the major regulations governing investment companies, and how do they affect the financial management of investment companies?

14. Investment companies have grown at an exceptionally rapid rate in recent years. Do you expect this growth to continue? Why or why not?

15. Explain how timing and security selection influence the decisions of investment company managers. Are the influences the same for money market and other mutual funds? In general, do you think investment companies offer shareholders higher rates of return than they could receive through direct investment? Why or why not?

16. What are sector funds? What are the advantages and disadvantages of investing in sector funds versus other types of investment companies?

17. What are the major functions of investment bankers? What risk management techniques can investment bankers use to hedge against changes in financial market conditions?

18. How do the services of securities firms compare to those offered by depositories? Does one industry have a clear advantage over the other in attracting customers? If so, which industry and why? Would you recommend regulatory changes? If so, what are they?

19. Regulation has had an especially great impact on the securities industry in the last 15 years. Explain the effect of the SEC's May Day ruling and of Rule 415 on the industry.

20. Explain why securities firms' profits are affected by changes in interest rates. What are the pros and cons of diversification for the securities industry?

21. What difficulties are encountered in evaluating the financial performance of securities firms?

Problems

1. The Sun Coast Manufacturing Company, which has a rather small pension fund, has hired a consulting firm to provide advice on asset/liability management. The following information has been collected:

Financial Data (Thousands)

Cash	$101.50
Obligations	$885.75
Duration of obligations	4.5 years
Obligations/total assets	0.86

Calculate the current amount of earning assets on the balance sheet, and the average asset duration needed to immunize the net worth position of the pension fund.

2. Return to the example in Table 24.2. Assume that market yields rise to 8% from the original level of 5%. Show that the value of net worth is unchanged if the balance sheet is immunized. Repeat the analysis under the assumption that yields fall from 5% to 4%. (*Hint:* Use Equation 4A.7 to find asset and obligation values.)

3. A pension fund currently has earning assets of $25,750,000, and financial obligations of $22,950,000. The cash balance is $3,250,000. The current market rate for assets and liabilities is 7.5 percent. The fund currently has a duration GAP of 1.1 years. If market rates rise to 8.25 percent, what will be the resulting change in the fund's net worth? (*Note:* Equations introduced in Chapter 18 are useful for answering this question.)

4. GBP Manufacturers estimates the future cash flow obligations of its pension fund at $450,000 per year for the next five years. Using a required discount rate of 6 percent, the value of the obligations is $1,895,564. The net worth of the fund currently stands at $400,000, and the cash balance is $180,000. If management wants to immunize net worth from an unexpected shift in market yields, what average duration must it achieve for its portfolio of earning assets?

Selected References

Arnott, Robert D. "The Pension Sponsor's View of Asset Allocation." *Financial Analysts Journal* 41 (September–October 1985): 17-23.

Bodie, Zvi, et al. "Corporate Pension Policy: An Empirical Investigation." *Financial Analysts Journal* 41 (September/ October 1985): 10-16.

Chen, Carl R., and Steve Stockum. "Selectivity, Market Timing, and Random Beta Behavior of Mutual Funds: A Generalized Model." *Journal of Financial Research* 9 (Spring 1986): 87-96.

Chua, Jess H., and Richard S. Woodward. *Gains from Stock Market Timing.* New York: Salomon Brothers Center for the Study of Financial Institutions, 1986.

Cummins, J. David, et al. "Effect of ERISA on the Investment Policies of Private Pension Plans: Survey Evidence." *Journal of Risk and Insurance* 47 (September 1980): 447-476.

Ehrlich, Edna E. "International Diversification by United States Pension Funds." *Quarterly Review* (Federal Reserve Bank of New York) 6 (Autumn 1981): 1-14.

Ezra, D. Don, and Keith P. Ambachtsheer. "Pension Funds: Rich or Poor?" *Financial Analysts Journal* 41 (March/April 1985): 43-56.

Ferri, Michael G., and H. Dennis Oberhelman. "A Study of the Management of Money Market Mutual Funds: 1975-1980." *Financial Management* 10 (August 1981): 24-29.

Friend, Irwin, Marshall Blume, and Jean Crockett. *Mutual Funds and Other Institutional Investors.* New York: McGraw-Hill, 1970.

Friend, Irwin, et al. *Investment Banking and the New Issues Market.* Cleveland: World Publishing Co., 1967.

Hayes, Samuel L. III. "The Transformation of Investment Banking." *Harvard Business Review* 57 (January/February 1979): 153-170.

Investment Company Institute. *Mutual Fund Fact Book.* Various issues.

Jensen, Michael C. "The Performance of Mutual Funds in the Period 1945–1964." *Journal of Finance* 23 (May 1968): 389–416.

Kidwell, David S., et al. "SEC Rule 415: The Ultimate Competitive Bid." *Journal of Financial and Quantitative Analysis* 19 (June 1984): 183–196.

Kientz, Richard J., and Clyde P. Stickney. "Immunization of Pension Funds and Sensitivity to Actuarial Assumptions." *Journal of Risk and Insurance* 47 (June 1980): 223–239.

Kon, Stanley, and Frank C. Jen. "The Investment Performance of Mutual Funds: An Empirical Investigation of Timing, Selectivity, and Market Efficiency." *Journal of Business* 42 (April 1979): 263–289.

Logue, Dennis E., and Richard J. Rogalski. *Managing Corporate Pension Plans: The Impact of Inflation.* Washington, DC: American Enterprise Institute, 1984.

Lynn, Robert J. *The Pension Crisis.* Lexington, MA: Lexington Books, 1983.

McKenna, Fred W., and Yong H. Kim. "Managerial Risk Preferences, Real Pension Costs, and Long-Run Corporate Pension Fund Investment Policy." *Journal of Risk and Insurance* 53 (March 1986): 29–48.

Munnell, Alicia H. "Guaranteeing Private Pension Benefits: A Potentially Expensive Business." *New England Economic Review* (Federal Reserve Bank of Boston) (March/April 1982), pp. 24–47.

Pozen, Robert C. "The Prudent Person Rule and ERISA: A Legal Perspective." *Financial Analysts Journal* 33 (March/April 1977): 30–35.

Rogowski, Robert J., and Eric H. Sorenson. "Deregulation in Investment Banking: Shelf Registrations, Structure and Performance." *Financial Management* 14 (Spring 1985): 5–15.

Securities Industry Association. *Securities Industry Trends.* Various issues.

Sharpe, William F. "Mutual Fund Performance." *Journal of Business* 39 (January 1966): 119–138.

Treynor, Jack L. "How to Rate Management of Investment Funds." *Harvard Business Review* (January/February 1965): 131–136.

Veit, E. Theodore, and John M. Cheney. "Managing Investment Portfolios: A Survey of Mutual Funds." *Financial Review* 19 (November 1984): 321–338.

Webb, James R., and Willard McIntosh. "Real Estate Investment Rules for REITs: A Survey." *The Journal of Real Estate Research* 1 (Fall 1986): 77–91.

Chapter 25

DIVERSIFIED FINANCIAL SERVICES FIRMS

We don't want Sears in the banking business.

Paul Volcker
Chairman
Federal Reserve Board (1984)

THE term "cold cash" took on vivid meaning to a broker for the securities firm of Dean Witter Reynolds working out of a Sears department store in Dallas in January 1984. A local butcher who had never before felt comfortable contacting a stock broker had just handed him $25,000 in cash to open an account. Until just minutes before his arrival at the Sears store, the butcher kept his savings in a freezer.[1]

Attracting customers who have never had a relationship with a financial institution was the dream behind Sears's journey into diversified financial services. Sears's plan, and that of several other financial giants, are the subjects of this chapter.

---

[1]Steve Weiner and Frank E. James, "Sears, a Powerhouse in Many Fields Now, Looks into New Ones," *The Wall Street Journal,* February 10, 1984, p. 7.

FINANCIAL SERVICES FIRMS: WHAT ARE THEY?

Financial services is a term encompassing all the deposit, credit, investment, and insurance operations discussed in this book. Traditionally, of course, subgroups of financial services were the focus, voluntarily or involuntarily, of specific institutions. Because of that specialization, earlier chapters emphasize identifying risk/expected return factors that make each service a unique problem in asset/liability management, with implications for the net interest margin and return on net worth. In the 1980s, however, individual firms have increasingly tended to expand their range of services, becoming providers of financial services in the broad sense.

Some experts believe that, eventually, all businesses now grouped together as "financial institutions" will offer the entire range of financial services. If so, the need to emphasize historical and regulatory differences between firms will disappear, and asset/liability management will no longer be partially segmented by type of institution. For now, however, the move to provide virtually all financial services is confined to large firms with origins in a variety of industries, including retailing, manufacturing, banking, insurance, and consumer finance.

This chapter explores diversified financial services firms and examines the implications for asset/liability management in the future. Included are profiles of five companies (originally from different industries), now offering a similar range of diversified financial services: American Express (travel and entertainment services), Citicorp (commercial banking), Merrill Lynch (securities), Prudential (insurance), and Sears (retailing).

DEVELOPMENT OF FINANCIAL SERVICES FIRMS: WHEN AND WHY

Although the rise of financial services firms has occurred in the 1980s, their roots extend to an earlier time. Sears offered consumer credit to promote the sale of goods as early as 1911. By 1931, the firm was selling car insurance in its stores through its Allstate Insurance subsidiary. In 1960, Sears acquired an S&L in California, entering the field of real estate finance. General Electric, a manufacturer of industrial and consumer goods, became involved in commercial finance through its captive finance company in 1932; it began making personal loans in the 1960s and entered the insurance field in the 1970s.[2]

Still, the extent to which financial services firms now exist is a function of factors identified in this book as recent phenomena: deregulation, a changing economy, and new customer preferences. Table 25.1 shows how depositories, nondepositories, and nonfinancial firms have moved into financial services. In 1960, for example, insurance firms, retailers, and securities dealers offered a small group of financial products, and only those not offered by banks and S&Ls. By 1984, nearly all financial products were offered by firms in each industry.[3]

Financial institutions are not the only firms to be affected by deregulation, a changing economy, and changing customer attitudes. The trucking industry, for example, also faced similar phenomena. Yet the rush in the 1980s has been to financial services, not to trucking. Why? There are four main reasons.

Ease of Entry

It is expensive to purchase a fleet of trucks and to train long-haul drivers. The cost of entering

---

[2]These developments are identified in Robert A. Eisenbeis, "Regulation and Financial Innovation: Implications for Financial Structure and Competition among Depository and Non-Depository Institutions," *Issues in Bank Regulation* 4 (Winter 1981): 15-23. Eisenbeis's data are drawn from Cleveland A. Christophe, *Competition in Financial Services* (New York: First National City Corporation, March 1974).

[3]Of course, not all products offered in 1984 were perfect substitutes for one another. For example, the term *checking account* could be interpreted to mean a demand deposit at a bank, a universal life insurance policy at an insurer, and a cash management account at a securities firm. Nonetheless, the "checking" row of Table 25.1 illustrates the much wider availability of some form of transaction account in 1984 than in 1960. The same interpretation can be offered for other rows in the table.

Table 25.1
Financial Services Offered, 1960 and 1984

	Banks		Savings and Loan Associations		Insurance Companies		Retailers		Securities Dealers	
	1960	1984	1960	1984	1960	1984	1960	1984	1960	1984
Checking	★	★		★		★		★		★
Savings	★	★	★	★		★		★		★
Time deposits	★	★	★	★		★		★		★
Installment loans	★	★	★	★		★		★		★
Business loans	★	★		★		★		★		★
Mortgage loans	★	★	★	★		★		★		★
Credit cards	★	★		★		★	★	★		★
Insurance					★	★		★		
Stocks, bonds, brokerage, underwriting		★		★		★		★	★	★
Mutual funds				★		★		★	★	★
Real estate		★		★		★		★		★
Interstate facilities		★				★		★		★

Source: Donald L. Koch, "The Emerging Financial Services Industry: Challenge and Innovation," *Economic Review,* Federal Reserve Bank of Atlanta 69 (April 1984): 26.

the financial services industry *de novo* (starting a new firm) is lower because the required investment in real assets is small. Although start-up costs, such as chartering or registration fees, arise with financial services, they are usually smaller than the investment required to enter other industries. Some nonfinancial firms, such as retailers already offering credit cards, find it particularly easy to expand their financial services. Financial institutions specializing in one service find it possible to move relatively quickly into others.

Substitutability of Products

A second reason the move to financial services has occurred quickly is that financial products have commodity-like characteristics. It is hard to tell one ear of corn from another, and one savings account is similar to another, as is one whole life policy to another, and so on. A single provider rarely can corner a market at the expense of competitors, and all firms offering a service have an equal opportunity to succeed—or fail.

Perceived Profitability

Some firms have entered the financial services business because they perceive it to be more profitable than their primary lines of business. An executive with J. C. Penney Company, a leading retailer with insurance and thrift subsidiaries, noted recently, "In general, financial services are more profitable than retailing."[4] Although executives of many thrifts, agricultural banks, and insurance companies might quarrel with this thought, it has led several nonfinancial firms into finance.

Synergy

A final motivation for the move toward diversified financial services, espoused by firms that have diversified by purchasing other firms, is a belief that the earnings of a diversified firm will exceed those of two or more firms operating separately. As a reporter for *The Wall Street Journal* put it in a recent article on diversified financial services firms in the 1980s: "With each acquisition, the word 'synergy' was used to the point of exhaustion."[5] Whether synergy has materialized in some of these diversified firms is a subject of debate, but one cannot dismiss synergy as a motivation for offering a broad range of financial services.

PROFILES OF MAJOR DIVERSIFIED FINANCIAL SERVICES FIRMS

Table 25.2 summarizes data from five major diversified financial services firms as of year-end 1985 and ranks them according to various data items. Because Prudential is a mutually owned company, data on net income and total net worth, including all the firm's subsidiaries, are unavailable. It is possible to infer from what is available, however, that Prudential's total net income and net worth would be in the lower part of the rankings, rather than in first or second place.

No firm ranked at the top or bottom on all data items. The reason lies partly in the fact that these firms came to financial services from different origins. For example, Sears's emphasis on retailing makes it less leveraged than firms that are entirely financially-oriented, and it has higher net worth. The labor intensiveness of retailing is also shown by the figures for number of employees, assets per employee, and revenue per employee. Merrill Lynch has the next-lowest ratio of revenues per employee, reflecting the large staffs traditional in the secur-

---

[4]Steve Weiner and Hank Gilman, "Debate Grows on Retailers' Bank Services," *The Wall Street Journal,* May 18, 1984.

[5]David B. Hilder and Steve Weiner, "Big Brokerage Houses Are Problem Children for Their New Parents," *The Wall Street Journal,* September 13, 1985, p. 1. (Synergy is first discussed in Chapter 19.) Emphasis on synergy in public statements may also be attributed to the fact that, according to finance theory, shareholders are not well served by nonsynergistic mergers; they can diversify their personal stock portfolios more easily and cheaply than firms can diversify their asset portfolios.

Table 25.2
Selected Data on Five Diversified Financial Services Firms, Year-End 1985
(Millions Unless Otherwise Specified)

	Revenues	Rank	Net Income	Rank	Total Assets	Rank	Common Equity	Rank	Employees (Number)	Rank	Assets per Employee	Rank	Revenues per Employee	Rank
American Express	$11,850	4	$ 810	3	$ 74,777	3	$ 5,369	3	70,536	4	$1.060	4	$0.168	3
Citicorp	22,504	3	998	2	173,597	1	6,550	2	81,300	2	2.135	1	0.277	2
Merrill Lynch	7,117	5	224	4	48,117	5	2,341	4	44,900	5	1.072	3	0.159	4
Prudential	27,418	2	NA	—	115,728	2	NA	—	80,000	3	1.447	2	0.343	1
Sears	40,715	1	1,303	1	66,417	4	11,794	1	460,000	1	0.144	5	0.089	5

Note: In 1985, the insurance operations of Prudential posted a $51 million loss; net worth (including security valuation reserves) of insurance operations only was $3,749 million at year-end.

Source: 1985 annual reports.

ities industry. The rankings also reflect performance differences as the five firms have struggled for preeminence.

Much of the remainder of the chapter is devoted to case histories of these firms. Although they have chosen different strategies and have met varying degrees of success, they have one thing in common: They have changed their own industries and other financial institutions forever.

MERRILL LYNCH AND COMPANY

Although Sears entered financial services long ago, many observers attribute the recent race to become the prototype diversified financial services firm not to Sears but to Merrill Lynch (ML). In the early 1970s, its Chairman Donald Regan, who once was Chief of Staff to President Ronald Reagan, announced a plan to transform ML into, as *Business Week* termed it, a "womb to tomb" financial services firm.[6] The first step was to create a publicly owned holding company, Merrill Lynch and Company, to acquire the assets of a privately held securities firm, Merrill Lynch Pierce Fenner and Smith. The latter firm, founded in 1820, is still the holding company's largest subsidiary, with nearly 500 offices in the United States and 29 foreign countries.

Expansion of Consumer Financial Services

One of the company's first major forays into product diversification was the Cash Management Account (CMA), offered through its brokerage subsidiary and described in the previous chapter. Introduced in 1977, the CMA had captured an estimated 70 percent of the market for that deposit-like service by 1985, despite the entry of other major competitors.[7] CMA holders

have access to cash-dispensing machines in over 6,000 locations nationwide.

For individuals who do not wish to make stock and bond selections but do want to participate in the securities markets, ML's brokerage arm has stressed mutual funds in recent years. All types are available, from money market to foreign currency funds.

ML, the Real Estate Company.   Besides expansion of securities products, ML sought to make progress toward its womb-to-tomb goal by establishing Merrill Lynch Realty, Inc. This holding company was formed in 1979 to acquire local real estate agencies, especially in fast-growing Sun Belt states. By 1981, 13 agencies with 250 offices had been acquired, and by the end of 1986, additional acquisitions had increased ML Realty's total residential real estate offices to 500. In addition, Merrill Lynch Realty operated a relocation subsidiary, through which it assisted newcomers to communities in which it had offices, and a mortgage subsidiary, offering homebuyers alternatives to borrowing from a local depository.

In late 1986, however, ML officials admitted that the synergy expected from adding real estate to its product offerings had not materialized. Management initially announced plans to sell the entire real estate unit, but later decided to sell shares to the public and retain majority ownership. Analysts noted that the unit was the least profitable of all ML subsidiaries.[8]

ML, the Insurance Company.   Merrill Lynch offers insurance products, often designed to appeal to customers with ML broker relationships. These products fit with a previous addition to ML's fold, Family Life Insurance Company, acquired in 1974. Family specializes

---

[6]"How They Manage the New Financial Conglomerates," *Business Week,* December 20, 1982, p. 50.

[7]Walt Bogdanich, "All-in-One Asset Accounts Offer Variety of Options, and Complexity," *The Wall Street Jour-*

nal, July 9, 1985, p. 31. Ironically, the CMA was initially offered through a bank, Bank One of Ohio, which was considered a "traitor" by other bankers at the time.

[8]Merrill Lynch, *Annual Report 1985,* p. 22; Steve Swartz and Laurie P. Cohen, "Merrill Lynch Will Sell Units in Real Estate," *The Wall Street Journal,* September 30, 1986, pp. 3–4; Steve Swartz, "Merrill Lynch Real Estate Line Will Go Public," *The Wall Street Journal,* December 23, 1986, p. 2.

in mortgage insurance and whole life, disability, and annuity products. ML agents also sell insurance products for nonsubsidiary underwriters and, in 1985, led the nation in sales of variable life insurance policies. At the beginning of 1987, the insurance unit was among ML's most successful subsidiaries, having more than doubled premium revenues each year for the previous five years.

Development of the Retail Financial Center.   In 1985, ML unveiled the first of its retail "financial centers" in downtown Manhattan. The largest in ML's nationwide chain, the center was a consolidation of five offices in the same area, considerably reducing operating costs. Cost reduction, however, was not the major strategic rationale for the center. Staffed with "financial consultants" (no longer called brokers) and on-site specialists in taxation, insurance, and other aspects of personal finance, the objective is to convince clients that ML employees are no longer salespeople, but professionals trained in a range of financial services that can be purchased from ML and Company. To serve customers while controlling personnel costs, ML has also hired "sales assistants" lacking the stature of financial consultants and intended to serve small-account customers.

ML, the Banker.   ML's retail services are enhanced by a nonbank bank, Merrill Lynch Bank and Trust Company, near Princeton, New Jersey, from which it sells insured CDs, provides clearing and support functions for the CMA program, and lends to customers and other ML subdiaries. It plans to convert the institution to a full-service bank if and when permitted to do so by Congress.

Cultivation of the Commercial Customer

Merrill Lynch has not neglected commercial and governmental customers in its pursuit of the retail dollar, having been a leader in investment banking for decades. In 1984, it acquired the firm of Becker Paribus, an investment banking house, but more importantly, a major commercial paper dealer, thereby becoming the leading participant in that market. ML has also been the largest underwriter of municipal bonds throughout the 1980s.

ML's investment banking has emphasized two additional specialty areas in recent years: corporate mergers and interest rate swaps. ML is also active in underwriting internationally, with investment banking operations in Canada, Great Britain, and Japan.

ML, the Business Lender.   Although prohibited from direct involvement in domestic commercial banking, ML is involved in international banking through subsidiaries in London, Panama, and Switzerland, and through an Edge Act branch in New York.

In 1982, ML added domestic commercial lending to its offerings when it unveiled the Capital Resources service, designed to attract medium-sized corporate borrowers, investors buying companies with borrowed money (so-called *leveraged buyouts*), and entrepreneurs seeking venture capital. Loans for these purposes are funded by ML's own commercial paper, avoiding Glass-Steagall prohibitions against securities firms' simultaneously taking deposits and making commercial loans. By 1985, assisting in leveraged buyouts had become such an important part of ML's operations that it formed a subsidiary, Merrill Lynch Capital Partners, Inc., solely devoted to that activity. The firm also began emphasizing cash management services for small businesses and investment management for corporate pension funds.

Merrill Lynch: Knows No Boundaries?

ML has many strengths. Its worldwide offices give it a major geographic presence, and its potential retail customer base is huge. Its CMA strongly resembles a transaction account, it owns a nonbank bank, and its international banking operations are already full-service.

In addition, the role of ML in investment banking strengthens its image in wholesale financial services. If and when unrestricted investment banking and commercial banking coexist in a single organization, ML's relationships with corporate customers will make it a fierce competitor for their banking business. ML's growing emphasis on financial services for medium-sized businesses offers the same promise, as does its ownership of a nonbank bank.

The firm is not "home free," however. Initially, ML's greatest challenge was retraining its large force of brokers unaccustomed to the new responsibilities required as financial consultants. Friction among securities, insurance, and real estate personnel prevented coordinated relationships with customers, a problem addressed by the formation of a Consumer Market sector within the business in 1985. The firm also overhauled its compensation structure in 1986 to reward financial consultants not only for trades executed but also for total assets brought under ML's management. The system radically departs from tradition in the securities industry. Although the system was considered a modest success in its first year, it will take time to implement fully.

High operating costs have kept ML from being as profitable as some competitors, although the firm has made strides to become more efficient in recent years. The firm embarked on a staff-reduction plan in 1984, attempting to reduce nonincome generating personnel (that is, researchers) while increasing the number of financial consultants. Table 25.2 demonstrates that ML still has a considerable distance to go, however, before achieving the staffing efficiencies of an organization such as Citicorp.

Finally, the firm's initial goal of serving everyone in every way made it difficult to structure the organization to achieve superior levels of profitability. Although ML's top management said the firm did not want to be a "financial supermarket," where customers "grab their products and services from a shelf," the objective at one time was described as being a "department store." By 1986, however, the firm's CEO stated its strategy differently, saying, "The idea is that we aren't going to be all things to all people. We're going to be some things to

some people."[9] Early evidence suggests that this more limited objective may also be more profitable, because earnings for 1986 were up sharply from previous years.

PRUDENTIAL INSURANCE COMPANY OF AMERICA

A second major player to enter the financial services scene was Prudential Insurance (Pru), the nation's largest life insurer, operating since 1875. In 1981, Pru sent "shock waves" through the financial community with its purchase of Bache Group, Inc., the nation's sixth-largest securities firm. Negotiations lasted only 13 days, astonishing observers of the usually conservative insurer. One noted that it was a case of "a 900-pound gorilla going after a banana."[10]

The Bache Acquisition: *This* Is Synergy?

For several years, Pru's chairman was interested in taking the firm beyond insurance. Although the plan did not initially include commercial banking, securities activities had been high on the list since 1974. When Bache became available, Pru's management agreed to pay $385 million for it. At the time, Bache was in turmoil, because it was involved in a controversial 1980 incident in which two wealthy Texans were accused of trying to corner the silver market.[11] Nonetheless, Pru's management was optimistic that Bache's problems were past and believed the acquisition was an ideal way to en-

[9]Stephen Taub, "Sizing Up the Brokers," *Financial World,* January 8-21, 1986, pp. 1-4; Swartz and Cohen, "Merrill Lynch Will Sell Units in Real Estate."

[10]Carol J. Loomis, "The Fight for Financial Turf," *Fortune* 104 (December 28, 1981): 55.

[11]Thomas Moore, "Ball Takes Bache and Runs with It," *Fortune* 107 (January 24, 1983): 97-100. The New York Stock Exchange imposed a $400,000 fine on Bache for the incident, the largest fine ever for a member firm. See "New Bache Chief Pushes a Host of Changes, Including New Name, to Lift Firm's Image," *The Wall Street Journal,* October 29, 1982.

ter the brokerage, mutual fund, and underwriting businesses with one giant step.

The Best-Laid Plans Often Go Awry.

Unfortunately for Pru, by 1985, the Bache acquisition had failed to live up to the expectations of Pru's management. One of Bache's major problems was its low productivity. In 1982, for example, commissions and fees per employee were nearly $15,000 less at Bache than at other leading brokers. Initially, new management Pru brought in to turn Bache around increased salaries even more and made costly cosmetic changes to the firm's offices. In 1984, Prudential-Bache, the renamed securities firm, posted the largest loss ever for a brokerage house, exceeding $110 million, at least partly attributed to high overhead costs. Wall Street analysts estimated that, from 1981 through 1984, Pru's average annual return on the Bache deal was −12.5 percent.[12] Things improved slightly in 1985, however, when Prudential-Bache posted a profit for the year.

During this time, life insurers had their own problems, a phenomenon from which the insurance division of Pru was not exempt. To address changing customer preferences, Pru introduced the industry's first combination universal/variable life policy in 1985. Although popular with customers, this and other nontraditional products were less profitable than whole life policies, squeezing the firm's overall margin. In addition, problems plagued Pru's P&C subsidiary, PRUPAC, and the firm's reinsurance subsidiary, Pru Re, had significant losses through the mid-1980s.

The original strategic plan at the time of the Bache acquisition called for brokers and insurance agents to work side by side, sharing client lists to increase sales; by 1985, only 15 percent were doing so. As did Merrill Lynch, Pru underestimated the difficulty of merging different cultures and found that brokers and insurance agents do not necessarily cooperate just because they work for the same firm. Con-

sequently, the outlook for synergy in Prudential's retail services remains cloudy.

The Move to Business Lending

On another front, like Merrill Lynch, Pru has declared its intention to become active in business lending by forming a holding company that owns three business-related financial services firms. One, PruCapital, Inc., specializes in lending to medium-sized companies and public utilities. Its major activities are leveraged buyouts and asset-based financing. In 1984, a new commercial unit, Prudential Venture Capital Management, Inc., was established to make equity investments in emerging firms. In addition, Pru is involved in investment banking through the Bache subsidiary. It also owns a limited-service bank called Prudential Bank and Trust Company. Cryptically, the bank is mentioned only once in Pru's recent annual reports, and a top Prudential manager is quoted as saying that limited-service banking "is an issue we'd prefer not to discuss or address."[13]

Prudential: Too Many Pieces of the Rock?

Because the insurance industry, which remains Pru's primary line of business, has had especially difficult times in the 1980s, Pru's road to becoming a preeminent financial services provider has been rough. In addition, Pru's securities subsidiary has been among the worst performers in a sometimes glittering industry. Fundamental improvements in each of these basic lines of business is necessary before the future envisioned at the time of the merger becomes reality. As at Merrill Lynch before 1986, the firm's strategic focus is fuzzy, having been vaguely articulated as being "Number One in each of our chosen major business lines."[14] Also as at ML, organizational restructuring has

---

[12]Hilder and Weiner, "Big Brokerage Houses Are Problem Children for Their Parents."

[13]Karen Langevin, "Court Throws Cold Water on Nonbank Frenzy," *National Underwriter* 89 (August 10, 1985): 41.

[14]Prudential, *Annual Report 1985,* p. 3.

been common in the years since the move to diversification. The firm continues to acquire a varied group of subsidiaries, adding a farm management organization, two investment management firms, and a home mortgage subsidiary in recent years. In 1988, Pru plans to open a nationwide network of residential real estate brokerage offices.

Still, Pru has features that make it a major force in the financial markets. Because of the insurance subsidiary's huge asset portfolio, the firm has substantial expertise in portfolio management, including real estate development. Pru has established relationships with many major corporations whose bonds it holds in private placements. The firm also enjoys relative freedom from geographic restrictions.

In addition, management argues that the mutual form of organization gives it an edge over competitors. According to this argument, the lack of stockholder scrutiny allows management to avoid a myopic eye on the immediate future, focusing instead on the year 2000.[15] Based on this view, in fact, management invested another $100 million in the securities subsidiary in 1984, the same year it reported its record-breaking loss. Pru is clearly in the financial services business for the long haul.

AMERICAN EXPRESS

When Prudential bought Bache, Sanford Weill, Chairman of Shearson Loeb Rhoades, the third-largest brokerage firm, saw the handwriting on the wall. To avoid being captured by a giant not of his own choosing, Weill approached the leading travel services firm, American Express (AmEx), and asked it to buy Shearson. In April 1981, within a month after the Pru-Bache deal, AmEx paid $930 million for Shearson, renaming it Shearson/American Express.

Like Merrill Lynch and Prudential, AmEx was hardly a newcomer to financial products. Founded in 1850 to transport packages and money across the American frontier, the firm invented the traveler's check in 1891. By the 1960s, AmEx's famous green credit card and its best-selling traveler's checks made the company a household word. The 1981 Shearson acquisition was the first of $3 billion spent recently to turn AmEx into a contender for the title of financial services leader.

Shearson/AmEx: Maybe *This* Is Synergy

Weill's goal was to obtain the AmEx cardholder list for Shearson brokers, a seemingly natural marketing tool to increase the company's ability to serve wealthy customers. AmEx executives did not agree to share, however, fearing that cardholders might become disenchanted if their Shearson-managed stock accounts went sour. Weill also hoped to capitalize on the acknowledged strength of AmEx's marketing department to enable Shearson to develop a distinctive image like those of rivals Merrill Lynch and E. F. Hutton. But AmEx continued to place more emphasis on credit card marketing than on the image of the brokerage firm.

Not that the Shearson/AmEx deal was unprofitable: Analysts estimated that AmEx's annual return on the Shearson investment from 1981 to 1984 averaged 10.9 percent.[16] As in the Prudential organization, however, problems emerged in the attempt to combine corporate cultures. By 1985, Weill and others had quit the company, unable to merge their management styles with that of AmEx's chairman and CEO, James Robinson.

Happily for AmEx, the managers Robinson brought in to replace Weill succeeded in increasing cooperation among personnel. Although by 1986, the firm was touted as a "state of the art financial services conglomerate," AmEx sought to reduce its exposure to cyclical swings in the securities business by selling partial ownership of Shearson to other investors in 1987. AmEx retained controlling interest.[17]

[15]"How They Manage the New Financial Conglomerates."

[16]Hilder and Weiner, "Big Brokerage Houses Are Problem Children for Their Parents."

[17]Anthony Bianco, "American Express: A Financial Supermarket That Works," *Business Week,* June 2, 1986, pp. 78-79, Steve Swartz, "American Express Co. Sets Shearson Issue;" *The Wall Street Journal,* March 24, 1987, p. 3.

AmEx and the Middle-Income Customer

In 1983, the upper-income marketing strategy that AmEx had initially pursued took an abrupt turn when AmEx acquired Investors Diversified Services (IDS), a mutual fund and financial planning group headquartered in Minneapolis. At a cost of nearly $800 million, IDS gave AmEx access to millions of middle-income consumers who were either ineligible for or uninterested in AmEx cards and Shearson brokerage accounts.

The IDS purchase had features of strategic importance to AmEx. Unlike many investment companies, IDS had a nationwide sales force. Most personnel were in small or medium-sized communities, unlike Shearson brokers who were concentrated in large cities. In addition, IDS had a life insurance subsidiary, adding a previously unavailable product to the AmEx line. The IDS acquisition permitted the company to simultaneously diversify along customer, geographic, and product lines.

Initially, however, operating costs for the new sales force were higher than AmEx anticipated, and reorganization was necessary. On the positive side, cross-selling efforts between Shearson and IDS products have been successful. In addition, increased emphasis has been placed on financial planning services available through IDS, and AmEx's management views the acquisition as a long-run asset.

AmEx and Consumer Credit

In 1986, AmEx expanded consumer lending operations by opening banks in Delaware and Minnesota. Using the customer base of its credit card and IDS account holders, the banks provide personal and mortgage loans. AmEx is also positioned to enter consumer banking through its network of over 17,500 point-of-sale authorization terminals and cash-dispensing machines.

AmEx and International Banking

AmEx is not a newcomer to banking. In 1919, to facilitate the traveler's check business, AmEx formed American Express International Banking Corporation (AEIBC), which by 1985 had 85 offices in 39 countries. For much of its recent history, the unit stressed international investment banking through its London office, but AmEx's interest was so low that AEIBC was put up for sale in early 1981. There were no takers.

After the Shearson acquisition, AmEx again turned its attention to developing commercial and retail banking products, and AEIBC received renewed emphasis. In 1983, AmEx added the Trade Development Bank of Switzerland to its international banking group, acquiring an institution with over $4.5 billion in deposits. Since then, AEIBC has been the "crown jewel" of AmEx. It has stressed three major banking strategies: services for wealthy individuals (called *private banking*), arrangement of international loan agreements, and international correspondent banking. All three services are fee-based, consistent with AmEx's historical emphasis on fee income from traveler's checks and credit cards, and with Shearson's fee-based securities operations.

AmEx and P&C Insurance

In 1968, for tax reasons, AmEx acquired Fireman's Fund, one of the nation's ten largest P&C insurers. By the early 1980s, the acquisition seemed to fit conveniently into AmEx's plan to become a diversified financial services firm. But the outlook for insurance changed rapidly in the early 1980s, and in 1983, AmEx posted its first earnings downturn in 36 years, attributed to severe underwriting losses at Fireman's.

Although Fireman's is a stock company, it had been privately held by AmEx since 1968. In 1984, with no quick access to external capital for Fireman's, AmEx was forced to inject $200 million into Fireman's to meet the requirements of California regulators. In 1985, AmEx distanced itself from Fireman's considerably by selling 85 percent of its stock to the public. AmEx's management noted that Fireman's mostly commercial customers did not mesh with the strong retail financial services unit resulting from the Shearson and IDS acquisitions.

Before the public sale, however, AmEx transferred Fireman's life insurance operations to IDS, consistent with the retail focus of the conglomerate.

AmEx and Investment Banking

Evidently some commercial operations can find a home at AmEx, because in 1984, Shearson/ AmEx paid $360 million for the investment banking firm of Lehman Brothers Kuhn Loeb, renaming the newly merged securities unit Shearson Lehman/American Express. The objectives of the acquisition were to make Shearson competitive with leading investment banking firms and to bring a primary government securities dealership into the AmEx fold. AmEx's investment banking operations were not initially successful, however, as partners in the previously privately held Lehman left and the firm fell behind competitors in the markets for mergers and private placements. Nevertheless, leadership at Shearson succeeded in turning things around after a period of adjustment, and, in 1986, investment banking was one of AmEx's most profitable units.

AmEx: Hoping No One Leaves Home without It

AmEx has many competitive strengths. Its image among consumers is unsurpassed: According to a 1984 survey, 75 percent of all Americans knew of American Express financial products, versus 66 percent for Merrill Lynch, 54 percent for Sears, and 53 percent for Citicorp. Interestingly, AmEx's closest rival for recognition was Prudential, with 72 percent. AmEx's retail product offerings are designed to appeal to virtually every middle- or upper-income household. It is possible that someday few Americans in these income categories will leave home without an AmEx connection.

Although early difficulties plagued almost all its acquisitions, AmEx has thus far been the most successful of the major financial services firms. Its strategic markets are clearer and narrower than those of Merrill Lynch or Prudential, enabling management to focus the firm's resources to achieve synergy among product lines.[18] AmEx's acquisitions also have been strong firms, not those going through difficult periods. In addition, AmEx has been willing to divest itself of operations that do not seem to work. A potential cloud on the horizon is the credit card division, which had lower growth in 1986 than AmEx's other units. Still, AmEx's new services may more than compensate for this decline. In 1987, AmEx announced a new credit card called Optimia, designed to compete with bank cards by charging a lower interest rate on outstanding balances.

SEARS, ROEBUCK AND COMPANY

If any year can be identified as the year diversified financial services firms emerged, it is 1981. Not only did the Pru-Bache and Shearson-AmEx deals occur, but in 1981, the world's largest retailer declared its intention to become the world's largest financial services firm. Sears, founded as a mail-order watch company in 1886, laid the groundwork for this move in 1980 by reorganizing as a holding company, of which only one subsidiary was department store and catalog operations. The firm acted on its new intentions swiftly, acquiring two major financial subsidiaries within a month.

Emergence of the Sears Financial Network

The first of these purchases, in October 1981, was Dean Witter Reynolds, then the fifth-largest brokerage firm. Only a few days later, Sears startled the financial community by announcing the purchase of Coldwell Banker, the nation's largest commercial real estate agency, with a residential division as well. Total price

---

[18]For more information on AmEx's reputation and financial performance, see American Express Company, *Annual Report 1984*, p. 4; Monci Jo Williams, "Synergy Works at American Express," *Fortune* 115 (February 16, 1987): 79-80.

tag for the two firms: $812 million. With its existing Allstate Insurance subsidiary, and its Allstate S&L in California (later renamed the Sears Savings Bank), the new acquisitions formed the Sears Financial Network.

Adding to the existing offices of Dean Witter and Coldwell Banker, Sears announced plans to open one-stop financial centers in at least half of its 800-plus retail outlets. By mid-1982, the first 8 prototype centers were in operation, and 308 were open by 1985. The firm has announced that no major expansion of these centers is anticipated.

Sears, the Broker

Initial reaction to the Dean Witter acquisition was skepticism. Unlike Prudential and AmEx, which were parent companies accustomed to wealthy individuals and corporations, Sears' retail customers were thought to be primarily middle- or lower-income families. *Institutional Investor,* a leading Wall Street trade publication, published a cartoon depicting the unlikely sight of a Rolls Royce parked in front of a Sears store. Critics forgot that selling financial products in department stores was nothing new for Sears. The Allstate Insurance Company had been selling policies in stores since 1933 and, in fact, was originally named after a best-selling brand of Sears tires. With the addition of Dean Witter and Coldwell Banker, the in-store list of available financial products was simply expanded.

Sears's management did not seem worried about the alleged incongruity of "stocks and socks." In fact, Sears had no real intention of pursuing the high-income customer as a major target market. Instead, the butcher who kept his money in a freezer was the person Sears was cultivating. Still, market research indicated that 45 percent of young affluent households shopped at Sears monthly, and that 65 percent had Sears credit cards, versus only 36 percent with American Express cards.[19]

Evidence on Stocks and Socks Accumulates.   Early evidence from Dean Witter brokers assigned to Sears stores seemed to confirm that the untapped savings of Sears customers was limitless. Stories of thousands—and, in some cases, millions—of dollars pouring into Dean Witter offices were common. In addition, the company's profits were up 130 percent in the first quarter of 1983, prompting many to think that the synergy that seemed to elude other financial service giants had been realized at Sears.

Despite this optimistic beginning, by 1985 it was clear that integrating Dean Witter had been rockier than had first been claimed. Part of the reason is familiar from Prudential-Bache's problems: Employee characteristics and management styles differ among industries and cannot be combined easily. To staff its in-store financial centers, Sears trained over 4,000 new salespeople between 1983 and 1985. But, because of defections by experienced Dean Witter brokers during the period, total brokerage employment increased by only 1,700.[20]

Investment bankers at Dean Witter were dissatisfied with the more conservative philosophy of Sears executives and left the company, and Dean Witter's position in investment banking slipped considerably between 1981 and 1986. Remaining managers were regarded lightly by others on Wall Street.[21]

Unprofitable Accounts.   In addition, brokerage accounts generated by the Dean Witter-Sears relationship were not initially profitable. When the firm did a mass mailing to 19 million credit card holders, encouraging them to open individual retirement accounts through Dean Witter, only a few thousand responded. Not only was the expense of the campaign consid-

---

[19]Alfred G. Haggerty, "Financial Centers a Big Success for Sears," *National Underwriter,* November 23, 1984, p. 56.

[20]Hilder and Weiner, "Big Brokerage Houses Are Problem Children for Their Parents"; Steve Cocheo, "How Sears Mixes Finance, Retailing," *ABA Banking Journal* 77 (April 1985): 70.

[21]Monci Jo Williams, "Sears Roebuck's Struggling Financial Empire," *Fortune* 112 (October 14, 1985): 40-44; Lenny Glynn, "The Dismantling of Dean Witter," *Institutional Investor* 19 (August 1985): 80-92.

erable, the company later determined that IRAs are not especially profitable, because they rarely involve commission-generating trades.

Sears customers were initially very interested in Dean Witter's mutual funds, but these, too, are low-profit relationships. The lucrative aspects of brokering, such as lending through margin accounts, did not materialize. By 1985, the productivity of Dean Witter brokers, measured by average commissions generated, had fallen to only 70 percent of the industry average, and was almost $30,000 lower than in 1983. These problems resulted in an estimated annual return on the Dean Witter acquisition of just 3.3 percent, not considering the additional $300 million Sears loaned Dean Witter in 1984 to shore up its capital.[22]

Sears, the Real Estate Company

The second 1981 acquisition, Coldwell Banker, has fared better. Coldwell Banker did not break totally new ground because of Sears' historic involvement in real estate. The company actually sold houses through the mail from 1908 to 1937, and some towns today boast entire neighborhoods in which homes were purchased from a Sears catalog.[23] Less unusual were the firm's California S&L and PMI Mortgage Insurance Corporation, one of the nation's largest, which Sears had owned since 1973. Starting in 1983, however, Sears added a new twist to real estate brokerage by offering discounts on home furnishings and appliances to homebuyers using Coldwell Banker's services. Although competitors objected, the practice has been upheld in most states.

Coldwell's profits increased steadily from 1981 through 1985. Its position in the residential real estate market was especially impressive, as the volume of houses sold increased to 7.5 percent of the national market in 1985, up from

only 1.3 percent at the time of acquisition. By 1986, it was second in residential real estate sales and the leader in commercial real estate.

Sears's plans for the residential mortgage market are grand. The objective by the mid-1990s is for Coldwell to be involved in over one-quarter of all home sales in the country, and for mortgages on these homes to be originated by financial institutions owned by Sears, insured by PMI, Inc., and packaged and brokered for resale by Dean Witter.

Sears, the Banker

Sears's ownership of an S&L since 1960 made it no stranger to deposit taking as it began its campaign to become the world's leading financial services company. Through this subsidiary, Sears has developed an ATM network that positions it to go nationwide when permitted to do so. In 1985, the firm moved more deeply into banking by purchasing a small Delaware bank, the Greenwood Trust Company, and selling the commercial loan portfolio to avoid violating bank holding company regulations. The opening quotation of the chapter indicates the reaction of at least one major banking regulator to Sears's entry into nonbank banking. The purpose of owning tiny Greenwood ($11 million total assets) is really to facilitate Sears's most ambitious effort to become the dominant retail financial services company: the Discover card.

Discover What? The Discover card, issued through Greenwood Trust to customers mostly drawn from Sears's credit card holders, is the world's first general-purpose financial services card.[24] Test-marketed in five states in 1985 and offered nationally in 1986, the card is intended to give a holder instant access to virtually any

---

[22]Williams, "Sears Roebuck's Struggling Financial Empire"; Hilder and Weiner, "Big Brokerage Houses Are Problem Children for Their Parents."

[23]For more information, see David M. Schwartz, "When Home Sweet Home Was Just a Mailbox Away," *Smithsonian* 16 (November 1985): 91–100.

[24]For information on Discover at the time it was announced, see Williams, "Sears Roebuck's Struggling Financial Empire"; "Mighty Sears Tests Its Clout in Credit Cards," *Business Week,* September 2, 1985, pp. 62–63; and Janet Key, "New Card Chief Focus for Sears," *Chicago Tribune,* October 3, 1985, Section 3, pp. 1, 6. Much of the information in this section is drawn from these articles.

financial service—from making a deposit, to buying stock, to charging merchandise at a store, to taking out a home equity loan. Launching the Discover card was a massive effort, viewed by analysts as Sears's riskiest venture ever.

Sears had to obtain agreement from merchants everywhere to accept the card as readily as they accept Visa, MasterCard, or American Express. Although some merchants agreed immediately (Holiday Inns, American Airlines, and Denny's Restaurants, for example), many were reluctant. Why should J. C. Penney, Macy's, or Marshall Field's help the Sears Financial Network earn additional interest income? To entice merchants into accepting the card, Sears charges lower processing fees than rival Visa, MasterCard, and American Express. Even so, acceptance has not been instantaneous. As of mid-1986, 380,000 accepting merchants were estimated, compared to over 2.5 million accepting Visa cards.[25]

Sears also had to build a base of customers willing to use the card, not only as a credit card, but also to take advantage of features Sears believes distinguish Discover from rival cards. Holding a Discover card now permits someone to tap a savings account at Greenwood Trust and, in some states, to make deposits into a Greenwood account through an ATM. Sears says that by 1990 cardholders will be able to buy CDs, take out loans, or trade securities, all through a member of the Sears Financial Network.

To entice potential cardholders, most of whom already carry bank cards, AmEx cards, or both, no annual fees were charged for the first two years of Discover's existence; discounts on Sears merchandise were provided for using the card; and a prearranged line of credit was awarded to the 28 million Sears cardholders active in 1985.

Early evidence suggests, however, that Discover cardholders view the card more as a substitute for a Sears credit card than as a financial services card. Not one of the respondents to a 1986 survey had used the card to open a savings account at Greenwood, and only 8 percent had used it at a cash-dispensing machine. In addition, no respondent considered Discover to be a substitute for a bank card or other national credit card.[26]

Sears's losses on the Discover card in 1985 were over $15 million after taxes and were estimated at over $115 million in 1986, making it a costly venture indeed.[27] It is too early to assess the impact of Discover on Sears—even Sears itself projected losses until 1988—but much of Sears's image as the premier provider of financial services to middle-income families rests with the success of Discover.

Sears: More for Everybody's Life?

The next several years are critical for the Sears Financial Network. Integrating the merchandising subsidiary and the Network has proved more difficult than anticipated, and management's attention continues to be divided. This has been a strain in recent years, as changing consumer preferences have presented major problems for both merchandising and financial services.

Sears's management has stated repeatedly that it intends to focus its Financial Network entirely on consumer finance. Although the firm has made modest ventures into commercial services, such as processing receivables for corporations, the almost exclusively middle-income consumer focus it has chosen differentiates Sears from Merrill Lynch, Prudential, and American Express. Should the Discover plan fail, Sears may have difficulty recovering its momentum in financial services. This, coupled with Dean Witter's slide in the usually profitable investment banking business, could spell trouble. In early 1987, Sears decided to sell over half of the branches of Sears Savings Bank to

[25]Eugene Johnson, "Non-Bank Challengers Are Changing Faces, Too," *Credit Union Magazine* 52 (February 1986): 50-54; James E. Ellis, "Sears' Discover Card Finds Its Way," *Business Week,* September 15, 1986, pp. 166-167.

[26]"Sears Discover Card Use Studied," *ABA Banking Journal* 78 (June 1986): 115.

[27]Sears, Roebuck and Company, *1985 Annual Report,* p. 4.

rival Citicorp, providing evidence of continued difficulties in the firm's financial network.

On the other hand, Sears has many established strengths. The strong capital position of the merchandising business has been used to bolster the weaker capital positions of finance subsidiaries, permitting Sears to be more patient in achieving financial success with new acquisitions than it might be otherwise. In addition, Allstate Insurance has consistently been one of the lowest-cost producers in the P&C industry, managing to escape the severe profit downturn suffered by most P&C firms in the 1980s.

Although the Dean Witter acquisition caused early difficulties, there are positive signs. A recent analysis indicated that between 35 percent and 40 percent of new Dean Witter accounts had been opened at Sears stores, and that 80 percent of the accounts were opened by individuals without a prior brokerage relationship. Household incomes averaged $36,000, encouraging Sears in its belief that it is building relationships that will prove profitable in time.[28] Because the company estimates that 75 percent of all American adults come to a Sears store each year, there is potential for building a large volume of business for the entire network.

CITICORP

The role of Citicorp as a trend setter in commercial banking is noted at various points in this book. The giant bank's relentless push against regulatory barriers is legendary. This strategic posture allowed Citicorp to develop into a nationwide diversified financial services firm in an era when many commercial banks felt bound both geographically and by product line. Founded in 1812, and the oldest of the contenders for financial services leader, Citicorp epitomizes a firm whose management engaged in "deregulated thinking" long before deregulation was a reality.

---

[28]Cocheo, "How Sears Mixes Finance, Retailing," p. 72.

Citicorp, the Innovator

Citicorp's recent history as an innovator dates at least to 1961, when First National City Bank developed the negotiable CD, an event discussed in Chapter 4. Thereafter, the bank pioneered liability management through its aggressive use of large CDs, Eurodollar deposits, and repos to evade the shackles of Reg Q.

Until 1968, First National City was not organized as a holding company, and almost all its business was in commercial banking. With the formation of Citicorp, the holding company that now owns the renamed Citibank, a new corporate strategy emerged, including aggressive pursuit of retail banking and product diversification to the full extent allowed. Management decided to attach the "Citi" prefix to virtually every product and service. To a large extent, these strategies remain in place today.

Every City Should Have a Citi. At the time the move to retail banking was initiated, the cost of retail funds was lower and the deposit base more stable than that of wholesale depositors. Competition for corporate business was fierce, not only from other commercial banks but also from finance companies and the commercial paper market. Soon, Citibank had opened hundreds of banking offices and ATMs in New York City, later expanding (but less successfully than management had hoped) into upstate New York as branching restrictions were loosened in that state.

By the mid-1970s, the central means of accomplishing Citicorp's strategy was well established: geographic expansion at home and abroad to spread the "Citi" trademark. Branches, ATMs, loan production offices, Edge Act offices, International Banking Facilities, and every other means of obtaining a physical presence as an interstate and international institution were employed. Citicorp also used mass mailings to garner new credit card applicants for Citibank's own Diners' Club and for Visa and MasterCard. Some reports state that the research alone required to direct Citicorp's retail strategy cost $200 million, a marketing expenditure unprecedented among financial institutions.[29]

A Temporary Setback. In 1980, the outlook for the retail strategy took a dismal turn. The advent of the money market certificate had driven up the cost of retail funds; the 1978 bankruptcy law revision produced skyrocketing losses on credit cards and consumer loans; usury ceilings held down profits on good loans; and the market value of Citicorp's large residential mortgage portfolio dropped precipitously as rates rose.

Furthermore, Citicorp's GAP managers in the international division engaged in deliberate asset/liability mismatching that year to compensate for poor results in the consumer segment; when their rate forecasts were wrong, the result was a loss of over $35 million. Although the commercial side of the firm had a good year, and the firm had an overall net profit, critics of the institution charged that the retail strategy had backfired. Net losses on consumer banking exceeded $79 million in 1980 and improved only slightly to $42 million the following year.

Citicorp, the Lawmaker

Undeterred, Citicorp's management set out to change laws it believed had prevented the retail strategy from being profitable, beginning aggressively and successfully with usury laws. Unable to persuade New York legislators, it looked to other states. Aware of Citicorp's dissatisfaction with New York laws, South Dakota lifted its usury ceiling in late 1980. Citicorp moved its credit card operations there in 1981, instituting an annual fee for cardholders at the same time. The credit card division is now among the firm's most profitable, and renewed efforts at expanding its customer base have continued in the 1980s.

Citicorp, Rescuer of Thrifts (and Regulators?)

In 1982, Citicorp removed itself from two regulations that large banks complained were the

most restrictive they faced: prohibitions against interstate deposit taking and against BHCs having thrift subsidiaries. Early in the year, the FSLIC was seeking merger partners for hundreds of thrifts to avoid running out of cash. When the nation's 20th-largest thrift, Fidelity Savings and Loan of Oakland, became insolvent, the FHLBB made an emergency rule permitting out-of-state institutions, including commercial banks, to bid for it. Although two rounds of bids were taken, the second at the insistence of Citicorp's opponents, the New York giant prevailed in August 1982.

The FSLIC stated that Citicorp's bid for Fidelity, immediately renamed Citicorp Savings, would save the insurance fund $143 million, a sum it could ill afford to lose in the worst year ever for thrift industry failures. The regulators argued that no S&L anywhere, and no California-based bank, had the financial strength to assume Fidelity, considering the severe losses the institution was experiencing. In return for an $80 million capital injection by Citicorp, the FSLIC agreed to subsidize negative spreads on the thrift for up to 12 years.[30]

Shortly thereafter, the Garn-St Germain bill was passed, clarifying Congress's view that interindustry, interstate mergers such as the Citicorp-Fidelity combination were the least desirable of all. Citicorp's size and aggressiveness, however, allowed it to expand to Illinois and Florida in 1984, when it made offers the FSLIC could not refuse for two failing thrifts, acquiring 104 deposit-taking facilities in those populous states. Among the most disappointed of the losing bidders for First Federal of Chicago was Sears. In 1986, regulators also accepted a Citicorp offer for a failing Washington, D. C., thrift.

Citicorp, the Securities Firm

Glass-Steagall prohibitions against underwriting domestic corporate securities did not

---

[29]"The New Banking Forces New Strategies," *Business Week,* July 13, 1981, p. 57.

[30]More details on this controversial decision can be found in Christopher Conte, "Citicorp Wins Bank Board Nod to Acquire S&L," *The Wall Street Journal,* August 17, 1982; and John Andrew, "Fidelity Federal Says Bid for Fidelity S&L Should Have Won Over Citicorp's Proposal," *The Wall Street Journal,* August 23, 1982.

prevent Citicorp from establishing a large investment banking division in the late 1970s, through which it underwrites substantial amounts of government and international corporate securities. The firm is positioned to enter domestic investment banking when the law allows, and management makes no secret of its intention to do so. Citicorp regularly seeks Fed approval to conduct some form of underwriting that the firm argues conforms to the letter of the Glass–Steagall Act. Just as regularly, the Fed rebuffs the proposals. Meanwhile, Citicorp's securities division is active in interest rate swaps, private placements, and foreign currency markets.

On the retail side, Citicorp was among the first commercial banks (but, for once, not *the* first) to offer discount brokerage services to its banking customers. It actively pursues full-line brokerage services abroad, and was one of a handful of non-Japanese firms to win a seat on the Tokyo Stock Exchange in 1986, a move viewed as a major step for its securities activities. Merrill Lynch and Shearson–AmEx were two other winners.

Citicorp, the Insurer

Prohibited from entering insurance on a large scale at home, Citicorp began its insurance activities overseas and, over the years, has increased the products offered and locales served. In 1984, buoyed by its success at influencing state laws or evading the letter of existing regulations, Citicorp planned an experimental life insurance operation in the United States. The experiment was based on a change in South Dakota law, permitting out-of-state banks with South Dakota subsidiaries to offer all types of insurance products. In 1985, however, the Fed refused to approve Citicorp's application to acquire a South Dakota bank from which to conduct insurance operations. The decision was viewed as a "major assertion of power" by the Fed, not only against Citicorp but against all banks seeking to enter insurance.[31]

Where Will Citi Go? Everywhere. What Will It Do? Everything.

The Fed's 1985 ruling on insurance shows that Citicorp has some disadvantages in comparison to its rivals. Chief among them is that it consistently faces greater federal regulation. Especially onerous, of course, are Glass–Steagall prohibitions against the mingling of investment and commercial banking and regulations against the underwriting and sale of most types of insurance. As if Glass–Steagall were not enough, the investment and commercial banking divisions of Citicorp have been fierce rivals in recent years. Personnel in the two divisions have been reluctant to refer customers to one another and have engaged in aggressive price competition for the same customers.[32]

In addition, as it seeks to expand, Citicorp faces weaknesses in its original lines of business, as do Sears and Prudential. The firm's brick-and-mortar investment in facilities, once the cornerstone of its entire strategy, is increasingly expensive in a deregulated environment. Citicorp also has substantial exposure to international credit risk from billions of dollars of loans to developing countries, and management has warned shareholders to expect losses in the years ahead.[33] Few of its diversified financial rivals have this risk exposure.

Still, it is difficult to ignore the BHC's great strengths. Citicorp's commitment to retail financial services is firmly entrenched with the appointment of John Reed, the strategy's chief architect, as chairman of the board in 1984, succeeding long-time chairman Walter Wriston, who spearheaded the formation of the holding company. It has a head start on many of its bank and nonbank rivals, having formulated its retail strategy relatively early. With well over 1,000 domestic banking offices and ownership or sharing of over 15,000 ATMs, its

---

[31]Monica Langley, "Federal Reserve Rejects Citicorp's Bid to Build National Insurance Business," *The Wall Street Journal,* August 2, 1985, p. 2.

[32]Sarah Bartlett et al., "Is This Any Way to Run an Investment Bank? Citicorp Thinks So," *Business Week,* July 28, 1986, pp. 56–58; Edward Boyer, "Citicorp: What the New Boss Is Up To," *Fortune* 113 (February 17, 1986): 42–44.

[33]*Citicorp Reports 1984,* p. 3; Boyer, "Citicorp: What the New Boss Is Up To"; Sarah Bartlett, "John Reed's Citicorp," *Business Week,* December 8, 1986, pp. 90–96.

geographic presence exceeds that of its competitors by a wide margin. By the end of 1984, in fact, Citicorp claimed it had relationships with one in every seven American households. Adding its 1,500-plus international offices, the totals are indeed impressive.[34]

The firm's asset base, over half again as large as Prudential, its nearest diversified rival, has been an advantage on several occasions, exemplified by the bidding wars for failing thrifts. Size also enhances the firm's ability to raise funds of all types. Further, the majority of Citicorp's liabilities enjoy the protection of federal deposit insurance, an opportunity unavailable on a large scale to the other firms profiled here.

But perhaps Citicorp's greatest advantage is its rich tradition of creativity and leadership in finance. Year after year, corporate executives and analysts recognize it as among the most innovative firms in any industry.[35] Citicorp has elevated evading regulation to an art. Its very existence guarantees that the regulatory dialectic will continue.

MANAGERIAL IMPLICATIONS OF DIVERSIFIED FINANCIAL SERVICES FIRMS

In 1982, William F. Ford, president of the Federal Reserve Bank of Atlanta, assessed then-emerging financial services firms such as Prudential, AmEx, and Sears.[36] His remarks challenged the common wisdom of that time, but he has since proved to have remarkable insight. Ford cautioned depository institutions, especially commercial banks, against concluding that these emerging firms would be the major providers of financial services. Instead, he noted that they were entering banking's traditional territory from positions of weakness in their basic businesses. Thus, said Ford, the success of diversified financial firms should not be taken for granted, and bankers should not necessarily enter nonbanking fields in order to compete.

Four years later, having earlier trumpeted the rise of diversified financial service firms, *Business Week* flatly stated, ". . . the financial supermarket has been a conspicuous bust. . . . the supermarket's advent was catalyzed not by the arguments of think-tank strategists but by such basic human emotions as insecurity, fear, and greed."[37] Although it is too early to abandon thoughts of diversified financial services firms as viable, and perhaps even formidable, players in the financial markets in the future, one can identify at least some lessons from their first decade.[38]

The National Delivery Firm Is Only One of Several Models

A phenomenon observed in other recently deregulated industries has occurred in financial services: More than one delivery system is successful. A study of deregulation in the trucking, airlines, and communications industries noted that three types of organizations are best at surviving the increased competition that comes from lowering barriers to entry in a product or service market: the national distribution firm, the low-cost, cut-rate producer, and the specialty firm.[39]

---

[34]*Citicorp Reports 1984,* p. 17; Citicorp, *Citicorp Reports 1985,* pp. 13, 38.

[35]See, for example, Cynthia Hutton, "America's Most Admired Corporations," *Fortune* 113 (January 6, 1986): 17.

[36]William F. Ford, "Banking's New Competition: Myths and Realities," *Economic Review,* Federal Reserve Bank of Atlanta 67 (January 1982): 4-11.

[37]Anthony Bianco, "How a Financial Supermarket Was Born," *Business Week,* December 23, 1985, p. 10.

[38]Two discussions of some of the early lessons of deregulation in financial services are Harvey Rosenblum and Christine Pavel, "Financial Services in Transition: The Effects of Nonbank Competitors," Federal Reserve Bank of Chicago, Staff Memorandum 84-1, 1984; and Jon C. Poppen, "Demystifying the Nonbank Financial Supermarket," *Magazine of Bank Administration* 61 (April 1985): 58-64. Further discussion is provided in Joel R. Friedman, "Who Won the Great Financial Services Wars?" *Magazine of Bank Administration* 62 (May 1986): 82-88.

[39]A summary of this study was published in Donald C. Waite III, "Deregulation and the Banking Industry," *The Bankers Magazine* 165 (January-February 1982): 26-35.

In financial services, these delivery systems can readily be seen. The national delivery firm is exemplified by the five firms discussed in this chapter. The low-cost producer is embodied in the numerous money market mutual funds that prosper by conducting business through 800-numbers and the U.S. Postal Service, despite fierce competition from MMDAs at local depository institutions. The continuing existence of specialty firms is seen among the thousands of successful credit unions. None of these institutions is likely to drive the others out of business.

Synergy Is Not Automatic

The case histories in this chapter indicate that synergy in financial services is easier to promise than to achieve. Managing diversified firms profitably is challenging. Thus far, none of the five firms profiled has been the most profitable among financial institutions, and, in fact, some have suffered financial and managerial setbacks on the path to diversification. Integrating and cross-selling services has been elusive. As long as integration is not achieved, synergy, which depends on a unified operating plan, will not be realized. Only AmEx, and to a lesser extent ML and Citicorp, show signs of achieving synergy soon.[40]

Cost Consciousness Is Essential

Another lesson from diversified financial services firms is the necessity of superior cost control. Narrow net interest margins are a way of life, and financial goals can be met only through careful attention to noninterest revenues and expenses. Initially, the sheer size of financial conglomerates provoked great concern from smaller competitors, who argued that size was somehow synonymous with efficiency. Time has proved that this is definitely not the case.

In fact, each of the five firms profiled here has been forced to engage in cost-cutting programs, including the streamlining of staffs and offices.

Financial Services Are Customer-Driven

Perhaps the most important lesson from the study of diversified financial services firms is that the customer is in the driver's seat. This was not always so, when price and service competition were limited and one firm seldom encroached on another. A decade into deregulation, however, customers are sending messages to diversified and nondiversified firms alike.

People May Not Want One-Stop Financial Shopping.   An analogy can be drawn between financial supermarkets and traditional supermarkets. Despite predictions to the contrary, Kroger, Safeway, and other large food chains have not put ethnic grocery stores or corner bakeries out of business. In fact, the popularity of specialty food stores has increased in recent years, even though grocery chains have tried to become all things to all people. Many consumers simply enjoy shopping around, seeing first-hand what products and services are available before they buy.

But They Do Want Control over Their Finances.   In the case of financial supermarkets, an added dimension of consumer behavior is important. Information on an individual's financial status and money management habits is intensely personal. Most people want to control the sharing of that information. Even people willing to buy all their groceries at Kroger may be reluctant to place all their money in a single financial institution. To the extent that this attitude toward personal finance persists, financial supermarkets may not only fail to supplant traditional delivery systems, they may become dinosaurs.

Price and Quality Are Important.   Commercial relationships between financial institu-

[40]Economists at the Federal Reserve Bank of New York examined other diversified financial services firms over the period 1980-1984 and drew similar conclusions. See Federal Reserve Bank of New York, *Recent Trends in Commercial Bank Profitability* (New York: Federal Reserve Bank of New York, 1986), pp. 297-302.

tions and other businesses work similarly. Large corporations have many financial connections, around the country and around the world. They conduct transactions through the institution providing the best service at the best price. The fact that one company can do everything is immaterial unless it offers competitive prices and quality.

Consumers respond to price and quality, too. Although most are less price-sensitive than business customers—for example, consumer deposits are less volatile than commercial ones, even without Reg Q—they will also sever relationships with institutions whose prices and services are unsatisfactory. Citibank's short-lived effort to force low-balance depositors to use ATMs by charging them to see a human teller is a case in point. Massive exodus to competing depositories quickly caused a reversal in the policy. If diversified financial services firms succeed, it will be because the marketplace desires it, not because their managers or owners do.

Fundamental Determinants of Value Are Unchanged

These lessons, and those throughout the book, point to a final conclusion. Institutional value is not created with words, intentions, or publicity. Value emerges from careful identification of market opportunities; thorough analysis of those opportunities, including risk-assessment and the expected impact on financial targets; and skillful execution, including the use of

available risk management tools. These principles hold regardless of the type, size, and location of an institution or of its historical origins. In fact, financial deregulation has not changed the determinants of value at all; it has merely broadened the range of opportunities available to individual firms.

SUMMARY

This chapter focuses on five prominent diversified financial services firms. Several factors have attracted companies to financial services, including the low cost of entry, the similarity of products offered, the expected profitability, and hopes for synergy. Yet even the leading providers of diversified financial services have so far not achieved the expected level of profitability and synergy.

Several conclusions can be drawn about the experience of diversified financial services firms. First, more than one type of firm will thrive in a deregulated environment. Another lesson is that synergy is elusive. Integration of established operations is difficult at best, and cooperation among former competitors does not develop quickly. Cost effectiveness is also elusive. Perhaps the most important lesson is that meeting the needs of customers is the key to success. Unless diversified financial services firms respond to the marketplace, they will not achieve their promise—nor, for that matter, will any financial institution.

Questions

1. Discuss the economic and competitive factors that have attracted companies to the financial services industry. Do you believe the industry will continue to be as attractive to potential entrants in the future as it has been in the 1980s? Why or why not?

2. Based on the overview of Merrill Lynch, Prudential, Sears, American Express, and Citicorp, identify the strategies each used to enter diversified financial services. What problems has each company encountered in its bid to reach the top of the financial services industry? Which company do you think appears to have the best strategy and implementation?

3. Do you think all financial services will someday be provided by companies such as the ones discussed in the chapter? Why or why not?

4. In recent years, research has identified three types of organizations which seem to be well suited for coping with deregulation. Identify these three types of organizations and give an example of each from the financial services industry.

5. For the five companies discussed in the chapter, what roadblocks to synergy were encountered following acquisitions of other firms?

6. Do you agree with Paul Volcker's statement, "We don't want Sears in the banking business"? Do you agree with *Business Week* that "the financial supermarket has been a conspicuous bust"? Why or why not?

Selected References

Bartlett, Sarah. "John Reed's Citicorp." *Business Week,* December 8, 1986, pp. 90-96.

Boyer, Edward. "Citicorp: What the New Boss Is Up To." *Fortune* 113 (February 17, 1986): 40-44.

Eisenbeis, Robert A. "Regulation and Financial Innovation: Implications for Financial Structure and Competition among Depository and Non-Depository Institutions." *Issues in Bank Regulation* 4 (Winter 1981): 15-23.

Ford, William F. "Banking's New Competition: Myths and Realities." *Economic Review* (Federal Reserve Bank of Atlanta) 67 (January/February 1982): 4-11.

Friedman, Joel C. "Who Won the Great Financial Services War?" *Magazine of Bank Administration* 62 (May 1986): 82-88.

Gardner, Robert M. "Sears' Role in Consumer Banking." *Bankers Magazine* 168 (January–February 1985): 6-10.

Glynn, Lenny. "The Dismantling of Dean Witter." *Institutional Investor* 19 (August 1985): 80-92.

"The Golden Plan of American Express." *Business Week,* April 30, 1984, pp. 118-122.

Johnson, Eugene. "Non-Bank Challengers Are Changing Faces Too." *Credit Union Magazine* 52 (February 1986): 50-54.

Laursen, Eric. "The New Order at Merrill." *Institutional Investor* 20 (January 1986): 257-260.

Poppen, Jon C. "Demystifying the Nonbank Financial Supermarket." *Magazine of Bank Administration* 61 (April 1985): 58-64.

Pavel, Christine, and Harvey Rosenblum. "Banks and Nonbanks: The Horserace Continues." *Economic Perspectives* (Federal Reserve Bank of Chicago) 9 (May/June 1985): 3-17.

Selby, Beth. "Can Shearson Save Its Lehman Legacy?" *Institutional Investor* 19 (December 1985): 57-60.

Waite, Donald C. III. "Deregulation and the Banking Industry." *The Bankers Magazine* 165 (January-February 1982): 26-35.

Williams, Monci Jo. "Sears Roebuck's Struggling Financial Empire." *Fortune* 112 (October 14, 1985): 40-44.

Appendix A

CASES

Case 1

FIRST NATIONAL CORPORATION

In 1986, Robert Huenephy, senior vice president in charge of the Special Lending Division at First National Corporation advocated establishing an asset-based lending department at the BHC's lead bank. He had periodically discussed the idea with other loan officers and with senior management. Loan officers were generally enthusiastic; senior management was generally cautious. Neither response surprised Bob. Loan officers wanted new loan products to offer their customers and more ways to meet loan goals. Senior management, while aware of the importance of meeting customer loan needs, as well as the competition in the marketplace, was concerned about the potential for higher loan losses.

First National, a conservative bank in a conservative Ohio city, was the anchor bank and the largest subsidiary by far of the parent First National Corporation. Founded in the mid-1800s, the bank had the distinction of holding one of the first 25 national charters.

Acquisitions, mergers, or other changes had moved it to fifth-oldest on the national roster. Its favorite historical reflection came from 1933 when, during the Depression, the Clearing House authorized banks to limit withdrawals to 5 percent of the customer's account. First National was the only bank in town to honor deposits in full to all comers.

During its first century, First National concentrated on doing business with corporations and other banks rather than on services to individuals. This strategy was consistent with its long history of fiscal soundness, solid capitalization, customer service, and community involvement. While in recent decades the bank had moved extensively into all aspects of retail banking, it had not abandoned its heritage.

First National was fortunate to be located in a market with a strong and diverse economic base. That market had helped the bank to generate a quality loan portfolio. It had also provided a stable deposit base and assisted in maintaining the bank's strong capital position. In 1986, the city's economy, like that of so many other cities, was moving from manufacturing to service-related jobs, but both manufacturing and services were expected to be important to the city's future. The city's business profile ranged from some of the nation's largest corporations to successful start-up enterprises. While the city's economic diversity did not make it recession-proof, it certainly helped it withstand economic downturns.

At the same time, more rapid growth in southern and western states challenged the city's economic future. It was not a part of the Sun Belt. Further, regulatory changes and a constant stream of new competitors continued to threaten the bank's loan growth and overall market share. In 1980, the Depository Institutions Deregulation and Monetary Control Act permitted savings associations and credit unions to offer their customers additional services in direct competition with banks. In 1982, the Garn-St Germain Depository Institutions Act permitted banks to pay interest without rate limitations on certain types of deposit accounts. In Ohio, legislation permitting statewide banking by 1989 had been passed in the 1970s. By 1985, Ohio law also allowed interstate banking on a reciprocal basis with 14 adjacent or nearby states. By then, First National was already competing for loans with numerous other Ohio commercial banking organizations, savings and loan associations, credit unions, securities firms, insurance companies, retail firms, commercial finance companies, and loan production offices of many out-of-state banks.

The continually growing competition, along with the bank's desire for continued loan growth and improved margins, concerned senior management. Consequently, Fred Yehger, executive vice president of lending, and George Kassidy, president, requested an analysis and development of a business plan for an asset-based lending department.

First National's Financial Position

Bob and a newly formed task force felt that their first job was to review the BHC's financial information to analyze ways asset-based lending might affect the balance sheet and profit position. This review would also provide a basis for comparison when they developed a projected balance sheet and income statement for the proposed product. From the information in Exhibits 1.1 and 1.2, plus other information, they developed Exhibit 1.3. Bob knew that the ways asset-based lending affected RONW or return on assets would be important to senior management and the board of directors.

Fiscal 1985 had been another successful year, with net income increasing by 15 percent to $34.1 million. Return on assets of 1.12 percent and RONW of 14.19 percent were both improvements over 1984. Assets had grown 23 percent and were expected to be nearly $4 billion by December 31, 1986. Deposits had risen 32 percent, and total loans by 39 percent. Bob wondered how much an asset-based lending department could add to that performance.

Loans and Credit Risk

Based on an existing loan-to-deposit ratio of under 80 percent and low reliance on volatile deposits, Bob felt senior management would not be concerned about whether the bank could handle the potential loan growth that asset-based lending might produce. At the same time, he knew of the bank's traditional sensitivity to credit risk, and asset-based loans certainly carried a higher degree of risk. His analysis would need to demonstrate that the risk was reasonable and that it would provide commensurate return. Bob would need to convince senior management that years of experience by commercial finance companies and other banks had resulted in improved techniques of monitoring and auditing collateral, greatly reducing the traditional risks of asset-based lending. Besides, some loans already in the bank's portfolio could benefit from the closer control that an asset-based department could provide. Risk assumptions would be important in gaining a total commitment from senior management, and since first National had historically followed a more conventional lending practice and structure, a new department could not succeed without that commitment.

Efficiency, Productivity, and Profitability

Bob knew higher costs were involved in asset-based lending than in conventional short-term or long-term commercial lending. More people were needed to conduct field audits of collateral and to monitor the loans internally. At the same time, he thought that existing loan officers could provide a more than adequate sales force, as long as a department head with experience in asset-based lending was hired to monitor loan quality and servicing. Costs might also be lowered by engaging a nationally recognized accounting firm to handle the field audits. Perhaps the accounting firm's fees could be passed on to the borrower, if competition would allow it.

Bob and his committee talked with a number of other banks that already had asset-based lending departments. They were frequently discouraged by reports of the lower loan rates now charged because of increased competition. Formerly, a loan priced at 3 percent to 5 percent over prime, not including other fees, was common. Now 1 percent to 2.5 percent over prime was the norm, and sometimes rates were lower. Bob knew that senior management increasingly emphasized higher margins and larger fees. He would need to substantiate that asset-based lending could contribute to those goals.

The Market

A major reason asset-based lending had grown more popular in recent years was that financial institutions were emphasizing the middle market. Asset-based lending offers access to a wider range of companies, enabling increased market share and profitability. First National knew the growing importance of the middle-market companies to its profitability, and Bob was convinced that to effectively serve the middle market, the bank needed to offer asset-based lending.

He no longer viewed asset-based lending as a unique industry, but as a product that could fit comfortably into the larger product line of the bank. First National would also have marketing advantages over commercial finance companies or loan production offices from out-of-town financial institutions. These advantages included knowledge of local companies, a network of contacts, cost savings from market proximity, and cultural similarities with borrowers. First National would need all these advantages to effectively sell against the list of 23 asset-based lending competitors the committee had compiled.

On the other hand, Bob knew that some members of senior management would argue that a "bandwagon" effect was occurring, setting the stage for future problems in the asset-based lending industry. Major concerns included too many lenders chasing too few loans, a shortage of qualified people, and an erosion of margins due to increased competition. Bob had already begun preparing for that argument. Asset-based lending should be handled by experts in the field who know the industries and techniques and insist on spending the time and money to do the job right. The institution would have to offer more than a good job done by professionals skilled in more conventional bank lending. The keys were proper margin evaluation, collateral valuation, and ongoing monitoring. Bob needed to convince senior management that an experienced staff that knew how to appraise and monitor collateral and to conduct financial analysis would provide the assurances they sought, as well as the higher yields.

Bob's committee prepared a product description (Exhibit 1.4), an executive summary (Exhibit 1.5), and supporting documentation on the financial implications to the BHC of establishing an asset-based lending product (Exhibits 1.6–1.10). A member of the committee from the bank's investment department prepared Exhibits 1.11–1.13 to enable further competitive analysis of all the major banks in First National's region. Finally, committee members knew they should be prepared to defend their analysis and recommendations to senior management and, subsequently, to the board of directors.

Exhibit 1.1

First National Corporation and Subsidiaries, Consolidated Statements of Condition as of December 31, 1983-1985
(Thousands)

Assets

	1985		1984		1983	
Cash and due from banks	$ 244,079	7.14%	$ 215,830	7.76%	$ 209,700	7.97%
Investment securities:						
U.S. Treasury and agencies	$ 437,225		$ 334,429		$ 378,095	
States and political subdivisions	121,191		122,759		134,128	
Other securities	4,069		3,903		3,907	
Total investment securities	562,485	16.45	461,091	16.59	516,130	19.60
Federal funds sold and reverse repos	452,475	13.23	545,305	19.61	521,530	19.81
Loans:						
Commercial and agricultural	$ 740,798		$ 452,258		$ 488,960	
Real estate—construction	68,583		39,408		27,924	
Real estate—mortgage	368,242		324,203		275,493	
Installment and credit card	622,935		453,502		325,455	
Other	214,358		181,910		149,763	
Total loans	$2,014,916		$1,451,281		$1,267,595	
Less unearned interest	(47,001)		(37,841)		(39,776)	
Less allowance for possible loan losses	(23,325)		(16,734)		(13,440)	
Net loans	1,944,590	56.88	1,396,706	50.24	1,214,379	46.13
Premises and equipment	63,697	1.86	56,589	2.04	57,565	2.19
Acceptances, customers' liability	49,297	1.44	36,797	1.32	43,111	1.64
Other assets	102,232	2.99	67,813	2.44	70,332	2.67
Total assets	$3,418,855	100.00%	$2,780,131	100.00%	$2,632,747	100.00%

Liabilities and Net Worth

Deposits:						
Noninterest-bearing deposits	$ 692,392		$ 557,159		$ 540,736	
Interest-bearing deposits:						
Savings	804,788		585,056		555,157	
Time	1,085,157		810,641		659,151	
Total deposits	$2,582,337	75.53%	$1,952,856	70.24%	$1,755,044	66.66%
Short-term borrowings (primarily fed funds purchased and repos)	405,693	11.87	476,595	17.14	533,783	20.27
Long-term debt	54,807	1.60	45,166	1.62	52,242	1.98
Acceptances executed	49,297	1.44	36,797	1.32	43,111	1.64
Other liabilities	66,836	1.95	47,962	1.73	44,924	1.71
Total liabilities	$3,158,970		$2,559,376		$2,429,104	
Preferred stock	$ 0	0.00	$ 0	0.00	$ 0	0.00
Common stock	52,824	1.55	24,750	0.89	22,500	0.85
Surplus	54,349	1.59	66,625	2.40	52,000	1.98
Undivided profits	152,712	4.47	129,380	4.65	129,143	4.91
Total net worth	$ 259,885		$ 220,755		$ 203,643	
Total liabilities and net worth	$3,418,855	100.00%	$2,780,131	100.00%	$2,632,747	100.00%
Market value of securities at year-end	$ 568,208		$ 458,777		$ 508,723	

Exhibit 1.2

First National Corporation and Subsidiaries, Consolidated Statements of Earnings for Years Ending December 31, 1983-1985 (Thousands)

	1985	% of Total Operating Income[a]	1984	% of Total Operating Income	1983	% of Total Operating Income
Interest income:						
Interest and fees on loans	$187,405	60.05%	$162,417	54.81%	$128,255	50.57%
Interest on federal funds sold	33,307	10.67	51,032	17.22	46,142	18.19
Interest on investment securities:						
Taxable	43,614	13.98	39,511	13.33	37,462	14.77
Nontaxable	7,045	2.26	7,220	2.44	7,754	3.06
Other interest income	629	0.20	1,033	0.35	2,897	1.14
Total interest income	$272,000		$261,213		$222,510	
Noninterest income:						
Trust income	$ 13,064	4.19	$ 11,460	3.87	$ 9,855	3.89
Service charges and fees	22,390	7.17	17,802	6.01	16,173	6.38
Other operating income	4,612	1.48	5,866	1.98	5,088	2.01
Total noninterest income	40,066		35,128		31,116	
Interest expense:						
Interest on savings deposits	$ 19,086	6.12	$ 16,035	5.41	$ 13,120	5.17
Interest on time deposits	113,524	36.38	100,476	33.91	82,213	32.42
Interest on short-term borrowings	28,740	9.21	50,420	17.01	43,632	17.20
Interest on long-term debt	5,531	1.77	5,023	1.70	4,846	1.91
Total interest expense	166,881		171,954		143,811	
Provision for possible loan losses	9,083	2.91	6,543	2.21	5,915	2.33

Noninterest expense:						
Salaries	$ 38,419	12.31	$ 32,966	11.12	$ 30,264	11.93
Pension and other employee benefits	6,612	2.12	5,951	2.01	5,142	2.03
Equipment expense	9,693	3.11	8,160	2.75	7,603	3.00
Occupancy expense	5,692	1.82	4,609	1.56	4,550	1.79
State taxes	4,102	1.31	3,887	1.31	3,719	1.47
Other operating expense	30,516	9.78	25,144	8.48	21,380	8.43
Total noninterest expense	95,034		80,717		72,658	
Net operating income before tax	$ 41,068	13.16	$ 37,127	12.53	$ 31,242	12.32
Taxes	9,843	3.15	7,539	2.54	5,712	2.25
Income before securities gains or losses (IBSGL)	$ 31,225	10.01	$ 29,588	9.98	$ 25,530	10.07
Other income (primarily security gains and losses)	2,906	0.93	101	0.03	102	0.04
Net income	$ 34,131	10.94	$ 29,689	10.02	$ 25,632	10.11
Per share:						
Net income	$3.31		$3.00		$2.59	
Dividends	$1.40		$1.27		$1.18	

ᵃTotal Operating Income = Total Interest Income + Total Noninterest Income

Exhibit 1.3
Selected Financial Information, First National Corporation
(Thousands Except Per-Share Data)

	1985	1984	1983
Results of Operations			
Net interest income	$105,119	$89,259	$78,699
Provision for possible loan losses	9,083	6,543	5,915
Net income	34,131	29,689	25,632
Net income per share[a]	$3.31	$3.00	$2.59
Cash dividends per share[a]	$1.40	$1.27	$1.18
Selected Average Balances			
Total assets	$ 3,043,513	$2,704,906	$2,448,121
Investment securities	540,719	487,980	480,870
Loans—net of unearned interest	1,699,148	1,341,416	1,086,585
Total deposits	2,254,461	1,835,720	1,624,227
Long-term debt	49,627	45,976	46,880
Stockholders' equity	240,508	211,952	196,197
Average number of outstanding shares[a]	10,316,961	9,900,000	9,900,000
Performance Ratios			
Return on average total assets	1.12%	1.10%	1.05%
Return on average interest-earning assets	1.28	1.27	1.22
Return on average equity	14.19	14.01	13.06
Average equity to average total assets	7.90	7.84	8.01
Average equity to average total deposits	10.67	11.55	12.08
Average total loans—net of unearned interest to average total deposits	75.37	73.07	66.90
Dividend payout	42.31	42.36	45.65
Book value per share at year-end[a]	$24.60	$22.30	$20.57

[a]Prior years' amounts are restated to reflect a 2-for-1 stock split in 1985 and a 10% stock dividend in 1984.

Exhibit 1.4
The Business Product Description

Loans from $500,000 to $10,000,000

Primary collateral	Accounts receivable
	Inventory (raw materials and finished goods)
Secondary collateral	Plant and equipment
	Land and buildings

Pricing

Rates from prime + 1.0% to prime + 4.0% (average: prime + 1.75%)
1-time fees to average 0.5% of committed lines

continued

Exhibit 1.4
The Business Product Description (*continued*)

Selling
Department head
Commercial lending staff and sales group
Branch offices

Staffing
Department head at vice president level
Assistant department head (credit and monitoring)
National accounting firm for auditing (at least initially)
Addition of clerical personnel as volume grows
Secretarial assistance

Processing
Lockbox account required for processing accounts receivable
Demand deposit cash collateral control account required for processing accounts receivable
Loans located in commercial loan portfolio
IBM PC-based asset-based lending system for monitoring the status of the account (sales, gross collections, aging, trends) and establishing the current credit availability

Appraisals (Equipment, Land, Buildings)
Situation will dictate the appraiser

Participations
Participate in loans that exceed our size guidelines or our willingness to accept the credit risk as the sole lender

Liquidations
Type of loan and location of business will dictate liquidator

---

Exhibit 1.5
Executive Summary of Assumptions

- Have identified the market for an asset-based lending product to:
  1. Fill a gap in our product line to the middle market
  2. Properly monitor the asset-based loans currently booked

- Asset-based lending has become a mainstream product for banks. Currently 70% of the members of the National Commercial Finance Association, a trade group of asset-based lenders, are banks, versus only 27% in 1982.

- Currently have 50% participation in credit lines of $23.8 million with commercial finance companies.

- Currently have 374 loans for $85 million secured by accounts receivable and/or inventory. Of these loans, 14 totaling $45 million would benefit from the discipline of asset-based lending.

- Pro forma financial statements for the asset-based lending function indicate the following (from Exhibits 1.9 and 1.10):
  1. Marginal earnings per share (EPS) of $0.055 at the end of 1990, averaging $0.025 over the next 5 years
  2. Marginal RONW of 16.0% by 1990, averaging 12.9% over the next 5 years
  3. Operating expenses/net revenue to average 32% over the next 5 years
  4. Net interest margin on asset-based loans to average 4.1% over the next 5 years
  5. Accumulated cash flow to reach $1.3 million by the end of 1990

- Product launch date to be June 1, 1986.

Exhibit 1.6
Financial Analysis:
Cost/Benefit Assumptions

Startup	June 1, 1986
Average loan size	$1,250,000
Interest income, interest expense, and loan losses	
Average loan rate	1.75% over prime
Average cost of funds	8.12% 90-day CD rate adjusted for reserves and FDIC insurance premium
Average deposit yield	8.12% 90-day CD rate
Net chargeoffs	1.25%
Commitment fees	0.50% of committed line (one-time)
All lockbox processing fees charged to operating account	
Startup expense	
Product development	$ 5,000
Computerized information system development	5,000
Operations	3,000
Marketing	16,000
Recruiting	19,500
Legal	5,000
Initial setup	5,000
Ongoing operating expense	
Salaries	
Department head	65,000
Assistant department head	30,000
Verification clerk	22,000 (as required by growth)
Secretary (1/3)	6,500
Performance bonus	
Department head	0% (up to 30%)
Assistant department head	0% (up to 20%)
Monitoring expense	
Cost bundled into loan rate and fee structure	
Loans per individual monitor	25
Average field audits	4
Average field audit cost	$1,390

Exhibit 1.7
Financial Analysis:
Capital Expenditure Schedule (May 1986)

IBM PC/AT	$10,000
Asset-based software	20,000
Department workstation	7,500
Assistant workstation	6,000
	$43,500

Exhibit 1.8
Asset–Based Lending,
Product Balance Sheet (December 31)
(Thousands)

	1986	1987	1988	1989	1990
Assets					
Cash and due from banks					
Float	$ 41	$ 229	$ 351	$ 445	$ 565
Reserve requirements	10	55	84	106	134
Net loans	4,711	24,083	36,346	46,095	58,460
Premises and equipment	39	31	23	15	7
Total Assets	$4,801	$24,398	$36,803	$46,661	$59,166
Liabilities and Net Worth					
Liabilities					
Demand deposits	$ 62	$ 342	$ 524	$ 664	$ 843
Funding requirement	4,408	22,373	33,741	42,779	54,243
Total Liabilities	$4,470	$22,715	$34,265	$43,443	$55,086
Net Worth Accounts					
Undivided profits					
Beginning balance	$ 0	$ (124)	$ (53)	$ 114	$ 363
Plus net income	(124)	123	288	430	585
Less cash dividends (@ 42%)	0	52	121	181	246
Ending balance	(124)	(53)	114	363	703
Capital requirement	456	1,736	2,424	2,855	3,377
Total Net Worth	$ 331	$ 1,683	$ 2,538	$ 3,218	$ 4,080
Total Liabilities and Net Worth	$4,801	$24,398	$36,803	$46,661	$59,166

Exhibit 1.9
Asset–Based Lending
Product Income Statement and Cash Flow
(Thousands)

	1986	1987	1988	1989	1990
Projections					
Average number of accounts	2	13	26	34	43
Average outstandings	$2,691	$16,418	$32,023	$41,938	$53,188
Average lines	$4,486	$27,363	$53,371	$69,897	$88,647
Average funding requirement	$2,488	$15,082	$29,377	$38,459	$48,764
Average investable demand deposits	$ 40	$ 263	$ 530	$ 699	$ 887
Ending number of accounts	4	20	29	37	47
Capital expenditures	$ 43.5	0	0	0	0

continued

Exhibit 1.9
Asset–Based Lending
Product Income Statement and Cash Flow[b]
(Thousands) (*continued*)

	1986	1987	1988	1989	1990
Income and Expenses					
Interest income:					
Interest on loans	$177	$1,847	$3,603	$4,718	$5,984
Commitment fees	40	163	103	82	104
Interest on deposits	4	28	57	76	96
Field audit income	0	0	0	0	0
Total Interest Income	$221	$2,038	$3,763	$4,876	$6,184
Interest expense:					
Funding cost	$205	$1,243	$2,422	$3,170	$4,020
Total Interest Expense	205	1,243	2,422	3,170	4,020
Net interest income	$ 16	$ 795	$1,341	$1,706	$2,164
Loan loss expense	52	286	422	448	534
Net Interest Income after Loan Loss Expense	$ (37)	$ 509	$ 919	$1,258	$1,630
Other Income:					
Lockbox fees	$ 1	$ 9	$ 17	$ 23	$ 29
Total Other Income	$ 1	$ 9	$ 17	$ 23	$ 29
Operating expense:					
1-time startup expense					
Product development	$ 5				
Computerized information system					
development	5				
Operations	3				
Marketing	16				
Recruiting/legal/setup	30				
Ongoing expense					
Product management	3	$ 3	$ 3	$ 3	$ 3
Computer systems	0	1	1	1	1
Lockbox cost	1	6	11	14	18
Marketing	1	1	1	1	1
User department					
Salaries and benefits	70	121	122	130	139
Other	3	20	35	45	56
Field audit expense	12	74	144	189	240
Depreciation/amortization	5	8	8	8	8
Occupancy	6	6	6	6	6
Overhead allocation (@ 22%)	35	52	73	87	104
Total Operating Expense	$195	$ 291	$ 404	$ 483	$ 575
Marginal Analysis					
Net income before tax	($231)	$ 228	$ 533	$ 797	$1,084
Tax (@ 46%)	(107)	105	245	367	498
Net income after tax[a]	($124)	$ 123	$ 288	$ 430	$ 585

[a]Negative tax figure in 1986 reflects the bank's ability to save taxes on profits from other operations because of the loss on asset-based lending.
[b]Cash flow = Net Income after Tax + Depreciation.

Exhibit 1.10
Asset–Based Lending,
Product Profitability Analysis

Product-to-Date Analysis		1986	1987	1988	1989	1990
Earnings per Share (EPS)						
Net income	Marginal	$ (124)	$ 123	$ 288	$ 430	$ 585
	Average	(124)	(1)	95	179	260
Number of shares		10,565	10,565	10,565	10,565	10,565
EPS	Marginal	$(0.012)	$ 0.012	$ 0.027	$ 0.041	$ 0.055
	Average	(0.012)	(.000)	0.009	0.017	0.025
Return on Equity (ROE)						
Net income	Marginal	$ (124)	$ 123	$ 288	$ 430	$ 585
	Average	(124)	(1)	95	179	260
Equity	Marginal	187	1,134	2,210	2,893	3,668
	Average	187	661	1,177	1,606	2,018
ROE	Marginal	−66.5%	10.8%	13.0%	14.9%	16.0%
	Average	−66.5%	−0.1%	8.1%	11.2%	12.9%
Operating Expense/Net Revenue (OE/NR)						
Operating expense	Marginal	$ 195	$ 291	$ 404	$ 483	$ 575
	Average	195	243	297	343	390
Net revenue	Marginal	17	804	1,359	1,728	2,193
	Average	17	411	727	977	1,220
OE/NR	Marginal	1,148%	36%	30%	28%	26%
	Average	1,148%	59%	41%	35%	32%
Net Interest Margin (NIM)						
Interest income	Marginal	$ 221	$ 2,039	$ 3,763	$ 4,876	$ 6,184
	Average	221	1,130	2,008	2,725	3,416
Interest expense	Marginal	205	1,243	2,422	3,170	4,020
	Average	205	724	1,290	1,760	2,212
Average investment in earning assets	Marginal	2,691	16,418	32,023	41,938	53,188
	Average	2,691	9,555	17,044	23,268	29,252
NIM	Marginal	0.6%	4.8%	4.2%	4.1%	4.1%
	Average	0.6%	4.2%	4.2%	4.1%	4.1%

Exhibit 1.11
Loan Analysis (December 1985 Data)

Name of Bank	Loans to Deposits	Rank	Loan Percentage Change	Rank	Allowance for Loan Losses to Total Loans	Rank	Net Chargeoffs to Average Loans	Rank	Nonperforming[a] Loans to Primary Capital	Rank
City A:										
Bank One	91.4%	17	18.9%	5	1.43%	15	0.34%	9	15.9%	12
Bank Two	90.2	13	28.9	2	1.61	20	0.46	12	3.3	1
First National Bank	83.6	7	24.4	3	1.25	7	0.28	5	3.8	2
Bank Three	80.5	3	20.2	4	0.86	1	0.47	14	16.1	13
Average for City A	86.4		23.1		1.29		0.39		9.8	
City B:										
Bank One	87.5	11	7.3	16	1.18	6	0.74	19	24.2	20
Bank Two	85.4	9	(3.9)	21	1.33	12	0.29	7	18.4	15
Bank Three	73.2	1	33.2	1	1.06	2	0.18	2	8.9	5
Average for City B	82.0		12.2		1.19		0.40		17.2	
City C:										
Bank One	81.4	4	4.6	19	1.90	21	1.22	20	38.3	21
Bank Two	93.0	18	7.6	15	1.52	17	2.28	21	21.9	18
Bank Three	90.5	15	14.5	11	1.14	5	0.43	11	21.0	17
Average for City C	88.3		8.9		1.52		1.31		27.1	
City D:										
Bank One	99.6	21	17.8	6	1.29	9	0.24	3	23.3	19
Bank Two	83.4	6	15.2	9	1.30	10	0.72	18	11.1	6
Bank Three	90.4	14	2.9	20	1.60	19	0.39	10	15.3	10
Bank Four	97.4	20	10.8	13	1.09	3	0.01	1	7.4	3
Bank Five	74.9	2	6.3	18	1.43	14	0.27	4	7.9	4
Average for City D	89.1		10.6		1.34		0.33		13.0	
City E:										
Bank One	94.1	19	16.0	8	1.50	16	0.47	13	18.4	14
Bank Two	87.4	10	14.6	10	1.33	13	0.29	6	13.8	9
Bank Three	84.6	8	11.7	12	1.58	18	0.33	8	13.3	7
Average for City E	88.7		14.1		1.47		0.36		15.2	
City F:										
Bank One	83.0	5	16.5	7	1.12	4	0.60	17	13.7	8
Bank Two	91.2	16	7.3	17	1.26	8	0.52	15	15.6	11
Bank Three	89.6	12	8.7	14	1.31	11	0.56	16	19.9	16
Average for City F	87.9		10.8		1.23		0.56		16.4	
Average for all banks	87.3		13.5		1.34		0.53		15.8	

[a]Nonperforming loans are those on which interest payments, principal payments, or both are not being received but which have not yet been written off.

Exhibit 1.12
Margin Analysis (December 1985 Data)

Name of Bank	% of Average Earning Assets					
	Interest Revenues	Rank	Interest Cost	Rank	Net Interest	Rank
City A						
Bank One	10.62%	19	6.46%	10	4.16%	16
Bank Two	11.88	4	5.94	2	5.94	2
First National Bank	10.75	17	5.93	1	4.82	8
Bank Three	11.05	13	6.74	15	4.31	15
Average for City A	11.08		6.27		4.81	
City B						
Bank One	12.77	2	6.57	13	6.20	1
Bank Two	12.20	3	6.43	9	5.77	3
Bank Three	11.49	7	6.08	3	5.41	5
Average for City B	12.15		6.36		5.79	
City C						
Bank One	11.12	12	6.42	7	4.70	11
Bank Two	13.59	1	7.93	21	5.66	4
Bank Three	11.39	10	6.61	14	4.78	9
Average for City C	12.03		6.99		5.05	
City D						
Bank One	10.12	21	6.28	4	3.84	21
Bank Two	11.72	5	6.40	5	5.32	6
Bank Three	10.95	14	6.41	6	4.54	13
Bank Four	10.61	20	6.50	12	4.11	18
Bank Five	11.50	6	6.79	18	4.71	10
Average for City D	10.98		6.48		4.50	
City E						
Bank One	10.89	15	6.91	19	3.98	19
Bank Two	10.79	16	6.46	11	4.33	14
Bank Three	11.43	9	6.75	16	4.68	12
Average for City E	11.04		6.71		4.33	
City F						
Bank One	10.68	18	6.78	17	3.90	20
Bank Two	11.43	8	6.43	8	5.00	7
Bank Three	11.30	11	7.16	20	4.14	17
Average for City F	11.14		6.79		4.35	
Average for all banks	11.35		6.57		4.78	

Exhibit 1.13
Deposit Analysis (December 1985 Data)

Name of Bank	Demand IPC	Rank	% of Total Domestic Deposits Bearing a Regulated Rate	Rank	Bearing a Market Rate	Rank	Deposit Percentage Change from Last Year	Rank
City A								
Bank One	20.5%	12	12.0%	12	64.4%	4	9.6%	11
Bank Two	22.3	9	11.3	15	61.5	8	12.8	6
First National Bank	29.2	2	11.6	14	52.5	21	19.9	2
Bank Three	24.9	4	16.9	4	56.6	16	19.0	3
Average for City A	24.2		13.0		58.8		15.3	
City B								
Bank One	19.8	13	18.5	2	59.5	13	4.3	18
Bank Two	21.7	10	15.3	11	60.1	11	10.7	9
Bank Three	24.7	6	16.1	6	56.8	15	23.7	1
Average for City B	22.1		16.6		58.8		12.9	
City C								
Bank One	22.5	8	17.2	3	56.4	17	(3.6)	20
Bank Two	16.2	21	8.5	17	68.0	1	5.6	15
Bank Three	17.7	20	16.0	8	63.1	5	15.4	5
Average for City C	18.8		13.9		62.5		5.8	
City D								
Bank One	19.0	16	15.4	10	61.8	7	4.5	17
Bank Two	18.3	17	19.3	1	60.1	10	6.0	14
Bank Three	24.8	5	16.4	5	54.1	19	(14.2)	21
Bank Four	25.2	3	15.8	9	53.3	20	6.4	13
Bank Five	19.5	15	16.1	7	60.3	9	4.9	16
Average for City D	21.4		16.6		57.9		1.5	
City E								
Bank One	17.7	19	5.8	20	66.4	2	9.3	12
Bank Two	29.9	1	8.5	18	54.6	18	3.3	19
Bank Three	17.9	18	11.7	13	58.3	14	10.2	10
Average for City E	21.8		8.7		59.8		7.6	
City F								
Bank One	21.0	11	6.6	19	65.9	3	12.6	7
Bank Two	19.7	14	4.2	21	59.6	12	16.5	4
Bank Three	22.8	7	9.5	16	62.5	6	12.0	8
Average for City F	21.2		6.8		62.7		13.7	
Average for all banks	21.7		13.0		59.8		9.0	

Case 2

HEART OF AMERICA STATE BANK

In late spring of 1981, Benjamin P. Charles, newly appointed loan officer at the Heart of America State Bank, was examining the file of Gold-Tones, Inc., a retailer of musical instruments and supplies. The owner-manager of Gold-Tones, Sam Jameson, had approached Mr. George Lanza, the bank president, about a long-term loan of $145,000, the proceeds of which were to be used to reduce accounts payable. While the final decision would be made by Mr. Lanza, Ben knew that his recommendation would be influential and that his own opportunities for advancement in the bank depended upon the quality of his analysis of this credit application.

The Heart of America Bank was a small institution that was struggling to build a strong customer base. Although it was viewed as an innovative institution, Heart of America faced strong competition from the old, established bank that was located only blocks away. Mr. Lanza had assumed the presidency just two years earlier, and viewed his primary goal as the achievement of profitable growth for the bank. To meet this goal, the bank had to attract new deposit sources, and Mr. Lanza realized that the move toward deregulation of deposit instruments gave him more freedom to compete for funds. For example, despite the 5¼ percent ceiling for interest payable on NOW accounts, he had latitude to establish service charges and account minimums. However, Mr. Lanza also recognized that incurring high costs to increase deposits would not help the bank unless those funds could be invested in assets earning a rate of return high enough to cover all costs. The bank's deposit structure was already changing to a higher-cost one, as customers gradually shifted funds into accounts paying higher rates.

In addition to these concerns, Mr. Lanza viewed the bank's future as also dependent upon growth in sound and profitable commercial loans. Trends in deregulation were threatening to complicate this aspect of the bank's operating environment, too, since thrift institutions were lobbying strongly for commercial lending powers, and nearby S&Ls were already making consumer loans. In light of this growing competition, the bank could not afford to alienate customers.

Ben had talked with Mr. Lanza frequently about these priorities, and recognized their impact on the decision to lend to Gold-Tones. The bank needed additional loans but could not afford to absorb many loan losses. Consequently, its lending policies had to remain conservative.

Gold-Tones was a long-standing and highly valued customer of the bank. The firm was a family-owned and -managed operation; the family was well-respected in the community, and the store had a good reputation for service and quality of merchandise. The family had run the business for some time, and had borrowed from Heart of America before. In fact, all of its bank obligations were loans negotiated with Mr. Lanza. The bank president expressed to Ben his confidence in the Jameson family, although he had some reservations about their financial acuity. Mr. Jameson tended to view marketing and sales growth as his first priority; his son, who worked full-time with the business, also had little interest in financial management issues. Mr. Jameson did not monitor their cash flow position carefully, and Ben was not even confident that the loan terms they had requested were appropriate.

The Jamesons wanted to borrow $145,000 for seven years, to be repaid in equal monthly installments over that same period. (This would increase the firm's total obligation to the bank to approximately $225,000.) The owners had no other alternative for raising capital; they had contributed almost everything possible, including proceeds from second mortgages on their homes. One of the strongest points in favor of the loan was the accountant the applicants had hired. It was their CPA who had suggested they look for sources of additional long-term funding.

The Metropolitan Area

Heart of America Bank and Gold-Tones were located in a midsized metropolitan area in the Midwest. The city benefited from a diversified group of employers, including two universities, home offices for two insurance companies, and several manufacturing firms. This mix of service and industry jobs protected the local economy to a certain extent from the severe downturns felt in heavily industrialized areas during a recession. The performance of an individual business, however, especially one marketing discretionary items, could be severely hurt in periods of faltering economic performance or unusual interest rate movements.

The Economic Environment

Nationally, the rate of growth in economic activity in the second quarter of 1981 had declined to a level far lower than that achieved in three previous quarters. Forecasts issued by the Federal Reserve Bank of St. Louis predicted that consumers would be less willing to spend in the coming months. This forecast was in part based on the recent pattern of retail sales nationwide (given in Exhibit 2.1). Although many other economists endorsed this forecast, still others predicted an increase in consumer spending during the latter part of 1981 and throughout 1982. The basis for these more optimistic forecasts was the possibility that a major tax reduction package would be passed by Congress and signed by the new President within another month, leaving more disposable income in the hands of consumers.

Local conditions were reflected in recent reports on retail sales compiled by the Association of Commerce and Industry (to which the bank subscribed), which are also in Exhibit 2.1.

Complicating all economic forecasts were interest rates. Ben knew that since October 1979, the Federal Reserve Open Market Committee had changed the focus of its monetary policy and had vowed to keep monetary growth under control. The long-run goal of this new approach was to bring down inflation and interest rates. Since that time, however, interest rate volatility and the general level of interest rates had been at an all-time high (see Exhibits 2.2 and 2.3), even though predictions of the rate of inflation for 1981 were well below actual inflation rates for the past two years. High interest rates were taking their toll on consumers and businesses alike. And, while the Republican administration predicted confidently that rates had peaked and would decline by 1981, many private economists predicted continuing high interest rates.

Gold-Tones: Financial Position

Mr. Jameson, manager of Gold-Tones, had provided Ben with the firm's financial statements as of March 31, 1981, and for the preceding two years (see Exhibits 2.4-2.7). Ben had already obtained the industry average figures in Exhibit 2.8. The shop owner discussed his past and potential performance with the loan officer in detail. Mr. Jameson explained to the loan officer that the increase in receivables occurred because he was no longer selling his accounts receivable to a finance company, but instead had resumed responsibility for their collection. He had no plans to return to the previous arrangement. Jameson believed the firm could increase sales by 6 percent per year for the next two fiscal years, and indicated that expenses (exclusive of interest on the new loan) should remain approximately the same percentage of sales as in fiscal 1981. However, Ben felt these forecasts should be reviewed carefully, because tax rates for small businesses were anticipated to be slightly lower than their 1981 levels, and economic predictions were so uncertain that the sales growth should not be taken for granted.

Further complicating Ben's task was the interest rate environment. His final evaluation must include a recommendation for the rate of interest to charge on the loan if it were approved. The bank's prime rate had fluctuated between 16 and 18 percent in recent months. Because the loan was to be a long-term obligation, a variable rate of interest would offer more protection against variability in the bank's earnings. Trends in the bank's deposit structure indicated that future interest costs paid on deposits could rise, and earnings on invested assets would have to increase accordingly to protect profits (see Exhibit 2.9.) Of course, a variable rate of interest would place more pressure on Gold–Tones, particularly if rates continued their rapid, upward trend. There was also the question of whether the loan terms should include any restrictive provisions. Ben had to consider all these alternatives before presenting his final recommendations to George Lanza.

Exhibit 2.1
Retail Sales Information

Compound Annual Rate of Change, U.S. Retail Sales		Midwest City Retail Sales (Thousands)	
January 1980	37.6%	November 1979	$42.64
February	(9.5)	December	48.55
March	(18.0)	January 1980	37.69
April	(17.0)	February	34.55
May	6.5	March	36.79
June	33.8	April	37.30
July	28.6	May	38.10
August	5.2	June	37.97
September	12.6	July	38.28
October	14.8	August	41.01
November	19.4	September	43.94
December	10.3	October	N/A
January 1981	33.2	November	43.67
February	20.6	December	54.70
March	11.6	January 1981	39.16
April	(21.5)	February	38.16
May	(7.3)	March	41.51
June	16.0	April	44.68
		May	42.10
		June	41.89

Source: National Economic Trends, Federal Reserve Bank of St. Louis, July 31, 1981.

Source: Midwest County Economic Indicators, Monthly Reports, Association of Commerce and Industry, 1981

Exhibit 2.2
Selected Interest Rates, 1973–mid–1981

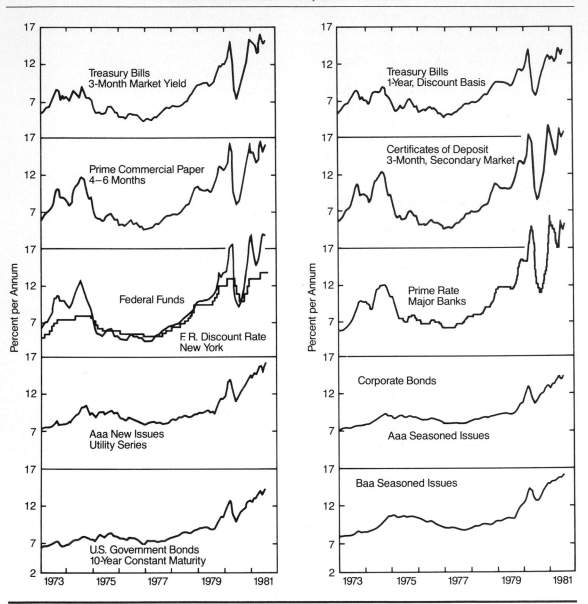

Source: Board of Governors of the Federal Reserve System, *Federal Reserve Monthly Chart Book,* August 1981.

Exhibit 2.3
Prime and Commercial Paper Rates, 1979–mid-1981

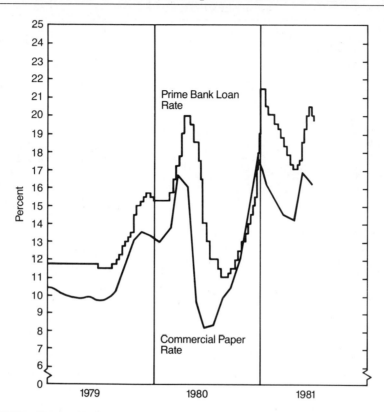

Source: Illinois Business Review, Vol. 38, No. 5 (July 1981) p. 3. Reprinted with permission.

Exhibit 2.4
**Comparative Balance Sheets for Gold–Tones, Inc.,
as of March 31, 1979–1981**

	At March 31		
	1981	1980	1979
Assets:			
Cash	$ 11,121	$ 13,147	$ 9,118
Accounts receivable—trade	76,621	28,956	41,549
Accounts receivable—other	1,000	—	—
Merchandise inventories	254,855	176,889 ·	187,251
Prepaid expenses	—	31	403
Total current assets	343,597	219,023	238,321
Leasehold improvements and equipment:			
Furniture, fixtures, and vehicles	32,297	25,100	23,759
Other equipment	9,092	9,092	9,092
	41,389	34,192	32,851
Less accumulated depreciation	22,029	25,194	20,882
	19,360	8,998	11,969
Leasehold improvements, less accumulated amortization of $1,636 in 1981 and $1,560 in 1980	37	113	193
	19,397	9,111	12,162
Other assets—cash surrender value of life insurance (net of loans $865 and $915 for 1981 and 1980, respectively)	1,457	877	—
Total Assets	$364,451	$229,011	$250,483
Liabilities:			
Current maturities of long-term debt	$ 46,976	$ 36,977	$ 37,931
Accounts payable	152,255	49,000	52,011
Accrued liabilities			
Taxes	12,003	5,896	4,394
Interest	13,093	12,634	12,065
Total current liabilities	224,327	104,507	106,401
Long-term debt—less current maturities	90,976	99,836	134,552
Total Liabilities	$315,303	$204,343	$240,953
Stockholders' equity			
Common stock—authorized 2,490 shares of $10 par value; issued and outstanding 2,250 shares	$ 22,500	$ 22,500	$ 22,500
Capital in excess of par value	2,500	2,500	2,500
	25,000	25,000	25,000
Retained earnings (accumulated deficit)	24,148	(333)	(15,470)
Total Stockholders' Equity	$ 49,148	$ 24,667	$ 9,530
Total Liabilities and Stockholders' Equity	$364,451	$229,010	$250,483

Exhibit 2.5
Comparative Income Statements of Gold–Tones, Inc., for the Years Ending March 31, 1979–1981

	Year Ended March 31		
	1981	1980	1979
Sales, net of returns and allowance and sales tax	$600,332	$575,699	$550,883
Cost of goods sold	354,718	340,290	319,240
Gross margin on sales	245,614	235,409	231,643
Operating expenses	205,583	203,529	187,071
Operating profit	40,031	31,880	44,572
Other income or (deductions)			
Interest income	7,904	895	2,389
Interest expense	(14,688)	(16,104)	(18,640)
Loss on disposal of fixed assets	(1,160)	—	—
Income before income taxes	32,087	16,671	28,321
Provision for income tax:			
Federal	5,353	1,482	4,900
State	2,253	731	1,130
Earnings before extraordinary item	24,481	14,458	22,291
Extraordinary item[a]	—	—	6,030
Net income	$ 24,481	$ 14,458	$ 28,321

[a]Reduction of taxes on income due to loss carryforward from previous year.

Exhibit 2.6
Comparative Statements of Changes in Financial Position of Gold–Tones, Inc., for the Years Ending March 31, 1979–1981

	1981	1980	1979
Working capital was provided from:			
Operations:			
Income	$ 24,481	$ 14,458	$28,321
Add (deduct) items not affecting working capital			
Depreciation and amortization	5,807	4,311	5,088
Loss on disposal of equipment	1,160	80	296
Working capital provided from operations	31,448	18,849	33,705
Proceeds from sale of equipment	1,000	—	—
Total working capital provided	32,448	18,849	33,705
Working capital was applied to:			
Purchase of equipment	18,253	1,340	8,990
Retirement of long-term debt	8,860	34,716	26,185
Increase in cash surrender value of life insurance	580	198	—
Total working capital applied	27,693	36,254	35,174
Increase (decrease) in working capital	$ 4,755	$(17,405)	$(1,469)

continued

Exhibit 2.6

Comparative Statements of Changes in Financial Position of Gold–Tones, Inc., for the Years Ending March 31, 1979–1981 (*continued*)

Changes in items forming working capital are included in the following analysis:	1981	1980	1979
Current assets:			
Cash	$ (2,026)	$ 4,029	$(3,778)
Accounts receivable	48,666	(12,593)	(5,103)
Merchandise inventories	77,966	(10,362)	3,850
Prepaid expenses	(31)	(372)	403
Total	$124,575	$(19,298)	$(4,628)
Current liabilities:			
Current maturities of long-term debt	9,998	(953)	(9,670)
Accounts payable	103,255	(3,011)	2,949
Accrued liabilities	1,878	172	3,562
Income taxes payable	4,689	1,899	—
Total	$119,820	$ (1,893)	$(3,159)
Increase (decrease) in working capital	$ 4,755	$(17,405)	$(1,469)

Exhibit 2.7

Supplemental Information on Long-Term Debt Obligations of Gold–Tones, Inc.

	1981	1980
Long-term debt consists of:		
Note payable to bank (SBA loan)	$ 73,229	$ 96,977
Other notes payable to bank	8,500	6,000
Installment notes payable	14,398	274
Due to stockholders	41,825	33,562
	137,952	136,813
Less current maturities	46,976	36,977
	$ 90,976	$ 99,836

Notes: The note payable to bank (SBA loan) is due in monthly installments of $3,370 through November 1982, including interest payable at the rate of 10% per year. The note is collateralized by inventory, certain term life insurance policies with a face amount of $225,000, by second mortgages on the homes of the officers of the company, and by the Small Business Administration.

Other notes payable consist of a note collateralized by the merchandise inventory payable from March 31, 1981, through March 31, 1982.

The installment notes are payable in monthly installments of $568 including interest at effective interest rates ranging from 10.30% to 16.24% per year. The maturity dates of these notes range from April 1980 to September 1984. These notes are collateralized by autos and trucks.

The stockholder notes are unsecured, payable on demand, and pay interest at the rate of 7% per annum. The notes payable to stockholders are subordinated to the SBA loan previously noted.

Exhibit 2.8
Median Financial Ratios for
the Retail Musical Instruments and Supplies Industry

Asset Size $250,000-$1 Million 3/31/80	Ratio	Entire Industry		
		3/31/80	3/31/79	3/31/78
1.6	Current Assets/Current Liabilities	1.6	1.7	1.5
0.3	Quick Ratio	0.3	0.5	0.5
16.3	Sales/Receivables	20.2	19.3	18.1
1.8	Cost of Sales/Inventory	2.0	2.1	2.3
2.2	Income before Interest and Taxes/Interest	2.1	3.2	3.2
1.8	Debt/Net Worth	2.0	1.9	1.9
16.2%	Income before Taxes/Net Worth	16.2%	23.5%	21.7%
6.0%	Income before Taxes/Total Assets	5.6%	7.2%	6.8%
1.8	Sales/Total Assets	2.0	2.1	2.2
64.4%	Total Debt/Total Assets	66.7%	62.0%	64.9%
36.2%	Operating Expenses/Sales	35.5%	33.6%	33.9%

Source: Robert Morris Associates, Annual Statement Studies 1980.

Exhibit 2.9
Selected Liabilities of Heart of America State Bank
(Quarterly Data in Thousands)

	1980				1981	
	Q1	Q2	Q3	Q4	Q1	Q2
IPC demand	$ 4,183	$ 4,163	$ 4,428	$ 4,455	$ 3,855	$ 3,656
IPC time and savings	8,548	8,472	9,108	9,481	8,155	7,637
Total deposits	17,184	15,535	16,381	16,363	14,096	13,790
Federal funds and repurchase agreements	-0-	60	-0-	-0-	1,024	914
Total liabilities	$17,346	$15,941	$17,189	$17,929	$15,450	$14,988

Case 3

CONSTRUCTION EQUIPMENT CREDIT UNION

John Siefkin, Managing Director and Treasurer of the Construction Equipment Credit Union (CECU)[1] was preparing for an important board meeting in December 1979. At this meeting, the board was to consider a major policy decision: the development of a shared automatic teller machine (ATM) network that would join the credit union with two other large financial institutions—a commercial bank and a savings and loan association. The board had requested that senior management prepare a complete analysis of advantages and disadvantages and recommend a course of action. Since CECU was one of the ten largest credit unions in the United States, and since no other credit union had taken leadership in a shared system, Mr. Siefkin knew that the board's decision could have industrywide ramifications in addition to its potential impact on his own institution's future. Furthermore, Mr. Siefkin himself and his colleagues were prominent in the industry, so their opinions were likely to influence managers across the country.

The common bond on which CECU was founded in the late 1930s was affiliation with the Caterpillar Tractor Company (now Caterpillar, Incorporated), a large manufacturing firm with headquarters in Peoria, Illinois, and numerous plants throughout the world. The firm was one of the nation's largest, ranking in the top 25 of the Fortune 500. With assets in excess of $5 billion, the company was among the 40 largest employers in the United States, and its operations were expected to continue growing at a steady rate. CECU, whose offices were also concentrated in Peoria, had earned the

loyalty of company employees. The firm employed almost 90,000 persons, and over 90 percent of these were members of the credit union.

Peoria, a city of 150,000 in central Illinois, was one whose economy in 1979 could be described as a microcosm of the U.S. economy, one that was highly diversified and paralleled national trends in labor force distribution. The Peoria metropolitan area exhibited similar characteristics. In the past, such diversity had enabled the area to withstand economic downturns better than other regions. Nevertheless, Illinois had seen its employment rate grow more slowly than the national average throughout the 1970s. In the United States, employment increased by 8.9 percent from 1971 to 1976, but the state's growth rate was only 4.2 percent. However, of four major metropolitan areas in the state, Peoria exhibited the most constant and sustained growth pattern in employment over the decade. The unfavorable comparison to national trends was because of a greater concentration of manufacturing than of service jobs. Some economists predicted this would not bode well for the region, since services were beginning to dominate the U.S. economy.

Mr. Siefkin knew that an important consideration in the current dilemma was the role CECU played in the local market for consumer financial services. From 1972 to 1979, its assets had grown from $43 million to $254 million; deposits had grown from $41 million to $222 million over the same period. (For comparison purposes, Exhibit 3.1 provides information from December 1978 and December 1979 on the deposits in commercial banks in Peoria County—the relevant metropolitan area.) In addition to the credit union's deposit position relative to local commercial banks, the senior management team would also review the insti-

---

[1]The credit union, established in 1937, operated under the name Caterpillar Employees Credit Union until 1981, when the name was changed to Construction Equipment Credit Union.

tution's array of consumer services. Unlike local banks, which were prevented by state law from having more than one full-service branch, the credit union stressed convenience by operating several branches in the metropolitan area. It was also among the first credit unions to offer credit card services to members, affiliating with Visa in 1977.

CECU had also moved aggressively to provide its members with interest-bearing transaction accounts (share drafts) as early as 1976. The accounts were popular, and the dollar volume of share draft balances grew 72 percent from 1977 to 1978. While the fate of share drafts was in the hands of the U.S. Congress as Mr. Siefkin pondered his management team's current recommendation, CECU had actively encouraged members to express grassroots support for share drafts through letters to legislators. (Nationwide, the credit union industry had launched an "S.O.S."—Save Our Share Drafts—campaign, which had resulted in 150,000 letters and telegrams to legislators. All but the largest banks opposed the extension of credit union share draft powers beyond their scheduled expiration date of December 31, 1979, and had lobbied hard in Congress to this effect.)

CECU's Financial Position

The credit union was also facing new financial challenges as the organization considered the network proposal. A federal usury ceiling of 12 percent on all credit union loans had been established in 1934 and was still in effect. However, since 1978, credit unions had been able to offer share certificates (called class of share accounts) with interest rates tied to six-month Treasury bills. Currently, the rate being paid on the certificates exceeded 13 percent. These certificates had proved very popular with members but had squeezed earnings. Their impact on the financial operations of the credit union was significant, as revealed in the financial statements in Exhibits 3.2 and 3.3. (A strike by Caterpillar workers in the fall of 1979 that lasted almost three months had put further pressure on CECU's financial position.) Because forecasts

of continued high interest rates made this situation likely to continue for some time, management personnel were especially concerned that any new projects cover their costs. Preferably, of course, they should generate surplus funds that could be used to offset the rising cost of deposits.

CECU and Electronic Funds Transfers

The greatest source of pride for the organization was its involvement in electronic funds transfer systems. In October 1978, the credit union installed three ATMs. This move had been preceded in 1977 by a significant investment in a new computer and other supporting equipment. By November 1979, several more ATMs had been added, some of which were at locations other than credit union offices. In addition, a new headquarters building for CECU had been completed in June 1979. It contained the most up-to-date data-processing equipment available. Almost all routine tasks of the credit union, including loan application and approval, already had been automated or were scheduled to be automated shortly.

Since local banks had been prohibited from installing ATMs up until this time, CECU believed its move to greater electronic banking was competitively wise. A new state law would permit banks to install up to eight ATMs at the rate of two per year, beginning January 1, 1980.

The Sharing Proposal

The current proposal would involve converting the credit union's proprietary ATM system to a shared network. The credit union initially would service the system through its recently expanded computer facilities. Financial institutions desiring to join the system would pay the credit union an original access fee and would be required to purchase their own additional ATMs and access cards. Interchange fees would be paid to a machine's owner if another institution's customer used that machine. A common network name and logo were to be developed, and advertising for the system would be funded jointly by participating institutions. Eventually, a service corporation, separate from any member institution, would be founded to operate the network.

Mr. Siefkin's staff had prepared a fee analysis for the proposed network (see Exhibit 3.4). Initial contacts had been made with the second largest bank in the county. Its response had been generally favorable. This bank, which served as correspondent to several smaller banks in the region, was to be a major force in drawing other banks into the network. A third sponsor, the area's largest S&L, was also being sought. It was moving cautiously, however. High interest rates and usury ceilings on mortgages were squeezing profits in the savings and loan industry, and the institution was seeking guidance on the proposal from the Federal Home Loan Bank Board.

Volume estimates for transactions to be processed through the proposed network were uncertain due to those unresolved issues. The technology involved in electronic banking had also changed so rapidly in the last five years that it was difficult to identify its likely state even five years hence, making long-run planning difficult. Mr. Siefkin's staff had prepared short-run cost estimates for CECU's ATMs, without assuming involvement in the network (see Exhibit 3.5). Mr. Siefkin wondered how these would change by 1985.

Legal and Regulatory Issues

Mr. Siefkin also planned to review recent articles on shared EFT systems collected for him by his staff. He knew that the National Commission on Electronic Funds Transfers had endorsed "procompetitive" sharing in its 1978 report. The commission went on to define procompetitive sharing as that which

maximizes consumer choice; ensures the lowest costs to consumers; encourages innovation; allows for all types of EFT systems, both shared and unshared; preserves competition by ensuring access to those who are not able to provide their own EFT systems; promotes competition by not allowing sharing where it would inhibit the growth of viable competition; permits flexibility in that it is not tied to present technology; and, as compared to mandatory sharing, it does not require a special antitrust law exemption for this industry.

In the eyes of the Department of Justice, shared networks that did not promote competition risked being charged with violation of antitrust laws. In particular, if sharing agreements were struck between significant competitors in a market area, they were likely to be questioned. Furthermore, any agreements that might even indirectly force small institutions to join one network over another were in danger of being labeled anti-competitive.

Beyond these legal questions were those involving regulation. While credit unions enjoyed relative freedom in their operation of EFT systems (other than compliance with consumer protection provisions of Regulation E), banks in the state were regulated about as tightly as anywhere in the nation. The regulatory environment of the savings and loan industry was different still. Finally, two competing bills on the financial system had been introduced in the U.S. Congress. If either bill passed, some believed it would substantially alter the existing relationship among consumer-oriented financial institutions.

Mr. Siefkin knew that the senior staff would have to evaluate all these concerns before preparing the report and recommendations. He also knew that, even if they identified specific benefits to the credit union from the shared network, they must also consider the benefits accruing to cooperating institutions and the possible adverse impact of these benefits on their own organization.

Exhibit 3.1
Deposits in Peoria County (Thousands)

Commercial Banks

Bank	1978		1979	
	Deposits	% of Total	Deposits	% of Total
A	$303,439.972	39.48%	$337,675.000	40.55%
B	125,874.455	16.38	131,701.069	15.83
C	113,458.876	14.76	123,673.505	14.85
D	27,468.045	3.57	29,479.270	3.54
E	16,046.971	2.09	17,508.127	2.10
F	14,650.000	1.92	15,900.000	1.90
G	38,099.511	4.96	40,270.571	4.84
H	40,556.239	5.28	41,700.132	5.01
I	44,684.169	5.81	50,187.920	6.03
J	35,847.754	4.66	36,581.076	4.39
K	8,377.000	1.09	8,015.856	0.96
Bank Total	$768,502.950		$832,692.490	

Construction Equipment Credit Union

$190,955.000		$222,152.000	

Exhibit 3.2
Construction Equipment Credit Union,
Comparative Statements of Condition
as of December 31, 1977–1979

	1977	1978	1979
Assets			
Cash	$ 1,645,941	$ 1,877,196	$ 142,095
Investments	23,958,838	15,450,769	27,978,552
Stock in NCUA Central Liquidity Facility	-0-	-0-	429,540
Consumer loans to members[a] (net of loan loss reserve)	108,798,336	141,017,837	169,021,535
First mortgage loans to members	26,082,130	38,320,130	46,660,997
Accrued interest receivable	811,305	945,221	3,247,383
Payroll deduction receivable	-0-	265,261	577,641
Land	-0-	480,000	487,334
Construction in progress	-0-	875,739	-0-
Building, equipment and leasehold improvements, net	2,405,514	2,363,461	5,204,274
Prepaid expenses	17,874	22,860	15,040
Other assets	18,180	45,749	46,694
Total Assets	$163,738,118	$201,664,223	$253,811,085

continued

Exhibit 3.2
**Construction Equipment Credit Union,
Comparative Statements of Condition
as of December 31, 1977–1979** (*continued*)

	1977	1978	1979
Liabilities and Members' Ownership			
Advance from NCUA Central Liquidity Facility	$ -0-	$ -0-	$ 10,000,000
Notes payable	-0-	-0-	9,045,000
Accrued salaries and expenses	249,077	193,872	259,877
Members' certificates of debt	32,232,000	39,619,000	29,261,000
Accrued interest and dividends	1,461,740	2,180,185	3,093,322
Shares owned by members			
Regular shares	104,585,160	111,880,945	102,045,466
Share drafts	5,767,557	9,932,360	11,070,697
Deposit certificates	12,633,000	29,523,000	79,775,000
Statutory reserve for loan losses	4,262,399	5,641,107	7,433,535
Undivided earnings	2,547,185	2,693,754	1,827,188
Total Liabilities and Ownership	$163,738,118	$201,664,223	$253,811,085

ªIncludes second mortgage loans.

Exhibit 3.3
**Construction Equipment Credit Union,
Comparative Statements of Income
for the Years Ended December 31, 1977–1979**

	1977	1978	1979
Income:			
Interest earned:			
Loans to members	$11,744,018	$15,602,187	$20,139,384
Investments	1,987,646	1,851,440	2,332,598
Loan fees	201,442	289,758	195,393
Gain (loss) on sale of investments	142,370	(86,177)	(4,271)
Other	4,846	8,170	10,328
Total income	$14,080,322	$17,665,378	$22,673,432
Expenses:			
Dividends to members	$ 5,919,561	$ 8,418,246	$ 9,919,827
CD interest to members	2,330,635	2,197,988	4,464,573
Interest on borrowed funds	-0-	56,318	367,331
Operating expenses	4,100,078	5,467,549	6,995,839
Total expenses	$12,350,274	$16,140,101	$21,747,570
Net income	$ 1,730,048	$ 1,525,277	$ 925,862

Exhibit 3.4
Anticipated Fee Schedule for
ATM Network

Interchange Fees:[a]	
Balance inquiry	$ 0.10
Withdrawal	0.25
Deposit	0.80
Transfer	0.15
Processing fee (per transaction)	[b]
Initial user fee	$6,000.00
Hookup fee per ATM	300.00

[a]Fee paid to an ATM owner when another institution's customer conducts business on that machine.

[b]The processing fee was set as a sliding schedule, with the maximum charge at $0.40 for a deposit. A minimum monthly fee also would be established.

Exhibit 3.5
ATM Usage and Cost Data
(Estimated for Mid-1980 without Sharing Agreement)

Average monthly transactions (total system)	71,000
Number of ATMs	12
Initial costs	
Cost of machine	$30,000
Installation[a]	6,000
User cards	4,000
Monthly operating costs (per ATM)	
Maintenance service and security (includes depreciation)	$ 2,300
Other expenses (including data-processing costs)	1,400
Human teller cost per transaction	$ 0.88

[a]Installation costs for a free-standing ATM (kiosk) would be approximately $20,000.

Case 4

TURNER FEDERAL SAVINGS AND LOAN

Ellen Adams, assistant vice president at Turner Federal Savings and Loan, was facing a difficult assignment in July 1983. She had been asked by her manager, the senior vice president of finance, to recommend whether to continue or to abandon the S&L's pilot program for futures hedging. Turner Federal was under increasing regulatory scrutiny because of its low net worth, and Ellen knew that her professional advancement at Turner depended upon this analysis.

Turner Federal was a large, mutually owned urban institution with assets in excess of $6 billion. Like many S&Ls, Turner was founded as a neighborhood home financing association in the 1920s. As the city had grown, particularly after World War II, so had Turner. By 1983, it was the second-largest S&L in the city, and one of the 30 largest in the United States. Unlike other institutions, however, when interest rates had risen dramatically in 1980 and 1981, Turner had continued to make fixed-rate mortgages at lower rates than those offered by competitors. Its long-time CEO, affiliated with Turner Federal since shortly after its founding, continually stressed the institution's community responsibility.

By April 1982, the combination of high deposit interest rates and continued fixed-rate lending had led the District Federal Home Loan Bank to become concerned about Turner's extremely low net worth position. Observers from the bank frequently attended meetings of Turner's Asset/Liability and Investment committees. Management knew that it must formulate specific plans for improving the deteriorating capital position. In the summer of 1982, an out-of-state consulting firm was hired to analyze Turner's rate-sensitivity GAP position. Because of Turner's size and its lack of a system for coordinated data collection, the consulting firm's first report, submitted in September 1982, was based on the balance sheet as of April 30, 1982. Ellen planned to review a copy of this GAP analysis (Exhibit 4.1), as well as the most recent analysis (Exhibit 4.2), based on data from April 30, 1983.

After several weeks of meetings and discussions with the consultants, a hedging policy was developed and submitted to the board of directors for approval. Ellen had outlined the key features of the policy in preparation for her analysis (Exhibit 4.3). After approving the policy, Turner's management had decided to institute a pilot program, based on the sale of one GNMA contract and one T-bill contract. The plan was simply to watch the behavior of the two contracts over time, including the impact of margin calls on Turner's cash flow.

The incident that had prompted Ellen's current assignment was the recent price behavior of the GNMA futures contract. Although GNMA cash prices and futures prices normally were highly correlated, the basis had been much larger and more erratic than usual. The consultants had interpreted this price behavior as the result of what they called a "short squeeze." GNMA futures contracts were based on a standardized $100,000 par value, with an 8 percent coupon rate. In 1981 and 1982, however, extraordinarily high interest rates had caused new GNMAs to be issued with 16 percent and 17 percent coupons. Although interest rates had fallen since then, for technical reasons related to the nature of GNMA futures contracts and associated delivery procedures, holders of short contracts who were forced to deliver securities at the September 1983 contract expiration date would find it cheaper to deliver GNMAs with 16 and 17 percent coupons than those with other coupons. The consultants believed that with $2.5 billion in September futures contracts outstanding in the market, but only $1.4 billion total in GNMAs with 16 percent or 17 percent coupons, some holders of short contracts who could not obtain the high-coupon GNMAs to fulfill their delivery obligations would be at a disadvantage. The phrase *short squeeze* referred to the potential shortage of 16 percent and 17 percent GNMAs.

Because the price of the single GNMA contract Turner had sold had increased during the last week, the association had experienced several margin calls. As a result, some of the S&L's managers had concluded that hedging was too risky to be used as a serious financial management tool. In addition, some managers argued that the S&L was too large to use the futures markets. They believed that the volume of transactions Turner would require in order to significantly incorporate futures into the overall asset/liability management plan was larger than the futures markets could handle successfully. To support their argument, they pointed to data on the volume of open-interest GNMA and T-bill futures contracts at selected points during the past year (Exhibit 4.4).

Before deciding whether to continue the program, the chief financial officer wanted one more close look at the current policy and pilot program, and Ellen had been selected for the assignment. She realized that, although her ultimate task was to recommend whether or not the pilot program should be continued, she would have to consider many important issues before coming to her decision. In particular, she believed she must analyze the following issues:

- What types of hedges were appropriate
- Whether concern about the size of Turner's hedging needs relative to the market were well-founded
- Whether Turner's current policy statement (on which the pilot hedging program was based) adequately covered all the important decisions involved in a typical hedging transaction
- Whether hedging, if maintained as a part of asset/liability management, should be internally managed or should continue to be externally managed by consultants and brokerage firms

Exhibit 4.1
Turner Federal Savings and Loan
GAP Analysis as of April 30, 1982 (Thousands)

	Month 1	Month 2	Month 3	Month 4	Month 5	Month 6	Quarter 3	Quarter 4	Quarters 5 and 6	Quarters 7 and 8	Years 3 and 4	Years 5+	Nonearning/Noninterest-Bearing	Total
Assets														
Cash													$ 5,581	$ 5,581
Fed funds sold	$ 600													600
Investments	13,500	$ 18,045	$ 7,000	$ 8,000	$ 2,500	$ 6,560	$ 10,000	$ 24,100	$ 12,090	$ 114,001	$ 198,363	$ 118,704		532,863
Mortgages	22,420	23,420	23,620	24,620	24,920	25,120	72,460	72,460	144,920	144,920	579,680	3,219,705		4,378,265
Mortgage-backed securities	1,550	1,550	1,550	1,550	1,550	1,550	4,650	4,650	9,300	9,300	37,200	760,816		835,216
Other loans	2,175	2,175	2,175	2,175	2,175	2,175	6,525	6,525	13,050	13,050	52,200	19,368		123,768
Fixed assets													67,185	67,185
Other assets	1,400	1,400	1,400	1,400	1,400	1,400	4,200	3,000	6,000	6,210	22,509	50,749	205,219	306,287
Total assets	$ 41,645	$ 46,590	$ 35,745	$ 37,745	$ 32,545	$ 36,805	$ 97,835	$ 110,735	$ 185,360	$ 287,481	$ 889,952	$4,169,342	$277,985	$6,249,765
Average rate (%)	10.56%	10.09%	10.35%	11.08%	9.92%	10.13%	10.05%	10.44%	9.84%	10.80%	10.46%	9.82%		10.00%
Liabilities and Net Worth														
NOWs	$ 125	$ 125	$ 125	125	125	125	375	375	$ 750	750	$ 4,022	$ 63,200		$ 70,222
Passbooks	2,000	2,000	2,000	2,000	2,000	2,000	6,000	6,000	12,000	12,000	52,473	904,258		1,004,731
Fixed-term CDs	313,890	275,430	521,453	318,841	366,330	606,833	201,195	146,271	157,349	323,119	272,010	38,320		3,541,041
IRAs									27,036					27,036
Jumbo CDs	63,166	41,779	39,768	30,867	16,534	20,316	3,750	561	1,100	200	941			218,982
Reverse repos	522,050	20,312												542,362
Other borrowings	93,500	66,760	60,500	59,100	46,125	40,500	62,300	74,125	68,405	50,000	47,000	13,659		681,974
Net worth													$163,417	163,417
Total liabilities and net worth	$994,731	$ 406,406	$ 623,846	$ 410,933	$ 431,114	$ 669,774	$ 273,620	$ 227,332	$ 266,640	$ 386,069	$ 376,446	$1,019,437	$163,417	$6,249,765
Average rate (%)	13.93%	12.05%	12.99%	14.25%	12.96%	12.75%	10.40%	10.71%	11.31%	13.72%	11.82%	5.50%		11.58%
GAP	($953,086)	($ 359,816)	($ 588,101)	($ 373,188)	($ 398,569)	($ 632,969)	($ 175,785)	($ 116,597)	($ 81,280)	($ 98,588)	$ 513,506	$3,149,905	$114,568	
Cumulative GAP	($953,086)	($1,312,902)	($1,901,003)	($2,274,191)	($2,672,760)	($3,305,729)	($3,481,514)	($3,598,111)	($3,679,391)	($3,777,979)	($3,264,473)	($ 114,568)		
Rate differential	–3.37%	–1.96%	–2.64%	–3.17%	–3.04%	–2.62%	–0.35%	–0.27%	–1.47%	–2.92%	–1.36%	4.32%		–1.58%

Exhibit 4.2
Turner Federal Savings and Loan
GAP Analysis as of April 30, 1983 (Thousands)

	Month 1	Month 2	Month 3	Month 4	Month 5	Month 6	Quarter 3	Quarter 4	Quarters 5 and 6	Quarters 7 and 8	Years 3 and 4	Years 5+	Nonearning/Noninterest-Bearing	Total
Assets														
Cash													$ 73,123	$ 73,123
Fed funds sold	$ 181,400													181,400
Investments	1,500	$ 595			$ 50		$ 1		$ 8,000	$ 36,032	$ 131,429	$ 83,680		261,287
Mortgages	17,747	17,747	$ 17,747	17,747	18,137	18,927	62,112	$ 114,600	201,067	176,734	582,133	2,262,818		3,507,516
Mortgage-backed securities	3,340	3,340	3,340	3,340	3,340	3,340	10,025	10,025	20,050	20,050	80,210	1,135,888		1,296,288
Other loans	214	214	214	214	214	214	636	636	1,066	1,281	135,442			140,345
Fixed assets													76,857	76,857
Other assets	73,063	1,184	1,184	1,184	1,184	1,184	3,553	2,513	5,025	5,244	18,839	53,791	717,899	885,847
Total assets	$ 277,264	$ 23,080	$ 22,485	$ 22,485	$ 22,925	$ 23,665	$ 76,327	$ 127,774	$ 235,208	$ 239,341	$ 948,053	$3,536,177	$867,879	$6,422,663
Average rate (%)	9.87%	9.70%	9.76%	9.76%	9.76%	9.77%	9.95%	10.56%	10.73%	10.52%	10.54%	10.45%		10.43%
Liabilities and Net Worth														
MMDAs	$ 756,000													$ 756,000
NOWs	262	$ 262	$ 262	$ 262	$ 262	$ 262	$ 786	$ 786	$ 1,575	$ 1,575	$ 8,521	$ 133,185		148,000
Passbooks	9,200	9,200	18,400	46,000	46,000	46,000	73,600	36,800	55,200	55,200	110,400	414,000		920,000
Fixed-term CDs	336,114	188,727	285,541	231,698	284,308	359,464	60,432	333,600	330,148	315,018	247,049	21,601		2,993,700
IRAs		10,500	21,500	2,364	2,129	2,799	3,880	5,532	59,969					108,673
Jumbo CDs	22,169	49,867	33,662	14,356	12,006	10,048	4,251	1,771	100		2,343			150,573
Reverse repos	346,688	28,666										805		376,159
Other borrowings	88,650	110,949	14,500	10,000	36,000	45,300	119,900	99,625	84,300	17,000	7,991	11,086		645,301
Net worth													324,257	324,257
Total liabilities and net worth	$1,559,083	$ 398,171	$ 373,865	$ 304,680	$ 380,705	$ 463,873	$ 262,849	$ 478,114	$ 531,292	$ 388,793	$ 376,304	$ 580,677	$324,257	$6,422,663
Average rate (%)	8.90%	9.48%	8.90%	8.59%	8.77%	8.86%	8.60%	13.40%	11.70%	10.83%	8.12%	5.00%		9.20%
GAP	($1,281,819)	($ 375,091)	($ 351,380)	($ 282,195)	($ 357,780)	($ 440,208)	($ 186,522)	($ 350,340)	($ 296,084)	($ 149,452)	$ 571,749	$2,955,500	$543,622	
Cumulative GAP	($1,281,819)	($1,656,910)	($2,008,290)	($2,290,485)	($2,648,265)	($3,088,473)	($3,274,995)	($3,625,335)	($3,921,419)	($4,070,871)	($3,499,122)	($ 543,622)		
Rate differential	0.97%	0.22%	0.86%	1.17%	0.99%	0.91%	1.35%	-2.84%	-0.97%	-0.31%	2.42%	5.45%		1.23%

Exhibit 4.3
Key Features of Turner Federal's Financial Futures Hedging Policy

---

I. The objectives of using interest rate futures to manage interest rate risk include:
- A.   To protect the value of mortgage loans, securities, and other rate-sensitive assets
- B.   To fix liability costs
- C.   To protect against other risks resulting from an imbalance between rate-sensitive assets and liabilities

[The policy then went on to specify what futures instruments would be considered; virtually all then available were named.]

II. The size of position limits will be determined by the amount of unmatched rate-sensitive assets and liabilities. Initially, positions less than or equal to 25 percent of mismatched rate-sensitive assets or liabilities are authorized.

III. Each hedge shall be accompanied by a statement providing the following information:
- A.   Purpose of the hedge (for example: "to protect asset value in the securities portfolio")
- B.   Contract to be used (the one with the highest price correlation to the cash instrument)
- C.   Number of contracts (determined by the cash position being hedged)

Exhibit 4.4
Open Interest in Selected Futures Contracts

Date	Type of Contract	Open Interest (Number of Contracts)
7/14/82	September GNMA	18,871
	September T-bill	29,403
10/14/82	December GNMA	18,796
	December T-bill	26,410
1/14/83	March GNMA	15,569
	March T-bill	33,101
4/14/83	June GNMA	20,886
	June T-bill	26,042
7/14/83	September GNMA	29,020
	September T-bill	26,730

Appendix B

MATHEMATICAL TABLES

Table B.1
Present Value of $1 Due at the End of n Periods

$$PVIF_{k,n} = \frac{1}{(1 + k)^n}$$

Period	1%	2%	3%	4%	5%	6%	7%	8%	9%	10%
1	.9901	.9804	.9709	.9615	.9524	.9434	.9346	.9259	.9174	.9091
2	.9803	.9612	.9426	.9246	.9070	.8900	.8734	.8573	.8417	.8264
3	.9706	.9423	.9151	.8890	.8638	.8396	.8163	.7938	.7722	.7513
4	.9610	.9238	.8885	.8548	.8227	.7921	.7629	.7350	.7084	.6830
5	.9515	.9057	.8626	.8219	.7835	.7473	.7130	.6806	.6499	.6209
6	.9420	.8880	.8375	.7903	.7462	.7050	.6663	.6302	.5963	.5645
7	.9327	.8706	.8131	.7599	.7107	.6651	.6227	.5835	.5470	.5132
8	.9235	.8535	.7894	.7307	.6768	.6274	.5820	.5403	.5019	.4665
9	.9143	.8368	.7664	.7026	.6446	.5919	.5439	.5002	.4604	.4241
10	.9053	.8203	.7441	.6756	.6139	.5584	.5083	.4632	.4224	.3855
11	.8963	.8043	.7224	.6496	.5847	.5268	.4751	.4289	.3875	.3505
12	.8874	.7885	.7014	.6246	.5568	.4970	.4440	.3971	.3555	.3186
13	.8787	.7730	.6810	.6006	.5303	.4688	.4150	.3677	.3262	.2897
14	.8700	.7579	.6611	.5775	.5051	.4423	.3878	.3405	.2992	.2633
15	.8613	.7430	.6419	.5553	.4810	.4173	.3624	.3152	.2745	.2394
16	.8528	.7284	.6232	.5339	.4581	.3936	.3387	.2919	.2519	.2176
17	.8444	.7142	.6050	.5134	.4363	.3714	.3166	.2703	.2311	.1978
18	.8360	.7002	.5874	.4936	.4155	.3503	.2959	.2502	.2120	.1799
19	.8277	.6864	.5703	.4746	.3957	.3305	.2765	.2317	.1945	.1635
20	.8195	.6730	.5537	.4564	.3769	.3118	.2584	.2145	.1784	.1486
21	.8114	.6598	.5375	.4388	.3589	.2942	.2415	.1987	.1637	.1351
22	.8034	.6468	.5219	.4220	.3418	.2775	.2257	.1839	.1502	.1228
23	.7954	.6342	.5067	.4057	.3256	.2618	.2109	.1703	.1378	.1117
24	.7876	.6217	.4919	.3901	.3101	.2470	.1971	.1577	.1264	.1015
25	.7798	.6095	.4776	.3751	.2953	.2330	.1842	.1460	.1160	.0923
26	.7720	.5976	.4637	.3604	.2812	.2198	.1722	.1352	.1064	.0839
27	.7644	.5859	.4502	.3468	.2678	.2074	.1609	.1252	.0976	.0763
28	.7568	.5744	.4371	.3335	.2551	.1956	.1504	.1159	.0895	.0693
29	.7493	.5631	.4243	.3207	.2429	.1846	.1406	.1073	.0822	.0630
30	.7419	.5521	.4120	.3083	.2314	.1741	.1314	.0994	.0754	.0573
35	.7059	.5000	.3554	.2534	.1813	.1301	.0937	.0676	.0490	.0356
40	.6717	.4529	.3066	.2083	.1420	.0972	.0668	.0460	.0318	.0221
45	.6391	.4102	.2644	.1712	.1113	.0727	.0476	.0313	.0207	.0137
50	.6080	.3715	.2281	.1407	.0872	.0543	.0339	.0213	.0134	.0085
55	.5785	.3365	.1968	.1157	.0683	.0406	.0242	.0145	.0087	.0053

Table B.1 (*continued*)

Period	12%	14%	15%	16%	18%	20%	24%	28%	32%	36%
1	.8929	8772	.8696	.8621	.8475	.8333	.8065	.7813	.7576	.7353
2	.7972	.7695	.7561	.7432	.7182	.6944	.6504	.6104	.5739	.5407
3	.7118	.6750	.6575	.6407	.6086	.5787	.5245	.4768	.4348	.3975
4	.6355	.5921	.5718	.5523	.5158	.4823	.4230	.3725	.3294	.2923
5	.5674	.5194	.4972	.4761	.4371	.4019	.3411	.2910	.2495	.2149
6	.5066	.4556	.4323	.4104	.3704	.3349	.2751	.2274	.1890	.1580
7	.4523	.3996	.3759	.3538	.3139	.2791	.2218	.1776	.1432	.1162
8	.4039	.3506	.3269	.3050	.2660	.2326	.1789	.1388	.1085	.0854
9	.3606	.3075	.2843	.2630	.2255	.1938	.1443	.1084	.0822	.0628
10	.3220	.2697	.2472	.2267	.1911	.1615	.1164	.0847	.0623	.0462
11	.2875	.2366	.2149	.1954	.1619	.1346	.0938	.0662	.0472	.0340
12	.2567	.2076	.1869	.1685	.1372	.1122	.0757	.0517	.0357	.0250
13	.2292	.1821	.1625	.1452	.1163	.0935	.0610	.0404	.0271	.0184
14	.2046	.1597	.1413	.1252	.0985	.0779	.0492	.0316	.0205	.0135
15	.1827	.1401	.1229	.1079	.0835	.0649	.0397	.0247	.0155	.0099
16	.1631	.1229	.1069	.0980	.0708	.0541	.0320	.0193	.0118	.0073
17	.1456	.1078	.0929	.0802	.0600	.0451	.0258	.0150	.0089	.0054
18	.1300	.0946	.0808	.0691	.0508	.0376	.0208	.0118	.0068	.0039
19	.1161	.0829	.0703	.0596	.0431	.0313	.0168	.0092	.0051	.0029
20	.1037	.0728	.0611	.0514	.0365	.0261	.0135	.0072	.0039	.0021
21	.0926	.0638	.0531	.0443	.0309	.0217	.0109	.0056	.0029	.0016
22	.0826	.0560	.0462	.0382	.0262	.0181	.0088	.0044	.0022	.0012
23	.0738	.0491	.0402	.0329	.0222	.0151	.0071	.0034	.0017	.0008
24	.0659	.0431	.0349	.0284	.0188	.0126	.0057	.0027	.0013	.0006
25	.0588	.0378	.0304	.0245	.0160	.0105	.0046	.0021	.0010	.0005
26	.0525	.0331	.0264	.0211	.0135	.0087	.0037	.0016	.0007	.0003
27	.0469	.0291	.0230	.0182	.0115	.0073	.0030	.0013	.0006	.0002
28	.0419	.0255	.0200	.0157	.0097	.0061	.0024	.0010	.0004	.0002
29	.0374	.0224	.0174	.0135	.0082	.0051	.0020	.0008	.0003	.0001
30	.0334	.0196	.0151	.0116	.0070	.0042	.0016	.0006	.0002	.0001
35	.0189	.0102	.0075	.0055	.0030	.0017	.0005	.0002	.0001	*
40	.0107	.0053	.0037	.0026	.0013	.0007	.0002	.0001	*	*
45	.0061	.0027	.0019	.0013	.0006	.0003	.0001	*	*	*
50	.0035	.0014	.0009	.0006	.0003	.0001	*	*	*	*
55	.0020	.0007	.0005	.0003	.0001	*	*	*	*	*

*The factor is zero to four decimal places.

Table B.2
Present Value of an Annuity of $1 per Period for n Periods

$$\text{PVIFA}_{k,n} = \sum_{t=1}^{n} \frac{1}{(1 + k)^t} = \frac{1 - \dfrac{1}{(1 + k)^n}}{k} = \frac{1}{k} - \frac{1}{k(1 + k)^n}$$

Number of Periods	1%	2%	3%	4%	5%	6%	7%	8%	9%
1	0.9901	0.9804	0.9709	0.9615	0.9524	0.9434	0.9346	0.9259	0.9174
2	1.9704	1.9416	1.9135	1.8861	1.8594	1.8334	1.8080	1.7833	1.7591
3	2.9410	2.8839	2.8286	2.7751	2.7232	2.6730	2.6243	2.5771	2.5313
4	3.9020	3.8077	3.7171	3.6299	3.5460	3.4651	3.3872	3.3121	3.2397
5	4.8534	4.7135	4.5797	4.4518	4.3295	4.2124	4.1002	3.9927	3.8897
6	5.7955	5.6014	5.4172	5.2421	5.0757	4.9173	4.7665	4.6229	4.4859
7	6.7282	6.4720	6.2303	6.0021	5.7864	5.5824	5.3893	5.2064	5.0330
8	7.6517	7.3255	7.0197	6.7327	6.4632	6.2098	5.9713	5.7466	5.5348
9	8.5660	8.1622	7.7861	7.4353	7.1078	6.8017	6.5152	6.2469	5.9952
10	9.4713	8.9826	8.5302	8.1109	7.7217	7.3601	7.0236	6.7101	6.4177
11	10.3676	9.7868	9.2526	8.7605	8.3064	7.8869	7.4987	7.1390	6.8052
12	11.2551	10.5753	9.9540	9.3851	8.8633	8.3838	7.9427	7.5361	7.1607
13	12.1337	11.3484	10.6350	9.9856	9.3936	8.8527	8.3577	7.9038	7.4869
14	13.0037	12.1062	11.2961	10.5631	9.8986	9.2950	8.7455	8.2442	7.7862
15	13.8651	12.8493	11.9379	11.1184	10.3797	9.7122	9.1079	8.5595	8.0607
16	14.7179	13.5777	12.5611	11.6523	10.8378	10.1059	9.4466	8.8514	8.3126
17	15.5623	14.2919	13.1661	12.1657	11.2741	10.4773	9.7632	9.1216	8.5436
18	16.3983	14.9920	13.7535	12.6593	11.6896	10.8276	10.0591	9.3719	8.7556
19	17.2260	15.6785	14.3238	13.1339	12.0853	11.1581	10.3356	9.6036	8.9501
20	18.0456	16.3514	14.8775	13.5903	12.4622	11.4699	10.5940	9.8181	9.1285
21	18.8570	17.0112	15.4150	14.0292	12.8212	11.7641	10.8355	10.0168	9.2922
22	19.6604	17.6580	15.9369	14.4511	13.1630	12.0416	11.0612	10.2007	9.4424
23	20.4558	18.2922	16.4436	14.8568	13.4886	12.3034	11.2722	10.3711	9.5802
24	21.2434	18.9139	16.9355	15.2470	13.7986	12.5504	11.4693	10.5288	9.7066
25	22.0232	19.5235	17.4131	15.6221	14.0939	12.7834	11.6536	10.6748	9.8226
26	22.7952	20.1210	17.8768	15.9828	14.3752	13.0032	11.8258	10.8100	9.9290
27	23.5596	20.7069	18.3270	16.3296	14.6430	13.2105	11.9867	10.9352	10.0266
28	24.3164	21.2813	18.7641	16.6631	14.8981	13.4062	12.1371	11.0511	10.1161
29	25.0658	21.8444	19.1885	16.9837	15.1411	13.5907	12.2777	11.1584	10.1983
30	25.8077	22.3965	19.6004	17.2920	15.3725	13.7648	12.4090	11.2578	10.2737
35	29.4086	24.9986	21.4872	18.6646	16.3742	14.4982	12.9477	11.6546	10.5668
40	32.8347	27.3555	23.1148	19.7928	17.1591	15.0463	13.3317	11.9246	10.7574
45	36.0945	29.4902	24.5187	20.7200	17.7741	15.4558	13.6055	12.1084	10.8812
50	39.1961	31.4236	25.7298	21.4822	18.2559	15.7619	13.8007	12.2335	10.9617
55	42.1472	33.1748	26.7744	22.1086	18.6335	15.9905	13.9399	12.3186	11.0140

Table B.2 (*continued*)

Number of Periods	10%	12%	14%	15%	16%	18%	20%	24%	28%	32%
1	0.9091	0.8929	0.8772	0.8696	0.8621	0.8475	0.8333	0.8065	0.7813	0.7576
2	1.7355	1.6901	1.6467	1.6257	1.6052	1.5656	1.5278	1.4568	1.3916	1.3315
3	2.4869	2.4018	2.3216	2.2832	2.2459	2.1743	2.1065	1.9813	1.8684	1.7663
4	3.1699	3.0373	2.9137	2.8550	2.7982	2.6901	2.5887	2.4043	2.2410	2.0957
5	3.7908	3.6048	3.4331	3.3522	3.2743	3.1272	2.9906	2.7454	2.5320	2.3452
6	4.3553	4.1114	3.8887	3.7845	3.6847	3.4976	3.3255	3.0205	2.7594	2.5342
7	4.8684	4.5638	4.2883	4.1604	4.0386	3.8115	3.6046	3.2423	2.9370	2.6775
8	5.3349	4.9676	4.6389	4.4873	4.3436	4.0776	3.8372	3.4212	3.0758	2.7860
9	5.7590	5.3282	4.9464	4.7716	4.6065	4.3030	4.0310	3.5655	3.1842	2.8681
10	6.1446	5.6502	5.2161	5.0188	4.8332	4.4941	4.1925	3.6819	3.2689	2.9304
11	6.4951	5.9377	5.4527	5.2337	5.0286	4.6560	4.3271	3.7757	3.3351	2.9776
12	6.8137	6.1944	5.6603	5.4206	5.1971	4.7932	4.4392	3.8514	3.3868	3.0133
13	7.1034	6.4235	5.8424	5.5831	5.3423	4.9095	4.5327	3.9124	3.4272	3.0404
14	7.3667	6.6282	6.0021	5.7245	5.4675	5.0081	4.6106	3.9616	3.4587	3.0609
15	7.6061	6.8109	6.1422	5.8474	5.5755	5.0916	4.6755	4.0013	3.4834	3.0764
16	7.8237	6.9740	6.2651	5.9542	5.6685	5.1624	4.7296	4.0333	3.5026	3.0882
17	8.0216	7.1196	6.3729	6.0472	5.7487	5.2223	4.7746	4.0591	3.5177	3.0971
18	8.2014	7.2497	6.4674	6.1280	5.8178	5.2732	4.8122	4.0799	3.5294	3.1039
19	8.3649	7.3658	6.5504	6.1982	5.8775	5.3162	4.8435	4.0967	3.5386	3.1090
20	8.5136	7.4694	6.6231	6.2593	5.9288	5.3527	4.8696	4.1103	3.5458	3.1129
21	8.6487	7.5620	6.6870	6.3125	5.9731	5.3837	4.8913	4.1212	3.5514	3.1158
22	8.7715	7.6446	6.7429	6.3587	6.0113	5.4099	4.9094	4.1300	3.5558	3.1180
23	8.8832	7.7184	6.7921	6.3988	6.0442	5.4321	4.9245	4.1371	3.5592	3.1197
24	8.9847	7.7843	6.8351	6.4338	6.0726	5.4509	4.9371	4.1428	3.5619	3.1210
25	9.0770	7.8431	6.8729	6.4641	6.0971	5.4669	4.9476	4.1474	3.5640	3.1220
26	9.1609	7.8957	6.9061	6.4906	6.1182	5.4804	4.9563	4.1511	3.5656	3.1227
27	9.2372	7.9426	6.9352	6.5135	6.1364	5.4919	4.9636	4.1542	3.5669	3.1233
28	9.3066	7.9844	6.9607	6.5335	6.1520	5.5016	4.9697	4.1566	3.5679	3.1237
29	9.3696	8.0218	6.9830	6.5509	6.1656	5.5098	4.9747	4.1585	3.5687	3.1240
30	9.4269	8.0552	7.0027	6.5660	6.1772	5.5168	4.9789	4.1601	3.5693	3.1242
35	9.6442	8.1755	7.0700	6.6166	6.2153	5.5386	4.9915	4.1644	3.5708	3.1248
40	9.7791	8.2438	7.1050	6.6418	6.2335	5.5482	4.9966	4.1659	3.5712	3.1250
45	9.8628	8.2825	7.1232	6.6543	6.2421	5.5523	4.9986	4.1664	3.5714	3.1250
50	9.9148	8.3045	7.1327	6.6605	6.2463	5.5541	4.9995	4.1666	3.5714	3.1250
55	9.9471	8.3170	7.1376	6.6636	6.2482	5.5549	4.9998	4.1666	3.5714	3.1250

Table B.3
Future Value of $1 at the End of n Periods

$$FVIF_{k,n} = (1 + k)^n$$

Period	1%	2%	3%	4%	5%	6%	7%	8%	9%	10%
1	1.0100	1.0200	1.0300	1.0400	1.0500	1.0600	1.0700	1.0800	1.0900	1.1000
2	1.0201	1.0404	1.0609	1.0816	1.1025	1.1236	1.1449	1.1664	1.1881	1.2100
3	1.0303	1.0612	1.0927	1.1249	1.1576	1.1910	1.2250	1.2597	1.2950	1.3310
4	1.0406	1.0824	1.1255	1.1699	1.2155	1.2625	1.3108	1.3605	1.4116	1.4641
5	1.0510	1.1041	1.1593	1.2167	1.2763	1.3382	1.4026	1.4693	1.5386	1.6105
6	1.0615	1.1262	1.1941	1.2653	1.3401	1.4185	1.5007	1.5869	1.6771	1.7716
7	1.0721	1.1487	1.2299	1.3159	1.4071	1.5036	1.6058	1.7138	1.8280	1.9487
8	1.0829	1.1717	1.2668	1.3686	1.4775	1.5938	1.7182	1.8509	1.9926	2.1436
9	1.0937	1.1951	1.3048	1.4233	1.5513	1.6895	1.8385	1.9990	2.1719	2.3579
10	1.1046	1.2190	1.3439	1.4802	1.6289	1.7908	1.9672	2.1589	2.3674	2.5937
11	1.1157	1.2434	1.3842	1.5395	1.7103	1.8983	2.1049	2.3316	2.5804	2.8531
12	1.1268	1.2682	1.4258	1.6010	1.7959	2.0122	2.2522	2.5182	2.8127	3.1384
13	1.1381	1.2936	1.4685	1.6651	1.8856	2.1329	2.4098	2.7196	3.0658	3.4523
14	1.1495	1.3195	1.5126	1.7317	1.9799	2.2609	2.5785	2.9372	3.3417	3.7975
15	1.1610	1.3459	1.5580	1.8009	2.0789	2.3966	2.7590	3.1722	3.6425	4.1772
16	1.1726	1.3728	1.6047	1.8730	2.1829	2.5404	2.9522	3.4259	3.9703	4.5950
17	1.1843	1.4002	1.6528	1.9479	2.2920	2.6928	3.1588	3.7000	4.3276	5.0545
18	1.1961	1.4282	1.7024	2.0258	2.4066	2.8543	3.3799	3.9960	4.7171	5.5599
19	1.2081	1.4568	1.7535	2.1068	2.5270	3.0256	3.6165	4.3157	5.1417	6.1159
20	1.2202	1.4859	1.8061	2.1911	2.6533	3.2071	3.8697	4.6610	5.6044	6.7275
21	1.2324	1.5157	1.8603	2.2788	2.7860	3.3996	4.1406	5.0338	6.1088	7.4002
22	1.2447	1.5460	1.9161	2.3699	2.9253	3.6035	4.4304	5.4365	6.6586	8.1403
23	1.2572	1.5769	1.9736	2.4647	3.0715	3.8197	4.7405	5.8715	7.2579	8.9543
24	1.2697	1.6084	2.0328	2.5633	3.2251	4.0489	5.0724	6.3412	7.9111	9.8497
25	1.2824	1.6406	2.0938	2.6658	3.3864	4.2919	5.4274	6.8485	8.6231	10.835
26	1.2953	1.6734	2.1566	2.7725	3.5557	4.5494	5.8074	7.3964	9.3992	11.918
27	1.3082	1.7069	2.2213	2.8834	3.7335	4.8223	6.2139	7.9881	10.245	13.110
28	1.3213	1.7410	2.2879	2.9987	3.9201	5.1117	6.6488	8.6271	11.167	14.421
29	1.3345	1.7758	2.3566	3.1187	4.1161	5.4184	7.1143	9.3173	12.172	15.863
30	1.3478	1.8114	2.4273	3.2434	4.3219	5.7435	7.6123	10.063	13.268	17.449
40	1.4889	2.2080	3.2620	4.8010	7.0400	10.286	14.974	21.725	31.409	45.259
50	1.6446	2.6916	4.3839	7.1067	11.467	18.420	29.457	46.902	74.358	117.39
60	1.8167	3.2810	5.8916	10.520	18.679	32.988	57.946	101.26	176.03	304.48

Table B.3 (*continued*)

Period	12%	14%	15%	16%	18%	20%	24%	28%	32%	36%
1	1.1200	1.1400	1.1500	1.1600	1.1800	1.2000	1.2400	1.2800	1.3200	1.3600
2	1.2544	1.2996	1.3225	1.3456	1.3924	1.4400	1.5376	1.6384	1.7424	1.8496
3	1.4049	1.4815	1.5209	1.5609	1.6430	1.7280	1.9066	2.0972	2.3000	2.5155
4	1.5735	1.6890	1.7490	1.8106	1.9388	2.0736	2.3642	2.6844	3.0360	3.4210
5	1.7623	1.9254	2.0114	2.1003	2.2878	2.4883	2.9316	3.4360	4.0075	4.6526
6	1.9738	2.1950	2.3131	2.4364	2.6996	2.9860	3.6352	4.3980	5.2899	6.3275
7	2.2107	2.5023	2.6600	2.8262	3.1855	3.5832	4.5077	5.6295	6.9826	8.6054
8	2.4760	2.8526	3.0590	3.2784	3.7589	4.2998	5.5895	7.2058	9.2170	11.703
9	2.7731	3.2519	3.5179	3.8030	4.4355	5.1598	6.9310	9.2234	12.166	15.917
10	3.1058	3.7072	4.0456	4.4114	5.2338	6.1917	8.5944	11.806	16.060	21.647
11	3.4785	4.2262	4.6524	5.1173	6.1759	7.4301	10.657	15.112	21.199	29.439
12	3.8960	4.8179	5.3503	5.9360	7.2876	8.9161	13.215	19.343	27.983	40.037
13	4.3635	5.4924	6.1528	6.8858	8.5994	10.699	16.386	24.759	36.937	54.451
14	4.8871	6.2613	7.0757	7.9875	10.147	12.839	20.319	31.691	48.757	74.053
15	5.4736	7.1379	8.1371	9.2655	11.974	15.407	25.196	40.565	64.359	100.71
16	6.1304	8.1372	9.3576	10.748	14.129	18.488	31.243	51.923	84.954	136.97
17	6.8660	9.2765	10.761	12.468	16.672	22.186	38.741	66.461	112.14	186.28
18	7.6900	10.575	12.375	14.463	19.673	26.623	48.039	85.071	148.02	253.34
19	8.6128	12.056	14.232	16.777	23.214	31.948	59.568	108.89	195.39	344.54
20	9.6463	13.743	16.367	19.461	27.393	38.338	73.864	139.38	257.92	468.57
21	10.804	15.668	18.822	22.574	32.324	46.005	91.592	178.41	340.45	637.26
22	12.100	17.861	21.645	26.186	38.142	55.206	113.57	228.36	449.39	866.67
23	13.552	20.362	24.891	30.376	45.008	66.247	140.83	292.30	593.20	1178.7
24	15.179	23.212	28.625	35.236	53.109	79.497	174.63	374.14	783.02	1603.0
25	17.000	26.462	32.919	40.874	62.669	95.396	216.54	478.90	1033.6	2180.1
26	19.040	30.167	37.857	47.414	73.949	114.48	268.51	613.00	1364.3	2964.9
27	21.325	34.390	43.535	55.000	87.260	137.37	332.95	784.64	1800.9	4032.3
28	23.884	39.204	50.066	63.800	102.97	164.84	412.86	1004.3	2377.2	5483.9
29	26.750	44.693	57.575	74.009	121.50	197.81	511.95	1285.6	3137.9	7458.1
30	29.960	50.950	66.212	85.850	143.37	237.38	634.82	1645.5	4142.1	10143.
40	93.051	188.88	267.86	378.72	750.38	1469.8	5455.9	19427.	66521.	*
50	289.00	700.23	1083.7	1670.7	3927.4	9100.4	46890.	*	*	*
60	897.60	2595.9	4384.0	7370.2	20555.	56348.	*	*	*	*

*FVIF > 99,999.

Author Index

SUBJECT INDEX